P9-CSA-718

FOURTH CANADIAN EDITION

FINANCIAL ACCOUNTING

WALTER T. HARRISON, JR.
BAYLOR UNIVERSITY

CHARLES T. HORNGREN
STANFORD UNIVERSITY

C. WILLIAM (BILL) THOMAS
BAYLOR UNIVERSITY

W. MORLEY LEMON
UNIVERSITY OF WATERLOO

CATHERINE SEGUIN
UNIVERSITY OF TORONTO

SANDRA ROBERTSON LEMON
CONSULTANT

Pearson Canada
Toronto

To Jake, Max, Meg, Ben, and Tessa

—Sandra R. Lemon and W. Morley Lemon

To Dennis, Andrea, Allison, and Mark

—Catherine I. Seguin

Library and Archives Canada Cataloguing in Publication

Financial accounting / Walter T. Harrison Jr. ... [et al.]. — 4th Canadian ed.

Includes index.
ISBN 978-0-13-138433-0

1. Accounting—Textbooks. I. Harrison, Walter T. II. Title.

HF5636.F545 2011 657'.044 C2010-906784-3

ISBN 978-0-13-138433-0

Vice-President, Editorial Director: Gary Bennett
Editor-in-Chief: Nicole Lukach
Executive Marketing Manager: Cas Shields
Developmental Editor: Victoria Naik
Project Managers: Cheryl Jackson and Imee Salumbides
Production Editor: Leanne Rancourt
Copy Editor: Lu Cormier
Proofreader: Laurel Sparrow
Compositor: Nelson Gonzalez
Photo Researcher: The Editing Company
Art Director: Julia Hall
Cover and Interior Designer: Opus House Inc./Sonya Thursby
Cover Image: Super Stock

Photo Credits
1 Courtesy of Gildan Inc. **60** BlackBerry®, RIM®, Research In Motion®, SureType®, SurePress™ and related trademarks, names and logos are the property of Research In Motion Limited and are registered and/or used in the U.S. and countries around the world. **117** Courtesy of Le Château Inc. **182** Image source/Getty Images. **195** David R. Frazier/Photolibrary, Inc./Photo Researchers, Inc. **208** iStockPhoto. **237** CP/Mario Beauregard. **283** CP/Boris Spremo. **337** CP/Bayne Stanley. **390** CP/Bayne Stanley. **452** Courtesy of Potash Corp. **513** Courtesy of ATCO Group Ltd. **554** CP/Francis Vachon. **596** Courtesy of Gildan Inc. **666** Toronto Star/GetStock.com

2 3 4 5 14 13 12

Printed and bound in the United States of America.

Contents

Inventory and Cost of Goods Sold ... 283

SPOTLIGHT: LEON'S FURNITURE ... 283

Property, Plant, and Equipment, and Intangible Assets ... 337

SPOTLIGHT: CANADIAN TIRE ... 337

The Statement of Cash Flows ... 596

SPOTLIGHT: GILDAN ACTIVEWEAR INC. ... 596

Financial Statement Analysis ... 666

SPOTLIGHT: METRO INC. ... 666

About the Authors

Walter T. Harrison, Jr. is Professor of Accounting at the Hankamer School of Business, Baylor University. He received his B.B.A. degree from Baylor University, his M.S. from Oklahoma State University, and his Ph.D. from Michigan State University.

Professor Harrison, recipient of numerous teaching awards from student groups as well as from university administrators, has also taught at Cleveland State Community College, Michigan State University, the University of Texas, and Stanford University.

A member of the American Accounting Association and the American Institute of Certified Public Accountants, Professor Harrison has served as Chairman of the Financial Accounting Standards Committee of the American Accounting Association, on the Teaching/Curriculum Development Award Committee, on the Program Advisory Committee for Accounting Education and Teaching, and on the Notable Contributions to Accounting Literature Committee.

Professor Harrison has lectured in several foreign countries and published articles in numerous journals, including *The Accounting Review*, *Journal of Accounting Research*, *Journal of Accountancy*, *Journal of Accounting and Public Policy*, *Economic Consequences of Financial Accounting Standards*, *Accounting Horizons*, *Issues in Accounting Education*, and *Journal of Law and Commerce*. He is coauthor of *Financial Accounting*, Seventh Edition, 2006 (with Charles T. Horngren) and *Accounting*, Eighth Edition (with Charles T. Horngren and Linda S. Bamber) published by Pearson Prentice Hall. Professor Harrison has received scholarships, fellowships, research grants, or awards from Price Waterhouse & Co., Deloitte & Touche, the Ernst & Young Foundation, and the KPMG Peat Marwick Foundation.

Charles T. Horngren is the Edmund W. Littlefield Professor of Accounting, Emeritus, at Stanford University. A graduate of Marquette University, he received his MBA from Harvard University and his Ph.D. from the University of Chicago. He is also the recipient of honourary doctorates from Marquette University and DePaul University.

A Certified Public Accountant, Horngren served on the Accounting Principles Board for six years, the Financial Accounting Standards Board Advisory Council for five years, and the Council of the American Institute of Certified Public Accountants for three years. For six years, he served as a trustee of the Financial Accounting Foundation, which oversees the Financial Accounting Standards Board and the Government Accounting Standards Board.

Horngren is a member of the Accounting Hall of Fame.

A member of the American Accounting Association, Horngren has been its President and its Director of Research. He received its first annual Outstanding Accounting Educator Award.

The California Certified Public Accountants Foundation gave Horngren its Faculty Excellence Award and its Distinguished Professor Award. He is the first person to have received both awards.

Horngren was named Accountant of the Year, Education, by the national professional accounting fraternity, Beta Alpha Psi.

Horngren is also a member of the Institute of Management Accountants, where he has received its Distinguished Service Award. He was a member of the Institute's Board of Regents, which administers the Certified Management Accountant examinations.

Horngren is the author of other accounting books published by Pearson Prentice Hall and Pearson Canada Inc.: *Cost Accounting: A Managerial Emphasis*, Fifth Canadian Edition, 2010 (with George Foster, Srikant Datar, and Maureen Gowing) and *Accounting*, Canadian Eighth Edition, 2010 (with Walter T. Harrison, Linda S. Bamber, W. Morley Lemon, Peter R. Norwood, and Jo-Ann Johnston).

Horngren is the Consulting Editor of the Charles T. Horngren Series in Accounting.

W. Morley Lemon is Professor Emeritus, University of Waterloo where he was a faculty member for 24 years. He served as Director of the School of Acountancy 1987-1988 and 1998-2002. He obtained his BA from the University of Western Ontario, his MBA from the University if Toronto, and his PhD from the University of Texas at Austin. Professor Lemon obtained his CA in Ontario. In 1985, he was honoured by that Institute, which elected him a Fellow; in 2003 he received that Institute's ICAO Award of Outstanding Merit. Professor Lemon received his CPA in Texas.

Professor Lemon was awarded the University of Waterloo Distinguished Teacher Award at the 1998 University of Waterloo convocation. In 2004 he was awarded the L.S. Rosen Outstanding Educator award ' the Canadian Academic Accounting Association. In 2010, Professor Lemon was awarded the 2010 Distinguished Service Award by the Auditing Section, American Accounting Association. He has been a Visiting Professor at the University of Texas in Austin and at the University of Auckland, New Zealand several times over the past few years.

Professor Lemon is coauthor, with Arens, Loebbeke, and Splettstoesser, of *Auditing and Other Assurance Services*, Canadian Ninth Edition, published by Pearson Canada, and coauthored five previous Canadian editions of that text. He is also coauthor, with Horngren, Harrison, Bamber, and Norwood, of *Accounting*, Canadian Sixth Edition, published by Pearson Canada. He coauthored the five previous Canadian editions of that text. Professor Lemon was co-author , with Harrison, Horngren and Lemon of *Financial Accounting* Canadian Third Edition, published by Pearson Canada. He also coauthored the first two Canadian editions of that text

He was a member of the Canadian Institute of Chartered Accountants' Assurance Standards Board. He has also served on the Institute of Chartered Accountants of Ontario Council, as well as a number of committees for both bodies. He has chaired and served on a number of committees of the Canadian Academic Accounting Association. Professor Lemon has served on Council and chaired and served on a number of committees of the American Accounting Association.

Professor Lemon has presented lectures and papers at a number of universities and academic and professional conferences and symposia in Canada, the United States and China. He has chaired and organized six audit symposia held at the University of Waterloo. He has served on the editorial board of and reviewed papers for a number of academic journals including *The Accounting Review, Contemporary Accounting Research, Journal of Business Ethics, Issues in Accounting Education, Auditing: A Journal of Practice and Theory, Advances in Accounting, Journal of Accounting and Public Policy*, and *CA Magazine*. Professor Lemon has coauthored two monographs and has had papers published in *Contemporary Accounting Research, Auditing: A Journal of Practice and Theory, Research on Accounting Ethics, Journal of Accounting, Auditing and Finance, The Chartered Accountant in Australia* and *CA Magazine*. He has had a chapter published in *Research Opportunities in Internal Auditing* and papers published in the following collections: *Educating the Profession of Accountancy in the Twenty-First Century, Comparative International Accounting Education Standards, Comparative* [illegible]*nal Auditing Standards*, and *The Impact of Inflation on* [illegible] *A Global View.*

[illegible] Lemon has received a number of research [illegible] served as the Director of the Centre for Accounting Ethics, School of Accountancy, University of Waterloo. He has written a number of ethics cases published by the Centre.

Catherine I. Seguin, MBA, CGA, teaches accounting at the University of Toronto Mississauga. In addition to her books, *Accounting for Not-for-Profit Organizations* for Carswell (Thomson-Reuters) and *Not-for-Profit Accounting*, published by CGA Canada, she has co-authored a practice book on management accounting for McGraw-Hill Ryerson and revised the 3rd edition of the study guide that accompanies this textbook.

At the University of Toronto Mississauga, Catherine initiated, organized and continues to run an internship course where 4th year Bachelor of Commerce and Bachelor of Business Administration students are given an opportunity to gain business experience to complement their studies. She has also organized, co-hosted, and chaired ongoing workshops inviting all University of Toronto Mississauga instructors teaching first year classes to discuss and learn what pedagogical and organizational issues they face.

In the business community, she has participated in a consultation on the reform of the Canada Corporations Act for not-for-profit organizations. Currently, she serves on several boards of not-for-profit organizations and has been a Professional Development speaker for CGA Ontario on the topic of Not-for-Profit Accounting.

Sandra Robertson Lemon presently is a consultant providing accounting and financial services to owner-managed businesses. A graduate of McGill University, she also obtained a Diploma in Accounting from Wilfrid Laurier University. Her experience provides her with a knowledge of the requirements and responsibilities of external reporting as well as an understanding of the value of accounting in providing relevant and reliable information to management.

Ms. Lemon was a staff accountant for an international public accounting firm. In this capacity, she was involved in the conduct of review engagements and audits of financial statements. Following that, she assumed the position of Chief Financial Officer for a Canadian owner-managed business through its growth phase and subsequent merger with an international company. Her responsibilities as a member of the management team included all the accounting systems and reporting, the tax and legal issues, and the treasury function.

Ms. Lemon was co-author , with Harrison, Horngren, and Lemon of *Financial Accounting* Canadian Third Edition, published by Pearson Canada. She also coauthored the first two Canadian editions of that text

Ms. Lemon has served on the board of a number of community organizations; some of this service included executive responsibility.

Preface

Financial Accounting Helps Students "Nail" the Accounting Cycle!

Financial Accounting helps students "nail" the accounting cycle up front in order to increase success and retention later on. The concepts and mechanics students learn in the critical accounting cycle chapters are used consistently and repetitively—and with clear-cut details and explanations—throughout the remainder of the text, minimizing confusion.

The Fourth Canadian Edition features new coauthor Catherine Seguin of the University of Toronto Mississauga who brings her financial accounting teaching experience to key sections of the book.

Better Coverage of the Accounting Cycle from Start to Finish

Chapter 1 introduces the accounting cycle with a brief financial statement overview, using the financial statements of Gildan Activewear Inc. This first exposure to accounting explores financial statements in depth, familiarizes students with using real business data, and points out basic relationships between the different types of statements. Chapter 1 also includes a discussion of financial accounting reporting standards and how these standards are set. The role of ethics in business and accounting decisions is examined.

Chapter 2 continues the discussion of the accounting cycle by explaining how to analyze and record basic transactions, and builds in repetition to ensure that students understand the fundamentals when they prepare the trial balance.

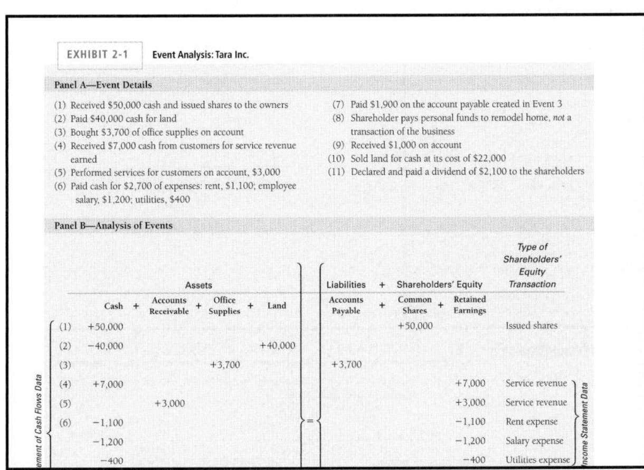

EXHIBIT 2-1 Event Analysis: Tara Inc.

Panel A—Event Details

(1) Received $50,000 cash and issued shares to the owners
(2) Paid $40,000 cash for land
(3) Bought $3,700 of office supplies on account
(4) Received $7,000 cash from customers for service revenue earned
(5) Performed services for customers on account, $3,000
(6) Paid cash for $2,700 of expenses: rent, $1,100; employee salary, $1,200; utilities, $400
(7) Paid $1,900 on the account payable created in Event 3
(8) Shareholder pays personal funds to remodel home, *not* a transaction of the business
(9) Received $1,000 on account
(10) Sold land for cash at its cost of $22,000
(11) Declared and paid a dividend of $2,100 to the shareholders

Panel B—Analysis of Events

	Assets				=	Liabilities +	Shareholders' Equity		Type of Shareholders' Equity Transaction
	Cash +	Accounts Receivable +	Office Supplies +	Land		Accounts Payable +	Common Shares +	Retained Earnings	
(1)	+50,000						+50,000		Issued shares
(2)	−40,000			+40,000					
(3)			+3,700			+3,700			
(4)	+7,000							+7,000	Service revenue
(5)		+3,000						+3,000	Service revenue
(6)	−1,100							−1,100	Rent expense
	−1,200							−1,200	Salary expense
	−400							−400	Utilities expense

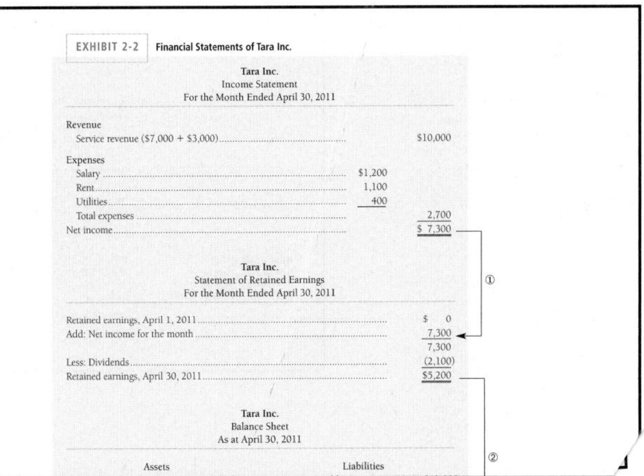

EXHIBIT 2-2 Financial Statements of Tara Inc.

Tara Inc.
Income Statement
For the Month Ended April 30, 2011

Revenue		
Service revenue ($7,000 + $3,000)		$10,000
Expenses		
Salary	$1,200	
Rent	1,100	
Utilities	400	
Total expenses		2,700
Net income		$ 7,300

①

Tara Inc.
Statement of Retained Earnings
For the Month Ended April 30, 2011

Retained earnings, April 1, 2011	$ 0
Add: Net income for the month	7,300
	7,300
Less: Dividends	(2,100)
Retained earnings, April 30, 2011	$5,200

②

Tara Inc.
Balance Sheet
As at April 30, 2011

Assets	Liabilities

Chapter 3 concludes the discussion of the accounting cycle with adjusting and closing entries, and preparation of the related trial balances to close the loop for students.

Consistency, Repetition, and a High Level of Detail

Throughout the text, the core concepts and mechanics are brought together using consistent language, format, and formulas. Students also receive thorough explanations and details that show the meaning behind each concept and how to do the computation following it, providing an in-depth understanding of the fundamentals. Basic procedures and concepts are placed in a business context.

Whether it's the first transaction or the last, students perform the analysis in the same way, thus reinforcing their understanding, reducing the level of confusion and frustration, and helping them capture those "I get it!" moments.

For example, in Chapter 2 students see the impact of transactions and how the transactions are eventually summarized into the income statement, statement of retained earnings, and balance sheet.

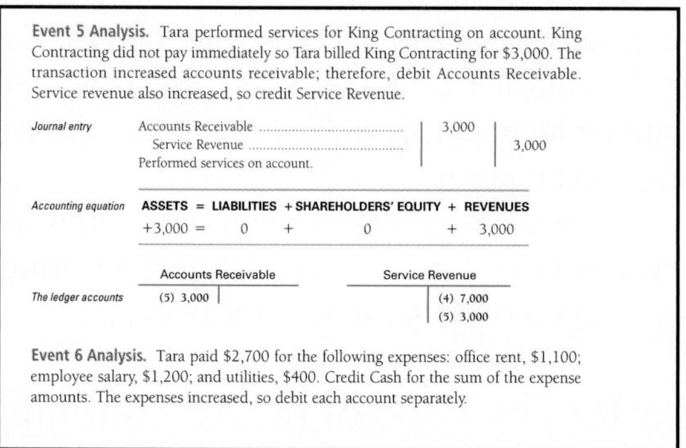

Event 5 Analysis. Tara performed services for King Contracting on account. King Contracting did not pay immediately so Tara billed King Contracting for $3,000. The transaction increased accounts receivable; therefore, debit Accounts Receivable. Service revenue also increased, so credit Service Revenue.

Journal entry

	Debit	Credit
Accounts Receivable	3,000	
Service Revenue		3,000
Performed services on account.		

Accounting equation

ASSETS	=	LIABILITIES	+ SHAREHOLDERS' EQUITY	+	REVENUES
+3,000	=	0	+ 0	+	3,000

The ledger accounts

Accounts Receivable		Service Revenue	
(5) 3,000			(4) 7,000
			(5) 3,000

Event 6 Analysis. Tara paid $2,700 for the following expenses: office rent, $1,100; employee salary, $1,200; and utilities, $400. Credit Cash for the sum of the expense amounts. The expenses increased, so debit each account separately.

A **Mid-Chapter Summary Problem** provides a stopping point for students—it gives them an opportunity to repeat the entire process again, using data from a different company, to make sure they've "got it." **The End-of-Chapter Summary Problem** closes out the chapter and allows students to practise the process again and really "nail" these fundamental skills. By presenting these problems and solutions twice in one chapter, this text breaks up the information, enabling students to absorb and master the material in more manageable pieces.

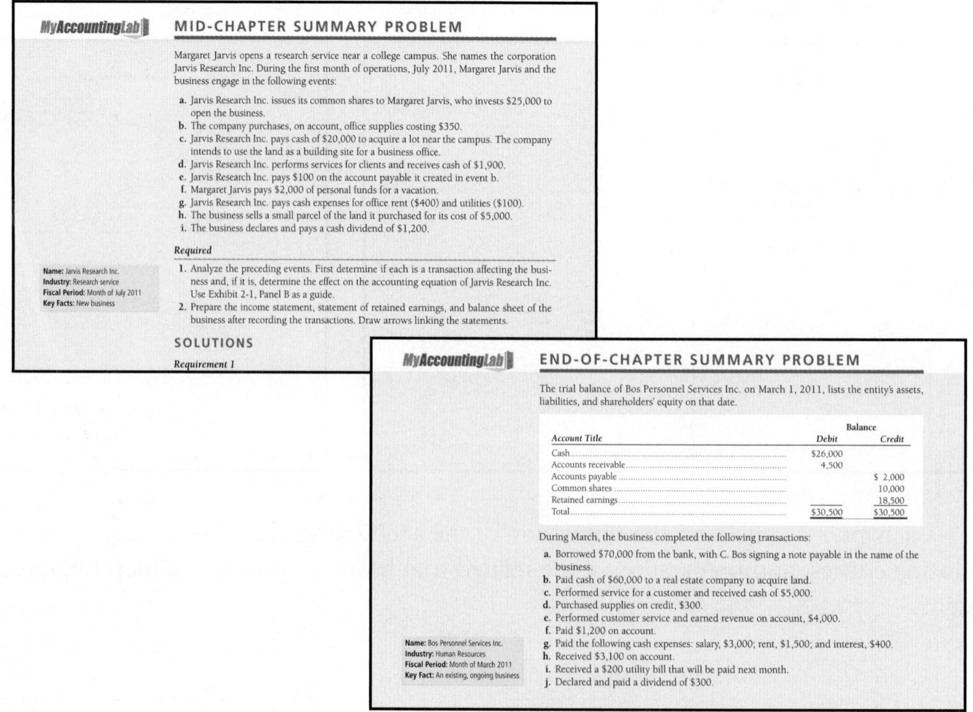

MyAccountingLab

MID-CHAPTER SUMMARY PROBLEM

Margaret Jarvis opens a research service near a college campus. She names the corporation Jarvis Research Inc. During the first month of operations, July 2011, Margaret Jarvis and the business engage in the following events:

a. Jarvis Research Inc. issues its common shares to Margaret Jarvis, who invests $25,000 to open the business.
b. The company purchases, on account, office supplies costing $350.
c. Jarvis Research Inc. pays cash of $20,000 to acquire a lot near the campus. The company intends to use the land as a building site for a business office.
d. Jarvis Research Inc. performs services for clients and receives cash of $1,900.
e. Jarvis Research Inc. pays $100 on the account payable it created in event b.
f. Margaret Jarvis pays $2,000 of personal funds for a vacation.
g. Jarvis Research Inc. pays cash expenses for office rent ($400) and utilities ($100).
h. The business sells a small parcel of the land it purchased for its cost of $5,000.
i. The business declares and pays a cash dividend of $1,200.

Required

1. Analyze the preceding events. First determine if each is a transaction affecting the business and, if it is, determine the effect on the accounting equation of Jarvis Research Inc. Use Exhibit 2-1, Panel B as a guide.
2. Prepare the income statement, statement of retained earnings, and balance sheet of the business after recording the transactions. Draw arrows linking the statements.

Name: Jarvis Research Inc.
Industry: Research service
Fiscal Period: Month of July 2011
Key Facts: New business

SOLUTIONS

Requirement 1

MyAccountingLab

END-OF-CHAPTER SUMMARY PROBLEM

The trial balance of Bos Personnel Services Inc. on March 1, 2011, lists the entity's assets, liabilities, and shareholders' equity on that date.

Account Title	Balance *Debit*	Balance *Credit*
Cash	$26,000	
Accounts receivable	4,500	
Accounts payable		$ 2,000
Common shares		10,000
Retained earnings		18,500
Total	$30,500	$30,500

During March, the business completed the following transactions:

a. Borrowed $70,000 from the bank, with C. Bos signing a note payable in the name of the business.
b. Paid cash of $60,000 to a real estate company to acquire land.
c. Performed service for a customer and received cash of $5,000.
d. Purchased supplies on credit, $300.
e. Performed customer service and earned revenue on account, $4,000.
f. Paid $1,200 on account.
g. Paid the following cash expenses: salary, $3,000; rent, $1,500; and interest, $400.
h. Received $3,100 on account.
i. Received a $200 utility bill that will be paid next month.
j. Declared and paid a dividend of $300.

Name: Bos Personnel Services Inc.
Industry: Human Resources
Fiscal Period: Month of March 2011
Key Fact: An existing, ongoing business

New to the Fourth Canadian Edition

New Financial Reporting Standards

Canadian accounting standards have undergone and will continue to undergo significant changes in the next few years. Publicly accountable enterprises (public companies) in Canada must issue financial statements based on **International Financial Reporting Standards** (IFRS) after January 1, 2011. Private enterprises (private companies) in Canada must issue financial statements based on **Accounting Standards for Private Enterprises** (ASPE) after January 1, 2011. To ensure that students are learning the most current information and are ready for the new standards they will encounter, we have based the discussion of accounting in the text on IFRS. We have also included key references and explanations of ASPE where the requirements under ASPE differ from IFRS.

When students practise or complete their homework in **MyAccountingLab**, they will be working on questions based on IFRS that are designed to be a companion for the IFRS text coverage.

New User and Preparer Features

We recognize that students take a financial accounting course for a number of reasons. Some will go on to higher level accounting courses, while others will use the fundamental accounting concepts they've learned in financial accounting as they pursue other business fields. In the Fourth Canadian Edition of *Financial Accounting*, we have taken care to highlight accounting concepts from both the user and preparer perspectives to ensure that students understand the value of accounting regardless of the path they take after the course.

Using Accounting in Decision Making Boxes

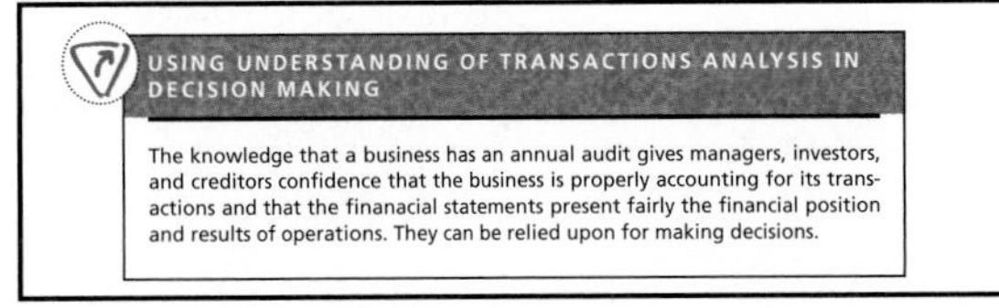
USING UNDERSTANDING OF TRANSACTIONS ANALYSIS IN DECISION MAKING

The knowledge that a business has an annual audit gives managers, investors, and creditors confidence that the business is properly accounting for its transactions and that the finanacial statements present fairly the financial position and results of operations. They can be relied upon for making decisions.

Throughout the text, we have included new 'Using Accounting' boxes that demonstrate how specific concepts such as accounting transactions apply to decision-makers such as managers, investors, and creditors. For example, the new Using Understanding of Transactions Analysis in Decision Making box on page 85 explains that when managers, investors, and creditors know a business has an annual audit, this knowledge gives them confidence that the business is properly accounting for its transactions and that the financial statements can therefore be relied upon.

Accounting for... Boxes

Complimenting our user-focused boxes are new preparer-oriented boxes that highlight how key accounting concepts relate to the individuals responsible for preparing accounting information. For example, in our new Accounting for Transactions Part 2 box on page 83, we discuss how accountants must follow the *rules of debit and credit* when recording transactions in the journal.

These new boxes show how the key terms, concepts, and formulas introduced in the text are used in the context of business decisions by both users and preparers.

ACCOUNTING FOR TRANSACTIONS PART 2

I. The accountant must decide where and how to record the transaction.

The transaction is recorded in the journal, which is the chronological record of transactions.

The transaction in the *journal* must include a debit and a credit and follow the *rules of debit and credit:*

	Increase	Decrease
Asset	Debit	Credit
Liability	Credit	Debit
Shareholders' equity	Credit	Debit
Revenue	Credit	Debit
Expense	Debit	Credit

II. The accountant must decide where to store the account information in the journal.

The account information is recorded in the respective accounts in the ledger.

New and Updated Content on Ethics

Sound ethical judgment is important for every major financial decision—which is why this text provides consistent ethical reinforcement. A new decision-making model is introduced in Chapter 1 and integrated throughout the text.

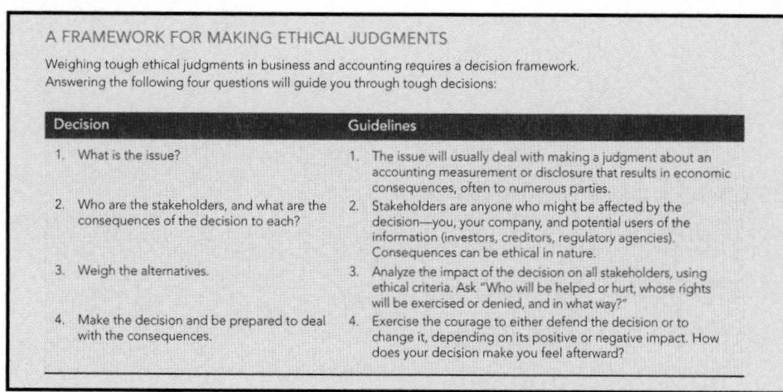

A FRAMEWORK FOR MAKING ETHICAL JUDGMENTS

Weighing tough ethical judgments in business and accounting requires a decision framework. Answering the following four questions will guide you through tough decisions:

Decision	Guidelines
1. What is the issue?	1. The issue will usually deal with making a judgment about an accounting measurement or disclosure that results in economic consequences, often to numerous parties.
2. Who are the stakeholders, and what are the consequences of the decision to each?	2. Stakeholders are anyone who might be affected by the decision—you, your company, and potential users of the information (investors, creditors, regulatory agencies). Consequences can be ethical in nature.
3. Weigh the alternatives.	3. Analyze the impact of the decision on all stakeholders, using ethical criteria. Ask "Who will be helped or hurt, whose rights will be exercised or denied, and in what way?"
4. Make the decision and be prepared to deal with the consequences.	4. Exercise the courage to either defend the decision or to change it, depending on its positive or negative impact. How does your decision make you feel afterward?

New End-of-Chapter Summaries

Each chapter concludes with a chapter summary that is keyed to the Learning Objectives of the chapter. The summary highlights the major topics discussed in the chapter. The student will have the opportunity to review the concepts presented in a clear, concise way. Terms introduced and discussed in the chapter are highlighted for quick cross-reference.

SUMMARY OF CHAPTER 1

Learning Objective ❶: Learn that financial statements are the product of accounting

Accounting is an information system that measures business activities, processes data into reports, and communicates results to decision makers. These **decision makers or users** include investors and creditors (primary users), managers, government and regulatory agencies, taxing authorities, and individuals.

A business can be **organized** as a **proprietorship**, a **partnership**, or a **public** or **private corporation.** A public corporation's shares are traded on a stock exchange while a private corporation's shares are privately held.

Learning Objective ❷: Apply the accounting equation to business organizations

The financial statements are based on the **accounting equation** whereby a**ssets equal liabilities and owners' equity**. **Assets** are the resources of the business and include cash, accounts receivable, inventory, and property, plant, and equipment.

Enhanced Coverage of Cash Flows

The current economy has created a shift in how we view money—specifically, cash. Cash flow is the lifeblood of any business, so in the Fourth Canadian Edition of *Financial Accounting*, coverage of cash flows has been increased and highlighted in selected chapters so that students can easily see the connections and understand the significance.

Reporting Property, Plant, and Equipment Transactions on the Statement of Cash Flows

OBJECTIVE

❻ **Report** long-lived assets on the statement of cash flows

Three main types of capital asset transactions appear on the statement of cash flows:

- Acquisitions
- Sales
- Depreciation, and amortization

Acquisitions and sales of property, plant, and equipment are *investing* activities. A company invests in property, plant, and equipment by paying cash or incurring a liability. The cash payments for buildings and equipment are investing activities that appear on the statement of cash flows. The sale of property, plant, and equipment results in a cash receipt, as illustrated in Exhibit 7-9, which excerpts data from the

New Fraud Coverage

In an age of public scandals, understanding fraud is a key component of Financial Accounting. Chapter 4 now includes the concept of fraud, and introduces students to the "fraud triangle" (motivation, opportunity, and rationalization) and a discussion of internal controls as the primary way companies prevent fraud.

Examples of real fraud cases have been included in relevant sections throughout the text, giving students real-life business context. Examples include the following:

ETHICS ALERT!

Is That Cost Really an Asset?

There is a world of difference between a capital expenditure and an expense. Just ask MCI. MCI WorldCom (now just MCI) got into hot water by missing the mark in its accounting for capital expenditures.

A few years ago—before cellular phones became so popular—long-distance (LD) phone service was extremely profitable for Sprint and MCI. These companies invested huge amounts on LD phone networks. MCI was one of the hottest stocks on Wall Street.

Almost overnight, cellular companies Cingular and Verizon began to siphon profits away from MCI. Profits grew thin and then turned to losses. MCI needed to protect its pacesetter image. But how?

- Livent (Chapter 4)
- Datapoint and MiniScribe (Chapter 6)
- WorldCom (MCI) (Chapters 7 and 13)
- Bristol-Myers Squibb (Chapter 11)

Features

Learning Objectives are listed on the first page of each chapter. This "roadmap" shows you what will be covered and what is especially important. Each learning objective is repeated in the side margin where the material is first covered in the chapter.

Chapter-Opening Vignettes immerse you in the real world of accounting, where business decisions affect the future of actual organizations. These stories show why the chapter topics are important to real companies. Some of the companies you'll read about include Canadian companies such as RIM, Canadian Tire, Leon's Furniture, and WestJet.

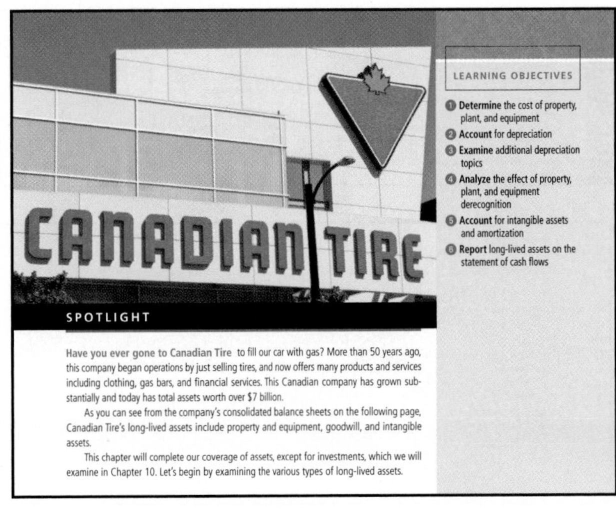

Objectives in the margins signal the beginning of the section that covers the learning objective topic. Look for this feature when you are studying and want to review a particular topic.

> **Measuring the Cost of Property, Plant, and Equipment**
>
> Here is a basic working rule for determining the cost of an asset:
>
> *The cost of any asset is the sum of all the costs incurred to bring the asset to its location and intended use.* The cost of property, plant, and equipment includes its purchase price (less any purchase discounts), plus any taxes, commissions, and other amounts paid to make the asset ready for use. Because the specific costs differ for the various categories of property, plant, and equipment, we discuss the major groups individually.
>
> OBJECTIVE
> 1 **Determine** the cost of property, plant, and equipment

Accounting Vocabulary key terms are highlighted in boldface within the text and their full definitions are given at the end of each chapter. These terms are collected in the glossary at the end of the text.

MyAccountingLab icons in the first three chapters direct readers to an online **Accounting Cycle Tutorial** that can be found through the MyAccountingLab site at **www.myaccountinglab.com**. These icons appear whenever a topic is covered in a tutorial or application. When readers enter the tutorial, they'll find three buttons on the opening page of each module: Tutorial provides a review of the major concepts, Application provides practice exercises, and Glossary reviews important terms.

> MyAccountingLab
> Accounting Cycle Tutorial
> Income Statement Accounts and Transactions Tutorial
>
> • A debit decreases a liability or a shareholders' equity account.
>
> Dividends and Expenses accounts are exceptions to the rule. Dividends and Expenses are equity accounts that are increased by a debit. Dividends and Expenses accounts are negative (or *contra*) equity accounts.
>
> Revenues and Expenses are often treated as separate account categories because they appear on the income statement. Exhibit 2-7 shows Revenues and Expenses below the other equity accounts.

Mid-Chapter and **End-of-Chapter Summary Problems** give you the opportunity to pause and assess your understanding of chapter concepts at two locations within each chapter—midway and at the end of the chapter. Full solutions appear with the problems for immediate feedback. Each problem has been enhanced with annotations to guide you through the thought processes involved in each step.

> MyAccountingLab
>
> **END-OF-CHAPTER SUMMARY PROBLEM**
>
> *Problem 1*
>
> The figures that follow appear in the *Answers to the Mid-Chapter Summary Problem*, Requirement 2, on page 350, for Canadian Tire.

	Method A: Straight-Line			Method B: Double-Diminishing-Balance		
Year	Annual Depreciation Expense	Accumulated Depreciation	Carrying amount	Annual Depreciation Expense	Accumulated Depreciation	Carrying Amount
Start			$44,000			$44,000
2010	$4,000	$ 4,000	40,000	$8,800	$ 8,800	35,200
2011	4,000	8,000	36,000	7,040	15,840	28,160
2012	4,000	12,000	32,000	5,632	21,472	22,528

> **Name:** Canadian Tire
> **Industry:** Retailer
> **Accounting Period:** The years 2010, 2011, 2012
>
> *Required*
>
> Suppose the income tax authorities permitted a choice between these two depreciation methods. Which method would Canadian Tire select for income tax purposes? Why?
>
> *Problem 2*
>
> Suppose Canadian Tire purchased the equipment described in the table on January 1, 2007.

Each of the summary problems can also be found on the MyAccountingLab that accompanies the text. MyAccountingLab provides students with the opportunity to practise these problems over and over with new values and data until they've mastered the underlying concepts.

Review the Chapter with These Features

Quick Check provides multiple-choice questions with answers included for quick self-assessment.

> **Review the Statement of Cash Flows**
>
> **Quick Check** (Answers are given on page 637.)
>
> 1. All the following activities are reported on the statement of cash flows, except
>   a. Operating activities c. Financing activities
>   b. Investing activities d. Marketing activities
> 2. Activities that create long-term liabilities are usually
>   a. Operating activities c. Financing activities
>   b. Investing activities d. Noncash investing and financing activities
> 3. Activities affecting long-term assets are
>   a. Operating activities c. Financing activities
>   b. Investing activities d. Marketing activities

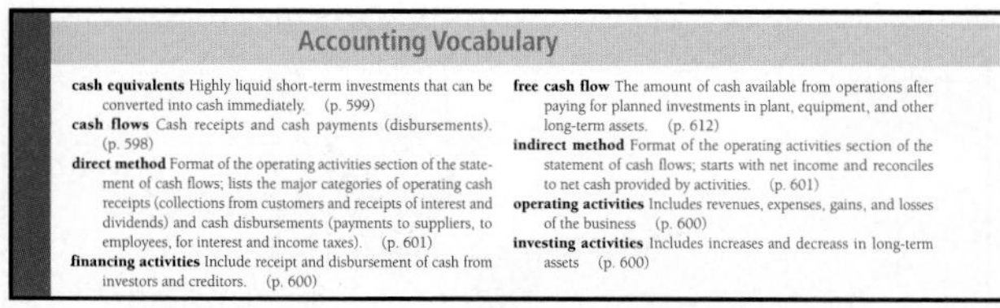

Accounting Vocabulary

cash equivalents Highly liquid short-term investments that can be converted into cash immediately. (p. 599)
cash flows Cash receipts and cash payments (disbursements). (p. 598)
direct method Format of the operating activities section of the statement of cash flows; lists the major categories of operating cash receipts (collections from customers and receipts of interest and dividends) and cash disbursements (payments to suppliers, to employees, for interest and income taxes). (p. 601)
financing activities Include receipt and disbursement of cash from investors and creditors. (p. 600)
free cash flow The amount of cash available from operations after paying for planned investments in plant, equipment, and other long-term assets. (p. 612)
indirect method Format of the operating activities section of the statement of cash flows; starts with net income and reconciles to net cash provided by activities. (p. 601)
operating activities Includes revenues, expenses, gains, and losses of the business (p. 600)
investing activities Includes increases and decreass in long-term assets (p. 600)

Accounting Vocabulary lists and defines the special accounting terms introduced in boldface in the text. Page numbers are given for your reference. These terms are also defined in the Glossary at the end of the book.

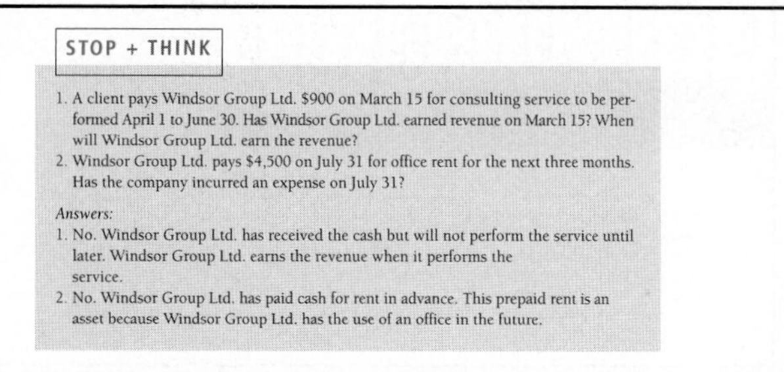

STOP + THINK

1. A client pays Windsor Group Ltd. $900 on March 15 for consulting service to be performed April 1 to June 30. Has Windsor Group Ltd. earned revenue on March 15? When will Windsor Group Ltd. earn the revenue?
2. Windsor Group Ltd. pays $4,500 on July 31 for office rent for the next three months. Has the company incurred an expense on July 31?

Answers:

1. No. Windsor Group Ltd. has received the cash but will not perform the service until later. Windsor Group Ltd. earns the revenue when it performs the service.
2. No. Windsor Group Ltd. has paid cash for rent in advance. This prepaid rent is an asset because Windsor Group Ltd. has the use of an office in the future.

Stop & Think sections relate concepts to everyday life so that students can see the immediate relevance.

Assess Your Progress with These Features

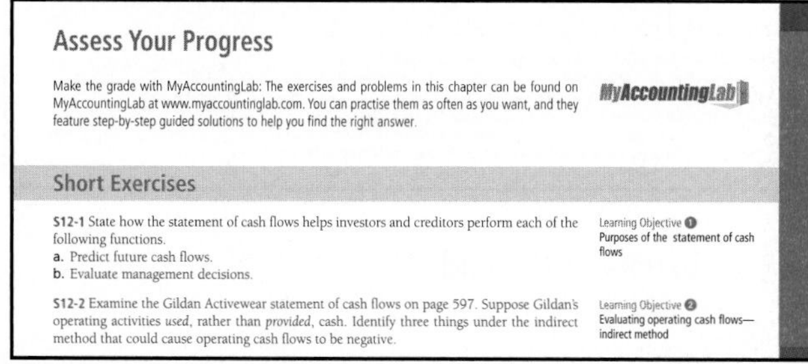

Assess Your Progress

Make the grade with MyAccountingLab: The exercises and problems in this chapter can be found on MyAccountingLab at www.myaccountinglab.com. You can practise them as often as you want, and they feature step-by-step guided solutions to help you find the right answer.

Short Exercises

S12-1 State how the statement of cash flows helps investors and creditors perform each of the following functions.
a. Predict future cash flows.
b. Evaluate management decisions.

Learning Objective 1
Purposes of the statement of cash flows

S12-2 Examine the Gildan Activewear statement of cash flows on page 597. Suppose Gildan's operating activities *used*, rather than *provided*, cash. Identify three things under the indirect method that could cause operating cash flows to be negative.

Learning Objective 2
Evaluating operating cash flows—indirect method

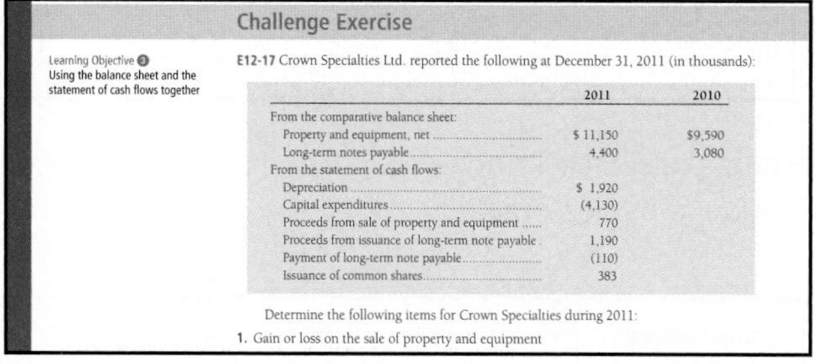

Challenge Exercise

Learning Objective 3
Using the balance sheet and the statement of cash flows together

E12-17 Crown Specialties Ltd. reported the following at December 31, 2011 (in thousands):

	2011	2010
From the comparative balance sheet:		
Property and equipment, net	$ 11,150	$9,590
Long-term notes payable	4,400	3,080
From the statement of cash flows:		
Depreciation	$ 1,920	
Capital expenditures	(4,130)	
Proceeds from sale of property and equipment	770	
Proceeds from issuance of long-term note payable	1,190	
Payment of long-term note payable	(110)	
Issuance of common shares	383	

Determine the following items for Crown Specialties during 2011:

1. Gain or loss on the sale of property and equipment

NEW Each of the exercises and problems can be found at **www.myaccountinglab.com**. Students can practise them as often as they want, and they feature step-by-step guided solutions to help them find the right answer.

Short Exercises are single-concept exercises designed to serve as warm-ups for homework assignments. The topic of the short exercise and the learning objectives covered are given in the margin.

Exercises on a single or a small number of topics require you to "do the accounting." The topic of the exercise and the learning objectives covered are given in the margin. The pencil icon in the margin indicates a writing exercise or problem.

NEW Some chapters also include **Serial Exercises** that involve an accounting cycle that spans several chapters.

Challenge Exercises provide a challenge for those students who have mastered the Exercises.

A multiple-choice **Quiz** follows the exercises in each chapter. This quiz asks students to think back to some of the key concepts from the chapter before moving on to solve some more complicated problems.

Problems are presented in two groups that mirror each other, "A" and "B." Many instructors work through problems from Group A in class to demonstrate accounting concepts, then assign problems from Group B for homework or extra practice. The topic of the problem and the learning objectives covered are provided in the margin.

Apply Your Knowledge with These Features

Decision Cases put you in business situations where you need to apply your accounting knowledge to make recommendations.

Ethical Issues are thought-provoking situations that help you recognize when ethics should affect an accounting decision.

Focus on Financials and **Focus on Analysis** cases give readers the opportunity to explore sections of the Gildan Annual Report, which is included as an Appendix at the back of the book. As students work with Gildan throughout the course, they will develop the ability to analyze actual financial statements.

Group Projects at the end of each chapter provide both in-class and homework assignments that require collaboration and cooperation among students.

Group Project

Select a company and research its business. Search the business press for articles about this company. Obtain its annual report by requesting it directly from the company or from the company's Web site.

Required

1. Based on your group's analysis, come to class prepared to instruct the class on six interesting facts about the company that can be found in its financial statements and the related notes. Your group can mention only the obvious, such as net sales or total revenue, net income, total assets, total liabilities, total shareholders' equity, and dividends, in conjunction with other terms. Once you use an obvious item, you may not use that item again.
2. The group should write a paper discussing the facts that it has uncovered. Limit the paper to two double-spaced word-processed pages.

Quick Check Answers

1. *b*

Changes to the Fourth Canadian Edition

Students and instructors will benefit from a variety of new content and features in the Fourth Canadian Edition of *Financial Accounting*. To reflect the most recent developments in the economy and in the accounting industry, the following content additions or changes have been made:

The first chapter has been rewritten to introduce the new **Joint Conceptual Framework for Accounting** from the Financial Accounting Standards Board (FASB) and the International Accounting Standards Board (IASB).

In order to ensure students are introduced to current accounting standards, International Financial Reporting Standards (IFRS), which are required for Canadian public companies for their financial statements for years beginning January 1, 2011, are discussed throughout the Fourth Canadian Edition. In addition, current accounting standards and Accounting Standards for Private Enterprises (ASPE) for private Canadian companies are discussed when there are key differences between ASPE and IFRS.

The Accounting Standards Board has been converging Canadian accounting standards with IFRS for several years and some Canadian companies have early adopted the new standards. (See the Gildan Activewear Inc. Annual Report in Appendix A).

With the recent changes and events in the economy, educating students on the importance of **ethics and ethical decision making** is critical. The discussion of ethics in accounting has been updated and moved to Chapter 1, placing greater emphasis on the importance of ethics at the very beginning of the text. The Fourth Canadian Edition also introduces an expanded decision-making model in Chapter 1 and integrates the model where appropriate throughout the text with economic, legal, and ethical dimensions. The Ethical Cases in the end-of-chapter material have been rewritten to unify and better integrate coverage on this important topic so that the material is reinforced consistently in every chapter.

In an age of public scandals, understanding **fraud** is a key component of financial accounting. Chapter 4 now includes the concept of fraud, and introduces students to the "fraud triangle" (motivation, opportunity, and rationalization) that leads to the discussion of internal controls as the primary way that companies prevent fraud—which has also been updated. The discussion of fraud in Chapter 4 also lays the foundation for the new ethical material, which adds real-life relevance and interest to otherwise dry accounting concepts by presenting real-world fraud cases, including Livent (Chapter 4), Datapoint and MiniScribe (Chapter 6), WorldCom (MCI) (Chapters 7 and 13), and Bristol-Myers Squibb (Chapter 11).

To help students understand accounting topics that are currently impacting **the global economy**, Chapter 11 includes a new discussion on quality of earnings, revenue recognition, and fraud. The quality of earnings section focuses on evaluating a company's financial position to help in decision making, which students will need when they enter the workforce. There is also an expanded discussion on the elements of the income statement and revenue recognition. The revenue recognition and other comprehensive income sections are key points, and are critical to understanding the new Canadian accounting standards.

To keep examples and data current and accurate, all **financial statements** for the companies covered have been updated. All real company financial data now refers to 2009 or 2010.

The **focus company is new** (Gildan Activewear Inc.) so that students see examples of statements and accounting practices that are as current as possible. As a result, the annual report in the book's appendices is new, and all the Focus on Financials and Focus on Analysis questions in the end-of-chapter material have been updated throughout the text.

Understanding cash flows is a critical concept for students in today's economy, which is why there is a new and increased emphasis on the use of cash flow information in selected chapters. By highlighting this coverage in selected chapters, this edition helps students make the connection between cash and other accounting concepts so they understand the significance of cash flow as the lifeblood of a business.

Every chapter of the Fourth Canadian Edition has a summary at the end of the chapter keyed to the Learning Objectives of the chapter.

To provide students with more opportunities to practise important concepts, and to provide instructors with additional choices of material to assign, all of the **end-of-chapter content** has been updated.

- Every end-of-chapter question in the Assess Your Progress sections is now available in **MyAccountingLab** for students to complete and receive immediate tutorial feedback and help when they need it.
- IFRS terminology and accounting requirements have been incorporated in the end-of-chapter questions.

Student Resources

MyAccountingLab

MyAccountingLab is a powerful online learning tool that not only provides opportunities for limitless practice, but recreates the "I get it" moments from the classroom. MyAccountingLab provides a rich suite of learning tools including

- Static and algorithmic versions of exercises and problems from the textbook
- An online, interactive Accounting Cycle Tutorial
- Mini-Cases
- Help Me Solve It question-specific interactive coaching
- A dynamic ebook with links to a multimedia library
- Excel application problems
- Access to StudyLife, a social networking site designed to help students find their ideal study partner
- Multiple Pathways to Learning Assessments to help students discover their personal learning style

Instructor Supplements

Instructor's Resource CD-ROM: This resource CD includes the following instructor supplements:

- **Instructor's Solutions Manual:** This manual contains full solutions for all end-of-chapter material.
- **Instructor's Resource Manual:** This manual contains valuable resources including chapter outlines, teaching tips, and assignment grids.
- **Pearson TestGen:** Over 1500 test questions, including multiple-choice, true/false, and essay questions, are provided in TestGen format. TestGen is a testing software that enables instructors to view and edit the existing questions, add questions, generate tests, and distribute the tests in a variety of formats. Powerful search and sort functions make it easy to locate questions and arrange them in any order desired. TestGen also enables instructors to administer tests on a local area network, have the tests graded electronically, and have the results prepared in electronic or printed reports. TestGen is compatible with Windows and Macintosh operating systems, and can be downloaded from the TestGen website located at www.pearsoned.com/testgen. Contact your local sales representative for details and access.
- **PowerPoints:** PowerPoint presentations offer an outline of the key points for each chapter.
- **Personal Response System**: These multiple-choice questions are created in PowerPoint for use in Personal Response Systems. Also known as "clickers," these systems allow instructors to poll students in class and to display aggregated results of answers.

These instructor supplements are also available for download from a password-protected section of Pearson Canada's online catalogue (vig.pearsoned.ca). Navigate to your book's catalogue page to view a list of those supplements that are available. See your local sales representative for details and access.

Pearson Advantage: For qualified adopters, Pearson Education is proud to introduce the **Pearson Advantage**. The Pearson Advantage is the first integrated Canadian service program committed to meeting the customization, training, and support needs for your course. Our commitments are made in writing and in consultation with faculty. Your local Pearson Education sales representative can provide you with more details on this service program.

Innovative Solutions Team: Pearson's Innovative Solutions Team works with faculty and campus course designers to ensure that Pearson technology products, assessment tools, and online course materials are tailored to meet your specific needs. This highly qualified team is dedicated to helping schools take full advantage of a wide range of educational technology, by assisting in the integration of a variety of instructional materials and media formats.

Acknowledgments

Thanks are extended to Gildan Activewear Inc. for permission to include portions of their annual report in Appendix A and Canadian Tire Corporation, Limited for allowing us to include their annual report on MyAccountingLab. Appreciation is also expressed to the following individuals and organizations:

Canadian Institute of Chartered Accountants
Shikha Gandhi, CA, Deloitte
Gord Fowler, FCA, CICA
KPMG LLP
Deloitte LLP
Professor Stan Laiken, University of Waterloo
Professor Irene Weicek, University of Toronto
SEDAR (see acknowledgement from previous edition
The Globe and Mail
The annual reports of a number of Canadian companies
Professors Tom Harrison, Charles Horngren, and Bill Thomas

Particular thanks are also due to the following instructors for reviewing the manuscript for the Fourth Canadian Edition and offering many useful suggestions:

David J McConomy, *Queen's University*
Robert G. Ducharme, *University of Waterloo*
Clifton Philpott, *Kwantlen Polytechnic University*
Scott Laing, *Dalhousie University*
Greg Berberich, *Wilfrid Laurier University*
Catherine Fortin, *McGill University*
Meredith Delaney, *Seneca College*
Ann Clarke-Okah, *Carlton University*
Hilary Becker, *Carlton University*
Eloisa T. Perez, *Grant MacEwan University*
Betty Wong, *Athabasca University*
Majidul Islam, *Concordia University*
Patricia Zima, *Mohawk College*

The authors acknowledge with gratitude the professional support received from Pearson Canada. In particular we thank Nicole Lukach, Editor in Chief, Business and Economics; Victoria Naik, Senior Developmental Editor; Jennifer Parks; Media Content Developer; Jordanna Caplan, Media Content Editor; Cheryl Jackson and Imee Salumbides, Project Managers; Leanne Rancourt, Production Editor; Lu Cormier, Copy Editor; and Cas Shields, Executive Marketing Manager.

Prologue

Accounting Careers: Much More Than Counting Things

What kind of career can you have in accounting? Almost any kind you want. A career in accounting lets you use your analytical skills in a variety of ways, and it brings both monetary and personal rewards. According to the *Jobs Rated Almanac*, "accountant" was the fifth best job in terms of low stress, high compensation, lots of autonomy, and tremendous hiring demand.[1]

Accounting as an art is widely believed to have been invented by Fra Luca Bartolomeo de Pacioli, an Italian mathematician and Franciscan friar in the 16th century. Pacioli was a close friend of Leonardo da Vinci, and collaborated with him on many projects.

Accounting as the profession we know today has its roots in the Industrial Revolution during the 18th and 19th centuries, mostly in England. However, accounting did not attain the stature of other professions such as law, medicine, or engineering until early in the 20th century. Professions are distinguished from trades by the following characteristics: (1) a unifying body of technical literature; (2) standards of competence; (3) codes of professional conduct; and (4) dedication to service to the public.

Today's accountants obtain years of formal education at the university level which, for most, culminates in a very rigorous professional qualification process that qualifies them to hold the designation *chartered accountant* (CA), *certified management accountant* (CMA), or *certified general accountant* (CGA). There are other professional designations that accountants may obtain as well, each with its own professional exam and set of professional standards. Examples are *certified internal auditor* (CIA) and *certified fraud examiner* (CFE).

Where Accountants Work

Where can you work as an accountant? There are four kinds of employers.

Public Practice

You can work for a public accounting (PA) firm, which could be a large international firm or a variety of medium to small-sized firms. Within the PA firm, you can specialize in areas such as audit, tax, or consulting. In this capacity, you'll be serving as an external accountant to many different clients. At present, the largest six international firms are Deloitte, Ernst & Young, KPMG, PricewaterhouseCoopers, Grant Thornton, and BDO Dunwoody. However, there are many other firms with international and national scope of practice. Many PAs start their career at a large PA firm. From there, they move on to obtain positions of leadership in the corporate finance world, industry, or just about anywhere there is a demand for persons who like solving complex problems.

Managerial Accounting

Instead of working for a wide variety of clients, you can work within one corporation or not-for-profit enterprise. Your role may be to analyze financial information and communicate that information to managers, who use it to plot strategy and make decisions. You may be called upon to help allocate corporate resources or improve financial performance. For example, you might do a cost-benefit analysis to help decide whether to acquire a company or build a factory. Or you might describe the financial implications of choosing one strategy over another. You might work in areas such as internal auditing, financial management, financial reporting, treasury management, and tax planning. The highest position in management accounting is the chief financial officer (CFO) position, with some CFOs rising to become chief executive officers (CEOs).

Government and Not-for-Profit Entities

As an accountant, you might work for the government—federal, provincial, or local. Like your counterparts in public accounting and business, your role as a government accountant includes responsibilities in the areas of auditing, financial reporting, and management accounting. You'll evaluate how government agencies are being managed. You may advise decision makers on how to allocate resources to promote efficiency. The RCMP hires CAs, CMAs, and CGAs to investigate the financial aspects of white-collar crime. You might find yourself working for the Canadian Revenue Agency, one of the provincial securities commissions, or a federal or provincial government department.

The Auditor General of Canada is appointed by the federal government, while the provincial auditors general are appointed by the provincial government. "The Office of the Auditor General of Canada is an independent and reliable source of the objective, fact-based information that Parliament needs to fulfill one of its most important roles: holding the federal government accountable for its stewardship of public funds. The Office audits departments and agencies, most Crown corporations, and many other federal organizations; it is also the auditor for the governments of Nunavut, the Yukon, and the Northwest Territories."[2]

As an accountant, you might also decide to work in the not-for-profit sector. Colleges, universities, public and private primary and secondary schools, hospitals, and charitable organizations such as churches and the United Way all have accounting functions. Accountants for these types of entities prepare financial statements as well as budgets and projections. Most have special training in accounting standards specially designed for work in the not-for-profit sector.

Education

Finally, you can work at a college or university, advancing the thought and theory of accounting and teaching future generations of new accountants. On the research side of education, you might study how companies use accounting information. You might develop new ways of categorizing financial data, or study accounting practices in different countries. You then publish your ideas in journals and books and present them to colleagues at meetings around the world. On the education side, you can help others learn about accounting and give them the tools they need to be their best.

CA, CMA, CGA: Letters That Speak Volumes

When employers see the CA, CMA, or CGA designation, they know what to expect about your education, knowledge, abilities, and personal attributes. They value your analytic skills and extensive training. Your CA, CMA, or CGA credential gives you a distinct advantage in the job market and instant credibility and respect in the workplace. It's a plus when dealing with other professionals such as bankers, lawyers, auditors, and federal regulators. In addition, your colleagues in private industry tend to defer to you when dealing with complex business matters, particularly those involving financial management.

The Hottest Growth Areas in Accounting

Recent legislation, such as the Sarbanes-Oxley Act of 2002, has brought rising demand for accountants of all kinds. In addition to strong overall demand, certain areas of accounting are especially hot.

Sustainability Reporting

Sustainability reporting involves reporting on an organization's performance with respect to health, safety, and environmental (HSE) issues. As businesses take a greater interest in environmental issues, PAs are getting involved in reporting on such matters as employee health, on-the-job accident rates, emissions of certain pollutants, spills, volumes of waste generated, and initiatives to reduce and minimize such incidents and releases. Utilities, manufacturers, and chemical companies are particularly affected by environmental issues. As a result, they turn to PAs to set up a preventive system to ensure compliance and avoid future claims or disputes or to provide assistance once legal implications have arisen.

Corporate social responsibility (CSR) reporting is similar to HSE reporting but with a broadened emphasis on social matters such as ethical labour practices, training, education, and diversity of workforce and corporate philanthropic initiatives. Most of the world's largest corporations have extensive CSR initiatives.

Assurance Services

Assurance services are services provided by a PA that improve the quality of information, or its context, for decision makers. Such information can be financial or nonfinancial, and it can be about past events or about ongoing processes or systems. This broad concept includes audit and attestation services and is distinct from consulting because it focuses primarily on improving information rather than on providing advice or installing systems. You can use your analytical and information-processing expertise by providing assurance services in areas ranging from electronic commerce to elder care, comprehensive risk assessment, business valuations, entity performance measurement, and information systems quality assessment.

Information Technology Services

Companies can't compete effectively if their information technology systems don't have the power or flexibility to perform essential functions. Companies need accountants with strong computer skills who can design and implement advanced systems to fit a company's specific needs and to find ways to protect and insulate data. PAs skilled in software research and development (including multimedia technology) are also highly valued.

International Accounting

Globalization means that cross-border transactions are becoming commonplace. Countries in Eastern Europe and Latin America, which previously had closed economies, are opening up and doing business with new trading partners. The passage of the North American Free Trade Agreement (NAFTA) and the General Agreement on Tariffs and Trade (GATT) facilitates trade, and the economic growth in areas such as the Pacific Rim further brings greater volumes of trade and financial flows. Organizations need accountants who understand international trade rules, accords, and laws; cross-border merger and acquisition issues; and foreign business customs, languages, cultures, and procedures.

Forensic Accounting

Forensic accounting is in growing demand after scandals such as the collapse of Enron and WorldCom, which are featured in this text. Forensic accountants look at a company's financial records for evidence of criminal activity. This could be anything from securities fraud to overvaluation of inventory to money laundering and improper capitalization of expenses.

Whether you seek a career in business, government, the not-for-profit sector, or a charity, **accounting** has a career for you. Every organization, from the smallest mom-and-pop music retailer to the biggest government in the world, needs accountants to help manage its resources. Global trade demands accountability, and evermore complex tax laws mean an ever-increasing need for the skills and services of accountants.

Endnotes

[1]Alba, Jason, and Manisha Bathija. *Vault Career Guide to Accounting*. (New York: Vault, 2002).
[2]http://www.oag-bvg.gc.ca/internet/English/admin_e_41.html

The Financial Statements

LEARNING OBJECTIVES

1. **Learn** that financial statements are the product of accounting
2. **Apply** the accounting equation to business organizations
3. **Understand** financial statements and how to use them
4. **Explain** the relationships among the financial statements
5. **Understand** financial accounting standards
6. **Understand** the role of ethics in business and accounting decisions

SPOTLIGHT

Gildan Activewear Inc. is a Canadian clothing company that manufactures and markets products such as T-shirts, socks, fleeces, sport shirts, and underwear. If you have purchased a T-shirt with your school's logo on it, the T-shirt was probably manufactured by Gildan and sold as a "blank" to the company that printed your school's logo.

Gildan was incorporated in 1984. While Gildan's head office is in Montreal, it is truly an international company. Gildan's products are manufactured in a number of countries and sold in 34 countries around the world through sales offices in the Barbados, the United States, the United Kingdom, and China. Gildan reports the results of its business activity in its annual report, which includes Gildan's financial statements.

The terms *financial statements, International Financial Reporting Standards, revenues,* and *expenses* may be foreign to you now. But as you work your way through this book, these terms and many other accounting and business terms and concepts will become familiar to you. Welcome to the world of accounting.

OBJECTIVE

1 **Learn** that financial statements are the product of accounting

Financial statements are the business documents that companies use to report the results of their activities to various user groups, which can include managers, investors, creditors and regulatory agencies. These parties use the reported information to make a variety of economic decisions. The system of accounting produces financial statements. In this chapter you will consider

- The objectives of different user groups
- The different forms of business organizations
- The underlying assumptions, principles, and concepts of generally accepted accounting principles and the bodies responsible for issuing accounting standards
- The judgment process necessary to make good accounting decisions
- The contents of the four basic financial statements and how different user groups use the information to make business decisions

In later chapters you will learn in more detail how to construct the four financial statements outlined below and how to apply your knowledge to make economic decisions.

The end result of financial accounting is the basic financial statements:

- Income statement (the statement of operations)
- Statement of retained earnings
- Balance sheet (the statement of financial position)
- Statement of cash flows

The October 4, 2009, financial statements of Gildan Activewear Inc. will be used as a basis for discussion throughout this chapter.

Most of you are taking this course to learn about accounting in a way that will serve you either as an accountant or as a manager such as vice-president of marketing, director of purchasing, or as a financial institution loan officer or investment manager. Accordingly, we have structured the text to prepare you for either career stream.

As an accountant you might find yourself

- Preparing financial statements for the organization that employs you
- Auditing financial statements as a public accountant
- Analyzing financial statements as a financial analyst working for an investment firm or a lending officer at a financial institution

MyAccountingLab For more practice and review of accounting cycle concepts, use ACT, the Accounting Cycle Tutorial, online at **www.myaccountinglab.com**. Margin logos like this one, directing you to the appropriate ACT section and material, appear throughout Chapters 1, 2, and 3. When you enter the tutorial, you'll find three buttons on the opening page of each chapter module. Here's what the buttons mean: **Tutorial** gives you a review of the major concepts, **Application** gives you practice exercises, and **Glossary** reviews important terms.

As a manager you might find yourself

- Having to certify the accuracy of financial statements presented by your company to a regulator
- Using financial statements of a company to determine whether or not to acquire shares of stock in a company
- Using information produced by your company's financial system to decide whether or not to increase production of a product the company produces or to move into a new market
- Using financial statements provided by a potential customer or borrower in deciding whether to grant credit to the potential customer or borrower

Economic Decisions

Gildan's managers have to make many business decisions. Should they introduce a new line of fleeces? Should the company set up a regional sales office in Australia or South Africa? Should Gildan consider acquiring a competitor such as Hanes? Should the company extend credit to a potential major customer? Accounting helps managers make these decisions.

Investors use accounting information to make the economic decision as to whether they should buy or sell Gildan shares. Creditors need accounting information to make the economic decision as to whether or not to grant credit to or make a loan to Gildan.

Suppose you have \$5,000 to invest or you are a bank and Gildan has come to you for a loan. What information would you need in order to make your decision? Let's see how accounting works.

A Model of Business

All organizations have a business cycle that describes their operation. Gildan's model begins with the acquisition of materials to make the T-shirts, socks, fleeces, and underwear. The finished products are then sold to Gildan's customers. The customers pay Gildan for their purchases and the cycle begins again. The financial statements report the results of this business cycle.

Accounting Is the Language of Business

Accounting is the information system that measures business activities, processes data into reports, and communicates results to decision makers. Accounting is "the language of business." The better you understand the language, the better you can manage your own finances.

Accounting produces the financial statements that report information about a business entity. The financial statements measure performance and tell us where a business stands in financial terms. In this chapter we focus on Gildan Activewear Inc. After completing this chapter, you will begin to understand financial statements.

Don't confuse bookkeeping and accounting. Bookkeeping is a mechanical part of accounting, just as arithmetic is a part of mathematics. Exhibit 1-1 illustrates the flow of accounting information and helps illustrate accounting's role in business. The accounting process starts and ends with people making decisions.

EXHIBIT 1-1 **The Flow of Accounting Information**

Who Uses Accounting Information?

Decision makers need information. A banker decides who gets a loan. Gildan Activewear decides whether to add a new product line. Let's see how some others use accounting information.

Investors and Creditors. Investors and creditors, such as shareholders and bankers, are the primary users of accounting information since they provide the money to finance Gildan Activewear Inc. An investor earns a return when the price of the company's shares increases and they sell their shares and when they receive a cash dividend on their shares. A banker decides who gets a loan and expects to be repaid. Banks earn money by charging the company interest.

The investor wants to be able to assess whether the company has been profitable in the past and thus is likely to earn future profits so that the share price will increase and the company will be able to pay dividends. The banker wants to determine whether the company will be able to pay the interest on the loan and will be able to repay the loan when it comes due. Both investor and creditor use accounting data to make their decisions.

Government and Regulatory Agencies. Most organizations face government regulation. For example, the Ontario Securities Commission (OSC), a provincial agency, requires public companies to report to the investing public. Gildan Activewear Inc., Potash Corporation of Saskatchewan, Magna International Inc., and other companies publish annual reports.

Taxing Authorities. There are all kinds of taxes. Gildan Activewear pays property tax on its assets and income tax on profits. Retailers collect tax from customers on purchases based on federal and provincial regulation. Most taxes are based on accounting data. Taxing authorities use the accounting information provided to them to determine if companies are paying the correct amount of taxes.

Individuals. People such as you manage bank accounts and decide whether to rent an apartment or buy a house. They budget the monthly income and expenditures of their businesses. Accounting provides the information to allow individuals to make these decisions.

Not-for-Profit Organizations. Not-for-profit organizations—churches, hospitals, and charities, such as Habitat for Humanity and the Canadian Red Cross—base their decisions on accounting data. In addition, accounting data is the basis of a not-for-profit's reporting on the organization's stewardship of funds received and its compliance with the reporting requirements of the Canada Revenue Agency.

Two Kinds of Accounting: Financial Accounting and Management Accounting

Both *external users* and *internal users* make use of accounting information. We can therefore classify accounting into two branches.

Financial accounting provides information for decision makers outside the organization, such as investors, creditors, government agencies, and the public. This information must be relevant for the needs of decision makers and must provide a faithful representation of the entity's economic activities. This textbook focuses on financial accounting.

Management accounting generates inside information for the managers of the organization. Examples of management accounting information include budgets, forecasts, and projections that are used in making strategic decisions of the organization. Internal information must be accurate and relevant for the decision needs of managers. Management accounting is covered in a separate course.

Organizing a Business

Accounting is used in every type of business. A business generally takes one of the following forms:

- Proprietorship
- Partnership
- Corporation

Exhibit 1-2 compares ways to organize a business.

Proprietorships. A **proprietorship** has a single owner, called the proprietor. Dell Computer started out in the college dorm room of Michael Dell, the owner. Proprietorships tend to be small businesses or individual professional organizations, such as physicians, lawyers, and accountants. From a legal perspective, the business

EXHIBIT 1-2 **The Various Forms of Business Organization**

	Proprietorship	Partnership	Corporation
Owner(s)	Proprietor—one owner	Partners—two or more owners	Shareholders—generally many owners
Life of entity	Limited by owner's choice or death	Limited by owners' choices or death	Indefinite
Personal liability of owner(s) for business debts	Proprietor is personally liable	Partners are usually personally liable	Shareholders are not personally liable
Accounting status	Accounting entity is separate from proprietor	Accounting entity is separate from partners	Accounting entity is separate from shareholders

is the proprietor, and the proprietor is personally liable for all business debts. But for accounting, a proprietorship is an entity separate from its proprietor. Thus, the business records do not include the proprietor's personal finances.

Partnerships. A **partnership** joins two or more persons as co-owners, and each owner is a partner. Individuals, corporations, partnerships, or other types of entities can be partners. Income and loss of the partnership "flows through" to the partners and they recognize it based on their agreed-upon percentage interest in the business. The partnership is not a taxpaying entity. Instead, each partner takes a proportionate share of the entity's taxable income and pays tax according to that partner's individual or corporate rate. Many retail establishments and some professional organizations of physicians, lawyers, and accountants are partnerships. Most partnerships are small or medium-sized, but some are gigantic, with several hundred partners. Accounting treats the partnership as a separate organization, distinct from the personal affairs of each partner. But the law views a partnership as the partners: Normally, each partner is personally liable for all the partnership's debts. For this reason, partnerships can be quite risky. Recently, professional partnerships such as public accounting firms and law firms have become **limited liability partnerships** (LLP), which limits claims against the partners to the partnership assets.

Corporations. A **corporation** is an incorporated business owned by **shareholders**. These people own shares of **stock**, which represent shares of ownership in a corporation. Corporations dominate business activity in Canada even though proprietorships and partnerships are more numerous. Corporations transact much more business and are larger in terms of total assets, income, and number of employees. Corporation names (in their entirety) include *Limited*, *Incorporated*, or *Corporation* (abbreviated *Ltd.*, *Inc.*, and *Corp.*, respectively) to indicate that they are corporations—for example, The Forzani Group Ltd., Gildan Activewear Inc., and Lions Gate Entertainment Corp. Some bear the name "Company," such as Hudson's Bay Company. A proprietorship and a partnership can also bear the name "Company."

A corporation is a business entity formed under federal or provincial law. From a legal perspective, unlike proprietorships and partnerships, a corporation is distinct from its owners. The corporation is like an artificial person and possesses many of the rights that a person has. Unlike proprietors and partners, the shareholders who own a corporation have no personal obligation for its debts. So we say shareholders have limited liability, as do partners in an LLP. Also unlike the other forms of organization, a corporation pays income taxes. In the other two cases, income tax is paid personally by the proprietor or partners.

A corporation's ownership is divided into shares of stock. One becomes a shareholder by purchasing the corporation's shares. Gildan Activewear Inc., for example, has issued more than 10,000,000 shares of stock. Any investor can become a co-owner by buying 1, 30, 100, 5,000, or any number of shares of its stock through the Toronto Stock Exchange (TSX), a national stock exchange. Gildan is an example of a public corporation. A corporation may be private, which means that the corporation's shares are privately held among either its founders or its family members.

Shares of a public corporation (publicly accountable enterprise) are widely held and publicly traded. Shares of a private corporation (private enterprise) are privately held among either its founders and or its family members.

Ultimate control of a corporation rests with the shareholders. They normally get one vote for each common share they own. Shareholders elect the members of the

board of directors, which sets policy for the corporation and appoints officers. The board elects a chairperson, who is the most powerful person in the corporation and may also carry the title chief executive officer (CEO), the top management position. Most corporations also have vice-presidents in charge of sales, manufacturing, accounting and finance, and other key areas.

Others. Accounting is also used to produce financial statements in other organizations such as not-for-profit organizations and government and other entities in the public sector.

The Accounting Equation

OBJECTIVE

❷ **Apply** the accounting equation to business organizations

Gildan Activewear Inc.'s financial statements tell us how the business is performing and where it stands. They are the final product of financial accounting. But how do we arrive at the financial statements? Let's examine the *elements of financial statements,* which are the building blocks on which these statements rest.

Assets and Liabilities

The financial statements are based on the **accounting equation**. This equation presents the resources of the business and the claims to those resources.

- **Assets** are the economic resources of a business that are expected to produce a benefit in the future. Gildan Activewear's cash, accounts receivable, inventories, and property, plant, and equipment are examples of assets. Claims on assets come from two sources.
- **Liabilities** are "outsider claims." They are debts payable to outsiders, called *creditors*. For example, a creditor who has loaned money to Gildan has a claim—a legal right—to a part of Gildan's assets until Gildan Activewear repays the debt.
- **Owners' equity** (also called **net assets** or **shareholders' equity** for a corporation or **capital**) represents the "insider claims" of a business. Equity means ownership, so shareholders' equity is the owners' interest in the assets of a corporation.

The accounting equation shows the relationship among assets, liabilities, and owners' equity. Assets appear on the left side of the equation and liabilities and owners' equity on the right side. As Exhibit 1-3 shows, the two sides must be equal.

EXHIBIT 1-3 **The Accounting Equation**

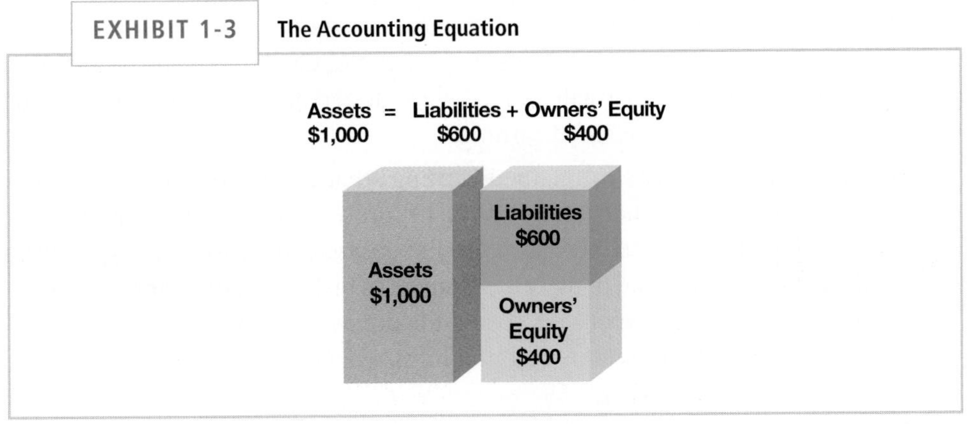

What are some of Gildan's assets? The first assets are **cash and cash equivalents**, the liquid (cash) assets that are the medium of exchange. Another important Gildan asset is **accounts receivable**, which primarily represents amounts due from customers who have purchased Gildan's products on account (credit). **Inventory** is another major asset; it includes the raw materials that go into Gildan's products and finished products that Gildan produces. Gildan also has assets in the form of **property, plant, and equipment**. These are the long-lived assets that the company uses to do business—manufacturing equipment, buildings, computers, and so on. Land, buildings, and equipment are also called tangible **capital assets**, **fixed assets**, or **plant assets**.

Gildan's liabilities include a number of payables, such as accounts payable and accrued liabilities. The word *payable* always signifies a liability. An **account payable** is a liability for goods or services purchased on credit and supported by the credit standing of the purchaser. **Long-term debt** is a liability that falls due beyond one year from the date of the financial statements.

Owners' Equity

Accounting Cycle Tutorial: Balance Sheet Accounts and Transactions - Tutorial

The owners' equity of any business is its assets minus its liabilities. We can write the accounting equation to show that the owners' claim to assets is a residual—what is left over after subtracting liabilities from assets.

$$\text{Assets} - \text{Liabilities} = \text{Owners' Equity}$$

The owners' equity of a corporation—called **shareholders' equity**, or simply *equity*—is divided into two main subparts:

- Contributed capital
- Retained earnings

The accounting equation can be written as

$$\text{Assets} = \text{Liabilities} + \text{Shareholders' Equity}$$
$$\text{Assets} = \text{Liabilities} + \text{Contributed Capital} + \text{Retained Earnings}$$

Contributed capital is the amount the shareholders have invested in the corporation. The basic component of contributed capital is **common shares**, which the corporation issues to shareholders as evidence of ownership.

Retained earnings are the amount earned by income-producing activities and kept for use in the business.

Typically, three types of transactions affect retained earnings:

- **Revenues** are inflows of resources that increase retained earnings from delivering goods or services to customers. For example, Gildan's sale of T-shirts to a screenprint company that will add a college design and logo brings in revenue and increases Gildan's retained earnings.
- **Expenses** are decreases in retained earnings that result from operations. For example, the wages that Gildan pays its production people constitute an expense and decrease retained earnings. Expenses are the cost of doing business and are thus the opposite of revenues. Expenses include office supplies, salaries, and utility payments. Expenses also include depreciation of property, plant, and equipment such as computers and buildings.

- **Dividends** decrease retained earnings, because they are distributions to shareholders of assets (usually cash) generated by net income. A successful business may pay dividends to shareholders as a return on their investments. Remember: **Dividends are not expenses. Dividends never affect net income. Instead of being subtracted from revenues to compute net income, dividends are recorded as direct reductions of retained earnings.**

Businesses strive for **profit**, the excess of revenues over expenses.

- When total revenues exceed total expenses, the result is called **net income**, or **net earnings** or **net profit**.
- When expenses exceed revenues, the result is a **net loss**.
- Net income or net loss is the "bottom line" on an income statement.

Exhibit 1-4 shows the relationships among

- Retained earnings
- Revenues − Expenses = Net income (or Net loss)
- Dividends

The owners' equity of proprietorships and partnerships is different from that of corporations. Proprietorships and partnerships don't identify contributed capital and retained earnings separately. Instead, they use a single heading—Capital—for example, Walker, Capital, for a proprietorship; and Chin, Capital, and Muesli, Capital, for a partnership.

EXHIBIT 1-4 **The Components of Retained Earnings**

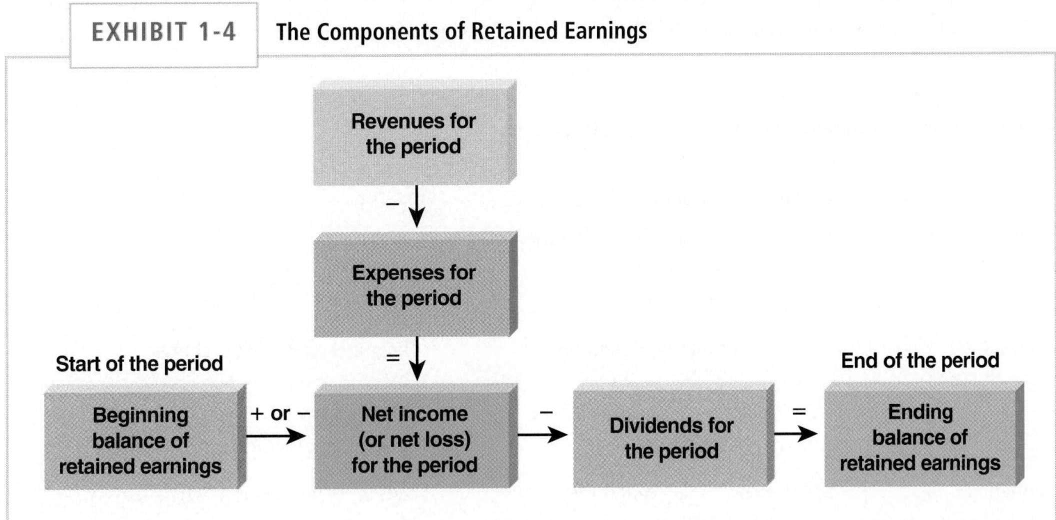

STOP + THINK

1. If the assets of a business are $240,000 and the liabilities are $80,000, how much is the owners' equity?
2. If the owners' equity in a business is $160,000 and the liabilities are $130,000, how much are the assets?
3. A company reported monthly revenues of $129,000 and expenses of $85,000. What is the result of operations for the month?
4. If the beginning balance of retained earnings is $100,000, revenue is $75,000, expenses total $50,000, and the company pays a dividend of $10,000, what is the ending balance of retained earnings?

Answers:
1. $160,000 ($240,000 − $80,000)
2. $290,000 ($160,000 + $130,000)
3. Net profit of $44,000 ($129,000 − $85,000); revenues minus expenses
4. $115,000 [$100,000 beginning balance + net income $25,000 ($75,000 − $50,000) − dividends $10,000]

OBJECTIVE

3 **Understand** financial statements and how to use them

The Financial Statements

The financial statements present a company to users in financial terms. Each financial statement relates to a specific date or a particular time period. What would creditors and investors want to know about Gildan Activewear Inc. at the end of a fiscal period? Exhibit 1-5 summarizes four questions decision makers may ask. The answers come from one of the financial statements.

EXHIBIT 1-5 How Information Is Reported on the Financial Statements

Question	Financial Statement	Answer
1. How well did the company perform during the year?	Income statement (also called the statement of operations)	Revenues − Expenses Net income (or Net loss)
2. Why did the company's retained earnings change during the year?	Statement of retained earnings*	Beginning retained earnings + Net income (or − Net loss) − Dividends Ending retained earnings
3. What is the company's financial position at the end of the year?	Balance sheet (also called the statement of financial position)	Assets = Liabilities + Owners' equity
4. How much cash did the company generate and spend during the year?	Statement of cash flows	Operating cash flows ± Investing cash flows ± Financing cash flows Increase (or decrease) in cash

* Negative retained earnings are called a **deficit**. A deficit would be incurred if accumulated losses exceed accumulated profits.

The following diagram shows how the data flow from one financial statement to the next. The order is important.

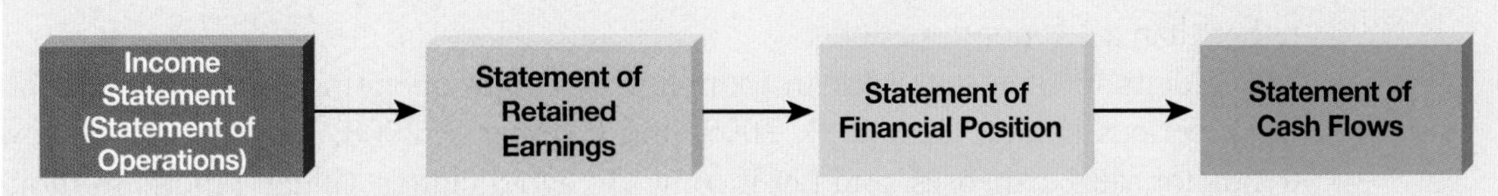

We begin with the income statement in Exhibit 1-6. The dollar amounts in the following discussion of Gildan's financial statements are in thousands of U.S. dollars, as are the dollar amounts reported in their financial statements.

The Income Statement Measures Operating Performance

The **income statement, statement of operations**, or **statement of earnings** reports the company's revenues, expenses, and net income or net loss for a period. The bottom line is net income or net loss for the period. At the top of Exhibit 1-6 is the company's name, Gildan Activewear Inc. On the second line is the term "Consolidated Statements of Earnings and Comprehensive Income." Gildan Activewear Inc. is actually made up of several corporations that are owned by a common group of shareholders. Commonly controlled corporations like this are required to combine, or consolidate, all of their revenues, expenses, assets, liabilities, and shareholders' equity, and to report them all as one.

Most companies use the calendar year as their accounting year. Examples are EnCana Corporation, Magna International Inc., and Great-West Lifeco Inc. Other companies have year-ends during the year; for example, almost all of Canada's major

EXHIBIT 1-6 Consolidated Statement of Earnings and Comprehensive Income (Adapted)

Gildan Activewear Inc.
Consolidated Statements of Earnings and Comprehensive Income (Adapted)
(in thousands of U.S. dollars)

	Year ended October 4, 2009	Year ended October 5, 2008*
1. **Net sales**	**$1,038,319**	$1,249,711
2. Cost of sales	**807,986**	911,242
3. Gross profit	**230,333**	338,469
4. Selling, general, and administrative expenses	**134,785**	142,760
5. Restructuring and other charges	**6,199**	5,489
6. Operating income	**89,349**	190,220
7. Financial (income) expense, net**	**(304)**	9,240
8. Non-controlling interest in consolidated joint venture	**110**	230
9. Earnings before income taxes	**89,543**	180,750
10. Income taxes	**(5,786)**	34,400
11. **Net earnings and comprehensive income**	**95,329**	146,350

*The *CICA Handbook* Section 3031 "Inventories" was issued in 2007 and was effective for companies with fiscal years beginning on or after January 1, 2008. As a result, the company applied Section 3031 for the 2009 statements and recast the 2008 statements.

**Financial (income) expenses (net) includes interest expense of $1,824 in 2009 and $7,422 in 2008.

banks have October 31 year-ends. Companies usually adopt an accounting year that ends on the low point of their operations. For example. Gildan and the Forzani Group report their income based on a 52-week (or 53-week as Gildan did in 2007) rather than a 12-month period.

Gildan's income statement in Exhibit 1-6 reports operating results for two 52-week periods ending October 4, 2009, and October 5, 2008, respectively, to show trends for sales, expenses, and net income. To avoid clutter, Gildan reports in thousands of dollars. Note that Gildan reports in U.S. dollars because so much of its business is in the United States,* and its shares are listed on the New York Stock Exchange as well as on the Toronto Stock Exchange.

During the year ended October 4, 2009, Gildan's net sales declined from $1,249,711 for the 52 weeks ended October 5, 2008, to $1,038,319 (see line 1). Net earnings and comprehensive income declined from $146,350 to $95,329 (see line 11).

USING FINANCIAL STATEMENTS IN DECISION MAKING

It is important to view financial statements in context; during the latter part of 2008 and throughout most of 2009, the whole world was in an economic crisis. Many companies lost money and many others became bankrupt. So, in fact, Gildan's performance was relatively good. The company's annual report reveals that its decline in sales in all four product lines was significantly less than the industry averages for those product lines and Gildan increased the market share in all four product lines. As you work your way through this text, you will see that financial statements are one, albeit an important one, of the sources decision makers use as inputs to their decisions.

The income statement reports two main categories:

- Revenues and gains
- Expenses and losses

We measure net income as follows:

$$\text{Net Income} = \text{Total Revenues and Gains} - \text{Total Expenses and Losses}$$

In accounting, the word *net* means the result after a subtraction. *Net* income is the profit left over after subtracting expenses and losses from revenues and gains. **Net income is the single most important item in the financial statements.**

Revenues. Companies do not always use the term *revenue* in their statement titles. For example, net sales revenue is often abbreviated as *net sales*. *Net* sales means sales revenue after subtracting all the goods customers have returned to the company. The Bay, Canadian Tire, and Jean Coutu get some goods back from customers due to product defects, or items that customers do not want for other reasons. Swiss Chalet and other restaurateurs don't have much in the way of sales returns. In Gildan's case, revenue comes from wholesale sales through the manufacturing and marketing of

*International accounting and foreign currency transactions are discussed in Chapter 10.

activewear primarily to companies that screenprint Gildan's T-shirts and to mass-market retailers.

Expenses. *Cost of sales* (also called *cost of goods sold*) represents the cost to Gildan Activewear Inc. of such expenses as raw materials, manufacturing costs, and depreciation of manufacturing equipment and facilities.

USING FINANCIAL ACCOUNTING IN DECISION MAKING

Since different companies have different ways of categorizing expenses, it is important that you understand how the company whose financial statements you are examining categorizes or groups its expenses. The notes to the financial statements are an integral part of the financial statements and often provide the information the user requires.

In Gildan's case, Note 1, *Significant Accounting Policies* (n), discloses that depreciation expense is a cost of sales, Note 17, *Other Information* (b), reports the actual depreciation expense during the year. Other companies, such as Magna International, show depreciation as a separate item on the Statement of Income and Comprehensive Income.

Selling, general, and administrative expenses (line 4) includes such costs as warehousing and handling costs, selling and administrative personnel expenses, professional fees, non-manufacturing depreciation expense, and bad debt expense.

Restructuring and other charges (line 5) includes primarily the costs incurred during the year related to the closure, relocation and consolidation of manufacturing and distribution facilities.

Financial (income) expense, net (line 7) includes interest expense, bank and other financial charges and (gain) or loss on foreign exchange transactions.

Non-controlling interest in consolidated joint venture (line 8) is the other partner in the joint venture's share of the joint venture's operating income. Gildan includes the joint venture's net sales, cost of sales, and selling, general and administrative expenses in the amounts reported on lines 1, 2, and 4 and so must deduct the amount on line 8 so that the amount on line 9 reflects only Gildan's share of the joint venture's income. Restructuring and other charges do not apply to the joint venture and so are not included in the calculation of the non-controlling interest.

Often, companies have other categories of revenue and expenses on their income statements. These revenues and expenses arise from activities outside a company's central, ongoing operations. For example, a company might dispose of property, plant, and equipment and suffer a loss (a loss has the same effect as an expense). Conversely, the company might have a gain (a gain has the same effect as a revenue item).

Accounting Cycle Tutorial: Income Statement Accounts and Transactions - Tutorial

Income tax expense (line 10). Corporations pay income tax just as individuals do. During 2009, Gildan's income tax expense was a recovery of $5,786 thousand as a result of different tax rates on earnings of foreign subsidiaries.

USING THE INCOME STATEMENT IN DECISION MAKING

The manager, the investor and the creditor are interested in evaluating the profitability of the corporation.

How well did Gildan Activewear Inc. do during 2009?

- The company was profitable. The bottom line reported a net income of $95,329.

Did sales increase?

- Sales decreased. This must be considered in the context of difficult economic conditions and above-average comparison to industry standards.

What trends are evident in gross profit and net income?

- Gross profit decreased from 27% to 22%; earnings before tax decreased from 14% to 9%. These decreases are directly related to the decrease in sales revenue.

What percentage of sales revenue ended up as profit?

- $\frac{\$95,329}{\$1,038,319} = 0.09$ That is, $0.09 of every sales dollar contributed to the profit.

Manager—Were performance goals achieved? The company was profitable but not as profitable as the previous year. It will be management's responsibility to develop strategies to increase net income by improving sales and/or reducing costs in fiscal 2010.

Investor—Is there sufficient income for dividend distribution and/or company expansion? Yes. In Gildan's example, the company is still expanding and not paying dividends. The investor would be aware of market conditions and company strategy for expansion, which would contribute to any investment decision.

Creditor—Will the company be able to pay interest costs? Note 2 reports that interest expense was $1,824. There is sufficient profit to cover current and increased interest costs.

Now let's move to the statement of retained earnings and Exhibit 1–7.

Statement of Retained Earnings

Retained earnings represent exactly what the term implies: that portion of net income the company has retained. Net income from the income statement also appears on the **statement of retained earnings** (line 2 in Exhibit 1-7). Net income increases retained earnings, and dividends decrease retained earnings. If Gildan had paid dividends during the year to its shareholders, retained earnings would have decreased. Why the decrease? Because the company did not retain the net income it gave to shareholders.

Gildan's statement of retained earnings needs explanation. Start with 2008. At October 5, 2008, Gildan had retained earnings of $689,190 (line 1). During 2009, Gildan earned net income of $95,329 (line 2). Gildan ended 2009 with retained earnings of $784,519 (line 3).

EXHIBIT 1-7 Statement of Retained Earnings (Partial, Adapted)

Gildan Activewear Inc.
Consolidated Statements of Shareholders' Equity (Partial, Adapted)
(in thousands of U.S. dollars)

	Year ended October 4, 2009	Year ended October 5, 2008*
Retained earnings:		
1. Balance, beginning of year	$689,190	$542,840
2. Net earnings	95,329	146,350
3. Balance, end of year	$784,519	$689,190

* The *CICA Handbook* Section 3031 "Inventories" was issued in 2007 and was effective for companies with fiscal years beginning on or after January 1, 2008. As a result, the company applied Section 3031 for the 2009 statements and recast the 2008 statements.

Which item on the statement of retained earnings comes directly from the income statement? It's net income. Line 2 of the retained earnings statement comes directly from line 11 of the income statement. Trace this amount from one statement to the other.

Give yourself a pat on the back. You're already learning how to analyze financial statements!

After a company earns net income, the board of directors decides whether to pay a dividend to the shareholders. Corporations are not obligated to pay dividends unless their boards decide to pay (i.e., declare) them. Usually, companies who are in development stages or growth mode (like Gildan Activewear Inc.) elect not to pay dividends, opting instead to plow the money back into the company to expand operations or purchase property, plant, and equipment. Established companies usually have enough accumulated retained earnings (and cash) to pay dividends.

USING THE STATEMENT OF SHAREHOLDERS' EQUITY IN DECISION MAKING

The manager, the investor, and the creditor are interested in seeing how much of Gildan's income was paid in dividends and how much was invested back (retained) in the business.

Manager—As Gildan is following a strategy of acquisition and debt repayment, management would choose to retain income in the business. This decision would also be influenced by the fact that economic conditions are just beginning to improve.

Investor—Gildan did not pay dividends, which should increase the share value of Gildan's shares. The individual investor's investment strategy will determine how the investor views this information.

Creditor—Gildan chose to retain cash in the business, which provides a creditor with a positive basis for review of Gildan's financial position.

The Balance Sheet Measures Financial Position

A company's **balance sheet**, also called the **statement of financial position**, reports three main categories: assets, liabilities, and shareholders' or owners' equity. Gildan Activewear Inc.'s Consolidated Balance Sheets, shown as Exhibit 1-8, are dated at the *moment in time* when the accounting periods end.

EXHIBIT 1-8 **Balance Sheet (Adapted)**

Gildan Activewear Inc.
Consolidated Balance Sheets
(in thousands of U.S. dollars)

	As at October 4, 2009	As at October 5, 2008*
Current Assets		
1. Cash and cash equivalents	$ 99,732	$ 12,357
2. Accounts receivable	166,762	215,833
3. Inventories	301,867	316,172
4. Prepaid expenses and deposits	11,604	10,413
5.	579,965	554,775
6. Property, plant, and equipment	414,538	436,516
7. Intangible assets	56,757	59,954
8. Other assets	9,985	17,277
9. Assets held for sale	6,544	10,497
10. Goodwill	6,709	6,709
11. Future income taxes	7,910	9,283
12. Total assets	$1,082,408	$1,095,011
Current Liabilities		
13. Accounts payable and accrued liabilities	$ 124,378	$ 149,344
14. Income taxes payable	11,822	46,627
15. Current portion of long-term debt	2,803	3,556
16.	139,003	199,527
17. Long-term debt	1,584	49,448
18. Future income taxes	23,764	27,331
19.Non-controlling interest in consolidated joint venture	7,272	7,162
	171,623	283,468
Commitments and contingencies		
Shareholders' equity		
20. Share capital	93,042	89,377
21. Contributed surplus	6,976	6,728
22. Retained earnings	784,519	689,190
23. Accumulated other comprehensive income	26,248	26,248
24.	810,767	715,438
25.	910,785	811,543
26. Total liabilities and shareholders' equity	$1,082,408	$1,095,011

* The *CICA Handbook* Section 3031 "Inventories" was issued in 2007 and was effective for companies with fiscal years beginning on or after January 1, 2008. As a result, the company applied Section 3031 for the 2009 statements and recast the 2008 statements.

Assets. Assets are subdivided into two categories: current and long-term. **Current assets** include cash and cash equivalents as well as those assets the company expects to convert to cash, sell, or consume during the next 12 months or within the business's normal operating cycle if longer than a year. Current assets for Gildan consist of cash and cash equivalents, accounts receivable, inventories, prepaid expenses, and deposits (lines 1 to 4). Gildan's current assets total $579,965 at October 4, 2009 (line 5).

Cash is a liquid asset that is a medium of exchange and *cash equivalents* include money market funds and other instruments that are easily convertible to cash. Gildan has $99,732 in cash and cash equivalents at October 4, 2009 (line 1).

Accounts receivable, $166,762 (line 2), are the amounts due to Gildan primarily for products purchased from the company on account (credit) and are amounts the company expects to collect from customers.

Inventory (Inventories) (line 3) are the company's second biggest current asset, totalling $301,867. Inventory is a common abbreviation for *merchandise inventory*; the two names are used interchangeably.

Prepaid expenses and deposits, $11,604 (line 4), represent prepayments for advertisements and for rent, insurance, and supplies that have not yet been used up. Prepaid expenses are assets because Gildan will benefit from these expenditures in the future.

Property, plant, and equipment of $414,538 (line 6) includes Gildan's land, buildings, computers, and production equipment. Gildan reports property, plant, and equipment at its carrying amount (historical cost minus accumulated depreciation). The actual Gildan financial statements have a footnote for property, plant, and equipment that shows the costs and accumulated depreciation of all the property, plant, and equipment owned by Gildan Activewear Inc. The note shows that Gildan deducts the accumulated depreciation from the total costs of the property, plant, and equipment to calculate the carrying amount of $414,538 thousand shown on the balance sheet. That amount is the portion of the property, plant, and equipment that has not yet been depreciated (used up). *Cost* means the acquisition price to Gildan. It does not mean that Gildan could sell its property, plant, and equipment at the cost prices. After all, the company may have acquired the assets several years ago.

Intangible assets, $56,757 (line 7), are assets with no physical form. Gildan's intangible assets include customer contracts and customer relationships. They are being amortized on a straight-line basis over 20 years.

Other assets, $9,985 (line 8), include long-term prepaid expenses, a long-term receivable, and restricted cash related to an acquisition.

Assets held for sale, $6,544 (line 9), includes property, plant, and equipment from closed facilities that are being held for sale.

Goodwill, $6,709 (line 10), represents the excess of the purchase price of a subsidiary over the net identifiable assets acquired.

Future income taxes, $7,910 (line 11), represents long-term tax benefits.

Overall, Gildan Activewear Inc. reports total assets of $1,082,408 (line 12) at October 4, 2009.

Liabilities. Liabilities are also divided into two categories: current and long-term. **Current liabilities** (lines 13 to 15) are debts payable within one year or within the entity's normal operating cycle if longer than a year. Current liabilities for Gildan Activewear Inc. at October 4, 2009, consist of accounts payable and accrued liabilities, income taxes payable, and the current portion (due in 2010) of the long-term debt. Gildan's current liabilities total $139,003 (line 16).

Accounts payable and accrued liabilities of $124,378 (line 13) represents amounts owed for goods and services that Gildan has purchased but not yet paid for.

Income taxes, $11,822 (line 14), represent income taxes payable for the fiscal year ended October 4, 2009.

Current portion of long-term debt of $2,803 (line 15) represents the current portion of the long-term debt reported in line 17.

Long-term liabilities are those liabilities that are due beyond one year after the balance sheet date. The long-term liabilities include long-term debt, future income taxes, and non-controlling interest in consolidated joint venture.

Long-term debt of $1,584 (line 17) represents debt due in future years.

Future income taxes of $23,764 (line 18) on the liability side represent taxes payable in future years. They arise because of timing differences between income for accounting purposes and income for tax purposes.

Non-controlling interest in consolidated joint venture of $7,272 (line 19) is the other partner in the joint venture's share of the joint venture's net assets. Gildan includes the joint venture's assets and liabilities in the amounts shown on the Consolidated Balance Sheets and so must deduct the amount on line 19 so that the amount on line 12 minus the amounts on lines 13 to 18 reflect only Gildan's share of the joint venture's net assets.

At October 4, 2009, total liabilities are $171,623 (total assets of $1,082,408 minus total shareholders' equity of $910,785). This is just 15.8% of total assets.

STOP + THINK

Examine Gildan's balance sheet in Exhibit 1-8. Look at total assets on line 12. What is your opinion of the change in total assets and total liabilities during fiscal 2009? Is it good news, bad news, or no news? Why? To what other item should you relate the change in total assets? Identify that item, its change during 2009, and state why it too is important.

Answer:

It is important to look at the complete picture and not to focus just on a part. Total assets declined from $1,095,011 to $1,082,408, a decrease of $12,603, but total liabilities must have declined more as shareholders' equity increased from $811,543 to $910,785, an increase of $99,242. Gildan is in a stronger financial position at October 4, 2009, than it was at October 5, 2008.

Owners' Equity. The accounting equation states that

$$\text{Assets} - \text{Liabilities} = \text{Owners' Equity}$$

The assets (resources) and the liabilities (debts) of Gildan are fairly easy to understand. Owners' equity is harder to understand. Owners' equity is simple to calculate, but what does it *mean*?

Accounting Cycle Tutorial: Income Statement Accounts and Transactions - Tutorial

Gildan Activewear Inc. calls its owners' equity *shareholders' equity*, and this title is descriptive. Remember that a company's owners' equity represents the shareholders' ownership of business assets. Owners' equity for Gildan consists of common shares, represented by almost 121 million shares issued to shareholders for approximately $93,042 through October 4, 2009 (line 20).

Contributed surplus of $6,976 (line 21) results from transactions related to stock options. The subject is dealt with in an advanced accounting course.

Retained earnings are $784,519 (line 22). Trace the $784,519 ending balance of retained earnings from the statement of retained earnings in Exhibit 1-7 (line 3) to the balance sheet in Exhibit 1-8 (line 22). Retained earnings links the statement of retained earnings to the balance sheet.

Accumulated other comprehensive income of $26,248 (line 23) is the accumulated change in shareholders' equity from all sources other than from the owners of the business. For example, unrealized foreign currency translation gains and losses are included in accumulated other comprehensive income. Retained earnings and other comprehensive income total $810,767 (line 24).

At October 4, 2009, Gildan has total shareholders' equity of $910,785 (line 24). We can now prove that Gildan's total assets equal the company's total liabilities and equity (amounts in thousands):

Total assets (line 12)		$1,082,408 ←	Must equal
Current liabilities (line 16)	$139,003		
Long-term liabilities (lines 17 to 19)	32,620		
Total liabilities		$171,623	
+ Total shareholders' equity (line 25)		910,785	
Total liabilities and shareholders' equity (line 26)		$1,082,408 ←	

USING THE BALANCE SHEET IN DECISION MAKING

By examining the balance sheet, investors and creditors are able to determine whether or not the company is able to pay its debts.

Is Gildan collecting receivables?

- Yes. Accounts receivable for 2009 are less than 2008, which reflects the decrease in sales revenue year over year and indicates that accounts receivable are being collected on a timely basis.

Can Gildan pay its current liabilities?

- Yes. Current assets are more than 4 times greater than current liabilities in 2009, whereas the difference was 2.75 times in 2008.

Can Gildan pay its current and long-term liabilities?

- Yes. Total assets of $1,082,408 are greater than total liabilities of $171,623.

Manager—Will cash flow be available to cover costs of business in the next year? What is our debt obligation over the next fiscal period? Cash and accounts receivable will provide funds to pay current accounts payable, enabling management to purchase resources required for ongoing business activity. The current portion of long-term debt is $2,803, which will be paid in the next fiscal period.

Investor—Are retained earnings increasing? Has an investor's investment been diluted through the issuance of more shares? Retained earnings have increased, reflecting an increased value of the company's net worth. Some additional shares have been issued, however, an investor's position would not be materially diluted.

Creditor—Does Gildan have debt? Will it be able to repay any debt currently held?

Yes. Gildan does have current debt of $2,803 plus long-term debt of $1,584 thousand totalling $4,387. Gildan has sufficient funds to carry and pay this debt. A request for funds to expand the business would be considered positively in context of the October 4, 2009, balance sheet

The statement of cash flows is the last required financial statement.

The Statement of Cash Flows Measures Cash Receipts and Payments

Companies engage in three basic types of activities:

1. **Operating activities**
2. **Investing activities**
3. **Financing activities**

The **statement of cash flows** reports cash flows under these three categories. Think about the cash flows (cash receipts and cash payments) in each category:

- *Companies operate by buying, and then selling, goods and services to customers.* **Operating activities** result in net income or net loss, and they either increase or decrease cash. The income statement tells whether the company is profitable. The statement of cash flows reports whether operations provided cash or used cash. Operating activities are most important and they should be the company's main source of cash. Continuing negative cash flows from operations can lead to bankruptcy.
- *Companies invest in long-term assets.* Gildan buys buildings and equipment. When these assets wear out, the company disperses of them. These are investing activities. Both purchases and sales of property, plant, and equipment are investing cash flows. Investing cash flows are next most important after operations.
- *Companies need money for financing.* **Financing activities** include both issuing and repurchasing shares of stock and borrowing and repaying funds. Gildan issues shares to its shareholders and repays long-term debt. These receipts and payments are financing cash flows.

Overview. Each category of cash flows—operating, financing, and investing—either increases or decreases cash. In Exhibit 1-9, which shows Gildan Activewear Inc.'s Consolidated Statement of Cash Flows, operating activities provided cash of \$169,179 (line 16) in the year ended October 4, 2009. This signals strong cash flow from operations. Fiscal 2009's financing activities used \$47,711 (line 23). Fiscal 2009's investing activities (purchase of property, plant, and equipment) used cash of \$34,198 (line 29). That signals expansion. On a statement of cash flows, cash receipts appear as positive amounts. Cash payments are negative and enclosed by parentheses.

Overall Gildan Activewear Inc.'s cash increased by \$87,375 in the year ended October 4, 2009 (line 31), and ended the year at \$99,732 (line 33). Trace ending cash back to the balance sheet in Exhibit 1-8 (line 1). Cash links the statement of cash flows to the balance sheet. You've just performed more financial statement analysis.

EXHIBIT 1-9 **Statement of Cash Flows**

Gildan Activewear Inc.
Consolidated Statements of Cash Flows
(in thousands of U.S. dollars)

	Year ended October 4, 2009	Year ended October 5, 2008*
Cash flows from (used in) operating activities		
1. Net earnings	$ 95,329	$146,350
Adjustments for:		
2. Depreciation and amortization	65,407	57,135
3. Variation of depreciation included in inventories	(2,437)	(957)
4. Restructuring charges related to assets held for sale and property, plant, and equipment	976	2,174
5. Loss on disposal of property, plant, and equipment	561	1,369
6. Stock-based compensation costs	3,007	2,965
7. Future income taxes	(2,434)	(15,885)
8. Non-controlling interest	110	230
9. Unrealized net (gain) loss on foreign exchange and financial derivatives	(1,012)	(2,222)
10.	159,507	191,159
Changes in non-cash working capital balances:		
11. Accounts receivable	48,351	10,263
12. Inventories	16,742	(31,178)
13. Prepaid expenses and deposits	(1,191)	(881)
14. Accounts payable and accrued liabilities	(22,731)	25,700
15. Income taxes payable	(31,499)	43,802
16.	169,179	238,865
Cash flows from (used in) financial activities		
17. (Decrease) increase in amounts drawn under revolving long-term credit facility	(45,000)	(4,000)
18. Decrease in bank indebtedness	—	(2,739)
19. Increase in other long-term debt	44	2,805
20. Repayments of other long-term debt	(3,661)	(5,461)
21. Proceeds from the issuance of shares	906	1,138
22. Repurchase of shares	—	(12)
23.	(47,711)	(8,269)
Cash flows from (used in) investing activities		
24. Purchase of property, plant, and equipment	(44,938)	(97,030)
25. Business acquisition	(1,196)	(126,819)
26. Restricted cash related to business acquisition	3,958	(10,000)
27. Proceeds on disposal of assets held for sale	6,349	3,736
28. Net decrease (increase) in other assets	1,629	2,826
29.	(34,198)	(227,287)
30. Effect of exchange rate changes on cash and cash equivalents denominated in foreign currencies	105	(202)
31. Net increase (decrease) in cash and cash equivalents during the year	87,375	3,107
32. Cash and cash equivalents, beginning of year	12,357	9,250
33. Cash and cash equivalents, end of year	$ 99,732	$ 12,357

* The *CICA Handbook* Section 3031 "Inventories" was issued in 2007 and was effective for companies with fiscal years beginning on or after January 1, 2008. As a result, the company applied Section 3031 for the 2009 statements and recast the 2008 statements.

USING THE STATEMENT OF CASH FLOWS IN DECISION MAKING

Investors and creditors can examine the statement of cash flows to see the decisions management made in terms of receiving and spending the company's cash.

Did Gildan's operating activities provide strong cash flow?

- Yes. Most of the increase in funds was provided by operating activities.

Did Gildan invest during the fiscal period?

- Yes. Property, plant, and equipment were purchased.

Did Gildan increase its debt or issue shares?

- Debt was reduced as amounts drawn under revolving long-term credit facility were decreased and payment was made on long-term debt.
- Some shares were issued, proceeds of which were $906.

Manager—Can inventories be increased to increase sales levels? Yes, operating cash is available. Can the purchase of equipment for a new product line be finaced? Yes. As debt is being repaid, there is a good possibility for additional loans. There is opportunity to issue shares to raise capital for investment.

Investor—Does business have a strong base to go forward on? Yes. Operating activities are providing cash flow. Is the company investing its cash effectively? Yes. The company is purchasing property, plant, and equipment. Is the company issuing shares? Yes. The company continues to build a strong shareholder base.

Creditor—Is the company borrowing to provide operating cash flow? No. The company has borrowed to finance the purchase of assets and acquire other operating companies. Is the company paying down its debt? Yes. The revolving long-term credit facility has decreased and payment was made on long-term debt.

The Notes to the Financial Statements Provide Additional Information

The notes to the financial statements are an integral part of the financial statements and should be read carefully as part of a review of the financial statements. The notes provide information that cannot be reported conveniently on the face of the financial statements. For example, the notes tell the readers information such as what accounting policies were used in preparing the financial statements, and what methods were used to account for inventories and depreciation. An example of these notes can be found in Appendix A: Annual Report for Gildan Activewear Inc. Note that each of Gildan's financial statements carries the statement "See accompanying notes to the consolidated financial statements."

Let's now summarize the relationships that link the financial statements.

Relationships Among the Financial Statements

Huron Ltd. (Exhibit 1-10) provides a simple example of the relationships among the financial statements. These statements are summarized with all amounts assumed for the illustration. Study the exhibit carefully because these relationships apply to all organizations.

OBJECTIVE

4 **Explain** the relationships among the financial statements

EXHIBIT 1-10 Relationships Among the Financial Statements

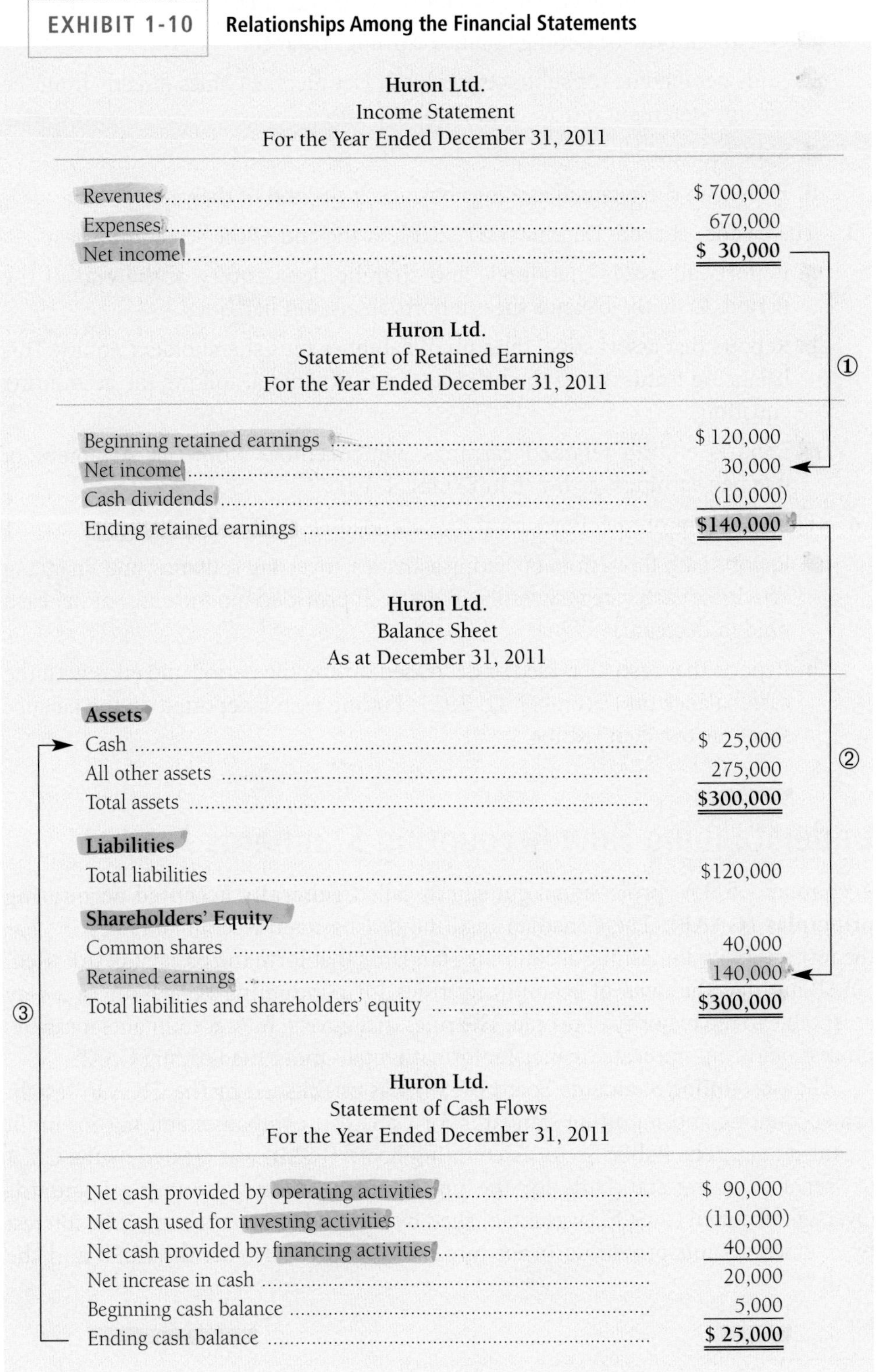

Huron Ltd.
Income Statement
For the Year Ended December 31, 2011

Revenues	$ 700,000
Expenses	670,000
Net income	$ 30,000

Huron Ltd.
Statement of Retained Earnings
For the Year Ended December 31, 2011

Beginning retained earnings	$ 120,000
Net income	30,000 ①
Cash dividends	(10,000)
Ending retained earnings	$140,000

Huron Ltd.
Balance Sheet
As at December 31, 2011

Assets	
Cash	$ 25,000
All other assets	275,000
Total assets	$300,000
Liabilities	
Total liabilities	$120,000
Shareholders' Equity	
Common shares	40,000
Retained earnings	140,000 ②
Total liabilities and shareholders' equity	$300,000

Huron Ltd.
Statement of Cash Flows
For the Year Ended December 31, 2011

Net cash provided by operating activities	$ 90,000
Net cash used for investing activities	(110,000)
Net cash provided by financing activities	40,000
Net increase in cash	20,000
Beginning cash balance	5,000
Ending cash balance ③	$ 25,000

Specifically, note the following.

1. The income statement for the year ended December 31, 2011,
   a. Reports all revenues and all expenses during the period. Revenues and expenses are reported *only* on the income statement.
   b. Reports net income if total revenues exceed total expenses. If expenses exceed revenues, there is a net loss.
2. The statement of retained earnings for the year ended December 31, 2011,
   a. Opens with the beginning retained earnings balance.
   b. Adds net income (or subtracts net loss). Net income comes directly from the income statement (arrow ① in Exhibit 1-10).
   c. Subtracts dividends.
   d. Ends with the retained earnings balance at the end of the year.
3. The balance sheet at December 31, 2011, at the end of the accounting year
   a. Reports all assets, liabilities, and shareholders' equity at the end of the period. Only the balance sheet reports assets and liabilities.
   b. Reports that assets equal the sum of liabilities plus shareholders' equity. This balancing feature gives the balance sheet its name; it follows the accounting equation.
   c. Reports ending retained earnings, which comes from the statement of retained earnings (arrow ② in Exhibit 1-10).
4. The statement of cash flows for the year ended December 31, 2011,
   a. Reports cash flows from operating activities, investing activities, and financing activities. Each category results in net cash provided (an increase) or net cash used (a decrease).
   b. Reports that cash increased or decreased during the period and ends with the cash balance on December 31, 2011. Ending cash is reported on the balance sheet (arrow ③ in Exhibit 1-10).

Understanding How Accounting Standards Are Set

OBJECTIVE

⑤ **Understand** financial accounting standards

Accountants follow professional guidelines called **generally accepted accounting principles (GAAP)**. The Canadian Institute of Chartered Accountants (CICA) has the responsibility for issuing accounting standards that form the basis of GAAP used. GAAP are like the laws of accounting: rules for conducting behaviour in a way acceptable to the majority of people. The rules that govern how accountants measure, process, and communicate financial information fall under the heading GAAP.

The Accounting Standards Board (AcSB) was established by the CICA to "establish accounting and reporting standards for Canadian companies and not-for-profit organizations." The Public Sector Accounting Board (PSAB) was created by the CICA to "set accounting standards for the public sector." The Accounting Standards Oversight Council (AcSOC) was established by the CICA to "serve the public interest by overseeing and providing input into the activities of both the AcSB and the PSAB."*

---

* See www.cica.ca.

The Canadian Securities Administrators, a body composed of officials appointed by the provincial and territorial governments with securities exchanges to set securities law, issued National Policy Statement 27 (NP 27) designating the *CICA Handbook* as generally accepted accounting principles. The *Canada Business Corporations Act* also designated the *CICA Handbook* as GAAP, and the *Ontario Securities Act* followed suit. In these ways, the CICA became the official promulgator of generally accepted accounting principles. Exhibit 1-11 illustrates how the authority for setting GAAP is delegated to the CICA by the federal and provincial and territorial governments and the Securities Administrators.

The world of commerce is becoming more global and as accounting became more complex, the existence of different GAAP in each of the countries of the world made comparisons between companies almost impossible. The global accounting profession, international banks, multinational corporations, and organizations such as the World Bank recognized the need for international accounting standards. In response, the International Accounting Standards Board (IASB) was set up in 2001 in London, England. The IASB issues **International Financial Reporting Standards (IFRS)**, which are being adopted as generally accepted accounting principles in Canada and around the world (Exhibit 1-12).

In 2006, the AcSB made the decision to converge Canadian GAAP for Canadian publicly accountable enterprises with IFRS. The last year for reporting under Canadian GAAP will be the year ending December 31, 2010. Reporting under IFRS standards will be required for annual periods beginning on or after January 1, 2011.

EXHIBIT 1-11 Flow of Authority for Developing GAAP

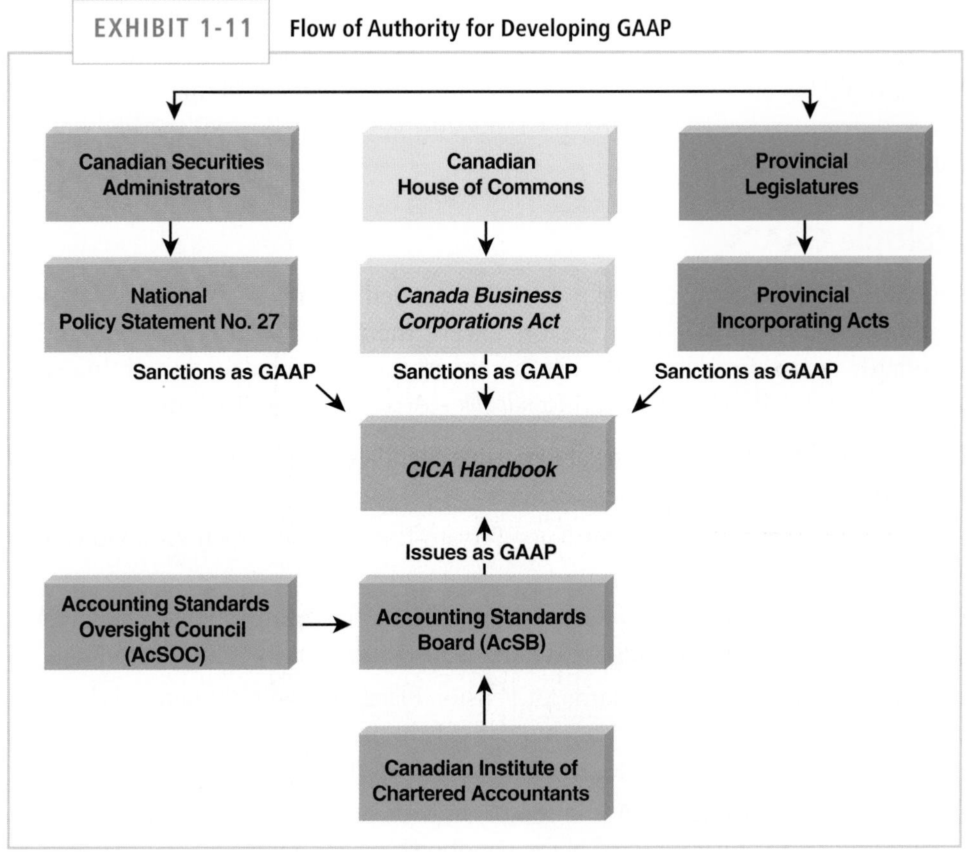

EXHIBIT 1-12 **Creation and Convergence of International Financial Reporting Standards**

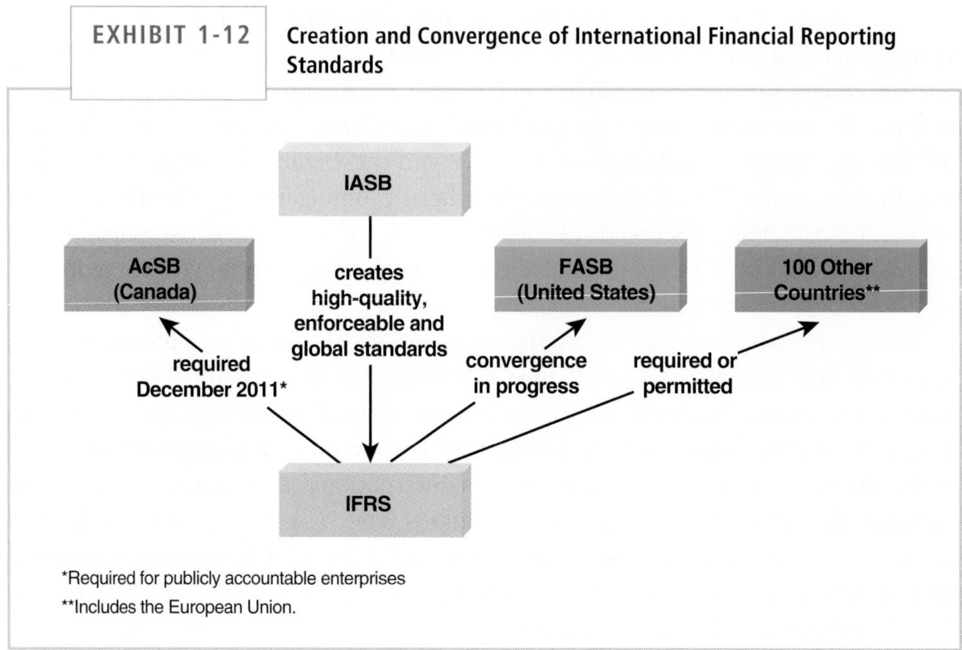

Publicly accountable enterprises (PAEs) are corporations that have issued or plan to issue shares or debt in public markets. PAEs are required to follow International Financial Reporting Standards established by the IASB. **Private enterprises (PEs)** are required to follow the accounting standards in Part II of the *CICA Handbook* entitled "Accounting Standards for Private Enterprises," (ASPE). These standards were developed by the AcSB. Since the financial information of private enterprises is not released or used by the public, requiring them to follow IFRS exclusively would be too time consuming and costly. While the focus of this text will be on IFRS, differences between GAAP for PAEs and GAAP for PEs will be highlighted throughout the book.

Multiple GAAPs

The *CICA Handbook – Accounting* previously included accounting principles that generally applied to entities in all sectors except the public sector. The Accounting Standards Board, in order to deal with convergence of Canadian accounting standards with IFRS, divided the *CICA Handbook – Accounting* into five parts:

- Part I: International Financial Reporting Standards, which must be followed by PAEs.
- Part II: Accounting Standards for Private Enterprises, which are followed by PEs.

ASPE

- Part III: Accounting Standards for Not-for-Profit Organizations. The CICA is presently revising accounting standards for not-for-profit entities.
- Part IV: Accounting Standards for Pension Plans. Accounting standards for pension plans will be added to this part of the handbook once the Accounting Standards Board completes its deliberations on this topic.
- Part V: Pre-changeover Accounting Standards are applied by an entity prior to its adoption of parts I to IV of the handbook.

In addition, there is a *CICA Public Sector Accounting Handbook*, which includes standards and guidance issued by the Public Sector Accounting Board regarding federal, provincial and territorial, and municipal reporting units. This text will discuss the standards in Part I and the standards in Part II where applicable.

The Accounting Conceptual Framework and Accounting Characteristics and Assumptions

Financial standards follow a conceptual framework. Exhibit 1-13 gives an overview of the joint conceptual framework developed by the IASB and the Financial Accounting Standards Board (FASB) as adopted in Canada (note that the Canadian framework differs slightly from that used in the U.S.). The overall *objective* of accounting is to provide financial information that is useful to present and future capital providers in making investment and lending decisions. In this sense capital means resources (usually cash). The two basic external providers of capital include investors (who exchange cash for shares) and creditors (who loan cash) to the entity.

To be useful, information must have the fundamental qualitative characteristics. Those include:

- Relevance
- Faithful representation

To have **relevance**, information must be capable of making a difference to the decision maker, having predictive or confirming value, *within the limits of materiality*. *Materiality* means that the information must be important enough to the informed

EXHIBIT 1-13 **Conceptual Foundation of Accounting**

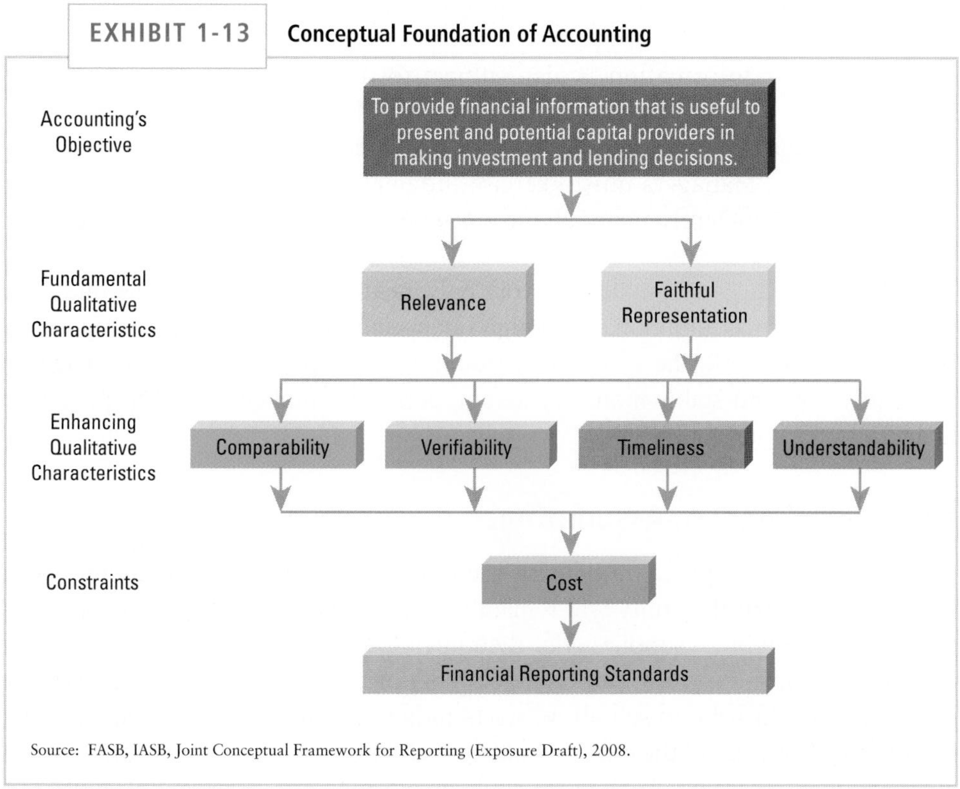

Source: FASB, IASB, Joint Conceptual Framework for Reporting (Exposure Draft), 2008.

user so that if it were omitted or erroneous, it would make a difference in the user's decision. Only information that is material needs to be separately *disclosed* (listed or discussed) in the financial statements. If not, it does not need separate disclosure, but may be combined with other information. **Faithful representation** means that decision-useful information about an economic phenomenon is complete, neutral (free from bias), and not materially misstated (accurate). Accounting information must focus on the *economic substance* of a transaction, event, or circumstance, which may or may not always be the same as its legal form.

Accounting information must also have a number of *enhancing qualitative characteristics*. These include

- Comparability
- Verifiability
- Timeliness
- Understandability

Comparability means that the accounting information for a company must be prepared in such a way as to be capable of being both compared with information from other companies in the same period, and *consistent* with similar information for that company in previous periods. *Verifiability* means that the information must be capable of being checked for accuracy, completeness, and faithful representation. The process of verifying information is often done by *internal* as well as *external auditors*. Verifiability enhances the faithful representation of information, and thus makes the information more representative of economic reality. *Timeliness* means that the information must be made available to users early enough to help them make decisions, thus making the information more relevant to their needs. *Understandability* means that the information must be sufficiently transparent so that it makes sense to reasonably informed users of the information (investors, creditors, regulatory agencies, and managers).

Accounting information is also subject to the cost constraint accounting information is costly to produce, and the *cost should not exceed the expected benefits* to users. Management of companies is primarily responsible for preparing accounting information. Managers must exercise judgment in determining whether the information is sufficiently material and not excessively costly to warrant separate disclosure.

The Canadian conceptual framework only includes one underlying assumption: the going concern assumption. Although not specifically included in the Canadian conceptual framework, the additional accounting assumptions included on page 29 (the entity, cost and stable-monetary assumptions) are implicitly used in preparing financial statements in Canada.

The Going-Concern Assumption

The Canadian conceptual framework includes the **going-concern assumption,** which assumes that the entity will remain in operation long enough to use existing assets—land, buildings, supplies—for their intended purposes. Consider the alternative to the going-concern assumption: going out of business. An entity that was not continuing would have to sell all its assets rather than use them. In that case, the most *relevant* measure of the assets would be their liquidation values (the amount the company would receive for the assets when sold in a forced sale). But going out of business is the exception rather than the rule. Therefore, the going-concern assumption takes for granted that a business will stay in business long enough to recover the cost of its assets by using those assets for their intended purpose.

The Entity Assumption

The **entity assumption** states that the organization stands apart as a separate economic unit. Sharp boundaries are drawn around each entity so as not to confuse its affairs with those of others.

Consider John Forzani, chairman of the board of The Forzani Group Ltd., the sporting goods chain. Mr. Forzani owns a home and automobiles, among other family possessions. He may owe money on some personal loans. All these assets and liabilities belong to John Forzani and have nothing to do with The Forzani Group Ltd. Likewise, The Forzani Group Ltd.'s cash, computers, and store equipment belong to the company, not to John Forzani. Why? Because the entity concept draws a sharp boundary around each entity. In this case The Forzani Group Ltd. is one entity and John Forzani is a separate entity.

Let's consider Gildan, which has several product lines—T-shirts, fleeces, underwear, and socks. Gildan management evaluates each product line as a separate entity. If socks sales are dropping, Gildan can identify the reason. But if sales figures from all product lines of the company are combined, then management cannot tell how many pairs of socks the company is selling. To correct the problem, managers need data for each product line of the company. The transactions of different units should not be accounted for together. Each unit should be evaluated separately.

The Cost Assumption

The **cost assumption** requires that assets and liabilities be measured at their cost when they are acquired or assumed. Cost is the amount paid for the asset. For example, if Gildan buys a building for $590,000 that the owner is offering for sale at $645,000 and that has an appraised value of $620,000, the purchase should be recorded at $590,000. The amount of the $590,000 would be the fair value of the asset *at the time of acquisition.*

The Stable-Monetary-Unit Assumption

In Canada, we record transactions in Canadian dollars, the medium of exchange. British accountants record transactions in pounds sterling, and Japanese accountants in yen. Europeans who belong to the European Union price goods and services in euros.

Unlike a litre or a kilometre, the value of a Canadian dollar or a Mexican peso changes over time against other currencies. A rise in the general price level is called *inflation*. During inflation, a dollar will purchase less milk, less toothpaste, and less of other goods. When prices are stable—when there is little inflation—a dollar's purchasing power is also stable.

Accountants assume that the dollar's purchasing power is relatively stable under the **stable-monetary-unit assumption**. We ignore inflation, and this allows us to add and subtract dollar amounts as though each dollar had the same purchasing power.

STOP + THINK

You are considering the purchase of land for future expansion. The seller is asking $50,000 for land that cost the seller $35,000. An appraisal shows a value of $47,000. You first offer $44,000, the seller makes a counter-offer of $48,000, and you agree on $46,000. What dollar value is recorded for the land in your accounting records?

Answer:
Record the land at $46,000, which is its cost.

ACCOUNTING FOR FINANCIAL STATEMENTS

I. The accountant must be aware of the objective of accounting, which is to provide financial information that is useful to present and potential capital providers in making investment and lending decisions.

In order to provide financial statements that contain such information, the fundamental qualitative characteristics of *relevance* and *faithful representation*, and the enhancing qualitative characteristics of *comparability, verifiability, timeliness*, and *understandability*, must be considered subject to the constraints of *materiality* and *cost*.

II. The accountant must be aware of certain assumptions that underlie the financial statements.

One of the more significant assumptions is that the business will remain a going concern for the foreseeable future (usually one year from the balance sheet date). The *going-concern assumption* means that the company will remain in business long enough to use its assets for their intended purposes.

Another assumption is the *entity* assumption, which states that all transactions included in the financial statements are transactions of the company and that no transactions are included that are not company transactions.

Ethics in Business and Accounting Decisions

OBJECTIVE

❻ **Understand** the role of ethics in business and accounting decisions

Ethical behaviour by those who prepare financial statements and those who audit the financial statements is very important because so many decision makers—managers, investors, creditors, regulators, and many others—rely on those financial statements. All those users rely on the competence and integrity of the preparers and the auditors. Financial markets in Canada, the United States, the United Kingdom, and many other countries operate as efficiently and effectively as they do because of the quality of the complex services provided by accountants within the companies and the auditors outside the companies who audit the financial statements. The market runs smoothly because participants have confidence in the quality of these services.

Companies need money to operate. To attract investors and obtain loans, companies must provide information to the public. Without that information, people won't invest. The Canadian and provincial governments have laws that require companies to report relevant information to outsiders. Relevant information has predictive value or feedback value and is timely and thus can influence a decision. Faithful representation means the information is verifiable and is free from bias.

Occasionally, a company will report biased information. It may overstate profits or understate the company's debts. In recent years, Livent Inc., the theatrical production company, allegedly kept two sets of books and falsified its financial reports. Several well-known U.S. companies were charged with reporting misleading information. Enron Corporation, at the time one of the largest companies in the United States, admitted understating its liabilities (debts). Xerox and WorldCom were accused of overstating profits. If these accusations were true, the published financial data of these companies were not a faithful representation and thus failed the basic test of good ethics. The result? People invested in them, lost money, and filed lawsuits to recover their losses. Reporting relevant information that is a faithful representation to the public is the ethical course of action.

Standards of Professional Conduct for Accountants. What are the criteria for ethical judgments in accounting? The three professional accounting bodies discussed below, other professional organizations, and large companies have codes of conduct that require high levels of ethical conduct. There is a need for high standards of ethical behaviour by accountants if people are going to rely on information for decision making produced by or audited by those accountants.

The influence of accounting in today's business world has emphasized the need for high professional, educational, and ethical standards for accountants. Through statutes passed by provincial legislatures, the three accounting organizations in Canada have received the authority to set educational requirements and professional standards for their members and to discipline members who fail to adhere to their codes of conduct. The acts make them self-regulating bodies, just as provincial associations of doctors and lawyers are.

The *Canadian Institute of Chartered Accountants (CICA)*, whose members are Chartered Accountants or CAs, is the oldest accounting organization in Canada. CAs belong to a provincial institute (*ordre* in Quebec) and through that body to the CICA. The provincial institutes and *ordre* grant the right to use the professional designation CA and have the responsibility for developing and enforcing the code of professional conduct that guides the actions of the CAs in that province.

Members of the *Certified General Accountants Association of Canada (CGAAC)* are allowed to use the designation Certified General Accountant or CGA. They belong to provincial associations (*ordre* in Quebec) and, in turn, to the CGAAC. The provincial associations and *ordre* grant the right to use the professional designation CGA and are responsible for developing and administering the code of professional conduct that guides the actions of the CGAs in that province.

Members of the *Society of Management Accountants of Canada (SMAC)* are permitted to use the designation Certified Management Accountant or CMA. They belong to provincial societies (*ordre* in Quebec) and, in turn, to the SMAC. The provincial societies and *ordre* grant the right to use the professional designation CMA and are responsible for developing and administering the code of professional conduct that guides the actions of CMAs in that province.

The recent corporate failures have driven home the need for good ethics among accountants as never before.

We Need an Audit to Validate the Financial Statements

Throughout this book we use actual examples to show how accounting relates to your daily activities.

Gildan Activewear Inc. reports that it is profitable. But did the company really sell that much activewear, underwear, and socks? Were profits really $95,329? Who reports these figures?

Gildan's top management is responsible for both (a) company operations—how well the company *really* performs—and (b) the information Gildan *reports* to the public. Can you see the conflict of interests here? A company's real performance may differ from what gets reported to the public. Company management has a built-in motivation to make the company look strong, especially when times are tough. Most managers are highly principled men and women, but a few managers have "cooked the books" to overstate their companies' *reported* profits.

How does society deal with this conflict of interests? Canadian and provincial regulation and securities acts require all companies that sell shares to the public to have an annual audit by independent accountants. Audits are intended to protect the public by ensuring that accounting data are relevant and a faithful representation. It turns out that Gildan Activewear Inc. passed the audit test. The accounting firm of KPMG LLP audited the financial statements of Gildan Activewear Inc. and stated that in its opinion, "the consolidated financial statements ... present fairly, in all material respects, the financial position of the Company and subsidiaries as at October 4, 2009, and October 5, 2008, and the results of their operations and their cash flows for the years ended October 4, 2009, and October 5, 2008 ...."

The take-away lesson is this: Avoid a company if its auditor does not state that the company's financial statements "present fairly ..."

Good business requires decision making, which in turn requires the exercise of good judgment, at both the individual and corporate levels. Perhaps, as an accountant, you may have to decide whether to record a $50,000 expenditure for a piece of equipment as an asset on the balance sheet or an expense on the income statement. Alternatively, as a sales manager for a company like CHC Helicopter Corporation, you may have to decide whether $25 million of goods and services delivered to customers in 2010 would be more appropriately recorded as revenue in 2010 or 2011. Depending on the type of business, the facts and circumstances surrounding accounting decisions may not always make them clear cut, and yet the decision may determine whether the company shows a profit or a loss in a particular period! What are the factors that influence business and accounting decisions, and how should these factors be weighed? Generally, three factors influence business and accounting decisions: economic, legal, and ethical.

The ***economic*** factor states that often the decision being made is designed to maximize the economic benefits to the decision maker. Sometimes the legal and/or ethical dimensions of the economic decision are ignored—the decision is illegal and/or unethical.

The ***legal*** factor is based on the proposition that free societies are governed by laws. Laws are written to provide clarity and to prevent abuse of the rights of individuals or society. Democratically enacted laws both contain and express society's collective moral standards. Legal analysis involves applying the relevant laws to each decision, and then choosing the action that complies with those laws. A complicating factor for a global business may be that what is legal in one country might not be legal in another. In that case, it is usually best to abide by the laws of the most restrictive country.

The ***ethical*** factor recognizes that while certain actions might be both economically profitable and legal, they may still not be right. Therefore, most companies, and many individuals, have established standards for themselves to enforce a higher level of conduct than that imposed by law. These standards govern how we treat others and the way we restrain our selfish desires. This behavior and its underlying beliefs are the essence of ethics. **Ethics** are shaped by our cultural, socioeconomic, and religious backgrounds. An *ethical analysis* is needed to guide judgment for making decisions.

The decision rule in an ethical analysis is to choose the action that fulfills ethical duties—responsibilities of the members of society to each other. The challenge in an ethical analysis is to identify specific ethical duties and stakeholders to whom you owe these duties. As with legal issues, a complicating factor in making global ethical decisions may be that what is considered ethical in one country is not considered ethical in another.

Ethical training starts at home and continues throughout our lives. It is reinforced by the teaching that we receive in our church, synagogue, or mosque; the schools we attend; and by the persons and companies we associate with.

A thorough understanding of ethics requires more study than we can accomplish in this book. However, remember that, when making accounting decisions, do not check your ethics at the door!

A FRAMEWORK FOR MAKING ETHICAL JUDGMENTS

Weighing tough ethical judgments in business and accounting requires a decision framework. Answering the following four questions will guide you through tough decisions:

Decision	Guidelines
1. What is the issue?	1. The issue will usually deal with making a judgment about an accounting measurement or disclosure that results in economic consequences, often to numerous parties.
2. Who are the stakeholders, and what are the consequences of the decision to each?	2. Stakeholders are anyone who might be affected by the decision—you, your company, and potential users of the information (investors, creditors, regulatory agencies). Consequences can be ethical in nature.
3. Weigh the alternatives.	3. Analyze the impact of the decision on all stakeholders, using ethical criteria. Ask "Who will be helped or hurt, whose rights will be exercised or denied, and in what way?"
4. Make the decision and be prepared to deal with the consequences.	4. Exercise the courage to either defend the decision or to change it, depending on its positive or negative impact. How does your decision make you feel afterward?

To simplify, we might ask three questions:

1. Is the action legal? If not, steer clear, unless you want to go to jail or pay monetary damages to injured parties. If the action is legal, go on to questions (2) and (3).
2. Who will be affected by the decision and how? Be as thorough about this analysis as possible, and analyze it from an ethical standpoint.
3. How will this decision make me feel afterward? How would it make me feel if my family read about it in the newspaper?

In later chapters throughout the book, we will apply this model to different accounting decisions.

In the business setting, ethics work best when modelled "from the top." Corporate Knights Inc. (www.corporateknights.ca) is a Canadian media company that "publishes the world's largest circulation magazine with an explicit focus on corporate responsibility," *Corporate Knights*. The company also publishes reports listing the most socially responsible corporations on a number of different dimensions. Of particular interest for our purposes is Corporate Knights' 2009 report entitled "8th Annual Best 50 Corporate Citizens in Canada." The company's website lists the criteria that were used in compiling the list, which includes such companies as Hydro One, Petro-Canada, TELUS, RONA Inc., Mountain Equipment Co-op,, and Bombardier Inc. As you begin to make your decisions about future employers, put these companies on your list! It's easier to act ethically when those you work for recognize the importance of ethics in business practices. These companies have learned from experience that in the long run, ethical conduct pays big rewards, not only socially, morally, and spiritually, but economically as well!

Chapter Summaries

Each chapter ends with a summary that identifies the major issues raised in the chapter. Read it carefully to ensure that you are familiar with the contents of the chapter.

SUMMARY OF CHAPTER 1

Learning Objective ❶: **Learn that financial statements are the product of accounting**

Accounting is an information system that measures business activities, processes data into reports, and communicates results to decision makers. These **decision makers or users** include investors and creditors (primary users), managers, government and regulatory agencies, taxing authorities, and individuals.

A business can be **organized** as a **proprietorship**, a **partnership**, or a **public** or **private corporation.** A public corporation's shares are traded on a stock exchange while a private corporation's shares are privately held.

Learning Objective ❷: **Apply the accounting equation to business organizations**

The financial statements are based on the **accounting equation** whereby a**ssets equal liabilities and owners' equity**. **Assets** are the resources of the business and include cash, accounts receivable, inventory, and property, plant, and equipment. Financing for these resources comes from two sources: creditors (liabilities) and owners (shareholders). **Liabilities** include accounts payable, notes payable, and long-term debt. **Owners' equity** includes the capital contributed by the owners and retained earnings.

Retained earnings are increased by revenues and decreased by expenses and dividends.

Learning Objective ❸: **Understand financial statements and how to use them**

The **financial statements** include the **income statement**, **statement of retained earnings**, **balance sheet**, and **statement of cash flows.**

The **income statement** shows how well the company has performed by reporting the revenue minus all expenses. Users are interested in seeing if the company can sell its products or services and they watch for trends and what percentage of sales revenue ends up as profit.

The **statement of retained earnings** shows users what a company did with its net income and if any amount was distributed by way of dividends to its shareholders.

The **balance sheet** reports the financial position of a company at a point in time. It includes three main categories: assets, liabilities, and shareholders' equity. Users are interested in knowing if the company can collect its receivables and pay both its current and its long-term liabilities.

The **statement of cash flows** reports cash receipts and cash payments classified according to the company's major activities: operating, investing, and financing. Users want to know where the company's cash is coming from and how it is being used.

The **notes to the financial statements** are an integral part of the financial statements and provide information that cannot be reported conveniently on the face of the financial statements.

Learning Objective ❹: **Explain the relationships among the financial statements**

The relationships between the income statement and the statement of retained earnings, between the statement of retained earnings and the balance sheet, and between the statement of cash flows and the balance sheet apply to all organizations.

Learning Objective ❺: **Understand financial accounting standards**

Accountants follow professional guidelines called **generally accepted accounting principles (GAAP).** In Canada, accounting standards are set by boards established by the **Canadian Institute of Chartered Accountants (CICA). The Accounting Standards Oversight Committee (AcSOC)** oversees and provides insight to the deliberations of the **Accounting Standards Board (AcSB),** which sets accounting standards for Canadian companies and not-for-profit organizations, and the **Public Sector Accounting Board (PSAB),** which sets standards for the public sector.

The **International Accounting Standards Board (IASB)** develops and issues **International Financial Reporting Standards (IFRS)** that are used in many countries around the world. The AcSB is converging IFRS with Canadian accounting standards. All **publicly accountable enterprises (PAEs)** in Canada are required to use IFRS for reporting in their financial statements. The AcSB has developed A**ccounting Standards for Private Enterprises (ASPE),** which must be used by **private enterprises (PE)** in Canada.

IFRS rest on a conceptual framework. The framework begins with the **objective** of financial reporting and includes the **fundamental qualitative characteristics** of **relevance** and **faithful representation,** as well as the **enhancing qualitative characteristics** of **comparability, verifiability, timeliness,** and **understandability,** all of which make accounting information useful. Accounting concepts include **the entity assumption, going-concern assumption, the cost assumption,** and **the stable-monetary-unit assumption. Multiple GAAPs** are discussed.

Learning Objective ❻: **Understand the role of ethics in business and accounting decisions**

Ethical behaviour by those who prepare financial statements and those who audit the financial statements is very important because so many decision makers—managers, investors, creditors, regulators, and many others—rely on those financial statements.

The **Canadian Institute of Chartered Accountants (CICA),** the **Certified General Accountants Association of Canada (CGAAC)** and the **Society of Management Accountants of Canada (SMAC)** have **codes of conduct** that require high levels of ethical conduct.

Audits are performed by independent accountants to ensure that financial statements are relevant and a faithful representation.

MyAccountingLab

END-OF-CHAPTER SUMMARY PROBLEM

J. J. Booth and Marie Savard incorporated Tara Inc., a consulting engineering company, and began operations on April 1, 2011. During April, the business provided engineering services for clients. It is now April 30, and J. J. and Marie wonder how well Tara Inc. performed during its first month. They also want to know the business's financial position at the end of April 30 and cash flows during the month.

The following data are listed in alphabetical order.

Accounts payable	$ 1,800	Land	$ 18,000
Accounts receivable	2,000	Office supplies	3,700
Adjustments to reconcile net income to net cash provided by operating activities	(3,900)	Payments of cash:	
		Acquisition of land	40,000
		Dividends	2,100
Cash balance at beginning of April	0	Rent expense	1,100
Cash balance at end of April	33,300	Retained earnings at beginning of April	0
Cash receipts:		Retained earnings at end of April	?
Issuance (sale) of shares	50,000	Salary expense	1,200
Sale of land	22,000	Service revenue	10,000
Common shares (contributed capital)	50,000	Utilities expense	400

Required

Name: Tara Inc.
Industry: Consulting engineering corporation
Fiscal Period: Month of April 2011

Review the list of accounts provided and determine whether each account is an asset, liability, shareholders' equity, revenue, or expense. Then group the accounts by financial statement.

1. Prepare the income statement, the statement of retained earnings, and the statement of cash flows for the month ended April 30, 2011, and the balance sheet at April 30, 2011. Draw arrows linking the pertinent items in the statements.
2. Answer the investors' underlying questions.
   a. How well did Tara Inc. perform during its first month of operations?
   b. Where does Tara Inc. stand financially at the end of the first month?
3. If you were a banker, would you be willing to lend money to Tara Inc.?
4. What additional information would you want to have before investing in Tara?

ANSWERS

Requirement 1

Financial Statements of Tara Inc.

The title must include the name of the company, "Income Statement," and the specific period of time covered. It is critical that the time period be defined.

Gather all the revenue and expense accounts from the account listing. List the revenue accounts first. List the expense accounts next.

Tara Inc.
Income Statement
For the Month Ended April 30, 2011

Revenue:		
Service revenue		$10,000
Expenses:		
Salary expense	$1,200	
Rent expense	1,100	
Utilities expense	400	
Total expenses		2,700
Net income		$ 7,300 ①

Tara Inc.
Statement of Retained Earnings
For the Month Ended April 30, 2011

Retained earnings, April 1, 2011	$ 0
Add: Net income for the month	7,300
	7,300
Less: Dividends	(2,100)
Retained earnings, April 30, 2011	$5,200

The title must include the name of the company, "Statement of Retained Earnings," and the specific period of time covered. It is critical that the time period be defined.

The net income amount (or net loss amount) is transferred from the income statement. Retained earnings at the end of the period is the result of a calculation, and is an accumulation of the corporation's performance since it began.

Tara Inc.
Balance Sheet
As at April 30, 2011

②

Assets		Liabilities	
Cash	$33,300	Accounts payable	$ 1,800
Accounts receivable	2,000	**Shareholders' Equity**	
Office supplies	3,700	Common shares	50,000
Land	18,000	Retained earnings	5,200
		Total shareholders' equity	55,200
		Total liabilities and	
Total assets	$57,000	shareholders' equity	$57,000

The title must include the name of the company, "Balance Sheet," and the date of the balance sheet. It shows the financial position at the end of the day.

Gather all the asset, liability, and equity accounts from the account listing. List assets first, then liabilities, then equity accounts. The retained earnings amount is transferred from the statement of retained earnings.

It is imperative that total assets = total liabilities + shareholders' equity.

Tara Inc.
Statement of Cash Flows
For the Month Ended April 30, 2011

③

Cash flows from operating activities:		
Net income		$ 7,300
Adjustments to reconcile net income to net cash provided by operating activities		(3,900)
Net cash provided by operating activities		3,400
Cash flows from investing activities:		
Acquisition of land	$(40,000)	
Sale of land	22,000	
Net cash used for investing activities		(18,000)
Cash flows from financing activities:		
Issuance (sale) of shares	$ 50,000	
Payment of dividends	(2,100)	
Net cash provided by financing activities		47,900
Net increase in cash		$33,300
Cash balance, April 1, 2011		0
Cash balance, April 30, 2011		$33,300

The title must include the name of the company, "Statement of Cash Flows," and the specific period of time covered. It is critical that the time period be defined.

Net income comes from the income statement. The adjustments amount was provided. In later chapters, you will learn how to calculate this amount.

Include all transactions that involve investing the company's cash, which involve any changes in the property, plant, and equipment.

Include all cash transactions relating to shares and long-term debt obligations.

Requirements 2, 3, and 4

2. a. The company performed rather well in April. Net income was $7,300—very good in relation to service revenue of $10,000. Tara was able to pay cash dividends of $2,100.
   b. The business ended April with cash of $33,300. Total assets of $57,000 far exceed total liabilities of $1,800. Shareholders' equity of $55,200 provides a good cushion for borrowing. The business's financial position at April 30, 2011, is strong.
   c. The company has plenty of cash, and assets far exceed liabilities. Operating activities generated positive cash flow in the first month of operations. Lenders like to see these features before making a loan.
3. Most bankers would be willing to lend to Tara Inc. at this time.
4. What would you like to know in addition to the information provided in the financial statements?

Consider the net income from the income statement.

Consider net worth, which is total assets minus total liabilities.

Review the Financial Statements

Quick Check (Answers are given on page 59.)

1. All of the following statements are true except one. Which statement is false?
   a. Bookkeeping is only a part of accounting.
   b. A proprietorship is a business with several owners.
   c. Professional accountants are held to a high standard of ethical conduct.
   d. The organization that formulates generally accepted accounting principles is the Canadian Institute of Chartered Accountants (CICA).
2. The recorded cost of assets at time of purchase is based on
   a. The amount paid for the assset.
   b. What it would cost to replace the asset.
   c. Current fair value as established by independent appraisers.
   d. Selling price.
3. The accounting equation can be expressed as
   a. Assets + Liabilities = Shareholders' Equity
   b. Shareholders' Equity − Assets = Liabilities
   c. Assets = Liabilities − Shareholders' Equity
   d. Assets − Liabilities = Shareholders' Equity
4. The nature of an asset is best described as
   a. Something with physical form that's valued at cost of purchase in the accounting records.
   b. An economic resource representing cash or the right to receive cash in the near future.
   c. An economic resource that's expected to benefit future operations.
   d. Something owned by a business that has a ready market value.
5. Which financial statement covers a period of time?
   a. Balance sheet
   b. Income statement
   c. Statement of cash flows
   d. Both b and c
6. How would net income be most likely to affect the accounting equation?
   a. Increase assets and increase shareholders' equity.
   b. Increase liabilities and decrease shareholders' equity.
   c. Increase assets and increase liabilities.
   d. Decrease assets and decrease liabilities.
7. During the year, ChemDry Ltd. has $100,000 in revenues, $40,000 in expenses, and $3,000 in dividend payments. Shareholders' equity changed by
   a. +$27,000
   b. +$57,000
   c. +$12,000
   d. −$8,000
8. ChemDry Ltd. in Question 7 had
   a. Net income of $100,000
   b. Net income of $57,000
   c. Net income of $60,000
   d. Net loss of $40,000
9. Leah Corporation holds cash of $5,000 and owes $25,000 on accounts payable. Leah has accounts receivable of $30,000, inventory of $20,000, and land cost of $50,000. How much are Leah's total assets and shareholders' equity?

	Total assets	Shareholders' equity
a.	$100,000	$25,000
b.	$105,000	$80,000
c.	$105,000	$25,000
d.	$25,000	$105,000

10. Which item(s) is (are) reported on the balance sheet?
    a. Retained earnings
    b. Accounts payable
    c. Inventory
    d. All of the above

11. During the year, Mason Inc.'s shareholders' equity increased from $30,000 to $40,000. Mason earned net income of $15,000. How much in dividends did Mason declare in the year?
    a. $6,000
    b. $0
    c. $8,000
    d. $5,000
12. Stuebs Corporation had total assets of $300,000 and total shareholders' equity of $100,000 at the beginning of the year. During the year assets increased by $50,000 and liabilities increased by $40,000. Shareholders' equity at the end of the year is
    a. $90,000
    b. $110,000
    c. $140,000
    d. $150,000

Accounting Vocabulary

accounting The information system that measures business activities, processes that information into reports and financial statements, and communicates the results to decision makers. (p. 3)

accounting equation The most basic tool of accounting: Assets = Liabilities + Owners' Equity. (p. 7)

account payable A liability for goods or services purchased on credit and backed by the general reputation and credit standing of the debtor. (p. 8)

accounts receivable An asset, amounts due from customers to whom a business has sold goods or services. (p. 8)

asset An economic resource that is expected to produce a benefit in the future. (p. 7)

balance sheet List of an entity's assets, liabilities, and owners' equity as of a specific date. Also called the *statement of financial position*. (p. 16)

board of directors Group elected by the shareholders to set policy for a corporation and to appoint its officers. (p. 7)

capital Another name for the *owners' equity* of a business. (p. 7)

capital assets Another name for *property, plant, and equipment*. (p. 8)

cash and cash equivalents Money and any medium of exchange that a bank accepts at face value. (p. 8)

common shares The most basic form of share capital. Common shareholders own a corporation. (p. 8)

contributed capital The amount of shareholders' equity that shareholders have invested in the corporation. (p. 8)

corporation A business owned by shareholders. A corporation is a legal entity, an "artificial person" in the eyes of the law. (p. 6)

cost assumption Assumption that assets and services should be recorded at their actual cost when acquired. (p. 29)

current asset An asset that is expected to be converted to cash, sold, or consumed during the next 12 months, or within the business's normal operating cycle if longer than a year. (p. 17)

current liability A debt due to be paid within one year or within the entity's operating cycle if the cycle is longer than a year. (p. 17)

deficit Negative balance in retained earnings caused by net losses over a period of years. (p. 10)

dividends Distributions (usually cash) by a corporation to its shareholders. (p. 9)

entity An organization or a section of an organization that, for accounting purposes, stands apart from other organizations and individuals as a separate economic unit. (p. 28)

ethics Standards of right and wrong that transcend economic and legal boundaries. Ethical standards deal with the way we treat others and restrain our own actions because of the desires, expectations, or rights of others and our obligations to them. (p. 33)

expenses Decrease in retained earnings that results from operations; the cost of doing business; opposite of revenues. (p. 8)

faithful representation The fundamental qualitative characteristic that accounting information is complete, free from bias, and without material error. (p. 28)

financial accounting The branch of accounting that provides information to people outside the firm. (p. 5)

financial statements Business documents that report financial information about a business entity to decision makers. (p. 2)

financing activities Activities that obtain from investors and creditors the cash needed to launch and sustain the business; a section of the statement of cash flows. (p. 20)

fixed assets Another name for *property, plant, and equipment*. (p. 8)

generally accepted accounting principles (GAAP) Accounting standards, issued by the Canadian Institute of Chartered Accountants (CICA) Accounting Standards Board, that govern how accounting is practised in Canada. (p. 24)

going-concern assumption Holds that the entity will remain in operation for the foreseeable future. (p. 29)

income statement A financial statement listing an entity's revenues, expenses, and net income or net loss for a specific period. Also called the *statement of operations* or the *statement of earnings*. (p. 11)

International Financial Reporting Standards (IFRS) International accounting standards issued by the International Accounting Standards Board (IASB). Canada is converging Canadian GAAP with IFRS for Publicly Accountable Enterprises (PAEs) effective January 2011. (p. 25)

inventory The merchandise that a company sells; also includes raw materials for use in a manufacturing process. (p. 8)

investing activities Activities that increase or decrease the capital assets available to the business; a section of the statement of cash flows. (p. 20)

liability An economic obligation (a debt) payable to an individual or an organization outside the entity. (p. 7)

limited liability partnership A business organization in which the business partnership (not the partners) is liable for the partnership's debts. (p. 6)

long-term debt A liability that falls due beyond one year from the date of the financial statements. (p. 8)

long-term liabilities Liabilities that are due beyond one year after the balance sheet date. (p. 18)

management accounting The branch of accounting that generates information for the internal decision makers of a business, such as top executives. (p. 5)

net assets Another name for *owners' equity*. (p. 7)

net earnings Another name for *net income*. (p. 9)

net income Excess of total revenues over total expenses. Also called *net earnings* or *net profit*. (p. 9)

net loss Excess of total expenses over total revenues. (p. 9)

net profit Another name for *net income*. (p. 9)

operating activities Activities that create revenue or expense in the entity's major line of business; a section of the statement of cash flows. Operating activities affect the income statement. (p. 20)

owners' equity The claim of the owners of a business to the assets of the business. Also called *capital*, *shareholders' equity*, or *net assets*. (p. 7)

partnership An association of two or more persons who co-own a business. (p. 6)

plant assets Another name for *property, plant, and equipment*. (p. 8)

private enterprises (PEs) Corporations whose shares are privately held either by its founders and/or by family members. (p. 26)

profit The excess of revenues over expenses. (p. 9)

property, plant, and equipment Long-lived assets, such as land, buildings, and equipment, used in the operation of the business. Also called *plant assets*, *fixed assets*, or *tangible capital assets*. (p. 8)

proprietorship A business with a single owner. (p. 5)

publicly accountable enterprises (PAEs) Corporations that have issued or plan to issue shares or debt in a public market. (p. 26)

relevance The fundamental qualitative characteristic of accounting information that is capable of making a difference to the decision maker and has predictive or confirming value. (p. 27)

retained earnings The amount of shareholders' equity that the corporation of the business has earned through profitable operation and has not given back to shareholders. (p. 8)

revenues Increase in retained earnings from delivering goods or services to customers or clients. (p. 8)

shareholder A person who owns shares of stock in a corporation. (p. 6)

shareholders' equity The shareholders' ownership interest in the assets of a corporation. Also called *owners' equity*. (p. 7)

stable-monetary-unit assumption The reason for ignoring the effect of inflation in the accounting records, based on the assumption that the dollar's purchasing power is relatively stable. (p. 29)

statement of cash flows Reports cash receipts and cash payments classified according to the entity's major activities: operating, investing, and financing. (p. 20)

statement of earnings Another name for the *income statement*. (p. 11)

statement of financial position Another name for the *balance sheet*. (p. 16)

statement of operations Another name for the *income statement*. (p. 11)

statement of retained earnings Summary of the changes in the retained earnings of a corporation during a specific period. (p. 14)

stock Shares into which the owners' equity of a corporation is divided. (p. 6)

Assess Your Progress

Make the grade with MyAccountingLab: The exercises and problems in this chapter can be found on MyAccountingLab at www.myaccountinglab.com. You can practise them as often as you want, and they feature step-by-step guided solutions to help you find the right answer.

Short Exercises

Learning Objective 1
Financial statements are the product of accounting

S1-1 Accounting definitions are precise, and you must understand the vocabulary to properly use accounting. Sharpen your understanding of key terms by answering the following questions:

1. How do the *assets* and *shareholders' equity* of Gildan Activewear Inc. differ from each other? Which one (assets or shareholders' equity) must be at least as large as the other? Which one can be smaller than the other?
2. How are Gildan Activewear Inc.'s *liabilities* and *shareholders' equity* similar? How are they different?

S1-2 Use the accounting equation to show how to determine the amount of the missing term in each of the following situations.

Learning Objective 2
Applying the accounting equation

Total Assets	=	Total Liabilities	+	Shareholders' Equity
a. $?		$150,000		$150,000
b. 290,000		90,000		?
c. 220,000		?		120,000

S1-3 Review the accounting equation on page 7.

Learning Objective 2
Using the accounting equation

1. Use the accounting equation to show how to determine the amount of a company's owners' equity. How would your answer change if you were analyzing your own household or a single IHOP restaurant?
2. If you know assets and owners' equity, how can you measure liabilities? Give the equation.

S1-4 Consider Walmart, the world's largest retailer. Classify the following items as an asset (A), a liability (L), or an owners' equity (E) item for Walmart:

Learning Objective 2
Classifying assets, liabilities, and owners' equity

_____ **a.** Accounts payable
_____ **b.** Common shares
_____ **c.** Cash
_____ **d.** Retained earnings
_____ **e.** Land
_____ **f.** Prepaid expenses
_____ **g.** Accounts receivable
_____ **h.** Long-term debt
_____ **i.** Merchandise inventories
_____ **j.** Notes payable
_____ **k.** Accrued expenses payable
_____ **l.** Equipment

S1-5

Learning Objective 3
Using the income statement

1. Identify the two basic categories of items on an income statement.
2. What do we call the bottom line of the income statement?

S1-6 Split Second Wireless Inc. began 2011 with total assets of $110 million and ended 2011 with assets of $160 million. During 2011 Split Second earned revenues of $90 million and had expenses of $20 million. Split Second paid dividends of $10 million in 2011. Prepare the company's income statement for the year ended December 31, 2011, complete with the appropriate heading.

Learning Objective 3
Preparing an income statement

S1-7 Mondala Ltd. began 2011 with retained earnings of $200 million. Revenues during the year were $400 million and expenses totalled $300 million. Mondala declared dividends of $40 million. What was the company's ending balance of retained earnings? To answer this question, prepare Mondala's statement of retained earnings for the year ended December 31, 2011, complete with its appropriate heading.

Learning Objective 3
Preparing a statement of retained earnings

S1-8 At December 31, 2011, Skate Sharp Limited has cash of $13,000, receivables of $2,000, and inventory of $40,000. The company's equipment totals $75,000, and other assets amount to $10,000. Skate Sharp owes accounts payable of $10,000 and short-term notes payable of $5,000, and also has long-term debt of $70,000.

Contributed capital is $15,000.

Prepare Skate Sharp Limited's balance sheet at December 31, 2011, complete with its appropriate heading.

Learning Objective 3
Preparing a balance sheet

S1-9 Brazos Medical, Inc., ended 2010 with cash of $24,000. During 2011, Brazos earned net income of $120,000 and had adjustments to reconcile net income to net cash provided by operations totalling $20,000 (this is a negative amount).

Brazos paid $300,000 for equipment during 2011 and had to borrow half of this amount on a long-term note. During the year, the company paid dividends of $15,000 and sold old equipment, receiving cash of $60,000.

Learning Objective 3
Preparing a statement of cash flows

Prepare Brazos' statement of cash flows with its appropriate heading for the year ended December 31, 2011. Follow the format in the summary problem on page 36.

Learning Objective 5
Applying accounting assumptions

S1-10 John Grant is chairman of the board of The Grant Group Ltd. Suppose Grant has just founded this company, and assume that he treats his home and other personal assets as part of The Grant Group Ltd. Answer these questions about the evaluation of The Grant Group Ltd.

1. Which accounting assumption governs this situation?
2. How can the proper application of this accounting assumption give John Grant a realistic view of The Grant Group Ltd.? Explain in detail.

Learning Objective 6
Making ethical judgments

S1-11 Accountants follow ethical guidelines in the conduct of their work. What are these standards of professional conduct designed to produce? Why is this goal important?

Learning Objective 4
Relationships among the financial statements

S1-12 Suppose you are analyzing the financial statements of a Canadian company. Identify each item with its appropriate financial statement, using the following abbreviations: income statement (IS), statement of retained earnings (SRE), balance sheet (BS), and statement of cash flows (SCF).

Three items appear on two financial statements, and one item shows up on three statements.

a. Dividends __________
b. Salary expense __________
c. Inventory __________
d. Sales revenue __________
e. Retained earnings __________
f. Net cash provided by operating activities __________
g. Net income __________
h. Cash __________
i. Net cash provided by financing activities __________
j. Accounts payable __________
k. Common shares __________
l. Interest revenue __________
m. Long-term debt __________
n. Net increase or decrease in cash __________

Exercises

Learning Objective 1
Organizing a business

E1-13 Quality Environmental Inc. needs funds, and Mary Wu, the president, has asked you to consider investing in the business. Answer the following questions about the different ways in which Wu might organize the business. Explain each answer.

a. What form of organization will enable the owners of Quality Environmental to limit their risk of loss to the amount they have invested in the business?
b. What form of business organization will give Wu the most freedom to manage the business as she wishes?
c. What form of organization will give creditors the maximum protection in the event that Quality Environmental fails and cannot pay its liabilities?

If you were Wu and could organize the business as you wish, what form of organization would you choose for Quality Environmental? Explain your reasoning.

Learning Objective 3
Evaluating business operations

E1-14 Ed Eisler wants to open a café in Digby, Nova Scotia. In need of cash, he asks the Bank of Montreal for a loan. The bank requires financial statements to show likely results of operations for the year and the expected financial position at year-end. With little knowledge of accounting, Eisler doesn't understand the request. Explain to him the information provided by the income statement and the balance sheet. Indicate why a lender would require this information.

Learning Objective 2
Applying accounting assumptions

E1-15 Identify the accounting assumption that best applies to each of the following situations.

a. Wendy's, the restaurant chain, sold a store location to Burger King. How can Wendy's determine the sale price of the store—by a professional appraisal, Wendy's cost, or the amount actually received from the sale?

b. If Trammel Crow Realtors had to liquidate its assets, their value would be less than carrying amounts of the assets.
c. Toyota wants to determine which division of the company—Toyota or Lexus—is more profitable.
d. You get an especially good buy on a laptop, paying only $399 for a computer that normally costs $799. What is your accounting value for this computer?

Learning Objective 2
Using the accounting equation

E1-16 Compute the missing amount in the accounting equation for each company (amounts in millions):

	Assets	Liabilities	Shareholders' Equity
TELUS	$?	$10,061	$ 6,926
Scotiabank	411,510	?	18,804
Shoppers Drugmart	5,644	2,434	?

Which company appears to have the strongest financial position? Explain your reasoning.

Learning Objective 2 3
Accounting equation; evaluating business

E1-17 Assume Maple Leaf Foods Inc. has current assets of $633.6 million; capital assets of $1,126.7 million; and other assets totalling $1,237.5 million. Current liabilities are $591.2 million and long-term liabilities total $1,245.2 million.

Required

1. Use these data to write Maple Leaf Foods' accounting equation.
2. How much in resources does Maple Leaf Foods have to work with?
3. How much does Maple Leaf Foods owe creditors?
4. How much of the company's assets do the Maple Leaf Foods shareholders actually own?

Learning Objective 2
Applying the accounting equation

E1-18 We Store For You Ltd.'s comparative balance sheets at December 31, 2011, and December 31, 2010, report (in millions):

	2011	2010
Total assets	$40	$30
Total liabilities	10	8

Required

Below are three situations about We Store For You's issuance of shares and payment of dividends during the year ended December 31, 2011. For each situation, use the accounting equation and statement of retained earnings to compute the amount of We Store For You's net income or loss during the year ended December 31, 2011.

1. We Store For You issued shares for $2 million and paid no dividends.
2. We Store For You issued no shares and paid dividends of $3 million.
3. We Store For You issued shares for $11 million and paid dividends of $2 million.

Learning Objective 2
Applying the accounting equation to business operations

E1-19 Answer these questions about two companies.

1. Mortimer Limited began the year with total liabilities of $400,000 and total shareholders' equity of $300,000. During the year, total assets increased by 20%. How much are total assets at the end of the year?
2. Aztec Associates began a year with total assets of $500,000 and total liabilities of $200,000. Net income for the year was $100,000 and no dividends were paid. How much is shareholders' equity at the end of the year?

Learning Objective ❸
Identifying financial statement information

E1-20 Assume MySpace Inc. is expanding into the United States. The company must decide where to locate, and how to finance the expansion. Identify the financial statement where decision makers can find the following information about MySpace Inc. In some cases, more than one statement will report the needed data.

a. Common shares
b. Income tax payable
c. Dividends
d. Income tax expense
e. Ending balance of retained earnings
f. Total assets
g. Long-term debt
h. Revenue
i. Cash spent to acquire equipment
j. Selling, general, and administrative expenses
k. Adjustments to reconcile net income to net cash provided by operations
l. Ending cash balance
m. Current liabilities
n. Net income
o. Cost of goods sold

Learning Objective ❷❸
Applying the accounting equation; understand the balance sheet

E1-21 Amounts of the assets and liabilities of Torrance Associates Inc., as of December 31, 2011, are given as follows. Also included are revenue and expense figures for the year ended on that date (amounts in millions):

Property and equipment, net	$ 4	Total revenue	$ 35
Investment	72	Receivables	253
Long-term liabilities	73	Current liabilities	290
Other expenses	14	Common shares	12
Cash	28	Interest expense	3
Retained earnings, beginning	19	Salary and other employee expense	9
Retained earnings, ending	?	Other assets	43

Required
Prepare the balance sheet of Torrance Associates Inc. at December 31, 2011. Use the accounting equation to compute ending retained earnings.

Learning Objective ❸
Understanding the income statement

E1-22 This exercise should be worked only in connection with Exercise 1-21. Refer to the data of Torrance Associates Inc. in Exercise 1-21.

Required
1. Prepare the income statement of Torrance Associates Inc. for the year ended December 31, 2011.
2. What amount of dividends did Torrance declare during the year ended December 31, 2011? Hint: Prepare a statement of retained earnings.

Learning Objective ❸
Using the financial statements

E1-23 Groovy Limited began 2011 with $95,000 in cash. During 2011, Groovy earned net income of $300,000, and adjustments to reconcile net income to net cash provided by operations totalled $60,000, a positive amount. Investing activities used cash of $400,000, and financing activities provided cash of $70,000. Groovy ended 2011 with total assets of $250,000 and total liabilities of $110,000.

Required
Prepare Groovy Limited's statement of cash flows for the year ended December 31, 2011. Identify the data items that do not appear on the statement of cash flows and indicate which financial statement reports these items.

E1-24 Assume a FedEx Kinko's at the University of Saskatchewan ended the month of July 2011 with these data:

Learning Objective 3
Preparing an income statement and a statement of retained earnings

Payments of cash:		Issuance (sale) of shares to owners	$35,000
Acquisition of equipment	$36,000	Rent expense	700
Dividends	2,000	Common shares	35,000
Retained earnings at July 1, 2011	0	Equipment	36,000
Retained earnings at July 31, 2011	?	Office supplies expense	1,200
Utilities expense	200	Accounts payable	3,200
Adjustments to reconcile net income to cash provided by operations	3,200	Service revenue	14,000
Salary expense	4,000		
Cash balance July 1, 2011	0		
Cash balance July 31, 2011	8,100		
Cash receipts:			

Required

Prepare the income statement and the statement of retained earnings of this FedEx Kinko's for the month ended July 31, 2011.

E1-25 Refer to the data in the preceding exercise. Prepare the balance sheet of the FedEx Kinko's at July 31, 2011.

Learning Objective 3
Preparing a balance sheet

E1-26 Refer to the data in Exercise 1-24. Prepare the statement of cash flows of the FedEx Kinko's at the University of Saskatchewan for the month ended July 31, 2011. Draw arrows linking the pertinent items in the statements you prepared for Exercises 1-24 through 1-26.

Learning Objective 3
Preparing a statement of cash flows

E1-27 This exercise should be used in conjunction with Exercises 1-24 through 1-26. The owner of the FedEx Kinko's now seeks your advice as to whether the University of Saskatchewan store should cease operations or continue operating. Write a report giving the owner your opinion of operating results, dividends, financial position, and cash flows during the company's first month of operations. Cite specifics from the financial statements to support your opinion. Conclude your report with advice on whether to stay in business or cease operations.

Learning Objective 3
Using financial statements for decision making

E1-28 Apply your understanding of the relationships among the financial statements to answer these questions.

a. How can a business earn large profits but have a small balance of retained earnings?
b. Give two reasons why a business can have a steady stream of net income over a five-year period and still experience a cash shortage.
c. If you could pick a single source of cash for your business, what would it be? Why?
d. How can a business lose money several years in a row and still have plenty of cash?

Learning Objective 5
Relationships among financial statements

Quiz

Test your understanding of the financial statements by answering the following questions. Select the best choice from among the possible answers given.

Q1-29 The *primary* objective of financial reporting is to provide information

a. Useful for making investment and credit decisions
b. About the profitability of the enterprise
c. On the cash flows of the company
d. To the federal government

Q1-30 For a business of a certain size, which type of business organization provides the least amount of protection for bankers and other creditors of the company?

a. Proprietorship
b. Partnership
c. Both a and b
d. Corporation

Q1-31 International Financial Reporting Standards (IFRS) were developed because
a. Canadian GAAP were outdated
b. Corporations wanted to change their reporting
c. Different GAAP in countries of the world made global comparisons difficult
d. New assumptions were defined

Q1-32 During January, assets increased by $20,000 and liabilities increased by $4,000. Shareholders' equity must have
a. Increased by $16,000
b. Increased by $24,000
c. Decreased by $16,000
d. Decreased by $24,000

Q1-33 The amount a company expects to collect from customers appears on the
a. Income statement in the expenses section
b. Balance sheet in the current assets section
c. Balance sheet in the shareholders' equity section
d. Statement of cash flows

Q1-34 All of the following are current assets except
a. Cash
b. Accounts receivable
c. Inventory
d. Sales revenue

Q1-35 Revenues are
a. Increases in share capital resulting from the owners investing in the business
b. Increases in retained earnings resulting from selling products or performing services
c. Decreases in liabilities resulting from paying off loans
d. All of the above

Q1-36 The financial statement that reports revenues and expenses is called the
a. Statement of retained earnings
b. Income statement
c. Statement of cash flows
d. Balance sheet

Q1-37 Another name for the balance sheet is the
a. Statement of operations
b. Statement of earnings
c. Statement of profit and loss
d. Statement of financial position

Q1-38 Baldwin Corporation began the year with cash of $35,000 and a computer that cost $20,000. During the year Baldwin earned sales revenue of $140,000 and had the following expenses: salaries, $59,000; rent, $8,000; and utilities, $3,000. At year-end Baldwin's cash balance was down to $16,000. How much net income (or net loss) did Baldwin experience for the year?
a. ($19,000)
b. $70,000
c. $107,000
d. $140,000

Q1-39 Quartz Instruments had retained earnings of $145,000 at December 31, 2010. Net income for 2011 totalled $90,000, and dividends for 2011 were $30,000. How much retained earnings should Quartz report at December 31, 2011?
a. $205,000
b. $235,000
c. $140,000
d. $175,000

Q1-40 Net income appears on which financial statement(s)?
a. Income statement
b. Statement of retained earnings
c. Both a and b
d. Balance sheet

Q1-41 Cash paid to purchase a building appears on the statement of cash flows among the
a. Operating activities
b. Financing activities
c. Investing activities
d. Shareholders' equity

Q1-42 The shareholders' equity of Chernasky Company at the beginning and end of 2011 totalled $15,000 and $18,000, respectively. Assets at the beginning of 2011 were $25,000. If the liabilities of Chernasky Company increased by $8,000 in 2011, how much were total assets at the end of 2011? Use the accounting equation.

a. $36,000
b. $16,000
c. $2,000
d. Some other amount (fill in the blank)

Q1-43 Drexler Company had the following on the dates indicated:

	12/31/11	12/31/10
Total assets	$750,000	$520,000
Total liabilities	300,000	200,000

Drexler had no share transactions in 2011 and, thus, the change in shareholders' equity for 2011 was due to net income and dividends. If dividends were $50,000, how much was Drexler's net income for 2011? Use the accounting equation and the statements of retained earnings.

a. $100,000
b. $130,000
c. $180,000
d. Some other amount (fill in the blank)

Problems

(Group A)

Learning Objective 1 3 4
Using financial statements and applying assumptions and characteristics to the income statement

P1-44A Assume that the Special Contract Division of FedEx Kinko's experienced the following transactions during the year ended December 31, 2011.

a. Suppose the division provided copy services to TELUS for the discounted price of $250,000. Under normal conditions, Kinko's would have provided these services for $280,000. Other revenues totalled $50,000.
b. Salaries cost the division $20,000 to provide these services. The division had to pay employees overtime. Ordinarily the salary cost for these services would have been $18,000.
c. Other expenses totalled $240,000. Income tax expense was 30% of income before tax.
d. FedEx Kinko's has two operating divisions. Each division is accounted for separately to indicate how well each is performing. At year-end, FedEx Kinko's combines the statements of divisions to show results for FedEx Kinko's as a whole.
e. Inflation affects the amounts that FedEx Kinko's must pay for copy machines. To show the effects of inflation, net income would drop by $3,000.
f. If FedEx Kinko's were to go out of business, the sale of its assets would bring in $150,000 in cash.

Required

1. Prepare the Special Contracts Division income statement for the year ended December 31, 2011.
2. As CEO, identify the accounting assumption or characteristics used in accounting for the items described in a through f. State how you have applied the assumption or characteristic in preparing the division income statement.

Learning Objective 2 3
Applying the accounting equation; understanding financial statements

P1-45A Compute the missing amounts (shown by a ?) for each company (in millions).

	Link Ltd.	Chain Inc.	Fence Corp.
Beginning			
Assets	$ 78	$ 30	?
Liabilities	47	19	$ 2
Common shares	6	1	2
Retained earnings	?	10	3
Ending			
Assets	?	$ 48	$ 9
Liabilities	$ 48	30	?
Common shares	6	1	2
Retained earnings	27	?	4
Owners' equity			
Dividends	$ 3	$ 2	$ 0
Income statement			
Revenues	$216	?	$20
Expenses	211	$144	19
Net income	?	9	1

At the end of the year, which company has the

- Highest net income?
- Highest percentage of net income to revenues?

Hint: Prepare a statement of retained earnings to help with your calculations.

Learning Objective 3
Balance sheet

P1-46A Dan Shoe, the manager of STRIDES Inc., prepared the company's balance sheet while the accountant was ill. The balance sheet contains numerous errors. In particular, Shoe knew that the balance sheet should balance, so he plugged in the shareholders' equity amount needed to achieve this balance. The shareholders' equity amount is *not* correct. All other amounts are accurate.

STRIDES Inc.
Balance Sheet
For the Month Ended July 31, 2011

Assets		Liabilities	
Cash	$ 25,000	Accounts receivable	$ 20,000
Store fixtures	10,000	Sales revenue	80,000
Accounts payable	16,000	Interest expense	800
Rent expense	4,000	Note payable	9,000
Salaries expense	15,000	Total	109,800
Land	44,000		
Advertising expense	3,000	Shareholders' Equity	
		Shareholders' equity	7,200
Total assets	$117,000	Total liabilities and shareholders' equity	$117,000

Required

1. Prepare the correct balance sheet and date it properly. Compute total assets, total liabilities, and shareholders' equity.
2. Is STRIDES Inc. actually in better or worse financial position than the erroneous balance sheet reports? Give the reason for your answer.

3. Identify the accounts listed on the incorrect balance sheet that are not reported on the balance sheet. State why you excluded them from the correct balance sheet you prepared for Requirement 1. On which financial statement should these accounts appear?

Learning Objective 3 4
Balance sheet, entity assumption

P1-47A Alexa Markowitz is a realtor. She buys and sells properties on her own, and she also earns commission as an agent for buyers and sellers. She organized her business as a corporation on March 16, 2011. The business received $60,000 cash from Markowitz and issued common shares. Consider the following facts as of March 31, 2011:

a. Markowitz has $5,000 in her personal bank account and $14,000 in the business bank account.
b. Office supplies on hand at the real estate office total $1,000.
c. Markowitz's business spent $25,000 for a ReMax franchise, which entitles her to represent herself as an agent. ReMax is a national affiliation of independent real estate agents. This franchise is a business asset.
d. The business owes $60,000 on a note payable for some undeveloped land acquired for a total price of $110,000.
e. Markowitz owes $100,000 on a personal mortgage on her personal residence, which she acquired in 2002 for a total price of $350,000.
f. Markowitz owes $1,800 on a personal charge account with Holt Renfrew.
g. Markowitz acquired business furniture for $10,000 on March 25. Of this amount, the business owes $6,000 on accounts payable at March 31.

Required

1. Prepare the balance sheet of the real estate business of Alexa Markowitz Realtor Inc. at March 31, 2011.
2. Does it appear that the realty business can pay its debts? How can you tell?
3. Explain why some of the items given in the preceding facts were not reported on the balance sheet of the business.

Learning Objective 3
Income statement, statement of retained earnings, balance sheet

P1-48A The assets and liabilities of Web Services Inc. as of December 31, 2011, and revenues and expenses for the year ended on that date are listed here.

Land	$ 8,000	Equipment	$ 11,000
Note payable	32,000	Interest expense	4,000
Property tax expense	2,000	Interest payable	2,000
Rent expense	15,000	Accounts payable	15,000
Accounts receivable	25,000	Salary expense	40,000
Service revenue	150,000	Building	126,000
Supplies	2,000	Cash	8,000
Utilities expense	3,000	Common shares	15,000

Beginning retained earnings were $60,000, and dividends totalled $30,000 for the year.

Required

1. Prepare the income statement of Web Services Inc. for the year ended December 31, 2011.
2. Prepare the company's statement of retained earnings for the year.
3. Prepare the company's balance sheet at December 31, 2011.
4. As CEO of Web Services Inc., after answering these questions, will you be pleased by Web Services's performance in 2011?
   a. Was Web Services profitable during 2011? By how much?
   b. Did retained earnings increase or decrease? By how much?
   c. Which is greater, total liabilities or total equity? Who owns more of Web Services's assets, creditors or Web Services's shareholders?

Learning Objective 3
Preparing a statement of cash flows

P1-49A The following data are from financial statements of Stuart Inc. for the fiscal year ended March 1, 2011 (in millions):

Purchases of capital assets and other assets	$ 144	Accounts receivable	$168
Issuance of long-term debt	164	Redemption of common shares	177
Net loss	(251)	Payment of dividends	31
Adjustments to reconcile net income (loss) to cash provided by operations	397	Common shares	715
Revenues	1,676	Issuance of common shares	1
Cash, beginning of year	41	Sales of capital assets and other assets	1
end of year	0	Retained earnings	752
Cost of goods sold	1,370	Repayment of long-term debt	1

Required

1. Prepare a statement of cash flows for the fiscal year ended March 1, 2011. Follow the format of the summary problem on page 36. Not all items given are reported in the statement of cash flows.
2. What was the largest source of cash? Is this a sign of financial strength or weakness?

Learning Objective 3 4
Analyzing a company's financial statements; relationships among the financial statements

P1-50A Summarized versions of the Gonzales Corporation's financial statements are given below for two years.

	(in thousands) 2011	2010
Statement of Operations		
Revenues	$ k	$16,000
Cost of goods sold	11,500	a
Other expenses	1,300	1,200
Earnings before income taxes	4,000	3,700
Income taxes (35% tax rate)	l	1,300
Net earnings	$ m	$ b
Statement of Retained Earnings		
Beginning balance	$ n	$ 3,500
Net earnings	o	c
Dividends	(300)	(200)
Ending balance	$ p	$ d
Balance Sheet		
Assets:		
Cash	$ q	$ e
Capital assets	3,000	1,800
Other assets	r	11,200
Total assets	$ s	$15,000
Liabilities:		
Current liabilities	$ t	$ 5,600
Notes payable and long-term debt	4,500	3,200
Other liabilities	80	200
Total liabilities	$ 9,100	$ f

Shareholders' Equity:		
Common shares	$ 300	$ 300
Retained earnings	u	g
Total shareholders' equity	v	6,000
Total liabilities and shareholders' equity	$ w	$ h
Statement of Cash Flows		
Net cash provided by operating activities	$ x	$ 1,900
Net cash used for investing activities	(1,000)	(900)
Net cash used for financing activities	(700)	(1.010)
Increase (decrease) in cash	400	i
Cash at beginning of year	y	2,010
Cash at end of year	$ z	$ j

Required

1. Determine the missing amounts denoted by the letters.
2. As Gonzales Corporation's CEO, use financial statements to answer these questions about the company. Explain each of your answers, and identify the financial statement where you found the information.
   a. Did operations improve or deteriorate during 2011?
   b. What is the company doing with most of its income—retaining it for use in the business or using it for dividends?
   c. How much in total resources does the company have to work with as it moves into the year 2012?
   d. At the end of 2010, how much did the company owe outsiders? At the end of 2011, how much did the company owe? Is this trend good or bad in comparison to the trend in assets?
   e. What is the company's major source of cash? Is cash increasing or decreasing? What is your opinion of the company's ability to generate cash?

(Group B)

Learning Objective 1 3 4
Applying assumptions and characteristics to the income statement

P1-51B Snap Fasteners Inc. experienced the following transactions during the year ended December 31, 2011:

a. All other expenses, excluding income taxes, totalled $14.9 million for the year. Income tax expense was 35% of income before tax.
b. Snap has several operating divisions. Each division is accounted for separately to show how well each division is performing. However, Snap's financial statements combine the statements of all the divisions to report on the company as a whole.
c. Inflation affects Snap's cost to manufacture goods. If Snap's financial statements were to show the effects of inflation, assume the company's reported net income would drop by $0.250 million.
d. If Snap were to go out of business, the sale of its assets might bring in over $5 million in cash.
e. Snap sold products for $56.2 million. Company management believes that the value of these products is approximately $60.5 million.
f. It cost Snap $40.0 million to manufacture the products it sold. If Snap had purchased the products instead of manufacturing them, Snap's cost would have been $43.0 million.

Required

1. Prepare Snap's income statement for the year ended December 31, 2011.
2. For items a through f, identify the accounting assumption or characteristic that determined how you accounted for the item described. State how you have applied the assumption or characteristic in preparing Snap's income statement.

Learning Objective 2 3
Applying the accounting equation; understanding the financial statements

P1-52B Compute the missing amounts (?) for each company (in millions).

	Gas Limited	Groceries Inc.	Bottlers Corp.
Beginning			
Assets	$11,200	$ 3,256	$ 909
Liabilities	4,075	1,756	564
Ending			
Assets	$12,400	$?	$1,025
Liabilities	4,400	1,699	565
Owners' Equity			
Issuance/(Repurchase) of shares	$ (36)	$ (0)	$?
Dividends	341	30	0
Income Statement			
Revenues	$11,288	$11,099	$1,663
Expenses	?	10,879	1,568

Which company has the

- Highest net income?
- Highest percentage of net income to revenues?

Hint: Prepare a statement of owners' equity, which begins with opening shareholders' equity and adds and subtracts changes to conclude with closing shareholders' equity.

Learning Objective 3
Balance sheet

P1-53B Ned Robinson, the manager of Lunenberg Times Inc., prepared the balance sheet of the company while the accountant was ill. The balance sheet contains numerous errors. In particular, the manager knew that the balance sheet should balance, so he plugged in the shareholders' equity amount needed to achieve this balance. The shareholders' equity amount, however, is *not* correct. All other amounts are accurate.

Lunenberg Times Inc.
Balance Sheet
For the Month Ended October 31, 2011

Assets		Liabilities	
Cash	$ 25,000	Accounts receivable	$ 10,000
Office furniture	15,000	Sales revenue	70,000
Note payable	16,000	Salary expense	20,000
Rent expense	4,000	Accounts payable	8,000
Inventory	30,000		
Land	34,000	**Shareholders' Equity**	
Advertising expense	2,500	Shareholders' equity	18,500
Total assets	$126,500	Total liabilities	$126,500

Required

1. Prepare the correct balance sheet and date it properly. Compute total assets, total liabilities, and shareholders' equity.
2. Is Lunenberg Times Inc. actually in better or worse financial position than the erroneous balance sheet reports? Give the reason for your answer.
3. Identify the accounts listed in the incorrect balance sheet that are *not* reported on the corrected balance sheet. State why you excluded them from the correct balance sheet you prepared for Requirement 1. Which financial statement should these accounts appear on?

Learning Objective 3 5
Balance sheet; entity assumption

P1-54B Luis Fantano is a realtor. He buys and sells properties on his own and also earns commission as an agent for buyers and sellers. Fantano organized his business as a corporation on July 10, 2011. The business received $75,000 from Fantano and issued common shares. Consider these facts as of July 31, 2011:

a. Fantano owes $5,000 on a personal charge account with Visa.
b. Fantano's business owes $80,000 on a note payable for some undeveloped land acquired for a total price of $135,000.
c. Fantano has $5,000 in his personal bank account and $10,000 in the business bank account.
d. Office supplies on hand at the real estate office total $1,000.
e. Fantano's business spent $35,000 for a Century 21 real estate franchise, which entitles him to represent himself as a Century 21 agent. Century 21 is a national affiliation of independent real estate agents. This franchise is a business asset.
f. Fantano owes $125,000 on a personal mortgage on his personal residence, which he acquired in 2001 for a total price of $300,000.
g. Fantano acquired business furniture for $18,000 on July 15. Of this amount, his business owes $10,000 on open account at July 31.

Required

1. Prepare the balance sheet of the realty business of Luis Fantano Realtor Inc. at July 31, 2011.
2. Does it appear that Fantano's realty business can pay its debts? How can you tell?
3. Identify the personal items given in the preceding facts that would not be reported on the balance sheet of the business.

Learning Objective 3 4
Income statement, statement of retained earnings, balance sheet; relationships among the financial statements

P1-55B The assets and liabilities of Auto Mechanics Ltd. as of December 31, 2011, and revenues and expenses for the year ended on that date follow.

Interest expense	$ 4,000	Accounts receivable	$ 25,000
Land	95,000	Advertising expense	10,000
Note payable	95,000	Building	140,000
Accounts payable	21,000	Salary expense	85,000
Rent expense	6,000	Salary payable	12,000
Cash	10,000	Service revenue	210,000
Common shares	75,000	Supplies	3,000
Furniture	20,000	Property tax expense	5,000

Beginning retained earnings were $40,000, and dividends totalled $50,000 for the year.

Required

1. Prepare the income statement of Auto Mechanics Ltd. for the year ended December 31, 2011.
2. Prepare the Auto Mechanics Ltd. statement of retained earnings for the year.
3. Prepare Auto Mechanics' balance sheet at December 31, 2011.
4. Using the information prepared in Requirements 1 through 3:
   a. Was Auto Mechanics Ltd. profitable during 2011? By how much?
   b. Did retained earnings increase or decrease? By how much?
   c. Which is greater, total liabilities or total equity? Who has a claim against more of Auto Mechanics Ltd.'s assets, the creditors or the shareholders?

Learning Objective 3
Preparing a statement of cash flows

P1-56B The data below are adapted from the financial statements of Long Boat Ltd. at the end of a recent year (in thousands).

Adjustments to reconcile net income to cash provided by operations	$ 65	Sales of capital assets	$ 2
Revenues	3,870	Payment of long-term debt	26
Bank overdraft, beginning of year	(11)	Cost of goods sold	3,182
Cash, end of year	23	Common shares	212
Purchases of capital assets	123	Accounts receivable	271
Long-term debt	234	Issuance of common shares	4
Net income	180	Change in bank loan	(44)
Retained earnings	1,000	Payment of dividends	24

Required

1. Prepare Long Boat's statement of cash flows for the year. Follow the solution to the summary problem starting on page 36. Not all the items given appear on the statement of cash flows.
2. Which activities provided the bulk of Long Boat's cash? Is this a sign of financial strength or weakness?

Learning Objective 3 5
Analyzing a company's financial statements; relationships among the financial statements

P1-57B Condensed versions of Your Phone Ltd.'s financial statements, with certain amounts omitted, are given for two years.

	(thousands) 2011	2010
Statement of Income		
Revenues	$94,500	$ a
Cost of goods sold	k	65,400
Other expenses	15,660	13,550
Income before income taxes	5,645	9,300
Income taxes	1,975	3,450
Net income	$ l	$ b
Statement of Retained Earnings		
Beginning balance	$ m	$10,000
Net income	n	c
Dividends	(480)	(450)
Ending balance	$ o	$ d
Balance Sheet		
Assets:		
Cash	$ p	$ 400
Capital assets	23,790	e
Other assets	q	17,900
Total assets	$ r	$38,500
Liabilities:		
Current liabilities	$11,100	$10,000
Long-term debt and other liabilities	s	12,500
Total liabilities	24,500	f
Shareholders' Equity:		
Common shares	$ 400	$ 600
Retained earnings	t	g
Total shareholders' equity	u	16,000
Total liabilities and shareholders' equity	$ v	$ h

Statement of Cash Flows		
Net cash provided by operating activities	$ w	$ 3,600
Net cash used for investing activities	(2,700)	(4,150)
Net cash provided by financing activities	250	900
Increase (decrease) in cash	50	i
Cash at beginning of year	x	50
Cash at end of year	$ y	$ j

Required

1. Determine the missing amounts denoted by the letters.
2. Use Your Phone's financial statements to answer these questions about the company. Explain each of your answers.
   a. Did operations improve or deteriorate during 2011?
   b. What is the company doing with most of its income—retaining it for use in the business or using it for dividends?
   c. How much in total resources does the company have to work with as it moves into 2012? How much in total resources did the company have at the end of 2010?
   d. At the end of 2010, how much did the company owe outsiders? At the end of 2011, how much did the company owe?
   e. What is the company's major source of cash? What is your opinion of the company's ability to generate cash? How is the company using most of its cash? Is the company growing or shrinking?

Apply Your Knowledge

Decision Cases

Learning Objective 3
Evaluating business operations; using financial statements

Case 1. Two businesses, Web Services and PC Providers, have sought business loans from you. To decide whether to make the loans, you have requested their balance sheets.

Web Services
Balance Sheet
October 31, 2011

Assets		Liabilities	
Cash	$ 11,000	Accounts payable	$ 13,000
Accounts receivable	4,000	Notes payable	377,000
Furniture	36,000	Total liabilities	390,000
Software	79,000	**Shareholders' Equity**	
Computers	300,000	Shareholders' equity	40,000
		Total liabilities and	
Total assets	$430,000	shareholders' equity	$430,000

PC Providers Inc.
Balance Sheet
October 31, 2011

Assets		Liabilities	
Cash	$ 9,000	Accounts payable	$ 12,000
Accounts receivable	24,000	Note payable	28,000
Merchandise inventory	85,000	Total liabilities	40,000
Furniture and fixtures	9,000		
Building	82,000	**Shareholders' Equity**	
Land	14,000	Shareholders' equity	183,000
		Total liabilities and	
Total assets	$223,000	shareholders' equity	$223,000

Required

1. Using only these balance sheets, to which entity would you be more comfortable lending money? Explain fully, citing specific items and amounts from the respective balance sheets.
2. Is there other financial information you would consider before making your decision? Be specific.

Learning Objective 3
Analyzing a company's financial statements

Case 2. After you have been out of college for a year, you have $5,000 to invest. A friend has started My Dream Inc., and she asks you to invest in her company. You obtain My Dream Inc.'s financial statements, which are summarized at the end of the first year as follows:

My Dream Inc.
Income Statement
For the Year Ended December 31, 2011

Revenues	$80,000
Expenses	60,000
Net income	$20,000

My Dream Inc.
Balance Sheet
December 31, 2011

Cash	$13,000	Liabilities	$35,000
Other assets	67,000	Equity	45,000
Total assets	$80,000	Total liabilities and equity	$80,000

Visits with your friend turn up the following facts:

a. The company owes an additional $10,000 for TV ads that was incurred in December but not recorded in the books.

b. Software costs of $20,000 were recorded as assets. These costs should have been expensed. My Dream paid cash for these expenses and recorded the cash payment correctly.

c. Revenues and receivables of $10,000 were overlooked and omitted.

Required

1. Prepare corrected financial statements.
2. Use your corrected statements to evaluate My Dream's results of operations and financial position.
3. Will you invest in My Dream? Give your reason.

Ethical Issue

During 2002, Enron Corporation admitted excluding large liabilities from its balance sheet. WorldCom confessed to recording expenses as assets. In 2002, Livent Inc.'s senior executives were charged with reducing expenses and inflating profits. All of these companies needed to improve their appearance as reported in their financial statements.

Required

1. What is the fundamental ethical issue in these situations?
2. Who are the stakeholders and what are the consequences of the actions taken by the three companies? Use the accounting equation to explain your answer.
3. What alternatives should these companies have considered?
4. The actions in all three cases were illegal. What do you think were the consequences of the three companies' management decisions?

Focus on Financials

Gildan Activewear Inc.

Learning Objective 3
Evaluating business operations

This case is based on the financial statements of Gildan Activewear Inc. (www.gildan.com). As you work with Gildan Activewear Inc. throughout this course, you will develop the ability to use actual financial statements.

Required

Refer to the Gildan Activewear Inc. financial statements in Appendix A at the end of the book.

1. Suppose you own shares in Gildan. If you could pick one item on the company's income statement to increase year after year, what would it be? Why is this item so important? Did this item increase or decrease during the year ended October 4, 2009? Is this good news or bad news for the company?
2. What was Gildan's largest expense each year? In your own words, explain the meaning of this item. Give specific examples of items that make up this expense. Why is this expense less than sales revenue?
3. Use the balance sheet as at October 4, 2009, of Gildan Activewear Inc. in Appendix A to answer these questions. At the end of October 4, 2009, how much in total resources did Gildan have to work with? How much did the company owe? How much of its assets did the company's shareholders actually own? Use these amounts to write Gildan's accounting equation at October 4, 2009 (express all items in thousands of dollars).
4. How much cash did Gildan have at October 5, 2008? How much cash did it have at October 4, 2009? Where does Gildan get most of its cash? How does the company spend its cash?

Focus on Analysis

Gildan Activewear Inc.

Learning Objective 3
Evaluating by using financial statements

This case is based on the financial statements of Gildan Activewear Inc. (www.gildan.com). As you work with Gildan Activewear Inc. throughout this course, you will develop the ability to analyze financial statements of actual companies.

Required

Refer to the Gildan Activewear Inc. financial statements in Appendix A at the end of the book. (Note: All 2009 references are to Gildan's 2009 fiscal year—October 6, 2008, through October 4, 2009.)

1. Write Gildan's accounting equation at October 4, 2009 (express all items in thousands of dollars). Does Gildan's financial condition look strong or weak? How can you tell?
2. What was the result of Gildan's operations during 2009? Identify both the name and the dollar value of the result of operations for 2009. Does an increase (decrease) signal good news or bad news for the company and its shareholders?
3. Examine shareholders' equity on the balance sheet and the statement of retained earnings. What were the changes in shareholders' equity during 2009? What caused these changes?
4. Which statement reports cash as part of Gildan's financial position? Which statement tells why cash increased (or decreased) during the year? What items caused Gildan's cash to change the most in 2009?
5. Which two items on the balance sheet changed the most compared to 2008? What management decisions likely led to the change?

Group Project

Project 1. As instructed by your professor, obtain an annual report of a Canadian company.

Required

1. Take the role of a loan committee of the Royal Bank of Canada. Assume the company has requested a loan from your bank. Analyze the company's financial statements and any other information you need to reach a decision regarding the largest amount of money you would be willing to lend. Go as deeply into the analysis and the related decision as you can. Specify the following:
   a. Any restrictions you would impose on the borrower.
   b. The length of the loan period (that is, over what period will you allow the company to pay you back).

Note: The long-term debt note to the financial statements gives details of the company's liabilities.

2. Write your group decision in a report addressed to the bank's board of directors. Limit your report to two double-spaced word-processed pages.
3. If your professor directs you to, present your decision and analysis to the class. Limit your presentation to 10 to 15 minutes.

Project 2. You are the owner of a company that is about to "go public" (that is, issue its shares to outside investors). You wish to make your company look as attractive as possible to raise $1 million in cash to expand the business. At the same time, you want to give potential investors a reliable and relevant picture of your company.

Required

1. Design a presentation to portray your company in a way that will enable outsiders to reach an informed decision as to whether to invest in your company. The presentation should include the following:

a. Name and location of your company
b. Nature of the company's business (be specific and detailed to provide a clear picture of the nature, history, and future goals of the business)
c. How you plan to spend the money you raise
d. The company's comparative income statement, statement of retained earnings, balance sheet, and statement of cash flows for two years: the current year and the preceding year. Make the data as realistic as possible with the intent of receiving $1 million.

2. Prepare a word-processed presentation that does not exceed five pages.
3. If directed by your professor, distribute copies of your presentation to the class with the intent of interesting your classmates in investing in your company. Make a 10- to 15-minute investment pitch to the class. Measure your success by the amount of investment commitment you receive.

Quick Check Answers

1. *b*
2. *a*
3. *d*
4. *c*
5. *d*
6. *a*
7. *b ($100,000 − $40,000 − $3,000 = $57,000)*
8. *c ($100,000 − $40,000 = $60,000)*
9. *b [Total assets = $105,000 ($5,000 + $30,000 + $20,000 + $50,000). Shareholders' equity: $80,000 ($105,000 − $25,000)]*
10. *d*
11. *d [$30,000 + Net income ($15,000) − Dividends = $40,000; Dividends = $5,000]*
12. *b*

	Assets	=	Liabilities	+	Equity
Beginning	$300,000	=	$200,000	+	$100,000
Increase	50,000	=	40,000	+	10,000*
Ending	350,000	=	240,000	+	110,000*

*Must solve for these amounts.

2 Transaction Analysis

LEARNING OBJECTIVES

1. **Analyze** transactions
2. **Understand** how accounting works
3. **Record** transactions in the journal
4. **Use** a trial balance
5. **Analyze** transactions using only T-accounts

SPOTLIGHT

In the year ended February 28, 2009, Research In Motion® (RIM) celebrated the tenth anniversary of the introduction of the BlackBerry® wireless system. The year 2009 was also a banner year for the company; the subscriber account base reached 25 million, and the 50 millionth BlackBerry smartphone was shipped. Revenue reached a record US$11 billion.

How does RIM determine the amount of its revenues, expenses, and net income? Like all other companies, RIM has a comprehensive accounting system. RIM's income statement (statement of operations) is given at the beginning of this chapter. The income statement shows that during the year ended February 28, 2009, RIM made over $11 billion in sales and earned net income of $1.9 billion. Where did those figures come from? In this chapter, we'll show you.

Research In Motion Limited
Consolidated Statement of Operations (Adapted)
For the Year Ended February 28, 2009

	US$ in thousands
Revenue	
Devices and other	$ 9,410,755
Service and software	1,654,431
	11,065,186
Cost of sales	
Devices and other	5,718,041
Service and software	249,847
	5,967,888
Gross margin	5,097,298
Expenses	
Research and development	684,702
Selling, marketing, and administration	1,495,697
Amortization	194,803
	2,375,202
Income from operations	2,722,096
Investment income	78,267
Income before income taxes	2,800,363
Provision for (recovery of) income taxes	
Current	948,536
Deferred	(40,789)
	907,747
Net income	$ 1,892,616

Chapter 1 introduced the basic financial statements. Chapter 2 will show you how companies actually record the transactions that eventually become part of the financial statements.

MyAccountingLab For more practice and review of accounting cycle concepts, use ACT, the Accounting Cycle Tutorial, online at **www.myaccountinglab.com**. Margin logos like this one, directing you to the appropriate ACT section and material, appear throughout Chapters 1, 2, and 3. When you enter the tutorial, you'll find three buttons on the opening page of each chapter module. Here's what the buttons mean: **Tutorial** gives you a review of the major concepts, **Application** gives you practice exercises, and **Glossary** reviews important terms.

Transactions

Business activity is all about transactions. A **transaction** is any event that has a financial impact on a business and can be measured. For example, Research In Motion Limited (RIM) pays programmers to create software for its various smartphones such as the BlackBerry Curve or the Blackberry Bold. RIM sells smartphones and borrows money and repays the loan—three separate transactions.

But not all events qualify as transactions. An advertisement on television may feature a BlackBerry Pearl Flip smartphone, motivating you to consider buying one. The ad may create lots of new business for RIM. But no transaction occurs until someone actually buys a RIM product. A transaction must occur before RIM records anything.

Transactions provide objective information about the financial impacts on a company. Every transaction has two sides.

In accounting we always record both sides of a transaction. We must be able to measure the financial effect of the event on the business before recording it as a transaction. You must be able to assign a dollar amount to the transaction to record it on the books.

The Account

As we saw in Chapter 1, the accounting equation expresses the basic relationships of accounting:

Assets = Liabilities + Shareholders' (Owners') Equity

For each asset, each liability, and each element of shareholders' equity, we use a record called an account. An **account** is the record of all the changes in a particular asset, liability, or shareholders' equity during a period. The account is the basic summary device of accounting. Before launching into transaction analysis, let's review the accounts that a company such as RIM uses.

Assets

Assets are economic resources that provide a future benefit for a business. Most firms use the following asset accounts:

Cash and Cash Equivalents. Cash and cash equivalents means money and any medium of exchange including bank account balances, paper currency, coins, GICs, and cheques.

Accounts Receivable. RIM, like most other companies, sells its goods or services and receives a promise for future collection of cash. The Accounts Receivable account holds these amounts.

Notes Receivable. RIM may receive a note receivable from a customer, who signed the note promising to pay RIM. A note receivable is similar to an account receivable, but a note receivable is more binding because the customer signed the note. Notes receivable usually specify an interest rate.

Inventory. RIM's most important asset is its inventory: the products the company sells to customers. Other titles for this account include Merchandise and Merchandise Inventory.

Prepaid Expenses. RIM pays certain expenses in advance. A **prepaid expense** is an asset because the payment provides a future benefit for the business. Prepaid Rent, Prepaid Insurance, and Office Supplies are prepaid expenses.

Land. The Land account includes the land RIM uses in its operations.

Buildings. The Buildings account includes RIM's buildings—office buildings, manufacturing factory, and the like.

Equipment, Furniture, and Fixtures. Businesses have separate asset accounts for each type of equipment, for example, Office Equipment, Manufacturing Equipment, and Store Equipment. The Furniture and Fixtures account includes these assets, which are similar to equipment.

Liabilities

Recall that a *liability* is a debt. A receivable is always an asset; a payable is always a liability. The most common types of liabilities include the following:

Accounts Payable. The Accounts Payable account is the direct opposite of Accounts Receivable. RIM's promise to pay a debt arising from a credit purchase of inventory appears in the Accounts Payable account.

Notes Payable. The Notes Payable account is the opposite of the Notes Receivable account. Notes Payable includes the amounts that RIM must pay because RIM signed promissory notes that require future payments. Notes payable, like notes receivable, also carry interest.

Accrued Liabilities. An **accrued liability** is a liability for an expense you have not yet paid. Interest Payable and Salary Payable are accrued liability accounts for most companies. Income Taxes Payable is another accrued liability.

Shareholders' (Owners') Equity

The owners' claims to the assets of a corporation are called shareholders' equity or simply owners' equity. A corporation uses Contributed Capital, Retained Earnings, and Dividends accounts to record changes in the company's shareholders' equity. In a proprietorship, there is a single Capital account. For a partnership, owners' equity is held in separate accounts for each owner's capital balance.

Contributed Capital. The Contributed Capital section shows the owners' investment in the corporation. Common Shares or Share Capital are typical contributed capital account titles. A corporation receives cash and issues common shares to the investor. A company's common shares are its most basic element of equity. All for-profit corporations have common shares with the exception of income trusts, which have trust units.

Retained Earnings. The Retained Earnings account shows the cumulative net income earned by the corporation over its lifetime, minus its cumulative net losses and dividends.

Dividends. After profitable operations, the board of directors of RIM may (or may not) declare and pay a cash dividend. Dividends are optional: they are decided by the board of directors. The corporation may keep a separate account titled Dividends, which indicates a decrease in Retained Earnings.

Revenues. The increase in shareholders' equity that results from delivering goods or services to customers is called revenue. The company uses as many revenue accounts as needed. RIM has two revenue accounts: "Devices and Other" and "Service and Software." A lawyer provides legal services for clients and uses a Service Revenue account. Scotiabank loans money to an outsider and uses an Interest Revenue account. If the business rents a building to a tenant, it needs a Rent Revenue account.

Expenses. An expense is the cost of operating a business. Expenses decrease shareholders' equity, the opposite of revenues. A business needs a separate account for each type of expense, such as Cost of Sales, Salary Expense, Rent Expense, Advertising Expense, and Utilities Expense. Businesses strive to minimize expenses and thereby maximize net income.

STOP + THINK

You were reading RIM's financial statements for the year ended February 28, 2009, and wondered to yourself:
1. What transactions would increase RIM's shareholders' equity?
2. What transactions would decrease RIM's shareholders' equity?

Answer:
1. Sale of shares and net income (revenue greater than expenses)
2. Declaration and payment of dividends and net loss (expenses greater than revenue)

OBJECTIVE

1 **Analyze** transactions

Accounting for Business Transactions

Example: Tara Inc.

To illustrate accounting for business transactions, let's return to J.J. Booth and Marie Savard. You met them in Chapter 1 when they opened a consulting engineering company on April 1, 2009, and incorporated it as Tara Inc.

We consider 11 events and analyze each in terms of its effect on the accounting equation of Tara Inc. We begin by using the accounting equation. In the second half of the chapter, we record transactions using the journal and ledger of the business.

Event 1. Booth, Savard, and several fellow engineers invest $50,000 to begin Tara Inc., and the business issues common shares to the shareholders. The effect of this transaction on the accounting equation of the business entity Tara Inc. is a receipt of $50,000 cash and issuance of common shares:

	ASSETS Cash	=	LIABILITIES	+	SHAREHOLDERS' EQUITY Common Shares	TYPE OF SHAREHOLDERS' EQUITY TRANSACTION
(1)	+ 50,000				+ 50,000	Issued shares

Every transaction's net amount on the left side of the equation must equal the net amount on the right side. The first transaction increases both the cash and the issued common shares of the business. To the right of the transaction we write "Issued shares" to record the reason for the $50,000 increase in shareholders' equity.

Tara Inc.
Balance Sheet
April 1, 2011

Assets		Liabilities	
Cash	$50,000	None	
		Shareholders' Equity	
		Common shares	$50,000
		Total shareholders' equity	50,000
		Total liabilities and	
Total assets	$50,000	shareholders' equity	$50,000

Every transaction affects the financial statements, and we can prepare the statements after one, two, or any number of transactions. For example, Tara Inc. could report the company's balance sheet after its first transaction, shown above.

This balance sheet shows that Tara Inc. holds cash of $50,000 and owes no liabilities. The company's equity (ownership) is denoted as *Common Shares* on the balance sheet. A bank would look favourably on the Tara Inc. balance sheet because the business has $50,000 cash and no debt—a strong financial position.

As a practical matter, most entities report their financial statements at the end of an accounting period—not after each transaction. But an accounting system can produce statements whenever managers need to know where the business stands.

Event 2. Tara Inc. purchases land for an office location and pays cash of $40,000. The effect of this transaction on the accounting equation is:

	ASSETS			LIABILITIES +	SHAREHOLDERS' EQUITY	TYPE OF SHAREHOLDERS' EQUITY TRANSACTION
	Cash	**+ Land**			**Common Shares**	
Bal.	50,000		=		50,000	Issued shares
(2)	−40,000	+40,000				
Bal.	10,000	40,000			50,000	
	50,000				50,000	

The purchase increases one asset (Land) and decreases another asset (Cash) by the same amount. After the transaction is completed, Tara Inc. has cash of $10,000, land of $40,000, and no liabilities. Shareholders' equity is unchanged at $50,000. Note that total assets must always equal total liabilities plus equity.

Event 3. The business buys stationery and other office supplies on account, agreeing to pay $3,700 within 30 days. This transaction increases both the assets and the liabilities of the business. Its effect on the accounting equation is as follows:

	ASSETS				LIABILITIES	+ SHAREHOLDERS' EQUITY
	Cash	**+ Office Supplies +**	**Land**		**Accounts Payable +**	**Common Shares**
Bal.	10,000		40,000	=		50,000
(3)		+3,700			+3,700	
Bal.	10,000	3,700	40,000		3,700	50,000
	53,700				53,700	

The new asset is Office Supplies, and the liability is Accounts Payable. Tara signs no formal promissory note, so the liability is an account payable, not a note payable.

Event 4. Tara Inc. earns service revenue by providing engineering services. Assume the business earns $7,000 and collects this amount in cash. The effect on the accounting equation is an increase in the asset Cash and an increase in Retained Earnings, as follows:

	ASSETS				LIABILITIES +	SHAREHOLDERS' EQUITY		TYPE OF SHAREHOLDERS' EQUITY TRANSACTION
	Cash +	Office Supplies +	Land		Accounts Payable +	Common Shares +	Retained Earnings	
Bal.	10,000	3,700	40,000	=	3,700	50,000		
(4)	+7,000						7,000	Service revenue
Bal.	17,000	3,700	40,000		3,700	50,000	7,000	
		60,700				60,700		

To the right we record "Service revenue" to show where the $7,000 of increase in retained earnings came from.

Event 5. Tara Inc. performs service on account, which means that Tara lets customers pay later. Tara earns revenue but doesn't receive the cash immediately. In Event 5, Tara provides engineering service for King Contracting Ltd., and King promises to pay Tara within one month. This promise is an account receivable—an asset—of Tara Inc.

The King Contracting Ltd. transaction record follows:

	ASSETS					LIABILITIES +	SHAREHOLDERS' EQUITY		TYPE OF SHAREHOLDERS' EQUITY TRANSACTION
	Cash +	Accounts Receivable +	Office Supplies +	Land		Accounts Payable +	Common Shares +	Retained Earnings	
Bal.	17,000		3,700	40,000	=	3,700	50,000	7,000	
(5)		+3,000						+3,000	Service revenue
Bal.	17,000	3,000	3,700	40,000		3,700	50,000	10,000	
		63,700					63,700		

It's performing the service that earns the revenue—not collecting the cash. Therefore, Tara records revenue when it performs the service—regardless of whether Tara receives the cash now or later.

Event 6. During the month, Tara Inc. pays $2,700 for the following expenses: office rent, $1,100; employee salary, $1,200; and utilities, $400. The effect on the accounting equation is:

	ASSETS					LIABILITIES +	SHAREHOLDERS' EQUITY		TYPE OF SHAREHOLDERS' EQUITY TRANSACTION
	Cash +	Accounts Receivable +	Office Supplies +	Land		Accounts Payable +	Common Shares +	Retained Earnings	
Bal.	17,000	3,000	3,700	40,000		3,700	50,000	10,000	
(6)	−1,100				=			−1,100	Rent expense
	−1,200							−1,200	Salary expense
	− 400							− 400	Utilities expense
Bal.	14,300	3,000	3,700	40,000		3,700	50,000	7,300	
	61,000					61,000			

The expenses decrease Tara's Cash and Retained Earnings. List each expense separately to keep track of its amount.

Event 7. Tara pays $1,900 on account, which means to make a payment on an account payable. In this transaction, Tara pays part of the balance owing to the store from which it purchased Office Supplies in Event 3. The transaction decreases Cash and also decreases Accounts Payable as follows:

	ASSETS					LIABILITIES +	SHAREHOLDERS' EQUITY	
	Cash +	Accounts Receivable +	Office Supplies +	Land		Accounts Payable +	Common Shares +	Retained Earnings
Bal.	14,300	3,000	3,700	40,000		3,700	50,000	7,300
(7)	−1,900				=	−1,900		
Bal.	12,400	3,000	3,700	40,000		1,800	50,000	7,300
	59,100					59,100		

Event 8. J.J. Booth paid $30,000 to remodel his home. This event is a personal transaction of J.J. Booth and is not a transaction for Tara so it is not recorded by Tara Inc. We focus solely on the business entity, not its owners. The transaction illustrates the entity assumption concept from Chapter 1.

Event 9. In Event 5, Tara Inc. performed service for King Contracting on account. The business now collects $1,000 from King Contracting. We say that Tara Inc. *collects the cash on account*, which means Tara will record an increase in Cash and a decrease in Accounts Receivable. This is not service revenue now because Tara already recorded the revenue in Event 5. The effect of collecting cash on account is:

	ASSETS					LIABILITIES +	SHAREHOLDERS' EQUITY	
	Cash +	Accounts Receivable +	Office Supplies +	Land		Accounts Payable +	Common Shares +	Retained Earnings
Bal.	12,400	3,000	3,700	40,000		1,800	50,000	7,300
(9)	+1,000	−1,000			=			
Bal.	13,400	2,000	3,700	40,000		1,800	50,000	7,300
	59,100					59,100		

Event 10. Tara Inc. sells part of the land purchased in Event 2 for $22,000, which is the same amount Tara paid for that part of the land it sold. Tara Inc. receives $22,000 cash, and the effect on the accounting equation is:

	ASSETS					LIABILITIES	+ SHAREHOLDERS' EQUITY	
	Cash +	Accounts Receivable +	Office Supplies +	Land		Accounts Payable +	Common Shares +	Retained Earnings
Bal.	13,400	2,000	3,700	40,000		1,800	50,000	7,300
(10)	+22,000			−22,000	=			
Bal.	35,400	2,000	3,700	18,000		1,800	50,000	7,300
	59,100					59,100		

Note that the company did not sell all its land; Tara still owns $18,000 worth of land.

Event 11. Tara Inc. declares a dividend and pays the shareholders $2,100 cash. The effect on the accounting equation is:

	ASSETS					LIABILITIES +	SHAREHOLDERS' EQUITY		TYPE OF SHAREHOLDERS' EQUITY TRANSACTION
	Cash +	Accounts Receivable +	Office Supplies +	Land		Accounts Payable +	Common Shares +	Retained Earnings	
Bal.	35,400	2,000	3,700	18,000		1,800	50,000	7,300	
(11)	−2,100				=			−2,100	Dividends
Bal.	33,300	2,000	3,700	18,000		1,800	50,000	5,200	
	57,000					57,000			

The dividend decreases both the asset Cash and the Retained Earnings of the business. *But dividends are not an expense.*

ACCOUNTING FOR TRANSACTIONS PART 1

The accountant must make a series of decisions with respect to transactions.

The first decision is deciding whether an event is or is not a transaction of the business:

- If the event affects the entity's financial position and can be measured, it should be recorded as a transaction. Tara Inc.'s Event 5 above is an example of such an event and so it should be treated as a transaction by Tara Inc.
- If either condition is absent, it should not be recorded as a transaction. Tara Inc.'s Event 8 above is an example of an event that is not a business transaction.

The second decision is made by establishing how the accounting equation is affected by the transaction.

The accountant must determine how the accounting equation (*Assets = Liabilities + Shareholders' Equity*) is affected by the debits and credits of the transaction.

Transactions and Financial Statements

Exhibit 2-1 summarizes the 11 preceding events. Panel A gives the details of the events, and Panel B shows the transaction analysis for the events that affect the business. As you study the exhibit, note that every transaction on Panel B maintains the following equality:

Assets = Liabilities + Shareholders' Equity

EXHIBIT 2-1 **Event Analysis: Tara Inc.**

Panel A—Event Details

(1) Received $50,000 cash and issued shares to the owners
(2) Paid $40,000 cash for land
(3) Bought $3,700 of office supplies on account
(4) Received $7,000 cash from customers for service revenue earned
(5) Performed services for customers on account, $3,000
(6) Paid cash for $2,700 of expenses: rent, $1,100; employee salary, $1,200; utilities, $400
(7) Paid $1,900 on the account payable created in Event 3
(8) Shareholder pays personal funds to remodel home, *not* a transaction of the business
(9) Received $1,000 on account
(10) Sold land for cash at its cost of $22,000
(11) Declared and paid a dividend of $2,100 to the shareholders

Panel B—Analysis of Events

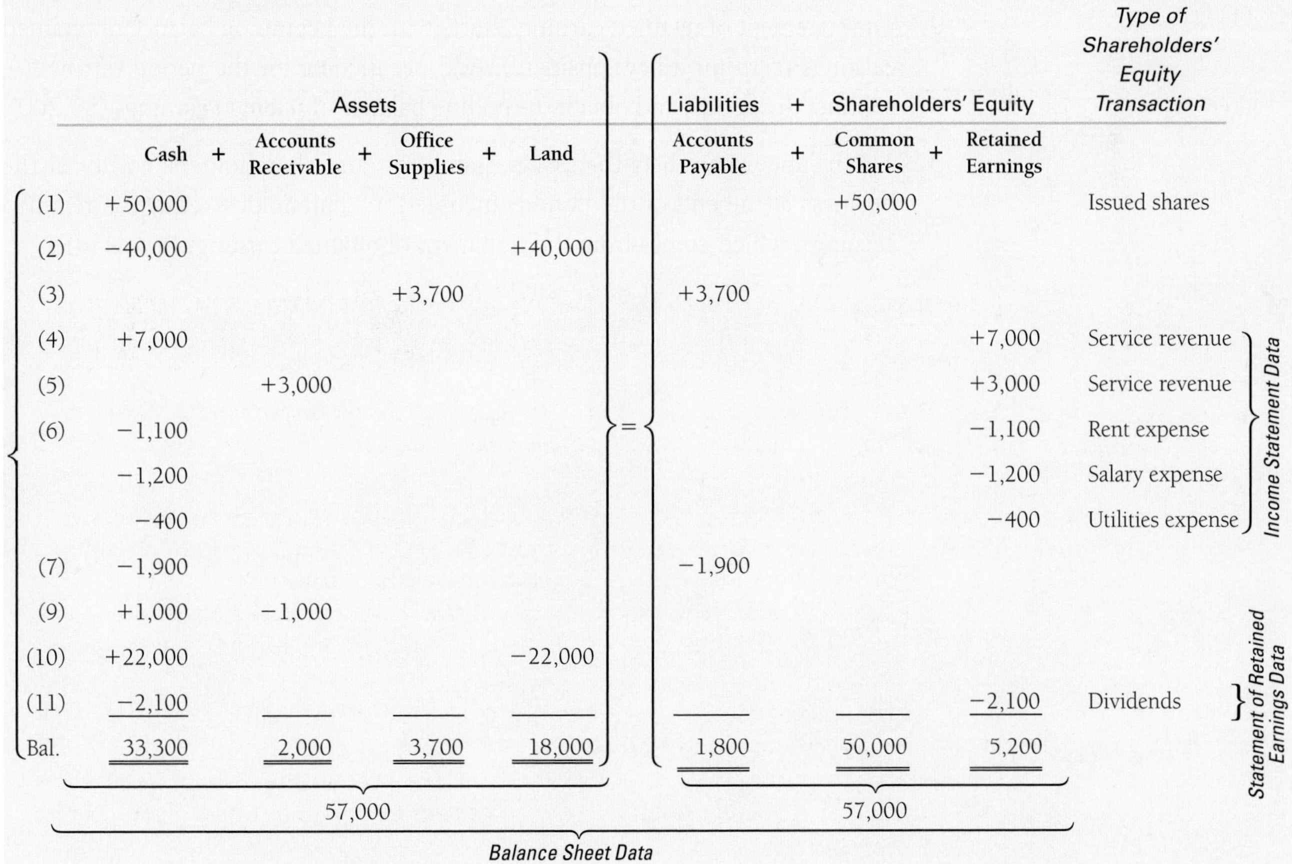

	Assets				=	Liabilities +	Shareholders' Equity		Type of Shareholders' Equity Transaction
	Cash +	Accounts Receivable +	Office Supplies +	Land		Accounts Payable +	Common Shares +	Retained Earnings	
(1)	+50,000						+50,000		Issued shares
(2)	−40,000			+40,000					
(3)			+3,700			+3,700			
(4)	+7,000							+7,000	Service revenue
(5)		+3,000						+3,000	Service revenue
(6)	−1,100							−1,100	Rent expense
	−1,200							−1,200	Salary expense
	−400							−400	Utilities expense
(7)	−1,900					−1,900			
(9)	+1,000	−1,000							
(10)	+22,000			−22,000					
(11)	−2,100							−2,100	Dividends
Bal.	33,300	2,000	3,700	18,000		1,800	50,000	5,200	
	57,000					57,000			

Panel B in Exhibit 2-1 provides the data for Tara Inc.'s financial statements:

- *Income statement* data appear as revenues and expenses under Retained Earnings. The revenues increase Retained Earnings; the expenses decrease Retained Earnings.
- The *balance sheet* data are composed of the ending balances of the assets, liabilities, and shareholders' equity shown at the bottom of the exhibit. The accounting equation shows that total assets ($57,000) equal total liabilities plus shareholders' equity ($57,000).
- The *statement of retained earnings* repeats net income (or net loss) from the income statement. Dividends are subtracted. Ending retained earnings is the final result.
- Data for the *statement of cash flows* are aligned under the Cash account. Cash receipts increase cash, and cash payments decrease cash.

Exhibit 2-2 shows the Tara Inc. financial statements at the end of April, the company's first month of operations. Follow the flow of data to observe the following:

1. The income statement reports revenues, expenses, and either a net income or a net loss for the period. During April, Tara Inc. earned a net income of $7,300. Compare the Tara Inc. income statement with that of Research In Motion Limited at the beginning of the chapter. The income statement includes only two types of accounts: revenues and expenses.
2. The statement of retained earnings starts with the beginning balance of retained earnings (zero for a new business). Add net income for the period (arrow ①), subtract dividends, and obtain the ending balance of retained earnings ($5,200).
3. The balance sheet lists the assets, liabilities, and shareholders' equity of the business at the end of the period. Included in shareholders' equity is retained earnings, which comes from the statement of retained earnings (arrow ②).

EXHIBIT 2-2 **Financial Statements of Tara Inc.**

Tara Inc.
Income Statement
For the Month Ended April 30, 2011

Revenue		
Service revenue ($7,000 + $3,000)		$10,000
Expenses		
Salary	$1,200	
Rent	1,100	
Utilities	400	
Total expenses		2,700
Net income		$ 7,300

①

Tara Inc.
Statement of Retained Earnings
For the Month Ended April 30, 2011

Retained earnings, April 1, 2011	$ 0
Add: Net income for the month	7,300
	7,300
Less: Dividends	(2,100)
Retained earnings, April 30, 2011	$5,200

②

Tara Inc.
Balance Sheet
As at April 30, 2011

Assets		Liabilities	
Cash	$33,300	Accounts payable	$ 1,800
Accounts receivable	2,000		
Office supplies	3,700	Shareholders' Equity	
Land	18,000	Common shares	50,000
		Retained earnings	5,200
		Total shareholders' equity	55,200
		Total liabilities and	
Total assets	$57,000	shareholders' equity	$57,000

MID-CHAPTER SUMMARY PROBLEM

Margaret Jarvis opens a research service near a college campus. She names the corporation Jarvis Research Inc. During the first month of operations, July 2011, Margaret Jarvis and the business engage in the following events:

a. Jarvis Research Inc. issues its common shares to Margaret Jarvis, who invests $25,000 to open the business.
b. The company purchases, on account, office supplies costing $350.
c. Jarvis Research Inc. pays cash of $20,000 to acquire a lot near the campus. The company intends to use the land as a building site for a business office.
d. Jarvis Research Inc. performs services for clients and receives cash of $1,900.
e. Jarvis Research Inc. pays $100 on the account payable it created in event b.
f. Margaret Jarvis pays $2,000 of personal funds for a vacation.
g. Jarvis Research Inc. pays cash expenses for office rent ($400) and utilities ($100).
h. The business sells a small parcel of the land it purchased for its cost of $5,000.
i. The business declares and pays a cash dividend of $1,200.

Required

Name: Jarvis Research Inc.
Industry: Research service
Fiscal Period: Month of July 2011
Key Facts: New business

1. Analyze the preceding events. First determine if each is a transaction affecting the business and, if it is, determine the effect on the accounting equation of Jarvis Research Inc. Use Exhibit 2-1, Panel B as a guide.
2. Prepare the income statement, statement of retained earnings, and balance sheet of the business after recording the transactions. Draw arrows linking the statements.

SOLUTIONS

Requirement 1

PANEL B—*Analysis of Events*

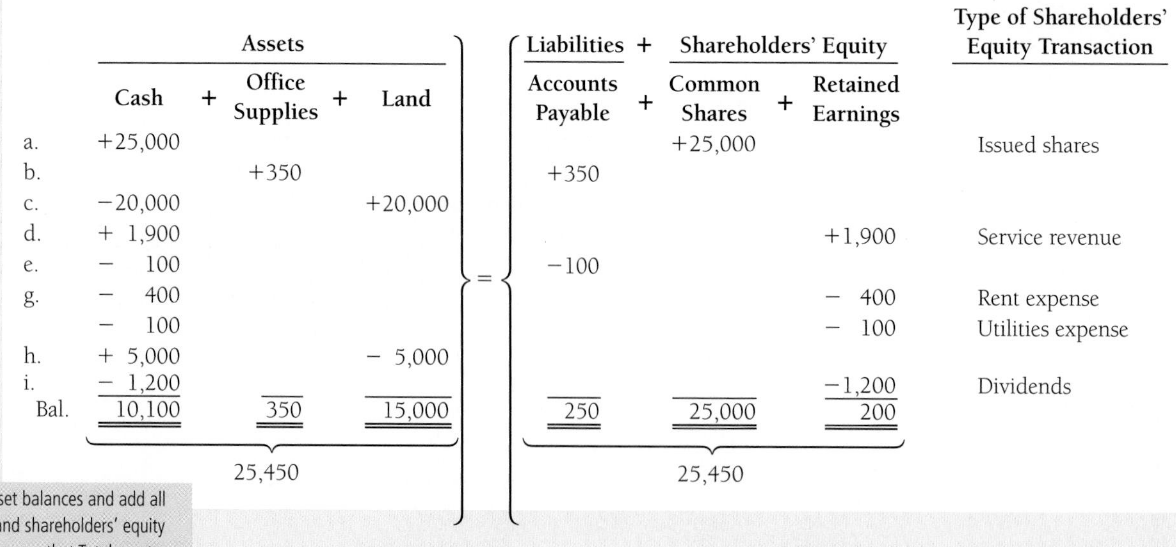

	Assets			=	Liabilities +	Shareholders' Equity		Type of Shareholders' Equity Transaction
	Cash +	Office Supplies +	Land		Accounts Payable +	Common Shares +	Retained Earnings	
a.	+25,000					+25,000		Issued shares
b.		+350			+350			
c.	−20,000		+20,000					
d.	+ 1,900						+1,900	Service revenue
e.	− 100				−100			
g.	− 400						− 400	Rent expense
	− 100						− 100	Utilities expense
h.	+ 5,000		− 5,000					
i.	− 1,200						−1,200	Dividends
Bal.	10,100	350	15,000		250	25,000	200	
	25,450				25,450			

Add all the asset balances and add all the liabilities and shareholders' equity balances. Make sure that Total assets = Total liabilities + Shareholders' equity.

Requirement 2

Jarvis Research Inc.
Income Statement
For the Month Ended July 31, 2011

Revenue		
Service revenue		$1,900
Expenses		
Rent	$400	
Utilities	100	
Total		500
Net income		$1,400

The title must include the name of the company, "Income Statement," and the specific period of time covered. It is critical that the time period be defined.

Use the revenue and expense amounts data from the Retained Earnings column and names from the Type of Shareholders' Equity Transaction column.

Jarvis Research Inc.
Statement of Retained Earnings
For the Month Ended July 31, 2011

Retained earnings, July 1, 2011	$ 0
Add: Net income for the month	1,400 ①
	1,400
Less: Dividends	(1,200)
Retained earnings, July 31, 2011	$ 200

The title must include the name of the company, "Statement of Retained Earnings," and the specific period of time covered. It is critical that the time period be defined.

Beginning retained earnings is $0 because this is the first year of operations. The net income amount is transferred from the income statement. The dividends amount is from the Retained Earnings column of Panel B.

Jarvis Research Inc.
Balance Sheet
As at July 31, 2011

Assets		Liabilities	
Cash	$10,100	Accounts payable	$ 250
Office supplies	350		
Land	15,000	**Shareholders' Equity**	
		Common shares	25,000
		Retained earnings	200 ②
		Total shareholders' equity	25,200
		Total liabilities and	
Total assets	$25,450	shareholders' equity	$25,450

The title must include the name of the company, "Balance Sheet," and the date of the balance sheet. It shows the financial position at the end of business on a specific date.

Gather the asset, liability, and common shares accounts from the heading of Panel B. Insert the final balances for each account from the Bal. row in Panel B. The retained earnings amount is transferred from the statement of retained earnings. It is imperative that Total assets = Total liabilities + Shareholders' equity.

The analysis in the first half of this chapter can be used, but it is cumbersome. Research In Motion Limited has hundreds of accounts and millions of transactions. The spreadsheet to account for RIM's transactions would be huge! In the second half of this chapter we discuss double-entry accounting as it is actually used in business.

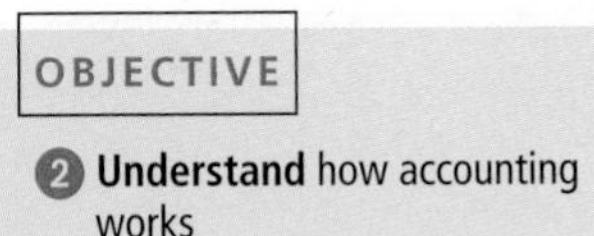

2 **Understand** how accounting works

Double-Entry Accounting

Accounting is based on a **double-entry system**, which records the *dual effects* on the entity.

Each transaction affects at least two accounts. For example, Tara Inc.'s receipt of $50,000 cash and issuance of shares increased both the Cash and the Common Shares. It would be incomplete to record only the increase in Cash or only the increase in Common Shares.

The T-Account

An account can be represented by the letter T. We call this a *T-account*. The vertical line in the letter divides the account into its two sides: left and right. The account title rests on the horizontal line at the top of the T. For example, the Cash account of a business can appear as follows:

Cash	
(Left side)	(Right side)
Debit	*Credit*

The left side of the account is called the **debit** side, and the right side is called the **credit** side. Often, students are confused by the words *debit* and *credit*. To become comfortable using them, remember that for every account

Debit = Left side	Credit = Right side

Every business transaction involves both a debit and a credit.

Increases and Decreases in the Accounts: The Rules of Debit and Credit

The type of account determines how we record increases or decreases. *The rules of debit and credit* follow in Exhibit 2-3.

- Increases in *assets* are recorded on the left (debit) side of the account. Decreases in *assets* are recorded on the right (credit) side. You receive cash and debit the Cash account. You pay cash and credit the Cash account
- Conversely, increases in *liabilities* and *shareholders' equity* are recorded by credits. Decreases in *liabilities* and *shareholders' equity* are recorded by debits.

EXHIBIT 2-3 **Accounting Equation and the Rules of Debit and Credit**

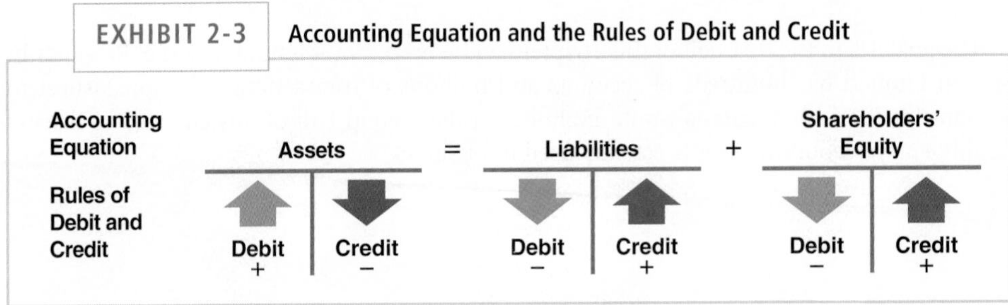

To illustrate the ideas diagrammed in Exhibit 2-3, let's review the first transaction. Tara Inc. received $50,000 and issued (gave) shares. Which accounts are affected? How will the accounts appear after the transaction? The Cash account and the Common Shares account will hold these amounts.

The amount remaining in an account is called its balance. This first transaction gives Cash a $50,000 debit balance and Common Shares a $50,000 credit balance. Exhibit 2-4 shows this relationship.

Tara Inc.'s second transaction is a $40,000 cash purchase of land. This transaction decreases Cash with a credit and increases Land with a debit, as shown in the following T-accounts (focus on Cash and Land):

Cash

	Debit	Credit
Bal.	50,000	Credit for decrease, 40,000
Bal.	10,000	

Common Shares

Debit	Credit	
	Bal.	50,000

Land

Debit		Credit
Debit for increase, 40,000		
Bal.	40,000	

After this transaction, Cash has a $10,000 debit balance. Land has a debit balance of $40,000, and Common Shares has a $50,000 credit balance, as shown in Exhibit 2-5.

MyAccountingLab

Accounting Cycle Tutorial: Balance Sheet Accounts and Transactions - Tutorial

EXHIBIT 2-4 The Accounting Equation After Tara's First Transaction

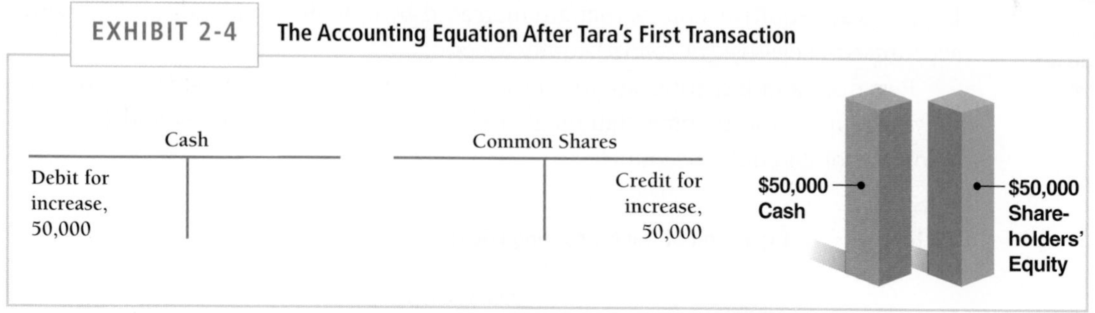

EXHIBIT 2-5 The Accounting Equation After Tara Inc.'s First Two Transactions

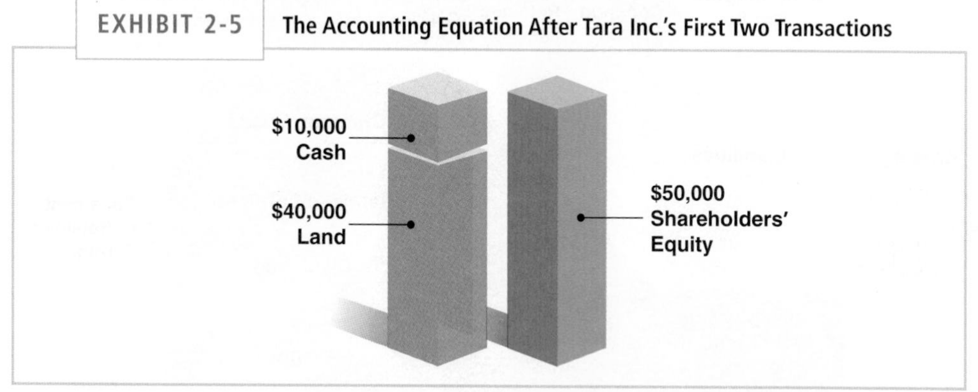

MyAccountingLab

Accounting Cycle Tutorial: Balance Sheet Accounts and Transactions - Application Exercise 2

Additional Shareholders' Equity Accounts: Revenues and Expenses

Shareholders' equity also includes the two types of income statement accounts, Revenues and Expenses:

- *Revenues* are increases in shareholders' equity that result from delivering goods or services to customers.
- *Expenses* are decreases in shareholders' equity due to the cost of operating the business.

Therefore, the accounting equation may be expanded as shown in Exhibit 2-6. Revenues and expenses appear in parentheses because their net effect—revenues minus expenses—equals net income, which increases shareholders' equity. If expenses exceed revenues, there is a net loss, which decreases shareholders' equity.

We can now express the rules of debit and credit in final form, as shown in Exhibit 2-7. *You should not proceed until you have learned these rules.* For example, you must remember the following:

- A debit increases an asset account.
- A credit decreases an asset account.

Liabilities and shareholders' equity are the opposite:

- A credit increases a liability account or a shareholders' equity account.
- A debit decreases a liability or a shareholders' equity account.

Accounting Cycle Tutorial: Income Statement Accounts and Transactions - Tutorial

Dividends and Expenses accounts are exceptions to the rule. Dividends and Expenses are equity accounts that are increased by a debit. Dividends and Expenses accounts are negative (or *contra*) equity accounts.

Revenues and Expenses are often treated as separate account categories because they appear on the income statement. Exhibit 2-7 shows Revenues and Expenses below the other equity accounts.

EXHIBIT 2-6 Expansion of the Accounting Equation

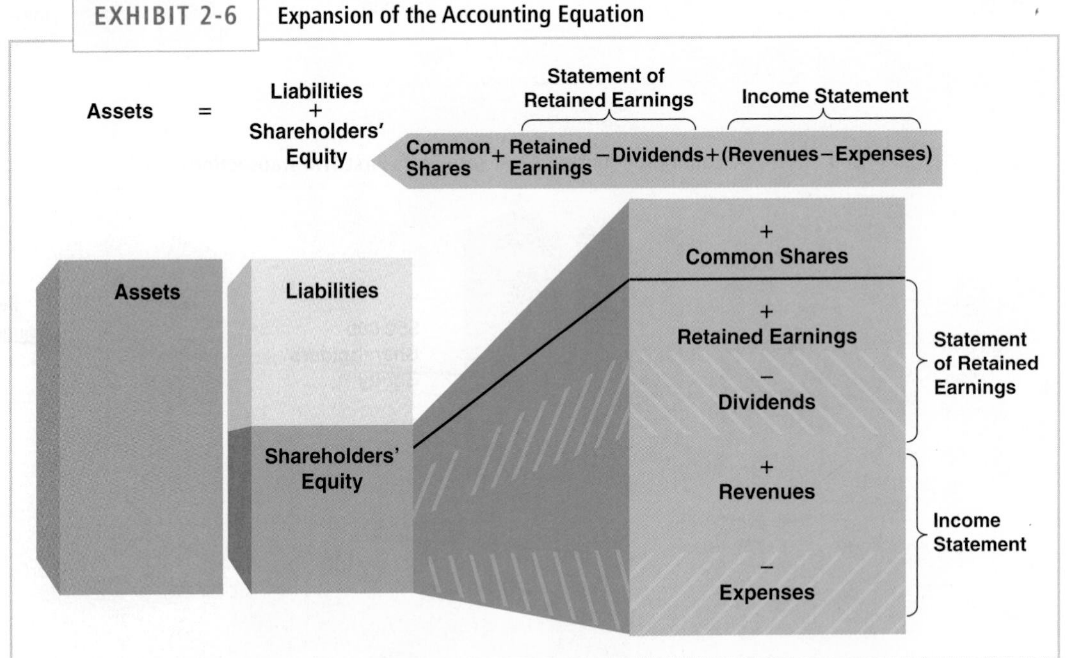

EXHIBIT 2-7 **Final Form of the Rules of Debit and Credit**

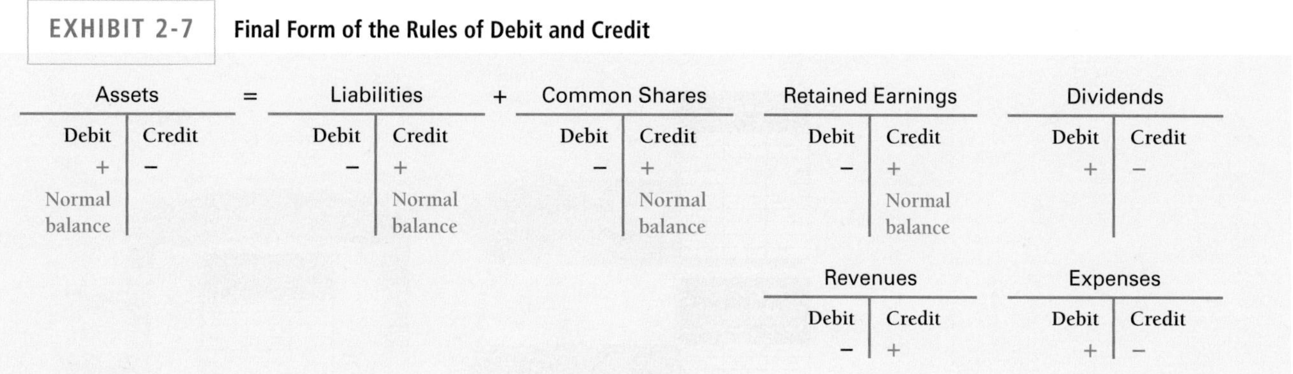

Recording Transactions

3 **Record** transactions in the journal

Accountants use a chronological record of transactions called a **journal**. The journalizing process follows three steps:

1. Specify each account affected by the transaction, and classify each account by type (asset, liability, shareholders' equity, revenue, or expense).
2. Determine whether each account is increased or decreased by the transaction. Use the rules of debit and credit to increase or decrease each account.
3. Record the transaction in the journal, including a brief explanation for the entry. The debit side is entered on the left margin, and the credit side is indented to the right. Date the journal entry.

Step 3 is also called "making the journal entry" or "journalizing the transaction." Let's apply the steps to journalize the first transaction of Tara Inc.

Step 1 The business receives cash and issues shares. Cash and Common Shares are affected. Cash is an asset and Common Shares is equity.

Step 2 Both Cash and Common Shares increase. Debit Cash to record an increase in this asset. Credit Common Shares to record an increase in this equity account.

Step 3 Journalize the transaction:

Date	Accounts and Explanation	Debit	Credit
Apr. 1, 2011	Cash	50,000	
	Common shares		50,000
	Issued common shares.		

When analyzing a transaction, first pinpoint its effects (if any) on Cash. Did Cash increase or decrease? Typically, it is easiest to identify a transaction's cash effects. Then identify the effects on other accounts.

Copying Information (Posting) From the Journal to the Ledger

The journal is a chronological record of all company transactions listed by date. But the journal does not indicate how much cash or accounts receivable the business has.

The **ledger** is a grouping of all the T-accounts with their balances. For example, the balance of the Cash account indicates how much cash the business has. The balance of Accounts Receivable shows the amount due from customers. The balance

EXHIBIT 2-8 **The Ledger (Asset, Liability, and Shareholders' Equity Accounts)**

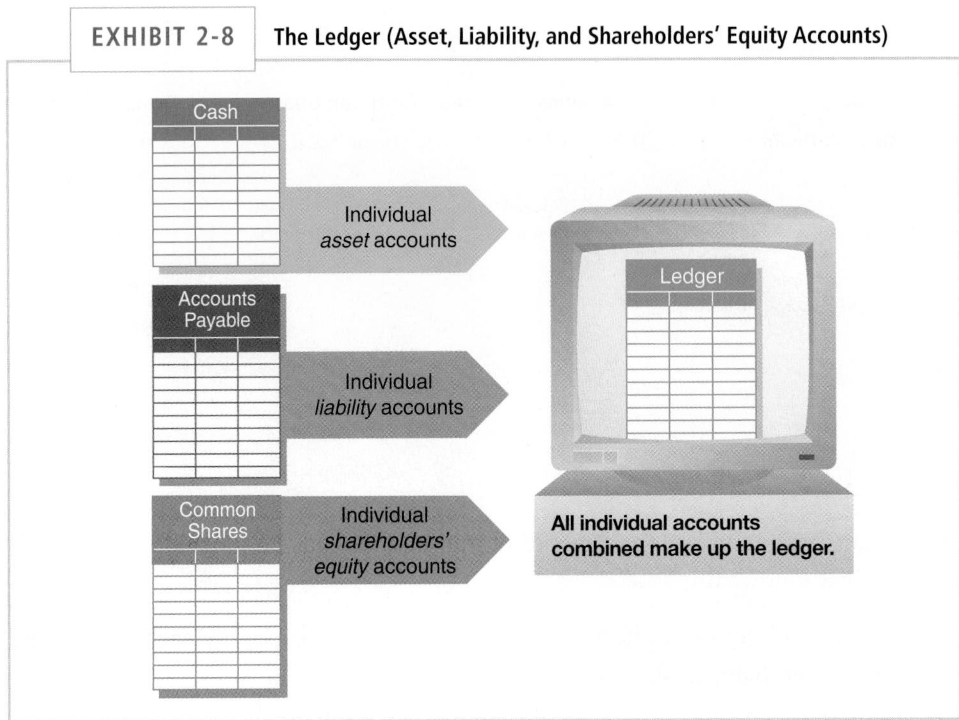

of Accounts Payable tells how much the business owes suppliers on open account, and so on.

In the phrase "keeping the books," *books* refers to the accounts in the ledger. In most accounting systems, the ledger is computerized. Exhibit 2-8 shows how the asset, liability, and shareholders' equity accounts are grouped in the ledger.

Entering a transaction in the journal does not get the data into the ledger. Data must be copied to the ledger—a process called **posting**. Debits in the journal are posted as debits in the accounts, and likewise for credits. Exhibit 2-9 shows how Tara Inc.'s share issuance transaction is posted to the accounts.

The Flow of Accounting Data

Exhibit 2-10 summarizes the flow of accounting data from the business transaction to the ledger.

EXHIBIT 2-9 **Journal Entry and Posting to the Accounts**

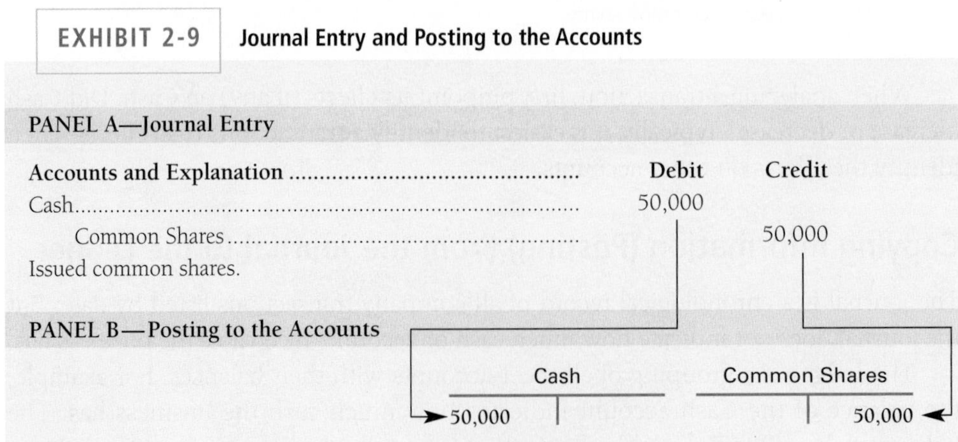

PANEL A—Journal Entry

Accounts and Explanation	Debit	Credit
Cash	50,000	
Common Shares		50,000
Issued common shares.		

PANEL B—Posting to the Accounts

EXHIBIT 2-10 Flow of Accounting Data

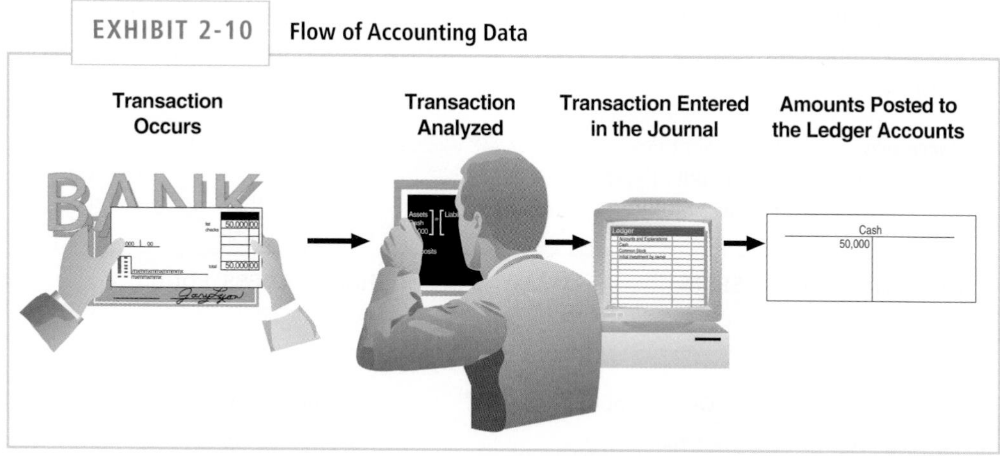

Let's continue the example of Tara Inc. and account for the same 11 events we illustrated earlier. Here we use the journal and the accounts. Each journal entry posted to the accounts is keyed by date or by transaction number. This linking allows you to locate any information you may need.

Event 1 Analysis. Tara Inc. received $50,000 cash from shareholders and in turn issued common shares to them. The journal entry, accounting equation, and ledger accounts follow:

Journal entry

	Debit	Credit
Cash	50,000	
Common Shares		50,000
Issued common shares.		

Accounting equation

ASSETS	=	LIABILITIES	+	SHAREHOLDERS' EQUITY
+50,000	=	0	+	50,000

The ledger accounts

Cash		Common Shares	
(1)* 50,000			(1)* 50,000

* The numbers in parentheses indicate the transaction number for purposes of this illustration.

Event 2 Analysis. The business paid $40,000 cash for land. The purchase decreased cash; therefore, credit Cash. The purchase increased the asset land; to record this increase, debit Land.

Journal entry

	Debit	Credit
Land	40,000	
Cash		40,000
Paid cash for land.		

Accounting equation

ASSETS	=	LIABILITIES	+	SHAREHOLDERS' EQUITY
+40,000 −40,000	=	0	+	0

The ledger accounts

Cash		Land	
(1) 50,000	(2) 40,000	(2) 40,000	

Event 3 Analysis. The business purchased office supplies for $3,700 on account payable. The purchase increased Office Supplies, an asset, and Accounts Payable, a liability.

Journal entry

	Debit	Credit
Office Supplies	3,700	
Accounts Payable		3,700
Purchased office supplies on account.		

Accounting equation

ASSETS	=	LIABILITIES	+	SHAREHOLDERS' EQUITY
+3,700	=	+3,700	+	0

The ledger accounts

Office Supplies	
(3) 3,700	

Accounts Payable	
	(3) 3,700

Event 4 Analysis. The business performed engineering services for clients and received cash of $7,000. The transaction increased cash and service revenue. To record the revenue, credit Service Revenue.

Journal entry

	Debit	Credit
Cash	7,000	
Service Revenue		7,000
Performed services for cash.		

Accounting equation

ASSETS	=	LIABILITIES	+	SHAREHOLDERS' EQUITY	+	REVENUES
+7,000	=	0	+	0	+	7,000

The ledger accounts

Cash	
(1) 50,000	(2) 40,000
(4) 7,000	

Service Revenue	
	(4) 7,000

Event 5 Analysis. Tara performed services for King Contracting on account. King Contracting did not pay immediately so Tara billed King Contracting for $3,000. The transaction increased accounts receivable; therefore, debit Accounts Receivable. Service revenue also increased, so credit Service Revenue.

Journal entry

	Debit	Credit
Accounts Receivable	3,000	
Service Revenue		3,000
Performed services on account.		

Accounting equation

ASSETS	=	LIABILITIES	+	SHAREHOLDERS' EQUITY	+	REVENUES
+3,000	=	0	+	0	+	3,000

The ledger accounts

Accounts Receivable	
(5) 3,000	

Service Revenue	
	(4) 7,000
	(5) 3,000

Event 6 Analysis. Tara paid $2,700 for the following expenses: office rent, $1,100; employee salary, $1,200; and utilities, $400. Credit Cash for the sum of the expense amounts. The expenses increased, so debit each account separately.

Journal entry

	Debit	Credit
Rent Expense	1,100	
Salary Expense	1,200	
Utilities Expense	400	
Cash		2,700
Paid expenses.		

Accounting equation

ASSETS	=	LIABILITIES	+	SHAREHOLDERS' EQUITY	−	EXPENSES
−2,700	=	0	+	0	−	2,700

The ledger accounts

Cash

(1) 50,000	(2) 40,000
(4) 7,000	(6) 2,700

Rent Expense

(6) 1,100	

Salary Expense

(6) 1,200	

Utilities Expense

(6) 400	

Event 7 Analysis. The business paid $1,900 on the account payable created in Event 3. Credit Cash for the payment. The payment decreased a liability, so debit Accounts Payable.

Journal entry

	Debit	Credit
Accounts Payable	1,900	
Cash		1,900
Paid cash on account.		

Accounting equation

ASSETS	=	LIABILITIES	+	SHAREHOLDERS' EQUITY
−1,900	=	−1,900	+	0

The ledger accounts

Cash

(1) 50,000	(2) 40,000
(4) 7,000	(6) 2,700
	(7) 1,900

Accounts Payable

(7) 1,900	(3) 3,700

Event 8 Analysis. J.J. Booth, a shareholder of Tara Inc., remodelled his personal residence. This is not a transaction of the engineering consultancy, so Tara does not record the event.

Event 9 Analysis. The business collected $1,000 cash on account from the client in Event 5. Cash increased so debit Cash. The asset accounts receivable decreased; therefore, credit Accounts Receivable.

Journal entry

	Debit	Credit
Cash	1,000	
Accounts Receivable		1,000
Collected cash on account.		

Accounting equation

ASSETS	=	LIABILITIES	+	SHAREHOLDERS' EQUITY
+1,000	=	0	+	0
−1,000				

The ledger accounts

Cash

(1) 50,000	(2) 40,000
(4) 7,000	(6) 2,700
(9) 1,000	(7) 1,900

Accounts Receivable

(5) 3,000	(9) 1,000

Event 10 Analysis. Tara sold a portion of its land for its cost of $22,000, receiving cash. The asset cash increased; debit Cash. The asset land decreased; credit Land.

Journal entry

	Debit	Credit
Cash	22,000	
Land		22,000
Sold land.		

Accounting equation

ASSETS	=	LIABILITIES	+	SHAREHOLDERS' EQUITY
+22,000	=	0	+	0
−22,000				

The ledger accounts

Cash		Land	
(1) 50,000	(2) 40,000	(2) 40,000	(10) 22,000
(4) 7,000	(6) 2,700		
(9) 1,000	(7) 1,900		
(10) 22,000			

Event 11 Analysis. Tara Inc. paid its shareholders cash dividends of $2,100. Credit Cash for the payment. The transaction also decreased shareholders' equity and requires a debit to an equity account; therefore, debit Dividends.

Journal entry

	Debit	Credit
Dividends	2,100	
Cash		2,100
Declared and paid dividends.		

Accounting equation

ASSETS	=	LIABILITIES	+	SHAREHOLDERS' EQUITY	−	DIVIDENDS
−2,100	=	0	+	0	−	2,100

The ledger accounts

Cash		Dividends	
(1) 50,000	(2) 40,000	(11) 2,100	
(4) 7,000	(6) 2,700		
(9) 1,000	(7) 1,900		
(10) 22,000	(11) 2,100		

Accounts After Posting to the Ledger

MyAccountingLab

Accounting Cycle Tutorial: The Journal and the Ledger – Application Exercise 1

Exhibit 2-11 shows the accounts after all transactions have been posted. Group the accounts under assets, liabilities, and shareholders' equity.

Each account has a balance, denoted as Bal., which is the difference between the account's total debits and its total credits. For example, the Accounts Payable balance is the difference between the credit ($3,700) and the debit ($1,900). Thus, the Accounts Payable balance is a credit of $1,800. The cash account has a debit balance of $33,300.

MyAccountingLab

Accounting Cycle Tutorial: The Journal and the Ledger – Application Exercise 2

A horizontal line separates the transaction amounts from the account balance. If the sum of an account's debits is greater than the sum of its credits, that account has a debit balance, as for Cash. If the sum of its credits is greater, that account has a credit balance, as for Accounts Payable.

EXHIBIT 2-11 Tara Inc.'s Ledger Accounts After Posting

Assets = **Liabilities** + **Shareholders' Equity**

Cash

(1)	50,000	(2)	40,000
(4)	7,000	(6)	2,700
(9)	1,000	(7)	1,900
(10)	22,000	(11)	2,100
Bal.	33,300		

Accounts Receivable

(5)	3,000	(9)	1,000
Bal.	2,000		

Office Supplies

(3)	3,700		
Bal.	3,700		

Land

(2)	40,000	(10)	22,000
Bal.	18,000		

Accounts Payable

(7)	1,900	(3)	3,700
		Bal.	1,800

Common Shares

		(1)	50,000
		Bal.	50,000

Dividends

(11)	2,100		
Bal.	2,100		

REVENUE

Service Revenue

		(4)	7,000
		(5)	3,000
		Bal.	10,000

EXPENSES

Rent Expense

(6)	1,100		
Bal.	1,100		

Salary Expense

(6)	1,200		
Bal.	1,200		

Utilities Expense

(6)	400		
Bal.	400		

ACCOUNTING FOR TRANSACTIONS PART 2

I. The accountant must decide where and how to record the transaction.

The transaction is recorded in the journal, which is the chronological record of transactions.

The transaction in the *journal* must include a debit and a credit and follow the *rules of debit and credit:*

	Increase	Decrease
Asset	Debit	Credit
Liability	Credit	Debit
Shareholders' equity	Credit	Debit
Revenue	Credit	Debit
Expense	Debit	Credit

II. The accountant must decide where to store the account information in the journal.

The account information is recorded in the respective accounts in the ledger.

The Trial Balance

A **trial balance** lists all accounts with their balances—assets first, followed by liabilities and then shareholders' equity. The trial balance summarizes all the account balances for the financial statements and shows whether total debits equal total credits. A trial balance may be taken at any time, but the most common time is at the end of the period. Exhibit 2-12 is the trial balance of Tara Inc. after its first 11 transactions have been journalized and posted at the end of April.

OBJECTIVE

Use a trial balance

EXHIBIT 2-12 Trial Balance

MyAccountingLab

Accounting Cycle Tutorial: The Journal and the Ledger – Glossary Terminology

MyAccountingLab

Accounting Cycle Tutorial: The Journal and the Ledger – Glossary Quiz

Tara Inc.
Trial Balance
April 30, 2011

Account Title	Balance Debit	Balance Credit
Cash	$33,300	
Accounts receivable	2,000	
Office supplies	3,700	
Land	18,000	
Accounts payable		$ 1,800
Common shares		50,000
Dividends	2,100	
Service revenue		10,000
Rent expense	1,100	
Salary expense	1,200	
Utilities expense	400	
Total	$61,800	$61,800

Analyzing Accounts

You can often tell what a company did by analyzing its accounts. This is a powerful tool for a manager who knows accounting. For example, if you know the beginning and ending balance of Cash, and if you know total cash receipts, you can compute your total cash payments during the period.

In our chapter example, suppose Tara Inc. began May with cash of $1,000. During May, Tara received cash of $8,000 and ended the month with a cash balance of $3,000. You can compute total cash payments by analyzing Tara's Cash account as follows:

Cash			
Beginning balance	1,000		
Cash receipts	8,000	Cash payments	$x = 6,000$
Ending balance	3,000		

Or, if you know Cash's beginning and ending balances and total payments, you can compute cash receipts during the period—for any company!

You can compute either sales on account or cash collections on account by analyzing the Accounts Receivable account as follows (using assumed amounts):

Accounts Receivable			
Beginning balance	6,000		
Sales on account	10,000	Collections on account	$x = 11,000$
Ending balance	5,000		

Also, you can determine how much you paid on account by analyzing Accounts Payable as follows (using assumed amounts):

Accounts Payable			
		Beginning balance	9,000
Payments on account	$x = 4,000$	Purchases on account	6,000
		Ending balance	11,000

Please master this powerful technique. It works for any company and for your own personal finances! You will find this tool very helpful when you become a manager.

USING UNDERSTANDING OF TRANSACTIONS ANALYSIS IN DECISION MAKING

The knowledge that a business has an annual audit gives managers, investors, and creditors confidence that the business is properly accounting for its transactions and that the financial statements present fairly the financial position and results of operations. They can be relied upon for making decisions.

ACCOUNTING FOR TRANSACTIONS PART 3

I. The accountant must list all the accounts and their balances and also determine whether the debits in the ledger equal the credits.

The trial balance is a list of all the accounts in the ledger. The debits should equal the credits; if they don't, the accountant must determine which account or accounts are incorrect.

II. The accountant completes the process by reporting the financial position of the organization and the results of its operations in the financial statements you learned about in Chapter 1. The accountant must determine that assets, liabilities, revenues, and expenses are correctly reported.

Revenues, *Expenses*, and *Net Income* or *Net Loss* are reported in the Income Statement.

Assets, *Liabilities*, and *Shareholders' Equity* are reported on the Balance Sheet.

Correcting Accounting Errors

Accounting errors can occur even in computerized systems. Input data may be wrong, or they may be entered twice or not at all. In a manual system, a debit may be entered as a credit, and vice versa. You can detect the reason or reasons behind many out-of-balance conditions by computing the difference between total debits and total credits. Then perform one or more of the following actions:

1. Search the records for a missing account. Trace each account back and forth from the journal to the ledger. A \$200 transaction may have been recorded incorrectly in the journal or posted incorrectly to the ledger. Search the journal for a \$200 transaction.
2. Divide the out-of-balance amount by 2. A debit treated as a credit, or vice versa, doubles the amount of error. Suppose Tara Inc. added \$300 to Cash instead of subtracting \$300. The out-of-balance amount is \$600, and dividing by 2 identifies \$300 as the amount of the transaction. Search the journal for the \$300 transaction, and trace it to the account affected.
3. Divide the out-of-balance amount by 9. If the result is an integer (no decimals), the error may be a
   - *slide* (writing \$400 as \$40).The accounts would be out of balance by \$360 (\$400 − \$40 = \$360). Dividing \$360 by 9 yields \$40. Scan the trial balance

in Exhibit 2-12 for an amount similar to $40. An account with a balance of $400 would be the misstated account.

- *transposition* (writing $2,100 as $1,200). The accounts would be out of balance by $900 ($2,100 − $1,200 = $900). Dividing $900 by 9 yields $100. Trace all amounts on the trial balance back to the T-accounts. An account with a balance of $2,100 would be the misstated account.

Chart of Accounts

As you know, the ledger contains the business accounts grouped under these headings:

1. **Balance sheet accounts: Assets, Liabilities, and Shareholders' Equity**
2. **Income statement accounts: Revenues and Expenses**

Organizations use a **chart of accounts** to list all accounts and account numbers. Account numbers usually have two or more digits. Assets are often numbered beginning with 1, liabilities with 2, shareholders' equity with 3, revenues with 4, and expenses with 5. The second, third, and higher digits in an account number indicate the position of the individual account within the category. For example, Cash may be account number 101, which is the first asset account. Accounts Payable may be number 201, the first liability account. All accounts are numbered by this system.

Organizations with many accounts use lengthy account numbers. For example, the chart of accounts of Research In Motion may use seven-digit account numbers. The chart of accounts for Tara Inc. appears in Exhibit 2-13. The gap between the account numbers 111 and 141 leaves room to add another category of receivables, for example, Notes Receivable, which may be numbered 121.

The Normal Balance of an Account

An account's *normal balance* falls on the side of the account—debit or credit—where increases are recorded. The normal balance of assets is on the debit side, so assets are called *debit-balance accounts*. Conversely, liabilities and shareholders' equity usually have a credit balance, so their normal balances are on the credit side. They are called *credit-balance accounts*. Exhibit 2-14 illustrates the normal balances of all the assets, liabilities, and shareholders' equities, including revenues and expenses.

EXHIBIT 2-13 **Chart of Accounts—Tara Inc.**

Balance Sheet Accounts		
Assets	**Liabilities**	**Shareholders' Equity**
101 Cash	201 Accounts Payable	301 Common Shares
111 Accounts Receivable	231 Notes Payable	311 Dividends
141 Office Supplies		312 Retained Earnings
151 Office Furniture		
191 Land		

Income Statement Accounts (Part of Shareholders' Equity)	
Revenues	**Expenses**
401 Service Revenue	501 Rent Expense
	502 Salary Expense
	503 Utilities Expense

EXHIBIT 2-14 **Normal Balances of the Accounts**

Assets	Debit	
Liabilities		Credit
Shareholders' equity—overall		Credit
Common shares		Credit
Retained earnings		Credit
Dividends	Debit	
Revenues		Credit
Expenses	Debit	

As explained earlier, shareholders' equity usually contains several accounts. But there are exceptions. Dividends and Expenses carry debit balances because they represent decreases in shareholders' equity. Overall, these accounts show a normal credit balance.

Account Formats

So far we have illustrated accounts in a two-column T-account format, with the debit column on the left and the credit column on the right. Another format has three *amount* columns, as illustrated for the Cash account in Exhibit 2-15. The first two amount columns are for the debit and credit amounts. The third amount column is for the account balance. A debit balance is denoted by "Dr.," the abbreviation of debit. A credit balance is denoted by "Cr.," the abbreviation for credit. This three-column format keeps a running balance in the third column.

MyAccountingLab

Accounting Cycle Tutorial: The Journal and the Ledger – Tutorial

EXHIBIT 2-15 **Account in Three-Column Format**

Account: Cash **Account No. 101**

Date	Item	Debit	Credit	Balance
2011				
Apr. 1		50,000		50,000 Dr.
3			40,000	10,000 Dr.

Analyzing Transactions Using Only T-Accounts

OBJECTIVE

5 **Analyze** transactions using only T-accounts

Business people must often make decisions without the benefit of a complete accounting system. For example, assume the manager of Kinney Fitness Equipment Inc. may consider borrowing $100,000 to buy equipment. To see how the two transactions [(a) borrowing cash and (b) buying equipment] affect Kinney, the manager can go directly to T-accounts, as follows:

T-accounts:

Cash	
(a) 100,000	

Note Payable	
	(a) 100,000

T-accounts:

Cash	
(a) 100,000	(b) 100,000

Equipment	
(b) 100,000	

Note Payable	
	(a) 100,000

This informal analysis shows immediately that Kinney will add $100,000 of equipment and a $100,000 note payable to its financial position. Assuming that

MyAccountingLab

Accounting Cycle Tutorial: The Journal and the Ledger – Application Exercises 4 and 5

MyAccountingLab

Accounting Cycle Tutorial: The Journal and the Ledger – Application Exercise 4

Kinney began with zero balances, the equipment and note payable transactions would result in the following balance sheet:

Kinney Fitness Equipment Inc.
Balance Sheet
As at September 12, 2011

Assets		Liabilities	
Cash	$ 0	Note payable	$100,000
Equipment	100,000	Total liabilities	100,000
		Shareholders' Equity	0
		Total liabilities and	
Total assets	$100,000	shareholders' equity	$100,000

Companies do not actually keep records in this shortcut fashion. But a decision maker who needs information immediately does not have time to journalize, post to the accounts, take a trial balance, and prepare financial statements. A manager who knows accounting can analyze the transaction and make a decision quickly.

SUMMARY OF CHAPTER 2

Learning Objective ❶: **Analyze transactions**

A **transaction** is any event that has a financial impact on a business and can be measured.

Recall from Chapter 1 that the **accounting equation** (Assets = Liabilities + Shareholders' Equity) expresses the basic relationships of accounting. We use the accounting equation as the focus for our discussion in this chapter.

An **account** is the record of all the changes in a particular asset, liability, or shareholders' equity during a period. The account is the basic summary device of accounting.

Accounting for business transactions involves considering business-related events and determining if each is a transaction or not. The next step is to analyze each event that is determined to be a transaction in terms of the accounting equation.

The accounting equation must balance for each transaction so that the transaction's net amount on the left side of the equation must equal the net amount on the right side. This means that some transactions may be recorded on both sides of the equation (for example, purchase of supplies on account affects both assets and liabilities). Other transactions may be recorded on only one side in two different accounts so that the effect on the equation is zero (for example, collection of an account receivable [an asset] increases cash and decreases accounts receivable [an asset] by the same amount on the left side of the equation).

Learning Objective ❷: **Understand how accounting works**

Each transaction affects at least two accounts. Each account can be represented by a **T-account**. The left side of the T is a **debit**; the right side is a **credit. Every business transaction involves both a debit and a credit.**

The rule of debit and credit states that

- Assets are increased by a debit and decreased by a credit
- Liabilities are decreased by a debit and increased by a credit
- Shareholders' equity is decreased by a debit and increased by a credit

The accounting equation can be expanded as follows:

Shareholders' Equity = Common Shares* + Retained Earnings – Dividends + (Revenues – Expenses)

The **balance sheet** includes the assets, liabilities, and shareholders' equity. The **statement of retained earnings** includes the retained earnings balance at the beginning of the year plus net income (or minus net loss) for the year minus dividends paid during the year. The **income statement** includes income for the year minus expenses for the year. If income exceeds expense, the income statement shows net income, a positive number; if expense exceeds revenue, the income statement shows net loss, a negative number.

Learning Objective ❸: **Record transactions in a journal**

Transactions are recorded in a **journal.** The journal is a chronological record of all the business's transactions listed by date.

The entries are **posted** from the journal to a **ledger**; that is, the entries from the journal are entered in the ledger. The ledger is a grouping of all the T-accounts. Each T-account shows the current balance of that particular account after all debit and credit entries from the journal for that account have been posted. For example, the Accounts Receivable ledger account shows the total amount due from customers.

Organizations use a **chart of accounts** to list all accounts and account numbers. The chart begins with asset accounts, then liability accounts, and next come the shareholders' equity accounts, followed by revenue accounts, and finally the expense accounts.

In summary, a business transaction occurs, and the transaction is analyzed and then entered in a journal. Finally, the amounts in the journal are posted in the ledger in the appropriate accounts.

Learning Objective ❹: **Use a trial balance**

A **trial balance** lists all accounts in the ledger with their balances. The trial balance is the starting point for the preparation of the financial statements, as you will learn in Chapter 3.

The various accounts have normal balances:

- Asset accounts are debits.
- Liability accounts are credits.
- Shareholders' equity accounts are credits (except for dividends, which are debits).
- Revenue accounts are credits.
- Expense accounts are debits.

Learning Objective ❺: **Analyze transactions using only T-accounts**

Business decisions can be analyzed using T-accounts. Managers who understand accounting can analyze a transaction and make a decision using only T-accounts.

---

*Shareholders' equity would also include preferred shares if issued by the business.

MyAccountingLab

END-OF-CHAPTER SUMMARY PROBLEM

The trial balance of Bos Personnel Services Inc. on March 1, 2011, lists the entity's assets, liabilities, and shareholders' equity on that date.

	Balance	
Account Title	*Debit*	*Credit*
Cash	$26,000	
Accounts receivable	4,500	
Accounts payable		$ 2,000
Common shares		10,000
Retained earnings		18,500
Total	$30,500	$30,500

During March, the business completed the following transactions:

a. Borrowed $70,000 from the bank, with C. Bos signing a note payable in the name of the business.
b. Paid cash of $60,000 to a real estate company to acquire land.
c. Performed service for a customer and received cash of $5,000.
d. Purchased supplies on credit, $300.
e. Performed customer service and earned revenue on account, $4,000.
f. Paid $1,200 on account.
g. Paid the following cash expenses: salary, $3,000; rent, $1,500; and interest, $400.
h. Received $3,100 on account.
i. Received a $200 utility bill that will be paid next month.
j. Declared and paid a dividend of $300.

Name: Bos Personnel Services Inc.
Industry: Human Resources
Fiscal Period: Month of March 2011
Key Fact: An existing, ongoing business

Required

1. Open the following accounts, with the balances indicated, in the ledger of Bos Personnel Services Inc. Use the T-account format.
    - Assets—Cash, $26,000; Accounts Receivable, $4,500; Supplies, no balance; Land, no balance
    - Liabilities—Accounts Payable, $2,000; Note Payable, no balance
    - Shareholders' Equity—Common Shares, $10,000; Retained Earnings, $18,500; Dividends, no balance
    - Revenues—Service Revenue, no balance
    - Expenses—(none have balances) Salary Expense, Rent Expense, Interest Expense, Utilities Expense

Prepare a T-account for each account name. Place the opening balance in the T-account, remembering that the normal balance in an asset account is a debit, in a liability or equity account is a credit, in a revenue account is a credit, and in an expense account is a debit.

For each transaction, ensure that Assets = Liabilities + Shareholders' equity.

2. Journalize the transactions listed above. Key journal entries by transaction letter.
3. Post to the ledger and show the balance in each account after all the transactions have been posted.
4. Prepare the trial balance of Bos Personnel Services Inc. at March 31, 2011.
5. To determine the net income or net loss of the entity during the month of March, prepare the income statement for the month ended March 31, 2011. List expenses in order from the largest to the smallest.
6. Suppose the organizers of Bos Personnel Services Inc. ask you to purchase shares in the company. Cite specifics from the income statement and the trial balance to support your decision.

Refer to the rules of debit and credit shown in Exhibit 2-7 on page 77.

ANSWERS

Requirement 1

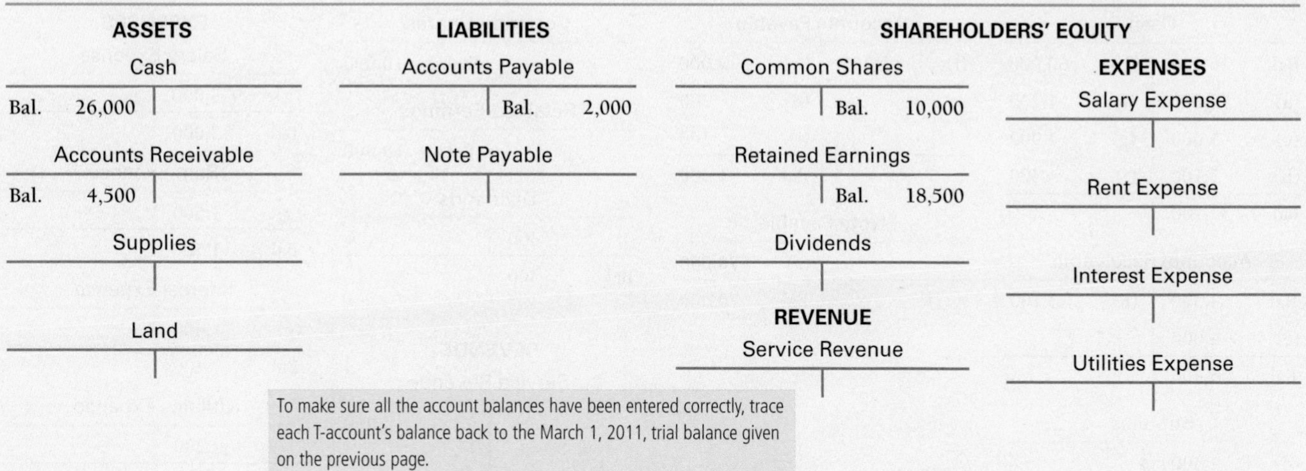

To make sure all the account balances have been entered correctly, trace each T-account's balance back to the March 1, 2011, trial balance given on the previous page.

Requirement 2

Accounts and Explanation	Debit	Credit
a. Cash	70,000	
Note Payable		70,000
Borrowed cash on note payable.		
b. Land	60,000	
Cash		60,000
Purchased land for cash.		
c. Cash	5,000	
Service Revenue		5,000
Performed service and received cash.		
d. Supplies	300	
Accounts Payable		300
Purchased supplies on account.		
e. Accounts Receivable	4,000	
Service Revenue		4,000
Performed service on account.		
f. Accounts Payable	1,200	
Cash		1,200
Paid on account.		

Accounts and Explanation	Debit	Credit
g. Salary Expense	3,000	
Rent Expense	1,500	
Interest Expense	400	
Cash		4,900
Paid cash expenses.		
h. Cash	3,100	
Accounts Receivable		3,100
Received on account.		
i. Utilities Expense	200	
Accounts Payable		200
Received utility bill.		
j. Dividends	300	
Cash		300
Declared and paid dividends.		

Selected transactions are explained more fully:

d. Increase Supplies (asset) and increase Accounts Payable (liability), since supplies were purchased on credit. Cash will be paid for the supplies in the future.

e. Increase Accounts Receivable (asset) and increase Service Revenue (income) since the service was performed on account. Cash will be received for the service in the future.

g. This transaction could also have been recorded with three journal entries, with a debit to the expense and a credit to Cash for each of the expenses.

i. Increase Utilities Expense (expenses) and increase Accounts Payable (liability), since cash will be paid for the utility bill in the future.

Requirement 3

ASSETS

Cash

Bal. 26,000	(b) 60,000		
(a) 70,000	(f) 1,200		
(c) 5,000	(g) 4,900		
(h) 3,100	(j) 300		
Bal. 37,700			

Accounts Receivable

Bal. 4,500	(h) 3,100
(e) 4,000	
Bal. 5,400	

Supplies

(d) 300	
Bal. 300	

Land

(b) 60,000	
Bal. 60,000	

LIABILITIES

Accounts Payable

(f) 1,200	Bal. 2,000
	(d) 300
	(i) 200
	Bal. 1,300

Note Payable

	(a) 70,000
	Bal. 70,000

SHAREHOLDERS' EQUITY

Common Shares

	Bal. 10,000

Retained Earnings

	Bal. 18,500

Dividends

(j) 300	
Bal. 300	

REVENUE

Service Revenue

	(c) 5,000
	(e) 4,000
	Bal. 9,000

EXPENSES

Salary Expense

(g) 3,000	
Bal. 3,000	

Rent Expense

(g) 1,500	
Bal. 1,500	

Interest Expense

(g) 400	
Bal. 400	

Utilities Expense

(i) 200	
Bal. 200	

Make sure each transaction is posted to the proper T-account, and make sure no transactions were missed. Make sure that Assets = Liabilities + Shareholders' Equity for each transaction before going to the next transaction.

Requirement 4

The title must include the name of the company, "Trial Balance," and the date of the trial balance. It shows the account balances on one specific date.

List all the accounts that have a balance in their T-accounts. Write the "Bal." amount for each account from Requirement 3 into the debit or credit column of the trial balance. Make sure that the total of the Debit column equals the total of the Credit column. Double underline the totals to show that the columns have been added and the totals are final.

Bos Personnel Services Inc.
Trial Balance
March 31, 2011

Account Title	Balance *Debit*	*Credit*
Cash	$ 37,700	
Accounts receivable	5,400	
Supplies	300	
Land	60,000	
Accounts payable		$ 1,300
Note payable		70,000
Common shares		10,000
Retained earnings		18,500
Dividends	300	
Service revenue		9,000
Salary expense	3,000	
Rent expense	1,500	
Interest expense	400	
Utilities expense	200	
Total	$108,800	$108,800

Requirement 5

Bos Personnel Services Inc.
Income Statement
For the Month Ended March 31, 2011

Revenue		
Service revenue		$9,000
Expenses		
Salary expense	$3,000	
Rent expense	1,500	
Interest expense	400	
Utilities expense	200	
Total expenses		5,100
Net income		$3,900

The title must include the name of the company, "Income Statement," and the specific period of time covered. It is critical that the time period be defined. Prepare the income statement by listing the revenue and expense account names from the trial balance. Then transfer the amounts from the trial balance to the income statement.

Requirement 6

An investment in Bos appears to be warranted because

a. The company earned net income of $3,900, so the business appears profitable.

b. Total assets of $103,400 ($37,700 + $5,400 + $300 + $60,000) far exceed total liabilities of $71,300 ($1,300 + $70,000), which suggests that Bos can pay its debts and remain in business.

c. Bos is paying a small dividend, so an investment in the shares may yield a return in the form of dividends.

Items to consider when answering a question like this are

a. Net income

b. The excess of assets over liabilities

c. Whether dividends were distributed during the year

Review the Transaction Analysis

Quick Check (Answers are given on page 116.)

1. A debit entry to an account
   a. Increases liabilities
   b. Increases shareholders' equity
   c. Increases assets
   d. Both a and c
2. Which of the following account types normally have a credit balance?
   a. Liabilities
   b. Revenues
   c. Expenses
   d. Both a and b
3. An attorney performs services of $800 for a client and receives $200 cash with the rest on account. The journal entry for this transaction would be which of the following?
   a. Debit Cash, debit Accounts Receivable, credit Service Revenue
   b. Debit Cash, credit Accounts Receivable, credit Service Revenue
   c. Debit Cash, credit Service Revenue
   d. Debit Cash, debit Service Revenue, credit Accounts Receivable
4. Accounts Payable had a normal beginning balance of $1,000. During the period, there were debit postings of $400 and credit postings of $600. What was the ending balance?
   a. $800 debit
   b. $800 credit
   c. $1,200 debit
   d. $1,200 credit
5. The list of all accounts with their balances is the
   a. Trial balance
   b. Chart of accounts
   c. Journal
   d. Balance sheet
6. The basic summary device used in accounting is the
   a. Ledger
   b. Account
   c. Journal
   d. Trial balance
7. The beginning Cash balance was $5,000. At the end of the period, the balance was $6,000. If total cash paid out during the period was $24,000, the amount of cash receipts was
   a. $23,000
   b. $13,000
   c. $25,000
   d. $35,000
8. In a double-entry accounting system
   a. A debit entry is recorded on the left side of a T-account
   b. Half of all the accounts have a normal credit balance
   c. Liabilities, owners' equity, and revenue accounts all have normal debit balances
   d. Both a and c are correct
9. Which accounts appear on which financial statement?

	Balance sheet	*Income statement*
a.	Cash, revenues, land	Expenses, payables
b.	Receivables, land, payables	Revenues, supplies
c.	Expenses, payables, cash	Revenues, receivables, land
d.	Cash, receivables, payables	Revenues, expenses

10. A doctor purchases medical supplies of $670 and pays $200 cash with the rest on account. The journal entry for this transaction would be
    a. Supplies
       Accounts Payable
          Cash
    b. Supplies
       Cash
          Accounts Payable
    c. Supplies
       Accounts Receivable
          Cash
    d. Supplies
          Accounts Payable
          Cash
11. Which is the correct sequence of accounting procedures?
    a. Journal, ledger, trial balance, financial statements
    b. Ledger, trial balance, journal, financial statements
    c. Financial statements, trial balance, ledger, journal
    d. Ledger, journal, trial balance, financial statements

12. The error of posting $100 as $10 can be detected by
    a. Dividing the out-of-balance amount by 2
    b. Totalling each account's balance in the ledger
    c. Dividing the out-of-balance amount by 9
    d. Examining the chart of accounts

Accounting Vocabulary

account The record of the changes that have occurred in a particular asset, liability, or shareholders' equity during a period. The basic summary device of accounting. (p. 62)

accrued liability A liability for an expense that has not yet been paid by the company. (p. 63)

chart of accounts List of a company's accounts and their account numbers. (p. 85)

credit The right side of an account. (p. 74)

debit The left side of an account. (p. 74)

double-entry system An accounting system that uses debits and credits to record the dual effects of each business transaction. (p. 74)

journal The chronological accounting record of an entity's transactions. (p. 77)

ledger The book of accounts and their balances. (p. 77)

posting Copying amounts from the journal to the ledger. (p. 78)

prepaid expense A category of miscellaneous assets that typically expire or get used up in the near future. Examples include Prepaid Rent, Prepaid Insurance, and Supplies. (p. 62)

transaction Any event that has a financial impact on the business and can be measured. (p. 61)

trial balance A list of all the ledger accounts with their balances. (p. 84)

Assess Your Progress

Make the grade with MyAccountingLab: The exercises and problems in this chapter can be found on MyAccountingLab at www.myaccountinglab.com. You can practise them as often as you want, and they feature step-by-step guided solutions to help you find the right answer.

Short Exercises

S2-1 Sue Deliveau opened a software consulting firm that immediately paid $2,000 for a computer. Was this event a transaction for the business?

Learning Objective 1
Analyzing a transaction

S2-2 Hourglass Software began with cash of $10,000. Hourglass then bought supplies for $2,000 on account. Separately, Hourglass paid $5,000 for a computer. Answer these questions.
a. How much in total assets does Hourglass have?
b. How much in liabilities does Hourglass owe?

Learning Objective 1
Analyzing the effects of transactions

S2-3 Marsha Solomon, a physiotherapist, opened a practice. The business completed the following transactions:

Learning Objective 1
Analyzing transactions

May	1	Solomon invested $25,000 cash to start her practice. The business issued shares to Solomon.
	1	Purchased medical supplies on account totalling $9,000.
	2	Paid monthly office rent of $4,000.
	3	Recorded $8,000 revenue for service rendered to patients, received cash of $2,000, and sent bills to patients for the remainder.

After these transactions, how much cash does the business have to work with? Use T-accounts to show your answer.

S2-4 Refer to Short Exercise 2-3. Which of the transactions of Marsha Solomon, P.T., increased the total assets of the business? For each transaction, identify the asset or liability that was increased or decreased.

Learning Objective 1
Analyzing transactions

Learning Objective ❷❸
Recording transactions

S2-5 After operating for several months, artist Paul Marciano completed the following transactions during the latter part of June:

June	15	Borrowed $25,000 from the bank, signing a note payable.
	22	Painted a portrait for a client on account totalling $9,000.
	28	Received $5,000 cash on account from clients.
	29	Received a utility bill of $600, which will be paid during July.
	30	Paid monthly salary of $2,500 to gallery assistant.

Journalize the transactions of Paul Marciano, artist. Include an explanation with each journal entry.

Learning Objective ❷❸
Journalizing transactions; posting

S2-6 Architect Sonia Biaggi purchased supplies on account for $5,000. Later Biaggi paid $3,000 on account.

1. Journalize the two transactions on the books of Sonia Biaggi, architect. Include an explanation for each transaction.
2. Open a T-account for Accounts Payable and post to Accounts Payable. Compute the balance and denote it as Bal.
3. How much does Biaggi's business owe after both transactions? In which account does this amount appear?

Learning Objective ❷❸
Journalizing transactions; posting

S2-7 Family Services Centre (The Centre) performed service for a client who could not pay immediately. The Centre expected to collect the $500 the following month. A month later, The Centre received $100 cash from the client.

1. Record the two transactions on the books of Family Services Centre. Include an explanation for each transaction.
2. Open these T-accounts: Cash, Accounts Receivable, and Service Revenue. Post to all three accounts. Compute each account balance and denote as Bal.
3. Answer these questions based on your analysis:
   a. How much did The Centre earn? Which account shows this amount?
   b. How much in total assets did The Centre acquire as a result of the two transactions? Show the amount of each asset.

Learning Objective ❹
Preparing and using a trial balance

S2-8 Assume that lululemon athletica inc. reported the following summarized data at December 31, 2011. Accounts appear in no particular order; dollar amounts are in millions.

Revenues	$275
Other liabilities	38
Other assets	101
Cash and other current assets	53
Accounts payable	5
Expenses	244
Shareholders' equity	80

Prepare the trial balance of lululemon at December 31, 2011. List the accounts in their proper order, as on page 84. How much was lululemon's net income or net loss?

S2-9 Blackberry's trial balance follows:

Learning Objective 4
Using a trial balance

Blackberry Inc.
Trial Balance
June 30, 2011

	Debit	*Credit*
Cash	$ 6,000	
Accounts receivable	13,000	
Supplies	4,000	
Equipment	22,000	
Land	50,000	
Accounts payable		$ 19,000
Note payable		20,000
Common shares		10,000
Retained earnings		8,000
Service revenue		70,000
Salary expense	21,000	
Rent expense	10,000	
Interest expense	1,000	
Total	$127,000	$127,000

Compute these amounts for Blackberry:

1. Total assets
2. Total liabilities
3. Total shareholders' equity
4. Net income or loss during June

S2-10 Refer to Blackberry's trial balance in Short Exercise S2-9. The purpose of this exercise is to help you learn how to correct three common accounting errors:

Learning Objective 4
Using a trial balance

Error 1. Slide: Suppose the trial balance lists Land as $5,000 instead of $50,000. Recompute column totals, take the difference, and divide by 9. The result is an integer (no decimals), which suggests that the error is either a transposition or a slide.

Error 2. Transposition: Assume the trial balance lists Accounts Receivable as $31,000 instead of $13,000. Recompute column totals, take the difference, and divide by 9. The result is an integer (no decimals), which suggests that the error is either a transposition or a slide.

Error 3. Mislabelling an item: Assume that Blackberry accidentally listed Accounts Receivable as a credit balance instead of a debit. Recompute the trial balance totals for debits and credits. Then take the difference between total debits and total credits, and divide the difference by 2. You get back to the original amount of Accounts Receivable.

S2-11 Accounting has its own vocabulary and basic relationships. Match the accounting terms at left with the corresponding definition or meaning at right.

Learning Objective 2
Using key accounting terms

___	1. Debit	A. The cost of operating a business; a decrease in shareholders' equity
___	2. Expense	B. Always a liability
___	3. Net income	C. Revenues – Expenses
___	4. Ledger	D. Grouping of accounts
___	5. Posting	E. Assets – Liabilities
___	6. Normal balance	F. Record of transactions
___	7. Payable	G. Always an asset
___	8. Journal	H. Left side of an account
___	9. Receivable	I. Side of an account where increases are recorded
___	10. Owners' equity	J. Copying data from the journal to the ledger

Learning Objective 5
Analyzing transactions without a journal

S2-12 Canadian Prairies Investments began by issuing common shares for cash of $100,000. The company immediately purchased computer equipment on account for $60,000.

1. Set up the following T-accounts for the company: Cash, Computer Equipment, Accounts Payable, Common Shares.
2. Record the transactions directly in the T-accounts without using a journal.
3. Show that total debits equal total credits.

Exercises

Learning Objective 1
Analyzing transactions

E2-13 Assume The Gap has opened a store in Ottawa. Starting with cash and shareholders' equity (common shares) of $100,000, Susan Harper, the store manager, signed a note payable to purchase land for $40,000 and a building for $130,000. She also paid $50,000 for store fixtures and $40,000 for inventory to use in the business. All these were paid for in cash.

Suppose the head office of Gap requires a weekly report from store managers. Write Harper's memo to the head office to report on her borrowing and purchases. Include the store's balance sheet as the final part of your memo. Prepare a T-account to compute the balance for cash.

Learning Objective 1
Transactions and the accounting equation

E2-14 During April, Spokes Ltd. completed a series of transactions. For each of the following items, give an example of a business transaction that has the described effect on the accounting equation of Spokes Ltd.

a. Increase one asset, and decrease another asset.
b. Decrease an asset, and decrease shareholders' equity.
c. Decrease an asset, and decrease a liability.
d. Increase an asset, and increase shareholders' equity.
e. Increase an asset, and increase a liability.

Learning Objective 1
Transaction analysis

E2-15 The following selected events were experienced by either Problem Solvers Inc., a corporation, or Pierce Laflame, the major shareholder. State whether each event (1) increased, (2) decreased, or (3) had no effect on the total assets of the business. Identify any specific asset affected.

a. Received $9,000 cash from customers on account
b. Laflame used personal funds to purchase a swimming pool for his home
c. Sold land and received cash of $60,000 (the land was carried on the company's books at $60,000)
d. Borrowed $50,000 from the bank
e. Made cash purchase of land for a building site, $85,000
f. Received $20,000 cash and issued shares to a shareholder
g. Paid $60,000 cash on accounts payable
h. Purchased equipment and signed a $100,000 promissory note in payment
i. Purchased supplies on account for $15,000
j. The business paid Laflame a cash dividend of $4,000

Learning Objective 1
Transaction analysis; accounting equation

E2-16 Joseph Ohara opens a dental practice. During the first month of operation (March), the practice, titled Joseph Ohara Dental Clinic Ltd., experienced the following events:

March 6	Ohara invested $50,000 in the business, which in turn issued its common shares to him.
9	The business paid cash for land costing $30,000. Ohara plans to build a professional services building on the land.
12	The business purchased dental supplies for $3,000 on account.
15	Joseph Ohara Dental Clinic Ltd. officially opened for business.
15–31	During the rest of the month, Ohara treated patients and earned service revenue of $10,000, receiving cash for half the revenue earned.
15–31	The practice paid cash expenses: employee salaries, $1,400; office rent, $1,000; utilities, $300.
31	The practice used dental supplies with a cost of $250.
31	The practice borrowed $10,000, signing a note payable to the bank.
31	The practice paid $2,000 on account.

Required

1. Analyze the effects of these events on the accounting equation of the practice of Joseph Ohara Dental Clinic Ltd. Use a format similar to that of Exhibit 2-1, Panel B, with headings for Cash, Accounts Receivable, Dental Supplies, Land, Accounts Payable, Note Payable, Common Shares, and Retained Earnings.
2. After completing the analysis, answer these questions about the business.
   a. How much are total assets?
   b. How much does the business expect to collect from patients?
   c. How much does the business owe in total?
   d. How much of the business's assets does Ohara really own?
   e. How much net income or net loss did the business experience during its first month of operations?

E2-17 Refer to Exercise 2-16. Record the transactions in the journal of Joseph Ohara Dental Clinic Ltd. List the transactions by date, and give an explanation for each transaction.

Learning Objective ❷❸
Journalizing transactions

E2-18 Perfect Printers Inc. completed the following transactions during October 2011, its first month of operations:

Learning Objective ❶
Journalizing transactions

Oct.	1	Received $25,000, and issued common shares
	2	Purchased $800 of office supplies on account
	4	Paid $20,000 cash for land to use as a building site
	6	Performed service for customers, and received cash of $5,000
	9	Paid $100 on accounts payable
	17	Performed service for Waterloo School Board on account totalling $1,500
	23	Collected $1,000 from Waterloo School Board on account
	31	Paid the following expenses: salary, $1,000; rent, $500

Required

1. Record the transactions in the journal of Perfect Printers Inc. Key transactions by date and include an explanation for each entry, as illustrated in the chapter.

E2-19 Refer to Exercise 2-18.

Learning Objective ❸❹
Posting to the ledger and preparing and using a trial balance

Required

1. After journalizing the transactions of Exercise 2-18, post the entries to the ledger, using T-accounts. Key transactions by date. Date the ending balance of each account October 31, 2011.
2. Prepare the trial balance of Perfect Printers Inc., at October 31, 2011.
3. How much are total assets, total liabilities, and total shareholders' equity on October 31, 2011?

E2-20 The first seven transactions of Splash Water Park Ltd. have been posted to the company's accounts as follows:

Learning Objective ❷❸
Journalizing transactions

Cash

(1)	20,000	(3)	8,000
(2)	7,000	(6)	8,000
(5)	100	(7)	400

Supplies

(4)	1,000	(5)	100

Equipment

(6)	8,000		

Land

(3)	31,000		

Accounts Payable

(7)	400	(4)	1,000

Note Payable

		(2)	7,000
		(3)	23,000

Common Shares

		(1)	20,000

Required

Prepare the journal entries that served as the sources for the seven transactions. Include an explanation for each entry. As Splash Water Park moves into the next period, how much cash does the business have? How much does Splash Water Park owe?

Learning Objective 4
Preparing and using a trial balance

E2-21 The accounts of Victoria Garden Care Ltd. follow with their normal balances at September 30, 2011. The accounts are listed in no particular order.

Account	Balance	Account	Balance
Dividends	6,000	Common shares	8,500
Utilities expense	1,400	Accounts payable	4,300
Accounts receivable	17,500	Service revenue	24,000
Delivery expense	300	Equipment	29,000
Retained earnings	21,400	Note payable	13,000
Salary expense	8,000	Cash	9,000

Required

1. Prepare the company's trial balance at September 30, 2011, listing accounts in proper sequence, as illustrated in the chapter. For example, Accounts Receivable comes before Equipment. List the expense with the largest balance first, the expense with the next largest balance second, and so on.
2. Prepare the financial statement for the month ended September 30, 2011, that will tell the company's top managers the results of operations for the month.

Learning Objective 4
Correcting errors in a trial balance

E2-22 The trial balance of Sam's Deli Inc. at October 31, 2011, does not balance:

Cash	$ 4,200	
Accounts receivable	13,000	
Inventory	17,000	
Supplies	600	
Land	55,000	
Accounts payable		$12,000
Common shares		47,900
Sales revenue		32,100
Salary expense	1,700	
Rent expense	800	
Utilities expense	700	
Total	$93,000	$92,000

The accounting records hold the following errors:

a. Recorded a $1,000 cash revenue transaction by debiting Accounts Receivable. The credit entry was correct.
b. Posted a $1,000 credit to Accounts Payable as $100.
c. Did not record utilities expense or the related account payable in the amount of $200.
d. Understated Common Shares by $1,100.
e. Omitted insurance expense of $1,000 from the trial balance.

Required

Prepare the correct trial balance at October 31, 2011, complete with a heading. Journal entries are not required.

Learning Objective 5
Recording transactions without a journal

E2-23 Set up the following T-accounts: Cash, Accounts Receivable, Office Supplies, Office Furniture, Accounts Payable, Common Shares, Dividends, Service Revenue, Salary Expense, and Rent Expense.

Record the following transactions directly in the T-accounts without using a journal. Use the letters to identify the transactions. Calculate the account balances and denote as Bal.

a. In the month of May 2011, Sonia Rothesay opened an accounting firm by investing $10,000 cash and office furniture valued at $5,000. Organized as a professional corporation, the business issued common shares to Rothesay.
b. Paid monthly rent of $1,600
c. Purchased office supplies on account, $600
d. Paid employees' salaries of $2,000
e. Paid $200 of the account payable created in transaction c
f. Performed accounting service on account, $12,100
g. Declared and paid dividends of $2,000

E2-24 Refer to Exercise 2-23.

Learning Objective ❹
Preparing and using a trial balance

1. After recording the transactions in Exercise 2-23, prepare the trial balance of Sonia Rothesay, Accountant, at May 31, 2011.
2. How well did the business perform during its first month? Give the basis for your answer.

Serial Exercise

Exercise 2-25 begins an accounting cycle that is completed in Chapter 3.

E2-25 Web Marketing Services Inc. completed these transactions during the first part of January 2011:

Learning Objective ❷❸❹
Recording transactions and preparing a trial balance

Jan.	2	Received $5,000 cash from investors, and issued common shares
	2	Paid monthly office rent, $500
	3	Paid cash for a Dell computer, $3,000, with the computer expected to remain in service for five years
	4	Purchased office furniture on account, $6,000, with the furniture projected to last for five years
	5	Purchased supplies on account, $900
	9	Performed marketing service for a client, and received cash for the full amount of $800
	12	Paid utility expenses, $200
	18	Performed marketing service for a client on account, $1,700

Required

1. Set up T-accounts for Cash, Accounts Receivable, Supplies, Equipment, Furniture, Accounts Payable, Common Shares, Dividends, Service Revenue, Rent Expense, Utilities Expense, and Salary Expense.
2. Journalize the transactions. Explanations are not required.
3. Post to the T-accounts. Key all items by date and denote an account balance on January 18 as Bal.
4. Prepare a trial balance at January 18. In the Serial Exercise of Chapter 3, we add transactions for the remainder of January and will require a trial balance at January 31, 2011.

Challenge Exercises

E2-26 The manager of Canadiana Gallery Ltd. needs to compute the following information:

Learning Objective ❺
Computing financial statement amounts

a. Total cash paid during March. Analyze Cash.
b. Cash collections from customers during March. Analyze Accounts Receivable.
c. Cash paid on a note payable during March. Analyze Notes Payable.

Here are additional data you need to analyze.

Account	Balance Feb. 28	Balance Mar. 31	Additional Information for the Month of March
1. Cash	10,000	5,000	Cash receipts, $80,000
2. Accounts Receivable	26,000	24,000	Sales on account, $50,000
3. Note Payable	13,000	21,000	New borrowing, $25,000

Prepare a T-account to compute each amount a through c.

Learning Objective 1 4
Analyzing transactions; using a trial balance

E2-27 The trial balance of You Build Inc. at December 31, 2011, does not balance.

Cash	$ 3,900	Common shares	$20,000
Accounts receivable	7,200	Retained earnings	7,300
Land	34,000	Service revenue	9,100
Accounts payable	5,800	Salary expense	3,400
Note payable	5,000	Advertising expense	900

Required

1. How much out of balance is the trial balance? Determine the out-of-balance amount. The error lies in the Accounts Receivable account. Add the out-of-balance amount to, or subtract it from, Accounts Receivable to determine the correct balance of Accounts Receivable.
2. You Build Inc. also failed to record the following transactions during December:
   a. Purchased additional land for $60,000 by signing a note payable
   b. Earned service revenue on account, $10,000
   c. Paid salary expense of $1,400
   d. Purchased a TV advertisement for $1,000 on account. This account will be paid during January.

   Add these amounts to, or subtract them from, the appropriate accounts to properly include the effects of these transactions. Then prepare the corrected trial balance of You Build Inc.
3. After correcting the accounts, advise the top management of You Build Inc. on the company's
   a. Total assets
   b. Total liabilities
   c. Net income or loss

Learning Objective 1
Analyzing transactions

E2-28 This question concerns the items and the amounts that two entities, City of Regina and Public Health Organization, Inc. (PHO), should report in their financial statements.

During August, PHO provided City of Regina with medical checks for new school pupils and sent a bill for $30,000. On September 7, Regina sent a cheque to PHO for $25,000. Regina began August with a cash balance of $50,000; PHO began with cash of $0.

Required

For this situation, show everything that both Regina and PHO will report on their August and September income statements and on their balance sheets at August 31 and September 30. Use the following format for your answer:

Regina:		
Income statement	August	September
Balance sheet	August 31	September 30
PHO:		
Income statement	August	September
Balance sheet	August 31	September 30

After showing what each company should report, briefly explain how the City of Regina and Public Health Organization, Inc. data relate to each other. Be specific.

Quiz

Test your understanding of transaction analysis by answering the following questions. Select the best choice from among the possible answers.

Q2-29 An investment of cash into the business will
a. Decrease total assets
b. Decrease total liabilities
c. Increase shareholders' equity
d. Have no effect on total assets

Q2-30 Purchasing a computer on account will
a. Increase total assets
b. Increase total liabilities
c. Have no effect on shareholders' equity
d. All of the above

Q2-31 Performing a service on account will
a. Increase total assets
b. Increase shareholders' equity
c. Both a and b
d. Increase total liabilities

Q2-32 Receiving cash from a customer on account will
a. Have no effect on total assets
b. Increase total assets
c. Decrease liabilities
d. Increase shareholders' equity

Q2-33 Purchasing computer equipment for cash will
a. Increase both total assets and total liabilities
b. Decrease both total assets and shareholders' equity
c. Decrease both total liabilities and shareholders' equity
d. Have no effect on total assets, total liabilities, or shareholders' equity

Q2-34 Purchasing a building for $100,000 by paying cash of $20,000 and signing a note payable for $80,000 will
a. Increase both total assets and total liabilities by $100,000
b. Increase both total assets and total liabilities by $80,000
c. Decrease total assets, and increase total liabilities by $20,000
d. Decrease both total assets and total liabilities by $20,000

Q2-35 What is the effect on total assets and shareholders' equity of paying the electric bill as soon as it is received each month?

	Total assets	Shareholders' equity
a.	Decrease	No effect
b.	No effect	No effect
c.	Decrease	Decrease
d.	No effect	Decrease

Q2-36 Which of the following transactions will increase an asset and increase a liability?
a. Buying equipment on account
b. Purchasing office equipment for cash
c. Issuing shares
d. Making a payment on account

Q2-37 Which of the following transactions will increase an asset and increase shareholders' equity?
a. Collecting cash from a customer on an account receivable
b. Performing a service on account for a customer
c. Borrowing money from a bank
d. Purchasing supplies on account

Q2-38 Where do we first record a transaction?
a. Ledger
b. Trial balance
c. Account
d. Journal

Q2-39 Which of the following is not an asset account?

a. Common Shares
b. Salary Expense
c. Service Revenue
d. None of the above accounts is an asset.

Q2-40 Which of the following statements is false?

a. Revenues are increased by credits.
b. Assets are increased by debits.
c. Dividends are increased by credits.
d. Liabilities are decreased by debits.

Q2-41 The journal entry to record the receipt of land and a building and issuance of common shares

a. Debits Land and Building, and credits Common Shares
b. Debits Land, and credits Common Shares
c. Debits Common Shares, and credits Land and Building
d. Credits Land and Building, and debits Common Shares

Q2-42 The journal entry to record the purchase of supplies on account

a. Credits Supplies, and debits Cash
b. Debits Supplies, and credits Accounts Payable
c. Debits Supplies Expense, and credits Supplies
d. Credits Supplies, and debits Accounts Payable

Q2-43 If the credit to record the purchase of supplies on account is not posted,

a. Liabilities will be understated.
b. Expenses will be overstated.
c. Assets will be understated.
d. Shareholders' equity will be understated.

Q2-44 The journal entry to record a payment on account will

a. Debit Accounts Payable, and credit Retained Earnings
b. Debit Cash, and credit Expenses
c. Debit Expenses, and credit Cash
d. Debit Accounts Payable, and credit Cash

Q2-45 If the credit to record the payment of an account payable is not posted,

a. Liabilities will be understated.
b. Expenses will be understated.
c. Cash will be overstated.
d. Cash will be understated.

Q2-46 Which statement is false?

a. A trial balance lists all the accounts with their current balances.
b. A trial balance is the same as a balance sheet.
c. A trial balance can verify the equality of debits and credits.
d. A trial balance can be taken at any time.

Q2-47 A business's purchase of a $100,000 building with an $85,000 mortgage payable and issuance of $15,000 of common shares will

a. Increase shareholders' equity by $15,000
b. Increase assets by $15,000
c. Increase assets by $85,000
d. Increase shareholders' equity by $100,000

Q2-48 A new company completed these transactions.

1. Shareholders invested $50,000 cash and inventory worth $25,000.
2. Sales on account, $12,000

What will total assets equal?

a. $75,000
b. $87,000
c. $63,000
d. $62,000

Problems

(Group A)

P2-49A The trial balance of Amusement Specialties Inc. follows:

Learning Objective 4
Analyzing a trial balance

Amusement Specialties Inc. Trial Balance December 31, 2011		
Cash	$ 14,000	
Accounts receivable	11,000	
Prepaid expenses	4,000	
Equipment	171,000	
Building	100,000	
Accounts payable		$ 30,000
Note payable		120,000
Common shares		102,000
Retained earnings		40,000
Dividends	22,000	
Service revenue		86,000
Rent expense	14,000	
Advertising expense	3,000	
Wage expense	32,000	
Supplies expense	7,000	
Total	$378,000	$378,000

Sue Sibalius, your best friend, is considering investing in Amusement Specialties Inc. She seeks your advice in interpreting this information. Specifically, she asks how to use this trial balance to compute the company's total assets, total liabilities, and net income or net loss for the year.

Required

Write a short note to answer Sue's questions. In your note, state the amounts of Amusement Specialties' total assets, total liabilities, and net income or net loss for the year. Also show how you computed each amount.

P2-50A The following amounts summarize the financial position of Blythe Spirit Consulting, Inc. on May 31, 2011:

Learning Objective 1 4
Analyzing transactions with the accounting equation and preparing the financial statements

	ASSETS				=	LIABILITIES	+	SHAREHOLDERS' EQUITY	
	Cash +	Accounts Receivable +	Supplies +	Land	=	Accounts Payable	+	Common Shares +	Retained Earnings
Bal.	1,300	1,000		12,000		8,000		4,000	2,300

During June 2011, the business completed these transactions:

a. Received cash of $5,000, and issued common shares
b. Performed services for a client, and received cash of $7,600
c. Paid $4,000 on accounts payable
d. Purchased supplies on account, $1,500
e. Collected cash from a customer on account, $1,000
f. Consulted on the design of a business report, and billed the client for services rendered, $2,500
g. Recorded the following business expenses for the month: paid office rent, $900; paid advertising, $300
h. Declared and paid a cash dividend of $2,000

Required

1. Analyze the effects of the preceding transactions on the accounting equation of Blythe Spirit Consulting, Inc. Adapt the format of Exhibit 2-1, Panel B.
2. Prepare the income statement of Blythe Spirit Consulting, Inc. for the month ended June 30, 2011. List expenses in decreasing order by amount.
3. Prepare the entity's statement of retained earnings for the month ended June 30, 2011.
4. Prepare the balance sheet of Blythe Spirit Consulting, Inc. at June 30, 2011.

Learning Objective ❷❸
Recording transactions, posting

P2-51A Use this problem in conjunction with Problem 2-50A.

Required

1. Journalize the transactions of Blythe Spirit Consulting, Inc. Explanations are not required.
2. Set up the following T-accounts: Cash, Accounts Receivable, Supplies, Land, Accounts Payable, Common Shares, Retained Earnings, Dividends, Service Revenue, Rent Expense, and Advertising Expense. Insert in each account its balance as given (example: Cash $1,300). Post the transactions to the accounts.
3. Compute the balance in each account. For each asset account, each liability account, and for Common Shares, compare its balance to the ending balance you obtained in Problem 2-50A. Are the amounts the same or different? (In Chapter 3, we complete the accounting process. There you will learn how the Retained Earnings, Dividends, Revenue, and Expense accounts work together in the processing of accounting information.)

Learning Objective ❶❷
Analyzing transactions with the accounting equation

P2-52A Mountain View Estates Ltd. experienced the following events during the organizing phase and its first month of operations. Some of the events were personal and did not affect the business. Others were business transactions.

Sept.	4	Gayland Jet, the major shareholder of the company, received $50,000 cash from an inheritance.
	5	Jet deposited $50,000 cash in a new business bank account titled Mountain View Estates Ltd. The business issued common shares to Jet.
	6	The business paid $300 cash for letterhead stationery for the new office.
	7	The business purchased office furniture. The company paid cash of $20,000 and agreed to pay the account payable for the remainder, $5,000, within three months.
	10	Jet sold TELUS shares, which he had owned for several years, receiving $30,000 cash from his stockbroker.
	11	Jet deposited the $30,000 cash from sale of the TELUS shares in his personal bank account.
	12	A representative of a large company telephoned Jet and told him of the company's intention to put a down payment of $10,000 on a lot.
	18	Jet finished a real estate deal on behalf of a client and submitted his bill for services, $10,000. Jet expects to collect from this client within two weeks.
	21	The business paid half its account payable for the furniture purchased on September 7.
	25	The business paid office rent of $4,000.
	30	The business declared and paid a cash dividend of $2,000.

Required

1. Classify each of the preceding events as one of the following:
   a. A business-related event but not a transaction to be recorded by Mountain View Estates Ltd.
   b. A personal transaction for a shareholder, not to be recorded by Mountain View Estates Ltd.
   c. A business transaction to be recorded by the business of Mountain View Estates Ltd.

2. Analyze the effects of the preceding events on the accounting equation of Mountain View Estates Ltd. Use a format similar to that in Exhibit 2-1, Panel B.
3. At the end of the first month of operations, Jet has a number of questions about the financial standing of the business. Explain the following to him:
   a. How the business can have more cash than retained earnings.
   b. How much in total resources the business has, how much it owes, and what Jet's ownership interest is in the assets of the business.
4. Record the transactions of the business in its journal. Include an explanation for each entry.

Learning Objective ❶❷❸
Analyzing and recording transactions

P2-53A During October, All Pets Veterinary Clinic Ltd. completed the following transactions:

Oct.	1	Dr. Squires deposited $8,000 cash in the business bank account. The business issued common shares to her.
	5	Paid monthly rent, $1,000
	9	Paid $5,000 cash, and signed a $25,000 note payable to purchase land for an office site
	10	Purchased supplies on account, $1,200
	19	Paid $600 on account
	22	Borrowed $10,000 from the bank for business use. Dr. Squires signed a note payable to the bank in the name of the business.
	31	Revenues earned during the month included $7,000 cash and $5,000 on account
	31	Paid employees' salaries ($2,000), advertising expense ($1,500), and utilities ($1,100)
	31	Declared and paid a cash dividend of $3,000

The clinic uses the following accounts: Cash, Accounts Receivable, Supplies, Land, Accounts Payable, Notes Payable, Common Shares, Dividends, Service Revenue, Salary Expense, Rent Expense, Utilities Expense, and Advertising Expense.

Required

1. Journalize each transaction of All Pets Veterinary Clinic Ltd. Explanations are not required.
2. Prepare T-accounts for Cash, Accounts Payable, and Notes Payable. Post to these three accounts.
3. After these transactions, how much cash does the business have? How much in total does it owe?

Learning Objective ❷❸❹
Journalizing transactions, posting, and preparing and using a trial balance

P2-54A During the first month of operations, May 2011, New Pane Windows Inc. completed the following transactions:

May	2	New Pane received $30,000 cash and issued common shares to shareholders.
	3	Purchased supplies, $1,000, and equipment, $2,600, on account
	4	Performed services, and received cash, $1,500
	7	Paid cash to acquire land for an office site, $22,000
	11	Repaired a window, and billed the customer $500
	16	Paid for the equipment purchased May 3 on account
	17	Paid the telephone bill, $95
	18	Received partial payment from client on account, $250
	22	Paid the water and electricity bills, $400
	29	Received $2,000 cash for installing a new window
	31	Paid employee salary, $1,300
	31	Declared and paid dividends of $1,500

Required

Set up the following T-accounts: Cash, Accounts Receivable, Supplies, Equipment, Land, Accounts Payable, Common Shares, Dividends, Service Revenue, Salary Expense, and Utilities Expense.

1. Record each transaction in the journal, using the account titles given. Key each transaction by date. Explanations are not required.
2. Post the transactions to the T-accounts, using transaction dates as posting references. Label the ending balance of each account Bal., as shown in the chapter.
3. Prepare the trial balance of New Pane Windows, at May 31, 2011.
4. The manager asks you how much in total resources the business has to work with, how much it owes, and whether May 2011 was profitable (and by how much).

Learning Objective 3 4
Recording transactions directly in T-accounts; preparing and using a trial balance

P2-55A During the first month of operations (January 2011), Music Services Ltd. completed the following selected transactions:

a. The business has cash of $10,000 and a building valued at $50,000. The corporation issued common shares to the shareholders.
b. Borrowed $50,000 from the bank, and signed a note payable
c. Paid $60,000 for music equipment
d. Purchased supplies on account, $1,000
e. Paid employees' salaries, $1,500
f. Received $800 for service performed for customers
g. Performed service to customers on account, $4,500
h. Paid $100 of the account payable created in transaction d
i. Received a $600 utility bill that will be paid in the near future
j. Received cash on account, $3,100
k. Paid the following cash expenses: rent, $1,000; advertising, $800

Required

1. Set up the following T-accounts: Cash, Accounts Receivable, Office Supplies, Music Equipment, Building, Accounts Payable, Note Payable, Common Shares, Service Revenue, Salary Expense, Rent Expense, Advertising Expense, and Utilities Expense.
2. Record the foregoing transactions directly in the T-accounts without using a journal. Use the letters to identify the transactions.
3. Prepare the trial balance of Music Services Ltd. at January 31, 2011.
4. The bank manager is afraid that the total liabilities of the business exceed the total assets. He also fears that the business suffered a net loss during January. Compute the amounts needed to answer his questions.

(Group B)

Learning Objective 4
Analyzing a trial balance

P2-56B The owners of Opera Tours Inc. are selling the business. They offer the trial balance that appears at the top of the next page to prospective buyers.

Your best friend is considering buying Opera Tours. She seeks your advice in interpreting this information. Specifically, she asks whether this trial balance provides the data to prepare a balance sheet and an income statement.

Required

Write a memo to answer your friend's questions. Indicate which accounts go on the balance sheet and which accounts go on the income statement. State the amount of net income that Opera Tours earned in 2011 and explain your computation.

Opera Tours Inc.
Trial Balance
December 31, 2011

Cash	$ 12,000	
Accounts receivable	45,000	
Prepaid expenses	4,000	
Equipment	231,000	
Accounts payable		$105,000
Note payable		92,000
Common shares		30,000
Retained earnings		32,000
Service revenue		139,000
Salary expense	69,000	
Tour expenses	26,000	
Rent expense	7,000	
Advertising expense	4,000	
Total	$398,000	$398,000

Learning Objective 1
Analyzing transactions with the accounting equation and preparing the financial statements

P2-57B Doug Hanna operates and is the major shareholder of an interior design studio called DH Designers, Inc. The following amounts summarize the financial position of the business on April 30, 2011:

	ASSETS				=	LIABILITIES +	SHAREHOLDERS' EQUITY	
	Cash +	Accounts Receivable +	Supplies +	Land	=	Accounts Payable +	Common Shares +	Retained Earnings
Bal.	1,700	2,200		24,100		5,400	10,000	12,600

During May 2011, the business completed these transactions:

a. Hanna received $30,000 as a gift and deposited the cash in the business bank account. The business issued common shares to Hanna.
b. Paid $1,000 on accounts payable
c. Performed services for a client and received cash of $5,100
d. Collected cash from a customer on account, $700
e. Purchased supplies on account, $800
f. Consulted on the interior design of a major office building and billed the client for services rendered, $15,000
g. Received cash of $1,700 and issued common shares to a shareholder
h. Recorded the following expenses for the month: paid office rent, $2,100; paid advertising, $1,600
i. Declared and paid a cash dividend of $2,000

Required

In order to guide Doug Hanna,

1. Analyze the effects of the preceding transactions on the accounting equation of DH Designers, Inc. Adapt the format of Exhibit 2-1, Panel B.
2. Prepare the income statement of DH Designers, Inc. for the month ended May 31, 2011. List expenses in decreasing order by amount.
3. Prepare the statement of retained earnings of DH Designers, Inc. for the month ended May 31, 2011.
4. Prepare the balance sheet of DH Designers, Inc. at May 31, 2011.

Learning Objective 2 3
Recording transactions, posting

P2-58B Use this problem in conjunction with Problem 2-57B.

Required

1. Journalize the transactions of DH Designers, Inc. Explanations are not required.
2. Set up the following T-accounts: Cash, Accounts Receivable, Supplies, Land, Accounts Payable, Common Shares, Retained Earnings, Dividends, Service Revenue, Rent Expense, and Advertising Expense. Insert in each account its balance as given (example: Cash $1,700). Post to the accounts.
3. Compute the balance in each account. For each asset account, each liability account, and for Common Shares, compare its balance to the ending balance you obtained in Problem 2-57B. Are the amounts the same or different? (In Chapter 3, we complete the accounting process. There you will learn how the Retained Earnings, Dividends, Revenue, and Expense accounts work together in the processing of accounting information.)

Learning Objective 1 2
Analyzing transactions with the accounting equation

P2-59B Lane Kohler opened a consulting practice that he operates as a corporation. The name of the new entity is Lane Kohler, Consultant, Inc. Kohler experienced the following events during the organizing phase of his new business and its first month of operations. Some of the events were personal transactions of the shareholder and did not affect the consulting practice. Others were transactions that should be accounted for by the business.

March 1	Kohler sold 1,000 shares of RIM stock and received $100,000 cash from his stockbroker.
2	Kohler deposited in his personal bank account the $100,000 cash from sale of the RIM shares.
3	Kohler received $150,000 cash through an inheritance from his grandfather.
5	Kohler deposited $50,000 cash in a new business bank account titled Lane Kohler, Consultant, Inc. The business issued common shares to Kohler.
6	A representative of a large company telephoned Kohler and told him of the company's intention to give $15,000 of consulting business to Kohler.
7	The business paid $450 cash for letterhead stationery for the consulting office.
9	The business purchased office furniture. Kohler paid cash of $5,000 and agreed to pay the account payable for the remainder, $10,500, within three months.
23	Kohler finished an analysis for a client and submitted his bill for services, $4,000. He expected to collect from this client within one month.
29	The business paid $5,000 of its account payable on the furniture purchased on March 9.
30	The business paid office rent of $2,100.
31	The business declared and paid a cash dividend of $1,000.

Required

1. Classify each of the preceding events as one of the following:
   a. A personal transaction of a shareholder not to be recorded by the business of Lane Kohler, Consultant, Inc.
   b. A business transaction to be recorded by the business of Lane Kohler, Consultant, Inc.
   c. A business-related event but not a transaction to be recorded by the business of Lane Kohler, Consultant, Inc.
2. Analyze the effects of the preceding events on the accounting equation of the business of Lane Kohler, Consultant, Inc. Use a format similar to Exhibit 2-1, Panel B.
3. At the end of the first month of operations, Kohler has a number of questions about the financial standing of the business. Answer the following questions for him:
   a. How can the business have more cash than retained earnings?
   b. How much in total resources does the business have? How much does it owe? What is Kohler's ownership interest in the assets of the business?
4. Record the transactions of the business in its journal. Include an explanation for each entry.

Learning Objective 2 3
Analyzing and recording transactions

P2-60B Wimberley Glass, Inc. has shops in the shopping malls of a major metropolitan area. The business completed the following transactions:

June	1	Received cash of $25,000, and issued common shares to a shareholder
	2	Paid $10,000 cash, and signed a $30,000 note payable to purchase land for a new glassworks site
	7	Received $20,000 cash from sales, and deposited that amount in the bank
	10	Purchased supplies on account, $1,000
	15	Paid employees' salaries, $2,800, and rent on a shop, $1,800
	15	Paid advertising expense, $1,100
	16	Paid $1,000 on account
	17	Declared and paid a cash dividend of $2,000

Wimberley Glass, Inc. uses the following accounts: Cash, Supplies, Land, Accounts Payable, Note Payable, Common Shares, Dividends, Sales Revenue, Salary Expense, Rent Expense, and Advertising Expense.

Required

1. Journalize each transaction. Explanations are not required.
2. Prepare T-accounts for Cash, Accounts Payable, and Notes Payable. Post to these three accounts.
3. After these transactions, how much cash does the business have? How much does it owe in total?

Learning Objective 2 3 4
Journalizing transactions, posting, and preparing and using a trial balance

P2-61B During the first month of operations, October 2011, Barron Environmental Services Inc. completed the following transactions:

Oct.	3	Received $20,000 cash, and issued common shares
	4	Performed services for a client, and received $5,000 cash
	6	Purchased supplies, $300, and furniture, $2,500, on account
	7	Paid $15,000 cash to acquire land for an office site
	7	Worked for a client, and billed the client $1,500
	16	Received partial payment from a client on account, $500
	24	Paid the telephone bill, $110
	24	Paid the water and electricity bills, $400
	28	Received $2,500 cash for helping a client meet environmental standards
	31	Paid secretary's salary, $1,200
	31	Paid $2,500 of the account payable created on October 6.
	31	Declared and paid dividends of $2,400

Required

Set up the following T-accounts: Cash, Accounts Receivable, Supplies, Furniture, Land, Accounts Payable, Common Shares, Dividends, Service Revenue, Salary Expense, and Utilities Expense.

1. Record each transaction in the journal, using the account titles given. Key each transaction by date. Explanations are not required.
2. Post the transactions to the T-accounts, using transaction dates as posting references. Label the ending balance of each account Bal., as shown in the chapter.
3. Prepare the trial balance of Barron Environmental Services Inc. at October 31, 2011.
4. Report to the shareholder how much in total resources the business has to work with, how much it owes, and whether October was profitable (and by how much).

Learning Objective 3 4
Recording transactions directly in T-accounts; preparing and using a trial balance

P2-62B During the first month of operations (June 2011), Schulich Graphics Service Inc. completed the following selected transactions:

a. Began the business with an investment of $20,000 cash and a building valued at $60,000. The corporation issued common shares to the shareholders.
b. Borrowed $90,000 from the bank, and signed a note payable
c. Paid $35,000 for computer equipment
d. Purchased office supplies on account for $1,300
e. Performed computer graphic service on account for a client, $2,500
f. Received $1,200 cash on account
g. Paid $800 of the account payable created in transaction d
h. Received a $500 bill for advertising expense that will be paid in the near future
i. Performed service for clients, and received $1,100 in cash
j. Paid employees' salaries totalling $2,200
k. Paid the following cash expenses: rent, $700; utilities, $400

Required

1. Set up the following T-accounts: Cash, Accounts Receivable, Office Supplies, Computer Equipment, Building, Accounts Payable, Note Payable, Common Shares, Service Revenue, Salary Expense, Advertising Expense, Rent Expense, and Utilities Expense.
2. Record each transaction directly in the T-accounts without using a journal. Use the letters to identify the transactions.
3. Prepare the trial balance of Schulich Graphics Service Inc. at June 30, 2011.

Apply Your Knowledge

Decision Cases

Learning Objective 4 5
Recording transactions directly in T-accounts, preparing a trial balance, and measuring net income or loss

Case 1. A friend named Tom Tipple has asked what effect certain transactions will have on his company. Time is short, so you cannot apply the detailed procedures of journalizing and posting. Instead, you must analyze the transactions without the use of a journal. Tipple will continue the business only if he can expect to earn monthly net income of $10,000. The following transactions occurred this month:

a. Tipple deposited $10,000 cash in a business bank account, and the corporation issued common shares to him.
b. Paid $300 cash for supplies
c. Purchased office furniture on account, $4,400
d. Earned revenue on account, $7,000
e. Borrowed $5,000 cash from the bank, and signed a note payable due within one year
f. Paid the following cash expenses for one month: employee's salary, $1,700; office rent, $600.
g. Collected cash from customers on account, $1,200
h. Paid on account, $1,000
i. Earned revenue, and received $2,500 cash
j. Purchased advertising in the local newspaper for cash, $800

Required

1. Set up the following T-accounts: Cash, Accounts Receivable, Supplies, Furniture, Accounts Payable, Notes Payable, Common Shares, Service Revenue, Salary Expense, Advertising Expense, and Rent Expense.

2. Record the transactions directly in the accounts without using a journal. Key each transaction by letter.
3. Prepare a trial balance at the current date. List expenses with the largest amount first, the next largest amount second, and so on. The business name will be Tipple Networks, Inc.
4. Compute the amount of net income or net loss for this first month of operations. Why would you recommend that Tipple continue or not continue in business?

Case 2. Barbara Boland opened a flower shop. Business has been good, and Boland is considering expanding with a second shop. A cousin has produced the following financial statements at December 31, 2011, the end of the first three months of operations:

Learning Objective 2
Correcting financial statements; deciding whether to expand a business

Barbara Boland Blossoms Inc.
Income Statement
Quarter Ended December 31, 2011

Sales revenue	$36,000
Common shares	10,000
Total revenue	46,000
Accounts payable	8,000
Advertising expense	5,000
Rent expense	6,000
Total expenses	19,000
Net income	$27,000

Barbara Boland Blossoms Inc.
Balance Sheet
December 31, 2011

Assets	
Cash	$ 6,000
Cost of goods sold (expense)	22,000
Flower inventory	5,000
Store fixtures	10,000
Total assets	$43,000
Liabilities	
None	
Owners' Equity	$43,000

In these financial statements all amounts are correct, except for Owners' Equity. Boland's cousin heard that total assets should equal total liabilities plus owners' equity, so he plugged in the amount of owners' equity at $43,000 to make the balance sheet come out evenly.

Required

Barbara Boland has asked whether she should expand the business. Her banker says Boland may be wise to expand if (a) net income for the first quarter reaches $5,000 and (b) total assets are at least $25,000. It appears that the business has reached these milestones, but Boland doubts her cousin's understanding of accounting. Boland needs your help in making this decision. Prepare a corrected income statement and balance sheet. (Remember that Retained Earnings, which was omitted from the balance sheet, should equal net income for the period; there were no dividends.) After preparing the statements, give Boland your recommendation as to whether she should expand the flower shop.

Ethical Issues

Issue 1. Scruffy Murphy is the president and principal shareholder of Scruffy's Bar and Grill Limited. To expand, the business is applying for a $250,000 bank loan. The bank requires the company to have shareholders' equity of at least as much as the loan. Currently, shareholders' equity is $150,000. To get the loan, Murphy is considering two options for beefing up the shareholders' equity of the business:

Option 1. Issue $100,000 common shares for cash. A friend has been wanting to invest in the company. This may be the right time to extend the offer.

Option 2. Transfer $100,000 of Murphy's personal land to the business, and issue common shares to Murphy. Then, after obtaining the loan, Murphy can transfer the land back to himself and cancel the common shares.

Requirement 1

Journalize the transactions required by each option.

Requirement 2

Use the Framework for Making Ethical Judgments in Chapter 1 (p. 33) to determine which plan would be ethical.

Issue 2. Community Charities has a standing agreement with Royal Bank of Canada (RBC). The agreement allows Community Charities to overdraw its cash balance at the bank when donations are running low. In the past, Community Charities managed funds wisely and rarely used this privilege. Recently, however, Beatrice Grand has been named president of Community Charities. To expand operations, she is acquiring office equipment and spending a lot for fundraising. During Grand's presidency, Community Charities has maintained a negative bank balance of about $3,000.

Required

What is the ethical issue in this situation? Do you approve or disapprove of Grand's management of Community Charities' and RBC's funds? Why? Use the Framework for Making Ethical Judgments in Chapter 1 (p. 33) in answering this question.

Focus on Financials

Learning Objective 2 5
Analyzing a leading company's financial statements

Gildan Activewear Inc.

Refer to the Gildan Activewear Inc. financial statements in Appendix A at the end of the book. Assume that Gildan completed the following selected transactions during the year ended October 4, 2009 (amounts in $ thousands).

a. Made sales on account, $1,038.3
b. Incurred cost of goods sold (an expense) of $808.0. Credit the Inventories account.
c. Paid selling, general and administrative expenses of $134.8
d. Paid restructuring and other expense, $6.2
e. Collected accounts receivable, $1,087.3
f. Paid cash for inventory, $793.6
g. Received cash for other assets, $7.3
h. Repaid long-term debt, $47.8
i. Paid $24.9 of accounts payable

Required

1. Set up T-accounts for Cash and Cash Equivalents (debit balance of $12.4); Accounts Receivable (debit balance of $215); Inventories (debit balance of $316.2); Other Assets ($17.2 debit balance); Net Sales ($0 balance); Cost of Goods Sold ($0 balance); Operating and Other Expenses ($0 balance); Restructuring and Other Expense ($0 balance); Long-Term Debt ($49.4 credit balance); Accounts Payable ($149.3 credit balance).
2. Journalize Gildan's transactions a through i. Explanations are not required.
3. Post to the T-accounts, and compute the balance for each account. Key postings by transaction letters a through i.
4. For each of the following accounts, compare your computed balance to Gildan's actual balance as shown on Gildan's income statement or balance sheet dated October 4, 2009. All your amounts should agree to the actual figures, rounded to the nearest thousand dollars. There may be a slight rounding error.
   a. Cash
   b. Accounts Receivable

c. Inventories
d. Net Sales
e. Cost of Goods Sold
f. Selling, General and Administrative Expenses

5. Use the relevant accounts from requirement 4 to prepare a summary income statement for Gildan for the year ended October 4, 2009. Compare the operating income you computed to Gildan's actual operating income. The two operating income amounts should be equal.

Focus on Analysis

Gildan Activewear Inc.

Learning Objective 3 4
Recording transactions and computing net income

Refer to the Gildan Activewear Inc. financial statements in Appendix A at the end of the book. Suppose you are an investor considering buying Gildan's shares. The following questions are important:

1. Explain which of Gildan's sales or collections from customers was the largest amount during the year ended October 4, 2009. Analyze net receivables to answer this question.
2. A major concern of lenders, such as banks, is the amount of long-term debt a company owes. How much long-term debt does Gildan owe at October 4, 2009? What must have happened to Gildan's long-term debt during the 2009 fiscal year?
3. Investors are vitally interested in a company's revenues and profits, and its trends of revenues and profits over time. Consider Gildan's revenues and net income during the period from October 5, 2008 to October 4, 2009. Compute the percentage change in revenue and also in net income or loss during this period. Which item changed more during this period, revenue or net income? (For convenience, show dollar amounts in thousands.) Which provides a better indicator of business success? Give the reason for your answer.

Group Projects

Project 1. You are promoting a concert in your area. Your purpose is to earn a profit, so you need to establish the formal structure of a business entity. Assume you organize as a corporation.

Required

1. Make a detailed list of 10 factors you must consider as you establish the business.
2. Describe 10 of the items your business must arrange to promote and stage the concert.
3. Identify the transactions that your business can undertake to organize, promote, and stage the concert. Journalize the transactions, and post to the relevant T-accounts. Set up the accounts you need for your business ledger.
4. Prepare the income statement, statement of retained earnings, and balance sheet immediately after the concert, that is, before you have had time to pay all the business bills and collect all receivables.
5. Assume that you will continue to promote concerts if the venture is successful. If it is unsuccessful, you will terminate the business within three months after the concert. Discuss how to evaluate the success of your venture and how to decide whether to continue in business.

Project 2. Contact a local business, and arrange with the owner to learn what accounts the business uses.

Required

1. Obtain a copy of the business's chart of accounts.
2. Prepare the company's financial statements for the most recent month, quarter, or year.

You may use either made-up account balances or balances supplied by the owner.

If the business has a large number of accounts within a category, combine related accounts and report a single amount on the financial statements. For example, the company may have several cash accounts. Combine all cash amounts and report a single Cash amount on the balance sheet.

You will probably encounter numerous accounts that you have not yet learned. Deal with these as best you can.

Quick Check Answers

1. *c*
2. *d*
3. *a*
4. *d*
5. *a*
6. *b*
7. *c*
8. *a*
9. *d*
10. *d*
11. *a*
12. *c*

Accrual Accounting and the Financial Statements

LEARNING OBJECTIVES

1. **Relate** accrual accounting and cash flows
2. **Recognize** revenue and record expenses
3. **Adjust** the accounts
4. **Prepare** the financial statements
5. **Close** the books
6. **Use** the financial statements in decision making

SPOTLIGHT

Le Château has been selling fashion apparel and more recently accessories and footwear to both men and women in Canada for 50 years. The company's merchandise is sold through 221 retail stores; four of the stores are in New York City, and nine stores are in the Middle East.

As you can see from Le Château's income statement, the company sold more than $345 million in merchandise during the year. How does Le Château know whether these revenues translated into profits? By looking at the income statement, you can see that Le Château's revenue exceeded its expenses by $38 million. Not bad for a Canadian company, eh?

Le Château Inc.
Consolidated Statement of Earnings
For the Year Ended January 31, 2009

	thousands
Sales	$345,614
Cost of sales and expenses:	
Cost of sales and selling, general and administrative	271,119
Depreciation and amortization	16,705
Write-off of fixed assets (note 5)	585
Interest on long-term debt and capital lease obligations	1,798
Interest income	(2,299)
Total expenses	$287,908
Earnings before income taxes:	$ 57,706
Provisions for income taxes (note 9)	19,085
Net earnings	$ 38,621

Chapter 2 focused on measuring and recording transactions up to the trial balance. This chapter completes our coverage of the accounting cycle by discussing the adjustment process, the preparation of financial statements, and the closing of the books at the end of the period. It also includes a discussion of accounting principles and concepts that govern the timing and recognition of revenue and expenses.

Accrual Accounting Versus Cash-Basis Accounting

Managers want to earn a profit. Investors search for companies whose share prices will increase. Banks seek borrowers who'll pay their debts. Accounting provides the information these people use for decision making. Accounting can be based on either of the following:

- Accrual basis
- Cash basis

Accrual accounting records the impact of a business transaction as it occurs. When the business performs a service, makes a sale, or incurs an expense, the accountant records the transaction even if it receives or pays no cash.

Cash-basis accounting records only cash transactions—cash receipts and cash payments. Cash receipts are treated as revenues, and cash payments are handled as expenses.

Corporations use accrual accounting to record their transactions. This means that businesses record revenues as the revenues are earned and expenses as the expenses are incurred—not necessarily when cash changes hands. Consider a sale on account. Which transaction increases your wealth—making an $800 sale on account, or collecting the $800 cash? Making the sale increases your wealth by $300 because you gave up inventory that cost you $500 and you got a receivable worth $800. Collecting cash later merely swaps your $800 receivable for $800 cash—no gain on this transaction. Making the sale—not collecting the cash—increases your wealth.

The basic defect of cash-basis accounting is that the cash basis ignores important information. That makes the financial statements incomplete. As a result, people using cash-basis financial statements make bad decisions.

Suppose your business makes a sale *on account*. The cash basis does not record the sale because you received no cash. You may be thinking, "Let's wait until we collect cash and then record the sale. After all, we pay the bills with cash, so ignore transactions that don't affect cash."

What's wrong with this argument? There are two defects—one on the balance sheet and the other on the income statement.

Balance-Sheet Defect. Assume that a company sold its product to a customer on account for $500. If we fail to record that sale, the balance sheet reports no account receivable. Why is this so bad? The revenue has been earned and the company owns the receivable and it should appear on the balance sheet. Without this information, your assets are understated as shown on the balance sheet.

Income-Statement Defect. Continuing on with the above example, a sale on account provides revenue that increases the company's wealth. Revenue has been earned since the customer purchased the product in exchange for a promise to pay the company later. Ignoring the sale understates your revenue and net income on the income statement.

The take-away lessons from this discussion are:

- Watch out for companies that use the cash basis of accounting. Their financial statements omit important information.
- All but the smallest businesses use the accrual basis of accounting.

Accrual Accounting and Cash Flows

OBJECTIVE

1 **Relate** accrual accounting and cash flows

Accrual accounting is more complex—and more complete—than cash-basis accounting. Accrual accounting records *cash* transactions, including:

- Collecting from customers
- Receiving cash from interest earned
- Paying salaries, rent, and other expenses
- Borrowing money
- Paying off loans
- Issuing shares

Accrual accounting also records *noncash* transactions such as:

- Purchases of inventory on account
- Sales on account
- Accrual of expenses incurred but not yet paid
- Depreciation expense
- Usage of prepaid rent, insurance, and supplies
- Earning of revenue when cash was collected in advance

We will look at transactions that are handled differently using cash-basis accounting and accrual accounting to illustrate the different impact each has on the income statement.

Pointz Corporation has the following transactions in July 2010:

1. Provided services to Customer A for $500 cash.
2. Provided services on account to Customer B for $800.
3. Paid employee's salary, $450.
4. Received a $50 hydro bill for electricity used during July.

The transactions and their impact on the income statement are shown below using both accrual accounting and cash-basis accounting.

Pointz Corporation
Income Statement Using Accrual Accounting
For the month ended July 31, 2010

Revenue $500 + $800	$1,300
Expenses:	
Salaries	450
Hydro	50
Net income	$ 800

Pointz Corporation
Income Statement Using Cash-Basis Accounting
For the month ended July 31, 2010

Revenue	$500
Expenses:	
Salaries	450
Hydro	0
Net income	$ 50

Consider the income statement. The accrual accounting statement includes both sales for a total of $1,300, whereas the cash-basis statement includes only the cash sale for $500. As you would expect, net income on an accrual basis reflects the profit earned on both the cash sale and the sale on account, that is, $800. The hydro expense was included under the accrual basis since the company used the electricity during the month to produce revenue. Since it has not been paid, it was not included under the cash basis. Which net income is more realistic, accrual accounting or cash basis? The accrual accounting income is more realistic because it includes all revenue earned and all expenses incurred.

Accrual accounting is based on a framework of concepts and principles. We turn now to the time-period concept, the revenue principle, and guidelines for recording expenses.

The Time-Period Concept

The only way for a business to know for certain how well it performed is to close its doors, sell the assets, pay the liabilities, and return any leftover cash to the owners. This process, called *liquidation*, means going out of business. Ongoing businesses cannot measure income this way. Instead, they need regular progress reports. Accountants, therefore, prepare financial statements for specific periods. The **time-period concept** ensures that accounting information is reported at regular intervals.

The basic accounting period is one year, and virtually all businesses prepare annual financial statements. Around 60% of large companies, including TransCanada Corporation, use the calendar year from January 1 through December 31.

A *fiscal year* ends on a date other than December 31. Most retailers, including Le Château, use a fiscal year that ends on January 31 because the low point in their business activity falls after Christmas. Le Château Inc.'s fiscal year is 52 weeks, ending on the last Saturday in January.

Companies prepare financial statements for interim periods of less than a year, such as a month, a quarter (three months), or a semi-annual period (six months). Most of the discussions in this text are based on an annual accounting period.

The Revenue Principle

❷ **Recognize** revenue and record expenses

The **revenue principle** governs two things:

1. *When* to record revenue (make a journal entry)
2. The *amount* of revenue to record

When should you record revenue? After it has been earned—and not before. In most cases, revenue is earned when the business has delivered a good or service to a customer. It has done everything required to earn the revenue by transferring the good or service to the customer.

For example, a customer walks into Le Château to shop. If the customer buys an item of clothing, Le Château has earned revenue. If the customer leaves the store without buying anything, no revenue has been earned.

The *amount* of revenue to record is the cash value of the good or service transferred to the customer. Suppose that in order to obtain golfer Lorie Kane's travel business, Marlin Travel arranges a trip for the price of $500. Ordinarily, Marlin would charge $600 for this service. How much revenue should it record? The answer is $500—the cash value of the transaction.

Recording Expenses

As revenue is earned, companies incur expenses during the normal day-to-day operations. They occur when inventory is sold or salaries are paid or payable to employees. Other examples include the usage of prepaid rent, insurance, and supplies, depreciation, as well as an accrual of expenses incurred but not yet paid.

Expenses have no future benefit to the company and should be identified as they are incurred during the accounting period. They are subtracted from revenues to compute net income or net loss.

Some expenses are paid in cash. Other expenses arise from using up an asset such as supplies. Still other expenses occur when a company creates a liability. For example, Le Château may pay the salary expense immediately, or it may record a liability for the expense. In either case, Le Château has a salary expense. The critical event for recording an expense is the occurrence of the expense, not the payment of cash.

MyAccountingLab

Accounting Cycle Tutorial: Income Statement Accounts and Transactions - Tutorial

STOP + THINK

1. A client pays Windsor Group Ltd. $900 on March 15 for consulting service to be performed April 1 to June 30. Has Windsor Group Ltd. earned revenue on March 15? When will Windsor Group Ltd. earn the revenue?
2. Windsor Group Ltd. pays $4,500 on July 31 for office rent for the next three months. Has the company incurred an expense on July 31?

Answers:
1. No. Windsor Group Ltd. has received the cash but will not perform the service until later. Windsor Group Ltd. earns the revenue when it performs the service.
2. No. Windsor Group Ltd. has paid cash for rent in advance. This prepaid rent is an asset because Windsor Group Ltd. has the use of an office in the future.

Ethical Issues in Accrual Accounting

Accrual accounting provides some ethical challenges that cash accounting avoids. For example, suppose that in 2010, Shop Online Inc. (SOL) prepays a $3 million advertising campaign to be conducted by Ogilvy & Mather (Canada) Ltd., a leading advertising agency. The advertisements are scheduled to run during December, January, and February. SOL is buying an asset, a prepaid expense. Suppose SOL pays for the advertisements on December 1 and the ads start running immediately. SOL should record one-third of the expense ($1 million) during the year ended December 31, 2010, and two-thirds ($2 million) during 2011.

Suppose 2010 is a great year for SOL—net income is better than expected. SOL's top managers believe that 2011 will not be as profitable. In this case, the company has a strong incentive to expense the full $3 million during 2010 in order to report all the expense in the 2010 income statement. This unethical action would keep $2 million of advertising expense off the 2011 income statement and make 2011's net income look better.

Another ethical challenge in accrual accounting arises because it is easy to overlook an expense at the end of the period. Suppose it is now December 31, 2010, and the year has not turned out very well for Highfield Computer Products Ltd. If top managers are unethical, the company can "manufacture" net income by failing to record some expenses. Suppose the company owes $40,000 in interest expense that it will pay in January 2011. At December 31, 2010, company accountants can "overlook" the $40,000 interest expense and increase the 2010 net income substantially.

Updating the Accounts: The Adjusting Process

At the end of a period, the business prepares its financial statements. This process begins with the trial balance introduced in Chapter 2. We refer to this trial balance as *unadjusted* because the accounts are not yet ready for the financial statements. In most cases, the simple label "Trial Balance" means "unadjusted."

Since companies are required to use accrual accounting, adjusting entries are needed to ensure that all revenue is recorded in the period it is earned and expenses are recorded in the same period the revenue was generated. These entries are recorded at the end of the accounting period before the financial statements are prepared.

Which Accounts Need to Be Updated (Adjusted)?

OBJECTIVE

❸ **Adjust** the account

The shareholders need to know how well Moreau Ltd. is performing. The financial statements report this information, and all accounts must be up to date. That means some accounts must be adjusted. Exhibit 3-1 gives the trial balance of Moreau Ltd. at April 30, 2011.

This trial balance is unadjusted. That means it's not completely up to date. It's not quite ready for preparing the financial statements for presentation to external users.

Cash, Accounts Payable, Common Shares, and Dividends are up to date and need no adjustment at the end of the period. Why? Because the day-to-day transactions provide all the data for these accounts.

Accounts Receivable, Supplies, Prepaid Rent, Furniture, and the other accounts are another story. These accounts are not yet up to date on April 30. Why? Because certain transactions have not yet been recorded. Consider Supplies. During April, Moreau Ltd. used stationery and other supplies to serve clients. But Moreau Ltd. did not make a journal entry every time someone printed a proposal for a client. That would waste time and money. Instead, Moreau Ltd. waits until the end of the period and then accounts for the supplies used up during the month.

The cost of supplies used up is an expense. An adjusting entry at the end of April updates both Supplies (an asset) and Supplies Expense. We must adjust all other accounts whose balances are not yet up to date.

Categories of Adjusting Entries

Accounting adjustments fall into three basic categories: deferrals, depreciation, and accruals.

Deferrals. A **deferral** is an adjustment for which the business paid or received cash in advance. TELUS Corporation purchases supplies for use in its operations. During the period, some supplies (assets) are used up and thus become expenses. At the end of the period, an adjustment is needed to decrease the Supplies account for the supplies

EXHIBIT 3-1 **Unadjusted Trial Balance**

Moreau Ltd.
Unadjusted Trial Balance
April 30, 2011

Cash	$24,800	
Accounts receivable	2,250	
Supplies	700	
Prepaid rent	3,000	
Furniture	16,500	
Accounts payable		$13,100
Unearned service revenue		450
Common shares		20,000
Retained earnings		11,250
Dividends	3,200	
Service revenue		7,000
Salary expense	950	
Utilities expense	400	
Total	$51,800	$51,800

used up. This is Supplies Expense. Prepaid Rent, Prepaid Insurance, and all other prepaid expenses require deferral adjustments.

There are also deferral adjustments for liabilities. Companies such as TELUS collect cash in advance of earning the revenue. TELUS collects cash up front and then provides wireless phone service. When TELUS receives cash up front, the company has a liability to provide a service for the client. This liability is called Unearned Service Revenue. Then, over the course of the contract period, TELUS earns Service Revenue by providing the phone service. This earning process requires an adjustment at the end of the period. The adjustment decreases the liability account and increases the revenue account for the revenue earned. Publishers such as Rogers Publishing Limited, publisher of *Maclean's* magazine, and your local newspaper sell subscriptions and collect cash in advance. They too must make adjusting entries for revenues earned later.

Depreciation. **Depreciation** is the allocation of the cost of a capital (long-lived) asset to expense over the asset's useful life. Depreciation is the most common long-term deferral. Le Château buys long-term capital assets, such as buildings, equipment, and furniture. As Le Château uses the assets, it records depreciation. The accounting adjustment records Depreciation Expense, which decreases the carrying amount of the asset over its life. The process is identical to a deferral-type adjustment; the only difference is the type of asset involved.

Accruals. An **accrual** is the opposite of a deferral. For an accrued *expense*, TELUS records an expense before paying cash. For an accrued *revenue*, TELUS records the revenue before collecting cash.

Salary Expense can create an accrual adjustment. As employees work for TELUS, the company's salary expense accrues with the passage of time. Suppose that at December 31, 2010, TELUS owes employees some salaries to be paid after the year-end. It will pay them on January 2, 2011. At December 31, 2010, TELUS recorded Salary Expense and Salary Payable for the amount owed. Other examples of expense accruals include interest expense and income tax expense.

An accrued revenue is a revenue that the business has earned and will collect next year. At year-end, TELUS must accrue the revenue. The adjustment debits a receivable and credits a revenue. For example, accrual of interest revenue debits Interest Receivable and credits Interest Revenue.

Let's see how the adjusting process actually works for Moreau Ltd. at April 30, 2011. We begin with prepaid expenses.

Deferrals—Prepaid Expenses

A prepaid expense is an expense paid in advance. Therefore, prepaid expenses are assets, because they provide a future benefit for the owner. Let's do the adjustment for prepaid rent and supplies.

Prepaid Rent. Rent is usually paid in advance. This prepayment creates an asset for the renter, who can then use the rented item in the future. Suppose Moreau Ltd. prepays three months' office rent ($3,000) on April 1. The entry for the prepayment of three months' rent debits Prepaid Rent as follows:

Apr. 1	Prepaid Rent ($1000 × 3)	3,000	
	Cash		3,000
	Paid three months' rent in advance.		

The accounting equation shows that one asset increases and another decreases. Total assets are unchanged.

ASSETS	=	LIABILITIES	+	SHAREHOLDERS' EQUITY
3,000	=	0	+	0
−3,000				

After posting, the Prepaid Rent account appears as follows:

Prepaid Rent			
Apr. 1	3,000		

Throughout April, the Prepaid Rent account maintains this beginning balance, as shown in Exhibit 3-1 (page 123). The adjustment transfers $1,000 from Prepaid Rent to Rent Expense as follows:*

Date	Account	Debit	Credit
Apr. 30	Rent Expense ($1000 × 1/3)	1,000	
	Prepaid Rent		1,000
	To record rent expense.		

Adjusting entry a

Both assets and shareholders' equity decrease.

ASSETS	=	LIABILITIES	+	SHAREHOLDERS' EQUITY	−	EXPENSES
−1,000	=	0			−	1,000

After posting, Prepaid Rent and Rent Expense appear as follows:

Prepaid Rent					Rent Expense		
Apr. 1	3,000	Apr. 30	1,000	→	Apr. 30	1,000	
Bal.	2,000				Bal.	1,000	

We record an expense in order to measure net income.

Supplies. Supplies are another type of prepaid expense. On April 2, Moreau Ltd. paid cash of $700 for office supplies:

Date	Account	Debit	Credit
Apr. 2	Supplies	700	
	Cash		700
	Paid cash for supplies.		

ASSETS	=	LIABILITIES	+	SHAREHOLDERS' EQUITY
700	=	0	+	0
−700				

The cost of the supplies Moreau Ltd. used is supplies expense. To measure supplies expense for April, the business counts the supplies on hand at the end of the month. The count shows that supplies costing $400 remain. Subtracting the $400 of supplies on hand at the end of April from the supplies available ($700) measures supplies expense for the month ($300) as follows:

*See Exhibit 3-7, page 135, for a summary of adjustments a through g.

ASSET AVAILABLE DURING THE PERIOD	–	ASSET ON HAND AT THE END OF THE PERIOD	=	ASSET USED (EXPENSE) DURING THE PERIOD
$700	–	$400	=	$300

The April 30 adjusting entry debits the expense and credits the asset, as follows:

Apr. 30	Supplies Expense ($700 – $400).	300	
	Supplies		300
	To record supplies expense.		

Adjusting entry b

ASSETS	=	LIABILITIES	+	SHAREHOLDERS' EQUITY	–	EXPENSES
–300	=	0			–	300

After posting, the Supplies and Supplies Expense accounts appear as follows:

Supplies

Apr. 2	700	Apr. 30	300
Bal.	400		

→

Supplies Expense

Apr. 30	300		
Bal.	300		

The Supplies account then enters the month of May with a $400 balance, and the adjustment process is repeated each month.

STOP + THINK

At the beginning of the month, supplies were $5,000. During the month, $7,000 of supplies were purchased. At month's end, $3,000 of supplies were still on hand. What are the adjusting entry and the ending balance in the Supplies account?

Answer:

Supplies Expense ($5,000 + $7,000 – $3,000)	9,000	
Supplies		9,000

Ending balance of supplies = $3,000 (the supplies still on hand)

Deferrals—Unearned Revenues

Some businesses collect cash from customers before earning the revenue. This creates a liability called **unearned revenue**, which is an obligation arising from receiving cash before providing a service. Only when the job is completed can the business earn the revenue. Suppose Circle Four Farms Ltd. engaged Moreau Ltd. to provide ongoing consulting services for the next year, agreeing to pay the consultancy $450 monthly, beginning immediately. If Moreau Ltd. collects the first amount on April 20, Moreau Ltd. records this transaction as follows:

Apr. 20	Cash	450	
	Unearned Service Revenue		450
	Received cash for revenue in advance.		

ASSETS	=	LIABILITIES	+	SHAREHOLDERS' EQUITY
450	=	450	+	0

After posting, the liability account appears as follows:

Unearned Service Revenue			
		Apr. 20	450

Unearned Service Revenue is a liability because Moreau Ltd. is obligated to perform services for the client. The April 30 unadjusted trial balance (Exhibit 3-1, p. 123) lists Unearned Service Revenue with a $450 credit balance. During the last 10 days of the month—April 21 through April 30—the consultancy will *earn* one-third (10 days divided by April's total of 30 days) of the $450, or $150. Therefore, the accountant makes the following adjustment on April 30:

Apr. 30	Unearned Service Revenue	150	
	Service Revenue		150
	To record unearned service revenue that has been earned ($450 × 1/3).		

Adjusting entry f

ASSETS	=	LIABILITIES	+	SHAREHOLDERS' EQUITY	+	REVENUES
0	=	−150			+	150

This adjusting entry shifts $150 of the total amount received ($450) from liability to revenue. After posting, Unearned Service Revenue is reduced to $300, and Service Revenue is increased by $150, as follows:

Unearned Service Revenue			
Apr. 30	150	Apr. 20	450
		Bal.	300

Service Revenue			
			7,000
		Apr. 30	150
		Bal.	7,150

All revenues collected in advance are accounted for in this way. An unearned revenue is a liability, not a revenue.

One company's prepaid expense is the other company's unearned revenue. For example, Circle Four Farms Ltd.'s prepaid expense is Moreau Ltd.'s liability for unearned revenue.

Depreciation of Property, Plant, and Equipment

Property, plant, and equipment (also referred to as tangible capital assets) are long-lived tangible assets, such as land, buildings, furniture, machinery, and equipment. All capital assets but land decline in usefulness as they age, and this decline is an expense. Accountants spread the cost of each capital asset, except land, over its useful life. Depreciation is the process of allocating cost to expense for a long-term capital asset.

To illustrate depreciation, consider Moreau Ltd. Suppose that on April 3 the business purchased furniture including several computers, a printer, a fax machine, and a copier, on account for $16,500:

Apr. 3	Furniture	16,500	
	Accounts Payable		16,500
	Purchased office furniture on account.		

ASSETS	=	LIABILITIES	+	SHAREHOLDERS' EQUITY
16,500	=	16,500	+	0

After posting, the Furniture account appears as follows:

Furniture		
Apr. 3	16,500	

Moreau Ltd. records an asset when it purchases furniture. Then, as the asset is used, a portion of the asset's cost is transferred to Depreciation Expense each period the asset is used. Accounting records the expenses incurred and deducts it from revenue. Computerized systems program the depreciation for automatic entry each period.

Moreau Ltd.'s furniture is expected to remain useful for five years and then be worthless. One way to compute the amount of depreciation for each year is to divide the cost of the asset ($16,500 in our example) by its expected useful life (five years). This procedure—called the straight-line depreciation method—gives annual depreciation of $3,300. The depreciation amount is an *estimate*. (Chapter 7 covers property, plant, and equipment and depreciation in more detail.)

Annual depreciation = $16,500/5 years = $3,300 per year

Depreciation for April is $275.

Monthly depreciation = $3,300/12 months = $275 per month

The Accumulated Depreciation Account. Depreciation expense for April is recorded as follows:

Apr. 30	Depreciation Expense—Furniture	275	
	Accumulated Depreciation—Furniture		275
	To record depreciation.		

Adjusting entry c

Note that assets decrease by the amount of the expense:

ASSETS	=	LIABILITIES	+	SHAREHOLDERS' EQUITY	−	EXPENSES
−275	=	0			−	275

The Accumulated Depreciation account (not Furniture) is credited to preserve the original cost of the furniture in the Furniture account. Managers can then refer to the Furniture account if they need to know how much the asset cost.

The **Accumulated Depreciation** account shows the sum of all depreciation expense from the date of acquiring the asset. Therefore, the balance in the Accumulated Depreciation account increases over the asset's life.

Accumulated Depreciation is a contra asset account—an asset account with a normal credit balance. A **contra account** has two distinguishing characteristics:

1. It always has a companion account.
2. Its normal balance is opposite that of the companion account.

In this case, Accumulated Depreciation is the contra account to Furniture, so Accumulated Depreciation appears directly after Furniture in the financial statements. A business carries an accumulated depreciation account for each depreciable asset, for example, Accumulated Depreciation—Building and Accumulated Depreciation—Machinery.

After posting, the accounts of Moreau Ltd. related to furniture are as follows:

Furniture			
Apr. 3	16,500		
Bal.	16,500		

Accumulated Depreciation—Furniture			
		Apr. 30	275
		Bal.	275

Depreciation Expense—Furniture			
Apr. 30	275		
Bal.	275		

Carrying Amount. The net amount of a capital asset (cost minus accumulated depreciation) is called that asset's **carrying amount** or *book value*. Exhibit 3-2 shows how Moreau Ltd. would report the carrying amount of its furniture at April 30, 2011. At April 30, 2011, the carrying amount of furniture is $16,225.

While some companies report the cost, the accumulated depreciation, and the difference, carrying amount, on the balance sheet, many others report that information in the notes to the financial statements and simply the carrying amount on the balance sheet.

Exhibit 3-3 shows how TELUS Corporation shows capital assets in its December 31, 2008, annual report. The second column from the left shows the cost of property, plant, and equipment. Assets under construction means construction in process; when completed it will be included with the buildings. Leasehold improvements are renovations to leased property.

The middle column shows the sum of the accumulated depreciation for each type of asset, and the column on the right shows the carrying amount of each type of asset.

EXHIBIT 3-2 **Capital Assets on the Balance Sheet of Moreau, Ltd. (April 30, 2011)**

Moreau Ltd.
Property, Plant, and Equipment
April 30, 2011

Furniture	$16,500
Less Accumulated Depreciation	(275)
Carrying amount of capital assets	$16,225

EXHIBIT 3-3 **TELUS Corporation Reporting of Property, Plant, and Equipment and Other (Adapted, in Millions), as at December 31, 2008**

	Cost	Accumulated Depreciation	Carrying Amount
Property, plant, equipment, and other			
Network assets	$20,609	$15,119	$5,490
Buildings and leasehold improvements	2,110	1,232	878
Assets under capital lease	15	9	6
Other	1,681	1,272	409
Land	49	–	49
Assets under construction	485	–	485
	$24,949	$17,632	$7,317

STOP + THINK

What will the carrying amount of Moreau Ltd.'s furniture be at the end of May 2011?

Answer:
$16,500 – $275 – $275 = $15,950.

Accruals—Accrued Expenses

Businesses incur expenses before they pay cash. Consider an employee's salary. Big Rock Brewery Income Trust's salary expense and salary payable grow as the employee works, so the liability is said to accrue. Another example is interest expense on a note payable. Interest accrues as the clock ticks. The term **accrued expense** refers to a liability that arises from an expense that has not yet been paid.

Companies don't record accrued expenses daily or weekly. Instead, they wait until the end of the period and use an adjusting entry to update each expense (and related liability) for the financial statements. Let's look at salary expense.

Most companies pay their employees at set times. Suppose Moreau Ltd. pays its employee a monthly salary of $1,900, half on the 15th and half on the last day of the month. The calendar below is for illustrative purposes and is not that for April 2011. It has the paydays circled.

April

Sun.	Mon.	Tue.	Wed.	Thur.	Fri.	Sat.
					1	2
3	4	5	6	7	8	9
10	11	12	13	14	(15)	16
17	18	19	20	21	22	23
24	25	26	27	28	29	(30)

Assume that if a payday falls on the weekend, Moreau Ltd. pays the employee on the following Monday. During the April illustrated, Moreau Ltd. paid its employee's first half-month salary of $950 and made the following entry:

Apr. 15	Salary Expense	950	
	Cash		950
	To pay salary.		

ASSETS	=	LIABILITIES	+	SHAREHOLDERS' EQUITY	–	EXPENSES
–950	=	0			–	950

After posting, the Salary Expense account is

Salary Expense		
Apr. 15	950	

Because April 30, the second payday of the month illustrated, falls on a Saturday, the second half-month amount of $950 will be paid on Monday, May 2. At April 30, therefore, Moreau Ltd. adjusts for additional *salary expense* and *salary payable* of $950 as follows:

Apr. 30	Salary Expense	950	*Adjusting entry d*
	Salary Payable		950
	To accrue salary expense.		

The accounting equation shows that an accrued expense increases liabilities and decreases shareholders' equity:

ASSETS	=	LIABILITIES	+	SHAREHOLDERS' EQUITY	−	EXPENSES
0	=	950			−	950

After posting, the Salary Payable and Salary Expense accounts appear as follows:

Salary Payable

	Apr. 30	950
	Bal.	950

Salary Expense

Apr. 15	950	
Apr. 30	950	
Bal.	1,900	

The accounts at April 30 for this illustration now contain the full month's salary information. Salary Expense has a full month's salary, and Salary Payable shows the amount owed at April 30. All accrued expenses are recorded this way—debit the expense account and credit the liability account.

Computerized systems contain a payroll module. The adjustment for accrued salaries is automatically journalized and posted at the end of each accounting period.

Accruals—Accrued Revenues

Businesses often earn revenue before they receive the cash—collection occurs later. A revenue that has been earned but not yet received in cash is called an **accrued revenue**.

Assume that Parkin, Ghandi, and Lee Inc., project engineers for a new hospital in Lethbridge, Alberta, hire Moreau Ltd. on April 15, 2011, to do some consulting on the hospital project. Parkin, Ghandi, and Lee Inc. arrange to pay Moreau Ltd. $500 monthly, with the first payment on May 15. During April, Moreau Ltd. will earn half a month's fee, $250, for work done from April 15 through April 30. On April 30, Moreau Ltd. makes the following adjusting entry:

Apr. 30	Accounts Receivable	250	*Adjusting entry e*
	Service Revenue		250
	To accrue service revenue ($500 × 1/2).		

Revenue increases both total assets and shareholders' equity:

ASSETS	=	LIABILITIES	+	SHAREHOLDERS' EQUITY	+	REVENUES
250	=	0			+	250

Recall that Accounts Receivable has an unadjusted balance of $2,250, and Service Revenue's unadjusted balance is $7,000 (Exhibit 3-1, p. 123). This April 30 adjusting entry has the following effects:

Accounts Receivable

	2,250	
Apr. 30	250	
Bal.	2,500	

Service Revenue

		7,000
	Apr. 30	150
	Apr. 30	250
	Bal.	7,400

All accrued revenues are accounted for similarly—debit a receivable and credit a revenue.

STOP + THINK

Suppose Moreau Ltd. holds a note receivable from a client. At the end of April, $125 of interest revenue has been earned. Prepare the adjusting entry at April 30.

Answer:

Interest Receivable..	125	
Interest Revenue..		125
To accrue interest revenue.		

MyAccountingLab

Accounting Cycle Tutorial: Adjustments - Tutorial

Summary of the Adjusting Process

Two purposes of the adjusting process are to

- Measure income
- Update the balance sheet

Therefore, every adjusting entry affects at least one

- Revenue or expense—to measure income
- Asset or liability—to update the balance sheet

Also, adjusting entries never affect cash and they are recorded at the end of the accounting period before the financial statements are prepared.

Exhibit 3-4 diagrams the distinctive timing of prepaid and accrual adjustments. Study prepaid expenses all the way across. Then study unearned revenues, and so on.

EXHIBIT 3-4 Prepaid and Accrual Adjustments

PREPAIDS—Cash First							
	First				Later		
Prepaid expenses	*Pay cash and record an asset:*			→	*Record an expense and decrease the asset:*		
	Prepaid Expense	XXX			Expense	XXX	
	Cash		XXX		Prepaid Expense		XXX
Unearned revenues	*Receive cash and record unearned revenue:*			→	*Record a revenue and decrease unearned revenue:*		
	Cash	XXX			Unearned Revenue	XXX	
	Unearned Revenue		XXX		Revenue		XXX
ACCRUALS—The Cash Transaction Occurs Later							
	First				Later		
Accrued expenses	*Accrue expense and a payable:*			→	*Pay cash and decrease the payable:*		
	Expense	XXX			Payable	XXX	
	Payable		XXX		Cash		XXX
Accrued revenues	*Accrue revenue and a receivable:*			→	*Receive cash and decrease the receivable:*		
	Receivable	XXX			Cash	XXX	
	Revenue		XXX		Receivable		XXX

Exhibit 3-5 summarizes the standard adjustments.

EXHIBIT 3-5 Summary of Adjusting Entries

	Type of Account	
Category of Adjusting Entry	Debit	Credit
Prepaid expense	Expense	Asset
Depreciation	Expense	Contra asset
Accrued expense	Expense	Liability
Accrued revenue	Asset	Revenue
Unearned revenue	Liability	Revenue

Adapted from material provided by Beverly Terry.

Exhibit 3-6 on page 134 summarizes the adjustments of Moreau Ltd. at April 30, 2011—the adjusting entries we've examined over the past few pages.

MyAccountingLab
Accounting Cycle Tutorial: Adjustments - Application Exercise 1

- Panel A repeats the data for each adjustment.
- Panel B gives the adjusting entries.
- Panel C shows the accounts after posting the adjusting entries. The adjustments are keyed by letter.

Exhibit 3-6 includes an additional adjusting entry that we have not yet discussed—the accrual of income tax expense. Like individual taxpayers, corporations are subject to income tax. They typically accrue income tax expense and the related income tax payable as the final adjusting entry of the period. Moreau Ltd. accrues income tax expense with adjusting entry g, as follows:

Apr. 30	Income Tax Expense	540	*Adjusting entry g*
	Income Tax Payable		540
	To accrue income tax expense.		

The Adjusted Trial Balance

This chapter began with the unadjusted trial balance (see Exhibit 3-1, p. 123). After the adjustments are journalized and posted, the accounts appear as shown in Exhibit 3-6, Panel C. A useful step in preparing the financial statements is to list the accounts, along with their adjusted balances, on an **adjusted trial balance**. This document lists all the accounts and their final balances in a single place. Exhibit 3-7 shows the preparation of the adjusted trial balance of Moreau Ltd.

Note how clearly the adjusted trial balance presents the data. The Account Title and the Unadjusted Trial Balance data come from the trial balance. The two Adjustments columns summarize the adjusting entries. The Adjusted Trial Balance columns give the final account balances. Each amount on the *adjusted* trial balance of Exhibit 3-7 is the unadjusted balance plus or minus the adjustments. For example, Accounts Receivable starts with a balance of $2,250. Add the $250 debit adjustment to get Accounts Receivable's ending balance of $2,500. Spreadsheets are designed for this type of analysis.

MyAccountingLab
Accounting Cycle Tutorial: Adjustments - Application Exercise 3

EXHIBIT 3-6 **The Adjusting Process of Moreau Ltd.**

PANEL A—Information for Adjustments at April 30, 2011

(a) Prepaid rent expired, $1,000
(b) Supplies on hand, $400. (See Exhibit 3-1.)
(c) Depreciation on furniture, $275.
(d) Accrued salary expense, $950. This entry assumes the pay period ended April 30 and the employee was paid May 2.
(e) Accrued service revenue, $250
(f) Amount of unearned service revenue that has been earned, $150.
(g) Accrued income tax expense, $540. (Described on page 133.)

PANEL B—Adjusting Entries

	Account	Debit	Credit
(a)	Rent Expense	1,000	
	Prepaid Rent		1,000
	To record rent expense.		
(b)	Supplies Expense	300	
	Supplies		300
	To record supplies used.		
(c)	Depreciation Expense—Furniture	275	
	Accumulated Depreciation—Furniture		275
	To record depreciation.		
(d)	Salary Expense	950	
	Salary Payable		950
	To accrue salary expense.		
(e)	Accounts Receivable	250	
	Service Revenue		250
	To accrue service revenue.		
(f)	Unearned Service Revenue	150	
	Service Revenue		150
	To record unearned revenue that has been earned.		
(g)	Income Tax Expense	540	
	Income Tax Payable		540
	To accrue income tax expense.		

PANEL C—Ledger Accounts

Assets

Cash

Debit	Credit
Bal. 24,800	

Accounts Receivable

Debit	Credit
2,250	
(e) 250	
Bal. 2,500	

Supplies

Debit	Credit
700	(b) 300
Bal. 400	

Prepaid Rent

Debit	Credit
3,000	(a) 1,000
Bal. 2,000	

Furniture

Debit	Credit
Bal. 16,500	

Accumulated Depreciation—Furniture

Debit	Credit
	(c) 275
	Bal. 275

Liabilities

Accounts Payable

Debit	Credit
	Bal. 13,100

Salary Payable

Debit	Credit
	(d) 950
	Bal. 950

Unearned Service Revenue

Debit	Credit
(f) 150	450
	Bal. 300

Income Tax Payable

Debit	Credit
	(g) 540
	Bal. 540

Shareholders' Equity

Common Shares

Debit	Credit
	Bal. 20,000

Retained Earnings

Debit	Credit
	Bal. 11,250

Dividends

Debit	Credit
Bal. 3,200	

Revenue

Service Revenue

Debit	Credit
	7,000
	(e) 250
	(f) 150
	Bal. 7,400

Expenses

Rent Expense

Debit	Credit
(a) 1,000	
Bal. 1,000	

Salary Expense

Debit	Credit
950	
(d) 950	
Bal. 1,900	

Supplies Expense

Debit	Credit
(b) 300	
Bal. 300	

Depreciation Expense—Furniture

Debit	Credit
(c) 275	
Bal. 275	

Utilities Expense

Debit	Credit
Bal. 400	

Income Tax Expense

Debit	Credit
(g) 540	
Bal. 540	

EXHIBIT 3-7 **Worksheet for the Preparation of Adjusted Trial Balance**

Moreau Ltd.
Preparation of Adjusted Trial Balance
April 30, 2011

	Unadjusted Trial Balance		Adjustments		Adjusted Trial Balance	
Account Title	Debit	Credit	Debit	Credit	Debit	Credit
Cash	24,800				24,800	
Accounts receivable	2,250		(e) 250		2,500	
Supplies	700			(b) 300	400	
Prepaid rent	3,000			(a) 1,000	2,000	
Furniture	16,500				16,500	
Accumulated depreciation—furniture				(c) 275		275
Accounts payable		13,100				13,100
Salary payable				(d) 950		950
Unearned service revenue		450	(f) 150			300
Income tax payable				(g) 540		540
Common shares		20,000				20,000
Retained earnings		11,250				11,250
Dividends	3,200				3,200	
Service revenue		7,000		(e) 250		7,400
				(f) 150		
Rent expense			(a) 1,000		1,000	
Salary expense	950		(d) 950		1,900	
Supplies expense			(b) 300		300	
Depreciation expense—furniture			(c) 275		275	
Utilities expense	400				400	
Income tax expense			(g) 540		540	
	51,800	51,800	3,465	3,465	53,815	53,815

Balance Sheet *(Exhibit 3-10)* — Cash through Common shares

Statement of Retained Earnings *(Exhibit 3-9)* — Retained earnings and Dividends

Income Statement *(Exhibit 3-8)* — Service revenue through Income tax expense

Preparing the Financial Statements

The April 2011 financial statements of Moreau Ltd. can be prepared from the adjusted trial balance. At the far right, Exhibit 3-7 shows how the accounts are distributed to the financial statements.

- The income statement (Exhibit 3-8) lists the revenue and expense accounts.
- The statement of retained earnings (Exhibit 3-9) shows the changes in retained earnings.
- The balance sheet (Exhibit 3-10) reports assets, liabilities, and shareholders' equity.
- The arrows in Exhibits 3-8, 3-9, and 3-10 show the flow of data from one statement to the next.

OBJECTIVE

4 **Prepare** the financial statements

Why is the income statement prepared first and the balance sheet last?

1. The income statement reports net income or net loss, the result of revenues minus expenses. Revenues and expenses affect shareholders' equity, so net income is transferred to retained earnings. Arrow ① tracks net income.
2. Retained Earnings is the final balancing element of the balance sheet. To solidify your understanding, trace the $11,035 retained earnings figure from Exhibit 3-9 to Exhibit 3-10. Arrow ② tracks retained earnings.

MyAccountingLab

Accounting Cycle Tutorial: Financial Statements - Application Exercise 2

EXHIBIT 3-8 **Income Statement**

Moreau Ltd.
Income Statement
For the Month Ended April 30, 2011

Revenue:		
Service revenue		$7,400
Expenses:		
Salary	$1,900	
Rent	1,000	
Utilities	400	
Supplies	300	
Depreciation	275	3,875
Income before tax		3,525
Income tax expense		540
Net income		$2,985

①

EXHIBIT 3-9 **Statement of Retained Earnings**

Moreau Ltd.
Statement of Retained Earnings
For the Month Ended April 30, 2011

Retained earnings, April 1, 2011	$11,250
Add: Net income	2,985
	14,235
Less: Dividends	(3,200)
Retained earnings, April 30, 2011	$11,035

②

EXHIBIT 3-10 **Balance Sheet**

Moreau Ltd.
Balance Sheet
April 30, 2011

Assets			Liabilities	
Cash		$24,800	Accounts payable	$13,100
Accounts receivable		2,500	Salary payable	950
Supplies		400	Unearned service revenue	300
Prepaid rent		2,000	Income tax payable	540
Furniture	$16,500		Total liabilities	14,890
Less Accumulated depreciation	(275)	16,225	**Shareholders' Equity**	
			Common shares	20,000
			Retained earnings	11,035
			Total shareholders' equity	31,035
Total assets		$45,925	Total liabilities and shareholders' equity	$45,925

You will note that the statement of cash flows is not included in the list of statements that are prepared from the adjusted trial balance. The reason it is not included, as you will discover in Chapter 12, is that the statement of cash flows is not prepared, as the other three are, from the adjusted trial balance but rather from the comparative balance sheets, the income statement, and other sources.

MID-CHAPTER SUMMARY PROBLEM

MyAccountingLab

The trial balance of Goldsmith Inc. shown below pertains to December 31, 2011, which is the end of its year-long accounting period. Data needed for the adjusting entries include the following (all amounts in thousands):

a. Supplies on hand at year-end, $2.
b. Depreciation on furniture and fixtures, $20.
c. Depreciation on building, $10.
d. Salary owed but not yet paid, $5.
e. Accrued service revenue, $12.
f. Of the $45 balance of unearned service revenue, $32 was earned during the year.
g. Accrued income tax expense, $35.

Required

1. Open the ledger accounts with their unadjusted balances. Show dollar amounts in thousands, as shown for Accounts Receivable:

Accounts Receivable	
370	

2. Journalize the Goldsmith Inc. adjusting entries at December 31, 2011. Key entries by letter, as in Exhibit 3-6, page 134. Make entries in thousands.
3. Post the adjusting entries.
4. Enter the trial balance on a worksheet, enter the adjusting entries, and prepare an adjusted trial balance, as shown in Exhibit 3-7.
5. Prepare the income statement, the statement of retained earnings, and the balance sheet. (At this stage, it is not necessary to classify assets or liabilities as current or long term.) Draw arrows linking these three financial statements.

Name: Goldsmith Inc.
Industry: Service corporation
Fiscal Period: Year ended December 31, 2011
Key Fact: Existing, ongoing business

Goldsmith Inc.
Trial Balance
December 31, 2011

	(in thousands)	
Cash	$ 198	
Accounts receivable	370	
Supplies	6	
Furniture and fixtures	100	
Accumulated depreciation—furniture and fixtures		$ 40
Building	250	
Accumulated depreciation—building		130
Accounts payable		380
Salary payable		
Unearned service revenue		45
Income tax payable		
Common shares		100
Retained earnings		193
Dividends	65	
Service revenue		286
Salary expense	172	
Supplies expense		
Depreciation expense—furniture and fixtures		
Depreciation expense—building		
Income tax expense		
Miscellaneous expense	13	
Total	$1,174	$1,174

ANSWERS

Requirements 1 and 3 (amounts in thousands)

Assets

Cash

Bal. 198		

Accounts Receivable

Debit	Credit
370	
(e) 12	
Bal. 382	

Supplies

Debit	Credit
6	(a) 4
Bal. 2	

Furniture and Fixtures

Debit	Credit
Bal. 100	

Accumulated Depreciation—Furniture and Fixtures

Debit	Credit
	40
	(b) 20
	Bal. 60

Building

Debit	Credit
Bal. 250	

Accumulated Depreciation—Building

Debit	Credit
	130
	(c) 10
	Bal. 140

Liabilities

Accounts Payable

Debit	Credit
	Bal. 380

Salary Payable

Debit	Credit
	(d) 5
	Bal. 5

Unearned Service Revenue

Debit	Credit
(f) 32	45
	Bal. 13

Income Tax Payable

Debit	Credit
	(g) 35
	Bal. 35

For Requirement 1, create a T-account for each account name listed in the December 31, 2011, trial balance. Insert the opening balances into the T-accounts from the trial balance, ensuring debit and credit balances on the trial balance are debit and credit balances in the T-accounts. To make sure all the account balances have been entered correctly, trace each T-account's balance back to the December 31, 2011, trial balance.

For Requirement 3, make sure each transaction is posted to the proper T-account, and make sure no transactions were missed.

Shareholders' Equity

Common Shares

Debit	Credit
	Bal. 100

Retained Earnings

Debit	Credit
	Bal. 193

Dividends

Debit	Credit
Bal. 65	

Revenue

Service Revenue

Debit	Credit
	286
	(e) 12
	(f) 32
	Bal. 330

Expenses

Salary Expense

Debit	Credit
172	
(d) 5	
Bal. 177	

Supplies Expense

Debit	Credit
(a) 4	
Bal. 4	

Depreciation Expense—Furniture and Fixtures

Debit	Credit
(b) 20	
Bal. 20	

Depreciation Expense—Building

Debit	Credit
(c) 10	
Bal. 10	

Income Tax Expense

Debit	Credit
(g) 35	
Bal. 35	

Miscellaneous Expense

Debit	Credit
Bal. 13	

Requirement 2

Refer to the rules of debit and credit shown in Chapter 2, Exhibit 2-7, on page 77.

Make sure that Assets = Liabilities + Shareholders' Equity for each transaction before going to the next transaction.

	2011		amounts in thousands	
(a)	Dec. 31	Supplies Expense	4	
		Supplies		4
		To record supplies used ($6 − $2).		
(b)	Dec. 31	Depreciation Expense—Furniture and Fixtures	20	
		Accumulated Depreciation—Furniture and Fixtures		20
		To record depreciation expense on furniture and fixtures.		
(c)	Dec. 31	Depreciation Expense—Building	10	
		Accumulated Depreciation—Building		10
		To record depreciation expense on building.		
(d)	Dec. 31	Salary Expense	5	
		Salary Payable		5
		To accrue salary expense.		
(e)	Dec. 31	Accounts Receivable	12	
		Service Revenue		12
		To accrue service revenue.		
(f)	Dec. 31	Unearned Service Revenue	32	
		Service Revenue		32
		To record unearned service revenue that has been earned.		
(g)	Dec. 31	Income Tax Expense	35	
		Income Tax Payable		35
		To accrue income tax expense.		

Requirement 4

Goldsmith Inc.
Preparation of Adjusted Trial Balance
December 31, 2011

(amounts in thousands)

	Unadjusted Trial Balance		Adjustments		Adjusted Trial Balance	
	Debit	Credit	Debit	Credit	Debit	Credit
Cash	198				198	
Accounts receivable	370		(e) 12		382	
Supplies	6			(a) 4	2	
Furniture and fixtures	100				100	
Accumulated depreciation—furniture and fixtures		40		(b) 20		60
Building	250				250	
Accumulated depreciation—building		130		(c) 10		140
Accounts payable		380				380
Salary payable				(d) 5		5
Unearned service revenue		45	(f) 32			13
Income tax payable				(g) 35		35
Common shares		100				100
Retained earnings		193				193
Dividends	65				65	
Service revenue		286		(e) 12 (f) 32		330
Salary expense	172		(d) 5		177	
Supplies expense			(a) 4		4	
Depreciation expense—furniture and fixtures			(b) 20		20	
Depreciation expense—building			(c) 10		10	
Income tax expense			(g) 35		35	
Miscellaneous expense	13				13	
	1,174	1,174	118	118	1,256	1,256

Create a worksheet with columns for the original trial balance, adjustments, and the adjusted trial balance. List all the account names that have a balance in their T-accounts. Write the account balances from the December 31, 2011, trial balance in the first two columns. Write the adjustment amounts in the next two columns. Write the "Bal." amounts from the T-accounts in the Adjusted Trial Balance columns. Ensure total debits equal total credits for each pair of columns. Double-check the adjusted trial balance amounts by adding the adjustments to the original trial balance amounts. Double underline the totals to show that the columns have been added and the totals are final.

Requirement 5

The title must include the name of the company, "Income Statement," and the specific period of time covered. It is critical that the time period is defined.

Gather all the revenue and expense account names and amounts from the Debit and Credit Adjusted Trial Balance columns of the worksheet.

Notice that Income Tax Expense is always reported separately from the other expenses, and it appears as the last item before net income (or net loss).

Goldsmith Ltd.
Income Statement
For the Year Ended December 31, 2011

	(amounts in thousands)	
Revenue:		
Service revenue		$330
Expenses:		
Salary	$177	
Depreciation—furniture and fixtures	20	
Depreciation—building	10	
Supplies	4	
Miscellaneous	13	224
Income before tax		106
Income tax expense		35
Net income		$ 71

The title must include the name of the company, "Statement of Retained Earnings," and the specific period of time covered. It is critical that the time period is defined.

Beginning retained earnings and dividends are from the Adjusted Trial Balance columns of the worksheet.

The net income amount is transferred from the income statement.

Goldsmith Inc.
Statement of Retained Earnings
For the Year Ended December 31, 2011

	(amounts in thousands)
Retained earnings, January 1, 2011	$193
Add: Net income	71
	264
Less: Dividends	(65)
Retained earnings, December 31, 2011	$199

The title must include the name of the company, "Balance Sheet," and the date of the balance sheet. It shows the financial position on one specific date.

Gather all the asset, liability, and common shares accounts and amounts from the Adjusted Trial Balance columns of the worksheet. The retained earnings amount is transferred from the statement of retained earnings.

It is imperative that Total assets = Total liabilities + Shareholders' equity.

Goldsmith Inc.
Balance Sheet
December 31, 2011

(amounts in thousands)

Assets			**Liabilities**	
Cash		$198	Accounts payable	$380
Accounts receivable		382	Salary payable	5
Supplies		2	Unearned service revenue	13
Furniture and fixtures	$100		Income tax payable	35
Less accumulated			Total liabilities	433
depreciation	(60)	40		
			Shareholders' Equity	
Building	$250		Common shares	100
Less accumulated			Retained earnings	199
depreciation	(140)	110	Total shareholders' equity	299
			Total liabilities and	
Total assets		$732	shareholders' equity	$732

Which Accounts Need to Be Closed? It is now April 30, the end of the month. Ranjini Sivakumar, Moreau's manager, will continue operating the business into May, June, and beyond. But wait—the revenue and the expense accounts still hold amounts for April. At the end of each accounting period, it is necessary to close the books.

OBJECTIVE

5 Close the books

Closing the books means preparing the accounts for the next period's transactions. The **closing entries** set the balances of the revenue and expense accounts back to zero at the end of the period. The idea is the same as setting the scoreboard back to zero after a hockey game.

Closing is easily handled by computers. Recall that the income statement reports only one period's income. For example, net income for Le Château or Moreau Ltd. for 2011 relates exclusively to 2011. At each year-end, Le Château's accountants close the company's revenues and expenses for that year.

Temporary Accounts. Because revenues and expenses relate to a limited period, they are called **temporary accounts**. The Dividends account is also temporary. The closing process applies only to temporary accounts (revenues, expenses, and dividends).

Permanent Accounts. Let's contrast the temporary accounts with the **permanent accounts**: assets, liabilities, and shareholders' equity. The permanent accounts are not closed at the end of the period because they carry over to the next period. Consider Cash, Accounts Receivable, Buildings, Accounts Payable, Common Shares, and Retained Earnings. Their final balances at the end of one period become the beginning balances of the next period.

Closing entries transfer the revenue, expense, and dividends balances to Retained Earnings. Following are the steps to close the books of a corporation such as Le Château or Moreau Ltd.:

① Debit each revenue account for the amount of its credit balance. Credit Retained Earnings for the sum of the revenues. Now the sum of the revenues is in Retained Earnings.

② Credit each expense account for the amount of its debit balance. Debit Retained Earnings for the sum of the expenses. The sum of the expenses is also in Retained Earnings.

③ Credit the Dividends account for the amount of its debit balance. Debit Retained Earnings. This entry places the dividends amount on the debit side of Retained Earnings. Remember that dividends are not expenses. Dividends never affect net income.

After closing the books, the Retained Earnings account of Moreau Ltd. appears as follows (data from p. 136):

Retained Earnings

		Beginning balance	11,250
Expenses	4,415	Revenues	7,400
Dividends	3,200		
		Ending balance	11,035

MyAccountingLab

Accounting Cycle Tutorial: Adjustments and Closing Entries - Tutorial

MyAccountingLab

Accounting Cycle Tutorial: Adjustments and Closing Entries - Application Exercise 2

Assume that Moreau Ltd. closes the books at the end of April. Exhibit 3-11 presents the complete closing process for the business. Panel A gives the closing journal entries, and Panel B shows the accounts after closing.

EXHIBIT 3-11 **Journalizing and Posting and Closing Entries**

PANEL A—Journalizing the Closing Entries

Closing Entries

	Date		Accounts	Debit	Credit
①	Apr.	30	Service Revenue	7,400	
			Retained Earnings		7,400
②		30	Retained Earnings	4,415	
			Rent Expense		1,000
			Salary Expense		1,900
			Supplies Expense		300
			Depreciation Expense—Furniture		275
			Utilities Expense		400
			Income Tax Expense		540
③		30	Retained Earnings	3,200	
			Dividends		3,200

PANEL B—Posting to the Accounts

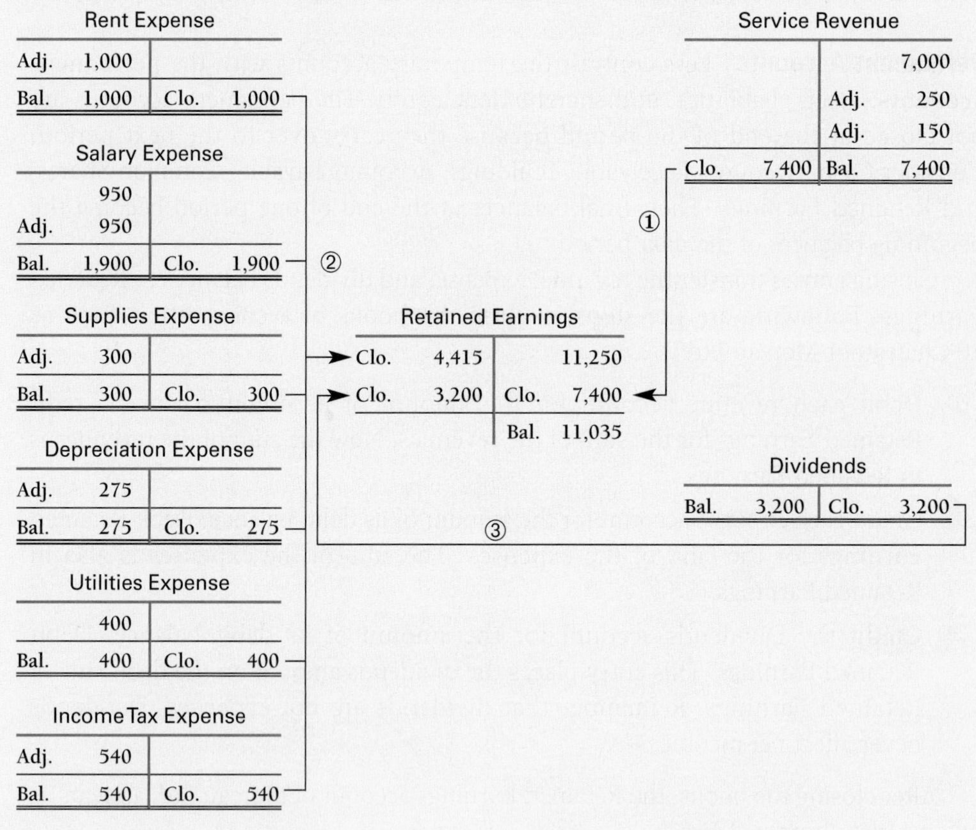

Adj. = Amount posted from an adjusting entry
Clo. = Amount posted from a closing entry
Bal. = Balance
As arrow ② in Panel B shows, it is not necessary to make a separate closing entry for each expense. In one closing entry, we record one debit to Retained Earnings and a separate credit to each expense account.

The Balance Sheet

The balance sheet reports the financial position of a company at a specific point in time. It lists the assets, liabilities, and shareholders' equity. These assets and liabilities are classified as either current or non-current.

OBJECTIVE

6 **Use** the financial statements in decsion making

Classifying Assets and Liabilities

On the balance sheet, assets and liabilities are classified as current or long-term to indicate their relative liquidity. **Liquidity** measures how quickly an item can be converted to cash. Cash is the most liquid asset. Accounts receivable are relatively liquid because the business expects to collect the cash quickly. Inventory is less liquid than accounts receivable because the company must first sell the goods. Furniture and buildings are even less liquid because these assets are held for use and not for sale. A balance sheet lists assets and liabilities in the order of their relative liquidity.

Current Assets. As we saw in Chapter 1, current assets are the most liquid assets. They will be converted to cash, sold, or consumed during the next 12 months or within the business's normal operating cycle if longer than a year. The **operating cycle** is the time span during which (1) cash is paid for goods and services, and (2) these goods and services are sold to bring in cash.

For most businesses, the operating cycle is a few months. Cash, Accounts Receivable, Merchandise Inventory, and Prepaid Expenses are current assets.

Long-Term Assets. Long-term assets are all assets not classified as current assets. One category of long-term assets is Property, Plant, and Equipment, sometimes called capital assets or fixed assets. Land, Buildings, Furniture and Fixtures, and Equipment are capital assets. Other types of long-term assets are Long-Term Investments, Intangible Assets, and Other Assets (a catch-all category for assets that are not classified more precisely but are also long-term).

Current Liabilities. As we saw in Chapter 1, current liabilities are debts that must be paid within one year or within the entity's operating cycle if longer than a year. Accounts Payable, Notes Payable due within one year, Salary Payable, Unearned Revenue, Interest Payable, and Income Tax Payable are current liabilities.

Bankers and other lenders are interested in the due dates of an entity's liabilities. The sooner a liability must be paid, the more pressure it creates for the company. Therefore, the balance sheet lists liabilities in the order in which they must be paid. Balance sheets usually report two liability classifications: current liabilities and long-term liabilities.

Long-Term Liabilities. All liabilities that are not current are classified as **long-term liabilities**. Many notes payable are long-term. Some notes payable are paid in installments, with the first installment due within one year, the second installment due the second year, and so on. The first installment would be a current liability, and the remainder would be long-term.

Let's see how Le Château Inc. reports these asset and liability categories on its balance sheet.

Reporting Assets and Liabilities: Le Château Inc.

Exhibit 3-12 shows the actual classified balance sheet of Le Château Inc. A **classified balance sheet** separates current assets from long-term assets and current liabilities from long-term liabilities. You should be familiar with most of Le Château's accounts. Study the Le Château statements all the way through—line by line.

Le Château's financial statements need two explanations:

1. *Consolidated* in the statement title means that Le Château owns a number of different companies and all of those companies' financial statements are combined, or consolidated, into a single set of statements.
2. The dates of the statements may look strange. Le Château, like many other companies, ends its accounting year on the Saturday nearest its basic year-end date,

EXHIBIT 3-12 **Financial Statements of Le Château Inc.**

Le Château Inc.
Consolidated Balance Sheets (Adapted)
(in thousands of dollars)

	Jan. 31, 2009	Jan. 26, 2008
Assets		
Current		
Cash and cash equivalents	$ 10,034	$ 3,846
Short-term investments	56,643	66,354
Accounts receivable and other assets	4,791	4,350
Derivative financial instruments	1,530	250
Inventories	54,012	45,903
Prepaid expenses	778	1,707
Total current assets	127,788	122,410
Fixed assets	88,643	84,466
	$216,431	$206,876
Liabilities and Shareholders' Equity		
Current		
Accounts payable and accrued liabilities	$ 25,403	$ 30,377
Dividend payable	4,239	3,133
Income taxes payable	2,285	5,092
Current portion of capital lease obligations	1,008	1,384
Current portion of long-term debt	8,746	7,113
Future income taxes	487	927
Total current liabilities	42,168	48,026
Capital lease obligations	—	1,008
Long-term debt	18,982	12,689
Future income taxes	3,176	2,975
Deferred lease inducements	9,691	8,573
Total liabilities	74,017	73,271
Shareholders' equity		
Capital stock	30,997	31,794
Contributed surplus	2,460	1,761
Retained earnings	107,914	99,884
Accumulated other comprehensive income	1,043	166
Total shareholders' equity	$142,414	$133,605
	$216,431	$206,876

which is January 31 each year. In 2008, that date fell on January 26. In 2009, the year-end date fell on January 31.

USING THE BALANCE SHEET IN DECISION MAKING

Accounting provides information for decision making.

Manager—Managers know they must have enough cash to pay the company's current liabilities.

Investor—Investors or shareholders know that a company that cannot pay its debts is not a good investment because it may go bankrupt.

Creditor—A creditor considering lending money must predict whether the borrower can repay the loan. If the borrower already has a lot of debt, the probability of repayment may be low.

To analyze a company's financial position, decision makers use ratios computed from various items in the balance sheet.

CURRENT RATIO

One of the most widely used financial ratios is the **current ratio**, which divides total current assets by total current liabilities.

$$\text{Current ratio} = \frac{\text{Total current assets}}{\text{Total current liabilities}}$$

The current ratio measures the company's ability to pay current liabilities with current assets. For Le Château (amounts in thousands for 2009, from page 144):

$$\frac{\$127{,}788}{\$42{,}168} = 3.03$$

The current ratio for Le Château indicates that the company has $3.03 in current assets for every $1.00 in current liabilities. A company prefers to have a high current ratio, which means that the business has plenty of current assets to pay current liabilities. An increasing current ratio from period to period indicates improvement in financial position.

What is a good value of the current ratio? It depends on the industry. Traditionally, a current ratio of 2.00 was considered ideal. However, a company with strong cash flows can operate successfully with a low current ratio of, say, 1.10 to 1.20. A company with weaker cash flows needs a higher current ratio of, say, 1.30 to 1.50.

DEBT RATIO

A second aid to decision making is the **debt ratio**, which is the ratio of total liabilities to total assets:

$$\text{Debt ratio} = \frac{\text{Total liabilities}}{\text{Total assets}}$$

For Le Château (amounts in thousands for 2009, from p. 144),

$$\frac{\$74{,}017}{\$216{,}431} = 0.341$$

The debt ratio indicates the proportion of a company's assets that is financed with debt. This ratio measures a business's ability to pay both current and long-term debts (total liabilities).

(continued)

For Le Château, the debt ratio is low. A lower ratio is safer than a higher debt ratio because a company with a small amount of liabilities has low required payments. This company is less likely to get into financial difficulty. By contrast, a business with a high debt ratio may have trouble paying its liabilities, especially when sales are low and cash is scarce.

When a company fails to pay its debts, the creditors can take the company away from its owners. Most bankruptcies result from high debt ratios.

What is a good value of the debt ratio? It depends on the industry. A profitable company with strong cash flows can operate successfully with a high debt ratio of, say, 0.70 to 0.80. A company with weak cash flows needs a lower debt ratio of, say, 0.50 to 0.60. Traditionally, a debt ratio of 0.50 was considered ideal. Recently, values have increased as companies have been able to operate more efficiently. Today, a normal value of the debt ratio is around 0.60 to 0.65.

The Income Statement

The income statement shows how profitable the company has been. It reports all revenue earned less all expenses incurred. A company is profitable if the revenue is greater than expenses; a company is running at a loss if the expenses exceed the revenue. A company may report the income statement using either a single-step format or a multi-step format.

A **single-step income statement** lists all the revenues together under a heading such as Revenues, or Revenues and Gains. The expenses are listed together in a single category titled Expenses, or Expenses and Losses. There is only one step, the subtraction of Expenses and Losses from the sum of Revenues and Gains, in arriving at net income. Le Château's income statement in the opening vignette is in single-step format.

A **multi-step income statement** contains a number of subtotals to highlight important relationships among revenues and expenses. For example, Tim Hortons' multi-step income statement in Exhibit 3-13 highlights gross margin (also called *gross profit*), earnings before other expenses and interest expense, and earnings before income taxes.

EXHIBIT 3-13 **Multi-Step Income Statement (Adapted, in millions)**

Tim Hortons Inc.
Consolidated Statement of Operations (Adapted)
For the Fiscal Year Ended December 28, 2008

Net revenue	$2,044
Cost of sales	1,181
Gross margin	863
Operating expenses	217
General and administrative expenses	131
Earnings before other expenses and interest expense	515
Other expenses	71
Interest expense, net	20
Earnings before income taxes	424
Income taxes	139
Net earnings for the year	$ 285

Many corporations using the multi-step income statement consider it important to report operating income separately from non-operating income. Typically they show non-operating income just before earnings before income taxes on the income statement.

Most actual company income statements do not conform to either a pure single-step format or a pure multi-step format. Today, business operations are too complex for all companies to conform to rigid reporting formats.

USING THE INCOME STATEMENT IN DECISION MAKING

When analyzing the income statement, managers, investors, and creditors are interested in knowing whether or not the company is profitable. They look to see if sales revenue has increased as well as net income. The manager's goal is to increase profit to satisfy both the investor and the creditor. For the investor, this signals that the selling price of their share could increase and the company will be able to distribute dividends. For the creditor, if a company is profitable, it will be able to pay its debts as they become due.

Tim Hortons' sales revenue and net income for the three fiscal years 2006, 2007, and 2008 (in millions) were as follows:

	2008	2007	2006
Sales revenue	2,043.6	1,895.8	1,659.5
Net income	284.7	269.6	259.6

This can also be expressed as a ratio called return on sales.

RETURN ON SALES (PROFIT MARGIN)

The **return on sales** ratio determines how much of the company's sales revenue ends up as net income. **Net income stated as a percentage of sales revenue** gives some idea about whether or not sales revenue was high enough to cover all of the company's costs. The higher the rate, the more sales dollars are providing income to the business and the fewer sales dollars are absorbed by expenses.

$$\text{Return on sales} = \frac{\text{Net income}}{\text{Sales revenue}}$$

For Tim Hortons, the return on sales for the past three years was as follows (amounts in millions of dollars):

2008	2007	2006
$\frac{\$284.7}{\$2,043.6} = 0.139$	$\frac{\$269.6}{\$1,895.8} = 0.142$	$\frac{\$259.6}{\$1,659.5} = 0.156$

For Tim Hortons in 2008, for every \$1.00 of sales, \$0.139 or \$0.14 ends up as net income. The difference between sales and net income or earnings is the expenses. Notice that for Tim Hortons, even though sales revenue and net income have increased over the years, net income as a percentage of sales has decreased. Companies try to control or reduce their expenses in order to increase net income, or they try to increase sales revenue by introducing a new product or by increasing the selling price.

MyAccountingLab

END-OF-CHAPTER SUMMARY PROBLEM

Refer to the mid-chapter summary problem that begins on page 137.

Required

1. Make Goldsmith Inc.'s closing entries at December 31, 2011. Explain what the closing entries accomplish and why they are necessary.
2. Post the closing entries to Retained Earnings and compare Retained Earnings' ending balance with the amount reported on the balance sheet on page 140. The two amounts should be the same.
3. Prepare Goldsmith Inc.'s classified balance sheet to identify the company's current assets and current liabilities. (Goldsmith Inc. has no long-term liabilities.) Then compute the company's current ratio and debt ratio at December 31, 2011.
4. The top management of Goldsmith Inc. has asked you for a $500,000 loan to expand the business. They propose to pay off the loan over a 10-year period. Recompute Goldsmith Inc.'s debt ratio assuming you make the loan. Use the company financial statements plus the ratio values to decide whether to grant the loan at an interest rate of 8%, 10%, or 12%. Goldsmith Inc.'s cash flow is strong. Give the reasoning underlying your decision.
5. Using Goldsmith's income statement from page 140, compute return on sales. If last year's rate was 23%, did this ratio improve or worsen? What would be the likely cause?

Name: Goldsmith Inc.
Industry: Service corporation
Fiscal Period: Year ended December 31, 2011
Key Fact: Existing, ongoing business

ANSWERS

Requirement 1

To close revenue accounts, debit each revenue account for the amounts reported on the income statement, and credit Retained Earnings for the total of the debits.

To close expense accounts, credit each expense account for the amounts reported on the income statement, and debit Retained Earnings for the total of the credits.

To close the dividend accounts, credit each dividend account for the amounts reported on the statement of retained earnings, and debit Retained Earnings for the total of the credits.

2011			(in thousands)	
Dec.	31	Service Revenue	330	
		Retained Earnings		330
	31	Retained Earnings	259	
		Salary Expense		177
		Depreciation Expense—Furniture and Fixtures		20
		Depreciation Expense—Building		10
		Supplies Expense		4
		Income Tax Expense		35
		Miscellaneous Expense		13
	31	Retained Earnings	65	
		Dividends		65

Explanation of Closing Entries

The closing entries set the balance of each revenue, expense, and Dividends account back to zero for the start of the next accounting period. We must close these accounts because their balances relate only to one accounting period.

Requirement 2

The balance in the Retained Earnings T-account should equal the Retained Earnings balance reported on the balance sheet.

Retained Earnings

Clo.	259		193
Clo.	65	Clo.	330
		Bal.	199

The balance in the Retained Earnings account agrees with the amount reported on the balance sheet, as it should.

Requirement 3

Goldsmith Inc.
Balance Sheet
December 31, 2011

(amounts in thousands)

Assets			Liabilities	
Current assets			Current liabilities	
Cash		$198	Accounts payable	$380
Accounts receivable		382	Salary payable	5
Supplies		2	Unearned service revenue	13
Total current assets		582	Income tax payable	35
Capital assets			Total current liabilities	433
Furniture and fixtures	$100			
Less Accumulated			**Shareholders' Equity**	
depreciation	(60)	40	Common shares	100
Building	$250		Retained earnings	199
Less Accumulated			Total shareholders' equity	299
depreciation	(140)	110	Total liabilities and	
Total assets		$732	shareholders' equity	$732

The title must include the name of the company, "Balance Sheet," and the date of the balance sheet. It shows the financial position on one specific date.

The classified balance sheet uses the same accounts and balances as those on the page 140 balance sheet. However, segregate current assets (assets expected to be converted to cash within one year) from capital assets, and segregate current liabilities (liabilities expected to be paid or settled within one year) from other liabilities.

$$\text{Current ratio} = \frac{\$582}{\$433} = 1.34 \qquad \text{Debt ratio} = \frac{\$433}{\$732} = 0.59$$

Current ratio = Current assets ÷ Current liabilities

Debt ratio = Current liabilities ÷ Total assets

Requirement 4

$$\text{Debt ratio assuming the loan is made} = \frac{\$433 + \$500}{\$732 + \$500} = \frac{\$933}{\$1{,}232} = 0.76$$

Decision: Make the loan at 10%.

Reasoning: Prior to the loan, the company's financial position and cash flow are strong. The current ratio is in a middle range, and the debt ratio is not too high. Net income (from the income statement) is high in relation to total revenue. Therefore, the company should be able to repay the loan.

The loan will increase the company's debt ratio from 59% to 76%, which is more risky than the company's financial position at present. On this basis, a midrange interest rate appears reasonable—at least as the starting point for the negotiation between Goldsmith Inc. and the bank.

You must add $500,000 to the current liabilities and total assets to account for the additional $500,000 loan. Factors to consider:

- The debt ratio increase. Creditors prefer a low debt ratio because it means creditors' claims are only a small percentage of total assets.
- Effect on future cash flows. More debt leads to greater debt repayments and greater interest payments in the future.

Requirement 5

$$\text{Return on sales} = \frac{\$71}{\$330} = 0.215$$

Compared to last year's rate of 0.230 or 23%, this ratio worsened. This would be caused by either a decline in sales, an increase in expenses, or both.

Return on sales = Net income ÷ Sales revenue

Investors and creditors prefer a high rate because it means the company is able to control its expenses

SUMMARY OF CHAPTER 3

Learning Objective ❶: **Relate accrual accounting and cash flows**

Accrual accounting records revenue as it is earned and expenses as they are incurred. **Cash-basis accounting** only records revenue when cash is received and expenses when cash is paid. Companies are required to use accrual accounting.

Accrual accounting is based on accounting concepts and principles such as the time-period concept, the revenue principle.

Learning Objective ❷: **Recognize revenue and record expenses**

The **time-period concept** ensures that accounting information is reported at regular intervals.

The **revenue principle** governs when to record revenue and at what amount.

Expenses are incurred during the normal day-to-day operations. Since they have no future benefit to the company, they should be identified and subtracted from revenue.

Learning Objective ❸: **Adjust the accounts**

Since companies are required to use accrual accounting, adjusting entries are needed to ensure that all revenue is recorded in the period it is earned and expenses are recorded in the same period the revenue was generated. These entries are recorded at the end of the accounting period before the financial statements are prepared. Adjusting entries include deferrals, depreciation, and accruals. **Deferrals** include adjustments for which the business paid or received cash in advance. Examples include prepaid rent, prepaid insurance, and supplies. **Depreciation** spreads the cost of property, plant, and equipment, except land, over its useful life. **Accruals** can be expenses or revenues that occur before the business pays or receives cash. Since accruals are not recorded, an adjusting entry is needed to update the account.

Learning Objective ❹: **Prepare the financial statements**

Once the adjusting entries are recorded and posted to the general ledger, the accounts are listed in an **adjusted trial balance.** The financial statements can be prepared from the adjusted trial balance. The financial statements include the income statement, the statement of retained earnings, and the balance sheet.

Learning Objective ❺: **Close the books**

At the end of the accounting period, **closing entries** are recorded to transfer all revenue, expenses, and the dividend accounts into the retained earnings. **Closing the books** prepares the accounts to begin recording the next period's transactions. Balance sheet accounts are permanent and never closed.

Learning Objective ❻: **Use the financial statements in decision making**

A **classified balance sheet** reports current assets from **long-term assets** and current liabilities from **long-term liabilities**. Managers, investors, and creditors analyze the balance sheet to determine if the company is able to pay its debts. The **current ratio** (current assets divided by current liabilities) measures the company's ability to pay short-term debt. The **debt ratio** (total liabilities divided by total assets) measures the company's ability to pay both current and long-term debt.

The income statement reports all revenue earned less all expenses incurred. When analyzing the income statement, investors and creditors look to see if sales revenue and net income have increased. For the investor, this signals that the selling price of their share could increase and the company will be able to distribute dividends. For the creditor, if a company is profitable, it means that it will be able to pay its debts as they become due.

Review Accrual Accounting and the Financial Statements

Quick Check (Answers are given on page 181.)

1. On September 1, LostForest Apartments Ltd. received $3,600 from a tenant for three months' rent. The receipt was credited to Unearned Rent Revenue. What adjusting entry is needed on September 30?

a. Unearned Rent Revenue	2,400	
Rent Revenue		2,400
b. Rent Revenue	1,200	
Unearned Rent Revenue		1,200
c. Unearned Rent Revenue	1,200	
Rent Revenue		1,200
d. Cash	1,200	
Rent Revenue		1,200

2. The following normal balances appear on the *adjusted* trial balance of Ojibway Industries:

Equipment	$90,000
Accumulated depreciation, equipment	15,000
Depreciation expense, equipment	5,000

The carrying amount of the equipment is
   a. $85,000
   b. $70,000
   c. $75,000
   d. $60,000
3. Jones Company Ltd. purchased supplies for $1,000 during 2011. At year-end Jones had $300 of supplies left. The adjusting entry should
   a. Debit Supplies, $700
   b. Debit Supplies Expense, $700
   c. Credit Supplies, $300
   d. Debit Supplies, $300
4. The accountant for Moreau Ltd. failed to make the adjusting entry to record depreciation for the current year. The effect of this error is
   a. Assets are overstated; shareholders' equity and net income are understated.
   b. Assets and expenses are understated, and net income is understated.
   c. Net income is overstated, and liabilities are understated.
   d. Assets, net income, and shareholders' equity are all overstated.
5. Interest due on a note payable at December 31 equals $125. What adjusting entry is required to accrue this expense?
   a. Dr. Interest Payable for $125, Cr. Interest Expense for $125
   b. Dr. Interest Expense for $125, Cr. Cash for $125
   c. Dr. Interest Receivable for $125, Cr. Interest Revenue for $125
   d. Dr. Interest Expense for $125, Cr. Interest Payable for $125
6. If a real estate company fails to accrue commission revenue,
   a. Liabilities are overstated, and owners' equity is understated.
   b. Assets are understated, and net income is understated.
   c. Net income is understated, and shareholders' equity is overstated.
   d. Revenues are understated, and net income is overstated.
7. All of the following statements are true except one. Which statement is false?
   a. Adjusting entries are required for a business that uses the cash basis.
   b. Accrual accounting produces better information than cash-basis accounting.
   c. Expenses are identified and recorded as they are incurred and deducted from revenue earned during the same period.
   d. A fiscal year ends on some date other than December 31.

8. The account Unearned Revenue is a(n)
   a. Revenue
   b. Expense
   c. Asset
   d. Liability
9. Adjusting entries
   a. Do not debit or credit Cash
   b. Are needed to measure the period's net income or net loss
   c. Update the accounts
   d. All of the above
10. An adjusting entry that debits an expense and credits a related liability is which type?
    a. Accrued expense
    b. Cash expense
    c. Prepaid expense
    d. Depreciation expense

Use the following data for Questions 11 and 12.

Here are key figures from the balance sheet of Davis Ltd. at the end of 2011 (in thousands):

	December 31, 2011
Total assets (of which 40% are current)	$4,000
Current liabilities	800
Bonds payable (long-term)	1,200
Common shares	1,500
Retained earnings	500
Total liabilities and shareholders' equity	$4,000

11. Davis's current ratio at the end of 2011 is
    a. 6.25
    b. 2.0
    c. 3.75
    d. 2.24
12. Davis's debt ratio at the end of 2011 is
    a. 42% (rounded)
    b. 17% (rounded)
    c. 60%
    d. 50%
13. On a trial balance, which of the following would indicate that an error has been made?
    a. Service Revenue has a debit balance.
    b. Salary Expense has a debit balance.
    c. Accumulated Depreciation has a credit balance.
    d. All of the above indicate errors.
14. The entry to close Management Fees Revenue would be
    a. Management Fees Revenue does not need to be closed out
    b. Dr. Retained Earnings Cr. Management Fees Revenue
    c. Dr. Management Fees Revenue Cr. Retained Earnings
    d. Dr. Management Fees Revenue Cr. Service Revenue
15. Which of the following accounts is not closed out?
    a. Accumulated Depreciation
    b. Depreciation Expense
    c. Dividends
    d. Interest Revenue
16. Suppose Starbucks Corporation borrows $50 million on a 10-year note payable. How does this transaction affect the company's current and debt ratios?
    a. Improves both ratios
    b. Improves the current ratio and hurts the debt ratio
    c. Hurts both ratios
    d. Hurts the current ratio and improves the debt ratio

S3-8 Return to the situation in Short Exercise 3-7. Here you are accounting for the same transactions on the books of Scotiabank, which lent the money to Schwartz & Associates Inc. Perform all three steps in Short Exercise 3-7 for Scotiabank using the bank's own accounts.

Learning Objective 3
Accruing and receiving cash from interest revenue

S3-9 Write a paragraph to explain why unearned revenues are liabilities instead of revenues. In your explanation, use the following actual example: *Maclean's* magazine collects cash from subscribers in advance and later delivers magazines to subscribers over a one-year period. Explain what happens to the unearned subscription revenue over the course of a year as *Maclean's* delivers magazines to subscribers. Into what account does the unearned subscription revenue go as *Maclean's* delivers magazines?

Learning Objective 3
Explaining unearned revenues

Give the journal entries that *Maclean's* would make to:

a. Collect $40,000 of subscription revenue in advance.
b. Record earning $10,000 of subscription revenue.

Include an explanation for each entry, as illustrated in the chapter.

S3-10 Birdie Golf Ltd. prepaid three months' rent ($6,000) on January 1. At March 31, Birdie prepared a trial balance and made the necessary adjusting entry at the end of the quarter. Birdie adjusts its accounts every quarter of the fiscal year, which ends December 31.

Learning Objective 4
Reporting prepaid expenses

What amount appears for Prepaid Rent on

a. Birdie's unadjusted trial balance at March 31?
b. Birdie's adjusted trial balance at March 31?

What amount appears for Rent Expense on

a. Birdie's unadjusted trial balance at March 31?
b. Birdie's adjusted trial balance at March 31?

S3-11 Josie Inc. collects cash from customers two ways:

Learning Objective 3
Updating the accounts

1. Accrued Revenue. Some customers pay Josie after Josie has performed service for the customer. During 2011, Josie made sales of $50,000 on account and later received cash of $40,000 on account from these customers.
2. Unearned Revenue. A few customers pay Josie in advance, and Josie later performs service for the customer. During 2011, Josie collected $7,000 cash in advance and later earned $6,000 of this amount.

Journalize the following for Josie:

a. Earning service revenue of $50,000 on account and then collecting $40,000 on account
b. Receiving $7,000 in advance and then earning $6,000 as service revenue

Explanations are not required.

S3-12 Entertainment Centre Ltd. reported the following data at March 31, 2011, with amounts adapted and in thousands:

Learning Objective 4
Preparing the financial statements

Retained earnings, March 31, 2010	$ 1,300	Cost of goods sold	$126,000
Accounts receivable	27,700	Cash	900
Net revenues	174,500	Property and equipment, net	7,200
Total current liabilities	53,600	Common shares	26,000
All other expenses	45,000	Inventories	33,000
Other current assets	4,800	Long-term liabilities	13,500
Other assets	24,300	Dividends	0

You are the CFO responsible for reporting Entertainment Centre Ltd. (ECL) results. Use these data to prepare ECL's income statement for the year ended March 31, 2011, the statement of retained earnings for the year ended March 31, 2011; and the classified balance sheet at March 31, 2011. Use the report format for the balance sheet. Draw arrows linking the three statements to explain the information flows between the statements.

Learning Objective 6
Using the financial statements in decision making

S3-13 Use the Entertainment Centre Ltd. data in Short Exercise 3-12 to make the company's closing entries at March 31, 2011. Then set up a T-account for Retained Earnings and post to that account. Compare Retained Earnings' ending balance to the amount reported on ECL's statement of retained earnings and balance sheet. What do you find? Why is this important?

Learning Objective 6
Using the financial statements

S3-14 Use the Entertainment Centre Ltd. data in Short Exercise 3-12 to compute ECL's

a. Current ratio
b. Debt ratio
c. Return on sales ratio

Round to two decimal places. Report to the CEO whether these values look strong, weak, or middle-of-the-road.

Learning Objective 6
Using the financial statements

S3-15 Use the Entertainment Centre Ltd. data in Short Exercise 3-12 to compute ECL' s return on sales.

1. Was the net revenue high enough to cover all of ECL's cost?
2. What could you do to increase this ratio?

Exercises

Learning Objective 1
Relating accrual accounting and cash flows

E3-16 During 2011, Organic Foods Inc. made sales of $4,000 (assume all on account) and collected cash of $4,100 from customers. Operating expenses totalled $800, all paid in cash. At December 31, 2011, Organic Foods' customers owed the company $400. Organic Foods owed creditors $700 on account. All amounts are in millions.

1. For these facts, show what Organic Foods Inc. would report on the following 2011 financial statements:
   - Income statement
   - Balance sheet
2. Suppose Organic Foods had used cash-basis accounting. What would Organic Foods Ltd. have reported for these facts?

Learning Objective 1
Relating accrual accounting and cash flows

E3-17 During 2011, Valley Sales Inc. earned revenues of $500,000 on account. Valley Sales collected $410,000 from customers during the year. Expenses totalled $420,000, and the related cash payments were $400,000. Show what Valley Sales would report on its 2011 income statement under the

a. Cash basis
b. Accrual basis

Compute net income under both bases of accounting. Which basis measures net income more appropriately? Explain your answer.

Learning Objective 1 2
Accrual basis of accounting, recognizing revenue and recording expenses

E3-18 During 2011, Dish Networks Inc. earned revenues of $700 million. Expenses totalled $540 million. Dish collected all but $20 million of the revenues and paid $530 million on its expenses. Dish's top managers are evaluating the year, and they ask you the following questions:

a. Under accrual accounting, what amount of revenue should the company report for 2011? Is the $700 million revenue earned or is it the amount of cash actually collected?
b. Under accrual accounting, what amount of total expense should Dish report for the year—$540 million or $530 million?
c. Which financial statement reports revenues and expenses? Which statement reports cash receipts and cash payments?

Learning Objective 2
Recognizing revenue and recording expenses

E3-19 Write a short paragraph to explain in your own words the concept of depreciation as used in accounting.

E3-20 Identify the basis on which to account for each of the following situations:

Learning Objective 2
Recognizing revenue and recording expenses

a. Salary expense of $20,000 is accrued at the end of the period to measure income properly.
b. October has been a particularly slow month, and the business will have a net loss for the third quarter of the year. Management is considering not following its customary practice of reporting quarterly earnings to the public.
c. A dentist performs a surgical operation and bills the patient's insurance company. It may take three months to collect from the insurance company. Should the dentist record revenue now or wait until cash is collected?
d. A construction company is building a highway system, and construction will take three years. How do you think it should record the revenue it earns over the year or over three years?
e. A utility bill is received on December 30 and will be paid next year. When should the company record utility expense?

E3-21 An accountant made the following adjustments at December 31, the end of the accounting period:

Learning Objective 1 3
Journalizing adjusting entries and analyzing their effects on net income; accrual versus cash basis

a. Prepaid insurance, beginning, $700. Payments for insurance during the period, $2,100. Prepaid insurance, ending, $800
b. Interest revenue accrued, $900
c. Unearned service revenue, beginning, $800. Unearned service revenue, ending, $300
d. Depreciation, $6,200
e. Employees' salaries owed for three days of a five-day work week; weekly payroll, $9,000
f. Income before income tax expense, $20,000. Income tax rate is 25%.

Required

1. Journalize the adjusting entries.
2. Suppose the adjustments were not made. Compute the overall overstatement or understatement of net income as a result of the omission of these adjustments.

E3-22 Green Leaf Fertilizer Ltd. experienced four situations for its supplies. Compute the amounts indicated by question marks for each situation. For situations 1 and 2, journalize the needed transaction. Consider each situation separately.

Learning Objective 2 3
Allocating supplies cost to the asset and the expenses, adjusting the accounts

	Situation			
	1	2	3	4
Beginning supplies	$ 500	$1,000	$ 300	$ 900
Payments for supplies during the year	?	3,100	?	1,100
Total amount to account for	$1,300	?	?	2,000
Ending supplies	400	500	700	?
Supplies expense	$ 900	$?	$ 700	$1,400

E3-23 Clark Motors Ltd. faced the following situations. Journalize the adjusting entry needed at year-end (December 31, 2011) for each situation. Consider each fact separately.

Learning Objective 3
Journalizing adjusting entries

a. The business has interest expense of $9,000 early in January 2012.
b. Interest revenue of $3,000 has been earned but not yet received.
c. When the business collected $12,000 in advance three months ago, the accountant debited Cash and credited Unearned Revenue. The client was paying for two cars, one delivered in December, the other to be delivered in February 2012.
d. Salary expense is $1,000 per day—Monday through Friday—and the business pays employees each Friday. For example purposes, assume that this year, December 31 falls on a Tuesday.
e. The unadjusted balance of the Supplies account is $3,100. The total cost of supplies on hand is $800.
f. Equipment was purchased at the beginning of this year at a cost of $60,000. The equipment's useful life is five years. Record the depreciation for this year and then determine the equipment's carrying amount.

Learning Objective 3
Making adjustments in T-accounts

E3-24 The accounting records of Lalonde Ltée include the following unadjusted balances at May 31: Accounts Receivable, $1,300; Supplies, $900; Salary Payable, $0; Unearned Service Revenue, $800; Service Revenue, $14,400; Salary Expense, $4,200; Supplies Expense, $0. As Lalonde's accountant you have developed the following data for the May 31 adjusting entries:

a. Supplies on hand, $300
b. Salary owed to employees, $2,000
c. Service revenue accrued, $600
d. Unearned service revenue that has been earned, $700

Open the foregoing T-accounts with their beginning balances. Then record the adjustments directly in the accounts, keying each adjustment amount by letter. Show each account's adjusted balance. Journal entries are not required.

Learning Objective 4
Preparing the financial statements

E3-25 The adjusted trial balance of Honeybee Hams Inc. follows.

Honeybee Hams Inc.
Adjusted Trial Balance
December 31, 2011

	Adjusted Trial Balance	
(in thousands)	Debit	Credit
Cash	$ 3,300	
Accounts receivable	1,800	
Inventories	1,100	
Prepaid expenses	1,900	
Capital assets	6,600	
Accumulated depreciation		$ 2,400
Other assets	9,900	
Accounts payable		7,700
Income tax payable		600
Other liabilities		2,200
Common shares		4,900
Retained earnings (December 31, 2010)		4,500
Dividends	1,700	
Sales revenue		41,000
Cost of goods sold	25,000	
Selling, administrative, and general expense	10,000	
Income tax expense	2,000	
	$63,300	$63,300

Required
Prepare Honeybee Hams' income statement and statement of retained earnings for the year ended December 31, 2011, and its balance sheet on that date. Draw arrows linking the three statements.

Learning Objective 3
Measuring financial statement amounts

E3-26 The adjusted trial balances of Tower Development Inc. for March 31, 2010, and March 31, 2011, include these amounts (in millions):

	2011	2010
Receivables	$300	$200
Prepaid insurance	180	110
Accrued liabilities (for other operating expenses)	700	600

Tower Development completed these transactions during the year ended March 31, 2011.

Collections from customers	$20,800
Payment of prepaid insurance	400
Cash payments for other operating expenses	4,100

Compute the amount of sales revenue, insurance expense, and other operating expense to report on the income statement for the year ended March 31, 2011.

E3-27 This question deals with the items and the amounts that two entities, Mountain Services Inc. (Mountain) and City of Squamish (Squamish), should report in their financial statements.

Learning Objective 4
Reporting on the financial statements

1. On March 31, 2011, Mountain collected $12,000 in advance from Squamish, a client. Under the contract, Mountain is obligated to provide consulting services for Squamish evenly during the year ended March 31, 2011. Assume you are Mountain.

   Mountain's income statement for the year ended December 31, 2011, will report _____ of $_____.

   Mountain's balance sheet at December 31, 2011, will report _____ of $_____.
2. Assume that you are Squamish. Squamish's income statement for the year ended December 31, 2011, will report _____ of $_____.

   Squamish's balance sheet at December 31, 2011, will report _____ of $_____.

E3-28 This exercise builds from a simple situation to a slightly more complex situation. Rogers, the Canadian wireless phone service provider, collects cash in advance from customers. All amounts are in millions.

Learning Objective 1 3
Relating deferrals and cash flows

Assume Rogers collected $400 in advance during 2011 and at year-end still owed customers phone service worth $90.

Required

1. Show what Rogers will report for 2011 on its
   - Income statement
   - Balance sheet
2. Use the same facts for Rogers as in Requirement 1. Further, assume Rogers reported unearned service revenue of $80 at the end of 2010.

Show what Rogers will report for 2011 on the same financial statements. Explain why your answer differs from your answer to Requirement 1.

E3-29 Prepare the required closing entries for the following selected accounts from the records of SouthWest Transport Inc. at December 31, 2011 (amounts in thousands):

Learning Objective 5
Closing the accounts

Cost of services sold	$11,600	Service Revenue	$23,600
Accumulated depreciation	17,800	Depreciatiation expense	4,100
Selling, general, and administrative expense	6,900	Other revenue	600
		Income tax expense	400
Retained earnings, December 31, 2010	1,900	Dividends	400
		Income tax payable	300

How much net income did SouthWest Transport Inc. earn during the year ended December 31, 2011? Prepare a T-account for Retained Earnings to show the December 31, 2011, balance of Retained Earnings.

Learning Objective 3 5
Identifying and recording adjusting and closing entries

E3-30 The unadjusted trial balance and income statement amounts from the December 31, 2011, adjusted trial balance of Yosaf Portraits Ltd. are given below.

Yosaf Portraits Ltd.
Trial Balance
December 31, 2011

Account Title	Unadjusted Trial Balance		From the Adjusted Trial Balance	
Cash	10,200			
Prepaid rent	1,100			
Equipment	32,100			
Accumulated depreciation		3,800		
Accounts payable		4,600		
Salary payable				
Unearned service revenue		8,400		
Income tax payable				
Note payable, long term		10,000		
Common shares		8,700		
Retained earnings		1,300		
Dividends	1,000			
Service revenue		12,800		19,500
Salary expense	4,000		4,900	
Rent expense	1,200		1,400	
Depreciation expense			300	
Income tax expense			1,600	
	49,600	49,600	8,200	19,500
Net income			11,300	
			19,500	19,500

Required
Journalize the adjusting and closing entries of Yosaf Portraits Ltd. at December 31, 2011. There was only one adjustment to Service Revenue.

Learning Objective 4 6
Preparing a classified balance sheet and using the financial statements

E3-31 Refer to Exercise 3-30.

Required
1. After solving Exercise 3-30, use the data in that exercise to prepare Yosaf Portraits Ltd.'s classified balance sheet at December 31, 2011. Use the report format. First you must compute the adjusted balance for several balance sheet accounts.
2. Compute Yosaf Portraits Ltd.'s current ratio and debt ratio at December 31, 2011. A year ago, the current ratio was 1.55 and the debt ratio was 0.45. Indicate whether the company's ability to pay its debts—both current and total—improved or deteriorated during the current year.

Learning Objective 6
Using the financial statements

E3-32 Le Gasse Inc. reported this information at December 31:

	2011	2010	2009
Current assets	$ 20	$ 15	$ 8
Total assets	50	57	35
Current liabilities	10	8	6
Total liabilities	20	20	10
Sales revenue	204	190	175
Net income	28	20	25

Required

1. Using this information, calculate the current ratio, the debt ratio, and the return on sales ratio for 2011, 2010, and 2009.
2. Explain whether each ratio improved or deteriorated over the three years. In each case, what does your answer indicate?

Serial Exercise

Exercise 3-33 continues the Web Marketing Services Inc. situation begun in Exercise 2-25 of Chapter 2 (p. 101).

E3-33

Learning Objective 3 4 5 6
Adjusting the accounts, preparing the financial statements, closing the accounts, and using financial statements to evaluate the business

Refer to Exercise 2-25 of Chapter 2. Start from the trial balance and the posted T-accounts prepared at January 18, 2011. Later in January, the business completed these transactions:

2011		
Jan.	21	Received $900 in advance for marketing work to be performed evenly over the next 30 days
	21	Hired a secretary to be paid on the 15th day of each month
	26	Paid $900 on account
	28	Collected $600 on account
	31	Declared and paid dividends of $1,000

Required

1. Open these T-accounts: Accumulated Depreciation—Equipment, Accumulated Depreciation—Furniture, Salary Payable, Unearned Service Revenue, Retained Earnings, Depreciation Expense—Equipment, Depreciation Expense—Furniture, and Supplies Expense. Also, use the T-accounts opened for Exercise 2-25.
2. Journalize the transactions of January 21 through 31.
3. Post the January 21 to January 31 transactions to the T-accounts, keying all items by date. Denote account balances as Bal.
4. Prepare a trial balance at January 31. Also set up columns for the adjustments and for the adjusted trial balance, as illustrated in Exhibit 3-7, on page 135.
5. At January 31, 2011, the following information is gathered for the adjusting entries:
   a. Accrued service revenue, $1,000
   b. Earned $300 of the service revenue collected in advance on January 21
   c. Supplies on hand, $300
   d. Depreciation expense—equipment, $100; furniture, $200
   e. Accrued expense for secretary's salary, $1,000.

   Make these adjustments directly in the adjustments columns and complete the adjusted trial balance at January 31, 2011.
6. Journalize and post the adjusting entries. Denote each adjusting amount as Adj. and an account balance as Bal.
7. Prepare the income statement and statement of retained earnings of Web Marketing Services Inc. for the month ended January 31, 2011, and the classified balance sheet at that date. Draw arrows to link the financial statements.
8. Journalize and post the closing entries at January 31, 2011. Denote each closing amount as Clo. and an account balance as Bal.
9. Using the information you have prepared, compute the current ratio and the debt ratio of Web Marketing Services Inc. (to two decimals) and evaluate these ratio values as indicative of a strong or weak financial position.
10. Using the information you have prepared, compute the return on sales of Web Marketing Services Inc. (to two decimals) and evaluate the ratio value as indicative of the company's profitability.

Challenge Exercises

Learning Objective ❸❹❻
Computing financial statement amounts, using the financial statements

E3-34 Valley Bleu Ltée reported the following current accounts at December 31, 2010 (amounts in thousands):

a. Cash	$1,700
b. Receivables	5,600
c. Inventory	1,800
d. Prepaid expenses	800
e. Accounts payable	2,400
f. Unearned revenue	1,200
g. Accrued expenses payable	1,700

During 2011, Valley Bleu completes these transactions:

- Used inventory of $3,800
- Sold services on account, $6,500
- Depreciation expense, $400
- Paid for accrued expenses, $500
- Collected from customers on account, $7,500
- Accrued expenses, $1,300
- Purchased inventory of $3,500 on account
- Paid on account, $5,000
- Used up prepaid expenses, $600

Compute Valley Bleu's current ratio at December 31, 2010, and again at December 31, 2011. Did the current ratio improve or deteriorate during 2011? Comment on the company's current ratio.

Learning Objective ❸❹
Computing financial statement amounts

E3-35 The accounts of Maritime Specialists Ltd. prior to the year-end adjustments are given below.

Cash	$ 4,000	Common shares	$ 10,000
Accounts receivable	7,000	Retained earnings	43,000
Supplies	4,000	Dividends	16,000
Prepaid insurance	3,000	Service revenue	155,000
Building	107,000	Salary expense	32,000
Accumulated depreciation—building	14,000	Depreciation expense—building	
Land	51,000	Supplies expense	
Accounts payable	6,000	Insurance expense	
Salary payable		Advertising expense	7,000
Unearned service revenue	5,000	Utilities expense	2,000

Adjusting data at the end of the year include:

a. Unearned service revenue that has been earned, $1,000
b. Accrued service revenue, $2,000
c. Supplies used in operations, $3,000
d. Accrued salary expense, $3,000
e. Prepaid insurance expired, $1,000
f. Depreciation expense, building, $2,000

Jon Whale, the principal shareholder, has received an offer to sell Maritime Specialists. He needs to know the following information within one hour:

a. Net income for the year covered by these data
b. Total assets
c. Total liabilities

d. Total shareholders' equity
e. Proof that Total assets = Total liabilities + Total shareholders' equity, after all items are updated

Required
Without opening any accounts, making any journal entries, or using a worksheet, provide Whale with the requested information. The business is not subject to income tax. Show all computations.

Quiz

Test your understanding of accrual accounting by answering the following questions. Select the best choice from among the possible answers given.

Questions 36 through 38 are based on the following facts:

Freddie Handel began a music business in July 2011. Handel prepares monthly financial statements and uses the accrual basis of accounting. The following transactions are Handel Company's only activities during July through October:

July 14	Bought music on account for $10, with payment to the supplier due in 90 days
Aug. 3	Performed a job on account for Joey Bach for $25, collectible from Bach in 30 days. Used up all the music purchased on July 14
Sept. 16	Collected the $25 receivable from Bach
Oct. 22	Paid the $10 owed to the supplier from the July 14 transaction

Q3-36 In which month should Handel record the cost of the music as an expense?
a. July
b. August
c. September
d. October

Q3-37 In which month should Handel report the $25 revenue on its income statement?
a. July
b. August
c. September
d. October

Q3-38 If Handel Company uses the *cash* basis of accounting instead of the accrual basis, in what month will Handel report revenue and in what month will it report expense?

	Revenue	Expense
a.	September	October
b.	September	July
c.	August	October
d.	September	August

Q3-39 In which month should revenue be recorded?
a. In the month that goods are ordered by the customer
b. In the month that goods are shipped to the customer
c. In the month that the invoice is mailed to the customer
d. In the month that cash is collected from the customer

Q3-40 On January 1 of the current year, Aladdin Company paid $600 rent to cover six months (January through June). Aladdin recorded this transaction as follows:

Prepaid Rent	600	
Cash		600

Aladdin adjusts the accounts at the end of each month. Based on these facts, the adjusting entry at the end of January should include

a. A credit to Prepaid Rent for $500
b. A debit to Prepaid Rent for $500
c. A debit to Prepaid Rent for $100
d. A credit to Prepaid Rent for $100

Q3-41 Assume the same facts as in the previous problem. Aladdin's adjusting entry at the end of February should include a debit to Rent Expense in the amount of

a. $0
b. $500
c. $200
d. $100

Q3-42 What effect does the adjusting entry in Question 3-41 have on Aladdin's net income for February?

a. Increase by $100
b. Increase by $200
c. Decrease by $100
d. Decrease by $200

Q3-43 An adjusting entry recorded March salary expense that will be paid in April. Which statement best describes the effect of this adjusting entry on the company's accounting equation at the end of March?

a. Assets are not affected, liabilities are decreased, and shareholders' equity is decreased.
b. Assets are decreased, liabilities are increased, and shareholders' equity is decreased.
c. Assets are not affected, liabilities are increased, and shareholders' equity is decreased.
d. Assets are decreased, liabilities are not affected, and shareholders' equity is decreased.

Q3-44 On April 1, 2011, Metro Insurance Company sold a one-year insurance policy covering the year ended April 1, 2012. Metro collected the full $1,200 on April 1, 2011. Metro made the following journal entry to record the receipt of cash in advance:

	Debit	Credit
Cash	1,200	
Unearned Revenue		1,200

Nine months have passed, and Metro has made no adjusting entries. Based on these facts, the adjusting entry needed by Metro at December 31, 2011, is

		Debit	Credit
a.	Unearned Revenue	300	
	Insurance Revenue		300
b.	Insurance Revenue	300	
	Unearned Revenue		300
c.	Unearned Revenue	900	
	Insurance Revenue		900
d.	Insurance Revenue	900	
	Unearned Revenue		900

Q3-45 The Unearned Revenue account of Dean Incorporated began 2011 with a normal balance of $5,000 and ended 2011 with a normal balance of $12,000. During 2011, the Unearned Revenue account was credited for $19,000 that Dean will earn later. Based on these facts, how much revenue did Dean earn in 2011?

a. $5,000
b. $19,000
c. $24,000
d. $12,000

Q3-46 What is the effect on the financial statements of *recording* depreciation on equipment?

a. Assets are decreased, but net income and shareholders' equity are not affected.
b. Net income, assets, and shareholders' equity are all decreased.
c. Net income and assets are decreased, but shareholders' equity is not affected.
d. Net income is not affected, but assets and shareholders' equity are decreased.

Q3-47 For 2011, Monterrey Company had revenues in excess of expenses. Which statement describes Monterrey's closing entries at the end of 2011?

a. Revenues will be debited, expenses will be credited, and retained earnings will be debited.
b. Revenues will be credited, expenses will be debited, and retained earnings will be debited.
c. Revenues will be debited, expenses will be credited, and retained earnings will be credited.
d. Revenues will be credited, expenses will be debited, and retained earnings will be credited.

Q3-48 Which of the following accounts would *not* be included in the closing entries?

a. Accumulated Depreciation
b. Service Revenue
c. Depreciation Expense
d. Retained Earnings

Q3-49 A major purpose of preparing closing entries is to

a. Zero out the liability accounts
b. Close out the Supplies account
c. Adjust the asset accounts to their correct current balances
d. Update the Retained Earnings account

Q3-50 Selected data for Austin Company follow:

Current assets	$50,000	Current liabilities	$40,000
Capital assets	70,000	Long-term liabilities	35,000
Total revenues	30,000	Total expenses	20,000

Based on these facts, what are Austin's ratios?

	Current ratio	Debt ratio	Net income as % of revenue
a.	2 to 1	0.5 to 1	0.25
b.	0.83 to 1	0.5 to 1	0.38
c.	1.25 to 1	0.625 to 1	0.33
d.	2 to 1	0.633 to 1	0.29

Problems

(Group A)

P3-51A Lewitas Ltd. earned revenues of $35 million during 2011 and ended the year with income of $8 million. During 2011, Lewitas Ltd. collected $33 million from customers and paid cash for all of its expenses plus an additional $1 million for accounts payable. Answer these questions about Lewitas's operating results, financial position, and cash flows during 2011:

Learning Objective 1
Relating accrual accounting and cash flows

Required

1. How much were the company's total expenses? Show your work.
2. Identify all the items that Lewitas will report on its 2011 income statement. Show each amount.
3. Lewitas began 2011 with receivables of $4 million. All sales were on account. What was the company's receivables balance at the end of 2011? Identify the appropriate financial statement, and show how Lewitas will report ending receivables in the 2011 annual report.
4. Lewitas began 2011 owing accounts payable totalling $9 million. How much in accounts payable did the company owe at the end of the year? Identify the appropriate financial statement, and show how Lewitas will report these accounts payable in its 2011 annual report.

Learning Objective 1
Cash basis versus accrual basis

P3-52A Prairies Consultants Inc. had the following selected transactions in August 2011:

Aug.	1	Prepaid insurance for August through December, $1,000
	4	Purchased software for cash, $800
	5	Performed service and received cash, $900
	8	Paid advertising expense, $300
	11	Performed service on account, $3,000
	19	Purchased computer on account, $1,600
	24	Collected for the August 11 service
	26	Paid account payable from August 19
	29	Paid salary expense, $900
	31	Adjusted for August insurance expense (see Aug. 1)
	31	Earned revenue of $800 that was collected in advance in July

Required

1. Show how each transaction would be handled using the cash basis and the accrual basis. Under each column, give the amount of revenue or expense for August. Journal entries are not required. Use the following format for your answer, and show your computations. Assume depreciation expense of $30 for software and $30 for the computer.

Prairies Consultants Inc.
Amount of Revenue (Expense) for August 2011

Date	Cash Basis	Accrual Basis

2. Compute August income (loss) before tax under each accounting method.
3. Indicate which measure of net income or net loss is preferable. Use the transactions on August 11 and 24 to explain.

Learning Objective 1 2
Applying accounting principles

P3-53A Write a memo to explain to a new employee the difference between the cash basis of accounting and the accrual basis. Mention the basis on which revenues and expenses are recorded under each method.

Learning Objective 3
Relating accrual accounting and cash flows, recognizing revenue and recording expenses

P3-54A Journalize the adjusting entry needed on December 31, 2011, the end of the current accounting period, for each of the following independent cases affecting Callaway Corp. Include an explanation for each entry.

a. Details of Prepaid Insurance are shown in the account:

Prepaid Insurance

Jan. 1	Bal.	400	
Mar. 31		3,600	

Callaway prepays insurance on March 31 each year. At December 31, $900 is still prepaid.

b. Callaway pays employees each Friday. The amount of the weekly payroll is $6,000 for a five-day work week. The current accounting period ends on Wednesday.
c. Callaway has a note receivable. During the current year, the company has earned accrued interest revenue of $500 that it will receive next year.
d. The beginning balance of Supplies was $2,600. During the year, Callaway purchased supplies costing $6,100, and at December 31 the cost of supplies on hand is $2,100.
e. Callaway is providing financial services for Manatawabi Investments Inc., and the owner of Manatawabi paid Callaway $12,000 for its annual service fee. Callaway recorded this amount as Unearned Service Revenue. Callaway estimates that it has earned one-third of the total fee during the current year.
f. Depreciation for the current year includes Office Furniture, $1,000, and Equipment, $2,700. Make a compound entry.

P3-55A The unadjusted trial balance of The Rock Industries Ltd. at January 31, 2011, appears below.

Learning Objective 3 4 6
Preparing an adjusted trial balance and the financial statements; using the financial statements to evaluate the business

The Rock Industries Ltd.
Trial Balance
January 31, 2011

Cash	$ 8,000	
Accounts receivable	10,000	
Prepaid rent	3,000	
Supplies	2,000	
Furniture	36,000	
Accumulated depreciation		$ 3,000
Accounts payable		10,000
Salary payable		
Common shares		26,000
Retained earnings (December 31, 2010)		13,000
Dividends	4,000	
Service revenue		14,000
Salary expense	2,000	
Rent expense		
Utilities expense	1,000	
Depreciation expense		
Supplies expense		
Total	$66,000	$66,000

Adjustment data:

a. Accrued service revenue at January 31, $2,000
b. Prepaid rent expired during the month. The unadjusted prepaid balance of $3,000 relates to the period January through March.
c. Supplies used during January, $2,000
d. Depreciation on furniture for the month. The estimated useful life of the furniture is three years.
e. Accrued salary expense at January 31 for Monday, Tuesday, and Wednesday. The five-day weekly payroll of $5,000 will be paid on Friday, February 2.

Required

1. Using Exhibit 3-7, page 135, as an example, prepare the adjusted trial balance of The Rock Industries Ltd. at January 31, 2011. Key each adjusting entry by letter.
2. Prepare the income statement, the statement of retained earnings, and the classified balance sheet. Draw arrows linking the three financial statements.
   a. Compare the business's net income for January using the information prepared in questions 1 and 2 to the amount of dividends paid to the owners. Suppose this trend continues each month for the remainder of 2011. What will be the effect on the business's financial position, as shown by its accounting equation?
   b. Will the trend make it easier or more difficult to borrow money if the business gets in a bind and needs cash? Why?
   c. Does either the current ratio or the cash position suggest the need for immediate borrowing? Explain.
   d. Does the return on sales suggest that services are appropriately priced? Explain.

Learning Objective 3
Analyzing and recording adjustments

P3-56A Sundance Apartments Inc.'s unadjusted and adjusted trial balance at April 30, 2011, follow:

Sundance Apartments Inc.
Adjusted Trial Balance
April 30, 2011

	Trial Balance		Adjusted Trial Balance	
Account Title	**Debit**	**Credit**	**Debit**	**Credit**
Cash	$ 8,300		$ 8,300	
Accounts receivable	6,300		6,800	
Interest receivable			300	
Note receivable	4,100		4,100	
Supplies	900		200	
Prepaid insurance	2,400		700	
Building	66,400		66,400	
Accumulated depreciation		$16,000		$ 18,200
Accounts payable		6,900		6,900
Wages payable				400
Unearned rental revenue		600		100
Common shares		18,000		18,000
Retained earnings		42,700		42,700
Dividends	3,600		3,600	
Rental revenue		9,900		10,900
Interest revenue				300
Wages expense	1,600		2,000	
Insurance expense			1,700	
Depreciation expense			2,200	
Property tax expense	300		300	
Supplies expense			700	
Utilities expense	200		200	
	$94,100	$94,100	$97,500	$97,500

Required

1. Make the adjusting entries that account for the differences between the two trial balances.
2. Compute Sundance Apartments Inc.'s total assets, total liabilities, total equity, and net income. Prove your answer with the accounting equation.

Learning Objective 4 6
Preparing the financial statements and using the financial statements to evaluate a business

P3-57A The adjusted trial balance of Marshall Ltd. at December 31, 2011, is given on page 169.

Required

1. Prepare Marshall Ltd.'s 2011 income statement, statement of retained earnings, and balance sheet. List expenses (except for income tax) in decreasing order on the income statement, and show total liabilities on the balance sheet. Draw arrows linking the three financial statements.
2. Marshall Ltd.'s lenders require that the company maintain a debt ratio no higher than 0.50. Compute Marshall Ltd.'s debt ratio at December 31, 2011, to determine whether the company is in compliance with this debt restriction. If not, suggest a way that Marshall Ltd. could have avoided this difficult situation.

Marshall Ltd.
Adjusted Trial Balance
December 31, 2011

Cash	$ 1,400	
Accounts receivable	8,900	
Supplies	2,300	
Prepaid rent	1,600	
Equipment	37,100	
Accumulated depreciation		$ 4,300
Accounts payable		3,700
Interest payable		800
Unearned service revenue		600
Income tax payable		2,100
Note payable		18,600
Common shares		5,000
Retained earnings		1,000
Dividends	24,000	
Service revenue		107,900
Depreciation expense	1,600	
Salary expense	39,900	
Rent expense	10,300	
Interest expense	3,100	
Insurance expense	3,800	
Supplies expense	2,900	
Income tax expense	7,100	
Total	$144,000	$144,000

Learning Objective 5
Closing the books and evaluating retained earnings

P3-58A The accounts of Marciano Services Ltd. at March 31, 2011, are listed in alphabetical order.

Accounts payable	$14,700	Insurance expense	600
Accounts receivable	16,500	Note payable, long-term	6,200
Accumulated depreciation—		Other assets	14,100
equipment	7,100	Prepaid expenses	5,300
Advertising expense	10,900	Retained earnings, March 31, 2010	20,200
Depreciation expense	1,900	Salary expense	17,800
Cash	7,500	Salary payable	2,400
Common shares	9,100	Service revenue	94,100
Current portion of note payable	800	Supplies	3,800
Dividends	31,200	Supplies expense	4,600
Equipment	43,200	Unearned service revenue	2,800

Required

1. All adjustments have been journalized and posted, but the closing entries have not been made. Journalize Marciano Ltd.'s closing entries at March 31, 2011.
2. Set up a T-account for Retained Earnings and post to that account. Compute Marciano's net income for the year ended March 31, 2011. What is the ending balance of Retained Earnings?
3. Did retained earnings increase or decrease during the year? What caused the increase or the decrease?

Learning Objective 4 6
Preparing a classified balance sheet and using the financial statements to evaluate the business

P3-59A Refer to Problem 3-58A.

1. Use the Marciano Ltd. data in Problem 3-58A to prepare the company's classified balance sheet at March 31, 2011. Show captions for total assets, total liabilities, and total liabilities and shareholders' equity.

2. Evaluate Marciano's debt position as strong or weak, giving your reason. Assess whether Marciano's ability to pay both current and total debts improved or deteriorated during 2011. In order to complete your evaluation, compute Marciano's current and debt ratios at March 31, 2011, rounding to two decimal places. At March 31, 2010, the current ratio was 1.30 and the debt ratio was 0.30.

Learning Objective 6
Using the financial statements to evaluate a business

P3-60A The balance sheet at December 31, 2009, 2010, and 2011 and income statement for the years ended December 31, 2009, 2010, and 2011 for Ojibway Inc. include the following data:

Ojibway Inc.
Balance Sheet
(in thousands)

	2011	2010	2009
Assets			
Current assets			
Cash	$ 3.0	$ 1.0	$ 0.5
Accounts receivable	8.0	5.0	3.5
Total current assets	11.0	6.0	4.0
Furniture and equipment, net	16.0	9.5	3.0
Total assets	$ 27.0	15.5	$ 7.0
Liabilities			
Current liabilities			
Accounts payable	$ 5.0	$ 4.5	$ 3.0
Salaries payable	1.5	1.0	0.5
Total current liabilities	6.5	5.5	3.5
Notes payable	9.0	5.0	3.5
Total liabilities	15.5	10.5	7.0
Shareholders' equity			
Shareholders' equity	11.5	5.0	0.0
Total liabilities and shareholders 'equity	$ 27.0	$ 15.5	$ 7.0

Ojibway Inc.
Income Statement
(in thousands)

	2011	2010	2009
Revenue			
Service revenue	$100.0	$ 90.0	$ 64.0
Expenses			
Salary	60.0	57.5	46.0
Rent	18.0	16.0	12.0
Supplies	4.0	3.0	2.0
Utilities	4.5	4.0	2.0
Depreciation	5.0	3.0	2.0
Total expenses	91.5	83.5	64.0
Income before taxes	8.5	6.5	0.0
Income tax expense	2.0	1.5	
Net income	$ 6.5	$ 5.0	$ 0.0

Required

Use the years of data to calculate the following:

1. The current ratio for 2009, 2010, and 2011
2. The debt ratio for 2009, 2010, and 2011

3. The return on sales for 2009, 2010, and 2011
4. Evaluate each ratio and determine if the ratio has improved or deteriorated over the three years. Explain what the changes mean.

(Group B)

Learning Objective 1
Relating accrual accounting and cash flows

P3-61B During 2011, Schubert Inc. earned revenues of $19 million from the sale of its products. Schubert ended the year with net income of $4 million. Schubert collected cash of $20 million from customers.

Answer these questions about Schubert's operating results, financial position, and cash flows during 2011:

1. How much were Schubert's total expenses? Show your work.
2. Identify all the items that Schubert will report on its income statement for 2011. Show each amount.
3. Schubert began 2011 with receivables of $6 million. All sales are on account. What was Schubert's receivables balance at the end of 2011? Identify the appropriate financial statement and show how Schubert will report its ending receivables balance in the company's 2011 annual report.
4. Schubert began 2011 owing accounts payable of $9 million. Schubert incurs all expenses on account. During 2011, Schubert paid $18 million on account. How much in accounts payable did Schubert owe at the end of 2011? Identify the appropriate financial statement and show how Schubert will report these accounts payable in its 2011 annual report.

Learning Objective 1
Cash basis versus accrual basis

P3-62B Fred's Catering Ltd. had the following selected transactions during May 2011:

May	1	Received $800 in advance for a banquet to be served later
	5	Paid electricity expenses, $700
	9	Received cash for the day's sales, $2,000
	14	Purchased two food warmers, $1,800
	23	Served a banquet, receiving a note receivable, $700
	31	Accrued salary expense, $900
	31	Prepaid $3,000 building rent for June and July

Required

1. Show how each transaction would be handled using the cash basis and the accrual basis. Under each column, give the amount of revenue or expense for May. Journal entries are not required. Use the following format for your answer, and show your computations. Ignore depreciation expense.

Fred's Catering Ltd.
Amount of Revenue (Expense) for May 2011

Date	Cash Basis	Accrual Basis

2. Compute income (loss) before tax for May under the two accounting methods.
3. Which method better measures income and assets? Use the last transaction to explain.

Learning Objective 1 2
Relating accrual accounting and cash flows, recognizing revenue and recording expenses

P3-63B As the controller of Stuart Enterprises Inc. you have hired a new employee, whom you must train. She objects to making an adjusting entry for accrued utilities at the end of the period. She reasons, "We will pay the utilities soon. Why not wait until payment to record the expense? In the end, the result will be the same." Write a reply to explain to the employee why the adjusting entry is needed for accrued utility expense.

Learning Objective 3
Making accounting adjustments

P3-64B Journalize the adjusting entry needed on December 31, 2011, the end of the current accounting period, for each of the following independent cases affecting Lee Computer Systems Inc. (LCSI). Include explanations for each entry.

a. Each Friday, LCSI pays employees for the current week's work. The amount of the payroll is $5,000 for a five-day work week. The current accounting period ends on Tuesday.
b. LCSI has received notes receivable from some clients for services. During the current year, LCSI has earned accrued interest revenue of $1,100, which will be received next year.
c. The beginning balance of Supplies was $1,800. During the year, LCSI purchased supplies costing $12,500, and at December 31 the inventory of supplies on hand is $2,900.
d. LCSI is developing software for a client and the client paid LCSI $20,000 at the start of the project. LCSI recorded this amount as Unearned Service Revenue. The software development will take several months to complete. LCSI executives estimate that the company has earned three-quarters of the total fee during the current year.
e. Depreciation for the current year includes Computer Equipment, $6,300, and Building, $3,700. Make a compound entry.
f. Details of Prepaid Insurance are shown in the Prepaid Insurance account. LCSI pays the annual insurance premium (the payment for insurance coverage is called a premium) on September 30 each year. At December 31, nine months of insurance is still prepaid.

Prepaid Insurance

Jan. 1	Bal.	1,800	
Sept. 30		3,600	

Learning Objective 3 4 6
Preparing an adjusted trial balance and the financial statements; using the current ratio to evaluate the business

P3-65B Consider the unadjusted trial balance of Creative Advertising Ltd. at October 31, 2011, and the related month-end adjustment data.

Creative Advertising Ltd.
Trial Balance
October 31, 2011

Cash	$16,300	
Accounts receivable	7,000	
Prepaid rent	4,000	
Supplies	600	
Computers	36,000	
Accumulated depreciation		$ 3,000
Accounts payable		8,800
Salary payable		
Common shares		15,000
Retained earnings (September 30, 2010)		21,000
Dividends	4,600	
Advertising revenue		25,400
Salary expense	4,400	
Rent expense		
Utilities expense	300	
Depreciation expense		
Supplies expense		
Total	$73,200	$73,200

Adjustment data:

a. Accrued advertising revenue at October 31, $2,900
b. Prepaid rent expired during the month. The unadjusted prepaid balance of $4,000 relates to the period October 2011 through January 2012.
c. Supplies used during October, $200

d. Depreciation on computers for the month. The computer's expected useful life is three years.

e. Accrued salary expense at October 31 for Monday through Thursday; the five-day weekly payroll is $2,000.

Required

1. Using Exhibit 3-7, page 135, as an example, prepare the adjusted trial balance of Creative Advertising Ltd. at October 31, 2011. Key each adjusting entry by letter.
2. Prepare the income statement, the statement of retained earnings, and the classified balance sheet. Draw arrows linking the three financial statements.
3. a. Compare the business's net income for October to the amount of dividends paid to the owners. Suppose this trend continues into November. What will be the effect on the business's financial position, as shown by its accounting equation?
   b. Will the trend make it easier or more difficult for Creative Advertising Ltd. to borrow money if the business gets in a bind and needs cash? Why?
   c. Does either the current ratio or the cash position suggest the need for immediate borrowing? Explain.

P3-66B Your Talent Agency Ltd.'s unadjusted and adjusted trial balances at December 31, 2011, are shown below.

Learning Objective 3
Analyzing and recording adjustments

Your Talent Agency Ltd.
Adjusted Trial Balance
December 31, 2011

	Trial Balance		Adjusted Trial Balance	
Account Title	**Debit**	**Credit**	**Debit**	**Credit**
Cash	$ 4,100		$ 4,100	
Accounts receivable	11,200		12,400	
Supplies	1,000		700	
Prepaid insurance	2,600		900	
Office furniture	21,600		21, 600	
Accumulated depreciation		$ 8,200		$ 9,300
Accounts payable		6,300		6,300
Salary payable				900
Interest payable				400
Note payable		6,000		6,000
Unearned commission revenue		1,500		1,100
Common shares		5,000		5,000
Retained earnings		3,500		3,500
Dividends	18,300		18,300	
Commission revenue		72,800		74,400
Depreciation expense			1,100	
Supplies expense			300	
Utilities expense	4,900		4,900	
Salary expense	26,600		27,500	
Rent expense	12,200		12,200	
Interest expense	800		1,200	
Insurance expense			1,700	
	$103,300	$103,300	$106,900	$106,900

Required

1. Make the adjusting entries that account for the difference between the two trial balances.
2. Compute Your Talent Agency Ltd.'s total assets, total liabilities, total equity, and net income.
3. Prove your answer with the accounting equation.

Learning Objective 4 6
Preparing the financial statements and using the debt ratio

P3-67B The adjusted trial balance of Reid and Campbell Ltd. at December 31, 2011, appears below.

Reid and Campbell Ltd.
Adjusted Trial Balance
December 31, 2011

Cash	$ 11,600	
Accounts receivable	41,400	
Prepaid rent	1,300	
Store furnishings	67,600	
Accumulated depreciation		$ 12,900
Accounts payable		3,600
Deposits		4,500
Interest payable		2,100
Salary payable		900
Income tax payable		8,800
Note payable		26,200
Common shares		12,000
Retained earnings, Dec. 31, 2010		20,300
Dividends	48,000	
Sales		165,900
Depreciation expense	11,300	
Salary expense	44,000	
Rent expense	12,000	
Interest expense	1,200	
Income tax expense	18,800	
Total	$257,200	$257,200

Required

1. Prepare Reid and Campbell Ltd.'s 2011 income statement, statement of retained earnings, and balance sheet. List expenses in decreasing order on the income statement and show total liabilities on the balance sheet. Draw arrows linking the three financial statements.
2. Compute Reid and Campbell Ltd.'s debt ratio at December 31, 2011, rounding to two decimal places. Evaluate the company's debt ratio as strong or weak.

Learning Objective 4 6
Preparing a classified balance sheet and using the ratios to evaluate the business

P3-68B The accounts of For You eTravel Inc. at December 31, 2011, are listed in alphabetical order.

Accounts payable	$ 5,100	Note payable, long-term	$10,600
Accounts receivable	6,600	Other assets	3,600
Accumulated depreciation—furniture	11,600	Retained earnings,	
Advertising expense	2,200	December 31, 2010	5,300
Depreciation expense	1,300	Salary expense	24,600
Cash	7,300	Salary payable	3,900
Common shares	15,000	Service revenue	93,500
Dividends	47,400	Supplies	7,700
Furniture	41,400	Supplies expense	5,700
Interest expense	800	Unearned service revenue	3,600

Required

1. All adjustments have been journalized and posted, but the closing entries have not been made. Journalize For You eTravel Inc.'s closing entries at December 31, 2011.
2. Set up a T-account for Retained Earnings and post to that account. Compute For You's net income for the year ended December 31, 2011. What is the ending balance of Retained Earnings?
3. Did Retained Earnings increase or decrease during the year? What caused the increase or the decrease?

Learning Objective 5
Closing the books and evaluating retained earnings

P3-69B Refer to Problem 3-68B.

1. Use the For You eTravel Inc. data in Problem 3-68B to prepare the company's classified balance sheet at December 31, 2011. Show captions for total assets, total liabilities, and total liabilities and shareholders' equity.
2. Evaluate For You's debt position as strong or weak, giving your reason. Assess whether For You's ability to pay both current and total debts improved or deteriorated during 2011. In order to complete your evaluation, compute For You's current and debt ratios at December 31, 2011, rounding to two decimal places. At December 31, 2010, the current ratio was 1.50 and the debt ratio was 0.45.

Learning Objective 6
Using the financial statements to evaluate a business

P3-70B A company's balance sheet at December 31, 2009, 2010, and 2011 and income statement for the years ended December 31, 2009, 2010, and 2011 include the data on page 176.

Required

Use the years of data to calculate the following:

1. The current ratio for 2009, 2010, and 2011
2. The debt ratio for 2009, 2010, and 2011
3. The return on sales for 2009, 2010, and 2011
4. Evaluate each ratio and determine if the ratio has improved or deteriorated over the three years. Explain what the changes mean.

Balance Sheet
(in thousands)

	2011	2010	2009
Assets			
Current assets			
Cash	$ 6.0	$ 4.0	$ 3.5
Accounts receivable	11.0	8.0	6.5
Total current assets	17.0	12.0	10.0
Furniture and equipment, net	19.0	12.5	6.0
Total assets	$36.0	$24.5	$16.0
Liabilities			
Current liabilities			
Accounts payable	$ 8.0	$ 7.0	$ 6.0
Salaries payable	4.5	4.0	3.5
Total current liabilities	12.5	11.0	9.5
Notes payable	12.0	6.0	5.5
Total liabilities	24.5	17.0	15.0
Shareholders' equity			
Shareholders' equity	11.5	7.5	1.0
Total liabilities and shareholders' equity	$36.0	$24.5	$16.0

Income Statement
(in thousands)

	2011	2010	2009
Revenue			
Service revenue	$110.0	$99.0	$75.0
Expenses			
Salary	65.0	59.0	48.0
Rent	20.0	18.0	17.0
Supplies	7.5	6.0	3.0
Utilities	6.0	4.5	3.5
Depreciation	6.0	3.0	2.0
Total expenses	104.5	90.5	73.5
Income before taxes	5.5	8.5	1.5
Income tax expense	1.5	2.0	.5
Net income	$ 4.0	$ 6.5	$ 1.0

Apply Your Knowledge

Decision Cases

Learning Objective 3 6
Adjusting and correcting the accounts; evaluating a business using financial statements

Case 1. On the next page is a list of accounts of Patel Consulting Ltd. at January 31, 2011. The unadjusted trial balance of Patel Consulting Ltd. at January 31, 2011, does not balance. In addition, the trial balance needs to be updated before the financial statements at January 31, 2011, can be prepared. The manager needs to know the current ratio of Patel Consulting Ltd.

Patel Consulting Ltd.
List of Accounts
January 31, 2011

Cash	$ 6,000	
Accounts receivable	2,200	
Supplies	800	
Prepaid rent	12,000	
Land	41,000	
Accounts payable		10,000
Salary payable		0
Unearned service revenue		1,500
Note payable, due in three years		25,400
Common shares		15,000
Retained earnings		7,300
Service revenue		9,100
Salary expense	3,400	
Rent expense	0	
Advertising expense	900	
Supplies expense	0	
	?	?

Required

1. How much *out of balance* is the trial balance? The error is in the Land account.
2. Patel Consulting Ltd. needs to make the following adjustments at January 31:
   a. Supplies of $600 were used during January.
   b. The balance of Prepaid Rent was paid on January 1 and covers the rest of 2011. No adjustment was made January 31.
   c. At January 31, Patel Consulting owes employees $400.
   d. Unearned service revenue of $800 was earned during January.

   Prepare a corrected, adjusted trial balance. Give Land its correct balance.
3. After the error is corrected and after these adjustments are made, compute the current ratio of Patel Consulting Ltd. If your business had this current ratio, could you sleep at night?

Learning Objective 3 4
Preparing financial statements; continue or close the business?

Case 2. On October 1, Sue Skate opened a restaurant named Silver Skates Ltd. After the first month of operations, Skate is at a crossroads. The October financial statements paint a glowing picture of the business, and Skate has asked you whether she should expand Silver Skates.

To expand the business, Sue Skate wants to be earning net income of $10,000 per month and have total assets of $35,000. Based on the financial information available to her, Skate believes she is meeting both goals.

To start the business, she invested $20,000, not the $10,000 amount reported as "Common shares" on the balance sheet. The bookkeeper plugged the $10,000 "Common shares" amount into the balance sheet to make it come out even. The bookkeeper made other mistakes too. Skate shows you the following financial statements that the bookkeeper prepared.

Silver Skates Ltd.
Income Statement
For the Month Ended October 31, 2011

Revenues:		
Investments by owner	$20,000	
Unearned banquet sales revenue	3,000	
		$23,000
Expenses:		
Wages expense	$ 5,000	
Rent expense	4,000	
Dividends	3,000	
Depreciation expense—fixtures	1,000	
		13,000
Net income (Net loss)		$10,000

Silver Skates Ltd.
Balance Sheet
October 31, 2011

Assets:		Liabilities:	
Cash	$ 6,000	Accounts payable	$ 5,000
Prepaid insurance	1,000	Sales revenue	32,000
Insurance expense	1,000	Accumulated depreciation—	
Food inventory	3,000	fixtures	1,000
Cost of goods sold (expense)	14,000		38,000
Fixtures (tables, chairs, etc.)	19,000	Owners' equity:	
Dishes and silverware	4,000	Common shares	10,000
	$48,000		$48,000

Required

Prepare corrected financial statements for Silver Skates Ltd.: income statement, statement of retained earnings, and balance sheet. Then, based on your corrected statements, recommend to Sue Skate whether she should expand her business.

Learning Objective 3 4
Valuing a business on the basis of its net income

Case 3. Walter Liu has owned and operated LW Media Inc. since its beginning 10 years ago. Recently, Liu mentioned that he would consider selling the company for the right price.

Assume that you are interested in buying this business. You obtain its most recent monthly trial balance, which follows on the next page. Revenues and expenses vary little from month to month, and June is a typical month. Your investigation reveals that the trial balance does not include the effects of monthly revenues of $5,000 and expenses totalling $1,100. If you were to buy LW Media Inc., you would hire a manager so you could devote your time to other duties. Assume that your manager would require a monthly salary of $6,000.

Required

1. Assume that the most you would pay for the business is 20 times the monthly net income *you could expect to earn* from it. Compute this possible price.
2. Walter Liu states that the least he will take for the business is 1.5 times shareholders' equity on June 30, 2011. Compute this amount.
3. Under these conditions, how much should you offer Liu? Give your reason.

LW Media Inc.
Trial Balance
June 30, 2011

Cash	$ 10,000	
Accounts receivable	4,900	
Prepaid expenses	3,200	
Equipment	115,000	
Accumulated depreciation		$ 76,500
Land	158,000	
Accounts payable		13,800
Salary payable		
Unearned revenue		56,700
Common shares		50,000
Retained earnings		88,000
Dividends	9,000	
Revenue		20,000
Rent expense		
Salary expense	4,000	
Utilities expense	900	
Depreciation expense		
Supplies expense		
Total	$305,000	$305,000

Ethical Issues

Issue 1. ARAS Inc. is in its third year of operations and the company has grown. To expand the business, ARAS borrowed $1 million from Royal Bank of Canada. As a condition for making this loan, the bank required that ARAS maintain a current ratio of at least 1.50 and a debt ratio of no more than 0.50.

Business recently has been worse than expected. Expenses have brought the current ratio down to 1.47 and the debt ratio up to 0.51 at December 15. Shane Rollins, the general manager, is considering the implication of reporting this current ratio to the bank. Rollins is considering recording this year some revenue on account that ARAS will earn next year. The contract for this job has been signed, and ARAS will perform the service during January.

Required

1. Journalize the revenue transaction, omitting amounts, and indicate how recording this revenue in December would affect the current ratio and the debt ratio.
2. State whether it is ethical to record the revenue transaction in December. Identify the accounting principle relevant to this situation.
3. Propose to ARAS a course of action that is ethical.

Issue 2. The net income of Accent Photography Company Ltd. decreased sharply during 2011. Mark Smith, owner of the company, anticipates the need for a bank loan in 2012. Late in 2011, he instructed the accountant to record a $20,000 sale of portraits to the Smith family, even though the photos will not be shot until January 2012. Smith also told the accountant *not* to make the following December 31, 2011, adjusting entries:

Salaries owed to employees	$5,000
Prepaid insurance that has expired	1,000

Required

1. Compute the overall effect of these transactions on the company's reported income for 2011. Is income overstated or understated?
2. Why did Smith take these actions? Are they ethical? Give your reason, identifying the parties helped and the parties harmed by Smith's action.
3. As a personal friend, what advice would you give the accountant?

Focus on Financials

Learning Objective 3 6
Tracing account balance to the financial statements

Gildan Activewear Inc.

Like all other businesses, Gildan adjusts accounts prior to year-end to measure assets, liabilities, revenues, and expenses for the financial statements. Examine Gildan's balance sheet in Appendix A, and pay particular attention to (a) Prepaid Expenses and (b) Accounts Payable and Accrued Liabilities.

Required

1. Why aren't Prepaid Expenses "true" expenses? What word could be added to "Accrued Liabilities" to make the nature of this account clear?
2. Open T-accounts for the Prepaid Expenses account and the Accounts Payable and Accrued Liabilities account. Insert Gildan's balances (in thousands) at October 5, 2008.
3. Journalize the following for the year ended October 4, 2009. Key entries by letter, and show accounts in thousands. Explanations are not required.
   a. Paid the beginning balance of Accounts Payable and Accrued Liabilities
   b. Allocated Prepaid Expenses of $10,413 to Selling and Administrative Expense
   c. Recorded Accounts Payable and Accrued Liabilities in the amount of $124,378. Assume this is a cost of sale expense.
   d. Recorded Selling and Administrative Expenses of $11,604 to Prepaid Expenses.
4. Post these entries and show that the balances in Prepaid Expenses and in Accounts Payable and Accrued Liabilities agree with the corresponding amounts reported in the October 4, 2009, balance sheet.
5. Compute the current ratios and debt ratios for Gildan at October 4, 2009, and at October 5, 2008. Did the ratio values improve, deteriorate, or hold steady during the year ended October 4, 2009? Do the ratio values indicate financial strength or weakness?

Focus on Analysis

Learning Objective 3
Explaining accruals and deferrals

Gildan Activewear Inc.

During the fiscal year ended October 4, 2009, Gildan Activewear (Appendix A) had numerous accruals and deferrals. As a new member of Gildan's accounting and financial staff, it is your job to explain the effects of accruals and deferrals on Gildan's net income for 2009. The accrual and deferral data follow, along with questions that Gildan's shareholders have raised (all amounts in thousands):

1. Beginning total receivables for 2009 were $215,833. Ending receivables for 2009 are $166,762. Which of these amounts did Gildan earn in 2008? Which amount did Gildan earn in 2009? Which amount is included in Gildan's revenue for 2009?
2. Accumulated depreciation on property, plant, and equipment stood at $177,026 at October 5, 2008, and at $235,236 at October 4, 2009. Accumulated depreciation was reduced by $1,361 for assets sold during the year. Calculate the depreciation expense for the year, and compare to the depreciation of property, plant, and equipment expense reported in Note 17 (b) Depreciation and amortization.
3. Certain income-statement accounts are directly linked to specific balance-sheet accounts other than cash. Examine Gildan's income statement in Appendix A. For each revenue and expense account that you can do so, excluding retained earnings, identify the related balance sheet account(s) (other than cash).

Group Project

Matt Davis formed a lawn service company as a summer job. To start the business on May 1, he deposited $1,000 in a new bank account in the name of the corporation. The $1,000 consisted of an $800 loan from his father and $200 of his own money. The corporation issued 200 common shares to Davis.

Davis rented lawn equipment, purchased supplies, and hired high-school students to mow and trim his customers' lawns. At the end of each month, Davis mailed bills to his customers. On August 31, Davis was ready to dissolve the business and return to Simon Fraser University for the fall semester. Because he had been so busy, he had kept few records other than his chequebook and a list of amounts owed by customers.

At August 31, Davis's chequebook shows a balance of $1,390, and his customers still owe him $560. During the summer, he collected $5,150 from customers. His chequebook lists payments for supplies totalling $400, and he still has gasoline, weedeater cord, and other supplies that cost a total of $50. He paid his employees wages of $1,900, and he still owes them $200 for the final week of the summer.

Davis rented some equipment from Ludwig Tool Company. On May 1, he signed a six-month lease on mowers and paid $600 for the full lease period. Ludwig will refund the unused portion of the prepayment if the equipment is in good shape. To get the refund, Davis has kept the mowers in excellent condition. In fact, he had to pay $300 to repair a mower that ran over a hidden tree stump.

To transport equipment to jobs, Davis used a trailer that he bought for $300. He figures that the summer's work used up one-third of the trailer's service potential. The business chequebook lists an expenditure of $460 for dividends paid to Davis during the summer. Also, Davis paid his father back during the summer.

Required

1. Prepare the income statement of Davis Lawn Service Inc. for the four months, May through August. The business is not subject to income tax.
2. Prepare the classified balance sheet of Davis Lawn Service Inc. at August 31.

Quick Check Answers

1. *c*	5. *d*	9. *d*	13. *a*
2. *c*	6. *b*	10. *a*	14. *c*
3. *b*	7. *a*	11. *b*	15. *a*
4. *d*	8. *d*	12. *d*	16. *b*

4 Internal Control and Cash

LEARNING OBJECTIVES

1. **Learn** about fraud and how much it costs
2. **Set up** an internal control system
3. **Prepare** and use a bank reconciliation
4. **Apply** internal controls to cash receipts and cash payments
5. **Use** a budget to manage cash
6. **Make** an ethical business judgment

SPOTLIGHT

Cooking the Books: GreBru Products Inc. Takes a Hit

The following is adapted from a true story:

"I've never been so shocked in my life!" exclaimed Lee Riffe, manager of the GreBru Products Inc. office in Vancouver, B.C. "I never thought this could happen to us. We are such a close-knit organization where everyone trusts everyone else. Why, people at GreBru feel like family! I feel betrayed, violated."

Riffe had just returned from the trial of Alec Jones, who had been convicted of embezzling over $600,000 from GreBru over a six-year period. Jones had been one of GreBru's most trusted employees for 10 years. A single father with two teenage daughters, Jones had pulled himself up by his own bootstraps, putting himself through community college where he had obtained an associate's degree in accounting. Riffe had hired him as a part-time bookkeeper at GreBru while Jones was in college to help him out. He had done such a good job that, when he completed his degree, Riffe asked him to stay on and assigned him the additional role of cashier, in charge of accumulating the daily cash receipts from customers and taking them to the night depository at the bank each day after work. Through the years, he also awarded him what he considered good raises, compensating him at a rate that was generally higher than other employees with his education and experience levels.

Jones rapidly became the company's "go-to" financial employee. He was eager to learn, dependable, responsible. In 10 years he never took a day of vacation, choosing instead to take advantage of the company's policy that allowed employees to draw additional compensation for vacation accrued but not taken at the end of each year. Riffe grew to depend on Jones more and more each month, as the business grew to serve over 1,000 customers. Jones's increased involvement on the financial side of the business freed Riffe to spend his time working on new business, spending less and less time on financial matters. Riffe had noticed that, in the past few years, Jones had begun to wear better clothes and drive a shiny late-model convertible around town. Both of his teenagers also drove late-model automobiles, and the family had recently moved into a new home in an upscale subdivision of the city. Riffe had been pleased that he had contributed to Jones's success. But in recent months, Riffe was becoming worried because, in spite of increasing revenues, the cash balances and cash flows from operations at GreBru had been steadily deteriorating, sometimes causing the company difficulty in paying its bills on time.

Jones, on the other hand, had felt underappreciated and underpaid for all of his hard work. Having learned the system well, and observing that no one was monitoring him, Jones fell into a simple but deadly trap. As cashier, he was in charge of receiving customer payments that came in by mail. Unknown to Riffe, Jones had been **lapping** accounts receivable, an embezzlement scheme nicknamed "robbing Peter to pay Paul." Jones began by misappropriating (stealing) some of the customers' cheques, endorsing them, and depositing them to his own bank account. To cover up the shortage in a particular customer's account, Jones would apply the collections received later from another customer's account. He would do this just before the monthly statements were mailed to the first customer, so that the customer wouldn't notice when she or he received the statement that someone else's payment was being applied to the amount owed GreBru. Of course, this left the second customer's account short, so Jones had to misapply the collection from a third customer to straighten out the discrepancy in the second customer's account. He did this for many customers, over a period of many months, boldly stealing more and more each month. With unlimited access to both cash and customer accounts, and with careful planning and constant diligence, Jones became very proficient at juggling entries in the books to keep anyone from discovering his scheme. This embezzlement went on for six years, allowing Jones to misappropriate $622,000 from the company. The customer accounts that were misstated due to the fraud eventually had to be written off.

What tipped off Riffe to the embezzlement? Jones was involved in a skiing accident and couldn't work for two weeks. The employee covering for Jones was swamped with telephone calls from customers wanting to discuss unexplained differences in their billing statements for amounts they could prove had been paid. The ensuing investigation pointed straight to Jones, and Riffe turned the case over to the authorities.

The excerpt from the GreBru Products Inc. balance sheet on the following page reports the company's assets. Focus on the top line, Cash and cash equivalents. At December 31, 2011, GreBru reported cash of $8,000. Due to Jones's scheme, the company had been cheated of $622,000 over several years that it could have used to buy new equipment, expand operations, or pay off debts.

GreBru Products has now revamped its internal controls. The company has hired a separate person, with no access to cash, to keep customer accounts receivable records. The company now uses a **lockbox system** for all cheques received by mail. They are sent to GreBru's bank lock box, where they are gathered by a bank employee and immediately deposited. The remittance advices accompanying the cheques are electronically scanned and forwarded to GreBru's accounts receivable bookkeeper

GreBru Products Inc.
Balance Sheet (Partial, Adapted)
As at December 31, 2011

Assets	
Cash and cash equivalents	$ 8,000
Accounts receivable	128,000
Inventories	247,000
Prepaid expenses	1,400
Property, plant, and equipment	
(net of accumulated depreciation of $97,000)	213,600
Other assets	15,000
Total assets	$613,000

where they are used as the source documents for posting amounts collected from customers. A summary of cash received goes to Riffe, who reviews it for reasonableness and compares it with the daily bank deposit total. Another employee, who has neither cash handling nor customer bookkeeping responsibilities, reconciles GreBru's monthly bank statement, and reconciles the total cash deposited per the daily listings with the total credits to customer accounts receivable. Now Riffe requires every employee to take time off for earned vacation, and rotates other employees through those positions while those employees are away.

Lapping is a type of fraud known as misappropriation of assets. Although it doesn't take a genius to accomplish, lapping requires some motivation, and is usually rationalized by distorted and unethical thinking. The opportunity to commit this type and other types of frauds arises through a weak internal control system. In this case, the fact that Jones had access to cash and the customer accounts receivable, along with the fact that Riffe failed to monitor Jones's activities, proved to be the deadly combination that provided the opportunity for this fraud.

This chapter begins with a discussion of fraud, its types, and common characteristics. We then discuss internal controls, which are the primary means by which fraud as well as unintentional financial statement errors are prevented. We also discuss how to account for cash. These three topics—fraud, internal control, and cash—go together. Internal controls help prevent fraud. Cash is probably the asset that is most often misappropriated through fraud.

The discussion of fraud in this chapter reinforces the notion that it is important for managers to understand accounting and internal control if they are to be effective in their job. Most frauds involve accounting manipulation of some sort that is successful because management senses something is wrong but don't understand accounting well enough to understand why. Well-designed and properly implemented internal controls can protect a company from fraud and error, but managers must have enough of an understanding of internal controls to determine if their internal controls are properly designed and implemented to be effective.

Fraud and Its Impact

OBJECTIVE

1 **Learn** about fraud and how much it costs

Fraud is an intentional misrepresentation of facts, made for the purpose of persuading another party to act in a way that causes injury or damage to that party. For example, in the chapter opening story, Alec Jones intentionally misappropriated money from GreBru and covered it up by making customer accounts look different than they actually were. In the end, his actions caused $622,000 in damages to GreBru.

ETHICS ALERT!

Fraud is a huge problem and is getting bigger, not only in Canada, but across the globe. Recent surveys of large and medium-sized companies revealed the following:

- Over 75% of businesses surveyed had experienced fraud.
- Over 50% of companies had experienced six or more instances of fraud in only one year.
- In 2007, companies lost an average of $2.4 million each to fraud (up from $1.7 million each in 2005).
- One out of every five workers indicated personal awareness of fraud in the workplace.

Since small businesses and those in countries outside Canada and the United States were omitted from these surveys, we can be sure that the actual incidence of fraud is even higher! Another recent survey taken by the Association for Certified Fraud Examiners (ACFE) reveals that occupational fraud and abuse results in losses equal to approximately 5% of total business revenue. When applied to the Canadian gross domestic product, this means that about $75 billion per year is lost due to fraud, an astonishing $4,500 per employee! If you think that fraud occurs only in the for-profit sector, think again. About 13.4% of the ACFE survey cases are not-for-profit organizations, amounting to millions in fraud through not-for-profit organizations each year.

Fraud has exploded with the expansion of e-commerce via the Internet. In addition, studies have shown that the percentage of losses related to fraud from transactions originating in "third world" or developing countries via the Internet is even higher than in economically developed countries.

What are the most common types of fraud? What causes fraud? What can be done to prevent it?

There are many types of fraud. Some of the most common types are insurance fraud, cheque forgery, credit card fraud, and identity theft. The two most common types of fraud that impact financial statements are:

- **Misappropriation of assets.** This type of fraud is committed by employees of an entity who steal money from the company and cover it up through erroneous entries in the books. The GreBru case is an example. Other examples of asset misappropriation include employee theft of inventory, bribery or kickback schemes in the purchasing function, or employee overstatement of expense reimbursement requests.
- **Fraudulent financial reporting.** This type of fraud is committed by company managers who make false and misleading entries in the books, making financial results of the company appear to be better than they actually are. The purpose of this type of fraud is to deceive investors and creditors into investing or loaning money to the company that they might not otherwise have invested or loaned.

The most common form of fraudulent financial reporting (also called management fraud) is **earnings management**. Research has indicated that managers engage in such fraud for a variety of reasons. Several such reasons and the related frauds are

- To meet profit targets set by market analysts so that the company's share price will increase. An example would be where the company's earnings are actually

$1.12 a share but analysts predicted $1.18 a share. The fraud: management reverses bad debt write-downs, reducing expenses to increase earnings to $1.18.

- To meet loan covenants so the lender won't demand payment of a loan. An example would be where the company has a loan covenant requiring it to maintain a working capital ratio (current assets/current liabilities) of 2:1 and the actual ratio at year-end is 1.8:1. The fraud: management reverses an inventory write-down to increase the value of inventory so that the new ratio is 2.1:1.
- To meet an earnings target that will result in a management bonus. The fraud: management overstates revenue by recording subsequent year sales in the current year, resulting in a misstated net income number so that the desired bonus is achieved.
- To convert a loss to a profit. The company suffers a net loss. The fraud: management overstates revenue to turn the loss into a profit.

Both misappropriation of assets and fraudulent financial reporting involve making false or misleading entries in the books of the company. We call this *cooking the books*. Of these two types, asset misappropriation is the most common, but fraudulent financial reporting is by far the most expensive. Perhaps two of the most notorious recent cases involving fraudulent financial reporting occurred in the United States and involved Enron Corporation in 2001 and WorldCom Corporation in 2002. These two scandals alone rocked the U.S. economy and impacted financial markets across the world. Enron (discussed in Chapter 10) committed fraudulent financial reporting by overstating profits through bogus sales of nonexistent assets with inflated values. When Enron's banks found out, they stopped loaning the company money to operate, causing it to go out of business almost overnight. WorldCom (discussed in Chapter 7) reported expenses as property, plant, and development and overstated both profits and assets. The company's internal auditor blew the whistle on WorldCom, resulting in the company's eventual collapse. Sadly, the same international accounting firm, Arthur Andersen, LLP, had audited both companies' financial statements. Because of these and other failed audits, the once mighty firm of Arthur Andersen was forced to close its doors in 2002.

Each of these frauds, and many others revealed about the same time, involved losses in the billions of dollars and thousands of jobs when the companies went out of business. Widespread media coverage sparked adverse market reaction, loss of confidence in the financial reporting system, and losses through declines in stock values that ran in the trillions of dollars!

Livent Inc. was a Canadian public company listed on the Toronto Stock Exchange. The company produced several successful musicals such as "The Phantom of the Opera," "Joseph and the Amazing Technicolor Dreamcoat," "Show Boat," and "Ragtime." In the late 1990s, Livent declared bankruptcy in the United States. There were criminal investigations in Canada and the U.S. Company co-founders Garth Drabinsky and Myron Gottlieb were indicted for fraud and misappropriation in the United States. In Canada, the co-founders and several other executives were charged with fraud. Drabinsky and Gottlieb were found guilty of fraud and forgery in an Ontario court for misstating the company's financial statements. In 2009, they were sentenced to time in prison.

We will discuss some of these cases throughout the remaining chapters of the text as examples of how accounting principles were deliberately misapplied, through cooking the books, in environments characterized by *weak internal controls*.

EXHIBIT 4-1 The Fraud Triangle

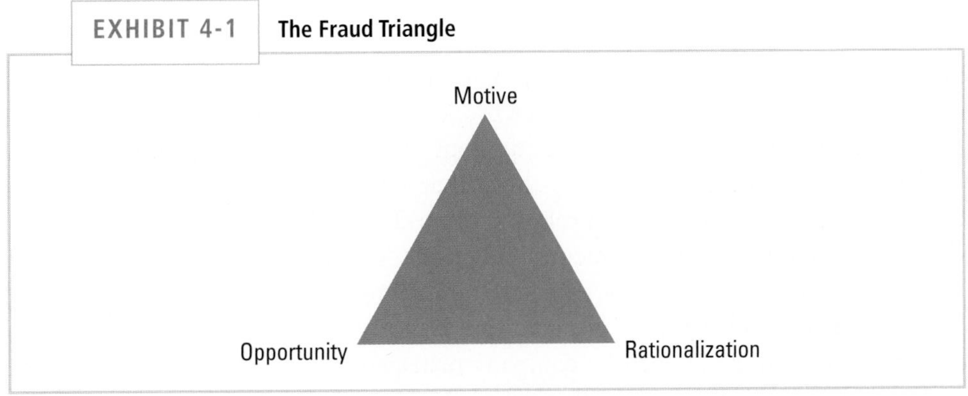

Exhibit 4-1 explains in graphic form the elements that make up virtually every fraud. We call it the **fraud triangle**.

The first element in the fraud triangle is *motive*. This usually results from either critical need or greed on the part of the person who commits the fraud (the perpetrator). Sometimes it is a matter of just never having enough (because some persons who commit fraud are already rich by most people's standards). Other times the perpetrator of the fraud might have a legitimate financial need, such as a medical emergency, but he or she uses illegitimate means to meet that need. A recent article in the *Wall Street Journal* indicated that employee theft was on the rise due to economic hard times. In any case, the prevailing attitude on the part of the perpetrator is, "I want it, and someone else has it, so I'm going to do whatever I have to do to get it."

The second element in the fraud triangle is *opportunity*. As in the case of GreBru, the opportunity to commit fraud usually arises through weak internal controls. It might be a breakdown in a key element of controls, such as improper *segregation of duties* and/or improper *access to assets*. Or it might result from a weak control environment, such as a domineering CEO, a weak or conflicted board of directors, or lax ethical practices, allowing top management to override whatever controls the company has placed in operation for other transactions.

The third element in the triangle is *rationalization*. The perpetrator engages in distorted thinking, such as: "I deserve this;" "Nobody treats me fairly;" "No one will ever know;" "Just this once, I won't let it happen again;" or "Everyone else is doing it."

KPMG Forensics recently produced a survey of Canadian executives entitled *Profile of a Canadian Fraudster* that provides interesting insights (www.kpmg.ca).

Fraud and Ethics

As we pointed out in our decision framework for making ethical accounting and business judgments introduced in Chapter 1, the decision to engage in fraud is an act with economic, legal, and ethical implications. The perpetrators of fraud usually do so for their own short-term *economic gain*, while others incur *economic losses* that may far outstrip the gains of the fraudsters. Moreover, fraud is defined by provincial, federal, and international law as *illegal*. Those who are caught and found guilty of fraud ultimately face penalties that include imprisonment, fines, and monetary damages. Finally, from an *ethical* standpoint, fraud violates the rights of many for the temporary betterment of a few, and for the ultimate betterment of no one. At the end of the day, everyone loses! Fraud is the ultimate unethical act in business!

Internal Control

The primary way that fraud, as well as unintentional errors, is prevented, detected, or corrected in an organization is through a proper system of internal control. How critical are internal controls? They're so important that the Ontario Legislature passed a law* to require public companies—those that sell their shares to the public—to maintain a system of internal controls. Exhibit 4-2 provides an excerpt from Loblaw Companies Limited's Management's Statement of Responsibility for Financial Reporting, taken from the January 2, 2010, annual report.

Internal control is a plan of organization and system of procedures designed, implemented, and maintained by company management and the board of directors to deal with risks to the business that have been identified and that relate to

- The reliability of the company's financial records and financial reporting
- The company's ability to operate effectively and efficiently
- The company's compliance with legal requirements

The Reliability of the Company's Financial Records and Financial Reporting. The system of internal control should be designed to ensure that the accounting records are accurate, reliable, and timely. Without reliable records, the business cannot know if it is profitable and investors and creditors cannot know if the financial statements are a faithful representation of the company's operations.

The Company's Ability to Operate Effectively and Efficiently. The system of internal control should be designed to ensure that assets and records are safeguarded. No company can afford to waste physical or reputational resources. It is important that employees follow company policy; everyone in the company must work toward the same goal. Company policies should be designed so that employees and customers are treated fairly.

The Company's Compliance With Legal Requirements. The system of internal control should be designed to ensure that those charged with governance of the company (for example, the board of directors) can be confident that employees of the

EXHIBIT 4-2 **Loblaw Companies Limited's Management's Statement of Responsibility for Financial Reporting (Partial)**

Management's Statement of Responsibility for Financial Reporting

Management is also responsible for establishing and maintaining adequate internal control over financial reporting to provide reasonable assurance regarding the reliability of financial reporting and the preparation of financial statements for external purposes in accordance with Canadian GAAP. A dedicated control compliance team reviews and evaluates internal controls, the results of which are shared with management on a quarterly basis. KPMG LLP, whose report follows, were appointed as independent auditors by a vote of the Company's shareholders to audit the consolidated financial statements.

*Bill 198 (Chapter 22, Statutes of Ontario, 2002) *An Act to Implement Budget Measures and Other Initiatives of the Government.*

company from management on down are complying with all laws and regulations that affect the company.

Those three issues may be interpreted as the following five objectives:

- Safeguard assets including records against waste, inefficiency, and fraud.
- Encourage all employees, managers, and staff to follow company policy.
- Promote operational efficiency to minimize waste.
- Ensure accurate, reliable accounting records.
- Comply with legal and regulatory requirements.

The *Sarbanes-Oxley Act* (SOX)

As the Enron and WorldCom scandals unfolded, many people asked, "How can these things happen? If such large companies that we have trusted commit such acts, how can we trust any company to be telling the truth in its financial statements? Where were the auditors?" To address public concern, U.S. Congress passed the *Sarbanes-Oxley Act of 2002*, abbreviated as SOX. SOX revamped corporate governance in the United States and also had sweeping effects on the accounting profession. It will take several years to determine how SOX has affected financial reporting. Securities regulators in Canada and around the world considered the SOX requirements in light of their own countries' capital markets.

Canadian-listed public companies are regulated by one of the 13 (10 provinces and 3 territories) securities commissions in Canada. The 13 securities commissions have formed an umbrella organization called the Canadian Securities Administrators (CSA), which issues Staff Notices and National Instruments on behalf of the 13 securities commissions.

A **public company** offers its securities, such as shares or debt, for sale to the general public. Three terms used in the ensuing discussion are often described by their acronyms:

- Internal control over financial reporting (ICFR)
- Disclosure controls and procedures (DC&P)
- Management Discussion and Analysis (MD&A)

National Instrument 52-109 (discussed below) describes ICFR as a process designed to provide reasonable assurance regarding the reliability of financial reporting. NI 52-109 describes DC&P as controls and other procedures that are designed to provide reasonable assurance that information required to be disclosed in filings required under securities regulation is accumulated and disclosed to management on a timely basis for disclosure decisions.

MD&A is designed to provide users of financial statements with an explanation of the company's past performance and financial condition and future prospects through the eyes of management. MD&A is not part of the financial statements but is included in the annual report (see the Gildan Activewear Inc. annual report in Appendix A).

The CSA began work on developing a Canadian strategy incorporating some or all of the rules in SOX for Canadian public companies. In August, 2008,* the CSA

*Source: "Certification of Internal Controls: Final Certification Rules" KPMG LLP, September 2008.

re-issued National Instrument 52-109 "Certification of Disclosure in Issuers' Annual and Interim [Quarterly] Filings." NI 52-109 has an effective date (that is, applies to filing companies with year-ends on or after the effective date) of December 15, 2008. Some of the requirements of interest of NI 52-109 are:

- "The [chief executive officer] CEO and [chief financial officer] CFO [certifying officers] must certify that they have evaluated the effectiveness of the issuer's ICFR and disclosed in the annual MD&A their conclusions about the effectiveness of ICFR at the financial year-end. The evaluation must be completed using a control framework.
- MD&A disclosure is required for each material weakness related to ICFR. Issuers are not required to remediate a material weakness; however, they must disclose plans or actions already taken to do so.
- Detailed guidance [in NI 52-109] outlines what should be considered when assessing the design and evaluating the effectiveness of DC&P and ICFR, including the extent of documentation to support the evaluation. The . . . rule requires the CEO and CFO to certify each quarter, among other things, that they have designed DC&P and ICFR and disclosed changes in ICFR that have materially affected or are reasonably likely to materially affect the issuer's ICFR.
- In addition, the annual certificate requires the certifying officers to evaluate the effectiveness of DC&P and disclose their conclusions in MD&A. [The] certifying officers [are also required] to disclose any ICFR weaknesses in MD&A."*
- Accountants learn about accounting and internal controls as part of their training, but even so, the requirements of certification required under N1 52-109 can be a challenge. It is important that managers understand accounting and internal control because as CEOs they too have to certify the numbers in the financial statements and the ICFRs. This course will provide you with the basic knowledge about both accounting and internal control so that you, as a manager, can function in the business world.

Exhibit 4-3 diagrams the shield that internal controls provide for an organization. Protected by this shield from fraud, waste, and inefficiency, companies can do business in a trustworthy manner that ensures public confidence, an extremely important element in maintaining the stability of financial markets around the world. The next section identifies the components of internal control.

OBJECTIVE

② **Set up** an internal control system

The Components of Internal Control

Internal control can be broken down into five components:

- Control environment
- Monitoring of controls
- Risk assessment
- Information system
- Control procedures

---

*Source: "Certification of Internal Controls: Final Certification Rules" KPMG LLP, September 2008.

EXHIBIT 4-3 **The Shield of Internal Control**

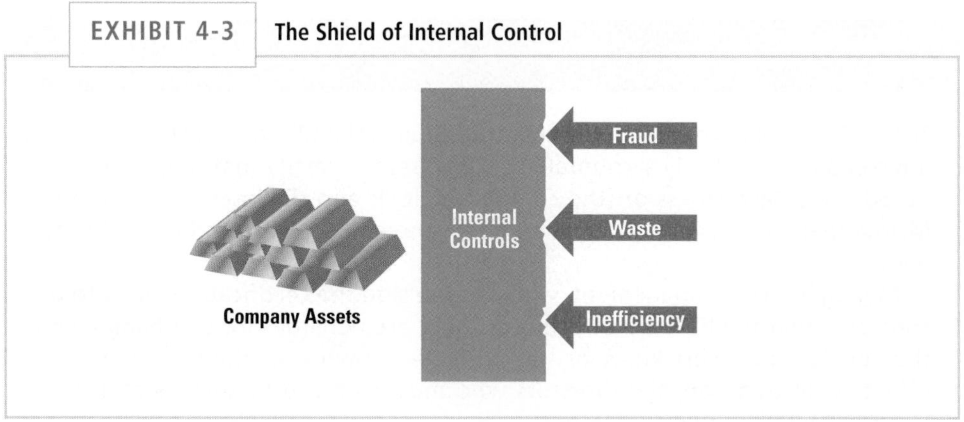

Control Environment. The control environment is the "tone at the top" of the business. It starts with the owner and the top managers. They must behave honourably to set a good example for company employees. They must demonstrate the importance of internal controls if they expect employees to take the controls seriously. A key ingredient in the control environment of many companies is a corporate code of conduct that communicates the company's policies on integrity and ethical values.

Risk Assessment. A company faces business risks, which are the risks that it will not achieve its objectives. The company must be able to identify its significant business risks as well as establish procedures for dealing with those risks to minimize their impact on the company, its employees, its owners, and its creditors. For example, CN Rail faces the risk of a derailment. Air Canada faces the risk of high fuel costs. All companies face business risks.

Information Systems. Management of a business needs accurate information to keep track of assets and measure profits and losses. Every system within the business that processes accounting data should have the ability to capture transactions as they occur, record (journalize) those transactions in an accurate and timely manner, summarize (post) those transactions in the books (ledgers), and report those transactions in the form of account balances or footnotes in the financial statements.

Control Procedures. Control procedures built into the control environment and information system are the means by which companies gain access to the five objectives of internal controls discussed previously. Examples include proper separation of duties, comparison and other checks, adequate records, proper approvals, and physical safeguards to protect assets from theft.

Monitoring of Controls. Monitoring provides "eyes and ears," so that no one person or group of persons can process a transaction completely without being seen and checked by another person or group. With modern computerized systems, much of the monitoring of day-to-day activity is done through controls programmed into a company's information technology. Computer programs dealing with such systems as cash receipts and cash disbursements can be automatically programmed to generate *exception reports* for transactions that exceed certain pre-defined guidelines (such as disbursements in excess of $15,000 in a payroll) for special management scrutiny. In addition, companies hire auditors to monitor their controls. Internal auditors monitor company controls from the inside to safeguard the company's assets, and external auditors test the controls from the outside to ensure that the accounting records are

USING INTERNAL CONTROL IN DECISION MAKING

NI 52-109 discussed earlier in the chapter requires the CEO and CFO of a reporting company (a publicly accountable enterprise) to "certify that they have evaluated the effectiveness of [the company's] ICFR and disclosed in the annual MD&A their conclusions about the effectiveness of IFCR at the financial year-end."

Manager—The management, who have to sign the certification, need to be confident that the IFCR are effective as there are penalties for certifying when the certifying officers knew or should have known that the ICFR were not effective. In addition, the directors who must sign the financial statements need to have the same confidence.

Investor—Investors would have more confidence that the financial statements present fairly the financial position of the company and the results of its operations.

Creditor—Creditors would have more confidence that the financial statements present fairly the financial position of the company and the results of its operations.

accurate and reliable. Audits were introduced in Chapter 1 and are discussed more thoroughly in the next section.

Internal Control Procedures

Whether the business is Gildan Activewear, Research In Motion, GreBru Products, or a Petro-Canada gas station, every major class of transactions needs to have the following *internal control procedures*.

Smart Hiring Practices and Separation of Duties. In a business with good internal controls, no important duty is overlooked. Each person in the information chain is important. The chain should start with hiring. Background checks should be conducted on job applicants. Proper training and supervision, as well as paying competitive salaries, helps ensure that all employees are sufficiently competent for their jobs. Employee responsibilities should be clearly laid out in position descriptions. For example, the **treasurer**'s department should be in charge of cash handling, as well as signing and approving cheques. Warehouse personnel should be in charge of storing and keeping track of inventory. With clearly assigned responsibilities, all important jobs get done.

In processing transactions, smart management *separates three key duties: asset handling, record keeping, and transaction approval*. For example, in the case of GreBru Products, separation of the duties of cash handling from record keeping for customer accounts receivable would have removed Alec Jones's incentive to engage in fraud, because it would have made it impossible for him to have lapped accounts receivable if another employee had been keeping the books. Ideally, someone else should also review customer accounts for collectability and be in charge of writing them off if they become completely uncollectible.

The accounting department should be completely separate from the operating departments, such as production and sales. What would happen if sales personnel, who were compensated based on a percentage of the amount of sales they made, approved the company's sales transactions to customers? Sales figures could be inflated and might not reflect the eventual amount collected from customers.

At all costs, accountants must not handle cash, and cash handlers must not have access to the accounting records. If one employee has both cash-handling and accounting duties, that person can steal cash and conceal the theft. This is what happened at GreBru Products.

For companies that are *too small* to hire separate persons to do all of these functions, the key to good internal control is *getting the owner involved*, usually by approving all large transactions, making bank deposits, or reconciling the monthly bank account.

Comparisons and Compliance Monitoring. No person or department should be able to completely process a transaction from beginning to end without being cross-checked by another person or department. For example, some division of the treasurer's department should be responsible for depositing daily cash receipts in the bank. The **controller**'s department should be responsible for recording customer collections to individual customer accounts receivable. A third employee (perhaps the person in the controller's department who reconciles the bank statement) should compare the treasurer's department's daily records of cash deposited with totals of collections posted to individual customer accounts by the controller's department.

One of the most effective tools for monitoring compliance with management's policies is the use of **operating budgets** and **cash budgets**. A **budget** is a quantitative financial plan that helps control day-to-day management activities. Management may prepare these budgets on a yearly, quarterly, monthly, or more frequent basis. Operating budgets are budgets of future periods' net income. They are prepared by line item of the income statement. Cash budgets, discussed in depth later in this chapter, are budgets of future periods' cash receipts and cash disbursements. Often these budgets are "rolling," being constantly updated by adding a time period a year away while dropping the time period that has just passed. Computer systems are programmed to prepare exception reports for data that are out of line with expectations. This data can include variances for each account from budgeted amounts. Department managers are required to explain the variances, and to take corrective actions in their operating plans to keep the budgets in line with expectations. This is an example of the use of **exception reporting**.

To validate the accounting records and monitor compliance with company policies, most companies have an audit. An **audit** is an examination of the company's financial statements and its accounting system, including its controls.

Audits can be internal or external. *Internal auditors* are employees of the business. They ensure that employees are following company policies and operations are running efficiently. Internal auditors also determine whether the company is following legal requirements.

External auditors are completely independent of the business. They are hired to determine whether or not the company's financial statements agree with generally accepted accounting principles. Auditors examine the client's financial statements and the underlying transactions in order to form a professional opinion on the accuracy and reliability of the company's financial statements.

Adequate Records. *Accounting records* provide the details of business transactions. The general rule is that all major groups of transactions should be supported by either hard copy documents or electronic records. Examples of documents include sales invoices, shipping records, customer remittance advices, purchase orders, vendor invoices, receiving reports, and cancelled (paid) cheques. Documents should be pre-numbered to assure completeness of processing and proper transaction cutoff, and to prevent theft and inefficiency. A gap in the numbered document sequence draws attention to the possibility that transactions might have been omitted from processing.

Limited Access. To complement segregation of duties, company policy should limit access to assets only to those persons or departments that have custodial responsibilities. For example, access to cash should be limited to persons in the treasurer's department. Cash receipts might be processed through a lock-box system. Access to inventory should be limited to persons in the company warehouse where inventories are stored, or to persons in the shipping and receiving functions. Likewise, the company should limit access to records to those persons who have record keeping responsibilities. All manual records of the business should be protected by lock and key, and electronic records should be protected by passwords. Only authorized persons should have access to certain records. Individual computers in the business should be protected by user identification and password. Electronic data files should be encrypted (processed through a special code) to prevent their recognition if accessed by a "hacker" or other unauthorized person.

Proper Approvals. No transaction should be processed without management's general or specific approval. The bigger the transaction, the more specific approval it should have. For individual small transactions, management might delegate approval to a specific department. For example:

- Sales to customers on account should all be approved by a separate credit department that reviews all customers for creditworthiness before goods are shipped to customers on credit. This helps assure that the company doesn't make sales to customers who cannot afford to pay their bills.
- Purchases of all items on credit should be approved by a separate purchasing department that specializes in that function. Among other things, a purchasing department should only buy from approved vendors, on the basis of competitive bids, to assure that the company gets the highest quality products for the most competitive prices.
- All personnel decisions, including hiring, firing, and pay adjustments, should be handled by a separate human resources (HR) department that specializes in personnel-related matters.

Very large (material) transactions should generally be approved by top management, and may even go to the board of directors.

Information Technology. Accounting systems are relying less on manual procedures and more on information technology (IT) than ever before for record keeping, asset handling, approval, and monitoring, as well as physically safeguarding the assets. For example, retailers such as The Bay and HMV control inventory by attaching an *electronic sensor* to merchandise. The cashier must remove or demagnetize the sensor before the customer can walk out of the store. If a customer tries to leave the store with the sensor attached, an alarm sounds. According to Checkpoint Systems, these devices reduce theft by as much as 50%. *Bar codes* speed checkout at retail stores, performing multiple operations in a single step. When the sales associate scans the merchandise at the register, the computer records the sale, removes the item from inventory, and computes the amount of cash to be tendered.

When a company employs sophisticated IT, the basic attributes of internal control do not change, but the procedures by which these attributes are implemented change substantially. For example, segregation of duties is often accomplished by separating mainframe computer departments from other user departments (e.g., controller, sales, purchasing, receiving, credit, HR, treasurer) and restricting access to the IT department only to authorized personnel. Within the computer department, programmers should be separated from computer operators and data librarians. Access to sensitive data files is protected by **password** and data encryption. Electronic records must be saved routinely, or they might be written over or erased. Comparisons of data (such as cash receipts with total credits to customer accounts) that might otherwise be done by hand are performed by the computer. Computers can monitor inventory levels by item, generating a purchase order for inventory when it reaches a certain level.

The use of computers has the advantage of speed and accuracy (when programmed correctly). However, a computer that is *not* programmed correctly can corrupt *all* the data, making it unusable. It is therefore important to hire experienced and competent people to run the IT department, to restrict access to sensitive data and the IT department only to authorized personnel, to check data entered into and retrieved from the computer for accuracy and completeness, and to test and retest programs on a regular basis to assure data integrity and accuracy.

Safeguard Controls. Businesses keep important documents in *fireproof vaults*. *Burglar alarms* safeguard buildings, and *security cameras* safeguard other property. *Loss-prevention specialists* train employees to spot suspicious activity.

Employees who handle cash are in a tempting position. Many businesses purchase **fidelity bonds** on cashiers. The bond is an insurance policy that reimburses the company for any losses due to employee theft. Before issuing a fidelity bond, the insurance company investigates the employee's background.

Mandatory vacations and *job rotation* improve internal control. Companies move employees from job to job. This improves morale by giving employees a broad view of the business. Also, knowing someone else will do your job next month keeps you honest. GreBru Products didn't rotate employees to different jobs, and it cost the company $622,000.

Internal Controls for E-Commerce

E-commerce creates its own risks. Hackers may gain access to confidential information such as account numbers and passwords.

Pitfalls

E-commerce pitfalls include

- Stolen credit-card numbers
- Computer viruses and Trojan horses
- Phishing expeditions

Stolen Credit-Card Numbers. Suppose you buy music from iTunes. To make the purchase, your credit-card number must travel through cyberspace. Wireless networks (Wi-Fi) are creating new security hazards.

Amateur hacker Carlos Salgado, Jr., used his home computer to steal 100,000 credit-card numbers with a combined limit exceeding $1 billion. Salgado was caught when he tried to sell the numbers to an undercover police woman.

Computer Viruses and Trojan Horses. A **computer virus** is a malicious program that (a) enters program code without consent and (b) performs destructive actions in the victim's computer files or programs. A **Trojan horse** is a malicious computer program that hides inside a legitimate program and works like a virus. Viruses can destroy or alter data, make bogus calculations, and infect files. Most firms have had a problem with viruses.

Phishing Expeditions. **Phishing** involves creating bogus Web sites, such as AOL4Free.com and freecds.com. The neat-sounding Web sites attract lots of visitors, and the thieves obtain account numbers and passwords from unsuspecting people. The thieves then use the data for illicit purposes.

Security Measures

To address the risks posed by e-commerce, companies have devised a number of security measures, including

- Encryption
- Firewalls

Encryption. The server holding confidential information may not be secure. One technique for protecting customer data is encryption. **Encryption** rearranges messages by a mathematical process. The encrypted message can't be read by those who don't know the code. An accounting example uses check-sum digits for account numbers. Each account number has its last digit equal to the sum of the previous digits. For example, consider Customer Number 2237, where 2 + 2 + 3 = 7. Any account number that fails this test triggers an error message.

Firewalls. A **firewall** limits access into a local network. Members can access the network but nonmembers can't. Usually several firewalls are built into the system. Think of a fortress with multiple walls protecting the company's computerized records in the centre. At the point of entry, passwords, PINs (personal identification numbers), and signatures are used. More sophisticated firewalls are used deeper in the network. Start with Firewall 1, and work toward the centre.

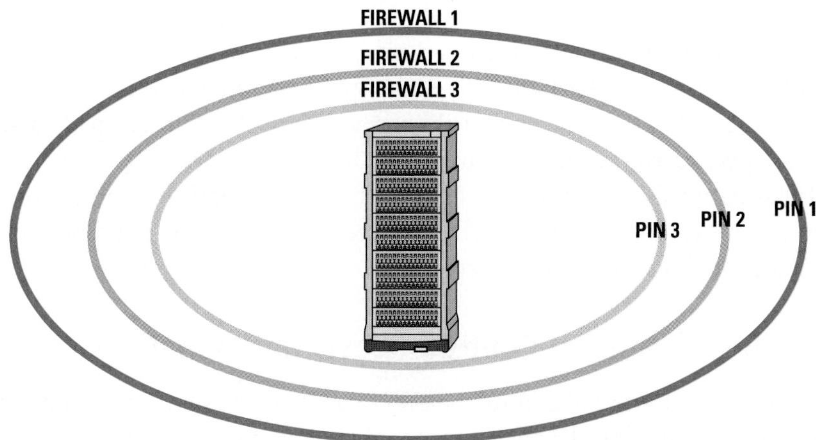

Two Faces of Internal Control

Internal controls are designed to safeguard assets, encourage adherence to company policies, promote operational efficiency, ensure accurate and reliable accounting records and comply with legal requirements. Two examples illustrate how things can go wrong.*

1. *Weak separation of duties* An employee of the *St. Catharines Standard* stole \$2.2 million from her employer. Lucy Magda apparently diverted cheques received in the mail and used them to conceal thefts of cash from the daily bank deposits. The theft was concealed by removing and destroying invoices for which the cheques were payment. Giving the advertising manager access to incoming receipts and the related invoices gave the manager the opportunity to steal and doctor the records to cover the theft.

The most obvious way to limit this risk is to deny the cashier access to accounting records. But in many companies, especially small businesses, it isn't feasible to separate all duties. To manage its risk, the *St. Catharines Standard* could do several things:

- Require employees to take vacations. That way other employees must review the work of the one on vacation. Discrepancies will probably come to light.
- Routinely check on the advertising manager's work. For example, another employee can reconcile customer accounts. Discrepancies can then be detected.
- Mail questionnaires to customers, and ask them to confirm their account balances to a responsible official of the company. Investigate all discrepancies.

2. *No proper authorization* Auditors at the Department of National Defence and the Department of Public Works uncovered a fraud that may have operated over 10 years and resulted in the government paying up to \$160 million for military computer hardware and support services it never received. Former Defence Minister David Pratt stated that there was a "very deliberate and well-crafted strategy to hide irregularities from audit teams at both Defence and Public Works."

**Sources:* www.ctv.ca, March 11, 2004; www.canada.com, September 17, 2007.

Good internal control systems include a system of authorizations for credit limits and approvals for purchases and payments, usually with a limit imposed. The *Financial Administration Act* had such limits; public servants could authorize payments up to $250,000. It seems that the perpetrators of the fraud made a series of fraudulent purchases for amounts under $250,000. In addition, the perpetrators argued that national security required that secrecy surround the transactions. Thus the transactions escaped detection. The three perpetrators of the fraud pleaded guilty in 2007 and were sentenced to jail terms.

Limitations of Internal Control—Costs and Benefits

Unfortunately, most internal control measures can be overcome. Systems designed to thwart one person's fraud can be beaten by two or more employees working together—*colluding*—to defraud the firm. Consider the Galaxy Theatre. Ralph, who sells tickets, and Lana, who takes the tickets, can design a scheme in which Ralph sells tickets and pockets the cash from 10 customers. Lana admits 10 customers without tickets. Ralph and Lana split the cash. To prevent this situation, Colleen, the manager, must take additional steps, such as matching the number of people in the theatre against the number of ticket stubs retained. But that takes time away from her other duties.

The stricter the internal control system, the more it costs. A too-complex system of internal control can strangle the business with red tape. How tight should the controls be? Internal controls must be judged in light of their costs and benefits. An example of a good cost/benefit relationship: A security guard at a Walmart store costs about $28,000 a year. On average, each guard prevents about $50,000 of theft. The net savings to Walmart is $22,000.

The Bank Account as a Control Device

Cash is the most liquid asset because it is the medium of exchange. Cash is easy to conceal and relatively easy to steal. As a result, most businesses have specific controls for cash.

Keeping cash in a bank account helps control cash. This is important because banks have established practices for safeguarding customers' money. The documents used to control bank accounts include the following:

- Signature card
- Bank statement
- Deposit slip
- Bank reconciliation
- Cheque

Signature Card

Banks require each person authorized to sign on an account to provide a *signature card*. This protects against forgery.

Deposit Slip

Banks supply standard forms such as *deposit slips*. The customer fills in the amount of each deposit. As proof of the transaction, the customer keeps a deposit receipt.

Cheque

To pay cash, the depositor can write a **cheque**, which tells the bank to pay the designated party a specified amount. There are three parties to a cheque:

- The maker, who signs the cheque
- The payee, to whom the cheque is paid
- The bank on which the cheque is drawn

Exhibit 4-4 shows a cheque drawn by Nixon Partners Inc., the maker. The cheque has two parts, the cheque itself and the **remittance advice** below. This optional attachment, which may often be scanned electronically, tells the payee the reason for the payment and is used as a source document for posting the proper accounts.

Bank Statement

Banks may send monthly statements to customers in paper form or the statements are available on the bank's Web site. A **bank statement** reports what the bank did with the customer's cash. The statement shows the account's beginning and ending balances, cash receipts, and payments. Exhibit 4-5 is the January 2011 bank statement of Nixon Partners Inc.

Electronic funds transfer (EFT) moves cash by electronic communication. It is cheaper for a company to pay employees by EFT (direct deposit) than by issuing payroll cheques. Many people pay their regular bills, such as mortgage, rent, and utilities, by EFT.

EXHIBIT 4-4 **Cheque With Remittance Advice**

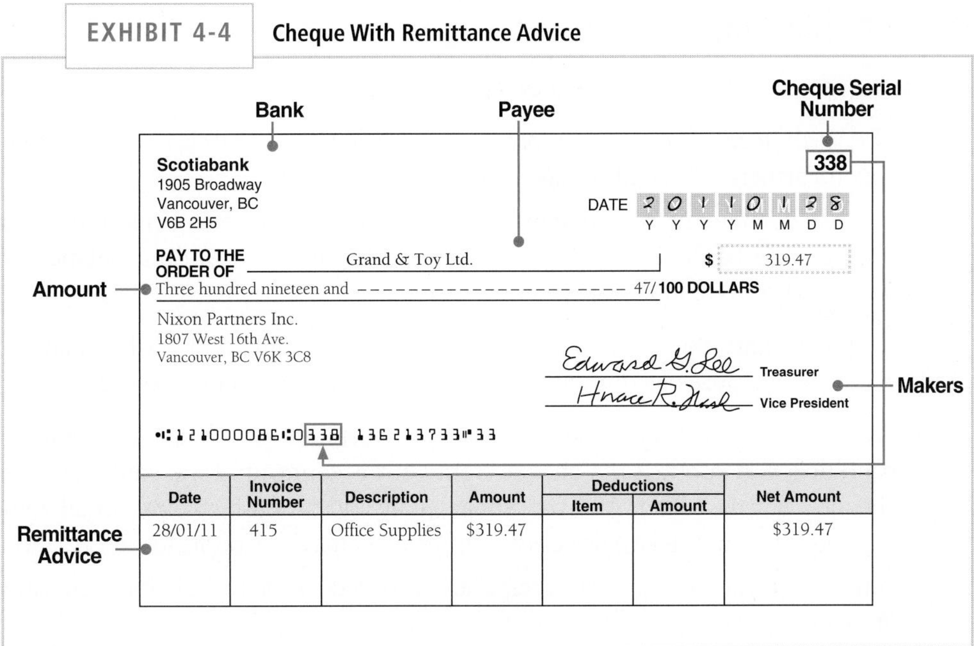

Scotiabank
1905 Broadway
Vancouver, BC
V6B 2H5

338

DATE 2 0 1 1 0 1 2 8
Y Y Y Y M M D D

PAY TO THE ORDER OF Grand & Toy Ltd. $ 319.47

Three hundred nineteen and ---- 47/100 DOLLARS

Nixon Partners Inc.
1807 West 16th Ave.
Vancouver, BC V6K 3C8

Edward G. Lee — Treasurer
Horace R. Hask — Vice President

Date	Invoice Number	Description	Amount	Deductions		Net Amount
				Item	Amount	
28/01/11	415	Office Supplies	$319.47			$319.47

EXHIBIT 4-5 **Bank Statement**

ACCOUNT STATEMENT

Scotiabank
1905 Broadway Vancouver, BC V6B 2H5

Nixon Partners Inc.
1807 West 16th Avenue
Vancouver, BC V6K 3C8

BUSINESS CHEQUING ACCOUNT 136–213733

CHEQUING ACCOUNT SUMMARY AS OF 31/01/11

BEGINNING BALANCE	TOTAL DEPOSITS	TOTAL WITHDRAWALS	SERVICE CHARGES	ENDING BALANCE
6,556.12	4,352.64	4,963.00	14.25	5,931.51

BUSINESS CHEQUING ACCOUNT TRANSACTIONS

DEPOSITS	DATE	AMOUNT
Deposit	Jan04	1,000.00
Deposit	Jan04	112.00
Deposit	Jan06	194.60
EFT—Collection of rent	Jan10	904.03
Bank Collection	Jan16	2,114.00
Interest	Jan20	28.01

CHARGES	DATE	AMOUNT
Service Charge	Jan31	14.25
Cheques:		

CHEQUES			BALANCES			
Number	Date	Amount	Date	Balance	Date	Balance
332	Jan06	3,000.00	Dec31	6,556.12	Jan16	7,378.75
656	Jan06	100.00	Jan04	7,616.12	Jan20	7,045.76
333	Jan10	150.00	Jan06	4,710.72	Jan25	5,945.76
334	Jan12	100.00	Jan10	5,464.75	Jan31	5,931.51
335	Jan12	100.00	Jan12	5,264.75		
336	Jan25	1,100.00				

OTHER CHARGES	DATE	AMOUNT
NSF	Jan04	52.00
EFT—Insurance	Jan20	361.00

MONTHLY SUMMARY

Withdrawals: 8 | Minimum Balance: 4,710.72 | Average Balance: 6,215.00

Bank Reconciliation

There are two records of a business's cash:

1. The Cash account in the company's general ledger. Exhibit 4-6 shows that Nixon Partners Inc.'s ending cash balance is $3,294.21.
2. The bank statement, which shows the cash receipts and payments transacted through the bank. In Exhibit 4-5, the bank shows an ending balance of $5,931.51 for Nixon Partners.

The books and the bank statement usually show different cash balances. Differences arise because of a time lag in recording transactions. Here are two examples:

- When you write a cheque, you immediately deduct it in your chequebook. But the bank does not subtract the cheque from your account until the bank pays the cheque a few days later. And you immediately add the cash receipts for all your deposits. But it may take a day or two for the bank to add deposits to your balance.
- Your EFT payments and cash receipts are recorded by the bank before you learn of them.

To ensure accurate cash records, you need to update your cash record—either online or after you receive your bank statement. The result of this updating process

EXHIBIT 4-6 **Cash Records of Nixon Partners Inc.**

ACCOUNT Cash

Date		Item	Debit	Credit	Balance
2011					
Jan.	1	Balance			6,556.12
	2	Cash receipt	1,112.00		7,668.12
	5	Cash receipt	194.60		7,862.72
	31	Cash payments		6,160.14	1,702.58
	31	Cash receipt	1,591.63		3,294.21

Cash Payments

Cheque No.	Amount	Cheque No.	Amount
332	$3,000.00	338	$ 319.47
333	510.00	339	83.00
334	100.00	340	203.14
335	100.00	341	458.53
336	1,100.00		
337	286.00	Total	$6,160.14

allows you to prepare a **bank reconciliation**. The bank reconciliation explains all differences between your cash records and your bank balance.

The person who prepares the bank reconciliation should have no other cash duties and be independent of cash activities. Otherwise, he or she can steal cash and manipulate the reconciliation to conceal the theft.

Preparing the Bank Reconciliation

OBJECTIVE

3 **Prepare** and use a bank reconciliation

Here are the items that appear on a bank reconciliation. They all cause differences between the bank balance and the book balance. We call your cash record (also known as a "chequebook") the "books."

Bank Side of the Reconciliation.

1. Items to show on the *Bank* side of the bank reconciliation include the following:
   a. *Deposits in transit* (outstanding deposits). You have recorded these deposits, but the bank has not. Add **deposits in transit** on the bank reconciliation.
   b. *Outstanding cheques.* You have recorded these cheques, but the bank has not yet paid them. Subtract **outstanding cheques.**
   c. *Bank errors.* Correct all bank errors on the Bank side of the reconciliation. For example, the bank may erroneously subtract from your account a cheque written by someone else.

Book Side of the Reconciliation.

2. Items to show on the *Book* side of the bank reconciliation include the following:
   a. *Bank collections.* **Bank collections** are cash receipts that the bank has recorded for your account. But you haven't recorded the cash receipt yet. Many businesses have their customers pay directly to their bank. This is called a *lockbox system* and reduces theft. An example is a bank collecting an account receivable for you. Add bank collections on the bank reconciliation.

b. *Electronic funds transfers.* The bank may receive or pay cash on your behalf. An electronic funds transfer (EFT) may be a cash receipt or a cash payment. Add EFT receipts and subtract EFT payments.

c. *Service charge.* This cash payment is the bank's fee for processing your transactions. Subtract service charges.

d. *Interest revenue on your chequing account.* On certain types of bank accounts, you earn interest if you keep enough cash in your account. The bank statement tells you of this cash receipt. Add interest revenue.

e. *Nonsufficient funds (NSF) cheques.* **Non-sufficient funds (NSF) cheques** are cash receipts from customers who do not have sufficient funds in their bank account to cover the amount. NSF cheques (sometimes called bad cheques) are treated as cash payments on your bank reconciliation. Subtract NSF cheques.

f. *The cost of printed cheques.* This cash payment is handled like a service charge. Subtract this cost.

g. *Book errors.* Correct all book errors on the Book side of the reconciliation. For example, you may have recorded a $120 cheque that you wrote as $210.

In a business, the bank reconciliation can be a part of internal control if it is done on a regular basis and if someone independent of the person preparing the bank reconciliation, for example, someone from another department, reviews the reconciliation.

Bank Reconciliation Illustrated. The bank statement in Exhibit 4-5 indicates that the January 31 bank balance of Nixon Partners Inc. is $5,931.51. However, Exhibit 4-6 shows that the company's Cash account on the books has a balance of $3,294.21. This situation calls for a bank reconciliation. Exhibit 4-7, Panel A, lists the reconciling items for easy reference, and Panel B shows the completed reconciliation.

After the reconciliation in Exhibit 4-7, the adjusted bank balance equals the adjusted book balance. This equality checks the accuracy of both the bank and the books.

Journalizing Transactions From the Bank Reconciliation. The bank reconciliation is an accountant's tool separate from the journals and ledgers. It does *not* account for transactions in the journal. To get the transactions into the accounts, we must make journal entries and post to the ledger. All items on the *Book* side of the bank reconciliation require journal entries.

The bank reconciliation in Exhibit 4-7 requires Nixon Partners to make journal entries to bring the Cash account up to date. Numbers in parentheses correspond to the reconciling items listed in Exhibit 4-7, Panel A.

(4) Jan.	31	Cash	904.03	
		Rent revenue		904.03
		Receipt of rent revenue.		
(5) Jan.	31	Cash	2,114.00	
		Notes receivable		1,900.00
		Interest revenue		214.00
		Note receivable collected by bank.		
(6) Jan.	31	Cash	28.01	
		Interest revenue		28.01
		Interest earned on bank balance.		
(7) Jan.	31	Cash	360.00	
		Accounts payable—Brown Company Ltd.		360.00
		Correction of cheque no. 333.		

(8) Jan.	31	Miscellaneous expense*	14.25	
		Cash		14.25
		Bank service charge.		
(9) Jan.	31	Accounts receivable—L. Ross	52.00	
		Cash		52.00
		NSF customer cheque returned by bank.		
(10) Jan.	31	Insurance expense	361.00	
		Cash		361.00
		Payment of monthly insurance.		

*Note: Miscellaneous Expense is debited for the bank service charge because the service charge pertains to no particular expense category.

EXHIBIT 4-7 Bank Reconciliation

PANEL A—Reconciling Items

Bank side:

1. Deposit in transit, $1,591.63
2. Bank error: The bank deducted $100.00 on January 6 for a cheque written by another company. Add $100.00 to the bank balance.
3. Outstanding cheques—total of $1,350.14

Cheque No.	Amount
337	$286.00
338	319.47
339	83.00
340	203.14
341	458.53

Book side:

4. EFT receipt of your rent revenue earned on an investment, $904.03.
5. Bank collection of your note receivable including interest of $214.00, $2,114.00.
6. Interest revenue earned on your bank balance, $28.01.
7. Book error: You recorded cheque no. 333 for $510.00 The amount you actually paid on account was $150.00. Add $360.00 to your book balance.
8. Bank service charge, $14.25.
9. NSF cheque from a customer, $52.00. Subtract $52.00 from your book balance.
10. EFT payment of insurance expense, $361.00.

PANEL B—Bank Reconciliation

Nixon Partners Inc.
Bank Reconciliation
January 31, 2011

Bank			Books		
Balance, January 31		$5,931.51	Balance, January 31		$3,294.21
Add:			Add:		
1. Deposit in transit		1,591.63	4. EFT receipt of rent revenue		904.03
2. Correction of bank error		100.00	5. Bank collection of note		
		7,623.14	receivable		2,114.00
			6. Interest revenue earned on		
			bank balance		28.01
			7. Correction of book error—		
Less:			overstated our cheque no. 333		360.00
3. Outstanding cheques					6,700.25
No. 337	$286.00				
No. 338	319.47		Less:		
No. 339	83.00		8. Service charge	$ 14.25	
No. 340	203.14		9. NSF cheque	52.00	
No. 341	458.53	(1,350.14)	10. EFT payment of insurance expense	361.00	(427.25)
Adjusted bank balance		$6,273.00	Adjusted bank balance		$6,273.00

These amounts should agree.

Summary of the Various Reconciling Items:

Bank Balance—Always

- *Add* deposits in transit.
- *Subtract* outstanding cheques.
- *Add* or *subtract* corrections of bank errors.

Book Balance—Always

- *Add* bank collections, interest revenue, and EFT receipts.
- *Subtract* service charges, NSF cheques, and EFT payments.
- *Add* or *subtract* corrections of book errors.

The entry for the NSF cheque (entry 9) needs explanation. Upon learning that a customer's $52.00 cheque to us was not good, we must credit Cash to update the Cash account. Unfortunately, we still have a receivable from the customer, so we must debit Accounts Receivable to reinstate our receivable.

Online Banking

Online banking allows you to pay bills and view your account electronically. You don't have to wait until the end of the month to get a bank statement. With online banking you can reconcile transactions at any time and keep your account current whenever you wish. Exhibit 4-8 shows a page from the account history of Toni Anderson's bank account.

The account history—like a bank statement—lists deposits, cheques, EFT payments, ATM withdrawals, and interest earned on Toni's bank balance.

But the account history doesn't show Toni's beginning balance, so Toni can't work from her beginning balance to her ending balance.

Using the Bank Reconciliation to Control Cash

The bank reconciliation is a powerful control device. Julie Brox is a CMA in Regina, Saskatchewan. She owns several apartment complexes that are managed by her uncle, Herman Klassen. Her uncle signs up tenants, collects the monthly rents, arranges custodial and maintenance work, hires and fires employees, writes the cheques, and

EXHIBIT 4-8 **Online Banking—Account History (Like a Bank Statement)**

Account History for Toni Anderson Chequing # 5401-632-9
as of Close of Business 07/27/2011

Account Details

Date ↓	Description	Withdrawals	Deposits	Balance
	Current Balance			**$4,136.08**
07/27/11	DEPOSIT		1,170.35	
07/26/11	28 DAYS INTEREST		2.26	
07/25/11	Cheque #6131 View Image	443.83		
07/24/11	Cheque #6130 View Image	401.52		
07/23/11	EFT PYMT ROGERS	61.15		
07/22/11	EFT PYMT	3,172.85		
07/20/11	Cheque #6127 View Image	550.00		
07/19/11	Cheque #6122 View Image	50.00		
07/16/11	Cheque #6116 View Image	2,056.75		
07/15/11	Cheque #6123 View Image	830.00		
07/13/11	Cheque #6124 View Image	150.00		
07/11/11	ATM 4900 16th AVE	200.00		
07/09/11	Cheque #6119 View Image	30.00		
07/05/11	Cheque #6125 View Image	2,500.00		
07/04/11	ATM 4900 16th AVE	100.00		
07/01/11	DEPOSIT		9,026.37	

E-Mail

STOP + THINK

You have been asked to prepare a bank reconciation and are given the following information. The bank statement balance is $4,500 and shows a service charge of $15, interest earned of $5, and an NSF cheque for $300. Deposits in transit total $1,200; outstanding cheques are $575. You recorded as $152 a cheque of $125 in payment of an account payable.

1. What is the adjusted bank balance?
2. What was the book balance of cash before the reconciliation?

Answers:

1. $5,125 ($4,500 + $1,200 − $575).
2. $5,408 ($5,125 + $15 − $5 + $300 − $27).

The adjusted book and bank balances are the same. The answer can be determined by working backward from the adjusted balance.

performs the bank reconciliation. In short, he does it all. This concentration of duties in one person is evidence of weak internal control. Brox's uncle could be stealing from her or making mistakes, and as a CMA she is aware of this possibility.

Brox trusts her uncle because he is a member of the family. Nevertheless, she exercises some controls over his management of her apartments. Brox periodically drops by her properties to see whether the custodial/maintenance staff is keeping the property in good condition. To control cash, Brox regularly examines the bank reconciliation that her uncle has performed. Brox would know immediately if her uncle were writing cheques to himself. By examining each cheque, Brox establishes control over cash payments.

Brox has a simple method for controlling cash receipts. She knows the occupancy level of her apartments. She also knows the monthly rent she charges. She multiplies the number of apartments—20—by the monthly rent (which averages $800 per unit) to arrive at an expected monthly rent revenue of $16,000. By tracing the $16,000 revenue to the bank statement, Brox can tell if all her rent money went into her bank account. To keep her uncle on his toes, Brox lets him know that she periodically audits his work.

Control activities such as these are critical. If there are only a few employees, separation of duties may not be feasible. The owner must control operations, or the assets may slip away. These controls are called *executive controls*.

MyAccountingLab

MID-CHAPTER SUMMARY PROBLEM

The Cash account of Chima Inc. at February 28, 2011, is as follows:

Cash

Feb. 1	Balance	3,995	Feb. 5	400
6		800	12	3,100
15		1,800	19	1,100
22		1,100	26	500
28		2,400	27	900
Feb. 28	Balance	4,095		

Aneil Chima deposits all cash receipts in the bank and makes all cash payments by cheque. Chima Inc. receives this bank statement on February 28, 2011 (as always, negative amounts are in parentheses):

Name: Chima Inc.
Accounting Period: Month of February 2011
Key Fact: Existing, ongoing business

Bank Statement for February 2011

Beginning balance		$ 3,995
Deposits:		
Feb. 7	$ 800	
15	1,800	
23	1,100	3,700
Cheques (total per day):		
Feb. 8	$ 400	
16	3,100	
23	1,100	(4,600)
Other items:		
Service charge		(10)
NSF cheque from M. E. Crown		(700)
Bank collection of note receivable		1,000*
EFT—monthly rent expense		(330)
Interest on account balance		15
Ending balance		$ 3,070

*Includes interest of $119

Required

1. Prepare the bank reconciliation of Chima Inc. at February 28, 2011.
2. Record the journal entries based on the bank reconciliation.

ANSWERS

Requirement 1

Chima Inc.
Bank Reconciliation
February 28, 2011

Bank:		
Balance, February 28, 2011		$3,070
Add: Deposit of February 28 in transit		2,400
		5,470
Less: Outstanding cheques issued on Feb. 26 ($500) and Feb. 27 ($900)		(1,400)
Adjusted bank balance, February 28, 2011		$4,070
Books:		
Balance, February 28, 2011		$4,095
Add: Bank collection of note receivable, including interest of $119		1,000
Interest earned on bank balance		15
		5,110
Less: Service charge	$ 10	
NSF cheque	700	
EFT—Rent expense	330	(1,040)
Adjusted book balance, February 28, 2011		$4,070

Before creating the bank reconciliation, compare the Cash account and the bank statement. Cross out all items that appear in both places. The items that remain are the reconciling items.

Begin with the ending balance on the bank statement.
- Add deposits (debits) from the Cash account not on the bank statement.
- Deduct cheques (credits) from the Cash account not on the bank statement.

Begin with the ending balance in the Cash general ledger account.
- Add money received by the bank on behalf of the company (increases to the bank statement balance).
- Deduct bank charges, NSF cheques, or pre-authorized payments (decreases to the bank statement balance).

Requirement 2

Feb. 28	Cash	1,000	
	Note receivable ($1,000 − $119)		881
	Interest revenue		119
	Note receivable collected by bank.		
28	Cash	15	
	Interest revenue		15
	Interest earned on bank balance.		
28	Miscellaneous expense	10	
	Cash		10
	Bank service charge.		

Feb. 28	Accounts receivable—M. E. Crown	700	
	Cash		700
	NSF cheque returned by bank.		
28	Rent expense	330	
	Cash		330
	Monthly rent expense.		

Prepare journal entries for all reconciling items from the "Books" section of the bank reconciliation.

OBJECTIVE

4 **Apply** internal controls to cash receipts and cash payments

Internal Control Over Cash Receipts

Cash requires some specific internal controls because cash is relatively easy to steal and it's easy to convert to other forms of wealth. Moreover, all transactions ultimately affect cash. That is why cash is called "the eye of the needle." Let's see how to control cash receipts.

All cash receipts should be deposited for safekeeping in the bank—quickly. Companies receive cash over the counter and through the mail. Each source of cash requires its own security measures.

Cash Receipts Over the Counter

Exhibit 4-9 illustrates a cash receipt over the counter in a grocery store. The point-of-sale terminal provides control over the cash receipts. Consider a Sobeys store. For each transaction, a Sobeys sales associate issues a receipt to the customer as proof of purchase. The cash drawer opens when all the purchases have been entered, and the machine electronically transmits a record of the sale to the store's main computer. At the end of each shift, the sales associate delivers his or her cash drawer to the office, where it is combined with cash from all other terminals and delivered by armoured car to the bank for deposit. Later, a separate employee in the accounting department

EXHIBIT 4-9 Cash Receipts Over the Counter

reconciles the electronic record of the sales per terminal to the record of the cash turned in. These measures, coupled with oversight by a manager, discourage theft.

Point-of-sale terminals also provide effective control over inventory. For example, in a restaurant, these devices track sales by menu item and total sales by cash, type of credit card, gift card redeemed, etc. They create the daily sales journal for that store, which, in turn, interfaces with the general ledger. Managers can use records produced by point-of-sale terminals to check inventory levels and compare them against sales records for accuracy. For example, in a restaurant, an effective way to monitor sales of expensive wine is for a manager to perform a quick count of the bottles on hand at the end of the day and compare it with the count at the end of the previous day, plus the record of any purchased. The count at the end of the previous day, plus the record of bottles purchased, minus the count at the end of the current day should equal the amount sold as recorded by the point-of-sale terminals in the restaurant.

An effective control for many chain retail businesses, such as restaurants, grocery stores, or clothing stores, to prevent unauthorized access to cash as well as to allow for more efficient management of cash, is the use of "depository bank accounts." Cash receipts for an individual store are deposited into a local bank account (preferably delivered by armoured car for security reasons) on a daily basis. The corporate headquarters arranges for its centralized bank to draft the local depository accounts on a frequent (perhaps daily) basis to get the money concentrated into the company's centralized account, where it can be used to pay the corporation's bills. Depository accounts are "one-way" accounts where the local management may only make deposits. They have no authority to write cheques on the account or take money out of the store's account.

Cash Receipts by Mail

Many companies receive cash by mail. Exhibit 4-10 shows how some companies control cash received by mail. All incoming mail is opened by a mailroom employee. The person opening the mail should also make a list of the receipts as an independent control from the treasurer/accounting department.The mailroom then sends all customer cheques to the treasurer, who has the cashier deposit the money in the bank. The remittance advices go to the accounting department for journal entries to Cash

EXHIBIT 4-10 **Receipts of Cheques by Mail**

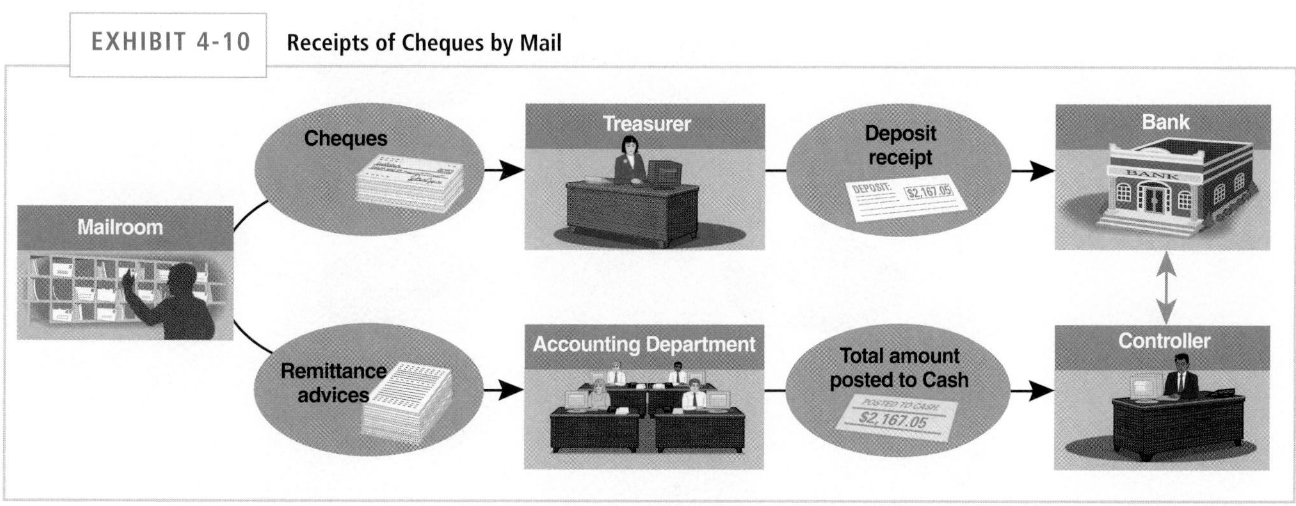

and to the appropriate customers' accounts receivable. As a final step, the controller compares the following records for the day:

- Bank deposit amount from the treasurer
- Debit to Cash from the accounting department

The debit to Cash should equal the amount deposited in the bank. All cash receipts are safe in the bank, and the company books are up to date.

Many companies use a lockbox system. Customers send their cheques directly to the company's bank account. Internal control is tight because company personnel never touch incoming cash. The lockbox system puts your cash to work immediately.

Internal Control Over Cash Payments

Companies make most payments by cheque. Let's see how to control cash payments by cheque.

Controls Over Payment by Cheque

As we have seen, you need a good separation of duties between (a) operations and (b) writing cheques for cash payments. Payment by cheque is an important internal control, as follows:

- The cheque provides a record of the payment.
- The cheque must be signed by an authorized official.
- Before signing the cheque, the official should study the evidence supporting the payment.

Controls Over Purchase and Payment. To illustrate the internal control over cash payments by cheque, suppose GreBru Products buys some of its inventory from Gildan Activewear Inc. The purchasing and payment process follows the steps shown in Exhibit 4-11. Start with the box for GreBru Products on the left side.

EXHIBIT 4-11 **The Purchasing/Paying Process**

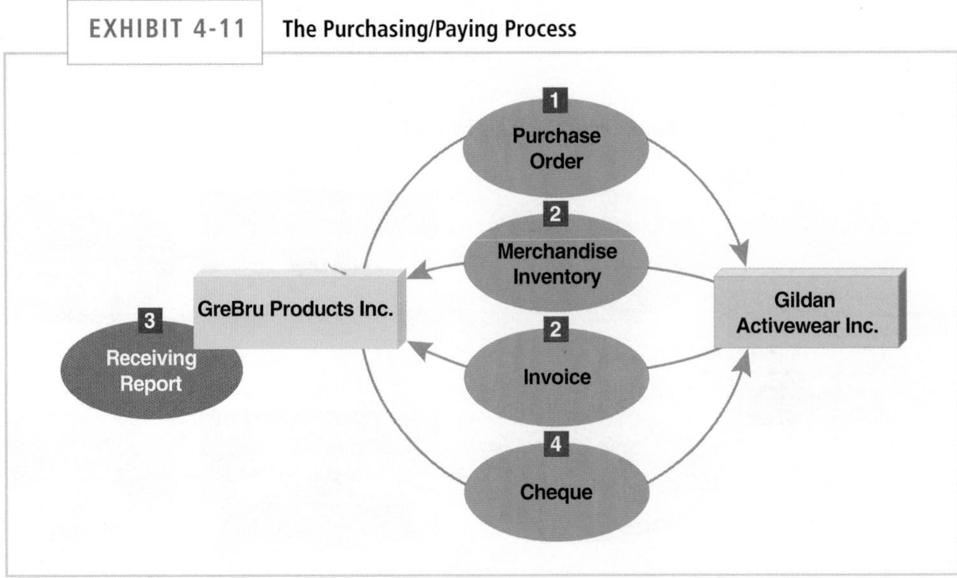

1 GreBru faxes a *purchase order* to Gildan. GreBru says, "Please send us 100 T-shirts."

2 Gildan ships the goods and faxes an *invoice* back to GreBru. Gildan sent the goods.

3 GreBru receives the *inventory* and prepares a *receiving report* to list the goods received. GreBru got its T-shirts.

4 After approving all documents, GreBru says, "Okay, we'll pay you" and sends a cheque to Gildan.

For good internal control, the purchasing agent should neither receive the goods nor approve the payment. If these duties aren't separated, a purchasing agent can buy goods and have them shipped to his or her home. Or a purchasing agent can spend too much on purchases, approve the payment, and split the excess with the supplier. To avoid these problems, companies distribute the following duties among different employees:

- Purchasing goods
- Receiving goods
- Approving the invoice for goods
- Signing the cheque or approving the EFT

Exhibit 4-12 shows GreBru's payment packet of documents.

Before approving the payment, the treasurer's department should examine the packet to ensure that all the documents agree. Only then does the company know:

1. It received the goods ordered.
2. It pays only for the goods received.

After payment, the person in the treasurer's department who has authorized the disbursement stamps the payment packet "paid" or punches a hole through it to prevent it from being submitted a second time. Dishonest people have tried to run a bill through twice for payment. The stamp or hole shows that the bill has been paid. If cheques are used, they should then be mailed directly to the payee without being allowed to return to the department that prepared them. To do so would violate separation of the duties of cash handling and record keeping, as well as unauthorized access to cash.

EXHIBIT 4-12 **Payment Packet**

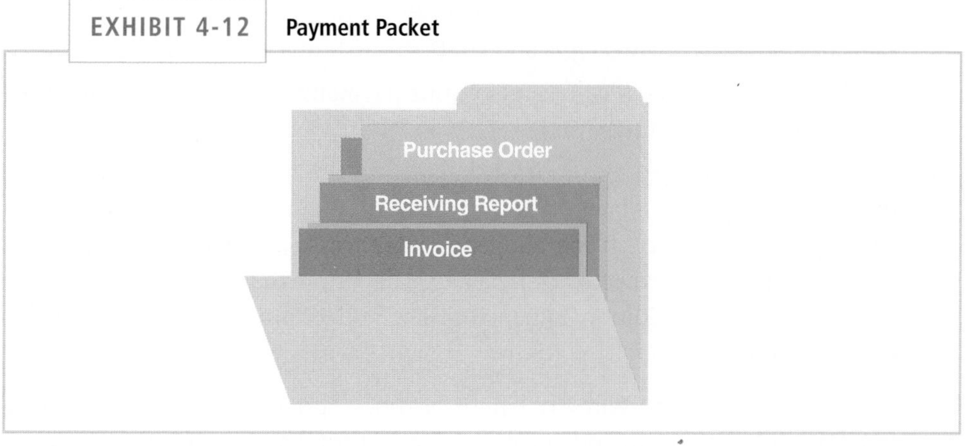

Petty Cash. It would be wasteful to write separate cheques for an executive's taxi fare, name tags needed right away, and delivery of a package across town. To pay such minor amounts, companies keep a small **petty cash** fund on hand in the care of a single employee.

The petty cash fund is opened with a particular amount of cash. A cheque for that amount is issued to Petty Cash. Assume that on February 28, CHC Helicopter Corp. establishes a petty cash fund of $500 in a sales department. The custodian of the petty cash fund cashes the cheque and places $500 in the fund, which may be a cash box or other device.

For each petty cash payment, the custodian prepares a petty cash slip to list the item purchased. The sum of the cash in the petty cash fund plus the total of the slip amounts should equal the opening balance at all times—in this case, $500. The Petty Cash account keeps its prescribed $500 balance at all times. Maintaining the Petty Cash account at this balance, supported by the fund (cash plus slips), is how an **imprest system** works. The control feature of an imprest system is that it clearly identifies the amount for which the custodian is responsible.

Using a Budget to Manage Cash

OBJECTIVE

5 **Use** a budget to manage cash

Managers control their organizations with an operating budget. As mentioned earlier in the chapter, a *budget* is a financial plan that helps managers coordinate business activities. Cash is the item that is budgeted most often.

How, for example, does TELUS Corp. decide when to invest millions in new wireless technology? How will TELUS Corp. decide how much to spend? Will borrowing be needed, or can TELUS Corp. finance the purchase with internally generated cash? What do ending cash balances need to be in order to provide a "safety margin" so the company won't unexpectedly run out of cash? A cash budget for a business works on roughly the same concept as a personal budget. Similarly, by what process do you decide how much to spend on your education? On an automobile? On a house? All of these decisions depend to some degree on the information that a cash budget provides.

A cash budget helps a company or an individual manage cash by planning receipts and payments during a future period. The company must determine how much cash it will need and then decide whether or not its operations will bring in the needed cash. Managers proceed as follows:

1. Start with the entity's cash balance at the beginning of the period. This is the amount left over from the preceding period.
2. Add the budgeted cash receipts and subtract the budgeted cash payments.
3. The beginning balance plus receipts minus payments equals the expected cash balance at the end of the period.
4. Compare the expected ending cash balance to the budgeted cash balance at the end of the period. Managers know the minimum amount of cash they need (the budgeted balance). If the budget shows excess cash, managers can invest the excess. But if the expected cash balance falls below the budgeted balance, the company will need additional financing. The budget is a valuable tool for helping the company plan for the future.

The budget period can span any length of time—a day, a week, a month, or a year. Exhibit 4-13 shows a hypothetical cash budget for The Country Store Ltd. for

EXHIBIT 4-13 **Cash Budget**

The Country Store Ltd.
Consolidated Cash Budget (Hypothetical)
For the Year Ended January 31, 2012

		(in millions)	
(1)	Cash balance, February 1, 2011		$ 12.0
	Estimated cash receipts:		
(2)	Collections from customers	$360.0	
(3)	Interest and dividends on investments	6.2	
(4)	Sale of store fixtures	4.9	371.1
			383.1
	Estimated cash payments:		
(5)	Purchases of inventory	245.0	
(6)	Operating expenses	82.5	
(7)	Expansion of existing stores	14.6	
(8)	Opening of new stores	12.4	
(9)	Payment of long-term debt	16.0	
(10)	Payment of dividends	8.0	(378.5)
(11)	Cash available (needed) before new financing		4.6
(12)	Budgeted cash balance, January 31, 2012		13.5
(13)	Cash available for additional investments (New financing needed)		$ (8.9)

the year ended January 31, 2012. Study it carefully, because at some point you will use a cash budget.

The Country Store Ltd.'s cash budget in Exhibit 4-13 begins with $12.0 million of cash (line 1). Then add budgeted cash receipts and subtract budgeted payments. In this case The Country Store expects to have $4.6 million of cash available at the year end (Line 11). The Country Store managers need to maintain a cash balance of at least $13.5 million (Line 12). Line 13 shows that The Country Store must arrange the financing of $8.9 million in order to achieve its goals for 2012.

Reporting Cash on the Balance Sheet

Most companies have numerous bank accounts, but they usually combine all cash amounts into a single total called "Cash and cash equivalents." **Cash equivalents** include liquid assets such as time deposits and guaranteed investment certificates, which are interest-bearing accounts that can be withdrawn with no penalty. Slightly less liquid than cash, cash equivalents are sufficiently similar to be reported along with cash. The balance sheet of GreBru Products Inc. reported the following at December 31, 2011.

GreBru Products Inc.
Consolidated Balance Sheet (Partial, Adapted)
As at December 31, 2011

Assets	
Current assets:	
Cash and cash equivalents	$8,000

Make an Ethical Business Judgment

OBJECTIVE

6 **Make** ethical business judgmenst

A REAL-WORLD EXAMPLE

ETHICS ALERT!

Sherron Watkins was a vice-president of Enron Corporation, one of the largest energy companies in the world in 2000. Watkins is a CPA (the Canadian equivalent of a CA). In the process of her work, she discovered that Enron's CFO, Andy Fastow, was involved in a significant fraud that resulted in Enron's financial statements being materially misstated. Watkins faced a tough decision that had an ethical dimension. The following discussion uses the framework for making ethical decisions developed in Chapter 1 to examine how Watkins worked through the ethical dilemma.

Question	Guideline
1. What is the issue?	**1.** Watkins' ethical dilemma was to decide what she should do with the information she had uncovered. *Specify the alternatives.* For Sherron Watkins, four alternatives are (a) express her concern about the outside partnerships to her boss, CFO Andrew Fastow; (b) express her concern to Kenneth Lay, CEO of Enron; (c) do nothing; or (d) resign.
2. Who are the important stakeholders?	**2.** *A*ll Enron employees (including Watkins), shareholders, creditors, and the U.S. Securities and Exchange Commission (SEC).
3. What are the alternatives and consequences?	**3.** **a.** If Watkins approached Fastow, he might have penalized her, or he might have rewarded her for careful work. This would have preserved her integrity and led Fastow to correct the situation and preserve Enron's public trust, but Fastow might have fired Watkins for insubordination. **b.** If Watkins took her concerns to the CEO, who was Fastow's boss—going over Fastow's head—her integrity would have been preserved. Her relationship with Fastow would surely have been strained and it might have been difficult for them to work together in the future. Watkins might have been rewarded for careful work, but if Fastow's boss had colluded with Fastow in setting up the partnerships, Watkins could have been penalized. If the situation was corrected and outsiders were notified, Enron could have been reprimanded by the SEC if the company's financial-statement data proved inaccurate. **c. and d.** If Watkins had done nothing, or resigned, she would have avoided a confrontation with Fastow or Lay. But, the public might have suffered if investors and creditors relied on faulty data and Watkins' conscience would likely have troubled her.
4. Decisions	**4.** Identifying the best choice is difficult. Watkins had to balance the likely effects on the various people against the dictates of her own conscience. This framework identifies the relevant factors. As it turned out, Watkins took her concerns to CEO Kenneth Lay, and he launched an investigation into the situation. Unfortunately, however, enough damage had already been done and Enron filed for Chapter 11 bankruptcy protection from its creditors. Enron fired Andrew Fastow who has since pleaded guilty to a number of charges and is now in jail.

SUMMARY OF CHAPTER 4

Learning Objective ❶: Learn about fraud and how much it costs

Fraud is the intentional misrepresentation of facts, made for the purpose of persuading another party to act in a way that causes injury or damage to that party. Fraud is a very important concern to any organization including not-for-profit organizations such as the Red Cross and religious organizations.

The two most common types of fraud are:

- **Misappropriation of assets.** This type of fraud is committed by an employee and is sometimes called fraud against the company.
- **Fraudulent financial reporting.** This type of fraud is committed by managers, who misstate a company's financial statements in order to mislead investors, creditors, and other users of financial statements.

Weak or non-existent **internal controls** permit both types of fraud to occur; strong internal controls are the best defence against fraud.

Motive, opportunity, and rationalization, the three corners of the **fraud triangle**, are the three elements that are present in almost every fraud.

Fraud is the ultimate unethical act in business.

Learning Objective ❷: Set up an internal control system

Internal control is a plan of organization and system of procedures designed, implemented, and maintained by company management and the board of directors to deal with risks to the business that have been identified and that relate to the reliability of the company's financial records and financial reporting, the company's ability to operate effectively and efficiently, and the company's compliance with legal requirements.

The components of internal control are the control environment, risk assessment, information system, control procedures, and monitoring of controls. Business risks are the risks that a company will not achieve its objectives.

Internal control procedures include smart hiring practices and separation of duties, comparisons and compliance monitoring, adequate records, limited access, proper approvals, information technology, and safeguard controls.

The discussion about internal control also applies to **e-commerce** and, in addition, e-commerce creates its own risks such as stolen credit-card numbers, **computer viruses**, **Trojan horses**, and **phishing**. E-commerce thus requires additional controls.

Learning Objective ❸: Prepare and use a bank reconciliation

Cash is the most liquid asset because it is a medium of exchange. Cash fraud is common as cash is relatively easy to steal.

Learning Objective ❹: Apply internal controls to cash receipts and cash payments

Bank accounts are controlled by various documents, including signature cards, **bank statements**, deposit slips, **cheques**, **electronic funds transfer (EFT)**, and **bank reconciliations**. Internal control over cash includes controls over cash receipts and cash disbursements.

Learning Objective ❺: Use a budget to manage cash

Budgets are a means by which managers control their organizations. The budget is a future-oriented financial plan that helps companies coordinate their business activities.

Learning Objective ❻: Make an ethical business judgment

The framework for making ethical judgments introduced in Chapter 1 is used in a real-world example.

MyAccountingLab

END-OF-CHAPTER SUMMARY PROBLEM

Assume the following situation and transactions for TransAlta Corporation. At December 31, 2009, TransAlta had total assets of $9,762 million, which included cash and cash equivalents of $82 million. At December 31, 2009, TransAlta had long-term obligations of $4,724 million, of which it expected to pay $63 million during 2010. Suppose at the end of 2009, Brian Burden, CFO of TransAlta, is preparing the budget for the next year.

Suppose Burden makes the following assumption. During 2010, Burden expects TransAlta to collect $2,103 million from customers. TransAlta expects to pay $1,100 million for fuel and purchased power, and $950 million for operations and other cash expenses. To remain competitive, TransAlta plans to spend $500 million to upgrade facilities and purchase new property, plant, and equipment. Sale of property, plant, and equipment will provide cash of $120 million. TransAlta will pay dividends of $225 million and distributions to a subsidiary's non-controlling limited partner of $50 million.

Because of the increased level of activity planned for 2011, Burden budgets the need for a minimum cash balance of $160 million at December 31, 2010.

Name: TransAlta Corporation
Industry: Energy corporation
Document: Cash budget
Fiscal Period: Year ended December 31, 2010

Required

1. How much must TransAlta borrow during 2010 to keep its cash balance from falling below $80 million? Prepare the 2010 cash budget to answer this important question.
2. Consider the company's need to borrow $643 million. TransAlta can avoid the need to borrow money in 2010 by delaying one particular cash payment until 2011 or later. Identify the item, and state why it might be unwise to delay its payment.

ANSWERS

Requirement 1

A cash budget helps a company estimate its cash inflows and cash outflows for a future period. The period of time covered must be specified in the heading of the cash budget.

Use only the cash amounts from the data that are given.

Cash receipts from:
- Ordinary sales
- Extraordinary sales

Cash payments for:
- Purchases from suppliers
- Cash dividends
- Debt repayments

TransAlta Corporation
Cash Budget (Hypothetical)
For the Year Ended December 31, 2010

	(in millions)	
Cash and cash equivalents, December 31, 2009		$ 82
Estimated cash receipts:		
Collections from customers		2,103
Sale of assets		120
		$2,305
Estimated cash payments:		
Purchases of operating expenses	$1,000	
Payment of fuel and purchased power	950	
Upgrading of facilities and purchase of property, plant, and equipment	500	
Payment of dividends and distributions	275	
Payment of long-term debt	63	(2,788)
Cash available (needed) before new financing		(483)
Budgeted cash balance, December 31, 2010		160
Cash available for additional investments, or (New financing needed)		$ (643)

Requirement 2

Consider delaying cash payments to upgrade facilities since the upgrades are not necessary to generate the current level of income.

TransAlta can eliminate the need for borrowing most of the $643 million by delaying the $500 million payment to *upgrade the company's facilities and purchase property, plant, and equipment*. Investors and creditors could consider the delay to be unwise because TransAlta needs the upgrading and new property, plant, and equipment to remain competitive.

Review Internal Control and Cash

Quick Check (Answers are given on page 236.)

1. Internal control has its own terminology. On the left are some key internal control concepts. On the right are some key terms. Match each internal control concept with its term by writing the appropriate letter in the space provided. Not all letters are used.

______	This procedure limits access to sensitive data.	a. Competent personnel
______	This type of insurance policy covers losses due to employee theft.	b. Encryption
______	Trusting your employees can lead you to overlook this procedure.	c. Separation of duties
______	The most basic purposes of internal control.	d. Safeguarding assets
______	Internal control cannot always safeguard against this problem.	e. Fidelity bond
______	Often mentioned as the cornerstone of a good system of internal control.	f. Collusion
______	Pay employees enough to require them to do a good job.	g. Firewalls
		h. Supervision
		i. External audits

2. Each of the following is an example of a control procedure, *except*
   a. Sound personnel procedures
   b. A sound marketing plan
   c. Separation of duties
   d. Limited access to assets
3. Which of the following is an example of poor internal control?
   a. The accounting department compares goods received with the related purchase order.
   b. Employees must take vacations.
   c. Rotate employees through various jobs.
   d. The mailroom clerk records daily cash receipts in the journal.
4. A not-for-profit organization has internal controls because
   a. It has a fiduciary responsibility to safeguard assets.
   b. It makes operations easier for employees.
   c. It wants to be businesslike.
   d. None of the above

Use the following information for Questions 5–8.

Lawrence Corporation has asked you to prepare its bank reconciliation at the end of the current month. Answer Questions 5–8 using the following code letters to indicate how the item described would be reported on the bank reconciliation.

a. Deduct from the book balance
b. Does not belong on the bank reconciliation
c. Add to the bank balance
d. Deduct from the bank balance
e. Add to the book balance

5. A cheque for $835 written by Lawrence during the current month was erroneously recorded as a $358 payment.
6. A $400 deposit made on the last day of the current month did not appear on this month's bank statement.
7. The bank statement showed interest earned of $65.
8. The bank statement included a cheque from a customer that was marked NSF.

9. Which of the following reconciling items does not require a journal entry?
   a. Bank service charge
   b. Bank collection of a note receivable
   c. NSF cheque
   d. Deposit in transit
10. A cheque was written for $542 to purchase supplies. The cheque was recorded in the journal as $425. The entry to correct the error would
    a. Increase Supplies, $117
    b. Decrease Cash, $117
    c. Decrease Supplies, $117
    d. Both a and b
11. A cash budget helps control cash by
    a. Helping to determine whether additional cash is available for investments or new financing is needed
    b. Developing a plan for increasing sales
    c. Ensuring accurate cash records
    d. All of the above

Accounting Vocabulary

audit A periodic examination of a company's financial statements and the accounting systems, controls, and records that produce them. (p. 193)

bank collections Collections of money by the bank on behalf of a depositor. (p. 201)

bank reconciliation A document explaining the reasons for the difference between a depositor's records and the bank's records about the depositor's cash. (p. 201)

bank statement Document showing the beginning and ending balances of a particular bank account listing the month's transactions that affected the account. (p. 199)

budget A quantitative expression of a plan that helps managers coordinate the entity's activities. (p. 193)

cash budget A budget that projects the entity's future cash receipts and cash disbursements. (p. 193)

cash equivalents Investments such as time deposits, certificates of deposit, or high-grade government securities that are considered so similar to cash that they are combined with cash for financial disclosure purposes on the balance sheet. (p. 213)

cheque Document instructing a bank to pay the designated person or business the specified amount of money. (p. 199)

computer virus A malicious program that enters a company's computer system by e-mail or other means and destroys program and data files. (p. 196)

controller The chief accounting officer of a business who accounts for cash. (p. 193)

deposits in transit A deposit recorded by the company but not yet by its bank. (p. 201)

earnings maganagement Occurs when managers record revenues and/or expenses inappropriately to meet profit objectives. (p. 185)

electronic funds transfer (EFT) System that transfers cash by electronic communication rather than by paper documents. (p. 199)

encryption Mathematical rearranging of data within an electronic file to prevent unauthorized access to information. (p. 196)

exception reporting Identifying data that is not within "normal limits" so that managers can follow up and take corrective action. Exception reporting is used in operating and cash budgets to keep company profits and cash flow in line with management's plans. (p. 193)

fidelity bond An insurance policy taken out on employees who handle cash. (p. 195)

firewall An electronic barrier, usually provided by passwords, around computerized data files to protect local area networks of computers from unauthorized access. (p. 196)

fraud An intentional misrepresentation of facts, made for the purpose of persuading another party to act in a way that causes injury or damage to that party. (p. 184)

fraud triangle The three elements that are present in almost all cases of fraud. These elements are motive, opportunity, and rationalization on the part of the perpetrator. (p. 187)

fraudulent financial reporting Fraud perpetrated by management by preparing misleading financial statements. (p. 185)

imprest system A way to account for petty cash by maintaining a constant balance in the petty cash account, supported by the fund (cash plus payment slips) totalling the same amount. (p. 212)

internal control Organizational plan and related measures adopted by an entity to safeguard assets, encourage adherence to company policies, promote operational efficiency, ensure accurate and reliable accounting records, and comply with legal requirements. (p. 188)

lapping A fraudulent scheme to steal cash through misappropriating certain customer payments and posting payments from other customers to the affected accounts to cover it up. Lapping is caused by weak internal controls (i.e., not segregating the duties of cash handling and accounts receivable bookkeeping, allowing the bookkeeper improper access to cash, and not appropriately monitoring the activities of those who handle cash). (p. 183)

lockbox system A system of handling cash receipts by mail whereby customers remit payment directly to the bank, rather than through the entity's mail system. (p. 183)

misappropriation of assets Fraud committed by employees by stealing assets from the company. (p. 185)

nonsufficient funds (NSF) cheque A cheque for which the payer's bank account has insufficient money to pay the cheque. NSF cheques are cash receipts that turn out to be worthless. (p. 202)

operating budget A budget of future net income. The operating budget projects a company's future revenue and expenses. It is usually prepared by line item of the company's income statement. (p. 193)

outstanding cheques Cheques issued by the company and recorded on its books but not yet paid by its bank. (p. 201)

password A special set of characters that must be provided by the user of computerized program or data files to prevent unauthorized access to those files. (p. 195)

petty cash Fund containing a small amount of cash that is used to pay minor amounts. (p. 212)

phishing Creating bogus Web sites for the purpose of stealing unauthorized data, such as names, addresses, social security numbers, bank account, and credit card numbers. (p. 196)

public company Company that offers its securities for sale to the general public. (p. 189)

remittance advice An optional attachment to a cheque (sometimes a perforated tear-off document and sometimes capable of being electronically scanned) that indicates the payer, date, and purpose of the cash payment. The remittance advice is often used as the source document for posting cash receipts or payments. (p. 199)

treasurer In a large company, the department that has total responsibility for cash handling and cash management. This includes cash budgeting, cash collections, writing cheques, investing excess funds, and making proposals for raising additional cash when needed. (p. 192)

Trojan horse A malicious program that hides within legitimate programs and acts like a computer virus. (p. 196)

Assess Your Progress

Make the grade with MyAccountingLab: The exercises and problems in this chapter can be found on MyAccountingLab at www.myaccountinglab.com. You can practise them as often as you want, and they feature step-by-step guided solutions to help you find the right answer.

Short Exercises

Learning Objective ❷
Setting up an internal control system

S4-1 What are some of the major requirements of NI 52–109?

Learning Objective ❷
Components of internal control

S4-2 List the components of internal control. In your own words briefly describe each component.

Learning Objective ❷
Characteristics of an effective system of internal control

S4-3 Explain in your own words why separation of duties is such an important procedure for safeguarding assets. Describe what can happen if the same person has custody of an asset and also accounts for it.

Learning Objective ❶
Learning about fraud

S4-4 Define "fraud." List and briefly discuss the three major components of the "fraud triangle."

Learning Objective ❸
Preparing a bank reconciliation

S4-5 The Cash account of SWITZER Ltd. reported a balance of $2,500 at August 31, 2011. Included were outstanding cheques totalling $900 and an August 31 deposit of $500 that did not appear on the bank statement. The bank statement, which came from HSBC Bank, listed an August 31, 2011, balance of $3,405. Included in the bank balance was an August 30 collection of $550 on account from a customer who pays the bank directly. The bank statement also shows a $20 service charge, $10 of interest revenue that SWITZER earned on its bank balance, and an NSF cheque for $35.

Prepare a bank reconciliation to determine how much cash SWITZER actually has at August 31, 2011.

Learning Objective ❸
Recording transactions from a bank reconciliation

S4-6 After preparing the SWITZER Ltd. bank reconciliation in Short Exercise 4-5, make the company's journal entries for transactions that arise from the bank reconciliation. Include an explanation with each entry.

Learning Objective ❸
Using a bank reconciliation as a control device

S4-7 Jordan Quinn manages the local Homeless Shelter. He fears that a trusted employee has been stealing from the shelter. This employee receives cash from supporters and also prepares the monthly bank reconciliation. To check on the employee, Quinn prepares his own bank reconciliation as in Exhibit 4-7 on page 203.

Homeless Shelter
Bank Reconciliation
August 31, 2011

Bank		Books	
Balance, August 31	$3,300	Balance, August 31	$2,820
Add		Add	
Deposits in transit	400	Bank collections	800
		Interest revenue	10
Less		Less	
Outstanding cheques	(1,100)	Service charge	(30)
Adjusted bank balance	$2,600	Adjusted book balance	$3,600

Does it appear that the employee has stolen from the shelter? If so, how much? Explain your answer. Which side of the bank reconciliation shows the shelter's true cash balance?

Learning Objective 4
Applying internal control over cash receipts

S4-8 Gina Rolande sells memberships to the symphony in Winnipeg. The symphony's procedure requires Rolande to write a patron receipt for all memberships sold. The receipt forms are pre-numbered. Rolande is having personal financial problems, and she stole $500 received from a member. To hide her theft, Rolande destroys the symphony copy of the receipt she gave the member. What will alert manager Tom Jelnick that something is wrong?

Learning Objective 4
Applying internal control over cash payments

S4-9 Answer the following questions about internal control over cash payments:

1. Payment by cheque carries three basic controls over cash. What are they?
2. Suppose a receptionist opens the mail, records payments received, and makes the bank deposit. How could a dishonest receptionist cheat the company? How do companies avoid this internal control weakness?

Learning Objective 5
Using a cash budget

S4-10 Briefly explain how a cash budget works and what it accomplishes with its last few lines of data.

Learning Objective 5
Preparing a cash budget

S4-11 Dairy Farmers of Ontario (DFO) is the marketing group for Ontario's dairy farms. Suppose the organization begins 2011 with cash of $28 million. DFO estimates cash receipts during the year will total $15 million. Planned payments for the year will total $14 million. To meet member commitment, DFO must maintain a cash balance of at least $25 million. Prepare the organization's cash budget for 2011.

Learning Objective 1 6
Learning about fraud and making an ethical judgment

S4-12 Jane Hill, an accountant for Stainton Hardware Inc., discovers that her supervisor, Drew Armour, made several errors last year. Overall, the errors overstated Stainton Hardware's net income by 20%. It is not clear whether the errors were deliberate or accidental. What should Jane Hill do?

Exercises

Learning Objective 2
E-commerce pitfalls

E4-13 How do computer viruses, Trojan horses, and phishing expeditions work? How can these e-commerce pitfalls hurt you? Be specific.

Learning Objective 2
Explaining the role of internal control

E4-14 Answer the following questions on internal control:

a. Separation of duties is an important internal control procedure. Why is this so?
b. Cash may be a small item on the financial statements. Nevertheless, internal control over cash is very important. Why is this true?

c. Crane Company requires that all documents supporting a cheque be cancelled by punching a hole through the packet. Why is this practice required? What might happen if it were not?

Learning Objective ❶❷
Learning about fraud, identifying internal control weaknesses

E4-15 Identify the internal control weakness in the following situations. State how the person can hurt the company.

a. Jerry Miller works as a security guard at U Park parking in Calgary. Miller has a master key to the cash box where commuters pay for parking. Each night Miller prepares the cash report that shows (a) the number of cars that parked on the lot and (b) the day's cash receipts. Sandra Covington, the U Park treasurer, checks Miller's figures by multiplying the number of cars by the parking fee per car. Covington then deposits the cash in the bank.
b. Sharon Fisher is the purchasing agent for Manatee Golf Equipment. Fisher prepares purchase orders based on requests from division managers of the company. Fisher faxes the purchase orders to suppliers who then ship the goods to Manatee. Fisher receives each incoming shipment and checks it for agreement with the purchase order and the related invoice. She then routes the goods to the respective division managers and sends the receiving report and the invoice to the accounting department for payment.
c. The external auditor for Mattson Financial Services takes a global view of the audit. To form his professional opinion of Mattson's financial statements, the auditor runs no tests of Mattson's financial statements or of the underlying transactions. Instead, the auditor computes a few ratios and compares the current-year ratio values to the ratio values a year ago. If the ratio values appear reasonable, the auditor concludes that Mattson's financial statements are okay.

Learning Objective ❷
Identifying internal control strengths and weaknesses

E4-16 The following situations describe two cash payment situations and two cash receipt situations. In each pair, one set of internal controls is better than the other. Evaluate the internal controls in each situation as strong or weak, and give the reason for your answer.

Cash payments:

a. Jim McCord Construction's policy calls for construction supervisors to request the equipment needed for their jobs. The home office then purchases the equipment and has it shipped to the construction site.
b. Granite & Marble Inc.'s policy calls for project supervisors to purchase the equipment needed for jobs. The supervisors then submit the paid receipts to the home office for reimbursement. This policy enables supervisors to get the equipment quickly and keep construction jobs moving.

Cash receipts:

a. At McClaren Chevrolet, cash received by mail goes straight to the accountant, who debits Cash and credits Accounts Receivable to record the collections from customers. The McClaren accountant then deposits the cash in the bank.
b. Cash received by mail at Fleur de Lys Orthopedic Clinic goes to the mailroom, where a mail clerk opens envelopes and totals the cash receipts for the day. The mail clerk forwards customer cheques to the cashier for deposit in the bank and forwards the remittance slips to the accounting department for posting credits to customer accounts.

Learning Objective ❶❷
Learning about fraud, correcting an internal control weakness

E4-17 In June 2008, it was reported in *The Globe and Mail* that Janet Donio, the former chief information officer of the Council of Ontario Universities (COU), was accused of embezzling $600,000 from the organization. Donio is alleged to have arranged the payment of funds for invoices for services never produced and which instead were allegedly siphoned off by Donio. In addition, her chief academic credentials—a Canadian university degree and a Ph.D. from the United States—were found to be bogus. The fraud was not discovered until after her departure from COU when an audit was launched due to irregularities noticed by her successor at COU.

How could Donio have embezzled the funds from COU? Give your opinion on how COU might have prevented the fraud, and the actions taken when irregularities were discovered.

Learning Objective 3
Classifying bank reconciliation items

E4-18 The following items appear on a bank reconciliation:

_______ 1. Outstanding cheques

_______ 2. Bank error: The bank credited our account for a deposit made by another bank customer

_______ 3. Service charge

_______ 4. Deposits in transit

_______ 5. NSF cheque

_______ 6. Bank collection of a note receivable on our behalf

_______ 7. Book error: We debited Cash for $100. The correct debit was $1,000

Classify each item as (a) an addition to the bank balance, (b) a subtraction from the bank balance, (c) an addition to the book balance, or (d) a subtraction from the book balance.

Learning Objective 3
Preparing a bank reconciliation

E4-19 LeAnn Bryant's chequebook lists the following:

Date	Cheque No.	Item	Cheque	Deposit	Balance
Nov. 1					$ 705
4	622	Direct Energy	$ 19		686
9		Dividends		$116	802
13	623	Canadian Tire	43		759
14	624	Petro-Canada	58		701
18	625	Cash	50		651
26	626	St. Mark's Church	25		626
28	627	Bent Tree Apartments	275		351
30		Paycheque		846	1,197

The November bank statement shows

Balance				$ 705
Add deposits				116
Deduct cheques	No.	Amount		
	622	$19		
	623	43		
	624	85*		
	625	50		(197)
Other charges:				
NSF cheque			$ 8	
Service charge			12	(20)
Balance				$ 604

*This is the correct amount for cheque number 624.

Required

Prepare Bryant's bank reconciliation at November 30.

Learning Objective 3
Preparing a bank reconciliation

E4-20 Tim Wong operates a FedEx Kinko's store. He has just received the monthly bank statement at May 31, 2011, from Royal Bank of Canada, and the statement shows an ending balance of $595. Listed on the statement are an EFT customer collection of $300, a service charge of $12, two NSF cheques totalling $120, and a $9 charge for printed cheques. In reviewing his cash records, Wong identifies outstanding cheques totalling $603 and a May 31 deposit in transit of $1,788. During May, he recorded a $290 cheque for the salary of a part-time employee as $29. Wong's Cash account shows a May 31 cash balance of $1,882. How much cash does Wong actually have at May 31?

E4-21 Use the data from Exercise 4-20 to make the journal entries that Wong should record on May 31 to update his Cash account. Include an explanation for each entry.

Learning Objective 3
Journalizing transactions from bank reconciliations

E4-22 A chain of shoe stores uses point-of-sale terminals as cash registers. The register shows the amount of each sale, the cash received from the customer, and any change returned to the customer. The machine also produces a customer receipt but keeps no record of transactions. At the end of the day, the clerk counts the cash in the register and gives it to the cashier for deposit in the company bank account. Write a memo to convince the store manager that there is an internal control weakness over cash receipts. Identify the weakness that gives an employee the best opportunity to steal cash and state how to prevent such a theft.

Learning Objective 4
Evaluating internal control over cash receipts

E4-23 Tee Golf Company manufactures a popular line of golf clubs. Tee Golf employs 140 workers and keeps their employment records on time sheets that show how many hours the employee works each week. On Friday, the shop foreman collects the time sheets, checks them for accuracy, and delivers them to the payroll department for preparation of paycheques. The treasurer signs the paycheques and returns the cheques to the payroll department for distribution to the employees.

Identify the main internal control weakness in this situation, state how the weakness can hurt Tee Golf, and propose a way to correct the weakness.

Learning Objective 4
Evaluating internal control over cash payments

E4-24 Wireless Communications Inc. is preparing its cash budget for 2012. Wireless ended 2011 with cash of $81 million, and managers need to keep a cash balance of at least $75 million for operations.

Collections from customers are expected to total $11,284 million during 2012, and payments for the cost of services and products should reach $6,166 million. Operating expense payments are budgeted at $2,543 million.

During 2012, Wireless expects to invest $1,825 million in new equipment and sell older assets for $115 million. Debt payments scheduled for 2012 will total $597 million. The company forecasts net income of $890 million for 2012 and plans to pay dividends of $338 million.

Prepare Wireless Communications' cash budget for 2012. Will the budgeted level of cash receipts leave Wireless with the desired ending cash balance of $75 million, or will the company need additional financing? If it does, how much will it need?

Learning Objective 5
Preparing a cash budget

E4-25 Sunbelt Bank recently appointed the accounting firm of Baker, Jackson, and Trent as the bank's auditor. Sunbelt quickly became one of Baker, Jackson, and Trent's largest clients. Subject to banking regulations, Sunbelt must provide for any expected losses on notes receivable that Sunbelt may not collect in full.

During the course of the audit, Baker, Jackson, and Trent determined that three large notes receivable of Sunbelt seem questionable. Baker, Jackson, and Trent discussed these loans with Stephanie Carson, controller of Sunbelt. Carson assured the auditors that these notes were good and that the makers of the notes will be able to pay their notes after the economy improves.

Baker, Jackson, and Trent stated that Sunbelt must record a loss for a portion of these notes receivable to account for the likelihood that Sunbelt may never collect their full amount. Carson objected and threatened to dismiss Baker, Jackson, and Trent if the auditor demands that the bank record the loss. Baker, Jackson, and Trent want to keep Sunbelt as a client. In fact, Baker, Jackson, and Trent were counting on the revenue from the Sunbelt audit to finance an expansion of the firm.

Apply the framework for making ethical decisions outlined on page 214 to decide how the accounting firm of Baker, Jackson, and Trent should proceed.

Learning Objective 6
Resolving an ethical challenge

E4-26 Assume Second Cup borrowed $1 million from Bank of Montreal and agreed to (a) pay an interest rate of 7% and (b) maintain a compensating balance amount equal to 5% of the loan. Determine Second Cup's actual effective interest rate on this loan.

Learning Objective 3
Compensating balance agreement

Challenge Exercises

Learning Objective ❶❷❸❻
Learning about fraud, evaluating internal controls over cash payments, making ethical judgments

E4-27 Morris Cody, the owner of Parkwood Apartments, has delegated management of the apartment building to Mario daSilva, a friend. Cody drops by to meet tenants and check up on rent receipts, but daSilva manages building maintenance and handles cash payments. Rentals have been very good lately, and cash receipts have kept pace with the apparent level of rent. However, for a year or so, the amount of cash on hand has been too low. When asked about this, daSilva explains that building maintenance has been required and suppliers are charging more for goods than in the past. During the past year, daSilva has taken two expensive vacations, and Cody wonders how daSilva can afford these trips on his $60,000 annual salary.

List at least three ways daSilva could be defrauding Cody of cash. In each instance also identify how Cody can determine whether daSilva's actions are ethical. Limit your answers to the building's cash payments. The business pays all suppliers by cheque (no EFTs).

Learning Objective ❺
Preparing and using a cash budget

E4-28 Dan Davis, the chief financial officer, is responsible for The Furniture Mart's cash budget for 2012. The budget will help Davis determine the amount of long-term borrowing needed to end the year with a cash balance of $150 thousand. Davis's assistants have assembled budget data for 2012, which the computer printed in alphabetical order. Not all the data items reproduced below are used in preparing the cash budget.

(Assumed Data)	(in thousands)
Actual cash balance December 31, 2011	$ 140
Budgeted total assets	22,977
Budgeted total current assets	7,776
Budgeted total current liabilities	4,860
Budgeted total liabilities	11,488
Budgeted total shareholders' equity	7,797
Collections from customers	18,527
Dividend payments	237
Issuance of shares	627
Net income	1,153
Payment of long-term and short-term debt	950
Payment of operating expenses	2,349
Purchases of inventory items	14,045
Purchase of property and equipment	1,518

Required

1. Prepare the cash budget of The Furniture Mart, Inc., for 2012.
2. Compute The Furniture Mart's budgeted current ratio and debt ratio at December 31, 2012. Based on these ratio values, and on the cash budget, would you lend $100,000 to The Furniture Mart? Give the reason for your decision.

Quiz

Test your understanding of internal control and cash by answering the following questions. Select the best choice from among the possible answers given.

Q4-29 All the following are objectives of internal control except

a. To comply with legal requirements
b. To safeguard assets
c. To maximize net income
d. To ensure accurate and reliable accounting records

Q4-30 All the following are internal control procedures except

a. Electronic devices
b. *Sarbanes-Oxley* reforms
c. Assignment of responsibilities
d. Internal and external audits

Q4-31 Requiring that an employee with no access to cash do the accounting is an example of which characteristic of internal control?

a. Separation of duties
b. Competent and reliable personnel
c. Mandatory vacations
d. Monitoring of controls

Q4-32 All the following are controls for cash received over the counter except

a. The customer should be able to see the amounts entered into the cash register.
b. A printed receipt must be given to the customer.
c. The cash drawer should open only when the sales clerk enters an amount on the keys.
d. The sales clerk must have access to the cash register tape.

Q4-33 In a bank reconciliation, an outstanding cheque is

a. Added to the book balance
b. Deducted from the book balance
c. Added to the bank balance
d. Deducted from the bank balance

Q4-34 In a bank reconciliation, a bank collection of a note receivable is

a. Added to the book balance
b. Deducted from the book balance
c. Added to the bank balance
d. Deducted from the bank balance

Q4-35 In a bank reconciliation, an EFT cash payment is

a. Added to the book balance
b. Deducted from the book balance
c. Added to the bank balance
d. Deducted from the bank balance

Q4-36 If a bookkeeper mistakenly recorded a $58 deposit as $85, the error would be shown on the bank reconciliation as a(n)

a. $27 addition to the book balance
b. $85 deduction from the book balance
c. $27 deduction from the book balance
d. $85 addition to the book balance

Q4-37 If a bank reconciliation included a deposit in transit of $670, the entry to record this reconciling item would include which of the following?

a. Credit to prepaid insurance for $670
b. Credit to cash for $670
c. Debit to cash for $670
d. No journal entry is required.

Q4-38 In a bank reconciliation, interest revenue earned on your bank balance is

a. Added to the book balance
b. Deducted from the book balance
c. Added to the bank balance
d. Deducted from the bank balance

Q4-39 Before paying an invoice for goods received on account, the controller or treasurer should ensure that

a. The company is paying for the goods it ordered
b. The company is paying for the goods it actually received
c. The company has not already paid this invoice
d. All of the above

Q4-40 La Petite France Bakery is budgeting cash for 2012. The cash balance at December 31, 2011, was $10,000. La Petite budgets 2012 cash receipts at $85,000. Estimated cash payments include $40,000 for inventory, $30,000 for operating expenses, and $20,000 to expand the store. La Petite needs a minimum cash balance of $10,000 at all times. La Petite expects to earn net income of $40,000 during 2012. What is the final result of the company's cash budget for 2012?

a. $10,000 is available for additional investments.
b. $5,000 is available for additional investments.
c. La Petite must arrange new financing for $5,000.
d. La Petite must pay off $10,000 of debt.

Problems

(Group A)

Learning Objective 1 2
Learning about fraud, identifying internal control weaknesses

P4-41A Avant Garde Imports is an importer of silver, brass, and furniture items from Mexico. Kay Jones is the general manager of Avant Garde Imports. Jones employs two other people in the business. Marco Gonzalez serves as the buyer for Avant Garde. He travels throughout Mexico to find interesting new products. When Gonzalez finds a new product, he arranges for Avant Garde to purchase and pay for the item. He helps the Mexican artisans prepare their invoices and then faxes the invoices to Jones in the company office.

Jones operates out of an office in Montreal, Quebec. The office is managed by Rita Bowden, who handles the mail, keeps the accounting records, makes bank deposits, and prepares the monthly bank reconciliation. Virtually all of Avant Garde's cash receipts arrive by mail—from sales made to Pier 1 Imports and Walmart.

Bowden also prepares cheques for payment based on invoices that come in from the suppliers who have been contacted by Gonzalez. To maintain control over cash payments, Jones examines the paperwork and signs all cheques.

Required

Identify all the major internal control weaknesses in Avant Garde's system and how the resulting action could hurt Avant Garde. Also state how to correct each weakness.

Learning Objective 1 4
Learning about fraud, identifying internal control weakness

P4-42A Each of the following situations reveals an internal control weakness.

a. Accounting firms use paraprofessional employees to perform routine tasks. For example, an accounting paraprofessional might prepare routine tax returns for clients. In the firm of Dunham & Lee, Rodney Lee, one of the partners, turns over a significant portion of his high-level accounting work to his paraprofessional staff.
b. In evaluating the internal control over cash payments of Butler Manufacturing, an auditor learns that the purchasing agent is responsible for purchasing diamonds for use in the company's manufacturing process, approving the invoices for payment, and signing the cheques. No supervisor reviews the purchasing agent's work.
c. Charlotte James owns an architecture firm. James's staff consists of 12 professional architects, and James manages the office. Often, James's work requires her to travel to meet with clients. During the past six months, James has observed that when she returns from a business trip, the architecture jobs in the office have not progressed satisfactorily. James learns that when she is away, two of her senior architects take over office management and neglect their normal duties. One employee could manage the office.
d. B.J. Tanner has been an employee of Crystal City for many years. Because the company is small, Tanner performs all accounting duties, plus opening the mail, preparing the bank deposit, and preparing the bank reconciliation.
e. Part of an internal auditor's job is to evaluate how efficiently the company is running. For example, is the company purchasing inventory from the least expensive supplier? After a particularly bad year, Long Photographic Products eliminates its internal audit department to reduce expenses.

Required

1. Identify the missing internal control characteristic in each situation.
2. Identify each firm's possible problem.
3. Propose a solution to the problem.

P4-43A The cash data of Alta Vista Toyota for June 2011 follow:

Learning Objective 3
Preparing the bank reconciliation and using it as a control device

Cash

Date	Item	Jrnl. Ref.	Debit	Credit	Balance
June 1	Balance				5,011
30		CR6	10,578		15,589
30		CP11		10,924	4,665

Cash Receipts (CR)		Cash Payments (CP)	
Date	Cash Debit	Cheque No.	Cash Credit
June 2	$ 4,174	3113	$ 891
8	407	3114	147
10	559	3115	1,930
16	2,187	3116	664
22	1,854	3117	1,472
29	1,060	3118	1,000
30	337	3119	632
Total	$10,578	3120	1,675
		3121	100
		3122	2,413
		Total	$10,924

Alta Vista received the following bank statement on June 30, 2011:

Bank Statement for June 2011

Beginning balance		$ 5,011
Deposits and other additions		
June 1	$ 326 EFT	
4	4,174	
9	407	
12	559	
17	2,187	
22	1,701 BC	
23	1,854	11,208
Cheques and other deductions		
June 7	$ 891	
13	1,390	
14	903 US	
15	147	
18	664	
21	219 EFT	
26	1,472	
30	1,000	
30	20 SC	(6,706)
Ending balance		$ 9,513

Explanation: EFT—electronic funds transfer, BC—bank collection, US—unauthorized signature, SC—service charge

Additional data for the bank reconciliation include the following:

a. The EFT deposit was a receipt of a monthly car lease. The EFT debit was a monthly insurance payment.
b. The bank collection was of a note receivable.
c. The unauthorized signature cheque was received from a customer.
d. The correct amount of cheque number 3115, a payment on account, is $1,390. (Alta Vista's accountant mistakenly recorded the cheque for $1,930.)

Required

1. Prepare the Alta Vista Toyota bank reconciliation at June 30, 2011.
2. Describe how a bank account and the bank reconciliation help the general manager control Alta Vista's cash.

Learning Objective 3
Preparing a bank reconciliation and the related journal entries

P4-44A The May 31 bank statement of Family Services Association (FSA) has just arrived from Scotiabank. To prepare the FSA bank reconciliation, you gather the following data:

a. FSA's Cash account shows a balance of $2,256.14 on May 31.
b. The May 31 bank balance is $4,023.05.
c. The bank statement shows that FSA earned $38.19 of interest on its bank balance during May. This amount was added to FSA's bank balance.
d. FSA pays utilities ($250) and insurance ($100) by EFT.
e. The following FSA cheques did not clear the bank by May 31:

Cheque No.	Amount
237	$ 46.10
288	141.00
291	578.05
293	11.87
294	609.51
295	8.88
296	101.63

f. The bank statement includes a donation of $850, electronically deposited to the bank for FSA.
g. The bank statement lists a $10.50 bank service charge.
h. On May 31, the FSA treasurer deposited $16.15, which will appear on the June bank statement.
i. The bank statement includes a $300 deposit that FSA did not make. The bank added $300 to FSA's account for another company's deposit.
j. The bank statement includes two charges for returned cheques from donors. One is a $395 cheque received from a donor with the imprint "Unauthorized Signature." The other is a nonsufficient funds cheque in the amount of $146.67 received from a client.

Required

1. Prepare the bank reconciliation for FSA.
2. Journalize the May 31 transactions needed to update FSA's Cash account. Include an explanation for each entry.

Learning Objective 4
Identifying internal control weakness in sales and cash receipts

P4-45A Sun Skin Care makes all sales on credit. Cash receipts arrive by mail, usually within 30 days of the sale. Nancy Brown opens envelopes and separates the cheques from the accompanying remittance advices. Brown forwards the cheques to another employee, who makes the daily bank deposit but has no access to the accounting records. Brown sends the remittance advices, which show the amount of cash received, to the accounting department for entry in the accounts receivable. Brown's only other duty is to grant allowances to customers. (An *allowance* decreases the amount that the customer must pay.) When Brown receives a customer cheque for less than the full amount of the invoice, she records the allowance in the accounting records and forwards the document to the accounting department.

Required

You are a new employee of Sun Skin Care. Write a memo to the company president identifying the internal control weakness in this situation. State how to correct the weakness.

P4-46A Kenneth Austin, chief financial officer of Morin Equipment Ltd., is responsible for the company's budgeting process. Austin's staff is preparing the Morin cash budget for 2012. A key input to the budgeting process is last year's statement of cash flows, which follows (amounts in thousands):

Learning Objective 5
Preparing a cash budget and using cash flow information

Morin Equipment Ltd.
Statement of Cash Flows
2011

	(in thousands)
Cash Flows From Operating Activities	
Collections from customers	$ 60,000
Interest received	100
Purchases of inventory	(44,000)
Operating expenses	(13,900)
Net cash provided by operations	2,200
Cash Flows From Investing Activities	
Purchases of equipment	(4,300)
Purchases of investments	(200)
Sales of investments	400
Net cash used for investing activities	(4,100)
Cash Flows From Financing Activities	
Payment of long-term debt	(300)
Issuance of shares	1,200
Payment of cash dividends	(500)
Net cash provided by financing activities	400
Cash	
Increase (decrease) in cash	(1,500)
Cash, beginning of year	2,700
Cash, end of year	$ 1,200

Required

1. Prepare the Morin Equipment Ltd. cash budget for 2012. Date the budget simply "2012" and denote the beginning and ending cash balances as "beginning" and "ending." Assume the company expects 2012 to be the same as 2011, but with the following changes:
   a. In 2012, the company expects a 15% increase in collections from customers and a 20% increase in purchases of inventory.
   b. There will be no sales of investments in 2012.
   c. Morin plans to issue no shares in 2012.
   d. Morin plans to end the year with a cash balance of $2,000 thousand.
2. Does the company's cash budget for 2012 suggest that Morin is growing, holding steady, or decreasing in size?

P4-47A Larry Raborn is a branch manager of HSBC. Active in community affairs, Raborn serves on the board of directors of The Salvation Army. The Salvation Army is expanding rapidly and is considering relocating. At a recent meeting, The Salvation Army decided to buy 200 hectares of land on the edge of town. The owner of the property is Freda Rader, a major depositor in his branch. Rader is completing a bitter divorce, and Raborn knows that Rader is eager to sell her property. In view of Rader's difficult situation, Raborn believes Rader would accept a low offer for the land. Realtors have appraised the property at $2.2 million.

Learning Objective 6
Making an ethical judgment

Required

Apply the framework for making the ethical decisions outlined in Chapter 1 to help Raborn decide what role he should play in The Salvation Army's attempt to buy the land from Rader.

(Group B)

Learning Objective ❶❷
Learning about fraud, identifying internal control weakness

P4-48B Trey Osborne, administrator of Valley View Clinic, seeks your advice. Valley View Clinic employs two people in the office, Jim Bates and Rhonda Clark. Osborne asks you how to assign the various office functions to the three people (including Osborne) to achieve good internal control. Here are the duties to be performed by the two office workers and Osborne:

a. Record cash payments
b. Record cash receipts
c. Receive incoming cash from patients
d. Reconcile the bank account
e. Deposit cash receipts
f. Sign cheques for payment

Required

1. Propose a plan that divides duties a through f to Bates, Clark, and Osborne. Your goal is to divide the duties so as to achieve good internal control for the clinic.
2. Identify several combinations of duties that should not be performed by the same person.

Learning Objective ❶❹
Learning about fraud, identifying internal control weaknesses

P4-49B Each of the following situations has an internal control weakness:

a. Retail stores such as Sobeys and Home Depot receive a significant portion of their sales revenue in cash. At the end of each day, sales clerks compare the cash in their own register with the record of sales kept within the register. They then forward the cash to a Brinks security officer for deposit in the bank.
b. The office supply company from which Martin Audiology Service purchases cash receipt forms recently notified Martin that the last-shipped sales receipts were not pre-numbered. Derek Martin, the owner, replied that he did not use the receipt numbers, so the omission is unimportant to him.
c. Azbell Electronics specializes in programs with musical applications. The company's most popular product prepares musical programs for large gatherings. In the company's early days, the owner and eight employees wrote the programs, lined up production of the programs, sold the products, and performed the general management of the company. As Azbell has grown, the number of employees has increased dramatically. Recently, the development of a new musical series stopped while the programmers redesigned Azbell's sound system. Azbell could have hired outsiders to do this task.
d. Paul Allen, who has no known sources of outside income, has been a trusted employee of Chapparall Cosmetics for 20 years. Allen performs all cash-handling and accounting duties, including opening the mail, preparing the bank deposit, accounting for cash and accounts receivable, and preparing the bank reconciliation. Allen has just purchased a new Lexus. Linda Altman, owner of the company, wonders how Allen can afford the new car on his salary.
e. Monica Wade employs three professional interior designers in her design studio. The studio is located in an area with a lot of new construction, and her business is booming. Ordinarily, Wade does all the purchasing of materials needed to complete jobs. During the summer, Wade takes a long vacation, and in her absence she allows each designer to purchase materials. On her return, Wade reviews operations and observes that expenses are higher and net income is lower than in the past.

Required

1. Identify the missing internal control characteristics in each situation.
2. Identify each firm's possible problem.
3. Propose a solution to the problem.

P4-50B The cash data of Navajo Products for September 2011 follow:

Learning Objective 3
Using the bank reconciliation as a control device

Cash

Date	Item	Jrnl. Ref.	Debit	Credit	Balance
Sept. 1	Balance				7,078
30		CR 10	9,106		16,184
30		CP 16		11,353	4,831

Cash Receipts (CR)		Cash Payments (CP)	
Date	Cash Debit	Cheque No.	Cash Credit
Sept. 1	$ 2,716	1413	$ 1,465
9	544	1414	1,004
11	1,655	1415	450
14	896	1416	8
17	367	1417	775
25	890	1418	88
30	2,038	1419	4,126
Total	$9,106	1420	970
		1421	200
		1422	2,267
		Total	$11,353

On September 30, 2011, Navajo received this bank statement:

Bank Statement for September 2011

Beginning balance		$ 7,078
Deposits and other additions:		
Sept. 1	$ 625 EFT	
5	2,716	
10	544	
12	1,655	
15	896	
18	367	
25	890	
30	1,400 BC	9,093
Cheques and other deductions		
Sept. 8	$ 441 NSF	
9	1,465	
13	1,004	
14	450	
15	8	
19	340 EFT	
22	775	
29	88	
30	4,216	
30	25 SC	(8,812)
Ending balance		$ 7,359

Explanation: BC—bank collection, EFT—electronic funds transfer, NSF—nonsufficient funds cheque, SC—service charge

Additional data for the bank reconciliation:

a. The EFT deposit was for monthly rent revenue. The EFT deduction was for monthly insurance expense.
b. The bank collection was of a note receivable.
c. The NSF cheque was received from a customer.
d. The correct amount of cheque number 1419, a payment on account, is $4,216. (The Navajo accountant mistakenly recorded the cheque for $4,126.)

Required

1. Prepare the bank reconciliation of Navajo Products at September 30, 2011.
2. Describe how a bank account and the bank reconciliation help managers control a firm's cash.

Learning Objective 3
Preparing a bank reconciliation and the related journal entries

P4-51B The January 31 bank statement of Bed & Bath Accessories has just arrived from Royal Bank of Canada. To prepare the Bed & Bath bank reconciliation, you gather the following data:

a. The January 31 bank balance is $8,400.82.
b. Bed & Bath's Cash account shows a balance of $7,391.55 on January 31.
c. The following Bed & Bath cheques are outstanding at January 31:

Cheque No.	Amount
616	$403.00
802	74.02
806	36.60
809	161.38
810	229.05
811	48.91

d. The bank statement includes two special deposits: $899.14, which is the amount of dividend revenue the bank collected from IBM on behalf of Bed & Bath, and $16.86, the interest revenue Bed & Bath earned on its bank balance during January.
e. The bank statement lists a $6.25 bank service charge.
f. On January 31 the Bed & Bath treasurer deposited $381.14, which will appear on the February bank statement.
g. The bank statement includes a $410.00 deduction for a cheque drawn by Bonjovi Music Company.
h. The bank statement includes two charges for returned cheques from customers. One is a nonsufficient funds cheque in the amount of $67.50 received from a customer. The other is a $195.03 cheque received from another customer. It was returned by the customer's bank with the imprint "Unauthorized Signature."
i. A few customers pay monthly bills by EFT. The January bank statement lists an EFT deposit for sales revenue of $200.23.

Required

1. Prepare the bank reconciliation for Bed & Bath Accessories at January 31.
2. Journalize the transactions needed to update the Cash account. Include an explanation for each entry.

Learning Objective 4
Identifying an internal control weakness in sales and cash receipts

P4-52B Nordhaus Energy Co. makes all sales on credit. Cash receipts arrive by mail, usually within 30 days of the sale. Dan Webster opens envelopes and separates the cheques from the accompanying remittance advices. Webster forwards the cheques to another employee, who makes the daily bank deposit but has no access to the accounting records. Webster sends the remittance advices, which show the amount of cash received, to the accounting department for entry in the accounts receivable. Webster's only other duty is to grant allowances to customers. (An *allowance* decreases the amount that the customer must pay.) When Webster receives a customer cheque for less than the full amount of the invoice, he records the allowance in the accounting records and forwards the document to the accounting department.

Required

You are a new employee of Nordhaus Energy Co. Write a memo to the company president identifying the internal control weakness in this situation. Explain how to correct the weakness.

Learning Objective 5
Preparing a cash budget and using cash flow information

P4-53B Melissa Becker is chief financial officer of Valero Machines. She is responsible for the company's budgeting process. Becker's staff is preparing the Valero cash budget for 2012. The starting point is the statement of cash flows of the current year, 2011, which follows:

Valero Machines
Statement of Cash Flows
2011

	(in thousands)
Cash Flows From Operating Activities	
Collections from customers	$ 35,600
Interest received	100
Purchases of inventory	(11,000)
Operating expenses	(16,600)
Net cash provided by operating activities	8,100
Cash Flows From Investing Activities	
Purchases of property and equipment	(5,000)
Purchases of investments	(7,500)
Sales of investments	8,100
Net cash used by investing activities	(4,400)
Cash Flows From Financing Activities	
Payment of dividends	(2,700)
Payment of short-term debt	(1,000)
Long-term borrowings by issuing notes payable	1,200
Issuance of common shares	300
Net cash used by financing activities	(2,200)
Increase (decrease) in Cash	1,500
Cash, beginning of year	2,600
Cash, end of year	$ 4,100

Required

1. Prepare the Valero Machines cash budget for 2012. Date the budget simply "2012" and denote the beginning and ending cash balances as "beginning" and "ending." Assume the company expects 2012 to be the same as 2011, but with the following changes:
   a. In 2012, the company expects a 10% increase in collections from customers, a 5% increase in purchases of inventory, and a doubling of additions to property and equipment.
   b. Operating expenses will drop by $2,000.
   c. There will be no sales of investments in 2012.
   d. Becker plans to end the year with a cash balance of $3,000.
2. Does the company's cash budget for 2012 suggest that Valero is growing, holding steady, or decreasing in size? (Challenge)

Learning Objective 6
Making an ethical judgment

P4-54B A community bank has a loan receivable from IMS Chocolates. IMS is six months late in making payments to the bank, and Jan French, a bank vice-president, is assisting IMS to restructure its debt.

French learns that IMS is depending on landing a contract with Snicker Foods, another bank client. French also serves as Snicker Foods' loan officer at the bank. In this capacity, French is aware that Snicker is considering bankruptcy. No one else outside Snicker Foods knows this. French has been a great help to IMS, and IMS's owner is counting on French's expertise in loan workouts to advise the company through this difficult process. To help the bank collect on this large loan, French has a strong motivation to alert IMS of Snicker's financial difficulties.

Required

Apply the framework for making an ethical decision outlined in Chapter 1 to help French plan her next action.

Apply Your Knowledge

Decision Cases

Learning Objective 1 3
Learning about fraud, using the bank reconciliation to detect a theft

Case 1. Green Construction Inc. has poor internal control. Recently Jean Ouimet, the owner, has suspected the cashier of stealing. Here are some details of the business's cash position at June 30, 2011.

a. The Cash account shows a balance of $10,402. This amount includes a June 30 deposit of $3,794 that does not appear on the June 30 bank statement.
b. The June 30 bank statement shows a balance of $8,224. The bank statement lists a $200 bank collection, an $8 service charge, and a $36 NSF cheque. The accountant has not recorded any of these items.
c. At June 30, the following cheques are outstanding:

Cheque No.	Amount
154	$116
256	150
278	853
291	990
292	206
293	145

d. The bookkeeper records all incoming cash and makes bank deposits. He also reconciles the monthly bank statement. Here is his June 30 reconciliation:

Balance per books, June 30		$10,402
Add: Outstanding cheques		1,460
Bank collection		200
Subtotal		12,062
Less: Deposits in transit	$3,794	
Service charge	8	
NSF cheque	36	(3,838)
Balance per bank, June 30		$ 8,224

Required

Ouimet has requested that you determine whether the cashier has stolen cash from the business and, if so, how much. He also asks you to explain how the cashier has attempted to conceal the theft. To make this determination, you perform your own bank reconciliation. There are no bank or book errors. Ouimet also asks you to evaluate the internal controls and to recommend any changes needed to improve them.

Learning Objective ❶❷
Learning about fraud, correcting an internal control weakness

Case 2. Gilead Construction Inc., which is headquartered in Calgary, Alberta, built a small apartment building in Red Deer. The construction foreman, whose name was Jon Machenko, moved to Red Deer in May to hire the 20 workers needed to complete the project. Machenko hired the construction workers, had them fill out the necessary tax forms, and sent the employment documents to the home office, which opened a payroll file for each employee.

Work on the building began on June 1. Each Friday evening, Jon Machenko filled out a time card that listed the hours worked for each employee during the five-day work week ended at 5:00 p.m. on Friday. Machenko faxed the time sheets to the home office, which prepared the payroll cheques on Monday morning. Machenko drove to the home office after lunch on Monday, picked up the payroll cheques, and returned to the construction site. At 5:00 p.m. on Monday, Machenko distributed the payroll cheques to the workers.

a. Describe in detail the internal control weakness in this situation. Specify what negative result could occur because of the internal control weakness.
b. Describe what you would do to correct the internal control weakness.

Ethical Issue

Eric Thorman owns shoe stores in Halifax and Lunenburg. Each store has a manager who is responsible for sales and store expenses, and runs advertisements in the local newspaper. The managers transfer cash to Thorman monthly and prepare their own bank reconciliations. The manager in Lunenburg has been stealing large sums of money. To cover the theft, he understates the amount of the outstanding cheques on the monthly bank reconciliation. As a result, each monthly bank reconciliation appears to balance. However, the balance sheet reports more cash than Thorman actually has in the bank. While negotiating the sale of the shoe stores, Thorman shows the balance sheet to prospective investors.

Required

1. Identify two parties other than Thorman who can be harmed by this theft. In what ways can they be harmed?
2. Discuss the role accounting plays in this situation.

Focus on Financials

Learning Objective ❷❹
Cash and internal control

Gildan Activewear Inc

Refer to the Gildan Activewear Inc. financial statements in Appendix A at the end of this book. Suppose Gildan's year-end bank statement, dated October 4, 2009, has just arrived at company headquarters. Further assume the bank statement shows Gildan's cash balance at $79,782 and that Gildan's Cash and Cash Equivalents account has a balance of $77,423 on the books.

1. You must determine how much to report for cash and cash equivalents on the October 4, 2009, balance sheet. Suppose you uncover these reconciling items (all amounts are assumed and in thousands):
   a. Interest earned on bank balance, $10
   b. Outstanding cheques, $15,050
   c. Bank collections of various items, $25,000
   d. Deposits in transit, $35,000
   e. Transposition error—Gildan overstated cash by $2,700
   f. Bank charges of $1

Prepare a bank reconciliation to show how Gildan arrived at the correct amount of cash and cash equivalents to report on its October 4, 2009, balance sheet. Prove that your answer is the actual amount Gildan reported. Journal entries are not required.

2. NI 52-109 requires the CEO and CFO to certify compliance with the disclosures required under the standard. Locate the statement of compliance in Gildan's MD&A in MyAccountingLab and compare it to the requirements under NI 52-109 reported in Chapter 4. Does Gildan meet the requirements with respect to
   a. Certification by the certifying officers? Who are identified as Gildan's certifying officers?
   b. Does the MD&A identify the control framework used? If so, what framework was used?

Focus on Analysis

Learning Objective 2 4
Analyzing internal control and cash flows

Gildan Activewear Inc.

Refer to the Gildan Activewear Inc. financial statements in Appendix A at the end of this book.

1. Focus on cash and cash equivalents. Why did cash change during the year ended October 4, 2009? The statement of cash flows holds the answer to this question. Analyze the seven largest *individual* items on the cash flow statement (exclude net (loss) income). For each of the seven individual items, state how Gildan's action affected cash. Show amounts in thousands.
2. Gildan's shares are listed on the Toronto Stock Exchange (TSX) and the New York Stock Exchange (NYSE). The U.S. listing requires Gildan to comply with *Sarbanes-Oxley*, which requires Gildan's auditors KPMG to provide an opinion on the effectiveness of Gildan's internal control over financial reporting. Locate the KPMG report in Gildan's annual report in Appendix A and compare it to the certification in Gildan's MD&A. What is the major difference between the two?

Group Project

You are promoting a rock concert in your area. Assume you organize as a corporation, with each member of your group purchasing $10,000 of the corporation's shares. Therefore, each of you is risking some hard-earned money on this venture. Assume it is April 1 and that the concert will be performed on June 30. Your promotional activities begin immediately, and ticket sales start on May 1. You expect to sell all the firm's assets, pay all the liabilities, and distribute all remaining cash to the group members by July 31.

Required

Write an internal control manual that will help safeguard the assets of the business. The manual should address the following aspects of internal control:

1. Assign responsibilities among the group members.
2. Authorize individuals, including group members and any outsiders that you need to hire, to perform specific jobs.
3. Separate duties among the group and any employees.
4. Describe all documents needed to account for and safeguard the business's assets.

Quick Check Answers

1. *g, e, h, d, f, c, a Unused: b, i*	5. *a*	9. *d*
2. *b*	6. *c*	10. *d*
3. *d*	7. *e*	11. *a*
4. *a*	8. *a*	

Short-Term Investments and Receivables

LEARNING OBJECTIVES

1. **Account** for short-term investments
2. **Account** for receivables
3. **Apply** internal controls to receivables
4. **Estimate** uncollectible receivables
5. **Account** for notes receivable
6. **Use** ratios to evaluate a business

SPOTLIGHT

Where do you go when you need groceries? Chances are you may have shopped at Loblaw. Most people, when they hear the name of Loblaw, automatically think of groceries. But did you know they also sell general merchandise, drugstore items, and financial products and services?

Take a look at Loblaw's comparative balance sheets (excerpt) for 2009 and 2008 on the following page. While inventories make up the majority of Loblaw's current assets, accounts receivable are the third largest current asset.

Another category of current assets is short-term investments. As you can see from Loblaw's comparative balance sheets for 2009 and 2008, Loblaw had about $397 million of short-term investments at the end of 2009. You'll notice that short-term investments are listed on the balance sheet immediately after cash and before receivables. Let's see why.

Loblaw
Consolidated Balance Sheets (Excerpt, Adapted)
As at January 2, 2010, and January 3, 2009

	($ millions) 2009	2008
Assets		
Current Assets		
Cash and cash equivalents	$ 993	$ 528
Short-term investments	397	225
Accounts receivable	774	867
Inventories	2,112	2,188
Income taxes	—	40
Future income taxes	38	41
Prepaid expenses and other assests	50	71
Total Current Assets	4,364	3,960
Fixed Assets	8,559	8,045
Goodwill and Intangible Assets	1,026	818
Other Assets	1,042	1,120
Total Assets	$14,991	$13,943

OBJECTIVE

1 **Account** for short-term investments

This chapter shows how to account for short-term investments and receivables, which are based in large part *but not completely* on International Accounting Standard (IAS) 32 "Financial Instruments: Presentation," IFRS 7 "Financial Instruments Disclosure," and IAS 39 "Financial Instruments: Recognition and Measurement."

For the private enterprise, *CICA Handbook* section 3856 deals with the recognition, measurement, presentation, and disclosure for all financial instruments. We cover short-term investments along with receivables to emphasize their relative liquidity. Short-term investments are the next-most-liquid current assets after cash. (Recall that liquid means close to cash.) We begin our discussion with short-term investments.

Short-Term Investments

Short-term investments, also called **marketable securities** or *temporary investments*, are investments that a company plans to hold for one year or less. These investments allow the company to invest excess cash for a short period of time and earn a return until the cash is needed.

Because short-term investments are the next most liquid asset after cash, we report short-term investments immediately after cash and before receivables on the balance sheet.

An investor, such as Loblaw Companies Limited, expects to sell a financial asset held for trading investment within a very short time—a few months at most. Therefore, all such investments are current assets. Other categories of investments are either short-term or long-term, depending on how long management intends to hold them. Let's begin with financial assets held for trading investment.

Trading Investments

The purpose of owning a financial asset held for **trading investment** is to hold it for a short time and then sell it for more than its cost. Trading investments can be shares or bonds in another company. Suppose Loblaw purchases shares in TransCanada Corporation, intending to sell the shares in a few months. If the fair value (or market price) of the TransCanada shares increases, Loblaw will have a gain; if TransCanada's share price decreases, Loblaw will have a loss. Along the way, Loblaw will receive dividend revenue from TransCanada.

Suppose Loblaw buys the TransCanada shares on December 18, 2010, paying $100,000 cash. Loblaw records the purchase of the investment at cost:

2010			
Dec. 18	Short-Term Investments	100,000	
	Cash		100,000
	Purchased investment.		

Short-Term Investments	
100,000	

Assume on December 27 Loblaw receives a cash dividend of $800 from TransCanada. Loblaw records the receipt of the dividend as follows:

2010			
Dec. 27	Cash	800	
	Dividend Revenue		800
	Received cash dividend.		

ASSETS	=	LIABILITIES	+	SHAREHOLDERS' EQUITY	+	REVENUES
+800	=	0	+	0	+	800

Unrealized Gains and Losses

Loblaw's fiscal year ends on January 1, 2011, and Loblaw prepares financial statements. Assume the TransCanada shares have risen in value, and on January 1, 2011, Loblaw's investment has a fair value (current market price) of $102,000. **Fair value** is the amount the owner can receive when selling the investment. Loblaw has an *unrealized gain* on the investment.

- *Gain* because the fair value ($102,000) is greater than Loblaw's investment cost. A gain has the same effect on owners' equity as a revenue.
- *Unrealized gain* because Loblaw has not yet sold the investment.

Trading investments are reported on the balance sheet at their fair value because that is the amount the investor can receive by selling the investment.

On January 1, 2011, Loblaw makes year-end adjustments to bring the TransCanada investment to its fair value (current market price) with the following entries:

2011			
Jan. 1	Short-Term Investments	2,000	
	Unrealized Gain on Investments		2,000
	Adjusted investment to fair value.		

Short-Term Investments	
100,000	
2,000	
102,000	

Unrealized Gain on Investments	
	2,000

After the adjustment, Loblaw's investment account appears as shown above. The Short-Term Investments account is ready to be reported on the balance sheet at fair value of $102,000.

If Loblaw's investment in TransCanada shares had decreased in value, say, to $95,000, then Loblaw would have reported an unrealized loss. A *loss* has the same effect on owners' equity as an expense. In this case, Loblaw would make a different entry at January 1, 2011, for an *unrealized loss* of $5,000.

2011			
Jan. 1	Unrealized Loss on Investments	5,000	
	Short-Term Investments		5,000
	Adjusted investment to fair value.		

Short-Term Investments	
100,000	5,000
95,000	

Unrealized Loss on Investments	
5,000	

Reporting on the Balance Sheet and the Income Statement

The Balance Sheet. Short-term investments are current assets. They appear on the balance sheet immediately after cash because short-term investments are almost as liquid as cash. (*Liquid* means close to cash.) Short-term investments are reported at their *fair value*.

Income Statement. Investments earn interest revenue and dividend revenue. Investments also create gains and losses. For short-term investments, these items are reported on the income statement as other revenue, gains, and losses as shown in Exhibit 5-1.

EXHIBIT 5-1 **Reporting Short-Term Investments and the Related Revenues, Gains, and Losses (amounts from the preceding example)**

Balance sheet		Income statement	
Current assets:		Revenues	$ XXX
Cash	$ XXX	Expenses	XXX
Short-term investments, at fair value	102,000	Other revenue, gains, and (losses)	
Accounts receivable	XXX	Interest revenue	XXX
		Dividend revenue	800
		Unrealized gain on investments	2,000
		Net income	$ XXX

Realized Gains and Losses

A *realized* gain or loss usually occurs only when the investor sells an investment. The gain or loss is different from the unrealized gain that we reported for Loblaw above. The result may be a:

- Realized gain → Sale price *greater than* investment carrying amount
- Realized loss → Sale price *less than* investment carrying amount

Suppose Loblaw sells its TransCanada shares on February 19, 2011. The sale price is $98,000, and Loblaw makes the following journal entry:

2011			
Feb. 19	Cash	98,000	
	Loss on Sale of Investments	4,000	
	Short-Term Investments		102,000
	Sold short-term investments at a loss.		

Loss on Sale of Investments	
4,000	

	Short-Term Investments	
	100,000	
	2,000	102,000
Bal.	0	

Accountants rarely use the word "Realized" in the account title. A gain (or a loss) is understood to be a realized gain (or loss) arising from a sale transaction. Unrealized gains and losses are clearly labelled as *unrealized*. Loblaw would report Gain (or Loss) on Sale of Investments among the "Other" items in the income statement.

Loblaw Corporation reported on its short-term investments at January 2, 2010, the following note:

> **Note 1. Summary of Significant Accounting Policies (Adapted)**
> **Short-term Investments.** Short-term investments consist primarily of government treasury bills, government-sponsored debt securities, corporate commercial paper, and bank term deposits. Short-term investments designated as held-for-trading financial assets approximate the fair value of these instruments.

Accounting Games That Companies Play

We wish to alert you to one of the accounting games that companies sometimes play. Suppose a company called Wood Products Ltd. (WPL) has some long-term investments (investments that WPL plans to hold for longer than a year). Before year-end WPL considers reclassifying these long-term investments as current assets. The investments increase WPL's current assets, which increases the current ratio. This strategy would be okay if WPL does in fact plan to sell the investments within the next year. But the strategy would be dishonest if WPL plans to keep the investments for longer than a year.

The above example illustrates that accounting is not cut and dried or all black and white. It takes good judgment—and honesty—to be a successful accountant.

MyAccountingLab

MID-CHAPTER SUMMARY PROBLEM

Research In Motion (RIM) Corporation is a leading Canadian communications company. Suppose one of the current assets on RIM's balance sheet is Short-Term Investments. Their cost is $41.8 million. Their fair value is $42.4 million.

What will RIM report on the balance sheet at February 27, 2010? What will RIM report on its 2010 income statement? Show the Short-Term Investments T-account.

Name: Research In Motion
Industry: Communications corporation
Accounting Period: Year ended February 27, 2010

Answer

Short-Term Investments, reported on the balance sheet as follows (amounts in millions):

Short-term investments are included in current assets (amounts assumed).

An unrealized gain is the excess of the market value over the cost (amounts assumed).

	(in millions)
Current assets	
Short-term investments at fair value	$42.4

RIM's income statement will report:

	(in millions)
Other revenue, gains, and (losses):	
Unrealized gain on investment ($42.4 − $41.8 million)	$ 0.6

Suppose RIM sells the investments on February 7, 2011, for $41.4 million. Journalize the sale and then show the Short-Term Investments account as it would appear after the sale.

Answer

2011			
Feb. 7	Cash	41,400,00	
	Loss on Sale of Short-Term Investments	1,00,000	
	Short-Term Investments		42,400,000
	Sold short-term investments at a loss.		

Short-Term Investments

	Debit	Credit
	41,800,000	
	600,000	42,400,000
Bal.	0	

Accounts and Notes Receivable

OBJECTIVE

❷ **Account** for receivables

Receivables are the third most liquid asset—after cash and short-term investments. Most of the remainder of the chapter shows how to account for receivables.

Types of Receivables

Receivables are monetary claims against others. They are acquired mainly by selling goods and services (accounts receivable) and by lending money (notes receivable). Journal entries to record receivables can be shown as follows:

Performing a Service on Account			Lending Money on a Note Receivable		
Accounts Receivable	XXX		Note Receivable	XXX	
Service Revenue		XXX	Cash		XXX
Performed a service on account.			Loaned money to another company.		

The two major types of receivables are accounts receivable and notes receivable. A business's *accounts receivable* are the amounts collectible from customers from the sale of goods and services. Accounts receivable, which are *current assets*, are sometimes called *trade receivables* or merely *receivables*.

The Accounts Receivable account in the general ledger serves as a *control account* that summarizes the total amount receivable from all customers. Companies also keep a *subsidiary ledger* of accounts receivable with a separate account for each customer, illustrated as follows:

GENERAL LEDGER		ACCOUNTS RECEIVABLE SUBSIDIARY LEDGER	
Accounts Receivable		**Aston Inc.**	
Bal.	9,000	Bal.	5,000
		Grand & Toy	
↑ Total $9,000		Bal.	1,000
		Purolator	
		Bal.	3,000

Notes receivable are more formal contracts than accounts receivable. The borrower signs a written promise to pay the creditor a definite sum at the *maturity* date. That is why notes receivable are also called promissory notes. The note may require the borrower to pledge *security* for the loan. This means that the borrower gives the lender permission to claim certain assets, called *collateral*, if the borrower fails to pay the amount due. We cover the details of notes receivable starting on page 252.

Other Receivables is a miscellaneous category that includes loans to employees and subsidiary companies. Some companies report other receivables under the heading Other Assets on the balance sheet.

Internal Controls Over Cash Collections on Account

OBJECTIVE

Apply internal controls to receivables

Businesses that sell on credit receive most of their cash payment on account by mail. Internal control over collections on account is important. Chapter 4 discussed control procedures for cash receipts, but another element of internal control deserves emphasis here—the separation of cash-handling and cash-accounting duties. Consider the following case:

> Franklin Supply Co. Ltd. is a small, family-owned business that takes pride in the loyalty of its workers. Most employees have been with Franklin for at least five years. The company makes 90% of its sales on account.
>
> The office staff consists of a bookkeeper and a supervisor. The bookkeeper maintains the general ledger and a subsidiary record of individual accounts receivable. He also makes the daily bank deposit. The supervisor prepares monthly financial statements and any special reports Franklin requires. She also takes sales orders from customers and serves as office manager.

Can you identify the internal control weakness here? The problem is that the bookkeeper makes the deposit. With this cash-handling duty, the bookkeeper could steal an incoming customer cheque and write off the customer's account as uncollectible. The customer doesn't complain because the bookkeeper has written the account off the books and Franklin, therefore, stops pursuing collection.

How can this weakness be corrected? The supervisor—not the bookkeeper—could open incoming mail and make the daily bank deposit. The bookkeeper should *not* be allowed to handle cash. Only the remittance advices would be forwarded to the bookkeeper to credit customer accounts receivable. Removing cash handling from the bookkeeper and keeping the accounts away from the supervisor separates duties and strengthens internal control.

Using a bank lockbox achieves the same separation of duties. Customers send their payments directly to Franklin Supply Co. Ltd.'s bank, which records and deposits the cash into Franklin's bank account. The bank then forwards the remittance advice to Franklin's bookkeeper, who credits the customer account. No Franklin employee ever touches incoming cash.

How Do We Manage the Risk of Not Collecting?

Most companies sell on credit and thus hold accounts receivable. By selling on credit, all companies run the risk of not collecting some receivables. Unfortunately, customers sometimes don't pay their debts. The prospect that we may fail to collect from a customer provides the biggest challenge in accounting for receivables.

MANAGING ACCOUNTS RECEIVABLE

Let's look at a business situation: Suppose you and a friend open a health club near your college. Assume you will let customers use the club and charge bills to their accounts. What challenges will you encounter by extending credit to customers?

The main issues in *managing* receivables, along with a plan of action, are

Issues	Plan of Action
1. What are the benefits and the costs of extending credit to customers?	**1.** Benefit—Increase in sales. Cost—Risk of not collecting.
2. Extend credit only to creditworthy customers.	**2.** Run a credit check on prospective customers.
3. Separate cash-handling and accounting duties to keep employees from stealing the cash collected from customers.	**3.** Design the internal control system to separate duties.
4. Pursue collection from customers to maximize cash flow.	**4.** Keep a close eye on customer paying habits. Send second, and third, statements to slow-paying customers, if necessary. Do not extend credit to overdue accounts.

These guidelines lead to our next topic, accounting for uncollectible receivables.

Accounting for Uncollectible Receivables

A company gets an account receivable only when it sells its product or service on credit (on account). You'll recall that the entry to record the earning of revenue on account is (amount assumed):

Accounts Receivable	1,000	
Sales Revenue (or Service Revenue)		1,000
Earned revenue on account.		

Ideally, the company would collect cash for all its receivables. But unfortunately the entry to record cash collections on account is for only $950.

Cash	950	
Accounts Receivable		950
Collections on account.		

You can see that companies rarely collect all of their accounts receivable. So companies must account for their uncollectible accounts—$50 in this example.

As stated above, selling on credit creates both a benefit and a cost:

- *Benefit*: Customers who cannot pay cash immediately can buy on credit, so company profits rise as sales increase.
- *Cost*: The company will be unable to collect from some credit customers. Accountants label this cost **uncollectible-account expense, doubtful-account expense**, or **bad-debt expense**.

Accounts receivable are reported in the financial statements at cost minus an appropriate allowance for uncollectible accounts (that is, net realizable value). This is the amount we expect to collect.

Bad debt expense is not shown as a separate line item on the income statement; it is usually included in Selling Expense or Administrative Expense.

A company that chose to present the allowance for uncollectible accounts could present the information in the notes to the financial statements or disclose the information on the balance sheet as follows:

Accounts receivable (net of allowance for uncollectible accounts of $120,000)	$2,005,234

Uncollectible-account expense is an expense associated with the failure to collect receivables. It is usually reported as an operating expense along with salary expense, rent expense, and utilities expense. To measure uncollectible-account expense, accountants use the allowance method or, in certain limited cases, the direct write-off method (which we discuss starting on page 250).

Allowance Method

OBJECTIVE

Use the allowance method for uncollectible receivables

The best way to measure bad debts is by the **allowance method**. This method records collection losses on the basis of estimates. Management does not wait to see which customers will not pay. Managers estimate bad-debt expense on the basis of the company's collection experience. The business records the estimated amount as Uncollectible-Account Expense and sets up an **Allowance for Uncollectible Accounts**. Other titles for this account are **Allowance for Doubtful Accounts** and **Allowance for Bad Debts**. This is a contra account to Accounts Receivable. The allowance shows the amount of the receivables that the business expects *not* to collect.

In Chapter 3 we used the Accumulated Depreciation account to show how much of a property, plant, and equipment asset has been expensed—the portion of the asset that is no longer a benefit to the company. Allowance for Uncollectible Accounts serves a similar purpose for accounts receivable. The allowance shows how much of the receivable has been expensed. You'll find the following table helpful (amounts are assumed).

Property, Plant, and Equipment......	$100,000	Accounts Receivable	$10,000
Less: Accumulated Depreciation..............................	(40,000)	Less: Allowance for Uncollectible Accounts	(900)
Property, Plant, and Equipment, net..	$ 60,000	Accounts Receivable, net	$ 9,100

Focus on Accounts Receivable. Customers owe this company $10,000, but the company expects to collect only $9,100. This amount is known as the net realizable value. Another way to report these receivables is:

Accounts receivable, net of allowance for uncollectible accounts of $900 .... $9,100

You can work backward to determine the full amount of the receivable, $10,000 (net realizable value of $9,100 plus the allowance of $900).

The income statement reports uncollectible-account expense among the operating expenses as follows (using assumed figures):

Income statement (partial):
Expenses:
Uncollectible-account expense... $2,000

STOP + THINK

You are considering an investment in Black Corporation and are looking at Black's June 30, 2010, financial statements, which are stated in thousands of U.S. dollars. In particular, you are focusing on Black's accounts receivable. The balance sheet includes the following:

	June 30	
	2010	2009
Accounts receivable trade, net of allowance for uncollectible accounts of $3,974 as of June 30, 2010, and $2,089 as of June 30, 2009	$134,396	$128,781

At June 30, 2010, how much did customers owe Black Corporation? How much did Black expect *not* to collect? How much of the receivables did Black expect to collect? What was the net realizable value of Black Corporation's receivables?

Answer:

	(in thousands)
Customers owed Black Corporation..	$138,370
Black expected not to collect...	3,974
Black expected to collect—net realizable value	$134,396

The best way to estimate uncollectibles uses the company's history of collections from customers. There are two basic ways to estimate uncollectibles:

- Percentage-of-sales method
- Aging-of-receivables method

Percentage-of-Sales. The **percentage-of-sales method** computes uncollectible-account expense as a percentage of revenue. This method takes an *income-statement approach* because it focuses on the amount of expense to be reported on the income statement. Assume it is June 30, 2010, and Black Corporation's accounts have these balances *before the year-end adjustments* (the following discussion expresses all amounts in thousands):

Accounts Receivable		Allowance for Uncollectible Accounts	
138,370			346

Customers owe Black Corporation $138,370, and the Allowance amount is $346. Suppose the economy slows down, and Black's top managers know that the company will fail to collect more than $346. Suppose Black's credit department estimates that uncollectible-account expense is 1/2 of 1% (0.005) of total revenues, which were $725,532 for 2010. The entry to record bad-debt expense for the year also updates the allowance as follows:

2010			
June 30	Uncollectible-Account Expense ($725,532 × 0.005)......	3,628	
	Allowance for Uncollectible Accounts		3,628
	Recorded expense for the year.		

The expense decreases assets, as shown by the accounting equation:

ASSETS	=	LIABILITIES	+	SHAREHOLDERS' EQUITY	−	EXPENSES
−3,628	=	0			−	3,628

Now the accounts are ready for reporting in the financial statements.

Accounts Receivable			Allowance for Uncollectible Accounts	
138,370				346
				3,628
				3,974

Net accounts receivable, $134,396

Compare these amounts to the Stop & Think answer on page 246. They are the same.

Customers still owe Black Corporation $138,370, but now the Allowance for Uncollectible Accounts balance is realistic. Black's balance sheet actually reported accounts receivable at their net realizable value amount of $134,396 ($138,370 − $3,974). Black's income statement included uncollectible-account expense among the operating expenses for the period.

Aging of Accounts Receivable. The other popular method for estimating uncollectibles is called **aging of accounts receivable**. This method is a *balance-sheet approach* because it focuses on Accounts Receivable. In the aging method, individual receivables from specific customers are analyzed based on how long they have been outstanding.*

Computerized accounting packages are programmed to age the company's accounts receivable. Exhibit 5-2 shows an assumed aging of receivables for Black at June 30, 2010. Black's receivables total $138,370 (in thousands of U.S. dollars). Of this amount, the aging schedule shows that the company will *not* collect $6,156, but the allowance for uncollectible accounts is not yet up to date. Suppose Black's accounts are as follows *before the year-end adjustment* (in thousands):

Accounts Receivable			Allowance for Uncollectible Accounts	
138,370				346

*Rather than preparing an aging schedule, the company could determine what the credit balance of the allowance for uncollectible accounts needs to be by calculating it as a percent of the total Accounts Receivable balance.

EXHIBIT 5-2 **Aging the Accounts Receivable of Black Corporation**

		Dollar Amounts (in thousands) Number of Days Past Due			
Customer	**Total**	**1–30**	**31–60**	**61–90**	**over 90**
City of Regina	$ 500	$ 500			
IBM Canada	1,000	1,000			
Keady Pipe Corp.	2,100		$ 1,000	$ 1,100	
TorBar Inc.	200			200	
Others	134,570	66,070	57,000	9,000	$2,500
	$138,370	$67,570	$58,000	$10,300	$2,500
Estimated % Uncollectible		2%	5%	10%	35%
Total Estimated Uncollectible Accounts	$ 6,156	$ 1,351	$ 2,900	$ 1,030	$ 875

The aging method will bring the balance of the allowance account ($346) to the needed amount ($6,156) as determined by the aging schedule in Exhibit 5-2. The lower left corner gives the needed balance in the allowance account. To update the allowance, Black Corporation would make this entry:

2010			
June 30	Uncollectible-Account Expense ($6,156 − $346)	5,810	
	Allowance for Uncollectible Accounts		5,810
	Recorded expense for the year.		

The expense decreases assets, as shown by the accounting equation.

ASSETS	=	LIABILITIES	+	SHAREHOLDERS' EQUITY	−	EXPENSES
−5,810	=	0			−	5,810

Now the balance sheet can report the amount that Black Corporation actually expects to collect from customers: $132,214 ($138,370 − $6,156). This is the net realizable value of Black's trade receivables. Black's accounts are now ready for the balance sheet, as follows:

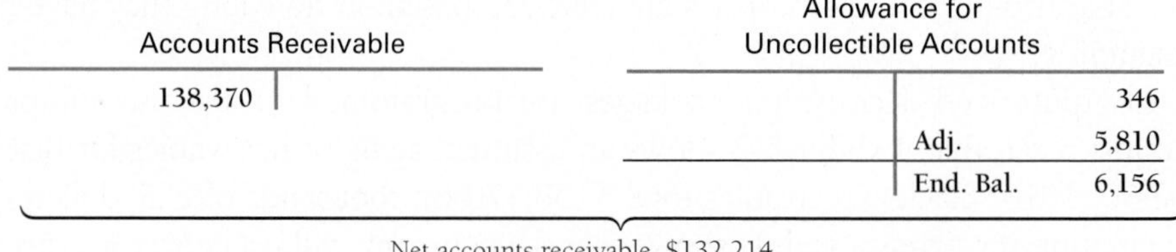

Writing Off Uncollectible Accounts. Suppose that early in July 2010, Black's credit department determines that Black cannot collect from customers Keady Pipe Corporation and TorBar Inc. (see Exhibit 5-2). Black Corporation then writes off the receivables from these two delinquent customers with the following entry (in thousands of U.S. dollars):

2010			
July 12	Allowance for Uncollectible Accounts	2,300	
	Accounts Receivable—Keady Pipe Corporation		2,100
	Accounts Receivable—TorBar Inc.		200
	Wrote off uncollectible receivables.		

After the write-off, Black's accounts show these amounts:

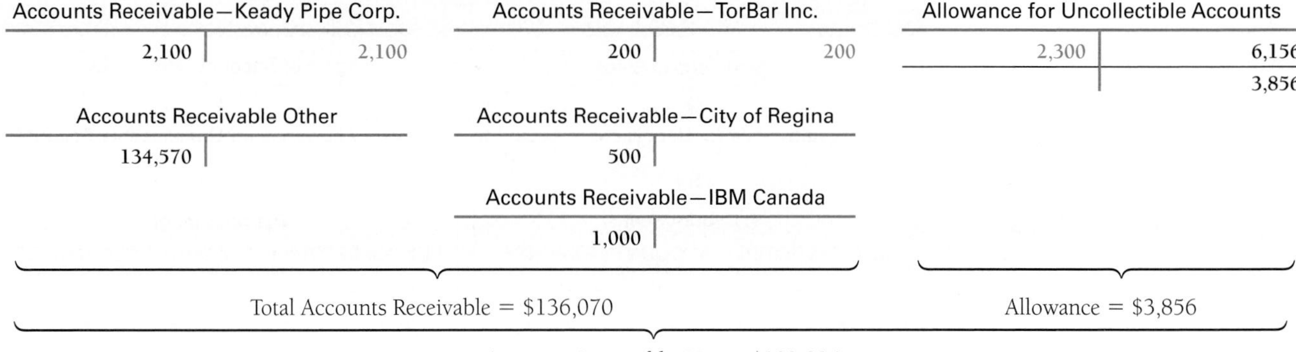

The accounting equation shows that the write-off of uncollectibles has no effect on total assets. The net realizable value of accounts receivable is still $132,214. There is no effect on net income either, because no income statement account is affected.

ASSETS	=	LIABILITIES	+	SHAREHOLDERS' EQUITY
+2,300 −2,300	=	0	+	0

STOP + THINK

In the preceding accounting equation (for the write-off of uncollectible receivables), why is there no effect on total assets? Why is there no effect on net income?

Answer:
There is no effect on total assets because the write-off of an uncollectible receivable decreases both Accounts Receivable and the Allowance for Uncollectible Accounts, a contra account. Both accounts are part of net receivables, so one effect offsets the other. The result is no effect on the net realizable value of the receivables and no effect on total assets. There is no effect on net income because the write-off of uncollectible accounts affects no expense account. (The expense account was affected when the Allowance for Uncollectible Accounts was created in an earlier period.)

Combining the Percentage-of-Sales and the Aging-of-Accounts-Receivable Methods. Most companies use the percentage-of-sales and aging-of-accounts-receivable methods together, as follows:

- For *interim statements* (monthly or quarterly), companies use the percentage-of-sales method because it is easier to apply. The percentage-of-sales method focuses on the uncollectible-account *expense*, but that is not enough.
- At the end of the year, companies use the aging-of-accounts-receivable method to ensure that Accounts Receivable is reported at *net realizable value* on the balance sheet. The aging-of-accounts-receivable method focuses on the amount of the receivables that is uncollectible.

- Using the two methods together provides good measures of both the expense and the asset. Exhibit 5-3 compares the two methods.

EXHIBIT 5-3 **Comparing the Percentage-of-Sales and Aging-of-Accounts-Receivable Methods for Estimating Uncollectible Accounts**

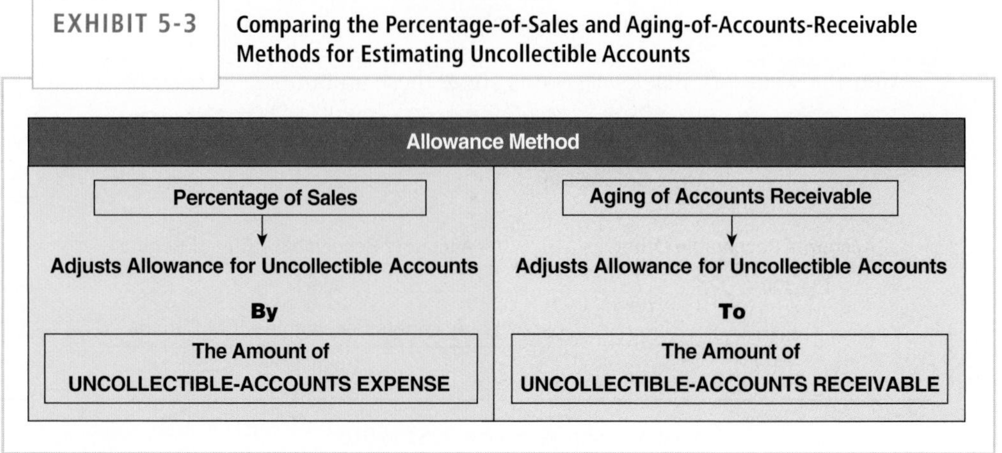

Recovery of an Uncollectible Account

When an account receivable is written off as uncollectible, the customer still owes the money. However, the company may stop pursuing collection and write off the account as uncollectible.

Some companies turn delinquent receivables over to a collection agency to help recover some of their cash. This is called *recovery of a bad account*. Recall that on July 12, 2010, Black Corporation wrote off the $200 account receivable from TorBar. Suppose it is now September 1, 2010, and the company unexpectedly receives the $200 from TorBar. To account for this recovery, the company makes two journal entries to (1) reverse the earlier write-off and (2) record the cash collection, as follows:

2010			
Sept. 1	Accounts Receivable—TorBar	200	
	Allowance for Uncollectible Accounts		200
	Reinstated TorBar's account receivable.		
	Cash	200	
	Accounts Receivable		200
	Collected on account.		

Direct Write-Off Method

There is another, less preferable, way to account for uncollectible receivables. Under the **direct write-off method**, the company waits until it decides that a specific customer's receivable is uncollectible. Then the accountant records uncollectible-account expense and writes off the customer's account receivable as follows (using assumed data):

2011			
Jan. 30	Uncollectible-Account Expense	2,000	
	Accounts Receivable—Jones Inc.		2,000
	Wrote off an uncollectible account by direct write-off method.		

This method is defective for two reasons:

1. The direct write-off method does not set up an allowance for uncollectible accounts. As a result, receivables are always reported at their full amount, which is more than the business expects to collect. *Assets on the balance sheet are overstated.*
2. In this example, the company made the sale to Jones Inc. in 2010 and should have recorded the expense during 2010. By recording the expense in 2011, the company overstates net income *in 2010*. Then, by recording the expense when it writes off the receivable in 2011, the company understates net income *in 2011*.

Expenses should be offset against the revenue of the same period. Thus, the direct write-off method is acceptable only when uncollectibles are so low that there is no significant difference between uncollectible account expense by the allowance method and the direct write-off method.

Computing Cash Collections From Customers

A company earns revenue and then collects the cash from customers. For Black Corporation and most other companies there is a time lag between earning the revenue and collecting the cash. Collections from customers are the single most important source of cash for any business. You can compute a company's collections from customers by analyzing its Accounts Receivable account. Receivables typically hold only five different items, as follows (amounts assumed):

Accounts Receivable

Beg. balance (left from last period)	200	Write-offs of uncollectible accounts	100**
		Collections from customers	X = 1,500†
Sales (or service) revenue	1,800*		
End. balance (carries over to next period)	400		

*The journal entry that places revenue into the receivable account is

Accounts Receivable	1,800	
Sales (or Service) Revenue		1,800

**The journal entry for write-offs is

Allowance for Uncollectible Accounts	100	
Accounts Receivable		100

†The journal entry that places collections into the receivable account is

Cash	1,500	
Accounts Receivable		1,500

Suppose you know all these amounts except collections from customers. You can compute collections by solving for X in the T-account.*

Often write-offs are not known and must be omitted. Then the computation of collections becomes an approximation.

*An equation may help you solve for X. The equation is $\$200 + \$1,800 - X - \$100 = \$400$. $X = \$1,500$.

Shifting Sales Into the Current Period Makes a Company Look Good Now, But You Pay for It Later

Suppose it is December 26. Late in the year a company's business dried up: Its profits are running below what everyone predicted. The company needs a loan and its banker requires financial statements to support the loan request. Unless the company acts quickly, it won't get the loan.

Fortunately, next year looks better. The company has standing orders for sales of $50,000. As soon as the company gets the merchandise, it can ship it to customers and record the sales. An old accounting trick can solve the problem. Book the $50,000 of sales in December. After all, the company will be shipping the goods on January 2 of next year. What difference does two days make?

It makes all the difference in the world. Shifting the sales into the current year will make the company look better immediately. Reported profits will rise, the current ratio will improve, and the company can then get the loan needed. But what are the consequences? If caught, the company will be prosecuted for fraud and its reputation will be ruined. Remember that the company shifted next year's sales into the current year. Next year's sales will be lower than the true amount, and profits will suffer. If next year turns out to be like this year, the company will be facing the same shortage again. Also, something may come up to keep the company from shipping the goods on January 2.

Very few companies pull these tricks, because these actions are dishonest, unethical, and illegal. Honesty is always the best policy.

The take-away lesson is this:

- Study a company's financial-statement notes to learn when it books revenue. If booked too early, the company's revenues aren't there yet and shouldn't be recognized.

Notes Receivable

OBJECTIVE

5 **Account** for notes receivable

As stated earlier, notes receivable are more formal than accounts receivable. Notes receivable due within one year or less are current assets. Notes due beyond one year are *long-term receivables* and are reported as capital assets. Some notes receivable are collected in installments. The portion due within one year is a current asset and the remainder is long-term. RONA Inc. may hold a $20,000 note receivable from a customer, but only the $6,000 the customer must pay within one year is a current asset of RONA.

Before launching into the accounting for notes receivable, let's define some key terms:

Creditor	The party to whom money is owed. The creditor is also called the *lender*.
Debtor	The party that borrowed and owes money on the note. The debtor is also called the *maker* of the note or the *borrower*.
Interest	Interest is the cost of borrowing money. The interest is stated in an annual percentage rate.
Maturity date	The date on which the debtor must pay the note.
Maturity value	The sum of principal and interest on the note.
Principal	The amount of money borrowed by the debtor.

Term The length of time from when the note was signed by the debtor to when the debtor must pay the note.

There are two parties to a note:

- The *creditor* has a note receivable.
- The *debtor* has a note payable.

The debtor signs the note and thereby creates a contract with the creditor. Exhibit 5-4 shows a typical promissory note.

The *principal* amount of the note ($1,000) is the amount borrowed by the debtor and lent by the creditor. This six-month note runs from July 1, 2010, to December 31, 2010, when Lauren Holland (the maker) promises to pay Canadian Western Bank (the creditor) the principal of $1,000 plus 9% interest per year. *Interest* is revenue to the creditor (Canadian Western Bank, in this case).

Accounting for Notes Receivable

Consider the promissory note shown in Exhibit 5-4. After Lauren Holland (the maker) signs the note, Canadian Western Bank gives her $1,000 cash. The bank's entries follow, assuming an October 31, 2010, year-end for Canadian Western Bank:

2010			
July 1	Note Receivable—L. Holland	1,000	
	Cash		1,000
	Made a loan.		

Note Receivable—L. Holland	
1,000	

The bank gave one asset, cash, in return for another asset, a note receivable, so the total assets did not change.

ASSETS	=	LIABILITIES	+	SHAREHOLDERS' EQUITY
+1,000 −1,000	=	0	+	0

EXHIBIT 5-4 **A Promissory Note**

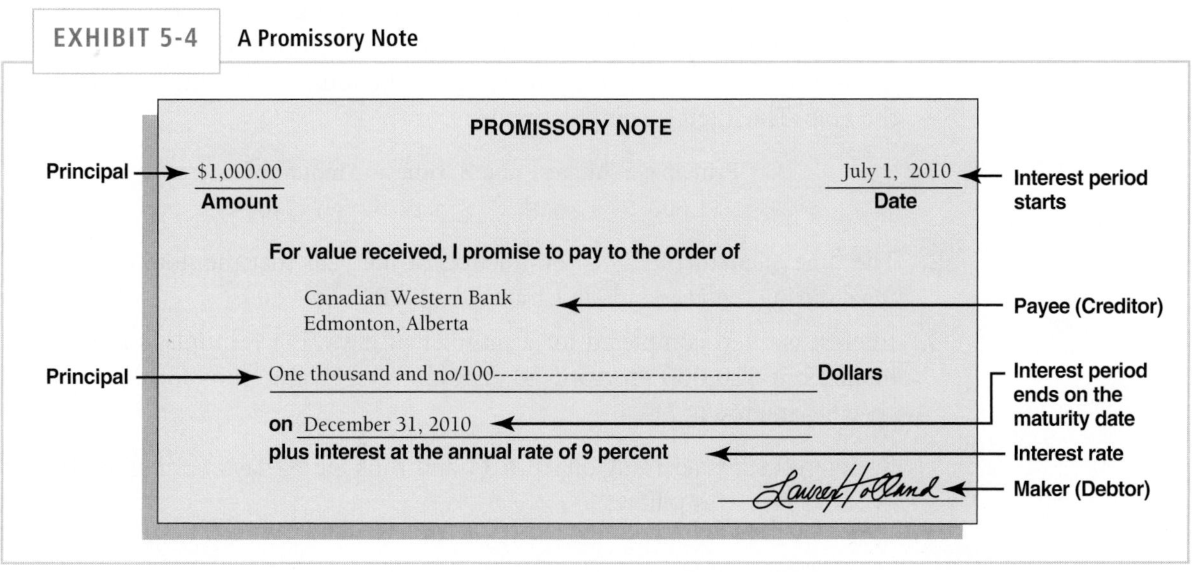

Canadian Western Bank earns interest revenue during July, August, September, and October. At October 31, 2010, the bank accrues interest revenue for four months as follows:

2010			
Oct. 31	Interest Receivable ($1,000 × 0.09 × 4/12)	30	
	Interest Revenue		30
	Accrued interest revenue.		

The bank's assets and its revenue increase.

The bank reports these amounts in its financial statements at October 31, 2010:

Balance sheet	
Current assets:	
Note receivable	$1,000
Interest receivable	30
Income statement	
Interest revenue	$30

The bank collects the note on December 31, 2010, and records:

2010			
Dec. 31	Cash	1,045	
	Note Receivable—L. Holland		1,000
	Interest Receivable		30
	Interest Revenue ($1,000 × 0.09 × 2/12)		15
	Collected note at maturity.		

This entry zeroes out Note Receivable and Interest Receivable and also records the interest revenue earned in the year ended October 31, 2010.

Note Receivable—L. Holland	
1,000	1,000

In its 2011 financial statements the only item that Canadian Western Bank will report is the interest revenue of $15 that was earned in 2011. There's no note receivable or interest receivable on the balance sheet because those items were zeroed out when the bank collected the note at maturity.

Three aspects of these entries deserve mention:

1. Interest rates are always for an annual period unless stated otherwise. In this example, the annual interest rate is 9%. At October 31, 2010, Canadian Western Bank accrues interest revenue for the four months the bank has held the note. The interest computation is:

Principal	× Interest rate	× Time	= Amount of Interest
$1,000 ×	0.09	× 4/12 =	$30

2. The time element (4/12) is the fraction of the year that the note has been in force during the year ended October 31, 2010.
3. Interest is often completed for a number of days. For example, suppose you loaned out $10,000 on April 10. The note receivable runs for 90 days and specifies interest at 8%.

    a. Interest starts accruing on April 11 and runs for 90 days, ending on the due date, July 9, as follows:

Month	Number of Days That Interest Accrues
April	20
May	31
June	30
July	9
Total	90

b. The interest computation is: $10,000 × 0.08 × 90/365 = $197

Some companies sell goods and services on notes receivable (versus selling on accounts receivable). This often occurs when the payment term extends beyond the customary accounts receivable period of 30 to 60 days.

Suppose that on March 20, 2010, West Fraser Timber Co. Ltd. sells lumber for $15,000 to Darmal Const. Inc. West Fraser receives Darmal's 90-day promissory note at 10% annual interest. The entries to record the sale and collection from Darmal follow the pattern illustrated previously for Canadian Western Bank and Lauren Holland, with one exception. At the outset, West Fraser would credit Sales Revenue (instead of Cash) because West Fraser is making a sale (and not lending money to Darmal).

Short-term notes receivable of the kind discussed in this chapter should be valued in the same way as accounts receivable in that an appropriate allowance should be set up for notes thought to be uncollectible.

Notes with a maturity of more than 365 days would be valued at amortized cost (that is, discounted to reflect the time value of money).

A company may also accept a note receivable from a trade customer whose account receivable is past due. The customer signs a note payable, and the company then credits the account receivable and debits a note receivable. We would say the company "received a note receivable from a customer on account."

For example, assume that on February 1, 2010, Power Ltd. purchased $5,000 of building supplies from Piercy's Building Supplies with 60-day credit terms. Piercy's records the sale as follows:

2010			
Feb. 1	Accounts Receivable	5,000	
	Sales		5,000
	To record sale to Power Ltd.		

If on April 1, 2010, Power Ltd. agrees to sign a 30-day note receivable to replace the account receivable due on that date, then Piercy's would record the following journal entry:

2010			
Apr. 1	Notes Receivable	5,000	
	Accounts Receivable—Power Ltd.		5,000
	To record conversion of account receivable to note receivable.		

Now let's examine some strategies to speed up cash flow.

How to Speed Up Cash Flow

All companies want speedy cash receipts. Rapid cash flow finances new products, new technology, research, and development. Thus, companies find ways to collect cash immediately. Two common strategies generate cash more quickly than waiting to collect from customers.

Credit Card Sales. The merchant sells merchandise and lets the customer pay with a credit card, such as VISA, MasterCard, or a company credit card such as HBC (Hudson's Bay Company). This strategy may dramatically increase sales, but the added revenue comes at a cost. Let's see how credit cards work from the seller's perspective. The merchant actually records the cash amount equal to the sale amount and each month the bank deducts the fee on that month's sales. The examples that follow are illustrative of the principle, not practice.

Suppose you purchase an iPhone from TELUS in Fredericton, New Brunswick, for $500 and you pay with a MasterCard. TELUS would record the sale as follows:

Cash	485	
Financing Expense	15	
Sales Revenue		500
Recorded credit card sale.		

ASSETS	=	LIABILITIES	+	SHAREHOLDERS' EQUITY	+	REVENUES	−	EXPENSES
+485	=	0	+		+	500	−	15

TELUS enters the transaction in the credit-card machine. The machine, linked to a MasterCard server, automatically credits TELUS's account for a discounted portion—say, $485—of the $500 sales amount. MasterCard gets 3%, or $15 ($500 × 0.03 = $15). To the merchant, the financing expense is an operating expense similar to interest expense.

Debit Card Sales. The merchant sells merchandise, and the customer pays by swiping a bank card such as a Scotiabank ScotiaCard or a TD Canada Trust Green Card using the Interac System. In this case, the bank card is being used as a debit card. To a merchant or service provider, a debit card is just like cash; when the card is swiped and the personal identification number (PIN) is entered, the merchant receives payment immediately as the Interac System takes money directly from the cardholder's bank account and transfers the money to the merchant's bank account less a processing fee. As with credit cards, the merchant is charged a fee. To record a sale of groceries for $65.48, Sobeys would record this entry:

Cash	64.48	
Interac Fee (assumed rate)	1.00	
Sales Revenue		65.48
Record sale paid using Interac.		

ASSETS	=	LIABILITIES	+	SHAREHOLDERS' EQUITY	+	REVENUE	−	EXPENSES
+64.48	=	0	+		+	65.48	−	1.00

One advantage for the merchant is that the payment is just like cash without the task of depositing the money. One advantage to the customer is that there is no need to carry cash. A second advantage to the cardholder is the cash-back feature; the cardholder can ask for cash back, and the merchant will record an entry that includes the purchase plus the requested cash. Using the above date and assuming the carholder requested $30.00 cash back, the entry would be:

Cash	94.48	
Interac Fee (assumed rate)	1.00	
Sales Revenue		65.48
Cash (to cardholder)		30.00
Record sale paid using Interac and cash back of $30.00.		

Selling (Factoring) Receivables. Suppose Black Corporation makes normal sales on account, debiting Accounts Receivable and crediting Sales Revenue. Black can then sell its accounts receivable to another business, called a *factor*. The factor earns revenue by paying a discounted price for the receivables and then collecting the full amount from the customers. The benefit to the company is the immediate receipt of cash.

To illustrate, suppose Black wishes to speed up cash flow and therefore sells $100,000 of accounts receivable, receiving cash of $95,000. Black would record the sale of the receivables as follows:

Cash	95,000	
Financing Expense	5,000	
Accounts Receivable		100,000
Sold accounts receivable.		

Again, Financing Expense is an operating expense, with the same effect as a loss. Some companies may debit a Loss account. Discounting a note receivable is similar to selling an account receivable; however, the credit is to Notes Receivable (instead of Accounts Receivable).

Using Ratios in Decisions Making

OBJECTIVE

6 **Use** ratios to evaluate a business

Managers, investors, and creditors use ratios to evaluate the financial health of a company. They care about the liquidity of assets. Liquidity is a measure of how quickly an item can be converted to cash. Remember a balance sheet lists assets in order of relative liquidity:

- *Cash and cash equivalents* come first because they are the most liquid asset.
- *Short-term investments* come next because they are almost as liquid as cash. They can be sold for cash whenever the owner wishes.
- *Current receivables* are less liquid than short-term investments because the company must collect the receivables.
- *Merchandise inventory* is less liquid than receivables because the goods must be sold first.
- *Prepaid expenses* are listed after inventories since they are expenses where cash has already been paid in advance.

We introduced the current ratio in Chapter 3. Recall that the current ratio is computed as follows:

$$\text{Current ratio} = \frac{\text{Total current assets}}{\text{Total current liabilities}}$$

The current ratio measures the company's ability to pay current liabilities with current assets. Other ratios, including the *acid-test* or *quick ratio* and the number of *days' sales (or revenues) in receivables*, also help investors measure liquidity. These measures help to build a picture of the strength of a business.

Acid-Test (or Quick) Ratio

The **acid-test ratio** (or **quick ratio**) is a more stringent measure of the company's ability to pay current liabilities. *The acid-test ratio is similar to the current ratio but it excludes inventory and prepaid expenses.*

Inventory takes time to sell before the company is able to collect its cash. A company with lots of inventory may have an acceptable current ratio but find it hard to pay its bills. Prepaid expenses are also excluded since the cash has already been paid for these assets that will be expensed as they are used up.

$$\text{Acid-test ratio} = \frac{\text{Cash} + \text{Short-term investments} + \text{Net current receivables}}{\text{Total current liabilities}}$$

Using Loblaw's balance sheet in the chapter opening story, the acid-test ratio is:

$$\text{2009 Loblaw} = \frac{\$993 + \$397 + \$774}{\$3,628^{*}} = 0.60$$

The higher the acid-test ratio, the easier it is to pay current liabilities. Loblaw's acid-test ratio of 0.60 means that Loblaw has \$0.60 of quick assets to pay each \$1.00 of current liabilities. In general, an acid-test ratio of 1.0 is considered safe. Does this mean that Loblaw's is in trouble? No, in the grocery industry, a low value is considered normal since companies depend upon selling their inventory quickly and turning that into cash.

What is an acceptable acid-test ratio? The answer depends on the industry. Auto dealers can operate smoothly with an acid-test ratio of 0.20. How can auto dealers survive with so low an acid-test ratio? GM, Toyota, and the other auto manufacturers help finance their dealers' inventory. Most dealers, therefore, have a financial safety net. Nike, the sports manufacturer, has a quick ratio of around 1.0.

Days' Sales in Receivables

After a business makes a credit sale, the *next* step is collecting the receivable. **Days' sales in receivables**, also called the *collection period*, tells how long it takes to collect the average level of receivables. Shorter is better because cash is coming in quickly. The longer the collection period, the less cash is available to pay bills and expand.

*Amount taken from 2009 balance sheet in annual report.

Days' sales in receivables can be computed in two logical steps, as follows. First, compute one day's sales (or one day's total revenues). Then divide one day's sales into average receivables for the period. We show days' sales in receivables for Loblaw Corporation.

For Loblaw Corporation (millions)

1. $$\text{One day's sale} = \frac{\text{Net sales}}{\text{365 days}} = \frac{\$30{,}735^{*}}{365} = \$84.20 \text{ per day}$$

2. $$\text{Days' sales in average accounts receivable} = \frac{\text{Average net accounts receivable}}{\text{One day's sales}} = \frac{\left(\text{Beginning net receivables} + \text{Ending net receivables}\right) \div 2}{\text{One day's sales}}$$

$$= \frac{(\$867 + \$774) \div 2}{\$84.20} = 9.7 \text{ or } 10 \text{ days}$$

*Taken from Loblaw's 2009 income statement.

Net sales come from the income statement and the receivables amounts are taken from the balance sheet. Average receivables is the simple average of the beginning and ending balances.

The length of the collection period depends on the credit terms of the company's sales. For example, sales on "net 30" terms should be collected within approximately 30 days. Loblaw's days' sales in average receivables was 10 days in the 2009 financial statements.

Companies watch their collection periods closely. Whenever the collections get slow, the business must find other sources of financing, such as borrowing cash or factoring receivables. During recessions, customers pay more slowly, and a longer collection period may be unavoidable.*

Reporting on the Statement of Cash Flows

Receivables and temporary investments appear on the balance sheet as assets. We saw these in Black Corporation's balance sheet at the beginning of the chapter. We've also seen how to report the related revenues, gains, and losses on the income statement. Because receivables and investment transactions affect cash, their effects must also be reported on the statement of cash flows.

Receivables bring in cash when the business collects from customers. These transactions are reported as *operating activities* on the statement of cash flows because they result from sales. Investment transactions are reported as *investing activities* on the statement of cash flows. Chapter 12 shows how companies report their cash flows to the public on the statement of cash flows. In that chapter, we will see exactly how to report cash flows related to receivables and investment transactions.

*Another ratio, **accounts receivable turnover**, captures the same information as days' sales in receivables. Receivable turnover is computed as follows: Net sales ÷ Average net accounts receivable. During 2010, Black Corporation had a receivable turnover rate of 5.5 times [$726 ÷ ([$134 + $129] ÷ 2)]. The authors prefer days' sales in receivables because it is easier to interpret. Days' sales in receivables can be compared directly to the company's credit sale terms.

SUMMARY OF CHAPTER 5

Learning Objective ❶: Learn about fraud and how much it costs

Short-term (trading) investments that a company plans to hold a **term** of for one year or less are classified as **current assets** on the balance sheet. When these investments are bought, they are recorded at cost but at year-end they are reported on the balance sheet at **fair value**. Any unrealized gain or loss resulting from the change in value is recorded and reported on the income statement. When the investment is sold, any realized gain or loss is also reported on the income statement.

Learning Objective ❷: Account for receivables

Accounts receivable (or **receivables**) result from a company selling its products or services on credit. They are recorded as a current asset because the company expects to collect cash from the customer within a short period of time. Notes receivable are more formal contracts than accounts receivable. A written agreement is made where the borrower agrees to pay a definite sum at a maturity date as well as **interest** over the life of the loan. Other receivables include loans to employees and subsidiary companies.

Learning Objective ❸: Apply internal controls to receivables

Internal control for receivables relates to cash collections on account where the cash-handling and cash-accounting duties are separated to prevent theft or fraud.

Learning Objective ❹: Use the allowance method for uncollectible receivables

Since some customers will not be able to pay their debts, the company estimates the amount of uncollectible accounts using the allowance method. Under the allowance method, the company can estimate uncollectibles using either the percentage-of-sales method or the aging of accounts receivable method. The **percentage-of-sales method** (income statement approach) computes uncollectible account expense as a percentage of revenue and adjusts the allowance account by this amount. Under the **aging of accounts receivable** method (balance sheet approach), individual accounts are analyzed according to the length of time they have been receivable from the customer and the allowance account is adjusted to this amount. An accounts receivable is written off when a company is not able to collect from the customer. Sometimes, an account receivable may be recovered after it has been written off.

Rather than estimating uncollectibles, a **direct write-off method** is used where the company decides that a specific customer's receivable is uncollectible and then writes it off. This is not acceptable unless the receivables are so low that there is no difference between using the allowance method or the direct write-off method.

Learning Objective ❺: Account for notes receivable

Notes receivable are formal arrangements in which the **debtor** signs a promissory note, agreeing to pay back both the **principal** borrowed plus a stated percentage of **interest** on a certain date. The **creditor** has a note receivable and the debtor has a note payable.

Learning Objective ❻: Use ratios to evaluate a business

Key ratios used in decision making include the current ratio, **acid-test** or **quick ratio**, and **days' sales in receivables**. These ratios help managers, investors, and creditors measure the liquidity of the company. Liquidity relates to how quickly a company can obtain and pay cash.

END-OF-CHAPTER SUMMARY PROBLEM

MyAccountingLab

CHC Helicopter Corporation is Vancouver-based and is the world's largest provider of helicopter services to the global offshore oil and gas industry. The company's balance sheet at April 30, 2010, adapted, reported:

	(in millions)
Trade accounts receivable	$240.6
Allowance for uncollectible accounts	(8.4)

Name: CHC Helicopter Corporation
Industry: Helicopter services
Accounting Period: Years ended April 30, 2010, and April 30, 2011

Required

1. How much of the April 30, 2010, balance of accounts receivable did CHC Helicopter Corporation expect to collect? Stated differently, what was the expected realizable value of these receivables?
2. Journalize, without explanations, 2011 entries for CHC Helicopter, assuming
   a. Estimated Uncollectible-Account Expense of $1.3 million, based on the percentage-of-sales method, all during the year.
   b. Write-offs of uncollectible accounts receivable totalling $8.0 million.
   c. April 30, 2011, aging of receivables, which indicates that $3.1 million of the total receivables of $303.4 million is uncollectible at year-end.
3. Show how CHC Helicopter's receivables and related allowance will appear on the April 30, 2011, balance sheet.
4. Show what CHC Helicopter's income statement will report for the foregoing transactions.

ANSWERS

Requirement 1

The expected realizable value of receivables is the full value less the allowance for uncollectible accounts.

	(in millions)
Expected realizable value of receivables ($240.6 − $8.4)	$232.2

Requirement 2

The estimate increases both the expense and the allowance for uncollectible accounts.

Write-offs reduce the allowance for uncollectible accounts and accounts receivable. They do *not* affect the uncollectible-account expense.

a. Uncollectible-Account Expense	1.3	
Allowance for Uncollectible Accounts		1.3
b. Allowance for Uncollectible Accounts	8.0	
Accounts Receivable		8.0

Allowance for Uncollectible Accounts

2011 Write-offs	8.0	April 30, 2010	8.4
		2011 Expense	1.3
		2011 Balance	1.7

First, determine the balance in Allowance for Uncollectible Accounts by filling in its T-account using the opening balance (given), adding the expense amount from 2 a, and deducting the write-offs from 2 b.

The final balance in the Allowance for Uncollectible Accounts must be $3.1 (estimated in 2 c). The balance in the T-account is already $1.7 (calculated above). Therefore, Uncollectible-Account Expense and Allowance for Uncollectible Accounts must be increased by the difference of $1.4.

c. Uncollectible-Account Expense ($3.1 − $1.7)	1.4	
Allowance for Uncollectible Accounts		1.4

Allowance for Uncollectible Accounts

	1.7
	1.4
	3.1

Accounts receivable are always shown at net realizable value, the amount actually expected to be collected.

Requirement 3

	(in millions)
Accounts receivable	$303.4
Allowance for uncollectible accounts	(3.1)
Accounts receivable, net	$300.3

Add all the Uncollectible-Account Expense amounts from Requirement 2 a, b, and c. The $2.7 includes estimates based on percentage of sales and aging of the receivables.

Requirement 4

	(in millions)
Expenses: Uncollectible-account expense for 2011 ($1.3 + $1.4)	$2.7

Review Short-Term Investments and Receivables

Quick Check **(Answers are given on page 282.)**

1. Harvey Penick Golf Academy held trading investments valued at $55,000 at December 31, 2010. These investments cost Penick $50,000. What is the appropriate amount for Penick to report for these investments on the December 31, 2010, balance sheet?
   a. $50,000
   b. $55,000
   c. $5,000 gain
   d. Cannot be determined from the data given
2. Return to Harvey Penick Golf Academy in Question 1. What should appear on the Penick income statement for the year ended December 31, 2010, for the trading investments?
   a. $50,000
   b. $55,000
   c. $5,000 unrealized gain
   d. Cannot be determined from the data given

Use the following information to answer Questions 3 through 7.

Neal Company had the following information relating to credit sales in 2010:

Accounts receivable December 31, 2010	$ 9,500
Allowance for uncollectible accounts December 31, 2010 (before adjustment)	900
Credit sales during 2010	46,000
Cash sales during 2010	15,000
Collections from customers on account during 2010	49,500

3. Uncollectible accounts are determined by the percentage-of-sales method to be 2% of credit sales. How much is uncollectible-account expense for 2010?
   a. $920
   b. $2,000
   c. $750
   d. $20
4. Using the percentage-of-sales method, what is the adjusted balance in the Allowance account at year-end 2010?
   a. $900
   b. $920
   c. $1,500
   d. $1,820
5. If uncollectible accounts are determined by aging of accounts receivable to be $1,350, the uncollectible account expense for 2010 would be
   a. $450
   b. $900
   c. $920
   d. $1,350

6. Using aging of accounts receivable, the balance of the Allowance account after the adjusting entry would be
   a. $450 c. $920
   b. $900 d. $1,350
7. Assuming aging of accounts receivable is used, the net realizable value of accounts receivable on the December 31, 2010, balance sheet would be
   a. $8,580 c. $8,600
   b. $8,150 d. $9,500
8. Accounts Receivable has a debit balance of $3,200, and the Allowance for Uncollectible Accounts has a credit balance of $300. A $100 account receivable is written off. What is the amount of net receivables (net realizable value) after the write-off?
   a. $2,800 c. $3,000
   b. $2,900 d. $3,100
9. Ridgewood Corporation began 2010 with accounts receivable of $800,000. Sales for the year totalled $2,500,000. Ridgewood ended the year with accounts receivable of $900,000. Ridgewood's bad-debt losses are minimal. How much cash did Ridgewood collect from customers in 2010?
   a. $3,400,000 c. $2,500,000
   b. $2,940,000 d. $2,400,000
10. Saturn Company received a four-month, 5%, $4,800 note receivable on December 1. The adjusting entry on December 31 will
    a. Debit Interest Receivable $20 c. Both a and b
    b. Credit Interest Revenue $20 d. Credit Interest Revenue $240
11. What is the maturity value of a $25,000, 5%, six-month note?
    a. $20,000 c. $25,625
    b. $25,000 d. $26,250
12. If the adjusting entry to accrue interest on a note receivable is omitted, then
    a. Liabilities are understated, net income is overstated, and shareholders' equity is overstated.
    b. Assets are overstated, net income is understated, and shareholders' equity is understated.
    c. Assets, net income, and shareholders' equity are overstated.
    d. Assets, net income, and shareholders' equity are understated.
13. Net sales total $730,000. Beginning and ending accounts receivable are $62,000 and $58,000, respectively. Calculate days' sales in receivables.
    a. 32 days c. 43 days
    b. 23 days d. 30 days
14. From the following list of accounts, calculate the quick ratio.

Cash	$3,000	Accounts payable	$ 8,000
Accounts receivable	6,000	Salary payable	3,000
Inventory	8,000	Notes payable (due in two years)	10,000
Prepaid insurance	2,000	Short-term investments	2,000

    a. 2.1 c. 1.0
    b. 1.3 d. 1.4

Accounting Vocabulary

accounts receivable turnover Net sales divided by average net accounts receivable. (p. 259)

acid-test ratio Ratio of the sum of cash plus short-term investments plus net current receivables to total current liabilities. Tells whether the entity can pay all its current liabilities if they come due immediately. Also called the *quick ratio*. (p. 258)

aging of accounts receivable A way to estimate bad debts by analyzing individual accounts receivable according to the length of time they have been receivable from the customer. Also called the *balance-sheet approach* because it focuses on accounts receivable. (p. 247)

Allowance for Bad Debts Another name for *Allowance for Uncollectible Accounts*. (p. 245)

Allowance for Doubtful Accounts Another name for *Allowance for Uncollectible Accounts*. (p. 245)

Allowance for Uncollectible Accounts A contra account, related to accounts receivable, that holds the estimated amount of collection losses. Another name for *Allowance for Doubtful Accounts*. (p. 245)

allowance method A method of recording collection losses based on estimates of how much money the business will not collect from its customers. (p. 245)

bad-debt expense Another name for *uncollectible-account expense*. (p. 245)

creditor The party to whom money is owed. (p. 252)

days' sales in receivables Tells the company how long it takes to collect the average level of receivables. (p. 258)

debtor The party who owes money. (p. 252)

direct write-off method A method of accounting for bad debts in which the company waits until a customer's account receivable proves uncollectible and then debits Uncollectible-Account Expense and credits the customer's Account Receivable. (p. 250)

doubtful-account expense Another name for *uncollectible-account expense*. (p. 245)

fair value The amount that a business could sell an asset for, or the amount that a business could pay to settle a liability. (p. 239)

interest The borrower's cost of renting money from a lender. Interest is revenue for the lender and expense for the borrower. (p. 252)

marketable securities Another name for *short-term investments*. (p. 238)

maturity date The date on which a debt instrument must be paid. (p. 252)

maturity value The sum of principal and interest on a note. (p. 252)

percentage-of-sales method Computes uncollectible-account expense as a percentage of net sales. Also called the *income statement approach* because it focuses on the amount of expense to be reported on the income statement. (p. 246)

principal The amount borrowed by a debtor and lent by a creditor. (p. 252)

quick ratio Another name for *acid-test ratio*. (p. 258)

receivables Monetary claims against a business or an individual, acquired mainly by selling goods or services and by lending money. (p. 242)

short-term investments Investments that a company plans to hold for one year or less. Also called *marketable securities*. (p. 238)

term The length of time from inception to maturity. (p. 253)

trading investment A share or bond investment that is to be sold in the near future with the intent of generating profits on the sale. (p. 239)

uncollectible-account expense Cost to the seller of extending credit. Arises from the failure to collect from credit customers. Also called *doubtful-account expense* or *bad-debt expense*. (p. 245)

Assess Your Progress

Make the grade with MyAccountingLab: The exercises and problems in this chapter can be found on MyAccountingLab at www.myaccountinglab.com. You can practise them as often as you want, and they feature step-by-step guided solutions to help you find the right answer.

Short Exercises

Learning Objective 1
Accounting for short-term investments

S5-1 Answer these questions about investments.

1. Why is a financial asset held for trading investment always a current asset? Explain.
2. What is the amount to report on the balance sheet for a financial asset held for trading investment?

Learning Objective 1
Accounting for a short-term investment

S5-2 Bannister Corp. holds short-term trading investments. On November 16, Bannister paid $80,000 for a short-term trading investment in RIM shares. At December 31, the fair value of the RIM shares is $84,000. For this situation, show everything that Bannister would report on its December 31 balance sheet and on its income statement for the year ended December 31.

Learning Objective 1
Accounting for a short-term investment

S5-3 Beckham Investments paid $104,000 for a short-term investment in RIM shares.

1. Suppose the RIM shares decreased in value to $98,000 at December 31. Make the Beckham journal entry to adjust the Short-Term Investment account to fair value.
2. Show how Beckham would report the short-term investment on its balance sheet and the unrealized gain or loss on its income statement.

Learning Objective 3
Internal control over the collection of receivables

S5-4 Don Roose keeps the accounts receivable records of Zachary & Polk, a partnership. What duty will a good internal control system withhold from Roose? Why?

Short Exercises 5-5 through 5-7 should be used together.

Learning Objective 4
Applying the allowance method (percentage-of-sales) to account for uncollectibles

S5-5 During its first year of operations, Environmental Products Inc. had sales of $875,000, all on account. Industry experience suggests that Environmental Products' uncollectibles will amount to 2% of credit sales. At December 31, 2010, Environmental Products' accounts receivable total $80,000. The company uses the allowance method to account for uncollectibles.

1. Make Environmental Products' journal entry for uncollectible-account expense using the percentage-of-sales method.
2. Show how Environmental Products could report accounts receivable on its balance sheet at December 31, 2010, by disclosing the allowance for uncollectible accounts. Follow the reporting format illustrated in the table at the top of page 246.

Learning Objective 4
Applying the allowance method (percentage-of-sales) to account for uncollectibles

S5-6 This exercise continues the situation of Short Exercise 5-5, in which Environmental Products ended the year 2010 with accounts receivable of $80,000 and an allowance for uncollectible accounts of $17,500. During 2011, Environmental Products completed the following transactions:

1. Credit sales, $1,000,000
2. Collections on account, $880,000
3. Write-offs of uncollectibles, $16,000
4. Uncollectible-account expense, 1.5% of credit sales

Journalize the 2011 transactions for Environmental Products. Explanations are not required.

Learning Objective 4
Applying the allowance method (percentage-of-sales) to account for uncollectibles

S5-7 Use the solution to Short Exercise 5-6 to answer these questions about Environmental Products Inc. for 2011.

1. Start with Accounts Receivable's beginning balance ($80,000) and then post to the Accounts Receivable T-account. How much do Environmental Products' customers owe the company at December 31, 2011?
2. Start with the Allowance account's beginning credit balance ($17,500) and then post to the Allowance for Uncollectible Accounts T-account. How much of the receivables at December 31, 2011, does the company expect *not* to collect?
3. At December 31, 2011, what is the net realizable value of the company's accounts receivable?

Learning Objective 4
Applying the allowance method (aging-of-accounts-receivable) to account for uncollectibles

S5-8 Gulig and Durham, a law firm, started 2011 with accounts receivable of $60,000 and an allowance for uncollectible accounts of $5,000. The 2011 service revenue on account was $400,000, and cash collections on account totalled $410,000. During 2011, Gulig and Durham wrote off uncollectible accounts receivable of $7,000. At December 31, 2011, the aging of accounts receivable indicated that Gulig and Durham will *not* collect $10,000 of its accounts receivable.

Journalize Gulig and Durham's (a) service revenue, (b) cash collections on account, (c) write-offs of uncollectible receivables, and (d) uncollectible-account expense for the year. Explanations are not required. Prepare a T-account for Allowance for Uncollectible Accounts to show your computation of uncollectible-account expense for the year.

Learning Objective 4
Applying the allowance method (aging-of-accounts-receivable) to account for uncollectibles

S5-9 Perform the following accounting for the receivables of Benoit, Brown & Hill, an accounting firm, at December 31, 2011.

1. Start with the beginning balances for these T-accounts:
   - Accounts Receivable, $80,000
   - Allowance for Uncollectible Accounts, $9,000

   Post the following 2011 transactions to the T-accounts:
   a. Service revenue of $850,000, all on account
   b. Collections on account, $790,000
   c. Write-offs of uncollectible accounts, $7,000
   d. Uncollectible-account expense (allowance method), $8,000

2. What are the ending balances of Accounts Receivable and Allowance for Uncollectible Accounts?
3. Show two ways Benoit, Brown & Hill could report accounts receivable on its balance sheet at December 31, 2011.

Learning Objective 5
Accounting for a note receivable

S5-10 Metro Credit Union in Charlottetown, Prince Edward Island, loaned $90,000 to David Mann on a six-month, 8% note. Record the following for Metro Credit Union:

a. Lending the money on March 6.
b. Collecting the principal and interest at maturity. Specify the date. Explanations are not required.

Learning Objective 5
Accounting for a note receivable

S5-11

1. Compute the amount of interest during 2009, 2010, and 2011 for the following note receivable: On June 30, 2009, Scotiabank loaned $100,000 to Heather Hutchison on a two-year, 8% note.
2. Which party has a (an)
   a. Note receivable?
   b. Note payable?
   c. Interest revenue?
   d. Interest expense?
3. How much in total would Scotiabank collect if Hutchison paid off the note early—say, on October 30, 2009?

Learning Objective 5
Accounting for a note receivable and interest thereon

S5-12 On May 31, 2010, Nancy Thomas borrowed $6,000 from Assiniboine Credit Union. Thomas signed a note payable, promising to pay the credit union principal plus interest on May 31, 2011. The interest rate on the note is 8%. The accounting year of Assiniboine Credit Union ends on December 31, 2010. Journalize Assiniboine Credit Union's (a) lending money on the note receivable at May 31, 2010, (b) accrual of interest at December 31, 2010, and (c) collection of principal and interest at May 31, 2011, the maturity date of the note.

Learning Objective 5
Reporting notes receivables

S5-13 Using your answers to Short Exercise 5-12, show how the Assiniboine Credit Union will report the following:

a. Whatever needs to be reported on the bank's classified balance sheet at December 31, 2010. Ignore Cash.
b. Whatever needs to be reported on the bank's income statement for the year ended December 31, 2010.
c. Whatever needs to be reported on the bank's classified balance sheet at December 31, 2011. Ignore Cash.
d. Whatever needs to be reported on the bank's income statement for the year ended December 31, 2011.

Learning Objective 6
Evaluating the acid-test ratio and days' sales in receivables

S5-14 Botany Clothiers reported the following amounts in its 2011 financial statements. The 2010 figures are given for comparison.

	2011		2010	
Current assets:				
Cash		$ 9,000		$ 7,000
Short-term investments		12,000		10,000
Accounts receivable	$60,000		$54,000	
Less allowance for uncollectibles	(5,000)	55,000	(5,000)	49,000
Inventory		170,000		172,000
Prepaid insurance		1,000		1,000
Total current assets		$247,000		$239,000
Total current liabilities		$ 80,000		$ 70,000
Net sales		$803,000		$750,000

Required

1. Compute Botany's acid-test ratio at the end of 2011. Round to two decimal places. How does the acid-test ratio compare with the industry average of 0.95?
2. Compare Botany's days' sales in receivables measure for 2011 with the company's credit terms of net 30 days.

S5-15 Victoria Medical Service reported the following selected items (amounts in thousands):

Learning Objective 2
Reporting receivables and other accounts in the financial statements

Unearned revenues (current)	$ 207	Service revenue	$8,613
Allowance for doubtful accounts	109	Other assets	767
Other expenses	2,569	Property, plant, and equipment	3,316
Accounts receivable	817	Operating expense	1,620
Accounts payable	385	Cash	239
		Notes payable (long-term)	719

1. Classify each item as (a) income statement or balance sheet and as (b) debit balance or credit balance.
2. How much net income (or net loss) did Victoria report for the year?
3. Compute Victoria's current ratio. Round to two decimal places.

Exercises

E5-16 Research Capital, the investment banking company, has extra cash to invest. Suppose Research Capital buys 1,000 shares of Potash Corporation of Saskatchewan at $185 per share. Assume Research Capital expects to hold the Potash shares for one month and then sell them. The purchase occurs on December 15, 2011. At December 31, the market price of a share of Potash is $195 per share.

Learning Objective 1
Accounting for a short-term investment

Required

1. What type of investment is this to Research Capital? Give the reason for your answer.
2. Record Research Capital's purchase of the Potash shares on December 15 and the adjustment to fair value on December 31.
3. Show how Research Capital would report this investment on its balance sheet at December 31 and any gain or loss on its income statement for the year ended December 31, 2011.

E5-17 On November 16, Edward Jones Co. paid $50,000 for a trading investment in shares of Royal Bank of Canada (RBC). On November 27, Edward Jones received a $500 cash dividend from RBC. It is now December 31, and the fair value of the RBC shares is $49,500. For this investment, show what Edward Jones should report in its income statement and balance sheet.

Learning Objective 1
Accounting for a short-term investment

E5-18 TELUS reports short-term investments on its balance sheet. Suppose a division of TELUS completed the following short-term investment transactions during 2010 and 2011:

Learning Objective 1
Accounting for a short-term investment

2010	
Nov. 6	Purchased 1,000 shares of Canadian Pacific Railway Limited (CPR) for $60,000. TELUS plans to sell the shares at a profit in the near future.
27	Received a cash dividend of $0.25 per share on the CPR shares.
Dec. 31	Adjusted the investment in CPR shares. Current fair value is $65,000. TELUS plans to sell the shares in early 2011.
2011	
Jan. 11	Sold the CPR shares for $66,000.

Required

1. Prepare T-accounts for Cash, Short-Term Investment, Dividend Revenue, Unrealized Loss or Gain on Investment, and Gain on Sale of Investment. Show the effects of TELUS's investment transactions. Start with a cash balance of $75,000. All the other accounts start at zero.

Learning Objective 3
Applying internal control to receivables

E5-19 As a recent college graduate, you land your first job in the customer collections department of Backroads Publishing. Shawn Dugan, the manager, asks you to propose a system to ensure that cash received from customers by mail is handled properly. Draft a short memorandum to explain the essential element in your proposed plan. State why this element is important. Refer to Chapter 4 if necessary.

Learning Objective 4
Reporting uncollectible accounts by the allowance method

E5-20 At December 31, 2011, Credit Valley Nissan has an Accounts Receivable balance of $101,000. Allowance for Uncollectible Accounts has a credit balance of $2,000 before the year-end adjustment. Service revenue for 2011 was $800,000. Credit Valley estimates that uncollectible-account expense for the year is 1% of sales. Make the December 31 entry to record uncollectible-account expense. Show how the accounts receivable and the allowance for uncollectible accounts are reported on the balance sheet. Use the reporting format "Accounts receivable, net of allowance for uncollectible accounts $ - - -" in 2011. Insert the value you've calculated for the allowance.

Learning Objective 4
Using the allowance method for uncollectible accounts

E5-21 On June 30, 2011, Perfect Party Planners (PPP) had a $40,000 balance in Accounts Receivable and a $3,000 credit balance in Allowance for Uncollectible Accounts. During July, PPP made credit sales of $75,000. July collections on account were $60,000, and write-offs of uncollectible receivables totalled $2,200, and an account of $1,000 was recovered. Uncollectible-account expense is estimated as 2% of revenue.

Required

1. Journalize sales, collections, write-offs of uncollectibles, recovery of accounts receivable, and uncollectible-account expense by the allowance method during July. Explanations are not required.
2. Show the ending balances in Accounts Receivable, Allowance for Uncollectible Accounts, and *Net* Accounts Receivable at July 31. How much does PPP expect to collect?
3. Show how PPP will report Accounts Receivable on its July 31 balance sheet. Use the format "Accounts Receivable, net of allowance for uncollectible accounts of $ - - -" at July 31, 2011. Insert the value you've calculated for the allowance.

Learning Objective 4
Using the direct write-off method for uncollectible accounts

E5-22 Refer to Exercise 5-21.

Required

1. Record uncollectible-account expense for July by the direct write-off method.
2. What amount of accounts receivable would Perfect Party Planners (PPP) report on its July 31 balance sheet under the direct write-off method? Does PPP expect to collect the full amount?

Learning Objective 4
Using the aging method to estimate uncollectible accounts

E5-23 At December 31, 2011, before any year-end adjustments, the Accounts Receivable balance of Sunset Hills Clinic is $235,000. Allowance for Uncollectible Accounts has a $6,500 credit balance. Sunset Hills prepares the following aging schedule for accounts receivable:

	Age of Accounts			
Total Balance	1–30 Days	31–60 Days	61–90 Days	Over 90 Days
$235,000	$110,000	$60,000	$50,000	$15,000
Estimated uncollectible	0.5%	1.0%	6.0%	40%

Required

1. Based on the aging of accounts receivable, is the unadjusted balance of the allowance account adequate? Is it either too high or too low?

2. Make the entry required by the aging schedule. Prepare a T-account for the allowance.
3. Show how Sunset Hills Clinic will report Accounts Receivable on its December 31 balance sheet. Include the two accounts that come before receivables on the balance sheet, using assumed amounts.

E5-24 University Travel experienced the following revenue and accounts receivable write-offs.

Learning Objective 4
Measuring and accounting for uncollectibles

		Accounts Receivable Write-Offs in Month			
Month	**Service Revenue**	January	February	March	Total
January	$ 6,800	$53	$ 86		$139
February	7,000		105	$ 33	138
March	7,500			115	115
	$21,300	$53	$191	$148	$392

University Travel estimates that 2% of revenues will become uncollectible.

Journalize service revenue (all on account), uncollectible-account expense, and write-offs during March. Include explanations. Is an estimate of 2% of revenues being uncollectible reasonable?

E5-25 Record the following note receivable transactions in the journal of Town & Country Realty. How much interest revenue did Town & Country earn this year? Use a 365-day year for interest computations, and round interest amounts to the nearest dollar.

Learning Objective 5
Recording notes receivable and accruing interest revenue

Oct.	1	Loaned $50,000 cash to Springfield Co. on a one-year, 9% note.
Nov.	3	Performed service for Joplin Corporation, receiving a 90-day, 12% note for $10,000.
Dec.	16	Received a $2,000, six-month, 12% note on account from Afton, Inc.
	31	Accrued interest revenue for the year.

E5-26 Mattson Loan Company completed these transactions:

Learning Objective 5
Reporting the effects of note receivable transactions on the balance sheet and income statement

2010		
Apr.	1	Loaned $20,000 to Charlene Baker on a one-year, 5% note.
Dec.	31	Accrued interest revenue on the Baker note.
2011		
Apr.	1	Collected the maturity value of the note from Baker (principal plus interest).

Show what Mattson would report for these transactions on its 2010 and 2011 balance sheets and income statements. Mattson's accounting year ends on December 31.

E5-27 Answer these questions about receivables and uncollectibles. For the true-false questions, explain any answers that are false.

Learning Objective 4 5
Practical questions about receivables

1. True or false? Credit sales increase receivables. Collections and write-offs decrease receivables.
2. Which receivables figure, the *total* amount that customers *owe* the company, or the *net* amount the company expects to collect, is more interesting to investors as they consider buying the company's shares? Give your reason.
3. Show how to determine net accounts receivable.
4. True or false? The direct write-off method of accounting for uncollectibles understates assets.
5. Caisse Desjardins lent $100,000 to Chicoutimi Ltée on a six-month, 6% note. Which party has interest receivable? Which party has interest payable? Which party has interest expense, and which has interest revenue? How much interest will these organizations record one month after Chicoutimi Ltée signs the note?
6. When Caisse Desjardins accrues interest on the Chicoutimi Ltée note, show the directional effects on the bank's assets, liabilities, and equity (increase, decrease, or no effect).

Learning Objective 6
Using the acid-test ratio and days' sales in receivables to evaluate a company

E5-28 Research In Motion Limited (RIM) reported the following items at year-ends 2008 and 2007.

Research In Motion Limited
Consolidated Balance Sheets (Summarized)
(amounts in millions)

	March 1, 2008	March 3, 2007		March 1, 2008	March 3, 2007
Current assets:			Current liabilities:		
Cash	$1,184.4	$ 677.1	Accounts payable	$ 271.1	$ 130.3
Short-term investments	420.7	310.1	Other current liabilities	1,203.3	416.3
Accounts receivable, net	1,174.7	572.6	Long-term liabilities	103.2	58.8
Inventories	396.3	255.9			
Other current assets	301.3	103.6	Shareholders' equity	3,933.6	2,483.5
Capital assets	2,033.8	1,169.6			
Total assets	$5,511.2	$3,088.9	Total liabilities and equity	$5,511.2	$3,088.9
Income Statement (partial): 2008					
Revenue		$6,009.4			

Compute RIM's (a) acid-test ratio and (b) days' sales in average receivables for 2008. Evaluate each ratio value as strong or weak. Assume RIM sells on terms of net 30 days.

Learning Objective 2
Analyzing a company's financial statements

E5-29 Loblaw Companies Limited reported these figures in millions of dollars:

	2007	2006
Net sales	$29,384	$28,640
Receivables at end of year	885	728

Required

1. Compute Loblaw's average collection period during 2007.
2. Was Loblaw's collection period long or short? Potash Corporation of Saskatchewan takes 36 days to collect its average level of receivables. FedEx, the overnight shipper, takes 40 days. What causes Loblaw's collection period to be so different?

Challenge Exercises

Learning Objective 2
Determining whether to sell on credit cards

E5-30 Ripley Shirt Company sells on credit and manages its own receivables. Average experience for the past three years has been as follows:

	Cash	Credit	Total
Sales	$300,000	$300,000	$600,000
Cost of goods sold	165,000	165,000	330,000
Uncollectible-account expense	—	10,000	10,000
Other expenses	84,000	84,000	168,000

John Ripley, the owner, is considering whether to accept credit cards (VISA, MasterCard). Ripley expects total sales to increase by 10% but cash sales to remain unchanged. If Ripley switches to credit cards, the business can save $8,000 on other expenses, but VISA and MasterCard charge 2% on credit card sales. Ripley figures that the increase in sales will be due to the increased volume of credit card sales.

Required
Should Ripley Shirt Company start selling on credit cards? Show the computations of net income under the present plan and under the credit card plan.

Learning Objective 4
Reconstructing receivables and uncollectible-account amounts

E5-31 Nixtel Inc. reported net receivables of $2,583 million and $2,785 million at December 31, 2011, and 2010, after subtracting allowances of $62 million and $88 million at these respective dates. Nixtel earned total revenue of $10,948 million (all on account) and recorded uncollectible-account expense of $2 million for the year ended December 31, 2011.

Required
Use this information to measure the following amounts for the year ended December 31, 2011.
a. Write-offs of uncollectible receivables
b. Collections from customers

Quiz

Test your understanding of short-term investments and receivables by answering the following questions. Select the best choice from among the possible answers given.

Q5-32 HSBC Bank Canada owns lots of investments. Assume that HSBC paid $600,000 for trading investments on December 3, 2011. Two weeks later, HSBC received a $45,000 cash dividend. At December 31, 2011, these trading investments were quoted at a market price of $603,000. HSBC's December income statement should report
a. Dividend revenue of $45,000
b. Unrealized gain of $3,000
c. Both a and b
d. None of the above

Q5-33 Refer to the HSBC data in Question 5-32. At December 31, the HSBC balance sheet should report
a. Dividend revenue of $45,000
b. Unrealized gain of $3,000
c. Short-term investment of $603,000
d. Short-term investment of $600,000

Q5-34 Under the allowance method for uncollectible receivables, the entry to record uncollectible-account expense has what effect on the financial statements?
a. Increases expenses and increases owners' equity
b. Decreases assets and has no effect on net income
c. Decreases owners' equity and increases liabilities
d. Decreases net income and decreases assets

Q5-35 Snead Company uses the aging method to adjust the allowance for uncollectible accounts at the end of the period. At December 31, 2011, the balance of accounts receivable is $210,000 and the allowance for uncollectible accounts has a credit balance of $3,000 (before adjustment). An analysis of accounts receivable produced the following age groups:

Current	$150,000
60 days past due	50,000
Over 60 days past due	10,000
	$210,000

Based on past experience, Snead estimates that the percentages of accounts that will prove to be uncollectible within the three groups are 2%, 8%, and 20%, respectively. Based on these facts, the adjusting entry for uncollectible accounts should be made in the amount of
a. $3,000
b. $6,000
c. $9,000
d. $13,000

Q5-36 Refer to Question 5-35. The net receivables on the balance sheet are ____________.

Q5-37 Harper Company uses the percentage-of-sales method to estimate uncollectibles. Net credit sales for the current year amount to $100,000 and management estimates 2% will be uncollectible. Allowance for Uncollectible Accounts prior to adjustment has a credit balance of $2,000. The amount of expense to report on the income statement will be

a. $30,000
b. $32,000
c. $28,000
d. $2,000

Q5-38 Refer to Question 5-37. The balance of Allowance for Uncollectible Accounts, after adjustment, will be

a. $2,000
b. $4,000
c. $6,000
d. $12,000
e. Impossible to determine from the information given

Q5-39 Draw a T-account to illustrate the information in Questions 5-37 and 5-38. Early the following year, Harper wrote off $3,000 of old receivables as uncollectible. The balance in the Allowance account is now ____________.

The next four questions use the following data:

On August 1, 2011, Maritimes Ltd. sold equipment and accepted a six-month, 9%, $10,000 note receivable. Maritimes' year-end is December 31.

Q5-40 How much interest revenue should Maritimes Ltd. accrue on December 31, 2011?

a. $225
b. $450
c. $375
d. Some other amount ____________

Q5-41 If Maritimes Ltd. fails to make an adjusting entry for the accrued interest, which of the following will happen?

a. Net income will be understated, and liabilities will be overstated.
b. Net income will be understated, and assets will be understated.
c. Net income will be overstated, and liabilities will be understated.
d. Net income will be overstated, and assets will be overstated.

Q5-42 How much interest does Maritimes Ltd. expect to collect on the maturity date (February 1, 2012)?

a. $450
b. $280
c. $75
d. Some other amount ____________

Q5-43 Which of the following accounts will Maritimes Ltd. credit in the journal entry at maturity on February 1, 2012, assuming collection in full?

a. Interest Receivable
b. Note Payable
c. Interest Payable
d. Cash

Q5-44 Write the journal entry for Question 5-43.

Q5-45 Which of the following is included in the calculation of the acid-test ratio?

a. Cash and accounts receivable
b. Prepaid expenses and cash
c. Inventory and short-term investment
d. Inventory and prepaid expenses

Q5-46 A company with net sales of $1,217,000, beginning net receivables of $90,000, and ending net receivables of $110,000, has a days' sales in accounts receivable value of

a. 50 days
b. 55 days
c. 30 days
d. 33 days

Q5-47 The company in Question 5-46 sells on credit terms of "net 30 days." Its days' sales in receivables figure is

a. Too high
b. Too low
c. About right
d. Impossible to evaluate from the data given

Problems

(Group A)

Learning Objective 1
Accounting for a short-term investment

P5-48A During the fourth quarter of 2010, Cablevision Inc. generated excess cash, which the company invested in securities, as follows:

Nov.	12	Purchased 1,000 common shares as a trading investment, paying $9 per share.
Dec.	14	Received cash dividend of $0.26 per share on the trading investment.
	31	Adjusted the trading investment to its fair value of $7.50 per share.

Required

1. Prepare T-accounts for Cash, beginning balance of $20,000; Short-Term Investment; Dividend Revenue; and Unrealized Gain on Investment or Unrealized Loss on Investment.
2. Journalize the foregoing transactions, and post to the T-accounts.
3. Show how to report the short-term investment on the Cablevision balance sheet at December 31.
4. Show how to report whatever should appear on Cablevision's income statement.
5. Cablevision sold the trading investment for $8,000 on January 10, 2011. Journalize the sale.

Learning Objective 3
Internal control of cash receipts from customers

P5-49A Computer Giant Inc. makes all sales on account. Susan Phillips, accountant for the company, receives and opens incoming mail. Company procedure requires Phillips to separate customer cheques from the remittance slips, which list the amounts that Phillips posts as credits to customer accounts receivable. Phillips deposits the cheques in the bank. At the end of each day she computes the day's total amount posted to customer accounts and matches this total to the bank deposit slip. This procedure ensures that all receipts are deposited in the bank.

Required

As a consultant hired by Computer Giant Inc., write a memo to management evaluating the company's internal controls over cash receipts from customers. If the system is effective, identify its strong features. If the system has flaws, propose a way to strengthen the controls.

Learning Objective 2 4
Accounting for receivables, collections, and uncollectibles by the percentage-of-sales method

P5-50A This problem takes you through the accounting for sales, receivables, and uncollectibles for FedEx Corporation, the overnight shipper. By selling on credit, FedEx cannot expect to collect 100% of its accounts receivable. Assume that at May 31, 2011, and 2010, respectively, FedEx reported the following on its balance sheet (adapted and in millions of U.S. dollars):

	May 31	
	2011	2010
Accounts receivable	$4,517	$4,078
Less: Allowance for uncollectibles	(316)	(136)
Accounts receivable, net	$4,201	$3,942

During the year ended May 31, 2011, FedEx earned service revenue and collected cash from customers. Assume uncollectible-account expense for the year was 1% of service revenue and that FedEx wrote off uncollectible receivables.

Required

1. Prepare T-accounts for Accounts Receivable and Allowance for Uncollectibles, and insert the May 31, 2011, balances as given.

2. Journalize the following assumed transactions of FedEx for the year ended May 31, 2011. Explanations are not required.
   a. Service revenue on account, $37,953 million
   b. Collections on account, $37,314 million
   c. Uncollectible-account expense, 1% of service revenue
   d. Write-offs of uncollectible accounts receivable, $200 million
   e. Recovered an account receivable, $2 million
3. Post your entries to the Accounts Receivable and the Allowance for Uncollectibles T-accounts.
4. Compute the ending balances for the two T-accounts, and compare your balances to the actual May 31, 2011 amounts. They should be the same.
5. Show what FedEx would report on its income statement for the year ended May 31, 2011.

Learning Objective 4
Using the aging approach for uncollectibles

P5-51A The December 31, 2011, records of First Data Communications include these accounts:

Accounts Receivable	$230,000
Allowance for Uncollectible Accounts	(8,500)

At year-end, the company ages its receivables and adjusts the balance in Allowance for Uncollectible Accounts to correspond to the aging schedule. During the last quarter of 2011, the company completed the following selected transactions:

2011	
Nov. 30	Wrote off as uncollectible the $1,100 account receivable from Rainbow Carpets and the $600 account receivable from Show-N-Tell Antiques.
Dec. 31	Adjusted the Allowance for Uncollectible Accounts, and recorded Uncollectible-Account Expense at year-end, based on the aging of receivables, which follows.

	Age of Accounts			
Total Balance	**1–30 Days**	**31–60 Days**	**61–90 Days**	**Over 90 Days**
$230,000	$150,000	$40,000	$14,000	$26,000
Estimated uncollectible	0.2%	0.5%	5.0%	30.0%

Required
1. Record the transactions in the journal. Explanations are not required.
2. Prepare a T-account for Allowance for Uncollectible Accounts, and post to that account.
3. Show two ways First Data could report its accounts receivable on a comparative balance sheet for 2010 and 2011. At December 31, 2010, the company's Accounts Receivable balance was $212,000 and the Allowance for Uncollectible Accounts stood at $4,200.

Learning Objective 1 4 6
Accounting for short-term investments, uncollectibles, and use ratios to evaluate the business

P5-52A Assume Deloitte & Touche, the accounting firm, advises Pappadeaux Seafood that Pappadeaux's financial statements must be changed to conform to GAAP. At December 31, 2011, Pappadeaux's accounts include the following:

Cash	$ 51,000
Short-term trading investments, at cost	19,000
Accounts receivable	37,000
Inventory	61,000
Prepaid expenses	14,000
Total current assets	$182,000
Accounts payable	$ 62,000
Other current liabilities	41,000
Total current liabilities	$103,000

Deloitte & Touche advised Pappadeaux that

- Cash includes $20,000 that is deposited in a compensating balance account that is tied up until 2013.
- The fair value of the short-term trading investments is $17,000. Pappadeaux purchased the investments a couple of weeks ago.
- Pappadeaux has been using the direct write-off method to account for uncollectible receivables. During 2011, Pappadeaux wrote off bad receivables of $7,000. Deloitte & Touche determines that uncollectible-account expense for the year should be 2.5% of sales revenue, which totalled $600,000 in 2011.
- Pappadeaux reported net income of $92,000 in 2011.

Required

1. Restate Pappadeaux's current accounts to conform to GAAP.
2. Compute Pappadeaux's current ratio and acid-test ratio both before and after your corrections.
3. Determine Pappadeaux's correct net income for 2011.

Learning Objective 5
Accounting for notes receivable and accrued interest revenue

P5-53A Assume that General Mills Canada, famous for Cheerios, Chex snacks, and Yoplait yogurt, completed the following selected transactions.

2011	
Nov. 30	Sold goods to Sobeys Inc., receiving a $50,000, three-month, 5% note.
Dec. 31	Made an adjusting entry to accrue interest on the Sobeys note.
2012	
Feb. 28	Collected the Sobeys note.
Mar. 1	Received a 90-day, 5%, $6,000 note from Louis' Joli Goût on account.
1	Sold the Louis note to Caisse Populaire, receiving cash of $5,900.
Dec. 16	Loaned $25,000 cash to Betty Crocker Brands, receiving a 90-day, 8% note.
31	Accrued the interest on the Betty Crocker Brands note.

Required

1. Record the transactions in General Mills' journal. Round interest amounts to the nearest dollar. Explanations are not required.
2. Show what General Mills will report on its comparative classified balance sheet at December 31, 2011, and December 31, 2012.

Learning Objective 6
Using ratio data to evaluate a company's financial position

P5-54A The comparative financial statements of Sunset Pools Inc., for 2011, 2010, and 2009 included the following selected data.

	(in millions)		
	2011	2010	2009
Balance sheet:			
Current assets:			
Cash	$ 86	$ 60	$ 70
Short-term investments	130	174	112
Receivables, net of allowance for uncollectible accounts of $27, $21, and $15, respectively	243	245	278
Inventories	330	375	362
Prepaid expenses	10	25	26
Total current assets	$ 799	$ 879	$ 848
Total current liabilities	$ 403	$ 498	$ 413
Income statement:			
Net sales	$2,898	$2,727	$2,206

Required

1. Compute these ratios for 2011 and 2010:
   a. Current ratio
   b. Acid-test ratio
   c. Days' sales in receivables
2. Write a memo explaining to top management which ratio values improved from 2010 to 2011 and which ratio values deteriorated. State whether the overall trend is favourable or unfavourable, and give the reason for your evaluation.

(Group B)

Learning Objective 1
Accounting for a short-term investment

P5-55B During the fourth quarter of 2011, the operations of Baris Carpet Centre generated excess cash, which the company invested in securities, as follows:

Dec.	10	Purchased 2,500 common shares as a trading investment, paying $15 per share.
	17	Received cash dividend of $0.50 per share on the trading investment.
	31	Adjusted the trading investment to its fair value of $40,000.

Required

1. Prepare T-accounts for Cash, balance of $85,000; Short-Term Investment; Dividend Revenue; and Unrealized Gain on Investment or Unrealized Loss on Investment.
2. Journalize the foregoing transactions, and post to the T-accounts.
3. Show how to report the short-term investment on Baris's balance sheet at December 31.
4. Show how to report whatever should appear on Baris's income statement.
5. On January 6, 2012, Baris sold the trading investment for $36,000. Journalize the sale.

Learning Objective 3
Internal control of cash receipts from customers

P5-56B Mountainview Software Sales makes all sales on credit, so virtually all cash receipts arrive in the mail. Shatel Patel, the company president, has just returned from a trade association meeting with new ideas for the business. Among other things, Patel plans to institute stronger internal controls over cash receipts from customers.

Required

Take the role of Shatel Patel, the company president. Write a memo to employees outlining procedures to ensure that all cash receipts are deposited in the bank and that the total amounts of each day's cash receipts are posted to customer accounts receivable.

Learning Objective 2 4
Accounting for receivables, collections, and uncollectibles by the percentage-of-sales method

P5-57B Brubacher Service Company sells for cash and on account. By selling on credit, Brubacher cannot expect to collect 100% of its accounts receivable. At December 31, 2011, and 2010, respectively, Brubacher reported the following on its balance sheet (in thousands of dollars):

	December 31,	
	2011	2010
Accounts receivable	$500	$400
Less: Allowance for uncollectibles	(95)	(60)
Accounts receivable, net	$405	$340

During the year ended December 31, 2011, Brubacher earned service revenue and collected cash from customers. Uncollectible-account expense for the year was 5% of service revenue and Brubacher wrote off uncollectible accounts receivable.

Required

1. Prepare T-accounts for Accounts Receivable and Allowance for Uncollectibles, and insert the December 31, 2010, balances as given.

2. Journalize the following transactions of Brubacher for the year ended December 31, 2011. Explanations are not required.
   a. Service revenue on account, $6,700 thousand
   b. Collections from customers on account, $6,300 thousand
   c. Uncollectible-account expense, 5% of service revenue
   d. Write-offs of uncollectible accounts receivable, $300 thousand
   e. Recovered an account receivable, $5,000
3. Post to the Accounts Receivable and Allowance for Uncollectibles T-accounts.
4. Compute the ending balances for the two T-accounts, and compare to the Brubacher Service amounts at December 31, 2011. They should be the same.
5. Show what Brubacher should report on its income statement for the year ended December 31, 2011.

P5-58B The December 31, 2011, records of Synetics Computers include these accounts:

Learning Objective 4
Using the aging approach for uncollectibles

Accounts Receivable	$114,000
Allowance for Uncollectible Accounts	(4,100)

At year-end, Synetics ages its receivables and adjusts the balance in Allowance for Uncollectible Accounts to correspond to the aging schedule. During the last quarter of 2011, Synetics completed the following selected transactions:

2011	
Oct. 31	Wrote off the following accounts receivable as uncollectible: Cisco Foods, $300; Tindall Storage, $400; and Tiffany Energy, $1,100.
Dec. 31	Adjusted the Allowance for Uncollectible Accounts and recorded uncollectible-account expense at year-end, based on the aging of receivables, which follows.

	Age of Accounts			
Total Balance	**1–30 Days**	**31–60 Days**	**61–90 Days**	**Over 90 Days**
$114,000	$80,000	$20,000	$4,000	$10,000
Estimated uncollectible	0.5%	1.0%	5.0%	40.0%

Required

1. Record the transactions in the journal. Explanations are not required.
2. Prepare a T-account for Allowance for Uncollectible Accounts, and post to that account.
3. Show two ways Synetics Computers could report its accounts receivable in a comparative balance sheet for 2010 and 2011. At December 31, 2010, the company's Accounts Receivable balance was $111,000 and the Allowance for Uncollectible Accounts stood at $3,700.

P5-59B The top managers of Whelan Gift Stores seek the counsel of Ernst & Young, the accounting firm, and learn that Whelan must make some changes to bring its financial statements into conformity with GAAP. At December 31, 2011, Whelan Gift Stores accounts include the following:

Learning Objective 1 4 6
Accounting for short-term investments, uncollectibles by the percentage-of-sales method

Cash	$ 23,000
Short-term trading investments, at cost	24,000
Accounts receivable	54,000
Inventory	45,000
Prepaid expenses	17,000
Total current assets	$163,000
Accounts payable	46,000
Other current liabilities	69,000
Total current liabilities	$115,000

As the accountant from Ernst & Young, you draw the following conclusions:

- Cash includes $6,000 that is deposited in a compensating balance account that will be tied up until 2013.
- The fair value of the short-term trading investments is $32,000. Whelan Gift Stores purchased the investments in early December.
- Whelan Gift Stores has been using the direct write-off method to account for uncollectibles. During 2011, the company wrote off bad receivables of $4,000. Ernst & Young determines that uncollectible-account expense should be 2% of sales, which for 2011 totalled $450,000.
- Whelan Gift Stores reported net income of $81,000 for 2011.

Required

1. Restate all current accounts to conform to GAAP. (Challenge)
2. Compute Whelan Gift Stores' current ratio and acid-test ratio both before and after your corrections.
3. Determine Whelan Gift Stores' correct net income for 2011. (Challenge)

Learning Objective 5
Accounting for notes receivable and accrued interest revenue

P5-60B Lilley & Taylor, partners in an accounting practice, completed the following selected transactions:

2010		
Oct.	31	Performed service for Berger Manufacturing Inc., receiving a $30,000, three-month, 5% note.
Dec.	31	Made an adjusting entry to accrue interest on the Berger note.
2011		
Jan.	31	Collected the Berger note.
Feb.	18	Received a 90-day, 8%, $10,000 note from Emerson Ltd., on account.
	19	Sold the Emerson note to a financial institution, receiving cash of $9,700.
Nov.	11	Loaned $20,000 cash to Diaz Insurance Agency, receiving a 90-day, 9% note.
Dec.	31	Accrued the interest on the Diaz note.

Required

1. Record the transactions in Lilley & Taylor's journal. Round all amounts to the nearest dollar. Explanations are not required.
2. Show what Lilley & Taylor will report on its comparative classified balance sheet at December 31, 2011, and December 31, 2010.

P5-61B The comparative financial statements of New World Piano Company for 2011, 2010, and 2009 included the following selected data:

Learning Objective 6
Using ratio data to evaluate a company's financial position

	(in millions)		
	2011	2010	2009
Balance sheet:			
Current assets:			
Cash	$ 67	$ 66	$ 62
Short-term investments	73	81	70
Receivables, net of allowance for uncollectible accounts of $7, $6, and $4, respectively	226	174	195
Inventories	398	375	349
Prepaid expenses	22	19	16
Total current assets	$ 786	$ 715	$ 692
Total current liabilities	$ 420	$ 405	$ 388
Income statement:			
Net sales	$2,071	$2,005	$1,965

Required

1. As a financial advisor to an investor in New World Piano Company, compute these ratios for 2011 and 2010.
   a. Current ratio
   b. Acid-test ratio
   c. Days' sales in receivables
2. Write a memo explaining to your client which ratio values showed improvement from 2010 to 2011 and which ratio values deteriorated. State whether the overall trend is favourable or unfavourable for the company, give the reason for your evaluation, and advise your client regarding its investment.

Apply Your Knowledge

Decision Cases

Case 1. A fire during 2011 destroyed most of the accounting records of Morris Financial Services Inc. The only accounting data for 2011 that Morris can come up with are the following balances at December 31, 2011. The general manager also knows that uncollectible-account expense should be 5% of service revenue.

Learning Objective 2 4
Accounting for receivables, collections, and uncollectible accounts on receivables

Accounts receivable	$180,000
Less: Allowance for uncollectibles	(22,000)
Total expenses, excluding uncollectible-account expense	670,000
Collections from customers	840,000
Write-offs of bad receivables	30,000
Accounts receivable, December 31, 2010	110,000

As the insurance claims officer, prepare a summary income statement for Morris Financial Services Inc., for the year ended December 31, 2011. The insurance claim will be affected by whether the company was profitable in 2011. Use a T-account for Accounts Receivable to compute service revenue.

Learning Objective ④
Estimating the collectibility of accounts receivable

Case 2. Suppose you work in the loan department of CIBC. Dean Young, owner of Dean Young Sports Equipment, has come to you seeking a loan for $500,000 to expand operations. Young proposes to use accounts receivable as collateral for the loan and has provided you with the following information from the company's most recent financial statements:

	(in thousands)		
	2011	2010	2009
Sales	$1,475	$1,001	$902
Cost of goods sold	876	647	605
Gross profit	599	354	297
Other expenses	518	287	253
Net profit or (loss) before taxes	$ 81	$ 67	$ 44
Accounts receivable	$ 128	$ 107	$ 94
Allowance for uncollectible accounts	13	11	9

Required
Analyze the trends of sales, days' sales in receivables, and cash collections from customers for 2011 and 2010. Would you make the loan to Young? Support your decision with facts and figures.

Ethical Issue

Sunnyvale Loan Company is in the consumer loan business. Sunnyvale borrows from banks and loans out the money at higher interest rates. Sunnyvale's bank requires Sunnyvale to submit quarterly financial statements to keep its line of credit. Sunnyvale's main asset is Notes Receivable. Therefore, Uncollectible-Account Expense and Allowance for Uncollectible Accounts are important accounts for the company. Kimberly Burnham, the company's owner, prefers for net income to increase in a smooth pattern, rather than increase in some periods and decrease in other periods. To report smoothly increasing net income, Burnham underestimates Uncollectible-Account Expense in some periods. In other periods, Burnham overestimates the expense. She reasons that the income overstatements roughly offset the income understatements over time.

Required
Is Sunnyvale Loan's practice of smoothing income ethical? Why or why not?

Focus on Financials

Learning Objective ①②④
Accounting for short-term investments and accounts receivable

Gildan Activewear Inc.

Refer to Gildan's financial statements in Appendix A at the end of this book.

1. In the notes to the financial statements are the following:

1. Significant Accounting Policies:
   d) Cash and cash equivalents:
   The Company considers all liquid investments with maturities of three months or less when acquired to be cash equivalents.
   r) Financial instruments and hedging relationships:
   All financial instruments.... Held-for-trading financial investments are measured at fair value and all gains and losses are included in net earnings in the period in which they arise....

Assume that cash and cash equivalents included short-term money market instruments at October 4, 2009, of $100 (and at October 5, 2008, of $200). Further assume that there were no fair value adjustments in 2009 and that the statement of cash flows reports that Gildan sold money market instruments for $150. How much gain or loss would Gildan have on the sale of the money market instruments?

2. How much were Gildan's receivables at October 4, 2009, and October 5, 2008? What can you assume from this information?
3. Assume that Gildan wrote off 1% of 2009 sales as uncollectible. How much did Gildan collect from customers during 2009?

Focus on Analysis

Learning Objective 4
Analyzing accounts receivable

Gildan Activewear Inc.

Refer to Gildan Activewear Inc.'s financial statements in Appendix A.

In the notes to the financial statements is the following:

> 1. Significant Accounting Policies:
>
> m) Trade accounts receivable:
>
> Trade accounts receivable consist of amounts due from our normal business activities. We maintain an allowance for uncollectible accounts to reflect expected credit losses. We provide for bad debts based on collection history and specific risks identified on a customer-by-customer basis. Uncollected accounts are written off through the allowance for doubtful accounts.**

Required

1. Does Gildan disclose the Allowance for Uncollectible Accounts in its financial statements? How can you determine what Gildan expects to collect from its reported Accounts Receivable?
2. What decision ratios can you calculate with the information reported in Gildan's financial statements? Calculate for 2009.
3. Would you conclude that Gildan's uncollectible-account expense will include large write-offs in 2009? What basis do you have for this conclusion?

** Note: Gildan uses the term allowance for doubtful accounts in their financial statements; this is another term for allowance for uncollectible accounts.

Group Project

Jillian Michaels and Dee Childress worked for several years as sales representatives for Xerox Corporation. During this time, they became close friends as they acquired expertise with the company's full range of copier equipment. Now they see an opportunity to put their expertise to work and fulfill lifelong desires to establish their own business. Northern Lights College has a campus in their community, Fort St. John, British Columbia, and there is no copy centre within eight kilometres of the campus. Business in the area is booming, office buildings and apartments are springing up, and the population of the Fort St. John section of the city is growing.

Michaels and Childress want to open a copy centre, similar to FedEx Kinko's, near the campus. A small shopping centre across the street from the college has a vacancy that would fit their needs. Michaels and Childress each have $35,000 to invest in the business, but they forecast the need for $200,000 to renovate the store and purchase some of the equipment they will need. Xerox Corporation will lease two large copiers to them at a total monthly rental of $6,000. With enough cash to see them through the first six months of operation, they are confident they can make the business succeed. The two women work very well together, and both have excellent credit ratings. Michaels and Childress must borrow $130,000 to start the business, advertise its opening, and keep it running for its first six months.

Required

Assume two roles: (1) Michaels and Childress, the partners who will own Fort St. John Copy Centre; and (2) loan officers at North Peace Savings and Credit Union (NPSCU).

1. As a group, visit a copy centre to familiarize yourselves with its operations. If possible, interview the manager or another employee. Then write a loan request that Michaels and Childress will submit to NPSCU with the intent of borrowing $130,000 to be paid back over three years. The loan will be a personal loan to the partnership of Michaels and Childress, not to Fort St. John Copy Centre. The request should specify all the details of Michaels's and Childress's plan that will motivate the bank to grant the loan. Include a budget for each of the first six months of operation of the proposed copy centre.
2. As a group, interview a loan officer in a bank. Write NPSCU's reply to the loan request. Specify all the details that the bank should require as conditions for making the loan.
3. If necessary, modify the loan request or the bank's reply in order to reach agreement between the two parties.

Quick Check Answers

1. *b*
2. *c*
3. *a ($46,000 × 0.02)*
4. *d ($900 + $920)*
5. *a ($1,350 − $900)*
6. *d*
7. *b ($9,500 − $1,350)*
8. *b ($3,200 − $100) − ($300 − $100)*
9. *d ($800,000 + $2,500,000 − $900,000)*
10. *c ($4,800 × 0.05 × 1/12)*
11. *c $25,000 + ($25,000 × 0.05 × 6/12)*
12. *d*
13. *d [($62,000 + $58,000)/2 ÷ ($730,000/365)]*
14. *c [($3,000 + $6,000) ÷ ($8,000 + $3,000)]*

Inventory and Cost of Goods Sold

LEARNING OBJECTIVES

1. **Account** for inventory
2. **Understand** the various inventory methods
3. **Show** how accounting standards relate to inventory
4. **Use** inventory in decision making
5. **Estimate** inventory by the gross profit method
6. **Show** how inventory errors affect the financial statements

SPOTLIGHT

You have just graduated from university, taken a job, and are moving into an apartment. The place is unfurnished so you will need a bed, dresser, sofa, table, and chairs to go with your TV and sound system. Where will you find these things? Leon's Furniture is a good source.

Leon's Furniture is known for its contemporary-styled, well-priced furnishings—just about right for a new graduate. The company operates 35 company stores and has 28 franchised locations.

Leon's Furniture Limited's balance sheet is summarized on the next page. You can see that merchandise inventory (labelled simply as Inventory) is one of Leon's Furniture's biggest assets. That's not surprising since Leon's, like other retailers, attracts customers with goods they can purchase and take home immediately.

Leon's Furniture Limited
Consolidated Balance Sheets (Adapted)
As at December 31

	(millions)	
	2009	**2008**
Assets		
Current		
Cash and cash equivalents	$ 58.3	$ 39.5
Short-term investments	112.4	99.8
Accounts receivable (net)	31.5	30.3
Inventory	84.0	92.9
Future tax assets	1.1	2.2
Total current assets	287.3	264.7
Property, plant, and equipment (net)	212.2	219.3
Other long-term assets	29.7	29.4
	$529.2	$513.4
Liabilities and Shareholders' Equity		
Current		
Accounts payable and accrued liabilities	$ 83.9	$ 95.2
Other current liabilities	38.7	34.4
Total current liabilities	122.6	129.6
Future tax liabilities	8.8	8.5
Other liabilities	22.6	22.0
Total liabilities	154.0	160.1
Shareholders' equity		
Common shares	17.7	16.5
Retained earnings	357.6	339.0
Other equity	(0.1)	(2.2)
Total shareholders' equity	375.2	353.3
	$529.2	$513.4

We also present Leon's Furniture Limited's income statement. The year 2009 was not a good year; sales and net income were down.

Leon's Furniture Limited
Consolidated Statements of Income (Adapted)
For the Years Ended December 31

	(millions)	
	2009	**2008**
Sales	$703.2	$740.3
Cost of sales	419.8	440.3
Gross profit	283.4	300.0
Selling, general, and administrative expenses	145.0	148.0
Depreciation	16.6	16.3
Other operating expenses	42.4	46.4
Interest income	(3.2)	(4.8)
	200.8	205.9
Income before income taxes	82.6	94.1
Provision for income taxes	25.7	30.7
Net income for the year	$ 56.9	$ 63.4

You can see that the *cost of sales* (another name for **cost of goods sold**) is by far Leon's Furniture's largest expense. The account titled Cost of Sales perfectly describes that expense. In short,

- Leon's buys inventory, an asset carried on the books at cost.
- The goods that Leon's sells are no longer Leon's Furniture's assets. The cost of inventory that's sold gets shifted into the expense account, Cost of Sales.

Merchandise inventory is the heart of a merchandising business, and cost of goods sold is the most important expense for a company that sells goods rather than services. This chapter covers the accounting for inventory and cost of goods sold. It also shows you how to analyze financial statements. Here we focus on inventory, cost of goods sold, and gross profit.

We begin by showing how the financial statements of a merchandiser such as Leon's Furniture Limited or The Forzani Group Ltd. differ from those of service entities such as Purolator or Royal LePage Real Estate. The financial statements in Exhibit 6-1 highlight how service entities differ from merchandisers.

EXHIBIT 6-1 **Contrasting a Service Company With a Merchandiser**

Service Company
Royal LePage Real Estate
Income Statement
For the Year Ended December 31, 2009

Service revenue	$XXX
Expenses	
Operating and administrative	X
Depreciation	X
Income tax	X
Net income	$ X

Merchandising Company
Leon's Furniture Ltd.
Income Statement
For the Year Ended December 31, 2009

Amounts in millions	
Sales revenue	$703.2
Cost of goods sold	419.8
Gross profit	283.4
Operating *expenses*	
Operating and administrative	X
Depreciation	X
Income tax	X
Net income	$ 56.9

Royal LePage Real Estate
Balance Sheet
As at December 31, 2009

Assets	
Current assets	
Cash	$X
Temporary investments	X
Accounts receivable, net	X
Prepaid expenses	X

Leon's Furniture Ltd.
Balance Sheet
As at December 31, 2009

Assets	
Amounts in thousands	
Current assets	
Cash	$ X
Temporary investments	X
Accounts receivable, net	X
Inventory	84
Prepaid expenses	X

Accounting for Inventory

The value of inventory affects two financial statement accounts: inventory reported as a current asset on the balance sheet; and cost of goods sold shown as an expense on the income statement. This basic concept of accounting for merchandise inventory can be illustrated with an example. Suppose Leon's Furniture has in stock three chairs that cost $300 each. Leon's Furniture marks the chairs up by $200 and sells two of the chairs for $500 each.

- Leon's Furniture's balance sheet reports the one chair that the company still holds in inventory at $300.
- The income statement reports the cost of the two chairs sold at $500 each for a total of $1,000, as shown in Exhibit 6-2.

Here is the basic concept of how we identify inventory, the asset, from cost of goods sold, the expense.

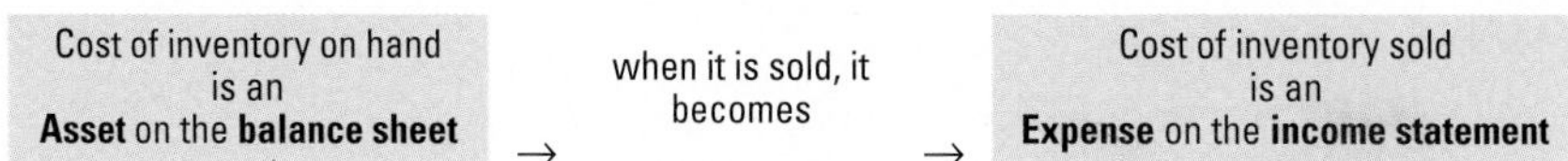

Inventory's cost shifts from asset to expense when the seller delivers the goods to the buyer.

Merchandisers have two accounts that service entities don't need: Inventory on the balance sheet and Cost of Goods Sold on the income statement.

Other Categories of Inventory

While the focus of this chapter is on merchandise inventory, other categories of inventory should also be mentioned:

- Manufacturing companies have inventories of raw materials, work in process, and finished goods. Raw materials are items used in the manufacturing process. Work in process includes partially finished goods, and finished goods are manufactured products that are ready for sale.
- Service companies have inventories of office supplies and other such items on hand at their year-end, which may be described as inventory or prepaid expenses.

EXHIBIT 6-2 **Inventory and Costs of Goods Sold When Inventory Cost Is Constant**

Balance Sheet (Partial)		**Income Statement (Partial)**	
Current assets		Sales revenue	
Cash	$XXX	(2 chairs @ sales price of $500	$1,000
Short-term investments	XXX	Cost of goods sold	
Accounts receivable	XXX	(2 chairs @ cost of $300)	600
Inventory (1 chair @ cost of $300)	300	Gross profit	$ 400
Prepaid expenses	XXX		

Sales Price Versus Cost of Inventory

Note the difference between the sale price of inventory and the cost of inventory. In our Leon's Furniture example,

- Sales revenue is based on the *sale price* of the inventory sold ($500 per chair).
- Cost of goods sold is based on the cost of the inventory sold ($300 per chair).
- Inventory on the balance sheet is based on the *cost* of the inventory still on hand ($300 per chair).

Exhibit 6-2 shows the items.

Gross profit, also called **gross margin**, is the excess of sales revenue over cost of goods sold. It is called *gross profit* because operating expenses have not yet been subtracted. Exhibit 6-3 shows actual inventory and cost of goods sold data (cost of sales) from the financial statements of Leon's Furniture Limited.

Leon's inventory of $84 million represents

$$\frac{\text{Inventory}}{\text{(balance sheet)}} = \frac{\text{Number of units of}}{\text{inventory } \textit{on hand}} \times \frac{\text{Cost per unit}}{\text{of inventory}}$$

Leon's cost of goods sold ($419.8 million) represents

$$\frac{\text{Cost of goods sold}}{\text{(income statement)}} = \frac{\text{Number of units of}}{\text{inventory sold}} \times \frac{\text{Cost per unit}}{\text{of inventory}}$$

Let's see what "units of inventory" and "cost per unit" mean.

Number of Units of Inventory. The number of inventory units on hand is determined from accounting records, backed up by a physical count of the goods at year-end.

EXHIBIT 6-3 **Leon's Furniture Limited Inventory and Cost of Goods Sold (Cost of Sales)**

Leon's Furniture Limited
Consolidated Balance Sheets (Partial, Adapted)
As at December 31

	(millions)	
Assets	**2009**	**2008**
Cash and cash equivalents	$ 58.3	$39.5
Short-term investments	112.4	99.8
Accounts receivable (net)	31.5	30.3
Inventory	84.0	92.9

Leon's Furniture Limited
Consolidated Statements of Income (Partial, Adapted)
For the Years Ended December 31

	(millions)	
	2009	**2008**
Sales	$703.2	$740.3
Cost of sales	419.8	440.3
Gross profit	$283.4	$300.0

Determining the ownership of inventory at the time of shipment depends on who has legal title. If inventory is shipped FOB (free on board) shipping point, it should be included on the books of the buyer, who has legal title, as soon as it leaves the shipper's dock. If the goods are shipped FOB destination, the inventory in transit still belongs on the books of the seller until it is delivered to the buyer.

Sometimes inventory is delivered by a company, say, Able Company, to another company, say, Baker Company, with the understanding that payment for the goods is only to be made once Baker Company sells the merchandise. Such goods are said to be held on consignment and, for financial reporting purposes, belong on the books of Able Company.

Cost per Unit of Inventory. The cost per unit of inventory poses a challenge because companies purchase goods at different prices throughout the year. Which unit costs go into the ending inventory for the balance sheet? Which unit costs go to cost of goods sold?

The next section shows how the different accounting methods determine ending inventory on the balance sheet and cost of goods sold for the income statement. First, however, you need to understand how inventory accounting systems work.

Accounting for Inventory in the Perpetual System

OBJECTIVE

① **Account** for inventory

There are two main types of inventory accounting systems: the periodic system and the perpetual system. The **periodic inventory system** is mainly used by businesses that sell inexpensive goods. A dollar store or a convenience store, for example, may not keep a running record of every one of the hundreds of items they sell. Instead, these stores count their inventory periodically—at least once a year—to determine the quantities on hand. Businesses such as some restaurants and hometown nurseries also use the periodic inventory system because the accounting cost is low. For details on the periodic inventory system, refer to Appendix 6A beginning on page 333.

A **perpetual inventory system** uses computer software to keep a running record of inventory on hand. This system achieves control over goods such as parts at a Buick dealer, lumber at RONA, furniture at Leon's Furniture, and all the various groceries and other items that a Loblaw store sells. Today, most businesses use the perpetual inventory system.

Even with a perpetual system, the business still counts the inventory on hand annually. The physical count serves as a check on the accuracy of the perpetual records and confirms the accuracy of the inventory records for preparing the financial statements. The chart below compares the perpetual and periodic systems.

Perpetual Inventory System	*Periodic Inventory System*
• Used for all types of goods	• Used for inexpensive goods
• Keeps a running record of all goods bought, sold, and on hand	• Does not keep a running record of all goods bought, sold, and on hand
• Inventory counted at least once a year	• Inventory counted at least once a year

EXHIBIT 6-4 **Bar Code for Electronic Scanner**

How the Perpetual System Works. Let's use an everyday situation to show how a perpetual inventory system works. Suppose you are buying a pair of Nike cross-trainer shoes from Forzani. The clerk scans the bar code on the product label of your purchase. Exhibit 6-4 illustrates a typical bar code. The bar code on the product or product label holds lots of information. The optical scanner reads the bar code, and the computer records the sale and updates the inventory records.

Recording Transactions in the Perpetual System. All accounting systems record each purchase of inventory as a debit to Inventory and a credit to either Cash or Accounts Payable.

When Leon's Furniture makes a sale, two entries are needed in the perpetual system:

- The company records the sale—debits Cash or Accounts Receivable and credits Sales Revenue for the sale price of the goods.
- Leon's Furniture also debits Cost of Goods Sold and credits Inventory for the cost of the inventory sold.

Exhibit 6-5 shows the accounting for inventory in a perpetual system. Panel A gives the journal entries and the T-accounts, and Panel B presents the income statement and the balance sheet. All amounts are assumed. (Exhibit 6A-1 illustrates the accounting for these transactions in a periodic inventory system while Exhibit 6A-2 compares the journal entries required for the two types of inventory systems.)

In Exhibit 6-5, Panel A, the first entry to Inventory summarizes a lot of detail. The cost of the inventory, $560,000,* is the net amount of the purchases, determined as follows (using assumed amounts):

Purchase price of the inventory from the seller	$600,000
+ **Freight-in** (Transportation cost to move the goods from the seller to the buyer)	4,000
− **Purchase returns** for unsuitable goods returned to the seller	(25,000)
− **Purchase allowances** granted by the seller	(5,000)
− **Purchase discounts** for early payment	(14,000)
= Net purchases of inventory	$560,000

Freight-in is the transportation cost paid by the buyer to move goods from the seller to the buyer. Freight-in is accounted for as part of the cost of inventory. A **purchase return** is a decrease in the cost of inventory because the buyer returned the goods to the seller. A **purchase allowance** also decreases the cost of inventory because the buyer got an allowance (a deduction) from the amount owed—often because of a merchandise defect. Throughout this book, we often refer to net purchases simply as purchases.

A **purchase discount** is a decrease in the cost of inventory that is earned by paying quickly. A common arrangement states payment terms of 2/10 n/30. This means the buyer can take a 2% discount for payment within 10 days, or pay the full amount within 30 days. Another common credit term is "net 30," which directs the customer to pay the full amount within 30 days. In summary,

NET PURCHASES = PURCHASES
− PURCHASE RETURNS AND ALLOWANCES
− PURCHASE DISCOUNTS
+ FREIGHT-IN

*The price shown does *not* include Canada's goods and services tax (GST)/harmonized sales tax (HST).

EXHIBIT 6-5 **Recording and Reporting Inventory—Perpetual System (Amounts Assumed)**

Perpetual System

PANEL A—Recording Transactions and the T-accounts

1. Inventory	560,000	
Accounts Payable		560,000
Purchase of inventory on account.		
2. Accounts Receivable	900,000	
Sales Revenue		900,000
Sold inventory on account.		
Cost of Goods Sold	540,000	
Inventory		540,000
Recorded cost of goods sold.		

The T-accounts show the following:

Inventory

Beginning balance	100,000*	Cost of goods sold	540,000
Purchases	560,000		
Ending balance	120,000		

*Beginning inventory was $100,000.

Cost of Goods Sold

Cost of goods sold	540,000	

PANEL B—Reporting in the Financial Statements

Income Statement (Partial)

Sales revenue	$900,000
Cost of goods sold	540,000
Gross profit	$360,000

Ending Balance Sheet (Partial)

Current assets:	
Cash	$ XXX
Temporary investments	XXX
Accounts receivable	XXX
Inventory	120,000
Prepaid expenses	XXX

Net sales are computed exactly the same way as net purchases, but with no freight-in.

NET SALES = SALES REVENUE
− SALES RETURNS AND ALLOWANCES
− SALES DISCOUNTS

Freight-out paid by the *seller* is not part of the cost of inventory. Instead, freight-out is a delivery expense. It is the seller's expense of delivering merchandise to customers. (Appendix 6A shows the accounting for these same transactions in a periodic accounting system.) Now study Exhibit 6-5 above and the dated illustration on the following page.

The first entry in Exhibit 6-5 is a summary entry. Since the various transactions that make up the $560,000 may occur on different dates, it is instructive to now view each entry separately with assumed dates as follows:

General Journal

Date	Account Titles and Explanation	Ref.	Debit	Credit
2011				
Jan. 4	Inventory		600,000	
	Accounts Payable			600,000
	To record purchase of merchandise.			
6	Inventory		4,000	
	Cash			4,000
	To record freight costs.			
11	Accounts Payable		25,000	
	Inventory			25,000
	To record purchase returns.			
13	Accounts Payable		5,000	
	Inventory			5,000
	To record purchase allowances.			
16	Accounts Payable		14,000	
	Inventory			14,000
	To record purchase discounts.			

Inventory Costing

Inventory is the first asset for which a manager can decide which accounting method to use. The accounting method selected affects the profits to be reported and the amount of income taxes to be paid and the values of the ratios derived from the balance sheet.

What Goes Into Inventory Cost?

The cost of merchandise in Leon's Furniture Limited's balance sheet represents all the costs that Leon's Furniture incurred to bring the inventory to the point of sale. Both the International Accounting Standards Board and the accounting standards for private enterprise state the following:

> *The cost of inventories shall comprise all costs of purchase, costs of conversion and other costs incurred in bringing the inventories to their present location and condition.*

Inventory's cost includes its basic purchase price, plus freight-in, insurance while in transit, and any costs paid to get the inventory ready to sell, less returns, allowances, and discounts.

Once a product is sitting in a Leon's Furniture showroom, other costs incurred, such as advertising and delivery costs, are not included as the cost of inventory. Advertising, sales commissions, and delivery costs are expenses.

What items to include in inventory is determined not by the nature of the assets but by the nature of the business. For example, a delivery truck would be inventory for a truck dealership but would be a capital asset for Purolator Courier Ltd.

The Various Inventory Costing Methods

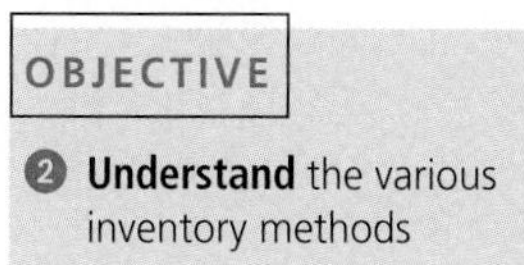

Determining the cost of inventory is easy when the unit cost remains constant, as in Exhibit 6-2. But unit cost usually changes. For example, prices often rise. Salomon snowboards that cost Intrawest $150 in October may cost $160 in November and

$180 in December. Intrawest sells 50 snowboards in November. How many of the Salomon snowboards sold cost $150, how many cost $160, and how many cost $180?

To compute cost of goods sold and the cost of ending inventory still on hand, we must assign a unit cost to the items. Three generally accepted inventory methods are the following:

1. Specific unit cost
2. Weighted-average cost
3. First-in, first-out (FIFO) cost

A company can use any of these methods. As we shall see, these methods can have very different effects on reported profits, income taxes, and cash flow. Therefore, companies select their inventory method with great care.

Specific Unit Cost. Some businesses deal in unique inventory items, such as antique furniture, jewels, and real estate. These businesses cost their inventories at the specific cost of the particular unit. For instance, a Chevrolet dealer may have two vehicles in the showroom—a "stripped-down" model that cost $22,000 and a "loaded" model that cost $29,000. If the dealer sells the loaded model, cost of goods sold is $29,000. The stripped-down auto will be the only unit left in inventory, so ending inventory is $22,000.

The **specific-unit-cost method** is also called the *specific identification method.* This method is too expensive to use for inventory items that have common characteristics, such as metres of lumber, litres of paint, or automobile tires.

The other acceptable inventory accounting methods—weighted-average and FIFO—do not use the specific cost of a particular unit. Instead, they assume different flows of inventory costs.

Illustration of Weighted-Average and FIFO Costing. To illustrate weighted-average and FIFO costing, we use a common set of data, given in Exhibit 6-6.

In Exhibit 6-6, Leon's began the period with 10 lamps that cost $10 each; the beginning inventory was therefore $100. During the period, Leon's bought 50 more lamps, sold 40 lamps, and ended the period with 20 lamps, summarized in the T-account in Exhibit 6-6 and as follows:

	Number of Units	Total Cost
Goods available for sale	= 10 + 25 + 25 = 60 units	$100 + $350 + $450 = $900
Cost of goods sold	= 40 units	?
Ending inventory	= 20 units	?

EXHIBIT 6-6 **Inventory Data Used to Illustrate Inventory Costing Methods**

Inventory				
Begin. bal.	(10 units @ $10)	100		
Purchases:			Cost of goods sold	
No. 1	(25 units @ $14)	350	(40 units @ $?)	?
No. 2	(25 units @ $18)	450		
Ending bal.	(20 units @ $?)	?		

The big accounting questions are

1. What is the cost of goods sold for the income statement?
2. What is the cost of the ending inventory for the balance sheet?

The answers to these questions depend on which inventory method Leon's uses. Leon's actually uses FIFO, but we will look at weighted-average costing first.

Weighted-Average Cost. The **weighted-average-cost method**, sometimes called the average-cost method, is based on the average cost of inventory for the period. The weighted-average cost per unit is determined as follows (data from Exhibit 6-6):

$$\text{Weighted-average cost per unit} = \frac{\text{Cost of goods available}^{*}}{\text{Number of units available}} = \frac{\$900}{60} = \$15$$

*Goods available = Beginning inventory + Purchases

Cost of goods sold = Number of units sold × Weighted-average cost per unit
= 40 units × $15 = $600

Ending inventory = Number of units on hand × Weighted-average cost per unit
= 20 units × $15 = $300

The following T-account shows the effects of weighted-average costing:

Inventory (at weighted-average cost)

Begin. bal.	(10 units @ $10)	100		
Purchases:				
No. 1	(25 units @ $14)	350		
No. 2	(25 units @ $18)	450	Cost of goods sold (40 units @ average cost of $15 per unit)	600
Ending bal.	(20 units @ average cost of $15 per unit)	300		

Under the perpetual inventory system, a new average cost is computed each time a new purchase is made. Using the same example as above, assume that after the sale, the company bought 10 new units at a cost of $20. A new average cost would be computed as follows:

Balance 20 units @ $15 per unit	= $300
Purchase No. 3: 10 units @ $20 per unit	= $200
Total cost	$500 divided by 30 units = $16.67 per unit

Therefore, the new weighted-average cost would be $16.67 per unit.

FIFO Cost. Under the **first-in, first-out (FIFO) cost method**, the first costs into inventory are the first costs assigned to cost of goods sold—hence, the name *first-in, first-out*. The following T-account shows how to compute FIFO cost of goods sold and ending inventory for Leon's lamps (data from Exhibit 6-6):

Inventory (at FIFO cost)

Begin. bal.	(10 units @ $10)	100			
Purchases:			Cost of goods sold (40 units):		
No. 1	(25 units @ $14)	350	(10 units @ $10)	100	
No. 2	(25 units @ $18)	450	(25 units @ $14)	350	540
			(5 units @ $18)	90	
Ending bal. (20 units @ $18)		360			

Under FIFO, the cost of ending inventory is always based on the latest costs incurred—in this case $18 per unit.

The Effects of FIFO and Weighted-Average Cost on Cost of Goods Sold, Gross Profit, and Ending Inventory

In our Leon's example, the cost of inventory rose from $10 to $14 to $18. When inventory unit costs change this way, the various inventory methods produce different cost-of-goods-sold figures. Exhibit 6-7 summarizes the income effects (Sales − Cost of goods sold = Gross profit) of the two inventory methods (remember that prices are rising). Study the exhibit carefully, focusing on cost of goods sold and gross profit.

EXHIBIT 6-7 **Effects of the FIFO and Weighted-Average Inventory Methods**

	FIFO	Weighted-Average
Sales revenue (assumed)	$1,000	$1,000
Cost of goods sold	540 (lowest)	600 (highest)
Gross profit	$ 460 (highest)	$ 400 (lowest)

Let's use the gross profit data from Exhibit 6-7 to illustrate the potential tax effects of the two methods in a period of rising prices:

	FIFO	Weighted-Average
Gross profit	$460	$400
Operating expenses (assumed)	260	260
Income before income tax	$200	$140
Income tax expense (35%)	$ 70	$ 49

Income tax expense is lower under weighted-average ($49) and higher under FIFO ($70).

Exhibit 6-8 demonstrates the effect of increasing and decreasing costs of inventory on cost of goods sold and ending inventory. Study this exhibit carefully; it will help you really understand FIFO and weighted-average.

In Canada, approximately the same number of companies use FIFO as use weighted-average. In a period of rising prices, FIFO will generally lead to higher profits and higher taxes than weighted-average while the opposite is true in a period of falling prices. The difference between the two methods on profit and income taxes may be small, and each of the two methods is appropriate for certain types of inventory. In addition, some companies use a mixture of specific unit cost, FIFO, and weighted-average. The authors have therefore concluded that a company does not place much emphasis on potential tax savings when it decides which of the three methods is appropriate for its organization (especially given that a company may use

EXHIBIT 6-8 **Cost of Goods Sold and Ending Inventory—FIFO and Weighted-Average; Increasing Costs and Decreasing Costs**

When inventory costs are decreasing,

	Income Statement Effects Cost of Goods Sold (COGS)	Balance Sheet Effects Ending Inventory (EI)	Cash Flow Effects Cost of Goods Sold (COGS)
FIFO	FIFO COGS is highest because it's based on the oldest costs, which are high. Gross profit is, therefore, the lowest.	FIFO EI is lowest because it's based on the most recent costs, which are low.	Less cash paid for taxes so could be used by firms seeking to minimize taxes.
Weighted-Average	Weighted-average is lowest because it's based on an average of the costs for the period, which is lower than the oldest costs. Gross profit is, therefore, the highest.	Weighted-average is highest because the average cost for the period is higher than the most recent ones.	More cash paid for taxes but still may be popular for firms seeking to maximize reported income.

When inventory costs are increasing,

	Income Statment Effects Cost of Goods Sold (COGS)	Balance Sheet Effects Ending Inventory (EI)	Cash Flow Effects Cost of Goods Sold (COGS)
FIFO	FIFO COGS is lowest because it's based on oldest costs, which are low. Gross profit is, therefore, the highest.	FIFO EI is highest because it's based on the most recent costs, which are high.	More cash paid for taxes but still may be popular for firms seeking to maximize reported income.
Weighted-Average	Weighted-average is highest because it's based on an average of the costs for the period, which is higher than the oldest costs. Gross profit is, therefore, the lowest.	Weighted-average is lowest because the average cost for the period is lower than the most recent ones.	Less cash paid for taxes so could be used by firms seeking to minimize taxes.

a different inventory costing method for tax purposes than the one used for financial reporting).

Comparison of the Inventory Methods

Let's compare the weighted-average and FIFO inventory methods.

1. How well does each method measure income by allocating inventory expense—cost of goods sold—against revenue? Weighted-average results in the most realistic net income figure. Weighted-average is an average that combines all costs (old costs and recent costs). In contrast, FIFO uses old inventory costs against revenue. FIFO income is therefore less realistic than income under weighted-average.
2. Which method reports the most up-to-date inventory cost on the balance sheet? FIFO reports the most current inventory cost on the balance sheet. Weighted-average can value inventory at very old costs because weighted-average leaves the oldest prices in ending inventory.
3. What effects do the methods have on income taxes? Weighted-average is an average that combines all costs (old costs and recent costs).

Managing Inventory

PetSmart Tropical Fish Inc. stocks two basic categories of merchandise:

- Tropical fish that are unique
- Fish tanks and related equipment and prepackaged fish foods and supplies

Jacob Stiles, the owner of PetSmart Tropical Fish Inc., is considering how accounting will affect the business. Let's examine several decisions that Stiles must make to achieve his goals for his company.

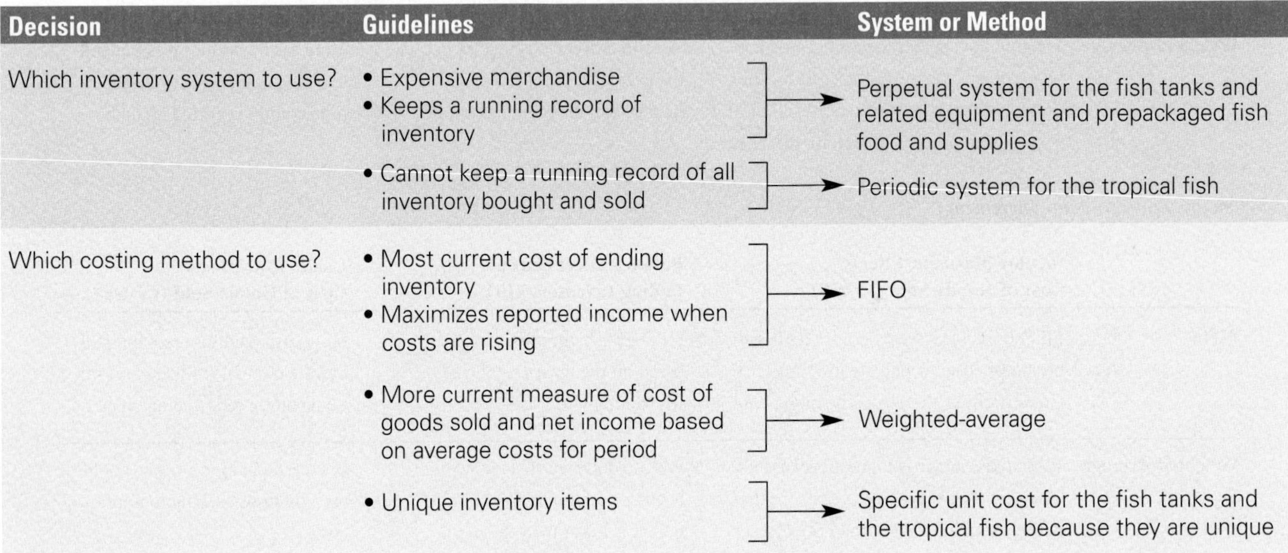

Decision	Guidelines	System or Method
Which inventory system to use?	• Expensive merchandise • Keeps a running record of inventory	Perpetual system for the fish tanks and related equipment and prepackaged fish food and supplies
	• Cannot keep a running record of all inventory bought and sold	Periodic system for the tropical fish
Which costing method to use?	• Most current cost of ending inventory • Maximizes reported income when costs are rising	FIFO
	• More current measure of cost of goods sold and net income based on average costs for period	Weighted-average
	• Unique inventory items	Specific unit cost for the fish tanks and the tropical fish because they are unique

MyAccountingLab

MID-CHAPTER SUMMARY PROBLEM

Suppose a division of DIY Building Products Inc. has these inventory records for January 2011:

Date	Item	Quantity	Unit Cost
Jan. 1	Beginning inventory	100 units	$ 8
6	Purchase	60 units	9
21	Purchase	150 units	9
27	Purchase	90 units	10

Name: DIY Building Products Inc.
Industry: Building products
Fiscal Period: Month of January 2011
Key Fact: Perpetual inventory system

Operating expense for January was $1,900, and sales of 310 units generated sales revenue of $6,770.

Required

1. Prepare the January income statement, showing amounts for FIFO and weighted-average cost. Label the bottom line "Operating income." (Round figures to whole-dollar amounts.) Show your computations, and compute cost of goods sold.
2. Explain which inventory method would result in:
   a. Reporting the highest operating income
   b. Reporting inventory on the balance sheet at the most current cost
   c. Attaining the best measure of net income for the income statement

ANSWERS

Requirement 1

DIY Building Products Inc.
Income Statement for Division
For the Month Ended January 31, 2011

	FIFO		Weighted-Average	
Sales revenue		$6,770		$6,770
Cost of goods sold:				
Beginning inventory	$ 800		$ 800	
Purchases	2,790		2,790	
Cost of goods available for sale	3,590		3,590	
Ending inventory	(900)		(808)	
Cost of goods sold		2,690		2,782
Gross profit		4,080		3,988
Operating expenses		1,900		1,900
Operating income		$2,180		$2,088

Computations

Beginning inventory: 100 × $8 = $800
Purchases: (60 × $9) + (150 × $9) + (90 × $10) = $2,790
Ending inventory—FIFO: 90* × $10 = $900
Weighted-average: 90 × $8.975** = $808 (rounded from $807.75)

*Number of units in ending inventory = 100 + 60 + 150 + 90 − 310 = 90
**$3,590/400 units† = $8.975 per unit
†Number of units available = 100 + 60 + 150 + 90 = 400

Margin notes:
- Sales revenue is given.
- Beginning inventory is given.
- See the Computations section.
- Beginning inventory + Purchases
- See the Computations section.
- Cost of goods available for sale − Ending inventory
- Sales revenue − Cost of goods sold
- Operating expenses are given.
- Gross profit − Operating expenses

Use the quantities and unit costs given in the question to calculate beginning inventory and purchases. Recall that FIFO ending inventory calculations use the most current purchase prices. Weighted-average ending inventory calculations use the average purchase prices (including the price of the beginning inventory).

Requirement 2

Since beginning inventory, purchases, and operating expense are the same for all three inventory methods, use the ending inventory and operating income amounts you calculated in Requirement 1 to help you answer these questions.

a. Use FIFO to report the highest operating income. Income under FIFO is highest when inventory unit costs are increasing, as in this situation.

b. Use FIFO to report inventory on the balance sheet at the most current cost. The oldest inventory costs are expensed as cost of goods sold, leaving the most recent (most current) costs of the period in ending inventory.

c. Use weighted-average to attain the best measure of net income. Weighted-average inventory costs, which are expensed as part of goods sold, are closer to the most recent (most current) inventory costs than FIFO costs are.

Accounting Standards and Inventories

OBJECTIVE

❸ **Show** how accounting standards relate to inventory

It is important at this point that you consider two characteristics of accounting that have special relevance to inventories:

- Comparability
- Disclosure

Comparability

Investors like to compare a company's financial statements from one period to the next so they can use this information to make a decision. In order to do this, the company must use the same accounting method for inventory consistently from one accounting period to another.

Suppose you are analyzing Leon's Furniture's net income pattern over a two-year period. Now, suppose Leon's Furniture switched from one inventory method to another during that time and its net income increased dramatically, but only because of the change in inventory method. If you did not know about the change, you might believe that Leon's Furniture's income increased due to improved operations, which is not the case.

Comparability including **consistency** is an enhancing qualitative characteristic that helps make accounting information useful. It allows the user to distinguish between similarities and differences by comparing a company's financial statements from one period to the next. This does not mean that a company is not permitted to change its accounting methods. International Financial Reporting Standards require that a change in accounting method, such as a change in the method of valuing inventory, be disclosed. International Accounting Standard (IAS) 8 "Accounting Policies, Changes in Accounting Estimates and Errors" indicates that such a change is acceptable if it "results in the financial statements providing reliable and more relevant information." The change should normally be applied retrospectively, which means that prior years' financial statements should be restated to reflect the change. In addition, the effect of the change on the current financial statements should be disclosed.

Such an accounting change might be disclosed in the notes to the financial statements according to the disclosure principle.

Disclosure Principle

The **disclosure principle** holds that a company's financial statements should report enough information for outsiders to make informed decisions about the company. Companies are required to provide notes at the end of their financial statements to *disclose* the accounting policies used along with other *relevant* information about a company. That means disclosing inventory accounting methods. Without knowledge of the accounting method being used, a user such as a banker could make an unwise lending decision.

Suppose the banker is comparing two companies—one uses one inventory method and the other uses another method that leads to higher income. The latter reports higher net income, but only because of the inventory method being used. Without knowing the reason for the higher income, the banker could loan money to the wrong business.

Lower of Cost and Net Realizable Value. The **lower-of-cost-and-net-realizable-value (LCNRV) rule** is based on the premise that inventory can become obsolete or damaged or its selling price can decline. IAS 2-9 requires that inventory be reported in the financial statements at whichever is lower—the inventory's cost or its **net realizable value** (that is, the amount the business could get if it sold the inventory less the costs of selling it). If the net realizable value of inventory falls below its historical cost, the business must write down the value of its goods to market value. On the balance sheet, the business reports ending inventory at its LCNRV. All this can be done automatically by a computerized accounting system. How is the write-down accomplished?

Suppose Klassen Furniture Inc. paid $3,000 for inventory on September 26. By December 31, the inventory can be replaced for $2,000. Klassen's December 31 balance sheet must report the inventory at the LCNRV value of $2,000. Exhibit 6-9 presents the effects of LCNRV on the balance sheet and the income statement. Before any LCNRV effect, cost of goods sold is $9,000.

An LCNRV write-down decreases Inventory and increases Cost of Goods Sold, as follows (see also Exhibit 6-9):

Dec. 31	Cost of Goods Sold	1,000	
	Inventory		1,000
	Write inventory down to net realizable value.		

Inventory	
Sept. 26 $3,000	
	$1,000 Dec. 31
Balance $2,000	

Inventory that has been written down to net realizable value should be reassessed each period. If the net realizable value has increased, the previous write-down should be reversed up to the new net realizable value. Of course, the inventory cannot be written up to a value that exceeds its original cost.

Assume that Klassen's inventory described above was still on hand at the end of the next period and that the net realizable value had increased to $2,400. The journal entry to reverse a previous write-down would be as follows:

Inventory	400	
Cost of Goods Sold		400
Write inventory up to the net realizable value.		

EXHIBIT 6-9 **Lower-of-Cost-and-Net-Realizable-Value (LCNRV) Effects on Inventory and Cost of Goods Sold**

Balance Sheet	
Current assets:	$ XXX
Cash	XXX
Short-term investments	XXX
Accounts receivable	XXX
Inventories, at market (which is lower than $3,000 cost)	2,000
Prepaid expenses	XXX
Total current assets	$ X,XXX

Income Statement	
Sales revenue	$21,000
Cost of goods sold ($9,000 + $1,000)	10,000
Gross profit	$11,000

Companies disclose how they apply LCNRV in a note to their financial statements as shown in the following excerpt from Sobeys Inc.'s 2009 audited annual report.

> ***Summary of Significant Accounting Policies***
>
> **Inventories**
>
> Warehouse inventories are valued at the lower of cost and net realizable value with cost being determined on a weighted average cost basis. . . .

OBJECTIVE

4 **Use** inventory in decision making

Decision Making: Using Inventory

Detailed Income Statement

Exhibit 6-10 provides an example of a detailed income statement, complete with all the discounts and expenses in their proper places. Study it carefully.

EXHIBIT 6-10 **Detailed Income Statement**

Valley Software Company
Income Statement
For the Year Ended December 31, 2011

Sales revenue	$100,000	
Less: Sales discounts	(2,000)	
Sales returns and allowances	(3,000)	
Net sales		$95,000*
Cost of goods sold		45,000
Gross profit		50,000
Operating expenses:		
Selling:		
Sales commission expense	$ 5,000	
Freight-out (delivery expense)	1,000	
Other expenses (detailed)	6,000	12,000
Administrative:		
Salary expense	$ 2,000	
Depreciation expense	2,000	
Other expenses (detailed)	4,000	8,000
Income before income tax		30,000
Income tax expense (40%)		12,000
Net income		$18,000

*Most companies report only the net sales figure.

Analyzing Financial Statements

Managers, investors, and creditors use ratios to evaluate a business. Two ratios relate directly to inventory: the gross profit percentage and the rate of inventory turnover.

USING INVENTORY TURNOVER IN DECISION MAKING

Manager—Managers are keeping their eye on inventory to make sure it is selling quickly. Slow-moving inventory could be a sign that it is outdated or no longer in demand. Also, determining the selling price for inventory affects gross profit and ultimately net income. If the gross profit is too low, it may indicate that the inventory is costing too much or the selling price is not high enough.

Investor—Investors look to see if inventory is selling quickly because it affects revenue as well as net income. They also examine gross profit to see if it is high enough to cover all the other expenses and still provide for a reasonable profit.

Creditor—Creditors are interested in how inventory is selling because the faster inventory is sold, the sooner the cash is flowing in and the company can pay its debts.

Gross Profit Percentage. Gross profit—sales minus cost of goods sold—is a key indicator of a company's ability to sell inventory at a profit. Merchandisers strive to increase **gross profit percentage**, also called the *gross margin percentage*. Gross profit percentage is markup stated as a percentage of sales. Gross profit percentage is computed as follows for Leon's Furniture. Data (in millions) for 2009 are taken from Exhibit 6-3, page 287.

$$\text{Gross profit percentage} = \frac{\text{Gross profit}}{\text{Net sales revenue}} = \frac{\$283.4}{\$703.2} = 0.403 = 40.3\%$$

Managers and investors watch the gross profit percentage carefully. A 40.3% gross margin means that each dollar of sales generates 40.3 cents of gross profit. On average, cost of goods sold consumes 59.7 cents of each sales dollar for Leon's. For most firms, the gross profit percentage changes little from year to year, so a small downturn may signal trouble.

Leon's gross profit percentage of 40.3% compares very favourably with those of other retailers. Exhibit 6-11 shows the gross profit percentages for Leon's, Pier 1, and Home Depot.

EXHIBIT 6-11 Gross Profit Percentages of Three Leading Retailers

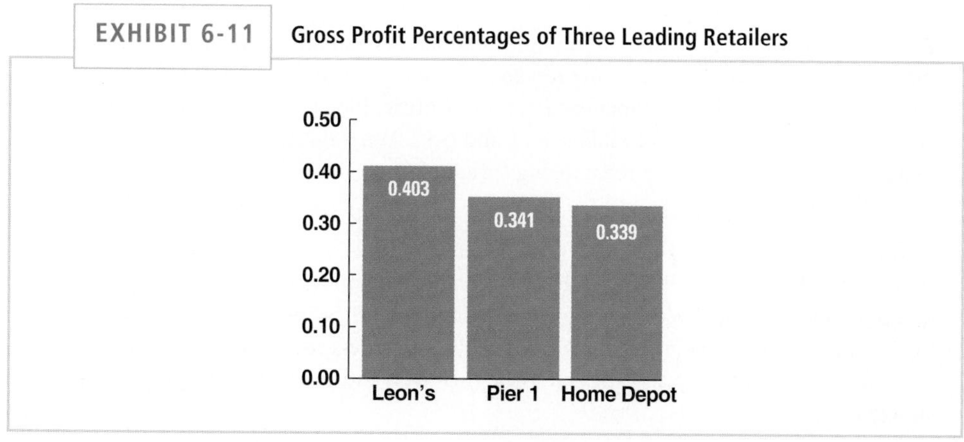

Inventory Turnover. Leon's strives to sell its inventory as quickly as possible because furniture and fixtures generate no profit until they are sold. The faster the sales, the higher the company's income, and the slower the sales, the lower the company's income. Ideally, a business could operate with zero inventory, but most businesses, especially retailers, must keep some goods on hand. **Inventory turnover**, the ratio of cost of goods sold to average inventory, indicates how rapidly inventory is sold. The 2009 computation for Leon's follows (data in millions from Exhibit 6-3, page 287):

$$\text{Inventory turnover} = \frac{\text{Cost of goods sold}}{\text{Average inventory}} = \frac{\text{Cost of goods sold}}{\left(\text{Beginning inventory} + \text{Ending inventory}\right) \div 2}$$

$$= \frac{\$419.8}{(\$84 + \$92.9)/2} = \text{4.75 or 4.8 times per year (every 76 days)}$$

The inventory turnover statistic shows how many times the company sold (or turned over) its average level of inventory during the year. Inventory turnover varies from industry to industry.

Leon's and other specialty retailers turn their inventory over slowly. Retailers must keep lots of inventory on hand because visual appeal is critical in retailing. Department stores such as The Bay and discounters such as Walmart and Zellers also keep a lot of inventory on hand. Exhibit 6-12 shows the inventory turnover rates for three leading retailers.

EXHIBIT 6-12 **Inventory Turnover Rates of Three Leading Retailers**

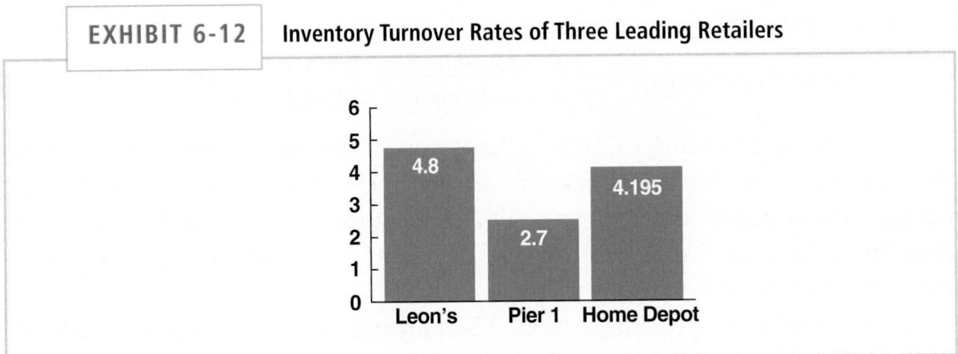

STOP + THINK

You have received a gift of cash from your grandparents and are considering investing in the stock market. You have carefully researched the market and have decided that you will invest in one of three companies: Leon's Furniture, Pier 1, or Home Depot. Assume your analysis has resulted in Exhibits 6-11 and 6-12. What do the ratio values in the two exhibits say about the merchandising (pricing) strategies of Leon's, Pier 1, and Home Depot?

Answer:

It's obvious that Leon's sells higher-end merchandise. Leon's gross profit percentage is much higher than those of Pier 1 and Home Depot. At the same time, Leon's has a higher turnover ratio. Home Depot's gross profit percentage is lower than Leon's. Generally, the lower the price, the faster the turnover, and the higher the price, the slower the turnover.

Additional Inventory Issues

Using the Cost-of-Goods-Sold Model

Exhibit 6-13 presents the **cost-of-goods-sold model**. Some accountants view this model as related to the periodic inventory system. But it's used by all companies, including those with perpetual inventory systems. The model is extremely powerful because it captures all the inventory information for an entire accounting period. Study this model carefully (all amounts are assumed).

EXHIBIT 6-13 **The Cost-of-Goods-Sold Model**

Cost of goods sold:	
Beginning inventory	$ 92.9
+ Purchases	410.9
= Goods available for sale	503.8
− Ending inventory	(84.0)
= Cost of goods sold	$419.8

Leon's Furniture uses a perpetual inventory accounting system. Let's see how Leon's can use the cost-of-goods-sold model to manage the business effectively.

1. What's the single most important question for Leon's to address?
   - What merchandise should Leon's offer to its customers? This is a *marketing* question that requires market research. If Leon's continually stocks the wrong merchandise, sales will suffer and profits will drop.
2. What's the second most important question for Leon's?
   - How much inventory should Leon's buy? **This is an accounting question faced by all merchandisers**. If Leon's buys too much merchandise, it will have to lower prices, the gross profit percentage will suffer, and it may lose money. If Leon's buys too little inventory, customers will go elsewhere. Buying the right quantity of inventory is critical for success. This question can be answered with the cost-of-goods-sold model. Let's see how it works.

We must rearrange the cost-of-goods-sold formula. Then we can help a Leon's store manager know how much inventory to buy, as follows (using amounts from Exhibit 6-13):

		(millions)
1	Cost of goods sold (based on the budget for the next period)	$419.8
2	+ Ending inventory (based on the budget for the next period)	84.0
3	= Goods available for sale as budgeted	503.8
4	− Beginning inventory (actual amount left over from the prior period)	92.9
5	= Purchases (how much inventory the manager needs to buy)	$410.9

In this case, the manager should buy $410.9 million of merchandise to work his plan for the upcoming period.

Estimating Inventory by the Gross Profit Method

OBJECTIVE

5 **Estimate** inventory by the gross profit method

Often a business must *estimate* the value of its goods. For example, if a fire destroys inventory, an insurance company will require an estimate of the loss. In this case, the business must estimate the cost of ending inventory because it was destroyed.

The **gross profit method**, also known as the *gross margin method*, is widely used to estimate ending inventory. This method uses the familiar cost-of-goods-sold model (amounts are assumed):

Beginning inventory	$ 4,000
+ Purchases	16,000
= Goods available for sale	20,000
− Ending inventory	(5,000)
= Cost of goods sold	$15,000

We rearrange *ending inventory* and *cost of goods sold* as follows:

Beginning inventory	$ 4,000
+ Purchases	16,000
= Goods available for sale	20,000
− Cost of goods sold	(15,000)
= Ending inventory	$ 5,000

Suppose a fire destroys some of Leon's inventory. To collect insurance, Leon's must estimate the cost of the ending inventory. Beginning inventory, net purchases, and net sales can be taken directly from the accounting records. Using Leon's *actual gross profit rate* of 40.3% (that is, gross profit divided by net sales), you can estimate the cost of goods sold. Then subtract cost of goods sold from goods available to estimate ending inventory. Exhibit 6-14 shows the calculations for the gross profit method with new amounts assumed for this illustration.

You can use the gross profit method to test the overall reasonableness of an ending inventory amount. This method also helps to detect large errors.

To ensure reliability, the gross profit rate should be based on historical trends adjusted for any current changes in pricing or product mix strategies that may have altered the historical range of the gross profit rate.

STOP + THINK

Assume your business had a bad fire and you wish to calculate your inventory loss. Beginning inventory is $70,000, net purchases total $365,000, and net sales are $500,000. With a normal gross profit rate of 30% of sales, how much is ending inventory?

Answer:
$70,000 + $365,000 – (0.70 x $500,000) = $85,000

Effects of Inventory Errors

OBJECTIVE

6 **Show** how inventory errors affect the financial statements

Inventory errors sometimes occur. In Exhibit 6-15, start with period 1, in which ending inventory is *overstated* by $5,000 and cost of goods sold is therefore *understated* by $5,000. Then compare period 1 with period 3, which is correct. *Period 1 should look exactly like period 3.*

EXHIBIT 6-14 **The Gross Profit Method of Estimating Inventory (amounts assumed)**

Beginning inventory		$18,000
Purchases		72,000
Goods available for sale		90,000
Cost of goods sold:		
Net sales revenue	$100,000	
Less estimated gross profit of 40.3%	(40,300)	
Estimated cost of goods sold		$59,700
Estimated cost of *ending inventory*		$30,300

EXHIBIT 6-15 **Inventory Errors: An Example**

	Period 1		Period 2		Period 3	
	Ending Inventory Overstated by $5,000		Beginning Inventory Overstated by $5,000		Correct	
Sales revenue		$100,000		$100,000		$100,000
Cost of goods sold:						
Beginning inventory	$10,000		**$ 15,000**		$10,000	
Purchases	50,000		50,000		50,000	
Cost of goods available for sale	60,000		**65,000**		60,000	
Ending inventory	**(15,000)**		(10,000)		(10,000)	
Cost of goods sold		**45,000**		**55,000**		50,000
Gross profit		**$ 55,000**		**$ 45,000**		$ 50,000

$100,000 (Periods 1 and 2 combined gross profit)

Source: The authors thank Professor Carl High for this example.

Inventory errors counterbalance in two consecutive periods. Why? Recall that period 1's ending inventory becomes period 2's beginning inventory amount. Thus, the error in period 1 carries over into period 2. Trace the ending inventory of $15,000 from period 1 to period 2. Then compare periods 2 and 3. *All periods should look exactly like period 3*. The amounts **in bold type** in Exhibit 6-15 are incorrect.

Beginning inventory and ending inventory have opposite effects on cost of goods sold (beginning inventory is added; ending inventory is subtracted); therefore, after two periods, an inventory accounting error "washes out" (counterbalances) as illustrated in Exhibit 6-15. Notice that total gross profit for periods 1 and 2 combined is correct ($100,000) even though each period's gross profit is wrong by $5,000. The correct gross profit is $50,000 for each period as shown in period 3.

Note that there is a direct relationship between ending inventory (EI) and gross profit (GP), but an inverse relationship between beginning inventory (BI) and gross profit; that is, an understatement of ending inventory results in an understatement of gross profit, but an understatement of beginning inventory results in an overstatement of gross profit. (COGS = cost of goods sold)

EI ↓ results in COGS ↑ results in GP ↓ (Direct relationship between EI and GP)

BI ↓ results in COGS ↓ results in GP ↑ (Inverse relationship between BI and GP)

Inventory Errors

Inventory errors cannot be ignored simply because they counterbalance. Suppose you are analyzing trends in the operations of the company presented above. Exhibit 6-15 shows a drop in gross profit from period 1 to period 2, followed by an increase in period 3. Did the company really get worse and then better again? No, that picture of operations is inaccurate because of the accounting error. The correct gross profit is $50,000 for each period. We must have accurate information for all periods. Exhibit 6-16 summarizes the effects of inventory accounting errors.

EXHIBIT 6-16 **Effects of Inventory Errors**

	Period 1		Period 2	
Inventory Error	Cost of Goods Sold	Gross Profit and Net Income	Cost of Goods Sold	Gross Profit and Net Income
Period 1 Ending inventory overstated	Understated	Overstated	Overstated	Understated
Period 1 Ending inventory understated	Overstated	Understated	Understated	Overstated

Ethical Issues: Cooking the Books

No area of accounting has a deeper ethical dimension than inventory. Managers of companies whose profits do not meet shareholder expectations are sometimes tempted to "cook the books" to increase reported income. The increase in reported income may lead investors and creditors into thinking the business is more successful than it really is.

What do managers hope to gain from fraudulent accounting? In some cases, they are trying to keep their jobs. In other cases, their bonuses are tied to reported income: the higher the company's net income, the higher the managers' bonuses. There are two main schemes for cooking the books.

- The easiest is simply to overstate ending inventory. The upward-pointing arrows in the accounting equation indicate an overstatement: reporting more assets and equity than are actually present.

ASSETS	=	LIABILITIES	+	SHAREHOLDERS' EQUITY
↑	=	0	+	↑

- The second way of using inventory to cook the books involves sales revenue. Sales schemes are more complex than overstating ending inventory. Consider two examples of real companies. Datapoint Corporation and MiniScribe, both computer-related companies, were charged with creating fictitious sales to boost reported profits. Datapoint is alleged to have hired drivers to transport its inventory around town so that the goods could not be physically counted. Datapoint tried to show that the goods had been sold. The scheme fell apart when the trucks returned the goods to Datapoint's warehouse, and Datapoint had unrealistic amounts of sales returns. What would you think of a company with $10 million in sales and $3 million of sales returns? No company produces that many defective computers.

MiniScribe is alleged to have shipped boxes of bricks labelled as computer parts to customers immediately before year-end. The bogus transactions increased the company's sales by $4 million—but only temporarily. The scheme boomeranged when MiniScribe had to record the returns. In virtually every area, accounting imposes a discipline that ultimately brings frauds to light.

Watch out for excessive sales returns. Some of the sales revenue may have been fictitious.

Reporting on the Statement of Cash Flows

Inventories appear on the balance sheet as current assets. Since inventory transactions affect cash, their effects are reported on the statement of cash flows.

Inventory transactions are *operating activities* because the purchase and sale of merchandise drives a company's operations. The purchase of inventory requires a cash payment and the sale of inventory requires a cash receipt. We will see in Chapter 12 how to report inventory transactions on the statement of cash flows.

SUMMARY OF CHAPTER 6

Learning Objective ❶: Account for inventory

When inventory is bought, it is a current asset on the balance sheet, and when it is sold, it is an expense on the income statement.

Learning Objective ❷: Understand the various inventory methods

A company can use either of the following methods to account for its inventory: A **perpetual inventory system** keeps a continuous record of inventory bought and sold. A **periodic inventory system** does not keep a continuous record of inventory and takes a physical count of inventory on hand to determine the cost of ending inventory. **Cost of goods sold** is computed.

To assign a cost to inventory, a company can use any of the following methods. The **specific-unit-cost method** is based on the specific cost of particular units. The **first-in, first-out (FIFO) cost method** assumes that the first costs into inventory are the first costs out to cost of goods sold. The **weighted-average cost method** is based on an average of the cost of inventory during the period.

Learning Objective ❸: Show how accounting standards relate to inventory

Comparability (including **consistency**) says that businesses should use the same accounting methods and procedures from period to period so users can compare information.

Disclosure says that a company's financial statements should report enough information for outsiders to be able to make knowledgeable decisions about the business.

The **lower-of-cost-and-net-realizable-value (LCNRV) rule** requires that inventory be reported in the financial statements at the lower of its cost and **net realizable value**.

Learning Objective ❹: Use inventory in decision making

Two ratios are used to analyze inventory:

Gross profit percentage = Gross profit/Net sales revenue

The gross profit percentage indicates the company's ability to sell inventory at a profit.

Inventory turnover = Cost of goods sold/Average inventory

Inventory turnover shows how rapidly inventory is sold.

Learning Objective ❺: **Estimate inventory by the gross profit method**

The **gross profit method** can be used to estimate ending inventory when records are lost or destroyed or to test the overall reasonableness of ending inventory.

Learning Objective ❻: **Show how inventory errors affect the financial statements**

Inventory errors affect the value of the following items: inventory on the balance sheet; cost of goods sold, gross profit and net income on the income statement.

MyAccountingLab

END-OF-CHAPTER SUMMARY PROBLEM

During February 2011, its first month of operations, Blanc Company reported the following transactions:

Feb. 1	Purchased 20,000 units on account for $2.50 each
Feb. 15	Purchased 25,000 units on account for $2.75 each
Feb. 20	Sold on account 35,000 units for $3.25 each
Feb. 23	Purchased 10,000 units on account for $2.70 each
Feb. 25	Paid for the purchases made on Feb. 1
Feb. 27	Collected $75,000 from customers on account
Feb. 28	Incurred on account $11,000 in operating expenses

The company uses the perpetual inventory method and pays 35% income tax.

Name: Blanc Company
Industry: Retail corporation
Fiscal Period: Year ended December 31, 2011
Key Fact: Perpetual inventory system

Since the company uses the perpetual inventory system, record inventory purchases and sales as they occur.

All merchandise is purchased on account.

Required

1. Prepare journal entries to record the transactions for the month of February assuming the company uses the FIFO inventory method. Explanations are not required.
2. Determine the ending inventory assuming the company uses the FIFO inventory method. (Hint: You might find it helpful to use a T-account.)
3. Prepare the company's multi-step income statement for the month of February.
4. Compute the company's gross profit percentage and the inventory turnover for the month. How does this company compare with the industry average of 17% for the gross profit and an inventory turnover of three times? Round to one decimal place.
5. Assume instead that the company uses the weighted-average method to value inventory; calculate the cost of goods sold and the ending inventory value.

ANSWERS

Requirement 1

All sales are made on account.

Use FIFO (oldest costs) to calculate cost of the 35,000 units sold:
Opening inventory: $0 (company just started)
From Feb. 1 purchase: $50,000 (20,000 units)
From Feb. 15 purchase: $68,750 (25,000 units)

Feb. 1	Inventory (20,000 units × $2.50)	50,000	
	Accounts payable		50,000
Feb. 15	Inventory (25,000 units × $2.75)	68,750	
	Accounts payable		68,750
Feb. 20	Accounts receivable (35,000 × $3.25)	113,750	
	Sales Revenue		113,750
	Cost of goods sold (20,000 × $2.50 + 15,000 × $2.75)	91,250	
	Inventory		91,250
Feb. 23	Inventory (10,000 units × $2.70)	27,000	
	Accounts payable		27,000

Feb. 25	Accounts payable	50,000	
	Cash		50,000
Feb. 27	Cash	75,000	
	Accounts receivable		75,000
Feb. 28	Operating expenses	11,000	
	Accounts payable		11,000
Feb. 28	Income tax expense (from Requirement 3)	4,025	
	Tax payable		4,025

Operating expenses were incurred ($11,000).

Income tax expense is 35% of net income before taxes (Sales revenue − Cost of goods sold − Operating expenses).

Requirement 2

FIFO − Ending inventory = $50,000 + $68,750 – $91,250 + $27,000 = $54,500

Inventory

	Debit	Credit	
Feb. 1	50,000		
Feb. 15	68,750	91,250	Feb. 20
Feb. 23	27,000		
Balance Feb. 28	54,500		

FIFO ending inventory:
Beginning inventory + Purchases − Cost of goods sold

Requirement 3

Blanc Company
Income Statement
For the Month Ended February 28, 2011

Sales revenue	$113,750
Cost of goods sold	91,250
Gross profit	$ 22,500
Operating expenses	11,000
Income before tax	$ 11,500
Income tax expense (35%)	4,025
Net income	$ 7,475

Beginning inventory must be the same amount as the inventory on the previous year's balance sheet.

Blanc Company is starting so there is no previous year's balance.

Ending inventory must be the same amount as the inventory on this year's balance sheet.

Sales revenue – Cost of goods sold

Gross margin – Operating expenses

GAAP require that income tax expense be presented separately from all other expenses.

Requirement 4

Gross profit percentage = $22,500/$113,750 = 19.8%
Inventory turnover = $91,250/$54,500* = 1.7 times

Compared to the industry averages, Blanc Company's gross profit percentage is higher, which suggests that the company is able to sell its inventory at a profit. However, the inventory turnover is low, which means that the company has too much inventory on hand.

Gross margin ÷ Sales revenue

Cost of goods sold ÷ Average inventory, where Average inventory = (Beginning inventory + Ending inventory) ÷ 2

Net income ÷ Sales revenue

Requirement 5

$$\text{Weighted average} - \text{calculate the unit cost} = \frac{\text{Cost of goods available for sale}}{\text{Number of units available for sale}}$$

A new unit cost must be calculated after a purchase is made.

*Since the company just started, there is no beginning inventory and, therefore, an average is not used.

$$\text{Feb. 15—New unit cost} = \frac{\$50{,}000\ (\text{Feb. 1}) + \$68{,}750\ (\text{Feb. 15})}{20{,}000 + 25{,}000} = \$2.64\ \text{each}$$

Feb. 20—Cost of goods sold = 35,000 units sold × $2.64 = $92,400

Feb. 23—New unit cost is calculated as follows:

Units left after the sale on Feb. 20 (45,000 available − 35,000 sold) = 10,000 × $2.64 = $26,400

Units bought on Feb. 23 = 10,000 × $2.70 = $27,000

Total cost = $53,400 ($26,400 + $27,000) divided by 20,000 (number of units on hand) = $2.67

Therefore, ending inventory = $2.67 × 20,000 units = $53,400

Review Inventory and Cost of Goods Sold

Quick Check (Answers are given on page 332.)

1. Which statement is true?
   a. The Sales account is used to record only sales on account.
   b. The invoice is the purchaser's request for collection from the customer.
   c. Gross profit is the excess of sales revenue over cost of goods sold.
   d. A service company purchases products from suppliers and then sells them.
2. Sales discounts should appear in the financial statements:
   a. As an addition to inventory
   b. As an addition to sales
   c. As an operating expense
   d. Among the current liabilities
   e. As a deduction from sales
3. How is inventory classified in the financial statements?
   a. As an asset
   b. As a liability
   c. As an expense
   d. As a revenue
   e. As a contra account to Cost of Goods Sold

Questions 4 through 6 use the following data of King Ltd.

	Units	Unit Cost	Total Cost	Units Sold
Beginning inventory	25	$5	$125	
Purchase on May 23	30	6	180	
Purchase on Nov. 5	10	7	70	
Sales	50	?	?	

4. King uses a FIFO inventory system. Cost of goods sold for the period is
   a. $275
   b. $347
   c. $255
   d. $375

5. King's FIFO cost of ending inventory would be
   a. $161
   b. $100
   c. $208
   d. $225

6. King's weighted-average cost of ending inventory is
   a. $87
   b. $104
   c. $100
   d. $330

7. When applying the lower-of-cost-and-net-realizable-value rule, "net realizable value" generally means
   a. Sales value
   b. Original cost
   c. Selling price less costs of selling
   d. Original cost, less physical deterioration

8. During a period of rising prices, the inventory method that will yield the highest net income and asset value is
   a. Specific identification
   b. Weighted-average cost
   c. FIFO

9. Which statement is true?
   a. When inventory costs are increasing, the gross profit using FIFO is lowest.
   b. Application of the lower-of-cost-and-net-realizable-value rule often results in a lower inventory value.
   c. An error overstating ending inventory in 2009 will understate 2009 net income.
   d. When prices are rising, the inventory method that results in the lowest ending inventory value is FIFO.

10. The ending inventory of LaVal Co. is $64,000. If beginning inventory was $70,000 and goods available for sale totalled $124,000, the cost of goods sold is
    a. $112,000
    b. $198,000
    c. $60,000
    d. $50,000
    e. None of the above ($_______)

11. Martin Company had cost of goods sold of $130,000. The beginning and ending inventories were $10,000 and $20,000, respectively. Purchases for the period must have been
    a. $82,000
    b. $94,000
    c. $132,000
    d. $140,000
    e. $138,000

Use the following information for Questions 12 through 14.

12. Tee Company had a $20,000 beginning inventory and a $24,000 ending inventory. Net sales were $180,000; purchases, $80,000; purchase returns and allowances, $4,000; and freight-in, $5,000. Cost of goods sold for the period is
    a. $69,000
    b. $49,000
    c. $85,000
    d. $77,000
    e. None of the above

13. What is Tee's gross profit percentage (rounded to the nearest percentage)?
    a. 57%
    b. 88%
    c. 47%
    d. None of the above

14. What is Tee's rate of inventory turnover?
    a. 3.4 times
    b. 3.5 times
    c. 6.4 times
    d. 6.2 times

15. Beginning inventory is $60,000, purchases are $180,000, and sales total $300,000. The normal gross profit is 30%. Using the gross profit method, how much is ending inventory?
    a. $120,000
    b. $106,400
    c. $244,000
    d. $30,000
    e. None of the above ($_______)

16. An overstatement of ending inventory in one period results in
    a. No effect on net income of the next period
    b. An understatement of net income of the next period
    c. An overstatement of net income of the next period
    d. An understatement of the beginning inventory of the next period

Accounting Vocabulary

comparability Investors like to compare a company's financial statements from one year to the next. Therefor, a company must consistently use the same accounting method each year. (p. 298)

consistency A business must use the same accounting methods and procedures from period to period. (p. 298)

cost of goods sold Cost of the inventory the business has sold to customers. Also called *cost of sales*. (p. 285)

cost-of-goods-sold model Formula that brings together all the inventory data for the entire accounting period: Beginning inventory + Purchases = Goods available for sale. Then, Goods available for sale − Ending inventory = Cost of goods sold. (p. 303)

disclosure principle A business's financial statements must report enough information for outsiders to make knowledgeable decisions about the business. The company should report relevant, reliable, and comparable information about its economic affairs. (p. 298)

first-in, first-out (FIFO) cost (method) Inventory costing method by which the first costs into inventory are the first costs out to cost of goods sold. Ending inventory is based on the costs of the most recent purchases. (p. 293)

gross margin Another name for *gross profit*. (p. 287)

gross profit Sales revenue minus cost of goods sold. Also called *gross margin*. (p. 287)

gross profit method A way to estimate inventory based on a rearrangement of the cost-of-goods-sold model: Beginning inventory + Net purchases = Goods available for sale − Cost of goods sold = Ending inventory. Also called the *gross margin method*. (p. 304)

gross profit percentage Gross profit divided by net sales revenue. Also called the *gross margin percentage*. (p. 300)

inventory turnover Ratio of cost of goods sold to average inventory. Indicates how rapidly inventory is sold. (p. 301)

lower-of-cost-and-net-realizable-value (LCNRV) rule Requires that an asset be reported in the financial statements at whichever is lower—its historical cost or its net realizable value. (p. 299)

net realizable value The amount a business could get if it sold the inventory less the costs of selling it. (p. 299)

periodic inventory system An inventory system in which the business does not keep a continuous record of the inventory on hand. Instead, at the end of the period, the business makes a physical count of the inventory on hand and applies the appropriate unit costs to determine the cost of the ending inventory. (p. 288)

perpetual inventory system An inventory system in which the business keeps a continuous record for each inventory item to show the inventory on hand at all times. (p. 288)

purchase allowance A decrease in the cost of purchases because the seller has granted the buyer a subtraction (an allowance) from the amount owed. (p. 289)

purchase discount A decrease in the cost of purchases earned by making an early payment to the vendor. (p. 289)

purchase return A decrease in the cost of purchases because the buyer returned the goods to the seller. (p. 289)

specific-unit-cost method Inventory costing method based on the specific cost of particular units of inventory. Also called the *specific identification method*. (p. 292)

weighted-average-cost method Inventory costing method based on the average cost of inventory for the period. Weighted-average cost is determined by dividing the cost of goods available by the number of units available. Also called the *average cost method*. (p. 293)

Assess Your Progress

MyAccountingLab

Make the grade with MyAccountingLab: The exercises and problems in this chapter can be found on MyAccountingLab at www.myaccountinglab.com. You can practise them as often as you want, and they feature step-by-step guided solutions to help you find the right answer.

Short Exercises

S6-1 Journalize the following assumed transactions for Shoppers Drug Mart Corporation. Show amounts in millions.

Learning Objective 1
Accounting for inventory transactions

- Cash purchases of inventory, $3,900 million
- Sales on account (including credit cards), $19,400 million
- Cost of goods sold (perpetual inventory system), $4,200 million
- Collections on account, $18,900 million

S6-2 Riley Kilgo Inc. purchased inventory costing $100,000 and sold 80% of the goods for $240,000. All purchases and sales were on account. Kilgo later collected 20% of the accounts receivable.

Learning Objective 1
Accounting for inventory transactions

1. Journalize these transactions for Kilgo, which uses the perpetual inventory system.
2. For these transactions, show what Kilgo will report for inventory, revenues, and expenses on its financial statements. Report gross profit on the appropriate statement.

S6-3 Allstate Sporting Goods started April with an inventory of 10 sets of golf clubs that cost a total of $1,500. During April Allstate purchased 20 sets of clubs for $3,200. At the end of the month, Allstate had six sets of golf clubs on hand. The store manager must select an inventory costing method, and he asks you to tell him both cost of goods sold and ending inventory under these two accounting methods:

Learning Objective 2
Applying the weighted-average cost and FIFO methods

a. Weighted-average cost
b. FIFO

S6-4 University Copy Centre Ltd. uses laser printers. The company started the year with 100 containers of ink (weighted-average cost of $9.20 each, FIFO cost of $9 each). During the year, University Copy Centre purchased 700 containers of ink at $10 and sold 600 units for $20 each. The company paid operating expenses throughout the year, to a total of $3,000. University Copy Centre is not subject to income tax. Prepare University Copy Centre Ltd.'s income statement for the year ended December 31, 2011, under the weighted-average and FIFO inventory costing methods. Include a complete statement heading.

Learning Objective 2
Applying the weighted-average cost and FIFO methods

S6-5 This exercise should be used in conjunction with Short Exercise S6-4. Now assume that University Copy Centre in Short Exercise S6-4 is a corporation subject to an 18% income tax. Compute University Copy Centre's income tax expense under the weighted-average cost and FIFO inventory costing methods. Which method would you select to (a) maximize income before tax and (b) minimize income tax expense? Format your answer as shown on page 292.

Learning Objective 2
Income tax effects of the inventory costing methods

S6-6 You are opening a new bookstore catering to the students at Queen's University. Once you have established this operation, you plan to approach investors to support an expansion to locations in other Canadian university communities. Explain to your accountant what characteristics you expect him to maintain in accounting for inventory and the reasons for your expectations.

Learning Objective 3
Accounting standards related to inventory

S6-7 It is December 31, 2011, end of year, and the controller of Garcia Corporation is applying the lower-of-cost-and-net-realizable-value (LCNRV) rule to inventories. Before any year-end adjustments Garcia has these data:

Learning Objective 3
Applying the lower-of-cost-and-net-realizable-value rule to inventory

Cost of goods sold	$410,000
Historical cost of ending inventory, as determined by a physical count	60,000

Garcia determines that the net realizable value of ending inventory is $49,000. Show what Garcia should report for ending inventory and for cost of goods sold. Identify the financial statement where each item appears.

Learning Objective 4
Using ratio data to evaluate operations

S6-8 Gildan Activewear Inc. made sales of $964.4 million during 2007. Cost of goods sold for the year totalled $655.3 million. At the end of 2006, Gildan's inventory stood at $200.7 million, and Gildan ended 2007 with inventory of $240 million. Compute Gildan's gross profit percentage and rate of inventory turnover for 2007.

Learning Objective 5
Estimating ending inventory by the gross profit method

S6-9 Provincial Technology Inc. began the year with inventory of $300,000 and purchased $1,600,000 of goods during the year. Sales for the year are $3,000,000, and Provincial's gross profit percentage is 40% of sales. Compute Provincial's estimated cost of ending inventory by using the gross profit method.

Learning Objective 6
Assessing the effect of an inventory error—one year only

S6-10 CWD Inc. reported these figures for its fiscal year (amounts in millions):

Net sales	$1,700
Cost of goods sold	1,180
Ending inventory	360

Suppose CWD later learns that ending inventory was overstated by $10 million. What are CWD's correct amounts for (a) net sales, (b) ending inventory, (c) cost of goods sold, and (d) gross profit?

Learning Objective 6
Assessing the effect of an inventory error on two years

S6-11 Suppose Staples Inc.'s $1.9 million cost of inventory at its fiscal year-end on February 3, 2011, was understated by $0.5 million.

1. Would 2011's reported gross profit of $5.2 million be overstated, understated, or correct? What would be the correct amount of gross profit for 2011?
2. Will 2012's gross profit of $5.6 million be overstated, understated, or correct? What would be the correct amount of gross profit for 2012?

Learning Objective 1 2
Ethical implications of inventory actions

S6-12 Determine whether each of the following actions in buying, selling, and accounting for inventories is ethical or unethical. Give your reason for each answer.

1. In applying the lower-of-cost-and-net-realizable-value rule to inventories, Terre Haute Industries recorded an excessively low net realizable value for ending inventory. This allowed the company to pay less income tax for the year.
2. Laminated Photo Film purchased lots of inventory shortly before year-end to increase the weighted-average cost of goods sold and decrease reported income for the year.
3. Madison Inc. delayed the purchase of inventory until after December 31, 2011, to keep 2011's cost of goods sold from growing too large. The delay in purchasing inventory helped net income of 2011 to reach the level of profit demanded by the company's investors.
4. Dover Sales Company deliberately overstated ending inventory in order to report higher profits (net income).
5. Roberto Corporation deliberately overstated purchases to produce a high figure for cost of goods sold (low amount of net income). The real reason was to decrease the company's income tax payments to the government.

Exercises

Learning Objective 1 2
Accounting for inventory transactions

E6-13 Accounting records for Red Deer Tire Ltd. yield the following data for the year ended December 31, 2011 (amounts in thousands):

Inventory, December 31, 2010	$ 550
Purchases of inventory (on account)	1,200
Sales of inventory—80% on account; 20% for cash (cost $900)	2,000
Inventory at FIFO cost, December 31, 2011	850

Required

1. Journalize Red Deer Tire's inventory transactions for the year under the perpetual system. Show all amounts in thousands. Use Exhibit 6-5 as a model, on page 290.
2. Report ending inventory, sales, cost of goods sold, and gross profit on the appropriate financial statement (amounts in thousands).

Learning Objective ❶❷
Analyzing inventory transactions

E6-14 Langley Inc. inventory records for a particular development program show the following at October 31, 2011:

Oct. 1	Beginning inventory	5 units @	$150	=	$ 750
15	Purchase	11 units @	160	=	1,760
26	Purchase	5 units @	170	=	850

At October 31, 10 of these programs are on hand.

Required

1. Journalize for Langley:
   a. Total October purchases in one summary entry. All purchases were on credit.
   b. Total October sales and cost of goods sold in two summary entries. The selling price was $500 per unit, and all sales were on credit. Langley uses the FIFO inventory method.
2. Under FIFO, how much gross profit would Langley earn on these transactions? What is the FIFO cost of Langley's ending inventory?

Learning Objective ❷
Determining ending inventory and cost of goods sold by three methods

E6-15 Use the data for Langley Inc. in Exercise E6-14 to answer the following.

Required

1. Compute cost of goods sold and ending inventory, using each of the following methods:
   a. Specific unit cost, with two $150 units, three $160 units, and five $170 units still on hand at the end
   b. Weighted-average cost
   c. First-in, first-out cost
2. Which method produces the highest cost of goods sold? Which method produces the lowest cost of goods sold? What causes the difference in cost of goods sold?

Learning Objective ❷
Computing the tax advantage of weighted-average cost over FIFO

E6-16 Use the data in Exercise E6-14 to illustrate Langley's income tax advantage from using weighted-average cost over FIFO cost. Sales revenue is $6,000, operating expenses are $1,100, and the income tax rate is 25%. How much in taxes would Langley save by using the weighted-average-cost method versus FIFO?

Learning Objective ❷
Determining ending inventory and cost of goods sold—FIFO versus weighted-average cost

E6-17 MusicBiz.net Ltd. specializes in sound equipment. Because each inventory item is expensive, MusicBiz uses a perpetual inventory system. Company records indicate the following data for a line of speakers:

Date	Item	Quantity	Unit Cost	Sale Price
June 1	Balance	6	$ 95	
10	Purchase	11	100	
21	Sale	3		$155
30	Sale	5		160

Required

1. Determine the amounts that MusicBiz should report for cost of goods sold and ending inventory in the following two ways:
   a. FIFO
   b. Weighted-average cost

2. MusicBiz uses the FIFO method. Prepare MusicBiz's income statement for the month ended June 30, 2011, reporting gross profit. Operating expenses totalled $319, and the income tax rate was 25%.

Learning Objective 2
Measuring gross profit—FIFO versus weighted-average cost, falling prices

E6-18 Suppose a Johnson store in Ottawa, Ontario, ended November 2011 with 800,000 units of merchandise that cost an average of $8 each. Suppose the store then sold 600,000 units for $5.0 million during December. Further, assume the store made two large purchases during December as follows:

December 6	100,000 units	@ $7	=	$ 700,000
26	400,000 units	@ 6	=	2,400,000

1. At December 31, the store manager needs to know the store's gross profit under both FIFO and weighted-average cost. Supply this information.
2. What caused the FIFO and weighted-average cost gross profit figures to differ?.

Learning Objective 2
Managing income taxes under the weighted-average-cost method

E6-19 Deitrick Guitar Company is nearing the end of its worst year ever. With three weeks until year-end, it appears that net income for the year will have decreased by 20% from last year. Jim Deitrick, the president and principal shareholder, is distressed with the year's results.

Deitrick asks you, the financial vice-president, to come up with a way to increase the business's net income. Inventory quantities are a little higher than normal because sales have been slow during the last few months. Deitrick uses the weighted-average-cost inventory method, and inventory costs have risen dramatically during the latter part of the year.

Required

Write a memorandum to Jim Deitrick to explain how the company can increase its net income for the year. Explain your reasoning in detail. Deitrick is a man of integrity, so your plan must be completely ethical.

Learning Objective 3 4
Identifying effects of the inventory methods and evaluating operations

E6-20 This exercise tests your understanding of accounting for inventory. Provide a word or phrase that best fits the description. Assume that the cost of inventory is rising.

___ 1. Generally associated with saving income taxes.

___ 2. Results in a cost of ending inventory that is close to the current cost of replacing the inventory.

___ 3. Used to account for automobiles, jewellery, and art objects.

___ 4. Maximizes reported income.

___ 5. Inventory system that keeps a running record of all goods bought, sold, and on hand.

___ 6. Characteristic that enables investors to compare a company's financial statements from one period to the next.

___ 7. Writes inventory down when net realizable value drops below historical cost.

___ 8. Key indicator of a company's ability to sell inventory at a profit.

___ 9. A decrease in the buyer's cost of inventory earned by paying quickly.

Learning Objective 2
Applying the lower-of-cost-and-net-realizable-value rule to inventories

E6-21 Tavistock Inc. uses a perpetual inventory system. Tavistock has these account balances at December 31, 2011, prior to making the year-end adjustments:

Inventory			Cost of Goods Sold			Sales Revenue	
Beg. bal.	12,400						
End bal.	14,000		Bal.	78,000		Bal.	125,000

A year ago, the net realizable value of Tavistock's ending inventory was $13,000, which exceeded cost of $12,400. Tavistock has determined that the net realizable value of the December 31, 2011, ending inventory is $12,000.

Required
Prepare Tavistock Inc.'s 2011 income statement through gross profit to show how the company would apply the lower-of-cost-and-net-realizable-value rule to its inventories.

E6-22 Supply the missing income statement amounts for each of the following companies (amounts in millions, at January 31, 2011):

Learning Objective 2
Determining amounts for the income statement; using the cost-of-goods-sold model

Company	Net Sales	Beginning Inventory	Purchases	Ending Inventory	Cost of Goods Sold	Gross Profit
Myers Confectionary	$543	$29	$470	$24	(a)	(b)
Canada Computers	74	7	(c)	8	(d)	19
Best Taste Beverages	(e)	(f)	16	2	16	19
Value for $	31	2	24	(g)	23	(h)

Prepare the income statement for Myers Confectionary Ltd., in millions of dollars, for the year ended January 31, 2011. Use the cost-of-goods-sold model to compute cost of goods sold. Myers's operating and other expenses for the year were $204. Ignore income tax.

Note: Exercise E6-23 builds on Exercise E6-22 with a profitability analysis of these actual companies.

E6-23 Refer to the data in Exercise E6-22. Compute all ratio values to answer the following questions:

Learning Objective 4
Measuring profitability

- Which company has the highest gross profit percentage? Which company has the lowest?
- Which company has the highest rate of inventory turnover? Which company has the lowest?

Based on your figures, which company appears to be the most profitable?

E6-24 Suppose a company you are considering as an investor made sales of $54.8 billion in the year ended December 31, 2011. Collections from customers totalled $55 billion. The company began the year with $6.6 billion in inventories and ended with $7.9 billion. During the year, purchases of inventory added up to $39.8 billion. Of the purchases, the company paid $37.9 billion to suppliers.

Learning Objective 5
Measuring gross profit and reporting cash flows

As an investor searching for a good investment, you would identify several critical pieces of information about the company's operations during the year.

Compute the company's gross profit, gross profit percentage, and rate of inventory turnover during 2011. Use the cost-of-goods-sold model as needed. Would the information help you make your investment decision?

E6-25 Your company, Home Products Ltd., prepares budgets to help manage the company. Home Products is budgeting for the fiscal year ended December 31, 2012. During the preceding fiscal year, 2011, sales totalled $1,777 million and cost of goods sold was $1,175 million. At December 31, 2011, inventory stood at $366 million.

Learning Objective 2
Budgeting inventory purchase

During the upcoming 2012 year, suppose you expect cost of goods sold to increase by 8%. The company budgets next year's ending inventory at $369 million.

Required
One of the most important decisions you make is how much inventory to buy. How much inventory will you purchase during the upcoming year to reach your budgeted figures?

E6-26 Vacation Properties began March with concession inventory of $36,000. The business made net purchases of concessions for $79,500 and had net sales of $150,000 before a break-in when its concession inventory was stolen. For the past several years, Vacation Properties' gross profit percentage has been 45%. Estimate the cost of the concession inventory stolen. Would a manager use the gross profit method to estimate ending inventory under normal circumstances?

Learning Objective 5
Estimating inventory by the gross profit method

Learning Objective 6
Correcting an inventory error

E6-27 Dijon Mustard Ltée. reported the following comparative income statement for the years ended September 30, 2011, and 2012:

Dijon Mustard Ltée
Income Statement
For the Years Ended September 30

	2012		2011	
Sales revenue		$194,000		$158,000
Cost of goods sold				
Beginning inventory	$ 23,000		$ 16,000	
Purchases	97,000		86,000	
Goods available for sale	120,000		102,000	
Ending inventory	(21,000)		(23,000)	
Cost of goods sold		99,000		79,000
Gross profit		95,000		79,000
Operating expenses		20,000		20,000
Net income		$ 75,000		$ 59,000

Dijon's shareholders are thrilled by the company's boost in sales and net income during 2012. Then they discover that the 2011 ending inventory was understated by $10,000. How well did Dijon really perform in 2012, as compared with 2011?

Challenge Exercises

Learning Objective 2
Inventory policy decisions

E6-28 For each of the following situations, identify the inventory method that you would use or, given the use of a particular method, state the strategy that you would follow to accomplish your goal:

a. Inventory costs are increasing. Your company uses weighted-average cost and is having an unexpectedly good year. It is near year-end, and you need to keep net income from increasing too much in order to save on income tax.
b. Suppliers of your inventory are threatening a labour strike, and it may be difficult for your company to obtain inventory. This situation could increase your income taxes.
c. Inventory costs are decreasing, and your company's board of directors wants to minimize income taxes.
d. Inventory costs are increasing, and the company prefers to report high income.
e. Inventory costs have been stable for several years, and you expect costs to remain stable for the indefinite future. (Give the reason for your choice of method.)

Learning Objective 2
Understanding inventory methods

E6-29 Suppose Holt Renfrew, the specialty retailer, had these records for ladies' evening gowns during 2011.

Beginning inventory (30 @ $1,000)	$ 30,000
Purchase in February (25 @ $1,100)	27,500
Purchase in June (60 @ $1,200)	72,000
Purchase in December (25 @ $1,300)	32,500
Goods available	$162,000

Assume sales of evening gowns totalled 130 units during 2011 and that Holt's uses the weighted-average-cost method to account for inventory. The income tax rate is 30%.

Required

1. Compute Holt's cost of goods sold for evening gowns in 2011.

2. Compute what cost of goods sold would have been if Holt's had purchased enough inventory in December—at $1,300 per evening gown—to keep year-end inventory at the same level it was at the beginning of the year, 30 units.

Learning Objective 4 5
Evaluating a company's profitability

E6-30 Cheri's Beauty Products Ltd. reported the figures below at December 31, 2011, 2010, and 2009. The business has declared bankruptcy. You have been asked to review the business and explain why it failed.

Cheri's Beauty Products Ltd.
Statement of Income
For the Years Ended December 31, 2011, 2010, and 2009

Thousands	2011	2010	2009
Sales	$41.0	$39.5	$37.1
Cost of sales	32.7	30.9	28.9
Selling expenses	8.0	7.2	6.8
Other expenses	0.4	1.0	0.8
Net income (net loss)	$ (0.1)	$ 0.4	$ 0.6
Additional data:			
Ending inventory	9.2	8.6	7.7

Required

Evaluate the trend of Cheri's Beauty Products' results of operations during 2009 through 2011. Consider the trends of sales, gross profit, and net income. Track the gross profit percentage (to three decimal places) and the rate of inventory turnover (to one decimal place) in each year—2009, 2010, and 2011. Also discuss the role that selling expenses must have played in Cheri's Beauty Products' difficulties.

Quiz

Test your understanding of accounting for inventory by answering the following questions. Select the best choice from among the possible answers given.

Q6-31 Riverside Software began January with $3,500 of merchandise inventory. During January, Riverside made the following entries for its inventory transactions:

Inventory	6,000	
Accounts Payable		6,000
Accounts Receivable	7,200	
Sales Revenue		7,200
Cost of Goods Sold	5,500	
Inventory		5,500

What was the value of Riverside's inventory at the end of January?

a. $0
b. $4,000
c. $4,500
d. $5,000

Q6-32 Use the data in Question Q6-31. What is Riverside's gross profit for January?

a. $0
b. $1,700
c. $5,000
d. $7,200

Q6-33 When does the cost of inventory become an expense?

a. When cash is collected from the customer
b. When inventory is purchased from the supplier
c. When payment is made to the supplier
d. When inventory is delivered to a customer

Questions Q6-34 and Q6-35 use the following facts. Leading Edge Frame Shop wants to know the effect of different inventory costing methods on its financial statements. Inventory and purchases data for April follow.

			Units	Unit Cost	Total Cost
April	1	Beginning inventory	2,000	$10.00	$20,000
	4	Purchase	1,000	10.60	10,600
	9	Sale	(1,500)		

Q6-34 If Leading Edge uses the FIFO method, the cost of the ending inventory will be

a. $10,600
b. $15,000
c. $15,300
d. $15,600

Q6-35 If Leading Edge uses the weighted-average-cost method, cost of goods sold will be

a. $10,600
b. $15,000
c. $15,300
d. $15,600

Q6-36 In a period of rising prices,

a. Gross profit under FIFO will be higher than under weighted-average cost.
b. Weighted-average-cost inventory will be greater than FIFO inventory.
c. Cost of goods sold under weighted-average cost will be less than under FIFO.
d. Net income under weighted-average cost will be higher than under FIFO.

Q6-37 The income statement for Heritage Health Foods shows gross profit of $144,000, operating expenses of $130,000, and cost of goods sold of $216,000. What is the amount of net sales revenue?

a. $274,000
b. $246,000
c. $360,000
d. $490,000

Q6-38 The words "net realizable value" as used in "the lower of cost and net realizable value" generally mean

a. Original cost
b. Market value
c. Retail market price
d. Liquidation price

Q6-39 The sum of ending inventory and cost of goods sold is

a. Goods available for sale
b. Net purchases
c. Gross profit
d. Beginning inventory

Q6-40 The following data come from the inventory records of Dodge Company:

Net sales revenue	$620,000
Beginning inventory	60,000
Ending inventory	40,000
Net purchases	400,000

Based on these facts, the gross profit for Dodge Company is

a. $150,000
b. $220,000
c. $190,000
d. Some other amount ($______)

Q6-41 Elizabeth Baker Cosmetics ended May with inventory of $20,000. Elizabeth Baker expects to end June with inventory of $15,000 after cost of goods sold of $90,000. How much inventory must Elizabeth Baker purchase during June to accomplish these results?

a. $85,000
b. $95,000
c. $105,000
d. Cannot be determined from the data given

Q6-42 Two financial ratios that clearly distinguish a discount chain such as Walmart from a high-end retailer such as Tiffany & Co. are the gross profit percentage and the rate of inventory turnover. Which set of relationships is most likely for Tiffany?

	Gross Profit Percentage	Inventory Turnover
a.	High	High
b.	Low	Low
c.	Low	High
d.	High	Low

Q6-43 Sales are $500,000, and cost of goods sold is $300,000. Beginning and ending inventories are $25,000 and $35,000, respectively. How many times did the company turn its inventory over during this period?

a. 16.7 times
b. 6.7 times
c. 8 times
d. 10 times

Q6-44 Tulsa Inc. reported the following data:

Freight-in	$ 20,000	Sales returns	$ 10,000
Purchases	205,000	Purchase returns	6,000
Beginning inventory	50,000	Sales revenue	490,000
Purchase discounts	4,000	Ending inventory	40,000

Tulsa's gross profit percentage is

a. 47.9%
b. 52.1%
c. 53.1%
d. 54.0%

Q6-45 Sherman Tank Company had the following for the first quarter of 2011:

Beginning inventory, $50,000 Net purchases, $75,000
Net sales revenue, $90,000 Gross profit rate, 30%

By the gross profit method, the ending inventory should be

a. $62,000
b. $63,000
c. $64,000
d. $65,000

Q6-46 An error understated Rice Corporation's December 31, 2011, ending inventory by $40,000. What effect will this error have on total assets and net income for 2011?

	Assets	Net Income
a.	No effect	No effect
b.	No effect	Overstate
c.	Understate	Understate
d.	Understate	No effect

Q6-47 What is the effect of Rice Corporation's 2011 inventory error on net income for 2012?

a. No effect
b. Understate
c. Overstate

Problems

(Group A)

Learning Objective 1 2
Accounting for inventory in a perpetual system

P6-48A Best Buy purchases merchandise inventory by the crate; each crate of inventory is a unit. The fiscal year of Best Buy ends each February 28.

Assume you are dealing with a single Best Buy store in Toronto, Ontario, and that the store experienced the following: The store began fiscal year 2011 with an inventory of 20,000 units that cost a total of $1,000,000. During the year, the store purchased merchandise on account as follows:

April (30,000 units @ cost of $60)	$1,800,000
August (50,000 units @ cost of $64)	3,200,000
November (60,000 units @ cost of $70)	4,200,000
Total purchases	$9,200,000

Cash payments on account totalled $8,800,000.

During fiscal year 2011, the store sold 150,000 units of merchandise for $14,400,000. Cash accounted for $5,000,000 of this, and the balance was on account. Best Buy uses the weighted-average-cost method for inventories.

Operating expenses for the year were $4,000,000. The store paid 80% in cash and accrued the rest as accrued liabilities. The store accrued income tax at the rate of 33%.

Required

1. Make summary journal entries to record the store's transactions for the year ended February 28, 2011. Best Buy uses a perpetual inventory system.
2. Prepare a T-account to show the activity in the Inventory account.
3. Prepare the store's income statement for the year ended February 28, 2011. Show totals for gross profit, income before tax, and net income.

Learning Objective 2
Measuring cost of goods sold and ending inventory—perpetual system

P6-49A Assume an outlet of The Runner's Store began August 2011 with 40 pairs of running shoes that cost the store $40 each. The sale price of these shoes was $70. During August, the store completed these inventory transactions:

			Units	Unit Cost	Unit Sale Price
Aug.	3	Sale	16	$40	$70
	8	Purchase	80	41	
	11	Sale	24	40	70
	19	Sale	9	41	72
	24	Sale	30	41	72
	30	Purchase	18	42	

Required

1. The preceding data are taken from the store's perpetual inventory records. Which cost method does the store use? Explain how you arrived at your answer.
2. Determine the store's cost of goods sold for August. Also compute gross profit for August.
3. What is the cost of the store's August 31 inventory of running shoes?

Learning Objective 2
Computing inventory by two methods—perpetual system

P6-50A Army-Navy Surplus Ltd. began March 2011 with 70 tents that cost $20 each. During the month, Army-Navy Surplus made the following purchases at cost:

March	4	100 tents	@ $22	=	$2,200
	19	160 tents	@ 24	=	3,840
	25	40 tents	@ 25	=	1,000

Army-Navy Surplus sold 320 tents, and at March 31 the ending inventory consists of 50 tents. The sale price of each tent was $45.

Required

1. Determine the cost of goods sold and ending inventory amounts for March under (a) weighted-average cost and (b) FIFO cost. Round weighted-average cost per unit to four decimal places, and round all other amounts to the nearest dollar.
2. Explain why cost of goods sold is highest under weighted-average cost. Be specific.
3. Prepare Army-Navy Surplus's income statement for March 2011. Report gross profit. Operating expenses totalled $4,000. Army-Navy Surplus uses weighted-average costing for inventory. The income tax rate is 21%.

P6-51A The records of Armstrong Aviation Supply Inc. include the following accounts for inventory of aviation fuel at December 31, 2011:

Learning Objective 2
Applying the different inventory costing methods—perpetual system

Inventory

Jan. 1	Balance	700 units @ $7.00	4,900		
Mar. 6	Purchase	300 units @ 7.05	2,115		
June 22	Purchase	8,400 units @ 7.50	63,000		
Oct. 4	Purchase	500 units @ 8.50	4,250		

Sales Revenue

	Dec. 31	9,000 units	127,800

Required

1. Prepare a partial income statement through gross profit under the weighted-average-cost and FIFO methods. Round weighted-average cost per unit to four decimal places and all other amounts to the nearest dollar.
2. Which inventory method would you use to minimize income tax? Explain why this method causes income tax to be the lowest.

P6-52A AMC Trade Mart has recently had lacklustre sales. The rate of inventory turnover has dropped, and the merchandise is gathering dust. At the same time, competition has forced AMC's suppliers to lower the prices that AMC will pay when it replaces its inventory. It is now December 31, 2011, and the current net realizable value of AMC's ending inventory is $80,000 below what AMC actually paid for the goods, which was $190,000. Before any adjustments at the end of the period, the Cost of Goods Sold account has a balance of $780,000.

Learning Objective 3
Applying the lower-cost-and-net-realizable-value rule to inventories—perpetual system

What accounting action should AMC take in this situation? Give any journal entry required. At what amount should AMC report Inventory on the balance sheet? At what amount should the company report cost of goods sold on the income statement? Discuss the accounting characteristic that is most relevant to this situation.

Are there circumstances that would allow AMC to increase the value of its inventory? Are there limits to which the value of the inventory may be increased?

P6-53A Chocolate Treats Ltd. and Coffee Bars Inc. are both specialty food chains. The two companies reported these figures, in thousands:

Learning Objective 4
Using gross profit percentage and inventory turnover to evaluate two companies

Chocolate Treats Ltd.
Statement of Operations

	Fiscal Year	
Thousands	**2011**	**2010**
Revenues:		
Net sales	$543	$708
Costs and Expenses:		
Cost of goods sold	475	598
General and administrative expenses	68	55

Chocolate Treats Ltd.
Balance Sheet

Thousands	January 31, 2011	2010
Assets		
Current assets:		
Cash and cash equivalents	$17	$28
Receivables	27	30
Inventories	24	29

Coffee Bars Inc.
Statement of Earnings

Thousands	Fiscal Year 2011	2010
Net sales	$7,787	$6,369
Cost of goods sold	3,179	2,605
Selling, general, and administrative expenses	2,948	2,363

Coffee Bars Inc.
Balance Sheet

Thousands	Year End 2011	2010
Assets		
Current assets:		
Cash and temporary investments	$313	$174
Receivables, net	224	191
Inventories	636	546

Required

1. Compute the gross profit percentage and the rate of inventory turnover for Chocolate Treats and for Coffee Bars for 2011.
2. Based on these statistics, which company looks more profitable? Why? What other expense category should we consider in evaluating these two companies?

Learning Objective 5
Estimating inventory by the gross profit method; preparing the income statement

P6-54A Suppose an Indigo bookstore lost inventory in a fire. To file an insurance claim, Indigo must estimate its inventory by the gross profit method. For the past two years, Indigo's gross profit has averaged 40% of net sales. Indigo's inventory records reveal the following data:

Inventory, July 1, 2011	$ 360,000
Transactions during July	
Purchases	628,000
Purchase discounts	4,500
Purchase returns	9,000
Sales revenue	1,000,000
Sales returns	170,000

Required

1. Estimate the cost of the lost inventory, using the gross profit method.
2. Prepare the July 2011 income statement through gross profit. Show the detailed computation of cost of goods sold in a separate schedule.

P6-55A Here are condensed versions of Pontiac Convenience Store's most recent income statement and balance sheet. Because the business is organized as a proprietorship, it pays no corporate income tax.

Learning Objective 1
Determining the amount of inventory to purchase

Pontiac Convenience Store
Income Statement
For the Year Ended December 31, 2011

Sales	$900,000
Cost of sales	700,000
Gross profit	200,000
Operating expenses	80,000
Net income	$120,000

Pontiac Convenience Store
Balance Sheet
December 31, 2011

Assets		Liabilities and Capital	
Cash	$ 70,000	Accounts payable	$ 35,000
Inventories	35,000	Note payable	280,000
Land and		Total liabilities	315,000
buildings, net	360,000	Owner, capital	150,000
Total assets	$465,000	Total liabilities and capital	$465,000

The owner is budgeting for 2012. She expects sales and cost of goods sold to increase by 8%. To meet customer demand for the increase in sales, ending inventory will need to be $50,000 at December 31, 2012. The owner hopes to earn a net income of $160,000 next year.

Required

1. One of the most important decisions a manager makes is the amount of inventory to purchase. Compute the amount of inventory to purchase in 2012.
2. Prepare the store's budgeted income statement for 2012 to reach the target net income of $160,000.

P6-56A Columbia Video Sales Ltd. reported the following data (millions). The shareholders are very happy with Columbia's steady increase in net income.

Learning Objective 6
Correcting inventory errors over a three-year period

Auditors discovered that the ending inventory for 2009 was understated by $1 million and that the ending inventory for 2010 was also understated by $1 million. The ending inventory for 2011 was correct.

Columbia Video Sales Ltd.
Income Statements for the Years Ended

(Amounts in millions)	2011		2010		2009	
Net sales revenue		$36		$33		$30
Cost of goods sold:						
Beginning inventory	$ 6		$ 5		$4	
Purchases	26		24		22	
Goods available for sale	32		29		26	
Less: Ending inventory	(7)		(6)		(5)	
Cost of goods sold		25		23		21
Gross profit		11		10		9
Total operating expenses		8		8		8
Net income		$ 3		$ 2		$ 1

Required

1. Show corrected income statements for each of the three years.
2. How much did these assumed corrections add to or take away from Columbia's total net income over the three-year period? How did the corrections affect the trend of net income?
3. Will Columbia's shareholders still be happy with the company's trend of net income? Give the reason for your answer.

(Group B)

Learning Objective ❶❷
Accounting for inventory in a perpetual system

P6-57B Italian Leather Goods Inc. began 2011 with an inventory of 50,000 units that cost $1,500,000. During the year the store purchased merchandise on account as follows:

March (40,000 units @ cost of $32)	$1,280,000
August (40,000 units @ cost of $34)	1,360,000
October (180,000 units @ cost of $35)	6,300,000
Total purchases	$8,940,000

Cash payments on account totalled $8,610,000.

During 2011, the company sold 260,000 units of merchandise for $12,900,000. Cash accounted for $4,700,000 of this, and the balance was on account. Italian Leather Goods uses the weighted-average-cost method for inventories.

Operating expenses for the year were $2,080,000. Italian Leather Goods paid 60% in cash and accrued the rest as accrued liabilities. The company accrued income tax at the rate of 32%.

Required

1. Make summary journal entries to record the Italian Leather Goods transactions for the year ended December 31, 2011. The company uses a perpetual inventory system.
2. Prepare a T-account to show the activity in the Inventory account.
3. Prepare the Italian Leather Goods Inc. income statement for the year ended December 31, 2011. Show totals for gross profit, income before tax, and net income.

Learning Objective ❷
Measuring cost of goods sold and ending inventory—perpetual system

P6-58B Whitewater Sports Ltd. began July 2011 with 50 backpacks that cost $19 each. The sale price of each backpack was $36. During July, Whitewater completed these inventory transactions:

			Units	Unit Cost	Unit Sale Price
July	2	Purchase	12	$20	
	8	Sale	37	19	$36
	13	Sale	13	19	36
		Sale	4	20	37
	17	Purchase	24	20	
	22	Sale	15	20	37

Required

1. The preceding data are taken from Whitewater's perpetual inventory records. Which cost method does Whitewater use? How can you tell?
2. Determine Whitewater's cost of goods sold for July. Also compute gross profit for July.
3. What is the cost of Whitewater's July 31 inventory of backpacks?

P6-59B Spice Inc. began October 2011 with 100 shirts that cost $76 each. During October, the store made the following purchases at cost:

Learning Objective 2
Computing inventory by two methods—perpetual system

Oct.	3	200 @	$81	=	$16,200
	12	90 @	82	=	7,380
	24	240 @	85	=	20,400

Spice sold 500 shirts and ended October with 130 shirts. The sale price of each shirt was $130.

Required

1. Determine the cost of goods sold and ending inventory amounts by the weighted-average-cost and FIFO cost methods. Round weighted-average cost per unit to three decimal places, and round all other amounts to the nearest dollar.
2. Explain why cost of goods sold is highest under weighted-average cost. Be specific.
3. Prepare Spice's income statement for October 2011. Report gross profit. Operating expenses totalled $10,000. Spice uses the weighted-average-cost method for inventory. The income tax rate is 23%.

P6-60B The records of Sonic Sound Systems Inc. include the following for cases of CDs at December 31, 2011:

Learning Objective 2
Applying the different inventory costing methods—perpetual system

Inventory

Jan.	1	Balance	300 cases	@ $300	121,500	
			100 cases	@ 315		
May	19	Purchase	600 cases	@ 335	201,000	
Aug.	12	Purchase	400 cases	@ 350	140,000	
Oct.	4	Purchase	700 cases	@ 370	259,000	

Sales Revenue

	Dec. 31	1,800 cases	910,000

Required

1. Prepare a partial income statement through gross profit under the weighted-average-cost and FIFO cost methods. Round weighted-average cost per unit to four decimal places and all other amounts to the nearest dollar.
2. Which inventory method would you use to report the highest net income? Explain why this method produces the highest reported income.

P6-61B Westside Copiers Ltd. has recently been plagued with lacklustre sales. The rate of inventory turnover has dropped, and some of the company's merchandise is gathering dust. At the same time, competition has forced some of Westside's suppliers to lower the prices that Westside will pay when it replaces its inventory. It is now December 31, 2011. The current net realizable value of Westside's ending inventory is $6,800,000, which is far less than the amount Westside paid for the goods, $8,900,000. Before any adjustments at the end of the period, Westside's Cost of Goods Sold account has a balance of $36,400,000.

Learning Objective 3
Applying the lower-of-cost-and-net-realizable-value rule to inventories—perpetual system

What accounting action should Westside Copiers take in this situation? Give any journal entry required. At what amount should Westside report Inventory on the balance sheet? At what amount should Westside report Cost of Goods Sold on the income statement? Discuss the accounting characteristic that is most relevant to this situation.

Are there circumstances that would allow Westside Copiers to increase the value of its inventory? Are there limits to which the value of inventory may be increased?

Learning Objective 4
Using gross profit percentage and inventory turnover to evaluate two leading companies

P6-62B Trans Canada Motors Ltd. and X Country Trucks Inc. are competitors. The companies reported these amounts, in millions. In January 2012, you wish to make an investment in one of these companies. Results for 2011 are not yet available.

Trans Canada Motors Ltd.
Statement of Earnings

		Fiscal Years	
Amounts in millions	**2010**	**2009**	**2008**
Net sales	$84.2	$73.6	$68.9
Cost of sales	63.4	55.2	52.6
Selling, general, and administrative expenses	12.2	11.3	11.2

Trans Canada Motors Ltd.
Balance Sheet

		Year-End	
Amounts in millions	**2010**	**2009**	**2008**
Assets			
Cash and cash equivalents	$11.3	$16.4	$13.9
Accounts receivable	13.4	10.9	9.9
Inventories	8.0	7.8	6.9

X Country Trucks Inc.
Statement of Operations

		Fiscal Years	
Amounts in millions	**2010**	**2009**	**2008**
Net sales	$24.0	$19.3	$13.9
Cost of sales	15.9	13.7	9.9
Selling, general, and administrative expenses	3.0	2.4	1.9

X Country Trucks Inc
Balance Sheet

		Year-End	
Amounts in millions	**2010**	**2009**	**2008**
Assets			
Cash and cash equivalents	$9.4	$6.4	$3.5
Accounts receivable	6.0	1.3	0.9
Inventories	0.4	0.3	0.2

Required

1. Compute both companies' gross profit percentage and their rates of inventory turnover during 2009 and 2008.
2. Can you tell from these statistics which company should be more profitable in percentage terms? Why? What other important category of expenses do the gross profit percentage and the inventory turnover ratio fail to consider?

P6-63B Assume McMillan Tire Ltd. lost some inventory in a fire. To file an insurance claim, McMillan must estimate its ending inventory by the gross profit method. Assume that, for the past two years, McMillan's gross profit has averaged 40% of net sales. Suppose the company's inventory records reveal the following data at June 15, 2011, the date of the fire.

Learning Objective 5
Estimating inventory by the gross profit method; preparing the income statement

Inventory, January 1	$1,200,000
Transactions during the year:	
Purchases	6,500,000
Purchase discounts	100,000
Purchase returns	10,000
Sales revenue	8,600,000
Sales returns	20,000

Required

1. Estimate the cost of the ending inventory lost in the fire using the gross profit method.
2. Prepare McMillan Tire Ltd.'s income statement through gross profit for the period up to the date of the fire. Date the statement "For the Period Up to the Fire." Show the detailed computations of cost of goods sold in a separate schedule.

P6-64B Margison Shoe Stores Ltd.'s income statement and balance sheet reported the following. The business is organized as a partnership, so it pays no corporate income tax. The owners are budgeting for 2012. They expect sales and cost of goods sold to increase by 10%. To meet customer demand, ending inventory will need to be $80,000 at December 31, 2012. The owners can lower operating expenses by $6,000 by doing some of the work themselves. They hope to earn a net income of $160,000 next year.

Learning Objective 1
Determining the amount of inventory to purchase

Margison Shoe Stores Ltd.
Income Statement
For the Year Ended December 31, 2011

Sales	$960,000
Cost of goods sold	720,000
Gross profit	240,000
Operating expenses	110,000
Net income	$130,000

Margison Shoe Stores Ltd.
Balance Sheet
December 31, 2011

Assets		Liabilities and Capital	
Cash	$ 40,000	Accounts payable	$ 30,000
Inventories	70,000	Note payable	190,000
Land and		Total liabilities	220,000
buildings, net	270,000	Owner, capital	160,000
Total assets	$380,000	Total liabilities and capital	$380,000

Required

1. One of the most important decisions a business owner makes is the amount of inventory to purchase. Compute the amount of inventory to purchase in 2012.
2. Prepare the store's budgeted income statement for 2012 to reach the target net income of $160,000.

P6-65B The accounting records of Oriental Rugs show these data (in thousands).

As the auditor, you discovered that the ending inventory for 2009 was overstated by $100,000 and that the ending inventory for 2010 was understated by $50,000. The ending inventory at December 31, 2011, was correct.

Learning Objective 6
Correcting inventory errors over a three-year period

Oriental Rugs
Income Statements for the Years Ended

(Amounts in thousands)	2011		2010		2009	
Net sales revenue		$1,400		$1,200		$1,100
Cost of goods sold:						
Beginning inventory	$ 400		$ 300		$200	
Purchases	800		700		600	
Goods available for sale	1,200		1,000		800	
Less ending inventory	(500)		(400)		(300)	
Cost of goods sold		700		600		500
Gross profit		700		600		600
Total operating expenses		500		430		450
Net income		$ 200		$ 170		$ 150

Required

1. Show correct income statements for each of the three years.
2. How much did these corrections add to, or take away from, Oriental Rugs' total net income over the three-year period? How did the corrections affect the trend of net income?

Apply Your Knowledge

Decision Cases

Learning Objective 1 2
Assessing the impact of a year-end purchase of inventory

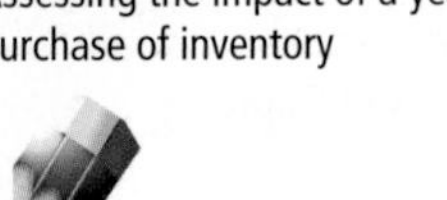

Case 1. Duracraft Corporation is nearing the end of its first year of operations. Duracraft made inventory purchases of $926,000 during the year, as follows:

January	1,500 units	@	$120.00	=	$ 180,000
July	3,000		142.00		426,000
November	2,000		160.00		320,000
Totals	6,500				$926,000

Sales for the year are 6,000 units for $1,800,000 of revenue. Expenses other than cost of goods sold and income taxes total $425,000. The president of the company is undecided about whether to adopt the FIFO method or the weighted-average-cost method for inventories. The income tax rate is 30%.

Required

1. To aid company decision making, prepare income statements under FIFO and under weighted-average cost.
2. Compare the net income under FIFO with net income under weighted-average cost. Which method produces the higher net income? What causes this difference? Be specific.

Learning Objective 2
Assessing the impact of the inventory costing method on the financial statements

Case 2. The inventory costing method a company chooses can affect the financial statements and, thus, the decisions of the people who use those statements.

Required

1. Company A uses the weighted-average-cost inventory method and discloses that in notes to the financial statements. Company B uses the FIFO method to account for its inventory.

Company B does not disclose which inventory method it uses. Company B reports a higher net income than Company A. In which company would you prefer to invest? Give your reason. Assume rising inventory costs.

2. The lower-of-cost-and-net-realizable-value rule is an accepted accounting concept. Would you want management to follow this rule in accounting for inventory if you were a shareholder or a creditor of a company? Give your reason.
3. Super Sports Company follows the lower-of-cost-and-net-realizable-value rule (LCNRV) and writes the value of its inventory of tents down to net realizable value, which has declined below cost. The following year, an unexpected camping craze results in a demand for tents that far exceeds supply, and the net realizable value increases above the previous cost. What effect will the LCNRV rule have on the income of Super Sports over the two years?

Ethical Issue

During 2010, Vanguard Inc. changed to the weighted-average-cost method of accounting for inventory. Suppose that during 2011, Vanguard changes back to the FIFO method and the following year Vanguard switches back to weighted-average cost again.

Required

1. What would you think of a company's ethics if it changed accounting methods every year?
2. What accounting characteristic would changing methods every year violate?
3. Who can be harmed when a company changes its accounting methods too often? How?

Focus on Financials

Gildan Activewear Inc.

Learning Objective ①③④
Analyzing inventories

The notes are part of the financial statements. They give details that would clutter the statements. This case will help you learn to use a company's inventory notes. Refer to Gildan Activewear Inc.'s statements and related notes in Appendix A at the end of the book and answer the following questions:

1. How much was Gildan's inventory at October 4, 2009? What about at October 5, 2008?
2. How does Gildan value its inventories? Which cost method does the company use?
3. Why may Gildan's gross profit not be comparable to other companies? Which accounting characteristic is referred to in your answer?
4. Did Gildan's gross profit percentage on company sales improve or deteriorate in 2009 compared to 2008?
5. Would you rate Gildan's rate of inventory turnover as fast or slow in comparison to most other companies? Explain your answer.

Group Project

Learning Objective ④
Comparing companies' inventory turnover ratios

Obtain the annual reports of 10 companies, two from each of five different industries. Most companies' financial statements can be downloaded from their Web sites.

1. Compute each company's gross profit percentage and rate of inventory turnover for the most recent two years. If annual reports are unavailable or do not provide enough data for multiple-year computations, you can gather financial statement data from SEDAR.
2. For the industries of the companies you are analyzing, obtain the industry averages for gross profit percentage and inventory turnover.

3. How well does each of your companies compare to the other company in its industry? How well do your companies compare to the average for their industry? What insight about your companies can you glean from these ratios?
4. Write a memo to summarize your findings, stating whether your group would invest in each of the companies it has analyzed.

Quick Check Answers

1. *c*
2. *e*
3. *a*
4. *a [(25 × $5) + (25 × $6) = $275]*
5. *b (10 × $7 + 5 × $6 =$100)*
6. *a (15 × [($125 + $180 + $70) ÷ 65] = $86.54)*
7. *c*
8. *c*
9. *b*
10. *c ($124,000 − $64,000 = $60,000)*
11. *d ($10,000 + X − $20,000 = $130,000; X = $140,000)*
12. *d ($20,000 + $80,000 − $4,000 + $5,000 − $24,000 = $77,000)*
13. *a [($180,000 − $77,000)/$180,000 = 0.572]*
14. *b [$77,000 ÷ ($20,000 + $24,000)/2 = 3.5]*
15. *d [$60,000 + $180,000 − ($300,000 × [1 − 0.30]) = $30,000]*
16. *b*

Appendix 6A

Accounting for Inventory in the Periodic System

In the periodic inventory system, the business keeps no running record of the merchandise. Instead, at the end of the period, the business counts inventory on hand and applies the unit costs to determine the cost of ending inventory. This inventory figure appears on the balance sheet and is used to compute cost of goods sold.

Recording Transactions in the Periodic System

In the periodic system, throughout the period the Inventory account carries the beginning balance left over from the preceding period. The business records purchases of inventory in the Purchases account (an expense). Then, at the end of the period, the Inventory

EXHIBIT 6A-1 Recording and Reporting Inventories—Periodic System (amounts assumed)

PANEL A—Recording Transactions and the T-accounts (all amounts are assumed)

		Debit	Credit
1.	Purchases	560,000	
	Accounts Payable		560,000
	Purchased inventory on account.		
2.	Accounts Receivable	900,000	
	Sales Revenue		900,000
	Sold inventory on account.		
3.	End-of-period entries to update Inventory and record Cost of Goods Sold (COGS):		
	a. Cost of Goods Sold	100,000	
	Inventory (beginning balance)		100,000
	Transferred beginning inventory to COGS.		
	b. Inventory (ending balance)	120,000	
	Cost of Goods Sold		120,000
	Set up ending inventory based on physical count.		
	c. Cost of Goods Sold	560,000	
	Purchases		560,000
	Transferred purchases to COGS.		

The T-accounts show the following:

Inventory	
100,000*	100,000
120,000	
120,000	

Cost of Goods Sold	
100,000	120,000
560,000	
540,000	

*Beginning Inventory was $100,000.

PANEL B—Reporting in the Financial Statements

Income Statement (Partial)

Sales revenue		$900,000
Cost of goods sold:		
Beginning inventory	$100,000	
Purchases	560,000	
Goods available for sale	660,000	
Ending inventory	(120,000)	
Cost of goods sold		540,000
Gross profit		$360,000

Ending Balance Sheet (Partial)

Current Assets:	
Cash	$ XXX
Temporary investments	XXX
Accounts receivable	XXX
Inventory	120,000
Prepaid expenses	XXX

account must be updated for the financial statements. A journal entry removes the beginning balance by crediting Inventory and debiting Cost of Goods Sold. A second journal entry sets up the ending inventory balance, based on the physical count. The final entry in this sequence transfers the amount of Purchases to Cost of Goods Sold. These end-of-period entries can be made during the closing process.

Exhibit 6A-1 illustrates the accounting in the periodic system. After the process is complete, Inventory has its correct ending balance of $120,000, and Cost of Goods Sold shows $540,000.

Exhibit 6A-2 illustrates the inventory-related journal entries for a perpetual inventory system and a periodic inventory system.

EXHIBIT 6A-2 **Inventory-Related Journal Entries Under a Perpetual Inventory System Versus a Periodic Inventory System**

	Perpetual Inventory System				Periodic Inventory System		
Date	Accounts	Debit	Credit	Date	Accounts	Debit	Credit
Jan. 2	Inventory	600,000		Jan. 2	Purchases	600,000	
	Accounts payable		600,000		Accounts payable		600,000
	Purchased 1,000 units on account.				Purchased 1000 units on account.		
3	Inventory	4,000		3	Freight-in	4,000	
	Accounts payable		4,000		Accounts Payable		4,000
	Record freight fee on purchases.				Record freight fee on purchases.		
9	Accounts payable	25,000		9	Accounts payable	25,000	
	Inventory		25,000		Purchase returns and allowance..		25,000
	Returned goods to supplier for credit.				Returned goods to supplier for credit.		
11	Accounts payable	5,000		11	Accounts payable	5,000	
	Inventory		5,000		Purchase allowance		5,000
	Record purchase allowance.				Record purchase allowance.		
16	Accounts payable	14,000		16	Accounts payable	14,000	
	Inventory		14,000		Purchase discount		14,000
	Record purchase discount.				Record purchase discount.		
16	Accounts payable	560,000		16	Accounts payable	560,000	
	Cash		560,000		Cash		560,000
	Record payment.				Record payment.		
31	Accounts receivable	900,000		31	Accounts receivable	900,000	
	Sales revenue		900,000		Sales revenue		900,000
	Record sales on account.				Record sales on account.		
31	Cost of goods sold	540,000		31	No entry.		
	Inventory		540,000				
	Update inventory and COGS.						
31	No adjustments required.			31	Cost of goods sold	540,000	
					Inventory,* ending balance	120,000	
					Purchase allowance	5,000	
					Purchase returns and allow. ..	25,000	
					Purchase discount	14,000	
					Purchases		600,000
					Freight-in		4,000
					Inventory, beginning		100,000
					Close out temporary accounts to COGS and record ending inventory.		

*Determined by physical count.

Appendix Assignments

Short Exercises

Recording inventory transactions in the periodic system

S6A-1 Capital Technologies Inc. began 2011 with inventory of $20,000. During the year, Capital purchased inventory costing $100,000 and sold goods for $140,000, with all transactions on account. Capital ended the year with inventory of $30,000. Journalize all the necessary transactions under the periodic inventory system.

Computing cost of goods sold and preparing the income statement—periodic system

S6A-2 Use the data in Short Exercise S6A-1 to do the following for Capital Technologies Inc.:

1. Post to the Inventory and Cost of Goods Sold accounts.
2. Compute cost of goods sold by the cost-of-goods-sold model.
3. Prepare the December 2011 income statement of Capital Technologies Inc. through gross profit.

Exercises

Computing amounts for the GAAP inventory methods—periodic system

E6A-3 Suppose a technology company's inventory records for a particular computer chip indicate the following at October 31:

Oct. 1	Beginning inventory....................	5 units	@ $160	=	$ 800
8	Purchase	4 units	@ 160	=	640
15	Purchase	11 units	@ 170	=	1,870
26	Purchase	5 units	@ 180	=	900

The physical count of inventory at October 31 indicates that 8 units of inventory are on hand.

Required

Compute ending inventory and cost of goods sold, using each of the following methods. Round all amounts to the nearest dollar.

1. Specific unit cost, assuming four $160 units and four $170 units are on hand
2. Weighted-average cost
3. First-in, first-out cost

Journalizing inventory transactions in the periodic system; computing cost of goods sold

E6A-4 Use the data in Exercise E6A-3 to journalize the following for the periodic system:

1. Total October purchases in one summary entry. All purchases were on credit.
2. Total October sales in a summary entry. Assume that the selling price was $300 per unit and that all sales were on credit.
3. October 31 entries for inventory. The company uses weighted-average cost. Post to the Cost of Goods Sold T-account to show how this amount is determined. Label each item in the account.
4. Show the computation of cost of goods sold by the cost-of-goods-sold model.

Problems

Computing cost of goods sold and gross profit on sales—periodic system

P6A-5 Assume a Roots outlet store began August 2011 with 40 units of inventory that cost $30 each. The sale price of these units was $60. During August, the store completed these inventory transactions:

			Units	Unit Cost	Unit Sale Price
Aug.	3	Sale	16	$30	$60
	8	Purchase	70	31	62
	11	Sale	24	30	60
	19	Sale	8	31	62
	24	Sale	30	31	62
	30	Purchase	28	32	73
	31	Sale	15	31	62

Required

1. Determine the store's cost of goods sold for August under the periodic inventory system. Assume the FIFO method.
2. Compute gross profit for August.

Recording transactions in the periodic system; reporting inventory items in the financial statements

P6A-6 Accounting records for Cookies for You Ltd. yield the following data for the year ended December 31, 2011 (amounts in thousands):

Inventory, December 31, 2010	$ 410
Purchases of inventory (on account)	3,200
Sales of inventory—80% on account; 20% for cash	4,830
Inventory at the lower of FIFO cost and net realizable value, December 31, 2011	600

Required

1. Journalize Cookies for You's inventory transactions for the year under the periodic system. Show all amounts in thousands. Use Exhibit 6A-1 as a model.
2. Report ending inventory, sales, cost of goods sold, and gross profit on the appropriate financial statement (amounts in thousands). Show the computation of cost of goods sold.

Property, Plant, and Equipment, and Intangible Assets

LEARNING OBJECTIVES

1. **Determine** the cost of property, plant, and equipment
2. **Account** for depreciation
3. **Examine** additional depreciation topics
4. **Analyze** the effect of property, plant, and equipment derecognition
5. **Account** for intangible assets and amortization
6. **Report** long-lived assets on the statement of cash flows

SPOTLIGHT

Have you ever gone to Canadian Tire to fill your car with gas? More than 50 years ago, this company began operations by just selling tires, and now offers many products and services including clothing, gas bars, and financial services. This Canadian company has grown substantially and today has total assets worth over $7 billion.

As you can see from the company's consolidated balance sheets on the following page, Canadian Tire's long-lived assets include property and equipment, goodwill, and intangible assets.

This chapter will complete our coverage of assets, except for investments, which we will examine in Chapter 10. Let's begin by examining the various types of long-lived assets.

Canadian Tire
Consolidated Balance Sheets
(Adapted)

($ in millions)	**As at January 3, 2009**	**As at December 29, 2007**
Current Assets		
1. Cash and cash equivalents	$ 429.0	$ —
2. Accounts receivable	824.1	715.0
3. Loans receivable	1,683.4	1,486.1
4. Merchandise inventories	917.5	778.7
5. Income taxes recoverable	64.2	53.2
6. Prepaid expenses and deposits	40.2	29.5
7. Future income taxes	20.2	75.7
8. Total current assets	3,978.6	3,138.2
9. Long-term receivables and other assets	265.4	231.2
10. Other long-term investments, net	25.2	7.6
11. Goodwill	70.7	51.8
12. Intangible assets	58.4	52.4
13. Property and equipment, net	3,389.8	3,283.6
14. Total assets	$7,788.1	$6,764.8

Types of Assets

Businesses use several types of assets that are classified as long-lived, such as property, plant, and equipment, and intangible assets. These assets are used in the business and are not held for sale.

Tangible long-lived assets are also called property, plant, and equipment. For example, buildings, airplanes, and equipment are tangible long-lived assets that decline in value while in use, and the expense associated with this is called depreciation. Of these assets, land is unique. Land is not expensed over time because its usefulness does not decrease. Many companies report tangible long-lived assets as property, plant, and equipment on the balance sheet. Canadian Tire calls them property and equipment.

Intangible assets are useful because of the special rights they carry. They have no physical form. Patents, copyrights, and trademarks are intangible assets, as is goodwill. Accounting for intangibles, except goodwill, is similar to accounting for tangible long-lived assets. Canadian Tire has several intangible assets on its balance sheet, including goodwill (line 11).

Accounting for long-lived tangible assets and intangibles has its own terminology. Different names apply to the individual assets and their corresponding expense accounts, as shown in Exhibit 7-1.

Unless stated otherwise, we describe accounting in accordance with International Financial Reporting Standards (IFRS) for financial-statement reporting to outsiders, as distinguished from reporting to the Canada Revenue Agency (CRA) for income tax purposes. Before examining the various types of capital assets, let's see how to value them.

EXHIBIT 7-1 **Long-Lived Asset Terminology**

Asset Account (Balance Sheet)	Related Expense Account (Income Statement)
Tangible Long-Lived Assets	
Land	None
Buildings, machinery and equipment, furniture and fixtures, and land improvements	Depreciation
Intangible Assets	Amortization (except goodwill)

Measuring the Cost of Property, Plant, and Equipment

OBJECTIVE

❶ **Determine** the cost of property, plant, and equipment

Here is a basic working rule for determining the cost of an asset:

The cost of any asset is the sum of all the costs incurred to bring the asset to its location and intended use. The cost of property, plant, and equipment includes its purchase price (less any purchase discounts), plus any taxes, commissions, and other amounts paid to make the asset ready for use. Because the specific costs differ for the various categories of property, plant, and equipment, we discuss the major groups individually.

Land

The cost of land includes its purchase price (cash plus any note payable given), real estate commission, survey fees, legal fees, and any back property taxes that the purchaser pays. Land cost also includes expenditures for grading and clearing the land and demolishing or removing unwanted buildings.

The cost of land does *not* include the cost of fencing, paving, sprinkler systems, and lighting. These are recorded in a separate account—called *land improvements*—and they are subject to depreciation.

Suppose Canadian Tire signs a $300,000 note payable to purchase 20 ha of land for a new retail store. Canadian Tire also pays $10,000 for real estate commission, $8,000 of back property tax, $5,000 for removal of an old building, a $1,000 survey fee, and $260,000 to pave the parking lot—all in cash. What is Canadian Tire's cost of this land?

Purchase price of land		$300,000
Add related costs:		
Real estate commission	$10,000	
Back property tax	8,000	
Removal of building	5,000	
Survey fee	1,000	
Total related costs		24,000
Total cost of land		$324,000

Note that the cost to pave the parking lot, $260,000, is *not* included in the land's cost, because the pavement is a land improvement. Canadian Tire would record the purchase of this land as follows:

Land	324,000	
Note Payable		300,000
Cash		24,000
To record the purchase of land.		

ASSETS	=	LIABILITIES	+	SHAREHOLDERS' EQUITY
+324,000 −24,000	=	+300,000	+	0

The purchase increases both assets and liabilities. There is no effect on equity.

Buildings, Machinery, and Equipment

The cost of constructing a building includes architectural fees, building permits, contractors' charges, and payments for material, labour, and overhead. The company may also include as cost the interest on money borrowed to construct a building or buy machinery and equipment for the building until the point in time when the building, machinery, and equipment are ready for their intended use.

When an existing building (new or old) is purchased, its cost includes the purchase price, brokerage commission, sales and other taxes paid, and all expenditures to repair and renovate the building for its intended purpose.

The cost of machinery and equipment includes its purchase price (less any discounts), plus transportation, insurance while in transit, sales and other taxes, purchase commission, installation costs, and any expenditures to test the asset before it is placed in service. The equipment cost will also include the cost of any special platforms used to support the equipment. After the asset is up and running, insurance, taxes, and maintenance costs are recorded as expenses, not as part of the asset's cost.

Land Improvements and Leasehold Improvements

For the Canadian Tire building, the cost to pave a parking lot ($260,000) would be recorded in a separate account titled Land Improvements. This account includes costs for other items such as driveways, signs, fences, and sprinkler systems. Although these assets are located on the land, they are subject to decay, and their cost should therefore be depreciated.

An airline such as WestJet leases some of its airplanes and other assets. The company customizes these assets to meet its special needs. For example, WestJet paints its logo on airplanes. These improvements are assets of WestJet Airlines Ltd., even though the company does not own the airplane. The cost of improvements to leased assets may appear under Property, Plant, and Equipment, or Other Long-Term Assets. The cost of leasehold improvements should be depreciated over the term of the lease or the life of the asset, whichever is shorter.

Lump-Sum (or Basket) Purchases of Assets

Businesses often purchase several assets as a group, or in a "basket," for a single lump-sum amount. For example, Great-West Lifeco Inc. may pay one price for land and a building. The company must identify the cost of each asset. The total cost is divided among the assets according to their relative fair values.

Suppose Great-West purchases land and a building in St. John's, Newfoundland, for a sales office. The building sits on 2 ha of land, and the combined purchase price of land and building is $2,800,000. An appraisal indicates that the land's fair value is $300,000 and that the building's market value is $2,700,000.

Great-West first calculates the ratio of each asset's fair value to the total fair value. Total appraised value is $2,700,000 + $300,000 = $3,000,000. Thus, the land, valued at $300,000, is 10% of the total fair value. The building's appraised value is 90% of the total. These percentages are then used to determine the cost of each asset, as follows:

Asset	Fair Value		Total Fair Value		Percentage of Total Fair Value		Total Cost		Cost of Each Asset
Land	$ 300,000	÷	$3,000,000	=	10%	×	$2,800,000	=	$ 280,000
Building	2,700,000	÷	3,000,000	=	90	×	2,800,000	=	2,520,000
Total	$3,000,000				100%				$2,800,000

If Great-West pays cash, the entry to record the purchase of the land and building is

Land	280,000	
Building	2,520,000	
Cash		2,800,000

ASSETS	=	LIABILITIES	+	SHAREHOLDERS' EQUITY
+280,000 +2,520,000 −2,800,000	=	0	+	0

Total assets don't change—merely the makeup of Great-West's assets.

STOP + THINK

How would WestJet Airlines Ltd. divide a $120,000 lump-sum purchase price for land, building, and equipment with estimated fair values of $40,000, $95,000, and $15,000, respectively?

Answer:

	Estimated Fair Value	Percentage of Total Fair Value	×	Total Cost	=	Cost of Each Asset
Land	$ 40,000	26.7%*	×	$120,000	=	$ 32,040
Building	95,000	63.3	×	120,000	=	75,960
Equipment	15,000	10.0	×	120,000	=	12,000
	$150,000	100.0%				$120,000

*$40,000/$150,000 = 0.267, and so on.

Capital Expenditure Versus an Immediate Expense

When a company spends money on property, plant, and equipment, it must decide whether to record an asset or an expense. Examples of these expenditures range from WestJet Airlines' purchase of a flight simulator from CAE Electronics to replacing a tire on a plane.

Expenditures that increase the asset's productivity or extend its useful life are called **capital expenditures**. For example, the cost of a major overhaul that extends the useful life of a Canadian Tire truck is a capital expenditure. Capital expenditures

EXHIBIT 7-2 Capital Expenditure or Immediate Expense for Costs Associated With a Van

Record an Asset for Capital Expenditures/Betterments	Record Repair and Maintenance Expense (Not an Asset) for an Expense
Extraordinary repairs:	*Ordinary repairs*:
Major engine overhaul	Repair of transmission or other mechanism
Modification of body for new use of van	Oil change, lubrication, and so on
Addition to storage capacity of van	Replacement tires, windshield, or a paint job

are said to be *capitalized,* which means the cost is added to an asset account and not expensed immediately. A major decision in accounting for property, plant, and equipment is whether to capitalize or expense a certain cost.

Costs that do not extend the asset's productivity or its useful life, but merely maintain the asset or restore it to working order, are considered repairs and are recorded as expenses. For example, Repair Expense is reported on the income statement. The costs of repainting a Canadian Tire truck, repairing a dented fender, and replacing tires are also expensed immediately. Exhibit 7-2 illustrates the distinction between capital expenditures and immediate expenses for van expenditures.

The distinction between a capital expenditure and an expense requires judgment: Does the cost extend the asset's usefulness or its useful life? If so, record an asset. If the cost merely repairs or maintains the asset or returns it to its prior condition, then record an expense.

Most companies expense all small costs, say, below $1,000. For higher costs, they follow the rule we gave above: they capitalize costs that extend the asset's usefulness or its useful life, and they expense all other costs. A conservative policy is one that avoids overstating assets and profits. A company that overstates its assets may get into trouble and have to defend itself in court. Whenever investors lose money because a company overstated its profits or its assets, the investors might file a lawsuit. The courts tend to be sympathetic to investor losses caused by shoddy accounting. The Ethics Alert below provides an example.

Accounting misstatements sometimes occur for asset costs. For example, a company may

- Expense a cost that should have been capitalized. This error overstates expenses and understates net income in the year of the error.
- Capitalize a cost that should have been expensed. This error understates expenses and overstates net income in the year of the error.

Is That Cost Really an Asset?

There is a world of difference between a capital expenditure and an expense. Just ask MCI. MCI WorldCom (now just MCI) got into hot water by missing the mark in its accounting for capital expenditures.

A few years ago—before cellular phones became so popular—long-distance (LD) phone service was extremely profitable for Sprint and MCI. These companies invested huge amounts on LD phone networks. MCI was one of the hottest stocks on Wall Street.

Almost overnight, cellular companies Cingular and Verizon began to siphon profits away from MCI. Profits grew thin and then turned to losses. MCI needed to protect its pacesetter image. But how?

MCI's chief financial officer, Scott Sullivan, made some highly unusual journal entries, as follows:

Line-Cost Assets	$billions	
Line-Cost Expenses		$billions
To reclassify expenses as assets.		

These line costs were payments MCI made to other companies (such as AT&T and Sprint) to transmit LD calls for MCI customers. It's a common practice for these companies to rent competitors' phone lines. But it's most unusual to record an expense and then later reclassify the expense as an asset.

The fundamental question is this: Is MCI's rental payment to transmit customer calls an expense or an asset?

Scott Sullivan rationalized that the rental payments were assets because they provided future business for MCI. Independent CPAs from KPMG disagreed. KPMG stated flat out that the rental payments were expenses because the LD calls lasted only minutes and provided no future benefit for MCI. KPMG was right. MCI was wrong. MCI's improper accounting created a scandal.

The take-away lesson from this is:

- Treat expenses as expenses and assets as assets!

Measuring Property, Plant, and Equipment Depreciation

As we've seen in previous chapters, property, plant, and equipment are reported on the balance sheet at carrying amount, which is

$$\text{Carrying amount of property, plant, and equipment} = \text{Cost} - \text{Accumulated depreciation}$$

Property, plant, and equipment wears out, grows obsolete, and loses value over time. To account for this process, we allocate an asset's cost to expense over its life—a process called **depreciation**. The depreciation process begins when an asset is availble for use, and continues (even if it is not being used) until the asset is removed. In the private enterprise sector, it is referred to as amortization. Exhibit 7-3 illustrates the depreciation process for the purchase of a Boeing 737 jet by WestJet Airlines.

EXHIBIT 7-3 Depreciation and the Allocation of Expense With Revenue

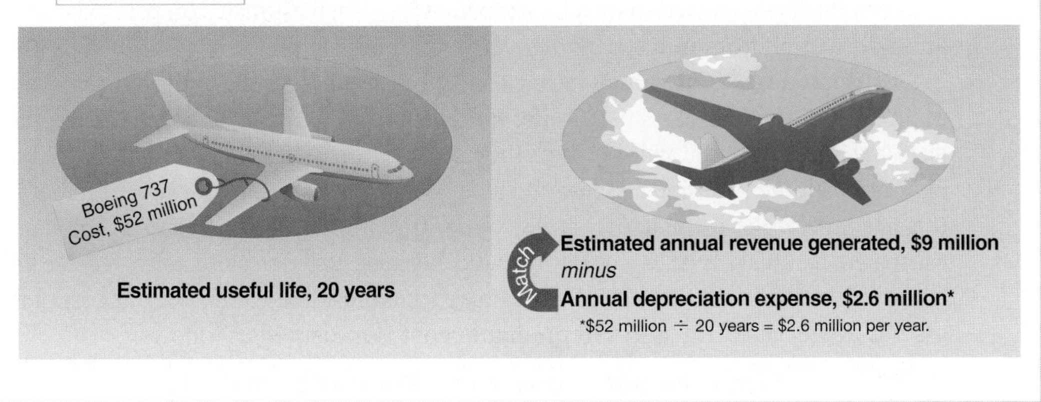

Recall that depreciation expense (not accumulated depreciation) is reported on the income statement.

Only land has an unlimited life and is not depreciated for accounting purposes. For most property, plant, and equipment, depreciation is caused by

- **Physical wear and tear.** For example, physical deterioration takes its toll on the usefulness of WestJet airplanes, vehicles, and buildings.
- **Obsolescence.** Computers and other electronic equipment may be *obsolete* before they deteriorate. An asset is obsolete when another asset can do the job more efficiently. An asset's useful life may be shorter than its physical life. WestJet and other companies depreciate their computers over a short period of time—perhaps four years—even though the computers will remain in working condition much longer.

Suppose WestJet buys a computer for use in scheduling flight crews. WestJet believes it will get four years of service from the computer, which will then be worthless. Under straight-line depreciation, WestJet expenses one-quarter of the asset's cost in each of its four years of use.

You've just seen what depreciation accounting is. Let's see what it is *not*.

1. **Depreciation is not a process of valuation.** Businesses do not record depreciation based on changes in the fair value of their property, plant, and equipment. Instead, businesses allocate the asset's cost to the periods of its useful life based on a specific depreciation method.
2. **Depreciation does not mean setting aside cash to replace assets as they wear out.** Any cash fund is entirely separate from depreciation.

How to Measure Depreciation

To measure depreciation for property, plant, and equipment, we must know its

1. Cost
2. Estimated useful life
3. Estimated residual value

We have already discussed cost, which is a known amount. The other two factors must be estimated.

Estimated useful life is the length of service expected from using the asset. Useful life may be expressed in years, units of output, kilometres, or some other measure. For example, the useful life of a building is stated in years. The useful life of a WestJet airplane or van may be expressed as the total number of kilometres the aircraft or vehicle is expected to travel. Companies base such estimates on past experience and information from industry and government publications.

Estimated residual value—also called *salvage value*—is the expected cash value of an asset at the end of its useful life. For example, WestJet may believe that a baggage-handling machine will be useful for seven years. After that time, WestJet may expect to sell the machine as scrap metal. The amount WestJet believes it can get for the machine is the estimated residual value. In computing depreciation, the asset's estimated residual value is *not* depreciated because WestJet expects to receive this amount from selling the asset. If there's no expected residual value, the full cost of the asset is depreciated. An asset's **depreciable cost** is measured as follows:

$$\text{Depreciable cost} = \text{Asset's cost} - \text{Estimated residual value}$$

Depreciation Methods

There are three main depreciation methods that will be discussed in this text:

- Straight-line
- Units-of-production
- Diminishing-balance—an accelerated depreciation method

These methods allocate different amounts of depreciation to each period. However, they all result in the same total amount of depreciation, which is the asset's depreciable cost. Exhibit 7-4 presents assumed data, which we will use to illustrate depreciation computations for a Canadian Tire van.

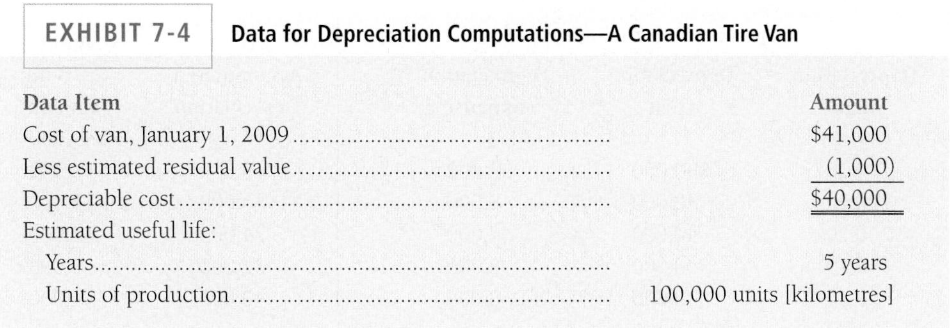

EXHIBIT 7-4 **Data for Depreciation Computations—A Canadian Tire Van**

Data Item	Amount
Cost of van, January 1, 2009	$41,000
Less estimated residual value	(1,000)
Depreciable cost	$40,000
Estimated useful life:	
Years	5 years
Units of production	100,000 units [kilometres]

Straight-Line Method. In the **straight-line (SL) method**, an equal amount of depreciation is assigned to each year (or period) of asset use. Depreciable cost is divided by useful life in years to determine the annual depreciation expense. Applied to the Canadian Tire van data from Exhibit 7-4, straight-line depreciation is

$$\text{Straight-line depreciation per year} = \frac{\text{Cost} - \text{Residual value}}{\text{Useful life, in years}}$$

$$= \frac{\$41{,}000 - \$1{,}000}{5}$$

$$= \$8{,}000$$

The entry to record depreciation is

Depreciation Expense	8,000	
Accumulated Depreciation		8,000

ASSETS	=	LIABILITIES	+	SHAREHOLDERS' EQUITY	−	EXPENSES
−8,000	=	0			−	8,000

Observe that depreciation decreases the asset (through Accumulated Depreciation) and also decreases equity (through Depreciation Expense). Let's assume that Canadian Tire purchased this van on January 1, 2009; Canadian Tire's fiscal year ends on December 31. Exhibit 7-5 gives a *straight-line depreciation schedule* for the van. The final column of the exhibit shows the *asset's carrying amount*, which is its cost less accumulated depreciation.

As an asset is used in operations, accumulated depreciation increases, and the carrying amount of the asset decreases. An asset's final carrying amount is its *residual value* ($1,000 in Exhibit 7-5). At the end of its useful life, the asset is said to be *fully depreciated*.

STOP + THINK

Imagine a company purchased a machine for $13,000 that had a useful life of five years and residual value of $3,000. If the asset's carrying amount was $7,000, how many more years of use would the machine have?

Answer:
The yearly depreciation would be $2,000 [($13,000 − $3,000)/5]. Therefore the years of use left would be 2 [($7,000 − $3,000)/$2,000)].

EXHIBIT 7-5 **Straight-Line Depreciation Schedule for a Canadian Tire Van**

		Depreciation for the Year							
Date	Asset Cost	Depreciation Rate		Depreciation Cost		Depreciation Expense	Accumulated Depreciation	Asset Carrying Amount
01-01-2009	$41,000							$41,000
31-12-2009		0.20*	×	$40,000	=	$8,000	$ 8,000	33,000
31-12-2010		0.20	×	40,000	=	8,000	16,000	25,000
31-12-2011		0.20	×	40,000	=	8,000	24,000	17,000
31-12-2012		0.20	×	40,000	=	8,000	32,000	9,000
31-12-2013		0.20	×	40,000	=	8,000	40,000	1,000

$^{*}\frac{1}{5\text{ years}} = 0.20$ per year

Units-of-Production Method. In the **units-of-production (UOP) method**, a fixed amount of depreciation is assigned to each *unit of output*, or service, produced by the asset. Depreciable cost is divided by useful life—in units of production—to determine this amount. This per-unit depreciation expense is then multiplied by the number of units produced each period to compute depreciation. The units-of-production depreciation for the Canadian Tire van data in Exhibit 7-4 is

$$\begin{aligned}\text{Units-of-production depreciation per unit of output} &= \frac{\text{Cost} - \text{Residual value}}{\text{Useful life, in units of production}}\\ &= \frac{\$41{,}000 - \$1{,}000}{100{,}000\text{ km}} = \$0.40/\text{km}\end{aligned}$$

Assume that the van is expected to be driven 20,000 km during the first year, 30,000 during the second, 25,000 during the third, 15,000 during the fourth, and 10,000 during the fifth. Exhibit 7-6 shows the UOP depreciation schedule.

The amount of UOP depreciation varies with the number of units the asset produces. In our example, the total number of units produced is 100,000. UOP depreciation does not depend directly on time, as do the other methods.

Diminishing-Balance Method. An **accelerated depreciation method** writes off a larger amount of the asset's cost near the start of its useful life than the straight-line method does. Double-diminishing-balance is the main accelerated depreciation method. The **double-diminishing-balance (DDB) method** computes annual depreciation by multiplying the asset's declining carrying amount by a constant percentage, which is two times the straight-line depreciation rate. Double-diminishing-balance amounts are computed as follows:

EXHIBIT 7-6 Units-of-Production Depreciation Schedule for a Canadian Tire Van

		Depreciation for the Year						
Date	Asset Cost	Depreciation Rate		Number of Units		Depreciation Expense	Accumulated Depreciation	Asset Carrying Amount
01-01-2009	$41,000							$41,000
31-12-2009		$0.40*	×	20,000	=	$ 8,000	$ 8,000	33,000
31-12-2010		0.40	×	30,000	=	12,000	20,000	21,000
31-12-2011		0.40	×	25,000	=	10,000	30,000	11,000
31-12-2012		0.40	×	15,000	=	6,000	36,000	5,000
31-12-2013		0.40	×	10,000	=	4,000	40,000	1,000

*($41,000 − $1,000)/100,000 km = $0.40/km.

- *First*, compute the straight-line depreciation rate per year. A five-year asset has a straight-line depreciation rate of 1/5, or 20% each year. A 10-year asset has a straight-line rate of 1/10, or 10%, and so on.
- *Second*, multiply the straight-line rate by 2 to compute the DDB rate. For a five-year asset, the DDB rate is 40% (20% × 2). A 10-year asset has a DDB rate of 20% (10% × 2).
- *Third*, multiply the DDB rate by the period's beginning asset carrying amount (cost less accumulated depreciation). Under the DDB method, ignore the residual value of the asset in computing depreciation, except during the last year. The DDB rate for the CanadianTire van in Exhibit 7-4 (page 345) is

$$\text{DDB depreciation rate per year} = \frac{1}{\text{Useful life, in years}} \times 2$$
$$= \frac{1}{5 \text{ years}} \times 2$$
$$= 20\% \times 2$$
$$= 40\%$$

- *Fourth,* determine the final year's depreciation amount—that is, the amount needed to reduce the asset carrying amount to its residual value. In Exhibit 7-7, the fifth and final year's DDB depreciation is $4,314: the carrying amount of $5,314 less the $1,000 residual value. *The residual value should not be depreciated* but should remain on the books until the asset is disposed of.

The DDB method differs from the other methods in two ways:

1. Residual value is ignored initially; in the first year, depreciation is computed on the asset's full cost.
2. Depreciation expense in the final year is whatever amount is needed to reduce the asset's carrying amount to its residual value.

EXHIBIT 7-7 **Double-Diminishing-Balance Depreciation Schedule for a Canadian Tire Van**

		Depreciation for the Year							
Date	Asset Cost	DDB Rate		Asset Carrying Amount		Depreciation Expense		Accumulated Depreciation	Asset Carrying Amount
01-01-2009	$41,000								$41,000
31-12-2009		0.40	×	$41,000	=	$16,400		$16,400	24,600
31-12-2010		0.40	×	24,600	=	9,840		26,240	14,760
31-12-2011		0.40	×	14,760	=	5,904		32,144	8,856
31-12-2012		0.40	×	8,856	=	3,542		35,686	5,314
31-12-2013						4,314*		40,000	1,000

*Last-year depreciation is the amount needed to reduce asset carrying amount to the residual value ($5,314 − $1,000 = $4,314).

STOP + THINK

What would you as a user of the company described in the Stop & Think on page 346 expect DDB depreciation to be for each year?

Answers:
Yr. 1: $5,200 ($13,000 × 40%)
Yr. 2: $3,120 ($7,800 × 40%)
Yr. 3: $1,680 ($13,000 − $5,200 − $3,120 − $3,000)*
Yr. 4: $0
Yr. 5: $0

*The asset is not depreciated below residual value.

Comparing Depreciation Methods

Let's compare the three methods in terms of the yearly amount of depreciation. The yearly amount of depreciation varies by method, but the total $40,000 depreciable cost is the same under all methods.

	Amount of Depreciation Per Year		
			Accelerated Method
Year	Straight-Line	Units-of-Production	Double-Diminishing-Balance
1	$ 8,000	$ 8,000	$16,400
2	8,000	12,000	9,840
3	8,000	10,000	5,904
4	8,000	6,000	3,542
5	8,000	4,000	4,314
Total	$40,000	$40,000	$40,000

IFRS (IAS 16) directs a business to choose a depreciation method that reflects the pattern in which the asset will be used. For an asset that generates revenue evenly over time, the straight-line method best meets this criterion. The units-of-production method best fits those assets that wear out because of physical use rather than obsolescence. The accelerated method (DDB) applies best to assets that generate greater amounts of revenue earlier in their useful lives and less in later years. For the private enterprise, depreciation should be recognized in a rational and systematic manner.

Exhibit 7-8 graphs annual depreciation amounts for the straight-line, units-of-production, and DDB methods. The graph of straight-line depreciation is flat through time because annual depreciation is the same in all periods. Units-of-production depreciation follows no particular pattern because annual depreciation depends on the use of the asset. Accelerated depreciation is greatest in the first year and less in the later years.

Recent surveys of companies in Canada and the United States indicate that straight-line depreciation is used by more than 80%. Around 10% use some form of accelerated depreciation and the rest use units of production and other methods. Many companies use more than one method.

For reporting in the financial statements, straight-line depreciation is most popular. As we shall see, however, many organizations use **capital cost allowance (CCA)**, a form of accelerated depreciation allowed for income-tax purposes by the *Income Tax Act*.

EXHIBIT 7-8 Depreciation Patterns Through Time

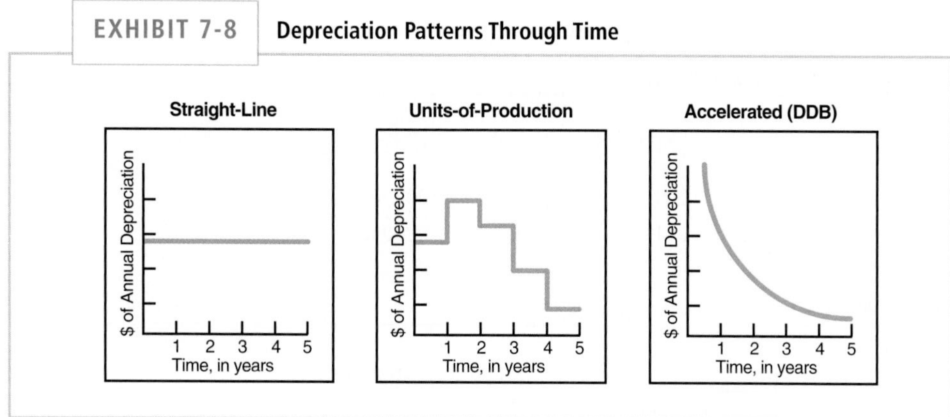

MID-CHAPTER SUMMARY PROBLEM

MyAccountingLab

Suppose you are a manager at Canadian Tire. The company purchased equipment on January 1, 2010, for $44,000. The expected useful life of the equipment is 10 years or 100,000 units of production, and its residual value is $4,000. Under three depreciation methods, the annual depreciation expense and the balance of accumulated depreciation at the end of 2010 and 2011 are as follows:

	Method A		Method B		Method C	
Year	Annual Depreciation Expense	Accumulated Depreciation	Annual Depreciation Expense	Accumulated Depreciation	Annual Depreciation Expense	Accumulated Depreciation
2010	$4,000	$4,000	$8,800	$ 8,800	$1,200	$1,200
2011	4,000	8,000	7,040	15,840	5,600	6,800

Required

1. Your assistant has provided you with the above information. Identify the depreciation method used in each instance, and show the equation and computation for each. (Round off to the nearest dollar.)

Name: Canadian Tire
Industry: Retailer
Accounting Period: The years 2010, 2011, 2012

2. Assume continued use of the same method through year 2012. Determine the annual depreciation expense, accumulated depreciation, and carrying amount of the equipment for 2010 through 2012 under each method, assuming 12,000 units of production in 2012.

Answers

Requirement 1

The straight-line method assigns the same depreciation expense to each year.

Method A: Straight-Line

Depreciable cost = $40,000 ($44,000 − $4,000)
Each year: $40,000/10 years = $4,000

The double-diminishing balance method assigns an expense amount that gets smaller every year. Do not include the residual value when using this method.

Method B: Double-Diminishing-Balance

$$\text{Rate} = \frac{1}{10 \text{ years}} \times 2 = 10\% \times 2 = 20\%$$

2010: 0.20 × $44,000 = $8,800

2011: 0.20 × ($44,000 − $8,800) = $7,040

With the units-of-production method, there is a direct correlation to the number of units produced.

Subtract the residual value from the original cost. Calculate the depreciation per unit. Then divide the annual depreciation expense by the unit cost to determine the number of units produced each year.

Method C: Units-of-Production

$$\text{Depreciation per unit} = \frac{\$44{,}000 - \$4{,}000}{100{,}000 \text{ units}} = \$0.40/\text{unit}$$

2010: $1,200 ÷ $0.40 = 3,000 units

2011: $5,600 ÷ $0.40 = 14,000 units

Requirement 2

Use the same $4,000 annual depreciation expense used for the prior years.

	Method A: Straight-Line		
Year	Annual Depreciation Expense	Accumulated Depreciation	Carrying Amount
Start			$44,000
2010	$4,000	$ 4,000	40,000
2011	4,000	8,000	36,000
2012	4,000	12,000	32,000

The depreciation expense is calculated as 20% of the prior year's carrying amount.

	Method B: Double-Diminishing-Balance		
Year	Annual Depreciation Expense	Accumulated Depreciation	Carrying Amount
Start			$44,000
2010	$8,800	$ 8,800	35,200
2011	7,040	15,840	28,160
2012	5,632	21,472	22,528

Use the same $0.40 per unit amount used for the prior years. Multiply by the number of units produced during 2012.

	Method C: Units-of-Production		
Year	Annual Depreciation Expense	Accumulated Depreciation	Carrying Amount
Start			$44,000
2010	$1,200	$ 1,200	42,800
2011	5,600	6,800	37,200
2012	4,800	11,600	32,400

Computations for 2012	
Straight-line	$40,000/10 years = $4,000
Double-diminishing-balance	0.20 × $28,160 = $5,632
Units-of-production	$0.40 × 12,000 units = $4,800

Additional Depreciation Topics

Depreciation for Partial Years

OBJECTIVE

3 **Examine** additional depreciation topics

Companies purchase property, plant, and equipment whenever they need them. They do not wait until the beginning of a year or a month. Therefore, companies must compute *depreciation for partial years*. Suppose the County Line Bar-B-Q restaurant in Edmonton purchases a building on April 1 for $500,000. The building's estimated life is 20 years, and its estimated residual value is $80,000. The restaurant's fiscal year ends on December 31. Let's consider how the company computes depreciation for April through December:

- First compute depreciation for a full year.
- Then multiply the full year's depreciation by the fraction of the year that you held the asset.

Assuming the straight-line method, the year's depreciation for County Line's building is $15,750, as follows:

$$\text{Full-year depreciation} = \frac{\$500{,}000 - \$80{,}000}{20} = \$21{,}000$$

$$\text{Partial year depreciation: } \$21{,}000 \times 9/12 = \$15{,}750$$

What if County Line bought the asset on April 18? Many businesses record no monthly depreciation on assets purchased after the 15th of the month, and they record a full month's depreciation on an asset bought on or before the 15th.

Most companies use computerized systems to account for property, plant, and equipment. Each asset has a unique identification number that links to the asset's cost, estimated life, residual value, and depreciation method. The system will automatically calculate the depreciation expense for each period. Accumulated Depreciation is automatically updated.

Changing the Useful Life of a Depreciable Asset

Managers must decide on an asset's useful life to compute its depreciation. After an asset is put into use, managers may refine their estimate on the basis of experience and new information. Such a change in accounting estimate is very rare in Canada; a senior partner of one of the Big Four chartered accountancy firms initiated a search of two large databases containing statements of public companies and could find only one such reported change in the past three years.

An example from the United States is illustrative. The Walt Disney Company made such a change, called a *change in accounting estimate*. Disney recalculated depreciation on the basis of revised useful lives of several of its theme park assets.

The following note in Walt Disney's financial statements reports this change in accounting estimate:

> *Note 5*
> . . . [T]he Company extended the estimated useful lives of certain theme park ride and attraction assets based upon historical data and engineering studies. The effect of this change was to decrease [depreciation] by approximately $8 million (an increase in net income of approximately $4.2 million . . .).

Assume that a Disney hot-dog stand cost $40,000 and that the company originally believed the asset had an eight-year useful life with no residual value. Using the straight-line method, the company would record $5,000 depreciation each year ($40,000/8 years = $5,000). Suppose Disney used the asset for two years. Accumulated depreciation reached $10,000, leaving a remaining depreciable carrying amount (cost *less* accumulated depreciation *less* residual value) of $30,000 ($40,000 − $10,000). From its experience, management believes the asset will remain useful for an additional 10 years. The company would spread the remaining depreciable carrying amount over the asset's remaining life as follows:

Asset's remaining depreciable carrying amount	÷	(New) Estimated useful life remaining	=	(New) Annual depreciation
$30,000	÷	10 years	=	$3,000

The yearly depreciation entry based on the new estimated useful life is

Depreciation Expense—Hot Dog Stand	3,000	
Accumulated Depreciation—Hot Dog Stand......		3,000

ASSETS	=	LIABILITIES	+	SHAREHOLDERS' EQUITY	−	EXPENSES
−3,000	=	0			−	3,000

STOP + THINK

1. Suppose a company was having a bad year—net income was well below expectations and lower than last year's income. For depreciation purposes, the company extended the estimated useful lives of its depreciable assets. How would this accounting change affect the company's (a) depreciation expense, (b) net income, and (c) owners' equity?
2. Suppose that the company's accounting change turned a loss year into a profitable year. Without the accounting change, the company would have reported a net loss for the year. The accounting change enabled the company to report net income. Under IFRS, the company's annual report must disclose the accounting change and its effect on net income. Would investors evaluate the company as better or worse for having made this accounting change?

Answers:

1. An accounting change that lengthens the estimated useful lives of depreciable assets
   (a) decreases depreciation expense and
   (b,c) increases net income and owners' equity.
2. Investor reactions are not always predictable. There is research to indicate that companies cannot fool investors. In this case, investment advisors would *probably* subtract from the company's reported net income the amount added by the accounting change. Investors could then use the remaining net *loss* figure to evaluate the company's lack of progress during the year. Investors would probably view the company as worse for having made this accounting change. It is probably for this reason that such changes in accounting estimates are so rare in Canada.

Exchanging Property, Plant, and Equipment. Managers often trade in old property, plant, and equipment for new ones. In such a transaction, the fair value of the asset given up is used to record the transaction unless the fair value of the asset received is more clearly evident (IAS 16.26).

A detailed discussion of exchanges of property, plant, and equipment and other long-lived assets is beyond the scope of this text.

Fully Depreciated Assets

A *fully depreciated asset* is an asset that has reached the end of its estimated useful life. Suppose Canadian Tire has fully depreciated equipment with zero residual value (cost was $40,000). Canadian Tire's accounts will appear as follows:

Equipment		Accumulated Depreciation	
40,000			40,000

The equipment's carrying amount is zero, but that doesn't mean the equipment is worthless. Canadian Tire may continue using the equipment for a few more years, but will not take any more depreciation.

When Canadian Tire disposes of the equipment, it will remove both the asset's cost ($40,000) and its accumulated depreciation ($40,000) from the books. The next section shows how to account for disposals of property, plant, and equipment.

Derecognition of Property, Plant, and Equipment

OBJECTIVE

❹ **Analyze** the effect of property, plant, and equipment derecognition

Derecognition is a term IAS 16 uses to refer to property, plant, and equipment that is either no longer useful or has been sold. When this occurs, the related accounts are removed from the company's books and a gain or loss is recorded.

Eventually, property, plant, and equipment ceases to serve a company's needs. The asset may wear out, become obsolete, or for some other reason cease to be useful. Before accounting for the disposal of the asset, the business should bring depreciation up to date to

- Record the expense up to the date of sale
- Measure the asset's final carrying amount

To account for disposal, remove the asset and its related accumulated depreciation from the books. Suppose the final year's depreciation expense has just been recorded to fully depreciate a machine that cost $50,000 and is estimated to have zero residual value. The machine's accumulated depreciation thus totals $50,000. Assuming that this asset is disposed of, not sold, the entry to record its disposal is:

Accumulated Depreciation—Machinery	50,000	
Machinery		50,000
To dispose of a fully depreciated machine.		

ASSETS	=	LIABILITIES	+	SHAREHOLDERS' EQUITY
+50,000 −50,000	=	0	+	0

There is no gain or loss on this disposal, so there is no effect on equity.

If assets are "junked" before being fully depreciated, the company incurs a loss on the disposal. Suppose M&M Meat Shops disposes of store fixtures that cost $4,000. Accumulated depreciation is $3,000, and the carrying amount is, therefore, $1,000. Junking these store fixtures results in a loss as follows:

Accumulated Depreciation—Store Fixtures	3,000	
Loss on Disposal of Store Fixtures	1,000	
Store Fixtures		4,000
To dispose of store fixtures.		

ASSETS	=	LIABILITIES	+	SHAREHOLDERS' EQUITY	−	LOSSES
+3,000 −4,000	=	0			−	1,000

M&M Meat Shops got rid of an asset with a $1,000 carrying amount and received nothing. The result is a $1,000 loss, which decreases both total assets and equity.

The Loss on Disposal of Store Fixtures is reported as Other Income (Expense) on the income statement. Losses decrease net income exactly as expenses do. Gains increase net income in the same manner as revenues.

Selling Property, Plant, and Equipment. Suppose M&M Meat Shops sells fixtures on September 30, 2010, that cost $10,000 when purchased on January 1, 2007, and have been depreciated on a straight-line basis. M&M Meat Shops originally estimated a 10-year useful life and no residual value. Prior to recording the sale, the M&M Meat Shops accountants must update the asset's depreciation. Suppose the business uses the calendar year as its accounting period. Partial-year depreciation must be recorded for the asset's expense from January 1, 2010, to the sale date. The straight-line depreciation entry at September 30, 2010, is

Sept. 30	Depreciation Expense ($10,000/10 years × 9/12)	750	
	Accumulated Depreciation—Fixtures		750
	To update depreciation.		

The Fixtures account and the Accumulated Depreciation—Fixtures account appear as follows. Observe that the fixtures' carrying amount is $6,250 ($10,000 – $3,750).

Fixtures

Jan. 1, 2007 10,000	

Accumulated Depreciation—Fixtures

	Dec. 31, 2007 1,000
	Dec. 31, 2008 1,000
	Dec. 31, 2009 1,000
	Sep. 30, 2010 750
	Balance 3,750

Suppose M&M Meat Shops sells the fixtures for $7,000 cash. The gain on the sale is $750, determined as follows:

Cash received from sale of the asset		$7,000
Carrying amount of asset sold:		
Cost	$10,000	
Less accumulated depreciation	(3,750)	6,250
Gain on sale of the asset		$ 750

The entry to record the sale of the fixtures for $7,000 cash is

Date	Accounts	Debit	Credit
Sept. 30	Cash	7,000	
	Accumulated Depreciation—Fixtures	3,750	
	Gain on Sale of Fixtures		750
	Fixtures		10,000
	To sell fixtures.		

ASSETS	=	LIABILITIES	–	SHAREHOLDERS' EQUITY	+	GAINS
+7,000 +3,750 −10,000	=	0			+	750

Gains are recorded as credits, in the same manner as revenues; losses are recorded as debits, in the same manner as expenses. Gains and losses on asset disposals appear on the income statement as other income (expense).

STOP + THINK

Suppose you are reviewing WestJet Airlines's comparative income statement for 2010 and 2009 and notice these items (amounts assumed):

	(in millions) 2010	2009
Net revenues	$1,600	$1,300
...		
Income from operations	150	165
Other income (expense)		
Gain on sale of maintenance building	20	
Income before income taxes	$ 170	$ 165

Which would you decide was a better year for WestJet, 2010 or 2009?

Answer:

From a revenue standpoint, 2010 was better because revenues were higher. But from an *income* standpoint, 2009 was better.

In 2009, the company's core business generated $165 million of income from operations. In 2010, operations produced only $150 million of operating income. Of the company's income in 2010, $20 million came from selling a maintenance building (gain of $20 million). A business cannot hope to continue on this path very long. This example shows why investors and creditors care about the sources of a company's profits, and not just the final amount of net income.

Using T-Accounts to Analyze Property, Plant, and Equipment Transactions

You can perform quite a bit of analysis if you know how transactions affect the property, plant, and equipment accounts. Here are the accounts with descriptions of the activity in each account.

Building (or Equipment)	
Beginning balance	
Cost of assets purchased	Cost of assets disposed of
Ending balance	

Accumulated Depreciation	
Accum. depreciation of assets disposed of	Beginning balance Depreciation expense for the current period
	Ending balance

Depreciation Expense	
Depreciation expense for the current period	

Gain on Sale of Building (or Equipment)	
	Gain on sale

Loss on Sale of Building (or Equipment)	
Loss on sale	

Example: Suppose you started the year with buildings that cost $100,000. During the year you bought another building for $150,000 and ended the year with buildings that cost $180,000. What was the cost of the building you sold?

Building			
Beginning balance	100,000		
Cost of assets purchased	150,000	Cost of assets sold	? = $70,000
Ending balance	180,000		

You can perform similar analyses to answer other interesting questions about what the business did during the period.

Other Issues in Accounting for Property, Plant, and Equipment

Long-lived assets such as property, plant, and equipment are complex because

- Depreciation affects income taxes
- Significant components of property, plant, and equipment should be depreciated separately
- Assets should be tested regularly for impairment
- The revaluation method could be used to measure property, plant, and equipment

Depreciation for Tax Purposes

Many businesses use the straight-line method for reporting property, plant, and equipment on the balance sheet and depreciation expense on the income statement. The *Income Tax Act* permits taxpayers to use accelerated depreciation (up to specified CCA maximums) for tax purposes. In other words, a taxpayer may use one method of depreciation for accounting purposes and another method for tax purposes.

Is It Ethical to Keep Two Sets of Depreciation Records?

Is it ethical for WestJet Airlines Ltd., The Jean Coutu Group (PJC) Inc., and Jazz Golf Equipment Inc. of Winnipeg to keep two sets of depreciation records—one for their financial statements and the other for reporting to CRA? Yes, that's perfectly okay because the two sets of depreciation records serve two very different purposes.

The depreciation records illustrated in this chapter are designed for the income statement and the balance sheet. The purpose here is to measure accounting income and asset values for reporting to shareholders and creditors. Accounting theory is the driving force behind these depreciation amounts to provide relevant information for investment and credit decisions.

Depreciation amounts for income tax purposes march to the beat of a different drummer. Parliament designs tax depreciation to raise tax revenue for the government. Political considerations enter the world of taxes, so tax depreciation is very different from basic accounting depreciation. Companies must comply with CCA regulations and so have two sets of records for depreciation.

The result of using one method for accounting and another method for tax purposes is that income tax expense and net income calculated for accounting purposes will usually be different from those calculated for tax purposes. In the early years of an asset's life, depreciation for tax purposes will be greater than depreciation for accounting purposes (and actual income tax expense will be less). In the later years, depreciation for accounting purposes will be greater than depreciation for tax purposes (and actual income tax will be more).

While the relationship is generally considered to be a topic for an advanced accounting course, the authors felt it important to introduce it in this text. There is more extensive coverage of the topic in Appendix 7A.

Depreciating Significant Components

ASPE

IFRS require that significant components of an item of property, plant, and equipment be depreciated separately. What does this mean? Take, for example, WestJet or British Airways, which buy aircraft for use in their operations. Their spare engines and parts may have a useful life different from their aircraft and, therefore, are depreciated separately. WestJet depreciates aircraft based on cycles, while the spare engines and parts are depreciated using the straight-line method over 20 years. In the private sector, depreciating separate components is done only when practicable.

Impairment

At each reporting date, a company should review its property, plant, and equipment to see if an asset is impaired. Impairment occurs when the carrying amount exceeds its recoverable amount (IAS 36.8). Recoverable amount is determined to be the higher of an asset's fair value (less costs to sell) and its value in use. Value in use is the present value of estimated future cash flows expected to be earned from the continuing use of an asset and from its disposal at the end of its useful life. Impairment may be caused by many factors including obsolescence, physical damage, and loss in market value. The journal entry to record impairment is

Loss on Impairment	XXX	
Accumulated Deprecation		XXX

If the situation changes, IFRS does permit a company to reverse the impairment loss by writing the asset up to its carrying amount. The accounting standards for private enterprises require a company to review its property, plant, and equipment only when impairment is suspected. No reversal of the write-off is allowed.

In a note to its financial statements, British Airways states that for its property, plant, and equipment

> The carrying value is reviewed for impairment when events or changes in circumstances indicate the carrying value may not be recoverable and the

cumulative impairment losses are shown as a reduction in the carrying value of property, plant and equipment.

Revaluation Model

Throughout this chapter, we have shown you what IFRS refers to as the cost model. This means that a company measures property, plant, and equipment at cost less any accumulated depreciation less any accumulated impairment losses.

Another method a company could choose to measure property, plant, and equipment is called the revaluation model. This asset would be recorded at cost when purchased but subsequently measured at its fair value less any accumulated depreciation less any accumulated losses. Fair value is the price at which the asset could be sold, and a professional valuator would do this revaluation regularly. It may be revalued at year-end or when the company believes a change in the asset value has taken place. With every new change in the asset account, depreciation has to be revised accordingly based on the new carrying amount. To keep the example simple, depreciation is ignored, and this topic is discussed in greater detail in an intermediate accounting course.

Example:
A company chooses to use the revaluation method for a building that was bought for $1.8 million and is being depreciated over 25 years, no residual value. Subsequently, if the appraised value is $2 million, the increase of $200,000 will be recognized through equity by the following journal entry:

Building	200,000	
Revaluation surplus		200,000

Revaluation Surplus is an equity account that is reported as other comprehensive income. Only the cost model is used for private enterprises.

USING PROPERTY, PLANT, AND EQUIPMENT IN DECISION MAKING

Manager—Managers choose which depreciation method to use to allocate the cost of property, plant, and equipment over its useful life. In this chapter, we looked at the straight-line method, units-of-production method, and diminishing-balance method. As discussed earlier, each method will produce varying amounts of depreciation expense every year, but overall they will result in the same total amount of depreciation. If the asset generates revenue evenly over time, the straight-line method is best; if it wears out over physical use, the units-of-production method should be used; if greater revenue is generated earlier in the asset's useful life, then diminishing-balance is the method to use.

Investor and creditor—Both investors and creditors read the notes to the financial statements to see which depreciation methods management used. Why do they do this? As we have already seen, the depreciation method chosen affects both the income statement and the balance sheet. Remember, if management chooses to use the straight-line method, then depreciation expense will be the same amount each year. However, if the double-diminishing-balance method is used, then depreciation expense is highest in the early years of the asset's life, causing net income to be lower. Let's look at an example.

Both Company A and Company B bought equipment costing $50,000 with no residual value and an estimated useful life of five years. Company A uses the straight-line method, while Company B uses the double-diminishing-balance method of depreciation. To keep the example simple, depreciation expense will be the only expense. Assume revenue for each company is $500,000 for the first year. Net income for each company would be as follows:

	Company A	Company B
Revenue	$500,000	$500,000
Depreciation expense	10,000	20,000
Net income	$490,000	$480,000

Even though revenue was the same for both companies, Company B's net income was lower. Investors and creditors look favourably upon a higher net income, and if they don't consider the impact of depreciation methods, they might choose Company B when in fact Company A might be the better choice.

Accounting for Natural Resources

EnCana is a leading North American energy company whose primary focus is natural gas production, but it is also involved in oil exploration and production. The company's property, plant, and equipment include long-lived assets such as refinery property, plant, and equipment, as well as costs directly associated with the acquisition of, exploration for, and development of natural gas and crude oil reserves.

All property, plant, and equipment for companies in this industry would be measured initially at cost and depreciated using either the cost model or the revaluation model as discussed earlier in this chapter.

However, the accounting guidelines for costs directly associated with exploration and development of natural gas and crude oil reserves, as found in IFRS 6, are complex and beyond the scope of this textbook.

Accounting for Intangible Assets

OBJECTIVE

5 **Account** for intangible assets and amortization

As we saw earlier, *intangible assets* are long-lived assets with no physical form. Intangibles are valuable because they carry special rights from patents, copyrights, trademarks, franchises, leaseholds, and goodwill. Like buildings and equipment, an intangible asset is recorded at its acquisition cost. Intangibles are often the most valuable assets of high-tech companies and other companies that depend on research and development. The residual value of most intangibles is zero.

Intangible assets fall into two categories:

- Intangibles with *finite lives* that can be measured. We record **amortization** for these intangibles. Amortization is usually computed on a straight-line basis, but one of the other methods could be used.
- Intangibles with *indefinite lives*. Record no amortization for these intangibles. Instead, check them annually for any loss in value (impairment), and record a loss when it occurs. Goodwill is the most prominent example of an intangible asset with an indefinite life.

In the following discussions, we illustrate the accounting for both categories of intangibles.

Accounting for Specific Intangibles

Each type of intangible asset is unique, and the accounting can vary from one intangible to another.

Patents. **Patents** are federal government grants giving the holder the exclusive right for 20 years to produce and sell an invention. The invention may be a product or a process—for example, Research In Motion's BlackBerry and IMAX's projection process. Like any other asset, a patent may be purchased. Suppose Bombardier pays $170,000 to acquire a patent on January 1, and the business believes the expected useful life of the patent is five years. Amortization expense is $34,000 per year ($170,000/5 years). Bombardier records the acquisition and amortization for this patent as follows:

Jan. 1	Patents	170,000	
	Cash		170,000
	To acquire a patent.		
Dec. 31	Amortization Expense—Patents ($170,000/5)	34,000	
	Accumulated amortization		34,000
	To amortize the cost of a patent.		

ASSETS	=	LIABILITIES	+	SHAREHOLDERS' EQUITY	–	EXPENSES
−34,000	=	0			–	34,000

Amortization for an intangible decreases both assets and equity exactly as it does for equipment.

Copyrights. **Copyrights** are exclusive rights to reproduce and sell a book, musical composition, film, or other work of art. Copyrights also protect computer software programs, such as Corel's WordPerfect. Issued by the federal government, copyrights extend 50 years beyond the author's (composer's, artist's, or programmer's) death. The cost of obtaining a copyright from the government is low, but a company may pay a large sum to purchase an existing copyright from the owner. For example, a publisher may pay the author of a popular novel $1 million or more for the book copyright. A copyright is usually amortized over 15 years of useful life.

Trademarks and Trade Names. **Trademarks** and **trade names** (or **brand names**) are distinctive identifications of products or services. You are probably familiar with the CBC's sectioned circle logo and CTV's red, blue, and green logo. You would also recognize MuchMusic's and TSN's logos. Tim Hortons and Roots are names we all recognize. Advertising slogans, such as Molson's "I am Canadian," are protected.

The cost of a trademark or trade name may be amortized over its useful life. But if the trademark is expected to generate cash flow for the indefinite future, the business should not amortize the trademark's cost.

Franchises and Licences. **Franchises and licences** are privileges granted by a private business or a government to sell a product or service in accordance with specified conditions. The Edmonton Oilers hockey organization is a franchise granted to its owner by the National Hockey League. Swiss Chalet restaurants and Canadian Tire are popular franchises. The useful lives of many franchises and licences are indefinite and, therefore, are not amortized.

Goodwill. In accounting, **goodwill** has a very specific meaning. It is defined as the excess of the cost of purchasing another company over the sum of the market values of its net assets (assets minus liabilities). A purchaser is willing to pay for goodwill when it buys another company with abnormal earning power.

Canadian Tire expanded into another line of business when it acquired Mark's Work Wearhouse Ltd. on February 1, 2002. The purchase price was $110.8 million. The fair value of the assets was $189.8 million, and the fair value of the liabilities was $97.9 million, so Canadian Tire paid $18.9 million for goodwill, computed as follows:

Purchase price paid for Mark's Work Wearhouse Ltd. (MWW)		$110.8 million
Sum of the fair values of MWW's assets	$189.8 million	
Less: Fair value of MWW's liabilities	97.9 million	
Value of MWW's net assets		91.9 million
Excess is called *goodwill*		$ 18.9 million

Canadian Tire would consolidate Mark's Work Wearhouse's financial statements, but if Canadian Tire were to combine Mark's records with its own, the entry, including goodwill, would be

Assets (Cash, Receivables, Inventories, Property, Plant, and Equipment, Other Assets all at fair value)	189,800,000	
Goodwill	18,900,000	
Liabilities		97,900,000
Cash		110,800,000

ASSETS	=	LIABILITIES	+	SHAREHOLDERS' EQUITY
+189,800,000 +18,900,000 −110,800,000	=	+97,900,000	+	0

Note that Canadian Tire has acquired both Mark's Work Wearhouse's assets and its liabilities.

Goodwill has special features, as follows:

1. Goodwill is recorded *only* when it is purchased in the acquisition of another company. A purchase transaction provides objective evidence of the value of goodwill. Companies never record goodwill that they have created for their own business.
2. Goodwill is not amortized because it has an indefinite life. As you will see below, if the value of goodwill is impaired it must be written down.

Accounting for the Impairment of an Intangible Asset

Some intangibles—such as goodwill, licences, and some trademarks—have indefinite lives and, therefore, are not subject to amortization. But all intangibles are subject to a write-down when their recoverable amount is less than the carrying amount. The annual report of Brampton Brick Limited for the year ended December 31, 2008, reports that "The Company performed its annual test for impairment of goodwill as at December 31, 2008 . . . [and] determined that there had been an impairment in the carrying value of goodwill . . . " As a result of the impairment test, the company wrote off the remaining value of its investment in Landscape Products' business by $6.7 million in fiscal 2008.

Brampton Brick recorded the write-down as follows:

2008			
Dec. 31	Goodwill Impairment	6.7	
	Goodwill		6.7

ASSETS	=	LIABILITIES	+	SHAREHOLDERS' EQUITY	−	EXPENSES
−6.7	=	0			−	6.7

Brampton Brick's financial statements reported the following (in millions of dollars):

	2008	2007
Balance sheet		
Intangible assets: Goodwill	$ 0	$ 6.7
Income statement		
Goodwill Impairment	(6.7)	(13.5)

For the private enterprise, impairment of intangible assets with an indefinite life is checked only when suspected.

Accounting for Research and Development Costs

Accounting for research and development (R&D) costs is one of the most difficult issues the accounting profession has faced. R&D is the lifeblood of companies such as Research In Motion, Open Text, TELUS, and Bombardier because it is vital to the development of new products and processes. The cost of R&D activities is one of these companies' most valuable (intangible) assets.

Canada requires *development costs* meeting certain criteria to be capitalized and then expensed over the life of the product, while other countries require such costs to be expensed in the year incurred. Canada and most other countries require *research costs* to be expensed as incurred.

Reporting Property, Plant, and Equipment Transactions on the Statement of Cash Flows

OBJECTIVE

6 **Report** long-lived assets on the statement of cash flows

Three main types of capital asset transactions appear on the statement of cash flows:

- Acquisitions
- Sales
- Depreciation and amortization

Acquisitions and sales of property, plant, and equipment are *investing* activities. A company invests in property, plant, and equipment by paying cash or incurring a liability. The cash payments for buildings and equipment are investing activities that appear on the statement of cash flows. The sale of property, plant, and equipment results in a cash receipt, as illustrated in Exhibit 7-9, which excerpts data from the statement of cash flows of WestJet Airlines Ltd. The acquisitions, sales, and depreciation of property, plant, and equipment are denoted in colour (lines 5, 6, and 2).

EXHIBIT 7-9 **Reporting Capital Asset Transactions on WestJet's Statement of Cash Flows**

WestJet Airlines Ltd.
Consolidated Statement of Cash Flows(partial, adapted)
For the Year Ended December 31, 2008

	amounts in millions
Operating Activities:	
1. Net earnings	$ 178.1
Adjustments to reconcile net income to cash provided by operating activities:	
2. Depreciation	136.5
3. Other items (summarized)	145.9
4. Cash provided by operating activities	460.5
Investing Activities:	
5. Purchases of aircraft and other capital assets	(205.0)
6. Proceeds from capital asset disposals	5.3
7. Cash used in investing activities	(199.7)
Financing Activities:	
8. Cash used in financing activities	(115.4)
9. Cash flows from operating, investing, and financing activities	145.4
10. Effect of exchange rate on cash	21.2
11. Net change in cash	166.6
12. Cash at beginning of year	653.5
13. Cash at end of year	$ 820.1

Let's examine the investing activities first. During the fiscal year ended December 31, 2008, WestJet paid $205 million for property, plant, and equipment (line 5). WestJet received $5.3 million from the disposal of these assets during the year. The $5.3 million is the amount of *cash* received from the disposal of the property, plant, and equipment. A gain or loss on the sale of these assets is not reported as an investing activity on the statement of cash flows. The gain or loss is reported on the income statement.

WestJet's statement of cash flows reports Depreciation in the operating activities section (line 2). Observe that "Depreciation" is listed as a positive item under Adjustments to Reconcile Net Income to Cash Provided by Operating Activities. You may be wondering why depreciation appears on the statement of cash flows. After all, depreciation does not affect cash.

In this format, the operating activities section of the statement of cash flows starts with net earnings (line 1) and reconciles to cash provided by operating activities (line 4). Depreciation decreases net income in the same way that all other expenses do. But it does not affect cash. Depreciation is therefore added back to net income to measure cash flows from operations. The add-back of depreciation to net income offsets the earlier subtraction of the expense. The sum of net income plus depreciation, therefore, helps to reconcile net income (on the accrual basis) to cash flows from operations (a cash-basis amount). We revisit this topic in the full context of the statement of cash flows in Chapter 12.

Incidentally, WestJet's cash flows are strong. Operations generated $460.5 million of cash, and WestJet spent $205 million on new aircraft, property, and equipment. The company is not standing still; it is continuing to expand.

STOP + THINK

Test your ability to understand the statement of cash flows.

1. How much cash did WestJet spend on purchases of aircraft and other capital assets during the year?
2. Suppose the carrying amount of the capital assets that WestJet sold for $5.3 million was $6 million (a cost of $50 million minus accumulated depreciation of $44 million). Write a sentence to explain why the sale transaction resulted in a loss for WestJet.
3. Where would WestJet report any gain or loss on the sale of the capital assets—on which financial statement, under which heading?

Answers:

1. WestJet spent $205 million.
2. The company sold for $5.3 million assets that had a carrying amount of $6 million. The result of the sale was a loss of $0.7 million ($5.3 million received and $6 million carrying amount).
3. Report the loss on the *income statement* under the heading *Non-operating income (expense)*.

SUMMARY OF CHAPTER 7

Learning Objective ❶: **Determine the cost of property, plant, and equipment**

Property, plant, and equipment such as building, land, and equipment are **tangible long-lived assets** that companies use in their business to help generate revenue. The asset account is debited for all costs incurred to get the asset to its location and ready for use.

Costs occurring after an asset has been placed in use are either capitalized (if it increases the asset's productivity or extends useful life) or expensed (if it maintains the asset and keeps it in good working order).

Learning Objective ❷: **Account for depreciation**

Since assets decline in value either from wearing out, becoming obsolete, or losing value, **depreciation** is used to allocate their cost to the periods of its useful life. Three depreciation methods discussed include the **straight-line (SL) method**, the **units-of-production (UOP) method**, and the **double-diminishing-balance (DDB) method**. The straight-line method assigns an equal amount of depreciation expense to each period; units of production measures depreciation based on output or service produced by the asset; while the diminishing balance depreciates a larger amount of the asset's cost at the beginning of its useful life.

If an asset is bought during the year, companies must compute depreciation for partial years.

Managers may revise their estimate of an asset's useful life and recalculate depreciation.

If a fully depreciated asset is still being used, it is left on the company's records.

Learning Objective ❸: **Examine additional depreciation topics**

Depreciation affects income taxes because Canada Revenue Agency allows an accelerated depreciation for tax purposes. Subsequent to the acquisition of property, plant, and equipment, a company can choose to measure these assets using either the cost method or the revaluation method. The cost method uses cost as its measurement while revaluation uses fair value. Also, IFRS requires significant components of property, plant, and equipment to be depreciated separately and to assess the impairment of these assets at each reporting date.

Learning Objective ❹: **Analyze the effect of property, plant, and equipment derecognition**

Before a company disposes of an asset, it must bring depreciation expense up to date. Other issues discussed with regards to property, plant, and equipment include income taxes, depreciating significant components, impairment, and using the revaluation method to measure assets.

Choosing a depreciation method affects the financial statements and this should be taken into consideration when analyzing the statements.

Learning Objective ❺: **Account for intangible assets and amortization**

Intangible assets are long-lived assets with no physical form and include **patents**, **copyrights**, **trademarks**, **franchises and licences**, leaseholds, and **goodwill**. Two categories of intangibles are those with finite lives (record amortization) and indefinite lives (no amortization is recorded but the asset is checked each year for impairment and a loss is recorded when it occurs).

Learning Objective ❻: **Report long-lived assets on the statement of cash flows**

On the statement of cash flows, acquisitions and sales of property, plant, and equipment are recorded under investing activities while the depreciation expense is added to net income under the operating activities.

MyAccountingLab

END-OF-CHAPTER SUMMARY PROBLEM

Problem 1

The figures that follow appear in the *Answers to the Mid-Chapter Summary Problem*, Requirement 2, on page 350, for Canadian Tire.

	Method A: Straight-Line			Method B: Double-Diminishing-Balance		
Year	Annual Depreciation Expense	Accumulated Depreciation	Carrying amount	Annual Depreciation Expense	Accumulated Depreciation	Carrying Amount
Start			$44,000			$44,000
2010	$4,000	$ 4,000	40,000	$8,800	$ 8,800	35,200
2011	4,000	8,000	36,000	7,040	15,840	28,160
2012	4,000	12,000	32,000	5,632	21,472	22,528

Name: Canadian Tire
Industry: Retailer
Accounting Period: The years 2010, 2011, 2012

Required

Suppose the income tax authorities permitted a choice between these two depreciation methods. Which method would Canadian Tire select for income tax purposes? Why?

Problem 2

Suppose Canadian Tire purchased the equipment described in the table on January 1, 2010. Management has depreciated the equipment by using the double-diminishing-balance method. On July 1, 2012, Canadian Tire sold the equipment for $27,000 cash.

Required

Record depreciation for 2012 and the sale of the equipment on July 1, 2012.

ANSWERS

Problem 1

If a choice were permitted, the greater depreciation expense leads to a lower net income and, therefore, a lower income tax expense. However, Canada's *Income Tax Act* does not allow depreciation as a deduction for income tax purposes. Canada Revenue Agency does allow capital cost allowance to be deducted.

For tax purposes, most companies select an accelerated method because it results in the most depreciation in the earliest years of the equipment's life. Accelerated depreciation minimizes taxable income and income tax payments in the early years of the asset's life, thereby maximizing the business's cash at the earliest possible time. Canadian Tire would use the maximum rate allowed by the Canada Revenue Agency.

Problem 2

Depreciation expense must first be recorded for the portion of the year that the asset was used before it was sold.

The gain on the sale is the excess of the cash received over the carrying amount of the asset.

To record depreciation to date of sale, and then the sale of the equipment:

2012			
July 1	Depreciation Expense—Equipment ($5,632 × 1/2 year)	2,816	
	Accumulated Depreciation—Equipment		2,816
	To update depreciation.		
July 1	Cash	27,000	
	Accumulated Depreciation—Equipment ($15,840 + $2,816)	18,656	
	Equipment		44,000
	Gain on Sale of Equipment		1,656
	To record sale of equipment.		

Review Property, Plant, and Equipment, and Intangible Assets

Quick Check (Answers are given on page 387.)

1. Argyle Corp. purchased a tract of land, a small office building, and some equipment for $1,500,000. The appraised value of the land was $850,000, the building $675,000, and the equipment $475,000. What is the cost of the land?
   a. $850,000
   b. $637,500
   c. $482,776
   d. None of the above
2. Which of the following statements about depreciation is false?
   a. Recording depreciation creates a fund to replace the asset at the end of its useful life.
   b. The cost of a building minus accumulated depreciation equals the building's carrying amount.
   c. Depreciation is a process of allocating the cost of property, plant, and equipment over its useful life.
   d. Depreciation is caused by physical wear and tear or obsolence.

Use the following data for Questions 3 through 6.

On August 1, 2010, Major Link Inc. purchased a new piece of equipment that cost $25,000. The estimated useful life is five years, and estimated residual value is $2,500.

3. Assume Major Link purchased the equipment on August 1, 2010. If Major Link uses the straight-line method for depreciation, what is the depreciation for the year ended December 31, 2010?
   a. $1,875
   b. $1,500
   c. $2,083
   d. $4,500
4. Assume Major Link purchased the equipment on January 1, 2010. If Major Link uses the straight-line method for depreciation, what is the asset's carrying amount at the end of 2011?
   a. $13,500
   b. $15,000
   c. $18,625
   d. $16,000
5. Assume Major Link purchased the equipment on January 1, 2010. If Major Link uses the double-diminishing-balance method of depreciation, what is the depreciation for the year ended December 31, 2011?
   a. $5,400
   b. $6,000
   c. $8,333
   d. $15,000
6. Return to Major Link's original purchase date of August 1, 2010. Assume that Major Link uses the straight-line method of depreciation and sells the equipment for $11,500 on August 1, 2014. Based on the result of the sale of the equipment, what benefit or cost will Major Link realize?
   a. $4,500
   b. $13,500
   c. $(9,000)
   d. $0
7. A company bought a new machine for $17,000 on January 1. The machine is expected to last four years and to have a residual value of $2,000. If the company uses the double-diminishing-balance method, what is the accumulated depreciation at the end of year 2?
   a. $10,880
   b. $11,250
   c. $12,750
   d. $15,000
8. Which of the following is *not* a capital expenditure?
   a. The addition of a building wing
   b. A complete overhaul of an air-conditioning system
   c. A tune-up of a company vehicle
   d. Replacement of an old motor with a new one in a piece of equipment
   e. The cost of installing a piece of equipment

9. Which of the following assets is *not* subject to a decreasing carrying amount through amortization?
   a. Goodwill
   b. Intangibles
   c. Land improvements
   d. Land
10. Why would a business select an accelerated method of depreciation for tax purposes?
    a. CCA depreciation follows a specific pattern of depreciation.
    b. Accelerated depreciation generates a greater amount of depreciation over the life of the asset than does straight-line depreciation.
    c. Accelerated depreciation is easier to calculate because residual value is ignored.
    d. Accelerated depreciation generates higher depreciation expense immediately, and therefore lower tax payments in the early years of the asset's life.
11. A company sells an asset that originally cost $300,000 for $100,000 on December 31, 2010. The accumulated depreciation account had a balance of $120,000 after the current year's depreciation of $30,000 had been recorded. The company should recognize a(n)
    a. $200,000 loss on disposal
    b. $80,000 loss on disposal
    c. $80,000 gain on disposal
    d. $50,000 loss on disposal
12. Which item among the following is *not* an intangible asset?
    a. A trademark
    b. A copyright
    c. A patent
    d. Goodwill
    e. All of the above are intangible assets

Accounting Vocabulary

accelerated depreciation method A depreciation method that writes off a relatively larger amount of the asset's cost nearer the start of its useful life than the straight-line method does. (p. 346).

amortization Allocation of the cost of an intangible asset with a finite life over its useful life (p. 359)

brand name A distinctive identification of a product or service. Also called a *trademark* or *trade name*. (p. 360)

capital cost allowance (CCA) Depreciation allowed for income tax purposes by the Canada Revenue Agency; the rates allowed are called *capital cost allowance rates*. (p. 349)

capital expenditure Expenditure that increases an asset's capacity or efficiency or extends its useful life. Capital expenditures are debited to an asset account. Also called *betterments*. (p. 341)

copyright Exclusive right to reproduce and sell a book, musical composition, film, other work of art, or computer program. Issued by the federal government, copyrights extend 50 years beyond the author's life. (p. 360)

depreciable cost The cost of a tangible asset minus its estimated residual value. (p. 344)

depreciation Allocation of the cost of property, plant, and equipment for its useful life. (p. 343)

double-diminishing-balance (DDB) method An accelerated depreciation method that computes annual depreciation by multiplying the asset's decreasing carrying amount by a constant percentage, which is two times the straight-line rate. (p. 346)

estimated residual value Expected cash value of an asset at the end of its useful life. Also called *scrap value* or *salvage value*. (p. 344)

estimated useful life Length of service that a business expects to get from an asset. May be expressed in years, units of output, kilometres, or other measures. (p. 344)

franchises and licences Privileges granted by a private business or a government to sell a product or service in accordance with specified conditions. (p. 360)

goodwill Excess of the cost of an acquired company over the sum of the market values of its net assets (assets minus liabilities). (p. 361)

intangible assets Long-lived assets with no physical form that convey a special right to current and expected future benefits. (p. 338)

patent A federal government grant giving the holder the exclusive right for 20 years to produce and sell an invention. (p. 360)

straight-line (SL) method Depreciation method in which an equal amount of depreciation expense is assigned to each year of asset use. (p. 345)

tangible long-lived assets Also called property, plant, and equipment. (p. 338)

trademark/trade name A distinctive identification of a product or service. Also called a *brand name*. (p. 360)

units-of-production (UOP) method Depreciation method by which a fixed amount of depreciation is assigned to each unit of output produced by the plant asset. (p. 346)

Assess Your Progress

Make the grade with MyAccountingLab: The exercises and problems in this chapter can be found on MyAccountingLab at www.myaccountinglab.com. You can practise them as often as you want, and they feature step-by-step guided solutions to help you find the right answer.

Short Exercises

Learning Objective 1
Cost and carrying amount of a company's property, plant, and equipment

S7-1 Examine the balance sheet of Canadian Tire at the beginning of this chapter on page 338. Answer these questions about the company:

1. What is Canadian Tire's largest category of assets?
2. If accumulated depreciation is $23.956 million at January 3, 2009, what was the cost of property, plant, and equipment? Why is carrying amount less than cost?

Learning Objective 1
Measuring the cost of property

S7-2 Page 339 of this chapter lists the costs included for the acquisition of land. First is the purchase price of the land, which is obviously included in the cost of the land. The reasons for including the related costs are not so obvious. For example, property tax is ordinarily an expense, not part of the cost of an asset. State why the related costs listed on page 339 are included as part of the cost of the land. After the land is ready for use, will these related costs be capitalized or expensed?

Learning Objective 1
Lump-sum purchase of assets

S7-3 Suppose you have purchased land, a building, and some equipment. At the time of the acquisition, the land has a current fair value of $75,000, the building's fair value is $60,000, and the equipment's fair value is $15,000. Journalize the lump-sum purchase of the three assets for a total cost of $140,000. Assume you sign a note payable for this amount.

Learning Objective 1
Capitalizing versus expensing equipment costs

S7-4 Assume WestJet repaired one of its Boeing 737 aircraft at a cost of $0.8 million, which WestJet paid in cash. Further, assume the WestJet accountant erroneously capitalized this cost as part of the cost of the plane.

Show the effects of the accounting error on WestJet's income statement and balance sheet. To answer this question, determine whether revenues, total expenses, net income, total assets, and shareholders' equity would be overstated or understated by the accounting error.

Learning Objective 2
Computing depreciation by three methods—first year only

S7-5 Assume that at the beginning of 2011, Porter Airlines purchased a Bombardier Q400 aircraft at a cost of $25,000,000. Porter expects the plane to remain useful for five years (5,000,000 km) and to have a residual value of $5,000,000. Porter expects the plane to be flown 750,000 km the first year and 1,250,000 km each year during years 2 through 4, and 500,000 km the last year.

1. Compute Porter's first-year depreciation on the plane using the following methods:
   a. Straight-line
   b. Units-of-production
   c. Double-diminishing-balance
2. Show the airplane's carrying amount at the end of the first year under each depreciation method.

Learning Objective 2
Computing depreciation by three methods—final year only

S7-6 Use the assumed Porter Airlines data in Short Exercise 7-5 to compute Porter's fifth-year depreciation on the plane using the following methods:

a. Straight-line
b. Units-of-production
c. Double-diminishing-balance

Learning Objective 2
Selecting the method that permits the greatest deduction for income tax purposes

S7-7 This exercise uses the assumed Porter Airlines data from Short Exercise 7-5. Assume Porter is trying to decide whether to use the maximum CCA allowed for income tax purposes.

1. Which depreciation method offers the tax advantage for the first year? Describe the nature of the tax advantage.
2. How much income tax will Porter save for the first year of the airplane's use compared with using the straight-line method? Canada Revenue Agency permits a maximum capital cost allowance rate of 25%. Porter's income tax rate is 35%. Ignore any earnings from investing the extra cash. Also ignore the 50% rule applicable to the year of acquisition.

Learning Objective 3
Partial-year depreciation

S7-8 Assume that on September 30, 2011, Swiss, the national airline of Switzerland, purchased an Airbus aircraft at a cost of €40,000,000 (€ is the symbol for the euro). Swiss expects the plane to remain useful for seven years (5,000,000 km) and to have a residual value of €5,000,000. Swiss expects the plane to be flown 500,000 km during the remainder of the first year ended December 31, 2011. Compute Swiss's depreciation on the plane for the year ended December 31, 2011, using the following methods:

a. Straight-line
b. Units-of-production
c. Double-diminishing-balance

Which method would produce the highest net income for 2011? Which method produces the lowest net income?

Learning Objective 3
Computing and recording depreciation after a change in useful life of the asset

S7-9 Canada's Wonderland paid $60,000 for a concession stand. Depreciation was recorded by the straight-line method over 10 years with zero residual value. Suppose that after using the concession stand for four years, Canada's Wonderland determines that the asset will remain useful for only three more years. How will this affect depreciation on the concession stand for year 5 by the straight-line method?

Learning Objective 4
Recording a gain or loss on derecognition under two depreciation methods

S7-10 On January 1, 2009, Big Rock Brewery purchased a van for $45,000. Big Rock expects the van to have a useful life of five years and a residual value of $5,000. The depreciation method used was straight-line. On December 31, 2012, the van was sold for $15,000 cash.

1. What was the carrying amount of the van on the date of sale?
2. Record the sale of the van on December 31, 2012.

Learning Objective 5
Accounting for the amortization of a company's intangible assets

S7-11 Define patents and goodwill, which are both intangible assets. Explain how the accounting differs between a patent and goodwill.

Learning Objective 5
Analyzing a company's goodwill

S7-12 Consider the purchase of a supplier by Canadian Tire.

1. Suppose the fair value of the net assets at the date of purchase (February 1, 2011) had been $180.3 million. What would the goodwill cost have been if Canadian Tire had paid $200 million?
2. Explain how Canadian Tire will have been accounting for this goodwill up to February 1, 2013.

Learning Objective 5
Accounting for patents and research cost

S7-13 This exercise summarizes the accounting for patents, which, like copyrights, trademarks, and franchises, provide the owner with a special right or privilege. It also covers research costs.

Suppose Jaguar Automobiles Ltd. paid $500,000 to research a new global positioning system. Jaguar also paid $1,200,000 to acquire a patent on a new motor. After readying the motor for production, Jaguar's sales revenue for the first year totalled $6,500,000. Cost of goods sold was $3,200,000, and selling expenses were $300,000. All these transactions occurred during fiscal 2011. Jaguar expects the patent to have a useful life of three years.

Prepare Jaguar's income statement for the fiscal year ended December 31, 2011, complete with a heading.

S7-14 You are reviewing the financial statements of Rising Yeast Co. During 2011, Rising Yeast purchased two other companies for $17 million. Also during fiscal 2011, Rising Yeast made capital expenditures of $2 million to expand its market share. During the year, the company sold operations, receiving cash of $25 million, and experienced a gain of $6 million on the disposal. Overall, Rising Yeast reported net income of $1 million during 2011. What would you expect the section for cash flows from investing activities on its statement of cash flows for 2011 to report? What total amount for net cash provided by (used in) investing activities do you anticipate?

Learning Objective 6
Reporting investing activities on the statement of cash flows

Exercises

E7-15 Moody Inc. purchased land, paying $150,000 cash as a down payment and signing a $100,000 note payable for the balance. Moody also had to pay delinquent property tax of $5,000, title insurance costing $3,000, and $25,000 to level the land and to remove an unwanted building. The company paid $70,000 to remove earth for the foundation and then constructed an office building at a cost of $3,750,000. It also paid $100,000 for a fence around the property, $10,500 for the company sign near the property entrance, and $18,000 for lighting of the grounds. Determine the cost of the company's land, land improvements, and building.

Learning Objective 1
Determining the cost of property

E7-16 Assume Trois Cuisines Manufacturing bought three machines in a $100,000 lump-sum purchase. An independent appraiser valued the machines as follows:

Learning Objective 1 4
Allocating costs to assets acquired in a lump-sum purchase; derecognizing equipment

Machine No.	Appraised Value
1	$27,000
2	45,000
3	36,000

Trois Cuisines paid one-third in cash and signed a note payable for the remainder. What is each machine's individual cost? Immediately after making this purchase, Trois Cuisines sold machine 2 for its appraised value. What is the result of the sale? Round to three decimal places.

E7-17 Assume Hershey Chocolate Ltd. purchased a piece of manufacturing machinery. Classify each of the following expenditures as an asset expenditure or an immediate expense related to machinery: (a) sales tax paid on the purchase price, (b) transportation and insurance while machinery is in transit from seller to buyer, (c) purchase price, (d) installation, (e) training of personnel for initial operation of the machinery, (f) special reinforcement to the machinery platform, (g) income tax paid on income earned from the sale of products manufactured by the machinery, (h) major overhaul to extend useful life by three years, (i) ordinary repairs to keep the machinery in good working order, (j) lubrication of the machinery before it is placed in service, and (k) periodic lubrication after the machinery is placed in service. What criteria differentiated an asset expenditure from an immediate expense?

Learning Objective 1
Distinguishing asset expenditures from expenses

E7-18 During 2011, Roberts Inc. paid $200,000 for land and built a restaurant in Collingwood, Ontario. Prior to construction, the City of Collingwood charged Roberts Inc. $2,250 for a building permit, which it paid. Roberts Inc. also paid $20,000 for architect's fees. The construction cost of $700,000 was financed by a long-term note payable issued on January 1, 2011, with interest cost of $29,000 paid at December 31, 2011. The building was completed September 30, 2011. Roberts Inc. will depreciate the building by the straight-line method over 25 years, with an estimated residual value of $60,000.

Learning Objective 1 2
Measuring, depreciating, and reporting property and plant

1. Journalize transactions for the following; explanations are not required.
   a. Purchase of the land
   b. All the costs chargeable to the building, in a single entry
   c. Depreciation on the building

2. Report this transaction in the capital assets on the company's balance sheet at December 31, 2011.

3. What will Roberts Inc.'s income statement for the year ended December 31, 2011, report for the building?

Learning Objective ❷❸
Determining depreciation amounts by three methods

E7-19 Assume you have a flower shop and you bought a delivery van for $30,000. You expect the van to remain in service for three years (150,000 km). At the end of its useful life, you estimate that the van's residual value will be $3,000. You estimate the van will travel 40,000 km the first year, 60,000 km the second year, and 50,000 km the third year. Prepare an estimate of the *depreciation expense* per year for the van under the three depreciation methods. Show your computations.

Which method do you think tracks the useful life cost on the van most closely? Would you use the maximum CCA for income tax purposes? The Canada Revenue Agency's maximum capital cost allowance rate is 30%. Explain in detail which method you chose.

Learning Objective ❶❷❻
Reporting property, plant, and equipment depreciation and investing cash flow

E7-20 In January 2011, suppose a Starbucks franchise in Regina purchased a building, paying $50,000 cash and signing a $100,000 note payable. The franchise paid another $50,000 to remodel the facility. Equipment and store fixtures cost $50,000; dishes and supplies—a current asset—were obtained for $10,000.

The franchise is depreciating the building over 25 years by the straight-line method, with estimated residual value of $50,000. The equipment and store fixtures will be replaced at the end of five years; these assets are being depreciated by the double-diminishing-balance method, with zero residual value. At the end of the first year, the franchise has dishes and supplies worth $2,000.

Show what the franchise will report for supplies, capital assets, and cash flows at the end of the first year on its

- Income statement
- Balance sheet
- Statement of cash flows (investing only)

Show all computations.

Note: The purchase of dishes and supplies is an operating cash flow because supplies are a current asset.

Learning Objective ❸
Comparing depreciation methods for income tax purposes

E7-21 On June 30, 2011, Baie Comeau Products Ltd. paid $210,000 for equipment that is expected to have a seven-year life. In this industry, the residual value of equipment is approximately 10% of the asset's cost. Baie Comeau Products Ltd.'s revenues for the year are $100,000, and expenses total $60,000 before depreciation.

Determine the extra amount of cash that Baie Comeau Products can invest by using CCA versus straight-line and claiming less than maximum CCA for the year ended December 31, 2011. The *Income Tax Act* CCA rate is 20%. The income tax rate is 30%. Apply the half-year rule.

Learning Objective ❷
Changing a building's useful life

E7-22 Assume The Salvation Army purchased a building for $900,000 and depreciated it on a straight-line basis over 30 years. The estimated residual value was $100,000. After using the building for 10 years, the Salvation Army realized that the building will remain useful for only 10 more years. Starting with the 11th year, the Salvation Army began depreciating the building over the newly revised total life of 20 years and decreased the estimated residual value to $75,000. What is the effect on depreciation expense on the building for years 11 and 12?

Learning Objective ❹
Analyzing the effect of a sale of equipment; DDB depreciation

E7-23 Assume that on January 2, 2011, a Pizza Hut franchise purchased fixtures for $15,000 cash, expecting the fixtures to remain in service five years. The shop has depreciated the fixtures on a double-diminishing-balance basis, with $1,000 estimated residual value. On June 30, 2012, Pizza Hut sold the fixtures for $5,000 cash. Record both the depreciation expense on the fixtures for 2012 and then the sale of the fixtures. Apart from your journal entry, also show how to compute the gain or loss on Pizza Hut's disposal of these fixtures.

Learning Objective ❶❷❹
Measuring equipment's cost, using UOP depreciation, and derecognizing a used asset

E7-24 Bison Transport is a large trucking company that operates from Ontario to British Columbia in Canada and in the United States. Bison uses the units-of-production (UOP) method to depreciate its trucks because its managers believe UOP depreciation best measures wear and tear.

Bison Transport trades in its trucks often to keep driver morale high and maximize fuel efficiency. Assume that in 2008, the company acquired a tractor-trailer rig costing $280,000 and expected it to remain in service for five years or 1,000,000 km. Estimated residual value would be $40,000. During 2008, the truck was driven 130,000 km; during 2009, 180,000 km; and during 2010, 180,000 km. After 90,000 km in 2011, the company wishes to trade in the tractor-trailer rig for a new rig. Determine the carrying value of the rig and prepare the journal entry to derecognize the rig.

Learning Objective ❺
Analyzing intangible assets

E7-25 Following is an excerpt from the balance sheet of On the Edge Technologies Inc.:

	(in thousands)	
	2011	2010
Goodwill (Note 4)	$60.7	$51.8
Intangible assets (Note 4)	48.4	42.4

A potential investor in On the Edge has asked you for advice. What information would you look for in the accompanying notes to the financial statements on which to base your advice about the investment decision?

Learning Objective ❺
Recording intangibles, amortization, and a change in the asset's useful life

E7-26 Holze Music Company purchased for $600,000 a patent for a new sound system. Although it gives legal protection for 20 years, the patent is expected to provide the company with a competitive advantage for only six years. Make journal entries to record (a) the purchase of the patent and (b) amortization for year 1.

After using the patent for two years, Holze Music Company's research director learns at a professional meeting that BOSE is designing a more powerful system. On the basis of this new information, Holze Music Company determines that the patent's total useful life is only four years. Record amortization for year 3.

Learning Objective ❺❻
Business acquisitions and statement of cash flows

E7-27 Research In Motion (RIM), the manufacturer of BlackBerry smartphones, recently reported in the statement of cash flows and notes to the financial statements in its annual report that it had made acquisitions of U.S.$6.2 million. Assume the balance sheet reported an increase in goodwill for the year in the amount of U.S.$4.5 million.

Required

1. What is the definition of goodwill?
2. Explain the meaning of (a) the $6.2 million that RIM reported on the statement of cash flows and (b) the $4.5 million increase in goodwill on the balance sheet.
3. RIM's income statement and statement of cash flows do not show any charges for amortization of goodwill during the year. Explain the reason for the lack of charges.

Learning Objective ❺
Measuring and recording goodwill

E7-28 Assume that Google paid $18 million to purchase MySpace.com. Assume further that MySpace had the following summarized data at the time of the Google acquisition (amounts in millions of U.S. dollars).

Assets		**Liabilities and Equity**	
Current assets	$10	Total liabilities	$24
Long-term assets	20	Shareholders' equity	6
	$30		$30

MySpace's long-term assets had a current value of only $15 million.

Required

1. Compute the cost of the goodwill purchased by Google.
2. Record the purchase of MySpace.
3. Explain how Google will account for goodwill in the future.

Learning Objective 6
Interpreting a statement of cash flows

E7-29 The following items are excerpted from an annual report of a large retailer.

Consolidated Statement of Cash Flows (Partial, Adapted)
For the Year Ended December 30, 2011

	amounts in millions
Cash flow from operating activities:	
Net income	$ 185.1
Noncash items:	
Depreciation	90.9
Cash flow from investing activities:	
Property, plant, and equipment	$(233.6)
Other investments	(0.6)
Disposal of assets	17.0

Required

1. Why is depreciation listed on the statement of cash flows?
2. Explain in detail each investing activity.

Learning Objective 6
Reporting cash flows for property and equipment

E7-30 Assume Flowers to Go Ltd., a chain of flower shops, completed the following transactions. For each transaction, show what the company would report for investing activities on its statement of cash flows. Show negative amounts in parentheses.

a. Sold a building for $600,000. The building had cost $1,000,000, and at the time of the sale its accumulated depreciation totalled $400,000.
b. Lost a store building in a fire. The warehouse cost $300,000 and had accumulated depreciation of $180,000. The insurance proceeds received were $120,000.
c. Renovated a store at a cost of $400,000, paying cash.
d. Purchased store fixtures for $60,000. The fixtures are expected to remain in service for five years and then be sold for $10,000. Flowers to Go uses the straight-line depreciation method.

Challenge Exercises

Learning Objective 2
Units-of-production depreciation

E7-31 Good Life Clubs purchased exercise equipment at a cost of $100,000 each. In addition, Good Life paid $2,000 for a special platform on which to stabilize the equipment for use. Freight costs of $2,500 to ship the equipment were paid by the equipment supplier. Good Life will depreciate the equipment by the units-of-production method, based on an expected useful life of 50,000 hours of exercise. The estimated residual value of the equipment is $10,000. How many hours of usage can Good Life expect from the equipment if budgeted depreciation expense is $10,304 for the year?

E7-32 Collicutt Energy Services Ltd. of Calgary, Alberta, reported the following for land, buildings, and equipment (in millions):

Learning Objective 4
Determining the gain or loss on sale of property and equipment

	December 31	
	2011	2010
Land, buildings, and equipment	$ 544.1	$ 575.1
Accumulated depreciation	(195.1)	(209.4)

During 2011, Collicutt Energy paid $74.2 million for new property and equipment. Depreciation for the year totalled $38.1 million. During 2011, Collicutt sold property and equipment for $20.2 million. How much was Collicutt's gain or loss on the sale of the property and equipment?

E7-33 Rindy Inc. has a popular line of beaded jewellery. Rindy Inc. reported net earnings of $21,000 for 2010. Depreciation expense for furniture, fixtures, equipment, and automotive totalled $1,000. Rindy depreciates furniture, fixtures, equipment, and automotive on a straight-line basis over five years and assumes no residual value. The company's income tax rate is 25%.

Learning Objective 2
Determining net income after a change in depreciation method

Assume that Rindy's furniture, fixtures, equipment, and automotive are three years old and that Rindy switches over to double-diminishing-balance (DDB) depreciation at the start of fiscal 2011. Further, assume that fiscal 2011 is expected to be the same as fiscal 2010 except for the change in depreciation method. How much net income can Rindy expect to earn during fiscal 2011?

E7-34 Air New Zealand (ANZ) is a Star Alliance member airline. Assume that early in 2011, ANZ purchased equipment at a cost of $200,000 (NZ). Management expects the equipment to remain in service four years and estimated residual value to be negligible. ANZ uses the straight-line depreciation method. Through an accounting error, ANZ expensed the entire cost of the equipment at the time of purchase.

Learning Objective 1
Capitalizing versus expensing; measuring the effect of an error

Required

Prepare a schedule to show the overstatement or understatement in the following items at the end of each year over the five-year life of the equipment. Ignore income taxes.

1. Total current assets 2. Equipment, net 3. Net income 4. Owners' equity

Quiz

Test your understanding of accounting for property, plant, and equipment, and intangibles by answering the following questions. Select the best choice from among the possible answers given.

Q7-35 A capital expenditure

a. Is expensed immediately
b. Records additional capital
c. Adds to an asset
d. Is a credit like capital (owners' equity)

Q7-36 Which of the following items should be accounted for as a capital expenditure?

a. Taxes paid in conjunction with the purchase of office equipment
b. The monthly rental cost of an office building
c. Costs incurred to repair leaks in the building's roof
d. Maintenance fees paid with funds provided by the company's capital

Q7-37 Suppose you buy land for $3,000,000 and spend $1,000,000 to develop the property. You then divide the land into lots as follows:

Category	Sale price per lot
10 Hilltop lots	$500,000
10 Valley lots	300,000

How much did each hilltop lot cost you?

a. $171,429
b. $228,571
c. $250,000
d. $400,000

Q7-38 Which statement about depreciation is false?

a. Depreciation is a process of allocating the cost of an asset to expense over its useful life.
b. Depreciation should not be recorded in years that the fair value of the asset has increased.
c. Residual value is the expected cash value of an asset at the end of its useful life.
d. Obsolescence as well as physical wear and tear should be considered when determining the period over which an asset should be depreciated.

Q7-39 A business would choose to use CCA for tax purposes for which of the following reasons?

a. It is easier to calculate.
b. The useful life of the asset is allocated appropriately.
c. Taxable income is lowest in the early years of the asset's life.
d. The Canada Revenue Agency requires this method.

Q7-40 The Blossom Shoppe's business activity fluctuates over its fiscal year, with December being its busiest month. Which method of depreciation would be most appropriate for its delivery van?

a. Straight-line
b. Diminishing-balance
c. Units-of-production
d. Some other method

Q7-41 Kramer Company failed to record depreciation of equipment. How does this omission affect Kramer's financial statements?

a. Net income is overstated, and assets are understated.
b. Net income is understated, and assets are understated.
c. Net income is understated, and assets are overstated.
d. Net income is overstated, and assets are overstated.

Q7-42 Jack's Stereo Inc. uses the double-diminishing-balance method for depreciation on its computers. Which item is not needed to compute depreciation for the first year?

a. Original cost
b. Estimated residual value
c. Expected useful life in years
d. All the above are needed

Q7-43 Which of the following costs is reported on a company's income statement?

a. Accumulated depreciation
b. Land
c. Accounts payable
d. Depreciation expense

Q7-44 Which of the following items is reported on the balance sheet? (Challenge)

a. Net sales revenue
b. Accumulated depreciation
c. Gain on disposal of equipment
d. Cost of goods sold

Q7-45 Which of the following transactions does not appear on a statement of cash flows?

a. Purchase of plant, property, and equipment
b. Accumulated depreciation
c. Cash receipts from sale of property, plant, and equipment
d. Depreciation expense

Q7-46 Intangible assets are different from other assets for which of the following reasons?
a. They have special rights to current and expected future benefits.
b. They do not become obsolete.
c. They have no physical form.
d. They are not amortized.

Q7-47 Your self-storage company has purchased a moving company for $400,000. The fair value of the moving company's net assets is $325,000. How do you record the $75,000 difference?
a. As an expense on the income statement
b. As a property, plant, and equipment cost
c. As a long-term asset named goodwill
d. None of the above

Q7-48 A company has purchased the rights to a patent valued at $850,000. The company expects the useful life of the patent to be five years. The correct amortization for this asset would be which of the following?
a. Straight-line over five years
b. Units-of-production method based on a capital asset of $850,000
c. Diminishing-balance method based on a capital asset of $850,000
d. Units-of-production method based on a capital asset determined by the company

Q7-49 Suppose The Globe and Mail paid $1 million for a rural newspaper in Ontario three years ago. The newspaper's assets were valued at $1,000,000 and its liabilities at $150,000. The company recorded $150,000 as goodwill at the time of the purchase. What *amortization* expense will be recorded for the current year?
a. $30,000 based on straight-line amortization over five years
b. No amortization, as review of the goodwill indicates there has been reduction in its value
c. No amortization, as the goodwill was fully expensed in the year of purchase
d. None of the above

Problems

(Group A)

P7-50A Assume Milne's Moving & Storage Ltd. (MMS) of Regina, Saskatchewan, incurred the following costs in acquiring land, making land improvements, and constructing and furnishing its own storage warehouse:

Learning Objective 1 2
Identifying the elements of property and plant's cost

Item	Amount
a. Purchase price of 4 acres of land, including an old building that will be used for an office (land fair value is $320,000, building fair value is $80,000)	$350,000
b. Landscaping (additional dirt and earth moving)	8,100
c. Fence around the land	31,600
d. Lawyer fee for title search on the land	1,000
e. Delinquent real estate taxes on the land to be paid by MMS	7,500
f. Company signs at front of the company property	3,400
g. Building permit for the warehouse	1,500
h. Architect fee for the design of the warehouse	24,500
i. Masonry, carpentry, roofing, and other labour to construct the warehouse	920,000
j. Renovation of the office building	50,200
k. Interest cost on construction loan for warehouse	9,700
l. Landscaping (trees and shrubs)	8,200
m. Parking lot, concrete walks, and lights on the property	57,600
n. Concrete, wood, and other materials used in the construction of the warehouse	234,300
o. Supervisory salary of construction supervisor (85% to warehouse, 5% to land improvements, 10% to office building)	60,000
p. Office furniture	115,700
q. Transportation and installation of furniture	2,300

Assume MMS depreciates buildings over 40 years, land improvements over 20 years, and furniture over eight years, all on a straight-line basis with zero residual value.

Required

1. Set up columns for Land, Land Improvements, Warehouse, Office Building, and Furniture. Show how to account for each of MMS's costs by listing the cost under the correct account. Determine the total cost of each asset.
2. Assuming that all construction was complete and the assets were placed in service on September 1, 2011, record depreciation for the year ended December 31, 2011. Round to the nearest dollar.
3. Identify the management issues included in this problem and what effect they have on business operations.

Learning Objective 2
Recording property, plant, and equipment transactions; reporting on the balance sheet

P7-51A Lifestyle Lighting Ltd. reported the following on its balance sheet at December 31, 2010:

Capital assets, at cost:	
Land	$ 150,000
Buildings	400,000
Less Accumulated depreciation	(87,500)
Equipment	600,000
Less Accumulated depreciation	(260,000)

In early July 2011, Lifestyle Lighting Ltd. expanded operations and purchased additional equipment at a cost of $100,000. The company depreciates buildings by the straight-line method over 20 years with residual value of $50,000. Due to obsolescence, the equipment has a useful life of only 10 years and is being depreciated by the double-diminishing-balance method with zero residual value.

Required

1. Journalize Lifestyle Lighting Ltd.'s capital equipment purchase and depreciation transactions for 2011.
2. Report capital assets on the December 31, 2011, balance sheet.

Learning Objective 1 2 4
Recording property, plant, and equipment transactions, derecognition, and changes in useful life

P7-52A Assume that Inter-Provincial Transport Ltd.'s balance sheet includes the following assets under Property, Plant, and Equipment: Land, Buildings, and Motor-Carrier Equipment. Inter-Provincial has a separate accumulated depreciation account for each of these assets except land. Further, assume that Inter-Provincial completed the following transactions:

2011	
Jan. 2	Sold motor-carrier equipment with accumulated depreciation of $67,000 (cost of $130,000) for $70,000 cash. Purchased similar new equipment with a cash price of $176,000.
July 3	Sold a building that had cost $650,000 and had accumulated depreciation of $145,000 through December 31 of the preceding year. Depreciation is computed on a straight-line basis. The building had a 40-year useful life and a residual value of $250,000. Inter-Provincial received $100,000 cash and a $400,000 note receivable.
Oct. 29	Purchased land and a building for a single price of $420,000. An independent appraisal valued the land at $150,000 and the building at $300,000.
Dec. 31	Recorded depreciation as follows: New motor-carrier equipment has an expected useful life of six years and an estimated residual value of 5% of cost. Depreciation is computed on the double-diminishing-balance method. Depreciation on buildings is computed by the straight-line method. The new building carries a 40-year useful life and a residual value equal to 10% of its cost.

Required

Record the transactions in Inter-Provincial Transport Ltd.'s journal.

Learning Objective 2
Explaining the concept of depreciation

P7-53A The board of directors of Special Services is reviewing its 2011 annual report. A new board member—a nurse with little business experience—questions the accountant about the depreciation amounts. The nurse wonders why depreciation expense has decreased from \$200,000 in 2009 to \$184,000 in 2010 to \$172,000 in 2011. She states that she could understand the decreasing annual amounts if the company had been disposing of buildings each year, but that has not occurred. Further, she notes that growth in the city is increasing the values of company buildings. Why is the company recording depreciation when the property values are increasing?

Required

Write a paragraph or two to explain the concept of depreciation to the nurse and to answer her questions.

Learning Objective 2 3
Computing depreciation by three methods and the cash-flow advantage of accelerated depreciation for tax purposes

P7-54A On January 3, 2011, B.W. Soffer Inc. paid \$224,000 for a computer system. In addition to the basic purchase price, the company paid a setup fee of \$6,200, \$6,700 sales tax, and \$3,100 for special installation. Management estimates that the computer will remain in service for five years and have a residual value of \$20,000. The computer will process 50,000 documents the first year, decreasing annually by 5,000 during each of the next four years (that is, 45,000 documents in 2012, 40,000 documents in 2013, and so on). In trying to decide which depreciation method to use, the company president has requested a depreciation schedule for each of three depreciation methods (straight-line, units-of-production, and double-diminishing-balance).

Required

1. Prepare a depreciation schedule for each of the three depreciation methods listed, showing asset cost, depreciation expense, accumulated depreciation, and asset carrying amount.
2. B.W. Soffer Inc. reports to shareholders and creditors in the financial statements using the depreciation method that maximizes reported income in the early years of asset use. For income tax purposes, however, the company uses the depreciation method that minimizes income. Consider the first year B.W. Soffer Inc. uses the computer system. Identify the depreciation method that meets the company's objectives. Discuss the advantages of each depreciation method.
3. Assume that cash provided by operations before income tax is \$150,000 for the computer system's first year. The income tax rate is 25%. For the method chosen by B.W. Soffer Inc. and for tax identified in Requirement 2, compare the net income and cash provided by operations (cash flow). Show which method gives the net-income advantage and which method gives the cash-flow advantage. (For purposes of this problem, assume the CCA rate of 30% and ignore the 50% CCA rule for year of purchase.)

Learning Objective 2 4 6
Analyzing property, plant, and equipment transactions from a company's financial statements

P7-55A The excerpts that follow are adapted from financial statements of a Canadian not-for-profit organization.

(amounts in thousands)	March 31	
Balance Sheet	2011	2010
Assets		
Total current assets	\$277,631	\$261,015
Property, plant, and equipment	68,406	61,225
Less accumulated depreciation	(26,909)	(22,725)
Long-term investments	108,302	147,165

Consolidated Statement of Cash Flows	For the Year Ended March 31 2011	2010
Operating excess of revenues over expense	$13,068	$15,321
Noncash items affecting net income:		
Depreciation	4,184	3,748
Cash flows from investing activities:		
Additions to property, plant, and equipment	(7,781)	(8,623)
Reduction of (additions to) long-term investments	38,863	(96,316)

Required

1. How much was the entity's cost of property, plant, and equipment at March 31, 2011? How much was the carrying amount of capital assets? Show computations.
2. The financial statements give four pieces of evidence that the entity purchased property, plant, and equipment and sold long-term investments during 2011. What is the evidence?
3. Prepare T-accounts for property, plant and equipment, Accumulated Depreciation, and Long-Term Investments. Then show all the activity in these accounts during 2011. Label each increase or decrease and give its dollar amount.
4. Why is depreciation added to net income on the statement of cash flows?

Learning Objective 5
Accounting for intangibles and the related expenses

P7-56A Part 1. Sobeys Inc.'s balance sheet reports the asset Cost in Excess of Net Assets of Purchased Businesses. Assume that Sobeys acquired another company, which carried these figures:

Carrying amount of net assets	$3.8 million
Fair value of assets	4.1 million

Required

1. What is the term used in Canadian financial reporting for the asset Cost in Excess of Net Assets of Purchased Businesses?
2. Record Sobeys Inc.'s purchase of the other company for $5.3 million cash.
3. Assume that Sobeys determined that the asset Cost in Excess of Net Assets of Purchased Businesses increased in value by $800,000. How would this transaction be recorded? Then, suppose Cost in Excess of Net Assets of Purchased Businesses decreased in value by $800,000. How would this transaction be recorded? Discuss the basis for your decision in each case.

Part 2. Suppose Ford paid $2.6 million for a patent related to an integrated system including hands-free cell phone, GPS, and iPod connectivity. The company expects to install this system in its automobiles for four years. Ford will sell this as an "extra" for $1,500. In the first year, 10,000 units were sold. All costs per unit totalled $835.

Required

1. As the CFO, how would you record transactions relating to the patent in the first year?
2. Prepare the income statement for the integrated system's operations for the first year. Evaluate the profitability of the integrated system's operations. Use an income tax rate of 38%.
3. Explain what items were recorded as assets and why.

Learning Objective 6
Reporting property, plant, and equipment transactions on the statement of cash flows

P7-57A At the end of 2010, Geothermal Heating Ltd. had total assets of $17.4 million and total liabilities of $9.2 million. Included among the assets were property, plant, and equipment with a cost of $4.8 million and accumulated depreciation of $3.4 million.

Assume that Geothermal Heating completed the following selected transactions during 2011. The company earned total revenues of $26.5 million and incurred total expenses of $21.3 million, which included depreciation of $1.7 million. During the year, Geothermal Heating paid $1.4 million for new equipment and sold old equipment for $0.3 million. The cost of the assets sold was $0.8 million, and their accumulated depreciation was $0.4 million.

Required

1. Explain how to determine whether Geothermal Heating had a gain or loss on the sale of old equipment during the year. What was the amount of the gain or loss, if any?
2. How will Geothermal Heating report property, plant, and equipment on the balance sheet at December 31, 2011, after all the year's activity? What will be the carrying amount of property, plant, and equipment?
3. How will Geothermal Heating report operating activities and investing activities on its statement of cash flows for 2011? The company's statement of cash flows starts with net income.

(Group B)

Learning Objective ❶❷
Identifying the elements of property, plant, and equipment cost

P7-58B McMillan Tire Inc. operates in several provinces. The head office incurred the following costs in acquiring land and a building, making land improvements, and constructing and furnishing a garage showroom.

a. Purchase price of land, including a building that will be enlarged to be a warehouse (land fair value is $150,000; building fair value is $50,000)	$180,000
b. Fence around the land	26,000
c. Company signs near front and rear approaches to the company property	25,000
d. Title insurance on the land acquisition	1,200
e. Renovation of the warehouse	21,300
f. Landscaping (additional dirt and earth moving)	3,550
g. Architect fee for the design of the garage/showroom	45,000
h. Building permit for the building	200
i. Delinquent real estate taxes on the land to be paid by McMillan	3,700
j. Concrete, wood, and other materials used in the construction of the garage/showroom	322,000
k. Supervisory salary of construction supervisor (90% to garage/showroom; 6% to land improvements, and 4% to building renovation)	55,000
l. Landscaping (trees and shrubs)	5,350
m. Masonry, carpentry, roofing, and other labour to construct the garage/showroom	234,000
n. Lights for the parking lot, walkways, and company signs	8,900
o. Parking lots and concrete walks on the property	17,450
p. Interest cost on construction loan for garage/showroom	3,300
q. Installation of equipment	8,000
r. Equipment for the garage/showroom	80,000

McMillan Tire depreciates buildings over 40 years, land improvements over 10 years, and equipment over eight years, all on a straight-line basis with zero residual value.

Required

1. Determine the total cost of each asset. Set up columns for Land, Land Improvements, Garage/Showroom, Warehouse, and Equipment. Decide how to account for each of McMillan's costs by listing the cost under the correct account.
2. All construction was complete and the assets were placed in service on March 29. Record depreciation for the year ended December 31. Round figures to the nearest dollar.
3. Identify the issues of this problem, and discuss how your decisions would affect the results of McMillan Tire Inc.

Learning Objective 1 2
Recording property, plant, and equipment transactions; reporting on the balance sheet

P7-59B Moreau Lock & Key Ltd. has a hefty investment in security equipment, as reported in the company's balance sheet at December 31, 2010:

Property, plant, and equipment, at cost:	
Land	$ 200,000
Buildings	310,000
Less Accumulated depreciation	(40,000)
Security equipment	620,000
Less Accumulated depreciation	(370,000)

In early October 2011, Moreau Lock & Key purchased additional security equipment at a cost of $80,000. The company amortizes buildings by the straight-line method over 20 years with a residual value of $70,000. Due to obsolescence, security equipment has a useful life of only eight years and is being depreciated by the double-diminishing-balance method with zero residual value.

Required

1. How will Moreau Lock & Key's equipment purchase be recorded? What will the 2011 depreciation expense be?
2. Report property, plant, and equipment on the company's December 31, 2011, balance sheet.

Learning Objective 1 2 4
Recording property, plant, and equipment transactions, derecognition and changes in useful life

P7-60B Schmaltz Cable Company's balance sheet reports the following assets under Property, Plant, and Equipment: Land, Buildings, Office Furniture, Communication Equipment, and Televideo Equipment. The company has a separate accumulated depreciation account for each of these assets except land. Assume that Schmaltz Cable completed the following transactions:

2011	
Jan. 4	Sold communication equipment with accumulated depreciation of $85,000 (cost of $96,000) for $18,000. Purchased new equipment for $118, 000.
June 30	Sold a building that had cost $495,000 and had accumulated depreciation of $255,000 through December 31 of the preceding year. Depreciation is computed on a straight-line basis. The building has a 40-year useful life and a residual value of $95,000. The company received $50,000 cash and a $250,000 note receivable.
Nov. 4	Purchased used communication and televideo equipment from Rogers Cable Company. Total cost was $80,000 paid in cash. An independent appraisal valued the communication equipment at $75,000 and the televideo equipment at $25,000.
Dec. 31	Depreciation is recorded as follows: Equipment is depreciated by the double-diminishing-balance method over a five-year life with zero residual value. Depreciation is recorded separately on the equipment purchased on January 4 and on November 4.

Required

If Schmaltz Cable has recorded these transactions correctly, what should your review of the company's records show?

Learning Objective 2
Explaining the concept of depreciation

P7-61B The board of directors of the Canadian Red Cross is having its regular quarterly meeting. Accounting policies are on the agenda, and depreciation is being discussed. A new board member, a social worker, has some strong opinions about two aspects of depreciation policy. The new board member argues that depreciation must be coupled with a fund to replace company assets. Otherwise, there is no substance to depreciation, he argues. He also challenges the three-year estimated life over which the Canadian Red Cross is depreciating association computers. He notes that the computers will last much longer and should be depreciated over at least 10 years.

Required

Write a paragraph or two to explain the concept of depreciation to the new board member and to answer his arguments.

Learning Objective ②③
Computing depreciation by three methods and the cash-flow advantage of accelerated depreciation for tax purposes

P7-62B On January 2, 2011, Yuki Sporting Goods Ltd. purchased branding equipment at a cost of $63,000. Before placing the equipment in service, the company spent $2,200 for delivery, $4,000 to customize the equipment, and $800 for installation. Management estimates that the equipment will remain in service for six years and have a residual value of $16,000. The equipment can be expected to brand 18,000 pieces in each of the first four years and 14,000 pieces in each of the next two years. In trying to decide which depreciation method to use, George Yuki requests a depreciation schedule for each method (straight-line, units-of-production, and double-diminishing-balance).

Required

1. Prepare a depreciation schedule for each of the depreciation methods listed, showing asset cost, depreciation expense, accumulated depreciation, and asset carrying value.
2. Yuki Sporting Goods reports to its banker in the financial statements using the depreciation method that maximizes reported income in the early years of asset use. For income tax purposes, however, the company uses maximum CCA, the method that minimizes income. Consider the first year that Yuki Sporting Goods uses the equipment. Identify the depreciation method that meets the company's objectives. Explain your choice. (The *Income Tax Act* permits maximum capital cost allowance for equipment of 30%. Ignore CRA's 50% rule in year of purchase.)
3. Cash provided by operations before income tax is $100,000 for the equipment's first year. The corporate income tax rate is 25%. For the two methods identified in Requirement 2, compare the net income and cash provided by operations (cash flow). Identify the method that gives the net-income advantage and identify the method that gives the cash-flow advantage.

Learning Objective ②④⑤⑥
Analyzing property, plant, and equipment transactions from a company's financial statements

P7-63B CrossCanada Transport Inc. (CC), provides warehouse and distribution services . The excerpts that follow are adapted from CC's financial statements for fiscal year 2011.

(amounts in thousands)	**October 31,**	
Balance Sheet	**2011**	**2010**
Assets		
Total current assets	$237,936	$208,530
Premises and equipment	5,941	5,246
Less Accumulated depreciation	(3,810)	(3,428)
Goodwill	4,752	4,304
	For the Year Ended October 31	
Statement of Cash Flows (in millions)	**2011**	**2010**
Cash provided from operating activities:		
Net income from continuing operations	$5,492	$4,757
Noncash items affecting net income:		
Depreciation	434	405
Cash used in investing activities:		
Acquisition of premises and equipment	(706)	(511)
Cash used in acquisitions (including $41 of premises and equipment)	(373)	(256)

Required

1. How much was CC's cost of property and equipment at October 31, 2011? How much was the carrying amount of premises and equipment? Show computations.

2. The financial statements give four pieces of evidence that CC purchased premises and equipment during 2011. What are they?
3. Prepare T-accounts for Premises and Equipment and Accumulated Depreciation. Then show all the activity in these accounts during 2011. Did CC dispose of any assets and, if so, what was the carrying amount?
4. Why has goodwill not been amortized?

Learning Objective 5
Accounting for intangibles, and the related expenses

P7-64B Part 1. The Coca-Cola Company's (CCC) balance sheet reports the asset Goodwill. Assume that CCC purchased an asset to be included in Goodwill as part of the acquisition of another company, which carried these figures (thousands of dollars):

Carrying amount of long-term assets	$34,550
Fair value of assets	49,000
Liabilities	4,500

Required

1. Explain the terms *carrying amount of assets*, *fair value of assets*, and *goodwill*. On what would you base the purchase price of the acquisition?
2. Make the journal entry to record CCC's purchase of the other company for $50,000 cash.

Part 2. Joshua Thomas has written a new dance song which Luv Sound Inc. would like to record. Joshua is negotiating the rights to the new song. It is estimated that Luv Sound will sell about 500,000 recordings either on CD, to radio station airings, or to iPod sales. Joshua would like to receive $2,000,000 for the copyright to this song.

Required

1. As the CFO of Luv Sound, decide whether $2,000,000 is an appropriate amount to pay for the copyright for Joshua Thomas's song.
2. If you chose to purchase the copyright, show how you would record the transaction.
3. What would be the accumulated amortization after 300,000 copies of song had been sold by Luv Sound Inc.?

Learning Objective 6
Reporting property, plant, and equipment transactions on the statement of cash flows

P7-65B At the end of 2010, a telecommunications company had total assets of $15.3 billion and total liabilities of $10.7 billion. Included among the assets were property, plant, and equipment with a cost of $16.4 billion and accumulated depreciation of $9.1 billion.

Suppose that the company completed the following selected transactions during 2011. The company earned total revenues of $11.6 billion and incurred total expenses of $9.89 billion, which included depreciation of $1.84 billion. During the year, the company paid $1.8 billion for new property, plant, and equipment and sold old property, plant, and equipment for $0.2 billion. The cost of the assets sold was $0.29 billion and their accumulated depreciation was $0.29 billion.

Required

1. Explain how to determine whether the company had a gain or a loss on the sale of the old property, plant, and equipment. What was the amount of the gain or loss, if any?
2. Show how the company would report property, plant, and equipment on the balance sheet at December 31, 2011.
3. Show how the company would report operating activities and investing activities on its statement of cash flows for 2011. The company's statement of cash flows starts with net income.

Apply Your Knowledge

Decision Cases

Learning Objective 2 3
Measuring profitability based on different depreciation methods

Case 1. Suppose you are considering investing in two businesses, La Petite France Bakery and Burgers Ahoy Inc. The two companies are virtually identical, and both began operations at the beginning of the current year.

In early January, both companies purchased equipment costing $175,000 that had a 10-year estimated useful life and a $10,000 residual value. La Petite France uses the depreciation method that maximizes reported income for both reporting and tax purposes. In contrast, Burgers Ahoy uses the double-diminishing-balance method for depreciation purposes. Assume that both companies' trial balances at December 31 included the following:

Sales revenue	$350,000
Cost of goods sold	94,000
Operating expenses before depreciation	50,000

The income tax rate is 25%. The maximum capital cost allowance rate is 20%.

Required

1. Prepare both companies' income statements.
2. Write an investment newsletter to address the following questions for your clients. Which company appears to be more profitable? Which company has more cash to invest in promising projects? If prices continue rising over the long term, in which company would you prefer to invest? Why?

Learning Objective 1 5
Property, plant, and equipment and intangible assets

Case 2. The following questions are unrelated except that they all apply to property, plant, and equipment and intangible assets:

1. The manager of Fashion Forward Ltd. regularly buys property, plant, and equipment and debits the cost to Repairs and Maintenance Expense. Why would she do that, since she knows this action violates IFRS?
2. The manager of Greytown Express Inc. regularly debits the cost of repairs and maintenance of property, plant, and equipment to Plant and Equipment. Why would he do that, since he knows he is violating IFRS?
3. It has been suggested that because many intangible assets have no value except to the company that owns them, they should be valued at $1.00 or zero on the balance sheet. Many accountants disagree with this view. Which view do you support? Why?

Ethical Issue

Vitner's Ltd. purchased land and a building for the lump sum of $6.0 million. To get the maximum tax deduction, Mary Drink allocated 80% of the purchase price to the building and only 20% to the land. A more realistic allocation would have been 60% to the building and 40% to the land.

Required

1. Explain the tax advantage of allocating too much to the building and too little to the land.
2. Was Vitner's allocation ethical? If so, state why. If not, why not? Identify who was harmed.

Focus on Financials

Learning Objective 2 4 6
Explaining property, plant, and equipment activity

Gildan Activewear Inc.

Refer to the Gildan financial statements in Appendix A at the end of this book, and answer the following questions.

1. Which depreciation method does Gildan use for reporting to shareholders and creditors in the financial statements? Would the company use the same method for income tax reporting? Give your reasons.
2. During 2009, Gildan sold property, plant, and equipment (assets). What were the proceeds? What was the cost of the property, plant and equipment disposed of?
3. How much did Gildan pay for property and equipment during 2009? What about in 2008? Evaluate the trend in these expenditures as to whether it conveys good news for Gildan.
4. During 2009, Gildan added new property, plant, and equipment. Therefore, it is possible that the company's property and equipment at the end of 2009 were proportionately newer than the assets the company held at the end of 2008. Were property and equipment proportionately newer or older at the end of 2009 (versus 2008)?

Focus on Analysis

Learning Objective 2 3 5 6
Analyzing property, plant, and equipment and intangible assets

Gildan Activewear Inc.

Refer to Gildan's financial statements in Appendix A at the end of the book, and answer the following questions:

1. In Note 4, Plant and Equipment, of the notes to the Gildan financial statements, an item "Assets not in service" is listed. Explain why these assets are not being depreciated.
2. How much was Gildan's depreciation and amortization expense during fiscal year 2009? How much was Gildan's accumulated depreciation and amortization at the end of year 2008? Explain why accumulated depreciation and amortization exceeds depreciation and amortization expense for the year 2009.
3. Explain why Gildan adds depreciation and amortization expenses back to net income in the computation of net cash from operating activities.
4. Does Gildan have any goodwill? How did it arise? In 2009, was amortization on goodwill charged? Gildan describes intangible assets. What are they? How much amortization of intangible assets did Gildan record in 2009?

Group Project

To do this project, choose and visit a local business or use your educational institution. If neither of these situations is appropriate, choose a type of business and develop the property, plant, and equipment, goodwill, and intangible assets as outlined below.

Required

1. List all the property, plant, and equipment assets for the business or organization you have chosen.
2. If possible, interview the manager. Gain as much information as you can about the company's property, plant, and equipment assets. For example, try to determine the assets' costs, the depreciation method the company is using, and the estimated useful life of each asset category. If an interview is impossible, then develop your own estimates of the assets' costs, useful lives, and book values, assuming appropriate depreciation methods.

3. Determine whether the business has any intangible assets. If it does, list them and find as much information as possible about their nature, cost, and estimated lives.
4. Write a detailed report of your findings, and be prepared to present your results to the class. Include your evaluation of the property, plant, and equipment of this business based on cost allocation, method of depreciation, and value to the business.

Quick Check Answers

1. *b [($850,000/[$850,000 + $675,000 + $475,000]) × $1,500,000 = $637,500]*
2. *a*
3. *a [($25,000 − $2,500)/5 × 5/12 = $1,875]*
4. *d [($25,000 − $2,500)/5 × 2 = $9,000; $25,000 − $9,000 = $16,000]*
5. *b [$25,000 × 2/5 = $10,000; ($25,000 − $10,000) × 2/5 = $6,000]*
6. *a [($25,000 − $2,500)/5 × 4 = $18,000; $25,000 − $18,000 = $7,000; $11,500 − $7,000 = gain of $4,500, therefore, a benefit will be realized]*
7. *c [$17,000 × 2/4 = $8,500; ($17,000 − $8,500) × 2/4 = $4,250; $8,500 + $4,250 = $12,750]*
8. *c*
9. *a*
10. *d*
11. *b*
12. *e*

Appendix 7A

Depreciation for Accounting Purposes and Capital Cost Allowance for Income Tax Purposes

This topic was introduced on page 357. The following discussion provides a more thorough investigation of the topic.

The majority of businesses use the straight-line method for reporting property, plant, and equipment values and depreciation expense to their owners and creditors on their financial statements. But businesses must keep a separate set of records for calculating the CCA they claim on their tax returns. This is because whatever depreciation method a business uses, depreciation expense on the income statement is different from CCA deducted for income tax purposes. The *Income Tax Act* allows corporations, as well as individuals earning business or professional income, to deduct from income **capital cost allowance (CCA)**, the term CRA uses to describe depreciation for tax purposes. CRA specifies the maximum capital cost allowance rate a taxpayer may use. Different classes of assets have different *capital cost allowance rates*. The capital cost allowance rates published by CRA are maximums. A taxpayer may claim from zero to the maximum capital cost allowance allowed in a year. Most taxpayers claim the maximum CCA since this provides the largest deduction from income as quickly as possible, thus decreasing the immediate tax payments. CCA rates tend to be similar to rates used for accelerated depreciation. Claiming the maximum CCA leaves more cash available for investment or other business uses.

To understand the relationships between cash flow, depreciation, and income tax, we use a van purchased by Bakal Corp. costing $40,000 with a five-year life and zero residual value:

- First-year depreciation is $8,000 under the straight-line depreciation method.
- CRA allows a maximum rate of 30% for vans, so Bakal would be allowed to claim a maximum of 30% or $12,000 in 2009.*

Assume that Bakal Corp. facility has $400,000 in revenue and $300,000 in cash operating expenses during the van's first year and an income tax rate of 30%. The cash flow analysis appears in Exhibit 7A-1.

Exhibit 7A-1 highlights an important fact: The higher the depreciation expense used for tax purposes, the lower the income before tax and thus the lower the tax payment. Therefore, accelerated depreciation helps conserve cash for use in the business. Exhibit 7A-1 shows that Bakal Corp. will have $1,200 (line 10) more cash at the end of the first year if it uses the maximum CCA rate instead of straight-line depreciation.

*Present CRA rules permit a taxpayer to deduct only 50% of the normal CCA in the year of acquisition of a capital asset. The authors have generally ignored that rule for purposes of this chapter to simplify the discussion. Where required to do so in the text, use the rule.

EXHIBIT 7A-1 **The Cash Flow Advantage of Accelerated Depreciation Over Straight-Line Depreciation for Income Tax Purposes**

	SL	CCA
1. Cash revenues	$400,000	$400,000
2. Cash operating expenses	300,000	300,000
3. Cash provided by operations before income tax	100,000	100,000
4. Depreciation/Capital cost allowance expense (a noncash expense)	8,000	12,000
5. Income before income tax	$ 92,000	$ 88,000
6. Income tax expense (30%)	$ 27,600	$ 26,400
Cash-flow analysis:		
7. Cash provided by operations before tax	$100,000	$100,000
8. Income tax expense	27,600	26,400
9. Cash provided by operations	$ 72,400	$ 73,600
10. Extra cash available for investment if maximum CCA is used ($73,600 − $72,400)		$ 1,200

STOP + THINK

Which depreciation method produces a higher net income? How much better? Show how you arrive at your answer.

Answer

Straight-line depreciation makes Bakal look better. Net income under

- Straight-line depreciation is $64,400 ($92,000 − $27,600).
- Accelerated depreciation (maximum CCA) is $61,600 ($88,000 − $26,400).

Under straight-line depreciation, Bakal reports $2,800 ($64,400 − $61,600) more net income. Therefore, most managers prefer to use straight-line depreciation for their financial statements.

8 Liabilities

LEARNING OBJECTIVES

1. **Account** for current liabilities and contingent liabilities
2. **Understand** bonds payable
3. **Account** for bonds payable
4. **Measure** interest expense
5. **Understand** the advantages and disadvantages of borrowing
6. **Account** for leases
7. **Report** liabilities on the balance sheet

SPOTLIGHT

WestJet Airlines Limited: A Success Story

WestJet began operations in 1996 serving five cities in Western Canada and now flies across Canada and to many destinations in the United States and the Caribbean. The airline decided at its start to operate with a single type of plane, the Boeing 737, in order to reduce operating costs. WestJet also decided to encourage share ownership by employees, so that the employee who checks you in, the pilots and cabin staff, and the baggage handlers are all "owners." This has led to a high level of service, which encourages passengers to "fly WestJet."

The airlines have some interesting liabilities. WestJet collects fares in advance and recognizes the revenue when the passenger actually takes the trip. Thus, WestJet had "advance ticket sales" of almost $300 million on its balance sheet at December 31, 2009. WestJet provides future travel credits that are non-refundable and have a fixed life to passengers for flight changes and cancelled flights. The liability was $65 million at December 31, 2009.

WestJet
Consolidated Balance Sheet (Adapted)
December 31, 2009 (in millions)

Assets		Liabilities and Shareholders' Equity	
Current Assets		Current Liabilities	
Cash and cash equivalents	$1,005	Accounts payable and accrued liabilities	$ 231
Other current assets	113	Advance ticket sales	286
Total current assets	1,118	Non-refundable guest credits	65
		Current portion of obligations under capital leases	1
		Current portion of long-term debt	171
		Total current liabilities	754
Property and equipment	2,308	Obligations under capital leases	3
Other long-lived assets	68	Long-term debt	1,048
		Other long-term liabilities	300
			2,105
		Shareholders' Equity	
		Shareholders' equity	1,389
Total assets	$3,494	Total liabilities and shareholders' equity	$3,494

This chapter shows how to account for liabilities—both current and long-term. We begin with current liabilities.

Current Liabilities

1 Account for current liabilities and contingent liabilities

Current liabilities are obligations due within one year or within the company's normal operating cycle if longer. Obligations due beyond that period of time are classified as *long-term liabilities.*

Current liabilities are of two kinds:

- Known amounts
- Estimated amounts

We look first at current liabilities of a known amount.

Current Liabilities of Known Amount

Current liabilities of known amount include accounts payable, short-term notes payable, GST/HST payable, sales tax payable, accrued liabilities, payroll liabilities, unearned revenues, and the current portion of long-term debt and capital leases.

Accounts Payable. Amounts owed for products or services purchased on account are *accounts payable*. For example, WestJet purchases soft drinks on account. We have seen many other examples of accounts payable in previous chapters. One of a merchandiser's most common transactions is the credit purchase of inventory. The Hudson's Bay Company and Sobeys buy their inventory on account.

Short-Term Notes Payable. Short-term notes payable, a common form of financing, are notes payable due within one year. Robertson Construction Inc. may issue short-term notes payable to borrow cash or to purchase assets. For its notes payable,

Robertson must accrue interest expense and interest payable at the end of the period. The following sequence of entries covers the purchase of inventory, accrual of interest expense, and payment of a short-term note payable:

2011			
Oct. 1	Inventory	8,000	
	Note Payable, Short-Term		8,000
	Purchase of inventory by issuing a six-month 10% note payable.		

This transaction increases both an asset and a liability.

ASSETS	=	LIABILITIES	+	SHAREHOLDERS' EQUITY
+8,000	=	+8,000	+	0

Assume Robertson Construction's year-end is December 31. At year-end, Robertson must accrue interest expense at 10% per year for October through December.

2011			
Dec. 31	Interest Expense ($8,000 × 0.10 × 3/12)	200	
	Interest Payable		200
	Adjusting entry to accrue interest expense at year-end.		

Liabilities increase and equity decreases because of the expense.

ASSETS	=	LIABILITIES	+	SHAREHOLDERS' EQUITY	−	EXPENSES
0	=	+200			−	200

The balance sheet at year-end will report the note payable of $8,000 and the related interest payable of $200 as current liabilities. The income statement will report interest expense of $200.

The following entry records the note's payment at March 31, 2012:

2012			
Mar. 31	Note Payable, Short-Term	8,000	
	Interest Payable	200	
	Interest Expense ($8,000 × 0.10 × 3/12)	200	
	Cash [$8,000 + ($8,000 × 0.10 × 6/12)]		8,400
	Payment of a note payable and interest at maturity.		

ASSETS	=	LIABILITIES	+	SHAREHOLDERS' EQUITY	−	EXPENSES
−8,400	=	−8,000 − 200			−	200

The debits zero out the two payables and also record Robertson's interest expense for January, February, and March.

Goods and Services Tax, Sales Tax, Harmonized Sales Tax Payable. Canada has three types of sales taxes:

- Goods and services tax (GST) is a value-added tax levied by the federal government. At the time of writing, the tax is 5%. It applies to most goods and services.

- Provincial or regional sales tax (PST) applies to goods and services purchased by a consumer such as an individual or a business for its own use. Note: Alberta, the Northwest Territories, Nunavut, and Yukon do not levy a provincial or regional sales tax.
- Harmonized sales tax (HST), which combines PST and GST, is also a value-added tax. British Columbia, New Brunswick, Newfoundland and Labrador, Nova Scotia, and Ontario levy an HST.

Goods and Services Tax Payable. The final consumer of a GST-taxable product or service bears the tax; entities farther up the supply chain from the final consumer pay GST on their purchases but get an input tax credit (ITC) equal to the GST they have paid.

GST payable is a current liability as it is payable annually, quarterly, or monthly to the Canada Revenue Agency (CRA) depending on the payer's volume of business.

Assume Kitchen Hardware Ltd., of Brandon, Manitoba, purchases lawn rakes for $3,000 plus 5% GST for a total of $3,150. Subsequently, Kitchen sells the rakes for $6,000 plus GST of $300 (provincial sales tax is ignored for this example but is covered below). The entries to record the purchase of the rakes, the sale of the rakes, and the remittance of the GST payable by Kitchen are as follows:

Inventory	3,000	
GST ITC	150	
Accounts Payable		3,150
To record purchase of inventory.		
Accounts Receivable	6,300	
Cost of Goods Sold	3,000	
Sales		6,000
Inventory		3,000
GST Payable		300
To record sale of inventory.		
GST Payable	300	
GST ITC		150
Cash		150
To record payment of GST collected less GST paid.		

Sales Tax Payable. PST is levied at the point of sale to the final consumer, unlike GST. It would apply to Kitchen Hardware when the company purchased a cash register and to Mary Fortin, a customer of Kitchen, when she purchased light bulbs.

- Alberta, the Northwest Territories, Nunavut, and Yukon do not charge the equivalent of a provincial sales tax.
- PST is charged on the sale to the final consumer and remitted to the provincial treasurer. Using the information in the example above, Kitchen Hardware would charge the Manitoba sales tax rate of 7% on the $6,000 sale and remit the tax collected of $420 to Manitoba Finance, Taxation Division.
- The company that sold the cash register to Kitchen would charge $72 on the sale and remit the tax collected to Manitoba Finance, Taxation Division.

PST payable is a current liability as it is payable quarterly or monthly depending on the payer's volume of business.

With respect to Kitchen Hardware's sale of rakes for $6,000, the GST would be $300 and the PST would be 7% or $420. So the total price to the consumer would be $6,720. The entries to record the sale of the rakes (including GST and PST payable) and the remittance of the PST payable by Kitchen are as follows:

Accounts Receivable	6,720	
Cost of Goods Sold	3,000	
Sales		6,000
Inventory		3,000
GST Payable		300
PST Payable		420
To record sale of inventory.		
PST Payable	420	
Cash		420
To record payment of PST collected.		

Harmonized Sales Tax Payable. The final consumer of an HST-taxable product or service bears the tax; entities farther up the supply chain from the final consumer pay HST on their purchases but get an input tax credit (ITC) equal to the HST they have paid.

HST payable is a current liability as it is payable to the Canada Revenue Agency annually, quarterly, or monthly. The CRA collects the provincial portion on behalf of the respective provinces and remits the amounts to each of the provinces for which it has collected the tax.

Assume Gillespie Hardware Inc., located in Orangeville, Ontario, buys wheelbarrows for $2,000 plus 13% HST (Ontario's provincial sales tax is 8% and GST is 5%) for a total of $2,260. Gillespie sells the wheelbarrows for $4,000 plus HST of $520. The entries to record the purchase and the sale of the wheelbarrows and the remittance of the HST payable are as follows:

Inventory	2,000	
HST ITC	260	
Accounts Payable		2,260
To record purchase of inventory.		
Accounts Receivable	4,520	
Cost of Goods Sold	2,000	
Sales		4,000
Inventory		2,000
HST Payable		520
To record sale of inventory.		
HST Payable	520	
HST ITC		260
Cash		260
To record payment of HST collected less HST paid.		

Accrued Liabilities (Accrued Expenses). An accrued liability usually results from an expense the business has incurred but not yet paid. Therefore, an accrued expense creates a liability, which explains why it is also called an *accrued expense*.

For example, WestJet's salaries and wages payable occur as employees work for the company. Interest expense accrues with the passage of time. There are several categories of accrued expenses:

- Salaries and Wages Payable
- Interest Payable
- Income Taxes Payable

Salaries and Wages Payable (also called Accrued Salaries and Wages Payable) is the liability for salaries, wages, and related payroll expenses not yet paid at the end of the period. This category also includes payroll deductions withheld from employee paycheques. *Interest Payable* is the company's interest payable on notes and bonds payable. *Income Taxes Payable* is the amount of income tax the company still owes at year-end.

Payroll Liabilities. **Payroll**, also called *employee compensation*, is a major expense. For service organizations—such as law firms, real estate brokers, and accounting firms—compensation is *the* major expense, just as cost of goods sold is the major expense for a merchandising company.

Employee compensation takes different forms. A *salary* is employee pay stated at a yearly or monthly rate. A *wage* is employee pay stated at an hourly rate. Sales employees earn a *commission*, which is a percentage of the sales the employee has made. A *bonus* is an amount over and above regular compensation. Accounting for all forms of compensation follows the same pattern, as illustrated in Exhibit 8-1 (using assumed figures).

Every expense accrual has the same effect: Liabilities increase and equity decreases because of the expense. The accounting equation shows these effects.

Salary expense represents *gross pay* (that is, pay before subtractions for taxes and other deductions). Salary expense creates several payroll entries, expenses, and liabilities:

- *Salary Payable to Employees* is their net (take-home) pay.
- *Employee Withheld Income Tax Payable* is the employees' income tax that has been withheld from paycheques.
- *Canada Pension Plan Payable* and *Employment Insurance Payable* are the employees' contributions to those two government programs.
- *Employee Union Dues Payable* are collected for the union by the employer.
- *Canada Pension Plan and Employment Insurance Expense* is the cost of the employer's contribution to those two government programs. The two credits to liabilities totalling $737 represent the liability for the employer's contribution.
- *Provincial Employer's Health and Post-Secondary Education Tax* is an employment expense levied on employers by some provinces.
- *Employment Dental Benefits Expense* is typical of employee benefits many employers provide. The payable represents the liability for those two expenses.

Unearned Revenues. *Unearned revenues* are also called *deferred revenues* and *revenues collected in advance*. For all unearned revenue the business has received cash from customers before earning the revenue. The company has a liability to provide goods or services to the customer. Let's consider an example.

WestJet sells tickets and collects cash in advance. WestJet therefore reports Advance Ticket Sales for airline tickets sold in advance. At December 31, 2009, WestJet owed customers $286 million of air travel (see page 391). Let's see how WestJet accounts for unearned ticket revenue.

EXHIBIT 8-1 Accounting for Payroll Expenses and Liabilities

Salary Expense	10,000	
Employee Withheld Income Tax Payable		1,350
Canada Pension Plan Payable		495
Employment Insurance Payable		173
Employee Union Dues Payable		272
Salary Payable to Employees [take-home pay]		7,710
To record salary expense and employee withholdings.		
Canada Pension Plan and Employment Insurance Expense	737	
Canada Pension Plan Payable		495
Employment Insurance Payable		242
To record employer's share of Canada Pension Plan and Employment Insurance.		
Provincial Employer's Health and Post-Secondary Education Tax	200	
Employee Dental Benefits Expense	182	
Employee Benefits Expense Payable		382
To record employee benefits payable by employer.		

ASSETS	=	LIABILITIES	+	SHAREHOLDERS' EQUITY	–	EXPENSES
		+1,350				
		+ 495				
0	=	+ 173				–10,000
		+ 272				
		+7,710				
0	=	+ 495				–737
		+ 242				
0	=	+ 382				–200
						–182

Assume that WestJet collects $800 for a round-trip ticket from Vancouver to Montreal (taxes and fees are not considered in this example). WestJet's entries would be as follows:

2011			
Sept. 1	Cash	800	
	Unearned Ticket Revenue		800
	To receive cash for plane fare (return) from Vancouver to Montreal.		

Advance Ticket Sales	
	800

WestJet's assets and liabilities increase equally. There is no revenue yet.

ASSETS	=	LIABILITIES	+	SHAREHOLDERS' EQUITY
+800	=	+800	+	0

Suppose the passenger flies from Vancouver to Montreal on September 26, 2011. WestJet records revenue as follows:

2011			
Sept. 26	Unearned Ticket Revenue	400	
	Ticket Revenue ($800/2)		400
	To record revenue earned that was collected in advance.		

The liability decreases and the revenue goes up:

Advance Ticket Sales		Ticket Revenue	
400	800		400

At December 31, 2011, West Jet reports:

- $400 of unearned ticket revenue (a liability) on the balance sheet
- $400 of ticket revenue on the income statement

The customer returns to Vancouver on January 28, 2012, and WestJet records the revenue earned with this journal entry:

2012			
Jan. 28	Unearned Ticket Revenue	400	
	Ticket Revenue ($800/2)		400
	Earned revenue that was collected in advance.		

Now the liability balance is zero because WestJet has earned all the revenue it collected in advance.

Current Portion of Long-Term Debt. Some long-term debt must be paid in installments. The **current portion of long-term debt** (also called *current installment of long-term debt*) is the amount of the principal that is payable within one year. At the end of each year, a company reclassifies (from long-term debt to a current liability) the amount of its long-term debt that must be paid during the upcoming year.

WestJet (page 391) reports Current Portion of Long-Term Debt among Current Liabilities on its balance sheet. WestJet also reports Long-Term Debt, which excludes the current maturities. *Long-term debt* refers to long-term notes payable and bonds payable, which we cover in the second half of this chapter.

STOP + THINK

You are thinking of purchasing WestJet shares and are concerned about WestJet's debt. You examine WestJet's balance sheet to answer the following questions about the company's current and long-term debt:

1. At December 31, 2009, how much in total did WestJet owe on current and long-term debt?
2. How much of the long-term debt did WestJet expect to pay during the year ended December 31, 2010? How much was the company scheduled to pay during later years?

Answers:

1. $1,219 million ($171 + $1,048)
2. Pay next year—$171 million; pay later—$1,048 million

Current Portion of Finance Leases. The accounting for finance leases is similar to the accounting for long-term debt. The portion of WestJet's capital (finance) leases due in 2010 ($1 million) is included with current liabilities while the portion due in 2011 and subsequent years ($3 million) is included with long-term liabilities.

Current Liabilities That Must Be Estimated

A business may know that a liability exists but may not know the amount. IAS 37 "Provisions, Contingent Liabilities and Contingent Assets" defines a *provision* as a liability of uncertain timing or amount. It requires a provision to be recognized in the financial statements when an entity has a present obligation as a result of a past event, the obligation can be reasonably estimated, and it is probable that the obligation will require resources to settle the obligation.

Estimated liabilities vary among companies. Estimated Warranty Payable is a liability account that most manufacturers have.

Estimated Warranty Payable. Many companies guarantee their products under *warranty* agreements. The warranty period may extend for 90 days to a year for consumer products. Automobile companies accrue liabilities for vehicle warranties, which usually extend for several years.

The IFRS "Framework for the Preparation and Presentation of Financial Statements" states "Expenses are recognised in the income statement on the basis of a direct association between the costs incurred and the earning of specific items of income." In other words, expenses incurred to earn income in a period must be recognized in the same period that the income is recognized. When a product is sold with a warranty, the cost of the warranty should be recognized in the same period that the revenue from the sale of the product is recognized whatever the warranty life. After all, the warranty motivates customers to buy products, so the company must record warranty expense. At the time of the sale, however, the company does not know which products will be defective. The exact amount of warranty expense cannot be known with certainty, so the business must estimate warranty expense and the related warranty liability.

Assume that Black & Decker Canada Inc., which manufactures power tools, made sales of $200,000 subject to product warranties. If, in past years, between 2% and 4% of products proved defective, Black & Decker could estimate that 3% of the products it sells this year will require repair or replacement. In that case, Black & Decker would estimate warranty expense of $6,000 ($200,000 × 0.03) for the period and make the following entry:

Warranty Expense	6,000	
Estimated Warranty Payable		6,000
To accrue warranty expense.		

Estimated Warranty Payable	
	6,000

Assume that defective merchandise totals $4,800. Black & Decker will replace the defective products and record the following:

Estimated Warranty Payable	4,800	
Inventory		4,800
To replace defective products sold under warranty.		

Estimated Warranty Payable		
4,800		6,000
	Bal.	1,200

At the end of the year, Black & Decker will report Estimated Warranty Payable of $1,200 as a current liability. The income statement reports Warranty Expense of $6,000 for the year. Then, next year Black & Decker will repeat this process. The Estimated Warranty Payable account probably won't ever zero out.

If Black & Decker paid cash to satisfy the warranty, then the credit would be to Cash rather than to Inventory.

Vacation pay is another expense that must be estimated. And income taxes must be estimated because the final amount isn't determined until early the next year.

Contingent Liabilities

IAS 37 "Provisions, Contingent Liabilities and Contingent Assets" defines a *contingent liability* as:

> "a possible obligation that arises from past events and whose existence will be confirmed only by the occurrence or non-occurrence of one or more uncertain future events not wholly within the control of the entity; or
>
> a present obligation that arises from past events but is not recognized [in the financial statements] because:
>
> (i) it is not probable that an outflow of resources embodying economic benefits will be required to settle the obligation; or
>
> (ii) the amount of the obligation cannot be measured with sufficient reliability."

Lawsuits in progress, guarantees of a subsidiary's debt, and audits by the Canada Revenue Agency are examples of contingent liabilities. Contingent liabilities are disclosed in the notes to the financial statements.

Canadian Tire Corporation reported on its contingencies at January 2, 2010, in the following note:

> ***Note 17.*** *GUARANTEES, COMMITMENTS AND CONTINGENCIES* (in part): **Other commitments and contingencies** As at January 2, 2010, [Canadian Tire] had the following other commitments and contingencies. In accordance with Canadian GAAP, the Company has not recognized a liability relating to these commitments and contingencies except for a provision for legal proceedings . . . .

A contingent liability could become an actual liability if the company lost a lawsuit, if the company had to make good on a guarantee, or if CRA ruled against the company. It would be misleading if the company omitted these disclosures in the notes to the financial statements. On the other hand, IAS 37 states that disclosure of a contingent liability is not appropriate if the chance that it will become an actual liability is remote.

Are All Liabilities Reported on the Balance Sheet or in the Notes?

The big danger with liabilities is that a company may fail to report a large debt on its balance sheet. What is the consequence of missing a large liability? The company would definitely understate its liabilities and its debt ratio and would probably overstate its net income. The company would probably overstate its net income. In short,

USING INFORMATION ABOUT PROVISIONS AND CONTINGENT LIABILITIES IN DECISION MAKING

IAS 37 "Provisions, Contingent Liabilities and Contingent Assets" clearly defines *provisions*, which, although estimated, must be recognized and reported in the financial statements, and *contingent liabilities*, which must be reported in the notes to the financial statements.

Manager—The management would appreciate that there are clear rules for accounting for estimated and contingent liabilities.

Investor and creditor—Investors and creditors would have confidence that estimated liabilities (and the related expenses) are properly recognized in the financial statements and that contingent liabilities are appropriately described in the notes to the financial statements.

its financial statements would make the company look stronger than it really is. Any such misstatement, if significant, hurts a company's credibility.

Contingent liabilities are very easy to overlook because they aren't actual debts. How would you feel if you owned shares in a company that failed to report a contingency that put the company out of business? If you had known of the contingency, you could have sold the shares and avoided the loss. In this case, you would hire a lawyer to file suit against the company for negligent financial reporting.

Summary of Current Liabilities

Let's summarize what we've covered thus far. A company can report its current liabilities on the balance sheet as follows:

Hudson Ltd.
Balance Sheet
December 31, 2011

Assets		Liabilities	
Current assets		**Current liabilities**	
Cash		Accounts payable	
Short-term investments		Salary payable*	
Etc.		Interest payable*	
		HST/GST payable*	
		Sales tax payable*	
		Income tax payable*	
Property, plant, and equipment:		Unearned revenue	
Land		Estimated warranty payable*	
Etc.		Notes payable, short-term	
		Current portion of long-term debt	
		Total current liabilities	
Other assets:		**Long-term liabilities**	
		Shareholders' Equity	
		Common shares	
		Retained earnings	
Total assets	$XXX	Total liabilities and shareholders' equity	$XXX

*These items are often combined and reported in a single total as "Accrued Liabilities" or "Accrued Expenses Payable."

IAS 39 "Financial Instruments: Recognition and Measurement" requires that all financial liabilities (with certain exceptions that are beyond the scope of this text) be measured for reporting purposes at amortized cost using the effective interest method. Practically speaking, current liabilities are due within the next year so their amortized cost would be the same as their actual cost.

On its income statement this company would report:

- *Expenses* related to some of the current liabilities. Examples include salary expense, interest expense, income tax expense, and warranty expense.
- *Revenue* related to the unearned revenue. Examples include service revenue and sales revenue that were collected in advance.

MID-CHAPTER SUMMARY PROBLEM

MyAccountingLab

Assume that Korvar Plastics Inc., a manufacturer of plastic pipe for the construction industry and located in Red Deer, Alberta, faced the following liability situations at June 30, 2011, the end of the company's fiscal year:

a. Long-term debt totals $10 million and is payable in annual installments of $1 million each. The interest rate on the debt is 7%, and interest is paid each December 31.

b. The company pays royalties on its purchased trademarks. Royalties for the trademarks are equal to a percentage of Korvar's sales. Assume that sales in 2011 were $40 million and were subject to a royalty rate of 3%. At June 30, 2011, Korvar owes two-thirds of the year's royalty, to be paid in July.

c. Salary expense for the last payroll period of the year was $90,000. Of this amount, employees' withheld income tax totalled $12,000, and other withholdings and employee benefits were $6,000. These payroll amounts will be paid early in July.

d. GST less ITC credits payable was $124,000.

e. On fiscal year 2011 sales of $40 million, management estimates warranty expense of 2%. One year ago, at June 30, 2010, Estimated Warranty Liability stood at $100,000. Warranty payments were $300,000 during the year ended June 30, 2011.

Show how Korvar Plastics Inc. would report these liabilities on its balance sheet at June 30, 2011.

Name: Korvar Plastics Inc.
Industry: Manufacturing
Accounting Period: June 30, 2011

Answer

a. Current liabilities:

Current portion of long-term debt	$1,000,000
Interest payable ($10,000,000 × 0.07 × 6/12)	350,000
Long-term debt ($10,000,000 − $1,000,000)	9,000,000

Current liabilities include the amount due to be paid within one year:
- Principal repayment
- Interest payment

b. Current liabilities:

Royalties payable ($40,000,000 × 0.03 × 2/3)	$ 800,000

Royalties are due to be paid within one year; thus, are a current liability.

c. Current liabilities:

Salary payable ($90,000 − $12,000 − $6,000)	$72,000
Employee withheld income tax payable	12,000
Other employee withholdings and benefits payable	6,000

Salaries payable to employees are net of all withholdings.

d. Current liabilities:

GST payable	$ 124,000

GST payable is net of applicable ITC credits.

e. Current liabilities:

Estimated warranty payable [$100,000 + ($40,000,000 × 0.02) − $300,000]	$ 600,000

Estimated warranty liability must be reduced by any warranty payments made during the year.

Long-Term Liabilities: Bonds

OBJECTIVE

② **Understand** bonds payable

Large companies, such as Bombardier, Canadian Tire, and TransCanada, cannot borrow billions of dollars from a single lender. So how do large corporations borrow huge amounts? They issue (sell) bonds to the public. **Bonds payable** are groups of notes issued to multiple lenders, called *bondholders*. Bombardier can borrow large amounts by issuing bonds to thousands of individual investors, who each lend a modest amount to Bombardier. Bombardier receives what it needs, and each investor limits his or her risk by diversifying investments—not putting all the investor's "eggs in one basket." Here we treat bonds and long-term notes that are payables together because their accounting is the same.

Bonds: An Introduction

Each bond that is issued is, in effect, a long-term note payable. Bonds payable are debts of the issuing company.

Purchasers of bonds receive a bond certificate, which carries the issuing company's name. The certificate also states the *principal*, which is typically stated in units of $1,000; principal is also called the bond's **face value** or *maturity value*. The bond obligates the issuing company to pay the debt at a specific future time called the *maturity date*.

Interest is the rental fee on money borrowed. The bond certificate states the interest rate that the issuer will pay the holder and the dates that the interest payments are due (generally twice a year). Exhibit 8-2 shows an actual bond certificate issued by the Bank of Montreal.

Issuing bonds usually requires the services of a securities firm, for example, RBC Dominion Securities, to act as the underwriter of the bond issue. The **underwriter** purchases the bonds from the issuing company and resells them to its clients, or it may hold some of the bonds for its own account and sell them at a later time.

Types of Bonds. All the bonds in a particular issue may mature at a specified time (**term bonds**) or in installments over a period of time (**serial bonds**). Serial bonds are like installment notes payable. Some of TransCanada Corporation's long-term debts are serial in nature because they come due in installments.

Secured, or *mortgage*, *bonds* give the bondholder the right to take specified assets of the issuer if the company *defaults*, that is, fails to pay interest or principal. *Unsecured bonds*, called **debentures**, are backed only by the good faith of the borrower. Debentures carry a higher rate of interest than secured bonds because debentures are riskier investments.

Bond Prices. Investors may buy and sell bonds through bond markets. The bond market in Canada is called the over-the-counter market. It is a network of investment dealers who trade bonds issued by the Government of Canada and Crown corporations, the provinces, municipalities and regions, and corporations. In addition, there is an electronic fixed-income trading system called CanDeal. It is owned by the 12 leading investment dealers in Canada. Bond prices are quoted at a percentage of their maturity value. For example,

- A $1,000 bond quoted at 100 is bought or sold for $1,000, which is 100% of its face value.

EXHIBIT 8-2 **Bond Certificate (a blank specimen)**

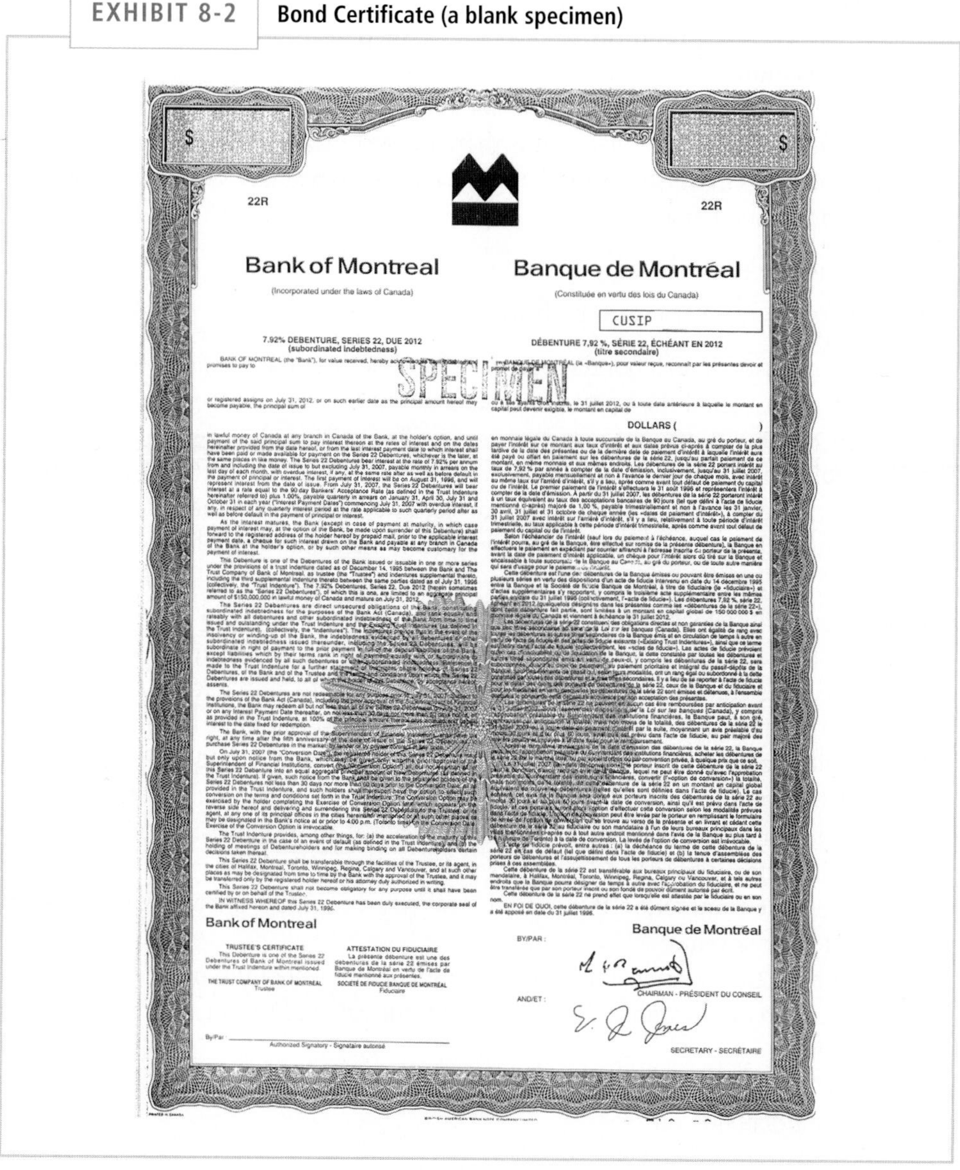
$ $

22R 22R

Bank of Montreal Banque de Montréal

(Incorporated under the laws of Canada) (Constituée en vertu des lois du Canada)

CUSIP

7.92% DEBENTURE, SERIES 22, DUE 2012 (subordinated indebtedness)

DÉBENTURE 7,92 %, SÉRIE 22, ÉCHÉANT EN 2012 (titre secondaire)

SPECIMEN

DOLLARS ( )

Bank of Montreal Banque de Montréal

TRUSTEE'S CERTIFICATE ATTESTATION DU FIDUCIAIRE

BY/PAR:

AND/ET:

CHAIRMAN - PRÉSIDENT DU CONSEIL

SECRETARY - SECRÉTAIRE

- The same bond quoted at 101.5 has a market price of \$1,015 (101.5% of face value = \$1,000 × 1.015).
- A \$1,000 bond quoted at 88.375 is priced at \$883.75 (\$1,000 × 0.88375).

Exhibit 8-3 contains actual price information for Province of Manitoba bonds taken from the *Globe and Mail* website on April 29, 2010. On this particular day, Province of Manitoba \$1,000 face value bonds with a coupon rate of 4.30% maturing in the year 2016 (maturity date, June 1, 2016) were traded. The bond's asking price was \$1,029.60 (\$1,000 × 1.0296). Bond prices may change daily due to changes in market demand and supply.

EXHIBIT 8-3 **Bond Price Information for Province of Manitoba**

Issuer Coupon	Maturity Date	Bid Price	Bid Yield
Manitoba 4.30	1-June-16	102.96	3.73

Bond Premium and Bond Discount. A bond issued at a price above its face value is said to be issued at a **premium**, and a bond issued at a price below face value is issued at a **discount**.

Premium on Bonds Payable has a *credit* balance and Discount on Bonds Payable carries a *debit* balance. Bond Discount is therefore a contra liability account.

As a bond nears maturity, its market price moves toward face value; therefore, the price of a bond issued at a

- Premium decreases toward maturity value
- Discount increases toward maturity value

On the maturity date, a bond's market value exactly equals its face value because the company that issued the bond pays that amount to retire the bond.

The Time Value of Money. A dollar received today is worth more than a dollar to be received in the future because you may invest today's dollar immediately and earn income from it. But if you must wait to receive the dollar, you forgo the interest revenue. Money earns income over time, a fact called the *time value of money*. Let's examine how the time value of money affects the pricing of bonds.

Assume that a bond with a face value of $1,000 reaches maturity three years from today and carries no interest. Would you pay $1,000 to purchase the bond? No, because the payment of $1,000 today to receive the same amount in the future provides you with no income on the investment. Just how much would you pay today to receive $1,000 at the end of three years? The answer is some amount *less* than $1,000. Let's suppose that you feel $750 is a good price. By investing $750 now to receive $1,000 later, you earn $250 interest revenue over the three years. The issuing company sees the transaction this way: It will pay you $250 interest for the use of your $750 for three years.

The amount to invest *now* to receive more later is called the **present value** of a future amount. In our example, $750 is the present value of the $1,000, which is the future amount.

Our $750 bond price is a reasonable estimate. The exact present value of any future amount depends on

1. The amount of the future payment ($1,000 in our example)
2. The length of time from the investment date to the date when the future amount is to be collected (three years)
3. The interest rate during the period (say, 10%)

In this case the present value is very close to $750. Present value is always less than the future amount. We discuss how present value is computed in Appendix B at the end of the book (pp. 757–765).

Bond Interest Rates Determine Bond Prices. Bonds are always sold at their *market price*, which is the amount investors are willing to pay. A **bond market price** *is the bond's present value*, which equals the present value of the principal payment plus the present value of the cash interest payments. Interest is usually paid semi-annually (twice a year). Some issuers pay annually or quarterly.

Two interest rates work to set the price of a bond:

- The **stated interest rate** is the interest rate printed on the bond certificate. The stated interest rate determines the amount of cash the borrower pays—and the investor receives—each year. For example, the Province of Saskatchewan's 6.35% bonds have a stated interest rate of 6.35%. Thus, Saskatchewan pays $6,350 of interest annually on each $100,000 bond. Each semi-annual interest payment is $3,175 ($100,000 × 0.0635 × 6/12).

- The **market interest rate**, or *effective interest rate*, is the rate that investors demand for loaning their money. The market rate varies by the minute.

An issuer may issue bonds with a stated interest rate that differs from the prevailing market interest rate. In fact, the two interest rates often differ because the issuer often has to finalize details of the bond weeks or months before the bonds are actually issued.

Exhibit 8-4 shows how the contract (stated) interest rate and the market interest rate interact to determine the issuance price of a bond payable for three separate cases.

Manitoba may issue 6.25% bonds when the market rate has risen to 7%. Will the Manitoba bonds attract investors in this market? No, because investors can earn 7% on other bonds of similar risk. Therefore, investors will purchase Manitoba bonds only at a price less than their face value. The difference between the lower price and face value is a *discount* (Exhibit 8-4). Conversely, if the market interest rate is 5%, Manitoba's 6.25% bonds will be so attractive that investors will pay more than face value for them. The difference between the higher price and face value is a *premium*. It is useful to remember that there is an inverse relationship between the market rate and bond prices—a higher market rate results in a lower bond price and a lower market rate results in a higher bond price.

EXHIBIT 8-4 **How the Contract Interest Rate and the Market Interest Rate Interact to Determine the Price of a Bond**

				Issuance Price of Bonds Payable
Case A:				
Contract (stated) interest rate on a bond payable	equals	Market interest rate	implies	Price of face, or maturity, value
Example: 6%	=	6%	→	*Face: $1,000 bond issued for $1,000*
Case B:				
Contract (stated) interest rate on a bond payable	less than	Market interest rate	implies	Discount price (price *below* face value)
Example: 6%	<	7%	→	*Discount: $1,000 bond issued for a price* below *$1,000*
Case C:				
Contract (stated) interest rate on a bond payable	greater than	Market interest rate	implies	Premium price (price *above* face value)
Example: 6%	>	5%	→	*Premium: $1,000 bond issued for a price* above *$1,000*

Issuing Bonds Payable at Face Value

Suppose Great-West Lifeco Inc. has $50,000 in 6% bonds that mature in five years. Assume that Great-West issues these bonds at face value on January 1, 2011. The issuance entry is as follows:

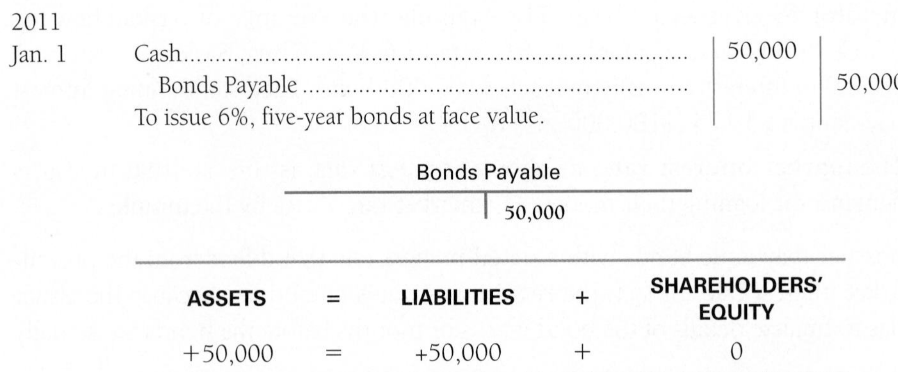

2011			
Jan. 1	Cash	50,000	
	Bonds Payable		50,000
	To issue 6%, five-year bonds at face value.		

Bonds Payable

	50,000

ASSETS	=	LIABILITIES	+	SHAREHOLDERS' EQUITY
+50,000	=	+50,000	+	0

Great-West, the borrower, makes a one-time entry to record the receipt of cash and the issuance of bonds. Afterward, investors buy and sell the bonds through the bond markets. These buy-and-sell transactions between outside investors do *not* involve Great-West at all.

Interest payments occur each January 1 and July 1. Great-West's entry to record the first semi-annual interest payment is as follows:

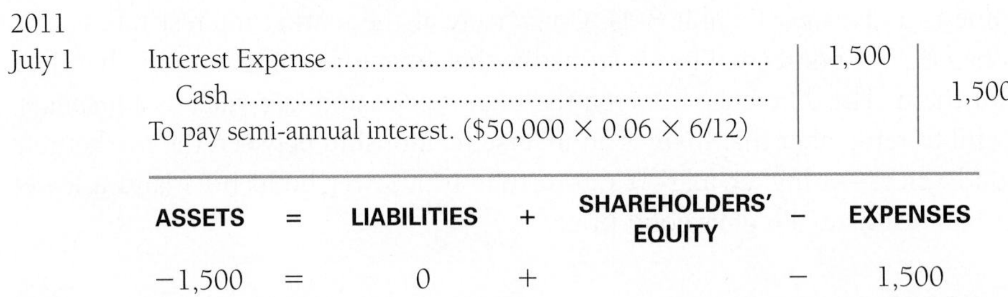

2011			
July 1	Interest Expense	1,500	
	Cash		1,500
	To pay semi-annual interest. ($50,000 × 0.06 × 6/12)		

ASSETS	=	LIABILITIES	+	SHAREHOLDERS' EQUITY	–	EXPENSES
−1,500	=	0	+		–	1,500

At year-end, Great-West must accrue interest expense and interest payable for six months (July through December), as follows:

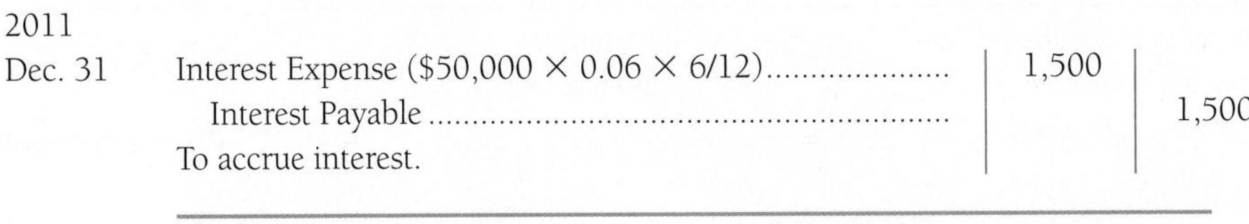

2011			
Dec. 31	Interest Expense ($50,000 × 0.06 × 6/12)	1,500	
	Interest Payable		1,500
	To accrue interest.		

ASSETS	=	LIABILITIES	+	SHAREHOLDERS' EQUITY	–	EXPENSES
0	=	+1,500	+		–	1,500

At maturity, Great-West will pay off the bonds as follows:

2016			
Jan. 1	Bonds Payable	50,000	
	Cash		50,000
	To pay bonds payable at maturity.		

Bonds Payable

50,000	50,000
	Bal. 0

ASSETS	=	LIABILITIES	+	SHAREHOLDERS' EQUITY
−50,000	=	−50,000		

Issuing Bonds Payable at a Discount

Market conditions may force a company to issue bonds at a discount. Suppose TELUS issues $100,000 of its 9% five-year bonds when the market interest rate is 10%. The market price of the bonds drops, and TELUS receives $96,149[1] at issuance. The transaction is recorded as follows:

2011			
Jan. 1	Cash	96,149	
	Discount on Bonds Payable	3,851	
	Bonds Payable		100,000
	To issue 9%, five-year bonds at a discount.		

ASSETS	=	LIABILITIES	+	SHAREHOLDERS' EQUITY
+96,149	=	−3,851 +100,000	+	0

Now the bond accounts have a net balance of $96,149 as follows:

Bonds Payable	+	Discount on Bonds Payable	= Net carrying amount of bonds payable
100,000		3,851	= $96,149

TELUS's balance sheet immediately after issuance of the bonds would report the following:

Total current liabilities		$ XXX
Long-term liabilities		
Bonds payable, 9%, due 2016	$100,000	
Less: Discount on bonds payable	(3,851)	96,149

Discount on Bonds Payable is a contra account to Bonds Payable, a decrease in the company's liabilities. Subtracting the discount from Bonds Payable yields the *carrying amount* of the bonds. Thus, TELUS's liability is $96,149, which is the amount the company borrowed.

What Is the Interest Expense on These Bonds Payable?

OBJECTIVE

Measure interest expense

TELUS pays interest on its bonds semi-annually, which is common practice. Each semi-annual interest *payment* remains the same over the life of the bonds:

$$\text{Semi-annual interest payment} = \$100{,}000 \times 0.09 \times 6/12 = \$4{,}500$$

This payment amount is fixed by the bond contract. But TELUS's interest *expense* increases from period to period as the bonds march toward maturity. Remember, these bonds were issued at a discount.

Panel A of Exhibit 8-5 repeats the TELUS bond data we've been using. Panel B provides an amortization table that

- Determines the periodic interest expense (column B)
- Shows the bond carrying amount (column E)

[1]Appendix B at the end of this book shows how to determine the price of this bond.

EXHIBIT 8-5 **Debt Amortization for a Bond Discount**

PANEL A—Bond Data

Issue date—January 1, 2011
Maturity (face) value—$100,000
Stated interest rate—9%
Interest paid—4 1/2% semi-annually, $4,500 = $100,000 × 0.09 × 6/12
Market interest rate at time of issue—10% annually, 5% semi-annually
Issue price—$96,149
Maturity date—January 1, 2016

PANEL B—Amortization Table

	A	B	C	D	E
Semi-Annual Interest Date	Interest Payment (4 1/2% of Maturity Value)	Interest Expense (5% of Preceding Bond Carrying Amount)	Discount Amortization (B − A)	Discount Account Balance (Preceding D − C)	Bond Carrying Amount ($100,000 − D)
Jan. 1, 2011				$3,851	$ 96,149
July 1	$4,500	$4,807	$307	3,544	96,456
Jan. 1, 2012	4,500	4,823	323	3,221	96,779
July 1	4,500	4,839	339	2,882	97,118
Jan. 1, 2013	4,500	4,856	356	2,526	97,474
July 1	4,500	4,874	374	2,152	97,848
Jan. 1, 2014	4,500	4,892	392	1,760	98,240
July 1	4,500	4,912	412	1,348	98,652
Jan. 1, 2015	4,500	4,933	433	915	99,085
July 1	4,500	4,954	454	461	99,539
Jan. 1, 2016	4,500	4,961*	461	0	100,000

*Adjusted for the effect of rounding.

Notes

- Column A The semi-annual interest payments are constant—fixed by the bond contract.
- Column B The interest expense each period = The preceding bond carrying amount × The market interest rate. Interest expense decreases as the bond carrying amount (E) decreases.
- Column C The excess of each interest payment (A) over interest expense (B) is the premium amortization (C) for the period.
- Column D The premium balance (D) decreases when amortized.
- Column E The bond carrying amount (E) decreases from $104,100 at issuance to $100,000 at maturity.

Study the exhibit carefully because the amounts we will be using come directly from the amortization table. This exhibit shows the *effective-interest method of amortization*, which is the correct way to measure interest expense as required by IFRS.

Interest Expense on Bonds Issued at a Discount

In Exhibit 8-5, TELUS Communications Inc. borrowed $96,149 cash but must pay $100,000 when the bonds mature. What happens to the $3,851 balance of the discount account over the life of the bond issue?

The $3,851 is additional interest expense to TELUS over and above the stated interest that TELUS pays each six months. Exhibit 8-6 graphs the interest expense and the interest payment on the TELUS bonds over their lifetime. Observe that the semi-annual interest payment is fixed—by contract—at $4,500 (column A in Exhibit 8-5), but the amount of interest expense (column B) increases each period as the bond carrying amount moves upward toward maturity.

EXHIBIT 8-6 **Interest Expense on Bonds Payable Issued at a Discount**

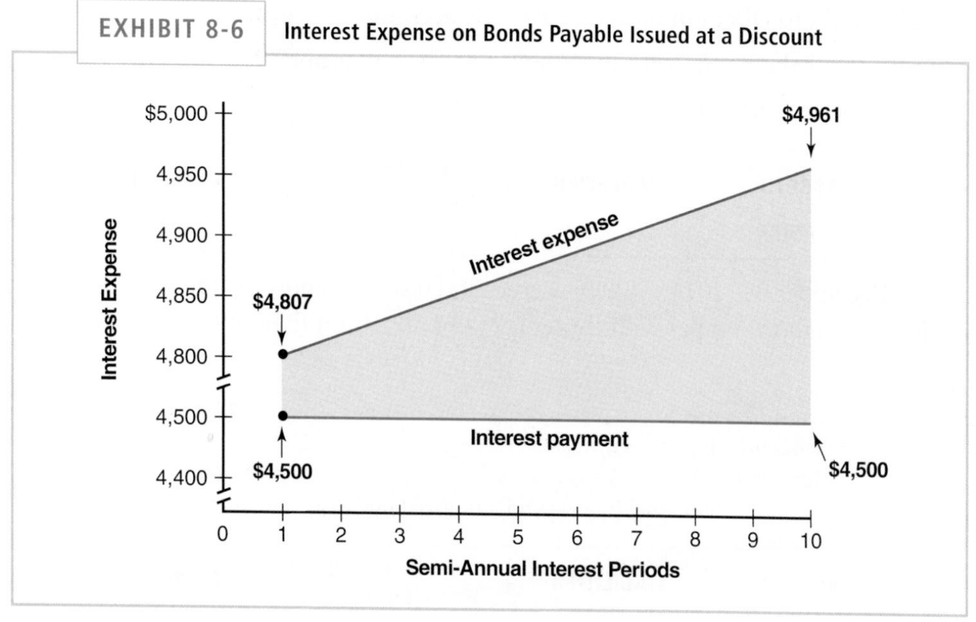

The discount is allocated to interest expense through amortization each period over the term of the bonds. Exhibit 8-7 illustrates the amortization of the bonds' carrying value from $96,149 at the start to $100,000 at maturity using the effective interest method required by IAS 39. These amounts come from Exhibit 8-5, column E.

Now let's see how to account for the TELUS bonds issued at a discount. In our example, TELUS issued its bonds on January 1, 2011, On July 1, TELUS made the first $4,500 semi-annual interest payment. But TELUS's interest expense is greater than $4,500. TELUS's journal entry to record interest expense and the interest payment for the first six months follows (with all amounts taken from Exhibit 8-5):

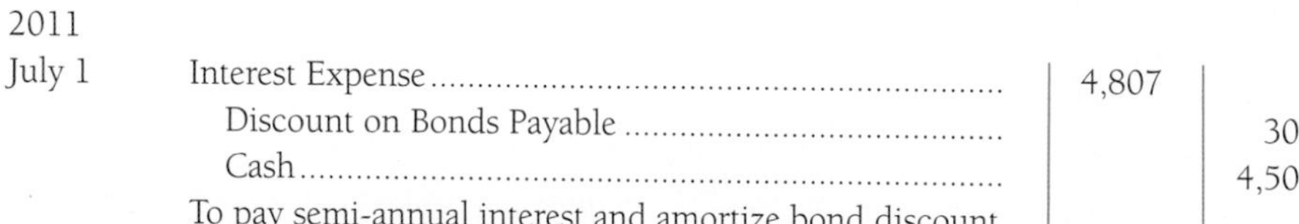

2011			
July 1	Interest Expense	4,807	
	Discount on Bonds Payable		307
	Cash		4,500
	To pay semi-annual interest and amortize bond discount.		

EXHIBIT 8-7 **Amortizing Bonds Payable Issued at a Discount**

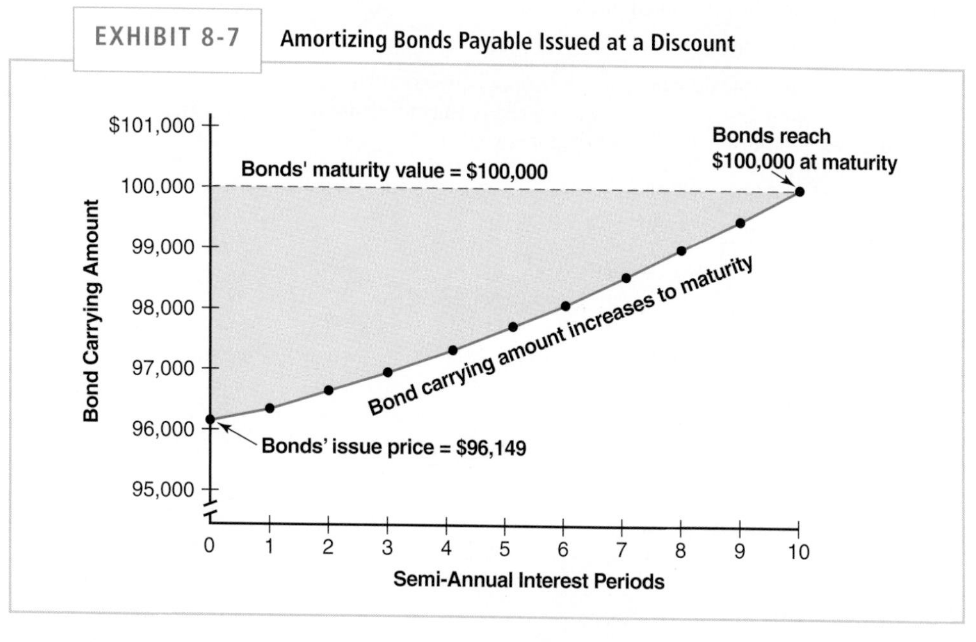

The credit to Discount on Bonds Payable accomplishes two purposes:

- It adjusts the bonds' carrying amount as the bonds approach maturity value.
- It allocates (amortizes) the discount to interest expense.

ASSETS	=	LIABILITIES	+	SHAREHOLDERS' EQUITY	–	EXPENSES
−4,500	=	+307			–	4,807

At December 31, 2011, TELUS accrues interest and amortizes the bond discount for July through December with this entry (amounts from Exhibit 8-5):

2011			
Dec. 31	Interest Expense	4,823	
	Discount on Bonds Payable		323
	Interest Payable		4,500
	To accrue semi-annual interest and amortize bond discount.		

ASSETS	=	LIABILITIES	+	SHAREHOLDERS' EQUITY	–	EXPENSES
0	=	+323 +4,500			–	4,823

At December 31, 2011, TELUS's bond accounts appear as follows:

Bonds Payable	
	100,000

Discount on Bonds Payable		
	3,851	307
		323
Bal.	3,221	

Bond carrying amount, $96,779 = $100,000 – $3,221 from Exhibit 8-5

STOP + THINK

You are analyzing the financial statements of a PAE company, and you note there is a difference between interest expense and the stated interest rate for the bonds. You wonder why interest expense is greater than the stated interest rate.

Answer:
Amortization of the bond discount is the difference between interest expense and the cash payment of interest. Interest expense exceeds the interest payment because the company issued the bonds at a discount and must pay the face amount at maturity.

STOP + THINK

What would you expect TELUS Communications Inc.'s 2011 income statement and year-end balance sheet to report for these bonds?

Answer:

Income Statement for 2011		
Interest expense ($4,807 + $4,823)		$ 9,630
Balance Sheet at December 31, 2011		
Current liabilities:		
Interest payable		$ 4,500
Long-term liabilities:		
Bonds payable	$100,000	
Less: Discount on bonds payable	(3,221)	96,779

At the bonds' maturity on January 1, 2016, the discount will have been amortized to zero, and the bonds' carrying amount will be $100,000. TELUS will retire the bonds by making a $100,000 payment to the bondholders.

Partial-Period Interest Amounts

Companies don't always issue bonds at the beginning or the end of their accounting year. They issue bonds when market conditions are most favourable, and that may be on May 16, August 1, or any other date. To illustrate partial-period interest, assume Goldcorp Inc. issues $100,000 of 8% bonds payable at 96 on August 31, 2011. The market rate of interest was 9%, and these bonds pay semi-annual interest on February 28 and August 31 each year. The first few lines of Goldcorp's amortization table are as follows:

Semi-Annual Interest Date	4% Interest Payment	$4\frac{1}{2}$% Interest Expense	Discount Amortization	Discount Account Balance	Bond Carrrying Amount
Aug. 31, 2011				$4,000	$96,000
Feb. 28, 2012	$4,000	$4,320	$320	3,680	96,320
Aug. 31, 2012	4,000	4,334	334	3,346	96,654

Goldcorp's accounting year ends on December 31, so at year-end Goldcorp must accrue interest and amortize bond discount for four months (September through December). At December 31, 2011, Goldcorp will make this entry:

2011			
Dec. 31	Interest Expense ($4,320 × 4/6)	2,880	
	Discount on Bonds Payable ($320 × 4/6)		213
	Interest Payable ($4,000 × 4/6)		2,667
	To accrue interest and amortize discount at year-end.		

The year-end entry at December 31, 2011, uses 4/6 of the upcoming semi-annual amounts at February 28, 2012. This example clearly illustrates the benefit of an amortization schedule.

Issuing Bonds at a Premium

Let's modify the TELUS bond example to illustrate issuance of the bonds at a premium. Assume that TELUS Communications Inc. issues $100,000 of five-year, 9% bonds that pay interest semi-annually. If the bonds are issued when the market interest rate is 8%, their issue price is $104,100.[2] The premium on these bonds is $4,100, and Exhibit 8-8 shows how to amortize the bonds by the effective-interest method. In practice, bond premiums are rare because few companies issue their bonds to pay cash interest above the market interest rate. We cover bond premiums for completeness.

TELUS's entries to record issuance of the bonds on January 1, 2011, and to make the first interest payment and amortize the bonds on July 1, are as follows:

2011			
Jan. 1	Cash	104,100	
	Bonds Payable		100,000
	Premium on Bonds Payable		4,100
	To issue 9%, five-year bonds at a premium.		

At the beginning, TELUS's liability is $104,100—not $100,000. The accounting equation makes this clear.

ASSETS	=	LIABILITIES	+	SHAREHOLDERS' EQUITY
104,100	=	100,000 +4,100	+	0

2011			
July 1	Interest Expense	4,164	
	Premium on Bonds Payable	336	
	Cash		4,500
	To pay semi-annual interest and amortize bond premium.		

ASSETS	=	LIABILITIES	+	SHAREHOLDERS' EQUITY	−	EXPENSES
−4,500	=	−336			−	4,164

Immediately after issuing the bonds at a premium on January 1, 2011, TELUS would report the bonds payable on the balance sheet as follows:

Total current liabilities		$ XXX
Long-term liabilities:		
Bonds payable	$100,000	
Premium on bonds payable	4,100	104,100

The premium is *added* to the balance of bonds payable to determine the carrying amount.

In Exhibit 8-8, TELUS borrowed $104,100 cash but must pay only $100,000 at maturity. The $4,100 premium on the bonds is a reduction in TELUS's interest expense over the term of the bonds. Exhibit 8-9 graphs TELUS's interest payments (column A from Exhibit 8-8) and interest expense (column B).

[2]Again, Appendix B at the end of the book shows how to determine the price of this bond.

EXHIBIT 8-8 **Debt Amortization for a Bond Discount**

PANEL A—Bond Data

Issue date—January 1, 2011	Market interest rate at time of issue—8% annually, 4% semi-annually
Maturity (face) value—$100,000	Issue price—$104,100
Contract interest rate—9%	Maturity date—January 1, 2016

Interest paid—4 1/2% semi-annually, $4,500 = $100,000 × 0.09 × 6/12

PANEL B—Amortization Table

	A	B	C	D	E
Semi-Annual Interest Date	Interest Payment (4 1/2% of Maturity Value)	Interest Expense (4% of Preceding Bond Carrying Amount)	Premium Amortization (A − B)	Premium Account Balance (Preceding D − C)	Bond Carrying Amount ($100,000 + D)
Jan. 1, 2011				$4,100	$104,100
July 1	$4,500	$4,164	$336	3,764	103,764
Jan. 1, 2012	4,500	4,151	349	3,415	103,415
July 1	4,500	4,137	363	3,052	103,052
Jan. 1, 2013	4,500	4,122	378	2,674	102,674
July 1	4,500	4,107	393	2,281	102,281
Jan. 1, 2014	4,500	4,091	409	1,872	101,872
July 1	4,500	4,075	425	1,447	101,447
Jan. 1, 2015	4,500	4,058	442	1,005	101,005
July 1	4,500	4,040	460	545	100,545
Jan. 1, 2016	4,500	3,955*	545	0	100,000

*Adjusted for the effect of rounding.

Notes

- Column A The semi-annual interest payments are constant—fixed by the bond contract.
- Column B The interest expense each period = The preceding bond carrying amount × The market interest rate. Interest expense increases as the bond carrying amount (E) increases.
- Column C The excess of interest expense (B) over interest payment (A) is the discount amortization (C) for the period.
- Column D The discount balance (D) decreases when amortized.
- Column E The bond carrying amount (E) increases from $96,149 at issuance to $100,000 at maturity.

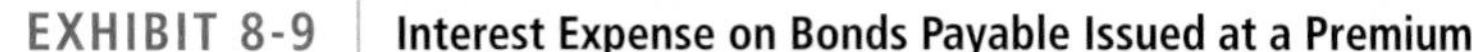

EXHIBIT 8-9 **Interest Expense on Bonds Payable Issued at a Premium**

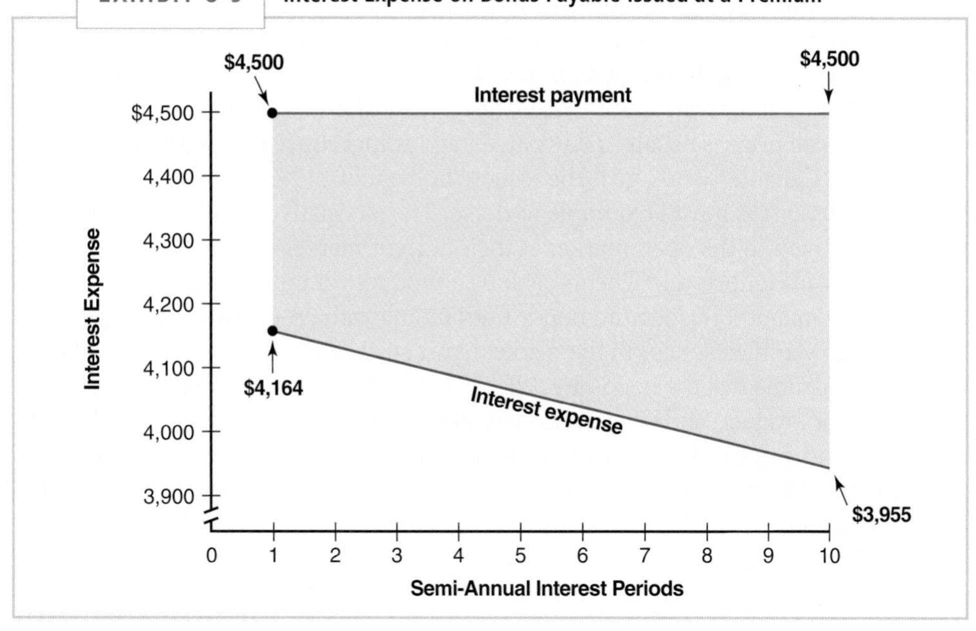

EXHIBIT 8-10 Amortizing Bonds Payable Issued at a Premium

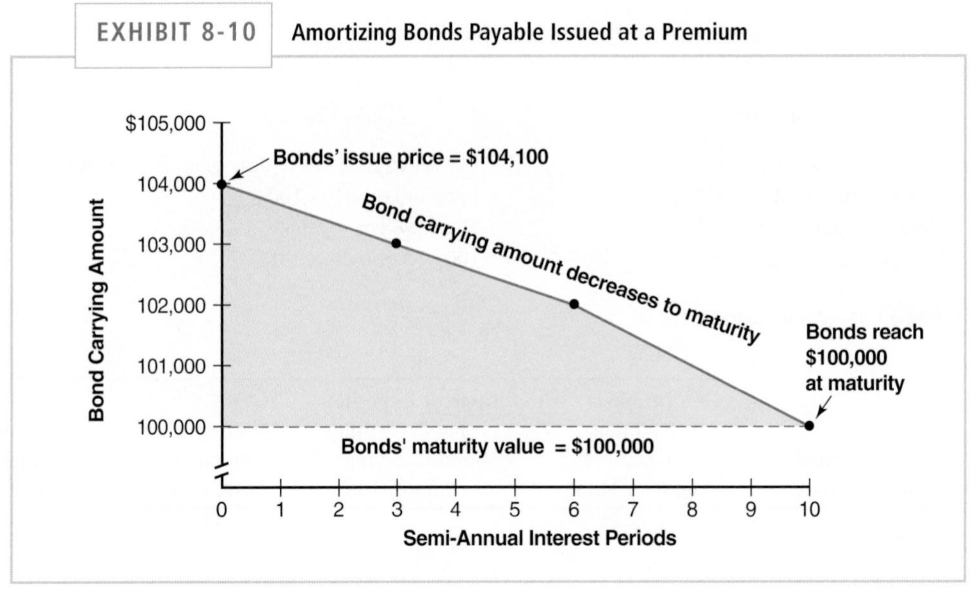

Through amortization the premium decreases interest expense each period over the term of the bonds. Exhibit 8-10 diagrams the amortization of the bond carrying amount from the issue price of $104,100 to the maturity value of $100,000. All amounts are taken from Exhibit 8-8.

TELUS's entry to record interest and amortization of the bond discount under the straight-line amortization method would be:

2011			
July 1	Interest Expense	4,164	
	Premium on Bonds Payable	336	
	Cash		4,500
	To pay semi-annual interest and amortize bond premium.		

Should We Derecognize Bonds Payable Before Their Maturity?

Normally, companies wait until maturity to pay off, or *retire*, their bonds payable. But companies sometimes retire bonds early. Such an action is termed **derecognition** by IAS 39. The main reason for retiring bonds early is to relieve the pressure of making interest payments. Also the company may be able to borrow at a lower interest rate.

Some bonds are **callable**, which means that the bonds' issuers may *call*, or pay off, those bonds at a prearranged price (this is the *call price)* whenever the issuers so choose. The call price is usually a few percentage points above the face value, perhaps 102 or 103. Callable bonds give the issuer the benefit of being able to pay off the bonds whenever it is most favourable to do so. The alternative to calling the bonds is to purchase them in the open market at their current market price.

Assume Air Products and Chemicals Inc., a producer of industrial gases and chemicals, has $70 million of debenture bonds outstanding with an unamortized discount of $350,000. Lower interest rates in the market may convince management to pay off these bonds now. Assume that the bonds are callable at 103. If the market price of the bonds is 99.25, will Air Products and Chemicals Inc. call the bonds or purchase them in the open market? Market price is the better choice because the market price is lower than the call price. Retiring the bonds on February 1, 2011, at 99.25 results in a gain of $175,000, computed as follows:

Face value of bonds being retired	$70,000,000
Less: Unamortized discount	(350,000)
Carrying amount of the bonds	69,650,000
Market price ($70,000,000 × 0.9925)	69,475,000
Gain on retirement of bonds payable	$ 175,000

Journal entry to record derecognition of the bonds:

2011			
Feb. 1	Bonds Payable	70,000,000	
	Discount on Bonds Payable		350,000
	Cash		69,475,000
	Gain on retirement of bonds		175,000
	To record the retirement of bonds.		

Gains and losses on early derecognition of debt are reported as a gain or loss on the income statement.

Convertible Bonds

Some corporate bonds may be converted into the issuing company's common shares. These bonds are called **convertible bonds** (or **convertible notes**). For investors, they combine (a) the safety of assured receipt of interest and principal on the bonds with (b) the opportunity for gains on the shares. The conversion feature is so attractive that investors usually accept a lower interest rate than they would for nonconvertible bonds. The lower cash interest payments benefit the issuer.

The holder of a convertible bond has the right to convert the bond into a specified number of common shares usually within a specified time period. The holder of the bond is likely to convert the bond into shares if the market price of the issuing company's shares gets high enough.

The subject of convertible bonds is mentioned for completeness; the accounting for convertible bonds and their presentation in the financial statements under the IFRS standards is complex and is beyond the scope of this text.

Financing Operations With Bonds or Shares?

OBJECTIVE

⑤ **Understand** the advantages and disadvantages of borrowing

Managers must decide how to get the money they need to pay for assets. There are three main ways to finance operations:

- By retained earnings
- By issuing shares
- By issuing bonds (or notes)

Each strategy has its advantages and disadvantages.

1. **Financing by retained earnings** means that the company already has enough cash to purchase the needed assets. There's no need to issue more shares or borrow money. This strategy is low-risk to the company.
2. **Issuing shares** creates no liabilities or interest expense and is less risky to the issuing corporation. But issuing shares is more costly, as we shall see.
3. **Issuing bonds or notes payable** does not dilute control of the corporation. It often results in higher earnings per share because the earnings on borrowed

money usually exceed interest expense. But creating more debt increases the risk of the company.

Earnings per share (EPS) is the amount of a company's net income for each of its outstanding shares. EPS is perhaps the single most important statistic used to evaluate companies because it is a standard measure of operating performance for comparing companies of different sizes and from different industries.

Suppose Athens Corporation needs $500,000 for expansion. Assume Athens has net income of $300,000 and 100,000 common shares outstanding. Management is considering two financing plans. Plan 1 is to issue $500,000 of 6% bonds, and plan 2 is to issue 50,000 common shares for $500,000. Management believes the new cash can be invested in operations to earn income of $200,000 before interest and taxes.

Exhibit 8-11 shows the earnings-per-share advantage of borrowing. As you can see, Athens Corporation's EPS amount is higher if the company borrows by issuing bonds (compare lines 9 and 10). Athens earns more on the investment ($102,000) than the interest it pays on the bonds ($30,000). This is called **trading on the equity** or using **leverage**. It is widely used to increase earnings per share of common shares.

In this case, borrowing results in higher earnings per share than issuing shares. Borrowing has its disadvantages, however. Interest expense may be high enough to eliminate net income and lead to losses. Also, borrowing creates liabilities that must be paid during bad years as well as good years. In contrast, a company that issues shares can omit its dividends during a bad year.

ACCOUNTING FOR EXPANSION

The accountant must make a decision as to how to finance the acquisition of new assets. In making that decision, the accountant must consider the pros and cons of each of the three choices:

- Using retained earnings may not be feasible unless the company has sufficient cash and cash equivalents and/or short-term investment to fund the acquisitions. If such is not the case, the following two alternatives must be considered.
- Issuing bonds may be an alternative if interest rates are relatively low and if the accountant believes that rates are not likely to rise to a level that would exceed the return generated by the assets purchased with the borrowed funds. How much financing/interest rate risk is the accountant willing to take? How good is the company's credit rating? The rating will determine the interest rate the company will have to pay.

  Another consideration is that interest must be paid annually, which could cause liquidity issues if cash flows won't support the annual payments. In addition, when the bonds mature, the principal must be repaid.
- Issuing shares is also an alternative. Dividends would be paid only if cash is available. On the other hand, bond interest is tax deductible.

  However, the number of shares issued and outstanding will increase and earnings per share will decrease. Is the company willing to give up some control of the company to the new shareholders?

In short, the accountant must carefully consider the three alternatives so that the decision provides the greatest benefit to the company. There are many issues to consider.

EXHIBIT 8-11 **Earnings-per-Share Advantage of Borrowing**

	Plan 1		Plan 2	
	Borrow $500,000 at 6%		Issue 50,000 Common Shares for $500,000	
1. Net income before expansion		$300,000		$300,000
2. Expected project income before interest and income tax	$200,000		$200,000	
3. Less interest expense ($500,000 × 0.06)	(30,000)		0	
4. Expected project income before income tax	170,000		200,000	
5. Less income tax expense (40%)	(68,000)		(80,000)	
6. Expected project net income		102,000		120,000
7. Total company net income		$402,000		$420,000
8. Earnings per share after expansion:				
9. Plan 1 Borrow ($402,000/100,000 shares)		$ 4.02		
10. Plan 2 ($420,000/150,000 shares)				$ 2.80

The Times-Interest-Earned Ratio

We have just seen how the wise use of borrowing can increase EPS. But too much debt can lead to bankruptcy if the business cannot pay liabilities as they come due. Managers and lenders use ratios to determine how much credit risk they are taking.

The debt ratio measures the effect of debt on the company's *financial position* but says nothing about the ability to pay interest expense. Analysts use a second ratio—the **times-interest-earned ratio**—to relate income to interest expense. To compute this ratio, we divide *income from operations* (also called *operating income*) by interest expense. This ratio measures the number of times that operating income can *cover* interest expense. The ratio is also called the **interest-coverage ratio**. A high times-interest-earned ratio indicates ease in paying interest expense; a low value suggests difficulty. Let's see how Sobeys Inc. and Loblaw Companies Limited, two leading grocery chains, compare on the times-interest-earned ratio (in millions of dollars).

		Sobeys Inc.	**Loblaw Companies Limited**
Times-interest-earned ratio	$= \frac{\text{Operating income}}{\text{Interest expense}} =$	$\frac{406}{60}$	$\frac{1,205}{269}$
		= 6.8 times	= 4.5 times

Sobeys' income from operations covers its interest expense 6.8 times. Loblaw's interest-coverage ratio is 4.5 times. Sobeys is less risky on this ratio than Loblaw.

STOP + THINK

As part of your review of the financial statements of Sobeys and Loblaw as a possible investment, which company would you expect to have the higher debt ratio?

Summarized balance sheet (amounts in millions)

	Sobeys Inc. May 2, 2009	**Loblaw Companies Limited.** January 2, 2010
Total assets	$4,858	$14,991
Total liabilities	$2,754	$ 8,718
Shareholders' equity	2,103	6,273
Total liabilities and equity	$4,858	$14,991

Answer:

Loblaw has a slightly higher debt ratio than Sobeys (in millions of dollars):

	Sobeys	**Loblaw**
$\text{Debt ratio} = \dfrac{\text{Total liabilities}}{\text{Total assets}} =$	$\dfrac{\$2,754}{\$4,858}$	$\dfrac{\$8,718}{\$14,991}$
	= 0.57	= 0.58

Further research would reveal that Sobeys' long-term (and interest-bearing) debt of $954 is 35% of Sobeys' total liabilities while Loblaw's long-term (and interest bearing) debt of $4,507 is 47% of Loblaw's total liabilities. This exercise demonstrates that a user must look deeply into the numbers on the financial statements to truly understand differences between companies.

USING A COMPANY'S FINANCING CHOICES IN DECISION MAKING

The text discussed financing expansion of a company's operations by using retained earnings or by seeking external funds through the issuing of bonds or shares. The choice the company makes affects managers, investors, and creditors differently.

Manager—The management would normally prefer that the company use retained earnings or issue shares because even though bond interest is tax deductible, it must be paid whether or not the company has the resources to pay it. Dividends may not be paid if the company does not have the cash to pay a dividend.

Investor—Investors would normally prefer that the company borrow funds to take advantage of leverage and to avoid the dilution of their share ownership if more shares were issued.

Creditor—Creditors would normally prefer that the company issue shares because dividends may or may not be paid. In addition, bondholders have a prior claim before shareholders to the assets if the company is wound up, and the larger the creditor pool the smaller the share for each creditor.

Long-Term Liabilities: Leases and Pensions

Leases

OBJECTIVE

6 **Account** for leases

A **lease** is a rental agreement in which the renter (**lessee**) agrees to make rent payments to the property owner (**lessor**) in exchange for the use of the asset for an agreed period of time. Leasing allows the lessee to acquire the use of a needed asset without having to make the large upfront payment that purchase agreements require. Accountants distinguish between two types of leases: finance leases and operating leases.

Lease Accounting for Publicly Accountable Enterprises

IAS 17 "Leases" is the basis for the following discussion of leases.

> "A *finance lease* is a lease that transfers substantially all the risks and rewards incidental to ownership of an asset. Title may or may not eventually be transferred." "An *operating lease* is a lease other than a finance lease." IAS 17 indicates that the substance of the transaction determines if a lease is a financing lease or an operating lease.

A **finance lease** generally has some or all of the following characteristics:

- The lessee is likely to obtain ownership of the leased asset at the end of the lease either because the lease transfers title of the leased asset to the lessee at the end of the lease term or the lease contains a purchase option at the end of the lease and it is likely that the price will be less than the fair value of the lease at that time and the lessee is likely to exercise the option.
- The lease term is for a major part of the economic life of the leased asset.
- The present value of the lease payments is substantially most of the fair value of the asset at the start of the lease.
- The asset is essentially specific to the lessee's needs.

There are other conditions that may also indicate that the lease is a finance lease.

IAS 17 requires the finance lease to be recognized (recorded on the lessee's books) at the fair value of the asset acquired, or, if lower, at the present value of the minimum lease payments over the term of the lease. The rate used to calculate the discount rate is the interest rate implicit in the lease or the lessee's incremental borrowing rate.

IAS 17 states that a company must disclose in the financial statements (including the notes to the financial statements):

- The recorded amount at the year-end for each class of finance lease.
- A schedule showing
  - The total future minimum finance lease payments due at the year-end, the interest included in the minimum payments, and the net minimum payments, and
  - The future minimum lease payments due within one year, within years two to five, and after five years.

An operating lease, as indicated above, is any lease that is not a finance lease. The operating lease is not recognized (recorded in the books of the company). The operating lease expense is generally recognized on a straight-line basis over the term of the lease.

IAS 17 states that a company must disclose in the notes to the financial statements the total future minimum non-cancellable operating lease payments due within one year, within years two to five, and after five years.

Lease Accounting for Private Enterprises

CICA Handbook, Section 3065, when considering the lessee, describes a finance lease as a capital lease. When considering the lessor, Section 3065 describes a finance lease as a sales-type lease or a direct financing lease depending on the characteristics of the lease from the lessor's perspective. A capital lease is defined as a lease that confers substantially all the benefits and risks of ownership to the lessee. A lease that does not transfer substantially all the risks and benefits is an operating lease.

Section 3065.03 defines a capital lease and an operating lease as follows:

> **Capital lease** is a lease that, from the point of view of the lessee, transfers substantially all the benefits and risks incident to ownership of property to the lessee.
>
> **Operating lease** is defined as a lease in which the lessor does not transfer substantially all the benefits and risks incident to ownership of property.

With respect to the recognizing of a capital lease by a lessee, Section 3065 states that a capital lease shall be recorded at the present value of the minimum lease payments using a discount rate that is the lower of the lessee's incremental borrowing rate or the interest rate implicit in the lease.

With respect to the disclosure of a capital lease's future payments, Section 3065 states that for a capital lease, the lessee must show the aggregate amount of payments required in each of the next five years as well as the related interest expense either separately or as part of interest on long-term liabilities.

With respect to disclosure of future payments for an operating lease by a lessee, Section 3065 states that the total of future minimum lease payments and the payments due for the following five years must be disclosed.

IFRS accounting for finance leases requires the lessee to set up the present value of the lease payments as an asset and a long-term liability. For example, suppose WestJet leased a Boeing 737-700 aircraft from The Boeing Company at December 31, 2010; the lease term is assumed to be 10 years. The lease payments starting December 31, 2011, are $8,500,000 annually.

The price from Boeing (fair value) for the aircraft (taxes are ignored) is $65,000,000. Using a discount rate of 6% and annual lease payments of $8,500,000, the present value of the annual lease payments would be ($8,500,000 × 7.360 [Exhibit B-6, Appendix B]) or $62,560,000.[3] Therefore, following IAS 17, the entry to record the lease the aircraft would be as follows:

2010			
Dec. 31	Leased Aircraft	62,560,000	
	Finance Lease Liability		62,560,000
	To record acquisition of a Boeing 737-700 using a finance lease with a 10-year term using a discount rate of 6% and annual payments of $8,500,000.		

Leased Aircraft would be a non-current asset within Property, Plant & Equipment. Finance Lease Liability would be classified as a long-term liability.

---

[3]Note that you are not expected to know how to calculate present value of future payments. The present value will be provided to you on examinations, if needed.

WestJet depreciates its aircraft over the number of cycles flown and assumes an aircraft will fly 30,000 to 50,000 cycles. Assume the aircraft leased above flies 5,000 cycles in 2011, that the estimated number of cycles is 40,000, and the estimated residual value is zero. The entry to record depreciation for 2011 would be recorded as follows:

2011			
Dec. 31	Depreciation expense	7,820,000	
	Accumulated depreciation		7,820,000
	To record depreciation expense for 2011 [($62,560,000) × (5,000/40,000)] $7,820,000.		

WestJet would record the lease payment of $8,500,000 on December 31, 2011. Using the data from Exhibit 8-12, WestJet would make the following journal entry at December 31, 2011, to record the payment:

2011			
Dec. 31	Lease Interest Expense	3,753,600	
	Finance Lease Liability	4,746,400	
	Cash		8,500,000
	To record lease payment, lease interest, and payment on lease principal at December 31, 2011.		

WestJet's balance sheet would show the principal payment of $5,031,184 due in 2012 under current liabilities (see Exhibit 8-12) and the balance of the lease due in 2013 and subsequently of $52,782,416 under long-term liabilities. WestJet's income statement for the year ended December 31, 2011, would show the depreciation expense of $7,820,000 and interest expense of $3,753,600.

As was mentioned above, operating leases are not recognized on the balance sheet as finance leases are. The annual lease payments are an expense on the income statement.

EXHIBIT 8-12 **Lease Amortization: Effective Interest Method of Amortization**

Date	Column A Lease Payment ($8,500,000)	Column B Interest Expense 6% × D	Column C Reduction of Obligation A – B	Column D Lease Obligation
12/31/2010	—	—	—	$62,560,000
12/31/2011	$8,500,000	$3,753,600	$4,746,400	57,813,600
12/31/2012	8,500,000	3,468,816	5,031,184	52,782,416
12/31/2013	8,500,000	3,166,945	5,333,055	47,449,361
12/31/2014	8,500,000	2,846,962	5,653,038	41,796,323
12/31/2015	8,500,000	2,507,779	5,992,221	35,804,102
12/31/2016	8,500,000	2,148,246	6,351,754	29,452,348
12/31/2017	8,500,000	1,767,141	6,732,859	22,719,489
12/31/2018	8,500,000	1,363,169	7,136,831	15,582,658
12/31/2019	8,500,000	934,960	7,565,041	8,017,618
12/31/2020	8,498,675*	481,057	8,017,618	0

* The last payment was adjusted to correct rounding error.

Many companies lease some of their property, plant, and equipment including computer software and other long-lived assets. WestJet's December 31, 2009, financial statements had the following note disclosures for its capital (finance) leases and operating leases respectively:

Note 8. Obligations under capital leases (partial, adapted)

The Corporation has entered into capital leases relating to a fuel storage facility and ground handling equipment. The obligations are as follows:

2010	$ 943
2011–2014	1,017
2015 and thereafter	4,862
Total minimum lease payments	$6,822
Less weighted average imputed interest at 5.28%	(2,720)
Net minimum lease payments	4,102
Less current portion of obligations under capital leases	(744)
Obligations under capital leases	$3,358

Note 12. Commitments and contingencies (partial, adapted)

(b) Operating leases and commitments

The Corporation has entered into operating leases and commitments for aircraft, land, buildings, equipment, computer hardware, software licences and satellite programming. As at December 31, 2009, the future payments in Canadian dollars, and where applicable, the US-dollar equivalents under operating leases and commitments, are as follows:

	US$	Cdn$
2010	$ 159,106	$ 189,892
2011–2014	749,919	828,608
2015 and thereafter	520,002	594,850
	$1,429,027	$1,613,350

Do Accountants Prefer Operating Leases or Finance Leases?

Suppose you were the accountant of Kepel Corporation. Kepel, whose assets total $504,000,000 and liabilities total $122,000,000, is considering leasing assets with a fair value of $11 million; the present value of the minimum lease payments discounted at the lease's implicit interest rate at $10 million. Kepel is the lessee (the renter) in the transaction. The lease can be structured either as an operating lease or as a finance lease. Which type of lease would you prefer for Kepel? Why? Computing Kepel's debt ratio two ways (new lease as an operating lease; new lease as a finance lease) will make your decision clear:

(Amounts in millions of dollars)	New Lease Is an Operating Lease	New Lease Is a Finance Lease
Debt ratio $= \dfrac{\text{Total liabilities}}{\text{Total assets}} =$	$\dfrac{\$122}{\$504}$	$\dfrac{\$122 + \$10}{\$504 + \$10} = \dfrac{\$132}{\$514}$
	$= 0.24$	$= 0.26$

You can see that a finance lease increases the debt ratio as both the asset and the liability are reported on the balance sheet. By contrast, operating leases don't affect the debt ratio. For this reason, the accountants would generally prefer operating leases.

USING A COMPANY'S LEASING CHOICES IN DECISION MAKING

The text discussed operating leases and finance leases as options available to companies when they wish to lease assets. The preference for managers, investors, and creditors would be to choose operating leases, but IFRS require leases that meet certain criteria to be accounted for as finance leases and to be recorded as assets and liabilities on the balance sheet.

Manager—The management would normally prefer that the company lease assets on an operating lease. The leased asset is not on the books although the operating lease obligation must appear in the notes to the financial statements. Finance leases increase expenses through depreciation and interest expense, while with operating leases the payment is the expense. Over the life of the lease, total recognized expenses will not differ if a lease is accounted for as an operating lease or a finance lease. In addition, finance leases increase the debt ratio and could make borrowing more expensive. Finance leases are non-cancellable, whereas operating leases may be cancellable.

Investor and creditor—Investors and creditors would normally prefer that the company lease assets on an operating lease because of the impact on the debt ratio.

Employee Benefits

IAS 19 "Employee Benefits" covers all of the various types of benefit plans provided to employees by a company in exchange for the services of the employees to the company. The principal forms of benefit plans are the following:

- Defined contribution **pension** plans. IAS 19 defines these plans as "...post-employment benefit plans under which an entity pays fixed contributions into a separate entity (a fund) and will have no legal or constructive obligation to pay further contributions if the fund does not hold sufficient assets to pay all employee benefits relating to employee service in the current and prior periods."
- Defined benefit pension plans. IAS 19 defines these plans as "...post-employment benefit plans other than defined contribution plans." Generally, in a defined benefit pension plan, the company promises the employee a specified monthly benefit on retirement that is based on age at retirement, length of service, and earnings during employment rather than on fund performance as is a defined contribution pension plan.
- Post-employment benefits. IAS 19 defines post-employment benefits as "... employee benefits (other than termination benefits) which are payable after the completion of employment." A post-employment benefit plan may be formal or informal. Post-retirement benefits include such things as medical insurance, dental insurance, and drug plans.

The accounting and reporting under IAS 19 for these plans is complex and beyond the scope of this text.

Reporting Liabilities

Reporting on the Balance Sheet

OBJECTIVE

7 **Report** liabilities on the balance sheet

This chapter began with the liabilities reported on the balance sheets of WestJet. Exhibit 8-13 repeats the liabilities section of West Jet's balance sheet.

Investors and creditors need the information illustrated in Exhibit 8-13 and discussed below in order to evaluate WestJet's balance sheet and the company.

Exhibit 8-13 includes Note 7 (adapted) from WestJet's December 31, 2009, financial statements, which gives additional information about the Company's long-term debt. Note 7 provides specific information about the details of the six tranches of term loans shown in Exhibit 8-13 and a schedule showing future repayments. The schedule shows that \$171 million is due in fiscal 2010 and \$1,048 million in subsequent years. Note 8 (adapted) is discussed on page 422; it provides information about the Company's capital leases.

EXHIBIT 8-13 **Reporting Liabilities of WestJet**

WestJet
Consolidated Balance Sheet (Partial, Adapted)
As at December 31, 2009

	(amounts in thousands)
Current Liabilities:	
Accounts payable and accrued liabilities	\$ 231,401
Advance ticket sales	286,361
Non-refundable guest credits	64,506
Current portion of obligations under capital leases	744
Current portion of long-term debt	171,223
Total current liabilities	754,235
Obligations under capital leases (Note 8)	3,358
Long-term debt (Note 7)	1,048,554
Other long-term liabilities	298,627
	\$2,104,744

7. LONG-TERM DEBT (Partial, Adapted)

	2009
Term loans—purchased aircraft	\$1,168,381
Term loan—purchased aircraft	33,631
Term loan—flight simulator	6,392
Term loans—live satellite television equipment	493
Term loan—Calgary Hangar facility	9,202
Term loan—Calgary Hangar facility	1,678
	1,219,777
Current portion	171,223
	\$1,048,554

Trace the current finance (capital) lease payments and long-term debt payments due in 2010 from the illustration on page 422 and Note 7 on Exhibit 8-13, respectively, to the WestJet balance sheet in Exhibit 8-13. Working back and forth between the financial statements and the notes to the financial statements is an important part of financial analysis. You now have the tools to understand the liabilities on an actual balance sheet.

Reporting the Fair Market Value of Long-Term Debt

IAS 39 requires that all financial liabilities (with certain exceptions that are beyond the scope of this text) be measured for reporting purposes at amortized cost using the effective-interest method. At December 31, 2009, WestJet's financial statements in Note 13 "Financial Instruments" (a) "Fair Value of Financial Assets and Financial Liabilities" reported capital leases and long-term debt as follows (amounts in millions) as required by IFRS 7:

	Amortized Cost	Carrying Amount	Fair Value
Long-term debt	$1,219	$1,219	$1,323
Obligations under capital leases	4	4	4

Overall, the fair value of WestJet's long-term debt was about $104 million higher than the amount carried on WestJet's books.

Reporting the Risks Related to Long-Term Debt

Companies face risks related to their financial assets and liabilities. IFRS 7 "Financial Instruments: Disclosures" requires reporting companies (PAEs) to provide information on the risks arising from their financial instruments to assist users in assessing the risks arising from those financial instruments. WestJet, in Note 13 (b) "Risk Management," discusses the foreign exchange risk, credit risk, interest rate risk, and liquidity risk the company faces.

SUMMARY OF CHAPTER 8

Learning Objective ❶: **Account for current liabilities and contingent liabilities**

Current liabilities are obligations due within one year or within the company's operating cycle if longer. Obligations due beyond that time period are **long-term liabilities**.

Current liabilities are of two kinds: (1) known amounts such as accounts payable, **short-term notes payable**, value-added taxes (such as sales taxes, GST, and HST), accrued liabilities, payroll liabilities, unearned revenues, **current portion of long-term debt**, and current portion of finance leases; and (2) estimated amounts such as estimated warranty payable and contingent liabilities.

Learning Objective ❷: **Understand bonds payable**

Bonds payable are groups of notes issued to multiple lenders. Bonds may be **term bonds**, which have a fixed maturity, or **serial bonds**, which are like installment notes payable. Bonds may also be secured by specified assets or be **debentures**, which are unsecured.

Bonds are bought and sold through bond markets; the price of a bond is dependent on the relationship between **stated interest rate** on the bond and the current **market interest rate**.

Bonds may be issued at a **premium** (above **face value**) or at a **discount** (below face value).

Learning Objective ❸: Account for bonds payable

When bonds are issued at face value, the stated interest rate is equal to the market interest rate when the bonds are issued.

When bonds are issued at a discount, the market interest rate is greater than the stated interest rate. The amount of money received is less than the face value of the bonds. The discount must be amortized over the life of the bonds using the effective interest rate method. When bonds are issued at a premium, the opposite is true.

Learning Objective ❹: Measure interest expense

The interest payment is the amount of cash paid and is the stated interest rate on the bond. The interest expense is equal to the interest payment plus the amortization of the discount. Interest expense is calculated using the effective interest method under which the interest expense equals the carrying value of a bond at the beginning of the accounting period times the market rate of interest at the time of issue.

In the case of bonds issued at a discount, the amount of amortization of the discount is equal to the interest expense minus the interest payment. In the case of bonds issued at a premium, the amortization of the premium is equal to interest payment minus the interest expense.

Learning Objective ❺: Understand the advantages and disadvantages of borrowing

A company that wishes to expand has three main ways to finance the expansion: by using retained earnings, by issuing shares, and by issuing bonds or notes. Each of the three methods has advantages and disadvantages which are discussed in the text.

Learning Objective ❻: Account for leases

A **lease** is a rental agreement in which the **lessee** agrees to make rent payments to the **lessor** (property owner) in exchange for the use of the asset. There are two types of leases: a **finance lease** where the lessee records the asset and lease liability on its books; and an **operating lease** where the lessor retains the asset leased on its books.

There are a number of characteristics, some or all of which, if present in the agreement, define the lease as a finance lease. An operating lease is a lease that is not a finance lease.

IAS 17 requires the finance lease to be recognized (recorded on the lessee's books) at the fair value of the asset acquired, or, if lower, at the **present value** of the minimum lease payments over the term of the lease. The rate used to calculate the discount rate is the interest rate implicit in the lease or the lessee's incremental borrowing rate.

With respect to finance leases, the company must disclose the discounted (interest excluded) lease payments due in the subsequent year as a current liability and the discounted (interest excluded) lease payments due in year two and onwards as a long-term liability. With respect to operating leases, the company must disclose future lease payments.

Learning Objective 7: **Report liabilities on the balance sheet**

The user of the financial statements must review current and long-term liabilities, which are reported on the balance sheet, and also review the notes related to those liabilities. IAS 39 requires companies to measure financial liabilities at amortized cost. IFRS 7 requires a company to report the fair value of liabilities comparing the fair values to the carrying amounts of the liabilities.

IFRS 7 requires companies to report the risks related to long-term debt. These risks include foreign exchange risk, credit risk, interest rate risk, and liquidity risk.

END-OF-CHAPTER SUMMARY PROBLEM

MyAccountingLab

TransCanada Corporation has a number of debt issues outstanding in various amounts with various interest rates and maturities. Assume TransCanada has outstanding an issue of 8% bonds that mature in 2021. Suppose the bonds are dated October 1, 2011, and pay interest each April 1 and October 1.

Required

1. Complete the following effective-interest amortization table through October 1, 2013:
   Bond Data
   Maturity value—$100,000
   Contract interest rate—8%
   Interest paid—4% semi-annually, $4,000 ($100,000 × 0.08 × 6/12)
   Market interest rate at the time of issue—9% annually, 4 1/2% semi-annually
   Issue price—93.80

Amortization Table

	A	B	C	D	E
Semi-Annual Interest Date	Interest Payment (4% of Maturity Amount)	Interest Expense (4 1/2% of Preceding Bond Carrying Amount)	Discount Amortization (B − A)	Discount Account Balance (Preceding D − C)	Bond Carrying Amount ($100,000 − D)
01-10-11					
01-04-12					
01-10-12					
01-04-13					
01-10-13					

2. Using the amortization table, record the following transactions:
   a. Issuance of the bonds on October 1, 2011.
   b. Accrual of interest and amortization of the bonds on December 31, 2011.
   c. Payment of interest and amortization of the bonds on April 1, 2012.
   d. Derecognition of two-thirds of the bonds payable on October 2, 2013. Purchase price of the bonds was based on their call price of 102.

Name: TransCanada Corporation
Industry: Pipeline provider
Accounting Period: The years 2011, 2012, 2013

ANSWERS

The semi-annual interest payment is constant ($4,000). The interest expense is calculated as 4.5% of the previous period's carrying value. The discount account balance reflects that the issue price of $93.80 is less than $100.00.

Requirement 1

	A	B	C	D	E
Semi-Annual Interest Date	Interest Payment (4% of Maturity Amount)	Interest Expense (4 1/2% of Preceding Bond Carrying Amount)	Discount Amortization (B − A)	Discount Account Balance (Preceding D − C)	Bond Carrying Amount ($100,000 − D)
01-10-11				$6,200	$93,800
01-04-12	$4,000	$4,221	$221	5,979	94,021
01-10-12	4,000	4,231	231	5,748	94,252
01-04-13	4,000	4,241	241	5,507	94,493
01-10-13	4,000	4,252	252	5,255	94,745

Requirement 2

The bonds were issued for less than $100,000, reflecting a discount. Use the amounts from columns D and E for 01-10-11 from the amortization table.

		Debit	Credit
a. 2011 Oct. 1	Cash	93,800	
	Discount on Bonds Payable	6,200	
	Bonds Payable		100,000
	To issue 8%, ten-year bonds at a discount.		

The accrued interest is calculated, and the bond discount is amortized. Use 3/6 of the amounts from columns A, B, and C for 01-04-12 from the amortization table.

		Debit	Credit
b. Dec. 31	Interest Expense ($4,221 × 3/6)	2,111	
	Discount on Bonds Payable ($121 × 3/6)		111
	Interest Payable ($4,000 × 3/6)		2,000
	To accrue interest and amortize the bonds.		

The semi-annual interest payment is made ($4,000 from column A). Only the January-to-March 2012 interest expense is recorded, since the October-to-December interest expense was already recorded in Requirement 2 b. The same is true for the discount on bonds payable. Reverse Interest Payable from Requirement 2 b, since cash is paid now.

		Debit	Credit
c. 2012 Apr. 1	Interest Expense	2,110	
	Interest Payable	2,000	
	Discount on Bonds Payable ($121 × 3/6)		110*
	Cash		4,000
	To pay semi-annual interest, part of which was accrued, and amortize the bonds.		

The cash paid on retirement was $102 for every $100 of bonds. Use 2/3 of the amount from column D for 01-10-13 to calculate Discount on Bonds Payable. The loss on retirement reflects the excess of the book value over the cash received and is the "plug" figure in the journal entry.

		Debit	Credit
d. 2013 Oct. 2	Bonds Payable ($100,000 × 2/3)	66,667	
	Loss on Retirement of Bonds	4,836	
	Discount on Bonds Payable ($5,255 × 2/3)		3,503
	Cash ($100,000 × 2/3 × 1.02)		68,000
	To retire bonds payable before maturity.		

*The total amortization was $221 of which $111 was recognized at December 31, 2011.

Review Liabilities

Quick Check (Answers are given on page 451.)

1. Which of the following is *not* an estimated liability?
   a. Allowance for bad debts
   b. Product warranties
   c. Income taxes
   d. Vacation pay
2. Recording estimated warranty expense in the current year *best* follows which accounting principle?
   a. Comparability
   b. Materiality
   c. Full disclosure
   d. Historical cost
   e. Relevance
3. Lotta Sound grants a 90-day warranty on all stereos. Historically, approximately 2 1/2% of all sales prove to be defective. Sales in June are $200,000. In July, $2,900 of defective units are returned for replacement. What entry must Lotta Sound make at the end of June to record the warranty expense?
   a. Debit Warranty Expense, and credit Estimated Warranty Payable, $2,900.
   b. Debit Warranty Expense, and credit Cash, $4,865.
   c. Debit Warranty Expense, and credit Estimated Warranty Payable, $5,000.
   d. No entry is needed at June 30.
4. Outback Camera Co. was organized to sell a single product that carries a 60-day warranty against defects. Engineering estimates indicate that 5% of the units sold will prove defective and require an average repair cost of $40 per unit. During Outback's first month of operations, total sales were 400 units; by the end of the month, six defective units had been repaired. The liability for product warranties at month-end should be which of the following?
   a. $270
   b. $530
   c. $560
   d. $810
   e. None of these
5. A contingent liability should be recorded in the accounts
   a. If the related future event will probably occur
   b. If the amount is due in cash within one year
   c. If the amount can be reasonably estimated
   d. Both a and b
   e Both a and c
6. An unsecured bond is a
   a. Registered bond
   b. Mortgage bond
   c. Term bond
   d. Serial bond
   e. Debenture bond
7. The Discount on Bonds Payable account
   a. Is a contra account to Bonds Payable
   b. Is a miscellaneous revenue account
   c. Is an expense account
   d. Is expensed at the bond's maturity
   e. Has a normal credit balance
8. The discount on a bond payable becomes
   a. Additional interest expense the year the bonds are sold
   b. Additional interest expense over the life of the bonds
   c. A reduction in interest expense the year the bonds mature
   d. A reduction in interest expense over the life of the bonds
   e. A liability in the year the bonds are sold

9. A bond that matures in installments is called a
   a. Secured bond
   b. Zero coupon
   c. Serial bond
   d. Term bond
   e. Callable bond
10. The carrying value of Bonds Payable equals
    a. Bonds Payable − Premium on Bonds Payable
    b. Bonds Payable − Discount on Bonds Payable
    c. Bonds Payable + Discount on Bonds Payable
    d. Bonds Payable + Accrued Interest
11. A corporation issues bonds that pay interest each March 1 and September 1. The corporation's December 31 adjusting entry may include a
    a. Debit to Cash
    b. Credit to Cash
    c. Credit to Interest Expense
    d. Debit to Interest Payable
    e. Credit to Discount on Bonds Payable

Use this information to answer Questions 12 through 16.

McLennan Corporation issued $200,000 of 9 1/2% five-year bonds. The bonds are dated and sold on January 1, 2011. Interest payment dates are January 1 and July 1. The bonds are issued for $196,140 to yield the market interest rate of 10%. Use the effective-interest method for Questions 12 through 15.

12. What is the amount of interest expense that McLennan Corporation will record on July 1, 2011, the first semi-annual interest payment date?
    a. $9,807
    b. $9,926
    c. $10,000
    d. $19,000
13. What is the amount of discount amortization that McLennan Corporation will record on July 1, 2011, the first semi-annual interest payment date?
    a. $0
    b. $74
    c. $193
    d. $307
14. What is the total cash payment for interest for each 12-month period?
    a. $10,000
    b. $19,000
    c. $19,614
    d. $20,000
15. What is the carrying amount of the bonds on the December 31, 2011, balance sheet?
    a. $196,140
    b. $196,526
    c. $196,769
    d. $196,912
16. Using straight-line amortization, the carrying amount of McLennan Corporation's bonds at December 31, 2011, is which of the following?
    a. $196,140
    b. $196,526
    c. $196,769
    d. $196,912

Accounting Vocabulary

bond market price The price investors are willing to pay for the bond. It is equal to the present value of the principal payment plus the present value of the interest payments. (p. 404)

bonds payable Groups of notes payable issued to multiple lenders called *bondholders*. (p. 402)

callable bonds Bonds that may be paid at a specified price whenever the issuer wants. (p. 414)

capital lease Lease agreement that meets any one of four criteria: (1) The lease transfers title of the leased asset to the lessee at the end of the lease term. (2) The lease contains a bargain purchase option. (3) The lease term is 75% or more of the estimated useful life of the leased asset. (4) The present value of the lease payments is 90% or more of the market value of the leased asset. (p. 420)

convertible bonds (or **convertible notes**) Bonds or notes that may be converted into the issuing company's common stock at the investor's option. (p. 415)

current portion of long-term debt The amount of the principal that is payable within one year. Also called *current installement of long-term debt*. (p. 397)

debentures Unsecured bonds—bonds backed only by the good faith of the borrower. (p. 402)

derecognition The decision to pay off a bond before maturity (p. 414)

direct financing lease Substantially similar to a sales-type lease, except it is negotiated through a financial institution. (p. 420)

discount (on a bond) Excess of a bond's face (par) value over its issue price. (p. 404)
earnings per share (EPS) Amount of a company's net income per outstanding common share. (p. 416)
face value of bond The principal amount payable by the issuer. Also called *maturity value*. (p. 402)
finance lease A lease defined by IFRS that transfers substantially all risks and rewards incidental to ownership of assets to the lessee. (p. 419)
interest-coverage ratio Another name for the *times-interest-earned ratio*. (p. 417)
lease Rental agreement in which the tenant (lessee) agrees to make rent payments to the property owner (lessor) in exchange for the use of the asset. (p. 419)
lessee Tenant in a lease agreement. (p. 419)
lessor Property owner in a lease agreement. (p. 419)
leverage Earning more income on borrowed money than the related interest expense, thereby increasing the earnings for the owners of the business. Also called *trading on the equity*. (p. 416)
market interest rate Interest rate that investors demand for loaning their money. Also called *effective interest rate*. (p. 405)
operating lease Usually a short-term or cancellable rental agreement. (p. 420)
payroll Employee compensation, a major expense of many businesses. (p. 395)
pension Employee benefit that will be received during retirement. (p. 423)
premium (on a bond) Excess of a bond's issue price over its face value. (p. 404)
present value Amount a person would invest now to receive a greater amount at a future date. (p. 404)
sales-type lease From the point of view of the lessor, transfers substantially all the benefits and risks of ownership of the asset (p. 420)
serial bonds Bonds that mature in installments over a period of time. (p. 402)
short-term notes payable Notes payable due within one year. (p. 391)
stated interest rate Interest rate printed on the bond certificate that determines the amount of cash interest the borrower pays and the investor receives each year. Also called the *coupon rate* or *contract interest rate*. (p. 404)
term bonds Bonds that all mature at the same time for a particular issue. (p. 402)
times-interest-earned ratio Ratio of income from operations to interest expense. Measures the number of times that operating income can cover interest expense. Also called the *interest-coverage ratio*. (p. 417)
trading on the equity Earning more income on borrowed money than the related interest expense, thereby increasing the earnings for the owners of the business. Also called *leverage*. (p. 416)
underwriter Organization that purchases the bonds from an issuing company and resells them to its clients or sells the bonds for a commission, agreeing to buy all unsold bonds. (p. 402)

Assess Your Progress

Make the grade with MyAccountingLab: The exercises and problems in this chapter can be found on MyAccountingLab at www.myaccountinglab.com. You can practise them as often as you want, and they feature step-by-step guided solutions to help you find the right answer.

Short Exercises

Learning Objective 1
Accounting for a note payable

S8-1 Jasper Sports Limited purchased inventory costing $10,000 by signing a 10% short-term note payable. The purchase occurred on March 31, 2011. Jasper pays annual interest each year on March 31. Journalize Jasper's (a) purchase of inventory, (b) accrual of interest expense on December 31, 2011, and (c) payment of the note plus interest on March 31, 2012.

Learning Objective 1
Reporting a short-term note payable and the related interest in the financial statements

S8-2 This short exercise works with Short Exercise 8-1.

1. Refer to the data in Short Exercise 8-1. Show what the company would report on its balance sheet at December 31, 2011, and on its income statement for the year ended on that date.
2. What one item will the financial statements for the year ended December 31, 2012, report? Identify the financial statement, the item, and its amount.

Learning Objective 1
Accounting for warranty expense and estimated warranty payable

S8-3 General Motors of Canada Limited guarantees automobiles against defects for five years or 160,000 km, whichever comes first. Suppose GM Canada can expect warranty costs during the five-year period to add up to 3% of sales.

Assume that Forbes Motors in Waterloo, Ontario, made sales of $2,000,000 on their Buick line during 2011. Forbes received cash for 10% of the sales and took notes receivable for the remainder. Payments to satisfy customer warranty claims totalled $50,000 during 2011.

1. Record the sales, warranty expense, and warranty payments for Forbes. Ignore any reimbursement that Forbes may receive from GM Canada.
2. Post to the Estimated Warranty Payable T-account. The beginning balance was $40,000. At the end of 2011, how much in estimated warranty payable does Forbes owe its customers?

Learning Objective 1
Reporting warranties in the financial statements

S8-4 Refer to the data given in Short Exercise 8-3. What amount of warranty expense will Forbes report during 2011? Does the warranty expense for the year equal the year's cash payments for warranties? Explain the relevant accounting principle as it applies to measuring warranty expense.

Learning Objective 1
Interpreting a company's contingent liabilities

S8-5 A major Canadian company included the following note in its financial statements:

> **NOTES TO CONSOLIDATED FINANCIAL STATEMENTS**
> **23. (In Part): Commitments, Contingencies, and Guarantees**
> c) Liability insurance
> The Company is self-insured for up to the first $5 million of costs incurred relating to a single liability claim in a year and to $10 million in aggregate claims arising during an annual policy period. The Company provides for unsettled reported losses and losses incurred but not reported based on an independent review of all claims made against the Company. Accruals for estimated losses related to self-insurance were not material at the date of these financial statements.

1. Why are these contingent (versus real) liabilities?
2. How can a contingent liability become a real liability for the company? What are the limits of self-insured liability claims? Explain how these limits work.
3. What is the meaning of the last sentence in the note?

Learning Objective 2 3
Pricing bonds

S8-6 Compute the price of the following bonds:

a. $1,000,000 quoted at 89.75
b. $500,000 quoted at 110.375
c. $100,000 quoted at 97.50
d. $400,000 quoted at 102.625

Learning Objective 2 3
Determining bond prices at face value, a discount, or a premium

S8-7 Determine whether the following bonds will be issued at face value, a premium, or a discount:

a. The market interest rate is 9%. Star Inc. issues bonds with a stated rate of 8 1/2%.
b. Charger Corporation issued 7 1/2% bonds when the market rate was 7 1/2%.
c. Explorer Corporation issued 8% bonds when the market interest rate was 6 7/8%.
d. Tundra Company issued bonds that pay cash interest at the stated interest rate of 7%. At the date of issuance, the market interest rate was 8 1/4%.

Learning Objective 2 3
Journalizing basic bond payable transactions; bonds issued at face value

S8-8 Suppose Scotiabank issued a six-year $10,000 bond with stated interest rate of 6.25% when the market interest rate was 6 1/4%. Assume that the accounting year of Scotiabank ends on October 31. Journalize the following transactions, including an explanation for each entry.

a. Issuance of the bond, payable on May 1, 2011
b. Accrual of interest expense on October 31, 2011 (rounded to the nearest dollar)
c. Payment of cash interest on November 1, 2011
d. Payment of the bonds at maturity (give the date)

Learning Objective 2 3
Issuing bonds and amortizing bonds by the effective-interest method

S8-9 Standard Autoparts Inc. issued $100,000 of 7%, 10-year bonds at a price of 87 on January 31, 2011. The market interest rate at the date of issuance was 9%, and the standard bonds pay interest semi-annually.

1. Prepare an effective-interest amortization table for the bonds through the first three interest payments. Use Exhibit 8-5, page 408, as a guide, and round amounts to the nearest dollar.
2. Record Standard's issuance of the bonds on January 31, 2011, and payment of the first semi-annual interest amount and amortization of the bonds on July 31, 2011. Explanations are not required.

S8-10 Use the amortization table that you prepared for Standard Autoparts in Short Exercise 8-9 to answer these questions about the company's long-term debt:

Learning Objective 4
Analyzing data on long-term debt

1. How much cash did Standard Autoparts borrow on January 31, 2011? How much cash will Standard Autoparts pay back at maturity on January 31, 2012?
2. How much cash interest will Standard Autoparts pay each six months?
3. How much interest expense will Standard Autoparts report on July 31, 2011, and on January 31, 2012? Why does the amount of interest expense increase each period? Explain in detail.

S8-11 Max Industries Ltd. borrowed money by issuing a $10,000 6.5%, 10-year bond. Assume the issue price was 94 on July 1, 2011.

Learning Objective 4
Determining bonds payable amounts: amortizing bonds by the straight-line method

1. How much cash did Max Industries receive when it issued the bond?
2. How much must Max Industries pay back at maturity? When is the maturity date?
3. How much cash interest will Max Industries pay each six months? Carry the interest amount to the nearest cent.
4. How much interest expense will Max Industries report each six months? Assume the straight-line amortization method, and carry the interest amount to the nearest cent.

S8-12 Return to the Max Industries bond in Short Exercise 8-11. Assume that Max Industries issued the bond on July 1, 2011, at a price of 90. Also assume that Max Industries' accounting year ends on December 31. Journalize the following transactions for Max Industries, including an explanation for each entry:

Learning Objective 4
Issuing bonds, accruing interest, and amortizing bonds by the straight-line method

a. Issuance of the bonds on July 1, 2011
b. Accrual of interest expense and amortization of bonds on December 31, 2011. (Use the straight-line amortization method, and round amounts to the nearest dollar.)
c. Payment of the first semi-annual interest amount on January 1, 2012.

S8-13 Assume that YouTube needs $1.5 million to expand the company. YouTube is considering the issuance of either

Learning Objective 5
Earnings-per-share effects of financing with bonds versus shares

- $1,500,000 of 5% bonds to borrow the money, or
- 100,000 common shares at $15 per share

Before any new financing, YouTube expects to earn net income of $500,000, and the company already has 200,000 common shares outstanding. YouTube believes the expansion will increase income before interest and income tax by $250,000. YouTube's income tax rate is 30%.

Prepare an analysis similar to Exhibit 8-11, page 416, to determine which plan is likely to result in the higher earnings per share. Based solely on the earnings-per-share comparison, which financing plan would you recommend for YouTube?

S8-14 Zigzag International Ltd. reported the following data in 2011 (in millions):

Learning Objective 5
Computing the times-interest-earned ratio

Net operating revenues	$29.2
Operating expenses	26.3
Operating income	2.9
Nonoperating items	
Interest expense	(1.6)
Other	(0.2)
Net income	$ 1.1

Compute Zigzag's times-interest-earned ratio, and write a sentence to explain what the ratio value means. Would you be willing to lend Zigzag $1 million? State your reason.

Learning Objective 7
Reporting liabilities, including capital lease obligations

S8-15 Trinidad Industries Inc. has the following selected accounts at December 31, 2011.

GST Payable (net of ITC)	$ 17,000
Bonds payable	300,000
Equipment	120,000
Current portion of bonds payable	40,000
Notes payable, long-term	100,000
Interest payable (due March 1, 2012)	10,000
Accounts payable	44,000
Discount on bonds payable (all long-term)	10,000
Accounts receivable	34,000

Prepare the liabilities section of Trinidad's balance sheet at December 31, 2011, to show how Trinidad would report these items. Report total current liabilities and total liabilities.

Exercises

Learning Objective 1
Accounting for warranty expense and the related liability

E8-16 The accounting records of Audio-Video Inc. included the following balances before the year-end adjustments:

Estimated Warranty Payable		Sales Revenue		Warranty Expense	
	Beg. bal. 8,000		150,000		

In the past, Audio-Video's warranty expense has been 6% of sales. During the current period, the business paid $9,400 to satisfy the warranty claims of customers.

Required

1. Record Audio-Video's warranty expense for the period and the company's cash payments to satisfy warranty claims. Explanations are not required.
2. Show everything Audio-Video will report on its income statement and balance sheet for this situation.
3. Which data item from Requirement 2 will affect Audio-Video's current ratio? Will Audio-Video's current ratio increase or decrease as a result of this item?

Learning Objective 1
Recording and reporting current liabilities

E8-17 *Ontario Traveller Magazine* completed the following transactions during 2011:

Aug.	31	Sold one-year subscriptions, collecting cash of $1,500, plus HST of 13%
Dec.	31	Remitted (paid) HST to Canada Revenue Agency (CRA)
	31	Made the necessary adjustment at year-end.

Journalize these transactions (explanations are not required). Then report any liability on the company's balance sheet at December 31.

Learning Objective 1
Reporting payroll expense and liabilities

E8-18 Penske Talent Search has an annual payroll of $150,000. At December 31, Penske owes salaries of $7,600 on which employee withholdings payable are $1,200 and employee benefits payable by the company are $1,000. The company has calculated its share of Canada Pension Plan, Employment Insurance, and other employee benefits to be 6% of payroll expense. The company will pay these amounts early next year. Show what Penske will report for the foregoing on its income statement and year-end balance sheet.

Learning Objective 1
Recording note-payable transactions

E8-19 Joy's Bar and Grill completed the following note-payable transactions.

2011		
Aug.	1	Purchased kitchen equipment costing $60,000 by issuing a one-year, 5% note
Dec.	31	Accrued interest on the note payable
2012		
Aug.	1	Paid the note payable at maturity

Answer these questions for Joy's Bar and Grill:

1. How much interest expense must be accrued at December 31, 2011?
2. Determine the amount of Joy's final payment on July 31, 2012.
3. How much interest expense will Joy's report for 2011 and for 2012?

Learning Objective 1
Accounting for income tax

E8-20 At December 31, 2010, Young Real Estate reported a current liability for income tax payable of $200,000. During 2011, Young earned income of $900,000 before income tax. The company's income tax rate during 2011 was 20%. Also during 2011, Young paid income taxes of $250,000. How much income tax payable did Young Real Estate report on its balance sheet at December 31, 2011? How much income tax expense did Young report on its 2011 income statement?

Learning Objective 1 7
Analyzing liabilities

E8-21 Mills Geothermal Ltd. installs environmental heating/cooling systems. The company's 2011 revenues totalled $360 million, and at December 31, 2011, the company had $65 million in current assets. The December 31, 2011, balance sheet reported the liabilities and shareholders' equity as follows.

	At Year-End (in millions)	
	2011	**2010**
Liabilities and Shareholders' Equity		
Current Liabilities		
Accounts payable	$ 29	$ 26
Accrued expenses	16	20
Employee compensation and benefits	9	11
Current portion of long-term debt	5	—
Total Current Liabilities	59	57
Long-Term Debt	115	115
Post-Retirement Benefits Payable	31	27
Other Liabilities	21	17
Shareholders' Equity	73	70
Total Liabilities and Shareholders' Equity	$299	$286

Required

1. Describe each of Mills Geothermal Ltd.'s liabilities, and state how the liability arose.
2. What were the company's total assets at December 31, 2011? Was the company's debt ratio at the end of 2011 high, low, or in a middle range?

Learning Objective 1
Reporting a contingent liability

E8-22 A Canadian industry leader in early phase drug development reported revenues of $470.3 million. At year-end, the company was a defendant in a number of lawsuits related to accounting issues.

NOTE G (in part): Litigation and Inquiries of the financial statements at year-end reported:

The [company] named as defendant[s] in the Federal Derivative Actions and the Province of Ontario Circuit Court Derivative Actions intend[s] to vigorously defend against the lawsuits. As the outcome of these matters is difficult to predict, significant changes in the Company's estimated exposures could occur.

Required

1. Suppose the company's lawyers believe a significant legal judgment against the company is reasonably possible. How should the company report this situation in its financial statements?
2. Suppose the company's lawyers believe it is probable that a $2 million judgment will be rendered against the company. How should this situation be reported in the company's financial statements? Journalize any entry required by IFRS. Explanations are not required.

Learning Objective ❶❼
Reporting current and long-term liabilities

E8-23 Assume that Premium Golf Equipment completed these selected transactions during December 2011.

a. Sales of $3,000,000 are subject to estimated warranty cost of 3%. The estimated warranty payable at the beginning of the year was $30,000, and warranty payments for the year totalled $60,000.
b. On December 1, 2011, Premium signed a $150,000 note that requires annual payments of $30,000 plus 5% interest on the unpaid balance each December 1.
c. Golf Town, a chain of golf stores, ordered $125,000 of golf equipment. With its order, Golf Town sent a cheque for $125,000, and Premium shipped $100,000 of the goods. Premium will ship the remainder of the goods on January 3, 2012.
d. The December payroll of $100,000 is subject to employee withheld income tax, Canada Pension Plan and Employment Insurance, and company share of Canada Pension Plan and Employment Insurance totalling $25,000 and benefits of $9,000. On December 31, Premium pays employees their take-home pay and accrues all tax amounts.

Required

Classify each liability as current or long-term and report the liability and its amount that would appear on the Premium Golf Equipment balance sheet at December 31, 2011. Show a total for current liabilities.

Learning Objective ❷❸
Issuing bonds, paying and accruing interest, and amortizing the bonds by the straight-line method

E8-24 On January 31, 2011, Triumph Sports Cars issued 10-year, 6% bonds with a face value of $100,000. The bonds were issued at 97 and pay interest on January 31 and July 31. Triumph amortizes bonds by the straight-line method. Record (a) issuance of the bonds on January 31, (b) the semi-annual interest payment and discount amortization on July 31, and (c) the interest accrual and discount amortization on December 31.

Learning Objective ❷❸❹
Measuring cash amounts for a bond; amortizing the bonds by the straight-line method

E8-25 Moreau Manufacturing Inc. has $200,000 of 8% debenture bonds outstanding. The bonds were issued at 102 in 2011 and mature in 2031.

Required

1. How much cash did Moreau receive when it issued these bonds?
2. How much cash *in total* will Moreau pay the bondholders through the maturity date of the bonds?
3. Take the difference between your answers to Requirements 1 and 2. This difference represents Moreau's total interest expense over the life of the bonds. (Challenge)
4. Compute Moreau's annual interest expense by the straight-line amortization method. Multiply this amount by 20. Your 20-year total should be the same as your answer to Requirement 3. (Challenge)

Learning Objective ❷❸❹
Issuing bonds (discount); recording interest payments and the related bond amortization

E8-26 Family General Stores Inc. is authorized to issue $500,000 of 7%, 10-year bonds. On December 31, 2011, when the market interest rate is 8%, the company issues $400,000 of the bonds and receives cash of $372,660. Family General amortizes bonds by the effective-interest method. The semi-annual interest dates are January 31 and July 31.

Required

1. Prepare a bond amortization table for the first four semi-annual interest periods.
2. Record issuance of the bonds on December 31, 2011, and the semi-annual interest payments on January 31, 2012, and on July 31, 2012.

Learning Objective ❷❸❹
Issuing bonds (premium); recording interest accrual and payment and the related bond amortization

E8-27 On June 30, 2011, the market interest rate is 7%. Dellaca Enterprises issues $500,000 of 8%, 20-year bonds at 110.625. The bonds pay interest on June 30 and December 31. Dellaca amortizes bonds by the effective-interest method.

Required

1. Prepare a bond amortization table for the first four semi-annual interest periods.
2. Record issuance of the bonds on June 30, 2011, the payment of interest at December 31, 2011, and the semi-annual interest payment on June 30, 2012.

Learning Objective ❸❹
Debt payment and bond amortization schedule

E8-28 Carlson Candies issued $300,000 of 8 3/8%, five-year bonds on January 1, 2011, when the market interest rate was 9 1/2%. The company pays interest annually at year-end. The issue price of the bonds was $287,041.

Required

Create a spreadsheet model to prepare a schedule to amortize the bonds. Use the effective-interest method of amortization. Round to the nearest dollar, and format your answer as shown here.

1	A	B	C	D	E	F
2						Bond
3		Interest	Interest	Discount	Discount	Carrying
4	Date	Payment	Expense	Amortization	Balance	Amount
5	1-1-2011					287,041
6	12-31-2011	$ ☐	$ ☐	$ ☐	$ ☐	$ ☐
7	12-31-2012	↓	↓	↓	↓	↓
8	12-31-2013					
9	12-31-2014					
10	12-31-2015					
		300,000 × 0.08375	+F5 × 0.095	+C6–B6	300,000–F5	+F5+D6

Learning Objective ❷❸❼
Recording derecognition of notes payable

E8-29 Montrose Corporation issued $300,000 of 8 1/2% notes on December 31, 2011, at a price of 98.5. The notes' term to maturity is 10 years. After three years, Montrose derecognizes the bonds when the market price per bond is 99.0.

Required

1. Without making journal entries, compute the carrying amount of the notes payable at December 31, 2014, immediately before the derecognition. Montrose uses the straight-line method to amortize bonds.
2. All amortization has been recorded properly. Journalize the derecognition transaction at December 31, 2014.

Learning Objective ❺
Using ratios to compare companies

E8-30 Companies that operate in different industries may have very different financial ratio values. These differences may grow even wider when we compare companies located in different countries.

Compare three leading companies on their current ratio, debt ratio, and times-interest-earned ratio. Compute three ratios for Sobeys (the Canadian grocery chain), Sony (the Japanese electronics manufacturer), and Daimler (the German auto company).

	(amounts in millions or billions)		
Income data	**Sobeys**	**Sony**	**Daimler**
Total revenues	$12,853	¥7,475	€151,589
Operating income	332	191	2,072
Interest expense	35	29	913
Net Income	197	124	3,227

	(amounts in millions or billions)		
Asset and liability data	Sobeys	Sony	Daimler
Total current assets	$1,235	¥3,770	€93,131
Long-term assets	2,504	6,838	96,891
Total current liabilities	1,230	3,200	59,977
Long-term liabilities	674	4,204	95,890
Shareholders' equity	1,835	3,204	34,155

Note: ¥ is the symbol for a Japanese yen; € for a euro.

Based on your computed ratio values, which company looks the least risky? (Challenge)

Learning Objective 5
Analyzing alternative plans for raising money

E8-31 Altman & Associates is considering two plans for raising $700,000 to expand operations. Plan A is to borrow at 5%, and plan B is to issue 100,000 common shares. Before any new financing, Altman has net income of $500,000 and 100,000 common shares outstanding. Assume you own most of Altman's existing shares. Management believes the company can use the new funds to earn additional income of $300,000 before interest and taxes. Altman's income tax rate is 30%.

Required

1. Analyze Altman's situation to determine which plan will result in higher earnings per share. Use Exhibit 8-11, page 416, as a model.
2. Which plan results in higher earnings per share? Which plan allows you to retain control of the company? Which plan creates more financial risk for the company? Which plan do you prefer? Why? Present your conclusion in a memo to Altman's board of directors.

Challenge Exercises

Learning Objective 1 7
Reporting current liabilities

E8-32 Assume the top management of Best Buy Inc. examines company accounting records at February 7, three weeks before the end of the fiscal year (amounts in billions):

Total current assets	$ 8.0
Noncurrent assets	3.9
	$ 11.9
Total current liabilities	6.0
Noncurrent liabilities	0.6
Shareholders' equity	5.3
	$11.9

Suppose Best Buy's top management wants to achieve a current ratio of 1.4. How much in current liabilities should Best Buy pay off within the next three weeks to achieve its goal?

Learning Objective 2 3 4 7
Refinancing old bonds with new bonds

E8-33 United Products completed one of the most famous debt refinancings in history. A debt refinancing occurs when a company issues new bonds to derecognize old bonds. The company debits the old bonds payable and credits the new bonds.

United had $125 million of 5 1/2% bonds payable outstanding, with 20 years to maturity. United derecognized these old bonds by issuing $75 million of new 9% bonds to the holders of the old bonds and paying the bondholders $13 million in cash. United issued both groups of bonds at par so there was no bond premium or discount. At the time of the debt refinancing, United had total assets of $600 million and total liabilities of $450 million. Net income for the most recent year was $6.5 million on sales of $1 billion.

Required

1. Journalize the debt refinancing transaction.
2. Compute annual interest expense for both the old and the new bond issues.

3. Why did United Products refinance the old 5 1/2% bonds with the new 9% bonds? Consider interest expense, net income, and the debt ratio.

E8-34 Mark IV Industries Inc. issued $100 million 13% debentures due March 15, 2016, with interest payable March 15 and September 15; the price was 96.5.

Learning Objective ❷❸❹
Analyzing bond transactions

Required
Answer these questions.

1. Journalize Mark IV Industries Inc.'s issuance of these bonds on March 15, 2011. No explanation is required, but describe the transaction in detail, indicating who received cash, who paid cash, and how much.
2. Why is the stated interest rate on these bonds so high?
3. Compute the semi-annual cash interest payment on the bonds.
4. Compute the semi-annual interest expense under the straight-line amortization method.
5. Compute both the first-year (from March 15, 2011, to March 15, 2012) and the second-year interest expense (March 15, 2012, to March 15, 2013) under the effective-interest amortization method. The market rate of interest at the date of issuance was 14%. Why is interest expense greater in the second year?

Quiz

Test your understanding of accounting for liabilities by answering the following questions. Select the best choice from among the possible answers given.

Q8-35 For the purpose of classifying liabilities as current or noncurrent, the term *operating cycle* refers to which of the following?
a. A period of one year
b. The time period between date of sale and the date the related revenue is collected
c. The time period between purchase of merchandise and the conversion of this merchandise back to cash
d. The average time period between business recessions

Q8-36 Failure to accrue interest expense results in which of the following?
a. An overstatement of net income and an overstatement of liabilities
b. An understatement of net income and an overstatement of liabilities
c. An understatement of net income and an understatement of liabilities
d. An overstatement of net income and an understatement of liabilities

Q8-37 Sportscar Warehouse operates in a province with a 6% sales tax. For convenience, Sportscar Warehouse credits Sales Revenue for the total amount (selling price plus sales tax) collected from each customer. If Sportscar Warehouse fails to make an adjustment for sales taxes, which of the following will be true?
a. Net income will be overstated, and liabilities will be overstated.
b. Net income will be overstated, and liabilities will be understated.
c. Net income will be understated, and liabilities will be overstated.
d. Net income will be understated, and liabilities will be understated.

Q8-38 What kind of account is *Unearned Revenue*?
a. Asset account
b. Liability account
c. Revenue account
d. Expense account

Q8-39 An end-of-period adjusting entry that debits Unearned Revenue will most likely credit which of the following?
a. A revenue
b. An asset
c. An expense
d. A liability

Q8-40 Adrian Inc. manufactures and sells computer monitors with a three-year warranty. Warranty costs are expected to average 8% of sales during the warranty period. The following table shows the sales and actual warranty payments during the first two years of operations:

Year	Sales	Warranty Payments
2010	$500,000	$ 4,000
2011	700,000	32,000

Based on these facts, what amount of warranty liability should Adrian Inc. report on its balance sheet at December 31, 2011?

a. $32,000
b. $36,000
c. $60,000
d. $96,000

Q8-41 Today's Fashions has a debt that has been properly reported as a long-term liability up to the present year (2011). Some of this debt comes due in 2011. If Today's Fashions continues to report the current position as a long-term liability, the effect will be to do which of the following?

a. Overstate the current ratio
b. Overstate net income
c. Understate total liabilities
d. Understate the debt ratio

Q8-42 A bond with a face amount of $10,000 has a current price quote of 102.875. What is the bond's price?

a. $1,028,750
b. $10,200.88
c. $10,028.75
d. $10,287.50

Q8-43 Bond carrying value equals Bonds Payable

a. Minus Premium on Bonds Payable
b. Plus Discount on Bonds Payable
c. Plus Premium on Bonds Payable
d. Minus Discount on Bonds Payable
e. Both a and b
f. Both c and d

Q8-44 What type of account is *Discount on Bonds Payable*, and what is its normal balance?

Type of account	Normal balance
a. Contra liability	Debit
b. Reversing account	Debit
c. Adjusting amount	Credit
d. Contra liability	Credit

Questions 8-45 through 8-48 use the following data:

Q8-45 Sweetwater Company sells $100,000 of 10%, 15-year bonds for 97 on April 1, 2011. The market rate of interest on that day is 10 1/2%. Interest is paid each year on April 1. The entry to record the sale of the bonds on April 1 would be which of the following?

	Account	Debit	Credit
a.	Cash	97,000	
	Bonds Payable		97,000
b.	Cash	100,000	
	Bonds Payable		100,000
c.	Cash	97,000	
	Discount on Bonds Payable	3,000	
	Bonds Payable		100,000
d.	Cash	100,000	
	Discount on Bonds Payable		3,000
	Bonds Payable		97,000

Q8-46 Sweetwater Company uses the straight-line amortization method. The sale price of the bonds was $97,000. The amount of interest expense on April 1 of each year will be which of the following?

a. $4,080
b. $4,000
c. $4,200
d. $10,200
e. None of these. The interest expense is _____.

Q8-47 Write the adjusting entry required at December 31, 2011.

Q8-48 Write the journal entry required at April 1, 2012.

Q8-49 McPherson Corporation issued $100,000 of 10%, five-year bonds on January 1, 2011, for $92,280. The market interest rate when the bonds were issued was 12%. Interest is paid semi-annually on January 1 and July 1. The first interest payment is July 1, 2011. Using the effective-interest amortization method, how much interest expense will McPherson record on July 1, 2011?

a. $6,000
b. $5,228
c. $6,772
d. $5,000
e. Some other amount ($_____)

Q8-50 Using the facts in the preceding question, McPherson's journal entry to record the interest expense on July 1, 2011, will include a

a. Debit to Bonds Payable
b. Credit to Interest Expense
c. Debit to Premium on Bonds Payable
d. Credit to Discount on Bonds Payable

Q8-51 Amortizing the discount on bonds payable does which of the following?

a. Increases the recorded amount of interest expense
b. Is necessary only if the bonds were issued at more than face value
c. Reduces the semi-annual cash payment for interest
d. Reduces the carrying value of the bond liability

Q8-52 The journal entry on the maturity date to record the payment of $1,000,000 of bonds payable that were issued at a $70,000 discount includes

a. A debit to Discount on Bonds Payable for $70,000
b. A credit to Cash for $1,070,000
c. A debit to Bonds Payable for $1,000,000
d. All of the above

Q8-53 The payment of the face amount of a bond on its maturity date is regarded as which of the following?

a. An operating activity
b. An investing activity
c. A financing activity

Problems

(Group A)

P8-54A Sea Spray Marina experienced these events during 2011.

Learning Objective 1
Measuring current liabilities

a. December revenue totalled $110,000 and, in addition, Sea Spray collected sales tax of 7%. The sales tax amount will be remitted to the province of Quebec early in January.
b. On October 31, Sea Spray signed a six-month, 7% note to purchase a boat costing $90,000. The note requires payment of principal and interest at maturity.
c. On August 31, Sea Spray received cash of $1,800 in advance for service revenue. This revenue will be earned evenly over six months.
d. Revenues of $900,000 were covered by Sea Spray's service warranty. At January 1, estimated warranty payable was $11,300. During the year, Sea Spray recorded warranty expense of $31,000 and paid warranty claims of $34,700.

e. Sea Spray owes $100,000 on a long-term note payable. At December 31, 6% interest for the year plus $20,000 of this principal are payable within one year.

Required
For each item, indicate the account and the related amount to be reported as a *current* liability on the Sea Spray Marina balance sheet at December 31, 2011.

Learning Objective 1
Recording liability-related transactions

P8-55A The following transactions of Smooth Sounds Music Company occurred during 2011 and 2012:

2011	
Mar. 3	Purchased a Steinway piano (inventory) for $40,000, signing a six-month, 5% note.
Apr. 30	Borrowed $50,000 on a 9% note payable that calls for annual installment payments of $25,000 principal plus interest. Record the short-term note payable in a separate account from the long-term note payable.
Sept. 3	Paid the six-month, 5% note at maturity.
Dec. 31	Accrued warranty expense, which is estimated at 2% of sales of $190,000.
31	Accrued interest on the outstanding note payable.
2012	
Apr. 30	Paid the first installment plus interest for one year on the outstanding note payable

Required
Record the transactions in Smooth Sounds' journal. Explanations are not required.

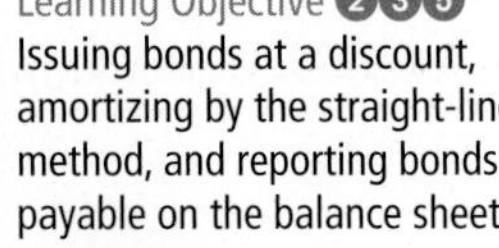
Learning Objective 2 3 5
Issuing bonds at a discount, amortizing by the straight-line method, and reporting bonds payable on the balance sheet

P8-56A On February 28, 2011, ETrade Inc. issues 8 $^{1}/_{2}$%, 20-year bonds with a face value of $200,000. The bonds pay interest on February 28 and August 31. ETrade amortizes bonds by the straight-line method.

Required
1. If the market interest rate is 7 $^{5}/_{8}$% when ETrade issues its bonds, will the bonds be priced at face value, a premium, or a discount? Explain.
2. If the market interest rate is 9% when ETrade issues its bonds, will the bonds be priced at face value, a premium, or a discount? Explain.
3. Assume that the issue price of the bonds is 97. Journalize the following bond transactions.
   a. Issuance of the bonds on February 28, 2011
   b. Payment of interest and amortization of the bonds on August 31, 2011
   c. Accrual of interest and amortization of the bonds on December 31, 2011
   d. Payment of interest and amortization of the bonds on February 28, 2012
4. Report interest payable and bonds payable as they would appear on the ETrade balance sheet at December 31, 2011.

P8-57A

Learning Objective ②③
Accounting for bonds payable at a discount and amortizing by the straight-line method

1. Journalize the following transactions of Trekker Boot Company:

2011	
Jan. 1	Issued $600,000 of 8%, 10-year bonds at 97
July 1	Paid semi-annual interest and amortized bonds by the straight-line method on the 8% bonds payable
Dec. 31	Accrued semi-annual interest expense and amortized bonds by the straight-line method on the 8% bonds payable
2012	
Jan. 1	Paid semi-annual interest
2021	
Jan 1	Paid the 8% bonds at maturity

2. At December 31, 2011, after all year-end adjustments, determine the carrying amount of Trekker's bonds payable, net.
3. For the six months ended July 1, 2011, determine for Trekker:
   a. Interest expense
   b. Cash interest paid

   What causes interest expense on the bonds to exceed cash interest paid?

P8-58A Notes to the Maritime Industries Ltd. financial statements reported the following data on December 31, 2011 (the end of the fiscal year):

Learning Objective ②③④⑦
Analyzing a company's long-term debt and reporting long-term debt on the balance sheet (effective-interest method)

Note 6, Indebtedness		
Bonds payable, 5%, due in 2016	$600,000	
Less Discount	(25,274)	$574,726
Notes payable, 8.3%, payable in $50,000 annual installments starting in Year 2015		250,000

Maritime Industries amortizes bonds by the effective-interest method.

Required

1. Answer the following questions about Maritime's long-term liabilities:
   a. What is the maturity value of the 5% bonds?
   b. What are Maritime's annual cash interest payments on the 5% bonds?
   c. What is the carrying amount of the 5% bonds at December 31, 2011?
2. Prepare an amortization table through December 31, 2014, for the 5% bonds. The market interest rate for these bonds was 6%. Maritime pays interest annually on December 31. How much is Maritime's interest expense on the 5% bonds for the year ended December 31, 2014?
3. Show how Maritime Industries would report the bonds payable and notes payable at December 31, 2014.

P8-59A On December 31, 2011, Digital Connections issued 8%, 10-year bonds payable with a maturity value of $500,000. The semi-annual interest dates are June 30 and December 31. The market interest rate is 9%, and the issue price of the bonds is 94. Digital Connections amortizes bonds by the effective-interest method.

Learning Objective ②③④⑦
Issuing bonds at a discount, amortizing by the effective-interest method, derecognizing bonds early, and reporting the bonds payable on the balance sheet

Required

1. Prepare an effective-interest-method amortization table for the first four semi-annual interest periods.

2. Journalize the following transactions:
   a. Issuance of the bonds on December 31, 2011. Credit Bonds Payable.
   b. Payment of interest and amortization of the bonds on June 30, 2012
   c. Payment of interest and amortization of the bonds on December 31, 2012
   d. Derecognition by the bondholders on July 1, 2013, of bonds with face value of $200,000 when the market price is 96.5
3. Show how Digital Connections would report the remaining bonds payable on its balance sheet at December 31, 2013.

Learning Objective 5
Financing operations with debt or with shares

P8-60A Outback Sporting Goods is embarking on a massive expansion. Assume plans call for opening 20 new stores during the next two years. Each store is scheduled to be 50% larger than the company's existing locations, offering more items of inventory, and with more elaborate displays. Management estimates that company operations will provide $1 million of the cash needed for expansion. Outback must raise the remaining $6 million from outsiders. The board of directors is considering obtaining the $6 million either through borrowing or by issuing common shares.

Required

Write a memo to Outback's management discussing the advantages and disadvantages of borrowing and of issuing common shares to raise the needed cash. Which method of raising the funds would you recommend?

Learning Objective 6
Account for a finance lease

P8-61A Surrey Heavy Equipment Rentals Inc. (SHERI), whose year-end is December 31, leased a Caterpillar 725 Articulated Truck from Finning International Inc. on January 2, 2011. The lease term is 10 years and the lease payments are $53,000 a year payable beginning January 2, 2012. SHERI's incremental borrowing rate is 8%. The price from Finning (fair value) for the truck (taxes are ignored) is $410,640.

Required

1. Give the journal entry to record the acquisition of the Caterpillar 725 Articulated Truck by Surrey Heavy Equipment Rentals Inc. on January 2, 2011.
2. Explain how the lease would be classified on the financial statements.
3. Assume SHERI depreciates its equipment for accounting purposes on a straight-line basis over the term of the lease and assumes a zero residual value. Give the journal entry to record the depreciation expense for the year ended December 31, 2011.
4. Give the journal entry to record lease interest expense for the year ended December 31, 2011.
5. Give the journal entry to record the lease payment on January 2, 2012.

Learning Objective 7
Reporting liabilities on the balance sheet; times-interest-earned ratio

P8-62A The accounting records of Pacer Foods Inc. include the following items at December 31, 2011.

Mortgage note payable, current	$ 50,000	Accumulated depreciation, equipment	$219,000
Bonds payable, long-term	490,000	Discount on bonds payable (all long-term)	7,000
Mortgage note payable, long-term	150,000	Operating income	291,000
Bonds payable current portion	70,000	Equipment	487,000
Interest expense	67,000	Interest payable	9,000

Required

1. Show how each relevant item would be reported on the Pacer Foods Inc. classified balance sheet, including headings and totals for current liabilities and long-term liabilities.

2. Answer the following questions about Pacer's financial position at December 31, 2011.
   a. What is the carrying amount of the bonds payable (combine the current and long-term amounts)?
   b. Why is the interest-payable amount so much less than the amount of interest expense?
3. How many times did Pacer cover its interest expense during 2011?

(Group B)

Learning Objective 1
Measuring current liabilities

P8-63B Goldwater Corporation experienced these five events during 2011:

a. December sales totalled $50,000, and Goldwater collected harmonized sales tax (HST) of 13%. The HST will be remitted to CRA in January 2012. Reporting requirements are the segregation of the provincial portion (8%) and federal portion (5%).
b. On November 30, Goldwater received rent of $6,000 in advance for a lease on unused store space. This rent will be earned evenly over three months.
c. On September 30, Goldwater signed a six-month, 9% note to purchase store fixtures costing $12,000. The note requires payment of principal and interest at maturity.
d. Sales of $400,000 were covered by Goldwater's product warranty. At January 1, estimated warranty payable was $12,400. During the year, Goldwater recorded warranty expense of $22,300 and paid warranty claims of $24,600.
e. Goldwater owes $100,000 on a long-term note. At December 31, 5% interest since July 31 and $20,000 of this principal are payable within one year.

Required

For each item, indicate the account and the related amount to be reported as a *current* liability on the Goldwater Corporation balance sheet at December 31, 2011.

Learning Objective 1
Recording liability-related transactions

P8-64B Assume that the following transactions of Sleuth Book Store occurred during 2011 and 2012.

Required

Record the transactions in the company's journal. Explanations are not required.

2011		
Jan.	9	Purchased store fixtures at a cost of $50,000, signing an 8% six-month note for that amount
June	30	Borrowed $200,000 on a 9% note that calls for annual installment payments of $50,000 principal plus interest. Record the short-term note payable in a separate account from the long-term note payable.
July	9	Paid the six-month, 8% note at maturity
Dec.	31	Accrued warranty expense, which is estimated at 3% of sales of $600,000
	31	Accrued interest on the outstanding note payable
2012		
June	30	Paid the first installment and interest for one year on the outstanding note payable

Learning Objective 2 3
Recording bond transactions (at face value) and reporting bonds payable on the balance sheet

P8-65B Assume the board of directors of The Saddledome Foundation authorizes the issue of $1 million of 8%, 20-year bonds. The semi-annual interest dates are March 31 and September 30. The bonds are issued on March 31, 2011, at face value.

Required

1. Journalize the following transactions:
   a. Issuance of the bonds on March 31, 2011
   b. Payment of interest on September 30, 2011

c. Accrual of interest on December 31, 2011
d. Payment of interest on March 31, 2012

2. Report interest payable and bonds payable as they would appear on the Saddledome Foundation balance sheet at December 31, 2011.

Learning Objective ❷❸❼
Issuing notes at a discount, amortizing by the straight-line method, and reporting notes payable on the balance sheet

P8-66B On February 28, 2011, Panorama Ltd. issues 7%, 10-year notes with a face value of $300,000. The notes pay interest on February 28 and August 31, and Panorama amortizes notes by the straight-line method.

Required

1. If the market interest rate is 6% when Panorama issues its notes, will the notes be priced at face value, a premium, or a discount? Explain.
2. If the market interest rate is 8% when Panorama issues its notes, will the notes be priced at face value, a premium, or a discount? Explain.
3. Assume that the issue price of the notes is 96. Journalize the following note payable transactions:
   a. Issuance of the notes on February 28, 2011
   b. Payment of interest and amortization of the bonds on August 31, 2011
   c. Accrual of interest and amortization of the bonds on December 31, 2011
   d. Payment of interest and amortization of the bonds on February 28, 2012
4. Report interest payable and notes payable as they would appear on Panorama's balance sheet at December 31, 2011.

Learning Objective ❷❸
Accounting for bonds payable at a discount and amortizing by the straight-line method

P8-67B

1. Journalize the following transactions of Farm Equipment Limited:

2011	
Jan. 1	Issued $100,000 of 8%, five-year bonds at 94
July 1	Paid semi-annual interest and amortized the bonds by the straight-line method on our 8% bonds payable
Dec. 31	Accrued semi-annual interest expense and amortized the bonds by the straight-line method on our 8% bonds payable
2012	
Jan. 1	Paid semi-annual interest
2016	
Jan. 1	Paid the 8% bonds at maturity

2. At December 31, 2011, after all year-end adjustments, determine the carrying amount of Farm Equipment Limited's bonds payable, net.
3. For the six months ended July 1, 2011, determine the following for Farm Equipment Limited:
   a. Interest expense
   b. Cash interest paid

   What causes interest expense on the bonds to exceed cash interest paid?

Learning Objective ❷❸❹❼
Analyzing a company's long-term debt and reporting the long-term debt on the balance sheet (effective-interest method)

P8-68B The notes to the Community Charities financial statements reported the following data on December 31, 2011 (end of the fiscal year):

Note D—Long-Term Debt		
7% bonds payable, due in 2017	$ 500,000	
Less: Discount	(26,032)	$473,968
$6^1/_2$% notes payable; principal due in annual amounts of $50,000 in 2015 through 2020		300,000

Community Charities amortizes bonds by the effective-interest method and pays all interest amounts at December 31.

Required

1. Answer the following questions about Community Charities' long-term liabilities:
   a. What is the maturity value of the 7% bonds?
   b. What is Community Charities' annual cash interest payment on the 7% bonds?
   c. What is the carrying amount of the 7% bonds at December 31, 2011?
2. Prepare an amortization table through December 31, 2014, for the 7% bonds. The market interest rate on the bonds was 8%. Round all amounts to the nearest dollar. How much is Community Charities' interest expense on the 7% bonds for the year ended December 31, 2014?
3. Show how Community Charities would report the 7% bonds payable and the 6 1/2% notes payable at December 31, 2014.

Learning Objective ❺
Financing operations with debt or shares

P8-69B Two businesses in very different circumstances are pondering how to raise $2 million.

HighTech.com has fallen on hard times. Net income has been low for the last three years, even falling by 10% from last year's level of profits, and cash flow also took a nose dive. Top management has experienced some turnover and has stabilized only recently. To become competitive again, High Tech needs $2 million to invest in new technology.

Decorator Services is in the midst of its most successful period since it began operations in 2009. Net income has increased by 25%. The outlook for the future is bright with new markets opening up and competitors unable to compete with Decorator. As a result, Decorator is planning a large-scale expansion.

Required

Propose a plan for each company to raise the needed cash. Which company should borrow? Which company should issue shares? Consider the advantages and disadvantages of raising money by borrowing and by issuing shares, and discuss them in your answer.

Learning Objective ❻
Account for a finance lease

P8-70B Argus Construction Ltd. of St. John's, Newfoundland, leased a Caterpillar 325DL Track Excavator from Toromont Industries Ltd. at January 2, 2011. The lease term is 10 years and the lease payments are $38,000 a year payable beginning January 2, 2012. Argus' incremental borrowing rate is 7%. The price from Toromont (fair value) for the truck (taxes are ignored) is $285,360.

Required

1. Give the journal entry to record the acquisition of the Caterpillar 325DL Track Excavator by Argus Construction Ltd. at January 2, 2011.
2. Explain how the lease would be classified on the financial statements.
3. Assume Argus Construction Ltd. depreciates its equipment for accounting purposes on a straight-line basis over the term of the lease and assumes a zero residual value. Give the journal entry to record the depreciation expense for the year ended December 31, 2011.

4. Give the journal entry to record lease interest expense for the year ended December 31, 2011.
5. Give the journal entry to record the lease payment on January 2, 2012.

Learning Objective 7
Reporting liabilities on the balance sheet, times-interest-earned ratio

P8-71B The accounting records of Toronto Financial Services include the following items at December 31, 2011.

Premium on bonds payable (all long-term)	$ 13,000
Interest payable	3,900
Operating income	104,000
Interest expense	39,000
Bonds payable, current portion	50,000
Accumulated depreciation, building	70,000
Mortgage note payable, long-term	215,000
Bonds payable long-term	250,000
Building	160,000

Required

1. Show how each relevant item would be reported on Toronto Financial Services' classified balance sheet. Include headings and totals for current liabilities and long-term liabilities.
2. Answer the following questions about the financial position of Toronto Financial Services at December 31, 2011.
   a. What is the carrying amount of the bonds payable (combine the current and long-term amounts)?
   b. Why is the interest payable amount so much less than the amount of interest expense? (Challenge)
3. How many times did Toronto cover its interest expense during 2011?

Apply Your Knowledge

Decision Cases

Learning Objective 2 3
Exploring an actual bankruptcy

Case 1. In 2002, Enron Corporation filed for Chapter 11 bankruptcy protection, shocking the business community: How could a company this large and this successful go bankrupt? This case explores the causes and the effects of Enron's bankruptcy.

At December 31, 2000, and for the four years ended on that date, Enron reported the following (amounts in millions):

Balance Sheet (summarized)				
Total assets				$65,503
Total liabilities				54,033
Total shareholders' equity				11,470
Income Statements (excerpts)				
	2000	1999	1998	1997
Net income	$979*	$893	$703	$105

*Operating Income = $1,953
Interest expense = $838

Unknown to investors and lenders, Enron also controlled hundreds of partnerships that owed vast amounts of money. These special-purpose entities (SPEs) did not appear on the Enron financial statements. Assume that the SPEs' assets totalled $7,000 million and their liabilities stood at $6,900 million; assume a 10% interest rate on these liabilities.

During the four-year period up to 2000, Enron's share price shot up from $17.50 to $90.56. Enron used its escalating share price to finance the purchase of the SPEs by guaranteeing lenders that Enron would give them Enron shares if the SPEs could not pay their loans.

In 2001, the SEC launched an investigation into Enron's accounting practices. It was alleged that Enron should have been including the SPEs in its financial statements all along. Enron then restated net income for years up to 2000, wiping out nearly $600 million of total net income (and total assets) for this four-year period. Enron's share price tumbled, and the guarantees to the SPEs' lenders added millions to Enron's liabilities (assume the full amount of the SPEs' debt). To make matters worse, the assets of the SPEs lost much of their value; assume that their market value is only $500 million.

Required

1. Compute the debt ratio that Enron reported at the end of 2000. Recompute this ratio after including the SPEs in Enron's financial statements. Also compute Enron's times-interest-earned ratio both ways for 2000. Assume that the changes to Enron's financial position occurred during 2000.
2. Why does it appear that Enron failed to include the SPEs in its financial statements? How do you view Enron after including the SPEs in the company's financial statements? (Challenge)

Learning Objective 5
Analyzing alternative ways of raising $5 million

Case 2. Business is going well for Park 'N Fly, the company that operates remote parking lots near major airports. The board of directors of this family-owned company believes that Park 'N Fly could earn an additional $2 million income before interest and taxes by expanding into new markets. However, the $5 million that the business needs for growth cannot be raised within the family. The directors, who strongly wish to retain family control of the company, must consider issuing securities to outsiders. The directors are considering three financing plans.

Plan A is to borrow at 6%. Plan B is to issue 100,000 common shares. Plan C is to issue 100,000 nonvoting, $3.75 preferred shares ($3.75 is the annual dividend paid on each preferred share).* Park 'N Fly currently has net income of $3.5 million and 1 million common shares outstanding. The company's income tax rate is 25%.

Required

1. Prepare an analysis to determine which plan will result in the highest earnings per common share.
2. Recommend one plan to the board of directors. Give your reasons.

Ethical Issues

Issue 1. Microsoft Corporation is the defendant in numerous lawsuits claiming unfair trade practices. Microsoft has strong incentives not to disclose these contingent liabilities; however, GAAP requires that companies report their contingent liabilities.

Required

1. Why would a company prefer not to disclose its contingent liabilities?
2. Describe how a bank could be harmed if a company seeking a loan did not disclose its contingent liabilities.
3. What is the ethical tightrope that companies must walk when they report their contingent liabilities?

*For a discussion of preferred shares, see Chapter 9.

Issue 2. The top managers of Medtech.com borrowed heavily to develop a prescription-medicine distribution system. Medtech's outlook was bright, and investors poured millions into the company. Sadly, Medtech never lived up to its potential, and the company is in bankruptcy. It can't pay about half of its liabilities.

Required

Is it unethical for managers to saddle a company with a high level of debt? Or is it just risky? Who could be hurt by a company's taking on too much debt? Discuss.

Focus on Financials

Learning Objective ❶❹❼
Analyzing current and contingent liabilities

Gildan Activewear Inc.

Refer to Gildan Activewear Inc.'s financial statements in Appendix A at the end of this book.

1. Gildan's balance sheet reports a current portion of long-term debt under current liabilities. Why is this portion of long-term debt reported as a current liability?
2. Gildan's Notes to the Financial Statements include the note, "Commitments and Contingencies." What information does this provide to the user of these financial statements?
3. Did Gildan borrow more or pay off more short-term and long-term debt in 2009? How can you tell?
4. How would you rate Gildan's overall debt position: risky, safe, or average? Compute the ratio at October 4, 2009, that answers the question.

Focus on Analysis

Learning Objective ❶❻❼
Analyzing current liabilities and long-term debt

Gildan Activewear Inc.

The Gildan Activewear Inc. financial statements report long-term debt owed by the company.

1. The statement of cash flows reports that Gildan completed a number of transactions in its financing activity during the year ended October 4, 2009. Journalize these transaction.
2. Use the data in Gildan's 2009 income statement and balance sheet to estimate Gildan's average interest rate during 2009 on all company borrowings. Use the average balance of long-term debt for the year ended October 4, 2009.

Group Projects

Project 1. Consider three different businesses:

1. A bank
2. A magazine publisher
3. A department store

For each business, list all its liabilities—both current and long-term. Then compare the three lists to identify the liabilities that the three businesses have in common. Also identify the liabilities that are unique to each type of business.

Project 2. Alcenon Corporation leases the majority of the assets that it uses in operations. Alcenon prefers operating leases (versus finance leases) in order to keep the lease liability off its balance sheet and maintain a low debt ratio.

Alcenon is negotiating a 10-year lease on an asset with an expected useful life of 15 years. The lease requires Alcenon to make 10 annual lease payments of $20,000 each, with the first payment due at the beginning of the lease term. The leased asset has a market value of

$135,180. The lease agreement specifies no transfer of title to the lessee and includes no bargain purchase option.

Write a report for Alcenon's management to explain what conditions must be present for Alcenon to be able to account for this lease as an operating lease.

Quick Check Answers

1. *a*
2. *e*
3. *c ($200,000 × 0.025 = $5,000)*
4. *c [400 × 0.05 × $40 = warranty expense of $800; repaired $40 × 6 = $240; year-end liability = $560 ($800 – $240)]*
5. *e*
6. *e*
7. *a*
8. *b*
9. *c*
10. *b*
11. *e*
12. *a ($196,140 × 0.10 × 6/12 = $9,807)*
13. *d [Int. exp. = $9,807 Int. payment = $9,500 ($200,000 × 0.095 × 6/12) $9,807 – $9,500 = $307]*
14. *b ($200,000 × 0.095 = $19,000)*
15. *c (See Amortization Schedule)*

Date	Interest Payment	Interest Expense	Discount Amortiz.	Bond Carry Amt.
1/1/11				$196,140
7/1/11	$9,500	$9,807	$307	196,447
1/1/12	9,500	9,822	322	196,769

16. *d {$196,140 + [($200,000 – $196,140) × 1/5] = $196,912}*

9 Shareholders' Equity

LEARNING OBJECTIVES

1. **Explain** the features of a corporation
2. **Account** for the issuance of shares
3. **Describe** how share repurchase transactions affect a company
4. **Account** for dividends
5. **Use** share values in decision making
6. **Compute** return on assets and return on equity
7. **Report** equity transactions on the statement of cash flows

SPOTLIGHT

Potash Corporation of Saskatchewan (PotashCorp) is one of the world's largest fertilizer enterprises. It has mines in Saskatchewan and New Brunswick and investments in Jordan, Israel, Chile, and China. As the demand for food grows in the world, the demand for fertilizer grows. PotashCorp is well positioned to meet that demand for fertilizer both in terms of its supply of raw materials and in terms of its strategic investments around the world.

Potash Corporation of Saskatchewan Inc.
Statement of Financial Position (Adapted)
As at December 31

	(in millions of US$)	
	2009	**2008**
Assets		
Current assets		
Cash and cash equivalents	$ 385.4	$ 276.8
Receivables	1,137.9	1,189.9
Inventory	623.5	714.9
Prepaid expenses and other current assets	124.9	85.6
	2,271.7	2,267.2
Property, plant, and equipment	6,413.3	4,812.2
Investments	3,760.3	2,750.7
Other assets	359.9	300.2
Intangible assets	20.0	21.5
Goodwill	97.0	97.0
	$12,922.2	$10,248.8
Liabilities		
Current liabilities		
Short-term debt and current portion of long-term debt	$ 728.8	$ 1,324.1
Payables and accrued charges	779.3	1,183.6
Current portion of derivative instrument liabilities	51.8	108.1
	1,559.9	2,615.8
Long-term debt	3,319.3	1,739.5
Derivative instrument liabilities	123.2	120.4
Future income tax liability	999.3	794.2
Accrued pension and other post-retirement benefits	280.8	253.4
Accrued environmental costs and assets retirement obligations	134.8	133.4
Other non-current liabilities and deferred credits	4.2	3.2
	6,421.5	5,659.9
Commitments, Contingencies, Guarantees		
Shareholders' Equity		
Share capital	1,430.3	1,402.5
Unlimited authorization of first preferred shares; none outstanding		
Unlimited authorization of common shares without par value; issued and oustanding 294,975,550 and 295,200,987 shares at December 31, 2009 and 2008 respectively		
Contributed surplus	149.5	126.2
Accumulated other comprehensive income	1,648.8	657.9
Retained earnings	3,272.1	2,402.3
	6,500.7	4,588.9
	$12,922.2	$10,248.8

Chapters 4 to 8 discussed accounting for assets and liabilities. By this time, you should be familiar with all the assets and liabilities listed on PotashCorp's balance sheet. Let's focus now on PotashCorp's shareholders' equity. In this chapter we discuss some of the decisions a company faces when:

- Paying dividends
- Issuing shares
- Buying back its shares

Let's begin with the organization of a corporation.

What Is the Best Way to Organize a Business?

Anyone starting a business must decide how to organize the company. Corporations differ from proprietorships and partnerships in several ways.

OBJECTIVE

1 **Explain** the features of a corporation

Separate Legal Entity. A corporation is a business entity formed under federal or provincial law. The federal or provincial government grants *articles of incorporation*, which consist of documents giving the governing body's permission to form a corporation. A corporation is a distinct entity, an artificial person that exists apart from its owners, the shareholders. The corporation has many of the rights that a person has. For example, a corporation may buy, own, and sell property. Assets and liabilities in the business belong to the corporation and not to its owners. The corporation may enter into contracts, sue, and be sued.

Nearly all well-known companies, such as Potash Corporation of Saskatchewan, Shoppers Drug Mart Corporation, TransCanada Corporation, Bombardier Inc., and Sobeys Inc., are corporations. Their full names include *Limited*, *Corporation*, or *Incorporated* (abbreviated *Ltd.*, *Corp.*, and *Inc.*) to indicate that they are corporations. However, some companies do not use those terms; Air Canada is an example.

Continuous Life and Transferability of Ownership. Corporations have *continuous lives* regardless of changes in their ownership. The shareholders of a corporation may transfer shares as they wish. They may sell or trade the shares to another person, give them away, bequeath them in a will, or dispose of them in any other way. The transfer of the shares from one person to another does not affect the continuity of the corporation. In contrast, proprietorships and partnerships terminate when ownership changes.

Limited Liability. Shareholders have **limited liability** for the corporation's debts. They have no personal obligation for corporate liabilities. The most that a shareholder can lose on an investment in a corporation's shares is the cost of the investment. Limited liability is one of the most attractive features of the corporate form of organization. It enables corporations to raise more capital from a wider group of investors than proprietorships and partnerships can. By contrast, proprietors and partners are personally liable for all the debts of their businesses (unless the business is organized as a limited liability partnership (LLP) or a limited liability company (LLC).

Separation of Ownership and Management. Shareholders own the corporation, but a *board of directors*—elected by the shareholders—appoints officers to manage the business. Thus, shareholders may invest \$1,000 or \$1 million in the corporation without having to manage it.

Management should act in the best interests of the shareholders, the owners of the company. The separation between owners and managers may create problems. Corporate officers may run the business for their own benefit and not for the shareholders'. For example, the chief financial officer (CFO) of Enron Corporation set up outside partnerships and paid himself millions of dollars to manage the partnerships—unknown to Enron shareholders. He subsequently went to prison.

Some managers believe that their goal is to maximize the firm's value. Other managers believe that they should consider some or all of the other stakeholders of the corporation such as employees, customers, the community where the company is located, and the environment. This topic, often referred to as corporate social responsibility or social accounting, will be discussed in more detail in Chapter 11.

Corporate Taxation. Corporations are separate taxable entities. They pay a variety of taxes not borne by proprietorships or partnerships, such as federal and provincial income taxes.

Corporate earnings are subject to **double taxation** of their income to the extent that the income is distributed to shareholders in the form of dividends.

- First, corporations pay income taxes on their corporate income.
- Then, shareholders pay personal income tax on the dividends that they receive from corporations. Canada's tax laws attempt to minimize double taxation so the tax rate on dividends is lower than the tax rate on regular income. Proprietorships and partnerships pay no business income tax. Instead, the tax falls solely on the owners, who are taxed on their share of the proprietorship or partnership income.

Government Regulation. Because shareholders have only limited liability for corporation debts, outsiders doing business with the corporation can look no further than the corporation if it fails to pay. To protect a corporation's creditors and the shareholders, both federal and provincial governments monitor corporations. This regulation consists mainly of ensuring that corporations disclose the information in financial statements that investors and creditors need to make informed decisions. Recall in Chapter 1 you learned that the federal and provincial governments through legislation require companies incorporated under their jurisdictions to prepare financial statements that adhere to IFRS (publicly accountable enterprises or PAEs) or Accounting Standards for Private Enterprises (private enterprises or PEs). Accounting is a source of much of this information in the financial statements..

Exhibit 9-1 summarizes the advantages and disadvantages of the corporate form of business organization.

EXHIBIT 9-1 Advantages and Disadvantages of a Corporation

Advantages	Disadvantages
1. Can raise more capital than a proprietorship or partnership can	1. Separation of ownership and management
2. Continuous life	2. Corporate taxation
3. Ease of transferring ownership	3. Government regulation
4. Limited liability of shareholders	

Organizing a Corporation

The creation of a corporation begins when its organizers, called the *incorporators*, submit articles of incorporation to the federal or provincial government for approval. The articles of incorporation include the authorization for the corporation to issue a certain number of shares of stock, which are shares of ownership in the corporation. The incorporators

- Pay fees
- Sign the articles of incorporation
- File the required documents with the incorporating jurisdiction
- Agree to a set of **bylaws**, which act as the constitution for governing the corporation

The corporation then comes into existence.

Ultimate control of the corporation rests with the shareholders. The shareholders elect a *board of directors*, which sets the company policy and appoints officers. The board elects a **chairperson**, who usually is the most powerful person in the organization. The board also designates the **president**, who is the chief executive officer (CEO) in charge of day-to-day operations. Most corporations also have a chief operating officer (COO), in which case the COO is responsible for administering day-to-day operations and reports to the CEO. The corporation also has vice-presidents in charge of sales, manufacturing, accounting and finance (the chief financial officer, or CFO), and other key areas. Exhibit 9-2 shows the authority structure in a corporation.

Shareholders' Rights

Ownership of shares entitles shareholders to five basic rights, unless specific rights are withheld by agreement with the shareholders:

1. *The right to sell the shares*. This right might be restricted in certain circumstances but such discussion is beyond the scope of this text.
2. *Vote*. The right to participate in management by voting on matters that come before the shareholders. This is the shareholder's sole voice in the management of the corporation. A shareholder is normally entitled to one vote for each common share owned. There are various classes of common shares that give the holder multiple votes or no vote.
3. *Dividends*. The right to receive a proportionate part of any distributed payment, or dividend. Each share in a particular class receives an equal dividend.

EXHIBIT 9-2 **Authority Structure in a Corporation**

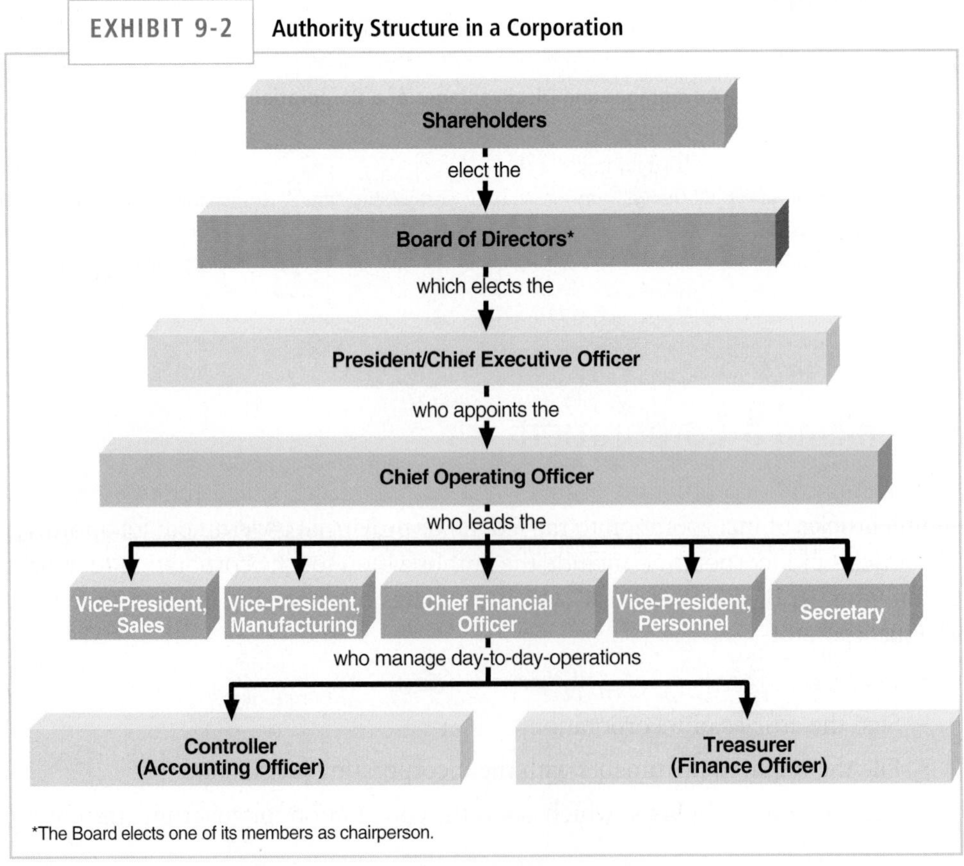

*The Board elects one of its members as chairperson.

4. *Liquidation*. The right to receive a proportionate share of any assets remaining after the corporation pays all liabilities in liquidation. Liquidation means to go out of business, sell the assets, pay its liabilities, and distribute any remaining cash to the owners.
5. *Preemption*. The right to maintain one's proportionate ownership in the corporation. Suppose you own 5% of a corporation's shares. If the corporation issues 100,000 new shares, it must offer you the opportunity to buy 5% (5,000) of the new shares. This right is called the *preemptive right*. This right might be specifically withheld.

Shareholders' Equity

As we saw in Chapter 1, *shareholders' equity* represents the shareholders' ownership interest in the assets of a corporation. Shareholders' equity is divided into three main parts:

1. *Contributed capital*, also called *capital stock* or *share capital*. This is the amount of shareholders' equity the shareholders have contributed to the corporation. The contributed surplus on PotashCorp's balance sheet is contributed capital.
2. *Retained earnings*. This is the amount of shareholders' equity the corporation has earned through profitable operations and has not used for dividends.
3. Under IAS 1 "Presentation of Financial Statements" companies have to calculate other comprehensive income (discussed in Chapter 11) and accumulate the changes each year in an account in Shareholders' Equity entitled Accumulated Other Comprehensive Income. PotashCorp's Statement of Financial Position at December 31, 2009, reports a balance of $1,648.8 million in the account Accumulated Other Comprehensive Income.

Private Enterprises
Accounting standards for private enterprises in Part II of the *CICA Handbook* do not require PEs to calculate comprehensive income, and so PEs do not have an account entitled Accumulated Other Comprehensive Income in their shareholders' equity.

Companies report shareholders' equity by source. They report contributed capital separately from accumulated other comprehensive income and retained earnings because most incorporating acts prohibit the declaration of cash dividends from contributed capital. Cash dividends are declared from retained earnings.

The owners' equity of a corporation is divided into shares of *stock*. A corporation issues *share certificates* to its owners in exchange for their investment in the business—usually cash. The basic unit of contributed capital is called a *share*. A corporation may issue a share certificate for any number of shares it wishes—one share, 100 shares, or any other number—but the total number of *authorized* shares is limited by charter. Exhibit 9-3 shows an actual common share certificate for Danier Leather Inc.

The terms *authorized*, *issued*, and *outstanding* are frequently used to describe a corporation's shares. *Authorized* refers to the maximum number of shares a corporation is allowed to distribute to shareholders. Companies incorporated under the *Canada Business Corporations Act* are permitted to issue an unlimited number of shares. *Issued* refers to the number of shares sold or transferred to shareholders. **Outstanding shares** are those actually in the hands of shareholders. Sometimes a company repurchases shares it has previously issued so that the number of shares outstanding will be less than the number of shares issued. For example, if a corporation issued 100,000 shares and later repurchased 20,000 shares, then the number of shares outstanding would be 80,000. The total number of shares outstanding at any time represents 100% ownership of the corporation.

EXHIBIT 9-3 Share Certificate

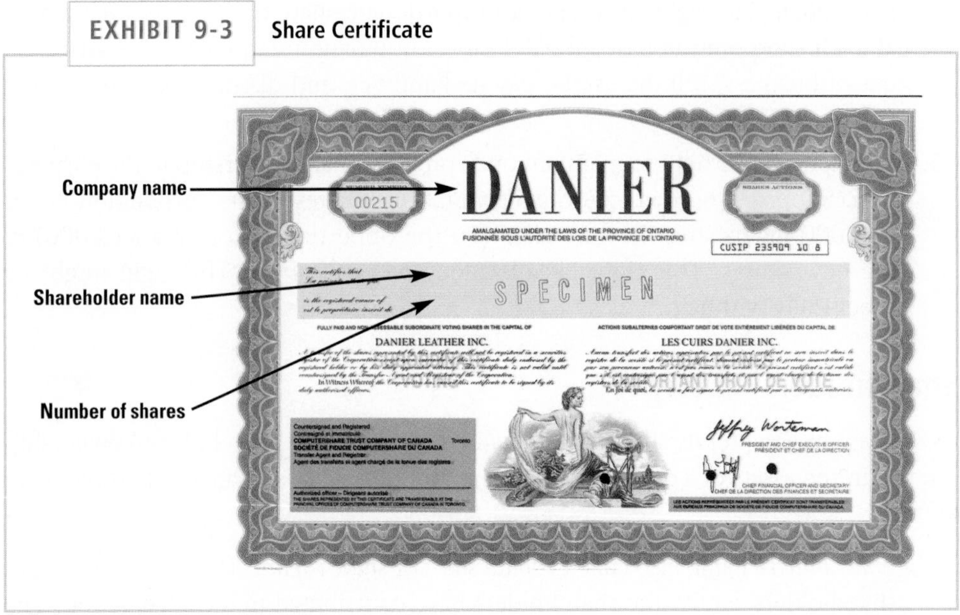

Classes of Shares

IAS 32 "Financial Instruments: Presentation" defines an equity instrument as "any contract that evidences a residual interest in the assets of an entity after deducting all of its liabilities." Accordingly, common shares and preferred shares, including convertible preferred shares, would be defined as equity instruments since they "own" any assets that are left over after all liabilities have been paid, as you learned in Chapter 1. The owners of those shares are residual claimants. Corporations issue different types of shares to appeal to a variety of investors. The shares of a corporation may be either

- Common
- Preferred

Every corporation issues *common shares*, the basic form of capital stock. IAS 33 defines a common share as "An ordinary share [that] is an equity instrument that is subordinate to all other classes of equity instruments." Unless designated otherwise, the word *share* is understood to mean "common share." Common shareholders have the five basic rights of share ownership, unless a right is specifically withheld. For example, some companies issue Class A common shares, which usually carry the right to vote, and Class B common shares, which may be nonvoting. In describing a corporation, we would say the common shareholders are the owners of the business. They stand to benefit the most if the corporation succeeds because they take the most risk by investing in common shares.

Preferred shares give their owners certain advantages over common shareholders. Preferred shareholders receive dividends before the common shareholders and receive assets before the common shareholders if the corporation liquidates. Owners of preferred shares also have the five basic shareholder rights, unless a right is specifically denied. Companies may issue different classes of preferred shares (Class A and Class B or Series A and Series B, for example). Each class is recorded in a separate account. The most preferred shareholders can expect to earn is their fixed dividend. Generally, preferred shares are nonvoting.

Preferred shares are a hybrid between common shares and long-term debt. Like debt, preferred shares pay a fixed dividend amount to the investor. Like common shares, the dividend is not required to be paid unless the board of directors has declared the dividend, although the preferred dividends may be cumulative. Also, companies have no obligation to pay back true preferred shares. Preferred shares that must be redeemed (paid back) by the corporation are a liability masquerading as a stock.

Preferred shares are not all that common. Surveys reveal that less than one-third of companies issue preferred shares. All corporations have common shares.

Exhibit 9-4 summarizes the similarities and differences among common shares, preferred shares, and long-term debt.

No-Stated-Value Shares. **No-stated-value shares** are shares of stock that do not have a value assigned to them by the articles of incorporation. The board of directors assigns a value to the shares when they are issued; this value is known as the **stated value**. For example, Dajol Inc. has authorization to issue 100,000 common shares, having no stated value assigned to them by the articles of incorporation. Dajol Inc. needs $50,000 at incorporation, and might issue 10,000 shares for $5.00 per share, 2,000 shares at $25.00 per share, or 1,000 shares at $50.00 per share, and so on. The point is that Dajol Inc. can assign whatever value to the shares the board of directors wishes. Normally, the stated value would be credited to Common Shares when the shares are issued.

The recorded value of a corporation's contributed capital or stated capital is the sum of the shares issued times the stated values of those shares at the time of issue. For example, if YDR Ltd. issued 1,000 common shares at a stated value of $8.00 per share, 2,000 shares at $12.00 per share, and 500 shares at $15.00 per share, its contributed capital or stated capital would be $39,500 [(1,000 × $8) + (2,000 × $12) + (500 × $15)].

The *Canada Business Corporations Act* and most provincial incorporating acts now require common and preferred shares to be issued without nominal or stated value. The full amount of the proceeds from the sale of shares by a company must be allocated to the capital account for those shares. For example, if Canadian Tire Corporation Ltd. were to issue 100 common shares for $2,500 (that is, the shares sold for $25.00 per share), $2,500 would be credited to Common Shares.

Issuing Shares

OBJECTIVE

❷ **Account** for the issuance of shares

Large corporations such as Hudson's Bay Company and EnCana Corp. need huge amounts of money to operate. Such corporations usually sell their newly issued shares though an *underwriter*, such as the brokerage firms ScotiaMcLeod and BMO Nesbitt Burns.

EXHIBIT 9-4 **Comparison of Common Shares, Preferred Shares, and Long-Term Debt**

	Common Shares	Preferred Shares	Long-Term Debt
1. Corporate obligation to repay principal	No	No	Yes
2. Dividends/interest	Dividends are not tax-deductible	Dividends are not tax-deductible	Interest expense is tax-deductable
3. Corporate obligation to pay dividends/interest	Only after declaration	Only after declaration	At fixed dates

Common Shares

Issuing Common Shares at a Stated Value. Suppose in the year ended December 31, 2011, George Weston Ltd. issues 100,000 common shares for cash, and the directors determine that the shares will be issued with a stated value (selling price) of $50 per share. The share issuance entry is

2011			
Jan. 8	Cash	5,000,000	
	Common Shares		5,000,000
	To issue common shares at $50.00 per share (100,000 × $50.00).		

We assume George Weston Ltd. received $5,000,000. The amount invested in the corporation, $5,000,000 in this case, is called *contributed capital*. The credit to Common Shares records an increase in the contributed capital of the corporation.

George Weston, in its annual report dated December 31, 2009, indicated there were 129,073,662 common shares outstanding with a stated value of $133 million. After this assumed transaction, George Weston would report $129,173,662 outstanding shares and the balance in its share capital account would be increased by $5 million.

All the transactions recorded in this section include a receipt of cash by the corporation as it issues *new* shares. These transactions are different from those reported in the financial press. In those transactions, one shareholder sells shares to another investor, and the corporation makes no journal entry. Note that issuances of shares are capital contributions and don't affect earnings.

STOP + THINK

You are thinking of investing in Shoppers Drug Mart Corporation, and have obtained a copy of its January 2, 2010, annual report. Your examination of the report reveals that Shoppers had share capital outstanding of $1,514 million at January 2, 2010, and $1,506 million at January 3, 2009.

1. Where would you look in the annual report to determine why the two numbers differ?
2. Assume that no shares were repurchased during the year. How would you determine the number of common shares issued during the year and the average price paid for those shares?

Answers:

1. The notes to the financial statements
2. The notes to the Shoppers Drug Mart financial statements disclose the number of shares issued and their stated value. If that information was not specifically provided you can calculate the change in common shares issued and outstanding and the stated value of the shares at each year-end.

Common Shares Issued for Assets Other Than Cash. IFRS 2 "Share-Based Payment" discusses the reporting of a transaction, described as a *share-based payment transaction*, where a company issues shares in exchange for goods or services. The company is required to measure the goods or services received and the resultant increase in shareholders' equity as the fair value of the goods or services received. If that fair value cannot be determined, the fair value of the shares given up will be the value assigned to the transaction.

IFRS's meaning is that the company debits the asset and credits common shares for the fair value of the asset acquired. If the fair value of the asset cannot be determined, the fair value of the shares given up becomes the value of the assets acquired. For example, if Kahn Corporation issued 15,000 common shares for equipment worth $4,000 and a building worth $120,000. Kahn Corporation's entry is

2011			
Nov. 12	Equipment	4,000	
	Building	120,000	
	Common Shares		124,000
	To issue common shares in exchange for equipment and a building.		

ASSETS	=	LIABILITIES	+	SHAREHOLDERS' EQUITY
+4,000 +120,000	=	0	+	+124,000

A Share Issuance for Other Than Cash Can Pose an Accounting Problem—Ethical Issue 1

IFRS say to record shares at the market price of whatever the corporation receives in exchange for the shares. When the corporation receives cash, the cash received provides clear evidence of the value of the shares because cash is worth its face amount.

Many entrepreneurs start up companies with an asset other than cash. They invest the asset and receive the new corporation's shares. A computer whiz may contribute some computer hardware and software. The software may be market-tested or it may be new. It may be worth millions or it may be worthless. An artist may contribute paintings or sculpture to start an art gallery. A real-estate agent may invest in a building to start a realty company.

The corporation must record the asset received and the shares given with a journal entry such as the following:

Software	XXX	
Common Shares		XXX
Issued shares in exchange for software.		

In effect, the new corporation is buying the software and paying for it by issuing common shares. Therefore, the business must assign a value to the software and to the common shares. The market price of the software determines the value assigned to the shares. What is the software really worth? Let's consider two possibilities:

Situation 1. The software has been on the market for several months and is selling well. The creator of the software has standing orders for 2,000 copies, and an industry expert values the software at $500,000. To start up the new corporation, the company makes this entry:

Software	500,000	
Common Shares		500,000
Issued shares in exchange for software.		

Situation 2. The software is new and untested. The entrepreneur believes it is worth millions but decides to be conservative and values it at $500,000. For its first transaction, the company makes this entry:

Software	500,000	
Common Shares		500,000
Issued shares in exchange for software.		

Suppose both entrepreneurs need $200,000 to market the software. They invite you to invest in their new business. Both companies' balance sheets will look like the balance sheet below:

Balance Sheet
December 31, 2011

Assets		**Liabilities**	
Computer software	$500,000		$ 0
		Shareholders' Equity	
		Common shares	500,000
Total assets	$500,000	Total liabilities and equity	$500,000

Both companies are debt-free and both appear to have a valuable asset. In which company will you invest? Here are two take-away lessons.

- Some accounting values are more solid than others.
- Not all financial statements mean exactly what they say, unless they are audited by independent public accountants who will require the preparers to follow IFRS.

Preferred Shares

Accounting for preferred shares follows the pattern we illustrated for common shares. The company records a Preferred Shares account at its stated value. When reporting shareholders' equity on the balance sheet, a corporation generally lists preferred shares, common shares, and retained earnings in that order. The example below is from Lambeth Plastics Ltd.

	(amounts in thousands)	
	2011	**2010**
Preferred shares, series I	$ 228	$ 228
Common shares	310	310
Share capital	538	538
Retained earnings	1,020	975
Total shareholders' equity	$1,558	$1,513

On April 18, 2012, Lambeth Plastics Ltd. announced the completion of the sale of 4,000 Series II Preferred Shares for proceeds of $200 thousand. The journal entry to record this issuance would be as follows:

2012			
Apr. 18	Cash	200,000	
	Preferred shares, Series II		200,000
	To record issuance of 4,000 Series II preferred shares.		

After this issuance, share capital in the shareholders' equity section would appear as follows (amounts in thousands):

Preferred shares, Series I	$228
Preferred shares, Series II	200
Common shares	310
Share capital	738

A Share Issuance for Other Than Cash Can Pose an Accounting Problem—Ethical Issue 2

As was pointed out earlier, issuance of shares for *cash* poses no serious ethical challenge. The company simply receives cash and records the shares at the amount received, as illustrated in the preceding sections of this chapter. There is no difficulty in valuing shares issued for cash because the value of the cash—and the shares—is obvious.

Issuing shares for assets other than cash can pose an ethical challenge. The company issuing the shares often wishes to record a large amount for the non-cash asset received (such as land or a building) and for the shares that it is issuing. Why? Because large asset and shareholders' equity amounts on the balance sheet make the business look more prosperous and more creditworthy.

A company is supposed to record an asset received at its current fair value. But one person's perception of a particular asset's fair value can differ from another person's opinion. One person may appraise land at a fair value of $400,000. Another may honestly believe the land is worth only $300,000. A company receiving land in exchange for its shares must decide whether to record the land received and the shares issued at $300,000, at $400,000, or at some amount in between.

The ethical course of action is to record the asset at its current fair value, as determined by a good-faith estimate of fair value from independent appraisers. It is rare for a corporation to be found guilty of *understating* the asset values on its balance sheet, but companies have been embarrassed by *overstating* these values. Investors who rely on the financial statements may be able to prove in court that an overstatement of asset values caused them to pay too much for the company's shares. Creditors who rely on financial statements may also be able to prove in court that an overstatement of asset values caused them to loan the corporation more than if the asset values were correctly stated. In both cases, the court may render a judgment against the company. For this reason, companies often value assets conservatively.

USING A COMPANY'S SHARE ISSUING CHOICES IN DECISION MAKING

Once the decision has been made to issue shares to raise funds by a company, the company must choose whether to issue common or preferred shares. The choice the company makes affects managers, investors, and creditors differently.

Manager—Management would likely prefer to issue common shares because preferred shares carry an explicit dividend. If preferred shares are issued and they are cumulative, management would be concerned about the impact on the cash flows of the company since the annual dividends would have to be paid sooner or later.

Investor—Investors of common shares would normally prefer that the company issued preferred shares as the issuance of common shares would dilute their share ownership unless they acquired additional shares to maintain their share percentage of ownership. In addition, earnings per share would likely decline because of the greater number of shares outstanding.

Creditor—Creditors would normally prefer that the company issued common shares especially if dividends on the preferred shares were cumulative.

ACCOUNTING FOR ISSUING SHARES

Once the accountant has decided to raise money by issuing shares, the accountant must make a decision as to whether to issue common shares or preferred shares.

- Common shares. The advantage of issuing common shares is that while there is an expectation of dividends on the part of investors, some companies do not pay dividends on common shares. Another advantage is that the amount the shareholders will receive per share is not fixed, as it generally is with preferred shares. The disadvantage of issuing common shares is that existing shareholders' ownership share will be diluted unless the existing owners buy additional shares to maintain their ownership share.
- Preferred shares. The advantage of issuing preferred shares is that the common shareholders' ownership share is not diluted. One disadvantage of issuing preferred shares is that preferred shares have a dividend rate attached and often the preferred dividends are cumulative.

MID-CHAPTER SUMMARY PROBLEM

MyAccountingLab

1. Test your understanding of the first half of this chapter by deciding whether each of the following statements is true or false.
   a. The policy-making body in a corporation is called the board of directors.
   b. The owner of 100 preferred shares has greater voting rights than the owner of 100 common shares.
   c. Issuance of 1,000 common shares at $12 per share increases contributed capital by $12,000.
   d. A corporation issues its preferred shares in exchange for land and a building with a combined fair value of $200,000. This transaction increases the corporation's owners' equity by $200,000 regardless of the assets' prior book values.
   e. Preferred shares are a riskier investment than common shares.
2. Adolfo Inc., an autoparts manufacturer, has two classes of common shares. Class A shares are entitled to one vote, whereas Class B shares are entitled to 100 votes. The two classes rank equally for dividends. The following is extracted from a recent annual report:

Shareholders' Equity

Capital stock	
Class A common shares, no stated value (authorized and issued 1,260 shares)...	$ 1,260
Class B common shares (authorized and issued 46,200)	11,000
	12,260
Retained earnings..	872,403
	$884,663

Required

a. Record the issuance of the Class A common shares. Use the Adolfo Inc. account titles.
b. Record the issuance of the Class B common shares. Use the Adolfo Inc. account titles.
c. How much of Adolfo Inc.'s shareholders' equity was contributed by the shareholders? How much was provided by profitable operations? Does this division of equity suggest that the company has been successful? Why or why not?
d. Write a sentence to describe what Adolfo Inc.'s shareholders' equity means.

Name: Adolfo Inc.
Industry: Auto parts manufacturing corporation
Fiscal Period: A recent fiscal year

Answers

1. a. True b. False c. True d. True e. False

b. Preferred shareholders typically do not have voting rights. e. Preferred shares are less risky because they usually have a fixed dividend rate.

2. a.

Cash........................	1,260	
Class A Common Shares..................		1,260
To record issuance of Class A common shares.		

b.

Cash........................	11,000	
Class B Common Shares..................		11,000
To record issuance of Class B common shares.		

a. and b. Share issuances increase assets (cash) and shareholders' equity.

c. Contributed by the shareholders: $12,260 ($1,260 + $11,000).
Provided by profitable operations: $872,403.
This division suggests that the company has been successful because almost all of its shareholders' equity has come from profitable operations.

Compare the fraction of shareholders' equity contributed by shareholders to the fraction contributed by retained earnings. A greater retained earnings fraction is positive.

d. Adolfo Inc.'s shareholders' equity of $884,663 means that the company's shareholders own $884,663 of the business's assets.

Shareholders' equity is the net worth of the company (Assets – Liabilities).

Repurchase of Shares by a Corporation

OBJECTIVE

❸ **Describe** how share repurchase transactions affect a company

Corporations may repurchase their own shares for several reasons:

1. The company needs the **repurchased shares** to fulfill future share issuance commitments, such as those related to share option plans and conversions of bonds and preferred shares into common shares.
2. The purchase may help support the share's current **market price** by decreasing the supply of shares available to the public; that is, repurchase is anti-dilutive.
3. Management wants to avoid a takeover by an outside party.

Private Enterprises

CICA Handbook Section 3240 states that the accounting for its own shares that a company reacquires may (under the two-transaction method) be cancelled, and a subsequent resale is treated as an original sale or (under the one-transaction method, which is the preferred method) share capital and the related accounts are not adjusted until the shares are resold. Under the one-transaction method, the cost of the shares is deducted from shareholders' equity.

IAS 32 "Financial Instruments: Presentation" discusses treasury shares which it defines as the shares a company has previously issued and then reacquired. The amount of the shares so acquired may be "disclosed separately either in the statement of financial position or in the notes...." IAS 32 states that a company cannot recognize a gain or loss on the purchase, sale, issue, or cancellation of its own shares.

If the shares are repurchased for cancellation and the price paid is more than the per-share paid-in capital, Capital Stock is debited for the per-share paid-in capital amount and Retained Earnings is debited for the excess. If the shares are repurchased for less than the per-share paid-in capital, Capital Stock is debited for the per-share paid-in capital amount and Contributed Surplus-Share Repurchase is credited for the difference. If the shares are repurchased pursuant to a share option plan, the amount paid for the shares by the company is debited to Treasury Shares, a contra account to Capital Stock.

The December 31, 2009, financial statements of Royal Dutch Shell plc, a U.K. company, provide an illustration of disclosure in the balance sheet (see Exhibit 9-5).

Should a Company Buy Back Its Own Shares?

Let's illustrate the accounting for repurchased shares by using the data of Ava Smallco Ltd. Before repurchasing any of its shares, the company reported the following shareholders' equity at December 31, 2010:

EXHIBIT 9-5 **Royal Dutch Shell plc Consolidated Balance Sheet as at December 31, 2009 (partial, adapted)**

Royal Dutch Shell plc
Consolidated Balance Sheet

	Amounts in U.S. dollars
Equity	
Ordinary share capital	527
Treasury shares	(1,711)
Other reserves	9,982
Retained earnings	127,633
Equity attributable to Royal Dutch Shell plc shareholders	136,431
Minority interest	1,704
Total equity	138,135

(Before Repurchase of Shares)	
Common shares (100,000 shares authorized; 10,000 shares issued)	$ 70,000
Retained earnings	193,632
Total equity	$263,632

During 2011, Ava Smallco Ltd. paid $12,000 to repurchase 1,000 of its common shares for cancellation. Ava Smallco Ltd. recorded the share repurchase as follows:

2011			
May 12	Common Shares	7,000	
	Retained Earnings	5,000	
	Cash		12,000
	Repurchased common shares for cancellation.		

When a company repurchases its shares for cancellation for more than the shares were issued for originally, it is deemed to be distributing profits (from Retained Earnings) to those shareholders who are selling their shares back to the company.

Ava Smallco Ltd.'s shareholders' equity would be shown as follows after the repurchase:

(After Repurchase of Shares)	
Common shares (100,000 shares authorized; 9,000 shares issued)	$ 63,000
Retained earnings	188,632
Total equity	$251,632

Compare Ava Smallco Ltd.'s total equity before the repurchase of shares ($263,632) and after ($251,632). You will see that Ava Smallco Ltd.'s total equity decreased by $12,000, the amount of cash the company paid to buy back its own shares. The repurchase of shares has the opposite effect of issuing shares:

- Issuing shares grows a company's assets and equity.
- Repurchasing shares *shrinks* assets and equity.

When the company repurchases its shares for less than the issue price, the difference is considered contributed surplus arising from the share repurchases, and Contributed Surplus—Share Repurchase is credited for the difference between the issue price and repurchase price.

Assume Ava Smallco Ltd. subsequently paid $10,000 to repurchase 1,000 of its common shares with the intention to re-issue the shares at some time in the future. Ava Smallco would record the share repurchase as follows:

2011			
Nov. 15	Treasury Shares	10,000	
	Cash		10,000
	Repurchased common shares that will be re-issued at a later date.		

Ava Smallco Ltd.'s shareholders' equity would be shown as follows after this second repurchase:

(After Second Repurchase of Shares)	
Common shares (100,000 shares authorized; 9,000 shares issued)	$ 63,000
Treasury shares	(10,000)
Retained earnings	188,632
Total equity	$241,632

Compare Ava Smallco Ltd.'s total equity after the first repurchase ($251,632) and after the second repurchase ($241,632). You will see that Ava Smallco Ltd.'s total equity decreased by $10,000, the amount of cash the company paid to buy back its own shares.

In most cases the company cancels the shares when they are repurchased. Shares that are reissued are accounted for in exactly the same way as shares that are issued for the first time.

STOP + THINK

You are examining the financial statements of SurCo Inc. and note that SurCo had net income of $5,000 for the year ended December 31, 2011, and paid dividends of the same amount during the year. The balance sheet provides the following additional information:

	December 31, 2011	December 31, 2010
Common shares (Issued and outstanding: 2011 1,800 shares; 2010 2,000 shares)	$18,000	$20,000
Retained earnings	36,800	40,800
Total shareholders' equity	$54,800	$60,800

Explain what caused the change in total shareholders' equity between December 31, 2010, and December 31, 2011.

Answer:

SurCo Inc. repurchased 200 common shares issued at $10.00 per share for $30.00 per share for cancellation.

Retained Earnings, Dividends, and Splits

The Retained Earnings account carries the balance of the business's net income less its net losses and less any declared dividends accumulated over the corporation's lifetime. *Retained* means "held onto." Successful companies grow by reinvesting back into the business the assets they generate through profitable operations. George Weston Limited is an example; about 88 percent of its equity comes from retained earnings.

The Retained Earnings account is not a reservoir of cash waiting for paying dividends to the shareholders. In fact, the corporation may have a large balance in Retained Earnings but not have the cash to pay a dividend. Cash and Retained Earnings are two entirely separate accounts with no particular relationship. A $500,000 balance in Retained Earnings says nothing about the company's Cash balance.

A *credit* balance in Retained Earnings is normal, indicating that the corporation's lifetime earnings exceed its lifetime losses and dividends. A *debit* balance in Retained Earnings arises when a corporation's lifetime losses and dividends exceed its lifetime earnings. Called a **deficit**, this amount is subtracted from the sum of the other equity accounts to determine total shareholders' equity. Retained earnings deficits are not uncommon.

Should the Company Declare and Pay Cash Dividends?

A *dividend* is a corporation's return to its shareholders of the benefits of earnings.

Dividends usually take one of three forms:

- Cash
- Shares
- Noncash assets

In this section we focus on cash dividends and stock dividends because noncash dividends are rare. For a noncash asset dividend, debit Retained Earnings and credit the asset (for example, Long-Term Investment) for the fair market value of the asset given.

Cash Dividends

Most dividends are cash dividends. Finance courses discuss how a company decides on its dividend policy. Accounting tells a company if it can pay a dividend. To do so, a company must have both

- Enough Retained Earnings to *declare* the dividend, and
- Enough Cash to *pay* the dividend

OBJECTIVE

4 **Account** for dividends

A corporation declares a dividend before paying it. Only the board of directors has the authority to declare a dividend. The corporation has no obligation to pay a dividend until the board declares one, but once declared, the dividend becomes a legal liability of the corporation. There are three relevant dates for dividends (using assumed amounts):

1. **Declaration date, June 19**. On the declaration date, the board of directors announces the dividend. Declaration of the dividend creates a liability for the corporation. Declaration is recorded by debiting Retained Earnings and crediting Dividends Payable. Assume a $50,000 dividend.

2011			
June 19	Retained Earnings*	50,000	
	Dividends Payable		50,000
	Declared a cash dividend.		

Liabilities increase, and equity goes down.

ASSETS	=	LIABILITIES	+	SHAREHOLDERS' EQUITY
0	=	+50,000		−50,000

2. **Date of record, July 1**. As part of the declaration, the corporation announces the record date, which follows the declaration date by a few weeks. The shareholders on the record date will receive the dividend. There is no journal entry for the date of record.
3. **Payment date, July 10**. Payment of the dividend usually follows the record date by a week or two. Payment is recorded by debiting Dividends Payable and crediting Cash.

July 10	Dividends Payable	50,000	
	Cash		50,000
	Paid cash dividend.		

Both assets and liabilities decrease. The corporation shrinks.

ASSETS	=	LIABILITIES	+	SHAREHOLDERS' EQUITY
−50,000	=	−50,000		

*In Chapter 2, we debited a Dividends account to clearly identify the purpose of the payment. From here on, we follow the more common practice of debiting the Retained Earnings account for dividend declarations.

Analyzing the Shareholders' Equity Accounts

By knowing accounting you can look at a company's comparative year-to-year financial statements and tell a lot about what the company did during the current year. For example, PotashCorp reported the following for Retained Earnings (in millions):

	December 31	
	2009	2008
Retained earnings	$3,272.1	$2,402.3

What do these figures tell you about PotashCorp's results of operations during 2009? Did PotashCorp have net income or net loss? How can you tell? PotashCorp had a net income. This is for certain, because

- Retained Earnings increased in 2009.
- Net income is the only item that increases Retained Earnings.

Was PotashCorp's net income $869.8 ($3,272.1 − $2,402.3 = $869.8)? Not necessarily. PotashCorp may have declared a dividend, and dividends decrease Retained Earnings.

If you know accounting—if you know PotashCorp's net income ($987.8 from PotashCorp's income statement)—you can compute PotashCorp's dividend declarations during 2009 as follows (in millions):

Retained Earnings

		Begin. bal.	2,402.3
Dividends	?	Net income	987.8
		Ending bal.	3,272.1

Dividends (x) were $118.0 ($2,402.3 + $987.8 − x = $3,272.1; x = $118.0). It really helps to know accounting!

Dividends on Preferred Shares

When a company has issued both preferred and common shares, the preferred shareholders receive their dividends first. The common shareholders receive dividends only if the total declared dividend is large enough to pay the preferred shareholders first.

Pinecraft Industries Inc. has 100,000 shares of $1.50 cumulative preferred shares outstanding in addition to its common shares. This $1.50 designation means that preferred dividends are paid at the annual amount of $1.50 per share. Assume that in 2011, Pinecraft declares an annual dividend of $1,000,000. The allocation to preferred and common shareholders is as follows:

Preferred dividend (100,000 shares × $1.50 per share)	$ 150,000
Common dividend (remainder: $1,000,000 − $150,000)	850,000
Total dividend	$1,000,000

If Pinecraft declares only a $200,000 dividend, preferred shareholders receive $150,000, and the common shareholders receive the remainder, $50,000 ($200,000 − $150,000).

Expressing the Dividend on Preferred Shares. Dividends on preferred shares are stated as a dollar amount since preferred shares do not have a nominal value stated on the face of the certificate. For example, preferred shares may be "$3 preferred," which means that shareholders receive an annual dividend of $3 per share.

Dividends on Cumulative and Noncumulative Preferred Shares. The allocation of dividends may be complex if the preferred shares are *cumulative*. Corporations sometimes fail to pay a dividend to preferred shareholders. This is called *passing the dividend*, and the passed dividends are said to be *in arrears*. The owners of **cumulative preferred shares** must receive all dividends in arrears plus the current year's dividend before the corporation can pay dividends to the common shareholders. *The law considers preferred shares noncumulative unless they are specifically labelled as cumulative.*

The preferred shares of Pinecraft Industries Inc. are cumulative. Suppose the company passed the 2010 preferred dividend of $150,000. Before paying dividends to its common shareholders in 2011, the company must first pay preferred dividends of $150,000 for both 2010 and 2011, a total of $300,000.

Assume that Pinecraft Industries Inc. did pass on its 2010 preferred dividend. In 2011, the company declares a $500,000 dividend. The entry to record the declaration is

2011			
Sept. 6	Retained Earnings	500,000	
	Dividends Payable, Preferred ($150,000 × 2)		300,000
	Dividends Payable, Common ($500,000 − $300,000)		200,000
	To declare a cash dividend.		

If the preferred shares are *noncumulative*, the corporation is not obligated to pay preferred dividends in arrears. A liability for dividends arises only when the board of directors declares the dividend.

Some preferred shares have a *participation feature*. The following events will occur when a company pays out extra dividends on participating preferred shares:

- Preferred shareholders receive their usual dividend.
- Common shareholders receive the dividend declared for the common shares.
- The excess above these amounts is shared by common and preferred in proportion to the total value of both classes of shares or according to some other agreed formula.

The details of determining dividends for participating preferred shares will be left to an intermediate accounting course.

Stock Dividends

A **stock dividend** is a proportional distribution by a corporation of its own shares to its shareholders. Stock dividends increase the shares account and decrease Retained Earnings. Total equity is unchanged, and no asset or liability is affected.

The corporation distributes stock dividends to shareholders in proportion to the number of shares they already own. If you own 300 common shares of PotashCorp and PotashCorp distributes a 10% common shares dividend, you will receive 30 (300 × 0.10) additional shares. You would then own 330 common shares. All other PotashCorp shareholders would also receive additional shares equal to 10% of their prior holdings.

In distributing a stock dividend, the corporation gives up no assets. Why, then, do companies issue stock dividends? A corporation may choose to distribute stock dividends for the following reasons:

1. **To continue dividends but conserve cash.** A company may want to keep cash for operations and yet wish to continue dividends in some form. So the corporation may distribute a stock dividend. Shareholders pay tax on stock dividends the same way they pay tax on cash dividends.
2. **To reduce the per-share market price of its shares.** Distribution of a stock dividend may cause the market price of a share of the company's stock to fall because of the increased supply of the shares. The objective is to make the shares less expensive and thus more attractive to more investors.

Suppose PotashCorp declared a 2% stock dividend in 2011. At the time, assume PotashCorp had 296 million common shares outstanding. PotashCorp is incorporated under the *Canada Business Corporations Act*, which suggests that the market price of the shares at the time of declaration be used to value the dividend. At the time of the stock dividend, assume PotashCorp's shares are trading for $120 per share. PotashCorp would record this stock dividend as follows, where SE stands for "shareholders' equity":

2011			
Nov. 19	Retained Earnings (296,000,000 common shares outstanding × 0.02 stock dividend × $120 market price per common share) (−SE)................................	710,400,000	
	Common Shares (+SE)..		710,400,000
	Distributed a 2% stock dividend.		

The accounting equation clearly shows that a stock dividend has no effect on total assets, liabilities, or equity. The increases in equity offset the decreases, and the net effect is zero.

ASSETS	=	LIABILITIES	+	SHAREHOLDERS' EQUITY
0	=	0		−710,400,000 +710,400,000

STOP + THINK

A corporation issued 1,000 common shares as a stock dividend when the share market price was $25. Assume that the 1,000 shares issued are (1) 10% of the outstanding shares and (2) 100% of the outstanding shares. Does either stock dividend change total shareholders' equity?

Answer:
No, neither a large stock dividend nor a small stock dividend affects total shareholders' equity because all the accounts affected by a stock dividend are part of shareholders' equity.

Stock Splits

A **stock split** is an increase in the number of authorized, issued, and outstanding shares of stock, coupled with a proportionate reduction in the share's book value. For example, if a company splits its stock 2 for 1, the number of outstanding shares is doubled and each share's book value is halved. A stock split, like a stock dividend, decreases the market price of the shares—with the intention of making the shares more attractive in the market. Leading companies in Canada—Bank of Nova Scotia, Canadian National Railway Company, Molson Coors Brewing Company, Suncor Energy Inc., and others—have split their stock.

The recent share price of PotashCorp on the Toronto Stock Exchange was $100. Assume PotashCorp wants to decrease the price to approximately $50. PotashCorp may decide to split its common shares.

A 2-for-1 stock split means that the company would have twice as many shares outstanding after the split as it had before and that each share's book value would be cut in half. Before the assumed split, PotashCorp had approximately 316 million common shares issued and outstanding. Compare PotashCorp's shareholders' equity before and after a 2-for-1 stock split:

Potash Corporation's Shareholders' Equity (Adapted)

Before 2-for-1 Stock Split:	**(in millions U.S. dollars)**	**After 2-for-1 Stock Split:**	**(in millions U.S. dollars)**
Common shares, unlimited number of shares authorized, 296 million shares issued	$1,480.3	Common shares, unlimited number of shares authorized, 592 million shares issued	$1,480.3
Retained earnings	3,272,1	Retained earnings	3,272,1
Other	1,748.3	Other	1,748.3
Total shareholders' equity	$6,500.7	Total shareholders' equity	$6,500.7

All account balances are the same after the stock split as before. Only the number of shares issued is affected. Total equity does not change.

Summary of the Effects on Assets, Liabilities, and Shareholders' Equity

We've seen how to account for the basic shareholders' equity transactions:

- Issuance of shares—common and preferred (pp. 459–464)
- Repurchase of shares (pp. 466–468)
- Cash dividends (pp. 468–471)
- Stock dividends and stock splits (pp. 471–473)

How do these transactions affect assets, liabilities, and equity? Exhibit 9-6 provides a helpful summary.

EXHIBIT 9-6 **Effects on Assets, Liabilities, and Equity**

	Effect on Total				
Transaction	**Assets**	=	**Liabilities**	+	**Shareholders' Equity**
Issuance of shares—common and preferred	Increase		No effect		Increase
Repurchase of shares	Decrease		No effect		Decrease
Declaration of cash dividend	No effect		Increase		Decrease
Payment of cash dividend	Decrease		Decrease		No effect
Stock dividend	No effect		No effect		No effect
Stock split	No effect		No effect		No effect

Retained Earnings Restrictions

As emphasized in previous chapters, retained earnings represent a corporation's lifetime earnings, including increases or decreases resulting from share repurchases discussed above, minus lifetime dividends to date (both cash dividends and stock dividends). In some cases restrictions to protect creditors are imposed that make a portion of the current Retained Earnings balance unavailable for dividends.

Restrictions are disclosed in the notes accompanying the financial statements and result from one or more of the following causes:

Legal	Regulatory agencies limit dividend payments to the balance of retained earnings.
Contractual	Debt covenants related to bank loans may restrict dividends to a specified percentage of retained earnings.
Voluntary	Corporate directors may limit dividends so that cash can be used in the business to take advantage of investment opportunities.

Measuring the Value of Shares

OBJECTIVE

5 **Use** share values in decision making

The business community measures *share values* in various ways, depending on the purpose of the measurement. These values include fair value, redemption value, liquidation value, and book value.

Fair, Redemption, Liquidation, and Book Value

The price of a share of stock traded on a market such as the Toronto Stock Exchange (TSX) is the **fair value** (market price) of that share. The fair value of a share is the price for which a person can buy or sell one share of stock. Fair value varies with the corporation's net income, financial position, and future prospects and the general economic conditions. *In almost all cases, shareholders are more concerned about the market price of a share than any other value.*

PotashCorp's recent share price was $101.10. Therefore, if PotashCorp were issuing 1,000 of its common shares, PotashCorp would receive cash of $101,100 (1,000 × $101.10 per share). This would be the fair value of the shares PotashCorp issued.

Preferred shares that require the company to redeem the shares at the holder's option at a set price are called *redeemable preferred shares*. The company is *obligated* to redeem the preferred shares. The price the corporation agrees to pay for the shares, which is set when the shares are issued, is called the *redemption value*. *Liquidation value* is the amount that a company must pay a preferred shareholder in the event the company liquidates and closes its doors if the necessary cash is available.

A company may issue *convertible preferred* shares that are convertible into common shares at a specified rate (for example, 4 common shares for 1 convertible preferred share). This feature allows the issuing company to pay a lower dividend of the convertible preferred shares. The accounting for the conversion of convertible preferred shares is complex and beyond the scope of this text.

The **book value** per common share is the amount of owners' equity on the company's books for each common share. If the company has only common shares outstanding, its book value is computed by dividing total equity by the number of common shares *outstanding*. For example, a company with shareholders' equity of $180,000 and 5,000 common shares outstanding has a book value of $36 per share ($180,000 ÷ 5,000 shares).

If the company has both preferred shares and common shares outstanding, the preferred shareholders have the first claim to owners' equity. Preferred shares often have a specified liquidation or redemption value. The value of the preferred equity is its redemption value plus any cumulative preferred dividends in arrears (assuming the preferred dividends are cumulative). Book value per common share is then computed as follows:

$$\text{Book value per common share} = \frac{\text{Total shareholders' equity} - \text{Preferred equity}}{\text{Number of common shares outstanding}}$$

Crusader Corp.'s balance sheet reports the following amounts:

Shareholders' Equity	
Preferred shares, $6.00, 400 shares issued, redemption value $130 per share	$ 40,000
Common shares, 5,000 shares issued	131,000
Retained earnings	70,000
Total shareholders' equity	$241,000

Suppose that four years (including the current year) of cumulative preferred dividends are in arrears and observe that Crusader's preferred shares have a redemption value of $130 per share. The book-value-per-share computations for Crusader Corp. are as follows:

Preferred equity	
Redemption value (400 shares × $130)	$ 52,000
Cumulative dividends (400 × $6.00 × 4 years)	9,600
Preferred equity	$61,600*
Common equity	
Total shareholders' equity	$241,000
Less preferred equity	(61,600)
Common equity	$179,400
Book value per share [$179,400 ÷ 5,000 shares outstanding]	$ 35.88

*If the preferred shares had no redemption value, then preferred equity would be $40,000 plus preferred dividends in arrears of $9,600 ($49,600).

Using Book Value Per Share

Some investors search for stocks whose share market value is below book value. They believe this indicates a good buy. Financial analysts often shy away from companies with a share price at or below book value. To them, such a company is in trouble. As you can see, not all users of financial statements agree on a share's value. Let's compare two companies, Canadian Tire Corporation Limited and RONA Inc.:

Company	Recent Share Price	Common Shareholders' Equity	Number of Common Shares Outstanding	Book Value
Canadian Tire Corporation Limited	$57.24	$3,687,900,000	78,178,066	$47.17
RONA Inc.	$15.77	$1,779,039,000	129,573,132	$13.73

$$^{*}\text{Book value} = \frac{\text{Common shareholders' equity}}{\text{Number of common shares outstanding}}$$

Neither company's shares are selling below their book value. But RONA's book value per share is somewhat closer to its market value than Canadian Tire's. Does this mean RONA's shares are the better investment? Not necessarily. In fact, wise investors base their decisions on more than a single ratio. In Chapter 13 you'll see the full range of financial ratios, plus a few more analytical techniques.

Relating Profitability to a Company's Shares

OBJECTIVE

6 **Compute** return on assets and return on equity

Investors search for companies whose shares are likely to increase in value. They're constantly comparing companies. But a comparison of PotashCorp with a new start-up is not meaningful. PotashCorp's profits run into the millions, which far exceed a new company's net income. Does this automatically make PotashCorp a better investment? Not necessarily. To compare companies of different sizes, investors use some standard profitability measures, including:

- Return on assets
- Return on equity

Return on Assets. The **rate of return on total assets**, or simply **return on assets (ROA)**, measures a company's success in using its assets to earn income for the two groups who finance the business:

- Creditors to whom the corporation owes money (creditors want interest)
- Shareholders who own the corporation's shares (shareholders want net income)

The sum of interest expense and net income is the return to the two groups who finance a corporation. This sum is the numerator of the return-on-assets ratio. The denominator is average total assets. Return on assets is computed as follows, using data from PotashCorp's financial statements for a recent year-end (dollar amounts in millions):

$$\text{Rate of return on total assets} = \frac{\text{Net income} + \text{Interest expense}}{\text{Average total assets}}$$

$$= \frac{\$987.8 + \$120.9}{(\$12{,}922.2 + \$10{,}248.8)/2} = \frac{\$1{,}108.7}{\$11{,}585.5} = 0.096$$

Net income and interest expense are taken from the income statement. Average total assets is computed from the beginning and ending balance sheets.

What is a good rate of return on total assets? Ten percent is considered strong for most companies. However, rates of return vary widely by industry. For example, high-technology companies earn much higher returns than do utility companies, retailers, and manufacturers of consumer goods such as toothpaste and paper towels. PotashCorp's return on assets is strong.

Return on Equity. Rate of return on common shareholders' equity, often called **return on equity (ROE)**, shows the relationship between net income and average common shareholders' equity. Return on equity is computed only on common shares because the return to preferred shareholders is their specified dividend (for example, \$1.50).

The numerator of return on equity is net income minus preferred dividends. The denominator is *average common shareholders' equity*—average total shareholders' equity minus preferred equity. A recent rate of return on common shareholders' equity for PotashCorp is computed as follows (dollar amounts in millions):

$$\text{Rate of return on common shareholders' equity} = \frac{\text{Net income} - \text{Preferred dividends}}{\text{Average common shareholders' equity}}$$

$$= \frac{\$987.8 - \$0}{(\$6{,}500.7 + \$4{,}588.9)/2} = \frac{\$987.8}{\$5{,}544.8} = 0.178$$

Because PotashCorp has no preferred shares, preferred dividends are zero. With no preferred shares outstanding, average *common* shareholders' equity is the same as average *total* equity—the average of the beginning and ending amounts.

PotashCorp's return on equity (17.8%) is higher than its return on assets (9.6%). This difference results from the interest-expense component of return on assets. Companies such as PotashCorp borrow at one rate (say, 6%) and invest the funds to earn a higher rate (say, 12%). Borrowing at a lower rate than the company's return on investments is called *using leverage*. Leverage increases net income as long as operating income exceeds the interest expense from borrowing.

ROE is always higher than ROA for a successful company. Shareholders take a lot more investment risk than bondholders, so the shareholders demand that ROE *exceed* ROA. If ROA were higher, that would mean that the return on debt—interest—is higher than the return on equity—net income. If that were true, there wouldn't be any shareholders. Everyone would be investing in bonds!

Investors and creditors use ROE in much the same way they use ROA—to compare companies. The higher the rate of return, the more successful the company. In most industries, 15% is considered good. Therefore, PotashCorp's 17.8% return on common shareholders' equity is good.

Using Information About a Company in Decision Making (About Share Investments)

Once an investor has decided to buy the shares of a particular company, the investor has to make a series of decisions:

Investor Decision	Guidelines
Which category of shares to buy for:	
• A safe investment?	Preferred shares are safer than common, but for even more safety, invest in blue chip stocks, high-grade corporate bonds, or government securities.
• Steady dividends?	Cumulative preferred shares. However, the company is not obligated to declare preferred dividends, and the dividends are unlikely to increase.
• Increasing dividends?	Common shares, as long as the company's net income is increasing and the company has adequate cash flow to pay a dividend after meeting all obligations and other cash demands.
• Increasing share price?	Common shares, but again only if the company's net income and cash flow are increasing.
• How to identify a good stock to buy?	There are many ways to pick share investments. One strategy that works reasonably well is to invest in companies that consistently earn higher rates of return on assets and on equity than competing firms in the same industry. Also, select industries that are expected to grow.

Reporting Shareholders' Equity Transactions

Statement of Cash Flows

OBJECTIVE

7 **Report** equity transactions on the statement of cash flows

Many of the transactions discussed in this chapter are reported on the statement of cash flows. Equity transactions are *financing activities* because the company is dealing with its owners. Financing transactions that affect both cash and equity fall into three main categories:

- Issuances of shares
- Repurchases of shares
- Cash dividends

Issuances of Shares. *Issuances of shares* include basic transactions in which a company issues its shares for cash. During 2009, PotashCorp issued 774,563 Class A common shares under options and a dividend reinvestment plan. The proceeds were $20.2 million. The sale was reported as a financing activity.

Repurchases of Shares. As we discussed earlier, a company can repurchase its shares. During the year ended December 31, 2009, PotashCorp did not repurchase any common shares either as treasury shares or for cancellation. However, during the year ended December 31, 2008, PotashCorp reported repurchasing 22,849,200 common shares for $3,356.4 million. The shares were cancelled.

Cash Dividends. Most companies pay cash dividends to their shareholders. Dividend payments are a type of financing transaction because the company is paying its shareholders for the use of their money. Stock dividends are not reported on the statement of cash flows because the company pays no cash. PotashCorp paid dividends in the amount of $116.9 million during 2009. See Exhibit 9-7.

Variations in Reporting Shareholders' Equity

Businesses often use terminology and formats in reporting shareholders' equity that differ from our examples. We use a more detailed format in this book to help you learn all the components of shareholders' equity.

One of the most important skills you will take from this course is the ability to understand the financial statements of real companies. Exhibit 9-8 is an example that presents a side-by-side comparison of our general teaching format and the format you are more likely to encounter in real-world balance sheets.

EXHIBIT 9-7 **PotashCorp Financing Activities (Adapted)**

	($ millions)
Financing activities:	
Dividends	(116.9)
Repurchase of common shares	—
Issuance of common shares	20.2

EXHIBIT 9-8 **Formats for Reporting Shareholders' Equity**

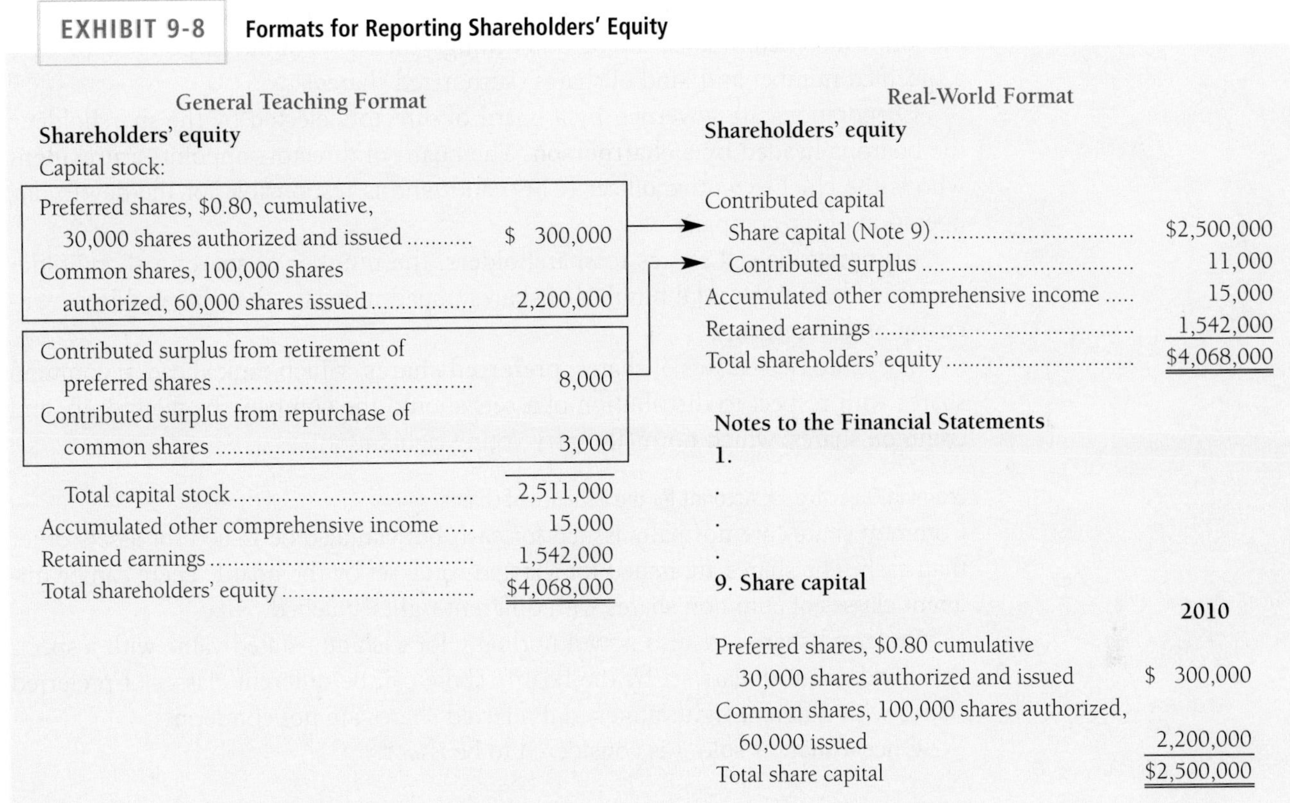

General Teaching Format

Shareholders' equity	
Capital stock:	
Preferred shares, $0.80, cumulative, 30,000 shares authorized and issued	$ 300,000
Common shares, 100,000 shares authorized, 60,000 shares issued	2,200,000
Contributed surplus from retirement of preferred shares	8,000
Contributed surplus from repurchase of common shares	3,000
Total capital stock	2,511,000
Accumulated other comprehensive income	15,000
Retained earnings	1,542,000
Total shareholders' equity	$4,068,000

Real-World Format

Shareholders' equity	
Contributed capital	
Share capital (Note 9)	$2,500,000
Contributed surplus	11,000
Accumulated other comprehensive income	15,000
Retained earnings	1,542,000
Total shareholders' equity	$4,068,000

Notes to the Financial Statements

1.

.

.

.

9. Share capital

	2010
Preferred shares, $0.80 cumulative 30,000 shares authorized and issued	$ 300,000
Common shares, 100,000 shares authorized, 60,000 issued	2,200,000
Total share capital	$2,500,000

In general:

- Preferred shares come first and the individual classes are listed separately. The dividend rate, features such as whether the dividend is cumulative and whether the shares are redeemable, and the number of shares authorized and issued are reported.
- Common shares come next and individual classes are listed separately. The number of shares authorized and issued is reported.
- Contributed surplus is listed next.
- Preferred shares, common shares, and contributed surplus are included in Contributed Capital.
- Accumulated other comprehensive income.
- Retained Earnings comes last.

SUMMARY OF CHAPTER 9

Learning Objective ❶: **Explain the features of a corporation**

A corporation is a legal entity that is separate from its owners. The owners of a corporation (shareholders) have **limited liability**.

Corporate earnings are subject to **double taxation**; the corporation pays taxes on its earnings and the shareholders pay taxes on dividends they receive.

Corporations are incorporated under federal or provincial jurisdiction and governed by government regulation.

The corporation receives articles of incorporation from the incorporating jurisdiction, which determines, among other things, the rights of the corporation to issue a specified number and kind of shares (authorized shares).

Corporations are governed by a board of directors elected by the shareholders; the board is headed by a **chairperson**. The board of directors appoints a **president** who is the chief executive officer (CEO) and who is responsible for the day-to-day operation of the company.

Corporations sell shares to shareholders; the number of shares a shareholder owns divided by the total number of shares issued indicates that shareholder's ownership of the company.

There are two classes of shares; **preferred shares**, which rank ahead of common shares with respect to distribution of assets should the company be wound up, and common shares, which normally carry voting rights.

Learning Objective ❷: Account for the issuance of shares

Common shares are normally issued for cash but can also be issued for assets other than cash. The shares are issued for a stated value set by the board. There can be different classes of common shares with different rights attached.

Preferred shares are also issued normally for cash at a stated value with a specified dividend in dollars set by the board. There can be different classes of preferred shares with different rights attached. Preferred shares are not common.

Once a share is sold it is considered to be *issued*.

Learning Objective ❸: Describe how share repurchase transactions affect a company

Companies may repurchase their shares for either cancellation or to hold for re-issue at a later date. The latter are referred to as Treasury shares. Shares that are repurchased for cancellation may be repurchased for a price equal to, greater than, or less than the issue price. The excess of the repurchase price over the issue price is debited to Retained Earnings. The deficiency under the issue price is credited to Retained Earnings.

The price paid for treasury shares is deducted from the issued share capital in the Shareholders' Equity section of the balance sheet.

Retained earnings is the sum of the earnings and gains minus the dividends and losses accumulated over the company's lifetime.

Learning Objective ❹: Account for dividends

The most common dividends are cash dividends although some companies issue **stock dividends** to conserve cash.

The relevant dates for a cash dividend are the declaration date, which is the date the dividend is declared; the *date of record*, which determines which shareholders will receive the dividend; and the *payment date*, which is the date when the dividend is paid.

The entry to record the declaration of a dividend is a debit to Retained Earnings and a credit to Dividends Payable. The entry to record payment of a dividend is a debit to Dividends Payable and a credit to Cash.

Preferred shares are normally preferred as to dividends and so must receive their designated dividend before common shareholders may receive a dividend. If the preferred shares have a cumulative feature, the preferred shareholders must also receive any unpaid back dividends before the common shareholders receive dividends.

When a company pays a stock dividend, each shareholder receives additional shares based on their shareholdings at the date of record.

A company may decide to split its shares. A 3-for-1 **stock split** would give each shareholder two additional shares for each share held. Needless to say, the **market prices** of the shares would fall to reflect the split.

Learning Objective ❺: **Use share values in decision making**
Fair value is the market price of a share of stock. Redemption value applies only to preferred shares and is the price the company agreed to pay to redeem the shares when the shares were issued. Liquidation value is the value of the shares if the company sold its assets, paid off its liabilities and distributed the cash remaining; remember preferred shareholders would be paid first. **Book value** is the amount of owners' equity on the books for each common share.

Learning Objective ❻: **Compute return on assets and return on equity**
Return on assets (ROA) measures a company's success in using its assets to earn income. The formula is Rate of return on total assets = (Net income + Interest expense)/Average total assets.

Return on equity (ROE) shows the relationship between net income and average return on shareholders' equity. The formula is Rate of return on common shareholders' equity = (Net income – Preferred dividends)/Average common shareholders' equity.

ROE is always higher than ROA for a successful company.

Learning Objective ❼: **Report equity transactions on the statement of cash flows**
There are three main categories of transactions that affect the Financing section of the statement of cash flows:

- Issuances of shares
- Repurchases of shares
- Cash dividends

END-OF-CHAPTER SUMMARY PROBLEM

MyAccountingLab

1. The balance sheet of Quetico Inc. reported the following at December 31, 2011:

Shareholders' Equity	
Preferred shares, $0.40, 10,000 shares authorized and issued (redemption value, $110,000)	$ 100,000
Common shares, 100,000 shares authorized*	400,000
Accumulated other comprehensive income	224,000
Retained earnings	476,500
Total shareholders' equity	$1,200,500

*The common shares were issued at a stated value of $8.00 per share.

Required

a. Are the preferred shares cumulative or noncumulative? How can you tell?
b. What is the total amount of the annual preferred dividend?
c. How many common shares are outstanding?
d. Compute the book value per share of the common shares. No preferred dividends are in arrears, and Quetico Inc. has not yet declared the 2011 dividend.

2. Use the following accounts and related balances to prepare the classified balance sheet of Gandhi Ltd. at September 30, 2011. Use the account format of the balance sheet.

Common shares, 50,000 shares authorized, 20,000 shares issued	$100,000	Property, plant, and equipment, net	$266,000
Dividends payable	4,000	Accounts receivable, net	23,000
Cash	9,000	Preferred shares, $3.75, 10,000 shares authorized, 2,000 shares issued	24,000
Accounts payable	28,000	Accrued liabilities	3,000
Long-term note payable	80,000	Retained earnings	104,000
Inventory	85,000		
Accumulated other comprehensive income	40,000		

All features must be specified in the financial statements.

Details given on the balance sheet.

Each common share was sold for the $8 stated value.

Book value per common share must exclude any amounts pertaining to preferred shares.

Answers

1. a. The preferred shares are not cumulative because they are not specifically labelled cumulative.
   b. Total annual preferred dividend: $4,000 (10,000 × $0.40).
   c. Common shares outstanding: 50,000 shares ($400,000 ÷ $8 stated value).
   d. Book value per common share:

Common:	
Total shareholders' equity	$1,200,500
Less shareholders' equity allocated to preferred	(110,000)*
Shareholders' equity allocated to common	$1,090,500
Book value per share ($1,090,500 ÷ 50,000 shares)	$ 21.81

*Redemption value ... $110,000

2.

The classified balance sheet must specify current assets and current liabilities. Make sure that Total assets = Total liabilities + Shareholders' equity.

Gandhi Ltd.
Balance Sheet
As at September 30, 2011

Assets		**Liabilities**		
Current		Current		
Cash	$ 9,000	Accounts payable	$ 28,000	
Accounts receivable, net	23,000	Dividends payable	4,000	
Inventory	85,000	Accrued liabilities	3,000	
Total current assets	117,000	Total current liabilities	35,000	
Property, plant, and equipment, net	266,000	Long-term note payable	80,000	
		Total liabilities		$115,000
		Shareholders' Equity		
		Preferred shares, $3.75, 10,000 shares authorized, 2,000 shares issued	$ 24,000	
		Common shares, 50,000 shares authorized, 20,000 shares issued	100,000	
		Accumulated other comprehensive income	40,000	
		Retained earnings	104,000	
		Total shareholders' equity		268,000
Total assets	$383,000	Total liabilities and shareholders' equity		$383,000

Review Shareholders' Equity

Quick Check (Answers are given on page 507.)

1. Copeland Company is authorized to issue 40,000 $10 common shares. On January 15, 2011, Copeland issued 10,000 shares at $15 per share. Copeland's journal entry to record these facts should include a
   a. Credit to Common Shares for $100,000
   b. Credit to Common Shares for $150,000
   c. Debit to Common Shares for $150,000
   d. Both a and b

Questions 2 through 5 use the following account balances of Casio Co. at March 31, 2011:

Number of common shares authorized	1,000,000	Number of common shares issued	180,000
Dividends Payable	$ 22,000	Cash	$ 74,000
Preferred Shares	100,000	Common Shares	180,000
		Retained Earnings	200,000

2. Casio has issued ______ common shares.
   a. 74,000
   b. 180,000
   c. 225,000
   d. Some other amount
3. Casio's total contributed capital at March 31, 2011, is
   a. $495,000
   b. $180,000
   c. $1,175,000
   d. Some other amount
4. Casio's total shareholders' equity as of March 31, 2011, is
   a. $1,406,000
   b. $1,249,000
   c. $480,000
   d. $1,480,000
5. What would Casio's total shareholders' equity be if there were $5,000 of common shares repurchased for cancellation? ______________
6. Woodstock Corporation repurchased common shares in 2011 at a price of $30 per share that had an average cost of $40 per share. What amount should Woodstock report on its income statement for 2011?
   a. $40
   b. $30
   c. $10
   d. $0
7. The shareholders' equity section of a corporation's balance sheet reports

Common Shares	*Discount on Bonds Payable*
a. Yes	No
b. No	Yes
c. Yes	Yes
d. No	No

8. The repurchase of a company's own shares
   a. Increases one asset, and decreases another asset
   b. Decreases total assets, and decreases total shareholders' equity
   c. Has no effect on total assets, total liabilities, or total shareholders' equity
   d. Decreases total assets, and increases total shareholders' equity
9. When does a cash dividend become a legal liability?
   a. On date of payment
   b. On date of record
   c. On date of declaration
   d. It never becomes a liability because it is paid.
10. When do dividends increase shareholders' equity?
    a. Never
    b. On date of declaration
    c. On date of record
    d. On date of payment
11. Willow Run Mall Inc. has 5,000 $2 cumulative preferred shares and 100,000 common shares outstanding. At the beginning of the current year, preferred dividends were three years in arrears. Willow Run's board of directors wants to pay a $1.25 cash dividend on each share of outstanding common shares. To accomplish this, what total amount of dividends must Willow Run declare?
    a. $170,000
    b. $185,000
    c. $165,000
    d. Some other amount $______
12. Which of the following is true of stock dividends?
    a. They have no effect on total shareholders' equity.
    b. They are distributions of cash to shareholders.
    c. They reduce the total assets of the company.
    d. They increase the corporation's total liabilities.
13. What is the effect of a stock split and a stock dividend on total assets?

Stock Split	*Stock Dividend*
a. Decrease	No effect
b. Decrease	Decrease
c. No effect	Decrease
d. No effect	No effect

14. A 2-for-1 stock split has the same effect on the number of shares being issued as a
   a. 20% stock dividend
   b. 50% stock dividend
   c. 100% stock dividend
   d. 200% stock dividend

15. The numerator for computing the rate of return on total assets is
   a. Net income
   b. Net income minus interest expense
   c. Net income plus interest expense
   d. Net income minus preferred dividends

16. The numerator for computing the rate of return on common equity is
   a. Net income minus preferred dividends
   b. Net income minus interest expense
   c. Net income plus preferred dividends
   d. Net income

Accounting Vocabulary

book value (of a share) Amount of owners' equity on the company's books for each share of its stock. (p. 474)

bylaws Constitution for governing a corporation. (p. 455)

chairperson Elected by a corporation's board of directors, usually the most powerful person in the corporation. (p. 456)

cumulative preferred shares Preferred shares whose owners must receive all dividends in arrears plus the current year's dividend before the corporation can pay dividends to the common shareholders. (p. 471)

deficit Debit balance in the Retained Earnings account. (p. 468)

double taxation Corporations pay income taxes on corporate income. Then, the shareholders pay personal income tax on the cash dividends that they receive from corporations. Canada's tax laws attempt to minimize double taxation. (p. 455)

fair value (of a share) Price for which a person could sell a share of stock. (p. 474)

limited liability No personal obligation of a shareholder for corporation debts. A shareholder can lose no more on an investment in a corporation's shares than the cost of the investment. (p. 454)

market price (of a share) Price for which a person could buy or sell a share of stock. (p. 466)

no-stated-value shares Shares of stock that do not have a value assigned to them by articles of the corporation. (p. 459)

outstanding shares Shares in the hands of shareholders. (p. 457)

preferred shares Shares that give their owners certain advantages, such as the priority to receive dividends before the common shareholders and the priority to receive assets before the common shareholders if the corporation liquidates. (p. 458)

president Chief executive officer in charge of managing the day-to-day operations of a corporation. (p. 456)

rate of return on common shareholders' equity Net income minus preferred dividends, divided by average common shareholders' equity. A measure of profitability. Also called *return on equity*. (p. 476)

rate of return on total assets Net income plus interest expense divided by average total assets. This ratio measures a company's success in using its assets to earn income for those who finance the business. Also called *return on assets*. (p. 476)

repurchased shares A corporation's own shares that it has issued and later reacquired. (p. 466)

return on assets Another name for *rate of return on total assets*. (p. 476)

return on equity Another name for *rate of return on common shareholders' equity*. (p. 476)

stated value An arbitrary amount assigned by a company to a share of its stock at the time of issue. (p. 459)

stock dividend A proportional distribution by a corporation of its own shares to its shareholders. (p. 471)

stock split An increase in the number of authorized, issued, and outstanding shares of stock coupled with a proportionate reduction in the share's book value. (p. 472)

Assess Your Progress

MyAccountingLab

Make the grade with MyAccountingLab: The exercises and problems in this chapter can be found on MyAccountingLab at www.myaccountinglab.com. You can practise them as often as you want, and they feature step-by-step guided solutions to help you find the right answer.

Short Exercises

Learning Objective 1
Advantages and disadvantages of a corporation

S9-1 What are two main advantages that a corporation has over a proprietorship and a partnership? What are two main disadvantages of a corporation?

Learning Objective 1
Authority structure in a corporation

S9-2 Consider the authority structure in a corporation, as diagrammed in Exhibit 9-2, page 456.

1. What group holds the ultimate power in a corporation?
2. Who is the most powerful person in the corporation? What's the abbreviation of this person's title?
3. Who's in charge of day-to-day operations? What's the abbreviation of this person's title?
4. Who's in charge of accounting and finance? What's the abbreviation of this person's title?

Learning Objective 1
Characteristics of preferred and common shares

S9-3 Answer the following questions about the characteristics of a corporation's shares:

1. Who are the real owners of a corporation?
2. What privileges do preferred shareholders have over common shareholders?
3. Which class of shareholders reaps greater benefits from a highly profitable corporation? Explain.

Learning Objective 2
Effect of a share issuance on net income

S9-4 Study George Weston Ltd.'s January 8, 2011, share issuance entry given on page 460, and answer these questions about the nature of the transaction.

1. If George Weston had sold the shares for $80, would the $30 ($80 − $50) be profit for George Weston?
2. Suppose the shares had been issued at different times and different prices. Will shares issued at higher prices have more rights than those issued at lower prices? Give the reason for your answer.

Learning Objective 2
Issuing shares and analyzing retained earnings

S9-5 On December 31, 2011, shareholders' equity accounts of Green Products Inc. (GPI) had the balances shown below. GPI paid dividends of $4,096 on December 1, 2011.

	2011	2010
Common shares	$82,968	$64,968
Retained earnings	80,435	78,881
Total shareholders' equity	$163,403	$143,849

1. GPI sold 10,000 common shares on June 30, 2011. What was the average selling price of these shares if this was the only common-shares transaction during 2011?
2. Journalize GPI's sale of the common shares on June 30, 2011.
3. Based only on the above information, did GPI earn a profit or loss during 2011? Calculate the profit or loss.

Learning Objective 2
Issuing shares to finance the purchase of assets

S9-6 This Short Exercise demonstrates the similarity and the difference between two ways to acquire capital assets.

Case A—Issue shares and buy the assets in separate transactions:	*Case B—Issue shares to acquire the assets in a single transaction:*
Longview Corporation issued 10,000 common shares for cash of $200,000. In a separate transaction, Longview used the cash to purchase a warehouse building for $160,000 and equipment for $40,000. Journalize the two transactions.	Tyler Corporation issued 10,000 common shares to acquire a warehouse valued at $160,000 and equipment worth $40,000. Journalize this transaction.

Compare the balances in all the accounts after making both sets of entries. Are the account balances the same or different?

Learning Objective 2
Preparing the shareholders' equity section of a balance sheet

S9-7 The financial statements of Eppley Employment Services Inc. reported the following accounts (adapted, with dollar amounts in thousands):

Common shares:		Total revenues	$1,390
600 shares issued	$600	Accounts payable	420
Long-term debt	25	Retained earnings	646
		Other current liabilities	2,566
		Total expenses	805

Prepare the shareholders' equity section of Eppley's balance sheet. Net income has already been closed to Retained Earnings.

Learning Objective 2
Using shareholders' equity data

S9-8 Use the Eppley Employment Services data in Short Exercise 9-7 to compute Eppley's

a. Net income
b. Total liabilities
c. Total assets (use the accounting equation)

Learning Objective 3
Accounting for the repurchase and sale of shares

S9-9 General Marketing Corporation reported the following shareholders' equity at December 31, 2011 (adapted and in millions):

Common shares	$ 257
Retained earnings	2,159
Total shareholders' equity	$2,416

During the next year, General Marketing repurchased common shares for cancellation at a cost of $38 million and issued shares for $5 million. The repurchased shares had a stated value of $40 million.

Record the repurchase and issuance of common shares. Overall, how much did shareholders' equity increase or decrease as a result of the two share transactions?

Learning Objective 4
Accounting for cash dividends

S9-10 Gleneagles Corporation earned net income of $70,000 during the year ended December 31, 2011. On December 15, Gleneagles had declared the annual cash dividend on its $0.50 preferred shares (10,000 shares issued for $100,000) and a $0.60 per share cash dividend on its common shares (25,000 shares issued for $50,000). Gleneagles then paid the dividends on January 4, 2012.

Journalize for Gleneagles Corporation:

a. Declaring the cash dividends on December 15, 2011
b. Paying the cash dividends on January 4, 2012

Did Retained Earnings increase or decrease during 2011? If so, by how much?

Learning Objective ❹
Dividing cash dividends between preferred and common shares

S9-11 Refer to the allocation of dividends for Pinecraft Industries Inc. on page 470. Answer these questions about Pinecraft's cash dividends.

1. How much in dividends must Pinecraft declare each year before the common shareholders receive any cash dividends for the year?
2. Suppose Pinecraft declares cash dividends of $300,000 for 2011. How much of the dividends go to preferred? How much go to common?
3. Are Pinecraft's preferred shares cumulative or noncumulative? How can you tell?
4. Pinecraft passed the preferred dividend in 2009 and 2010. Then in 2011, Pinecraft declares cash dividends of $800,000. How much of the dividends go to preferred? How much go to common?

Learning Objective ❹
Recording a small stock dividend

S9-12 Fidelity Software Ltd. has 80,000 common shares issued. Suppose Fidelity distributes a 10% stock dividend on May 11 when the market price (fair value) of its shares is $10.50 per share.

1. Journalize Fidelity's distribution of the shares dividend. An explanation is not required.
2. What was the overall effect of the stock dividend on Fidelity's total assets? What about on its total liabilities and its total shareholders' equity?

Learning Objective ❺
Computing book value per share

S9-13 Refer to the real-world format of shareholders' equity in Exhibit 9-8, page 479. That company has passed its preferred dividends for three years including the current year. Compute the book value of one of the company's common shares.

Learning Objective ❻
Computing and explaining return on assets and return on equity

S9-14 Give the formula for computing (a) rate of return on total assets (ROA) and (b) rate of return on common shareholders' equity (ROE). Then answer these questions about the rate-of-return computations.

1. Why is interest expense added to net income in the computation of ROA?
2. Why are preferred dividends subtracted from net income to compute ROE? Why are they not subtracted from net income in computing ROA?

Learning Objective ❻
Computing return on assets and return on equity

S9-15 Federated Machinery Ltd.'s 2011 financial statements reported the following items, with 2010 figures given for comparison (adapted and in millions). Compute Federated's return on assets and return on common equity for 2011. Evaluate the rates of return as strong or weak.

	2011	2010
Balance sheet		
Total assets	$10,608	$9,499
Total liabilities	$ 7,404	$6,629
Total shareholders' equity (all common)	3,204	2,870
Total liabilities and equity	$10,608	$9,499
Income statement		
Revenues and other income	$ 7,629	
Operating expense	7,284	
Interest expense	29	
Other expense	192	
Net income	$ 124	

Learning Objective ❼
Measuring cash flows from financing activities

S9-16 During 2011, Robertson Inc. earned net income of $5.6 billion and paid off $2.7 billion of long-term notes payable. Robertson Inc. raised $1.2 billion by issuing common shares, paid $3.0 billion to repurchase shares, and paid cash dividends of $1.9 billion. Report Robertson's *cash flows from financing activities* on the statement of cash flows for 2011.

Exercises

E9-17 Lance Brown and Monica Kobelsky are opening a Second Cup franchise. Brown and Kobelsky need outside capital, so they plan to organize the business as a corporation. They come to you for advice. Write a memorandum informing them of the steps in forming a corporation in the province of Alberta. Identify specific documents used in this process, and name the different parties involved in the ownership and management of a corporation.

Learning Objective 1
Organizing a corporation

E9-18 Burgers & Fries, Inc. is authorized to issue an unlimited number of common shares and 10,000 preferred shares. During its first year, the business completed the following share issuance transactions:

Learning Objective 2
Issuing shares and reporting shareholders' equity

July	19	Issued 10,000 common shares for cash of $6.50 per share
Oct.	3	Issued 500 $1.50 preferred shares for $50,000 cash
	11	Received inventory valued at $11,000 and equipment with fair value of $8,500 for 3,300 common shares

Required
1. Journalize the transactions. Explanations are not required.
2. Prepare the shareholders' equity section of Burgers & Fries' balance sheet. The ending balance of Retained Earnings is a deficit of $42,000.

E9-19 Citadel Sporting Goods is authorized to issue 5,000 preferred shares and 10,000 common shares. During a two-month period, Citadel completed these share-issuance transactions:

Learning Objective 2
Preparing the shareholders' equity section of a balance sheet

Sept.	23	Issued 1,000 common shares for cash of $16 per share
Oct.	2	Issued 300 $4.50 preferred shares for $20,000 cash
	12	Received inventory valued at $15,000 and equipment with fair value of $43,000 for 4,000 common shares

Required
Prepare the shareholders' equity section of the Citadel Sporting Goods balance sheet for the transactions given in this exercise. Retained Earnings has a balance of $49,000. Journal entries are not required.

E9-20 Trans World Publishing Inc. was recently organized. The company issued common shares to a lawyer who provided legal services of $15,000 to help organize the corporation. Trans World also issued common shares to an inventor in exchange for his patent with a fair value of $80,000. In addition, Trans World received cash both for the issuance of 5,000 of its preferred shares at $110 per share and for the issuance of 20,000 common shares at $20 per share. During the first year of operations, Trans World earned net income of $55,000 and declared a cash dividend of $20,000. Without making journal entries, determine the total contributed capital created by these transactions.

Learning Objective 2
Measuring the contributed capital of a corporation

E9-21 Sagebrush Software Ltd. had the following selected account balances at December 31, 2011 (in thousands). Prepare the shareholders' equity section of Sagebrush Software's balance sheet (in thousands).

Learning Objective 2 3
Shareholders' equity section of a balance sheet

Inventory	$ 653	Class A common shares, unlimited number authorized, 3,600 shares issued	$ 90
Property, plant, and equipment, net	857	Deficit	2,400
Contributed surplus – share repurchase	901	Accounts receivable, net	600
Class B common shares, unlimited number authorized, 5,000 shares issued	1,380	Notes payable	1,122

Explain what is meant by "deficit."

Learning Objective 2 3
Recording share transactions and measuring their effects on shareholders' equity

E9-22 Journalize the following transactions of Concilio Video Productions Inc.:

April 19	Issued 2,000 common shares at $10 per share
July 22	Repurchased 900 shares for re-issue at $11 per share
Nov. 11	Issued 800 common shares at $12 per share

What was the overall effect of these transactions on Concilio's shareholders' equity?

Learning Objective 2 3 4
Recording share issuance and dividend transactions

E9-23 At December 31, 2011, Blumenthall Corporation reported the shareholders' equity accounts shown here (as adapted, with dollar amounts in millions).

Common shares	
1,800 million shares issued	$ 2,700
Retained earnings	1,200
Total shareholders' equity	$3,900

Blumenthall's 2011 transactions included the following:

a. Net income, $350 million
b. Issuance of 6 million common shares for $12.50 per share
c. Repurchase of 1 million common shares for cancellation for $15 million
d. Declaration and payment of cash dividends of $25 million

Journalize Blumenthall's transactions. Explanations are not required.

Learning Objective 2 3 4
Reporting shareholders' equity after a sequence of transactions

E9-24 Use the Blumenthall Corporation data in Exercise 9-23 to prepare the shareholders' equity section of the company's balance sheet at December 31, 2011.

Learning Objective 2 3 4 5
Inferring transactions from a company's shareholders' equity

E9-25 Optical Products Company reported the following shareholders' equity on its balance sheet:

	December 31,	
Shareholders' Equity (dollars and shares in millions)	**2011**	**2010**
Preferred shares; authorized 20 shares;		
Convertible Preferred shares; issued and outstanding:		
2011 and 2010—0 and 2 shares, respectively	$ 0	$ 12
Common shares; authorized unlimited shares; issued:		
2011 and 2010—564 and 364 shares, respectively	3,270	1,900
Retained earnings	6,280	5,006
Total shareholders' equity	$ 9,550	$ 6,906
Total liabilities and shareholders' equity	$48,918	$45,549

Required

1. What caused Optical Products' preferred shares to decrease during 2011? Cite all the possible causes.
2. What caused Optical Products' common shares to increase during 2011? Identify all the possible causes.
3. How many shares of Optical Products were outstanding at December 31, 2011?
4. Optical Products' net income during 2011 was $1,410 million. How much were Optical Products' dividends during the year?
5. During 2011, the cost of repurchasing 10 million common shares for cancellation was $60 million. What average price did Optical Products pay for the shares the company repurchased during the year? Determine the amount received from new common shares issued during 2011.

E9-26 Great Lakes Manufacturing Inc. reported the following:

Learning Objective 4
Computing dividends on preferred and common shares

Shareholders' Equity	
Preferred shares, cumulative, $0.10, 80,000 shares issued	$ 80,000
Common shares, 8,130,000 shares issued	813,000

Great Lakes Manufacturing has paid all preferred dividends through 2007.

Required
Compute the total amounts of dividends to both preferred and common shareholders for 2010 and 2011 if total dividends are $50,000 in 2010 and $100,000 in 2011.

E9-27 The shareholders' equity for Best in Show Cinemas Ltd. (BSC) (adapted) at December 31, 2010, appears as follows:

Learning Objective 4
Recording a stock dividend and reporting shareholders' equity

Shareholders' Equity	
Common shares, 2,000,000 shares authorized, 500,000 shares issued	$1,012,000
Retained earnings	7,122,000
Total shareholders' equity	$8,134,000

On April 15, 2011, the market price of BSC common shares was $17 per share. Assume BSC distributed a 10% stock dividend on this date.

Required
1. Journalize the distribution of the stock dividend.
2. Prepare the shareholders' equity section of the balance sheet after the stock dividend.
3. Why is total shareholders' equity unchanged by the stock dividend?
4. Suppose BSC had a cash balance of $540,000 on April 16, 2011. What is the maximum amount of cash dividends BSC can declare?

E9-28 Identify the effects—both the direction and the dollar amount—of these assumed transactions on the total shareholders' equity of a large corporation. Each transaction is independent.

Learning Objective 2 3 4
Measuring the effects of share issuance, dividends, and share transactions

a. Declaration of cash dividends of $80 million
b. Payment of the cash dividend declared
c. 10% stock dividend. Before the dividend, 69 million common shares were outstanding; the market price was $7.625 at the time of the dividend.
d. A 50% stock dividend. Before the dividend, 69 million common shares were outstanding; the market price was $13.75 at the time of the dividend.
e. Repurchase of 2,000 common shares at $4.25 per share
f. Sale of 600 common shares for $5.00 per share
g. A 3-for-l stock split. Prior to the split, 69 million common shares were outstanding

E9-29 Solartech Inc. had the following shareholders' equity at January 31 (dollars in millions):

Learning Objective 4
Reporting shareholders' equity after a stock split

Common shares, 500 million shares authorized, 440 million shares issued	$ 318
Contributed surplus	44
Retained earnings	2,393
Total shareholders' equity	$2,755

Assume that on March 7, Solartech split its common shares 2 for 1. Prepare the shareholders' equity section of the balance sheet immediately after the split.

Learning Objective 5
Measuring the book value per share of common shares

E9-30 The balance sheet of Oriental Rug Company reported the following:

Redeemable preferred shares, $0.06, redemption value $10,000; outstanding 6,000 shares	$ 6,000
Common shareholders' equity:	
8,000 shares issued and outstanding	87,200
Total shareholders' equity	$93,200

Required

1. Compute the book value per share for the common shares, assuming all preferred dividends are fully paid up (none in arrears).
2. Compute the book value per share of the common shares, assuming that three years' preferred dividends, including the current year, are in arrears.
3. Oriental Rug's common shares recently traded at a market price of $7.75 per share. Does this mean that Oriental Rug's shares are a good buy at $7.75?

Learning Objective 6
Evaluating profitability

E9-31 Lexington Inns Limited reported these figures for 2011 and 2010 (in millions):

	2011	2010
Balance sheet		
Total assets	$15,695	$13,757
Common shares	43	388
Retained earnings	8,605	7,216
Income statement		
Operating income	$ 4,021	$ 3,818
Interest expense	219	272
Net income	1,486	1,543

Compute Lexington's return on assets and return on common shareholders' equity for 2011. Do these rates of return suggest strength or weakness? Give your reason.

Learning Objective 6
Evaluating profitability

E9-32 B.C. Pacific Company included the following items in its financial statements for 2011, the current year (amounts in millions):

Payment of long-term debt	$17,055	Dividends paid	$ 225
Proceeds from issuance of		Interest expense:	
common shares	8,425	Current year	1,437
Total liabilities:		Preceding year	597
Current year-end	32,320	Net income:	
Preceding year-end	38,023	Current year	1,882
Total shareholders' equity:		Preceding year	2,001
Current year-end	23,478	Operating income:	
Preceding year-end	14,048	Current year	4,884
Borrowings	6,582	Preceding year	4,012

Compute B.C. Pacific's return on assets and return on common equity during 2011 (the current year). B.C. Pacific has no preferred shares outstanding. Do the company's rates of return look strong or weak? Give your reason.

Learning Objective 7
Reporting cash flows from financing activities

E9-33 Use the B.C. Pacific Company data in Exercise 9-32 to show how the company reported cash flows from financing activities during 2011 (the current year). List items in descending order from largest to smallest dollar amount.

Challenge Exercises

Learning Objective ❷❸❹
Reconstructing transactions from the financial statements

E9-34 A-1 Networking Solutions Inc. began operations on January 1, 2011, and immediately issued its shares, receiving cash. A-1's balance sheet at December 31, 2011, reported the following shareholders' equity:

Common shares	$249,500
Contributed surplus	800
Retained earnings	38,000
Total shareholders' equity	$288,300

During 2011, A-1

a. Issued 50,000 common shares for $5 per share
b. Repurchased 800 of its own common shares for cancellation, paying $4 per share
c. Issued common shares for $7 each
d. Earned net income of $56,000 and declared and paid cash dividends. Revenues were $171,000 and expenses totalled $115,000.

Required

Journalize all A-1's shareholders' equity transactions during the year. A-1's entry in part (d) to close net income to Retained Earnings was:

Revenues	171,000	
Expenses		115,000
Retained Earnings		56,000

Learning Objective ❼
Reporting financing activities on the statement of cash flows

E9-35 Use the data in Challenge Exercise 9-34 to report all A-1 Networking Solutions' financing activities on the company's statement of cash flows for 2011 (journal entries and/or T-accounts may aid your approach to a solution).

Learning Objective ❷❸❹
Explaining the changes in shareholders' equity

E9-36 Startech Limited reported the following shareholders' equity data (all dollars in millions):

	December 31, 2011	December 31, 2010
Preferred shares	$ 604	$ 740
Common shares	2,390	2,130
Retained earnings	20,661	19,108

Startech earned net income of $2,960 during 2011. Common shares were issued for $20.00 each. For each account except Retained Earnings, one transaction explains the change from the December 31, 2010, balance to the December 31, 2011, balance. Two transactions affected Retained Earnings. Give a full explanation, including the dollar amount, for the change in each account.

Learning Objective ❷❸❹
Accounting for changes in shareholders' equity

E9-37 Fun City Inc. ended 2010 with 8 million common shares issued and outstanding. The average issue price was $1.50. Beginning retained earnings totalled $40 million.

- In March 2011, Fun City issued 2 million common shares at a price of $2 per share.
- In May, the company distributed a 10% stock dividend at a time when Fun City's common shares had a fair value of $3 per share.
- Then in October, Fun City's stock price dropped to $1 per share and the company repurchased 2 million shares.
- For the year, Fun City earned net income of $26 million and declared cash dividends of $17 million.

Complete the following tabulation to show what Fun City should report for shareholders' equity at December 31, 2011. Journal entries are not required.

(Amounts in millions)	Common Shares	+	Retained Earnings	−	Contributed Surplus Share Repurchase	=	Total Equity
Balance, Dec. 31, 2010	$12		$40		$0		$52
Issuance of shares 2011							
Stock dividend							
Repurchase of common shares							
Net income							
Cash dividends							
Balance, Dec. 31, 2011	$		$		$		$

Quiz

Test your understanding of shareholders' equity by answering the following questions. Select the best choice from among the possible answers given.

Q9-38 Which of the following is a characteristic of a corporation?

a. Mutual agency
b. No income tax
c. Limited liability of shareholders
d. Both a and b

Q9-39 Team Spirit Inc. issues 240,000 common shares for $5 per share. The journal entry is

	Account	Debit	Credit
a.	Cash	240,000	
	Common Shares		240,000
b.	Cash	1,200,000	
	Common Shares		240,000
	Gain on the Sale of Shares		960,000
c.	Cash	1,200,000	
	Common Shares		1,200,000
d.	Cash	1,200,000	
	Common Shares		480,000
	Contributed Surplus on Common Shares		720,000

Q9-40 Which of the following is true about stated value?

a. It represents what a share is worth.
b. It represents the original selling price for a share.
c. It is established for a share after it is issued.
d. It is an arbitrary amount assigned by a company to a share at the time of issue.
e. It may exist for common shares but not for preferred shares.

Q9-41 The contributed capital portion of shareholders' equity does not include

a. Preferred Shares
b. Contributed Surplus
c. Retained Earnings
d. Common Shares

Q9-42 Preferred shares are *least* likely to have which of the following characteristics?

a. Preference as to assets on liquidation of the corporation
b. Extra liability for the preferred shareholders
c. The right of the holder to convert to common shares
d. Preference as to dividends

Q9-43 Which of the following classifications represents the largest quantity of common shares?

a. Issued shares
b. Outstanding shares
c. Unissued shares
d. Authorized shares

Use the following information for Questions 9-44 through 9-46:

These account balances at December 31 relate to Sportaid Inc.

Accounts Payable	$ 51,700	Preferred shares, $0.10, 890,000 shares issued	89,000
Accounts Receivable	81,350	Retained Earnings	71,800
Common Shares	593,000	Notes Receivable	12,500
Bonds Payable	3,400		

Q9-44 What is total share capital for Sportaid Inc.?

a. $682,000
b. $701,345
c. $694,445
d. $753,800
e. None of the above

Q9-45 What is total shareholders' equity for Sportaid Inc.?

a. $766,300
b. $758,800
c. $753,800
d. $764,735
e. None of the above

Q9-46 Sportaid's net income for the period is $119,600 and beginning common shareholders' equity is $681,400. What is Sportaid's return on common shareholders' equity?

a. 15.7%
b. 16.4%
c. 17.5%
d. 18.6%

Q9-47 A company paid $20 per share to repurchase 500 common shares. The shares were originally issued at $15 per share. The journal entry to record the repurchase of common shares is

a.	Common Shares	10,000	
	Cash		10,000
b.	Common Shares	7,500	
	Retained Earnings	2,500	
	Cash		10,000
c.	Common Shares	5,000	
	Retained Earnings	5,000	
	Cash		10,000
d.	Retained Earnings	10,000	
	Cash		10,000

Q9-48 When common shares are repurchased for less than their stated value, the entry should include a credit to which of the following?

a. Gain on Sale of Shares
b. Loss on Sale of Shares
c. Contributed Surplus
d. Retained Earnings

Q9-49 A company repurchased 200 common shares at $55 per share. The stated value of each share is $50. The entry to record the repurchase includes which of the following?

a. Credit to Cash for $1,000
b. Credit to Common Shares for $11,000
c. Credit to Retained Earnings for $1,000
d. Debit to Retained Earnings for $1,000
e. Credit to Contributed Surplus for $11,000

Q9-50 Shareholders are eligible for a dividend if they own the shares on the date of

a. Declaration
b. Record
c. Payment
d. Issuance

Q9-51 Mario's Foods has outstanding 500 $7.00 preferred shares and 1,200 common shares. Mario's declares dividends of $14,300. The correct entry is

a.	Retained Earnings	14,300	
	Dividends Payable, Preferred		3,500
	Dividends Payable, Common		10,800
b.	Dividends Expense	14,300	
	Cash		14,300
c.	Retained Earnings	14,300	
	Dividends Payable, Preferred		7,150
	Dividends Payable, Common		7,150
d.	Dividends Payable, Preferred	3,500	
	Dividends Payable, Common	10,800	
	Cash		14,300

Q9-52 A corporation has 20,000 $8.00 preferred shares outstanding with a stated value of $2,000,000. Also, there are 20,000 common shares outstanding. If a $350,000 dividend is paid, how much goes to the preferred shareholders?

a. $0
b. $350,000
c. $160,000
d. $120,000
e. $320,000

Q9-53 Assume the same facts as in Question 9-52. What is the amount of dividends per share on common shares?

a. $9.50
b. $8.00
c. $17.50
d. $1.50
e. None of the above

Q9-54 Which of the following is *not* true about a 10% stock dividend?

a. Shareholders do not receive additional shares.
b. No assets are affected.
c. Retained Earnings decreases.
d. The market price of the share is needed to record the stock dividend.
e. Total shareholders' equity remains the same.

Q9-55 A company declares a 5% stock dividend. The debit to Retained Earnings is an amount equal to

a. The stated value of original shares
b. The excess of the market price over the original issue price of the shares to be issued
c. The book value of the shares to be issued
d. The fair value of the shares to be issued

Q9-56 Which of the following statements is *not* true about a 3-for-1 stock split?

a. Stated value is reduced to one-third of what it was before the split.
b. Total shareholders' equity increases.
c. The market price of each share will decrease.
d. A shareholder with 10 shares before the split owns 30 shares after the split.
e. Retained Earnings remains the same.

Q9-57 Franco Company's net income and interest expense are $44,000 and $4,000, respectively, and average total assets are $384,000. How much is Franco's return on assets?

a. 10.4%
b. 11.5%
c. 12.5%
d. 13.1%

Problems

(Group A)

Learning Objective 1 3 4
Explaining the features of a corporation's shares

P9-58A The board of directors of Freestroke Swim Centres Inc. is meeting to address the concerns of shareholders. Shareholders have submitted the following questions for discussion at the board meeting. Answer each question.

1. Why did Freestroke organize as a corporation if a corporation must pay an additional layer of income tax?
2. How are preferred shares similar to common shares? How are preferred shares similar to debt?
3. Freestroke repurchased common shares for $50,000 and a year later reissued them for $65,000. Explain to the shareholders whether the $15,000 excess is profit to be reported on the company's income statement. Explain your answer.
4. Would Freestroke investors prefer to receive cash dividends or stock dividends? Explain your reasoning.

Learning Objective 2
Recording corporate transactions and preparing the shareholders' equity section of the balance sheet

P9-59A The articles of incorporation from the province of Ontario authorize Challenger Canoes Inc. to issue 10,000 shares of $6 preferred shares and 100,000 common shares. In its first month, Challenger completed the following transactions:

2011		
Oct.	6	Issued 300 common shares to the lawyer for assistance with chartering the corporation. The lawyer's fee was $1,500. Debit Organization Expense.
	9	Issued 9,000 common shares to Jerry Spence and 12,000 shares to Sheila Markle in return for cash equal to the shares, market price of $5 per share. Spence and Markle are executives of the company.
	10	Issued 400 preferred shares to acquire a patent with a fair value of $40,000
	26	Issued 2,000 common shares for cash of $12,000

Required

1. Record the transactions in the journal.
2. Prepare the shareholders' equity section of the Challenger balance sheet at October 31, 2011. The ending balance of Retained Earnings is $49,000.

Learning Objective 2 4
Preparing the shareholders' equity section of the balance sheet

P9-60A Samuells' Sportswear's articles of incorporation authorize the company to issue 5,000 $5 preferred shares and 500,000 common shares. Samuells' issued 1,000 preferred shares at $100 per share. It issued 100,000 common shares for $427,000. The company's Retained Earnings balance at the beginning of 2011 was $61,000. Net income for 2011 was $80,000, and the company declared a $5 cash dividend on preferred shares for 2011.

Required

Prepare the shareholders' equity section of Samuells' Sportswear Inc.'s balance sheet at December 31, 2011. Show the computation of all amounts. Journal entries are not required.

Learning Objective 3
Fighting off a takeover of the corporation

P9-61A Calpak Winter Sports Ltd. is positioned ideally in the winter business. Located in Whistler B.C., Calpak is the only company with a distribution network for its imported goods. The company did a brisk business around the Winter Olympics held in Whistler in 2010. Calpak's recent success has made the company a prime target for a takeover. Against the wishes of Calpak's board of directors, an investment group from Vancouver is attempting to buy 51% of Calpak's outstanding shares. Board members are convinced that the Vancouver investors would sell off the most desirable pieces of the business and leave little of value. At the most recent board meeting, several suggestions were advanced to fight off the hostile takeover bid.

Required

Suppose you are a significant shareholder of Calpak Winter Sports. Write a short memo to the board to propose an action that would make it difficult for the investor group to take over Calpak. Include in your memo a discussion of the effect your proposed action would have on the company's assets, liabilities, and total shareholders' equity.

Learning Objective ❷❸❹
Measuring the effects of share issuance, repurchase of shares, and dividend transactions on shareholders' equity

P9-62A Wholegrain Health Foods Inc. is authorized to issue 5,000,000 common shares. In its initial public offering during 2007, Wholegrain issued 500,000 common shares for $7.00 per share. Over the next year, Wholegrain's share price increased and the company issued 400,000 more shares at an average price of $8.50.

During 2009, the price of Wholegrain's common shares dropped to $6.50, and the company repurchased 60,000 of its common shares to be held in Treasury.

During the five years 2007 through 2011, Wholegrain earned net income of $920,000 and declared and paid cash dividends of $140,000. A 10% stock dividend was distributed to the shareholders in 2011 on the shares outstanding. The market price was $8.00 per share when the stock dividend was distributed. At December 31, 2011, the company has total assets of $14,500,000 and total liabilities of $7,210,000.

Required

Show the computation of Wholegrain's total shareholders' equity at December 31, 2011. Present a detailed computation of each element of shareholders' equity.

Learning Objective ❷❹
Analyzing the shareholders' equity and dividends of a corporation

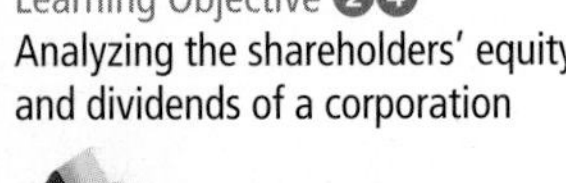

P9-63A Steeltrap Security Inc. included the following shareholders' equity on its balance sheet at December 31, 2011:

Shareholders' Equity	($ millions)
Preferred Shares:	
Authorized 20,000 shares in each class:	
$5.00 Cumulative Preferred Shares, 2,500 shares issued	$ 125,000
$2.50 Cumulative Preferred Shares, 4,000 shares issued	100,000
Common Shares:	
Authorized 80,000 shares, issued 48,000 shares	384,000
Retained earnings	529,000
	$1,138,000

Required

1. Identify the different issues of shares Steeltrap Security has outstanding.
2. What was the value at which the $2.50 Cumulative Preferred Shares were issued?
3. Suppose Steeltrap decided not to pay its preferred dividends for one year. Would the company have to pay these dividends in arrears before paying dividends to the common shareholders? Why?
4. What amount of preferred dividends must Steeltrap declare and pay each year to avoid having preferred dividends in arrears?
5. Assume preferred dividends are in arrears for 2010. Journalize the declaration of a $50,000 cash dividend for 2011. No explanation is needed.

Learning Objective ②③④
Accounting for share issuance, dividends, and share repurchase

P9-64A Exquisite Jewellery Limited reported the following summarized balance sheet at December 31, 2010:

Assets	
Current assets	$33,400
Property and equipment, net	51,800
Total assets	$85,200
Liabilities and Equity	
Liabilities	$37,800
Shareholders' equity:	
$0.50 cumulative preferred shares, 400 shares issued	2,000
Common shares, 6,000 shares issued	23,400
Retained earnings	22,000
Total liabilities and equity	$85,200

During 2011, Exquisite completed these transactions that affected shareholders' equity:

Feb. 13	Issued 5,000 common shares for $4 per share
June 7	Declared the regular cash dividend on the preferred shares
July 24	Paid the cash dividend
Aug. 9	Distributed a 10% stock dividend on the common shares. Market price of the common shares was $5 per share.
Oct. 26	Repurchased 500 common shares for cancellation, paying $6 per share
Nov. 20	Sold 200 common shares for $8 per share.

Required

1. Journalize Exquisite's transactions. Explanations are not required.
2. Report Exquisite Jewellery Limited's shareholders' equity at December 31, 2011. Net income for 2011 was $27,000.

Learning Objective ③④
Measuring the effects of dividend and share transactions on a company

P9-65A Niles Corporation completed the following selected transactions during the current year:

Mar. 3	Distributed a 10% stock dividend on the 90,000 common shares outstanding. The market price of the common shares was $25 per share.
May 16	Declared a cash dividend on the $5 preferred shares (5,000 shares outstanding)
30	Paid the cash dividends
Oct. 26	Repurchased 1,500 common shares at $24 per share
Dec. 8	Issued 1,500 common shares for $27 per share
19	Issued 10,000 common shares for $28 per share

Required

Analyze each transaction in terms of its effect (in dollars) on the accounting equation of Niles Corporation.

Learning Objective 3 6
Preparing a corporation's balance sheet; measuring profitability

P9-66A The following accounts and related balances of Kingston Appliances Inc. are arranged in no particular order.

Dividends payable	$ 3,000	Accounts payable	$ 31,000
Total assets, December 31, 2010	461,000	Retained earnings	?
Net income	36,200	Common shares,	
Common shareholders' equity		100,000 shares authorized,	
December 31, 2010	283,000	42,000 shares issued	171,000
Interest expense	3,800	Inventory	93,000
Prepaid expenses	13,000	Property, plant, and equipment, net	181,000
Patent, net	31,000	Goodwill	6,000
Accrued liabilities	17,000	Preferred shares, $4,	
Long-term note payable	79,000	25,000 shares authorized	
Accounts receivable, net	71,000	370 shares issued	37,000
Cash	44,000		

Required

1. Prepare Kingston's classified balance sheet in the account format at December 31, 2011.
2. Compute the rate of return on total assets and the rate of return on common shareholders' equity for the year ended December 31, 2011.
3. Do these rates of return suggest strength, weakness, or a midrange? Give your reason.

Learning Objective 7
Analyzing the statement of cash flows

P9-67A The statement of cash flows of Picture Perfect Photography reported the following for the year ended December 31, 2011:

Cash flows from financing activities	
Dividends [declared and] paid	$(8,300)
Proceeds from issuance of common shares	14,100
Payments of short-term notes payable	(6,900)
Payments of long-term notes payable	(1,300)
Proceeds from issuance of long-term notes payable	2,100
Repurchases of common shares at issue price for cancellation	(6,300)

Required

Make the journal entry that Picture Perfect used to record each of these transactions.

(Group B)

Learning Objective 1 2 5
Explaining the features of a corporation's shares

P9-68B Reinhart Industries Limited is conducting a special meeting of its board of directors to address some concerns raised by the shareholders. Shareholders have submitted the following questions. Answer each question.

1. Why are common shares and retained earnings shown separately in the shareholders' equity section of the balance sheet?
2. Lou Harris, a Reinhart shareholder, proposes to give some land she owns to the company in exchange for company shares. How should Reinhart Industries Limited determine the number of shares to issue for the land?
3. Preferred shares generally are preferred with respect to dividends and in the event of a liquidation. Why would investors buy *common* shares when *preferred* shares are available?
4. What does the redemption value of preferred shares require Reinhart to do?
5. One of the Reinhart shareholders owns 100 shares of Reinhart, and someone has offered to buy her shares for their book value. What formula should be used to compute the book value of her shares?

P9-69B The partners who own Bassett Furniture Co. wished to avoid the unlimited personal liability of the partnership form of business, so they incorporated as BFC Inc. The articles of incorporation from the province of Manitoba authorize the corporation to issue 10,000 $6 preferred shares and 250,000 common shares. In its first month, BFC completed the following transactions:

Learning Objective ❷
Recording corporate transactions and preparing the shareholders' equity section of the balance sheet

2011		
Jan.	3	Issued 1,000 common shares to the promoter for assistance with issuance of the common shares. The promotional fee was $10,000. Debit Organization Expense.
	6	Issued 5,000 common shares to Jo Bassett, and 3,800 shares to Mel Bassett in return for cash equal to the market price of $11 per share. (The Bassetts were partners in Bassett Furniture Co.)
	12	Issued 1,000 preferred shares to acquire a patent with a fair value of $110,000
	22	Issued 1,500 common shares for $12 cash per share

Required

1. Record the transactions in the journal.
2. Prepare the shareholders' equity section of the BFC Inc. balance sheet at January 31. The ending balance of Retained Earnings is $89,000.

P9-70B Northwest Territories Inc. has the following shareholders' equity information:

Learning Objective ❷❹
Preparing the shareholders' equity section of the balance sheet

Northwest's incorporation authorizes the company to issue 10,000 $5 cumulative preferred shares and 400,000 common shares. The company issued 1,000 preferred shares at $100 per share. It issued 100,000 common shares for a total of $370,000. The company's Retained Earnings balance at the beginning of 2011 was $40,000, and net income for the year was $90,000. During 2011, Northwest declared the specified dividend on preferred shares and a $0.50 per-share dividend on common shares. Preferred dividends for 2010 were in arrears.

Required

Prepare the shareholders' equity section of Northwest Territories Inc.'s balance sheet at December 31, 2011. Show the computation of all amounts. Journal entries are not required.

P9-71B Gary Swan Imports Inc. is located in Stratford, Ontario. Swan is the only company with reliable sources for its imported gifts. The company does a brisk business with specialty stores such as Bowrings. Swan's recent success has made the company a prime target for a takeover. An investment group from Toronto is attempting to buy 51% of Swan's outstanding shares against the wishes of Swan's board of directors. Board members are convinced that the Toronto investors would sell the most desirable pieces of the business and leave little of value.

Learning Objective ❸
Repurchasing common shares to fight off a takeover of the corporation

At the most recent board meeting, several suggestions were made to fight off the hostile takeover bid. The suggestion with the most promise is to repurchase a huge quantity of common shares. Swan has the cash to carry out this plan.

Required

1. Suppose you are a significant shareholder of Gary Swan Imports Inc. Write a memorandum to explain to the board how the repurchase of common shares would make it difficult for the Toronto group to take over Swan. Include in your memo a discussion of the effect that repurchasing common shares would have on shares outstanding and on the size of the corporation.
2. Suppose Swan management is successful in fighting off the takeover bid and later issues new shares at prices greater than the repurchase price. Explain what effect these sales will have on assets, shareholders' equity, and net income.

Learning Objective ❷❸❹
Measuring the effects of share issuance, share repurchase, and dividend transactions on shareholders' equity

P9-72B Western Agriculture Industries Ltd. is authorized by the province of Saskatchewan to issue 500,000 common shares.

In its initial public offering during 2007, Western Agricultural issued 200,000 of its common shares for $12 per share. Over the next year, Western Agricultural's common share price increased, and the company issued 100,000 more shares at an average price of $14.50.

During 2009, the price of Western Agricultural common shares dropped to $8, and Western Agricultural repurchased 30,000 of its common shares.

During the five years 2007 to 2011, Western Agricultural earned net income of $395,000 and declared and paid cash dividends of $119,000. Stock dividends of $135,000 were distributed to the shareholders in 2010, when the share market price was $10. At December 31, 2011, total assets of the company are $6,810,000, and liabilities add up to $2,924,000.

Required

Show the computation of Western Agricultural Industries Ltd.'s total shareholders' equity at December 31, 2011. Present a detailed computation of each element of shareholders' equity.

Learning Objective ❷❹
Analyzing the shareholders' equity and dividends of a corporation

P9-73B Teak Outdoor Furniture Limited included the following shareholders' equity on its year-end balance sheet at February 28, 2011:

Shareholders' Equity	
Preferred shares, $1.10 cumulative; authorized 100,000 shares in each class	
Class A—issued 75,000 shares	$ 1,500,000
Class B—issued 92,000 shares	1,840,000
Common shares; authorized 1,000,000 shares, issued 280,000 shares	6,940,000
Retained earnings	8,330,000
	$18,610,000

Required

1. Identify the different issues of shares Teak Outdoor Furniture Limited has outstanding.
2. Give the summary entries to record issuance of all the Teak shares. Assume that all the shares were issued for cash. Explanations are not required.
3. Suppose Teak did not pay its preferred dividends for three years. Would the company have to pay those dividends in arrears before paying dividends to the common shareholders? Give your reason.
4. What amount of preferred dividends must Teak declare and pay each year to avoid having preferred dividends in arrears?
5. Assume that preferred dividends are in arrears for 2010. Record the declaration of an $800,000 dividend on February 28, 2011. An explanation is not required.

Learning Objective ❷❸❹
Accounting for share issuance and dividends

P9-74B Winnipeg Enterprises Inc. reported the following summarized balance sheet at December 31, 2010:

Assets	
Current assets	$18,200
Property and equipment, net	34,700
Total assets	$52,900
Liabilities and Equity	
Liabilities	$ 6,200
Shareholders' equity:	
$5 cumulative preferred shares, 180 shares issued	1,800
Common shares, 2,400 shares issued	25,900
Retained earnings	19,000
Total liabilities and equity	$52,900

During 2011, Winnipeg Enterprise completed these transactions that affected shareholders' equity:

Feb.	22	Issued 1,000 common shares for $16 per share
May	4	Declared the regular cash dividend on the preferred shares
	24	Paid the cash dividend
July	9	Distributed a 10% stock dividend on the common shares. Market price of the common shares was $18 per share.
Nov.	19	Repurchased 800 common shares for cancellation paying $14 per share
Dec.	8	Issued 600 common shares for $15 per share

Required

1. Journalize Winnipeg Enterprise's transactions. Explanations are not required.
2. Report Winnipeg Enterprise's shareholders' equity at December 31, 2011. Net income for 2011 was $62,000.

P9-75B Cones Inc. of Baie-Comeau completed the following transactions during 2011, the company's 10th year of operations:

Learning Objective ③④
Measuring the effects of dividend and share transactions on a company

Feb.	2	Issued 10,000 common shares for cash of $250,000
Mar.	18	Repurchased 2,000 of the company's own common shares at $22 per share
Apr.	22	Sold 700 common shares for $26 per share
Aug.	6	Declared a cash dividend on the 10,000 $0.60 preferred shares
Sept.	1	Paid the cash dividends
Nov.	18	Distributed a 10% stock dividend on the 30,000 common shares outstanding. The market value of the common shares was $25 per share.

Required

Analyze each transaction in terms of its effect (in dollars) on the accounting equation of Cones Inc.

P9-76B The following accounts and related balances of Bluebird Designers Inc., as of December 31, 2011, are arranged in no particular order.

Learning Objective ③⑥
Preparing a corporation's balance sheet; measuring profitability

Cash	$ 41,000	Interest expense	$ 16,100
Accounts receivable, net	24,000	Property, plant, and equipment, net	357,000
Accrued liabilities	26,000	Common shares,	
Long-term note payable	98,000	500,000 shares authorized,	
Inventory	99,000	115,000 shares issued	112,000
Dividends payable	9,000	Prepaid expenses	10,000
Retained earnings	?	Common shareholders' equity,	
Accounts payable	131,000	December 31, 2010	222,000
Trademark net	9,000	Net income	31,000
Preferred shares, $0.50, 10,000 shares		Total assets, December 31, 2010	494,000
authorized and issued	27,000		
Goodwill	14,000		

Required

1. Prepare the company's classified balance sheet in the account format at December 31, 2011.
2. Compute the rate of return on total assets and the rate of return on common shareholders' equity for the year ended December 31, 2011.
3. Do these rates of return suggest strength or weakness? Give your reason.

Learning Objective 7
Analyzing the statement of cash flows

P9-77B The statement of cash flows of a large corporation reported the following (adapted) for the year ended December 31, 2011:

Cash flows from financing activities—*amounts in millions:*	
Cash dividends paid	$(1,854)
Issuance of common shares	1,194
Proceeds from issuance of long-term notes payable	51
Repurchase of common shares at issue price for cancellation	(3,010)
Payments of long-term notes payable	(157)

Required

Make the journal entry that the corporation would use to record each of these transactions.

Apply Your Knowledge

Decision Cases

Learning Objective 2
Evaluating alternative ways of raising capital

Case 1. Nate Smith and Darla Jones have written a computer program to advertise on text mail. They need additional capital to market the product, and they plan to incorporate their business. Smith and Jones are considering alternative capital structures for the corporation. Their primary goal is to raise as much capital as possible without giving up control of the business. Smith and Jones plan to receive 50,000 common shares of the corporation in return for the net assets of their old business. After the old company's books are closed and the assets adjusted to current fair value, Smith's and Jones's capital balances will each be $25,000.

The company's incorporation plans include an authorization to issue 10,000 preferred shares and 500,000 common shares. Smith and Jones are uncertain about the most desirable features for the preferred shares. Prior to incorporating, Smith and Jones are discussing their plans with two investment groups. The corporation can obtain capital from outside investors under either of the following plans:

- **Plan 1.** Group 1 will invest $80,000 to acquire 800 $6, nonvoting preferred shares.
- **Plan 2.** Group 2 will invest $55,000 to acquire 500 $5 preferred shares and $35,000 to acquire 35,000 common shares. Each preferred share receives 50 votes on matters that come before the shareholders.

Required

Assume that the company is incorporated.

1. Journalize the issuance of common shares to Smith and Jones. Debit each person's capital account for its balance.
2. Journalize the issuance of shares to the outsiders under both plans.
3. Assume that net income for the first year is $120,000 and total dividends are $30,000. Prepare the shareholders' equity section of the corporation's balance sheet under both plans.
4. Recommend one of the plans to Smith and Jones. Give your reasons.

Learning Objective 4
Analyzing cash dividends and stock dividends

Case 2. Suppose the balance sheet of the financial statements you are analyzing had the following shareholders' equity amounts on December 31, 2010 (adapted, in millions):

Common Shares; 1,135 shares issued	$ 278
Retained earnings	9,457
Total shareholders' equity	$ 9,735

During 2010, the corporation paid a cash dividend of $0.715 per share. Assume that, after paying the cash dividends, the corporation distributed a 10% stock dividend. Assume further that the following year the corporation declared and paid a cash dividend of $0.65 per share. Suppose you own 10,000 of this corporation's common shares acquired three years ago, prior to the 10% stock dividend. The market price of the shares was $61.02 per share before the stock dividend.

Required

1. How does the stock dividend affect your proportionate ownership in the corporation? Explain.
2. What amount of cash dividends did you receive last year? What amount of cash dividends will you receive after the above dividend action?
3. Assume that immediately after the stock dividend was distributed, the market price of the corporation's shares decreased from $61.02 per share to $55.473 per share. Does this decrease represent a loss to you? Explain.
4. Suppose the corporation announces at the time of the stock dividend that the company will continue to pay the annual $0.715 *cash* dividend per share, even after distributing the *stock* dividend. Would you expect the market price of the common shares to decrease to $55.473 per share as in Requirement 3? Explain.

Learning Objective 2 3 4 5
Evaluating financial position and profitability

Case 3. At December 31, 2011, Make It Limited reported the following data (condensed in millions):

Total assets	$65,503
Total liabilities	54,033
Shareholders' equity	11,470
Net income, as reported, for 2010	979

During 2011, Make It restated company financial statements for 2007 to 2010, after reporting that some data had been omitted from those prior-year statements. Assume that the startling events of 2011 included the following:

- Several related companies should have been, but were not, included in the Make It statements for 2010. These companies had total assets of $5,700 million, liabilities totalling $5,600 million, and net losses of $130 million.
- In January 2011, Make It's shareholders got the company to give them $2,000 million of 12% long-term notes payable in return for their giving up their common shares. Interest is accrued at year-end.

Take the role of a financial analyst. It is your job to analyze Make It Limited and rate the company's long-term debt.

Required

1. Measure Make It's expected net income for 2011 two ways:
   a. Assume 2011 net income should be the same as the amount of net income that was actually reported for 2010.
   b. Recompute expected net income for 2011 taking into account the new developments of 2011.
   c. Evaluate the likely trend of net income for the future. Discuss *why* this trend is developing. Ignore income tax.
2. Write Make It's accounting equation two ways:
   a. As actually reported at December 31, 2010
   b. As adjusted for the events of 2011
3. Measure Make It's debt ratio as reported at December 31, 2010, and again after making the adjustments for the events of 2011.
4. Based on your analysis, make a recommendation to the Debt-Rating Committee of Moody's Investor Services. Would you recommend upgrading, downgrading, or leaving Make It's debt rating undisturbed (currently, it is "high-grade")?

Ethical Issues

Ethical Issue 1. *Note:* This case is based on a real situation.
George Campbell paid $50,000 for a franchise that entitled him to market Success Associates software programs in the countries of the European Union. Campbell intended to sell individual franchises for the major language groups of Western Europe: German, French, English, Spanish, and Italian. Naturally, investors considering buying a franchise from Campbell asked to see the financial statements of his business.

Believing the value of the franchise to be greater than $50,000, Campbell sought to capitalize his own franchise at $500,000. The law firm of McDonald & LaDue helped Campbell form a corporation chartered to issue 500,000 common shares. Attorneys suggested the following chain of transactions:

a. A third party borrows $500,000 and purchases the franchise from Campbell.

b. Campbell pays the corporation $500,000 to acquire all its shares.

c. The corporation buys the franchise from the third party, who repays the loan.

In the final analysis, the third party is debt-free and out of the picture. Campbell owns all the corporation's shares, and the corporation owns the franchise. The corporation balance sheet lists a franchise acquired at a cost of $500,000. This balance sheet is Campbell's most valuable marketing tool.

Required

1. What is unethical about this situation?
2. Who can be harmed in this situation? How can they be harmed? What role does accounting play here?

Ethical Issue 2. St. Genevieve Petroleum Corp. is a public, independent oil producer. St. Genevieve's year-end is June 30. In February 2011, company geologists discovered a pool of oil that tripled the company's proven reserves. The March 31, 2011, interim financial statements did not disclose the new pool of oil. During February and March 2011, St. Genevieve's managers quietly purchased most of its shares. The June 30, 2011, annual financial statements did disclose the new pool of oil and the company's share price increased from $6 to $48.

Required

1. Did St. Genevieve's managers behave ethically? Explain your answer.
2. Identify the fundamental qualitative characteristic relevant to this situation.
3. Who was helped and who was harmed by management's actions?

Focus on Financials

Learning Objective ❷❸
Analyzing common shares and retained earnings

Gildan Activewear Ltd.
Gildan's financial statements appear in Appendix A at the end of this book. Use information in the financial statements and the notes to the financial statements to answer the following:

1. How many common shares were issued in 2009? Explain your answer.
2. Gildan has employee share purchase plans that allow eligible employees to purchase common shares of the company at a price of 90% of the current share price. What was the average current stock price of the shares purchased through the employee purchase plan in 2009?
3. What was the average price of the shares issued in 2009?
4. Did Gildan declare dividends during 2009? Explain your answer.

Focus on Analysis

Gildan Activewear Inc

Using Gildan Activewear Inc.'s financial statements that appear in Appendix A at the end of this book, answer the following: (Note: total assets were $867,700 and total shareholders' equity was $661,102 at October 2007 year-end.)

Learning Objective 5
Computing return on assets and return on equity

1. Compute Gildan's return on equity for the years ended October 4, 2009, and October 5, 2008.
2. Compute Gildan's return on assets for the years ended October 4, 2009, and October 5, 2008.
3. Interpret the relationship between return on equity and return on assets for each year and compare the results for the two years.

Group Project

Competitive pressures are the norm in business and corporate downsizing has occurred on a massive scale. Many companies or industries have pared down plant and equipment, laid off employees, or restructured operations.

Required

1. Identify all the stakeholders of a corporation. A *stakeholder* is a person or a group who has an interest (that is, a stake) in the success of the organization.
2. Identify several measures by which a company may be considered deficient and in need of downsizing. How can downsizing help to solve this problem?
3. Debate the downsizing issue. One group of students takes the perspective of the company and its shareholders, and another group of students takes the perspective of the other stakeholders of the company (the community in which the company operates and society at large).

Quick Check Answers

1. *b (10,000 shares × 15 = $150,000)*
2. *b*
3. *d ($180,000 + $100,000 = $280,000)*
4. *c ($180,000 + $200,000 + $100,000 = $480,000)*
5. *($480,000 − $5,000 = $475,000)*
6. *d [No gain or loss (for the income statement) on repurchased share transactions.]*
7. *a*
8. *b*
9. *c*
10. *a*
11. *c [annual preferred dividend = $10,000 (5,000 × $2)] [($10,000 × 4) + (100,000 × $1.25) = $165,000]*
12. *a*
13. *d*
14. *c*
15. *c*
16. *a*

Appendix 9A

Owners' Equity of Partnerships

In Chapter 1 you were introduced to the three main forms of business ownership: proprietorship, partnership, and corporation. Exhibit 1-2 on page 5 provides a concise summary of the essential features of these entities. In this appendix we expand on the basic principles of partnership accounting.

A partnership is an association of two or more persons who co-own a business. The legal life of a partnership terminates with the admission of a new partner, the withdrawal or death of a partner, voluntary dissolution by the partners, or involuntary dissolution. The essential characteristics of a partnership include the following features:

- Limited life—Life of a partnership is limited by the length of time that all partners continue to own a share of the business. When a partner withdraws from the partnership, the partnership must be dissolved.
- Unlimited personal liability—When a partnership cannot pay its debts with business assets, the partners must use their own personal assets to pay off this debt. Some professionals, such as accountants and lawyers, have organized their partnerships as limited liability partnerships (LLP) where liability is limited to partnership assets.
- Mutual agency—Every partner can bind the business to a contract within the scope of the partnership's regular business operations.
- Co-ownership of property—All assets that a partner invests in the partnership become the joint property of all the partners.
- No partnership income taxes—A partnership does not pay income taxes on the net income of the business. Instead, net income is divided among the partners and each partner is personally liable for the income taxes on his or her share of the business's net income, even if income is not withdrawn from the partnership.

A partnership may be formed by a simple oral agreement among two or more people to operate a business for profit. A partnership agreement should preferably be in writing to avoid misunderstandings and should specify information such as:

- The types of products and services to be provided
- Each partner's initial investment
- Additional investment conditions
- Each partner's rights and responsibilities
- Rules for withdrawing assets, such as cash, from the partnership
- Procedures for dissolving the partnership
- Profit and loss sharing formulas

Initial Investment by Partners

Assets contributed to a partnership are debited for their fair values. Fair values are also applied to any liabilities assumed by the partnership, and separate capital accounts and drawing accounts are maintained for each partner. Assume that on January 2, 2011, Jones and Wong establish a partnership whereby Jones contributes $80,000 cash and Wong contributes a building that has a fair value of $200,000 and an outstanding mortgage of $60,000. The journal entry to establish the partnership is as follows:

Date	Account	Debit	Credit
2011			
Jan. 2	Cash	80,000	
	Building	200,000	
	Mortgage Payable		60,000
	Jones, Capital		80,000
	Wong, Capital		140,000

Profit and loss sharing formulas may be based on contributions from the partners such as their relative investments, time and effort each plans to devote to the business, and the talents and expertise each partner brings to the business. Profits and losses must be divided equally among the partners if the partnership agreement does not specify a profit and loss formula. Usually, however, the partnership agreement will contain provisions that share profits and losses based on salary, percentage return on invested capital, and stated ratio for dividing up any balance remaining.

Assume Jones and Wong agree to share profits and losses in a 2:3 ratio. If net income during the first year of operations is $300,000, the following entry would be made to allocate net income to the partners:

2011			
Dec. 31	Income summary	300,000	
	Jones, Capital (2/5 × $300,000)		120,000
	Wong, Capital (3/5 × $300,000)		180,000
	To close income summary and allocate net income to the partners.		

Notice that we have debited an income summary account. In an earlier chapter the period-end closing process included closing all income statement accounts to the retained earnings account. An alternative approach is to close all income statement accounts to an income summary account. After closing all income statement accounts, the ending balance of the income summary account will equal the net income for the period. The income summary account would then be closed to the retained earnings account for a corporation. In this case, though, the income summary account would be closed to the partners' capital accounts, as shown in this journal entry.

If Jones and Wong withdrew cash of $30,000 and $40,000, respectively, these withdrawals would be recorded as follows:

2011			
Dec. 31	Jones, Drawings	30,000	
	Wong, Drawings	40,000	
	Cash		70,000

At the end of the period the statement of partners' equity would appear as follows:

Partners' Capital Statement
For the Year Ended December 31, 2011

	Jones	Wong	Total
Capital, January 2, 2011	$ 80,000	$140,000	$220,000
Add: Net income	120,000	180,000	300,000
	200,000	320,000	520,000
Less: Drawings	30,000	40,000	70,000
Capital, December 31, 2011	$170,000	$280,000	$450,000

Let's take a more complex example. Assume the partnership agreement specifies that Jones and Wong will receive a salary of $40,000 and $60,000, respectively, and each partner will receive an interest allowance equal to 10% of the balance of their beginning capital balance. Any remaining balance will be allocated equally.

Division of Net Income

	Jones	Wong	Total	Amount to Be Distributed
Partnership net income				$300,000
Salary allowance	$ 40,000	$ 60,000	$100,000	200,000
Interest allowance	8,000	14,000	22,000	178,000
Remainder	89,000	89,000	178,000	0
Total division	$137,000	$163,000	$300,000	

The following period-end entry transfers net income to the partners' capital accounts:

2011			
Dec. 31	Income Summary	300,000	
	Jones, Capital		137,000
	Wong, Capital		163,000
	To close Income Summary and allocate net income to the partners.		

Although Jones and Wong were allocated net incomes of $137,000 and $163,000, respectively, this does not indicate that the partners actually withdrew those amounts from the partnership. However, for income tax purposes Jones and Wong must record these amounts as income on their income tax returns whether they withdrew assets from the partnership or not.

Assume instead that the partnership had a net loss of $200,000. The net loss would be allocated as follows:

Division of Net Income

	Jones	Wong	Total	Amount to Be Distributed
Partnership net income				$(200,000)
Salary allowance	$ 40,000	$ 60,000	$ 100,000	(300,000)
Interest allowance	8,000	14,000	22,000	(322,000)
Remainder	(161,000)	(161,000)	(322,000)	0
Total division	$(113,000)	$ (87,000)	$(200,000)	

Since there was a net loss, income summary must have had a debit balance and the closing entry results in reductions to Jones's and Wong's capital accounts as follows:

2011			
Dec. 31	Jones, Capital	113,000	
	Wong, Capital	87,000	
	Income Summary		200,000

Problem

On January 2, 2011, B. Able, D. Nile, and R. Wright formed the ANW Partnership by making capital contributions of $91,875, $65,625, and $105,000, respectively. They anticipate annual net incomes of $300,000 and are considering the following alternative plans of sharing net incomes and losses: (a) equally; (b) in the ratio of their initial investments; (c) a ratio of 2:3:4; or (d) salary allowances of $45,000 to Able, $35,000 to Nile, and $50,000 to Wright; interest allowances of 10% on initial investments, with any remaining balance shared equally.

Required

1. For alternatives (a), (b), and (c), prepare a schedule showing the distribution of a $300,000 net income among the partners. Round your answers to the nearest whole dollar.
2. For alternative (d), prepare a schedule showing the distribution of a $40,000 net income.
3. Prepare a statement of changes in partners' equity showing the allocation of income to the partners, assuming they agree to use alternative (d) and the net income earned is $120,000. During the year, Able, Nile, and Wright withdraw $18,000, $20,000, and $35,000, respectively.
4. Prepare the December 31 journal entries to record the withdrawals by the partners, allocate profit or losses to the partners, and close the withdrawals accounts and the income summary using the information in Requirement 3.

Appendix 9A Solution

(1)(a) Division of Net Income

	B. Able	D. Nile	R. Wright	Total	Amount Yet to Be Distributed
Partnership net income					$300,000
Equally	$100,000	$100,000	$100,000	$300,000	0

(1)(b) Division of Net Income

Capital ratios*	0.35	0.25	0.40	1.00	

	B. Able	D. Nile	R. Wright	Total	Amount Yet to Be Distributed
Partnership net income					$300,000
Capital balance ratios*	$105,000	$75,000	$120,000	$300,000	0

*$91,875/($91,875 + $65,625 + $105,000) = 0.35

(1)(c) Division of Net Income

	B. Able	D. Nile	R. Wright	Total	Amount Yet to Be Distributed
Partnership net income					$300,000
2:3:4 ratio	$66,667	$100,000	$133,333	$300,000	0

2. Division of Net Income

	B. Able	D. Nile	R. Wright	Total	Amount Yet to Be Distributed
Partnership net income					$ 40,000
Salary allowance	$45,000	$35,000	$50,000	$130,000	(90,000)
Interest allowance	9,188	6,562	10,500	26,250	(116,250)
Remainder	(38,750)	(38,750)	(38,750)	(116,250)	0
Total division	$15,438	$ 2,812	$21,750	$ 40,000	

3. Division of Net Income

	B. Able	D. Nile	R. Wright	Total	Amount Yet to Be Distributed
Partnership net income					$120,000
Salary allowance	$45,000	$35,000	$50,000	$130,000	(10,000)
Interest allowance	9,188	6,562	10,500	26,250	(36,250)
Remainder	(12,083)	(12,083)	(12,084)	(36,250)	0
Total division	$42,105	$29,479	$48,416	$120,000	

ANW Partnership
Partners' Capital Statement
For the Year Ended December 31, 2011

	Able	Nile	Wright	Total
Capital, January 2	$ 91,875	$65,625	$105,000	$262,500
Add: Net income	42,105	29,479	48,416	120,000
	133,980	95,104	153,416	382,500
Less: Drawings	18,000	20,000	35,000	73,000
Capital, December 31	$115,980	$75,104	$118,416	$309,500

4.

Date	Account	Debit	Credit
2011			
Dec. 31	B. Able, Drawings	18,000	
	D. Nile, Drawings	20,000	
	R. Wright, Drawings	35,000	
	Cash		73,000
	To record withdrawals of cash from the partnership.		
2011			
Dec. 31	Income Summary	120,000	
	B. Able, Capital		42,105
	D. Nile, Capital		29,479
	R. Wright, Capital		48,416
	To close Income Summary and allocate net income to the partners.		
2011			
Dec. 31	B. Able, Capital	18,000	
	D. Nile, Capital	20,000	
	R. Wright, Capital	35,000	
	B. Able, Drawings		18,000
	D. Nile, Drawings		20,000
	R. Wright, Drawings		35,000
	To close the Drawings accounts to the partners' Capital accounts.		

Long-Term Investments and International Operations

10

ATCO

GROUP

LEARNING OBJECTIVES

1. **Account** for passive investments
2. **Use** the equity method for investments
3. **Understand** consolidated financial statements
4. **Account** for long-term investments in bonds
5. **Account** for international operations
6. **Report** investing transactions on the statement of cash flows

SPOTLIGHT

ATCO holds several different types of investments. Have you ever wondered what you will do with all the money you will be earning once you graduate? Maybe you will start investing through a retirement or savings plan at work, and you may make some investments on your own. The reasons people invest are for current income (interest and dividends) and appreciation of the investment's value (stocks, bonds, and real estate, for example).

Businesses like ATCO Ltd., Canadian Tire Corporation, and Great-West Life Assurance Company invest their money for the same reasons. In this chapter you'll learn how to account for investments of all types. We use ATCO Ltd. as our example company because ATCO has so many interesting investments.

You will also learn how companies like this do business across international borders and the impact that business has on their financial statements.

ATCO Ltd.
Consolidated Balance Sheet (Partial, Adapted)
December 31, 2009

	(millions of dollars)
1. **Assets**	
2. **Current assets**	
3. **Cash and short-term investments**	$1,024.6
4. Accounts receivable	480.2
5. Inventories	113.7
6. Other current assets	87.5
7. Total current assets	1706.0
8. Property, plant, and equipment	7250.0
9. Goodwill	71.2
10. Other long-term assets	927.4
	$9,954.6

Source: www.atco.com

ATCO Ltd. has been serving the people of Alberta and Canada since 1947. ATCO has grown from humble beginnings to become a multinational with operations across Canada and in the United States, South America, Europe, and Australia. Its operations include power generation; utilities including water, electricity, gas, and pipelines; work-force housing; industrial noise abatement; logistics technologies; facility management; and energy services. ATCO also either has controlling interest in or operates as joint ventures eight other enterprises. For example, Canadian Utilities Limited is a major subsidiary of ATCO. Canadian Utilities has a major subsidiary, CU Inc. Canadian Utilities and CU either have controlling interest in or operate as joint ventures more than 20 domestic and global enterprises. These investments are reflected in the various asset accounts such as inventory; property, plant, and equipment; and goodwill. The credit side of the ATCO balance sheet shows "Non-controlling interests $2,230.2 (millions)," which reflects the non-controlling or minority interests in the subsidiaries. In addition, ATCO has short-term investments.

Throughout this course, you have become increasingly familiar with the financial statements of companies such as Gildan Activewear Inc., Leon's Furniture, and Loblaw. You have seen most of the items that appear in a set of financial statements. One of your learning goals should be to develop the ability to interpret whatever you encounter in real-company statements. This chapter will help you advance toward that goal.

The first part of the chapter shows how to account for long-term investments, including a brief overview of consolidated financial statements. The second half of the chapter covers accounting for international operations.

Share Investments: A Review

Investments come in all sizes and shapes—from a few shares to the acquisition of an entire company. In earlier chapters, we discussed shares and bonds from the perspective of the company that issued the securities. In this chapter, we examine *long-term* investments.

To consider investments, we need to define two key terms. The entity that owns shares in a corporation is the *investor*. The corporation that issued the shares is the *investee*. If you own ATCO common shares, you are an investor and ATCO is the investee.

Share Prices

Investors buy more shares in transactions among themselves than directly from large companies, such as ATCO Ltd. Each share is issued only once, but it may be traded among investors many times thereafter. You may log onto the Internet or consult a newspaper to learn ATCO's current share price.

Exhibit 10-1 presents information on ATCO common shares from *The Globe and Mail Investor* for April 14, 2010. During the previous 52 weeks, ATCO shares reached a high price of $53.74 and a low price of $34.06 per share. The annual cash dividend is $1.06 per share. At the end of the previous day, the price of the shares closed at $50.34, down $0.40 from the closing price of the shares on April 13, 2010.

EXHIBIT 10-1 **Share Price Information for ATCO Ltd.**

52-Week		Stock			Net
Hi	Lo	Symbol	Div	Close	Change
$53.74	$34.06	ACO	$1.06	$50.34	–$0.40

Reporting Investments on the Balance Sheet

An investment is an asset to the investor. The investment may be short-term or long-term. *Short-term investments* are current assets and are sometimes called *temporary investments* or *marketable securities*. To be listed as short-term on the balance sheet,

- The investment must be *liquid* (readily convertible to cash).
- The investor must intend either to convert the investment to cash within one year or to use it to pay a current liability. We saw how to account for short-term investments in Chapter 5.

Investments that are not short-term are classified as **long-term investments**, a category of noncurrent assets. Long-term investments include shares and bonds that the investor expects to hold for longer than one year. Exhibit 10-2 shows the positions of short-term and long-term investments on the balance sheet.

EXHIBIT 10-2 **Reporting Investments on the Balance Sheet**

Current Assets:		
Cash	$X	
Short-term investments	X	
Accounts receivable	X	
Inventories	X	
Prepaid expenses	X	
Total current assets		$X
Long-term investments [or simply Investments]		X
Property, plant, and equipment (net)		X
Intangible assets (net)		X
Other assets		X

Assets are listed in the order of liquidity. Long-term investments are less liquid than current assets but more liquid than property, plant, and equipment. Many companies report short-term investments immediately after cash; ATCO, like many other companies, reports a total for cash plus short-term investments.

Accounting for Long-Term Investments in Shares

IFRS describe three categories of long-term share investments. The categories depend on the percentage of ownership by the investor.* They are:

1. *Investments in subsidiaries.* A subsidiary is a company controlled by another company (the parent), which is entitled to the rewards and bears the risks of the subsidiary. Generally a parent will own more than 50% of the voting shares of the subsidiary. The financial statements of the investee are consolidated with those of the investor. The private enterprise can choose to either consolidate its financial statements or account for its investment using either the equity method or the cost method. If the share investments are quoted in an active market, fair value replaces the cost method with any changes in fair value reported through net income.

2. *Investments subject to significant influence.* An investee is generally described as being subject to significant influence when the investor owns between 20% and 50% of the voting shares of the investee. Significant influence allows the investor to direct the affairs of the investee. The investor accounts for the investment using the *equity method* by which the investor's proportionate share of the investee's profits and losses are treated as income or loss by the investor. The investor's share of dividends paid by the investee are treated as a return of investment and are credited to the investment account. The private enterprise can choose to use either the equity method or the cost method. If the share investments are quoted in an active market, fair value replaces the cost method with any changes in fair value reported through net income.
3. *Passive investments.* These are investments where the investor owns less than 20% of the voting shares of the investee and thus is presumed to exercise no influence over the affairs of the investee. The investor records the investment at the price paid and adjusts the investment account for changes in fair value either through net income (fair value) or through other comprehensive income (passive). If the market price is not available, then the cost method is used. Until January 1, 2013, the investor accounts for the investment using the cost method by which the investor's share of dividends paid by the investee is treated as income by the investor. After this date, under IFRS 9, the investor will record the initial investment at cost and, at each reporting date, record any changes in fair value through either other comprehensive income or through profit or loss (net income). This chapter will illustrate IFRS 9 since many Canadian companies adopted this approach early. For the private enterprise, either the cost method can be used or fair value where any changes in fair value are reported through net income.

We begin our discussion with "passive investments."

---

*Both the International Accounting Standards Board and the Financial Accounting Standards Board in the U.S. have released an Exposure Draft that could change the way investments are accounted for in the future.

Accounting for Passive Investments

1 **Account** for passive investments

An investor may make a **passive investment** where the purpose is similar to that of short-term investing; the investor will hold the investment to earn dividend revenue and/or capital appreciation but has no long-term interest in the investee. The investor usually holds less than 20% of the voting shares and would normally play no important role in the investee's operations.

Passive investments are accounted for at fair value because the company expects to sell the investment at its current market price. *Cost* is used only as the initial amount for recording the investments. These investments are reported on the balance sheet at *fair value*.

Suppose ATCO Ltd. purchases 1,000 Agrium Inc. common shares at the market price of $50.00. ATCO intends to hold this investment for longer than a year and therefore classifies it as a passive investment. ATCO's entry to record the investment is:

2010			
July 10	Long-Term Investment (1,000 × $50.00)	50,000	
	Cash		50,000
	Purchased investment.		

ASSETS	=	LIABILITIES	+	SHAREHOLDERS' EQUITY
+50,000 −50,000	=	0	+	0

Assume that ATCO receives a $0.14 per share cash dividend on the Agrium Inc. shares. ATCO's entry to record receipt of the dividend is:

2010			
Oct. 5	Cash (1,000 × $0.14)	140	
	Dividend Revenue		140
	Received cash dividend.		

ASSETS	=	LIABILITIES	+	SHAREHOLDERS' EQUITY	+	REVENUES
140	=	0	+		+	140

What Value of an Investment Is Most Relevant?

Fair value is the amount for which you can buy or sell an investment. Because of the relevance of fair values for decision making, passive investments in shares are reported on the balance sheet at their fair value. On the balance sheet date we therefore adjust passive investments from their last carrying amount to current fair value. Assume that the fair value of the Agrium common shares is $53,000 on December 31, 2010, and the company chooses to report any changes in fair value through Other Comprehensive Income. In this case, ATCO makes the following entry to bring the investment to fair value.

2010			
Dec. 31	Long-Term Investment ($53,000 − $50,000)	3,000	
	Other Comprehensive Income		3,000
	Adjusted investment to fair value.		

The increase in the investment's fair value creates additional equity for the investor.

ASSETS	=	LIABILITIES	+	SHAREHOLDERS' EQUITY
+3,000	=	0		+3,000

The Long-Term Investment account and the Other Comprehensive Income account would appear as follows:

Long-Term Investment		Other Comprehensive Income	
50,000			
3,000			3,000

If the investment's fair value declines, the Long-Term Investment account is credited. The corresponding debit is to Other Comprehensive Income. *Unrealized* gains and losses result from changes in fair value, not from sales of investments.

Unrealized gains and unrealized losses on passive investments that occur in a fiscal year are reported in two places in the financial statements:

- *Other Comprehensive Income,* which can be reported on the *income statement* in a separate section below net income or on the *statement of comprehensive income*. For example, the Consolidated Statement of Comprehensive Income section of Leon's Furniture Limited's 2009 annual report states:

Other comprehensive income, net of tax	
Unrealized gain on financial assets arising during the year (net of tax of $45)	$223

- *Accumulated Other Comprehensive Income*, which is a separate section of shareholders' equity below retained earnings on the *balance sheet*. The Shareholders' Equity section of the Leon's Furniture Limited's 2009 balance sheet reports:

Accumulated other comprehensive income	$(142)

At December 31, 2010, ATCO would close the Other Comprehensive Income account to the shareholders' equity account Accumulated Other Comprehensive Income as follows:

2010			
Dec. 31	Other Comprehensive Income	3,000	
	Accumulated Other Comprehensive Income		3,000
	To close out the unrealized gain on the investment to Accumulated Other Comprehensive Income.		

For the private enterprise, all unrealized gains and losses flow through net income.

After the preceding entries are posted, the Other Comprehensive Income and the Accumulated Other Comprehensive Income would appear as follows:

Other Comprehensive Income		Accumulated Other Comprehensive Income	
	3,000		
3,000			3,000
			Bal. 3,000

If the company chooses to recognize the changes in fair value in the investment through income (called profit or loss), unrealized gains or unrealized losses would be used instead of other comprehensive income. These unrealized gains and losses are reported under Other Revenue on the income statement.

Selling a Passive Investment

The sale of a passive investment can result in a *realized* gain or loss. Realized gains and losses measure the difference between the amount received from the sale of the investment and the cost of the investment.

Suppose ATCO sells its investment in Agrium Inc. shares for $57,000 during 2011. ATCO would record the sale as follows:

2011			
May 19	Cash	57,000	
	Accumulated Other Comprehensive Income	3,000	
	Long-Term Investment		53,000
	Gain on Sale of Investment		7,000
	To record sale of investment.		

ASSETS	=	LIABILITIES	+	SHAREHOLDERS' EQUITY	+	GAINS
57,000 −53,000	=	0	−	3,000	+	7,000

ATCO would report the Gain on Sale of Investments as an "Other" item on the income statement. If the company chose to recognize the changes in fair value in the investment through net income, *unrealized gains and losses* would be used instead of *other comprehensive income*. This treatment is similar to the example shown for short-term investments in Chapter 5. If the cost method were used, the investment would be recorded at cost and any dividends received would be reported as income by the investor.

STOP + THINK

Suppose Ardnas Holdings Ltd. holds the following portfolio securities as long-term investments at March 31, 2011:

Shares	Cost	Current Market Value
Canadian Tire Corp.	$70,000	$47,500
Quebecor	26,000	16,000
	$96,000	$63,500

Show how Ardnas Holdings will report long-term investments on its March 31, 2011, balance sheet if the decline in value is thought not to be temporary.

Answer:

Assets	
Long-term investments	$63,500

Equity-Method Investments

We use the **equity method** to account for investments in which the investor owns 20% to 50% of the investee's shares.

Why Buy a Large Stake in Another Company?

An investor who holds less than 20% of the investee's voting shares usually plays no important role in the investee's operations. But an investor with a larger share holding—between 20% and 50% of the investee's voting shares—may significantly influence how the investee operates the business. Such an investor can probably affect the investee's decisions on dividend policy, product lines, and other important matters.

ATCO holds equity-method investments in the Barking Power Station in London, England, and in the Joffre Plant in Central Alberta. Because ATCO has a voice in shaping the policy and operations of these two power-generating facilities, some measure of their profits and losses should be included in ATCO's income.

Accounting for Equity-Method Investments

② **Use** the equity method for investments

Investments accounted for by the equity method are recorded initially at cost. Suppose NPC Corporation paid $611 million for 32% of the common shares of Bruce Power in Ontario. NPC's entry to record the purchase of this investment follows (in millions):

2010			
Jan. 2	Long-Term Investment	611	
	Cash		611
	To purchase equity investment.		

ASSETS	=	LIABILITIES	+	SHAREHOLDERS' EQUITY
+611 −611	=	0	+	0

The Investor's Percentage of Investee Income. Under the equity method, NPC, as the investor, applies its percentage of ownership (32% in our example) in recording its share of the investee's net income. Suppose Bruce reports net income of $100 million for 2010, NPC records 32% of this amount as follows (in millions):

Dec. 31	Long-Term Investment ($100 × 0.32)	32	
	Equity-Method Investment Revenue		32
	To record investment revenue.		

ASSETS	=	LIABILITIES	+	SHAREHOLDERS' EQUITY	+	REVENUES
32	=	0	+		+	32

Because of the close relationship between NPC and Bruce, the investor increases the Investment account and records Investment Revenue when the investee reports income. As Bruce's equity increases, so does the Investment account on NPC's books.

Receiving Dividends Under the Equity Method. NPC Corporation records its proportionate part of cash dividends received from Bruce. Assume Bruce declares and pays a cash dividend of $10 million. NPC receives 32% of this dividend and records this entry (in millions):

Dec. 31	Cash ($10 × 0.32)	3*	
	Long-Term Investment		3*
	To receive cash dividend on equity investment.		

*$3.2 million rounded to $3 million

ASSETS	=	LIABILITIES	+	SHAREHOLDERS' EQUITY
3 −3	=	0	+	0

The Investment account is *decreased* for the receipt of a dividend on an equity method investment. Why? Because the dividend decreases the investee's owners' equity and thus the investor's investment.

After the preceding entries are posted, NPC's Long-Term Investment account would include its equity in the net assets of Bruce as follows (in millions):

Long-Term Investment

2010	Jan. 2	Purchase	611	Dec. 31	Dividends	3
	Dec. 31	Net income	32			
	Dec. 31	Balance	640			

NPC reports long-term investments on the balance sheet and the equity-method investment revenue on the income statement as follows:

	millions
Balance sheet (partial):	
Assets	
Total current assets	$XXX
Long-term investments	640
Property, plant, and equipment, net	XXX
Income statement (partial):	
Income from operations	$XXX
Other revenue:	
Equity-method investment revenue	32
Net income	$XXX

Gain or loss on the sale of an equity-method investment is measured as the difference between the sale proceeds and the carrying amount of the investment. For example, NPC Corporation's financial statements show that the investment in Bruce Power at December 31, 2010, was $640 million. Suppose NPC sold 10% of its interest in Bruce Power on January 10, 2011, for $62 million. The entry to record the sale would be

2011			
Jan. 10	Cash	62	
	Loss on Sale of Investment	2	
	Long-Term Investment ($640 million × 0.10)		64
	Sold 10% of investment.		

ASSETS	=	LIABILITIES	+	SHAREHOLDERS' EQUITY	−	LOSSES
62 −64	=	0	+		−	2

When there has been a loss in value in an equity investment that is other than a temporary decline, the investment is written down to reflect the loss. This is different than adjusting the value to fair value, which is done whether the decline is temporary or other than temporary.

Summary of the Equity Method. The following T-account illustrates the accounting for equity-method investments.

Equity-Method Investment	
Original cost	Share of losses
Share of income	Share of dividends
Balance	

Consolidated Subsidiaries

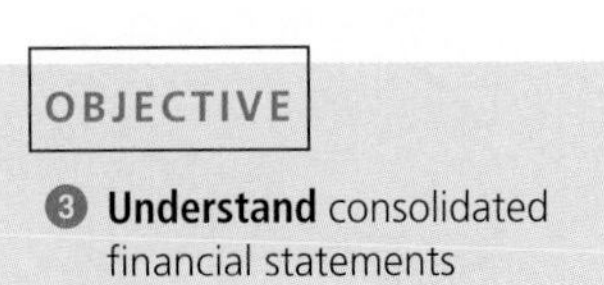

Companies buy a significant stake in another company to *influence* the other company's operations. In this section, we cover the situation in which a corporation buys enough of another company to actually *control* that company. ATCO's 100% ownership of Canadian Utilities Limited is an example.

Why Buy Another Company?

Most large corporations own controlling interests in other companies. A **controlling** (or **majority**) **interest** is the ownership of more than 50% of the investee's voting shares. Such an investment enables the investor to elect a majority of the members of the investee's board of directors and thus control the investee. The investor is called the **parent company**, and the investee company is called the **subsidiary company**. For example, ATCO Structures is a subsidiary of ATCO Ltd., the parent. Therefore, the shareholders of ATCO Ltd. control ATCO Structures, as shown in Exhibit 10-3. Exhibit 10-4 shows how ATCO operates worldwide.

EXHIBIT 10-3 Ownership Structure of ATCO Ltd. and ATCO Structures

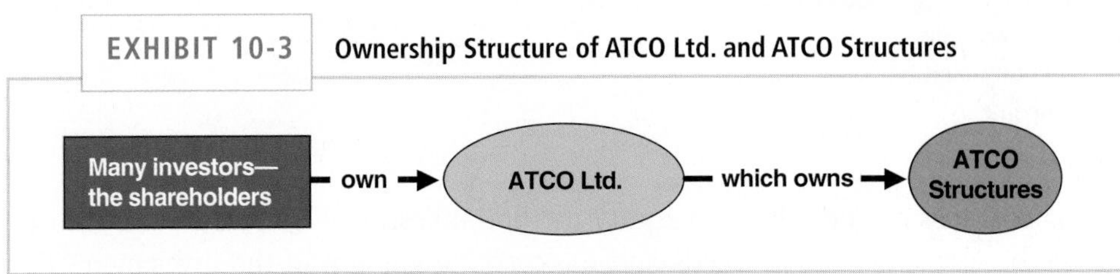

EXHIBIT 10-4 How ATCO Ltd. Operates Worldwide

ATCO Ltd. controls

- Some corporations directly
- Some corporations through Canadian Utilities Limited

ATCO groups its subsidiaries as follows:

- Power Generation
- Utilities
- Global Enterprises
  - ATCO Industrials Group

There are more than 40 companies in the ATCO Group.

Consolidation Accounting

Consolidation accounting is a method of combining the financial statements of all the companies controlled by the same shareholders. This method reports a single set of financial statements for the consolidated entity, which carries the name of the parent company. Exhibit 10-5 summarizes the accounting methods used for share investments.

Consolidated statements combine the balance sheets, income statements, and other financial statements of the parent company with those of its subsidiaries. The result is as if the parent and its subsidiaries were one company. Users can gain a better perspective on total operations than they could by examining the reports of the parent and each individual subsidiary.

In consolidated financial statements the assets, liabilities, revenues, and expenses of each subsidiary are added to the parent's accounts. For example, the balance in the Cash account of Canadian Utilities Limited is added to the balance in the ATCO Ltd. Cash account, and the sum of the two amounts is presented as a single amount in the ATCO consolidated balance sheet at the beginning of the chapter. Each account balance of a subsidiary loses its identity in the consolidated statements, which bear the name of the parent company, ATCO Ltd.

EXHIBIT 10-5 **Accounting Methods for Share Investment by Percentage of Ownership**

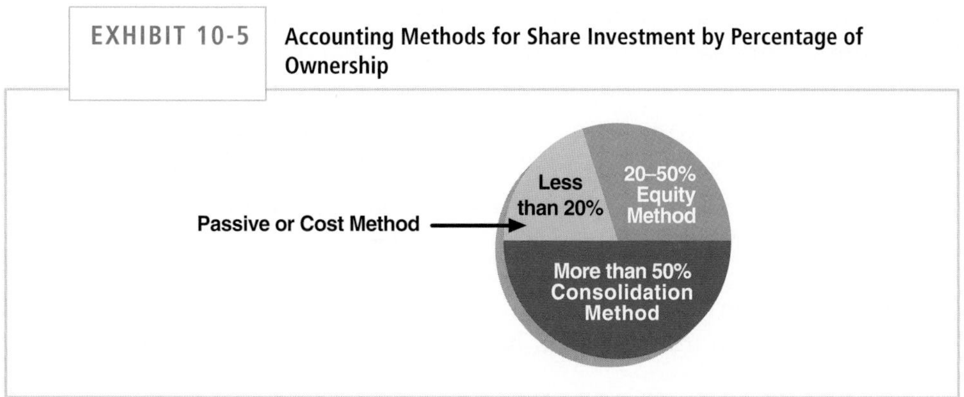

Goodwill and Non-Controlling Interests

Goodwill and Non-Controlling Interests are two accounts that only a consolidated entity can have. *Goodwill*, which we studied in Chapter 7 (see p. 361), arises when a parent company pays more to acquire a subsidiary company than the fair value of the subsidiary's net assets. As we saw in Chapter 7, goodwill is the intangible asset that represents the parent company's excess payment to acquire the subsidiary. ATCO reports goodwill of $71.2 million on its December 31, 2009, balance sheet.

Non-controlling interest arises when a parent company purchases less than 100% of the shares of a subsidiary company. For example, ATCO owns less than 100% of some of the companies it controls. The remainder of the subsidiaries' shares is a non-controlling interest to ATCO. Non-controlling interest is included within shareholders' equity on the balance sheet of the parent company. ATCO reports non-controlling interest on its balance sheet in the amount of $2,230.2 (millions).

Income of a Consolidated Entity

The income of a consolidated entity is the net income of the parent plus the parent's proportion of the subsidiaries' net income. Suppose Parent Company owns all the shares of Subsidiary S-1 and 60% of the shares of Subsidiary S-2. During the year just ended, Parent earned net income of $330,000, S-1 earned $150,000, and S-2 had a net loss of $100,000. Parent Company would report net income of $420,000, computed as follows:

	Net Income (Net Loss) of Each Company		Parent's Ownership of Each Company		Parent's Consolidated Net Income (Net Loss)
Parent Company	$ 330,000	×	100%	=	$330,000
Subsidiary S-1	150,000	×	100	=	150,000
Subsidiary S-2	(100,000)	×	60	=	(60,000)
Consolidated net income					$420,000

Intercompany sales and expenses must also be eliminated but that is a subject for an advanced accounting text.

Long-Term Investments in Bonds

OBJECTIVE

4 **Account** for long-term investments in bonds

The major investors in bonds are financial institutions, pension plans, mutual funds, and insurance companies, such as Manulife Financial Corporation. The relationship between the issuing corporation and the investor (bondholder) may be diagrammed as follows:

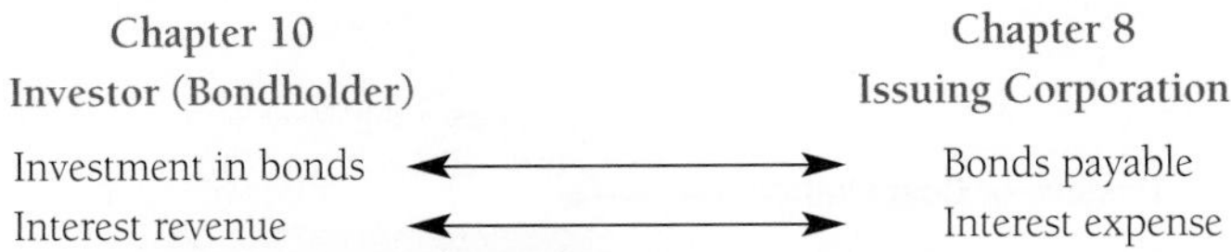

An investment in bonds is classified either as short-term (a current asset) or as long-term. Short-term investments in bonds are rare. Here, we focus on long-term investments in bonds.

Bond investments are recorded at cost. Years later, at maturity, the investor will receive the bond's face value. Often bond investments are purchased at a premium or a discount. When there is a premium or discount, **bond investments** are amortized to account for interest revenue and the bonds' carrying amount. Held-to-maturity investments are reported by the *amortized cost method*, which determines the carrying amount.

Suppose an investor purchases $100,000 of 5% Government of Canada bonds at a price of $95,735 on June 1, 2010. The bonds pay interest on June 1 and December 1. The investor intends to hold the bonds until their maturity on June 2, 2015. The bonds will be outstanding for five years (10 interest periods). The investor paid a discounted price for the bonds of $95,735 (an effective interest rate of 6%). The investor must amortize the bonds' carrying amount from cost of $95,735 up to $100,000 over their term to maturity.

ASPE

IAS 39 requires bond investments to be valued at amortized cost and also require the amortization to be calculated using the effective interest method (see Chapter 8, p. 408, and Appendix B). For the private enterprises, amortization is calculated using either the straight-line method or the effective interest method. The following are the entries for this long-term investment:

2010			
June 1	Long-Term Investment in Bonds ($100,000 × 95.735)	95,735	
	Cash		95,735
	To purchase bond investment.		
Dec. 2	Cash ($100,000 × 0.05 × 1/2)	2,500	
	Interest Revenue		2,500
	To receive semi-annual interest.		
Dec. 2	Long-Term Investment in Bonds (($95,735 × 0.06 × 1/2) − $2,500)	373*	
	Interest Revenue		373*
	To amortize bond investment.		

*Rounded

At December 31, the year-end adjustments are

2010			
Dec. 31	Interest Receivable ($100,000 × 0.05 × 1/12)	417*	
	Interest Revenue.		417*
	To accrue interest revenue.		
Dec. 31	Long-Term Investment in Bonds (($96,108 × 0.06 × 1/12) − $417)	64*	
	Interest Revenue		64*
	To amortize bond investment.		

*Rounded

This amortization entry has two effects:

1. It increases the Long-Term Investment account on its march toward maturity value.
2. It increases the interest by the amount of the increase in the carrying amount of the investment.

The financial statements at December 31, 2010, report the following for this investment in bonds:

Balance sheet at December 31, 2010:	
Current assets:	
Interest receivable	$ 417
Long-term investments in bonds ($95,735 + $373 + $64)	96,172
Property, plant, and equipment	X,XXX
Income statement for the year ended December 31, 2010:	
Other revenues:	
Interest revenue ($2,500 + $373 + $417 + $64)	$3,354

Using Insider Information to Generate a Profit

An investor who owns 20% to 50% of the voting stock of another company could use their influence to direct the affairs of the company (the investee). This also gives the investor access to all kinds of information about the investee. Lawsuits have been filed in recent years against people who had access to the investee's non-public information and used this to sell their shares at a profit.

USING LONG-TERM INVESTMENTS IN DECISION MAKING

As we have seen in this chapter, investments may be bought to earn dividend revenue and/or capital appreciation (called passive) or they are bought with the intention to either significantly influence or control the company's operations (referred to as strategic).

Manager—Managers buy investments with one or more of these intentions in mind. If the company has excess cash on hand, they may decide to invest this cash rather than have it sit in a bank account where it earns little interest. On the other hand, they may decide to buy another company's shares with a plan to be involved in the company's operations.

Investor—Investors would consider the type of investment. If the investment were passive, they would look at the statements and notes to see whether or not it increased or decreased in value and look at the amount of dividend revenue the company received. If it were a strategic investment, the investor would look at whether or not this investment generated a reasonable profit for the company.

Creditor—Creditors are always looking to see if a company would be a good candidate for a loan and whether there was sufficient profit from operations or investment income to cover current and increased interest costs.

MyAccountingLab

MID-CHAPTER SUMMARY PROBLEM

1. Identify the appropriate accounting method for each of the following long-term investment situations:
   a. Investment in 25% of investee's shares
   b. 10% investment in shares
   c. Investment in more than 50% of investee's shares
2. At what amount should the following long-term investment portfolio be reported on the June 30, 2010, balance sheet? All the investments are less than 5% of the investee's shares and are classified as passive. The investor chooses to record any changes in fair value through other comprehensive income.

Shares	Investment Cost	Fair Value
Bank of Montreal	$75,000	$52,000
Canadian Tire Corp.	24,000	31,000
Jean Coutu Group	32,000	36,000

   Journalize any adjusting entry required by these data.
3. Investor Corporation paid $67,900 to acquire a 40% equity-method investment in the common shares of Investee Corporation. At the end of the first year, Investee's net income was $80,000, and Investee declared and paid cash dividends of $55,000. What is Investor's ending balance in its Equity-Method Investment account? Use a T-account to answer.

	Parent Corporation	Subsidiary Corporation	Eliminations Debit	Eliminations Credit	Consolidated Amounts
Assets					
Cash	$ 7,000	$ 4,000			
Note receivable from Parent	—	20,000			
Investment in Subsidiary	85,000	—			
Other assets	108,000	99,000			
Total	$200,000	$123,000			
Liabilities and Shareholders' Equity					
Accounts payable	$ 15,000	$ 8,000			
Notes payable	20,000	30,000			
Common shares	120,000	60,000			
Retained earnings	45,000	25,000			
Total	$200,000	$123,000			

Answers

1. a. Equity
   b. Passive
   c. Consolidation

For investments:
Less than 20%→Passive;
20% to 50%→Equity;
Greater than 50%→Consolidation

2. Report the investments at fair value ($119,000) as follows:

Determine the fair value for each investment in the portfolio. Then create the journal entry for any change from investment cost to current fair value.

Shares	Investment Cost	Fair Value
Bank of Montreal	$ 75,000	$ 52,000
Canadian Tire	24,000	31,000
Jean Coutu Group	32,000	36,000
Totals	$131,000	$119,000

Adjusting entry:

Other Comprehensive Income ($131,000 − $119,000)	12,000	
Long-Term Investments		12,000
To adjust investments to current fair value.		

3. Equity-Method Investment

The equity-method investment T-account includes:
100% of the cost of the investment
+ 40% of the investee's net income
– 40% of the investee's cash dividends

Equity-Method Investment

Cost	67,900	Dividends	22,000**
Income	32,000*		
Balance	77,900		

*$80,000 × 0.40 = $32,000
**$55,000 × 0.40 = $22,000

Accounting for International Operations

Many Canadian companies do large parts of their business abroad. Bank of Nova Scotia, Magna International Inc., and Research In Motion Limited, among many others, are very active in other countries. Exhibit 10-6 shows the percentages of international sales for these companies.

Accounting for business activities across national boundaries is called *international accounting*. Electronic communication makes international accounting important because investors around the world need the same data to make decisions.

International trade is growing, as is the investment by Canadian companies in companies in other countries. It is the authors' belief that it is important you be provided with some exposure to the accounting for international trade and international operations.

The complexities of foreign currency translation are normally covered in an advanced accounting course. Accordingly, the following discussion is intended to provide you with a basic understanding of foreign currency translation in the context of international trade and the context of international investment by Canadian companies.

EXHIBIT 10-6 **Extent of International Business**

Company	Percentage of International Revenue
Bank of Nova Scotia	43%
Magna International Inc.	71
Research In Motion Limited	93

Foreign Currencies and Exchange Rates

Most countries use their own national currencies. An exception is a group of European nations, the European Union (EU)—France, Germany, Italy, Belgium, and others use a common currency, the *euro*, whose symbol is €. If Bombardier Inc., a Canadian company, sells aircraft to Air France, will Bombardier receive Canadian dollars or euros? If the transaction takes place in dollars, Air France must buy dollars to pay Bombardier in Canadian currency. If the transaction is in euros, Bombardier will collect euros and sell the euros for dollars.

The price of one nation's currency may be stated in terms of another country's monetary unit. This measure of one currency against another is called the **foreign-currency exchange rate**. In Exhibit 10-7, the dollar value of a euro is $1.35. This means that one euro can be bought for about $1.35. Other currencies are also listed in Exhibit 10-7.

We can convert the cost of an item in one currency to its cost in a second currency. We call this conversion a *translation*. Suppose an item costs 200 euros. To compute its cost in dollars, we multiply the amount in euros by the conversion rate: 200 euros × $1.35 = $270.00.

Two main factors determine the supply of and demand for a particular currency:

1. The ratio of a country's imports to its exports
2. The rate of return available in the country's capital markets

EXHIBIT 10-7 **Foreign-Currency Exchange Rates**

Country	Monetary Unit	Canadian Dollar Value	Country	Monetary Unit	Canadian Dollar Value
Hong Kong	Dollar	$0.129	Japan	Yen (¥)	0.010
France	Euro (€)	1.35	Mexico	Peso (P)	0.823
Germany	Euro (€)	1.35	United Kingdom	Pound (£)	1.544
Italy	Euro (€)	1.35	United States	Dollar ($)	1.00

Source: The Bank of Canada, April 9, 2010.

The Import/Export Ratio. Japanese exports often surpass Japan's imports. Customers of Japanese companies must buy yen (the Japanese unit of currency) in the international currency market to pay for their purchases. This strong demand drives up the price—the foreign exchange rate—of the yen. Canada also exports more than it imports. In contrast, the United States imports more goods than it exports.

The Rate of Return. The rate of return available in a country's capital markets affects the amount of investment funds flowing into the country. When rates of return are high in a politically stable country such as Canada, international investors buy shares, bonds, and real estate in that country. This activity increases the demand for the nation's currency and drives up its exchange rate.

Currencies are often described as *strong* or *weak*. The exchange rate of a **strong currency** is rising relative to other nations' currencies. The exchange rate of a **weak currency** is falling relative to other currencies.

The Bank of Canada's Web site listed the exchange rate for the British pound as $1.67 on January 15, 2010. On March 15, 2010, that rate was $1.54. We would say that the dollar has risen against—is stronger than—the British pound. Because the pound has become less expensive, the dollar now buys more pounds. A stronger dollar would make travel to England more attractive to Canadians.

Managing Cash in International Transactions. International transactions are common. Linamar Corporation, the original equipment automobile components supplier based in Guelph, Ontario, is an example. Linamar has factories in Canada, the United States, Mexico, China, Korea, and Europe. Sales are made to companies outside the Linamar family of companies and between Linamar companies in these geographic areas. For example, a transmission might be manufactured in Canada for General Motors in the United States using parts manufactured by Linamar in Europe. The European parts would be priced in euros while the transmission could be priced in Canadian dollars and sold to GM for U.S. dollars.

Do We Collect Cash in Dollars or in a Foreign Currency? Do We Pay in Dollars or in a Foreign Currency?

Linamar owns Skyjack Inc., which manufactures the Skyjack, a self-propelled scissor-type elevating work platform used mainly in construction. Consider the sale of an SJ8243 Skyjack to All-England Construction Ltd. for $65,000 Canadian. The sale can be conducted in dollars or in pounds. If All-England Construction agrees to pay in dollars, Skyjack avoids the complication of dealing in a foreign currency, and the transaction is the same as selling to Devlan Construction Ltd. across town. Suppose that All-England Construction demands to pay in pounds and that Skyjack agrees to receive pounds instead of dollars.

Because Skyjack will need to convert the pounds to dollars, the transaction poses a challenge. What if the pound loses value—weakens, taking fewer dollars to obtain each pound—before Skyjack collects from All-England Construction? In this case, Skyjack will not earn as much as expected on the sale. The following example shows how to account for international transactions that result in the receipt of a foreign currency. It also shows how to measure the effects of such transactions on a company's cash position and profits.

Skyjack sells goods to All-England Construction Ltd. for a price of £10,000 on January 15, 2010. On that date, a pound was worth $1.67, as quoted on the Bank of Canada exchange rate tables. On March 15, 2010, suppose the pound has weakened against the dollar so that a pound is worth $1.54. Skyjack receives £10,000 from All-England Construction on March 8 but the dollar value of Skyjack's receipt is $15,400 (£10,000 × $1.54), which is $1,300 less than expected. Skyjack ends up earning less than hoped for on the transaction. The following journal entries show how Skyjack would account for these transactions:

OBJECTIVE

5 Account for international operations

2010			
Jan. 15	Accounts Receivable—All-England Construction (£10,000 × $1.67)	16,700	
	Sales Revenue		16,700
	Sale on account.		

ASSETS	=	LIABILITIES	+	SHAREHOLDERS' EQUITY	+	REVENUES
16,700	=	0	+		+	16,700

Mar. 15	Cash (£10,000 × $1.54)	15,400	
	Foreign-Currency Transaction Loss	1,300	
	Accounts Receivable—All-England Construction		16,700
	Collection on account.		

ASSETS	=	LIABILITIES	+	SHAREHOLDERS' EQUITY	–	LOSSES
15,400 –16,700	=	0	+		–	1,300

If Skyjack had required All-England Construction to pay at the time of the sale, Skyjack would have received pounds worth $16,700. But by waiting the normal 60-day collection period to receive cash, Skyjack exposed itself to *foreign-currency exchange risk*, the risk of loss in an international transaction. In this case, Skyjack experienced a $1,300 foreign-currency transaction loss and received $1,300 less cash than expected, as shown in the collection entry.

If the pound had increased in value, Skyjack would have experienced a foreign-currency transaction gain. When a company holds a receivable denominated in a foreign currency, it wants the foreign currency to remain strong so that it can be converted into more dollars. Unfortunately, that did not occur for Skyjack.

Purchasing from a foreign company may also expose a company to foreign-currency exchange risk. To illustrate, assume Linamar buys a milling machine from Gesellschaft Ltd., a Swiss company. After lengthy negotiations, the two companies decide on a price of 20,000 Swiss francs. On January 11, 2010, when Linamar receives the machine, the Swiss franc is quoted in international currency markets at $1.02 Canadian. When Linamar pays two months later, on March 2, 2010, the Swiss franc has weakened against the dollar—decreased in value to $0.96. Linamar would record the purchase and payment as follows:

2010			
Jan. 11	Property, plant, and equipment (20,000 Swiss francs × $1.02)	20,400	
	Accounts Payable—Gesellschaft Ltd.		20,400
	Purchase on account.		

ASSETS	=	LIABILITIES	+	SHAREHOLDERS' EQUITY
20,400	=	20,400	+	0

Mar. 2	Accounts Payable—Gesellschaft Ltd.	20,400	
	Cash (20,000 Swiss francs × $0.96).		19,200
	Foreign-Currency Transaction Gain		1,200
	Payment on account.		

ASSETS	=	LIABILITIES	+	SHAREHOLDERS' EQUITY	+	GAINS
−19,200	=	−20,400	+		+	1,200

The Swiss franc could have strengthened against the dollar, in which case Linamar would have had a foreign-currency transaction loss. A company with a payable denominated in a foreign currency hopes that the dollar gets stronger: The payment then costs fewer dollars.

Reporting Gains and Losses on the Income Statement

The Foreign-Currency Transaction Gain account is the record of the gains on transactions settled in a currency other than the dollar. Likewise, the Foreign-Currency Transaction Loss account shows the amount of the losses on transactions conducted in foreign currencies. The company reports the *net amount* of these two accounts on the income statement as Other Revenues and Gains, or Other Expenses and Losses, as the case may be. For example, Linamar, on its consolidated statements, would combine the $1,300 foreign-currency loss and the $1,200 gain and report the net loss of $100 on the income statement as part of Selling, General, and Administrative Expenses.

These gains and losses are not included in Cost of Sales because they arise from buying and selling foreign currencies, not from the main line of the company's business (in the case of Linamar, selling automobile components and Skyjacks). Companies seek to minimize their foreign-currency losses by a strategy called *hedging*.

Should We Hedge Our Foreign-Currency Transaction Risk?

One way for Canadian companies to avoid foreign-currency transaction losses is to insist that international transactions be settled in dollars. This requirement puts the burden of currency translation on the foreign party. But this approach may alienate customers and decrease sales. Another way for a company to protect itself is by **hedging**. Hedging means to protect oneself from losing money in one transaction by engaging in a counterbalancing transaction.

A Canadian company selling goods to be collected in Mexican pesos expects to receive a fixed number of pesos in the future. If the peso is losing value, the Canadian company would expect the pesos to be worth fewer dollars than the amount of the receivable—an expected loss situation.

The Canadian company may have accumulated payables stated in a foreign currency in the normal course of its business, such as the amount payable by Linamar to the Swiss company. Losses on the receipt of pesos may be offset by gains on the payment of Swiss francs to Gesellschaft Ltd. Most companies do not have equal amounts of receivables and payables in foreign currency. To obtain a more precise hedge, some companies buy *futures contracts*, which are contracts for foreign currencies to be received in the future. Futures contracts can effectively create a payable to offset a receivable exactly, and vice versa. Many companies that do business internationally use hedging techniques. Accounting for hedges is covered in advanced accounting courses.

Consolidation of Foreign Subsidiaries

A Canadian company, such as Linamar, with a foreign subsidiary must consolidate the subsidiary's financial statements into its own statements for reporting to the public. The consolidation of a foreign subsidiary poses two special challenges:

1. Some countries outside Canada specify accounting treatments that differ from Canadian accounting principles. For reporting to the Canadian public, accountants must first bring the subsidiary's statements into conformity with IFRS.
2. The subsidiary statements are expressed in a foreign currency. First, we must translate the subsidiary statements into dollars, then the two companies' statements can be consolidated.

The process of translating a foreign subsidiary's financial statements into dollars usually creates a *foreign-currency translation adjustment*. This item appears in the financial statements of most multinational companies and is reported as other comprehensive income in a separate section below net income or on the statement of comprehensive income. Linamar Corporation's December 31, 2008, annual report shows a cumulative translation adjustment in the amount of $28.6 million on the statement of comprehensive income.

A translation adjustment arises due to changes in the foreign exchange rate over time. In general,

- *Assets* and *liabilities* are translated into dollars at the current exchange rate on the date of the statements.
- Income and expenses are translated into dollars at the current exchange rates on the dates of the transactions.

International Accounting Standards

In this text, we focus on the accounting principles that are generally accepted in Canada. Most accounting methods are consistent throughout the world. Double-entry accounting, the accrual system, and the basic financial statements are used worldwide. Differences, however, do exist among countries, as shown in Exhibit 10-8.

In discussing depreciation (Chapter 7), we emphasized that in Canada, the methods used for reporting to tax authorities differ from the methods used for reporting to

EXHIBIT 10-8 **Some International Accounting Differences**

Country	Inventories	Research and Development Costs	Goodwill
Canada	LIFO is unacceptable	Expense research costs Some development costs may be capitalized	Record an impairment
United States	Specific unit cost, FIFO, LIFO, weighted-average	Expensed as incurred	Similar to Canada
Germany	Similar to U.S.	Similar to U.S.	Amortized over 5 years
Japan	Similar to U.S.	May be capitalized and amortized over 5 years	Amortized over 5 years

shareholders. However, tax reporting and shareholder reporting are identical in many countries. For example, France has a "Plan Compatible," which specifies that a National Uniform Chart of Accounts be used for both tax returns and reporting to shareholders. German financial reporting is also determined primarily by tax laws.

USING INTERNATIONAL OPERATIONS IN DECISION MAKING

Many companies are involved with international operations, whether it is through transactions with a foreign company or because the company has a subsidiary in a foreign country. Either way, foreign currency exchange gains or losses affect a company's financial statements.

Manager—Managers seek ways to minimize the effects of foreign currency exchange risk when doing business with international companies. In the case of a subsidiary in foreign operations, managers are required to follow the rules of accounting when consolidating the financial statements and, as a result, a foreign exchange gain or loss may occur.

Investor—Investors examine the effects of foreign exchange gains or losses on the company's profits and whether or not the company is worth investing in.

Creditor—Creditors look to see if the company is able to handle the risk of foreign exchange gains or losses particularly if it involves repaying a loan.

Using the Statement of Cash Flows

OBJECTIVE

6 **Report** investing transactions on the statement of cash flows

Investing activities include many types of transactions. In Chapter 7, we covered investing transactions in which companies purchase and sell long-term assets, such as property, plant, and equipment. In this chapter, we examined another type of investing activity actually called *investment*. The purchase and sale of investments in shares and bonds of other companies are also investing activities reported on the statement of cash flows.

Investing activities are usually reported on the statement of cash flows as the second category, after operating activities and before financing activities. Exhibit 10-9 provides excerpts from ATCO Ltd.'s statement of cash flows. During 2009, ATCO

EXHIBIT 10-9 **ATCO Ltd. Consolidated Statement of Cash Flows**

ATCO Ltd.
Statement of Cash Flows (Partial, adapted)
For the Year Ended December 31, 2009

	(in millions)
Cash flows—Investing activities	
Purchase of property, plant, and equipment	$(922.5)
Proceeds (costs) on disposal of other property, plant, and equipment	15.1
Contributions by utility customers for extensions to plant	114.1
Purchase of intangibles	(64.3)
Changes in noncash working capital	(30.9)
Other	15.8
Cash used for investing activities	$(872.7)

spent $922.5 million on new property, plant, and equipment. Overall, ATCO invested $872.7 million. This is one reason ATCO stays ahead of competitors: it invests in the future.

SUMMARY OF CHAPTER 9

Learning Objective ❶: Account for passive investments

Passive investments are recorded at cost but reported on the balance sheet at fair value. Any changes in value are recorded under "other comprehensive income" or through net income (profit or loss). The cost method is used for investments where the market price is not available.

Learning Objective ❷: Use the equity method for investments

If the company **owns between 20% and 50%** of the voting shares of the investee, the **equity method** is used to account for the investment. This means that the investor recognizes their share of the investee's net income as their own. The investor's share of dividends is treated as a return of investment.

Learning Objective ❸: Understand consolidated financial statements

If the company **owns more than 50%** of the investee's shares, the financial statements of the investee are **consolidated** (combined) with those of the investor. The result is as if the parent and subsidiary are one company. Goodwill and Non-Controlling Interest are two accounts that only a consolidated entity would have. Goodwill results when a company pays more for the subsidiary company than the fair value of the subsidiary's net assets. **Non-controlling interest** occurs when a company buys less than 100% of the company they control.

Learning Objective ❹: Account for long-term investments in bonds

A company may buy a **long-term investment** in bonds. The company would initially record this type of investment at the price paid. It would be accounted for using the amortized cost method.

Learning Objective ❺: **Account for international operations**

Since many Canadian companies conduct business outside of Canada, the effects of **foreign-currency exchange rates**, resulting from a transaction, are recorded. Gains and losses resulting from foreign-currency exchange rates are reported in the income statement. If a company operates a **subsidiary** in a foreign country, the financial statements of the subsidiary must be translated into the reporting company's currency before the financial statements are consolidated.

Learning Objective ❻: **Report investing transactions on the statement of cash flows**

On the statement of cash flows, long-term investments are reported under investing activities.

END-OF-CHAPTER SUMMARY PROBLEM

MyAccountingLab

Translate the balance sheet of the Brazilian subsidiary of The Jean Shop Corporation, a Canadian company, into dollars. When The Jean Shop acquired this subsidiary, the exchange rate of the Brazilian currency, the real, was $0.45. The average exchange rate applicable to retained earnings is $0.52. The real's current exchange rate is $0.53.

Before performing the translation, predict whether the translation adjustment will be positive or negative. Does this situation generate a foreign-currency translation gain or loss? Give your reasons.

	Reals
Assets	900,000
Liabilities	600,000
Shareholders' equity:	
Common shares	30,000
Retained earnings	270,000
	900,000

Answers

Translation of foreign-currency balance sheet:

This situation will generate a *positive* translation adjustment, which is like a gain. The gain occurs because the real's current exchange rate, which is used to translate net assets (assets minus liabilities), exceeds the historical exchange rates used for shareholders' equity.

The calculation follows.

The current exchange rate is higher than the rate in effect at the time of the investment purchase. This results in an increase in the value of the investment and, accordingly, a gain.

	Reals	Exchange Rate	Dollars
Assets	900,000	$0.53	$477,000
Liabilities	600,000	0.53	$318,000
Shareholders' equity:			
Common shares	30,000	0.45	13,500
Retained earnings	270,000	0.52	140,400
Foreign-currency translation adjustment	—		5,100
	900,000		$477,000

The foreign-currency translation adjustment is the "plug" figure that makes total assets equal total liabilities plus shareholders' equity after translation. A positive figure is like a foreign-currency translation gain. A negative figure is like a foreign-currency translation loss.

Review Long-Term Investments and International Operations

Quick Check (Answers are given on page 553.)

1. A company's investment in less than 1% of GE's shares, which it expects to hold for two years and then sell, is which type of investment?
   a. Held-for-trading
   b. Equity
   c. Passive
   d. Consolidation
2. DuBois Corporation purchased a passive investment in 1,000 shares of Scotiabank (BNS) for $31 per share. On the next balance sheet date, BNS is quoted at $35 per share. DuBois' *balance sheet* should report
   a. Unrealized loss of $4,000
   b. Unrealized gain of $31,000
   c. Investments of $31,000
   d. Investments of $35,000
3. Use the DuBois Corporation data in Question 2. DuBois' *income statement* should report
   a. Unrealized gain of $4,000
   b. Unrealized loss of $4,000
   c. Investments of $31,000
   d. Nothing because DuBois hasn't sold the investment
4. Use the DuBois Corporation data in Question 2. DuBois sold the Scotiabank shares for $40,000 two years later. DuBois' *income statement* should report
   a. Unrealized gain of $4,000
   b. Gain on sale of $9,000
   c. Gain on sale of $5,000
   d. Investments of $40,000
5. Alexander Moving & Storage Inc. paid $100,000 for 20% of the common shares of Sellers Ltd. Sellers earned net income of $50,000 and paid dividends of $25,000. The carrying value of Alexander's investment in Sellers is
   a. $100,000
   b. $105,000
   c. $125,000
   d. $150,000
6. Tarrant Inc. owns 80% of Rockwall Corporation, and Rockwall owns 80% of Kaufman Company. During 2011, these companies' net incomes are as follows before any consolidations:
   - Tarrant, $100,000
   - Rockwall, $68,000
   - Kaufman, $40,000

   How much net income should Tarrant report for 2011?
   a. $100,000
   b. $164,000
   c. $180,000
   d. $204,000
7. TRULINE Inc. holds an investment in Manulife bonds that pay interest each June 30. TRULINE's *balance sheet* at December 31 should report
   a. Interest receivable
   b. Interest payable
   c. Interest revenue
   d. Interest expense
8. You are going on a vacation to France, and you buy euros for $1.60. On your return you cash in your unused euros for $1.50. During your vacation
   a. The dollar lost value
   b. The euro rose against the dollar
   c. The euro gained value
   d. The dollar rose against the euro
9. Grey County, Ontario, purchased earth-moving equipment from a U.S. company. The cost was $1,000,000 in U.S. dollars, and the U.S. dollar was quoted at $1.25. A month later, Grey County paid its debt, and the Canadian dollar was quoted at $1.27. What was Grey County's cost of the equipment?
   a. $20,000
   b. $1,250,000
   c. $950,000
   d. $1,020,000

10. ATCO owns numerous foreign subsidiary companies. When ATCO consolidates its Australian subsidiary, ATCO should translate the subsidiary's assets into Canadian dollars at the
    a. Historical exchange rate when ATCO purchased the Australian company
    b. Average exchange rate during the period ATCO owned the Australian subsidiary
    c. Current exchange rate
    d. None of the above. There's no need to translate the subsidiary's assets into Canadian dollars.

Accounting Vocabulary

bond investments Bonds and notes that an investor intends to hold until maturity. (p. 524)

consolidated statements Financial statements of the parent company plus those of majority-owned subsidiaries as if the combination were a single legal entity. (p. 523)

controlling (majority) interest Ownership of more than 50% of an investee company's voting shares. (p. 522)

equity method The method used to account for investments in which the investor has 20–50% of the investee's voting shares and can significantly influence the decisions of the investee. (p. 519)

foreign-currency exchange rate The measure of one country's currency against another country's currency. (p. 529)

hedging To protect oneself from losing money in one transaction by engaging in a counterbalancing transaction. (p. 532)

long-term investments Any investment that does not meet the criteria of a short-term investment; any investment that the investor expects to hold for longer than a year. (p. 515)

majority interest Ownership of more than 50% of an investee company's voting shares. (p. 522)

non-controlling interest A subsidiary company's equity that is held by shareholders other than the parent company. (p. 523)

parent company An investor company that owns more than 50% of the voting shares of a subsidiary company. (p. 522)

passive investments All investments held to earn dividend revenue and/or capital appreciation. (p. 516)

strong currency A currency whose exchange rate is rising relative to other nations' currencies. (p. 529)

subsidiary company An investee company in which a parent company owns more than 50% of the voting shares. (p. 522)

weak currency A currency whose exchange rate is falling relative to other nations' currencies. (p. 529)

Assess Your Progress

Make the grade with MyAccountingLab: The exercises and problems in this chapter can be found on MyAccountingLab at www.myaccountinglab.com. You can practise them as often as you want, and they feature step-by-step guided solutions to help you find the right answer.

Short Exercises

Learning Objective 1
Accounting for a passive investment; unrealized gain or loss

S10-1 Assume Knowlton Holdings Ltd. completed these long-term passive investment transactions during 2011:

2011		
Feb.	10	Purchased 300 shares of BCE, paying $25 per share. Knowlton intends to hold the investment for the indefinite future.
Dec.	1	Received a cash dividend of $0.36 per share on the BCE shares.
Dec.	31	Adjusted the BCE investment to its current fair value of $7,000.

1. Journalize Knowlton investment transactions. Explanations are not required.
2. Show how to report the investment and any unrealized gain or loss on Knowlton's balance sheet at December 31, 2011. Ignore income tax.

Learning Objective 1
Accounting for the sale of a passive investment

S10-2 Use the data given in Short Exercise 10-1. On May 19, 2012, Knowlton sold its investment in BCE shares for $26 per share.

1. Journalize the sale. No explanation is required.
2. How does the gain or loss that you recorded here differ from the gain or loss that was recorded at December 31, 2011?

Learning Objective 2
Accounting for a 40% investment in another company

S10-3 Suppose on February 1, 2011, General Motors paid $41 million for a 40% investment in ABC Ltd., an auto parts manufacturer. Assume ABC earned net income of $6 million and paid cash dividends of $2 million during 2011.

1. What method should General Motors use to account for the investment in ABC? Give your reason.
2. Journalize these three transactions on the books of General Motors. Show all amounts in millions of dollars, and include an explanation for each entry.
3. Post to the Long-Term Investment T-account. What is its balance after all the transactions are posted?

Learning Objective 2
Accounting for the sale of an equity-method investment

S10-4 Use the data given in Short Exercise 10-3. Assume that in November 2012, General Motors sold half its investment in ABC to Toyota. The sale price was $14 million. Compute General Motors' gain or loss on the sale.

Learning Objective 3
Understanding consolidated financial statements

S10-5 Answer these questions about consolidation accounting:

1. Define *parent company*. Define *subsidiary company*.
2. How do consolidated financial statements differ from the financial statements of a single company?
3. Which company's name appears on the consolidated financial statements? How much of the subsidiary's shares must the parent own before reporting consolidated statements?

Learning Objective 3
Understanding goodwill and minority interest

S10-6 Two accounts that arise from consolidation accounting are Goodwill and Non-Controlling Interest.

1. What is *goodwill*, and how does it arise? Which company reports goodwill, the parent or the subsidiary? Where is goodwill reported?
2. What is non-controlling interest and which company reports it, the parent or the subsidiary? Where is non-controlling interest reported?

Learning Objective 4
Working with a bond investment

S10-7 Suppose Prudential Bache (PB) buys $1,000,000 of CitiCorp bonds at a price of 101. The CitiCorp bonds pay cash interest at the annual rate of 7% and mature at the end of five years.

1. How much did PB pay to purchase the bond investment? How much will PB collect when the bond investment matures?
2. How much cash interest will PB receive each year from CitiCorp?
3. Will PB's annual interest revenue on the bond investment be more or less than the amount of cash interest received each year? Give your reason.
4. Compute PB's first-year interest revenue on this bond investment. Use the effective interest of 6.75% to amortize the investment.

Learning Objective 4
Recording bond investment transactions

S10-8 Return to Short Exercise 10-7, the Prudential Bache (PB) investment in CitiCorp bonds. Journalize on PB's books:

a. Purchase of the bond investment on January 2, 2011. PB expects to hold the investment to maturity.
b. Receipt of annual cash interest on December 31, 2011
c. Amortization of the bonds on December 31, 2011
d. Collection of the investment's face value at the maturity date on January 2, 2016. (Assume the receipt of 2015 interest and the amortization of bonds for 2015 have already been recorded, so ignore these entries.)

S10-9 Suppose Coca-Cola Canada (CCC) sells soft-drink syrup to a Russian company on September 14. CCC agrees to accept 2,000,000 Russian rubles. On the date of sale, the ruble is quoted at $0.0346. CCC collects half the receivable on October 19, when the ruble is worth $0.0339. Then, on November 10, when the foreign-exchange rate of the ruble is $0.035, CCC collects the final amount.

Journalize these three transactions for CCC.

Learning Objective 5
Accounting for transactions stated in a foreign currency

S10-10 Shipp Belting Ltd. sells goods for 1,000,000 Mexican pesos. The foreign-exchange rate for a peso is $0.085 on the date of sale, July 31, 2011. Shipp Belting then collects cash on August 28, when the exchange rate for a peso is $0.089. Record Shipp's cash collection.

Shipp Belting buys inventory for 20,000 Swiss francs. A Swiss franc costs $1.0826 on the purchase date, August 25, 2011. Record Shipp Belting's payment of cash on September 29, 2011, when the exchange rate for a Swiss franc is $1.0831.

In these two scenarios, which currencies strengthened and which weakened?

Learning Objective 5
Accounting for transactions stated in a foreign currency

S10-11 Exhibit 10-8, page 533, outlines some differences between accounting in Canada and accounting in other countries. Canadian companies conduct a lot of business with American companies. But there are important differences between American and Canadian accounting. In your own words, describe the differences and similarities for inventories, goodwill, and research and development among Canada, the United States, Japan, and Germany.

Learning Objective 5
International accounting differences

S10-12 Companies divide their cash flows into three categories for reporting on the statement of cash flows.

1. List the three categories of cash flows in the order they appear on the statement of cash flows. Which category of cash flows is most closely related to this chapter?
2. Identify two types of transactions that companies report as cash flows from investing activities.

Learning Objective 6
Reporting cash flows

Exercises

E10-13 Journalize the following long-term passive investment transactions of Solomon Brothers Department Stores:

a. Purchased 400 shares of Royal Bank of Canada at $40 per share, with the intent of holding the shares for the indefinite future
b. Received cash dividend of $0.50 per share on the Royal Bank of Canada investment
c. At year-end, adjusted the investment account to current fair value of $35 per share
d. Sold the shares for the market price of $30 per share

Learning Objective 1
Journalizing transactions for an investment

E10-14 Dow-Smith Ltd. bought 3,000 common shares of Shoppers Drug Mart at $50, 600 common shares of Bank of Montreal (BMO) at $42.50, and 1,400 common shares of EnCana at $93.36, all as passive investments. At December 31, TSX Online reports Shoppers' shares at $48.05, BMO's shares at $31.25, and EnCana's shares at $56.96.

Learning Objective 1
Accounting for long-term investments

Required

1. Determine the cost and the fair value of the long-term investment portfolio at December 31.
2. Record Dow-Smith's adjusting entry at December 31.
3. What would Dow-Smith report on its income statement and balance sheet for the information given? Make the necessary disclosures. Ignore income tax.

E10-15 Research In Motion (RIM) owns equity-method investments in several companies. Suppose RIM paid $1,000,000 to acquire a 25% investment in Thai Software Company. Thai Software reported net income of $640,000 for the first year and declared and paid cash dividends of $420,000.

1. Record the following in RIM's journal: (a) purchase of the investment, (b) RIM's proportion of Thai Software's net income, and (c) receipt of the cash dividends.
2. What is the ending balance in RIM's investment account?

Learning Objective 2
Accounting for transactions under the equity method

Learning Objective 2
Measuring gain or loss on the sale of an equity-method investment

E10-16 Without making journal entries, record the transactions of Exercise 10-15 directly in the RIM account, Long-Term Investment in Thai Software. Assume that after all the noted transactions took place, RIM sold its entire investment in Thai Software for cash of $2,700,000. How much is RIM's gain or loss on the sale of the investment?

Learning Objective 2
Applying the appropriate accounting method for a 25% investment

E10-17 Oaktree Financial Inc. paid $500,000 for a 25% investment in the common shares of eTrav Inc. For the first year, eTrav reported net income of $200,000 and at year-end declared and paid cash dividends of $100,000. On the balance sheet date, the fair value of Oaktree's investment in eTrav shares was $384,000.

Required

1. Which method is appropriate for Oaktree Financial to use in accounting for its investment in eTrav? Why?
2. Show everything that Oaktree would report for the investment and any investment revenue in its year-end financial statements.

Learning Objective 4
Recording bond investment transactions

E10-18 Assume that on September 30, 2011, Manulife Financial paid 91 for 7% bonds of Hydro-Québec as a long-term bond investment. The effective interest rate was 8%. The maturity value of the bonds will be $20,000 on September 30, 2016. The bonds pay interest on March 31 and September 30.

Required

1. What method should Manulife use to account for its investment in the Hydro-Québec bonds?
2. Using the effective interest method of amortizing the bonds, journalize all of Manulife's transactions on the bonds for 2011.
3. Show how Manulife would report everything related to the bond investment on its balance sheet at December 31, 2011.

Learning Objective 5
Managing and accounting for foreign-currency transactions

E10-19 Assume that Future Shop completed the following foreign-currency transaction:

Mar.	17	Purchased DVD players as inventory on account from Sony. The price was 300,000 yen, and the exchange rate of the yen was $0.01341.
Apr.	16	Paid Sony when the exchange rate was $0.0129
	19	Sold merchandise on account to Bon Temps, a French company, at a price of 60,000 euros. The exchange rate was $1.6051.
	30	Collected from Bon Temps when the exchange rate was $1.5903

1. Journalize these transactions for Future Shop. Focus on the gains and losses caused by changes in foreign-currency rates.
2. On March 18, immediately after the purchase, and on April 20, immediately after the sale, which currencies did Future Shop want to strengthen? Which currencies did in fact strengthen? Explain your reasoning in detail.

Learning Objective 5
Translating a foreign-currency balance sheet into dollars

E10-20 Translate into dollars the balance sheet of Assiniboine Leather Goods Inc.'s Spanish subsidiary. When Assiniboine Leather Goods acquired the foreign subsidiary, a euro was worth \$1.60. The current exchange rate is \$1.70. During the period when retained earnings were earned, the average exchange rate was \$1.58 per euro.

	Euros
Assets	500,000
Liabilities	300,000
Shareholders' equity:	
Common shares	50,000
Retained earnings	150,000
	500,000

During the period covered by this situation, which currency was stronger, the dollar or the euro?

Learning Objective 6
Preparing and using the statement of cash flows

E10-21 During fiscal year 2011, Donuts 'R' Us Inc. reported net loss of \$135.8 million. Donuts received \$1.0 million from the sale of other businesses. Donuts made capital expenditures of \$10.4 million and sold property, plant, and equipment for \$7.3 million. The company purchased long-term investments at a cost of \$12.2 million and sold other long-term investments for \$2.5 million.

Required

Prepare the investing activities section of the Donuts 'R' Us statement of cash flows. Based solely on Donuts' investing activities, does it appear that the company is growing or shrinking? How can you tell?

Learning Objective 6
Using the statement of cash flows

E10-22 At the end of the year, Blue Chip Properties Ltd.'s statement of cash flows reported the following for investment activities:

Blue Chip Properties Ltd.
Consolidated Statement of Cash Flows (Partial)

Cash Flows from Investing Activities	
Notes receivable collected	\$ 3,110,000
Purchases of short-term investments	(3,457,000)
Proceeds from sales of equipment	1,409,000*
Proceeds from sales of investments (cost of \$450,000)	461,000
Expenditures for property, plant, and equipment	(1,761,000)
Net cash used by investing activities	\$ (238,000)

*Cost \$5,100,000; Accumulated depreciation, \$3,691,000

Required

For each item listed, make the journal entry that placed the item on Blue Chip's statement of cash flows.

Challenge Exercises

Learning Objective ❶❷❸❺
Accounting for various types of investments

E10-23 This exercise summarizes the accounting for investments. Suppose YouTube.ca owns the following investment at December 31, 2011:

a. 100% of the common shares of YouTube United Kingdom, which holds assets of £800,000 and owes a total of £600,000. At December 31, 2011, the current exchange rate of the pound (£) is £1 = $1.80. The translation rate of the pound applicable to shareholders' equity is £1 = $1.70. During 2011, YouTube United Kingdom earned net income of £100,000 and the average exchange rate for the year was £1 = $1.85. YouTube United Kingdom paid cash dividends of £40,000 during 2011.
b. Investments that YouTube is holding for trade. These investments cost $900,000 and declined in value by $400,000 during 2011, but they paid cash dividends of $16,000 to YouTube. One year ago, at December 31, 2010, the fair value of these investments was $1,100,000.
c. 25% of the common shares of YouTube Financing Associates. During 2011, YouTube Financing earned net income of $300,000 and declared and paid cash dividends of $80,000. The carrying amount of this investment was $700,000 at December 31, 2010.

Required

1. Which method is used to account for each investment?
2. By how much did each of these investments increase or decrease YouTube's net income during 2011?
3. For investment b and c, show how YouTube would report these investments on its balance sheet at December 31, 2011.

Learning Objective ❶❻
Explaining and analyzing accumulated other comprehensive income

E10-24 Big-Box Retail Corporation reported shareholders' equity on its balance sheet at December 31, 2011, as follows:

Big-Box Retail Corporation
Balance Sheet (Partial)
December 31, 2011

	millions
Shareholders' Equity:	
Common shares, $0.10	
800 million shares authorized, 300 million shares issued	$1,113
Retained earnings	6,250
Accumulated other comprehensive income (loss)	(?)

Required

1. Identify the two components that typically make up accumulated other comprehensive income.
2. For each component of accumulated other comprehensive income, describe the event that can cause a *positive* balance. Also describe the events that can cause a negative balance for each component.
3. At December 31, 2010, Big-Box's accumulated other comprehensive loss was $53 million. Then, during 2011, Big-Box had a positive foreign-currency translation adjustment of $29 million and an unrealized loss of $16 million on passive investments. Assume Big-Box chooses to record any changes in fair value through other comprehensive income. What was Big-Box's balance of accumulated other comprehensive income (loss) at December 31, 2011?

Quiz

Test your understanding of long-term investments and international operations by answering the following questions. Select the best choice from among the possible answers given.

Questions 10-25 through 10-27 use the following data:

Assume that Maritimes Holdings Inc. owns the following long-term passive investment:

December 31, 2011				
Company	Number of Shares	Cost per Share	Current Fair Value per Share	Dividend per Share
Airbus Corp.	1,000	$60	$71	$2
Whole Grains Inc.	200	9	11	1.50
MySpace Ltd.	500	20	24	1

Q10-25 Maritime's balance sheet at December 31, 2011, should report

a. Investments of $85,200
b. Investments of $81,200
c. Dividend revenue of $2,800
d. Unrealized loss of $13,400

Q10-26 Maritime's 2011 income statement should report

a. Investments of $71,800
b. Gain on sale of investment of $13,400
c. Unrealized gain of $13,400
d. Dividend revenue of $2,800

Q10-27 Suppose Maritime sells the Airbus shares for $68 per share, February 2, 2012. Journalize the sale.

Q10-28 Dividends received on an equity-method investment

a. Increase the investment account
b. Decrease the investment account
c. Increase dividend revenue
d. Increase owners' equity

Q10-29 The starting point in accounting for all investments is

a. Fair value on the balance sheet date
b. Equity value
c. Cost
d. Cost minus dividends

Q10-30 Consolidation accounting

a. Combines the accounts of the parent company and those of the subsidiary companies
b. Eliminates all liabilities
c. Reports the receivables and payables of the parent company only
d. All of the above

Q10-31 On January 1, 2011, Vallée Bleue Ltée purchased $100,000 face value of the 7% bonds of Mail Frontier Inc. at 105. Interest is paid on January 1. The bonds mature on January 1, 2012. For the year ended December 31, 2011, Vallée Bleu received cash interest of

a. $5,000
b. $6,000
c. $6,400
d. $7,000

Q10-32 Return to Vallée Bleue's bond investment in Question 10-31. Assume an effective interest rate of 6%. For the year ended December 31, 2011, Vallée Bleu earned interest revenue of

a. $5,000
b. $6,300
c. $7,000
d. $7,700

Q10-33 Yukon Systems purchased inventory on account from Panasonic. The price was ¥100,000, and a yen was quoted at $0.0129. Yukon paid the debt in yen a month later, when the price of a yen was $0.0134. Yukon

a. Debited Inventory for $1,290
b. Debited Inventory for $1,340
c. Recorded a Foreign-Currency Transaction Loss of $50
d. None of the above

Q10-34 One way to avoid a foreign-currency transaction loss is to

a. Pay in the foreign currency
b. Collect in your own currency
c. Offset foreign-currency inventory and plant assets
d. Pay debts as late as possible

Q10-35 Foreign-currency transaction gains and losses are reported on the

a. Balance sheet
b. Consolidation worksheet
c. Statement of cash flows
d. Income statement

Q10-36 Consolidation of a foreign subsidiary usually results in a

a. Gain on consolidation
b. Loss on consolidation
c. Foreign-currency translation adjustment
d. Foreign-currency transaction gain or loss

Problems

(Group A)

Learning Objective 1 2
Reporting investments on the balance sheet and the related revenue on the income statement

P10-37A Winnipeg Exchanges Ltd. completed the following long-term investment transactions during 2011.

2011		
May	12	Purchased 20,000 shares, which make up 35% of the common shares of Fellingham Corporation at a total cost of $370,000
July	9	Received annual cash dividend of $1.26 per share on the Fellingham investment
Sept.	16	Purchased 800 common shares of Tomassini Inc. as a passive investment, paying $41.50 per share
Oct.	30	Received cash dividend of $0.30 per share on the Tomassini investment
Dec.	31	Received annual report from Fellingham Corporation. Net income for the year was $510,000.

At year-end the current fair value of the Tomassini shares is $30,600. The fair value of the Fellingham shares is $652,000.

Required

1. For which investment is current fair value used in the accounting? Why is fair value used for one investment and not the other?
2. Show what Winnipeg Exchange Ltd. would report on its year-end balance sheet and income statement for these investment transactions. It is helpful to use a T-account for the Long-Term Investment in Fellingham Shares account. Ignore income tax.

P10-38A The beginning balance sheet of New Technology Corporation included the following:

Learning Objective 1 2
Accounting for passive and equity-method investments

Long-Term Investment in MSC Software (equity-method investment)	$619,000

New Technology completed the following investment transactions during the year 2011:

Mar. 16	Purchased 2,000 shares of ATI Inc. as a long-term passive investment, paying $12.25 per share
May 21	Received cash dividend of $0.75 per share on the ATI investment
Aug. 17	Received cash dividend of $81,000 from MSC Software
Dec. 31	Received annual report from MSC Software. Net income for the year was $550,000. Of this amount, New Technology's proportion is 22%.

At year-end, the fair values of New Technology's investments are ATI, $25,700, and MSC, $700,000.

Required

1. Record the transactions in the journal of New Technology Corporation.
2. Post entries to the T-account for Long-Term Investment in MSC and determine its balance at December 31, 2011.
3. Show how to report the Long-Term Passive Investment and the Long-Term Investment in MSC accounts on New Technology's balance sheet at December 31, 2011.

P10-39A This problem demonstrates the dramatic effect that consolidation accounting can have on a company's ratios. ABC Company owns 100% of ABC Credit Corporation, its financing subsidiary. ABC's main operations consist of manufacturing automotive products. ABC Credit Corporation mainly helps people finance the purchase of automobiles from ABC and its dealers. The two companies' individual balance sheets are adapted and summarized as follows (amounts in billions):

Learning Objective 3
Analyzing consolidated financial statements

	ABC (Parent)	ABC Credit (Subsidiary)
Total assets	$94.8	$179.0
Total liabilities	$68.4	$164.7
Total shareholders' equity	26.4	14.3
Total liabilities and equity	$94.8	$179.0

Assume that ABC Credit's liabilities include $1.8 billion owed to ABC, the parent company.

Required

1. Compute the debt ratio of ABC Company considered alone.
2. Determine the consolidated total assets, total liabilities, and shareholders' equity of ABC Company after consolidating the financial statements of ABC Credit into the totals of ABC, the parent company.
3. Recompute the debt ratio of the consolidated entity. Why do companies prefer not to consolidate their financing subsidiaries into their own financial statements?

P10-40A Insurance companies and pension plans hold large quantities of bond investments. Prairie Insurance Corp. purchased $600,000 of 5% bonds of Eaton Inc. for 104.5 on March 1, 2011, when the effective interest rate was 4%. These bonds pay interest on March 1 and September 1 each year. They mature on March 1, 2016. At February 28, 2012, the market price of the bonds is 103.5.

Learning Objective 4
Accounting for a bond investment purchased at a premium

Required

1. Journalize Prairie's purchase of the bonds as a long-term investment on March 1, 2011 (to be held to maturity), receipt of cash interest and amortization of the bond investment on September 1, 2011, and accrual of interest revenue and amortization at February 28, 2012. Use the effective-interest method for amortizing the bond investment.
2. Show all financial statement effects of this long-term bond investment on Prairie Insurance Corp.'s balance sheet and income statement at February 28, 2012.

Learning Objective 5
Recording foreign-currency transactions and reporting the transaction gain or loss

P10-41A Suppose Bridgestone Corporation completed the following international transactions:

May	1	Sold inventory on account to Mezzo, an Italian company, for €82,000. The exchange rate of the euro is $1.60, and Mezzo demands to pay in euros.
	10	Purchased supplies on account from an American company at a price of $50,000 in U.S. dollars. The exchange rate of the U.S. dollar is $1.20, and payment will be in U.S. dollars.
	17	Sold inventory on account to an English firm for £100,000. Payment will be in British pounds. The exchange rate is £1 = $1.80.
	22	Collected from Mezzo. The exchange rate is €1 = $1.65.
June	18	Paid the American company. The exchange rate of the U.S. dollar is $1.22.
	24	Collected from the English firm: The exchange rate is £1 = $1.75.

Required

1. Record these transactions in Bridgestone's journal, and show how to report the transaction gain or loss on the income statement.
2. How will what you learned in this problem help you structure international transactions?

Learning Objective 5
Measuring and explaining the foreign-currency translation adjustment

P10-42A Assume that Research In Motion (RIM) has a subsidiary company based in Japan.

Required

1. Translate into dollars the foreign-currency balance sheet of the Japanese subsidiary of RIM.

	Yen
Assets	300,000,000
Liabilities	80,000,000
Shareholders' equity:	
Common shares	20,000,000
Retained earnings	200,000,000
	300,000,000

When RIM acquired this subsidiary, the Japanese yen was worth $0.0134. The current exchange rate is $0.0137. During the period when the subsidiary earned its income, the average exchange rate was $0.0135 per yen.

Before you perform the foreign-currency translation calculations, indicate whether RIM has experienced a positive or a negative translation adjustment. State whether the adjustment is a gain or a loss, and show where it is reported in the financial statements.

2. To which company does the foreign-currency translation adjustment "belong"? In which company's financial statements will the translation adjustment be reported?

P10-43A Excerpts from Smart Pro Inc.'s statement of cash flows appear as follows:

Learning Objective 6
Using a statement of cash flows

Smart Pro Inc.
Consolidated Statement of Cash Flows (Partial, Adapted)
For the Years Ended December 31

(In millions)	2011	2010
Cash and cash equivalents, beginning of year	$ 2,976	$ 3,695
Net cash provided by operating activities	8,654	12,827
Cash flows provided by (used for) investing activities:		
Additions to property, plant, and equipment	(7,309)	(6,674)
Acquisitions of other companies	(883)	(2,317)
Purchases of investments	(7,141)	(17,188)
Sales of investments	15,138	16,144
Net cash (used for) investing activities	(195)	(10,035)
Cash flows provided by (used for) financing activities:		
Borrowing	329	215
Repayment of long-term debt	(10)	(46)
Proceeds from issuance of shares	762	797
Repurchase of common shares	(4,008)	(4,007)
Payment of dividends to shareholders	(538)	(470)
Net cash (used for) financing activities	(3,465)	(3,511)
Net increase (decrease) in cash and cash equivalents	4,994	(719)
Cash and cash equivalents, end of year	$ 7,970	$ 2,976

Required

As the chief executive officer of Smart Pro Inc., your duty is to write the management letter to your shareholders to explain Smart Pro's investing activities during 2011. Compare the company's level of investment with the preceding year, and indicate the major way the company financed its investments during 2011. Net income for 2011 was $1,291 million.

(Group B)

P10-44B Homestead Financial Corporation owns numerous investments in the shares of other companies. Homestead Financial completed the following long-term investment transactions:

Learning Objective 1 2
Reporting investments on the balance sheet and the related revenue on the income statement

2011		
May	1	Purchased 8,000 shares, which make up 25% of the common shares of Mars Company at total cost of $450,000
Sept.	15	Received a cash dividend of $1.40 per share on the Mars investment
Oct.	12	Purchased 1,000 common shares of Mercury Corporation as a passive investment paying $22.50 per share
Dec.	14	Received a cash dividend of $0.75 per share on the Mercury investment
	31	Received annual report from Mars Company. Net income for the year was $350,000.

At year-end the current fair value of the Mercury shares is $19,200. The fair value of the Mars shares is $740,000.

Required

1. For which investment is current fair value used in the accounting? Why is fair value used for one investment and not the other?
2. Show what Homestead Financial will report on its year-end balance sheet and income statement for these investments. (It is helpful to use a T-account for the Long-Term Investment in Mars Shares account.) Ignore income tax.

Learning Objective 1 2
Accounting for passive and equity-method investments

P10-45B The beginning balance sheet of Dealmaker Securities Limited included the following:

Long-Term Investments in Affiliates (equity-method investments)........................	$409,000

Dealmaker completed the following investment transactions during the year:

Feb.	16	Purchased 10,000 shares of BCM Software common shares as a long-term passive investment, paying $9.25 per share
May	14	Received cash dividend of $0.82 per share on the BCM investment
Oct.	15	Received cash dividend of $29,000 from an affiliated company
Dec.	31	Received annual reports from affiliated companies. Their total net income for the year was $620,000. Of this amount, Dealmaker's proportion is 25%.

The fair values of Dealmaker's investments are BCM, $89,000, and affiliated companies, $947,000.

Required

1. Record the transactions in the journal of Dealmaker Securities.
2. Post entries to the Long-Term Investments in Affiliates T-account, and determine its balance at December 31.
3. Show how to report Long-Term Passive Investments and Long-Term Investments in Affiliates on Dealmaker's balance sheet at December 31.

Learning Objective 4
Accounting for a bond investment purchased at a discount

P10-46B Financial institutions hold large quantities of bond investments. Suppose Sun Life Financial purchases $500,000 of 6% bonds of General Components Corporation for 88 on January 1, 2011, when the effective interest rate was 8%. These bonds pay interest on January 1 and July 1 each year. They mature on January 1, 2019. At December 31, 2011, the market price of the bonds is 90.

Required

1. Journalize Sun Life's purchase of the bonds as a long-term investment on January 1, 2011 (to be held to maturity), receipt of cash interest and amortization of the bond investment on July 1, 2011, and accrual of interest revenue and amortization at December 31, 2011. Use the effective-interest method for amortizing the bond investment.
2. Show all financial statement effects of this long-term bond investment on Sun Life's balance sheet and income statement at December 31, 2011.

Learning Objective 5
Recording foreign-currency transactions and reporting the transaction gain or loss

P10-47B Sun Power Drinks Inc. (SPD) completed the following international transactions:

Apr.	4	Sold soft-drink syrup on account to a Mexican company for $81,000. The exchange rate of the Mexican peso is $0.085, and the customer agrees to pay in Canadian dollars.
	13	Purchased inventory on account from an American company at a price of 100,000 U.S. dollars. The exchange rate of the U.S. dollar is $1.20 and payment will be in U.S. dollars.
	20	Sold goods on account to an English firm for £70,000. Payment will be in British pounds, and the exchange rate of the pound is $1.80.
	27	Collected from the Mexican company.
May	21	Paid the American company. The exchange rate of the U.S. dollar is $1.22.
June	17	Collected from the English firm. The exchange rate of the British pound is $1.85.

Required

1. Record these transactions in Sun's journal and show how to report the transaction gain or loss on the income statement.
2. How will what you learned in this problem help you structure international transactions?

P10-48B Arte Fabrics Ltd. owns a subsidiary based in France.

Learning Objective 5
Measuring and explaining the foreign-currency translation adjustment

Required

1. Translate the foreign-currency balance sheet of the French subsidiary of Arte Fabrics Ltd. into dollars. When Arte Fabrics acquired this subsidiary, the euro was worth $1.60. The current exchange rate is $1.80 per euro. During the period when the subsidiary earned its income, the average exchange rate was $1.70 per euro.

	euros
Assets	3,000,000
Liabilities	1,000,000
Shareholders' equity:	
Common shares	300,000
Retained earnings	1,700,000
	3,000,000

   Before you perform the foreign-currency translation calculation, indicate whether Arte Fabrics has experienced a positive or a negative foreign-currency translation adjustment. State whether the adjustment is a gain or a loss, and show where it is reported in the financial statements.

2. To which company does the translation adjustment "belong"? In which company's financial statements will the translation adjustment be reported?

Learning Objective 6
Using a statement of cash flows

P10-49B Marine Transport Ltd.'s statement of cash flows, as adapted, appears as follows:

Marine Transport Ltd.
Consolidated Statement of Cash Flows
For the Years Ended December 31 (Stated in thousands of Canadian dollars)

	2011	2010
Cash flows from (used in):		
Operating activities:		
Net earnings	$192,833	$114,676
Items not involving cash:		
Depreciation and amortization	127,223	111,442
Amortization of other liabilities	(897)	(868)
Amortization of hedge settlements	1,400	1,427
Net realized loss on cash flow hedge	18	—
Loss on derecognition of property and equipment and ship parts	32,773	394
Stock-based compensation expense	20,058	21,205
Future income tax expense	41,775	46,635
Unrealized foreign exchange loss (gain)	13,813	(346)
Decrease in non-cash working capital	112,069	43,707
	541,065	338,272
Financing activities:		
Increase in long-term debt	141,178	418,581
Repayment of long-term debt	(156,516)	(132,559)
Decrease in obligations under capital lease	(356)	(480)
Share issuance costs	—	(10)
Shares repurchased	(21,250)	—
Issuance of common shares	1,551	—
Increase in other assets	(20,897)	(27,830)
Increase in non-cash working capital	(3,000)	(1,071)
	(59,290)	256,631
Investing activities:		
Ship additions	(191,437)	(438,906)
Ship disposals	1,975	3,822
Other property and equipment additions	(24,639)	(43,590)
Other property and equipment disposals	13,819	1,611
	(200,282)	(477,063)
Cash flow from operating, financing, and investing activities	281,493	117,840
Effect of exchange rate on cash	(5,452)	37
Net change in cash	276,041	117,877
Cash, beginning of year	377,517	259,640
Cash, end of year	$653,558	$377,517

Cash is defined as cash and cash equivalents.

Required

As a member of an investment club, you have been asked to review Marine Transport's major investing activities during 2011. Compare the company's level of investment with the previous year, and indicate how the company financed its investments during 2011.

Apply Your Knowledge

Decision Cases

Learning Objective 1 5
Making an investment decision

Case 1. Infografix Corporation's consolidated sales for 2011 were $26.6 million and expenses totalled $24.8 million. Infografix operates worldwide and conducts 37% of its business outside Canada. During 2011, Infografix reported the following items in its financial statements (amounts in millions):

Foreign-currency translation adjustments	$(202)
Unrealized holding on passive investments	(328)

As you consider an investment in Infografix shares, some concerns arise. Answer the following questions:

1. What do the parentheses around the two dollar amounts signify?
2. Are these items reported as assets, liabilities, shareholders' equity, revenues, or expenses? Are they normal-balance accounts, or are they contra accounts?
3. Are these items reason for rejoicing or sorrow at Infografix? Are Infografix's emotions about these items deep or only moderate? Why?
4. Did Infografix include these items in net income? Did it include these items in retained earnings? In the final analysis, how much net income did Infografix report for 2011?
5. Should these items scare you away from investing in Infografix shares? Why or why not?

Learning Objective 1 2 4
Making an investment sale decision

Case 2. Cathy Talbert is the general manager of Barham Ltd., which provides data-management services for physicians in the Regina, Saskatchewan, area. Barham is having a rough year. Net income trails projections for the year by almost $75,000. This shortfall is especially important. Barham plans to issue shares early next year and needs to show investors that the company can meet its earnings targets.

Barham holds several investments purchased a few years ago. Even though investing in shares is outside Barham's core business of data-management services, Talbert thinks these investments may hold the key to helping the company meet its net income goal for the year. She is considering what to do with the following investments:

1. Barham owns 50% of the common shares of Prairie Office Systems, which provides the business forms that Barham uses. Prairie Office Systems has lost money for the past two years but still has a retained earnings balance of $550,000. Talbert thinks she can get Prairie's treasurer to declare a $160,000 cash dividend, half of which would go to Barham.
2. Barham owns a bond investment with a 4% coupon rate and an annual interest payment. The bond was purchased eight years ago for $293,000. The purchase price represents a discount from the bonds' maturity value of $400,000 based on an effective rate of 8%. These bonds mature two years from now, and their current market value is $380,000. Ms. Talbert has checked with a Scotiabank investment representative and Talbert is considering selling the bonds. A charge of 1% commission would be made on the sale transaction.
3. Barham owns 5,000 Royal Bank of Canada (RBC) shares valued at $53 per share. One year ago, RBC was worth only $28 per share. Barham purchased the RBC shares for $37 per share. Talbert wonders whether Barham should sell the RBC shares.

Required

Evaluate all three actions as a way for Barham Ltd. to generate the needed amount of income. Recommend the best way for Barham to achieve its net income goal.

Ethical Issue

Media One owns 15% of the voting shares of Online Inc. The remainder of the Online shares are held by numerous investors with small holdings. Austin Cohen, president of Media One and a member of Online's board of directors, heavily influences Online's policies.

Under the fair value method of accounting for investments, Media One's net income increases as it receives dividend revenue from Online. Media One pays President Cohen a bonus computed as a percentage of Media One's net income. Therefore, Cohen can control his personal bonus to a certain extent by influencing Online's dividends.

A recession occurs in 2011, and Media One's income is low. Cohen uses his power to have Online pay a large cash dividend. The action requires Online to borrow in order to pay the dividend.

Required

1. In getting Online to pay the large cash dividend, is Cohen acting within his authority as a member of the Online board of directors? Are Cohen's actions ethical? Whom can his actions harm?
2. Discuss how using the equity method of accounting for investment would decrease Cohen's potential for manipulating his bonus.

Focus on Financials

Learning Objective 3 5 6
Analyzing investments, consolidated statements, and international operations

Gildan Activewear Inc.

Gildan's financial statements are given in Appendix A at the end of this book.

1. Does Gildan have any subsidiaries? How can you tell?
2. Is Gildan expanding or contracting its operations? How can you tell?
3. Does Gildan engage in foreign-currency transactions? If so, what is the nature of the transactions?

Focus on Analysis

Learning Objective 1 2 3 6
Analyzing goodwill, consolidated subsidiaries, and investments

Gildan Activewear Inc.

Gildan's financial statements are given in Appendix A at the end of this book.

1. Gildan has subsidiaries. What is Gildan's percentage of ownership? How can you tell?
2. Gildan reports intangible assets on its consolidated balance sheet. What are these assets and how are they accounted for?
3. Did Gildan's goodwill suffer any impairment during the year? How can you tell?

Group Project

Pick a stock from *The Globe and Mail* or other database or publication. Assume that your group purchases 1,000 shares as a long-term investment and that your 1,000 shares are less than 20% of the company's outstanding shares. Research the shares to determine whether the company pays cash dividends and, if so, how much and at what intervals.

Required

1. Track the shares for a period assigned by your professor. Over the specified period, keep a daily record of the share price to see how well your investment has performed. Keep a record of any dividends you would have received. End the period of your analysis with a month-end, such as September 30 or December 31.

2. Journalize all transactions that you have experienced, including the share purchase, dividends received (both cash dividends and stock dividends), and any year-end adjustment required by the accounting method that is appropriate for your situation. Assume you will prepare financial statements on the ending date of your study.
3. Show what you will report on your company's balance sheet, income statement, and statement of cash flows as a result of your investment transactions.

Quick Check Answers

1. *c*
2. *d (1,000 shares × \$35 = \$35,000)*
3. *a (\$35,000 − \$31,000 = \$4,000)*
4. *b [\$40,000 − (1,000 shares × \$31) = \$9,000]*
5. *b [\$100,000 + 0.20 (\$50,000 − \$25,000) = \$105,000]*
6. *c (\$100,000 + 0.80 [\$68,000 + 0.80(\$40,000)] = \$180,000)*
7. *a*
8. *d*
9. *b (\$1,000,000 in U.S. dollars × \$1.25 = \$1,250,000)*
10. *c*

11 The Comprehensive Income Statement and the Statement of Shareholders' Equity

LEARNING OBJECTIVES

1. **Analyze** a corporate comprehensive income statement
2. **Account** for a corporation's income tax
3. **Analyze** shareholders' equity
4. **Understand** managers' and auditors' responsibilities for the financial statements

SPOTLIGHT

TELUS Corporation is one of Canada's leading communication companies. It is a leader in wireless with its 3G+ network that covers most of Canada, as well as having a significant position in landlines in British Columbia, Alberta, and Quebec and in cable and satellite television. In addition, TELUS provides a wide range of IT services including IT healthcare services.

While 2009 was a difficult year in most industries because of the recession, you will see when you examine TELUS's consolidated statements of income and other comprehensive income below that TELUS performed very well. Robert McFarlane, TELUS's executive vice-president and chief financial officer, stated in the December 31, 2009, annual report, "Our solid financial foundation allowed us to stay the course in 2009 and invest prudently in our core businesses, despite the recessionary pressures we faced."

Source: TELUS Corporation 2009 Annual Report (http://about.telus.com/investors/annualreport2009/).

EXHIBIT 11-1 **TELUS Corporation Consolidated Statements of Income and Other Comprehensive Income**

TELUS Corporation
Consolidated Statements of Income
and Other Comprehensive Income (Adapted)

Years ended December 31 (millions except for share amounts)	2009	2008
1. **Operating Revenues**	$9,606	$9,653
Operating Expenses		
2. Operations	5,925	5,815
3. Restructuring costs	190	59
4. Depreciation	1,341	1,384
5. Amortization of intangible assets	381	329
6.	7,837	7,587
7. **Operating Income**	1,769	2,066
8. Other expense, net	32	36
9. Financing costs	532	463
10. **Income Before Income Taxes**	1,205	1,567
11. Income Taxes	203	436
12. **Net Income**	1,002	1,131
Other Comprehensive Income		
13. Change in unrealized fair value of derivatives designated as cash flow hedges	69	(26)
14. Foreign currency translation adjustment arising from translating financial statements of self-sustaining foreign operations	(12)	2
15. Change in unrealized fair value of available-for-sale financial assets	1	(2)
16.	58	(26)
17. **Comprehensive Income**	$1,060	$1,105
Net Income Attributable to:		
18. Common Shares and Non-Voting Shares	$ 998	$1,128
19. Non-controlling interests	4	3
20.	$1,002	$1,131
Total Comprehensive Income Attributable to:		
21. Common Shares and Non-Voting Shares	$1,056	$1,102
22. Non-controlling interests	4	3
23.	$1,060	$1,105
Net Income Per Common Share and Non-Voting Share		
24. Basic	$ 3.14	$ 3.52
25. Diluted	$ 3.14	$ 3.51
26. Dividends Declared Per Common Share and Non-Voting Share	$ 1.90	$1.825

This chapter rounds out your coverage of the corporate income statement. After studying this material, you will have seen all the types of items that typically appear on an income statement. You will learn about *income from operations* and **comprehensive income**. Income from continuing operations is often the basis for analysts' predictions about companies' future operations. You will also learn about earnings per share, the most often-mentioned statistic in business. Finally, you'll learn about the statement of shareholders' equity, of which a component is the changes to retained earnings. The knowledge you will get from this chapter will help you analyze financial statements and use the information in decision making.

We begin with a basic question: How do we evaluate the quality of a company's earnings? The term *quality of earnings* refers to the characteristics of an earnings number that make it most useful for decision making.

Evaluating the Quality of Earnings

OBJECTIVE

1 **Analyze** a corporate comprehensive income statement

A corporation's net income (including earnings per share) receives more attention than any other item in the financial statements. To shareholders, the larger the net income, the greater the likelihood of dividends. In addition, an upward trend in net income generally translates sooner or later to a higher price. To creditors, a larger net income indicates a better ability to pay debts.

Suppose you are considering investing in the stock of either TELUS, or Brand X Superstore. How do you make the decision? A knowledgeable investor will want to assess each company's **earnings quality**. The higher the quality of earnings in the current period compared to its recent past, the more likely it is that the company is executing a successful business strategy to generate healthy earnings in the future, which is a key component in its stock price.

There are many components of earnings quality. Among the most prominent are (1) proper revenue and expense recognition, (2) high and improving gross margin/sales ratio, (3) low operating expenses compared to sales, and (4) high and improving operating earnings/sales. To explore the makeup and the quality of earnings, let's examine its various sources. Exhibit 11-1 shows the Consolidated Statements of Income and Other Comprehensive Income of TELUS Corporation, for fiscal years 2009 and 2008. We'll use these statements as a basis for our discussion of earnings quality.

Revenue Recognition

The first component of earnings quality, and the top line of the income statement, is proper recognition of net revenue, or *net sales*. You learned a little about revenue in Chapters 3 through 6. As you learned in Chapter 3 (p. 118), under accrual accounting, revenue should be recognized when it is *earned*—that is, when the selling business has done everything it has to do to deliver either the product or the service to the customer. In recognizing revenue, several important events have to occur: (1) the seller delivers the product or service to the customer, (2) the customer takes both possession and ownership of the product or service, and (3) the seller either collects cash or is reasonably assured of collecting the cash in the near future. In Chapter 4 (p. 208) you learned the process by which cash collected over the counter is entered into the accounting system. In Chapter 5 (pp. 243 through 252), you learned that credit sales, or sales on account, have to go through the process of collection, that some will ultimately not be collectible, and that a company must make allowances for doubtful accounts. In Chapter 6 (p. 288), you studied the concept of *free on board* (FOB) terms, which govern the issue of who owns the goods during the shipment process, and therefore the timing of revenue. You must understand all of these concepts in order to grasp the meaning of revenue recognition.

Let's examine Exhibit 11-1 and analyze the trend in TELUS's operating revenues (line 1). A review of the TELUS 2004 annual report shows that operating revenues have increased steadily from $7,007 million in 2002 to $9,653 million in 2008. Operating revenues decreased by $47 million (0.5%) in 2009 to $9,606 million primarily due to the recession in 2009. The market price of TELUS shares did not react to the slight decrease in operating revenue.

It is important when analyzing revenue to try to understand whether a larger than expected increase occurred because the company did a better job of marketing its products or services or if, as the ethics material below explains, management has fraudulently overstated revenue. It is equally important when analyzing revenue to understand whether a larger than expected decrease occurred because the company is losing market share and the decrease indicates a trend. Another explanation is that offered by Gildan and TELUS. There was a recession in 2009, and despite a decline in revenue, both companies had strong performances.

Cooking the Books With Revenue

Research has shown that roughly half of all financial statement fraud over the past two decades has involved improper revenue recognition. Following are several of the more significant revenue recognition issues involving fraud:

- **Recognizing revenue prematurely (before it is earned).** One of the common fraud techniques is *channel stuffing*, where a company may ship inventory to regular customers in excess of amounts ordered. Bristol-Myers Squibb, a global pharmaceuticals company, was sued by the SEC in 2004 for channel stuffing during 2000 and 2001. The company allegedly stuffed its distribution channels with excess inventory near the end of every quarter in amounts sufficient to meet company sales targets (tied to executive bonuses), overstating revenue by about $1.5 billion. The company paid a civil fine of $100 million and established a $50 million fund to compensate shareholders for their losses.*
- **Providing incentives for customers to purchase more inventory than is needed**, in exchange for future discounts and other benefits.
- **Reporting revenue when significant services are still to be performed or goods delivered.**
- **Reporting sales to fictitious or nonexistent customers.** This may include falsified shipping and inventory records.

Expense Recognition—Continuing Operations

In Exhibit 11-1, in the topmost section of the consolidated statements of income and other comprehensive income, TELUS reports income from continuing operations (lines 1 to 12). Similarly, in Exhibit 11-2, in the topmost section of the statement of income and other comprehensive income, Westmount Concepts reports income from continuing operations (lines 1 to 10). This part of each business is expected to continue from period to period. We may use this information to predict that TELUS will earn income from continuing operations of approximately $1,000 million next year and Westmount will earn income from continuing operations of approximately $55,000 next year.

IFRS "Framework for the Preparation and Presentation of Financial Statements" defines an expense as " ...a decrease in future economic benefits related to a decrease in an asset or an increase of a liability...." The framework also states "Expenses are

*Accounting and Auditing Enforcement Release No. 2075, August 4, 2004. *Securities and Exchange Commission v. Bristol-Myers Squibb Company*, 04-3680 DNJ (2004). See www.sec.gov.

recognised in the income statement on the basis of a direct association between the costs incurred and the earning of specific items of income." That definition includes expenses such as cost of goods sold, wages and employee benefits, utilities, and depreciation. It is just as important that all expenses are accurately, completely, and transparently included in the computation of net income as it is important to avoid premature or improper revenue recognition.

After revenue, the next two important components in earnings quality are cost of goods sold and gross profit, in the case of a retailing or manufacturing company. Recall from Chapter 6 that cost of goods sold represents the direct cost of the goods sold to customers. Exhibit 11-2, from the December 31, 2011, financial statements of Westmount Concepts Inc., provides an example of a retailing company. Notice that Westmount's sales increased by 25% from 2010 to 2011 and gross profit increased by 30% for the same period. The sales increase is a good sign and the greater increase in gross profit suggests that although the company likely increased its prices, it still had a healthy increase in sales.

Companies that sell services, such as TELUS or WestJet Airlines, report earnings from operations, an important component of their earnings quality. TELUS's operating expenses increased by 3% from 2008 to 2009 and operating income decreased by 14% over the same period.

EXHIBIT 11-2 **Westmount Concepts Inc. Statement of Income and Other Comprehensive Income**

Westmount Concepts Inc.
Statement of Income and Other Comprehensive Income
For the Years Ended December 31

Group	#	Item		2011	2010
Total Comprehensive Income	1	Sales revenue		$500,000	$400,000
	2	Cost of goods sold		240,000	200,000
	3	Gross profit		260,000	200,000
	4	Operating expenses (includes interest expense 2011, $6,000; 2010, $4,800)		181,000	150,000
	5	Operating income		79,000	50,000
		Other gains (losses):			
	6	Loss on restructuring operations		(8,000)	—
	7	Gain on sale of computers		9,000	—
	8	Income from continuing operations before income tax		80,000	50,000
	9	Income tax expense		25,600	16,000
	10	Income from continuing operations		54,400	34,000
		Discontinued operations:			
	11	Operating loss (net of tax)	(5,000)		
	12	Gain on disposal of discontinued assets (net of tax)	5,000	—	—
	13	Net income		54,400	34,000
		Other comprehensive income:			
	14	Unrealized gain on derivatives (net of tax)		1,000	—
		Comprehensive income		$ 55,400	$ 34,000
Earnings per share	15	Earnings per share (12,500 shares outstanding)			
	16	Net income attributable to common shares		$ 4.35	$2.72
	17	Total comprehensive income attributable to common shares		$ 6.53	$2.72

TELUS's largest expense is operations; it increased by 2% in 2009. Restructuring costs increased from $59 million to $190 million as TELUS rationalized its operations to reduce costs to deal with the existing economic environment. Most of the restructuring costs related to the cost of workforce reductions. Depreciation decreased by 3%. Amortization increased from $329 million to $381 million largely because of increased amortization of software.

Financing costs increased by $69 million primarily due to losses on the derecognition of long-term debt, a subject dealt with in Chapter 8.

Income taxes decreased from $436 million to $203 million primarily due to decreased income before taxes. The expense shown is made up of two amounts (current taxes and deferred taxes), which will be discussed later in the chapter under Learning Objective 2.

It is important to consider the trending of the individual expenses for several reasons. Perhaps the most important reason is to ascertain whether the company is becoming more profitable or declining in profitability. For example, has wages expense declined despite increased production, leading to greater profitability? Or has commission expense increased despite decreased sales, leading to decreased profitability?

Another explanation for an unexpected decrease in an expense or expenses is earnings management where management deliberately misstates expenses. For example, management could overstate closing inventory, resulting in cost of goods sold being understated and net income being overstated. Or management could fail to record invoices received at the year-end and thus understate expenses and accounts payable. Earlier in this text you read how management at WorldCom capitalized several billion dollars of expenses to make the company seem profitable.

Statement of Comprehensive Income

IAS 1 "Presentation of Financial Statements" requires a company to provide either:

- Two statements, one of which will be a statement of comprehensive income and the other an income statement, or
- One statement of comprehensive income, which will include both an income statement and a statement of comprehensive income (showing categories of other comprehensive income). Exhibits 11-1 and 11-2 are examples of this second approach.

Other comprehensive income includes items of income and expense that are excluded from net income such as unrealized gains or losses from derivatives, foreign currency translation adjustments, and changes in the fair value of available-for-sale financial assets (Exhibit 11-1) and discontinued operations (Exhibit 11-2). Items included in other comprehensive income but that are not part of net income from continuing operations are close to accumulated other comprehensive income section of shareholders' equity.

TELUS reports three categories of other comprehensive income (lines 13 to 16) on its consolidated statements of income and other comprehensive income (Exhibit 11-1). Westmount Concepts reports one category of other comprehensive income (line 14) on its comprehensive income statement (Exhibit 11-2).

With respect to the three categories of other comprehensive income reported by TELUS, the accounting for derivatives and their presentation in the financial statements under IFRS is complex and beyond the scope of this text. Foreign currency translation adjustments were discussed in Chapter 10. Changes in unrealized fair value of financial assets were discussed in Chapter 5.

IFRS 5 "Non-Current Assets Held for Sale and Discontinued Operations" requires that information such as that presented by Westmount Concepts in Exhibit 11-2 be presented in the Statement of Comprehensive Income. Specifically, IFRS 5 requires a company to present the revenue, expenses, and pre-tax profit or loss and the related tax as well as the gain or loss on the fair value measurement less costs to sell off the assets of the discontinued operations. The topic of discounted operations is presented under a separate heading below.

Section 1520 "income statement" does not include a category "other comprehensive income" but does require the income statement to calculate income from continuing operations and then to add (deduct) income (loss) from discontinued operations.

Which Income Number Predicts Future Profits?

How is income from continuing operations used in investment analysis? Suppose Laney Gibbs, an analyst with BMO Nesbitt Burns in Halifax, is estimating the value of Westmount Concepts Inc.'s common shares. Gibbs believes that Westmount can earn annual income each year equal to its income from continuing operations, $54,000 (rounded).

To estimate the value of Westmount Concepts Inc.'s common shares, financial analysts determine the present value (present value means the value today) of Westmount Concepts Inc.'s stream of future income. Gibbs must use some interest rate to compute the present value. Assume that an appropriate interest rate (i) for the valuation of Westmount is 12%. This rate is determined subjectively, based on the risk that Westmount might not be able to earn annual income from continuing operations of $54,000 (rounded) for the indefinite future. The rate is also called the **investment capitalization rate** because it is used to estimate the value of an investment. The higher the risk, the higher the rate, and the lower the risk, the lower the rate. The computation of the estimated value of Westmount's common shares is

$$\begin{array}{c}\text{Estimated value of}\\ \text{Westmount Concepts Inc.}\\ \text{common shares}\end{array} = \frac{\begin{array}{c}\text{Estimated future}\\ \text{annual income from operations}\end{array}}{\text{Investment capitalization rate}} = \frac{\$54{,}000}{0.12} = \$450{,}000^{*}$$

*This valuation model has many forms, which are covered in finance classes. Here, we introduce the basic form.

Gibbs thus estimates that Westmount Concepts Inc. is worth $450,000. She would then compare this estimate to the current market price of Westmount Concepts Inc.'s shares, which is $513,000. Westmount's balance sheet reports that Westmount Concepts Inc. has 12,500 common shares outstanding. In addition, suppose *The Globe and Mail* reports that Westmount Concepts Inc. common shares are selling for \$41.04 per share. The current market price of Westmount Concepts Inc. is thus

Current market price of the company	=	Number of common shares outstanding	×	Current market price per share
\$513,000	=	12,500	×	\$41.04

The investment decision rule may take this form:

				DECISION:
If estimated value of the company (such as Westmount)	Exceeds →	Current market price of the company	→	Buy the shares because you think the share price will go up.
	Equals →		→	Hold the shares because you think the share price will hold steady
	Is less than →		→	Sell the shares because you think the share price will fall

In this case,

			DECISION:
Estimated value of Westmount \$450,000	Is less than	Current market price of the company \$513,000	Sell the shares
\$36.00 per share*	Is less than	\$41.04 per share	

*\$450,000 / 12,500 shares = \$36.00 per share

Gibbs believes the share price should fall to bring the current market price of \$513,000 to somewhere in a range near \$450,000. Based largely on Westmount's income from continuing operations, Gibbs thinks that Westmount Concepts Inc. would be more fairly valued at \$450,000. Based on this analysis, BMO Nesbitt Burns would recommend that investors sell their shareholdings of Westmount Concepts Inc.

Investors often make their decisions based on the value of a single share. They can estimate the value of one share by using earnings per share (EPS) of common shares, as follows:

$$\text{Estimated value of one common share} = \frac{\text{Estimated annual earnings per share}}{\text{Investment capitalization rate}}$$

The analysis based on one share follows the pattern illustrated for the company as a whole.

Discontinued Operations

Earlier in this chapter you learned that income from discontinued operations is to be shown separately from income from continuing operations under both IFRS 5 and ASPE 1520. Exhibit 11-2 showed what the income statement would look like under IFRS. Both IFRS and APSE require such disclosure because a discontinued operation is a one-time event and not part of a company's continuing operations. It is for that reason that financial analysts typically do *not* include discontinued operations in predictions of future corporate income.

In Chapter 10, you read about ATCO Ltd., which is involved with utilities, power generation, logistics and energy services, and technologies and industrials on a worldwide basis. We call each identifiable division of a company a **segment of the business**. A company may sell a segment of its business. The sale of a business segment is viewed as a one-time transaction. George Weston Limited reported in its December 31, 2009, financial statements that a U.S. subsidiary, Dunedin Holdings, disposed of its fresh bread and baked goods business for $3,107 million. The notes to the financial statements reported the following with respect to the disposal:

Sales	$145
Operating income	9
Gain on disposal	939
Interest income and other financing charges (this amount was added back to calculate Earnings of $949)	(1)
Earnings before the following	949
Income taxes	41
Earnings from discontinued operations	$908

Accounting for a Change in Accounting Policy

Companies sometimes change from one accounting policy or method to another, such as from double-diminishing-balance (DDB) to straight-line depreciation, or from first-in, first-out (FIFO) to weighted-average cost for inventory. An accounting change makes it difficult to compare one period's financial statements with those of preceding periods. Without detailed information, investors and creditors can be misled into thinking that the current year is better or worse than the preceding year when, in fact, the only difference is a change in accounting method. It is for this reason that IAS 8 states that a change in accounting policy should be made only if it is required by the IFRS or " . . . if the change . . . results in the financial statements providing reliable and more relevant information . . . on the entity's financial position, financial performance, or cash flows."

The objective of IAS 8 (in part) "...is to prescribe the criteria for selecting and changing accounting policies, together with the accounting treatment and disclosure of changes in accounting policies...." The standard differentiates between initial application of IFRS and voluntary changes.

A change in policy due to initial application of IFRS must follow the transitional provisions specified in the IFRS. However, if the IFRS does not specify transitional methods, the change should be applied retrospectively. Voluntary changes must be applied retrospectively.

ASPE ACCOUNTING STANDARDS FOR PRIVATE ENTERPRISES

The objective of Section 1506 "Accounting Changes" (in part) "is to prescribe the criteria for changing accounting policies, together with the accounting treatment and disclosure of changes in accounting policies...." Changes include changes required to comply with generally accepted accounting principles as found in Part II of the *CICA Handbook*, "Accounting Standards for Private Enterprise" and voluntary changes.

A change in policy due to initial application of GAAP must follow the transitional provisions specified in the ASPE. However, if the ASPE does not specify transitional methods, the change should be applied retrospectively. Voluntary changes must be applied retrospectively.

While the topic of accounting changes is complex and beyond the scope of this text, the following example is illustrative of the impact of retrospective application of an accounting change. Balmy Beach Boats Ltd. a PAE, has a machine that cost $20,000 in 2008 and Balmy Beach has been depreciating the machine at the rate of 10% ($2,000) per year on a straight-line basis.

In 2011, Balmy Beach decides to convert to double-diminishing-balance (DDB) depreciation using a rate of 20% as a more accurate allocation of the cost of using the machine. Net income after deducting depreciation expense of $2,048 was $25,952 for 2011. Balmy Beach provides comparatives below for the previous two years together with the current year's balances. Depreciation using the DDB method would be:

	2008	2009	2010	2011
DDB depreciation	$4,000	$3,200	$2,560	$2,048
Depreciation expense previously claimed	2,000	2,000	2,000	
Cumulative difference	2,000	3,200	3,760	

The (partial) comparative statement of retained earnings would be as follows:

	2009	2010	2011
Opening balance	$18,000	$36,800	$60,240
Restatement of depreciation expense	2,000*		
Revised opening balance	16,000	36,800	60,240
Net income	22,000	24,000	25,952
Less additional depreciation	1,200	560	
Restated net income	20,800	23,440	25,952
Restated closing balance	$36,800	$60,240	$86,192

*Restatement of 2008 closing balance is $16,000: $18,000 original − $2,000 (which is $4,000 DDB − $2,000 straight-line).

Watch Out for Voluntary Accounting Changes That Increase Reported Income

Investment analysts follow companies to see if they meet their forecast earnings targets. And managers sometimes take drastic action to increase reported earnings.

Assume it's late in November and earnings may fall *below* the target for the year. A reasonable thing to do is to try to increase sales and net income. Managers can also cut expenses. These actions are ethical and honest. Profits earned by these actions are real. Managers can take another action that is honest and legal, but its ethics are questionable. Suppose the company has been using the double-diminishing-balance method for depreciation. Changing to straight-line depreciation can increase reported income.

Accounting changes are a quick-and-dirty way to create reported profits when the company can't earn enough from continuing operations. This is why IFRS permits companies to change an accounting method only if the change results in more relevant and reliable information and requires companies to report changes in accounting methods, along with their effects on earnings—to let investors know where the income came from. In addition, the companies must restate all prior-year financial statements to show how they would have appeared if the new accounting method had been in effect all along. This helps investors compare all periods' profits and losses on the same accounting basis.

Earnings per Share

IAS 33 "Earnings Per Share" provides guidance in calculating and presenting earnings per share.

The final segment of a corporation's income statement presents the company's earnings per share. **Earnings per share (EPS)** is the amount of a company's *net* income per share of its *outstanding common shares*. EPS is a key measure of a business's success because it shows how much income the company earned for each common share. Share prices are quoted at an amount per share, and investors buy a certain number of shares. EPS is used to help determine the value of a share. EPS is computed as follows:

$$\text{Earnings per share} = \frac{\text{Net income} - \text{Preferred dividends}}{\text{Average number of common shares outstanding}}$$

The corporation lists its various sources of income separately: continuing operations, and other comprehensive income. It also lists the EPS figure separately for each element of net income. Consider the EPS calculations for Westmount Concepts Inc. The final section (lines 15 to 17) of Exhibit 11-2 shows how companies report EPS under IFRS. IFRS requires disclosure of basic and diluted EPS for net income available to ordinary shareholders and disclosure of basic and diluted EPS for discontinued operations.

When the number of common shares outstanding changes during the year, such as when a company issues shares or repurchases shares during the year, earnings per share is calculated based on the weighted average number of common shares outstanding during the year.

Effect of Preferred Dividends on Earnings per Share. Recall that EPS is earnings per *common* share. But holders of preferred shares have first claim on dividends. Therefore, preferred dividends must be subtracted from net income in the computation of EPS.

Suppose Westmount Concepts Inc. had 10,000 preferred shares outstanding, each with a \$1.00 dividend. The annual preferred dividend would be \$10,000

(10,000 × \$1.00). The \$10,000 would be subtracted from each of the different income subtotals, resulting in the following EPS computations:

Earnings per share of common shares (12,500 shares outstanding):	
Income before other comprehensive income (\$54,400 − \$10,000)/12,500	\$3.55
Income from discontinued operations (\$27,200/12,500)	2.18
Comprehensive income (\$81,600 − \$10,000)/12,500	\$5.73

Earnings per Share May Not Be What They Seem

Although EPS is widely used as a measure of profitability, it has some serious limitations. Two firms could have the same earnings and EPS, but they would not be equally profitable if one firm invested more assets or capital to generate those earnings. Another problem arises when firms boost their EPS by manipulating the denominator. A firm could actually have a decline in earnings but could increase EPS by simply repurchasing shares.

Earnings per Share Dilution. Some corporations make their bonds or preferred shares more attractive to investors by offering conversion privileges, which permit the holder to convert the bond or preferred shares into some specified number of common shares. Bombardier is one such company. If the bonds or preferred shares are converted to common shares, the EPS is diluted, or reduced, because more common shares are divided into net income. Corporations with complex capital structures present two sets of EPS figures:

- EPS based on actual outstanding common shares (*basic* EPS)
- EPS based on outstanding common shares plus the additional common shares that would arise from conversion of convertible bonds or preferred shares into common shares (*diluted* EPS)

The topic of earnings per share dilution is complex and beyond the scope of this text.

What Should You Analyze to Gain an Overall Picture of a Company?

Two key figures used in financial analysis are

- Net income (or income from continuing operations)
- Cash flow from operations

For any one period, Westmount Concepts Inc.'s net income and net cash flow from operating activities may chart different paths. Accounting income arises from the accrual process as follows:

Total revenues and gains − Total expenses and losses = Net income (or Net loss)

As we have seen, revenues and gains are recorded when they occur, regardless of when the company receives or pays cash.

Net cash flow, on the other hand, is based solely on cash receipts and cash payments. During any particular period, a company may have lots of revenues and expenses and a hefty net income. But the company may have weak cash flow because it has not yet collected from customers. The reverse may also be true: The company may have abundant cash but little income.

The income statement and the statement of cash flows often present different pictures of the company. Which one provides better information? Neither: Both statements are needed, along with the balance sheet and statement of shareholders' equity, for an overall view of the business. Chapter 12 will cover the statement of cash flows in detail.

ACCOUNTING FOR INCOME STATEMENT PREPARATION

The accountant must consider a number of issues when preparing the income statement under IFRS:

- Does the revenue used to calculate income from continuing operations include only transactions completed by the year-end and that are properly classified as revenue from continuing operations?
- Are all expenses used to calculate income from continuing operations for the period included? Are only current period expenses included? Are the expenses included properly classified as expenses from continuing operations?
- Is other comprehensive income properly presented? Does it include the changes in shareholders' equity other than income from continuing operations such as unrealized gains or losses from derivatives, foreign currency translation adjustments, and changes in the fair value of available-for-sale financial assets?
- Have any changes in accounting policy been accounted for retroactively?
- Has earnings per share been properly accounted for and properly presented?
- Have corporate income taxes been properly accounted for?
- Have any prior period errors that were discovered during the period been properly accounted for?

USING A COMPANY'S INCOME STATEMENT AND STATEMENT OF SHAREHOLDERS' EQUITY IN DECISION MAKING

The income statement and the statement of shareholders' equity are important sources of information for managers, investors, and creditors. The content of the two statements affects managers, investors, and creditors differently. The three groups would also be interested in the auditor's report if the auditor gave the company a reservation of opinion related to either statement.

Manager—The manager would be most concerned about income from continuing operations and prior period errors.

Investor—Investors look to income from continuing operations as a predictor of future income. The investor would also be interested in earnings per share. Other issues that would concern an investor are discontinued operations, changes in accounting policy, and prior period errors. The investor would have to consider the impact of each of the three issues on the company's future operations.

The investor would also be interested in the information provided by the statement of shareholders' equity. Did the company pay cash or stock dividends? Did the dividend change during the period? Did the company issue new shares or repurchase shares?

Creditor—Creditors would be most interested in income from continuing operations and interest or financing expense. Did the company generate significantly more net income than its interest costs? The creditor would also consider the impact of discontinued operations, changes in accounting policy, and prior period errors.

The creditor would also be interested in the statement of shareholders' equity: How much cash did the company pay out in dividends and to repurchase shares? Is the company likely to have to borrow to finance future operations as a result of its dividend and share repurchase policies?

Accounting for Corporate Income Taxes

OBJECTIVE

② **Account** for a corporation's income tax

Corporations pay income tax as individuals do, but corporate and personal tax rates differ. The 2011 federal tax rate is 11% for private corporations and 16.5% for other corporations. The provinces also levy corporate income taxes at varying rates. The combined rate in 2011 for other than private corporations varies from 26.5% to 32.5%. We will use 30% in the following discussion.

To account for income tax, the corporation measures the following for each period:

- *Income tax expense*, an expense on the income statement. Income tax helps measure net income.
- *Income tax payable*, a liability on the balance sheet. Income tax payable is the current year's unpaid income tax.

Accounting for income tax by a corporation follows the principles of accrual accounting. Suppose that in 2010 Red Lake Outfitters Ltd. reported income before tax (also called **pretax accounting income**) of $9 million. Assume Red Lake's combined income tax rate is 30%. To begin this discussion, let's assume income tax expense and income tax payable are the same. Then Red Lake Outfitters Ltd. would record income tax for the year as follows:

2010			
Dec. 31	Income Tax Expense	2,700,000	
	Income Tax Payable		2,700,000
	Recorded income tax for the year ($9,000,000 × 0.30).		

ASSETS	=	LIABILITIES	+	SHAREHOLDERS' EQUITY	–	EXPENSES
0	=	2,700,000	+		–	2,700,000

Red Lake Outfitters Ltd.'s 2010 financial statements would report these figures (partial, in thousands):

Income statement		**Balance sheet**	
Income before income tax	$9,000	Current liabilities:	
Income tax expense	(2,700)	Income tax payable	$2,700
Net income	$6,300		

In general, income tax expense and income tax payable can be computed as follows:*

Income tax *expense*	=	Income before income tax (from the *income statement*)	×	Income tax rate
Income tax *payable*	**=**	**Taxable income (from the *income tax return filed with tax authorities*)**	**×**	**Income tax rate**

*The authors thank Jean Marie Hudson for suggesting this presentation.

The income statement and the income tax return are entirely separate documents:

- The income statement reports the results of operations.
- The income tax return is filed with Canada Revenue Agency (CRA) or the province in the case of Alberta and Quebec, to report the company's estimate of how much tax to pay the government in the current period.

For most companies, income tax expense and income tax payable differ. Certain revenues and expenses affect income differently for accounting purposes and tax purposes. One of the most important differences between accounting income and **taxable income** occurs when a corporation uses straight-line depreciation for the financial statements and capital cost allowance rates for the tax return. For any one year, tax depreciation usually differs from accounting depreciation on the income statement.

Continuing with the Red Lake Outfitters Ltd. illustration, suppose for 2011 that Red Lake has:

- Pretax accounting income of $10 million on the income statement
- Taxable income of $9.2 million on the company's income tax return

Taxable income is $0.8 million less than accounting income because Red Lake Outfitters Ltd., like many other companies, uses straight-line depreciation for accounting purposes and capital cost allowance for income tax purposes. Red Lake Outfitters Ltd. will record income tax for 2011 as follows (dollar amounts in millions and an income tax rate of 30%):

2011			
Dec. 31	Income Tax Expense ($10 × 0.30)	3.00	
	Income Tax Payable ($9.2 × 0.30)		2.76
	Deferred Income Tax Liability		0.24
	Recorded income tax for the year.		

ASSETS	=	LIABILITIES	+	SHAREHOLDERS' EQUITY	–	EXPENSES
0	=	$2.76 + $0.24			–	$3.00

Income tax expense is reported on the income statement, and income tax payable and deferred income tax liability on the balance sheet, as follows for Red Lake Outfitters Ltd. at the end of 2011 (dollar amounts in millions):

*Capital cost allowance rates are maximum allowable rates set by the Canada Revenue Agency.

Income statement		**Balance sheet**	
Income before income tax	$10.00	Current liabilities:	
Income tax expense	(3.00)	Income tax payable	$2.76
Net income	$ 7.00	Long-term liabilities:	
		Deferred income tax liability	0.24*

*Assumes the beginning balance of Deferred Income Tax Liability was zero.

Early in 2012, Red Lake Outfitters Ltd. would pay its income tax payable of $2.76 million because this is a current liability. Deferred income tax liability, however, is usually long-term, and the company may pay this liability over a longer period.

For a given year, Income Tax Payable can exceed Income Tax Expense. When that occurs, the company records a Deferred Income Tax Asset.

Analyzing Retained Earnings

Prior Period Error Adjustments

OBJECTIVE

3 **Analyze** shareholders' equity

IAS 8 "Accounting Policies, Changes in Accounting Estimates and Errors," referred to previously when accounting changes were discussed, is also concerned with material prior period errors. IAS 8 requires the error to be corrected retrospectively in the financial statements issued at the year-end following the discovery of the error.

Let us consider the impact of a material prior period error. The error means that the income statement for the year when the error occurred is incorrect as are the retained earnings for that year and subsequent years. The correction of the prior period error will result in a restated income statement for the year involved and restated statements of retained earnings.

Corrections to Retained Earnings for errors of earlier periods are called **prior period error adjustments**. The prior period error adjustment appears on the statement of retained earnings. Assume that Darlind Corp. recorded 2010 income tax expense as $30,000. The correct amount was $40,000. This error understated 2010 expenses and current liabilities by $10,000 and overstated net income by $10,000. A re-assessment by CRA in 2011 for the additional $10,000 alerted Darlind Corp. to the mistake.

This accounting error requires a prior period error adjustment. Prior period error adjustments are not reported on the income statement because they relate to an earlier accounting period. This prior period error adjustment would appear on the statement of retained earnings, as shown in Exhibit 11-3, with all amounts assumed.

EXHIBIT 11-3 **Reporting a Prior Period Error Adjustment on the Statement of Retained Earnings**

Darlind Corp.
Statement of Retained Earnings
For the Year Ended December 31, 2011

Retained earnings balance, December 31, 2010, as originally reported	$390,000
Prior period error adjustment—debit to correct error in recording income tax expense of 2010	(10,000)
Retained earnings balance, December 31, 2010, as adjusted	380,000
Net income for 2011	114,000
	494,000
Dividends for 2011	(41,000)
Retained earnings balance, December 31, 2011	$453,000

Analyzing the Statement of Shareholders' Equity

Most companies report a statement of shareholders' equity, which includes retained earnings. The statement of shareholders' equity is formatted like a statement of retained earnings but with a column for each element of shareholders' equity. The **statement of shareholders' equity** thus reports reasons for the changes in equity during the period.

Exhibit 11-4 is the 2011 statement of shareholders' equity for Westmount Concepts Inc. Study its format. There is a column for each element of equity, with common shares on the left and the far right column reporting the total. The top row (line 1) reports the beginning balances taken from last period's balance sheet. The rows report the various transactions, starting with Net income (line 2). The statement ends with the December 31, 2011, balances (line 8), which appear on the ending balance sheet given in Exhibit 11-5.

Let's examine Westmount Concepts Inc.'s shareholders' equity during 2011 using Exhibit 11-4.

Net Income (Line 2). During 2011, Westmount Concepts Inc. earned net income of $54,400, which increased Retained Earnings. Trace net income from the income statement (Exhibit 11-2, page 558) to the statement of shareholders' equity (Exhibit 11-4). Then trace the ending amount of Retained Earnings to the balance sheet in Exhibit 11-5. Moving back and forth among the financial statements is an important part of financial analysis.

Declaration of Cash Dividends (Line 3). The statement of shareholders' equity reports the amount of cash dividends the company declared during the year. Westmount Concepts Inc.'s cash dividends were $1.68 per share or $21,000, roughly one-third of net income. Dividends of $0.42 per share were paid in March, June, September, and December, 2011. Exhibit 11-4 reports the decrease in retained earnings from the declaration of the cash dividends.

EXHIBIT 11-4 **Statement of Shareholders' Equity**

Westmount Concepts Inc.
Statement of Shareholders' Equity
For the Year Ended December 31, 2011

	Common Shares	Contributed Surplus—Share Repurchases	Retained Earnings	Unrealized Gain (Loss) on Investments	Accumulated Other Comprehensive Income	Total Shareholders' Equity
1 Balance, December 31, 2010*	$180,000		$136,000		$(4,000)	$312,000
2 Net income			54,400			54,400
3 Cash dividends			(21,000)			(21,000)
4 Repurchase of common shares	(15,000)	1,000				(14,000)
5 Share dividends—10%	14,300		(14,300)			0
6 Issuance of shares	6,000					6,000
7 Unrealized gain on derivatives					1,000	1,000
8 Balance, December 31, 2011	$185,300	1,000	$155,100		$(3000)	$338,400

*There were 12,000 shares outstanding at December 31, 2010.

EXHIBIT 11-5 As at Shareholders' Equity Section of the Balance Sheet

Westmount Concepts Inc.
Balance Sheet (Partial)
As at December 31, 2011

Total assets	$894,110
Total liabilities	$555,710
Shareholders' Equity	
Common shares, shares issued—12,500	185,300
Contributed surplus	1,000
Retained earnings	155,100
Accumulated other comprensive income	(3,000)
Total shareholders' equity	338,400
Total liabilities and shareholders' equity	$894,110

Repurchase of Shares (Line 4). The statement of shareholders' equity reports the repurchase of shares. Recall from Chapter 9 that when shares are repurchased for cancellation, Common Shares is debited for the issue price of the shares repurchased. On January 2, 2011, Westmount Concepts Inc. paid $14,000 to repurchase 1,000 company shares (line 4). This transaction decreased shareholders' equity by $14,000. The Common Shares account was debited in the amount of $15,000, the amount of the credit to Common Shares when the repurchased shares were first issued. The difference of $1,000 ($15,000 − $14,000) is credited to Contributed Surplus. Practically, the company gained on the repurchase since it paid less to reacquire the shares than it sold them for originally. But a company cannot profit from transactions in its own shares, so the "gain" is put into Contributed Surplus in Shareholders' Equity.

Distribution of Share Dividends (Line 5). On January 3, 2011, Westmount Concepts Inc. distributed a share dividend to its shareholders. Prior to the share dividend, Westmount Concepts Inc.'s Common Shares account had a balance of $165,000. The company issued a share dividend of 10%, which added 1,100 shares to the 11,000 shares outstanding at the beginning of the year, which resulted in 12,100 shares being outstanding. The shares were valued at $13.00 per share, the market price at the date the dividend was declared.

But there was more to this share dividend. Westmount decreased (debited) Retained Earnings for the market value of the new shares issued in the share dividend. This market price, $14,300, is reported under Retained Earnings in Exhibit 11-4. The market price of the dividend ($14,300) was credited to Common Shares.

Issuance of Shares (Line 6). On January 4, 2011, Westmount Concepts Inc. issued 400 common shares for $6,000, which went into the Common Shares account. The issuance of shares increased contributed capital and total equity by $6,000.

Accumulated Other Comprehensive Income. Categories of Other Comprehensive Income include changes in unrealized fair value of derivatives designated as cash flow hedges, foreign currency translation adjustments arising from translating financial statements of self-sustaining foreign operations, change in unrealized fair value of available-for-sale financial assets (Exhibit 11-1), and derivatives (Exhibit 11-2).

At December 31, 2010, Westmount Concepts Inc. had a negative foreign currency adjustment of $4,000. During 2011, Westmount Concepts Inc. recognized an unrealized gain on derivatives.

Responsibility for the Financial Statements

Management's Responsibility

OBJECTIVE

4 **Understand** managers' and auditors' responsibilities for the financial statements

Management issues a management report in the annual report in which it acknowledges its responsibility for the company's financial statements. Management also acknowledges its responsibility for internal controls. Exhibit 11-6 is an excerpt from the statements of management's responsibility for the financial statements and for internal controls over financial reporting included in the 2009 annual report of Thomson Reuters corporation, a media conglomerate whose business includes financial and media divisions as well as legal, tax, accounting, healthcare, and science.

EXHIBIT 11-6 **Excerpt from Management Reports—Thomson Reuters Corporation**

Management's Responsibility for the Consolidated Financial Statements

The management of Thomson Reuters Corporation (the "Company") is responsible for the accompanying consolidated financial statements and other information included in this annual report. The financial statements have been prepared in conformity with International Financial Reporting Standards, as issued by the International Accounting Standards Board, using the best estimates and judgments of management, where appropriate. Information presented elsewhere in this annual report is consistent with that in the financial statements.

The Company's board of directors is responsible for ensuring that management fulfills its responsibilities in respect of financial reporting and internal control....

Management's Report on Internal Control over Financial Reporting

Management is responsible for establishing and maintaining adequate internal control over financial reporting. Internal control over financial reporting is a process that was designed to provide reasonable assurance regarding the reliability of financial reporting and the preparation of financial statements for external purposes in accordance with International Financial Reporting Standards as issued by the International Accounting Standards Board ("IFRS"). Internal control over financial reporting includes those policies and procedures that (i) pertain to the maintenance of records that, in reasonable detail, accurately and fairly reflect the transactions and dispositions of the assets of Thomson Reuters Corporation (the "Company"); (ii) provide reasonable assurance that transactions are recorded as necessary to permit preparation of financial statements in accordance with IFRS, and that receipts and expenditures of the Company are being made only in accordance with authorizations of management and directors of the Company; and (iii) provide reasonable assurance regarding prevention or timely detection of unauthorized acquisition, use, or disposition of the Company's assets that could have a material effect on the financial statements.

Because of its inherent limitations, internal control over financial reporting may not prevent or detect misstatements. Also, projections of any evaluation of effectiveness to future periods are subject to the risk that controls may become inadequate because of changes in conditions, or that the degree of compliance with the policies and procedures may deteriorate....

Management declares its responsibility for the financial statements and states that they conform to IFRS. As we've seen throughout this book, IFRS are the standard for preparing the financial statements for publicly accountable enterprises and are designed to produce relevant, reliable, and useful information for making investment and credit decisions.

Auditor's Report

The various federal and provincial incorporating acts and, in the case of listed companies, the provincial securities commissions and the stock exchanges require companies that issue their shares or trust units publicly to file audited financial statements with the various bodies. To comply with this requirement, companies engage outside auditors who are usually chartered accountants, or, depending on the province, certified general accountants, to examine their statements. In some provinces, certified management accountants and others may perform the audit. The independent auditors decide whether the company's financial statements comply with IFRS for publicly accountable enterprises and ASPE for private entities and then issue an auditor's report. Auditors' reports usually fall into one of two categories:

1. **Unqualified (clean) opinion**. The statements are reliable.
2. Reservation of opinion:
   i. **Qualified opinion.** The statements are reliable except for one item for which the opinion is said to be qualified.
   ii. **Adverse opinion.** There is a significant deviation from IFRS or ASPE, and the statements do not present fairly.
   iii. **Denial of opinion.** The auditor was unable to reach a professional opinion because of scope limitations (inability to obtain sufficient appropriate evidential matter).

Exhibit 11-7 is the auditor's report on the financial statements of Thomson Reuters Corporation.

The auditor's report is addressed to the shareholders of the company. The auditing firm signs its name, in this case the Toronto office of PricewaterhouseCoopers LLP (LLP is the abbreviation for limited liability partnership).

The auditor's report typically contains three paragraphs:

- The first (introductory) paragraph identifies the audited financial statements. It also delineates the responsibilities of management and the auditor insofar as the financial statements are concerned.
- The second (scope) paragraph describes how the audit was performed, mentioning that generally accepted auditing standards are the benchmark for evaluating the audit's quality.
- The third (opinion) paragraph states PricewaterhouseCoopers's opinion that Thomson Reuters's financial statements conform to IFRS and that people can rely on them for decision making.

Thomson Reuters's auditor's report contains an unqualified opinion, which indicates that the financial statements are reliable.

The independent audit adds credibility to the financial statements. It is no accident that financial reporting and auditing are very advanced in Canada and the United States and that these two countries' capital markets are highly regarded.

EXHIBIT 11-7 **Excerpt from Auditor's Report on the Financial Statements of Thomson Reuters Corporation**

To the shareholders of Thomson Reuters Corporation:
We have completed integrated audits of Thomson Reuters Corporation's 2009 and 2008 consolidated financial statements and of its internal control over financial reporting as at December 31, 2009. Our opinions, based on our audits are presented below.

Consolidated Financial Statements
We have audited the accompanying consolidated statement of financial position of Thomson Reuters Corporation (the "Company") as at December 31, 2009, December 31, 2008 and January 1, 2008, and the related consolidated income statement and statements of comprehensive income, cash flow and changes in equity for each of the years ended December 31, 2009 and 2008. These financial statements are the responsibility of the Company's management. Our responsibility is to express an opinion on these financial statements based on our audits.

We conducted our audits of the Company's consolidated financial statements in accordance with Canadian generally accepted auditing standards and the standards of the Public Company Accounting Oversight Board (United States). Those standards require that we plan and perform an audit to obtain reasonable assurance about whether the financial statements are free of material misstatement. An audit of financial statements includes examining, on a test basis, evidence supporting the amounts and disclosures in the financial statements. A financial statement audit also includes assessing the accounting principles used and significant estimates made by management, and evalulating the overall financial statement presentation. We believe that our audits provide a reasonable basis for our opinion.

In our opinion, the consolidated financial statements referred to above present fairly, in all material respects, the financial position of the Company as at December 31, 2009, December 31, 2008 and January 1, 2008 and the results of its operations and its cash flows for each of the years ended December 31, 2009 and 2008 in accordance with International Financial Reporting Standards as issued by the International Accounting Standards Board....

/s/ PricewaterhouseCoopers LLP
Chartered Accountants, Licensed Public Accountants
Toronto, Canada
March 11, 2010

SUMMARY OF CHAPTER 11

Learning Objective 1: **Analyze a corporate comprehensive income statement**

A corporation's income statement including **earnings per share (EPS)** receives more attention than any other item in the financial statements. An important consideration for investors is **earnings quality**, which involves correctly recognizing both revenue and expenses.

Recognizing revenue when it is earned and not before is an important consideration. Premature recognition of revenue is a serious accounting fraud.

Two important components of earnings quality for a manufacturing company or a retail organization are cost of goods sold and gross profit. Earnings from operations is an important component of earnings for a service company such as an airline or a law firm.

Careful recording and reporting of the other expenses is also important to earnings quality. Understating of expenses is an area of accounting fraud.

Income from continuing operations includes revenue and expenses related to the company's regular business operations. Net income from continuing operations is the best predictor of future corporate income. The components of **other comprehensive income** are more volatile than income from continuing operations.

IAS 1 requires a company to provide either:

- Two statements, one of which will be a statement of comprehensive income and the other an income statement, or
- One statement of comprehensive income, which will include both an income statement and a statement of comprehensive income.

APSE Section 1520 does not require private enterprise companies to separate the income statement into income from continuing operations and other comprehensive income.

Analysts compare the value of a company's common shares with the market price of the company's shares in making a buy or hold decision or a sell decision.

The disposal of discontinued operations is a one-time decision. IFRS 5 and APSE Section 1520 requires transactions related to disposal of a discontinued operation to be shown separately from income from continuing operations.

A change in accounting policy must be undertaken only if required by a new accounting standard or if the change results in more relevant and reliable information. Such a change must be accounted for retrospectively.

Earnings per share is an important metric for users of financial statements. A publicly accountable enterprise must provide earnings per share information about continuing operations and also for discontinued operations. A private enterprise must provide information about continuing operations and also discontinued operations.

Learning Objective ❷: **Account for a corporation's income tax**

Taxpayers are allowed to deduct certain expenses such as depreciation at different rates for financial reporting purposes and for tax reporting purposes. The result is that Tax Expense reported on the income statement is different from Tax Payable reported on the balance sheet. The difference is recognized as a Deferred Tax Asset if Tax Payable exceeds Tax Expense and as a Deferred Tax Liability if Tax Expense exceeds Tax Payable.

Learning Objective ❸: **Analyze shareholders' equity**

Prior period errors are errors in the financial statements that were made in a prior period but which came to light in the current period. **Prior period error adjustments** must be accounted for retroactively.

The **statement of shareholders' equity** reports changes in shareholders' equity during the period under review. The statement discloses changes in common shares (and preferred shares if issued), retained earnings, contributed surplus (if applicable), and accumulated other comprehensive income.

Learning Objective ❹: **Understand managers' and auditors' responsibilities for the financial statements**

Management is responsible for the preparation of the financial statements and for the company's internal controls.

The independent auditor is responsible for auditing the financial statements and issuing an opinion called the auditor's report on the results of the audit. The work of the auditor adds credibility to the financial statements because of the independence and technical expertise the auditor brings to the task.

MyAccountingLab

END-OF-CHAPTER SUMMARY PROBLEM

The following information was taken from the ledger of Canmore Outdoor Products Ltd., a publicly accountable enterprise, as at December 31, 2011:

Prior period adjustment— credit to Retained Earnings	$ 5,000	Income tax expense (saving): Unrealized gain on derivatives	6,400
Gain on sale of property, plant, and equipment	21,000	Preferred shares, $8.00, 500 shares issued	50,000
Cost of goods sold	380,000	Dividends	16,000
Income tax expense (saving): Continuing operations	25,600	Unrealized gain on derivatives	20,000
Selling expenses	78,000	Loss due to lawsuit	11,000
Common shares, 40,000 shares issued	165,000	General expenses	62,000
Sales revenue	620,000	Retained earnings, beginning, as originally reported	103,000
Interest expense	30,000		

Name: Canmore Outdoor Products Ltd.
Industry: Outdoor products corporation
Fiscal Period: Year ended December 31, 2011

Required

Prepare a single-step income statement (with all revenues grouped together) and a statement of retained earnings for Canmore Outdoor Products Ltd. for the year ended December 31, 2011. Include the net income earnings-per-share presentation and show computations. Assume no changes in the share accounts during the year.

Answers

Sort the ledger items into those that appear on the statement of retained earnings and those that appear on the income statement.

Revenue includes gain on sale of property, plant, and equipment.

Expenses include all normal operating costs related to the revenue reported. Income tax expense is included here.

This is reported net of income tax.

Canmore Outdoor Products Ltd.
Income Statement
For the Year Ended December 31, 2011

Revenue and gains:		
Sales revenue		$620,000
Gain on sale of property, plant, and equipment		21,000
Total revenues and gains		641,000
Expenses and losses:		
Cost of goods sold	$380,000	
Selling expenses	78,000	
General expenses	62,000	
Interest expense	30,000	
Loss due to lawsuit	11,000	
Income tax expense	25,600	
Total expenses and losses		586,600
Net income		54,400
Other comprehensive income		
Unrealized gain on derivatives, $20,000, less income tax, $6,400		13,600
Comprehensive income		$ 68,000

Earnings per share: (40,000 shares outstanding)*
Net income [($54,400 − $4,000)/40,000 shares] $1.26

*Computations:

$$EPS = \frac{\text{Income} - \text{Preferred dividends}}{\text{Common shares outstanding}}$$

Preferred dividends: 500 × $8.00 = $4,000
Common shares outstanding: 40,000 shares

The earnings per share is calculated by using net income from various parts of the income statement less preferred dividends. Use the common shares and preferred shares information from the data given to calculate preferred dividends and the number of common shares outstanding.

Canmore Outdoor Products Ltd.
Statement of Retained Earnings
For the Year Ended December 31, 2011

Retained earnings balance, beginning, as originally reported	$103,000
Prior period adjustment	5,000
Retained earnings balance, beginning, as adjusted	108,000
Net income for current year	54,400
	162,400
Dividends for current year	(16,000)
Retained earnings balance, ending	$146,400

Prior period adjustments must be disclosed in a separate line in the statement of retained earnings.

Given in the list of data.

Review the Comprehensive Income Statement and the Statement of Shareholders' Equity

Quick Check (Answers are given on page 595.)

1. The quality of earnings suggests that
   a. Net income is the best measure of the results of operations.
   b. Income from continuing operations is better than income from one-time transactions.
   c. Continuing operations and one-time transactions are of equal importance.
   d. Shareholders want the corporation to earn enough income to be able to pay its debts.
2. Which statement is true?
   a. Discontinued operations are a separate category on the income statement.
   b. Extraordinary items are part of discontinued operations.
   c. Cumulative effect of accounting changes is combined with continuing operations on the income statement.
   d. All of the above are true.
3. Marshall Transportation Ltd. earned $5.94 per common share. Suppose you capitalize Marshall's income at 6%. How much are you willing to pay for a share of Marshall Transportation?
   a. $32.17
   b. $5.17
   c. $165.00
   d. Some other amount

4. Return to TELUS's income statement on page 555. TELUS has no preferred shares outstanding. How many common and nonvoting shares did TELUS have outstanding during fiscal year 2009? Focus on the bottom line, net income.
   a. 337 million
   b. 320 million
   c. 318 million
   d. 31 million

5. Why is it important for companies to report their accounting changes to the public?
   a. Accounting changes affect dividends, and investors want dividends.
   b. Some accounting changes are more extraordinary than others.
   c. Most accounting changes increase net income, and investors need to know why the increase in net income occurred.
   d. Without the reporting of accounting changes, investors could believe that all the company's income came from continuing operations.

6. Other comprehensive income
   a. Affects earnings per share
   b. Includes extraordinary gains and losses
   c. Includes unrealized gains and losses on investments
   d. Has no effect on income tax

7. OnStar GPS Systems earned income before tax of $50,000. Taxable income was $40,000, and the income tax rate was 25%. OnStar recorded income tax with this journal entry:

a.	Income Tax Expense	12,500	
	Income Tax Payable		10,000
	Deferred Income Tax Liability		2,500
b.	Income Tax Expense	12,500	
	Income Tax Payable		12,500
c.	Income Tax Payable	10,000	
	Income Tax Expense		10,000
d.	Income Tax Payable	12,500	
	Income Tax Expense		10,000
	Deferred Income Tax Liability		2,500

8. Deferred Income Tax Liability is usually

	Type of Account	*Reported on the*
a.	Short-term	Income statement
b.	Short-term	Statement of shareholders' equity
c.	Long-term	Income statement
d.	Long-term	Balance statement

9. The main purpose of the statement of shareholders' equity is to report
   a. Financial position
   b. Reasons for changes in the equity accounts
   c. Results of operations
   d. Comprehensive income

10. An auditor report by independent accountants
    a. Ensures that the financial statements are error-free
    b. Gives investors assurance that the company's shares are a safe investment
    c. Gives investors assurance that the company's financial statements conform to GAAP
    d. Is ultimately the responsibility of the management of the client company

Accounting Vocabulary

adverse opinion An audit opinion stating that the financial statements are unreliable. (p. 573)

clean opinion An *unqualified opinion*. The statements are reliable. (p. 573)

comprehensive income Includes net income and other comprehensive income. (p. 555)

denial of opinion An audit opinion stating that the auditor was unable to reach a professional opinion regarding the quality of the financial statements. (p. 573)

earnings per share (EPS) Amount of a company's net income per outstanding common share. (p. 564)

earnings quality Has many components, the most important being proper revenue and expense recognition (p. 556)

investment capitalization rate An earnings rate used to estimate the value of an investment in the share capital of a company. (p. 561)

other comprehensive income Includes amounts not included in continuing operations that affect shareholders' equity and are other than from owners of the business (p. 559)

pretax accounting income Income before tax on the income statement. (p. 567)

prior period error adjustment A correction to the beginning balance of Retained Earnings for an error of an earlier period. (p. 569)

qualified opinion An audit opinion stating that the financial statements are reliable, except for one or more items for which the opinion is said to be qualified. (p. 573)

segment of a business An identifiable division of a company. (p. 562)

statement of shareholders' equity Reports the changes in all categories of shareholders' equity during the period. (p. 570)

taxable income The basis for computing the amount of tax to pay the government. (p. 568)

unqualified (clean) opinion An audit opinion stating that the financial statements are reliable. (p. 573)

Assess Your Progress

Make the grade with MyAccountingLab: The exercises and problems in this chapter can be found on MyAccountingLab at www.myaccountinglab.com. You can practise them as often as you want, and they feature step-by-step guided solutions to help you find the right answer.

Short Exercises

S11-1 List the major parts of a complex corporate income statement for Omnibus Corporation Inc. for the year ended March 31, 2011. Include all the major parts of the income statement, starting with net sales revenue and ending with net income (net loss). You may ignore dollar amounts and earnings per share.

Learning Objective 1
Preparing a complex income statement

S11-2 Study the income statement of **TELUS Corporation.** (page 555), and answer these questions about the company:

1. How much operating income did TELUS earn on operating revenue? How much was income before taxes? How much was net income?
2. What dollar amount of net income would most sophisticated investors use to predict TELUS's net income for the next year? Name this item, give its amount, and state your reason.

Learning Objective 1
Explaining the items on a complex income statement

S11-3 Financial Resources Inc. reported the following items, listed in no particular order, at December 31, 2011 (in thousands):

Learning Objective 1
Preparing a complex income statement

Other gains (losses)	$ (2,000)	Cost of goods sold	$66,000
Net sales revenue	168,000	Operating expenses	56,000
Loss on discontinued operations	20,000	Accounts receivable	21,000

Income tax of 25% applies to all items.

Prepare Financial Resources' comprehensive income statement for the year ended December 31, 2011. Omit earnings per share.

S11-4 Return to the Financial Resources data in Short Exercise 11-3. Financial Resources had 10,000 common shares outstanding during 2011. Financial Resources declared and paid preferred dividends of $5,000 during 2011.

Report Financial Resources' earnings per share on the comprehensive income statement.

Learning Objective 1
Reporting earnings per share

S11-5 Use the Financial Resources data in Short Exercise 11-3. In addition, Financial Resources had unrealized gains of $1,000 on investments and a $2,000 foreign-currency translation adjustment (a gain) during 2011. Start with Financial Resources' comprehensive

Learning Objective 1
Reporting comprehensive income

income from Short Exercise 11-3 and show how the company could report additional comprehensive income on its 2011 comprehensive income statement.

Should Financial Resources report earnings per share for other comprehensive income? State why or why not.

Learning Objective 1
Valuing a company's shares

S11-6 For fiscal year 2009 (the year ended January 2, 2010) Shoppers Drug Mart Corporation reported net sales of $9,986 million and net income of $585 million from operations.

Earnings per share was $2.69. At a capitalization rate of 6%, how much should one share of Shoppers Drug Mart be worth? Compare your estimated share price to Shoppers Drug Mart's actual share price as quoted in *The Globe and Mail*, in your newspaper, or on the Internet. Based on your estimated market value, should you buy, hold, or sell Shoppers Drug Mart shares?

Learning Objective 1
Interpreting earnings-per-share data

S11-7 Marstaller Motor Limited has preferred shares outstanding and issued additional common shares during the year.

1. Give the basic equation to compute earnings per common share for net income.
2. List the income items for which Marstaller must report earnings-per-share data.
3. What makes earnings per share so useful as a business statistic?

Learning Objective 2
Accounting for a corporation's income tax

S11-8 PEI Marine Inc. had income before income tax of $110,000 and taxable income of $90,000 for 2011, the company's first year of operations. The income tax rate is 25%.

1. Make the entry to record PEI Marine's income taxes for 2011.
2. Show what PEI Marine will report on its 2011 income statement starting with income before income tax. Also show what PEI Marine will report for current and long-term liabilities on its December 31, 2011, balance sheet.

Learning Objective 3
Reporting a prior period adjustment

S11-9 Quick Pies Ltd. was set to report the following statement of retained earnings for the year ended December 31, 2011.

Quick Pies Ltd.
Statement of Retained Earnings
For the Year Ended December 31, 2011

Retained earnings, December 31, 2010	$140,000
Net income for 2011	91,000
Dividends for 2011	(14,000)
Retained earnings, December 31, 2011	$217,000

Before issuing its 2011 financial statements, Quick Pies learned that net income of 2010 was overstated by $16,000. Prepare Quick Pies' 2011 statement of retained earnings to show the correction of the error—that is, the prior period adjustment.

Learning Objective 4
Using the statement of shareholders' equity

S11-10 Use the statement of shareholders' equity in Exhibit 11-4 (p. 570) to answer the following questions about Westmount Concepts Inc.:

1. How much cash did the issuance of common shares bring in during 2011?
2. What was the effect of the share dividends on Westmount's retained earnings? What was the effect on total share capital, on total shareholders' equity, and on total assets?
3. What was the impact on shareholders' equity of the common shares that Westmount repurchased during 2011?

Exercises

E11-11 Mountain Cycles Inc. reported a number of special items on its income statement. The following data, listed in no particular order, came from Mountain's financial statements (amounts in thousands):

Learning Objective 1 — Preparing and using a complex income statement

Income tax expense (saving):		Net sales	$18,300
Continuing operations	$515	Foreign-currency translation adjustment	320
Discontinued operations	56	Income from discontinued operations	311
Unrealized gain on portfolio investments	15	Dividends declared and paid	860
Short-term investments	25	Total operating expenses	16,250

Required

Show how the Mountain Cycles Inc. comprehensive income statement for the year ended September 30, 2011, should appear. Omit earnings per share.

E11-12 The Golden Books Corporation accounting records include the following for 2011 (in thousands):

Learning Objective 1 — Preparing and using a complex income statement

Other revenues	$ 1,400
Income tax expense—discontinued operations	600
Income tax expense—income from continuing operations	2,150
Income from discontinued operations	1,500
Sales revenue	114,000
Total operating expenses	106,800

Required

1. Prepare Golden Books' single-step income statement for the year ended December 31, 2011, including earnings per share. Golden Books had 1,600 thousand common shares and no preferred shares outstanding during the year.
2. Assume investors capitalize Golden Books' earnings at 7%. Estimate the price of one common share of the company.

E11-13 High Seas Cruise Lines Inc. reported the following income statement for the year ended December 31, 2011.

Learning Objective 1 — Using an income statement

	millions
Operating revenues	$ 70,752
Operating expenses	60,258
Operating income	10,494
Other revenue (expense), net	985
Income from continuing operations	11,479
Discontinued operations, net of tax	935
Comprehensive income	$12,414

Required

1. Were High Seas' discontinued operations more like an expense or a revenue? How can you tell?
2. Should the discontinued operations be included in or excluded from income? State your reason.

3. Suppose you are working as a financial analyst and your job is to predict High Seas' net income for 2012 and beyond. Which item from the income statement will you use for your prediction? Identify its amount. Why will you use this item?

Learning Objective 1
Using income data for investment analysis

E11-14 During 2009, Canadian National Railway Company (CN) had sales of $7.4 billion, operating profit of $2.4 billion, and net income of $1.9 billion. Earnings per share (EPS) were $3.92. On July 19, 2010, a common share of CN was priced at $62.56 on the Toronto Stock Exchange.

What investment capitalization rate did investors appear to be using to determine the value of one common share of CN? The formula for the value of one common share uses EPS in the calculation.

Learning Objective 1
Computing earnings per share

E11-15 Tennyson Loan Corporation's balance sheet reports the following:

$6 Preferred shares, 10,000 shares issued	$500,000
Common shares, 1,200,000 shares issued	600,000

During 2011 Tennyson earned net income of $5,800,000. Compute Tennyson's EPS for 2011.

Learning Objective 1
Computing and using earnings per share

E11-16 Midtown Holding Limited operates numerous businesses, including motel, auto rental, and real estate companies. Year 2011 was interesting for Midtown, which reported the following on its income statement (in millions):

Net revenues	$3,930
Total expenses and other	3,354
Income from continuing operations	576
Other comprehensive income	
Discontinued operations, net of tax	84
Foreign currency translation adjustment	8
Comprehensive income	$ 668

During 2011, Midtown had the following (in millions, except for stated value per share):

Common shares 900 shares issued	$9

Required

Show how Midtown should report earnings per share for 2011.

Learning Objective 2
Accounting for income tax by a corporation

E11-17 For 2011, its first year of operations, Smartpages Advertising Ltd. earned pretax accounting income (on the income statement) of $600,000. Taxable income (on the tax return filed with the Canada Revenue Agency) is $550,000. The income tax rate is 25%. Record Smartpages' income tax for the year. Show what Smartpages will report on its 2011 income statement and balance sheet for this situation. Start the income statement with income before tax.

Learning Objective 2
Accounting for income tax by a corporation

E11-18 During 2011, the Castle Heights Corp. income statement reported income of $300,000 before tax. The company's income tax return filed with the Canada Revenue Agency showed taxable income of $250,000. During 2011, Castle Heights was subject to an income tax rate of 25%.

Required

1. Journalize Castle Heights' income taxes for 2011.
2. How much income tax did Castle Heights have to pay currently for 2011?

3. At the beginning of 2011, Castle Heights' balance of Future Income Tax Liability was $40,000. How much Future Income Tax Liability did Castle Heights report on its balance sheet at December 31, 2011?

E11-19 Roy Beaty Products Inc. reported a prior period error adjustment in 2011. An accounting error caused net income of 2010 to be understated by $10 million. Retained earnings at December 31, 2010, as previously reported, stood at $324 million. Net income for 2011 was $88 million, and 2011 dividends were $48 million.

Learning Objective 3
Reporting a prior period adjustment on the statement of retained earnings

Required
Prepare the company's statement of retained earnings for the year ended December 31, 2011. How does the prior period adjustment affect Roy Beaty's net income for 2011?

E11-20 At December 31, 2010, Lake Air Mall Inc. reported shareholders' equity as follows:

Learning Objective 3
Preparing a statement of retained earnings

Common shares, 500,000 shares authorized, 300,000 shares issued..................	$ 870,000
Retained earnings..	680,000
	$1,550,000

During 2011, Lake Air Mall completed these transactions (listed in chronological order):

a. Declared and issued a 5% stock dividend on the outstanding shares. At the time, Lake Air Mall shares were quoted at a market price of $10 per share
b. Issued 20,000 common shares at the price of $12 per share
c. Net income from operations for the year, $320,000
d. Declared cash dividends of $100,000

Required
Prepare Lake Air Mall's statement of shareholders' equity for 2011, using the format of Exhibit 11-4 (p. 570) as a model.

E11-21 Spring Water Limited reported the following items on its statement of shareholders' equity for the year ended December 31, 2011 (in thousands):

Learning Objective 3
Using a company's statement of shareholders' equity

	Common Shares	Retained Earnings	Accumulated Other Comprehensive Income	Total Shareholders' Equity
Balance, Dec. 31, 2010.............	$3,000	$5,000	$14	$8,014
Net earnings from operations		1,500		
Unrealized gain on investments .			2	
Issuance of 15 shares	150			
Cash dividends.........................		(220)		
Balance, Dec. 31, 2011				

Required
1. Determine the December 31, 2011, balances in Spring Water's shareholders' equity accounts and total shareholders' equity on this date.
2. Spring Water's total liabilities on December 31, 2011, are $7,500 thousand. What is Spring Water's debt ratio on this date?
3. Was there a profit or a loss for the year ended December 31, 2011? How can you tell?
4. At what price per share did Spring Water issue common shares during 2011?

Learning Objective 4
Identifying responsibility and standards for the financial statements

E11-22 The 2009 annual report of WestJet Airlines Ltd. included the following:

MANAGEMENT'S REPORT TO THE SHAREHOLDERS

The consolidated financial statements have been prepared by management in accordance with Canadian generally accepted accounting principles. When a choice between accounting methods exists, management has chosen those it deems conservative and appropriate in the circumstances. Financial statements will, by necessity, include certain amounts based on estimates and judgments. Management has determined such amounts on a reasonable basis to ensure that the consolidated financial statements are presented fairly in all material respects. Financial information contained in this report is consistent, where appropriate, with the information and data contained in the consolidated financial statements. All information in this report is the responsibility of management.

Management has established systems of internal control, including disclosure controls and procedures, which are designed to provide reasonable assurance that financial and non-financial information that is disclosed is timely, complete, relevant and accurate. These systems of internal control also serve to safeguard the Corporation's assets. The systems of internal control are monitored by management, and further supported by an internal audit department whose functions include reviewing internal controls and their applications.

The Board of Directors is responsible for the overall stewardship and governance of the Corporation, including ensuring management fulfills its responsibility for financial reporting and internal control, and reviewing and approving the consolidated financial statements. The Board carries out this responsibility principally through its Audit Committee.

The Audit Committee of the Board of Directors, composed of independent Directors, meets regularly with management, the internal auditors and the external auditors to satisfy itself that each is properly discharging its responsibilities, and to review the consolidated financial statements and management's discussion and analysis. The Audit Committee reports its findings to the Board of Directors prior to the approval of such statements for issuance to the shareholders. The Audit Committee also recommends, for review by the Board of Directors and approval of shareholders, the reappointment of the external auditors. The internal and external auditors have full and free access to the Audit Committee.

The consolidated financial statements have been audited by KPMG LLP, the independent external auditors, in accordance with generally accepted auditing standards on behalf of the shareholders. The auditors' report outlines the scope of their examination and sets forth their opinion.

/s/Sean Durfy
SEAN DURFY
President and
Chief Executive Officer

/s/Vito Culmone
VITO CULMONE
Executive Vice-President, Finance
and Chief Financial Officer

Calgary, Canada
February 16, 2010

AUDITORS' REPORT TO THE SHAREHOLDERS

We have audited the consolidated balance sheets of WestJet Airlines Ltd. as at December 31, 2009 and 2008, and the consolidated statements of earnings, comprehensive income, shareholders' equity and cash flows for the years then ended. These consolidated financial statements are the responsibility of the Corporation's management. Our responsibility is to express an opinion on these consolidated financial statements based on our audits.

We conducted our audits in accordance with Canadian generally accepted auditing standards. Those standards require that we plan and perform an audit to obtain reasonable assurance whether the financial statements are free of material misstatement. An audit includes examining, on a test basis, evidence supporting the amounts and disclosures in the financial statements. An audit also includes assessing the accounting principles used and significant estimates made by management, as well as evaluating the overall financial statement presentation.

In our opinion, these consolidated financial statements present fairly, in all material respects, the financial position of the Corporation as at December 31, 2009 and 2008 and the results of its operations and its cash flows for the years then ended in accordance with Canadian generally accepted accounting principles.

/s/KPMG LLP
Chartered Accountants

Calgary, Canada
February 16, 2010

1. Who is responsible for WestJet's financial statements?
2. By what accounting standard are the financial statements prepared?
3. Identify one concrete action that WestJet's management takes to fulfill its responsibility for the reliability of the company's financial information.
4. Which entity gave an outside, independent opinion on the WestJet financial statements? Where was this entity located, and when did it release its opinion to the public?
5. Exactly what did the audit cover? Give names and dates.
6. By what standard did the auditor conduct the audit?
7. What was the auditor's opinion of WestJet's financial statements?

Quiz

Test your understanding of the corporate income statement and the statement of shareholders' equity by answering the following questions. Select the best choice from among the possible answers given.

Q11-23 What is the best source of income for a corporation?

a. Prior period error adjustments
b. Continuing operations
c. Foreign currency exchange adjustment
d. Discontinued operations

Q11-24 Jergens Lotion Limited reports several earnings numbers on its current-year income statement (parentheses indicate a loss):

Gross profit	$140,000	Income from continuing operations	$35,000
Comprehensive income	41,000	Foreign currency translation adjustment	14,000
Income before income tax	60,000	Discontinued operations	(8,000)

How much net income would most investment analysts predict for Jergens to earn next year?

a. $14,000
b. $35,000
c. $49,000
d. $41,000

Q11-25 Refer to Question 11-24. Suppose you are evaluating Jergens Lotion Limited shares as an investment. You require a 10% rate of return on investments, so you capitalize Jergens' earnings at 10%. How much are you willing to pay for all of Jergens' common shares?

a. $1,400,000
b. $600,000
c. $410,000
d. $350,000

Q11-26 Hi-Valu Inc. had the following items:

Loss from discontinued operations	$ 90,000
Gain on sale of discontinued assets	110,000

Operating income before income tax and income before discontinued operations and gain on sale of discontinued assets totals $260,000, and the income tax rate is 25%. Hi-Valu's comprehensive income is

a. $210,000
b. $280,000
c. $380,000
d. $460,000

Q11-27 Hi-Valu Inc. in Question 11-26 has 10,000 $5 preferred shares and 100,000 common shares outstanding. Earnings per share for net income is

a. $1.02
b. $1.60
c. $1.68
d. $2.02

Q11-28 Earnings per share is based on

a. Continuing operations
b. Discontinued operations
c. Number of common shares outstanding
d. Comprehensive income

Q11-29 Copystar Corporation has income before income tax of $150,000 and taxable income of $100,000. The income tax rate is 25%. Copystar's income statement will report net income of

a. $40,000
b. $60,000
c. $112,500
d. $120,000

Q11-30 Copystar Corporation in the preceding question must immediately pay income tax of

a. $60,000
b. $8,000
c. $32,000
d. $25,000

Q11-31 Use the Copystar Corporation data in Question 11-29. At the end of its first year of operations, Copystar's deferred income tax liability is

a. $12,500
b. $28,000
c. $32,000
d. $40,000

Q11-32 Which of the following items is most closely related to prior period adjustments?

a. Earnings per share
b. Retained earnings
c. Accounting errors
d. Preferred share dividends

Q11-33 Examine the statement of shareholders' equity of Westmount Concepts Inc. in Exhibit 11-4 (p. 570). What was the fair value of each share that Westmount gave its shareholders in the stock dividend?

a. $8
b. $8,000
c. $34,000
d. $13

Q11-34 Which statement is true?

a. Management audits the financial statements.
b. Independent auditors prepare the financial statements.
c. IFRS will govern the form and content of the financial statements beginning in 2011.
d. The Public Company Oversight Board evaluates internal controls.

Problems

(Group A)

Learning Objective 1
Preparing a complex income statement

P11-35A The following information was taken from the records of Beauty Cosmetics Ltd. at December 31, 2011.

Prior period error adjustment— debit to Retained Earnings	$ 4,000	Dividends on common shares	$ 37,000
Income tax expense (saving):		Interest expense	23,000
		Gain on lawsuit settlement	8,000
Continuing operations	25,000	Dividend revenue	11,000
Income from discontinued operations	2,000	General expenses	71,000
Loss on sale of discontinued assets	(8,900)	Sales revenue	567,000
Cumulative effect of change in inventory method	2,500	Retained earnings, beginning, as originally reported	63,000
Loss on sale of plant assets	10,000	Selling expenses	87,000
Income from discontinued operations	7,000	Common shares	
Preferred shares $1.50 4,000 shares issued	100,000	20,000 shares authorized and issued	350,000
Cumulative effect of change in inventory method (credit) retrospective to 2010	7,600	Loss on sale of discontinued assets	27,000
		Cost of goods sold	319,000

Required

1. Prepare Beauty Cosmetics' single-step comprehensive income statement, which lists all revenues together and all expenses together, for the fiscal year ended December 31, 2011. Include earnings-per-share data.

2. Would the comprehensive income statement for 2011 require change from previous reporting? Why? By how much?
3. Evaluate income for the year ended December 31, 2011. Beauty Cosmetics' top managers hoped to earn income from continuing operations equal to 10% of sales.

Learning Objective 3
Preparing a statement of shareholder's equity

P11-36A Use the data in Problem 11-35A and the format of Exhibit 11-4 to prepare the Beauty Cosmetics statement of shareholders' equity for the year ended December 31, 2011. Assume Beauty Cosmetics adopted IFRS (Comprehensive Income) effective 2010.

Learning Objective 1
Using income data to make an investment decision

P11-37A Beauty Cosmetics in Problem 11-35A holds significant promise for carving a niche in its industry. A group of Canadian investors is considering purchasing the company's outstanding common shares. Beauty Cosmetics' common shares are currently selling for $32 per share.

A *Financial Markets Magazine* story predicted the company's income is bound to grow. It appears that Beauty Cosmetics can earn at least its current level of income for the indefinite future. Based on this information, the investors think that an appropriate investment capitalization rate for estimating the value of Beauty Cosmetics' common shares is 8%. How much will this belief lead the investors to offer for Beauty Cosmetics? Will Beauty Cosmetics' existing shareholders be likely to accept this offer? Explain your answers.

Learning Objective 1
Computing earnings per share and estimating the price of a common share

P11-38A Turnaround Specialists Ltd. (TSL) specializes in taking underperforming companies to a higher level of performance. TSL's capital structure at December 31, 2010, included 10,000 $2.50 preferred shares and 120,000 common shares. During 2011, TSL issued common shares and ended the year with 127,000 common shares outstanding. Average common shares outstanding during 2011 were 123,500. Income from continuing operations during 2011 was $219,000. The company discontinued a segment of the business at a loss of $69,000, and sale of discontinued assets generated a gain of $49,500. All amounts are after income tax.

Required

1. Compute TSL's earnings per share. Start with income from continuing operations.
2. Analysts believe TSL can earn its current level of income for the indefinite future. Estimate the market price of a common share of TSL at investment capitalization rates of 6%, 8%, and 10%. Which estimate presumes an investment in TSL is the most risky? How can you tell?

Learning Objective 1
Preparing a corrected income statement, including comprehensive income

P11-39A Richard Wright, accountant for Sweetie Pie Foods Inc., was injured in an auto accident. Another employee prepared the following income statement for the fiscal year ended June 30, 2011:

Sweetie Pie Foods Inc.
Income Statement
For the Year Ended June 30, 2011

Revenue and gains:		
Sales		$733,000
Contributed surplus on common shares		100,000
Total revenues and gains		833,000
Expenses and losses:		
Cost of goods sold	$383,000	
Selling expenses	103,000	
General expenses	74,000	
Sales returns	22,000	
Unrealized loss on investments	4,000	
Dividends paid	15,000	
Sales discounts	10,000	
Income tax expense	46,500	
Total expenses and losses		657,500
Income from operations		175,500
Other gains and losses:		
Gain on sale of discontinued assets	30,000	
Loss on discontinued operations	(15,000)	
Total other gains (losses)		15,000
Net income		$190,500
Earnings per share		$ 4.76

The individual *amounts* listed on the income statement are correct. However, some *accounts* are reported incorrectly, and some accounts do not belong on the income statement at all. Also, income tax (33%) has not been applied to all appropriate figures. Sweetie Pie Foods issued 44,000 common shares back in 2005 and repurchased 4,000 common shares all during the fiscal year 2011.

Required

Prepare a corrected statement of income (single-step, which lists all revenues together and all expenses together), including comprehensive income, for fiscal year 2011. Include earnings per share.

Learning Objective 2
Accounting for a corporation's income tax

P11-40A The accounting (not the income tax) records of Haynes Publications Inc. provide the comparative income statements for 2010 and 2011, respectively:

	2011	2010
Total revenue	$720,000	$600,000
Expenses:		
Cost of goods sold	$310,000	$290,000
Operating expenses	190,000	180,000
Total expenses before tax	500,000	470,000
Pretax accounting income	$220,000	$130,000

Taxable income for 2010 includes these modifications from pretax accounting income:

a. Additional taxable income of $10,000 for rent revenue earned in 2011, but collected in advance in 2010. Revenue collected in advance is included in the taxable income of the year when the cash is received. In calculating taxable income on the tax return, this revenue belongs in 2010.

b. There is additional capital cost allowance of $20,000 for depreciation expense. Canada Revenue Agency (CRA) capital cost allowance (CCA) rate is higher than the straight-line method used by Haynes Publications Inc.

The income tax rate is 33%.

Required

1. Compute Haynes' taxable income for 2010.
2. Journalize the corporation's income taxes for 2010.
3. Prepare the corporation's income statement for 2010.

Learning Objective 3
Using a statement of shareholders' equity

P11-41A Asian Food Specialties Inc. reported the following statement of shareholders' equity for the year ended June 30, 2011. The company was founded in 2007 and issued 455 million common shares. There had been no further share transactions until 2011.

Asian Food Specialties Inc.
Statement of Shareholders' Equity
For the Year Ended June 30, 2011

(In millions)	Common Shares	Retained Earnings	Total
Balance, June 30, 2010			
455 shares outstanding	$2,275	$1,702	$3,977
Net income		540	540
Cash dividends		(117)	(117)
Issuance of shares (5 shares)	50		50
Stock dividend (36 shares)	186	(186)	–
Issuance of shares (2 shares)	20		20
Balance, June 30, 2011	$2,531	$1,939	$4,470

Required

Answer these questions about Asian Food Specialties' shareholders' equity transactions.

1. The income tax rate is 33%. How much income before income tax did Asian Food Specialties report on the income statement?
2. What is the stated value of a common share at June 30, 2010?
3. At what price per share did Asian Food Specialties issue its common shares during the year?
4. Asian Food Specialties' statement of shareholders' equity lists the share transactions in the order in which they occurred. What was the percentage of the stock dividend? Round to the nearest percentage.

(Group B)

Learning Objective 1
Preparing a complex income statement

P11-42B The following information was taken from the records of Kendall Industries Ltd. at April 30, 2011. Kendall manufactures electronic controls for model airplanes.

Dividends	$ 15,000	Prior period error adjustment—credit to Retained Earnings	$ 6,000
Interest revenue	4,000	Interest expense	11,000
Foreign currency translation adjustment	5,000	Cost of goods sold	424,000
Income from discontinued operations	30,000	Cumulative effect of change in depreciation method (debit)	(18,000)
Loss on insurance settlement	12,000	Loss on sale of plant assets	8,000
General expenses	113,000	Income tax expense (saving):	
Preferred shares—$2, 10,000 shares authorized, 5,000 shares issued	200,000	Continuing operations	33,250
Retained earnings, beginning, as originally reported	88,000	Discontinued operations	7,500
Selling expenses	136,000	Cumulative effect of change in depreciation method	(4,500)
Common shares, 24,000 shares authorized and issued	240,000		
Sales revenue	833,000		

Required

1. Prepare Kendall's single-step comprehensive income statement, which lists all revenues together and all expenses together for the fiscal year ended April 30, 2011. Include earnings-per-share data.
2. Calculate the necessary changes to 2010 comparative income from operations based on retrospective reporting required by IFRS.
3. Evaluate income for the year ended April 30, 2011. Kendall's top managers hoped to earn income from continuing operations equal to 9% of sales.

Learning Objective 3
Preparing a statement of shareholders' equity

P11-43B Use the data in Problem 11-42B to prepare Kendall Industries Ltd.'s statement of shareholders' equity for the year ended April 30, 2011. Kendall Industries adopted IFRS in 2011.

Learning Objective 1
Using income data to make an investment decision

P11-44B Kendall Industries Ltd. in Problem 11-42B holds significant promise for carving a niche in the electronic controls industry, and a group of Swiss investors is considering purchasing Kendall's outstanding common shares. Kendall's common shares are currently selling for $50 per share.

A *Canadian Business* magazine story predicts that Kendall's income is bound to grow. It appears that the company can earn at least its current level of income for the indefinite future.

Based on this information, the investors think an appropriate investment capitalization rate for estimating the value of Kendall common shares is 9%. How much will this belief lead the investors to offer for Kendall Industries Ltd.? Will the existing shareholders of Kendall be likely to accept this offer? Explain your answers.

Learning Objective 1
Computing earnings per share and estimating the price of a share

P11-45B The capital structure of Morgan Products Inc. at December 31, 2010, included 20,000 $1.25 preferred shares and 44,000 common shares. During 2011, Morgan issued common shares and ended the year with 58,000 shares. The average number of common shares outstanding for the year was 51,000. Income from continuing operations during 2011 was $81,100. The company discontinued a segment of the business at a gain of $6,630, and unrealized losses on investments generated a loss of $16,000. All amounts are after income tax.

Required

1. Compute Morgan's earnings per share. Start with income from continuing operations.

2. Analysts believe Morgan can earn its current level of income for the indefinite future. Estimate the market price of a common share at investment capitalization rates of 7%, 9%, and 11%. Which estimate presumes an investment in Morgan shares is the most risky? How can you tell?

Learning Objective 1
Preparing a corrected income statement, including comprehensive income

P11-46B Rhonda Sparks, accountant for Canon Pet Supplies Ltd., was injured in a skiing accident. Another employee prepared the accompanying income statement for the year ended December 31, 2011.

The individual *amounts* listed on the income statement are correct. However, some *accounts* are reported incorrectly, and some accounts do not belong on the income statement at all. Also, income tax (30%) has not been applied to all appropriate figures. Canon issued 52,000 common shares in 2010 and repurchased 2,000 shares during 2011.

Canon Pet Supplies Ltd.
Income Statement
2011

Revenue and gains:		
Sales		$362,000
Unrealized gain on investments		10,000
Contributed surplus		80,000
Total revenues and gains		452,000
Expenses and losses:		
Cost of goods sold	$103,000	
Selling expenses	56,000	
General expenses	61,000	
Sales returns	11,000	
Dividends paid	7,000	
Sales discounts	6,000	
Income tax expense	37,500	
Total expenses and losses		281,500
Income from operations		170,500
Other gains and losses:		
Foreign currency translation adjustment	(3,000)	
Loss on discontinued operations	(20,000)	
Total other losses		(23,000)
Net income		$147,500
Earnings per share		$ 2.95

Required

Prepare a corrected statement of comprehensive income (single-step, which lists all revenues together and all expenses together), including comprehensive income for 2011. Include earnings per share.

Learning Objective 2
Accounting for a corporation's income tax

P11-47B The accounting (not the income tax) records of Ottawa Rafting Inc. provide the following comparative income statements for 2010 and 2011, respectively.

	2011	2010
Total revenue	$990,000	$900,000
Expenses:		
Cost of goods sold	$460,000	$430,000
Operating expenses	280,000	270,000
Total expenses before tax	740,000	700,000
Pretax accounting income	$250,000	$200,000

Taxable income for 2010 includes these modifications from pretax accounting income:

a. Additional taxable income of $15,000 for revenue earned in 2011, but collected in advance in 2010. Revenue collected in advance is included in the taxable income of the year when the cash is received. In calculating taxable income on the tax return, this revenue belongs in 2010.

b. There is additional capital cost allowance of $30,000 for depreciation expense. Canada Revenue Agency capital cost allowance rate is higher than the straight-line method used by Ottawa Rafting Inc.

The income tax rate is 25%.

Required

1. Compute Ottawa Rafting's taxable income for 2010.
2. Journalize the corporation's income taxes for 2010.
3. Prepare the corporation's income statement for 2010.

Learning Objective 3
Using a statement of shareholders' equity

P11-48B Datacom Services Inc. reported the following statement of shareholders' equity for the year ended October 31, 2011.

Datacom Services Inc.
Statement of Shareholders' Equity
For the Year Ended October 31, 2011

(in millions)	Common Shares	Retained Earnings	Total
Balance, Oct. 31, 2010, 675 shares outstanding	$2,025	$904	$2,929
Net income		360	360
Cash dividends		(194)	(194)
Issuance of shares (13 shares)	49		49
Stock dividend (55 shares)	166	(166)	–
Balance, Oct. 31, 2011	$2,240	$904	$3,144

Required

Answer these questions about Datacom Services' shareholders' equity transactions:

1. The income tax rate is 33%. How much income before income tax did Datacom report on the income statement?
2. What is the stated value of a common share at October 31, 2011?
3. At what price per share did Datacom Services issue its common shares during the year?
4. Datacom Services' statement lists the share transactions in the order they occurred. What was the percentage of the stock dividend?

Apply Your Knowledge

Decision Cases

Learning Objective 1
Evaluating the components of income

Case 1. Prudhoe Bay Oil Ltd. is having its initial public offering (IPO) of company shares. To create public interest in its shares, Prudhoe Bay's chief financial officer has blitzed the media with press releases. One, in particular, caught your eye. On September 19, Prudhoe Bay announced unaudited earnings per share (EPS) of $1.19, up 89% from last year's EPS of $0.63. An 89% increase in EPS is outstanding!

Before deciding to buy Prudhoe Bay stock, you investigated further and found that the company omitted several items from the determination of unaudited EPS:

- Unrealized loss on investments, $0.06 per share
- Gain on sale of building, $0.05 per share
- Cumulative effect of change in method of recognizing revenue, increase in retained earnings, $1.10 per share
- Restructuring expenses, $0.29 per share
- Loss on settlement of lawsuit begun five years ago, $0.12 per share
- Lost income due to employee labour strike, $0.24 per share
- Income from discontinued operations, $0.09 per share

Wondering how to treat these "special items," you called your stockbroker at Merrill Lynch. She thinks that these items are nonrecurring and outside Prudhoe Bay's core operations. Furthermore, she suggests that you ignore the items and consider Prudhoe Bay's earnings of $1.19 per share to be a good estimate of long-term profitability.

Required

What EPS number will you use to predict Prudhoe Bay's future profits? Show your work, and explain your reasoning for each item.

Learning Objective 1
Using the financial statements in investment analysis

Case 2. Mike Magid Toyota is an automobile dealership. Magid's annual report includes Note 1—Summary of Significant Accounting Policies, as follows:

> **Income Recognition**
>
> Sales are recognized when cash payment is received or, in the case of credit sales, which represent the majority of . . . sales, when a down payment is received and the customer enters into an installment sales contract. These installment sales contracts . . . are normally collectible over 36 to 60 months . . . .
>
> Revenue from auto insurance policies sold to customers is recognized as income over the life of the contracts.

Bay Area Nissan, a competitor of Mike Magid Toyota, includes the following note in its Summary of Significant Accounting Policies:

> **Accounting Policies for Revenues**
>
> Sales are recognized when cash payment is received or, in the case of credit sales, which represent the majority of . . . sales, when the customer enters into an installment sales contract. Customer down payments are rare. Most of these installment sales contracts are normally collectible over 36 to 60 months . . . . Revenue from auto insurance policies sold to customers is recognized when the customer signs an insurance contract. Expenses are recognized over the life of the insurance contracts.

Suppose you have decided to invest in an auto dealership and you've narrowed your choices to Magid and Bay Area. Which company's earnings are of higher quality? Why? Will their accounting policies affect your investment decision? If so, how? Mention specific accounts in the financial statements that will differ between the two companies.

Ethical Issue

The income statement of Transparency Accounting Services Ltd. reported the following results of operations:

Earnings from operations	$178,064
Income tax expense	58,761
Net earnings	119,303
Other comprehensive income:	
Income from discontinued operations, net of tax	149,755
Unrealized loss on investments	(32,961)
Comprehensive net income	$236,097

Suppose Transparency's management had reported the company's results of operations in this manner:

Earnings before income taxes	$352,384
Income tax expense	116,287
Net earnings	$236,097

Required

1. Does it really matter how a company reports its operating results? Why? Who could be helped by management's action? Who could be hurt?
2. Suppose Transparency's management decides to report its operating results in the second manner. Evaluate the ethics of this decision.

Focus on Financials

Learning Objective ❶❸❹
Analyzing a corporate income statement and statement of shareholders' equity, and understanding managers'/ auditors' responsibilities for financial statements

Gildan Activewear Inc.

Refer to the Gildan Activewear Inc. financial statements in Appendix A at the end of this book.

Required

1. Review Management's Responsibility for Financial Reporting and answer the following questions:
   a. Who prepared the consolidated financial statements?
   b. What was management responsible for?
   c. What is the Audit and Finance Committee's function?
2. Was there an audit of the consolidated financial statements? How did you confirm this? Provide details with your answer.
3. The Consolidated Statements of Earnings and Comprehensive Income
   a. Include restructuring and other charges (note 16) in operating income. Discuss these charges and explain why they are included in operating income.
   b. For the years 2008 and 2009 refer to "(recast-note 1)". Using the information in the Notes to the Financial Statements—Note 1(b), discuss the reason for this note and any changes that have been made to prior years' information.
4. The Consolidated Statements of Shareholders' Equity report recast net earnings for fiscal year-ends 2006, 2007, 2008, and 2009. Explain why these changes were made.

Focus on Analysis

Gildan Activewear Inc.
Refer to the Gildan Activewear Inc. financial statements in Appendix A at the end of this book.

Learning Objective 1 3
Evaluating the quality of earnings, valuing investments, and analyzing shares outstanding

Required

1. Using the earnings per share and the reported net earnings, calculate the number of common shares outstanding at October 4, 2009.
2. At October 4, 2009, and at October 5, 2008, how much would you have been willing to pay per share of Gildan Activewear Inc. if you had rated the investment as high risk? What about if you had rated it as low risk? Use even-numbered investment capitalization rates in the range of 4% to 10% for your analysis and use EPS for the calculation.
3. The quoted share price of Gildan Activewear Inc. on October 6, 2009, was $20.12 and on October 6, 2008, was $23.69. Which values that you estimated in Requirement 2 were closest to the actual share price? Would investment in the shares at October 4, 2009, be deemed a high- or low-risk investment? At October 5, 2008?

Group Project

Select a company and research its business. Search the business press for articles about this company. Obtain its annual report by requesting it directly from the company or from the company's Web site.

Required

1. Based on your group's analysis, come to class prepared to instruct the class on six interesting facts about the company that can be found in its financial statements and the related notes. Your group can mention only the obvious, such as net sales or total revenue, net income, total assets, total liabilities, total shareholders' equity, and dividends, in conjunction with other terms. Once you use an obvious item, you may not use that item again.
2. The group should write a paper discussing the facts that it has uncovered. Limit the paper to two double-spaced word-processed pages.

Quick Check Answers

1. *b*
2. *a*
3. *d ($5.94/0.06 = $99)*
4. *c ($998/$3.14 = 318 million)*
5. *d*
6. *c*
7. *a*
8. *d*
9. *b*
10. *c*

12 The Statement of Cash Flows

LEARNING OBJECTIVES

1. **Identify** the purposes of the statement of cash flows
2. **Distinguish** among operating, investing, and financing cash flows
3. **Prepare** a statement of cash flows by the indirect method

A-1 **Prepare** a statement of cash flows by the direct method

SPOTLIGHT

Gildan Activewear Inc.'s consolidated statement of cash flows shows how well Gildan coped with the world-wide economic downturn that began in 2008 and continued in 2009. Gildan's sales and net earnings declined in 2009 as did the sales and net earnings of many manufacturing companies. However, by good management, Gildan increased its cash and cash equivalents by US$87.4 million in the year ended October 4, 2009.

Gildan Activewear Inc.
Consolidated Statement of Cash Flows
For the Year Ended October 4, 2009

(Amounts in thousands of U.S. dollars)	**2009**
Cash flows from (used in) operating activities:	
Net earnings	$ 95,329
Adjustments for:	
Depreciation and amortization	65,407
Variation of depreciation included in inventories	(2,437)
Restructuring charges related to assets held for sale and property, plant and equipment	976
Loss on disposal of property, plant and equipment	561
Stock-based compensation costs	3,007
Future income taxes	(2,434)
Non-controlling interest	110
Unrealized net gain (loss) on foreign exchange and financial derivatives	(1,012)
	159,507
Changes in non-cash working capital balances:	
Accounts receivable	48,351
Inventories	16,742
Prepaid expenses and deposits	(1,191)
Accounts payable and accrued liabilities	(22,731)
Income taxes payable	(31,499)
	169,179
Cash flows from (used in) financing activities:	
(Decrease) increase in amounts drawn under revolving long-term credit facility	(45,000)
Decrease in bank indebtedness	—
Increase in other long-term debt	44
Repayment of other long-term debt	(3,661)
Proceeds from the issuance of shares	906
Repurchase of shares	—
	(47,711)
Cash flows from (used in) investing activities:	
Purchase of property, plant and equipment	(44,938)
Business acquisition	(1,196)
Restricted cash related to business acquisition	3,958
Proceeds on disposal of assets held for sale	6,349
Net decrease (increase) in other assets	1,629
	(34,198)
Effect of exchange rate changes on cash and cash equivalents denominated in foreign currencies	105
Net increase (decrease) in cash and cash equivalents during the year	87,375
Cash and cash equivalents, beginning of year	12,357
Cash and cash equivalents, end of year	$ 99,732

Source: Gildan Activewear Inc. 2009 Annual Report.

In this chapter, we show you how to prepare and use the statement of cash flows. We begin with the statement format used by the vast majority of companies, called the *indirect approach*. The appendix at the end of the chapter includes the alternative format of the statement of cash flows, the *direct approach*. After working through this chapter, you can analyze the cash flows of actual companies.

This chapter has three distinct sections:

- Basic Concepts, beginning on this page
- Preparing the Statement of Cash Flows: Indirect Method, page 601
- Preparing the Statement of Cash Flows: Direct Method, Appendix 12A, page 638

The introduction applies to all cash-flow topics. Professors who wish to cover only the indirect method can assign the first two parts of the chapter. Those interested only in the direct method can proceed from the introduction, which ends on page 601, to the direct method in the chapter appendix, on page 638.

Basic Concepts: The Statement of Cash Flows

OBJECTIVE

1 **Identify** the purposes of the statement of cash flows

International Accounting Standard (IAS) 7 "Statement of Cash Flows" explains that the information disclosed by a company about its cash flows provides decision-useful information to users of financial statements. The statement of cash flows includes information about operating, investing, and financing activities.

ASPE Section 1540 "Cash Flow Statement" is similar in concept to IAS 7 "Statement of Cash Flows."

The balance sheet reports financial position, and balance sheets from two periods show whether cash increased or decreased. But that doesn't tell why the cash balance changed. The income statement reports revenues, expenses, and net income and provides some clues about cash, but the income statement does not tell why cash increased or decreased. We need a third statement.

The statement of cash flows reports **cash flows**—cash receipts and cash payments—in other words, where cash came from (receipts) and how it was spent (payments). The statement covers a span of time and therefore is dated "For the Year Ended December 31, 2011" or "For the Month Ended June 30, 2011." Exhibit 12-1 illustrates the relative timing of the four basic statements.

EXHIBIT 12-1 Timing of the Financial Statements

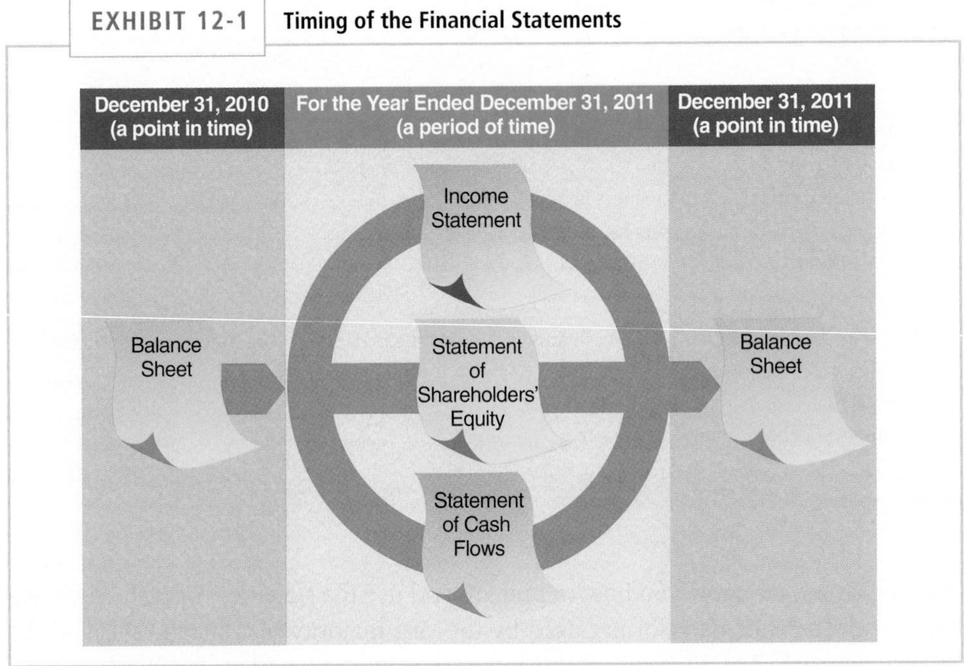

The statement of cash flows helps managers, investors, and creditors perform the following functions:

1. **Predict future cash flows.** Past cash receipts and payments are reasonably good predictors of future cash flows.
2. **Evaluate management decisions.** Businesses that make wise investment decisions prosper, and those that make unwise decisions suffer losses. The statement of cash flows reports how managers got cash and how they used cash to run the business.
3. **Determine ability to pay dividends and interest.** Shareholders want dividends on their investments. Creditors collect interest and principal on their loans. The statement of cash flows reports on the ability to make these payments.
4. **Show the relationship of net income to cash flows.** Usually, cash and net income move together. High levels of income tend to lead to increases in cash, and low levels of income tend to lead to decreases in cash. However, a company's cash flow can suffer even when net income is high.

On a statement of cash flows, *cash* means more than just cash in the bank. It includes cash equivalents, which are highly liquid short-term investments that can be converted into cash immediately. Investments with maturities of three months or less often qualify as cash equivalents. Examples include money-market accounts and investments in Canadian government securities. Throughout this chapter, the term *cash* refers to cash and cash equivalents.

How Is a Company's Cash Flow? Telltale Signs of Financial Difficulty

Companies want to earn net income because profit measures success. Without net income, a business sinks. There will be no dividends, and the share price will likely suffer. High net income helps attract investors, but companies can't pay bills with net income. That requires cash.

A company needs both net income and strong cash flow. Income and cash flow usually move together because net income generates cash. Sometimes, however, net income and cash flow follow different patterns. To illustrate, consider Fastech Company Ltd.:

Fastech Company Ltd.
Income Statement
For the Year Ended December 31, 2011

Sales revenue	$100,000
Cost of goods sold	30,000
Operating expenses	10,000
Net income	$ 60,000

Fastech Company Ltd.
Balance Sheet
December 31, 2011

Cash	$ 3,000	Total current liabilities	$ 50,000
Receivables	37,000	Long-term liabilities	20,000
Inventory	40,000		
PPE, net	60,000	Shareholders' equity	70,000
Total assets	$140,000	Total liabilities and equity	$140,000

What can we glean from Fastech's income statement and balance sheet?

- Fastech is profitable. Net income is 60% of revenue. Fastech's profitability looks outstanding.
- The current ratio is 1.6, and the debt ratio is only 50%. These measures suggest little trouble in paying bills.
- But Fastech is on the verge of bankruptcy. Can you spot the problem? Can you see what is causing the problem? Three trouble spots leap out to a financial analyst.

1. The cash balance is very low. Three thousand dollars isn't enough cash to pay the bills of a company with sales of $100,000.
2. Fastech isn't selling inventory fast enough. Fastech turned over its inventory only 0.75 times during the year. As we saw in Chapter 6, many companies have inventory turnover rates of 3 to 8 times a year. A turnover ratio of 0.75 times means it takes a very long time to sell inventory, and that delays cash collections.
3. Fastech's days' sales in receivables ratio is 135 days. Very few companies can wait that long to collect from customers. With standard credit terms of net 30 days, Fastech should collect cash within around 45 days. Fastech cannot survive with a collection period of 135 days.

   The take away lesson from this discussion is this:

   - A company needs both net income and strong cash flow to succeed in business.

Let's now turn to the different categories of cash flows.

Operating, Investing, and Financing Activities

A business engages in three types of business activities:

- Operating activities
- Investing activities
- Financing activities

OBJECTIVE

2 **Distinguish** among operating, investing, and financing cash flows

Gildan's statement of cash flows reports cash flows under these three headings, as shown on page 597.

Operating activities create revenues, expenses, gains, and losses—*net income,* which is a product of accrual-basis accounting. The statement of cash flows reports on operating activities.[1] Operating activities are the most important of the three categories because they reflect the core of the organization. *A successful business must generate most of its cash from operating activities.*

Investing activities increase and decrease *long-term assets,* such as computers and software, land, buildings, equipment, and investments in other companies. Purchases and sales of these assets are investing activities. Investing activities are important, but they are less critical than operating activities.

Financing activities obtain cash from investors and creditors. Issuing and repurchasing shares, borrowing money, and paying cash dividends to shareholders are financing activities.[2] Paying off a loan is another example. Financing cash flows relate to *long-term liabilities* and *owners' equity*. Financing activities are important but not as important as operating activities.

Exhibit 12-2 shows how operating, investing, and financing activities relate to the various parts of the balance sheet.

---

[1] A simplifying assumption has been made throughout this chapter that *all* current asset accounts and *all* current liability accounts and their related cash flows should be classified as operating activities on the statement of cash flows. There are, in fact, a number of current asset and current liability accounts that reflect investing and financing activities, respectively. For example, current assets may include short-term investments and short-term notes receivable. The cash flows from these accounts should be classified as investing activities on the statement of cash flows. Current liabilities may include short-term loans payable and related cash flows, which should be classified as financing activities on the statement of cash flows.

[2] While most companies classify payments of interest on loans and interest and dividends received as operating activities, and payments of dividends as financing activities, IAS 7 does permit companies to classify interest paid as a financing activity and interest and dividends received as investing activities. IAS 7 also permits dividends paid to be classified as operating activities. When completing assigned homework and exam questions, follow the classifications outlined in the textbook.

EXHIBIT 12-2 Operating, Investing, and Financing Cash Flows and the Balance Sheet

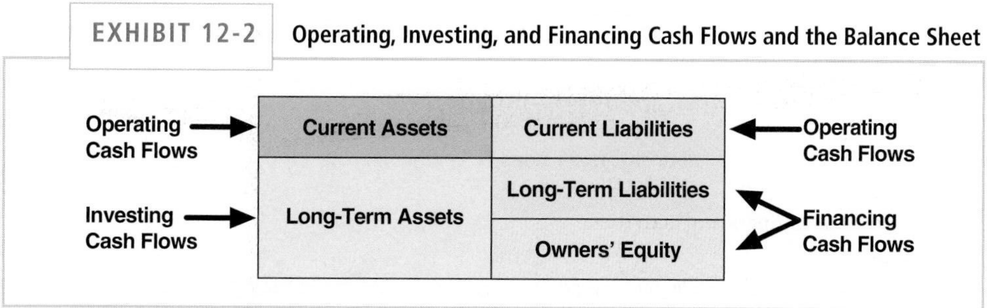

Examine Gildan Activewear's statement of cash flows on page 597. Focus on the final line of each section: Operating, Financing, and Investing. During the year ended October 4, 2009, Gildan's operating activities provided almost US$170 million of cash. Financing activities used almost US$48 million and investing activities used US$34 million.

These figures show that:

- *Operations* are Gildan's largest source of cash.
- The company is managing its debt.
- The company is investing in the future.

Two Formats for Operating Activities

There are two ways to format operating activities on the statement of cash flows:

- **Indirect method**, which reconciles net income to net cash provided by operating activities. (pp. 601 to 617)
- **Direct method**, which reports all cash receipts and cash payments from operating activities.(pp. 638 to 651)

The two methods use different computations, but they produce the same figure for cash from *operating activities*. The two methods do not affect *investing* or *financing* activities. The following table summarizes the differences between the two approaches:

Indirect Method		Direct Method	
Net income	$600	Collections from customers.........	$2,000
Adjustments:		*Deductions:*	
Depreciation added back, etc.	300	Payments to suppliers, etc.......	(1,100)
Cash provided by operating activities	$900	Cash provided by operating activities	$ 900

We begin with the indirect method because the vast majority of companies use it.

Preparing the Statement of Cash Flows: Indirect Method

To illustrate the statementof cash flows we use Bradshaw Corporation, a dealer in playground equipment. Proceed as shown in the following steps to prepare the statement of cash flows by the indirect method.

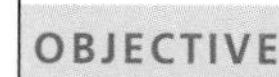

OBJECTIVE

❸ **Prepare** a statement of cash flows by the indirect method

STEP 1 Lay out the template as shown in Part 1 of Exhibit 12-3. The exhibit is comprehensive. The diagram in Exhibit 12-3 Part 2 (p. 603) gives a visual picture of the statement.

STEP 2 Use the comparative balance sheet to determine the increase or decrease in cash during the period. The change in cash is the "check figure" for the statement of cash flows. Exhibit 12-4 (p. 604) gives Bradshaw Corporation's

EXHIBIT 12-3 **Part 1—Template of the Statement of Cash Flows: Indirect Method**

Bradshaw Corporation
Statement of Cash Flows
For the Year Ended December 31, 2011

Cash flows from operating activities:
Net income
Adjustments to reconcile net income to net cash provided by operating activities:
+ Depreciation expense
+ Loss on sale of long-term assets
− Gain on sale of long-term assets
− Increases in current assets other than cash
+ Decreases in current assets other than cash
+ Increases in current liabilities
− Decreases in current liabilities
Net cash provided by operating activities

Cash flows from investing activities:
Proceeds from sales of long-term assets (investments, land, building, equipment, and so on)
− Purchases of long-term assets
+ Collections of long-term receivables
− Increases in long-term loans to others
Net cash provided by (used for) investing activities

Cash flows from financing activities:
Issuance of shares
− Repurchase of shares
+ Borrowing (issuance of notes or bonds payable)
− Payment of notes or bonds payable
− Payment of dividends
Net cash provided by (used for) financing activities

Net increase (decrease) in cash during the year
+ Cash at December 31, 2010
= Cash at December 31, 2011

comparative balance sheet with cash highlighted. Bradshaw's cash decreased by $20,000 during 2011. *Why* did cash decrease? The statement of cash flows provides the answer.

STEP 3 From the income statement, take net income, depreciation and amortization expense, and any gains or losses on the sale of long-term assets. Print these items on the statement of cash flows. Exhibit 12-5 (p. 604) gives Bradshaw Corporation's income statement, with relevant items highlighted.

STEP 4 Use the income statement and the balance sheet data to prepare the statement of cash flows. The statement of cash flows is complete only after you have explained the year-to-year changes in all the balance sheet accounts.

Cash Flows From Operating Activities

Operating activities are related to the transactions that make up net income.*

*The authors thank Alfonso Oddo for suggesting this summary.

EXHIBIT 12-3 **Part 2—Positive and Negative Items on the Statement of Cash Flows: Indirect Method**

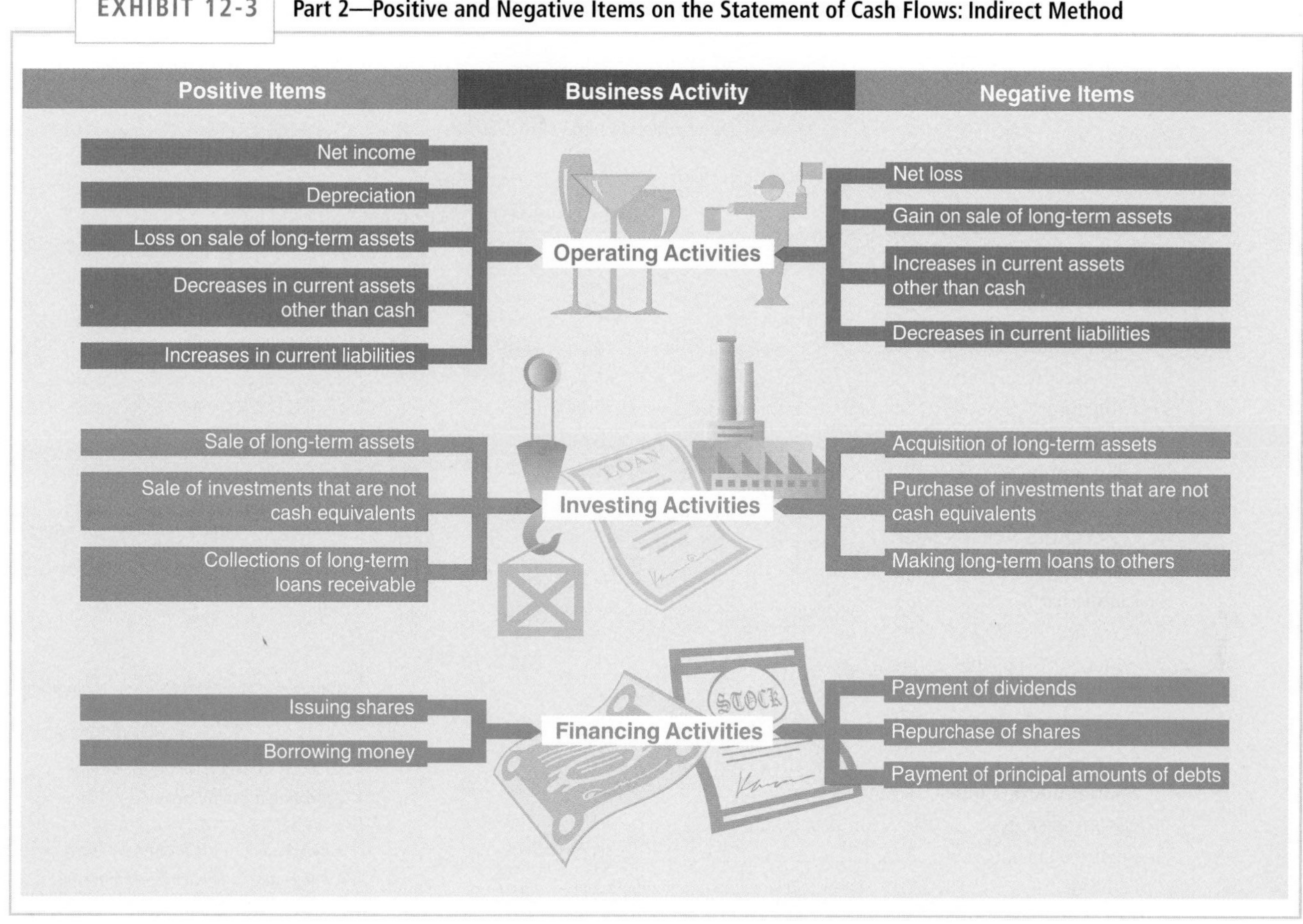

The operating section of the statement of cash flows begins with net income, taken from the income statement (Exhibit 12-5), and is followed by "Adjustments to reconcile net income to net cash provided by operating activities" (Exhibit 12-6). Let's discuss these adjustments.

Ⓐ **Depreciation Expense.** This expense is added back to net income when we go from net income to cash flow. Let's see why. Depreciation is recorded as follows:

Depreciation Expense	18,000	
Accumulated Depreciation		18,000

Depreciation expense has no effect on cash. However, depreciation expense, like all other expenses, decreases net income. Therefore, to convert net income to cash flow, we add depreciation back to net income. The add-back cancels the earlier deduction.

Example: Suppose you had only two transactions during the period, a \$1,000 cash sale and depreciation expense of \$300. Net income is \$700 (\$1,000 − \$300). Cash flow from operations is \$1,000. To go from net income (\$700) to cash flow (\$1,000), we must add back the depreciation (\$300).

Ⓑ **Gains and Losses on the Sale of Long-Term Assets.** Sales of long-term assets are *investing* activities, and there is often a gain or loss on the sale. On the statement of cash flows, a gain or loss on the sale is an adjustment to net income. Exhibit 12-6 includes an adjustment for a gain. During 2011, Bradshaw sold equipment for

EXHIBIT 12-4 **Comparative Balance Sheet for Bradshaw Corporation**

Bradshaw Corporation
Comparative Balance Sheet
As at December 31, 2011 and 2010

(Amounts in thousands)	2011	2010	Increase (Decrease)	
Assets				
Current:				
Cash	$ 22	$ 42	$ (20)	
Accounts receivable	93	80	13	*Changes in current assets—Operating*
Interest receivable	3	1	2	
Inventory	135	138	(3)	
Prepaid expenses	8	7	1	
Long-term note receivable from another company	11	—	11	*Changes in noncurrent assets—Investing*
Property, plant, and equipment assets, net of depreciation	353	219	134	
Total	$625	$487	$138	
Liabilities				
Current:				
Accounts payable	$ 91	$ 57	$ 34	*Changes in current liabilities—Operating*
Salary and wages payable	4	6	(2)	
Accrued liabilities	1	3	(2)	
Long-term debt	160	77	83	*Changes in long-term liabilities and contributed capital accounts—Financing*
Shareholders' Equity				
Common shares	259	258	1	
Retained earnings	110	86	24	*Changes due to net income—Operating* *Change due to dividends—Financing*
Total	$625	$487	$138	

EXHIBIT 12-5 **Income Statement for Bradshaw Corporation**

Bradshaw Corporation
Income Statement
For the Year Ended December 31, 2011

	(amounts in thousands)	
Revenues and gains:		
Sales revenue	$284	
Interest revenue	12	
Dividend revenue	9	
Gain on sale of property, plant, and equipment	8	
Total revenues and gains		$313
Expenses:		
Cost of goods sold	150	
Salary and wages expense	56	
Depreciation expense	18	
Other operating expense	17	
Interest expense	16	
Income tax expense	15	
Total expenses		272
Net income		$ 41

EXHIBIT 12-6 Statement of Cash Flows—Operating Activities by the Indirect Method

Bradshaw Corporation
Statement of Cash Flows
For the Year Ended December 31, 2011

			(amounts in thousands)
	Cash flows from operating activities:		
	Net income		$41
	Adjustments to reconcile net income to net cash provided by operating activities:		
Ⓐ	Depreciation	$ 18	
Ⓑ	Gain on sale of property, plant, and equipment	(8)	
Ⓒ	Increase in accounts receivable	(13)	
Ⓒ	Increase in interest receivable	(2)	
Ⓒ	Decrease in inventory	3	
Ⓒ	Increase in prepaid expenses	(1)	
Ⓒ	Increase in accounts payable	34	
Ⓒ	Decrease in salary and wages payable	(2)	
Ⓒ	Decrease in accrued liabilities	(2)	27
	Net cash provided by operating activities		$68

$62,000. The carrying amount was $54,000 (see calculation of carrying amount on page 607), so there was a gain of $8,000.

The $62,000 cash received from the sale is an investing activity; the $62,000 includes the $8,000 gain. Net income also includes the gain, so we must subtract the gain from net cash provided from operations, as shown in Bradshaw Corporation's statement of cash flows (Exhibit 12-6). (We explain investing activities in the next section.)

A loss on the sale of property, plant, and equipment also creates an adjustment in the operating section. Losses are *added back* to net income to compute cash flow from operations.

Ⓒ Changes in the Current Asset and Current Liability Accounts. Most current assets and current liabilities result from operating activities. For example, accounts receivable result from sales, inventory relates to cost of goods sold, and so on. Changes in the current accounts are reported as adjustments to net income on the statement of cash flows. The reasoning follows:

1. **An *increase* in another current asset decreases cash.** It takes cash to acquire assets. Suppose you make a sale on account. Accounts receivable are increased, but cash isn't affected yet. Exhibit 12-4 (page 604) reports that Bradshaw Corporation's Accounts Receivable increased by $13,000 during 2011. To compute cash flow from operations, we must subtract the $13,000 increase in Accounts Receivable, as shown in Exhibit 12-6. The reason is this: We have *not* collected this $13,000 in cash. The same logic applies to the other current assets. If they increase, cash decreases.
2. **A *decrease* in another current asset increases cash.** Suppose Bradshaw's Accounts Receivable balance decreased by $4,000. Cash receipts caused Accounts Receivable to decrease, so we add decreases in Accounts Receivable and the other current assets to net income.

3. **A *decrease* in a current liability decreases cash.** Payment of a current liability decreases both cash and the liability, so we subtract decreases in current liabilities from net income. In Exhibit 12-6, the $2,000 decrease in Accrued Liabilities is *subtracted* from net income to compute net cash provided by operations.
4. **An *increase* in a current liability increases cash.** Bradshaw's Accounts Payable increased. That can occur only if cash is not spent to pay this liability. Cash payments are therefore less than expenses and Bradshaw has more cash on hand. Thus, increases in current liabilities increase cash.

Evaluating Cash Flows From Operating Activities. Let's step back and evaluate Bradshaw's operating cash flows during 2011. Bradshaw Corporation's operations provided net cash flows of $68,000 (Exhibit 12-6). This amount exceeds net income, and it should because of the add-back of depreciation and the management of current assets and current liabilities. Now let's examine Bradshaw's investing and financing activities, as reported in Exhibit 12-7.

EXHIBIT 12-7 Statement of Cash Flows—Indirect Method

Bradshaw Corporation
Statement of Cash Flows
For the Year Ended December 31, 2011

		(amounts in thousands)	
	Cash flows from operating activities:		
	Net income		$ 41
	Adjustments to reconcile net income to net cash provided by operating activities:		
Ⓐ	Depreciation	$ 18	
Ⓑ	Gain on sale of property, plant, and equipment	(8)	
Ⓒ	Increase in accounts receivable	(13)	
Ⓒ	Increase in interest receivable	(2)	
Ⓒ	Decrease in inventory	3	
Ⓒ	Increase in prepaid expenses	(1)	
Ⓒ	Increase in accounts payable	34	
Ⓒ	Decrease in salary and wages payable	(2)	
Ⓒ	Decrease in accrued liabilities	(2)	27
	Net cash provided by operating activities		68
	Cash flows from investing activities:		
	Acquisition of property, plant, and equipment	(206)	
	Loan to another company	(11)	
	Proceeds from sale of property, plant, and equipment	62	
	Net cash used for investing activities		(155)
	Cash flows from financing activities:		
	Proceeds from issuance of common shares	1	
	Proceeds from issuance of long-term debt	94	
	Payment of long-term debt	(11)	
	Payment of dividends	(17)	
	Net cash provided by financing activities		67
	Net decrease in cash		(20)
	Cash balance, December 31, 2010		42
	Cash balance, December 31, 2011		$ 22

Cash Flows From Investing Activities

Investing activities affect long-term asset accounts, such as Long-Term Assets, Investments, and Notes Receivable.

Most of the data come from the balance sheet.

Computing Acquisitions and Sales of Property, Plant, and Equipment Assets. Companies keep separate accounts for each item of property, plant, and equipment. But for computing cash flows, it is helpful to combine these accounts into a single summary account. Also, we subtract accumulated depreciation from the assets' cost and use the net figure. It is easier to work with a single property, plant, and equipment asset account.

To illustrate, observe that Bradshaw Corporation's

- Balance sheet reports beginning property, plant, and equipment, net of depreciation, of \$219,000. The ending balance is \$353,000 (Exhibit 12-4).
- Income statement shows depreciation expense of \$18,000 and an \$8,000 gain on sale of property, plant, and equipment (Exhibit 12-5).

Bradshaw's purchases of property, plant, and equipment total \$206,000 (take this amount as given; see Exhibit 12-7). How much, then, are the proceeds from the sale of property, plant, and equipment? First, we must determine the carrying amount of property, plant, and equipment sold, as follows:

Property, plant, and equipment (net)

Beginning balance	+	Acquisitions	−	Depreciation	−	Carrying amount of assets sold	=	Ending balance
\$219,000	+	\$206,000	−	\$18,000		−X	=	\$353,000
						−X	=	\$353,000 − \$219,000 − \$206,000 + \$18,000
						X	=	\$54,000

The sale proceeds are \$62,000, determined as follows:

Sale proceeds =	Carrying amount of assets sold	+ Gain	− Loss
=	\$54,000	+ \$8,000	− \$0
=	\$62,000		

Trace the sale proceeds of \$62,000 to the statement of cash flows in Exhibit 12-7.

The Property, Plant, and Equipment T-account provides another look at the computation of the carrying amount of the assets sold.

Property, Plant, and Equipment, net of accumulated depreciation

Beginning balance	219,000	Amortization	18,000
Acquisitions	206,000	Carrying amount of assets sold	54,000
Ending balance	353,000		

If the sale had resulted in a loss of \$3,000, the sale proceeds would have been \$51,000 (\$54,000 – \$3,000), and the statement would report \$51,000 as a cash receipt from this investing activity.

Computing Acquisitions and Sales of Long-Term Investments, and Long-Term Loans and Collections. The cash amounts of investment transactions can be computed in the manner illustrated for property, plant, and equipment. Investments are easier because there is no depreciation to account for, as shown in the following equation:

Investments (amounts assumed for illustration only)

Beginning balance	+	Purchases	−	Carrying amount of investments sold	=	Ending balance
$100,000	+	$50,000		−X	=	$140,000
				−X	=	$140,000 − $100,000 − $50,000
				X	=	$10,000

The Investments T-account provides another look.

Investments

Beginning balance	100		
Purchases	50	Carrying amount of investments sold	10
Ending balance	140		

Bradshaw Corporation has a long-term note receivable, and the cash flows from loan transactions on notes receivable can be determined as follows (data from Exhibit 12-4 and the general ledger):

Notes Receivable

Beginning balance	+	New loans made	−	Collections	=	Ending balance
$0	+	$X		−0	=	$11,000
		X			=	$11,000

Notes Receivable

Beginning balance	0		
New loans made	11	**Collections**	0
Ending balance	11		

Exhibit 12-8 summarizes the cash flows from investing activities, highlighted in colour.

Cash Flows From Financing Activities

Financing activities affect liabilities and shareholders' equity accounts, such as Notes Payable, Bonds Payable, Long-Term Debt, Common Shares, and Retained Earnings.

Computing Issuances and Payments of Long-Term Debt. The beginning and ending balances of Long-Term Debt, Notes Payable, or Bonds Payable are taken from the balance sheet. If the amount of either the new issuances or the payments is known, the other amount can be computed. Bradshaw Corporation's new debt issuances total $94,000 (take this amount as given; Exhibit 12-7). Debt payments are computed from the Long-Term Debt account (see Exhibit 12-4).

Long-Term Debt (Notes Payable, Bonds Payable)

Beginning balance	+	Issuance of new debt	−	Payments of debt	=	Ending balance
$77,000	+	$94,000		−X	=	$160,000
				−X	=	$160,000 − $77,000 − $94,000
				X	=	$11,000

EXHIBIT 12-8 **Computing Cash Flows From Investing Activities**

Receipts

From sale of property, plant, and equipment	Beginning property, plant, and equipment (net) + Acquisition cost − Depreciation − Carrying amount of assets sold = Ending property, plant, and equipment (net)
	Cash received = Carrying amount of assets sold + Gain on sale − Loss on sale
From sale of investments	Beginning investments + Purchase cost of investments − Cost of investments sold = Ending investments
	Cash received = Cost of investments sold + Gain on sale − Loss on sale
From collection of notes receivable	Beginning notes receivable + New loans made − Collections = Ending notes receivable

Payments

For acquisition of property, plant, and equipment	Beginning property, plant, and equipment (net) + Acquisition cost − Depreciation − Carrying amount of assets sold = Ending property, plant, and equipment (net)
For purchase of investments	Beginning investments + Purchase cost of investments − Cost of investments sold = Ending investments
For new loans made	Beginning notes receivable + New loans made − Collections = Ending notes receivable

Long-Term Debt

		Beginning balance	77,000
Payments	11,000	Issuance of new debt	94,000
		Ending balance	160,000

Computing Issuances of Shares and Repurchases of Shares. These cash flows can be determined from the share accounts. For example, cash received from issuing common shares or the cash paid for repurchase of common shares is determined from the Common Shares account. We use a single summary account for shares as we do for property, plant, and equipment. Using data from Exhibits 12-4 and 12-7, we have

Common Shares

Beginning balance	+	Issuance of new shares	=	Ending balance
$258,000	+	$1,000	=	$259,000

Common Shares

	Beginning balance	258,000
	Issuance of new shares	1,000
	Ending	259,000

Apart from the Bradshaw Corporation example, cash flows affecting share repurchases for cancellation can be computed as follows:

Common Shares (amounts assumed for illustration only)

Beginning balance	−	Repurchase of shares	=	Ending balance
$16,000	−	$3,000	=	$13,000

Common Shares

		Beginning balance	16,000
Repurchase of shares	3,000		
		Ending balance	13,000

Computing Dividend Payments. If dividend payments are not given elsewhere, they can be computed. Bradshaw Corporation's dividends declared are as follows:

Retained Earnings

Beginning balance	+	Net income	−	Dividends declared	=	Ending balance				
$86,000	+	$41,000		−X	=	$110,000				
				−X	=	$110,000	−	$86,000	−	$41,000
				X	=	$17,000				

The T-accounts provide another view of the dividend declaration computation.

Retained Earnings

Dividend declarations	17,000	Beginning balance	86,000
		Net income	41,000
		Ending balance	110,000

The credit when a dividend is declared is to the current liability account Dividends Payable. If there is not a balance in the Dividends Payable account on the balance sheet, the dividends have been paid and there will be a financing cash outflow equivalent to the dividend declared calculated above and the dividend actually paid.

STOP + THINK

Classify each of the following as an operating activity, an investing activity, or a financing activity as reported on the statement of cash flows prepared by the *indirect* method.

a. Issuance of shares
b. Borrowing
c. Sales revenue
d. Payment of dividends
e. Purchase of land
f. Repurchase of shares
g. Paying bonds payable
h. Interest expense
i. Sale of equipment
j. Cost of goods sold
k. Purchase of another company
l. Making a loan

Answers:

a. Financing
b. Financing
c. Operating
d. Financing
e. Investing
f. Financing
g. Financing
h. Operating
i. Investing
j. Operating
k. Investing
l. Investing

Exhibit 12-9 summarizes the computation of cash flows from financing activities, highlighted in colour.

EXHIBIT 12-9 Computing Cash Flows From Financing Activities

Receipts	
From borrowing—issuance of long-term debt	Beginning long-term debt (notes payable) + Cash received from issuance of long-term debt − Payment of debt = Ending long-term debt
From issuance of shares	Beginning shares + Cash received from issuance of new shares = Ending shares
Payments	
Of long-term debt	Beginning long-term debt (notes payable) + Cash received from issuance of long-term debt − Payment of debt = Ending long-term debt
To repurchase shares	Beginning shares − Repurchase cost of shares = Ending shares
Of dividends	Beginning retained earnings + Net income − Dividend declarations and payments = Ending retained earnings

Noncash Investing and Financing Activities

Companies make investments that do not require cash. They also obtain financing other than cash. Our examples have included none of these transactions. Now suppose that Bradshaw Corporation issued common shares valued at $320,000 to acquire a warehouse. Bradshaw would journalize this transaction as follows:

Warehouse Building	320,000	
Common Shares		320,000

IAS 7 indicates that this transaction would not be reported on the statement of cash flows because Bradshaw paid no cash. But the investment in the warehouse and the issuance of shares are important. Noncash investing and financing activities like this transaction can be reported in a separate schedule that follows the statement of cash flows or can be disclosed in a note. Exhibit 12-10 illustrates noncash investing and financing activities (all amounts are assumed).

Now let's apply what you have learned about the statement of cash flows prepared by the indirect method.

EXHIBIT 12-10 Noncash Investing and Financing Activities (all amounts assumed)

	(amounts in thousands)
Noncash Investing and Financing Activities:	
Acquisition of building by issuing common shares	$320
Acquisition of land by issuing note payable	70
Acquisition of equipment by issuing note payable	30
Total noncash investing and financing activities	$420

Measuring Cash Adequacy: Free Cash Flow

Throughout this chapter, we have focused on cash flows from operating, investing, and financing activities. Some investors, creditors, and managers want to know how much cash a company can "free up" for new opportunities. The business world changes so quickly that new possibilities arise daily. The company with a significant free cash flow is better able to respond to new opportunities. **Free cash flow** is the amount of cash available from operations after paying for planned investments in property, plant, and equipment and other long-term assets. Free cash flow can be computed as follows:

$$\text{Free cash flow} = \begin{matrix}\text{Net cash flow provided by}\\ \text{operating activities}\end{matrix} - \begin{matrix}\text{Cash outflow earmarked for investment}\\ \text{in property, plant, and equipment}\\ \text{and other long-term assets}\end{matrix}$$

As an example, Research In Motion Limited is one of the world's leading technology companies. It depends on technological breakthroughs to maintain its competitive edge. RIM performs its own research and development and also acquires companies that have technology that advances RIM's products and services. Accordingly, RIM needs a large free cash flow to continue to grow.

In the year ended February 27, 2010, RIM generated cash flow from operations of US$3 billion while investing cash of US$1.8 billion. RIM had US$1.2 billion in free cash flow to invest if good investment opportunities came along.

USING INFORMATION FROM THE STATEMENT OF CASH FLOWS IN DECISION MAKING

Early in this chapter, you learned that a comparison of the balance of cash and cash equivalents reported on the balance sheet at the beginning of a period with the balance of cash and cash equivalents reported on the balance sheet at the end of the period will indicate whether cash and cash equivalents increased or decreased over the period. But the balance sheets do not indicate the reason for the change. Similarly, the income statement does not answer the question of why there was an increase or decrease. The statement of cash flows provides the missing information. It is for that reason that managers, investors, and creditors find the statement of cash flows a very useful tool for decision making.

Manager—The management is able to assess whether the cash flow from operations is sufficient to fund the company's investment activities or whether the company will have to seek additional funds from investors and/or creditors if it is to continue to expand.

Investor—Investors can use the statement of cash flows to assist them in deciding whether or not to invest in a company's shares. The statement of cash flows will provide information such as:

- How much is an investment in the company's shares likely to pay in future dividends?
- Is the share price likely to increase or decrease?
- Is the company growing by investing in the future or contracting by selling assets?
- Is the company borrowing money or issuing shares to pay for operations?

Creditor—Creditors can use the statement of cash flows to assess whether the company appears likely to be able to pay the periodic interest on its debt and if the company will have to borrow to repay its debt when it comes due.

ACCOUNTING FOR THE STATEMENT OF CASH FLOWS

IAS 7 expresses a preference for preparing the funds from operations section of the statement of cash flows using the direct method, as it is believed to be the more informative method. On the other hand, the text pointed out that most companies use the indirect method. The accountant must decide therefore whether to use the more informative direct method or the indirect method, which will allow investors and creditors to more easily compare the company's statement of cash flows with other companies' statements of cash flows.

SUMMARY OF CHAPTER 12

Learning Objective ❶: **Identify the purposes of the statement of cash flows**

IAS 7 "Statement of Cash Flows" explains that the information disclosed by a company about its **cash flows** provides decision-useful information to users of financial statements. The statement of cash flows includes information about operating, financing, and investing activities.

The **statement of cash flows** reports where cash came from and where cash went. It helps managers, investors, and creditors:

- Predict future cash flows
- Evaluate management decisions
- Determine the ability of the company to pay dividends and interest
- Understand the relationship between net income and cash flows

Cash means cash and cash equivalents. **Cash equivalents** are highly liquid short-term financial instruments.

Learning Objective ❷: **Distinguish among operating, investing, and financing cash flows**

Operating activities are related to the transactions that make up net income. A successful business must generate most of its cash from operating activities. Operating cash flows relate to current assets and liabilities.

Investing activities include purchases and sales of property, plant, and equipment, intangible assets, and investments in other companies. A company that is growing will have a negative cash flow from investing activities. Investing cash flows relate to long-term assets.

Financing activities include borrowing and repaying funds, issuing and repurchasing shares, and the payment of dividends. Financing activities relate to long-term liabilities and owner's equity.

There are two ways to format operating activities on the statement of cash flows:

- **Indirect method** reconciles net income to net cash provided by operating activities.
- **Direct method** reports all cash receipts and cash payments from operating activities.

Although the two methods use different processes to compute funds from operations, they both result in the same final figure.

IAS 7 permits either method but indicates that the direct method is its preferred choice. However most companies use the indirect method.

Learning Objective ❸: **Prepare a statement of cash flows by the indirect method**

Cash flows from operating activities under the indirect method begins with net income, which is adjusted as follows:

- Add back noncash expenses.
- Add loss/deduct gain on sales of long-term assets.
- Add decreases/deduct increases in current assets other than cash.
- Add increases/deduct decreases in current liabilities.

The sum of the above is the total funds provided by (if positive)/used from (if negative) operations for the period.

Cash flows from investing activities are calculated as follows:

- Add sales/deduct purchases of long-term assets.
- Add issue of/deduct collection of long-term loans to others.

The sum of the above is the total funds provided by (if positive)/used by (if negative) investing activities for the period. A negative investing funds flow indicates that the company is expanding.

Cash flows from financing activities are calculated as follows:

- Add issue of/deduct repurchase of shares.
- Add borrowing/deduct repayment of long-term debt.
- Deduct payment of cash dividends.

The sum of the above is the total funds provided by/used by financing activities for the period. A negative financing funds flow indicates that the company is reducing its debt and/or paying dividends.

Noncash activities such as the purchase of land and a building by issuing shares are not shown on the statement of cash flows but must be disclosed on a separate schedule that follows the statement of cash flows or in a note to the financial statements.

END-OF-CHAPTER SUMMARY PROBLEM

MyAccountingLab

Gorska Corporation, a private company reported the following income statement and comparative balance sheet, along with transaction data for 2011:

Gorska Corporation
Income Statement
For the Year Ended December 31, 2011

Sales revenue		$662,000
Cost of goods sold		560,000
Gross margin		102,000
Operating expenses		
Salary expense	$46,000	
Depreciation expense, equipment	7,000	
Amortization expense, patent	3,000	
Rent expense	2,000	
Total operating expenses		58,000
Income from operations		44,000
Other items:		
Loss on sale of equipment		(2,000)
Income before income tax		42,000
Income tax expense		16,000
Net income		$ 26,000

Gorska Corporation
Balance Sheet
As at December 31, 2011 and 2010

Assets	2011	2010	Liabilities and Shareholders' Equity	2011	2010
Current:			Current:		
Cash and equivalents	$ 19,000	$ 3,000	Accounts payable	$ 35,000	$ 26,000
Accounts receivable	22,000	23,000	Accrued liabilities	7,000	9,000
Inventories	34,000	31,000	Income tax payable	10,000	10,000
Prepaid expenses	1,000	3,000	Total current liabilities	52,000	45,000
Total current assets	76,000	60,000	Long-term note payable	44,000	—
Long-term investments	18,000	10,000	Bonds payable	40,000	53,000
Equipment, net	67,000	52,000	Shareholders' Equity		
Patent, net	44,000	10,000	Common shares	42,000	15,000
Total assets	$205,000	$132,000	Retained earnings	27,000	19,000
			Total liabilities and shareholders' equity	$205,000	$132,000

Transaction Data for 2011:	
Purchase of equipment	$98,000
Payment of cash dividends	18,000
Issuance of common shares to retire bonds payable	13,000
Purchase of long-term investment	8,000
Issuance of long-term note payable to purchase patent	37,000
Issuance of long-term note payable to borrow cash	7,000
Issuance of common shares for cash	19,000
Proceeds on sale of equipment (carrying amount, $76,000)	74,000
Repurchase of common shares for cancellation	5,000

Name: Gorska Corporation
Fiscal Period: Year ended December 31, 2011

Required

Prepare Gorska Corporation's statement of cash flows for the year ended December 31, 2011. Format operating cash flows by the indirect method. Follow the four steps outlined below. For Step 4, prepare a T-account to show the transaction activity in each long-term balance sheet account. For each capital asset, use a single account, net of accumulated depreciation or amortization (for example: Equipment, net).

STEP 1 Lay out the template of the statement of cash flows.

STEP 2 From the comparative balance sheet, determine the increase in cash during the year, $16,000.

STEP 3 From the income statement, take net income, depreciation and amortization, and the loss on sale of equipment, to the statement of cash flows.

STEP 4 Complete the statement of cash flows. Account for the year-to-year change in each balance sheet account.

Answer

The title must include the name of the company, "Statement of Cash Flows," and the specific period of time covered. There are three sections: Cash flows from operating, investing, and financing activities.

Add back noncash items: depreciation, amortization, and deduct gains/add loss from sales of long-term assets.

$2,000 = $76,000 − $74,000

Any changes in current assets and current liabilities are included in the operating activities section. Calculate as 2011 balance − 2010 balance from the balance sheets.

Any cash changes in the long-term assets are included in the investing activities section. Check "Transaction Data for 2011."

Any cash changes in the long-term liabilities and contributed capital accounts are included in the financing activities section. Check "Transaction Data for 2011."

This result should equal the Dec. 31, 2011 balance sheet Cash amount.

Check "Transaction Data for 2011."

Gorska Corporation
Statement of Cash Flows
For the Year Ended December 31, 2011

Cash flows from operating activities:		
Net income		$26,000
Adjustments to reconcile net income to net cash provided by operating activities:		
Depreciation	$ 7,000	
Amortization	3,000	
Loss on sale of equipment	2,000	
Decrease in accounts receivable	1,000	
Increase in inventories	(3,000)	
Decrease in prepaid expenses	2,000	
Increase in accounts payable	9,000	
Decrease in accrued liabilities	(2,000)	19,000
Net cash provided by operating activities		45,000
Cash flows from investing activities:		
Purchase of equipment	(98,000)	
Sale of equipment	74,000	
Purchase of long-term investment	(8,000)	
Net cash used for investing activities		(32,000)
Cash flows from financing activities:		
Issuance of common shares	19,000	
Payment of cash dividends	(18,000)	
Issuance of long-term note payable	7,000	
Repurchase of common shares	(5,000)	
Net cash provided by financing activities		3,000
Net increase in cash		16,000
Cash balance, December 31, 2010		3,000
Cash balance, December 31, 2011		$19,000
Noncash investing and financing activities:		
Issuance of long-term note payable to purchase patent		$37,000
Issuance of common shares to retire bonds payable		13,000
Total noncash investing and financing activities		$50,000

Long-Term Investments

	Debit		Credit
Bal.	10,000		
	8,000		
Bal.	18,000		

Equipment, Net

	Debit		Credit
Bal.	52,000		
	98,000		76,000
			7,000
Bal.	67,000		

Patent, Net

	Debit		Credit
Bal.	10,000		
	37,000		3,000
Bal.	44,000		

Long-Term Note Payable

	Debit		Credit
		Bal.	0
			37,000
			7,000
		Bal.	44,000

Bonds Payable

	Debit		Credit
		Bal.	53,000
	13,000		
		Bal.	40,000

Common Shares

	Debit		Credit
		Bal.	15,000
			13,000
	5,000		19,000
		Bal.	42,000

Retained Earnings

	Debit		Credit
		Bal.	19,000
	18,000		26,000
		Bal.	27,000

Use the 2010 and 2011 balance sheet amounts and the transaction data for 2011 to complete these T-accounts.

Review the Statement of Cash Flows

Quick Check (Answers are given on page 637.)

1. All the following activities are reported on the statement of cash flows, except
   a. Operating activities
   b. Investing activities
   c. Financing activities
   d. Marketing activities
2. Activities that create long-term liabilities are usually
   a. Operating activities
   b. Investing activities
   c. Financing activities
   d. Noncash investing and financing activities
3. Activities affecting long-term assets are
   a. Operating activities
   b. Investing activities
   c. Financing activities
   d. Marketing activities
4. Hilltop Company borrowed $50,000, paid dividends of $12,000, issued 2,000 shares for $30 per share, purchased land for $24,000, and received dividends of $6,000. Net income was $80,000 and depreciation for the year totalled $5,000. How much should be reported as net cash provided by financing activities?
   a. $85,000
   b. $98,000
   c. $110,000
   d. $104,000
5. Activities that obtain the cash needed to launch and sustain a company are
   a. Income activities
   b. Investing activities
   c. Financing activities
   d. Marketing activities
6. The exchange of shares for land would be reported as
   a. Exchanges are not reported on the statement of cash flows.
   b. Noncash investing and financing activities
   c. Investing activities
   d. Financing activities

Use the following Baycraft Ltd. information for Questions 7 through 10.

Net Income	$47,000	Decrease in Inventories	$ 2,000
Depreciation Expense	8,000	Increase in Accounts Payable	7,000
Payment of Dividends	2,000	Acquisition of Equipment	24,000
Increase in Accounts Receivable	4,000	Sale of Shares	3,000
Collection of Notes Receivable	6,000	Payment of Long-Term Debt	9,000
Loss on Sale of Land	12,000	Proceeds from Sale of Land	36,000

7. Under the indirect method, net cash provided by operating activities would be
   a. $72,000
   b. $76,000
   c. $83,000
   d. $84,000

8. Net cash provided by (used for) investing activities would be
   a. $18,000
   b. $(12,000)
   c. $(6,000)
   d. $24,000

9. Net cash provided by (used for) financing activities would be
   a. $4,000
   b. $2,000
   c. $(8,000)
   d. $(11,000)

10. The cost of land must have been
    a. $30,000
    b. $48,000
    c. $54,000
    d. Cannot be determined from the data given

11. Merryhill Industries began the year with $45,000 in accounts receivable and ended the year with $31,000 in accounts receivable. If sales for the year were $650,000, the cash collected from customers during the year amounted to
    a. $664,000
    b. $672,000
    c. $733,000
    d. $695,000

12. Mouton Cheese Ltée made sales of $690,000 and had cost of goods sold of $390,000. Inventory increased by $15,000, and accounts payable increased by $9,000. Operating expenses were $175,000. How much was Mouton's net income for the year?
    a. $110,000
    b. $116,000
    c. $125,000
    d. $300,000

13. Use the Mouton Cheese Ltée data from Question 12. How much cash did Mouton pay for inventory during the year?
    a. $374,000
    b. $390,000
    c. $396,000
    d. Some other amount ($fill in the blank)

Accounting Vocabulary

cash equivalents Highly liquid short-term investments that can be converted into cash immediately. (p. 599)

cash flows Cash receipts and cash payments (disbursements). (p. 598)

direct method Format of the operating activities section of the statement of cash flows; lists the major categories of operating cash receipts (collections from customers and receipts of interest and dividends) and cash disbursements (payments to suppliers, to employees, for interest and income taxes). (p. 601)

financing activities Include receipt and disbursement of cash from investors and creditors. (p. 600)

free cash flow The amount of cash available from operations after paying for planned investments in plant, equipment, and other long-term assets. (p. 612)

indirect method Format of the operating activities section of the statement of cash flows; starts with net income and reconciles to net cash provided by activities. (p. 601)

investing activities Include increases and decreases in long-term assets (p. 600)

operating activities Include revenues, expenses, gains, and losses of the business (p. 600)

Assess Your Progress

Make the grade with MyAccountingLab: The exercises and problems in this chapter can be found on MyAccountingLab at www.myaccountinglab.com. You can practise them as often as you want, and they feature step-by-step guided solutions to help you find the right answer.

Short Exercises

Learning Objective 1
Purposes of the statement of cash flows

S12-1 State how the statement of cash flows helps investors and creditors perform each of the following functions.

a. Predict future cash flows.
b. Evaluate management decisions.

Learning Objective 2
Evaluating operating cash flows—indirect method

S12-2 Examine the Gildan Activewear statement of cash flows on page 597. Suppose Gildan's operating activities *used*, rather than *provided*, cash. Identify three things under the indirect method that could cause operating cash flows to be negative.

Learning Objective 3
Reporting cash flows from operating activities—indirect method

S12-3 Canada Wide Transportation (CWT) began 2011 with accounts receivable, inventory, and prepaid expenses totalling $65,000. At the end of the year, CWT had a total of $78,000 for these current assets. At the beginning of 2011, CWT owed current liabilities of $42,000, and at year-end current liabilities totalled $40,000.

Net income for the year was $80,000. Included in net income were a $4,000 gain on the sale of land and depreciation expense of $9,000.

Show how CWT should report cash flows from operating activities for 2011. CWT uses the *indirect* method. Use Exhibit 12-6 (p. 605) as a guide.

Learning Objective 2
Identifying items for reporting cash flows from operations—indirect method

S12-4 Bewell Clinic Inc. is preparing its statement of cash flows (indirect method) for the year ended November 30, 2011. Consider the following items in preparing the company's statement of cash flows. Identify each item as an operating activity—addition to net income (O+), or subtraction from net income (O–); an investing activity (I); a financing activity (F); or an activity that is not used to prepare the statement of cash flows by the indirect method (N). Place the appropriate symbol in the blank space.

___ a. Loss on sale of land	___ h. Increase in accounts payable
___ b. Depreciation expense	___ i. Net income
___ c. Increase in inventory	___ j. Payment of dividends
___ d. Decrease in prepaid expense	___ k. Decrease in accrued liabilities
___ e. Decrease in accounts receivable	___ l. Issuance of common shares
___ f. Purchase of equipment	___ m. Gain on sale of building
___ g. Collection of cash from customers	___ n. Retained earnings

Learning Objective 3
Computing operating cash flows—indirect method

S12-5 (Short Exercise 12-6 is an alternative exercise.) Edwards Corporation Inc. accountants have assembled the following data for the year ended June 30, 2011.

Payment of dividends	$ 6,000	Cost of goods sold	$100,000
Proceeds from issuance of common shares	20,000	Other operating expenses	35,000
Sales revenue	224,000	Purchase of equipment	40,000
Increase in current assets other than cash	30,000	Decrease in current liabilities	5,000
Repurchase of common shares	5,000	Payment of note payable	30,000
		Proceeds from sale of land	60,000
		Amortization expense	8,000

Prepare the *operating activities section* of Edwards' statement of cash flows for the year ended June 30, 2011. Edwards uses the *indirect* method for operating cash flows.

Learning Objective 3
Preparing a statement of cash flows—indirect method

S12-6 Use the data in Short Exercise 12-5 to prepare Edwards Corporation's statement of cash flows for the year ended June 30, 2011. Edwards uses the *indirect* method for operating activities. Use Exhibit 12-7, page 606, as a guide, but you may stop after determining the net increase (or decrease) in cash.

Learning Objective 3
Computing investing cash flows

S12-7 Autos of Red Deer Inc. reported the following financial statements for 2011:

Autos of Red Deer Inc.
Income Statement
For the Year Ended December 31, 2011

(In thousands)	
Sales revenue	$710
Cost of goods sold	340
Salary expense	70
Depreciation expense	20
Other expenses	130
Total expenses	560
Net income	$150

Autos of Red Deer Inc.
Comparative Balance Sheet
As at December 31, 2011 and 2010

(In thousands)					
Assets	**2011**	**2010**	**Liabilities**	**2011**	**2010**
Current:			Current:		
Cash	$ 19	$ 16	Accounts payable	$ 47	$ 42
Accounts receivable	59	48	Salary payable	23	21
Inventory	75	84	Accrued liabilities	8	11
Prepaid expenses	3	2	Long-term notes payable	68	58
Long-term investments	55	75	**Shareholders' Equity**		
Property, plant, and equipment	225	185	Common shares	40	32
			Retained earnings	250	246
Total	$436	$410	Total	$436	$410

Compute the following investing cash flows.

a. Acquisitions of plant and equipment (all were for cash). Autos of Red Deer sold no plant and equipment.
b. Proceeds from the sale of investments. Autos of Red Deer purchased no investments.

Learning Objective 3
Computing financing cash flows

S12-8 Use the Autos of Red Deer data in Short Exercise 12-7 to compute:

a. New borrowing or payment of long-term notes payable. Autos of Red Deer had only one long-term note payable transaction during the year.
b. Issuance of common shares or repurchase of common shares. Autos of Red Deer had only one common share transaction during the year.
c. Payment of cash dividends (same as dividends declared).

Exercises

E12-9 B.C. Plating Inc. has experienced an unbroken string of 10 years of growth in net income. Nevertheless, the company is facing bankruptcy. Creditors are calling all B.C. Plating's loans for immediate payment, and the cash is simply not available. It is clear that the company's top managers overemphasized profits and gave too little attention to cash flow.

Learning Objective 1
Identifying the purposes of the statement of cash flows

Required

Write a brief memo, in your own words, to explain to the managers of B.C. Plating the purposes of the statement of cash flows.

E12-10 Tyler-Bolton Investments specializes in low-risk government bonds. Identify each of Tyler-Bolton's transactions as operating (O), investing (I), financing (F), noncash investing and financing (NIF), or a transaction that is not reported on the statement of cash flows. (N) Indicate whether each item increases (+) or decreases (−) cash. The indirect method is used for operating activities.

Learning Objective 2
Identifying activities for the statement of cash flows—indirect method

___ a. Net income
___ b. Payment of cash dividend
___ c. Sale of long-term investment
___ d. Loss on sale of equipment
___ e. Depreciation of intangible assets
___ f. Issuance of long-term note payable to borrow cash
___ g. Amortization of equipment
___ h. Repurchase of common shares
___ i. Issuance of common shares for cash
___ j. Increase in accounts payable
___ k. Acquisition of equipment by issuance of note payable
___ l. Payment of long-term debt
___ m. Acquisition of building by cash payment
___ n. Accrual of salary expense
___ o. Purchase of long-term investment
___ p. Decrease in merchandise inventory
___ q. Increase in prepaid expenses
___ r. Cash sale of land
___ s. Decrease in accrued liabilities

E12-11 Indicate whether each of the following transactions records an operating activity, an investing activity, a financing activity, or a noncash investing and financing activity. The statement of cash flows is prepared by the *indirect* method.

Learning Objective 2
Classifying transactions for the statement of cash flows—indirect method

a.	Equipment	18,000		h.	Cash	81,000	
	Cash		18,000		Common Shares		81,000
b.	Cash	7,200					
	Long-Term Investment		7,200	i.	Common Shares	13,000	
c.	Bonds Payable	45,000			Cash		13,000
	Cash		45,000	j.	Cash	60,000	
d.	Building	164,000			Accounts Receivable	10,000	
	Note Payable, Long-Term		164,000		Service Revenue		70,000
e.	Loss on Disposal of Equipment	1,400		k.	Salary Expense	22,000	
	Equipment, Net		1,400		Cash		22,000
f.	Dividends Payable	16,500		l.	Land	87,000	
	Cash		16,500		Cash		87,000
g.	Furniture and Fixtures	22,100		m.	Amortization Expense	9,000	
	Cash		22,100		Accumulated Amortization		9,000

Learning Objective 3
Computing cash flows from operating activities—indirect method

E12-12 The accounting records of North Central Distributors Inc. reveal the following:

Net income	$35,000	Depreciation	$18,000
Collection of dividend revenue	7,000	Decrease in current liabilities	20,000
Payment of interest	16,000	Increase in current assets other than cash	27,000
Sales revenue	9,000		
Loss on sale of land	5,000	Payment of dividends	7,000
Acquisition of land	37,000	Payment of income tax	13,000

Required

Compute cash flows from operating activities by the indirect method. Use the format of the operating activities section of Exhibit 12-6 (p. 605). Also evaluate the operating cash flow of North Central Distributors. Give the reason for your evaluation.

Learning Objective 3
Computing cash flows from operating activities—indirect method

E12-13 The accounting records of Saskatoon Fur Traders Ltd. include these accounts:

Cash

Mar. 1	5,000		
Receipts	447,000	Payments	448,000
Mar. 31	4,000		

Accounts Receivable

Mar. 1	18,000		
Receipts	443,000	Collections	447,000
Mar. 31	14,000		

Inventory

Mar. 1	19,000		
Purchases	337,000	Cost of sales	335,000
Mar. 31	21,000		

Equipment

Mar. 1	93,000		
Acquisition	6,000		
Mar. 31	99,000		

Accumulated Depreciation—Equipment

		Mar. 1	52,000
		Depreciation	3,000
		Mar. 31	55,000

Accounts Payable

		Mar. 1	14,000
Payments	332,000	Purchases	337,000
		Mar. 31	19,000

Accrued Liabilities

		Mar. 1	9,000
Payments	14,000	Receipts	11,000
		Mar. 31	6,000

Retained Earnings

		Mar. 1	64,000
Quarterly dividend	18,000	Net income	41,000
		Mar. 31	87,000

Compute Saskatoon's net cash provided by (used for) operating activities during March. Use the indirect method. Does Saskatoon have trouble collecting receivables or selling inventory? How can you tell?

Learning Objective 3
Preparing the statement of cash flows—indirect method

E12-14 The income statement and additional data of Noel Travel Products Inc. follow:

Noel Travel Products Inc.
Income Statement
For the Year Ended December 31, 2011

Revenues:		
Sales revenue	$229,000	
Dividend revenue	8,000	$237,000
Expenses:		
Cost of goods sold	$ 91,000	
Salary expense	45,000	
Depreciation expense	29,000	
Advertising expense	4,000	
Interest expense	2,000	
Income tax expense	9,000	180,000
Net income		$ 57,000

Additional data:

a. Acquisition of plant assets was $150,000. Of this amount, $100,000 was paid in cash and $50,000 by signing a note payable.
b. Proceeds from sale of land totalled $24,000.
c. Proceeds from issuance of common shares totalled $30,000.
d. Payment of long-term note payable was $15,000.
e. Payment of dividends was $11,000.
f. From the balance sheet:

	December 31, 2011	December 31, 2010
Current Assets:		
Cash	$47,000	$20,000
Accounts receivable	43,000	58,000
Inventory	83,000	77,000
Prepaid expenses	9,000	8,000
Current Liabilities:		
Accounts payable	35,000	22,000
Accrued liabilities	13,000	21,000

Required

1. Prepare Noel's statement of cash flows for the year ended December 31, 2011, using the indirect method.
2. Evaluate Noel's cash flows for the year. In your evaluation, mention all three categories of cash flows and give the reason for your evaluation.

Learning Objective 3
Interpreting a statement of cash flows—indirect method

E12-15 Consider three independent cases for the cash flows of 827 Boulevard Shoes Ltd. For each case, identify from the statement of cash flows how 827 Boulevard Shoes generated the cash to acquire new capital assets. Rank the three cases from the most financially healthy to the least healthy.

	Case A	Case B	Case C
Cash flows from operating activities:			
Net income	$ 30,000	$ 30,000	$ 30,000
Depreciation	11,000	11,000	11,000
Increase in current assets	(1,000)	(19,000)	(7,000)
Decrease in current liabilities	0	(6,000)	(8,000)
	$ 40,000	$ 16,000	$ 26,000
Cash flows from investing activities:			
Acquisition of capital assets	$(91,000)	$(91,000)	$ (91,000)
Sales of capital assets	8,000	97,000	4,000
	$(83,000)	$ 6,000	$ (87,000)
Cash flows from financing activities:			
Issuance of common shares	$ 50,000	$ 16,000	$104,000
Payment of debt	(9,000)	(21,000)	(29,000)
	$ 41,000	$ (5,000)	$ 75,000
Net increase (decrease) in cash	$ (2,000)	$ 17,000	$ 14,000

Learning Objective 3
Computing investing and financing amounts for the statement of cash flows

E12-16 Compute the following items for the statement of cash flows.

a. Beginning and ending Capital Assets, Net, are $103,000 and $107,000, respectively. Depreciation for the period was $21,500, and purchases of new plant and equipment were $27,000. Capital assets were sold at a $1,000 loss. What were the cash proceeds of the sale?

b. Beginning and ending Retained Earnings are $45,000 and $73,000, respectively. Net income for the period was $47,000, and stock dividends were $8,000. How much were cash dividends?

Challenge Exercise

Learning Objective 3
Using the balance sheet and the statement of cash flows together

E12-17 Crown Specialties Ltd. reported the following at December 31, 2011 (in thousands):

	2011	2010
From the comparative balance sheet:		
Property and equipment, net	$ 11,150	$9,590
Long-term notes payable	4,400	3,080
From the statement of cash flows:		
Depreciation	$ 1,920	
Capital expenditures	(4,130)	
Proceeds from sale of property and equipment	770	
Proceeds from issuance of long-term note payable	1,190	
Payment of long-term note payable	(110)	
Issuance of common shares	383	

Determine the following items for Crown Specialties during 2011:

1. Gain or loss on the sale of property and equipment
2. Amount of long-term debt issued for something other than cash

Quiz

Test your understanding of the statement of cash flows by answering the following questions. Select the best choice among the possible answers given.

Q12-18 Paying off bonds payable is reported on the statement of cash flows under

a. Operating activities
b. Investing activities
c. Financing activities
d. Noncash investing and financing activities

Q12-19 The sale of inventory for cash is reported on the statement of cash flows under

a. Operating activities
b. Investing activities
c. Financing activities
d. Noncash investing and financing activities

Q12-20 Selling equipment is reported on the statement of cash flows under

a. Operating activities
b. Investing activities
c. Financing activities
d. Noncash investing and financing activities

Q12-21 Which of the following terms appears on a statement of cash flows—indirect method?

a. Payments to suppliers
b. Amortization expense
c. Collections from customers
d. Cash receipt of interest revenue

Q12-22 On an indirect-method statement of cash flows, an increase in prepaid insurance would be

a. Included in payments to suppliers
b. Added to net income
c. Added to increases in current assets
d. Deducted from net income

Q12-23 On an indirect-method statement of cash flows, an increase in accounts payable would be

a. Reported in the investing activities section
b. Reported in the financing activities section
c. Added to net income in the operating activities section
d. Deducted from net income in the operating activities section

Q12-24 On an indirect-method statement of cash flows, a gain on the sale of plant assets would be

a. Ignored, since the gain did not generate any cash
b. Reported in the investing activities section
c. Deducted from net income in the operating activities section
d. Added to net income in the operating activities section

Q12-25 Paying cash dividends is a/an ______ activity.
Receiving cash dividends is a/an ______ activity.

Q12-26 Matlock Camera Co. sold equipment with a cost of $20,000 and accumulated depreciation of $8,000 for an amount that resulted in a gain of $3,000. What amount should Matlock report on the statement of cash flows as "proceeds from sale of plant and equipment"?

a. $9,000
b. $17,000
c. $15,000
d. Some other amount ($________)

Questions 27 through 35 use the following data. Trudeau Corporation formats operating cash flows by the indirect method.

Trudeau Corporation
Income Statement for the Year Ended December 31, 2011

Sales revenue	$180,000	
Gain on sale of equipment	8,000	$188,000
Cost of goods sold	110,000	
Depreciation	6,000	
Other operating expenses	25,000	141,000
Net income		$ 47,000

Trudeau Corporation
Comparative Balance Sheet as at December 31, 2011 and 2010

Assets	2011	2010	Liabilities and Shareholders' Equity	2011	2010
Cash	$ 4,000	$ 1,000	Accounts payable	$ 6,000	$ 7,000
Accounts receivable	7,000	11,000	Accrued liabilities	7,000	3,000
Inventory	10,000	9,000	Common shares	20,000	10,000
Plant and equipment, net	93,000	69,000	Retained earnings	81,000	70,000
	$114,000	$90,000		$114,000	$90,000

Q12-27 How many items enter the computation of Trudeau's net cash provided by operating activities?

a. 2
b. 3
c. 5
d. 7

Q12-28 How do Trudeau's accrued liabilities affect the company's statement of cash flows for 2011?

a. They don't because the accrued liabilities are not yet paid
b. Increase in cash provided by operating activities
c. Increase in cash used by investing activities
d. Increase in cash used by financing activities

Q12-29 How do accounts receivable affect Trudeau's cash flows from operating activities for 2011?

a. Increase in cash provided by operating activities
b. Decrease in cash provided by operating activities
c. They don't because accounts receivable result from investing activities
d. Decrease in cash used by investing activities

Q12-30 Trudeau's net cash provided by operating activities during 2011 was

a. $3,000
b. $47,000
c. $51,000
d. $58,000

Q12-31 How many items enter the computation of Trudeau's net cash flow investing activities for 2011?

a. 2
b. 3
c. 5
d. 7

Q12-32 The carrying amount of equipment sold during 2011 was $20,000. Trudeau's net cash flow from investing activities for 2011 was

a. Net cash used of $22,000
b. Net cash used of $28,000
c. Net cash used of $50,000
d. Net cash provided of $28,000

Q12-33 How many items enter the computation of Trudeau's net cash flow from financing activities for 2011?

a. 2
b. 3
c. 5
d. 7

Q12-34 Trudeau's largest financing cash flow for 2011 resulted from

a. Sale of equipment
b. Purchase of equipment
c. Issuance of common shares
d. Payment of dividends

Q12-35 Trudeau's net cash flow from financing activities for 2011 was

a. Net cash used of $25,000
b. Net cash used of $20,000
c. Net cash provided of $10,000
d. Net cash used of $26,000

Q12-36 Sales totalled $800,000, accounts receivable increased by $40,000, and accounts payable decreased by $35,000. How much cash did the company collect from customers?

a. $760,000
b. $795,000
c. $800,000
d. $840,000

Q12-37 Income Tax Payable was $5,000 at the end of the year and $2,800 at the beginning. Income tax expense for the year totalled $59,100. What amount of cash did the company pay for income tax during the year?

a. $56,900
b. $59,100
c. $61,300
d. $61,900

Problems

(Group A)

Learning Objective 1 2
Using cash flow data to evaluate performance

P12-38A Top managers of Relax Inns are reviewing company performance for 2011. The income statement reports a 20% increase in net income over 2010. However, most of the increase resulted from an extraordinary gain on insurance proceeds from fire damage to a building. The balance sheet shows a large increase in receivables. The statement of cash flows, in summarized form, reports the following:

Net cash used for operating activities	$(80,000)
Net cash provided by investing activities	40,000
Net cash provided by financing activities	50,000
Increase in cash during 2011	$ 10,000

Required

Write a memo giving Relax Inns' managers your assessment of 2011 operations and your outlook for the future. Focus on the information content of the cash flow data.

Learning Objective 2 3
Preparing an income statement, balance sheet, and statement of cash flows—indirect method

P12-39A Vintage Automobiles of Orangeville Ltd. was formed on January 1, 2011, when Vintage issued common shares for $300,000. Early in January 2011, Vintage made the following cash payments:

a. $150,000 for equipment
b. $120,000 for inventory (four cars at $30,000 each)
c. $20,000 for 2011 rent on a store building

In February 2011, Vintage purchased six cars for inventory on account. Cost of this inventory was $260,000 ($43,333.33 each). Before year-end, Vintage paid $208,000 of this debt. Vintage uses the FIFO method to account for inventory.

During 2011, Vintage sold eight vintage autos for a total of $500,000. Before year-end, Vintage collected 80% of this amount.

The business employs three people. The combined annual payroll is $95,000, of which Vintage owes $4,000 at year-end. At the end of the year, Vintage paid income tax of $10,000.

Late in 2011, Vintage declared and paid cash dividends of $11,000.

For equipment, Vintage uses the straight-line depreciation method over five years with zero residual value.

Required

1. Prepare Vintage Automobiles of Orangeville Ltd.'s income statement for the year ended December 31, 2011. Use the single-step format, with all revenues listed together and all expenses listed together.
2. Prepare Vintage's balance sheet at December 31, 2011.
3. Prepare Vintage's statement of cash flows for the year ended December 31, 2011. Format cash flows from operating activities by using the *indirect* method.
4. Comment on the business performance based on the statement of cash flows.

Learning Objective 2 3
Preparing the statement of cash flows—indirect method

P12-40A Primrose Software Inc. has assembled the following data for the year ended December 31, 2011.

	December 31, 2011	December 31, 2010
Current Accounts:		
Current assets:		
Cash and cash equivalents	$38,700	$22,700
Accounts receivable	69,700	64,200
Inventories	88,600	83,000
Prepaid expenses	5,300	4,100
Current liabilities:		
Accounts payable	57,200	55,800
Income tax payable	18,600	16,700
Accrued liabilities	15,500	27,200

Transaction Data for 2011:

Acquisition of land by issuing long-term note payable	$ 95,000	Repurchase of common shares	$14,300
Stock dividends	31,800	Loss on sale of equipment	11,700
Collection of loan	8,700	Payment of cash dividends	18,300
Depreciation expense	27,100	Issuance of long-term note payable to borrow cash	34,400
Purchase of building	125,300	Net income	45,100
Retirement of bonds payable by issuing common shares	65,000	Issuance of common shares for cash	41,200
Purchase of long-term investment	31,600	Proceeds from sale of equipment	58,000

Required

Prepare Primrose Software Inc.'s statement of cash flows using the *indirect* method to report operating activities. Include an accompanying schedule of noncash investing and financing activities. How much of the cash used for investing activities was provided by operations?

P12-41A The comparative balance sheet of Northern Movie Theatre Company at March 31, 2011, reported the following:

Learning Objective 2 3
Preparing the statement of cash flows—indirect method

	March 31, 2011	March 31, 2010
Current assets:		
Cash and cash equivalents	$ 9,900	$14,000
Accounts receivable	14,900	21,700
Inventories	63,200	60,600
Prepaid expenses	1,900	1,700
Current liabilities:		
Accounts payable	30,300	27,600
Accrued liabilities	10,700	11,100
Income tax payable	8,000	4,700

Northern's transactions during the year ended March 31, 2011, included the following:

Acquisition of land by issuing note payable	$101,000	Sale of long-term investment	$13,700
Payment of cash dividend	30,000	Depreciation expense	17,300
Cash purchase of equipment	78,700	Cash purchase of building	47,000
Issuance of long-term note payable to borrow cash	50,000	Net income	50,000
		Issuance of common shares for cash	11,000
		Stock dividend	18,000

Required

1. Prepare Northern Movie Theatre Company's statement of cash flows for the year ended March 31, 2011, using the *indirect* method to report cash flows from operating activities. Report noncash investing and financing activities in an accompanying schedule.
2. Evaluate Northern's cash flows for the year. Mention all three categories of cash flows and give the reason for your evaluation.

P12-42A The 2011 comparative balance sheet and income statement of 4 Seasons Supply Corp. follow. 4 Seasons had no noncash investing and financing transactions during 2011. During the year, there were no sales of land or equipment, no issuance of notes payable, and no repurchase of shares transactions.

Learning Objective 2 3
Preparing the statement of cash flows—indirect method

4 Seasons Supply Corp.
Comparative Balance Sheet
as at December 31, 2011 and 2010

	December 31, 2011	December 31, 2010	Increase (Decrease)
Current assets:			
Cash and cash equivalents	$ 17,600	$ 5,300	$12,300
Accounts receivable	27,200	27,600	(400)
Inventories	83,600	87,200	(3,600)
Prepaid expenses	2,500	1,900	600
Property, plant, and equipment:			
Land	89,000	60,000	29,000
Equipment, net	53,500	49,400	4,100
Total assets	$273,400	$231,400	$42,000
Current liabilities:			
Accounts payable	$ 35,800	$ 33,700	$ 2,100
Salary payable	3,100	6,600	(3,500)
Other accrued liabilities	22,600	23,700	(1,100)
Long-term liabilities:			
Notes payable	75,000	100,000	(25,000)
Shareholders' equity:			
Common shares	88,300	64,700	23,600
Retained earnings	48,600	2,700	45,900
Total liabilities and shareholders' equity	$273,400	$231,400	$42,000

4 Seasons Supply Corp.
Income Statement
for the Year Ended December 31, 2011

Revenues:		
Sales revenue		$228,700
Expenses:		
Cost of goods sold	$70,600	
Salary expense	27,800	
Depreciation expense	4,000	
Other operating expense	10,500	
Interest expense	11,600	
Income tax expense	29,100	
Total expenses		153,600
Net income		$ 75,100

Required

1. Prepare the 2011 statement of cash flows, formatting operating activities by using the *indirect* method.
2. How will what you learned in this problem help you evaluate an investment?

(Group B)

Learning Objective ❶❷
Using cash-flow information to evaluate performance

P12-43B Top managers of Culinary Imports Limited are reviewing company performance for 2011. The income statement reports a 15% increase in net income, the fourth consecutive year showing an income increase above 10%. The income statement includes a nonrecurring loss without which net income would have increased by 16%. The balance sheet shows modest increases in assets, liabilities, and shareholders' equity. The assets posting the largest increases are plant and equipment because the company is halfway through a five-year expansion program. No other asset and no liabilities are increasing dramatically. A summarized version of the statement of cash flows reports the following:

Net cash provided by operating activities	$ 310,000
Net cash used for investing activities	(290,000)
Net cash provided by financing activities	50,000
Increase in cash during 2011	$ 70,000

Required

Write a memo giving top managers of Culinary Imports Limited your assessment of 2011 operations and your outlook for the future. Focus on the net income and the cash flow data.

Learning Objective ❷❸
Preparing an income statement, balance sheet, and statement of cash flows—indirect method

P12-44B Cruise Canada Motorhomes Inc. (CCM) was formed on January 1, 2011, when the company issued its common shares for $200,000. Early in January, CCM made the following cash payments:

a. For showroom fixtures, $50,000
b. For inventory, two motorhomes at $60,000 each, a total of $120,000
c. For rent on a store building, $12,000

In February, CCM purchased three motorhomes on account. Cost of this inventory was $160,000 ($53,333.33 each). Before year-end, CCM paid $140,000 of this debt. CCM uses the FIFO method to account for inventory.

During 2011, CCM sold four motorhomes for a total of $560,000. Before year-end, CCM collected 90% of this amount.

The store employs three people. The combined annual payroll is $90,000, of which CCM owes $3,000 at year-end. At the end of the year, CCM paid income tax of $64,000.

Late in 2011, CCM declared and paid cash dividends of $40,000.

For showroom fixtures, CCM uses the straight-line depreciation method over five years with zero residual value.

Required

1. Prepare CCM's income statement for the year ended December 31, 2011. Use the single-step format, with all revenues listed together and all expenses listed together.
2. Prepare CCM's balance sheet at December 31, 2011.
3. Prepare CCM's statement of cash flows for the year ended December 31, 2011. Format cash flows from operating activities by the indirect method.
4. Comment on the business performance based on the statement of cash flows.

Learning Objective 2 3
Preparing the statement of cash flows—indirect method

P12-45B Accountants for Crowne Plaza Products Inc. have assembled the following data for the year ended December 31, 2011:

	December 31, 2011	December 31, 2010
Current Accounts:		
Current assets:		
Cash and cash equivalents	$29,100	$34,800
Accounts receivable	70,100	73,700
Inventories	90,600	96,500
Prepaid expenses	3,200	2,100
Current liabilities:		
Accounts payable	71,600	67,500
Income tax payable	5,900	6,800
Accrued liabilities	28,300	23,200

Transaction Data for 2011:

Payment of cash dividends	$48,300	Stock dividends	$ 12,600
Issuance of long-term note payable to borrow cash	71,000	Collection of loan	10,300
Net income	31,000	Purchase of equipment	69,000
Issuance of preferred shares for cash	36,200	Payment of note payable by issuing common shares	89,400
Sale of long-term investment	12,200	Purchase of long-term investment	44,800
Depreciation expense	30,300	Acquisition of building by issuing long-term note payable	201,000
Payment of long-term note payable	47,800		
Gain on sale of investment	3,500		

Required
Prepare Crowne Plaza Products' statement of cash flows using the *indirect* method to report operating activities. Include an accompanying schedule of noncash investing and financing activities. How much of the cash used for investing activities was provided by operations?

Learning Objective 2 3
Preparing the statement of cash flows—indirect method

P12-46B The comparative balance sheet of Crossbow Novelties Corp. at December 31, 2011, reported the following:

	December 31, 2011	December 31, 2010
Current Assets:		
Cash and cash equivalents	$28,800	$12,500
Accounts receivable	28,600	29,300
Inventories	51,600	53,000
Prepaid expenses	4,200	3,700
Current Liabilities:		
Accounts payable	31,100	28,000
Accrued liabilities	14,300	16,800
Income tax payable	11,000	14,300

Crossbow's transactions during 2011 included the following:

Cash purchase of building	$124,000	Depreciation expense	$17,800
Net income	52,000	Payment of cash dividends	17,000
Issuance of common shares for cash	105,600	Cash purchase of equipment	55,000
Stock dividend	13,000	Issuance of long-term note payable to borrow cash	32,000
Sale of long-term investment	6,000	Retirement of note payable by issuing common shares	30,000

Required

1. Prepare the statement of cash flows of Crossbow Novelties Corp. for the year ended December 31, 2011. Use the *indirect* method to report cash flows from operating activities. Report noncash investing and financing activities in an accompanying schedule.
2. Evaluate Crossbow's cash flows for the year. Mention all three categories of cash flows, and give the reason for your evaluation.

Learning Objective 2 3
Preparing the statement of cash flows—indirect method

P12-47B The 2011 comparative balance sheet and income statement of Riverbend Pools Inc. follow. Riverbend had no noncash investing and financing transactions during 2011. During the year, there were no sales of land or equipment, no issuances of notes payable, and no share repurchase transactions.

Required

1. Prepare the statement of cash flows of Riverbend Pools Inc. for the year ended December 31, 2011. Format operating activities by the indirect method.
2. How will what you learned in this problem help you evaluate an investment?

Riverbend Pools Inc.
Comparative Balance Sheet
December 31, 2011 and 2010

	2011	2010	Increase (Decrease)
Current assets:			
Cash and cash equivalents	$ 28,700	$ 15,600	$13,100
Accounts receivable	47,100	44,000	3,100
Inventories	94,300	89,900	4,400
Prepaid expenses	1,700	2,200	(500)
Property, plant, and equipment:			
Land	35,100	10,000	25,100
Equipment, net	100,900	93,700	7,200
Total assets	$307,800	$255,400	$52,400
Current liabilities:			
Accounts payable	$ 22,700	$ 24,600	$(1,900)
Salary payable	2,100	1,400	700
Other accrued liabilities	24,400	22,500	1,900
Long-term liabilities:			
Notes payable	55,000	65,000	(10,000)
Shareholders' equity:			
Common shares	131,100	122,300	8,800
Retained earnings	72,500	19,600	52,900
Total liabilities and shareholders' equity	$307,800	$255,400	$52,400

Riverbend Pools Inc.
Income Statement
For the Year Ended December 31, 2011

Revenues:		
Sales revenue		$438,000
Interest revenue		11,700
Total revenues		449,700
Expenses:		
Cost of goods sold	$185,200	
Salary expense	76,400	
Depreciation expense	15,300	
Other operating expense	49,700	
Interest expense	24,600	
Income tax expense	16,900	
Total expense		368,100
Net income		$ 81,600

Apply Your Knowledge

Decision Cases

Learning Objective 3
Preparing and using the statement of cash flows to evaluate operations

Case 1. The 2011 income statement and the 2011 comparative balance sheet of T-Bar-M Camp Inc. have just been distributed at a meeting of the camp's board of directors. The directors raise a fundamental question: Why is the cash balance so low? This question is especially troublesome since 2011 showed record profits. As the controller of the company, you must answer the question.

T-Bar-M Camp Inc.
Income Statement
For the Year Ended December 31, 2011

	(in thousands)
Revenues:	
Sales revenue	$436
Expenses:	
Cost of goods sold	$221
Salary expense	48
Depreciation expense	57
Interest expense	13
Total expenses	339
Net income	$ 97

T-Bar-M Camp Inc.
Comparative Balance Statement
December 31, 2011 and 2010

(in thousands)	2011	2010
Assets		
Cash	$ 17	$ 63
Accounts receivable, net	72	61
Inventories	194	181
Long-term investments	31	0
Property, plant, and equipment	369	259
Accumulated depreciation	(244)	(198)
Patents, net	177	188
Totals	$616	$554
Liabilities and Shareholders' Equity		
Accounts payable	$ 63	$ 56
Accrued liabilities	12	17
Notes payable, long-term	179	264
Common shares	149	61
Retained earnings	213	156
Totals	$616	$554

Required

1. Prepare a statement of cash flows for 2011 in the format that best shows the relationship between net income and operating cash flow. The company sold no plant and equipment or long-term investments and issued no notes payable during 2011. There were *no* noncash investing and financing transactions during the year. Show all amounts in thousands.
2. Answer the board members' question: Why is the cash balance so low? Point out the two largest cash payments during 2011.
3. Considering net income and the company's cash flows during 2011, was it a good year or a bad year? Give your reasons. Explain the format you chose for the statement of cash flows.

Learning Objective 1 2
Using cash-flow data to evaluate an investment

Case 2. Applied Technology Inc. and Four-Star Catering Ltd. are asking you to recommend their shares to your clients. Because Applied and Four-Star earn about the same net income and have similar financial positions, your decision depends on their statements of cash flows summarized as follows:

	Applied Technology Inc.		Four-Star Catering Ltd.	
Net cash provided by operating activities:		$ 30,000		$ 70,000
Cash provided by (used for) investing activities:				
Purchase of property, plant, and equipment	$(20,000)		$(100,000)	
Sale of property, plant, and equipment	40,000	20,000	10,000	(90,000)
Cash provided by (used for) financing activities:				
Issuance of common shares		—		30,000
Paying off long-term debt		(40,000)		—
Net increase in cash		$ 10,000		$ 10,000

Based on their cash flows, which company looks better? Give your reasons.

Ethical Issue

Columbia Industries is having a bad year. Net income is only $37,000. Also, two important overseas customers are falling behind in their payments to Columbia, and Columbia's accounts receivable are ballooning. The company desperately needs a loan. The Columbia board of directors is considering ways to put the best face on the company's financial statements. Columbia's bank closely examines cash flow from operations. Daniel Peavey, Columbia's controller, suggests reclassifying the receivables from the slow-paying clients as long-term. He explains to the board that removing the $80,000 rise in accounts receivable from current assets will increase net cash provided by operations. This approach may help Columbia get the loan.

Required

1. Using only the amounts given, compute net cash provided by operations, both without and with the reclassification of the receivables. Which reporting makes Columbia look better?
2. Under what condition would the reclassification of the receivables be ethical? Under what condition would it be unethical?

Focus on Financials

Learning Objective ❶❷❸❹
Using the statement of cash flows

Gildan Activewear Inc.
Use Gildan Activewear Inc.'s statement of cash flows along with the company's other financial statements, all in Appendix A at the end of the book, to answer the following questions.

Required

1. By which method does Gildan report cash flows from operating activities? Explain your answer.
2. Compute these amounts for the year ended October 4, 2009, using Gildan's income statement and balance sheet.
   a. Collections from customers
   b. Payments to suppliers. Cost of sales, selling, general, and administrative expenses incur costs with Gildan's suppliers. Depreciation is included in the cost of sales, selling, general, and administrative expenses.
3. Prepare a T-account for Property, Plant and Equipment, Net, and show all activity in this account for fiscal 2009. Use the depreciation amount in Note 17(b) as referenced in the statement of cash flows and assume that
   a. Gildan's assets held for sale are not property, plant, and equipment
   b. Gildan acquired property, plant, and equipment as reported on the statement of cash flows.
4. Evaluate the increase in cash in the fiscal year 2009 compared with fiscal years 2008 and 2007.

Focus on Analysis

Learning Objective ❶❷❸❹
Analyzing cash flows

Gildan Activewear Inc.
Refer to the Gildan Activewear Inc. financial statements in Appendix A at the end of this book. Focus on the fiscal year 2009.

Required

1. What was Gildan's main source of cash? Is this a positive result? What was Gildan's main use of cash? What sources of information contributed to your analysis?

2. Explain in detail the three main reasons why net cash from operations differs from net earnings.
3. There are two statements on which companies report declaration of dividends. Identify the two statements, review these statements, and determine what dividends Gildan paid shareholders in 2009.

Group Projects

Project 1. Each member of the group should obtain the annual report of a different company. Select companies in different industries. Evaluate each company's trend of cash flows for the most recent two years. In your evaluation of the companies' cash flows, you may use any other information that is publicly available—for example, the other financial statements (income statement, balance sheet, statement of shareholders' equity, and the related notes) and news stories from magazines and newspapers. Rank the companies' cash flows from best to worst and write a two-page report on your findings.

Project 2. Select a company and obtain its annual report, including all the financial statements. Focus on the statement of cash flows and, in particular, the cash flows from operating activities. Specify whether the company uses the direct method or the indirect method to report operating cash flows. As necessary, use the other financial statements (income statement, balance sheet, and statement of shareholders' equity) and the notes to prepare the company's cash flows from operating activities by using the *other* method.

Quick Check Answers

1. *d*
2. *c*
3. *b*
4. *b ($50,000 − $12,000 + $60,000 = $98,000)*
5. *c*
6. *b*
7. *a ($47,000 + $8,000 − $4,000 + $12,000 + $7,000 + $2,000 = $72,000)*
8. *a ($6,000 − $24,000 + $36,000 = $18,000)*
9. *c (−$2,000 + $3,000 − $9,000 = −$8,000)*
10. *b ($12,000 + $36,000 = $48,000)*
11. *a [$650,000 + ($45,000 − $31,000) = $664,000]*
12. *c ($690,000 − $390,000 − $175,000 = $125,000)*
13. *d ($390,000 − $15,000 + $9,000 = $384,000)*

Appendix 12A

Preparing the Statement of Cash Flows: Direct Method

OBJECTIVE

(A-1) **Prepare** a statement of cash flows by the direct method

IAS 7 "Statement of Cash Flows" in paragraph 19 reads "Entities are encouraged to report cash flows from operating activities using the direct method." The reason for the IAS 7 preference is that the International Accounting Standards Board believes the direct method provides clearer information about the sources and uses of cash. Very few companies use this method because it requires more computations than the indirect method. Investing and financing cash flows are unaffected by the method of formatting operating cash flows.

To illustrate the statement of cash flows, we use Bradshaw Corporation, a dealer in playground equipment. To prepare the statement of cash flows by the direct method, proceed as follows:

STEP 1 Lay out the template of the statement of cash flows by the direct method, as shown in Part 1 of Exhibit 12A-1. Part 2 (p. 640) gives a visual picture of the statement.

STEP 2 Use the comparative balance sheet to determine the increase or decrease in cash during the period. The change in cash is the "check figure" for the statement of cash flows. Bradshaw Corporation's comparative balance sheet indicates that Bradshaw's cash decreased by $20,000 during 2011 (Exhibit 12-4, p. 604). *Why* did Bradshaw's cash fall during 2011? The statement of cash flows explains.

STEP 3 Use the available data to prepare the statement of cash flows. Bradshaw's transaction data appear in Exhibit 12A-2. These transactions affected both the income statement (Exhibit 12-5, p. 604) and the statement of cash flows. Some transactions affect one statement and some, the other. For example, sales (item 1) are reported on the income statement. Cash collections (item 2) go on the statement of cash flows. Other transactions, such as the cash receipt of dividend revenue (item 5), affect both statements. *The statement of cash flows reports only those transactions with cash effects* (those with an asterisk in Exhibit 12A-2). Exhibit 12A-3 gives Bradshaw Corporation's statement of cash flows for 2011.

Cash Flows From Operating Activities

Operating cash flows are listed first because they are the most important. Exhibit 12A-3 (p. 642) shows that Bradshaw is sound; operating activities were the largest source of cash.

Cash Collections From Customers. Both cash sales and collections of accounts receivable are reported on the statement of cash flows as "Collections from customers... $271,000" in Exhibit 12A-3.

Cash Receipts of Interest. The income statement reports interest revenue. Only the cash receipts of interest appear on the statement of cash flows—$10,000 in Exhibit 12A-3.

EXHIBIT 12A-1 **Part 1—Template of the Statement of Cash Flows: Direct Method**

Bradshaw Corporation
Statement of Cash Flows
For the Year Ended December 31, 2011

Cash flows from operating activities:
Receipts:
Collections from customers
Interest received on notes receivable
Dividends received on investments in shares
Other operating receipts
Total cash receipts
Payments:
To suppliers
To employees
For interest
For income tax
Other operating payments
Total cash payments
Net cash provided by operating activities
Cash flows from investing activities:
Sales of long-term assets (investments, land, building, equipment, and so on)
− Purchases of long-term assets
+ Collections of long-term receivables
− Long-term loans to others
Net cash provided by (used for) investing activities
Cash flows from financing activities:
Issuance of shares
− Repurchase of shares
+ Borrowing (issuance of notes or bonds payable)
− Payment of notes or bonds payable
− Payment of dividends
Net cash provided by (used for) financing activities
Net increase (decrease) in cash during the year
+ Cash at December 31, 2010
= Cash at December 31, 2011

Cash Receipts of Dividends. Dividends are earned on investments in shares. Dividend revenue is reported on the income statement, and only cash receipts are reported on the statement of cash flows—$9,000 in Exhibit 12A-3. (Dividends *received* are operating activities, but dividends *paid* are financing.)

Payments to Suppliers. Payments to suppliers include all payments for inventory and operating expenses except employee compensation, interest, and income taxes. *Suppliers* are those entities that provide the business with its inventory and essential services. For example, a clothing store's suppliers may include Arrow Shirts, Gildan Activewear, and Levi Strauss. Other suppliers provide advertising, utilities, and various services that are operating expenses. Exhibit 12A-3 shows that Bradshaw Corporation paid suppliers $133,000.

Payments to Employees. This category includes payments for salaries, wages, commissions, and other forms of employee compensation. Accrued amounts are excluded

EXHIBIT 12A-1 **Part 2—Cash Receipts and Cash Payments on the Statement of Cash Flows: Direct Method**

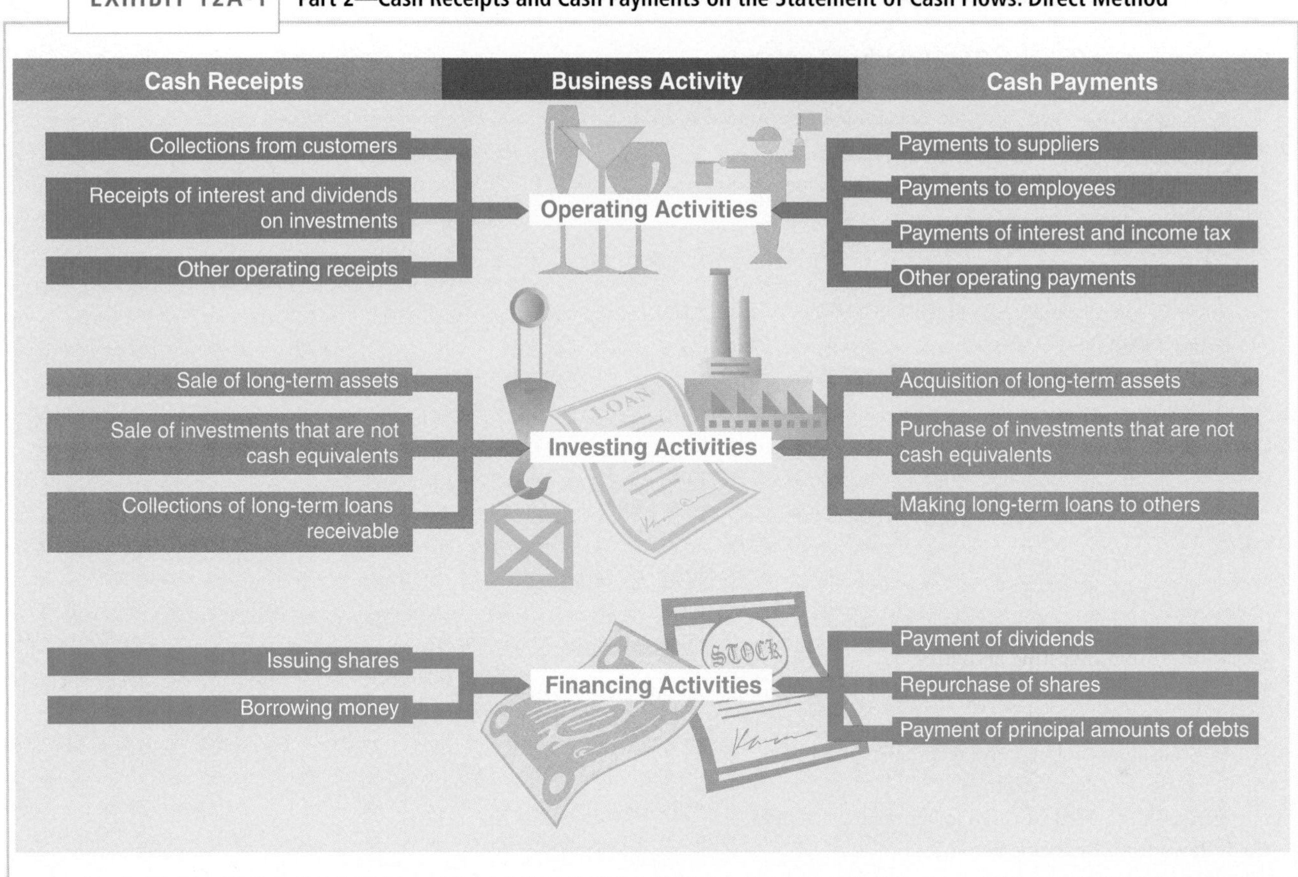

because they have not yet been paid. The statement of cash flows in Exhibit 12A-3 reports only the cash payments ($58,000).

Payments for Interest Expense and Income Tax Expense. Interest and income tax payments are reported separately. Bradshaw Corporation paid all its interest and income tax expenses in cash. Therefore, the same amount appears on the income statement and the statement of cash flows. Interest payments are operating cash flows because the interest is an expense.

Depreciation Expense. This expense is *not* listed on the statement of cash flows in Exhibit 12A-3 because it does not affect cash.

Gain on Sale of Property, Plant, and Equipment. The gain is not listed on the statement of cash flows in Exhibit 12A-3 because it does not affect cash. The proceeds from selling the property, plant, and equipment will be included as a cash inflow under investing activities.

Cash Flows From Investing Activities

Investing is critical because a company's investments determine its future course. Large purchases of capital assets signal expansion. Low levels of investing over a period indicate that the business is not growing.

Purchases of Long-Term Assets; Purchasing Investments and Making Loans to Other Companies. These cash payments acquire long-term assets. Bradshaw Corporation's first investing activity in Exhibit 12A-3 is the purchase of property,

EXHIBIT 12A-2 **Summary of Bradshaw Corporation's 2011 Transactions**

Operating Activities
1. Sales on credit, $284,000
*2. Collections from customers, $271,000
3. Interest revenue on notes receivable, $12,000
*4. Collection of interest receivable, $10,000
*5. Cash receipt of dividend revenue on investments in shares, $9,000
6. Cost of goods sold, $150,000
7. Purchases of inventory on credit, $147,000
*8. Payments to suppliers, $133,000
9. Salary and wages expense, $56,000
*10. Payments of salary and wages, $58,000
11. Depreciation expense, $18,000
12. Other operating expense, $17,000
*13. Interest expense and payments, $16,000
*14. Income tax expense and payments, $15,000

Investing Activities
*15. Cash payments to acquire property, plant, and equipment, $206,000
*16. Loan to another company, $11,000
*17. Proceeds from sale of property, plant, and equipment, $62,000, including $8,000 gain

Financing Activities
*18. Proceeds from issuance of common shares, $1,000
*19. Proceeds from issuance of long-term debt, $94,000
*20. Payment of long-term debt, $11,000
*21. Declaration and payment of cash dividends, $17,000

*Indicates a cash flow to be reported on the statement of cash flows.
Note: Income statement data are taken from Exhibit 12-A6, page 644.

plant, and equipment ($206,000). Bradshaw also made an $11,000 loan and got a note receivable.

Proceeds From Selling Long-Term Assets and Investments and From Collecting Notes Receivable. These cash receipts are also investing activities. The sale of the property, plant, and equipment needs explanation. Bradshaw Corporation received $62,000 cash from the sale of property, plant, and equipment, and there was an $8,000 gain on this transaction. What is the appropriate amount to show on the statement of cash flows? It is $62,000, the cash proceeds from the sale, not the $8,000 gain.

Investors are often critical of a company that sells large amounts of its property, plant, and equipment. That may signal an emergency. For example, budget cuts in the telecom industry required Nortel Networks Corporation to downsize significantly.

Cash Flows From Financing Activities

Cash flows from financing activities include the following:

Proceeds From Issuance of Shares and Debt. Issuing shares and borrowing money are two common ways to finance operations. In Exhibit 12A-3, Bradshaw Corporation issued common shares and received cash of $1,000. Bradshaw also issued long-term debt (notes payable) to borrow $94,000.

Payment of Debt and Repurchases of the Company's Own Shares. The payment of debt (notes payable) decreases cash, which is the opposite effect of borrowing.

EXHIBIT 12A-3 **Statement of Cash Flows—Direct Method**

Bradshaw Corporation
Statement of Cash Flows
For the Year Ended December 31, 2011

	(amounts in thousands)	
Cash flows from operating activities:		
Receipts:		
Collections from customers	$ 271	
Interest received on notes receivable	10	
Dividends received on investments in shares	9	
Total cash receipts		$ 290
Payments:		
To suppliers	(133)	
To employees	(58)	
For interest	(16)	
For income tax	(15)	
Total cash payments		(222)
Net cash provided by operating activities		68
Cash flows from investing activities:		
Acquisition of property, plant, and equipment	(206)	
Loan to another company	(11)	
Proceeds from sale of property, plant, and equipment	62	
Net cash used for investing activities		(155)
Cash flows from financing activities:		
Proceeds from issuance of common shares	1	
Proceeds from issuance of long-term debt	94	
Payment of long-term debt	(11)	
Payment of dividends	(17)	
Net cash provided by financing activities		67
Net decrease in cash		(20)
Cash balance, December 31, 2010		42
Cash balance, December 31, 2011		$ 22

Bradshaw Corporation reports long-term debt payments of $11,000. The repurchase of shares is another example.

Payment of Cash Dividends. The payment of cash dividends is a financing activity, as illustrated by Bradshaw's $17,000 payment in Exhibit 12A-3. A *stock* dividend has no effect on Cash and is *not* reported on the statement of cash flows.

Noncash Investing and Financing Activities

Companies make investments that do not require cash. They also obtain financing other than cash. Our examples thus far have included none of these transactions. Now suppose that Bradshaw Corporation issued common shares valued at $320,000 to acquire a warehouse. Bradshaw would journalize this transaction as follows:

Warehouse Building	320,000	
Common Shares		320,000

This transaction would not be reported on the statement of cash flows because Bradshaw paid no cash. But the investment in the warehouse and the issuance of shares are important. Noncash investing and financing activities like this transaction can be reported in a separate schedule that follows the statement of cash flows or can be disclosed in a note. Exhibit 12A-4 illustrates noncash investing and financing activities (all amounts are assumed).

EXHIBIT 12A-4 **Noncash Investing and Financing Activities (All Amounts Assumed)**

	thousands
Noncash Investing and Financing Activities:	
Acquisition of building by issuing common shares	$320
Acquisition of land by issuing note payable	70
Acquisition of equipment by issuing short-term note payable	30
Total noncash investing and financing activities	$420

STOP + THINK

Classify each of the following as an operating activity, an investing activity, or a financing activity. Also identify those items that are not reported on the statement of cash flows prepared by the *direct* method.

a. Net income
b. Payment of dividends
c. Borrowing
d. Payment of cash to suppliers
e. Making a loan
f. Receipt of cash dividends
g. Depreciation expense
h. Purchase of equipment
i. Issuance of shares
j. Purchase of another company
k. Payment of a note payable
l. Payment of income taxes
m. Collections from customers
n. Accrual of interest revenue
o. Expiration of prepaid expense

Answer:

a. Not reported
b. Financing
c. Financing
d. Operating
e. Investing
f. Operating
g. Not reported
h. Investing
i. Financing
j. Investing
k. Financing
l. Operating
m. Operating
n. Not reported
o. Not reported

Now let's see how to compute the amounts of the operating cash flows by the direct method.

Computing Operating Cash Flows by the Direct Method

To compute operating cash flows by the direct method, we use the income statement and the *changes* in the related balance sheet accounts. Exhibit 12A-5 diagrams the process. Exhibit 12A-6 is Bradshaw Corporation's income statement and Exhibit 12A-7 (page 645) is the comparative balance sheet.

Computing Cash Collections From Customers. Collections start with sales revenue (an accrual-basis amount). Bradshaw Corporation's income statement (Exhibit 12A-6) reports sales of $284,000. Accounts Receivable increased from $80,000 at the beginning of the year to $93,000 at year-end, a $13,000 increase (Exhibit 12A-7). Based on those amounts, Cash Collections equal $271,000. We must solve for cash collections (X).

Accounts Receivable

Beginning balance	+	Sales	−	Collections	=	Ending balance				
$80,000	+	$284,000		−X	=	$93,000				
				−X	=	$93,000	−	$80,000	−	$284,000
				−X	=	$271,000				

EXHIBIT 12A-5 **Direct Method of Computing Cash Flows From Operating Activities**

RECEIPTS/PAYMENTS	From Income Statement Account	Change in Related Balance Sheet Account	
RECEIPTS:			
From customers	Sales Revenue	+ Decrease in Accounts Receivable − Increase in Accounts Receivable	
Of interest	Interest Revenue	+ Decrease in Interest Receivable − Increase in Interest Receivable	
PAYMENTS:			
To suppliers	Cost of Goods Sold	+ Increase in Inventory − Decrease in Inventory	+ Decrease in Accounts Payable − Increase in Accounts Payable
	Operating Expense	+ Increase in Prepaids − Decrease in Prepaids	+ Decrease in Accrued Liabilities − Increase in Accrued Liabilities
To employees	Salary (Wages) Expense	+ Decrease in Salary (Wages) Payable − Increase in Salary (Wages) Payable	
For interest	Interest Expense	+ Decrease in Interest Payable − Increase in Interest Payable	
For income tax	Income Tax Expense	+ Decrease in Income Tax Payable − Increase in Income Tax Payable	

We thank Barbara Gerrity for suggesting this exhibit.

EXHIBIT 12A-6 **Income Statement for the Bradshaw Corporation**

Bradshaw Corporation
Income Statement
For the Year Ended December 31, 2011

	(amounts in thousands)	
Revenues and gains:		
Sales revenue	$284	
Interest revenue	12	
Dividend revenue	9	
Gain on sale of property, plant, and equipment	8	
Total revenues and gains		$313
Expenses:		
Cost of goods sold	150	
Salary and wages expense	56	
Depreciation expense	18	
Other operating expense	17	
Interest expense	16	
Income tax expense	15	
Total expenses		272
Net income		$ 41

EXHIBIT 12A-7 Comparative Balance Sheet for Bradshaw Corporation

Bradshaw Corporation
Comparative Balance Sheet
As at December 31, 2011 and 2010

(amounts in thousands)	2011	2010	Increase (Decrease)	
Assets				
Current:				
Cash	$ 22	$ 42	$(20)	
Accounts receivable	93	80	13	*Changes in current assets—Operating*
Interest receivable	3	1	2	
Inventory	135	138	(3)	
Prepaid expenses	8	7	1	
Long-term note receivable from another company	11	—	11	*Changes in noncurrent assets—Investing*
Property, plant, and equipment, net of amortization	353	219	134	
Total	$625	$487	$138	
Liabilities				
Current:				
Accounts payable	$ 91	$ 57	$ 34	*Changes in current liabilities—Operating*
Salary and wages payable	4	6	(2)	
Accrued liabilities	1	3	(2)	
Long-term debt	160	77	83	*Changes in long-term liabilities and contributed capital accounts—Financing*
Shareholders' Equity				
Common shares	259	258	1	
Retained earnings	110	86	24	*Change due to net income—Operating* *Change due to dividends—Financing*
Total	$625	$487	$138	

The T-account for Accounts Receivable provides another view of the same computation.

Accounts Receivable

Beginning balance	80,000		
Sales	284,000	Collections	271,000
Ending balance	93,000		

Accounts Receivable increased, so collections must be less than sales.

All collections of receivables are computed in this way. Let's turn now to other cash receipts. In our example, Bradshaw Corporation earned interest revenue. Interest Receivable's balance increased by $2,000 (Exhibit 12A-7). Cash receipts of interest were $10,000 (Interest Revenue of $12,000 minus the $2,000 increase in Interest Receivable). Exhibit 12A-5 shows how to make this computation.

Computing Payments to Suppliers. This computation includes two parts:

- Payments for inventory
- Payments for operating expenses (other than interest and income tax)

Payments for inventory are computed by converting cost of goods sold to the cash basis. We use Cost of Goods Sold, Inventory, and Accounts Payable. First, we must solve for purchases. All amounts come from Exhibits 12A-6 and 12A-7.

Cost of Goods Sold

Beginning inventory	+	Purchases	−	Ending inventory	=	Cost of good sold				
$138,000	+	X		$135,000	=	$150,000				
		X			=	$150,000	−	$138,000	+	$135,000
		X			=	$147,000				

Now we can compute cash payments for inventory (Y), as follows:

Accounts Payable

Beginning balance	+	Purchases	−	Payments for inventory	=	Ending balance				
$57,000	+	$147,000		−Y	=	$91,000				
				−Y	=	$91,000	−	$57,000	−	$147,000
				Y	=	$113,000				

The T-accounts show where the data come from: Start with Cost of Goods Sold.

Inventory

Beg. inventory	138,000	Cost of goods sold	150,000
Purchases	147,000		
End. inventory	135,000		

Accounts Payable

Payments for inventory	113,000	Beg. bal.	57,000
		Purchases	147,000
		End bal.	91,000

Accounts Payable increased, so payments are less than purchases.

Computing Payments for Operating Expenses. Payments for operating expenses other than interest and income tax can be computed from three accounts: Prepaid Expenses, Accrued Liabilities, and Other Operating Expenses. All Bradshaw Corporation data come from Exhibits 12A-6 and 12A-7.[3]

Prepaid Expenses

Beginning balance	+	Payments	−	Expiration of prepaid expense	=	Ending balance				
$7,000	+	X	−	$7,000	=	$8,000				
		X			=	$8,000	−	$7,000	+	$7,000
		X			=	$8,000				

Accrued Liabilities

Beginning balance	+	Accrual of expense at year-end	−	Payments	=	Ending balance				
$3,000	+	$1,000		−X	=	$1,000				
				−X	=	$1,000	−	$3,000	−	$1,000
				−X	=	$3,000				

Other Operating Expenses

Accrual of expense at year-end	+	Expiration of prepaid expense	+	Payments	=	Ending balance				
$1,000	+	$7,000	+	X	=	$17,000				
				X	=	$17,000	−	$1,000	−	$7,000
				X	=	$9,000				
Total payments for operating expenses					=	$8,000	+	$3,000	+	$9,000
					=	$20,000				

[3] A simplifying assumption has been made in this example that the entire opening prepaid expenses will expire during the year and that all opening accrued liabilities will be paid during the year.

The T-accounts give another picture of the same data.

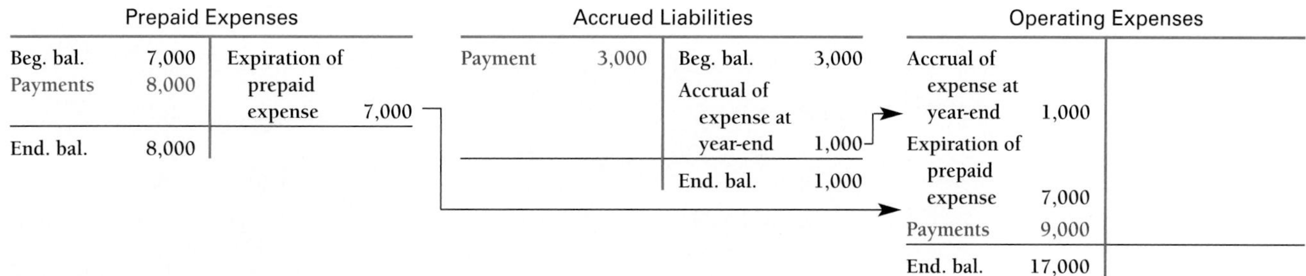

Prepaid Expenses

Beg. bal.	7,000	Expiration of prepaid expense	7,000
Payments	8,000		
End. bal.	8,000		

Accrued Liabilities

Payment	3,000	Beg. bal.	3,000
		Accrual of expense at year-end	1,000
		End. bal.	1,000

Operating Expenses

Accrual of expense at year-end	1,000		
Expiration of prepaid expense	7,000		
Payments	9,000		
End. bal.	17,000		

Computing Payments to Employees. It is convenient to combine all payments to employees into one account, Salary and Wages Expense. We then adjust the expense for the change in Salary and Wages Payable, as shown here.

Salary and Wages Payable

Beginning balance	+	Salary and wages expense	−	Payments	=	Ending balance				
\$6,000	+	\$56,000		−X	=	\$4,000				
				−X	=	\$4,000	−	\$6,000	−	\$56,000
				−X	=	\$58,000				

The T-account gives another picture of the same data.

Salary and Wages Payable

		Beginning balance	6,000
Payments to employees	58,000	Salary and wages expense	56,000
		Ending balance	4,000

Computing Payments of Interest and Income Taxes. Bradshaw Corporation's expense and payment amounts are the same for interest and income tax so no analysis is required. If the expense and the payment differ, the payment can be computed as shown in Exhibit 12A-5.

Computing Investing and Financing Cash Flows

Investing and financing cash flows are explained on pages 607–611. These computations are the same for both the direct and indirect methods.

STOP + THINK

Ouimet Energy Inc., reported the following for 2011 and 2010 (adapted, in millions):

At December 31,	2011	2010
Receivables, net	$1,416	$1,050
Inventory	608	589
Accounts payable	1,341	897
Income taxes payable	244	—

For the Year Ended December 31, 2011	
Revenues	$17,933
Cost of crude oil and products sold	5,935
Income tax expense	382

Based on these figures, how much cash did

- Ouimet collect from customers during 2011?
- Ouimet pay for purchases of crude oil and products during 2011?
- Ouimet pay for income taxes during 2011?

Answers (in millions):

		Beginning Receivables	+ Revenues	− Collections	= Ending Receivables
Collections from customers	= $17,567	$1,050	+ $17,933	− $17,567	= $1,416

		Cost of Crude Oil and Products Sold	+ Increase in Inventory	− Increase in Accounts Payable	= Payments
Payments for purchases of crude oil and products	= $5,510	$5,935	+ ($608 – $589)	− ($1,341 – $897)	= $5,510

		Beginning Income Taxes Payable	+ Income Tax Expense	− Payment	= Ending Income Taxes Payable
Payment of income taxes	= $138	—	+ $382	− $138	= $244

SUMMARY OF APPENDIX 12A

Learning Objective A-1: Prepare a statement of cash flows by the direct method

Cash flows from operating activities under the direct method begin with cash receipts from operations from which cash payments for operations are deducted:

- Receipts include collections from customers, interest received on notes receivable, dividends received on investments in shares, and other operating receipts.
- Disbursements include payments to suppliers, to employees, for interest, for income tax, and for other operating payments.

The sum of the above is the total funds provided by (if positive)/used from (if negative) operations for the period.

Cash flows from investing activities are calculated as follows:

- Add sales/deduct purchases of long-term assets.
- Deduct issue of/add collection of long-term loans to others.

The sum of the above is the total funds provided by (if positive)/used by (if negative) investing activities for the period. A negative investing funds flow indicates that the company is expanding.

Cash flows from financing activities are calculated as follows:

- Add issue of/deduct repurchase of shares.
- Add borrowing/deduct repayment of long-term debt.
- Deduct payment of cash dividends.

The sum of the above is the total funds provided by/used by financing activities for the period. A negative financing funds flow indicates that the company is reducing its debt and/or paying dividends.

Noncash activities such as the purchase of land and a building by issuing shares are not shown on the statement of cash flows but must be disclosed on a separate schedule that follows the statement of cash flows or in a note to the financial statements.

END-OF-APPENDIX SUMMARY PROBLEM

MyAccountingLab

Kapoor Products Inc. reported the following comparative balance sheet and income statement for 2011.

Kapoor Products Inc.
Balance Sheet
As at December 31, 2011 and 2010

	2011	2010
Cash	$ 19,000	$ 3,000
Accounts receivable	22,000	23,000
Inventories	34,000	31,000
Prepaid expenses	1,000	3,000
Equipment (net)	90,000	79,000
Intangible assets	9,000	9,000
	$175,000	$148,000
Accounts payable	$ 14,000	$ 9,000
Accrued liabilities	16,000	19,000
Income tax payable	14,000	12,000
Long-term debt	45,000	50,000
Common shares	22,000	18,000
Retained earnings	64,000	40,000
	$175,000	$148,000

Kapoor Products Inc.
Income Statement
For the Years Ended December 31, 2011 and 2010

	2011	2010
Sales revenue	$190,000	$165,000
Gain on sale of equipment	6,000	—
Total revenue and gains	196,000	165,000
Cost of goods sold	85,000	70,000
Depreciation expense	19,000	17,000
Other operating expenses	36,000	33,000
Total expenses	140,000	120,000
Income before income tax	56,000	45,000
Income tax expense	18,000	15,000
Net income	$ 38,000	$ 30,000

Assume that you are an investment analyst for Canmore Investments Ltd. and have been tasked with analyzing Kapoor Products Inc. as Canmore is considering purchasing it. You determine that you need the following Kapoor cash flow data for 2011. There were no non-cash investing and financing activities.

a. Collections from customers
b. Cash payments for inventory
c. Cash payments for operating expenses
d. Cash payment for income tax
e. Cash received from the sale of equipment, with Kapoor Products Inc. paying $40,000 for new equipment during the year
f. Issuance of common shares
g. Issuance of long-term debt, with Kapoor Products Inc. paying off $20,000 of long-term debt during the year
h. Cash dividends, with no stock dividends

Name: Kapoor Products Inc.
Fiscal Period: Year ended December 31, 2011

Provide your colleagues with the needed data. Show your work.

Answer

The change in Accounts Receivable of $1,000 ($22,000 – $23,000) is a result of sales and collections from customers.

a. Analyze Accounts Receivable (let X = Collections from customers):

Beginning	+	Sales	−	Collections	=	Ending
$23,000	+	$190,000	−	X	=	$22,000
				X	=	$191,000

First calculate the amount of purchases. Then calculate the change in Accounts Payable that relates to cash payments.

b. Analyze Inventory and Accounts Payable (let X = Purchases, and let Y = Payments for inventory):

Beginning Inventory	+	Purchases	−	Ending Inventory	=	Cost of Goods Sold
$31,000	+	X	−	$34,000	=	$85,000
		X			=	$88,000

Beginning Accounts Payable	+ Purchases	− Payments	=	Ending Accounts Payable
$9,000	+ $88,000	− Y	=	$14,000
		Y	=	$83,000

c. Start with Other Operating Expenses, and adjust for the changes in Prepaid Expenses and Accrued Liabilities:

Cash payments for operating expenses must account for the changes that relate to prepaid expenses and accrued liabilities.

Other Operating Expenses	+ Increase, or − Decrease in Prepaid Expenses	− Increase, or + Decrease in Accrued Liabilities	=	Payments for Operating Expenses
$36,000	− $2,000	+ 3,000	=	$37,000

d. Analyze Income Tax Payable (let X = Payments of income tax):

The change in Income Tax Payable of $2,000 ($14,000 − $12,000) is a result of income tax expense and income tax payments made.

Beginning	+ Income Tax Expense	− Payments	=	Ending
$12,000	+ $18,000	− X	=	$14,000
		X	=	$16,000

e. Analyze Equipment (Net) (let X = carrying amount of equipment sold. Then combine with gain or loss on sale to compute cash received from sale.)

Cash received from the sale of equipment is the carrying amount of the equipment plus the gain or minus the loss on the sale. First determine the carrying amount of the equipment sold.

Beginning	+ Acquisitions	− Depreciation	− Carrying Amount Sold	= Ending
$79,000	+ $40,000	− $19,000	− X	= $90,000
			X	= $10,000

Cash received from sale	=	Carrying Amount Sold	+ Gain, or − Loss on Sale
$16,000	=	$10,000	+ $6,000

f. Analyze Common Shares (let X = issuance):

The change in Common Shares of $4,000 ($22,000 − $18,000) is a result of issuing shares.

Beginning	+ Issuance	= Ending
$18,000 +	X	= $22,000
	X	= $4,000

g. Analyze Long-Term Debt (let X = issuance):

Long-Term Debt declined by $5,000 ($45,000 − $50,000). However, since a $20,000 payment was made during the year, $15,000 of long-term debt must have been issued.

Beginning	+ Issuance	− Payment	= Ending
$50,000 +	X	− $20,000	= $45,000
	X		= $15,000

h. Analyze Retained Earnings (let X = dividends):

The change in Retained Earnings of $24,000 ($64,000 − $40,000) is a result of net income ($38,000 from the 2011 income statement) and the payment of cash dividends. The same information is shown on the statement of retained earnings.

Beginning	+ Net Income	− Dividends	= Ending
$40,000 +	$38,000 −	X	= $64,000
		X	= $14,000

Assess Your Progress

Make the grade with MyAccountingLab: The exercises and problems in this appendix can be found on MyAccountingLab at www.myaccountinglab.com. You can practise them as often as you want, and they feature step-by-step guided solutions to help you find the right answer.

Short Exercises

Learning Objective A-1
Preparing a statement of cash flows—direct method

S12A-1 Tally-Ho Horse Farm Inc. began 2011 with cash of $44,000. During the year, Tally-Ho earned service revenue of $500,000 and collected $510,000 from customers. Expenses for the year totalled $420,000, with $400,000 paid in cash to suppliers and employees. Tally-Ho also paid $100,000 to purchase equipment and a cash dividend of $50,000 to shareholders. During 2011, Tally-Ho borrowed $20,000 by issuing a note payable.

Prepare the company's statement of cash flows for the year. Format operating activities by the direct method.

Learning Objective A-1
Computing operating cash flows—direct method

S12-A2 (Short Exercise S12A-3 is an alternative this appendix.) Maritime Fisheries Ltd. provides the following data for the year ended June 30, 2011.

Cost of goods sold	$100,000	Payment of dividends	$ 6,000
Payments to suppliers	87,000	Proceeds from issuance of	
Purchase of equipment	40,000	common shares	20,000
Payments to employees	70,000	Sales revenue	210,000
Payment of note payable	30,000	Collections from customers	180,000
Proceeds from sale of land	60,000	Payment of income tax	10,000
Depreciation expense	8,000	Repurchase of common shares	5,000

Prepare the *operating activities section* of Maritime Fisheries Ltd.'s statement of cash flows for the year ended June 30, 2011. Maritime Fisheries uses the *direct* method for operating cash flows.

Learning Objective A-1
Preparing a statement of cash flows—direct method

S12A-3 Use the data in Short Exercise 12A-2 to prepare Maritime Fisheries Ltd.'s statement of cash flows for the year ended June 30, 2011. Maritime Fisheries uses the *direct* method for operating activities. Use Exhibit 12A-3, page 642, as a guide, but you may stop after determining the net increase (or decrease) in cash.

Learning Objective A-1
Computing operating cash flows—direct method

S12A-4 Autos of Red Deer Inc. reported the following financial statements for 2011:

Autos of Red Deer Inc.
Income Statement
For the Year Ended December 31, 2011

(in thousands)	
Sales revenue	$710
Cost of goods sold	340
Salary expense	70
Depreciation expense	20
Other expenses	130
Total expenses	560
Net income	$150

Autos of Red Deer Inc.
Comparative Balance Sheet
As at December 31, 2011 and 2010

(in thousands)					
Assets	**2011**	**2010**	**Liabilities**	**2011**	**2010**
Current:			Current:		
Cash	$ 19	$ 16	Accounts payable	$ 47	$ 42
Accounts receivable	59	48	Salary payable	23	21
Inventory	75	84	Accrued liabilities	8	11
Prepaid expenses	3	2	Long-term notes payable	68	58
Long-term investments	55	75	**Shareholders' Equity**		
Property, plant, and			Common shares	40	32
equipment	225	185	Retained earnings	250	246
Total	$436	$410	Total	$436	$410

Compute the following:

a. Collections from customers

b. Payments for inventory

S12A-5 Use the Autos of Red Deer data in Short Exercise 12A-4 to compute the following:

Learning Objective A-1
Computing operating cash flows—direct method

a. Payments to employees

b. Payments of other expenses

Exercises

E12A-6 Identify each of the following transactions as operating (O), investing (I), financing (F), noncash investing and financing (NIF), or not reported on the statement of cash flows (N). Indicate whether each transaction increases (+) or decreases (−) cash. The *direct* method is used for operating activities.

Learning Objective A-1
Identifying activities for the statement of cash flows—direct method

___ a. Repurchase of common shares
___ b. Issuance of common shares for cash
___ c. Payment of accounts payable
___ d. Issuance of preferred shares for cash
___ e. Payment of cash dividend
___ f. Sale of long-term investment
___ g. Amortization of patent
___ h. Collection of accounts receivable
___ i. Issuance of long-term note payable to borrow cash
___ j. Depreciation of equipment
___ k. Acquisition of equipment by issuance of note payable
___ l. Payment of long-term debt
___ m. Acquisition of building by payment of cash
___ n. Accrual of salary expense
___ o. Purchase of long-term investment
___ p. Payment of wages to employees
___ q. Collection of cash interest
___ r. Cash sale of land
___ s. Distribution of stock dividend

E12A-7 Indicate where, if at all, each of the following transactions would be reported on a statement of cash flows prepared by the *direct* method and the accompanying schedule of noncash investing and financing activities.

Learning Objective A-1
Classifying transactions for the statement of cash flows—direct method

a.	Equipment	18,000		h.	Retained Earnings	36,000	
	Cash		18,000		Common Shares		36,000
b.	Cash	7,200		i.	Cash	2,000	
	Long-Term Investment		7,200		Interest Revenue		2,000
c.	Bonds Payable	45,000		j.	Land	87,700	
	Cash		45,000		Cash		87,700
d.	Building	164,000		k.	Accounts Payable	8,300	
	Cash		164,000		Cash		8,300
e.	Cash	1,400		l.	Salary Expense	4,300	
	Accounts Receivable		1,400		Cash		4,300
f.	Dividends Payable	16,500		m.	Cash	81,000	
	Cash		16,500		Common Shares		81,000
g.	Furniture and Fixtures	22,100			Common Shares	13,000	
	Note Payable, Short-Term		22,100	n.	Cash		13,000

Learning Objective A-1
Computing cash flows from operating activities—direct method

E12A-8 The accounting records of Jasmine Pharmaceuticals Inc. reveal the following:

Payment of salaries and wages	$34,000	Net income	$34,000
Depreciation	22,000	Payment of income tax	13,000
Decrease in current liabilities	20,000	Collection of dividend revenue	7,000
Increase in current assets other than cash	27,000	Payment of interest	16,000
Payment of dividends	12,000	Cash sales	38,000
Collection of accounts receivable	93,000	Loss on sale of land	5,000
		Acquisition of land	37,000
		Payment of accounts payable	54,000

Required

Compute cash flows from operating activities by the *direct* method. Use the format of the operating activities section of Exhibit 12A-3. Also evaluate Jasmine's operating cash flow. Give the reason for your evaluation.

Learning Objective A-1
Identifying items for the statement of cash flows—direct method

E12A-9 Selected accounts of Fishbowl Antiques Inc. show the following:

Salary Payable

		Beginning balance	9,000
Payments	40,000	Salary expense	38,000
		Ending balance	7,000

Buildings

Beginning balance	90,000	Depreciation	18,000
Acquisitions	145,000	Carrying amount of building sold	109,000*
Ending balance	108,000		

*Sale price was 140,000

Notes Payable

		Beginning balance	273,000
Payments	69,000	Issuance of note payable for cash	83,000
		Ending balance	287,000

Required

For each account, identify the item or items that should appear on a statement of cash flows prepared by the *direct* method. State where to report the item.

E12A-10 The income statement and additional data of Floral World Ltd. follow:

Learning Objective A-1
Preparing the statement of cash flows—direct method

Floral World Ltd.
Income Statement
For the Year Ended June 30, 2011

Revenues:		
Sales revenue	$229,000	
Dividend revenue	15,000	$244,000
Expenses:		
Cost of goods sold	103,000	
Salary expense	45,000	
Depreciation expense	29,000	
Advertising expense	11,000	
Interest expense	2,000	
Income tax expense	9,000	199,000
Net income		$ 45,000

Additional data:

a. Collections from customers are $30,000 more than sales.
b. Payments to suppliers are $1,000 more than the sum of cost of goods sold plus advertising expense.
c. Payments to employees are $1,000 more than salary expense.
d. Dividend revenue, interest expense, and income tax expense equal their cash amounts.
e. Acquisition of plant and equipment is $150,000. Of this amount, $101,000 is paid in cash and $49,000 by signing a note payable.
f. Proceeds from sale of land total $24,000.
g. Proceeds from issuance of common shares total $30,000.
h. Payment of long-term note payable is $15,000.
i. Payment of dividends is $11,000.
j. Cash balance, June 30, 2010, was $20,000.

Required

1. Prepare Floral World Ltd.'s statement of cash flows and accompanying schedule of noncash investing and financing activities. Report operating activities by the *direct* method.
2. Evaluate Floral World's cash flows for the year. In your evaluation, mention all three categories of cash flows and give the reason for your evaluation.

E12A-11 Compute the following items for the statement of cash flows.

Learning Objective A-1
Computing amounts for the statement of cash flows—direct method

a. Beginning and ending Accounts Receivable are $22,000 and $32,000, respectively. Credit sales for the period total $60,000. How much are cash collections from customers?
b. Cost of goods sold is $111,000. Beginning Inventory was $25,000, and ending Inventory is $21,000. Beginning and ending Accounts Payable are $14,000 and $8,000, respectively. How much are cash payments for inventory?

Challenge Exercise

Learning Objective 3 A-1
Computing cash-flow amounts

E12-A12 Morgan Industries Inc. reported the following in its financial statements for the year ended August 31, 2011 (in thousands):

	2011	2010
Income Statement		
Net sales	$24,623	$21,207
Cost of sales	18,048	15,466
Depreciation	269	230
Other operating expenses	3,883	4,248
Income tax expense	537	486
Net income	$ 1,886	$ 777
Balance Sheet		
Cash and cash equivalents	$ 17	$ 13
Accounts receivable	601	615
Inventory	3,100	2,831
Property and equipment, net	4,345	3,428
Accounts payable	1,547	1,364
Accrued liabilities	938	631
Income tax payable	201	194
Long-term liabilities	478	464
Common shares	519	446
Retained earnings	4,380	3,788

Determine the following cash receipts and payments for Morgan Industries Inc. during 2011.

a. Collections from customers
b. Payments for inventory
c. Payments for other operating expenses
d. Payment of income tax
e. Proceeds from issuance of common shares
f. Payment of cash dividends

Problems

(Group A)

Learning Objective 2 A-1
Preparing the statement of cash flows—direct method

P12A-13A World Mosaic Furniture Gallery Inc. provided the following data from the company's records for the year ended April 30, 2011:

a. Credit sales, $583,900
b. Loan to another company, $12,500
c. Cash payments to purchase property, plant, and equipment, $59,400
d. Cost of goods sold, $382,600
e. Proceeds from issuance of common shares, $8,000
f. Payment of cash dividends, $48,400
g. Collection of interest, $4,400
h. Acquisition of equipment by issuing short-term note payable, $16,400
i. Payments of salaries, $93,600
j. Proceeds from sale of property, plant, and equipment, $22,400, including $6,800 loss
k. Collections on accounts receivable, $428,600
l. Interest revenue, $3,800
m. Cash receipt of dividend revenue, $4,100
n. Payments to suppliers, $368,500
o. Cash sales, $171,900
p. Depreciation expense, $59,900
q. Proceeds from issuance of note payable, $19,600
r. Payments of long-term notes payable, $50,000
s. Interest expense and payments, $13,300
t. Salary expense, $95,300
u. Loan collections, $12,800
v. Proceeds from sale of investments, $9,100, including $2,000 gain
w. Payment of short-term note payable by issuing long-term note payable, $63,000
x. Amortization expense, $2,900
y. Income tax expense and payments, $37,900
z. Cash balance: April 30, 2010, $39,300; April 30, 2011, $36,600

Required

1. Prepare World Mosaic Furniture Gallery Inc.'s statement of cash flows for the year ended April 30, 2011. Use the *direct* method for cash flows from operating activities. Follow the format of Exhibit 12A-3 (p. 642), but do *not* show amounts in thousands. Include an accompanying schedule of noncash investing and financing activities.
2. Evaluate 2011 from a cash-flow standpoint. Give your reasons.

Learning Objective 2 A-1
Preparing an income statement, balance sheet, and statement of cash flows—direct method

P12A-14A Vintage Automobiles of Orangeville Ltd. was formed on January 1, 2011, when Vintage issued common shares for $300,000. Early in January 2011, Vintage made the following cash payments:

a. $150,000 for equipment
b. $120,000 for inventory (four cars at $30,000 each)
c. $20,000 for 2011 rent on a store building

In February 2011, Vintage purchased six cars for inventory on account. Cost of this inventory was $260,000 ($43,333.33 each). Before year-end, Vintage paid $208,000 of this debt. Vintage uses the FIFO method to account for inventory.

During 2011, Vintage sold eight vintage autos for a total of $500,000. Before year-end, Vintage collected 80% of this amount.

The business employs three people. The combined annual payroll is $95,000, of which Vintage owes $4,000 at year-end. At the end of the year, Vintage paid income tax of $10,000.

Late in 2011, Vintage declared and paid cash dividends of $11,000.

For equipment, Vintage uses the straight-line depreciation method over five years with zero residual value.

Required

1. Prepare Vintage's income statement for the year ended December 31, 2011. Use the single-step format, with all revenues listed together and all expenses listed together.
2. Prepare Vintage's balance sheet at December 31, 2011.
3. Prepare Vintage's statement of cash flows for the year ended December 31, 2011. Format cash flows from operating activities by using the *direct* method.

Learning Objective 2 A-1
Preparing the statement of cash flows—direct method

P12A-15A The 2011 comparative balance sheet and income statement of 4 Seasons Supply Corp. follow. 4 Seasons had no noncash investing and financing transactions during 2011. During the year, there were no sales of land or equipment, no issuance of notes payable, and no repurchase of shares transactions.

4 Seasons Supply Corp.
Comparative Balance Sheet as at December 31, 2011 and 2010

	December 31, 2011	December 31, 2010	Increase (Decrease)
Current assets:			
Cash and cash equivalents	$ 17,600	$ 5,300	$12,300
Accounts receivable	27,200	27,600	(400)
Inventories	83,600	87,200	(3,600)
Prepaid expenses	2,500	1,900	600
Property, plant, and equipment:			
Land	89,000	60,000	29,000
Equipment, net	53,500	49,400	4,100
Total assets	$273,400	$231,400	$42,000
Current liabilities:			
Accounts payable	$ 35,800	$ 33,700	$ 2,100
Salary payable	3,100	6,600	(3,500)
Other accrued liabilities	22,600	23,700	(1,100)
Long-term liabilities:			
Notes payable	75,000	100,000	(25,000)
Shareholders' equity:			
Common shares	88,300	64,700	23,600
Retained earnings	48,600	2,700	45,900
Total liabilities and shareholders' equity	$273,400	$231,400	$42,000

4 Seasons Supply Corp.
Income Statement for the Year Ended December 31, 2011

Revenues:		
Sales revenue		$228,700
Expenses:		
Cost of goods sold	$70,600	
Salary expense	27,800	
Depreciation expense	4,000	
Other operating expense	10,500	
Interest expense	11,600	
Income tax expense	29,100	
Total expenses		153,600
Net income		$ 75,100

Required

1. Prepare the 2011 statement of cash flows by using the *direct* method.
2. How will what you learned in this problem help you evaluate an investment?

Learning Objective 3 A-1
Preparing the statement of cash flows—direct and indirect methods

P12-16-A To prepare the statement of cash flows, accountants for Franklin Electric Limited have summarized 2011 activity in two accounts as follows:

Cash

Beginning balance	53,600	Payments on accounts payable	399,100
Sale of long-term investment	21,200	Payments of dividends	27,200
Collections from customers	661,700	Payments of salaries and wages	143,800
Issuance of common shares	47,300	Payments of interest	26,900
Receipts of dividends	17,100	Purchase of equipment	31,400
		Payments of operating expenses	34,300
		Payment of long-term note payable	41,300
		Repurchase of common shares	26,400
		Payment of income tax	18,900
Ending balance	51,600		

Common Shares

Repurchase of common shares for cancellation	26,400	Beginning balance	110,800
		Issuance for cash	47,300
		Issuance to acquire land	80,100
		Issuance to retire note payable	19,000
		Ending balance	230,800

Required

1. Prepare the statement of cash flows of Franklin Electric Limited for the year ended December 31, 2011, using the *direct* method to report operating activities. Also prepare the accompanying schedule of noncash investing and financing activities.

Franklin Electric Limited
Income Statement
For the Year Ended December 31, 2011

Revenues:		
Sales revenue		$689,300
Dividend revenue		17,100
Total revenue		706,400
Expenses and losses:		
Cost of goods sold	$402,600	
Salary and wage expense	150,800	
Depreciation expense	19,300	
Other operating expense	44,100	
Interest expense	28,800	
Income tax expense	16,200	
Loss on sale of investments	1,100	
Total expenses and losses		662,900
Net income		$ 43,500

Franklin Electric Limited
Selected Balance Sheet Data

	2011 Increase (Decrease)
Current assets:	
Cash and cash equivalents	$ (2,000)
Accounts receivable	27,600
Inventories	(11,800)
Prepaid expenses	600
Long-term investments	(22,300)
Equipment, net	12,100
Land	80,100
Current liabilities:	
Accounts payable	(8,300)
Interest payable	1,900
Salary payable	7,000
Other accrued liabilities	10,400
Income tax payable	(2,700)
Long-term note payable	(60,300)
Common shares	120,000
Retained earnings	16,300

Learning Objective 3 A-1
Preparing the statement of cash flows—direct method

P12A-17A The comparative balance sheet of Graphic Design Studio Inc. at June 30, 2011, included these amounts.

Graphic Design Studio Inc.
Balance Sheet
As at June 30, 2011 and 2010

	2011	2010	Increase (Decrease)
Current assets:			
Cash	$ 28,600	$ 8,600	$ 20,000
Accounts receivable	48,800	51,900	(3,100)
Inventories	68,600	60,200	8,400
Prepaid expenses	3,700	2,800	900
Long-term investment	10,100	5,200	4,900
Equipment, net	74,500	73,600	900
Land	42,400	96,000	(53,600)
	$276,700	$298,300	$(21,600)
Current liabilities:			
Notes payable, short-term	$ 13,400	$ 18,100	$ (4,700)
Accounts payable	42,400	40,300	2,100
Income tax payable	13,800	14,500	(700)
Accrued liabilities	8,200	9,700	(1,500)
Interest payable	3,700	2,900	800
Salary payable	900	2,600	(1,700)
Long-term note payable	47,400	94,100	(46,700)
Common shares	59,800	51,200	8,600
Retained earnings	87,100	64,900	22,200
	$276,700	$298,300	$(21,600)

Transaction data for the year ended June 30, 2011

a. Net income, $60,300
b. Depreciation expense on equipment, $13,400
c. Purchased long-term investment, $4,900
d. Sold land for $46,900, including $6,700 loss
e. Acquired equipment by issuing long-term note payable, $14,300
f. Paid long-term note payable, $61,000
g. Received cash for issuance of common shares, $3,900
h. Paid cash dividends, $38,100
i. Paid short-term note payable by issuing common shares, $4,700

Required

1. Prepare the statement of cash flows of Graphic Design Studio Inc. for the year ended June 30, 2011, using the *direct* method to report operating activities. Also prepare the accompanying schedule of noncash investing and financing activities. All current accounts except short-term notes payable result from operating transactions. The accounting records provide the following: collections from customers, $261,800; interest received, $1,300; payments to suppliers, $133,500; payments to employees, $40,500; payments for income tax, $10,600; and payment of interest $5,300.

(Group B)

Learning Objective 2 A-1
Preparing the statement of Cash flows—direct method

P12A-18B Rocco's Gourmet Foods Inc. provides the following data from the company's records for the year ended July 31, 2011:

a. Salary expense, $105,300
b. Cash payments to purchase property, plant, and equipment, $181,000
c. Proceeds from issuance of note payable, $44,100
d. Payments of long-term note payable, $18,800
e. Proceeds from sale of property, plant, and equipment, $59,700, including $10,600 gain
f. Interest revenue, $12,100
g. Cash receipt of dividend revenue on investments, $2,700
h. Payments to suppliers, $673,300
i. Interest expense and payments, $37,800
j. Cost of goods sold, $481,100
k. Collection of interest revenue, $11,700
l. Acquisition of equipment by issuing short-term note payable, $35,500
m. Payments of salaries, $104,000
n. Credit sales, $768,100
o. Loan to another company, $35,000
p. Income tax expense and payments, $56,400
q. Advertising expense, $27,700
r. Collections on accounts receivable, $741,100
s. Loan collections, $74,400
t. Proceeds from sale of investments, $34,700, including $3,800 loss
u. Payment of long-term note payable by issuing preferred shares, $107,300
v. Depreciation expense, $23,900
w. Cash sales, $146,000
x. Proceeds from issuance of common shares, $50,000
y. Payment of cash dividends, $50,500
z. Cash balance: July 31, 2010—$23,800; July 31, 2011—$31,400

Required

1. Prepare Rocco's Gourmet Foods Inc.'s statement of cash flows for the year ended July 31, 2011. Use the *direct* method for cash flows from operating activities. Follow the format of Exhibit 12A-3, but do *not* show amounts in thousands. Include an accompanying schedule of noncash investing and financing activities.
2. Evaluate 2011 in terms of cash flow. Give your reasons.

Learning Objective 2 A-1
Preparing an income statement, balance sheet, and statement of cash flows—direct method

P12A-19B Cruise Canada Motorhomes Inc. (CCM) was formed on January 1, 2011, when the company issued its common shares for $200,000. Early in January, CCM made the following cash payments:

a. For showroom fixtures, $50,000
b. For inventory, two motorhomes at $60,000 each, a total of $120,000
c. For rent on a store building, $12,000

In February, CCM purchased three motorhomes on account. Cost of this inventory was $160,000 ($53,333.33 each). Before year-end, CCM paid $140,000 of this debt. CCM uses the FIFO method to account for inventory.

During 2011, CCM sold four motorhomes for a total of $560,000. Before year-end, CCM collected 90% of this amount.

The store employs three people. The combined annual payroll is $90,000, of which CCM owes $3,000 at year-end. At the end of the year, CCM paid income tax of $64,000.

Late in 2011, CCM declared and paid cash dividends of $40,000.

For showroom fixtures, CCM uses the straight-line depreciation method over five years with zero residual value.

Required

1. Prepare CCM's income statement for the year ended December 31, 2011. Use the single-step format, with all the revenues listed together and all expenses listed together.
2. Prepare CCM's balance sheet at December 31, 2011.
3. Prepare CCM's statement of cash flows for the year ended December 31, 2011. Format cash flows from operating activities by using the *direct* method.

Learning Objective 2 A-1
Preparing the statement of cash flows—direct method

P12A-20B The 2011 comparative balance sheet and income statement of Riverbend Pools Inc. follow. Riverbend had no noncash investing and financing transactions during 2011. During the year, there were no sales of land or equipment, no issuances of notes payable, and no share repurchase transactions.

Riverbend Pools Inc.
Comparative Balance Sheet
December 31, 2011 and 2010

	2011	2010	Increase (Decrease)
Current assets:			
Cash and cash equivalents	$ 28,700	$ 15,600	$13,100
Accounts receivable	47,100	44,000	3,100
Inventories	94,300	89,900	4,400
Prepaid expenses	1,700	2,200	(500)
Property, plant, and equipment:			
Land	35,100	10,000	25,100
Equipment, net	100,900	93,700	7,200
Total assets	$307,800	$255,400	$52,400
Current liabilities:			
Accounts payable	$ 22,700	$ 24,600	$(1,900)
Salary payable	2,100	1,400	700
Other accrued liabilities	24,400	22,500	1,900
Long-term liabilities:			
Notes payable	55,000	65,000	(10,000)
Shareholders' equity:			
Common shares	131,100	122,300	8,800
Retained earnings	72,500	19,600	52,900
Total liabilities and shareholders' equity	$307,800	$255,400	$52,400

Riverbend Pools Inc.
Income Statement for 2011

Revenues:		
Sales revenue		$438,000
Interest revenue		11,700
Total revenues		449,700
Expenses:		
Cost of goods sold	$185,200	
Salary expense	76,400	
Depreciation expense	15,300	
Other operating expense	49,700	
Interest expense	24,600	
Income tax expense	16,900	
Total expense		368,100
Net income		$ 81,600

Required

1. Prepare the 2011 statement of cash flows by using the *direct* method.
2. How will what you learned in this problem help you evaluate an investment?

Learning Objective 3 A-1
Preparing the statement of cash flows—direct and indirect methods

P12A-21B To prepare the statement of cash flows, accountants for Powers Art Gallery Inc. have summarized 2011 activity in two accounts as follows:

Cash

Beginning balance	87,100	Payments of operating expenses	46,100
Issuance of common shares	60,800	Payment of long-term note payable	78,900
Receipts of dividends	1,900	Repurchase of common shares	10,400
Collection of loan	18,500	Payment of income tax	8,000
Sale of long-term investments	9,900	Payments on accounts payable	101,600
Receipts of interest	12,200	Payments of dividends	1,800
Collections from customers	308,100	Payments of salaries and wages	67,500
		Payments of interest	21,800
		Purchase of equipment	79,900
Ending balance	82,500		

Common Shares

		Beginning balance	103,500
		Issuance for cash	60,800
		Issuance to acquire land	62,100
		Issuance to retire long-term note payable	21,100
		Ending balance	247,500

Required

1. Prepare Powers' statement of cash flows for the year ended December 31, 2011, using the *direct* method to report operating activities. Also prepare the accompanying schedule of noncash investing and financing activities. Powers' 2011 income statement and selected balance sheet data follow.

Powers Art Gallery Inc.
Income Statement
For the Year Ended December 31, 2011

Revenues and gains:		
Sales revenue		$291,800
Interest revenue		12,200
Dividend revenue		1,900
Gain on sale of investments		700
Total revenues and gains		306,600
Expenses:		
Cost of goods sold	$103,600	
Salary and wage expense	66,800	
Depreciation expense	20,900	
Other operating expense	44,700	
Interest expense	24,100	
Income tax expense	2,600	
Total expenses		262,700
Net income		$ 43,900

Powers Art Gallery Inc.
Selected Balance Sheet Data

	2011 Increase (Decrease)
Current assets:	
Cash and cash equivalents	$ (4,600)
Accounts receivable	(16,300)
Inventories	5,700
Prepaid expenses	(1,900)
Loan receivable	(18,500)
Long-term investments	(9,200)
Equipment, net	59,000
Land	62,100
Current liabilities:	
Accounts payable	$ 7,700
Interest payable	2,300
Salary payable	(700)
Other accrued liabilities	(3,300)
Income tax payable	(5,400)
Long-term note payable	(100,000)
Common shares	133,600
Retained earnings	42,100

P12A-22B Arts de France Ltée's comparative balance sheet at September 30, 2011, included the following balances:

Learning Objective 3 A-1
Preparing the statement of cash flows—direct method

Arts de France Ltée
Balance Sheet
As at September 30, 2011 and 2010

	2011	2010	Increase (Decrease)
Current assets:			
Cash	$ 21,700	$ 17,600	$ 4,100
Accounts receivable	46,000	46,800	(800)
Inventories	121,700	116,900	4,800
Prepaid expenses	8,600	9,300	(700)
Long-term investments	51,100	13,800	37,300
Equipment, net	131,900	92,100	39,800
Land	47,100	74,300	(27,200)
	$428,100	$370,800	$ 57,300
Current liabilities:			
Notes payable, short-term	$ 22,000	$ 0	$ 22,000
Accounts payable	88,100	98,100	(10,000)
Accrued liabilities	17,900	29,100	(11,200)
Salary payable	1,500	1,100	400
Long-term note payable	123,000	121,400	1,600
Common shares	113,900	62,000	51,900
Retained earnings	61,700	59,100	2,600
	$428,100	$370,800	$ 57,300

Transaction data for the year ended September 30, 2011:

a. Net income, $66,900
b. Depreciation expense on equipment, $8,500
c. Purchased long-term investments, $37,300
d. Sold land for $38,100, including $10,900 gain
e. Acquired equipment by issuing long-term note payable, $26,300
f. Paid long-term note payable, $24,700
g. Received cash of $51,900 for issuance of common shares
h. Paid cash dividends, $64,300
i. Acquired equipment by issuing short-term note payable, $22,000

Required

1. Prepare Arts de France's statement of cash flows for the year ended September 30, 2011, using the *direct* method to report operating activities. Also prepare the accompanying schedule of noncash investing and financing activities. All current accounts except short-term notes payable result from operating transactions.Prepare a supplementary schedule showing cash flows from operations by using the *direct* method. The accounting records provide the following: collections from customers, $343,100; interest received, $8,600; payments to suppliers, $216,400; payments to employees, $63,000; payment of income tax, $21,200; payment of interest, $10,700.

13 Financial Statement Analysis

LEARNING OBJECTIVES

1. **Use** horizontal analysis to study comparative financial statements
2. **Perform** a vertical analysis of financial statements
3. **Prepare** common-size financial statements
4. **Use** the statement of cash flows in decision making
5. **Compute** and use financial ratios in decision making

SPOTLIGHT

This book began with the financial statements of Gildan Activewear Inc., a company that produces a wide range of clothing. Throughout this book we have shown how to account for the operations, financial position, and cash flows of a variety of companies, such as Le Château Inc., Loblaw Companies Limited, Canadian Tire, Leon's, and ATCO Ltd. Only one aspect of the course remains: the overall analysis of financial statements.

We have chosen Metro Inc., a leading Canadian grocery store chain, to illustrate different kinds of financial statement analysis. We begin with an analysis of Metro Inc.'s statement of earnings. In 2009, Metro had revenues of $11,196 million, and the company had net earnings of $354 million. These numbers look pretty good, but how good are they? We need to compare 2009 with prior years to see if Metro made progress during 2009. It could be that 2008 was a better year. We also need to compare Metro to its competitors.

Metro Inc.
Consolidated Statements of Earnings (Adapted)
For the Years Ended September 27, 2009, and September 26, 2008

In millions of dollars	**2009**	**2008**
Sales	$ 11,196	$ 10,725
Cost of sales and operating expenses	(10,481)	(10,103)
Share of earnings in a public company subject to significant influence	37	17
Banner conversion costs	(11)	—
Earnings before interest, taxes, and depreciation	741	639
Depreciation and amortization	(189)	(176)
Operating income	552	463
Financial costs, net	(48)	(58)
Earnings before income taxes	504	405
Income taxes	(150)	(114)
Earnings before minority interest	354	291
Minority interest	—	2
Net earnings	$ 354	$ 293

This chapter covers the basic tools of financial analysis. The first part of the chapter shows how to evaluate Metro from year to year and also how to compare Metro to different companies. For this comparison we use two of Canada's leading grocery chains, Metro and Sobeys. The second part of the chapter discusses the most widely used financial ratios. You have seen many of these ratios in earlier chapters: the current ratio, days' sales in receivables, inventory turnover, return on assets, and return on equity.

By studying all these ratios together, you will do the following:

- Learn the basic tools of financial analysis.
- Enhance your business education.

Regardless of your chosen field—marketing, management, finance, entrepreneurship, or accounting—you will find these analytical tools useful as you move through your career.

How Is a Company Evaluated?

Investors and creditors for both public and private corporations cannot evaluate a company by examining only one year's data. This is why most financial statements cover at least two periods, like the Metro Inc. statement of earnings that begins this chapter. In fact, most financial analysis covers trends of three to five years. The goal of financial analysis is to predict the future.

The graphs in Exhibit 13-1 show Metro's three-year trend of sales and operating income. Metro's sales and operating income increased steadily for the past three years. These are good signs. How would you predict Metro's sales and operating income for 2010 and beyond? Based on the recent past, you would probably extend the sales line and the operating income line upward.

Let's examine some of the tools of financial analysis: we begin with horizontal analysis.

EXHIBIT 13-1 Representative Financial Data of Metro Inc. (Adapted)

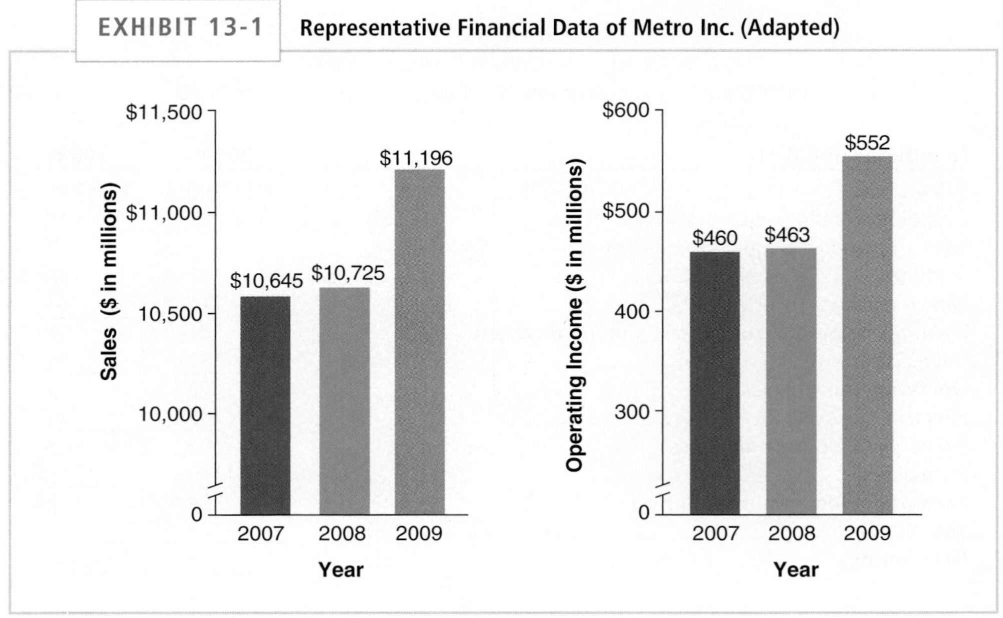

Horizontal Analysis

OBJECTIVE

1 **Use** horizontal analysis to study comparative financial statements

Many decisions hinge on the trend of the numbers in sales expenses, net income, and so on. Has the sales figure risen from last year? If so, by how much? Suppose that sales have increased by $200,000. Considered alone this fact is not very informative, but the *percentage change* in sales over time helps a lot. It is better to know that sales have increased by 20% than to know only that the increase is $200,000.

The study of percentage changes from year to year is called **horizontal analysis**. Computing a percentage change requires two steps:

1. Compute the dollar amount of the change from one period (the base period) to the next.
2. Divide the dollar amount of change by the base-period amount.

Illustration: Metro Inc.

Horizontal analysis is illustrated for Metro Inc. as follows (dollars in millions):

			Increase (Decrease)	
	2009	2008	Amount	Percentage
Sales	$11,196	$10,725	$471	4.4%

Metro's sales increased by 4.4% during 2009, computed as follows:

STEP 1 Compute the dollar amount of change in sales from 2008 to 2009:

$$2009 - 2008 = \text{Increase}$$
$$\$11{,}196 - \$10{,}725 = \$471$$

STEP 2 Divide the dollar amount of change by the base-period amount. This computes the percentage change for the period:

$$\text{Percentage change} = \frac{\text{Dollar amount of change}}{\text{Base-year amount}}$$

$$= \frac{\$471}{\$10,725} = 4.4\%$$

Exhibits 13-2 and 13-3 are detailed for Metro Inc. The income statements show that sales increased by 4.4% during 2009.

EXHIBIT 13-2 **Comparative Income Statement—Horizontal Analysis**

Metro Inc.
Consolidated Statement of Earnings (Adapted)
For the Years Ended September 26, 2009, and September 27, 2008

			Increase (Decrease)	
(In millions of dollars)	**2009**	**2008**	**Amount**	**Percentage**
Sales	$11,196	$10,725	$471	4.4%
Cost of sales and operating expenses	(10,481)	(10,103)	(378)	3.7
Share of earnings in a public company subject to significant influence	37	17	20	117.6
Banner conversion costs	(11)	—	(11)	100.0
Earnings before interest, taxes, and depreciation	741	639	102	15.9
Depreciation and amortzation	(189)	(176)	13	7.4
Operating income	552	463	89	19.2
Financial costs, net	(48)	(58)	10	(17.2)
Earnings before income taxes	504	405	99	24.4
Income taxes	(150)	(114)	36	31.6
Earnings before minority interest	354	291	63	21.6
Minority interest	—	2	(2)	(100.0)
Net earnings	$ 354	$293	$61	20.8

Note: Any increase from zero to a positive number is treated as an increase of 100%; any decrease to zero is treated as a decrease of 100%. Any decrease in a negative number is treated as an increase; any increase in a negative number is treated as a decrease.

STOP + THINK

Assume you are a financial analyst for an investment bank and have been charged with gathering information about Metro Inc. for a client. You have performed comparative analysis similar to Exhibit 13-2 of Metro's statements of earnings for 2009 and 2008. What do you think is the most important information for your analysis in Exhibit 13-2?

Answer:

Sales have increased by 4.4%, which is a modest increase but cost of sales and operating expenses have increased by only 3.7%. This information suggests that Metro is doing a good job of controlling expenses and that it is a well-run company.

EXHIBIT 13-3 **Comparative Balance Sheet—Horizontal Analysis**

Metro Inc.
Consolidated Balance Sheet (Adapted)
As at September 26, 2009, and September 27, 2008

			Increase (Decrease)	
(in millions of dollars)	**2009**	**2008**	**Amount**	**Percentage**
ASSETS				
Current assets				
Cash and cash equivalents	$ 241	$ 152	$ 89	58.5%
Accounts receivable	316	303	13	4.3
Inventories	681	641	40	6.2
Prepaid expenses	8	8	0	0.0
Income taxes receivable	7	25	(18)	(72.0)
Future income taxes	30	38	(8)	(21.1)
	1,283	1,167	116	9.9
Investments and other assets	204	176	28	15.9
Fixed assets	1,306	1,232	74	6.0
Intangible assets	325	328	(3)	(0.9)
Goodwill	1,479	1,479	—	(0.0)
Future income taxes	4	3	1	0.3
Accrued benefit assets	65	41	24	58.5
	$4,666	$4,426	$240	5.4
LIABILITIES AND SHAREHOLDERS' EQUITY				
Current liabilities				
Bank loans	$ 1	$ 1	$ 0	0.0%
Accounts payable	1,111	1,063	48	4.5
Income taxes payable	25	51	(26)	(51.0)
Future income taxes	9	6	3	50.0
Current portion of long-term debt	6	6	0	0.0
	1,152	1,127	25	2.2
Long-term debt	1,004	1,005	(1)	0.1
Accrued benefit obligations	49	51	(2)	(3.9)
Future income taxes	165	140	25	17.8
Other long-term liabilities	32	34	(2)	(5.9)
	2,402	2,357	45	1.9
Shareholders' equity				
Share capital	717	698	19	2.7
Contributed surplus	4	5	(1)	0.2
Retained earnings	1,545	1,367	178	13.0
Accumulated other comprehensive income	(2)	(1)	1	(100.0)
	2,264	2,069	195	9.4
	$4,666	$4,426	$240	5.4

Trend Percentages

Trend percentages are a form of horizontal analysis. Trends indicate the direction a business is taking. How have sales changed over a five-year period? What trend does income from continuing operations show? These questions can be answered by trend percentages over a representative period, such as the most recent five years.

Trend percentages are computed by selecting a base year whose amounts are set equal to 100%. The amount for each following year is expressed as a percentage of the base amount. To compute a trend percentage, divide an item for a later year by the base-year amount.

$$\text{Trend \%} = \frac{\text{Any-year \$}}{\text{Base-year \$}}$$

Metro Inc. showed operating income from continuing operations for the past five years as follows:

(in millions)	**2009**	**2008**	**2007**	**2006**	**2005**
Operating income	$552	$463	$460	$ 433	$279

We would like trend percentages for the four-year period 2006 to 2009. The base year is 2005. Trend percentages are computed by dividing each year's amount by the 2005 amount. The resulting trend percentages follow (2005 = 100%):

	2009	**2008**	**2007**	**2006**	**2005**
Operating income	198%	166%	165%	155%	100%

Looking at the trend percentages for Metro Inc., we can see that operating income rose sharply in 2006 and again in 2009.

You can perform a trend analysis on any item you consider important. Trend analysis is widely used for predicting the future.

Horizontal analysis highlights changes in an item over time. However, no single technique gives a complete picture of a business.

Vertical Analysis

❷ **Perform** a vertical analysis of financial statements

Vertical analysis shows the relationship of a financial statement item to its base, which is the 100% figure. All items on the financial statement are reported as a percentage of that base. For the income statement, total revenue is usually the base. Suppose under normal conditions a company's net income is 8% of revenue. A drop to 6% may cause the company's share price to fall.

Illustration: Metro Inc.

Exhibit 13-4 shows the vertical analysis of Metro's income statement as a percentage of sales. In this case,

$$\text{Vertical analysis \%} = \frac{\text{Each income statement item}}{\text{Sales}}$$

For Metro in 2009, the vertical-analysis percentage for operating income increased to 4.9% ($552 million/$11,196 million = 0.049) and as a result net income increased to 3.1% in 2009 compared to 2.7% in 2008.

Exhibit 13-5 shows the vertical analysis of Metro's balance sheet. The base amount (100%) is total assets. The vertical analysis of Metro's balance sheet reveals several things about the company's financial position:

- Current assets make up a slightly larger percentage of total assets (27.5% in 2009 compared to 26.3% in 2008). Cash and cash equivalents increased from 3.4% in 2008 to 5.2% in 2009 while accounts receivable stayed the same at 6.8% for both 2008 and 2009, which is a positive sign.

- Fixed assets (property, plant, and equipment) remain the second most significant asset. Metro is continuing to expand its capacity.
- Long-term debt decreased from 22.8% in 2008 to 21.5% in 2009.

How Do We Compare One Company to Another?

OBJECTIVE

3 **Prepare** common-size financial statements

The percentages in Exhibits 13-4 and 13-5 can be presented as a separate statement that reports only percentages (no dollar amounts). Such a statement is called a **common-size statement**.

On a common-size income statement, each item is expressed as a percentage of the net sales amount. Net sales is the *common size* to which we relate the other amounts. In the balance sheet, the common size is total assets. A common-size statement eases the comparison of different companies because their amounts are stated in percentages.

EXHIBIT 13-4 **Comparative Income Statement—Vertical Analysis Metro Inc.**

Metro Inc.
Consolidated Statement of Earnings (Adapted)
For the Years Ended September 26, 2009, and September 27, 2008

	2009		2008	
(in millions of dollars)	**Amount**	**Percentage of Sales***	**Amount**	**Percentage of Sales***
Sales	$11,196	100.0%	$10,725	100.0%
Cost of sales and operating expenses	(10,481)	(93.6)	(10,103)	(94.2)
Share of earnings in a public company subject to significant influence	37	0.3	17	0.2
Banner conversion costs	(11)	(0.1)	—	—
Earnings before interest, taxes, and depreciation.	741	6.6	639	6.0
Depreciation and amortization	(189)	(1.7)	(176)	(1.6)
Operating income	552	4.9	463	4.4
Financial costs, net	(48)	(0.4)	(58)	(0.6)
Earnings before income taxes	504	4.5	405	3.8
Income taxes	(150)	(1.4)	(114)	(1.1)
Earnings before minority interest	354	3.1	291	2.7
Minority interest	0	0.0	2	0.0
Net earnings	$354	3.1%	$ 293	2.7%

*Some percentages may not be exact because of rounding.

EXHIBIT 13-5 **Comparative Balance Sheet—Vertical Analysis**

Metro Inc.
Consolidated Balance Sheet (Adapted)
September 26, 2009, and September 27, 2008

	2009		2008	
(In millions of dollars)	**Amount**	**Percentage of Total***	**Amount**	**Percentage of Total***
ASSETS				
Current assets				
Cash and cash equivalents	$ 241	5.2%	$ 152	3.4%
Accounts receivable	316	6.8	303	6.8
Inventories	681	14.6	641	14.4
Prepaid expenses	8	0.2	8	0.2
Income taxes receivable	7	0.1	25	0.6
Future income taxes	30	0.6	38	0.9
	1,283	27.5	1,167	26.3
Investments and other assets	204	4.4	176	3.9
Fixed assets	1,306	28.0	1,232	27.9
Intangible assets	325	7.0	328	7.4
Goodwill	1,479	31.7	1,479	33.4
Future income taxes	4	0.1	3	0.1
Accrued benefit assets	65	1.3	41	1.0
	$4,666	100%	$4,426	100.0%
LIABILITIES AND SHAREHOLDERS' EQUITY				
Current liabilities				
Bank loans	$ 1	—%	$ 1	—%
Accounts payable	1,111	23.8	1,063	24.1
Income taxes payable	25	0.5	51	1.2
Future income taxes	9	0.2	6	0.1
Current portion of long-term debt	6	0.2	6	0.1
	1,152	24.7	1,127	25.5
Long-term debt	1,004	21.5	1,005	22.8
Accrued benefit obligations	49	1.1	51	1.2
Future income taxes	165	3.5	140	3.0
Other long-term liabilities	32	0.6	34	0.8
	2,402	51.4	2,357	53.3
Shareholders' equity				
Share capital	717	15.4	698	15.8
Contributed surplus	4	0.1	5	0.1
Retained earnings	1,545	33.1	1,367	30.8
Accumulated other comprehensive income	(2)	—	(1)	(—)
	2,264	48.6	2,069	46.7
	$4,666	100.0%	$4,426	100.0%

*Some percentages may not be exact because of rounding.

STOP + THINK

Assume you are a financial analyst for an investment bank and have been charged with gathering information about K-M Inc. for a client. You have been provided with the following 2010 income statement by K-M and have decided to calculate the common-size percentages. Show your calculations.

Net sales	$150,000
Cost of goods sold	60,000
Gross margin	90,000
Operating expense	40,000
Operating income	50,000
Income tax expense	15,000
Net income	$ 35,000

Answer:

Net sales	100%	(= $150,000 ÷ $150,000)
Cost of goods sold	40	(= $60,000 ÷ $150,000)
Gross margin	60	(= $90,000 ÷ $150,000)
Operating expense	27	(= $40,000 ÷ $150,000)
Operating income	33	(= $50,000 ÷ $150,000)
Income tax expense	10	(= $15,000 ÷ $150,000)
Net income	23%	(= $35,000 ÷ $150,000)

Benchmarking

Benchmarking is the comparison of a company to a standard set by others. Suppose you are a financial analyst for ScotiaMcLeod. You are considering an investment in the shares of a grocery chain, and you are choosing between Metro Inc. and Sobeys Inc. A direct comparison of their financial statements in dollar amounts is not meaningful because the amounts are so different; however, you can convert the two companies' income statements to common size and compare the percentages. The comparison is meaningful, as we shall see.

Benchmarking Against a Key Competitor

Exhibit 13-6 presents the common-size income statements of Metro Inc. and Sobeys Inc. Sobeys serves as an excellent benchmark because both are large, successful Canadian grocery chains. Although Sobeys is about a third bigger than Metro in terms of sales volume, the two companies are comparable in terms of operations.

Using the Statement of Cash Flows

OBJECTIVE

4 **Use** the statement of cash flows in decision making

The chapter has focused on the income statement and balance sheet. To continue our discussion of its role in decision making, let's use Exhibit 13-7, the statement of cash flows of SK Corporation.

Analysts find the statement of cash flows more helpful for spotting weakness than for gauging success. Why? Because a *shortage* of cash can throw a company into bankruptcy, but lots of cash doesn't ensure success. The statement of cash flows in Exhibit 13-7 reveals the following:

- SK Corporation's operations provide less cash than net income. Ordinarily, cash provided by operations exceeds net income because of the add-back of depreciation. The increases in current assets and current liabilities should cancel out over time. For SK Corporation, current assets increased far more than current

EXHIBIT 13-6 **Common-Size Income Statement Compared With a Key Competitor**

Metro Inc.
Common-Size Income Statement (Adapted) for Comparison With a Key Competitor
For the Years Ended as Indicated

	Metro Inc. (Adapted) September 26, 2009	Sobeys Inc. (Adapted) May 2, 2009
Sales	100.0%	100.0%
Cost of goods sold, operating and other expenses	95.5	95.3
Income before income tax	4.5	4.7
Income tax expense	1.4	0.7
Net earnings	3.1%	4.0%

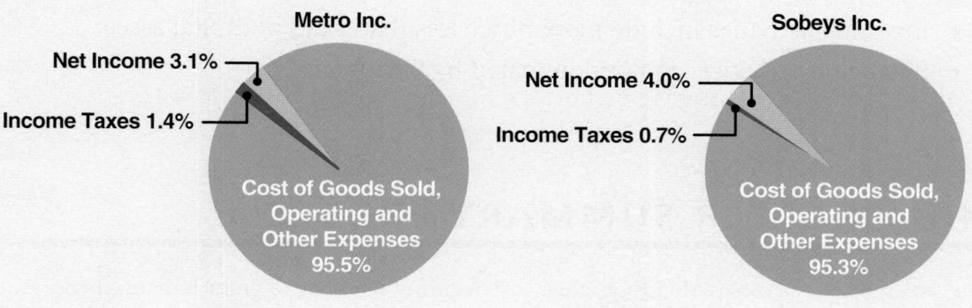

EXHIBIT 13-7 **Statement of Cash Flows**

SK Corporation
Statement of Cash Flows
For the Year Ended June 30, 2010

	Millions	
Operating activities:		
Net income		$ 35,000
Adjustments for noncash items:		
Depreciation	$ 14,000	
Net increase in current assets other than cash	(24,000)	
Net increase in current liabilities	8,000	(2,000)
Net cash provided by operating activities		33,000
Investing activities:		
Sale of property, plant, and equipment	91,000	
Net cash provided by investing activities		91,000
Financing activities:		
Borrowing	22,000	
Payment of long-term debt	(90,000)	
Repurchase of shares	(9,000)	
Payment of dividends	(23,000)	
Net cash used for financing activities		(100,000)
Increase in cash		$ 24,000

liabilities during the year. This may be harmless. But it may signal difficulty in collecting receivables or selling inventory. Either event may cause trouble.

- The sale of property, plant, and equipment is SK's major source of cash. This is okay if this is a one-time situation. SK may be shifting from one line of business to another, and it may be selling off old assets. But, if the sale of property, plant, and equipment is the major source of cash for several periods, SK will face a cash shortage. A company cannot continue to sell off its property, plant, and equipment forever. Soon, it will go out of business.
- The only strength shown by the statement of cash flows is that SK paid off more long-term debt than it did new borrowing. This will improve the debt ratio and SK's credit standing.

Here are some cash flow signs of a healthy company:

- Operations are a major *source* of cash (not a *use* of cash).
- Investing activities include more purchases than sales of capital assets.
- Financing activities are not dominated by borrowing.

MyAccountingLab

MID-CHAPTER SUMMARY PROBLEM

You, an employee at a bank lending office, are deciding whether to grant Jamate Corporation, which makes metal detectors, a large loan. You decide to perform a horizontal analysis and a vertical analysis of the comparative income statement of Jamate Corporation. State whether 2010 was a good year or a bad year and give your reasons.

Jamate Corporation
Comparative Income Statement
For the Years Ended December 31, 2010 and 2009

	2010	2009
Total revenues	$275,000	$225,000
Expenses:		
Cost of products sold	194,000	165,000
Engineering, selling, and administrative expenses	54,000	48,000
Interest expense	5,000	5,000
Income tax expense	9,000	3,000
Other expense (income)	1,000	(1,000)
Total expenses	263,000	220,000
Net earnings	$ 12,000	$ 5,000

Name: Jamate Corporation
Fiscal Period: Years ended December 31, 2010 and 2009

Answer

The horizontal analysis shows that total revenues increased 22.2%. This was greater than the 19.5% increase in total expenses, resulting in a 140% increase in net earnings.

Jamate Corporation
Horizontal Analysis of Comparative Income Statement
For the Years Ended December 31, 2010 and 2009

			Increase (Decrease)	
	2010	2009	Amount	Percent
Total revenues	$275,000	$225,000	$50,000	22.2%
Expenses:				
Cost of products sold	194,000	165,000	29,000	17.6
Engineering, selling, and administrative expenses	54,000	48,000	6,000	12.5
Interest expense	5,000	5,000	—	—
Income tax expense	9,000	3,000	6,000	200.0
Other expense (income)	1,000	(1,000)	2,000	—*
Total expenses	263,000	220,000	43,000	19.5
Net earnings	$ 12,000	$ 5,000	$ 7,000	140.0%

*Percentage changes are typically not computed for shifts from a negative to a positive amount, and vice versa.

Horizontal analysis compares 2010 with 2009 to determine the changes in each income statement item in dollar amounts and percent ($ and %). Large or unusual changes in $ or % should be investigated.

The net earnings increase of 140% occurred because the dollar amounts are quite small. Income tax expense increased 200%; this would be investigated.

The vertical analysis shows decreases in the percentages of net sales consumed by the cost of products sold (from 73.3% to 70.5%) and by the engineering, selling, and administrative expenses (from 21.3% to 19.6%). Because these two items are Jamate's largest dollar expenses, their percentage decreases are quite important. The relative reduction in expenses raised 2010's net earnings to 4.4% of sales, compared with 2.2% the preceding year. The overall analysis indicates that 2010 was significantly better than 2009.

Jamate Corporation
Vertical Analysis of Comparative Income Statement
For the Years Ended December 31, 2010 and 2009

	2010		2009	
	Amount	Percent	Amount	Percent
Total revenues	$275,000	100.0%	$225,000	100.0%
Expenses:				
Cost of products sold	194,000	70.5	165,000	73.3
Engineering, selling, and administrative expenses	54,000	19.6	48,000	21.3
Interest expense	5,000	1.8	5,000	2.2
Income tax expense	9,000	3.3	3,000	1.4*
Other expense (income)	1,000	0.4	(1,000)	(0.4)
Total expenses	263,000	95.6	220,000	97.8
Net earnings	$ 12,000	4.4%	$ 5,000	2.2%

*Number rounded up.

Vertical analysis expresses net earnings and expenses as a percentage of total revenues. The percentages for 2010 are compared with those of 2009. Any large or unexpected differences would be reviewed.

Using Ratios in Decision Making

OBJECTIVE

5 **Compute** and use financial ratios in decision making

Ratios are a major tool of financial analysis. A ratio expresses the relationship of one number to another. Suppose your balance sheet shows current assets of $100,000 and current liabilities of $50,000, the ratio of current assets to current liabilities is $100,000 to $50,000. We can express this ratio as 2 to 1, or 2:1. The current ratio is 2.0.

Many companies include ratios in a special section of their annual reports. RubberMate Corporation displays ratio data in the summary section of its annual report. Exhibit 13-8 shows data from that summary section. Investment services—such as Globe Interactive, with its online services, and the *Financial Post*—provide to subscribers data on public companies and industries in Canada. Credit agencies such as Dun & Bradstreet Canada (www.dnb.ca) offer industry averages as part of their financial services.

The ratios we discuss in this chapter may be classified as follows:

1. Ability to pay current liabilities
2. Ability to sell inventory and collect receivables
3. Ability to pay long-term debt
4. Profitability
5. Analysis of shares as an investment

How much can a computer help in analyzing financial statements for investment purposes? Time yourself as you perform one of the financial-ratio problems in this chapter. Multiply your efforts by 10 as though you were comparing 10 companies. Now rank these 10 companies on the basis of four or five ratios.

Online financial databases, such as SEDAR (www.sedar.com), offer complete information on all publicly filed data and reports by all Canadian public companies for the last several years. Assume that you want to compare companies' recent earnings histories. Use the database to compare several companies by doing vertical or horizontal analysis of their financial data or by computing the ratios discussed below for the companies in which you are interested. You might also review their press releases and other public statements. The investment services mentioned above are another source of information.

EXHIBIT 13-8 **Financial Summary of RubberMate Corporation (Dollar Amounts in Thousands Except Per-Share Amounts)**

Years Ended December 31	2010	2009	2008
Operating Results			
Net earnings	$ 218	$ 164	$ 163
Per common share	$1.32	$1.02	$1.02
Percent of sales	10.8%	9.1%	9.8%
Return on average shareholders' equity	20.0%	17.5%	19.7%
Financial Position			
Current assets	$570	$477	$419
Current liabilities	$359	$323	$345
Working capital	$211	$154	$ 74
Current ratio	1.59	1.48	1.21

Ethical Issue: Things May Not Always Be As They Seem

You will learn in the following pages that there are a number of ratios that managers and analysts, and other users of financial statements, use to assess the health and strength of a company. However, ratios can be and have been manipulated to present a picture of a business that is inaccurate and fraudulent.

The executives of WorldCom, one of the largest bankruptcies in history, manipulated both revenue and cost of sales in such a way that gross margin increased slightly every quarter to give the appearance of constant growth whereas, in fact, the gross margin was steadily declining. Such actions are a form of earnings management and are inappropriate. Earnings management is an important issue and one that you will cover in an advanced course.

Later in the chapter you will learn that it is important to consider all ratios over a period of years to get a more accurate picture of a company. Having said that, dishonest managers can and will, from time to time, present fraudulent information in an attempt to deceive users of that information.

Measuring Ability to Pay Current Liabilities

Sometimes a company buys inventory or supplies on credit or they may need to obtain a short-term loan.

Manager—Managers must make sure there is enough cash on hand to pay the company's current liabilities.

Investor—Investors know that a company that cannot pay its debts is not a good investment because it could go bankrupt.

Creditor—Creditors want to make sure they will be repaid if they loan the company money.

We will now examine several ratios that would indicate whether or not a company could pay back current liabilities.

Working capital is defined as follows:

$$\text{Working capital} = \text{Current assets} - \text{Current liabilities}$$

Working capital measures the ability to meet short-term obligations with current assets. In general, the larger the working capital, the better the ability to pay debts. Recall that capital is total assets minus total liabilities. Working capital is like a "current" version of total capital. Consider two companies with equal working capital:

	Company A	Company B
Current assets	$100,000	$200,000
Current liabilities	50,000	150,000
Working capital	$ 50,000	$ 50,000

Both companies have working capital of $50,000, but Company A's working capital is as large as its current liabilities. Company B's working capital is only one-third as large as its current liabilities. Two decision-making tools based on working-capital data are the *current ratio* and the *acid-test ratio*.

Current Ratio. The most common ratio evaluating current assets and current liabilities is the *current ratio*, which is current assets divided by current liabilities. The current ratio measures the company's ability to pay current liabilities with current assets. Exhibit 13-9 gives the income statement and balance sheet of Meben Furniture Ltd.

The current ratios of Meben Furniture Ltd. at December 31, 2010 and 2009, follow, along with the average for the retail furniture industry:

Formula	Meben's Current Ratio 2010	Meben's Current Ratio 2009	Industry Average
Current ratio = $\frac{\text{Current assets}}{\text{Cuttent liabilities}}$	$\frac{\$262,000}{\$142,000} = 1.85$	$\frac{\$236,000}{\$126,000} = 1.87$	1.50

The current ratio was virtually unchanged during 2010. In general, a higher current ratio indicates a stronger financial position. The business has sufficient liquid assets to maintain its operations. Meben's current ratio of 1.85 compares favourably with the current ratios of some well-known companies:

Company	Current Ratio
Enbridge Inc. (Utility)	0.94
Research In Motion (Hi-tech company)	2.39
Loblaw Companies Limited (Grocery stores)	1.20

What is an acceptable current ratio? The answer depends on the industry. The norm for companies in most industries is around 1.50, as reported by the Risk Management Association. Meben's current ratio of 1.85 is better than average.

The Limitations of Ratio Analysis

Business decisions are made in a world of uncertainty. As useful as ratios are, they aren't a cure-all. Consider a physician's use of a thermometer. A reading of 38.8° Celsius tells a doctor something is wrong with the patient, but doesn't indicate what the problem is or how to cure it.

In financial analysis, a sudden drop in the current ratio signals that something is wrong, but doesn't identify the problem. A user of financial information, such as a manager, an investor, a bank loan officer, or an analyst, must analyze the figures to learn what caused the ratio to fall. A drop in current assets may mean a cash shortage or that sales are slow. The user must evaluate all the ratios in the light of factors such as increased competition or a slowdown in the economy.

Legislation, international affairs, scandals, and other factors can turn profits into losses. To be useful, ratios should be analyzed over a period of years to consider all relevant factors. Any one year, or even any two years, may not represent the company's performance over the long term.

Acid-Test Ratio. The *acid-test* (or *quick*) *ratio* tells us whether the entity could pass the acid test of paying all its current liabilities if they came due immediately. The acid-test ratio uses a narrower base to measure liquidity than the current ratio does.

To compute the acid-test ratio, we add cash, short-term investments, and net current receivables (accounts and notes, net of allowances) and divide by current liabilities. Inventory and prepaid expenses are two current assets not included in the acid-test computations because they are less liquid. A business may not be able to convert inventory to cash immediately, and with prepaid expenses, the cash has already been spent.

EXHIBIT 13-9 **Comparative Financial Statements**

Meben Furniture Ltd.
Comparative Income Statement
For the Years Ended December 31, 2010 and 2009

	2010	2009
Net sales	$858,000	$803,000
Cost of goods sold	513,000	509,000
Gross margin	345,000	294,000
Operating expenses:		
Selling expenses	126,000	114,000
General expenses	118,000	123,000
Total operating expenses	244,000	237,000
Income from operations	101,000	57,000
Interest revenue	(4,000)	—
Interest expense	24,000	14,000
Income before income taxes	81,000	43,000
Income tax expense	33,000	17,000
Net income	$ 48,000	$ 26,000

Meben Furniture Ltd.
Comparative Balance Sheet
December 31, 2010 and 2009

	2010	2009
Assets		
Current assets:		
Cash	$ 29,000	$ 32,000
Accounts receivable, net	114,000	85,000
Inventories	113,000	111,000
Prepaid expenses	6,000	8,000
Total current assets	262,000	236,000
Long-term investments	18,000	9,000
Property, plant, and equipment, net	507,000	399,000
Total assets	$787,000	$644,000
Liabilities		
Current liabilities:		
Notes payable	$ 42,000	$ 27,000
Accounts payable	73,000	68,000
Accrued liabilities	27,000	31,000
Total current liabilities	142,000	126,000
Long-term debt	289,000	198,000
Total liabilities	431,000	324,000
Shareholders' Equity		
Common shares	185,500	185,500
Retained earnings	170,000	134,000
Accumulated other comprehensive income	500	500
Total shareholders' equity	356,000	320,000
Total liabilities and shareholders' equity	$787,000	$644,000

Meben Furniture Ltd.'s acid-test ratios for 2010 and 2009 follow:

Formula	Meben's Acid-Test Ratio 2010	2009	Industry Average
Acid-test ratio = (Cash + Short-term investments + Net current receivables) / Current liabilities	($29,000 + $0 + $114,000) / $142,000 = 1.01	($32,000 + $0 + $85,000) / $126,000 = 0.93	0.40

The company's acid-test ratio improved during 2010 and is significantly better than the industry average. Compare Meben's acid-test ratio with the values of some well-known companies.

Company	Acid-Test Ratio
Enbridge Inc. (Utility)	0.74
Research In Motion (Hi-tech company)	1.94
Loblaw Companies Limited (Grocery stores)	0.60

An acid-test ratio of 0.90 to 1.00 is acceptable in most industries. How can a leading company, such as Loblaw Companies Limited with its 0.60 acid-test ratio, function with such a low ratio? Loblaw has almost no receivables. Its inventory is priced to turn over very quickly. This points us to the next two ratios.

STOP + THINK

Assume you are a financial analyst for an investment bank and have been charged with analyzing Meben's Furniture Ltd.'s financial statements. You calculate that Meben's current ratio is 1.85, which looks strong, whereas the company's acid-test ratio is 1.01, also strong. Suppose Meben's acid-test ratio were low, say 0.48. What would be the most likely reason for the discrepancy between a high current ratio and a weak acid-test ratio?

Answers:

In such a situation, it would appear that the company is having difficulty selling its inventory. The level of inventory must be relatively high, and the inventory is propping up the current ratio. The rate of inventory turnover may be low.

Measuring Ability to Sell Inventory and Collect Receivables

In Chapter 3, we saw how the operating cycle is the time span during which (1) cash is paid for inventory and (2) these inventories are sold to bring in cash. This means the company's money is tied up in inventory until it is sold and cash is collected from its customers. This could take weeks, even months.

Manager—Managers need to know if there is too much or too little inventory on hand. This helps them decide how much inventory to buy. They also need to monitor their accounts receivable to ensure they are collecting cash from their customers in a timely fashion.

Investor—Investors are happy when inventory is sold quickly because selling inventory increases revenue and ultimately net income.

Creditor—Creditors know that collecting cash soon after the sale enables the company to pay its bills and loans on time.

The ability to sell inventory and collect receivables is critical to business success. We will now discuss these ratios.

Inventory Turnover. Companies generally strive to sell their inventory as quickly as possible. The faster inventory sells, the sooner cash comes in.

Inventory turnover is a measure of the number of times a company sells its average level of inventory during a year. A fast turnover indicates ease in selling inventory; a low turnover indicates difficulty. A value of 6 means that the company's average level of inventory has been sold six times during the year, and that's better than a turnover of three times. But too high a value can mean that the business is not keeping enough inventory on hand, which can result in lost sales if the company cannot fill orders. Therefore, a business strives for the most *profitable* rate of inventory turnover, not necessarily the *highest* rate.

To compute the inventory turnover ratio, divide cost of goods sold by the average inventory for the period. We use the cost of goods sold—*not sales*—in the computation because both cost of goods sold and inventory are stated *at cost*. Meben Furniture Ltd.'s inventory turnover for 2010 is:

	Formula	Meben's Inventory Turnover	Industry Average
Inventory turnover =	$\frac{\text{Cost of goods sold}}{\text{Average inventory}}$	$\frac{\$513{,}000}{\$112{,}000} = 4.6$	3.4

Cost of goods sold comes from the income statement (Exhibit 13-9). Average inventory is calculated by averaging the beginning inventory ($111,000) and ending inventory ($113,000). (See the balance sheet, Exhibit 13-9.) If inventory levels vary greatly from month to month, compute the average by adding the 12 monthly balances and dividing the sum by 12.

Inventory turnover varies widely with the nature of the business. For example, most manufacturers of farm machinery have an inventory turnover close to three times a year. In contrast, companies that remove natural gas from the ground hold their inventory for a very short period of time and have an average turnover of 30. Meben's turnover of 4.6 times a year is high for its industry, which has an average turnover of 3.4. Meben's high inventory turnover results from its policy of keeping little inventory on hand. The company sells directly but also takes customer orders and has its suppliers ship directly to some customers.

To evaluate a company's inventory turnover fully, compare the ratio over time. A sharp decline in the rate of inventory turnover or a steady decline over a long period suggests the need for corrective action.

Accounts Receivable Turnover. *Accounts receivable turnover* measures a company's ability to collect cash from credit customers. In general, the higher the ratio the better. However, a receivable turnover that is too high may indicate that credit is too tight, and that might cause you to lose sales to good customers.

To compute the accounts receivable turnover, divide net credit sales by average net accounts receivable. The ratio indicates how many times during the year the average level of receivables was turned into cash. Meben Furniture Ltd.'s accounts receivable turnover ratio for 2010 is:

	Formula	Meben's Accounts Receivable Turnover	Industry Average
Accounts receivable turnover =	$\frac{\text{Net credit sales}}{\text{Average net accounts receivable}}$	$\frac{\$858{,}000}{\$99{,}500} = 8.6$	51.0

Meben makes almost all sales on credit. It the company makes both cash and credit sales, this ratio is best computed by using only net credit sales. Average net accounts receivable is calculated by adding the beginning accounts receivable balance ($85,000) and the ending balance ($114,000), then dividing by 2. If the accounts receivable balances exhibit a seasonal pattern, compute the average by adding the 12 monthly balances and dividing the sum by 12.

Meben's receivable turnover of 8.6 times per year is much slower than the industry average. The explanation is simple: Meben is a hometown store that sells to local people who tend to pay their bills over a period of time. Many larger stores and chains of stores sell their receivables to other companies called *factors*, a practice that keeps receivables low and receivable turnover high. But companies that factor (sell) their receivables receive less than the face value of the receivables. Meben follows a different strategy.

Days' Sales in Receivables. Businesses must convert accounts receivable to cash. All else being equal, the lower the receivable balance, the better the cash flow.

The *days'-sales-in-receivables* ratio tells us how many days' sales remain in Accounts Receivable. Compute the ratio by a two-step process:

1. Divide net sales by 365 days to calculate the average sales for one day.
2. Divide average net accounts receivable by average sales per day.

The data to compute this ratio for Meben Furniture Ltd. for 2010 are taken from the income statement and the balance sheet (Exhibit 13-9):

	Formula	Meben's Days' Sales in Accounts Receivable	Industry Average
Days' sales in *average* accounts receivable:			
1. One day's sales =	$\frac{\text{Net sales}}{\text{365 days}}$	$\frac{\$858{,}000}{\text{365 days}} = \$2{,}351$	
2. Days' sales in average accounts receivable =	$\frac{\text{Average net accounts receivable}}{\text{One day's sales}}$	$\frac{\$99{,}500}{\$2{,}351} = \text{42 days}$	7 days

Days' sales in average receivables can also be computed in a single step: $99,500/($858,000/365 days) = 42 days. Meben's collection period is much longer (worse) than the industry average because Meben collects its own receivables. As was noted above, most furniture stores sell their receivables and carry fewer days' sales in receivables.

Meben's ratio tells us that 42 average days' sales remain in accounts receivable and need to be collected. The company will increase its cash flow if it can decrease this ratio. To detect any changes over time in the firm's ability to collect its receivables, let's compute the days'-sales-in-receivables ratio at the beginning and the end of 2010:

Days' Sales in ENDING 2009 Accounts Receivable:

One day's sales $= \dfrac{\$803{,}000}{365 \text{ days}} = \$2{,}200$ Days' sales in *ENDING* 2009 accounts receivable $= \dfrac{\$85{,}000}{\$2{,}200} =$ 39 days at the beginning of 2010

Days' Sales in ENDING 2010 Accounts Receivable:

One day's sales $= \dfrac{\$858{,}000}{365 \text{ days}} = \$2{,}351$ Days' sales in *ENDING* 2010 accounts receivable $= \dfrac{\$114{,}000}{\$2{,}351} =$ 48 days at the end of 2010

This analysis shows a slowdown in Meben's collection of receivables; days' sales in accounts receivable have increased from 39 at the beginning of the year to 48 at year-end. The credit and collection department should strengthen its collection efforts. Otherwise, the company may experience a cash shortage in 2011 and beyond.

Analyzing Changes in Receivables Ratios

A company's days' sales in receivables might increase because the company loosens its credit terms (for example, from net 30 to net 45) in an effort to increase sales. Another reason might be that the company is doing a poor job of collecting its receivables. As is true of all the other ratios you study here, changes in the ratio are important but so is understanding why the ratio changed.

Measuring Ability to Pay Long-Term Debt

A business may be generating a profit but still be low in cash. If a company is not able to pay its debts as they come due, it could soon be in serious financial difficulty and even forced into bankruptcy.

Manager—Managers must make sure they have enough assets to pay the company's debts.

Investor—Investors or shareholders want to make sure they are making a wise decision by investing in a profitable company.

Creditor—Creditors loan money with the anticipation of being paid back the principal plus interest.

The ratios discussed so far relate to current assets and current liabilities. They measure the ability to sell inventory, collect receivables, and pay current liabilities. Most businesses also have long-term debt. Two indicators of the ability to pay total liabilities are the *debt ratio* and the *times-interest-earned ratio*.

Debt Ratio. Suppose you are a loan officer at a bank, and you have received $500,000 loan applications from two similar companies. The first firm already owes $600,000, and the second owes only $250,000. Other things being equal, which company gets the loan? Company 2 would, because it owes less.

This relationship between total liabilities and total assets is called the *debt ratio*. It tells us the proportion of the company's assets that it has financed with debt. A debt ratio of 1 reveals that debt has financed all the assets. A debt ratio of 0.50 means that debt financed half the assets. The higher the debt ratio, the greater the pressure to pay interest and principal. The lower the ratio, the lower the risk.

The debt ratios for Meben Furniture Ltd. follow:

Formula	Meben's Debt Ratio 2010	Meben's Debt Ratio 2009	Industry Average
Debt ratio = $\frac{\text{Total liabilities}}{\text{Total assets}}$	$\frac{\$431,000}{\$787,000} = 0.55$	$\frac{\$324,000}{\$644,000} = 0.50$	0.64

Risk Management Association reports that the average debt ratio for most companies ranges around 0.62, with relatively little variation from company to company. Meben's 0.55 debt ratio indicates a fairly low-risk debt position compared with the retail furniture industry average of 0.64.

Times-Interest-Earned Ratio. Analysts use a second ratio—the *times-interest-earned ratio*—to relate income to interest expense. To compute the times-interest-earned ratio, divide income from operations (operating income) by interest expense. This ratio measures the number of times that operating income can *cover* interest expense and is also called the *interest-coverage ratio*. A high ratio indicates ease in paying interest; a low value suggests difficulty.

Meben's times-interest-earned ratios are:

Formula	Meben's Times-Interest-Earned Ratio 2010	Meben's Times-Interest-Earned Ratio 2009	Industry Average
Times-interest-earned ratio = $\frac{\text{Income from operations}}{\text{Interest expense}}$	$\frac{\$101,000}{\$24,000} = 4.21$	$\frac{\$57,000}{\$14,000} = 4.07$	2.80

The company's times-interest-earned ratio increased in 2010. This is a favourable sign.

Measuring Profitability

The fundamental goal of business is to earn a profit, and so the ratios that measure profitability are reported widely.

Manager—Managers are sometimes evaluated based on how well the company has performed.

Investor—,An investor buys shares in a company expecting to receive dividends as well as an increase in the market price of their share. They look to see if the company is able to earn a profit.

Creditor—Creditors know that a profitable company is able to pay back their debt.

Understanding Ratios That Measure Profitability

Suppose you are a personal financial planner who helps clients select share investments. Over the next few years, you might expect Metro Inc. to earn higher rates of return on a share investment than analysts are forecasting for Sobeys Inc. Which company's shares will you recommend? Perhaps Metro's—for reasons that you will better understand after studying four rate-of-return measurements.

Return on Sales. In business, *return* refers to profitability. Consider the **return on net sales**, or profit margin. (The word *net* is usually omitted for convenience.) This ratio shows the percentage of each sales dollar earned as net income. The return-on-sales ratios for Meben Furniture Ltd. are:

Formula			Meben's Return on Sales 2010	Meben's Return on Sales 2009	Industry Average
Return on net sales	=	$\frac{\text{Net income}}{\text{Net sales}}$	$\frac{\$48{,}000}{\$858{,}000} = 0.056$	$\frac{\$26{,}000}{\$803{,}000} = 0.032$	0.008

Companies strive for a high rate of return. The higher the percentage, the more profit is being generated by sales dollars. Meben's return on sales is higher than the average furniture store. Compare Meben's return on sales to the returns of some other companies:

Company	Return on Sales
Leon's Furniture Limited (Furniture stores)	0.081
Sobeys Inc. (Grocery stores)	0.016
Tim Hortons Inc. (Quick-service restaurant chain)	0.132

Return on Total Assets. The *return on total assets*, or simply **return on assets**, measures a company's success in using assets to earn a profit. Creditors have loaned money, and the interest they receive is their return on investment. Shareholders have bought the company's shares, and net income is their return. The sum of interest expense and net income is the return to the two groups that have financed the company. This sum is the numerator of the ratio. Average total assets is the denominator. The return-on-assets ratio for Meben Furniture Ltd. is:

Formula			Meben's 2010 Return on Total Assets	Industry Average
Return on total assets	=	$\frac{\text{Net income + Interest expense}}{\text{Average total assets}}$	$\frac{\$48{,}000 + \$24{,}000}{\$715{,}500} = 0.101$	0.078

To compute average total assets, add the beginning and ending balances and divide by 2. Compare Meben Furniture Ltd.'s return on assets to the rates of these leading companies:

Company	Rate of Return on Assets
Gildan Activewear Inc. (Clothing manufacturer)	0.892
RONA Inc. (Home improvement retailer and distributor)	0.062
Bombardier Inc. (Production of transportation equipment and services)	0.046

Return on Common Shareholders' Equity. A popular measure of profitability is the *return on common shareholders' equity*, often shortened to **return on equity**. This ratio shows the relationship between net income and common shareholders' investment in the company—how much income is earned for every $1 invested.

To compute this ratio, first subtract preferred dividends from net income to measure income available to the common shareholders. Then divide income available to common shareholders by the average common shareholders' equity during the year. Common shareholders' equity is total shareholders' equity minus preferred equity. The 2010 rate of return on common shareholders' equity for Meben Furniture Ltd. is:

Formula			Meben's 2010 Return on Common Shareholders' Equity	Industry Average
Return on common shareholders' equity	=	$\dfrac{\text{Net income} - \text{Preferred dividends}}{\text{Average common shareholders' equity}}$	$\dfrac{\$48{,}000 - \$0}{\$338{,}000} = 0.142$	0.121

Average common shareholders' equity uses the beginning and ending balances [($356,000 + $320,000)/2 = $338,000].

Observe that Meben's return on equity (0.142) is higher than its return on assets (0.101). This is a good sign. This difference results from borrowing at one rate—say, 8%—and investing the funds to earn a higher rate, such as the firm's 14.2% return on equity. This practice is called using *leverage* or *trading on the equity*. The higher the debt ratio, the higher the leverage. Companies that finance operations with debt are said to *leverage* their positions.

For Meben Furniture Ltd., leverage increases profitability. This is not always the case because leverage can hurt profits. If revenues drop, debt and interest expense still must be paid. Therefore, leverage is a double-edged sword. It increases profits during good times but compounds losses during bad times.

Compare Meben Furniture Ltd.'s rate of return on common shareholders' equity with the rates of some leading companies:

Company	Return on Common Equity
Gildan Activewear Inc. (Clothing manufacturer)	0.111
RONA Inc. (Home improvement retailer and distributor)	0.0851
Bombardier Inc. (Production of transportation equipment and services)	0.222

Earnings per Share of Common Stock. *Earnings per share of common stock*, or simply *earnings per share (EPS)*, is the amount of net income earned for each share of outstanding *common* stock. EPS is the most widely quoted of all financial statistics. It is the only ratio that appears on the income statement.

Earnings per share is computed by dividing net income available to common shareholders by the number of common shares outstanding during the year. Preferred dividends are subtracted from net income because the preferred shareholders have a prior claim to their dividends. Meben Furniture Ltd. has no preferred shares outstanding and thus has no preferred dividends. The firm's EPS for 2010 and 2009 follows (Meben had 10,000 common shares outstanding):

Formula			Meben's Earnings per Share 2010	Meben's Earnings per Share 2009
Earnings per share of common stock	=	$\dfrac{\text{Net income} - \text{Preferred dividends}}{\text{Average number of common shares outstanding}}$	$\dfrac{\$48{,}000 - \$0}{10{,}000} = \$4.80$	$\dfrac{\$26{,}000 - \$0}{10{,}000} = \$2.60$

Meben Furniture Ltd.'s EPS increased 85%, which is good news. Its shareholders should not expect such a significant boost in EPS every year. Most companies strive to increase EPS by 10% to 15% annually.

Analyzing Share Investments

Investors purchase shares to earn a return on their investment. This return consists of two parts: (1) gains (or losses) from selling the shares, and (2) dividends.

Price/Earnings Ratio. The **price/earnings ratio** is the ratio of the market price of a common share to earnings per share. This ratio, abbreviated P/E, is available, for example, in *The Globe and Mail* stock listings and online at www.tsx.com. It shows the market price of $1 of earnings.

Calculations for the P/E ratios of Meben Furniture Ltd. follow. Meben is not a real company and is not listed on a stock exchange, but assume the market price of its common shares was $60 at the end of 2010 and $35 at the end of 2009. Share prices can be obtained from a financial publication, a stockbroker, the company's Internet site, or the Internet site of a stock exchange such as the Toronto Stock Exchange.

	Meben's Price/Earnings Ratio	
Formula	**2010**	**2009**
$\text{P/E ratio} = \dfrac{\text{Market price per common share}}{\text{Earnings per share}}$	$\dfrac{\$60.00}{\$4.80} = 12.5$	$\dfrac{\$35.00}{\$2.60} = 13.5$

Given Meben's 2010 P/E ratio of 12.5, we would say that the company's shares are selling at 12.5 times earnings. Each $1 of Meben's earnings is worth $12.50 to the stock market.

Dividend Yield. Dividend yield is the ratio of dividends per share to the share's market price. This ratio measures the percentage of a share's market price that is returned annually to the shareholders as dividends. *Preferred* shareholders pay special attention to this ratio because they invest primarily to receive dividends.

Meben Furniture Ltd. paid annual cash dividends of $1.20 per common share in 2010 and $1.00 in 2009. Assume the market prices of the company's common shares were $60 in 2010 and $35 in 2009. The firm's dividend yields on common shares are:

	Dividend Yield on Meben's Common Shares	
Formula	**2010**	**2009**
$\text{Dividend yield on common share}^{*} = \dfrac{\text{Dividend per share of common stock}}{\text{Market price per share of common stock}}$	$\dfrac{\$1.20}{\$60.00} = 0.020$	$\dfrac{\$1.00}{\$35.00} = 0.029$

*Dividend yields may also be calculated for preferred shares.

An investor who buys Meben Furniture Ltd. common shares for $60 can expect to receive around 2% of the investment annually in the form of cash dividends. Dividend yields vary widely, from 3% to 9% for older, established firms (such as BCE and National Bank) down to the range of 0% to 3% for young, growth-oriented companies. Rogers Communications, for example, pays a cash dividend of $1.25 per share, for a dividend yield of 3.8%. Open Text and Research In Motion do not pay cash dividends.

Book Value per Share of Common Stock. *Book value per share of common stock* is simply common shareholders' equity divided by the number of shares outstanding. Common shareholders' equity equals total shareholders' equity less preferred equity.

Meben Furniture Ltd. has no preferred shares outstanding. Calculations of its book-value-per-share-of-common-stock ratios follow. Recall that 10,000 common shares were outstanding at the end of years 2010 and 2009.

	Formula	Book Value per Share of Meben's Common Stock 2010	2009
Book value per share of common stock =	$\frac{\text{Total shareholders' equity} - \text{Preferred equity}}{\text{Number of shares of common stock outstanding}}$	$\frac{\$356{,}000 - \$0}{10{,}000} = \$35.60$	$\frac{\$320{,}000 - \$0}{10{,}000} = \$32.00$

Book value indicates the recorded accounting amount for each common share outstanding. Many experts believe that book value is not useful for investment analysis because it bears no relationship to market price and provides little information beyond shareholders' equity reported on the balance sheet. But some investors base their investment decisions on book value. For example, some investors rank shares on the basis of the ratio of market price to book value. The lower the ratio, the more attractive the shares. These investors are called "value" investors, as contrasted with "growth" investors, who focus more on trends in a company's net income.

Red Flags in Financial Statement Analysis

Recent accounting scandals highlighted the importance of red flags in financial analysis. If the following conditions are present, the company may be too risky.

- **Earnings Problems.** Have income from continuing operations and net income decreased significantly for several years in a row? Has income turned into a loss? This may be okay for a company in a cyclical industry, such as an airline or a home builder, but most companies cannot survive consecutive loss years.

- **Decreased Cash Flow.** Cash flow validates earnings. Is cash flow from operations consistently lower than net income? Are the sales of capital assets a major source of cash? If so, the company may be facing a cash shortage.

- **Too Much Debt.** How does the company's debt ratio compare to that of major competitors and to the industry average? If the debt ratio is much higher than average, the company may be unable to pay debts during tough times.

- **Inability to Collect Receivables.** Are days' sales in receivables growing faster than for other companies in the industry? A cash shortage may be looming.

- **Buildup of Inventories.** Is inventory turnover slowing down? If so, the company may be unable to move products, or it may be overstating inventory. Recall from the cost-of-goods-sold model that one of the easiest ways to overstate net income is to overstate ending inventory.

- **Trends of Sales, Inventory, and Receivables.** Sales, receivables, and inventory generally move together. Increased sales lead to higher receivables and require more inventory to meet demand. Strange movements among these items may spell trouble.

Efficient Markets

An **efficient capital market** is one in which market prices fully reflect all information available to the public. Because share prices reflect all publicly accessible data, it can be argued that the stock market is efficient. Market efficiency has implications for management action and for investor decisions. It means that managers cannot fool the market with accounting gimmicks. If the information is available, the market as a whole can set a "fair" price for the company's shares.

Suppose you are the president of Kemble Corporation. Reported earnings per share are $4, and the share price is $40—so the P/E ratio is 10. You believe the corporation's shares are underpriced in comparison with other companies in the same industry. To correct this situation, you are considering changing your depreciation method from accelerated to straight-line. The accounting change will increase earnings per share to $5. Will the share price then rise to $50? Probably not; the company's share price will probably remain at $40 because the market can understand the accounting change. After all, the company merely changed its method of computing depreciation. There is no effect on the company's cash flows, and its economic position is unchanged. An efficient market interprets data in light of their true underlying meaning.

An appropriate investment strategy seeks to manage risk, diversify, and minimize transaction costs. Financial analysis consists mainly of identifying the risks of various shares to manage the risk.

Exhibit 13-10 summarizes the most widely used ratios.

SUMMARY OF CHAPTER 13

Learning Objective ❶: **Use horizontal analysis to study comparative financial statements**

A **horizontal analysis** is used to study percentage changes in sales, net income and so on from year to year. The dollar amount of the change from one period to the next is divided by the base-year amount. A form of horizontal analysis is a **trend percentage** that shows how sales or any other item have changed over a period of time. It is computed by selecting a base year whose amounts are set equal to 100%. The amount for each of the following years is expressed as a percentage of the base year.

Learning Objective ❷: **Perform a vertical analysis of financial statements**

A **vertical analysis** is used to compare each item on the income statement using sales as a base or each item on the balance sheet using total assets as its base. It reveals the percentage of an individual item to its base.

Learning Objective ❸: **Prepare common-size financial statements**

A **common-size statement** reports each item as a percentage of the total rather than in dollar amounts. It aids in comparing different companies because their amounts are stated in percentages.

Learning Objective ❹: **Use the statement of cash flows in decision making**

Analyzing a cash flow statement may help to reveal whether or not the company is experiencing cash problems. Generally speaking, a company's main source of cash should come from its operations. If the major source of cash over several periods is from investing, for example, selling property, plant and equipment, it may signal a cash shortage. Paying off debt helps to improve a company's debt ratio.

EXHIBIT 13-10 **Ratios Used in Financial Statement Analysis**

Ratio	Computation	Information Provided
Measuring ability to pay current liabilities:		
1. Current ratio	$\frac{\text{Current assets}}{\text{Current liabilities}}$	Measures ability to pay current liabilities with current assets
2. Acid-test (quick) ratio	$\frac{\text{Cash} + \text{Short-term investments} + \text{Net current receivables}}{\text{Current liabilities}}$	Shows ability to pay all current liabilities if they come due immediately
Measuring ability to sell inventory and collect receivables:		
3. Inventory turnover	$\frac{\text{Cost of goods sold}}{\text{Average inventory}}$	Indicates saleability of inventory—the number of times a company sells its average inventory level during a year
4. Accounts receivable turnover	$\frac{\text{Net credit sales}}{\text{Average net accounts receivable}}$	Measures ability to collect cash from credit customers
5. Days' sales in receivables	$\frac{\text{Average net accounts receivable}}{\text{One day's sales}}$	Shows how many days' sales remain in Accounts Receivable—how many days it takes to collect the average level of receivables
Measuring ability to pay long-term debt:		
6. Debt ratio	$\frac{\text{Total liabilities}}{\text{Total assets}}$	Indicates percentage of assets financed with debt
7. Times-interest-earned ratio	$\frac{\text{Income from operations}}{\text{Interest expense}}$	Measures the number of times operating income can cover interest expense
Measuring profitability:		
8. Return on net sales	$\frac{\text{Net income}}{\text{Net sales}}$	Shows the percentage of each sales dollar earned as net income
9. Return on total assets	$\frac{\text{Net income} + \text{Interest expense}}{\text{Average total assets}}$	Measures how profitably a company uses its assets
10. Return on common shareholders' equity	$\frac{\text{Net income} - \text{Preferred dividends}}{\text{Average common shareholders' equity}}$	Gauges how much income is earned with the money invested by common shareholders
11. Earnings per share of common stock	$\frac{\text{Net income} - \text{Preferred dividends}}{\text{Average number of common shares outstanding}}$	Gives the amount of net income earned for each share of the company's common stock
Analyzing shares as an investment:		
12. Price/earnings ratio	$\frac{\text{Market price per share of common stock}}{\text{Earnings per share}}$	Indicates the market price of $1 of earnings
13. Dividend yield	$\frac{\text{Dividend per share of common (or preferred) stock}}{\text{Market price per share of common (or preferred) stock}}$	Shows the percentage of a share's market price returned as dividends to shareholders each period
14. Book value per share of common stock	$\frac{\text{Total shareholders' equity} - \text{Preferred equity}}{\text{Number of common shares outstanding}}$	Indicates the recorded accounting amount for each share of common stock outstanding

Learning Objective ⑤: **Compute and use financial ratios in decision making**

Ratios studied in this chapter included the ability to pay current liabilities; ability to sell inventory and collect receivables; ability to pay long-term debt; profitability; and analysis of shares as an investment. Ratios are a major tool of financial analysis and should be considered as only one source of information when analyzing a company.

END-OF-CHAPTER SUMMARY PROBLEM

MyAccountingLab

The following financial data are adapted from the financial statements of Keppel Inc.

Keppel Inc.
Four-Years' Selected Financial Data
For the Years Ended June 30

	2010**	2009	2008	2007
Operating Results*				
Sales	$6,550	$3,043	$4,048	$3,586
Cost of goods sold	4,913	2,344	3,107	2,761
Income from operations	254	208	260	225
Interest expense	42	12	25	16
Net income	179	133	164	140
Cash dividends	22	20	27	21
Financial Position				
Inventory	$ 904	$ 392	$ 491	$ 515
Total assets	$2,440	$1,344	$1,724	$1,662
Current ratio	1.90	2.01	1.88	2.02
Shareholders' equity	$1,080	$ 853	$1,020	$ 946
Average number of common shares outstanding (in thousands)	244	227	226	225

*Dollar amounts are in thousands.
**Keppel Inc. purchased all the shares of a competitor, Bognor Ltd., in November 2009.

Name: Keppel Inc.
Fiscal Period: Years ended June 30, 2007 to 2010.

Required

Compute the following ratios for 2008 through 2010, and evaluate Keppel Inc.'s operating results. Are operating results strong or weak? Did they improve or deteriorate during the four-year period? Your analysis will reveal a clear trend.

1. Return on sales
2. Earnings per share
3. Inventory turnover
4. Times-interest-earned ratio
5. Return on shareholders' equity

Answer

Remember to use the previous year's inventory balance when calculating average inventory in the inventory turnover ratio. Use the previous year's shareholders' equity when calculating average shareholders' equity in the rate of return on shareholders' equity.

	2010	2009	2008
1. Return on sales	$\frac{\$179}{\$6{,}550} = 0.027$	$\frac{\$133}{\$3{,}043} = 0.044$	$\frac{\$164}{\$4{,}048} = 0.041$
2. Earnings per share	$\frac{\$179}{244} = \$0.73$	$\frac{\$133}{227} = \$0.59$	$\frac{\$164}{226} = \$0.73$
3. Inventory turnover	$\frac{\$4{,}913}{(\$904 + \$392)/2} = 7.58$ times	$\frac{\$2{,}344}{(\$392 + \$491)/2} = 5.31$ times	$\frac{\$3{,}107}{(\$491 + \$515)/2} = 6.18$ times
4. Times-interest-earned ratio	$\frac{\$254}{\$42} = 6.05$ times	$\frac{\$208}{\$12} = 17.33$ times	$\frac{\$260}{\$25} = 10.4$ times
5. Return on shareholders' equity	$\frac{\$179}{(\$1{,}080 + \$853)/2} = 0.185$	$\frac{\$133}{(\$853 + \$1{,}020)/2} = 0.142$	$\frac{\$164}{(\$1{,}020 + \$946)/2} = 0.167$

For the five ratios calculated, the higher the ratio, the better. Ratios that increase each year are a positive trend and indicate good news. Remember to evaluate all ratios along with other information about the company. One ratio will not tell the complete story.

Evaluation:

The first thing to notice is that Keppel Inc.'s total assets and inventory almost doubled from 2009 to 2010. A review of Keppel's financial statements reveals that the purchase of Bognor Ltd. was for cash and that the financial statements of the competitor were consolidated with those of Keppel effective the date of acquisition. Keppel borrowed the funds to pay for the acquisition which resulted in a significant increase in interest expense.

The analysis shows that Keppel Inc. continues to perform well. Ratio 1 improved from 2008 to 2009 but declined in 2010 probably as a result of the consolidation. Ratio 2 improved to the 2008 level. Ratio 3 declined in 2009 but improved in 2010. Even though inventory doubled from 2009 to 2010, it sold more quickly in 2010. Ratio 4 declined because of the increased debt taken on to finance the purchase. Ratio 5 improved from 2009 suggesting the acquisition of Bognor will provide enhanced value for shareholders in the future.

Review Financial Statement Analysis

Quick Check (Answers are given on page 721.)

Analyze the Donaldson Limited financial statements by answering the questions that follow. Donaldson owns a chain of restaurants.

Donaldson Limited
Consolidated Statement of Income (Adapted)
For the Years Ended December 31, 2011, 2010, and 2009

in millions, except per share data	2011	2010	2009
Revenues			
Sales by company-operated restaurants	$12,795.4	$11,499.6	$11,040.7
Revenues from franchised and affiliated restaurants	4,345.1	3,906.1	3,829.3
Total revenues	17,140.5	15,405.7	14,870.0
Operating Expenses			
Company-operated restaurant expenses			
Food & paper (Cost of goods sold)	4,314.8	3,917.4	3,802.1
Payroll & employee benefits	3,411.4	3,078.2	2,901.2
Occupancy & other operating expenses	3,279.8	2,911.0	2,750.4
Franchised restaurants—occupancy expenses	937.7	840.1	800.2
Selling, general & administrative expenses	1,833.0	1,712.8	1,661.7
Other operating expense, net	531.6	833.3	257.4
Total operating expenses	14,308.3	13,292.8	12,173.0
Operating income	2,832.2	2,112.9	2,697.0
Interest expense	388.0	374.1	452.4
Gain on sale of subsidiary	—	—	(137.1)
Non-operating expense, net	97.8	76.7	52.0
Income before income taxes and cumulative effect of accounting changes	2,346.4	1,662.1	2,329.7
Income tax expense	838.2	670.0	693.1
Income before cumulative effect of accounting changes	1,508.2	992.1	1,636.6
Cumulative effect of accounting changes, net of tax benefits of $9.4 and $17.6	(36.8)	(98.6)	—
Net income	$ 1,471.4	$ 893.5	$ 1,636.6
Per common share—basic:			
Income before cumulative effect of accounting changes	$ 1.19	$ 0.78	$ 1.27
Cumulative effect of accounting changes	(0.03)	(0.08)	
Net income	$ 1.16	$ 0.70	$ 1.27
Dividends per common share	$ 0.40	$ 0.24	$ 0.23

Donaldson Limited
Consolidated Balance Sheet
For the Years Ended December 31, 2011 and 2010

in millions, except per share data	**2011**	**2010**
Assets		
Current assets		
Cash and equivalents	$ 492.8	$ 330.4
Accounts and notes receivable	734.5	855.3
Inventories, at cost	129.4	111.7
Prepaid expenses and other current assets	528.7	418.0
Total current assets	1,885.4	1,715.4
Other assets		
Investments in affiliates	1,089.6	1,037.7
Goodwill, net	1,665.1	1,558.5
Miscellaneous	960.3	1,075.5
Total other assets	3,715.0	3,671.7
Property and equipment		
Property and equipment, at cost	28,740.2	26,218.6
Accumulated depreciation	(8,815.5)	(7,635.2)
Net property and equipment	19,924.7	18,583.4
Total assets	$25,525.1	$23,970.5
Liabilities and Shareholders' Equity		
Current liabilities		
Accounts payable	$ 577.4	$ 635.8
Income taxes	71.5	16.3
Other taxes	222.0	191.8
Accrued interest	193.1	199.4
Accrued restructuring and restaurant closing costs	115.7	328.5
Accrued payroll and other liabilities	918.1	774.7
Current maturities of long-term debt	388.0	275.8
Total current liabilities	2,485.8	2,422.3
Long-term debt	9,342.5	9,703.6
Other long-term liabilities and minority interests	699.8	560.0
Deferred income taxes	1,015.1	1,003.7
Total liabilities	13,543.2	13,689.6
Shareholders' equity		
Preferred shares authorized—165.0 million shares; issued—none		
Common shares authorized—3.5 billion shares; issued—1,261.9 million shares	1,854.1	1,763.9
Retained earnings	10,763.3	10,118.3
Accumulated other comprehensive income (loss)	(635.5)	(1,601.3)
Total shareholders' equity	11,981.9	10,280.9
Total liabilities and shareholders' equity	$25,525.1	$23,970.5

1. The trend precentage for selling, general and administrative expenses using 2010 as the base year for Donaldson is
   a. 1.14
   b. 1.10
   c. 1.07
   d. None of the above ($________)
2. Vertical analysis of Donaldson's income statement for 2010 would show which of the following for selling, general, and administrative expenses?
   a. 1.144
   b. 0.143
   c. 0.107
   d. None of the above ($________)

3. Which item on Donaldson's income statement has the most favourable trend during 2009–2011?
   a. Total revenues
   b. Net income
   c. Food & paper costs
   d. Payroll & employee benefits
4. On Donaldson's common-size balance sheet for 2011, goodwill would appear as
   a. 0.065
   b. Up by 6.8%
   c. $1,665.1 million
   d. 9.7% of total revenues
5. A good benchmark for Donaldson Limited would be
   a. Whataburger
   b. Boeing
   c. Intel
   d. All of the above
6. Donaldson's inventory turnover for 2011 was
   a. 91 times
   b. 62 times
   c. 21 times
   d. 36 times
7. Donaldson's acid-test ratio at the end of 2011 was
   a. 1.49
   b. 0.49
   c. 0.30
   d. 0.20
8. Donaldson's average collection period for accounts and notes receivables for 2011 is
   a. 1 day
   b. 2 days
   c. 30 days
   d. 17 days
9. Donaldson's total debt position looks
   a. Safe
   b. Middle-ground
   c. Risky
   d. Cannot tell from the financials
10. Donaldson's return on sales for 2011 was
    a. 13.2%
    b. $1.16
    c. 5.9%
    d. 8.6%
11. Donaldson's return on shareholders' equity for 2011 was
    a. 13.2%
    b. 8.6%
    c. 5.9%
    d. $1,471.4 million
12. On June 30, 2011, Donaldson's common shares sold for $26 per share. At that price, how much did investors say $1 of the company's net income was worth?
    a. $1.00
    b. $22.41
    c. $21.85
    d. $26.00
13. Use Donaldson's financial statements and the data in Question 12 to compute Donaldson's dividend yield during 2011.
    a. 3.1%
    b. 2.4%
    c. 2.2%
    d. 1.5%

Accounting Vocabulary

benchmarking The comparison of a company to a standard set by other companies, with a view toward improvement. (p. 674)

common-size statement A financial statement that reports only percentages (no dollar amounts). (p. 672)

dividend yield Ratio of dividends per share to the stock's market price per share. Tells the percentage of a share's market value that the company returns to shareholders as dividends. (p. 689)

efficient capital market A capital market in which market prices fully reflect all information available to the public. (p. 691)

horizontal analysis Study of percentage changes in comparative financial statements. (p. 668)

price/earnings ratio Ratio of the market price of a common share to the company's earnings per share. Measures the value that the stock market places on $1 of a company's earnings. (p. 689)

return on assets Net income plus interest expense, divided by average total assets. Measures a company's success in using assets to earn income for persons who fincance the business. (p. 687)

return on equity Net income minus preferred dividends, divided by average common shareholders' equity. A measure of profitability (p. 687)

return on net sales Ratio of net income to net sales. A measure of profitability. Also called *return on sales*. (p. 686)

trend percentages A form of horizontal analysis that indicates the direction a business is taking. (p. 670)

vertical analysis Analysis of a financial statement that reveals the relationship of each statement item to a specified base, which is the 100% figure. (p. 671)

working capital Current assets minus current liabilities; measures a business's ability to meet its short-term obligations with its current assets. (p. 679)

Assess Your Progress

Make the grade with MyAccountingLab: The exercises and problems in this chapter can be found on MyAccountingLab at www.myaccountinglab.com. You can practise them as often as you want, and they feature step-by-step guided solutions to help you find the right answer.

Short Exercises

Learning Objective 1
Horizontal analysis of revenues and net income

S13-1 Cannes Corporation reported the following amounts on its 2011 comparative income statement.

(in thousands)	2011	2010	2009
Revenues	$10,889	$10,095	$9,777
Total expenses	5,985	5,604	5,194

Perform a horizontal analysis of revenues and net income—both in dollar amounts and in percentages—for 2011 and 2010.

Learning Objective 1
Trend analysis of sales and net income

S13-2 Zoobilee Inc. reported the following sales and net income amounts:

(in thousands)	2011	2010	2009	2008
Sales	$9,180	$8,990	$8,770	$8,550
Net income	520	500	460	400

Show Zoobilee's trend percentages for sales and net income. Use 2008 as the base year.

Learning Objective 2
Vertical analysis to correct a cash shortage

S13-3 Vision Software Limited reported the following amounts on its balance sheets at December 31, 2011, 2010, and 2009.

	2011	2010	2009
Cash	$ 6,000	$ 6,000	$ 5,000
Receivables, net	30,000	22,000	19,000
Inventory	148,000	106,000	74,000
Prepaid expenses	2,000	2,000	1,000
Property, plant, and equipment, net	96,000	88,000	87,000
Total assets	$282,000	$224,000	$186,000

Sales and profits are high. Nevertheless, Vision is experiencing a cash shortage. Perform a vertical analysis of Vision Software's assets at the end of years 2011, 2010, and 2009. Use the analysis to explain the reason for the cash shortage.

Learning Objective 3
Common-size income statements of two companies

S13-4 Porterfield Inc. and Beasley Ltd. are competitors. Compare the two companies by converting their condensed income statements to common size.

(in millions)	Porterfield	Beasley
Net sales	$9,489	$19,536
Cost of goods sold	5,785	14,101
Selling and administrative expenses	2,690	3,846
Interest expense	59	16
Other expense	34	38
Income tax expense	331	597
Net income	$ 590	$ 938

Which company earned more net income? Which company's net income was a higher percentage of its net sales? Which company is more profitable? Explain your answer.

Learning Objective 5
Evaluating the trend in a company's current ratio

S13-5 Examine the financial data of RubberMate Corporation in Exhibit 13-8, page 678. Show how to compute RubberMate's current ratio for each year from 2008 through 2010. Is the company's ability to pay its current liabilities improving or deteriorating?

Learning Objective 5
Evaluating a company's acid-test ratio

S13-6 Use the Metro Inc. balance sheet data in Exhibit 13-3, page 670.

1. Compute Metro's acid-test ratio at September 26, 2009, and September 27, 2008.
2. Compare Metro's ratio values to those of Enbridge, Research In Motion, and Loblaw on page 682. Is Metro's acid-test ratio strong or weak? Explain.

Learning Objective 5
Computing inventory turnover and days' sales in receivables

S13-7 Use Metro Inc.'s 2009 income statement and balance sheet to compute the following:

a. Metro's inventory turnover for 2009. Assume 60% cost of sales.
b. Days' sales in receivables during 2009. (Round dollar amounts to one decimal place.)

Do these measures look strong or weak? Give the reason for your answer.

Learning Objective 5
Measuring ability to pay long-term debt

S13-8 Use the financial statements of Metro Inc.

1. Compute the company's debt ratio at September 26, 2009. In which text exhibit does this ratio value appear?
2. Compute the company's times-interest-earned ratio for 2009. Financial costs represent interest expense.
3. Is Metro's ability to pay liabilities and interest expense strong or weak? Comment on the value of each ratio computed for Requirements 1 and 2.

Learning Objective 5
Measuring profitability

S13-9 Use the financial statements of Metro Inc. to locate or, if necessary, to compute these profitability measures for 2009. Show each computation.

a. Return on sales.
b. Return on total assets
c. Return on equity

Are these rates of return strong or weak? Explain.

Learning Objective 5
Computing EPS and the price/earnings ratio

S13-10 The annual report of Classic Cars Inc. for the year ended December 31, 2011, included the following items (in thousands):

Preferred shares outstanding, $4,5,000 issued	$500
Net income	$990
Number of common shares outstanding	200

1. Compute earnings per share (EPS) and the price/earnings ratio for Classic Cars' common shares. Round to the nearest cent. The price of a common share of Classic Cars is $77.60.
2. How much does the stock market say $1 of Classic Cars' net income is worth?

Learning Objective 5
Using ratio data to reconstruct an income statement

S13-11 A skeleton of Hill Country Florist Limited's income statement appears as follows (amounts in thousands):

Income Statement	
Net sales	$7,278
Cost of goods sold	(a)
Selling expenses	1,510
Administrative expenses	351
Interest expense	(b)
Other expenses	126
Income before taxes	1,042
Income tax expense	(c)
Net income	$ (d)

Use the following ratio data to complete Hill Country Florist's income statement:

a. Inventory turnover was 5 (beginning inventory was $775, ending inventory was $767).
b. Return on sales is 0.12.

Learning Objective 5
Using ratio data to reconstruct a balance sheet

S13-12 A skeleton of Hill Country Florist Limited's balance sheet appears as follows (amounts in thousands):

Balance Sheet			
Cash	$ 253	Total current liabilities	$1,164
Receivables	(a)	Long-term debt	(e)
Inventories	555	Other long-term liabilities	826
Prepaid expenses	(b)		
Total current assets	(c)		
Property, plant, and equipment, net	(d)	Common shares	185
		Retained earnings	2,846
Other assets	1,150	Total liabilities and	
Total assets	$6,315	shareholders' equity	$ (f)

Use the following ratio data to complete Hill Country Florist's balance sheet:

a. Debt ratio is 0.52.
b. Current ratio is 1.20.
c. Acid-test ratio is 0.70.

Exercises

Learning Objective 1
Computing year-to-year changes in working capital

E13-13 What were the dollar amount of change and the percentage of each change in Rocky Mountain Lodge Limited's working capital during 2011 and 2010? Is this trend favourable or unfavourable?

	2011	2010	2009
Total current assets	$326,000	$290,000	$280,000
Total current liabilities	170,000	167,000	150,000

E13-14 Prepare a horizontal analysis of the comparative income statement of Stamps Music Ltd. Round percentage changes to the nearest one-tenth percent (three decimal places).

Learning Objective 1
Horizontal analysis of an income statement

Stamps Music Ltd.
Comparative Income Statement
For the Years Ended December 31, 2011 and 2010

	2011	2010
Total revenue	$403,000	$430,000
Expenses:		
Cost of goods sold	$188,000	$202,000
Selling and general expenses	93,000	90,000
Interest expense	4,000	10,000
Income tax expense	37,000	42,000
Total expenses	322,000	344,000
Net income	$ 81,000	$ 86,000

E13-15 Compute trend percentages for Carmel Valley Sales & Service Ltd. total revenue and net income for the following five-year period, using year 0 as the base year. Round to the nearest full percent.

Learning Objective 1
Computing trend percentages

(In thousands)	Year 4	Year 3	Year 2	Year 1	Year 0
Total revenue	$1,418	$1,287	$1,106	$1,009	$1,043
Net income	125	104	93	81	85

Which grew faster during the period, total revenue or net income?

E13-16 Cobra Golf Limited has requested that you perform a vertical analysis of its balance sheet to determine the component percentages of its assets, liabilities, and shareholders' equity.

Learning Objective 2
Vertical analysis of a balance sheet

Cobra Golf Limited
Balance Sheet
December 31, 2011

Assets	
Total current assets	$ 92,000
Property, plant, and equipment, net	247,000
Other assets	35,000
Total assets	$374,000
Liabilities	
Total current liabilities	$ 48,000
Long-term debt	108,000
Total liabilities	156,000
Shareholders' Equity	
Total shareholders' equity	218,000
Total liabilities and shareholders' equity	$374,000

E13-17 Prepare a comparative common-size income statement for Stamps Music Ltd. using the 2011 and 2010 data of Exercise 13-14 and rounding percentages to one-tenth percent (three decimal places).

Learning Objective 3
Preparing a common-size income statement

Learning Objective 4
Analyzing the statement of cash flows

E13-18 Identify any weaknesses revealed by the statement of cash flows of Holland Marsh Farms Limited.

Holland Marsh Farms Limited
Statement of Cash Flows
For the Current Year

Operating activities:		
Income from operations		$ 42,000
Add (subtract) noncash items:		
Depreciation	$ 23,000	
Net increase in current assets other than cash	(45,000)	
Net decrease in current liabilities exclusive of short-term debt	(7,000)	(29,000)
Net cash provided by operating activities		13,000
Investing activities:		
Sale of property, plant, and equipment		101,000
Financing activities:		
Issuance of bonds payable	$ 102,000	
Payment of short-term debt	(159,000)	
Payment of long-term debt	(79,000)	
Payment of dividends	(42,000)	
Net cash used for financing activities		(178,000)
Increase (decrease) in cash		$ (64,000)

Learning Objective 5
Computing five ratios

E13-19 The financial statements of National News Inc. include the following items:

	Current Year	Preceding Year
Balance Sheet:		
Cash	$ 17,000	$ 22,000
Short-term investments	11,000	26,000
Net receivables	64,000	73,000
Inventory	77,000	71,000
Prepaid expenses	16,000	8,000
Total current assets	$185,000	$200,000
Total current liabilities	$111,000	$ 91,000
Income Statement:		
Net credit sales	$654,000	
Cost of goods sold	327,000	

Required

Compute the following ratios for the current year:

a. Current ratio
b. Acid-test ratio
c. Inventory turnover
d. Accounts receivable turnover
e. Days' sales in receivables

Learning Objective 5
Analyzing the ability to pay current liabilities

E13-20 Patio Furniture Inc. has asked you to determine whether the company's ability to pay its current liabilities and long-term debts improved or deteriorated during 2011. To answer this question, compute the following ratios for 2011 and 2010.

a. Current ratio
b. Acid-test ratio
c. Debt ratio
d. Times-interest-earned ratio

Summarize the results of your analysis in a written report.

	2011	2010
Cash	$ 61,000	$ 47,000
Short-term investments	28,000	—
Net receivables	142,000	116,000
Inventory	286,000	263,000
Prepaid expenses	11,000	9,000
Total assets	643,000	489,000
Total current liabilities	255,000	221,000
Long-term debt	46,000	52,000
Income from operations	165,000	158,000
Interest expense	40,000	39,000

Learning Objective 5
Analyzing profitability

E13-21 Compute four ratios that measure ability to earn profits for PGI Decor Inc., whose comparative income statement follows:

PGI Decor Inc.
Comparative Income Statement
For the Years Ended December 31, 2011 and 2010

in thousands	**2011**	**2010**
Net sales	$174,000	$158,000
Cost of goods sold	93,000	86,000
Gross profit	81,000	72,000
Selling and general expenses	46,000	41,000
Income from operations	35,000	31,000
Interest expense	9,000	10,000
Income before income tax	26,000	21,000
Income tax expense	9,000	8,000
Net income	$ 17,000	$ 13,000

Additional data:

	2011	2010	2009
Total assets	$204,000	$191,000	$171,000
Common shareholders' equity	$ 96,000	$ 89,000	$ 79,000
Preferred dividends	$ 3,000	$ 3,000	$ 0
Common shares outstanding during the year	21,000	20,000	18,000

Did the company's operating performance improve or deteriorate during 2011?

Learning Objective 5
Evaluating shares as an investment

E13-22 Evaluate the common shares of Phillips Distributing Limited as an investment. Specifically, use the three share ratios to determine whether the common shares increased or decreased in attractiveness during the past year.

	2011	2010
Net income	$112,000	$ 96,000
Common share dividends	25,000	20,000
Total shareholders' equity at year-end		
(includes 80,000 common shares)	580,000	500,000
Preferred shares, $8, 1,000 shares issued	100,000	100,000
Market price per common share at year-end	$ 22.50	$ 16.75

Challenge Exercises

Learning Objective 2 3 5
Using ratio data to reconstruct a company's balance sheet

E13-23 The following data (dollar amounts in millions) are taken from the financial statements of Phase 1 Industries Inc.

Total liabilities	$11,800
Preferred shares	$ 0
Total current assets	$10,200
Accumulated depreciation	$ 1,400
Debt ratio	59%
Current ratio	1.50

Required

Complete the following condensed balance sheet. Report amounts to the nearest million dollars.

Current assets		$?
Property, plant, and equipment	$?	
Less accumulated depreciation	(?)	?
Total assets		$?
Current liabilities		$?
Long-term liabilities		?
Shareholders' equity		?
Total liabilities and shareholders' equity		$?

Learning Objective 2 3 5
Using ratio data to reconstruct a company's income statement

E13-24 The following data (dollar amounts in millions) are from the financial statements of Provincial Industry Limited.

Average shareholders' equity	$3,600
Interest expense	$ 400
Preferred shares	$ 0
Operating income as a percent of sales	25%
Return on equity	20%
Income tax rate	40%

Required

Complete the following condensed income statement. Report amounts to the nearest million dollars.

Sales	$?
Operating expense	?
Operating income	?
Interest expense	?
Pretax income	?
Income tax expense	?
Net income	$?

Quiz

Test your understanding of financial statement analysis by answering the following questions. Select the best choice from among the possible answers given. Use the Canada Technology Corporation (CTC) financial statements to answer the questions that follow.

Canada Technology Corporation
Consolidated Statements of Financial Position
(In millions)

	December 31, 2011	December 31, 2010
Assets		
Current assets:		
Cash and cash equivalents	$ 4,317	$ 4,232
Short-term investments	835	406
Accounts receivable, net	3,635	2,586
Inventories	327	306
Other	1,519	1,394
Total current assets	10,633	8,924
Property, plant, and equipment, net	1,517	913
Investments	6,770	5,267
Other noncurrent assets	391	366
Total assets	$19,311	$15,470
Liabilities and Shareholders' Equity		
Current liabilities:		
Accounts payable	$ 7,316	$ 5,989
Accrued and other	3,580	2,944
Total current liabilities	10,896	8,933
Long-term debt	505	506
Other noncurrent liabilities	1,630	1,158
Commitments and contingent liabilities	—	—
Total liabilities	13,031	10,597
Shareholders' equity:		
Preferred shares; shares issued: 0	—	—
Common shares; shares authorized: 7,000; shares issued; 2,556 and 2,579 respectively	284	1,479
Retained earnings	6,131	3,486
Other comprehensive loss	(83)	(33)
Other	(52)	(59)
Total shareholders' equity	6,280	4,873
Total liabilities and shareholders' equity	$19,311	$15,470

Canada Technology Corporation
Consolidated Statements of Income
(in millions, except per share amounts)

	Years Ended December 31,		
	2011	**2010**	**2009**
Net revenue	$41,444	$35,404	$31,168
Cost of goods sold	33,892	29,055	25,661
Gross profit	7,552	6,349	5,507
Operating expenses:			
Selling, general, and administrative	3,544	3,050	2,784
Research, development, and engineering	464	455	452
Special charges	—	—	482
Total operating expenses	4,008	3,505	3,718
Operating income	3,544	2,844	1,789
Investment and other income (loss), net	180	183	(58)
Income before income taxes	3,724	3,027	1,731
Income tax expense	1,079	905	485
Net income	$ 2,645	$ 2,122	$ 1,246
Earnings per common share:			
Basic	$ 1.03	$ 0.82	$ 0.48

Q13-25 During 2011, CTC's total assets
a. Increased by $8,341 million
b. Increased by 24.8%
c. Both a and b
d. Increased by 19.9%

Q13-26 CTC's current ratio at year-end 2011 is closest to
a. 1.2
b. 1.1
c. 1.0
d. 0.8

Q13-27 CTC's acid-test ratio at year-end 2011 is closest to
a. 0.80
b. 0.65
c. 0.47
d. $8,787 million

Q13-28 What is the largest single item included in CTC's debt ratio at December 31, 2011?
a. Cash and cash equivalents
b. Accounts payable
c. Investments
d. Common shares

Q13-29 Using the earliest year available as the base year, the trend percentage for CTC's net revenue during 2011 was
a. 117%
b. Up by $10,276 million
c. Up by 17.1%
d. 133%

Q13-30 CTC's common-size income statement for 2011 would report cost of goods sold as
a. $33,892 million
b. Up by 16.6%
c. 81.8%
d. 132.1%

Q13-31 CTC's days' sales in receivables during 2011 was
a. 22 days
b. 27 days
c. 32 days
d. 114 days

Q13-32 CTC's inventory turnover during fiscal year 2011 was
a. Very slow
b. 54 times
c. 107 times
d. 129 times

Q13-33 CTC's long-term debt bears interest at 6%. During the year ended December 31, 2011, CTC's times-interest-earned ratio was

a. 117 times
b. 110 times
c. 100 times
d. 125 times

Q13-34 CTC's trend of return on sales is

a. Improving
b. Declining
c. Stuck at 6%
d. Worrisome

Q13-35 How many common shares did CTC have outstanding, on average, during 2011? Hint: Use the earnings per share formula.

a. 2,721 million
b. 2,701 million
c. 2,645 million
d. 2,568 million

Q13-36 Book value per common share of CTC outstanding at December 31, 2011, was

a. $2.72
b. $4.37
c. $6,280
d. $2.46

Problems

(Group A)

P13-37A Net sales, net income, and total assets for Smart Pak Inc. for a five-year period follow:

Learning Objective 1 5
Trend percentages, return on sales, and comparison with the industry

(In thousands)	2011	2010	2009	2008	2007
Net sales	$367	$313	$266	$281	$197
Net income	37	21	11	18	16
Total assets	286	254	209	197	185

Required

1. Compute trend percentages for each item for 2008 through 2011. Use 2007 as the base year and round to the nearest percent.
2. Compute the return on net sales for 2009 through 2011, rounding to three decimal places.
3. How does Smart Pak's return on net sales compare with that of the industry? In the packaging industry, rates above 8% are considered good, and rates above 10% are outstanding.

P13-38A Top managers of Medical Products Inc. have asked for your help in comparing the company's profit performance and financial position with the average for the industry. The accountant has given you the company's income statement and balance sheet and also the following data for the industry:

Learning Objective 5
Evaluating a stock as an investment

Medical Products Inc.
Income Statement Compared with Industry Average
For the Year Ended December 31, 2011

	Medical Products	Industry Average
Net sales	$957,000	100.0%
Cost of goods sold	652,000	55.9
Gross profit	305,000	44.1
Operating expenses	200,000	28.1
Operating income	105,000	16.0
Other expenses	3,000	2.4
Net income	$102,000	13.6%

Medical Products Inc.
Balance Sheet Compared with Industry Average
December 31, 2011

	Medical Products	Industry Average
Current assets	$486,000	74.4%
Fixed assets, net	117,000	20.0
Intangible assets, net	24,000	0.6
Other assets	3,000	5.0
Total	$630,000	100.0%
Current liabilities	$245,000	45.6%
Long-term liabilities	114,000	19.0
Shareholders' equity	271,000	35.4
Total	$630,000	100.0%

Required

1. Prepare a common-size income statement and balance sheet for Medical Products. The first column of each statement should present Medical Products' common-size statement, and the second column should show the industry averages.
2. For the profitability analysis, compute Medical Products' (a) ratio of gross profit to net sales, (b) ratio of operating income to net sales, and (c) ratio of net income to net sales. Compare these figures with the industry average. Is Medical Products' profit performance better or worse than the average for the industry?
3. For the analysis of financial position, compute Medical Products' (a) ratios of current assets and current liabilities to total assets and (b) ratio of shareholders' equity to total assets. Compare these ratios with the industry averages. Is Medical Products' financial position better or worse than the average for the industry?

Learning Objective 4
Using the statement of cash flows for decision making

P13-39A You are evaluating two companies as possible investments. The two companies, similar in size, are commuter airlines that fly passengers up and down the West Coast. All other available information has been analyzed and your investment decision depends on the statement of cash flows.

Commonwealth Airlines (Comair) Limited
Statement of Cash Flows
For the Years Ended November 30, 2011 and 2010

	2011		2010	
Operating activities:				
Net income (net loss)		$(67,000)		$154,000
Adjustments for noncash items:				
Total		84,000		(23,000)
Net cash provided by operating activities		17,000		131,000
Investing activities:				
Purchase of property, plant, and equipment	$ (50,000)		$(91,000)	
Sale of long-term investments	52,000		4,000	
Net cash provided by (used for) investing activities		2,000		(87,000)
Financing activities:				
Issuance of short-term notes payable	122,000		143,000	
Payment of short-term notes payable	(179,000)		(134,000)	
Payment of cash dividends	(45,000)		(64,000)	
Net cash used for financing activities		(102,000)		(55,000)
Increase (decrease) in cash		(83,000)		(11,000)
Cash balance at beginning of year		92,000		103,000
Cash balance at the end of year		$ 9,000		$ 92,000

Jetway Inc.
Statement of Cash Flows
For the Years Ended November 30, 2011 and 2010

	2011		2010	
Operating activities:				
Net income		$184,000		$ 131,000
Adjustments for noncash items:				
Total		64,000		62,000
Net cash provided by operating activities		248,000		193,000
Investing activities:				
Purchase of property, plant, and equipment	$(303,000)		$(453,000)	
Sale of property, plant, and equipment	46,000		72,000	
Net cash used for investing activities		(257,000)		(381,000)
Financing activities:				
Issuance of long-term notes payable	174,000		118,000	
Payment of short-term notes payable	(66,000)		(18,000)	
Net cash provided by financing activities		108,000		100,000
Increase (decrease) in cash		99,000		(88,000)
Cash balance at beginning of year		116,000		204,000
Cash balance at end of year		$215,000		$ 116,000

Required
Discuss the relative strengths and weaknesses of Comair and Jetway. Conclude your discussion by recommending one of the companies' shares as an investment.

P13-40A Financial statement data of Metro Engineering Limited include the following items:

Learning Objective 5
Effects of business transactions on selected ratios

Cash	$ 47,000	Accounts payable	$142,000
Short-term investments	21,000	Accrued liabilities	50,000
Accounts receivable, net	102,000	Long-term notes payable	146,000
Inventories	274,000	Other long-term liabilities	78,000
Prepaid expenses	15,000	Net income	104,000
Total assets	933,000	Number of common shares	
Short-term notes payable	72,000	outstanding	22,000

Required
1. Compute Metro's current ratio, debt ratio, and earnings per share. Use the following format for your answer. (Use dollar and share amounts in thousands except for EPS.)

Requirement 1		
Current ratio	**Debt ratio**	**Earnings per share**

2. Compute the three ratios after evaluating the effect of each transaction that follows. Consider each transaction *separately*.
   a. Borrowed $27,000 on a long-term note payable
   b. Issued 10,000 common shares, receiving cash of $108,000
   c. Paid short-term notes payable, $51,000
   d. Purchased merchandise of $48,000 on account, debiting Inventory
   e. Received cash on account, $6,000

Format your answer as follows:

Requirement 2			
Transaction (letter)	**Current ratio**	**Debt ratio**	**Earnings per share**

Learning Objective 5
Using ratios to evaluate a share investment

P13-41A Comparative financial statement data of Crest Optical Inc. follow:

Crest Optical Inc.
Comparative Income Statement
For the Years Ended December 31, 2011 and 2010

	2011	**2010**
Net sales	$667,000	$599,000
Cost of goods sold	378,000	313,000
Gross profit	289,000	286,000
Operating expenses	129,000	147,000
Income from operations	160,000	139,000
Interest expense	37,000	41,000
Income before income tax	123,000	98,000
Income tax expense	44,000	43,000
Net income	$ 79,000	$ 55,000

Crest Optical Inc.
Comparative Balance Sheet
December 31, 2011 and 2010

	2011	**2010**	**2009***
Current assets:			
Cash	$ 37,000	$ 40,000	
Current receivables, net	208,000	151,000	$138,000
Inventories	152,000	186,000	144,000
Prepaid expenses	5,000	20,000	
Total current assets	402,000	397,000	
Property, plant, and equipment, net	287,000	256,000	
Total assets	$689,000	$653,000	607,000
Total current liabilities	$286,000	$217,000	
Long-term liabilities	145,000	185,000	
Total liabilities	431,000	402,000	
Preferred shareholders' equity, $4	50,000	50,000	
Common shareholders' equity	208,000	201,000	198,000
Total liabilities and shareholders' equity	$689,000	$653,000	

*Selected 2009 amounts.

Other information:

1. Market price of Crest common shares: $61 at December 31, 2011, and $45.50 at December 31, 2010
2. Common shares outstanding: 15,000 during 2011 and 14,000 during 2010
3. Preferred shares outstanding: 500 during 2011 and 2010
4. All sales on credit

Required

1. Compute the following ratios for 2011 and 2010:
   a. Current ratio
   b. Inventory turnover
   c. Times-interest-earned ratio
   d. Return on assets
   e. Return on equity
   f. Earnings per share
   g. Price/earnings ratio
2. Decide (a) whether Crest's financial position improved or deteriorated during 2011 and (b) whether the investment attractiveness of Crest's common shares appears to have increased or decreased.
3. How will what you learned in this problem help you evaluate an investment?

Learning Objective 5
Using ratios to decide between two share investments

P13-42A Assume that you are considering purchasing shares as an investment. You have narrowed the choice to two Internet firms, Video.com Inc. and On-Line Express Ltd., and have assembled the following data.

Selected income statement data for current year:

	Video	Express
Net sales (all on credit)	$603,000	$519,000
Cost of goods sold	454,000	387,000
Income from operations	93,000	72,000
Interest expense	—	12,000
Net income	56,000	38,000

Selected balance sheet and market price data at *end* of current year:

	Video	Express
Current assets:		
Cash	$ 25,000	$ 39,000
Short-term investments	6,000	13,000
Current receivables, net	189,000	164,000
Inventories	211,000	183,000
Prepaid expenses	19,000	15,000
Total current assets	$450,000	$414,000
Total assets	$974,000	$938,000
Total current liabilities	366,000	338,000
Total liabilities	667,000*	691,000*
Preferred shares $4.00 (250 shares)		25,000
Common shares (150,000 shares)	150,000	
(20,000 shares)		100,000
Total shareholders' equity	307,000	247,000
Market price per common share	$ 9.00	$ 47.50

*Includes long-term debt; Video $-0-, and Express $350,000

Selected balance sheet data at *beginning* of current year:

	Video	Express
Current receivables, net	$142,000	$193,000
Inventories	209,000	197,000
Total assets	842,000	909,000
Long-term debt	—	303,000
Preferred shares, $4.00 (250 shares)		25,000
Common shares (150,000 shares)	150,000	
(20,000 shares)		100,000
Total shareholders' equity	263,000	215,000

Your strategy is to invest in companies that have low price/earnings ratios but appear to be in good shape financially. Assume that you have analyzed all other factors and that your decision depends on the results of ratio analysis.

Required

1. Compute the following ratios for both companies for the current year and decide which company's shares better fit your investment strategy based on the
   a. Acid-test ratio
   b. Inventory turnover
   c. Days' sales in receivables
   d. Debt ratio
   e. Times-interest-earned ratio
   f. Return on equity
   g. Earnings per share
   h. Price/earnings ratio

Learning Objective 5
Analyzing a company based on its ratios

P13-43A Take the role of an investment analyst at Merrill Lynch. It is your job to recommend investments for your client. The only information you have is the following ratio values for two companies in the direct mail industry.

Ratio	Fast Mail Ltd.	Message Direct Inc.
Days' sales in receivables	51	43
Inventory turnover	9	7
Gross profit percentage	62%	71%
Net income as a percent of sales	16%	14%
Times interest earned	12	18
Return on equity	29%	36%
Return on assets	19%	14%

Write a report to the Merrill Lynch investment committee. Recommend one company's shares over the other. State the reasons for your recommendation.

(Group B)

Learning Objective 1 5
Trend percentages, return on common equity, and comparison with the industry

P13-44B Net revenues, net income, and common shareholders' equity for Accenté Ltée for a five-year period follow.

(in thousands)	2011	2010	2009	2008	2007
Net revenues	$781	$714	$681	$662	$581
Net income	41	35	32	28	20
Ending common shareholders' equity	386	354	330	296	263

Required

1. Compute trend percentages for each item for 2008 through 2011. Use 2007 as the base year. Round to the nearest percent.
2. Compute the return on equity for 2009 through 2011, rounding to three decimal places. Accenté has no preferred shares outstanding.
3. In this industry, rates of return on equity of 13% are average, returns above 16% are good, and returns above 20% are outstanding. How does Accenté's return on equity compare with the industry?

Learning Objective ❷❸❺
Common-size statements, analysis of profitability, and comparison with the industry

P13-45B Pathfinder Inc. has asked you to compare the company's profit performance and financial position with the industry average. The proprietor has given you the company's income statement and balance sheet as well as the industry average data for retailers.

Pathfinder Inc.
Income Statement Compared with Industry Average
For the Year Ended December 31, 2011

	Pathfinder	Industry Average
Net sales	$700,000	100.0%
Cost of goods sold	497,000	65.8
Gross profit	203,000	34.2
Operating expenses	163,000	19.7
Operating income	40,000	14.5
Other expenses	3,000	0.4
Net income	$ 37,000	14.1%

Pathfinder Inc.
Balance Sheet Compared with Industry Average
December 31, 2011

	Pathfinder	Industry Average
Current assets	$300,000	70.9%
Fixed assets, net	74,000	23.6
Intangible assets, net	4,000	0.8
Other assets	22,000	4.7
Total	$400,000	100.0%
Current liabilities	$206,000	48.1%
Long-term liabilities	64,000	16.6
Shareholders' equity	130,000	35.3
Total	$400,000	100.0%

Required

1. Prepare a common-size income statement and a balance sheet for Pathfinder. The first column of each statement should present Pathfinder's common-size statement, and the second column, the industry averages.
2. For the profitability analysis, compute Pathfinder's (a) ratio of gross profit to net sales, (b) ratio of operating income to net sales, and (c) ratio of net income to net sales. Compare these figures with the industry averages. Is Pathfinder's profit performance better or worse than the industry average?
3. For the analysis of financial position, compute Pathfinder's (a) ratio of current assets to total assets, and (b) ratio of shareholders' equity to total assets. Compare these ratios with the industry averages. Is Pathfinder's financial position better or worse than the industry averages?

Learning Objective ❹
Using the statement of cash flows for decision making

P13-46B You have been asked to evaluate two companies as possible investments. The two companies, Norfolk Industries Inc. and Strafford Crystal Limited, are similar in size. Assume that all other available information has been analyzed, and the decision concerning which company's shares to purchase depends on their cash flow data.

Required

Discuss the relative strengths and weaknesses of each company. Conclude your discussion by recommending one company's shares as an investment.

Norfolk Industries Inc.
Statement of Cash Flows
For the Years Ended September 30, 2011 and 2010

	2011		2010	
Operating activities:				
Net income		$ 17,000		$ 44,000
Adjustments for noncash items:				
Total		(14,000)		(4,000)
Net cash provided by operating activities		3,000		40,000
Investing activities:				
Purchase of property, plant, and equipment	$ (13,000)		$ (3,000)	
Sale of property, plant, and equipment	86,000		79,000	
Net cash provided by investing activities		73,000		76,000
Financing activities:				
Issuance of short-term notes payable	43,000		19,000	
Payment of short-term notes payable	(101,000)		(108,000)	
Net cash used for financing activities		(58,000)		(89,000)
Increase in cash		18,000		27,000
Cash balance at beginning of year		31,000		4,000
Cash balance at end of year		$ 49,000		$ 31,000

Strafford Crystal Limited
Statement of Cash Flows
For the Years Ended September 30, 2011 and 2010

	2011		2010	
Operating activities:				
Net income		$ 89,000		$ 71,000
Adjustments for noncash items:				
Total		19,000		—
Net cash provided by operating activities		108,000		71,000
Investing activities:				
Purchase of property, plant, and equipment	$(121,000)		$(91,000)	
Net cash used for investing activities		(121,000)		(91,000)
Financing activities:				
Issuance of long-term notes payable	46,000		43,000	
Payment of short-term notes payable	(15,000)		(40,000)	
Payment of cash dividends	(12,000)		(9,000)	
Net cash provided by (used for) financing activities		19,000		(6,000)
Increase (decrease) in cash		6,000		(26,000)
Cash balance at beginning of year		54,000		80,000
Cash balance at end of year		$ 60,000		$ 54,000

Learning Objective 5
Effects of business transactions on selected ratios

P13-47B Financial statement data of HiFlite Electronics Limited include the following items (dollars in thousands):

Cash	$ 22,000
Short-term investments	39,000
Accounts receivable, net	83,000
Inventories	141,000
Prepaid expenses	8,000
Total assets	677,000
Short-term notes payable	49,000
Accounts payable	103,000
Accrued liabilities	38,000
Long-term notes payable	160,000
Other long-term liabilities	31,000
Net income	91,000
Number of common shares outstanding	40,000

Required

1. Compute HiFlite's current ratio, debt ratio, and earnings per share. Use the following format for your answer:

Requirement 1		
Current ratio	**Debt ratio**	**Earnings per share**

2. Compute the three ratios after evaluating the effect of each transaction that follows. Consider each transaction *separately*.
   a. Purchased store supplies of $46,000 on account
   b. Borrowed $125,000 on a long-term note payable
   c. Issued 5,000 common shares, receiving cash of $120,000
   d. Paid short-term notes payable, $32,000
   e. Received cash on account, $19,000

   Format your answer as follows:

Requirement 2			
Transaction (letter)	**Current ratio**	**Debt ratio**	**Earnings per share**

Learning Objective 5
Using ratios to evaluate a share investment

P13-48B Comparative financial statement data of Mira TV Sales Ltd. follow.

Mira TV Sales Ltd.
Comparative Income Statement
For the Years Ended December 31, 2011 and 2010

	2011	2010
Net sales	$662,000	$527,000
Cost of goods sold	429,000	318,000
Gross profit	233,000	209,000
Operating expenses	136,000	134,000
Income from operations	97,000	75,000
Interest expense	9,000	8,000
Income before income tax	88,000	67,000
Income tax expense	30,000	27,000
Net income	$ 58,000	$ 40,000

Mira TV Sales Ltd.
Comparative Balance Sheet
December 31, 2011 and 2010

	2011	2010	2009*
Current assets:			
Cash	$ 96,000	$ 97,000	
Current receivables, net	162,000	116,000	$103,000
Inventories	147,000	162,000	207,000
Prepaid expenses	16,000	7,000	
Total current assets	421,000	382,000	
Property, plant, and equipment, net	214,000	178,000	
Total assets	$635,000	$560,000	598,000
Total current liabilities	$206,000	$223,000	
Long-term liabilities	119,000	117,000	
Total liabilities	325,000	340,000	
Preferred shareholders' equity, $6.00 (1,000 shares outstanding)	100,000	100,000	
Common shareholders' equity	210,000	120,000	90,000
Total liabilities and shareholders' equity	$635,000	$560,000	

*Selected 2009 amounts.

Other information:

1. Market price of Mira's common shares: $83 at December 31, 2010, and $62.50 at December 31, 2009
2. Common shares outstanding: 10,000 during 2011 and 9,000 during 2010
3. All sales on credit

Required

1. Compute the following ratios for 2011 and 2010:
   a. Current ratio
   b. Inventory turnover
   c. Times-interest-earned ratio
   d. Return on equity
   e. Earnings per share
   f. Price/earnings ratio
2. Decide (a) whether Mira's financial position improved or deteriorated during 2011 and (b) whether the investment attractiveness of Mira's common shares appears to have increased or decreased.
3. How will what you learned in this problem help you evaluate an investment?

Learning Objective 5
Using ratios to decide between two share investments

P13-49B Assume that you are purchasing an investment and have decided to invest in a company in the publishing business. You have narrowed the choice to Thrifty Nickel Corp. and The Village Cryer Limited and have assembled the following data.

Selected income statement data for the current year:

	Thrifty Nickel	Village Cryer
Net sales (all on credit)	$371,000	$497,000
Cost of goods sold	209,000	258,000
Income from operations	79,000	138,000
Interest expense	—	19,000
Net income	48,000	72,000

Selected balance sheet data at *beginning* of the current year:

	Thrifty Nickel	Village Cryer
Current receivables, net	$ 40,000	$ 48,000
Inventories	93,000	88,000
Total assets	259,000	270,000
Long-term debt	—	86,000
Preferred shares: 5%, $200 issued	—	20,000
Common shares: (10,000 shares)	10,000	
(5,000 shares)		12,500
Total shareholders' equity	118,000	126,000

Selected balance sheet and market price data at *end* of the current year:

	Thrifty Nickel	Village Cryer
Current assets:		
Cash	$ 22,000	$ 19,000
Short-term investments	20,000	18,000
Current receivables, net	42,000	46,000
Inventories	87,000	100,000
Prepaid expenses	2,000	3,000
Total current assets	$173,000	$186,000
Total assets	265,000	328,000
Total current liabilities	108,000	98,000
Total liabilities	108,000*	131,000*
Preferred shares: $5.00 (200 shares)		20,000
Common shares: (10,000 shares)	10,000	
(5,000 shares)		12,500
Total shareholders' equity	157,000	197,000
Market price per share of common share	$51	$112

*Includes long-term debt: Thrifty Nickel $-0- and Village Cryer $86,000

Your strategy is to invest in companies that have low price/earnings ratios but appear to be in good shape financially. Assume that you have analyzed all other factors and your decision depends on the results of ratio analysis.

Required

1. Compute the following ratios for both companies for the current year, and decide which company's shares better fit your investment strategy.
   a. Acid-test ratio
   b. Inventory turnover
   c. Days' sales in average receivables
   d. Debt ratio
   e. Times-interest-earned ratio
   f. Return on equity
   g. Earnings per share
   h. Price/earnings ratio

Learning Objective 5
Analyzing a company based on its ratios

P13-50B Take the role of an investment analyst at RBC Dominion Securities. It is your job to recommend investments for your clients. The only information you have is the following ratio values for two companies in the pharmaceuticals industry.

Ratio	Pain Free Ltd.	Remedy Inc.
Days' sales in receivables	36	42
Inventory turnover	6	8
Gross profit percentage	49%	51%
Net income as a percent of sales	7.2%	8.3%
Times interest earned	16	9
Return on equity	32.3%	21.5%
Return on assets	12.1%	16.4%

Write a report to your investment committee. Recommend one company's shares over the other's. State the reasons for your recommendation.

Apply Your Knowledge

Decision Cases

Learning Objective 5
Assessing the effects of transactions on a company

Case 1. Assume a major Canadian company had a bad year in 2011, when it suffered a $4.9 billion net loss. The loss pushed most of the return measures into the negative column and the current ratio dropped below 1.0. The company's debt ratio is still only 0.27. Assume top management is pondering ways to improve the company's ratios. In particular, management is considering the following transactions:

1. Sell off a segment of the business for $30 million (receiving half in cash and half in the form of a long-term note receivable). Book value of the segment business is $27 million.
2. Borrow $100 million on long-term debt.
3. Repurchase common shares for $500 million cash.
4. Write off one-fourth of goodwill carried on the books at $128 million.
5. Sell advertising at the normal gross profit of 60%. The advertisements run immediately.
6. Purchase trademarks from a competitor, paying $20 million cash and signing a one-year note payable for $80 million.

Required

1. Top management wants to know the effects of these transactions (increase, decrease, or no effect) on the following ratios of the company:
   a. Current ratio
   b. Debt ratio
   c. Times-interest-earned ratio
   d. Return on equity
   e. Book value per common share
2. Some of these transactions have an immediately positive effect on the company's financial condition. Some are definitely negative. Others have an effect that cannot be judged as clearly positive or negative. Evaluate each transaction's effect as positive, negative, or unclear.

Learning Objective 5
Analyzing the effects of an accounting difference on the ratios

Case 2. Company A uses the first-in, first-out (FIFO) method to account for its inventory, and Company B uses weighted-average cost. Analyze the effect of this difference in accounting methods on the two companies' ratio values. For each ratio discussed in this chapter, indicate which company will have the higher (and the lower) ratio value. Also identify those ratios that

are unaffected by the inventory valuation difference. Ignore the effects of income taxes, and assume inventory costs are increasing. Then, based on your analysis of the ratios, summarize your conclusions as to which company looks better overall.

Case 3. Suppose you manage The Runner's Store Inc., a sporting goods store that lost money during the past year. To turn the business around, you must analyze the company and industry data for the current year to learn what is wrong. The company's and industry average data follow:

Learning Objective 2 5
Identifying action to cut losses and establish profitability

The Runner's Store Inc.
Common-Size Balance Sheet Data

	Runner's Store	Industry Average
Cash and short-term investments	3.0%	6.8%
Trade receivables, net	15.2	11.0
Inventory	64.2	60.5
Prepaid expenses	1.0	0.0
Total current assets	83.4	78.3
Fixed assets, net	12.6	15.2
Other assets	4.0	6.5
Total assets	100.0%	100.0%
Notes payable, short-term 12%	17.1%	14.0%
Accounts payable	21.1	25.1
Accrued liabilities	7.8	7.9
Total current liabilities	46.0	47.0
Long-term debt, 11%	19.7	16.4
Total liabilities	65.7	63.4
Common shareholders' equity	34.3	36.6
Total liabilities and shareholders' equity	100.0%	100.0%

The Runner's Store Inc.
Common-Size Income Statement Data

	Runner's Store	Industry Average
Net sales	100.0%	100.0%
Cost of sales	(68.2)	(64.8)
Gross profit	31.8	35.2
Operating expense	(37.1)	(32.3)
Operating income (loss)	(5.3)	2.9
Interest expense	(5.8)	(1.3)
Other revenue	1.1	0.3
Income (loss) before income tax	(10.0)	1.9
Income tax (expense) saving	4.4	(0.8)
Net income (loss)	(5.6)%	1.1%

Required
On the basis of your analysis of these figures, suggest four courses of action The Runner's Store might take to reduce its losses and establish profitable operations. Give your reason for each suggestion.

Ethical Issue

Turnberry Golf Corporation's long-term debt agreements make certain demands on the business. For example, Turnberry may not repurchase common shares in excess of the balance of retained earnings. Also, long-term debt may not exceed shareholders' equity, and the current ratio may not fall below 1.50. If Turnberry fails to meet any of these requirements, the company's lenders have the authority to take over management of the company.

Changes in consumer demand have made it hard for Turnberry to attract customers. Current liabilities have mounted faster than current assets, causing the current ratio to fall to 1.47. Before releasing financial statements, Turnberry management is scrambling to improve the current ratio. The controller points out that an investment can be classified as either long-term or short-term, depending on management's intention. By deciding to convert an investment to cash within one year, Turnberry can classify the investment as short-term: a current asset. On the controller's recommendation, Turnberry's board of directors votes to reclassify long-term investments as short-term.

Required

1. What effect will reclassifying the investments have on the current ratio? Is Turnberry's financial position stronger as a result of reclassifying the investments?
2. Shortly after the financial statements are released, sales improve; so, too, does the current ratio. As a result, Turnberry management decides not to sell the investments it had reclassified as short-term. Accordingly, the company reclassifies the investments as long-term. Has management behaved unethically? Give the reasoning underlying your answer.

Focus on Financials

Learning Objective 5
Measuring profitability and analyzing shares as an investment

Gildan Activewear Inc.

Use the five-year summary of selected financial data for Gildan Activewear Inc. to answer the following questions.

	2009	2008	2007	2006	2005
Net sales	$1,038.3	$1,249.7	$964.4	$773.2	$653.9
Net earnings	95.3	146.4	129.1	106.3	85.8
Cash from operations	159.5	191.2	167.7	158.0	122.0
Total assets	1,082.4	1,095.0	867.7	718.9	596.5
Total long-term debt	4.4	53.0	59.7	33.9	47.1

Required

1. Using 2005 as the base year, perform trend analysis of Gildan's selected Financial Highlights for net sales, net earnings, and cash from operations for each year 2005 through 2009.
2. Evaluate Gildan's operating performance during 2005 through 2009. Comment on each item computed. In your overall evaluation of performance, consider this information from the Management's Discussion and Analysis in the 2009 Annual Report.

> "*ECONOMIC ENVIRONMENT*
> *During fiscal 2009, the severe downturn in the overall economic environment resulted in a dramatic curtailment of consumer and corporate spending which negatively impacted demand for our products....*
>
> *During fiscal 2009, we took a number of steps in response to the downturn in the economy, in order to prudently manage our receivables, inventory levels and capital expenditures.... At the end of the first quarter of 2009, we established a goal to be*

essentially debt free by the end of the fiscal year, and we exceeded this goal by accumulating a cash position of approximately $100 million at October 4, 2009.

The Company is currently planning for a fiscal 2010 on the basis of the continuation of weak macro economic conditions, although it believes it is in a position to take advantage of any unanticipated improvement in overall industry demand during fiscal 2010...."

Focus on Analysis

Gildan Activewear Inc.

Learning Objective 3
Prepare common-size statements

Use the Gildan Activewear Inc. financial statements in Appendix A to address the following questions.

Required

1. During fiscal 2009, Gildan's net earnings decreased over 2008. Prepare a common-size income statement for 2009 and 2008.
2. Discuss the results of Gildan based on the common-size income statement.
3. In your opinion, what is the company's outlook for the future?

Group Projects

Project 1. Select an industry in which you are interested, and use the leading company in that industry as the benchmark. Then select two other companies in the same industry. For each category of ratios in Exhibit 13-10 on page 692, compute at least two ratios for all three companies. Write a two-page report that compares the two companies with the benchmark company.

Project 2. Select a company and obtain its financial statements. Convert the income statement and the balance sheet to common size, and compare the company you selected to the industry average. Risk Management Association's *Annual Statement Studies*, Dun & Bradstreet's *Industry Norms & Key Business Ratios*, and Prentice Hall's *Almanac of Business and Industrial Financial Ratios* by Leo Troy publish common-size statements for most industries.

Quick Check Answers

1. *c ($1,833/$1,712.8 = 1.070)*
2. *c ($1,833/$17,140.5 = 0.107)*
3. *b (Net income: $1,471.4 – $893.5 = $577.9; $577.9/$893.5 = Increase of 64.7%)*
4. *a ($1,665.1/$25,525.1 = 0.065)*
5. *a*
6. *d* $\left[\frac{\$4,314.8}{(\$129.4 + \$111.7)/2}\right] = 35.8 \approx 36$ *times*
7. *b [($492.8 + $734.5)/$2,485.8 = 0.49]*
8. *d* $\left[\frac{(\$734.5 + \$855.3)/2)}{\$17,140.5/365}\right] = 16.9 \approx 17$ *days*
9. *a (Debt ratio is ($25,525.1 – $11,981.9)/$25,525.1 = 0.53. This debt ratio is lower than the average for most companies, given in the chapter as 0.62.)*
10. *d ($1,471.4/$17,140.5 = 0.086)*

11. $a\left[\dfrac{\$1{,}471.4}{(\$11{,}981.9 + \$10{,}280.9)/2}\right] = 0.132$

12. *b* (\$26/\$1.16 = \$22.41)

13. *d* (\$0.40/\$26.00 = 0.015)

GILDAN

MANAGEMENT'S RESPONSIBILITY FOR FINANCIAL REPORTING

The accompanying Consolidated Financial Statements have been prepared by management and approved by the Board of Directors of the Company. The Consolidated Financial Statements were prepared in accordance with Canadian generally accepted accounting principles and, where appropriate, reflect management's best estimates and judgments. Where alternative accounting methods exist, management has chosen those methods deemed most appropriate in the circumstances. Management is responsible for the accuracy, integrity and objectivity of the Consolidated Financial Statements within reasonable limits of materiality, and for maintaining a system of internal controls over financial reporting as described in "Management's Annual Report on Internal Control Over Financial Reporting" on page 32 of the 2009 Annual Management's Discussion and Analysis. Management is also responsible for the preparation and presentation of other financial information included in the 2009 Annual Report and its consistency with the Consolidated Financial Statements.

The Audit and Finance Committee, which is appointed annually by the Board of Directors and comprised exclusively of independent directors, meets with management as well as with the independent auditors and internal auditors to satisfy itself that management is properly discharging its financial reporting responsibilities and to review the Consolidated Financial Statements and the independent auditors' report. The Audit and Finance Committee reports its findings to the Board of Directors for consideration in approving the Consolidated Financial Statements for presentation to the shareholders. The Audit and Finance Committee considers, for review by the Board of Directors and approval by the shareholders, the engagement or reappointment of the independent auditors.

The Consolidated Financial Statements have been independently audited by KPMG LLP, Chartered Accountants, on behalf of the shareholders, in accordance with Canadian generally accepted auditing standards and the standards of the Public Company Accounting Oversight Board (United States). Their report outlines the nature of their audit and expresses their opinion on the Consolidated Financial Statements of the Company. In addition, our auditors have issued an attestation report on the Company's internal controls over financial reporting as at October 4, 2009. KPMG LLP has direct access to the Audit and Finance Committee of the Board of Directors.

Glenn J. Chamandy
President and Chief Executive Officer

Laurence G. Sellyn
Executive Vice-President,
Chief Financial and Administrative Officer

December 9, 2009

REPORT OF INDEPENDENT REGISTERED PUBLIC ACCOUNTING FIRM

To the Shareholders and Board of Directors of Gildan Activewear Inc.

We have audited the accompanying consolidated balance sheets of Gildan Activewear Inc. (the "Company") and subsidiaries as at October 4, 2009 and October 5, 2008 and the related consolidated statements of earnings and comprehensive income, shareholders' equity and cash flows for the years ended October 4, 2009, October 5, 2008 and September 30, 2007. These consolidated financial statements are the responsibility of the Company's management. Our responsibility is to express an opinion on these consolidated financial statements based on our audits.

We conducted our audits in accordance with Canadian generally accepted auditing standards and the standards of the Public Company Accounting Oversight Board (United States). Those standards require that we plan and perform the audit to obtain reasonable assurance about whether the financial statements are free of material misstatement. An audit includes examining, on a test basis, evidence supporting the amounts and disclosures in the financial statements. An audit also includes assessing the accounting principles used and significant estimates made by management, as well as evaluating the overall financial statement presentation. We believe that our audits provide a reasonable basis for our opinion.

In our opinion, the consolidated financial statements referred to above present fairly, in all material respects, the financial position of the Company and subsidiaries as at October 4, 2009 and October 5, 2008, and the results of their operations and their cash flows for the years ended October 4, 2009, October 5, 2008 and September 30, 2007, in conformity with Canadian generally accepted accounting principles.

We have also audited, in accordance with the standards of the Public Company Accounting Oversight Board (United States), the Company's internal control over financial reporting as at October 4, 2009, based on criteria established in *Internal Control - Integrated Framework issued by the Committee of Sponsoring Organizations of the Treadway Commission* (*COSO*), and our report dated December 8, 2009 expressed an unqualified opinion on the effectiveness of the Company's internal control over financial reporting.

KPMG LLP*

Chartered Accountants
Montréal, Canada
December 8, 2009

* CA Auditor permit no 20408
KPMG LLP is a Canadian limited liability partnership and a member firm of the KPMG network of independent member firms affiliated with KPMG International, a Swiss cooperative. KPMG Canada provides services to KPMG LLP.

REPORT OF INDEPENDENT REGISTERED PUBLIC ACCOUNTING FIRM

To the Shareholders and Board of Directors of Gildan Activewear Inc.

We have audited Gildan Activewear Inc.'s (the "Company") internal control over financial reporting as at October 4, 2009, based on the criteria established in *Internal Control - Integrated Framework issued by the Committee of Sponsoring Organizations of the Treadway Commission (COSO).* The Company's management is responsible for maintaining effective internal control over financial reporting and for its assessment of the effectiveness of internal control over financial reporting as presented in the section entitled "Management's Annual Report on Internal Control over Financial Reporting" included in Management's Discussion and Analysis. Our responsibility is to express an opinion on the Company's internal control over financial reporting based on our audit.

We conducted our audit in accordance with the standards of the Public Company Accounting Oversight Board (United States). Those standards require that we plan and perform the audit to obtain reasonable assurance about whether effective internal control over the financial reporting was maintained in all material respects. Our audit included obtaining an understanding of internal control over financial reporting, assessing the risk that a material weakness exists, and testing and evaluating the design and operating effectiveness of internal control based on the assessed risk. Our audit also included performing such other procedures as we considered necessary in the circumstances. We believe that our audit provides a reasonable basis for our opinion.

A company's internal control over financial reporting is a process designed to provide reasonable assurance regarding the reliability of financial reporting and the preparation of financial statements for external purposes in accordance with generally accepted accounting principles. A company's internal control over financial reporting includes those policies and procedures that (1) pertain to the maintenance of records that, in reasonable detail, accurately and fairly reflect the transactions and dispositions of the assets of the company; (2) provide reasonable assurance that transactions are recorded as necessary to permit preparation of financial statements in accordance with generally accepted accounting principles, and that receipts and expenditures of the Company are being made only in accordance with authorizations of management and directors of the Company; and (3) provide reasonable assurance regarding prevention or timely detection of unauthorized acquisition, use, or disposition of the Company's assets that could have a material effect on the financial statements.

Because of its inherent limitations, internal control over financial reporting may not prevent or detect misstatements. Also, projections of any evaluation of effectiveness to future periods are subject to the risk that controls may become inadequate because of changes in conditions, or that the degree of compliance with the policies or procedures may deteriorate.

In our opinion, the Company maintained, in all material respects, effective internal control over financial reporting as at October 4, 2009, based on criteria established in *Internal Control - Integrated Framework issued by the Committee of Sponsoring Organizations of the Treadway Commission (COSO).*

We also have conducted our audits on the consolidated financial statements in accordance with Canadian generally accepted auditing standards and the standards of the Public Company Accounting Oversight Board (United States). Our report dated December 8, 2009 expressed an unqualified opinion on those consolidated financial statements.

KPMG LLP*

Chartered Accountants
Montréal, Canada
December 8, 2009

* CA Auditor permit no 20408
KPMG LLP is a Canadian limited liability partnership and a member firm of the KPMG network of independent member firms affiliated with KPMG International, a Swiss cooperative. KPMG Canada provides services to KPMG LLP.

GILDAN

CONSOLIDATED FINANCIAL STATEMENTS

GILDAN ACTIVEWEAR INC.
CONSOLIDATED BALANCE SHEETS
As at October 4, 2009 and October 5, 2008
(in thousands of U.S. dollars)

	2009	2008 *(recast-note 1(b))*
Current assets:		
Cash and cash equivalents	$ 99,732	$ 12,357
Accounts receivable	166,762	215,833
Inventories (note 3)	301,867	316,172
Prepaid expenses and deposits	11,604	10,413
	579,965	554,775
Property, plant and equipment (note 4)	414,538	436,516
Intangible assets (note 5)	56,757	59,954
Other assets (note 6)	9,985	17,277
Assets held for sale (note 16)	6,544	10,497
Goodwill (note 2)	6,709	6,709
Future income taxes (note 14)	7,910	9,283
Total assets	$ 1,082,408	$ 1,095,011
Current liabilities:		
Accounts payable and accrued liabilities	$ 124,378	$ 149,344
Income taxes payable	11,822	46,627
Current portion of long-term debt (note 8)	2,803	3,556
	139,003	199,527
Long-term debt (note 8)	1,584	49,448
Future income taxes (note 14)	23,764	27,331
Non-controlling interest in consolidated joint venture	7,272	7,162
Commitments and contingencies (note 12)		
Shareholders' equity (note 9):		
Share capital	93,042	89,377
Contributed surplus	6,976	6,728
Retained earnings	784,519	689,190
Accumulated other comprehensive income	26,248	26,248
	810,767	715,438
	910,785	811,543
Total liabilities and shareholders' equity	$ 1,082,408	$ 1,095,011

See accompanying notes to consolidated financial statements.

On behalf of the Board of Directors:

Director
Glenn J. Chamandy

Director
William D. Anderson

GILDAN

CONSOLIDATED FINANCIAL STATEMENTS

GILDAN ACTIVEWEAR INC.
CONSOLIDATED STATEMENTS OF EARNINGS AND COMPREHENSIVE INCOME

Years ended October 4, 2009, October 5, 2008 and September 30, 2007
(in thousands of U.S. dollars, except per share data)

	2009	2008	2007
		(recast-note 1)	*(recast-note 1)*
Net sales	$ 1,038,319	$ 1,249,711	$ 964,429
Cost of sales	807,986	911,242	705,546
Gross profit	230,333	338,469	258,883
Selling, general and administrative expenses	134,785	142,760	99,926
Restructuring and other charges (note 16)	6,199	5,489	28,012
Operating income	89,349	190,220	130,945
Financial (income) expense, net (note 19(b))	(304)	9,240	5,420
Non-controlling interest in consolidated joint venture	110	230	1,278
Earnings before income taxes	89,543	180,750	124,247
Income taxes (note 14)	(5,786)	34,400	(4,815)
Net earnings and comprehensive income	$ 95,329	$ 146,350	$ 129,062
Earnings per share (note 15):			
Basic EPS	$ 0.79	$ 1.21	$ 1.07
Diluted EPS	0.79	1.20	1.06

See accompanying notes to consolidated financial statements.

GILDAN

CONSOLIDATED FINANCIAL STATEMENTS

GILDAN ACTIVEWEAR INC.
CONSOLIDATED STATEMENTS OF SHAREHOLDERS' EQUITY

Years ended October 4, 2009, October 5, 2008 and September 30, 2007
(in thousands or thousands of U.S. dollars)

	Share capital		Contributed	Accumulated other comprehensive	Retained	Total shareholders'
	Number	Amount	surplus	income	earnings	equity
Balance, October 1, 2006, as previously reported	120,228	$ 86,584	$ 2,365	$ 26,248	$ 415,368	$ 530,565
Cumulative effect of adopting a new accounting policy (note 1(b))	-	-	-	-	(1,590)	(1,590)
Balance, October 1, 2006, as recast	120,228	86,584	2,365	26,248	413,778	528,975
Stock-based compensation related to stock options and Treasury restricted share units	-	-	1,814	-	-	1,814
Shares issued under employee share purchase plan	18	530	-	-	-	530
Shares issued pursuant to exercise of stock options	149	786	-	-	-	786
Shares issued pursuant to vesting of Treasury restricted share units	27	226	(226)	-	-	-
Share repurchases	(3)	(65)	-	-	-	(65)
Net earnings, recast (note 1(b))	-	-	-	-	129,062	129,062
Balance, September 30, 2007, as recast	120,419	$ 88,061	$ 3,953	$ 26,248	$ 542,840	$ 661,102
Stock-based compensation related to stock options and Treasury restricted share units	-	-	2,965	-	-	2,965
Shares issued under employee share purchase plan	21	720	-	-	-	720
Shares issued pursuant to exercise of stock options	81	418	-	-	-	418
Shares issued pursuant to vesting of Treasury restricted share units	15	190	(190)	-	-	-
Share repurchases	-	(12)	-	-	-	(12)
Net earnings, recast (note 1(b))	-	-	-	-	146,350	146,350
Balance, October 5, 2008, as recast	120,536	$ 89,377	$ 6,728	$ 26,248	$ 689,190	$ 811,543
Stock-based compensation related to stock options and Treasury restricted share units	-	-	3,007	-	-	3,007
Shares issued under employee share purchase plan	58	781	-	-	-	781
Shares issued pursuant to exercise of stock options	54	125	-	-	-	125
Shares issued pursuant to vesting of Treasury restricted share units	315	2,759	(2,759)	-	-	-
Net earnings	-	-	-	-	95,329	95,329
Balance, October 4, 2009	120,963	$ 93,042	$ 6,976	$ 26,248	$ 784,519	$ 910,785

See accompanying notes to consolidated financial statements.

GILDAN

CONSOLIDATED FINANCIAL STATEMENTS

GILDAN ACTIVEWEAR INC.
CONSOLIDATED STATEMENTS OF CASH FLOWS
Years ended October 4, 2009, October 5, 2008 and September 30, 2007
(in thousands of U.S. dollars)

	2009	2008	2007
		(recast-note 1(b))	*(recast-note 1(b))*
Cash flows from (used in) operating activities:			
Net earnings	$ 95,329	$ 146,350	$ 129,062
Adjustments for:			
Depreciation and amortization (note 17(b))	65,407	57,135	37,268
Variation of depreciation included in inventories (note 17(b))	(2,437)	(957)	(1,837)
Restructuring charges related to assets held for sale and property, plant and equipment (note 16)	976	2,174	5,523
Loss on disposal of property, plant and equipment	561	1,369	332
Stock-based compensation costs	3,007	2,965	1,814
Future income taxes (note 14)	(2,434)	(15,885)	(8,919)
Non-controlling interest	110	230	1,278
Unrealized net (gain) loss on foreign exchange and financial derivatives	(1,012)	(2,222)	3,226
	159,507	191,159	167,747
Changes in non-cash working capital balances:			
Accounts receivable	48,351	10,263	(34,919)
Inventories	16,742	(31,178)	(37,473)
Prepaid expenses and deposits	(1,191)	(881)	(2,202)
Accounts payable and accrued liabilities	(22,731)	25,700	(4,800)
Income taxes payable	(31,499)	43,802	343
	169,179	238,865	88,696
Cash flows from (used in) financing activities:			
(Decrease) increase in amounts drawn under revolving long-term credit facility	(45,000)	(4,000)	49,000
Decrease in bank indebtedness	-	(2,739)	(3,500)
Increase in other long-term debt	44	2,805	-
Repayment of other long-term debt	(3,661)	(5,461)	(23,201)
Proceeds from the issuance of shares	906	1,138	1,316
Repurchase of shares	-	(12)	(65)
	(47,711)	(8,269)	23,550
Cash flows from (used in) investing activities:			
Purchase of property, plant and equipment	(44,938)	(97,030)	(134,282)
Business acquisition (note 2)	(1,196)	(126,819)	-
Restricted cash related to business acquisition (note 2)	3,958	(10,000)	-
Proceeds on disposal of assets held for sale	6,349	3,736	6,668
Net decrease (increase) in other assets	1,629	2,826	(4,608)
	(34,198)	(227,287)	(132,222)
Effect of exchange rate changes on cash and cash equivalents denominated in foreign currencies	105	(202)	219
Net increase (decrease) in cash and cash equivalents during the year	87,375	3,107	(19,757)
Cash and cash equivalents, beginning of year	12,357	9,250	29,007
Cash and cash equivalents, end of year	$ 99,732	$ 12,357	$ 9,250

Supplemental disclosure of cash flow information (note 17(a))

See accompanying notes to consolidated financial statements.

GILDAN

NOTES TO CONSOLIDATED FINANCIAL STATEMENTS

Years ended October 4, 2009, October 5, 2008 and September 30, 2007
(Tabular amounts in thousands or thousands of U.S. dollars except per share data, unless otherwise indicated)

Gildan Activewear Inc. (the "Company") is incorporated under the Canada Business Corporations Act. Its principal business activity is the manufacture and sale of activewear, socks and underwear. The Company's fiscal year ends on the first Sunday following September 28. All references to 2009, 2008 and 2007 represent the fiscal years ended October 4, 2009, October 5, 2008 and September 30, 2007, respectively.

1. SIGNIFICANT ACCOUNTING POLICIES:

The consolidated financial statements are expressed in U.S. dollars and have been prepared in accordance with Canadian generally accepted accounting principles. The Company's functional currency is the U.S. dollar. The principal accounting policies of the Company are summarized as follows:

(a) Basis of presentation:

The accompanying consolidated financial statements include the accounts of the Company and its subsidiaries. The consolidated financial statements also include the accounts of a yarn spinning joint venture with Frontier Spinning Mills, Inc., CanAm Yarns LLC ("CanAm"), as the Company is considered the primary beneficiary of this entity. All significant intercompany balances and transactions have been eliminated on consolidation.

Statement of earnings classification:
Effective the first quarter of fiscal 2009, the Company changed certain classifications of its statement of earnings and comprehensive income with retrospective application to comparative figures presented for prior periods. These new classifications align the results of operations by function and incorporate presentation requirements under the Canadian Institute of Chartered Accountants (CICA) Handbook Section 3031, *Inventories*, which has been adopted effective the first quarter of fiscal 2009. Pursuant to the requirements of Section 3031, depreciation expense related to manufacturing activities is now included in cost of sales. The remaining depreciation and amortization expense has been reclassified to selling, general and administrative expenses. Depreciation and amortization expense is therefore no longer presented as a separate caption on the statement of earnings and comprehensive income. In addition, the Company reclassified certain other items in its statement of earnings and comprehensive income. Outbound freight to customers, previously classified within selling, general and administrative expenses, is now reported within cost of sales. Also, a new caption is now presented for financial expenses and income, which includes interest income and expenses (including mark-to-market adjustments of interest rate swap contracts), foreign exchange gains and losses (including mark-to-market adjustments of forward foreign exchange contracts), and other financial charges. Interest expense net of interest income was previously reported as a separate caption, while foreign exchange gains and losses were previously included in cost of sales. Other financial charges were previously reflected in selling, general and administrative expenses. For the year ended October 5, 2008 these changes in classification have resulted in a decrease of $63.8 million (2007 - $47.8 million) and $8.7 million (2007 - $11.1 million) in gross profit and selling, general and administrative expenses, respectively, compared to the amounts previously reported. The decrease of $63.8 million (2007 - $47.8 million) in gross profit is due to reclassifications of $44.1 million (2007 - $30.4 million) of depreciation and amortization expense, $20.6 million (2007 - $16.7 million) of outbound freight to customers less $0.9 million (2007 – plus $0.7 million of foreign exchange gain) of foreign exchange loss and other financial income. There was no impact on net earnings as a result of these changes in classification.

GILDAN

NOTES TO CONSOLIDATED FINANCIAL STATEMENTS

1. SIGNIFICANT ACCOUNTING POLICIES (continued):

(b) Adoption of new accounting standards:

Inventories:

Effective the commencement of its 2009 fiscal year, the Company adopted CICA Handbook Section 3031, *Inventories*, which replaced Section 3030, *Inventories,* and harmonized the Canadian standards related to inventories with International Financial Reporting Standards (IFRS). This Section, which was issued in June 2007, provides changes to the measurement of, and more extensive guidance on, the determination of cost, including allocation of overhead; narrows the permitted cost formulas; requires impairment testing; clarifies that major spare parts not in use should be included in property, plant and equipment; and expands the disclosure requirements to increase transparency. The Company compared the requirements of this new Section with its current measurement and determination of costs and concluded that the new Section did not have a significant impact on the results of operations. The Company previously included and will continue to include the amount of depreciation related to manufacturing activities as a component of the cost of inventories. However, the new Section requires depreciation expense related to inventories which have been sold to be presented in cost of sales. As a result, effective the first quarter of fiscal 2009, depreciation expense related to manufacturing activities was reclassified to cost of sales.

See the section, Statement of earnings classification, in note 1(a) above and note 3 for the new disclosure requirements related to the adoption of Section 3031.

General Standards of Financial Statement Presentation:

Effective the commencement of its 2009 fiscal year, the Company adopted the amendment of CICA Handbook Section 1400, *General Standards of Financial Statement Presentation*, which is effective for fiscal year's beginning on or after October 1, 2008 and which includes requirements to assess and disclose the Company's ability to continue as a going concern. The adoption of the amended Section did not have an impact on the consolidated financial statements of the Company.

Goodwill and intangible assets:

In February 2008, Canada's Accounting Standard's Board (AcSB) issued CICA Handbook Section 3064, *Goodwill and Intangible Assets*, replacing Section 3062, *Goodwill and Other Intangible Assets*, and Section 3450, *Research and Development Costs*. Section 3064 establishes revised standards for the recognition, measurement, presentation and disclosure of goodwill and intangible assets. The new Section also provides guidance for the treatment of preproduction and start-up costs and requires that these costs be expensed as incurred. This Section applies to annual financial statements relating to the Company's fiscal year beginning on October 6, 2008 and has been adopted on a retrospective basis effective from the first quarter of fiscal 2009.

Prior to the adoption of Section 3064, the Company deferred and amortized plant start-up costs on a straight-line basis over two years. The impact of adopting this Section, on a retrospective basis, was an increase of $1.8 million in net earnings for fiscal 2008 (increase of $0.01 in basic and diluted earnings per share), and a decrease in net earnings of $1.0 million for fiscal 2007 (decrease of $0.01 in basic and diluted earnings per share). The adoption of this Section also resulted in a decrease of $0.8 million in other assets as at October 5, 2008 and a decrease of $1.6 million in shareholders' equity as at October 1, 2006.

Credit risk and the fair value of financial assets and financial liabilities:

On January 20, 2009, the Emerging Issues Committee (EIC) of the AcSB issued EIC Abstract 173, *Credit Risk and Fair Value of Financial Assets and Financial Liabilities*, which establishes that an entity's own credit risk and the credit risk of the counterparty should be taken into account in determining the fair value of financial assets and financial liabilities, including derivative instruments. EIC 173 should be applied retrospectively without restatement of prior years to all financial assets and liabilities measured at fair value in interim and annual financial statements for periods ending on or after January 20, 2009 and was applicable to the Company for its second quarter of fiscal 2009 with retrospective application, if any, to the beginning of its current fiscal year. The adoption of EIC 173 did not have an impact on the consolidated financial statements of the Company.

1. SIGNIFICANT ACCOUNTING POLICIES (continued):

(b) Adoption of new accounting standards (continued):

Financial Instruments – Disclosures:
In June 2009, the AcSB issued amendments to CICA Handbook Section 3862, *Financial Instruments – Disclosures* in order to align with International Financial Reporting Standard IFRS 7, *Financial Instruments: Disclosures*. This Section has been amended to include additional disclosure requirements about fair value measurements of financial instruments and to enhance liquidity risk disclosure. The amendments establish a three-tier fair value hierarchy, which prioritizes the inputs used in measuring fair value. These tiers include: Level 1, defined as observable inputs such as quoted prices in active markets; Level 2, defined as inputs other than quoted prices in active markets that are either directly or indirectly observable; and Level 3, defined as unobservable inputs in which little or no market data exists, therefore requiring an entity to develop its own assumptions. The amendments apply to annual financial statements relating to fiscal years ended after September 30, 2009 and are applicable to the Company as at October 4, 2009. The amended Section relates to disclosure only and did not impact the financial results of the Company. As at October 4, 2009, the Company held no assets or liabilities required to be measured at fair value except for cash and cash equivalents which was measured using Level 2 inputs in the fair value hierarchy.

(c) Future accounting standards:

Business combinations:
In January 2009, the AcSB issued CICA Handbook Section 1582, *Business Combinations*, which replaces Section 1581, *Business Combinations*, and provides the equivalent to IFRS 3, *Business Combinations* (January 2008). The new Section expands the definition of a business subject to an acquisition and establishes significant new guidance on the measurement of consideration given, and the recognition and measurement of assets acquired and liabilities assumed in a business combination. The new Section requires that all business acquisitions be measured at the full fair value of the acquired entity at the acquisition date even if the business combination is achieved in stages, or if less than 100 percent of the equity interest in the acquiree is owned at the acquisition date. The measurement of equity consideration given in a business combination will no longer be based on the average of the fair value of the shares a few days before and after the day the terms and conditions have been agreed to and the acquisition announced, but rather at the acquisition date. Subsequent changes in fair value of contingent consideration classified as a liability will be recognized in earnings and not as an adjustment to the purchase price. Restructuring and other direct costs of a business combination are no longer considered part of the acquisition accounting. Instead, such costs will be expensed as incurred, unless they constitute the costs associated with issuing debt or equity securities. The Section applies prospectively to business combinations for which the acquisition date is on or after the beginning of the first annual reporting period beginning on or after January 1, 2011. Earlier adoption is permitted. This new Section will only have an impact on our consolidated financial statements for future acquisitions that will be made in periods subsequent to the date of adoption. The Company is currently considering early adoption of Section 1582.

Consolidated financial statements and non-controlling interests:
In January 2009, the AcSB issued CICA Handbook Section 1601, *Consolidated Financial Statements*, and Handbook Section 1602, *Non-Controlling Interests*, which together replace Section 1600, *Consolidated Financial Statements*. These two Sections are the equivalent to the corresponding provisions of International Accounting Standard 27, *Consolidated and Separate Financial Statements* (January 2008) under IFRS. Section 1602 applies to the accounting for non-controlling interests and transactions with non-controlling interest holders in consolidated financial statements. The new Sections require that, for each business combination, the acquirer measure any non-controlling interest in the acquiree either at fair value or at the non-controlling interest's proportionate share of the acquiree's identifiable net assets. The new Sections also require non-controlling interest to be presented as a separate component of shareholders' equity. Under Section 1602, non-controlling interest in income is not deducted in arriving at consolidated net income or other comprehensive income. Rather, net income and each component of other comprehensive income are allocated to the controlling and non-controlling interests based on relative ownership interests. These Sections apply to interim and annual consolidated financial statements relating to fiscal years beginning on or after January 1, 2011, and should be adopted concurrently with Section 1582. Earlier adoption is permitted which would be effective as of the beginning of the fiscal year of adoption. The Company is currently considering early adoption of Section 1582, which would result in the reclassification of the non-controlling interest in consolidated joint venture from a separate item on the consolidated balance sheet to a separate component of shareholders' equity for all periods presented.

GILDAN

NOTES TO CONSOLIDATED FINANCIAL STATEMENTS

1. SIGNIFICANT ACCOUNTING POLICIES (continued):

(c) Future accounting standards (continued):

International Financial Reporting Standards
In February 2008, the AcSB confirmed that IFRS, as issued by the International Accounting Standards Board, will replace Canadian generally accepted accounting principles for publicly accountable enterprises effective for fiscal years beginning on or after January 1, 2011. As a result, the Company will be required to change over to IFRS for its fiscal 2012 interim and annual financial statements with comparative information for fiscal 2011.

In preparation for the changeover to IFRS, the Company has developed an IFRS transition plan. The Company has completed its initial phase, comprised of a diagnostic process, which involved a comparison of the Company's current accounting policies under Canadian generally accepted accounting principles with currently issued IFRS. The identified differences are being analyzed and will be addressed according to the level of impact they will have on the key elements of the transition plan. These key elements include: accounting policies, including choices among policies permitted under IFRS; information technology and data systems; internal control over financial reporting; disclosure controls and procedures, including investor relations and external communications plans; and business activities.

As the IFRS transition plan progresses, the Company will continue to report on the status of the transition plan and provide more detailed information of the impact on the key elements indicated above.

(d) Cash and cash equivalents:
The Company considers all liquid investments with maturities of three months or less when acquired to be cash equivalents.

(e) Inventories:
Inventories are stated at the lower of First-In First-Out cost and net realizable value. Inventory costs include the purchase price and other costs directly related to the acquisition of materials. Inventory costs also include the costs directly related to the conversion of materials to finished goods, such as direct labour, and a systematic allocation of fixed and variable production overhead, including manufacturing depreciation expense. The allocation of fixed production overheads to the cost of inventories is based on the normal capacity of the production facilities. Normal capacity is the average production expected to be achieved over a number of periods under normal circumstances.

(f) Property, plant and equipment:
Property, plant and equipment are recorded at cost. Depreciation and amortization are recorded on a straight-line basis over the estimated useful lives of the assets at the following annual rates:

Asset	Rate
Buildings and improvements	2 1/2% to 20%
Equipment	10% to 25%

Assets not in service include expenditures incurred to date for plant expansions which are still in process and equipment not yet in service as at the balance sheet date. Depreciation on these assets commences when the assets are put into service.

The cost of information technology projects including internally developed software is capitalized and included in equipment commencing at the point at which conceptual formulation, design and testing of possible software project alternatives are complete and management authorizes and commits to funding the project. The Company does not capitalize pilot projects where it believes that future economic benefits are less than probable. The costs of information technology projects that are capitalized include the cost of software tools and licenses used in the development of the projects as well as direct payroll and consulting costs.

GILDAN

1. SIGNIFICANT ACCOUNTING POLICIES (continued):

(g) Assets held for sale:
Long-lived assets are classified as held for sale when certain criteria are met, which include: the Company's commitment to a plan to sell the assets; the assets are available for immediate sale in their present condition; an active program to locate buyers and other actions to sell the assets have been initiated; the sale of the assets is probable and their transfer is expected to qualify for recognition as a completed sale within one year; the assets are being actively marketed at reasonable prices in relation to their fair value; and it is unlikely that significant changes will be made to the plan to sell the assets or that the plan will be withdrawn.

The Company measures assets held for sale at the lower of carrying amount or fair value less cost to sell. These assets are not depreciated.

(h) Intangible assets:
Intangible assets, which consist of acquired customer contracts and customer relationships, are being amortized on a straight-line basis over a period of twenty years.

(i) Goodwill:
Goodwill represents the excess of the purchase price over the fair value of net assets acquired. Goodwill is not amortized and is tested for impairment annually, or more frequently if events or changes in circumstances indicate that the asset might be impaired. When the carrying amount of a reporting unit exceeds the estimated fair value of the reporting unit, an impairment loss is recognized in an amount equal to the excess of the carrying value over the fair value of the goodwill, if any.

(j) Impairment of long-lived assets:
Long-lived assets, consisting of property, plant and equipment and intangible assets with finite lives, are reviewed for potential impairment whenever events or changes in circumstances indicate that the carrying amounts of such assets may not be recoverable. An impairment loss would be recognized when the estimated undiscounted future cash flows expected to result from the use of an asset and its eventual disposition are less than its carrying amount. The amount of the impairment loss recognized is measured as the amount by which the carrying value for an asset exceeds the fair value of the asset, with fair value being determined based upon discounted cash flows or appraised values, depending on the nature of the asset.

(k) Foreign currency translation:
Monetary assets and liabilities of the Canadian and foreign operations denominated in currencies other than U.S. dollars are translated at the rates of exchange at the balance sheet date. Other balance sheet items, denominated in currencies other than U.S. dollars, are translated at the rates prevailing at the respective transaction dates. Income and expenses, denominated in currencies other than U.S. dollars, are translated at average rates prevailing during the year. Gains or losses on foreign exchange are recorded in the consolidated statements of earnings.

The foreign subsidiaries are considered to be integrated foreign operations, and their accounts have been translated using the temporal method with translation gains and losses included in the consolidated statements of earnings. The Company does not currently have any self-sustaining foreign subsidiaries.

(l) Revenue recognition:
Revenue is recognized upon shipment of products to customers, since title passes upon shipment, and when the selling price is fixed or determinable. At the time of sale, estimates are made for customer price discounts and volume rebates based on the terms of existing programs. Accruals required for new programs, which relate to prior sales, are recorded at the time the new program is introduced. Sales are recorded net of these program costs and a provision for estimated sales returns, which is based on historical experience, current trends and other known factors, and exclude sales taxes.

(m) Trade accounts receivable:
Trade accounts receivable consist of amounts due from our normal business activities. We maintain an allowance for doubtful accounts to reflect expected credit losses. We provide for bad debts based on collection history and specific risks identified on a customer-by-customer basis. Uncollected accounts are written off through the allowance for doubtful accounts.

GILDAN

NOTES TO CONSOLIDATED FINANCIAL STATEMENTS

1. SIGNIFICANT ACCOUNTING POLICIES (continued):

(n) Cost of sales and gross profit:

Cost of sales includes all raw material costs, manufacturing conversion costs, including manufacturing depreciation expense, sourcing costs, transportation costs incurred until the receipt of finished goods at the Company's distribution facilities, and outbound freight to customers. Cost of sales also includes costs relating to purchasing, receiving and inspection activities, manufacturing administration, third-party manufacturing services, insurance, internal transfer of inventories and customs and duties.

Gross profit is the result of sales less cost of sales. The Company's gross profit may not be comparable to this metric as reported by other companies, since some entities exclude depreciation expense and outbound freight to customers from cost of sales.

(o) Selling, general and administrative expenses:

Selling, general and administrative (SG&A) expenses include warehousing and handling costs, selling and administrative personnel costs, advertising and marketing expenses, costs of leased facilities and equipment, professional fees, non-manufacturing depreciation expense, and other general and administrative expenses. SG&A expenses also include amortization of customer-related intangible assets and bad debt expense.

(p) Advertising and product introduction expenditures:

Advertising and co-op advertising expenses are expensed as incurred in selling, general and administrative expenses. Product introduction expenditures are one-time fees paid to retailers to allow the Company's products to be placed on store shelves. These fees are recognized as a reduction in revenue when incurred unless the Company receives a benefit over a period of time and certain other criteria are met, such as recoverability and enforceability. In this case, these fees are recorded as an asset and are amortized as a reduction of revenue over the term of the arrangement. The Company evaluates the recoverability of these assets on a quarterly basis.

(q) Cotton and yarn procurements:

The Company contracts to buy cotton and yarn with future delivery dates at fixed prices in order to reduce the effects of fluctuations in the prices of cotton used in the manufacture of its products. These contracts are not used for trading purposes. The Company commits to fixed prices on a percentage of its cotton and yarn requirements up to eighteen months in the future. If the cost of committed prices for cotton and yarn plus estimated costs to complete production exceed current selling prices, a loss is recognized for the excess as a charge to cost of sales.

(r) Financial instruments and hedging relationships:

All financial instruments are classified into one of the following five categories: held-for-trading, held-to-maturity investments, loans and receivables, available-for-sale financial assets or other financial liabilities. All financial instruments, including derivatives, are included on the consolidated balance sheet and are measured at fair market value with the exception of loans and receivables, held-to-maturity investments and other financial liabilities, which are measured at amortized cost. Subsequent measurement and recognition of changes in fair value of financial instruments depend on their initial classification. Held-for-trading financial investments are measured at fair value and all gains and losses are included in net earnings in the period in which they arise. Available-for-sale financial instruments are measured at fair value with revaluation gains and losses included in other comprehensive income until the asset is removed from the balance sheet.

1. SIGNIFICANT ACCOUNTING POLICIES (continued):

(r) Financial instruments and hedging relationships (continued):

Derivative instruments are recorded as either assets or liabilities measured at their fair value unless exempted from derivative treatment as a normal purchase and sale. Certain derivatives embedded in other contracts must also be measured at fair value. All changes in the fair value of derivatives are recognized in net earnings unless specific hedge criteria are met, which requires that a company must formally document, designate and assess the effectiveness of transactions that receive hedge accounting. Derivatives that qualify as hedging instruments must be designated as either a "cash flow hedge," when the hedged item is a future cash flow, or a "fair value hedge," when the hedged item is a recognized asset or liability. The effective portion of unrealized gains and losses related to a cash flow hedge are included in other comprehensive income. For a cash flow hedge, when hedging instruments become ineffective before their maturity or the hedging relationship is terminated, any gains, losses, revenues or expenses associated with the hedging item that had previously been recognized in other comprehensive income as a result of applying hedge accounting are carried forward to be recognized in net earnings in the same period as the hedged item affects net earnings to the extent that it is probable that the forecasted cash flows will occur. For a fair value hedge, both the derivative and the hedged item are recorded at fair value in the consolidated balance sheet and the unrealized gains and losses from both items are included in net earnings. Any derivative instrument that does not qualify for hedge accounting is marked-to-market at each reporting date and the gains or losses are included in net earnings.

The Company has classified cash equivalents as held-for-trading. The Company has also classified accounts receivable as loans and receivables, and accounts payable and long-term debt as other financial liabilities, all of which are measured at amortized cost.

The Company may periodically use derivative financial instruments to manage risks related to fluctuations in exchange rates, commodity prices and interest rates. Derivative financial instruments are not used for trading purposes. Forward foreign exchange contracts are entered into with maturities not exceeding twenty-four months.

When the Company utilizes derivatives in hedge accounting relationships, the Company formally documents all relationships between hedging instruments and hedged items, as well as its risk management objective and strategy for undertaking various hedge transactions. This process includes linking all derivatives to specific assets and liabilities on the balance sheet or to specific firm commitments or anticipated transactions. The Company also formally assesses, both at the hedge's inception and on an ongoing basis, whether the derivatives that are used in hedging transactions are effective in offsetting cash flows of hedged items.

As at October 4, 2009, there were no derivative financial instruments outstanding. As at October 5, 2008, all forward foreign exchange contracts were reported on a mark-to-market basis, and the gains or losses were included in net earnings. The Company elected not to apply hedge accounting for these derivatives.

(s) Comprehensive income:

Comprehensive income, which consists of net earnings and other comprehensive income, is defined as the change in shareholders' equity from transactions and other events from non-owner sources. Other comprehensive income refers to items recognized in comprehensive income but that are excluded from net earnings calculated in accordance with generally accepted accounting principles and includes unrealized gains and losses on financial assets classified as available for sale, unrealized foreign currency translation gains and losses arising from self-sustaining foreign subsidiaries and changes in the fair value of the effective portion of qualifying cash flow hedging instruments.

(t) Income taxes:

The Company utilizes the asset and liability method for accounting for income taxes which requires the establishment of future tax assets and liabilities, measured at substantively enacted tax rates, for all temporary differences caused when the tax bases of assets and liabilities differ from those reported in the financial statements. Future income tax assets are evaluated and a valuation allowance is provided to the extent that it is determined that it is no longer more likely than not that the asset will be realized.

GILDAN

NOTES TO CONSOLIDATED FINANCIAL STATEMENTS

1. SIGNIFICANT ACCOUNTING POLICIES (continued):

(t) Income taxes (continued):

The Company's income tax provision is based on interpretations of applicable tax laws, including income tax treaties between various countries in which the Company operates as well as underlying rules and regulations with respect to transfer pricing. These interpretations involve judgments and estimates and may be challenged through government taxation audits that the Company is regularly subject to. The Company recognizes the benefits of uncertain tax filing positions in its financial statements when it is considered likely that the tax position will be sustained upon examination by tax authorities, including the resolution of any related appeals or litigation processes, based on the technical merits of the position. The tax benefits recognized from such positions are measured at the best estimate of the amounts expected to be realized upon ultimate resolution. The Company periodically reviews and adjusts its estimates and assumptions of income tax assets and liabilities as circumstances warrant, such as changes to tax laws, administrative guidance, change in management's assessment of the technical merits of its positions due to new information, and the resolution of uncertainties through either the conclusion of tax audits or expiration of prescribed time limits within relevant statutes. Previously recognized tax benefits relating to uncertain tax filing positions are derecognized if it becomes likely that the Company's tax position will no longer be upheld.

(u) Stock-based compensation and other stock-based payments:

The Company follows the fair value-based method to account for all transactions where services are received in exchange for stock-based compensation and other stock-based payments. For stock options and Treasury restricted share units, compensation cost is measured at the fair value at the date of grant, net of estimated forfeitures, and is expensed over the award's vesting period. For non-Treasury restricted share units, the compensation cost is ultimately measured based on the market price of the Company's shares at the vesting date, net of estimated forfeitures, and is recognized by amortizing the cost over the vesting period. The offsetting liability is marked to the underlying market price until the vesting date with any changes in the market value of the Company's shares resulting in a change in the measure of compensation cost for these awards until vested, which is recorded in the periods in which these changes occur.

For employee share purchase plans, the Company's contribution, on the employee's behalf, is recognized as compensation expense with an offset to share capital, and consideration paid by employees on purchase of stock is also recorded as an increase to share capital.

(v) Employee future benefits:

The Company offers group defined contribution plans to eligible employees whereby the Company matches employees' contributions up to a fixed percentage of the employee's salary. Contributions by the Company to trustee-managed investment portfolios or employee associations are expensed as incurred.

The Company maintains a liability for statutory severance and pre-notice benefit obligations for active employees located in the Caribbean Basin and Central America which is payable to the employees in a lump sum upon termination of employment. The liability is based on management's best estimates of the ultimate costs to be incurred to settle the liability and is based on a number of assumptions and factors, including historical trends, actuarial assumptions and economic conditions.

(w) Earnings per share:

Basic earnings per share are computed by dividing net earnings by the weighted average number of common shares outstanding for the year. Diluted earnings per share are computed using the treasury stock method. Under the treasury stock method, the weighted average number of common shares outstanding for the period is increased to include additional shares from the assumed exercise of options and the issuance of Treasury restricted share units, if dilutive.

The number of additional shares is calculated by assuming that all outstanding options are exercised and all outstanding Treasury restricted share units have vested, and that the proceeds from such exercises, as well as the amount of unrecognized stock-based compensation which is considered to be assumed proceeds under the treasury stock method, are used to repurchase common shares at the average share price for the period. For Treasury restricted share units, only the unrecognized stock-based compensation is considered assumed proceeds since there is no exercise price paid by the holder.

GILDAN

1. SIGNIFICANT ACCOUNTING POLICIES (continued):

(x) Environmental expenditures:

Environmental expenditures that relate to current operations are expensed or capitalized as appropriate. Expenditures that extend the life of the related property or mitigate or prevent future environmental contamination are capitalized in property, plant and equipment and are generally amortized over the remaining useful life of the underlying asset. Expenditures that relate to an existing condition caused by past operations and which are not expected to contribute to current or future operations are expensed. Liabilities are recorded when environmental assessments and/or remedial efforts are likely, and when the costs, based on a specific plan of action in terms of the technology to be used and the extent of the corrective action required, can be reasonably estimated.

The Company may be obliged to incur certain costs should it decide to discontinue some of its activities. There were no liabilities recorded for such costs in the consolidated balance sheets because the Company plans to continue its activities for an indefinite period, and the information available is insufficient to reasonably estimate a schedule for future asset retirement. Where there is a legal obligation associated with the retirement of property, plant and equipment, a liability is initially recognized at its estimated fair value and a corresponding asset retirement cost is added to the carrying value of the related asset and amortized over the remaining life of the underlying asset. The Company had no asset retirement obligations as at October 4, 2009 and October 5, 2008.

(y) Business acquisitions:

The Company accounts for business acquisitions using the purchase method. Accordingly, the purchase price of a business acquisition is allocated to its identifiable net assets including identifiable intangible assets, on the basis of estimated fair values as at the date of purchase, with any excess being assigned to goodwill. When the amounts assigned to identifiable net assets exceed the cost of the purchase, resulting in negative goodwill, the excess is applied, to the extent possible, to certain non-current assets, with the balance recorded as an extraordinary gain.

(z) Use of estimates:

The preparation of financial statements in conformity with generally accepted accounting principles requires management to make estimates and assumptions that affect the reported amounts of assets and liabilities and disclosure of contingent assets and liabilities at the date of the financial statements and the reported amounts of revenues and expenses during the reporting period. Financial results as determined by actual events could differ materially from those estimates.

Significant areas requiring the use of management estimates and assumptions include the allowance for doubtful accounts, inventory valuation, income tax assets and liabilities, accruals for sales promotional programs, the fair value of identifiable tangible and intangible assets acquired in a business combination, impairment of assets and the recoverability of long-lived assets.

2. BUSINESS ACQUISITION:

On October 15, 2007, the Company acquired 100% of the capital stock of V.I. Prewett & Son, Inc. ("Prewett"), a U.S. supplier of basic family socks primarily to U.S. mass-market retailers. The acquisition is intended to enhance further the Company's position as a full-product supplier of socks, activewear and underwear for the retail channel.

The aggregate purchase price of $128.0 million was comprised of cash consideration of $125.3 million, a deferred payment of $1.2 million, which was disbursed in the fourth quarter of fiscal 2009, and transaction costs of $1.5 million. The purchase agreement provides for an additional purchase consideration of up to $10.0 million contingent on specified future events. This amount was paid into escrow by the Company, but events occurring subsequent to the acquisition have resulted in a reduction of the contingent purchase price and escrow balance to $6.0 million as at October 4, 2009. The escrow deposit of $6.0 million (October 5, 2008 - $10.0 million) is included in other assets on the consolidated balance sheet. The remaining contingent purchase price may be subject to further reductions during fiscal 2010 and 2011. Any further purchase price consideration paid by the Company will be accounted for as additional goodwill.

The Company accounted for this acquisition using the purchase method and the results of Prewett have been consolidated with those of the Company from the date of acquisition. The Company has allocated the purchase price to the assets acquired based on their fair values and taking into account all relevant information available at that time.

GILDAN

NOTES TO CONSOLIDATED FINANCIAL STATEMENTS

2. BUSINESS ACQUISITION (continued):

The following table summarizes the estimated fair value of assets acquired and liabilities assumed at the date of acquisition:

Assets acquired:	
Accounts receivable	$ 28,228
Inventories	44,074
Prepaid expenses	1,573
Property, plant and equipment	26,202
Customer contracts and customer relationships	61,000
Other assets	196
	161,273
Liabilities assumed:	
Bank indebtedness	(2,739)
Accounts payable and accrued liabilities	(12,800)
Future income taxes	(24,428)
	(39,967)
Net identifiable assets acquired	121,306
Goodwill	6,709
Purchase price	$ 128,015
Consideration:	
Cash	$ 125,294
Transaction costs	1,525
Deferred payment disbursed in fiscal 2009	1,196
	$ 128,015

Immediately following the acquisition, the Company repaid the entire amount of bank indebtedness assumed at the date of acquisition. Goodwill recorded in connection with this acquisition is not deductible for tax purposes.

3. INVENTORIES:

Inventories were comprised of the following:

	2009	2008
Raw materials and spare parts inventories	$ 43,078	$ 59,742
Work in process	24,576	29,086
Finished goods	234,213	227,344
	$ 301,867	$ 316,172

The amount of inventory recognized as an expense and included in cost of sales was $795.0 million (2008 - $890.6 million), which included an expense of $8.1 million (2008 - $9.4 million), related to the write-down of slow-moving or obsolete inventory.

GILDAN

NOTES TO CONSOLIDATED FINANCIAL STATEMENTS

4. PROPERTY, PLANT AND EQUIPMENT:

2009	Cost	Accumulated depreciation	Net book value
Land	$ 17,152	$ -	$ 17,152
Buildings and improvements	146,823	34,798	112,025
Equipment	460,616	200,438	260,178
Assets not in service	25,183	-	25,183
	$ 649,774	$ 235,236	$ 414,538

2008	Cost	Accumulated depreciation	Net book value
Land	$ 19,110	$ -	$ 19,110
Buildings and improvements	151,989	35,066	116,923
Equipment	420,893	141,960	278,933
Assets not in service	21,550	-	21,550
	$ 613,542	$ 177,026	$ 436,516

Assets not in service include expenditures incurred to date for plant expansions which are still in process and equipment not yet in service as at the balance sheet date.

5. INTANGIBLE ASSETS:

	2009	2008
Customer contracts and customer relationships	$ 63,526	$ 63,526
Accumulated amortization	(6,769)	(3,572)
	$ 56,757	$ 59,954

6. OTHER ASSETS:

	2009	2008
Long-term prepaid expenses and other	$ 2,689	$ 5,529
Long-term non-trade receivable	1,254	1,748
Restricted cash related to the acquisition of Prewett (note 2)	6,042	10,000
	$ 9,985	$ 17,277

7. REVOLVING LINE OF CREDIT:

The Company's joint venture, CanAm, has a revolving line of credit in the amount of $4.0 million. The borrowings are due on demand and bear interest at 30-day LIBOR plus 2.0% (2.26% at October 4, 2009; 4.49% at October 5, 2008). The line of credit is secured by a first ranking security interest on the assets of CanAm. There were no amounts drawn under the line of credit at October 4, 2009 (2008 – nil).

GILDAN

NOTES TO CONSOLIDATED FINANCIAL STATEMENTS

8. LONG-TERM DEBT:

	2009	2008
Secured:		
Term loan, repayable in monthly instalments, bearing interest at 30-day LIBOR plus 2.50% (2.76% at October 4, 2009; 4.99% at October 5, 2008) maturing in September 2012; secured by assets (b)	$ 3,162	$ 4,889
Municipal bonds, repayable in annual instalments, bearing interest at variable rates (3.05% at October 4, 2009; 2.60% at October 5, 2008) maturing in January 2010; secured by building and equipment (c)	714	1,429
Other term loans and notes payable to bank which matured during the year	-	478
	3,876	6,796
Current portion of secured debt	2,348	2,827
	$ 1,528	$ 3,969
Unsecured:		
Revolving term credit facility (a)	$ -	$ 45,000
Term loans, bearing interest at rates up to 4% per annum, maturing at various dates through 2011	511	1,208
	511	46,208
Current portion of unsecured debt	455	729
	56	45,479
Total secured and unsecured long-term debt	$ 1,584	$ 49,448

(a) The Company has a committed revolving term credit facility for a maximum of $400.0 million, which matures in June 2013. The facility is unsecured. There were no amounts drawn under this facility at October 4, 2009 (2008 - $45.0 million). In addition, an amount of $0.2 million (2008 - $3.6 million) has been committed against this facility to cover various letters of credit as described in note 13.

(b) The term loan has been entered into by CanAm. The property, plant and equipment of CanAm serve as collateral for the long-term borrowings of CanAm. Other creditors of CanAm do not have any recourse to the general credit of the Company.

(c) As a result of the acquisition of Kentucky Derby Hosiery Co., Inc. ("Kentucky Derby") in fiscal 2006, the Company assumed the obligations entered into by Kentucky Derby. The property, plant and equipment of Kentucky Derby serve as collateral for the long-term borrowings of Kentucky Derby.

Under various financing arrangements with its bankers and other long-term lenders, the Company is required to meet certain financial covenants. The Company was in compliance with all of these financial covenants as at October 4, 2009 and October 5, 2008.

GILDAN

NOTES TO CONSOLIDATED FINANCIAL STATEMENTS

8. LONG-TERM DEBT (continued):

Principal payments due on long-term debt as at October 4, 2009 are as follows:

Fiscal year		
2010	$	2,803
2011		1,584
	$	4,387

9. SHAREHOLDERS' EQUITY:

(a) The Company has a shareholder rights plan which provides the Board of Directors and the shareholders with additional time to assess any unsolicited take-over bid for the Company and, where appropriate, pursue other alternatives for maximizing shareholder value.

(b) On May 2, 2007, the Board of Directors of the Company declared a two-for-one stock split, effected in the form of a stock dividend, applicable to all of its issued and outstanding common shares, to shareholders of record on May 18, 2007. All share and per share data in these consolidated financial statements reflect the effect of the stock split on a retroactive basis.

(c) Accumulated other comprehensive income:

At the commencement of fiscal 2004, the Company adopted the U.S. dollar as its functional and reporting currency. The change in the functional currency for the prior periods resulted in a currency translation adjustment of $26.2 million, which is reflected in the accumulated other comprehensive income.

(d) Share capital:

Authorized:
First preferred shares, without limit as to number and without par value, issuable in series and non-voting. Second preferred shares, without limit as to number and without par value, issuable in series and non-voting. As at October 4, 2009 and October 5, 2008 none of the first and second preferred shares were issued. Common shares, authorized without limit as to number and without par value.

Issued:
As at October 4, 2009 there were 120,963,028 (2008 - 120,536,501) common shares issued and outstanding.

10. STOCK-BASED COMPENSATION:

(a) Employee share purchase plans:

The Company has employee share purchase plans which allow eligible employees to authorize payroll deductions of up to 10% of their salary to purchase from Treasury, common shares of the Company at a price of 90% of the then current stock price as defined in the plans. Shares purchased under the plans prior to January 1, 2008 must be held for a minimum of one year. Employees purchasing shares under the plans subsequent to January 1, 2008 must hold the shares for a minimum of two years. The Company has reserved 2,800,000 common shares for issuance under the plans. As at October 4, 2009, a total of 219,353 (2008 - 161,746) shares were issued under these plans. Included as compensation costs in selling, general and administrative expenses is $0.1 million (2008 - $0.1 million; 2007 - $0.1 million) relating to the employee share purchase plans.

GILDAN

NOTES TO CONSOLIDATED FINANCIAL STATEMENTS

10. STOCK-BASED COMPENSATION (continued):

(b) Stock options and restricted share units:

The Company's Long Term Incentive Plan (the "LTIP") includes stock options and restricted share units. The LTIP allows the Board of Directors to grant stock options, dilutive restricted share units ("Treasury RSUs") and non-dilutive restricted share units ("non-Treasury RSUs") to officers and other key employees of the Company and its subsidiaries. On February 2, 2006, the shareholders of the Company approved an amendment to the LTIP to fix at 6,000,316 the number of common shares that are issuable pursuant to the exercise of stock options and the vesting of Treasury RSUs. As at October 4, 2009, 3,404,045 common shares remained authorized for future issuance under this plan.

The exercise price payable for each common share covered by a stock option is determined by the Board of Directors at the date of the grant, but may not be less than the closing price of the common shares of the Company on the trading day immediately preceding the effective date of the grant. Stock options vest equally beginning on and after the second, third, fourth and fifth anniversary of the grant date and expire no more than seven or ten years after the date of the grant.

Changes in outstanding stock options were as follows:

	Number	Weighted average exercise price
		(in Canadian dollars)
Options outstanding, September 30, 2007	852	$ 10.08
Granted	128	39.37
Exercised	(81)	5.32
Forfeited	(21)	32.85
Options outstanding, October 5, 2008	878	14.23
Granted	233	23.48
Exercised	(54)	2.58
Forfeited	(47)	30.75
Options outstanding, October 4, 2009	1,010	$ 16.21

The weighted average fair value of each option granted in fiscal 2009 was estimated on the date of grant using the Black-Scholes pricing model with the following weighted average assumptions:

	2009	2008	2007
Risk-free interest rate	3.06%	4.17%	3.90%
Expected volatility	34.98%	30.73%	29.00%
Expected life	5.25 years	4.68 years	4.66 years
Expected dividend yield	-	-	-

The grant date weighted average fair value of options granted in fiscal 2009 was $9.24 (2008 – $13.02; 2007 – $7.70).

GILDAN

10. STOCK-BASED COMPENSATION (continued):

(b) Stock options and restricted share units (continued):

The following table summarizes information about stock options outstanding and exercisable at October 4, 2009:

	Options outstanding			Options exercisable	
Range of exercise prices	Number	Weighted average exercise price	Weighted average remaining contractual life (yrs)	Number	Weighted average exercise price
(in Canadian dollars)		(in Canadian dollars)			(in Canadian dollars)
$ 5.00 - $ 5.39	63	$ 5.25	2.09	63	$ 5.25
$ 6.06 - $ 6.88	301	6.34	0.98	301	6.34
$ 8.64 - $ 8.70	208	8.64	1.37	208	8.64
$11.41 - $23.49	214	23.48	6.01	-	-
$27.17 - $39.39	224	32.61	4.44	87	30.69
	1,010	$ 16.21		659	$ 10.17

A Treasury RSU represents the right of an individual to receive one common share on the vesting date without any monetary consideration being paid to the Company. With the exception of a special, one-time award, which vests at the end of an eight-year period, all other Treasury RSUs awarded to date vest at the end of a five-year vesting period. The vesting of 50% of the Treasury RSUs are dependent upon the fiscal performance of the Company relative to a benchmark group of Canadian publicly listed companies. Compensation expense relating to the Treasury RSUs is recognized in the financial statements over the vesting period based on the fair value of the Treasury RSUs on the date of the grant and estimates relating to forfeitures and the probability of the performance objectives being met. The fair value of the Treasury RSUs granted is equal to the market price of the common shares of the Company at the time of grant.

Changes in outstanding Treasury RSUs were as follows:

	Number	Weighted average fair value per unit
Treasury RSUs outstanding, September 30, 2007	941	$ 16.13
Granted	133	29.35
Settled through the issuance of common shares	(15)	12.87
Forfeited	(81)	22.69
Treasury RSUs outstanding, October 5, 2008	978	17.43
Granted	181	11.11
Settled through the issuance of common shares	(315)	8.75
Forfeited	(86)	26.75
Treasury RSUs outstanding, October 4, 2009	758	$ 18.48

As at October 4, 2009, 20,000 (2008 – nil) of the outstanding Treasury RSUs were vested for which shares will be issued in December 2009. The compensation expense included in selling, general and administrative expenses and cost of sales, in respect of the options and Treasury RSUs, was $3.0 million (2008 - $3.0 million; 2007 - $1.8 million). The counterpart has been recorded as contributed surplus. When the shares are issued to the employees, the amounts previously credited to contributed surplus are transferred to share capital.

GILDAN

NOTES TO CONSOLIDATED FINANCIAL STATEMENTS

10. STOCK-BASED COMPENSATION (continued):

(b) Stock options and restricted share units (continued):

Changes in outstanding non-Treasury RSUs were as follows:

	Number
Non-Treasury RSUs outstanding, September 30, 2007	56
Granted	50
Settled	(1)
Forfeited	(6)
Non-Treasury RSUs outstanding, October 5, 2008	99
Granted	106
Settled	(3)
Forfeited	(17)
Non-Treasury RSUs outstanding, October 4, 2009	185

Non-Treasury RSUs have the same features as Treasury RSUs, except that their vesting period is a maximum of three years and they will be settled in cash at the end of the vesting period. The settlement amount is based on the Company's stock price at the vesting date. As of October 4, 2009, the weighted average fair value per non-Treasury RSU was $18.55. No common shares are issued from treasury under such awards and they are, therefore, non-dilutive. As at October 4, 2009, 47,170 (2008 – nil) of the outstanding non-Treasury RSUs were vested, which were settled in cash subsequent to year-end.

The compensation expense included in selling, general and administrative expenses and cost of sales, in respect of the non-Treasury RSUs, was $0.8 million (2008 - $0.3 million; 2007 - $0.4 million). The total obligation under this plan as at October 4, 2009, is $1.7 million (2008 - $0.8 million) and is recorded in accounts payable and accrued liabilities.

11. DEFERRED SHARE UNIT PLAN:

The Company has a deferred share unit plan for independent members of the Company's Board of Directors who must receive 50% of their annual board retainers in the form of deferred share units ("DSUs"). The value of these DSUs is the market price of the Company's common shares at the time of payment of the retainers or fees. DSUs granted under the plan will be redeemable and the value thereof payable in cash only after the director ceases to act as a director of the Company. As at October 4, 2009, there were 36,086 (2008 - 19,499) DSUs outstanding at a value of $0.7 million (2008 - $0.4 million). This amount is included in accounts payable and accrued liabilities. The DSU obligation is adjusted each quarter based on the market value of the Company's common shares. The Company includes the cost of the DSU plan in selling, general and administrative expenses.

Changes in outstanding DSUs were as follows:

	Number
DSUs outstanding, September 30, 2007	11
Granted	8
DSUs outstanding, October 5, 2008	19
Granted	17
DSUs outstanding, October 4, 2009	36

12. COMMITMENTS AND CONTINGENCIES:

(a) The minimum annual lease payments under operating leases for premises, equipment and aircraft are approximately as follows:

Fiscal year	
2010	$ 7,976
2011	6,760
2012	5,058
2013	4,696
2014	3,954
Thereafter	11,398
	$ 39,842

(b) As at October 4, 2009, there were contractual obligations outstanding of approximately $60.0 million for the acquisition of property, plant and equipment (2008 - $14.1 million).

(c) During fiscal 2009, the United States Department of Agriculture advanced $4.3 million to CanAm in connection with a new subsidy program aimed at subsidizing qualifying capital expenditures. Amounts received under this program are initially based on U.S. cotton consumption. The assistance provided is not repayable, provided that the amounts received under the program are used to finance eligible capital expenditures over a certain period of time. As at October 4, 2009, the balance of financial assistance received in the amount of $4.1 million, which is to be disbursed no later than February 2011 to finance eligible capital expenditures, is included in accounts payable and accrued liabilities. Once the eligible capital expenditures are made, the balance included in accounts payable and accrued liabilities will be recognized as a reduction of the cost of the eligible capital expenditures.

(d) Securities Class Actions:

The Company and certain of its senior officers have been named as defendants in a number of proposed class action lawsuits filed in the United States District Court for the Southern District of New York. A proposed class action has also been filed in the Ontario Superior Court of Justice and a petition for authorization to commence a class action has been filed in the Quebec Superior Court. Each of these U.S. and Canadian lawsuits, which have yet to be certified as a class action by the respective courts at this stage, seek to represent a class comprised of persons who acquired the Company's common shares between August 2, 2007 and April 29, 2008 and allege, among other things, that the defendants misrepresented the Company's financial condition and its financial prospects in its financial guidance concerning the 2008 fiscal year, which was subsequently revised on April 29, 2008.

The U.S. lawsuits have been consolidated, and a consolidated amended complaint was filed alleging claims under the U.S. securities laws. On July 1, 2009, the District Court granted the motion by Gildan and other defendants to dismiss the U.S. action in its entirety, holding that the consolidated amended complaint failed to adequately allege the essential elements of a claim under the applicable provisions of the U.S. securities laws, including the existence of a material misstatement and fraudulent intent. On July 17, 2009, plaintiffs filed a motion seeking reconsideration of this decision only insofar as it declined to grant plaintiffs an opportunity to file a second amended complaint. On July 31, 2009, the Company and the other defendants filed a response to plaintiffs' motion seeking reconsideration. On December 4, 2009, the plaintiffs' motion seeking reconsideration was denied.

In addition to pursuing common law claims, the Ontario action proposes to seek leave from the Ontario court to also bring statutory misrepresentation civil liability claims under Ontario's Securities Act. A motion, along with affidavit evidence, for leave to pursue such statutory liability claims and class certification have been filed by the plaintiff. No date has been set yet for the hearing of that motion.

The Company strongly contests the basis upon which these actions are predicated and intends to vigorously defend its position. However, due to the inherent uncertainties of litigation, it is not possible to predict the final outcome of these lawsuits or determine the amount of any potential losses, if any. No provision for contingent loss has been recorded in the consolidated financial statements.

GILDAN

NOTES TO CONSOLIDATED FINANCIAL STATEMENTS

12. COMMITMENTS AND CONTINGENCIES (continued):

(e) The Company is a party to other claims and litigation arising in the normal course of operations. The Company does not expect the resolution of these matters to have a materially adverse effect on the financial position or results of operations of the Company.

13. GUARANTEES:

The Company, and some of its subsidiaries, have granted corporate guarantees, irrevocable standby letters of credit and surety bonds, to third parties to indemnify them in the event the Company and some of its subsidiaries do not perform their contractual obligations. As at October 4, 2009, the maximum potential liability under these guarantees was $10.0 million (2008 - $14.1 million), of which $4.7 million (2008 - $4.5 million) was for surety bonds and $5.3 million (2008 - $9.6 million) was for corporate guarantees and standby letters of credit. The standby letters of credit mature at various dates up to fiscal 2010, the surety bonds are automatically renewed on an annual basis and the corporate guarantees mature at various dates up to fiscal 2010.

As at October 4, 2009, the Company has recorded no liability with respect to these guarantees, as the Company does not expect to make any payments for the aforementioned items. Management has determined that the fair value of the non-contingent obligations requiring performance under the guarantees in the event that specified triggering events or conditions occur approximates the cost of obtaining the standby letters of credit and surety bonds.

14. INCOME TAXES:

The income tax provision differs from the amount computed by applying the combined Canadian federal and provincial tax rates to earnings before income taxes. The reasons for the difference and the related tax effects are as follows:

	2009	2008	2007
Combined basic Canadian federal and provincial income taxes	$ 27,884	$ 56,114	$ 40,291
(Decrease) increase in income taxes resulting from:			
Effect of different tax rates on earnings of foreign subsidiaries	(32,181)	(51,292)	(38,288)
Income tax (recovery) charge for prior taxation years	(6,085)	26,906	(7,601)
Effect of non-deductible expenses and other	4,596	2,672	783
	$ (5,786)	$ 34,400	$ (4,815)

For fiscal 2009 and 2007, the income tax recoveries of $6.1 million and $7.6 million, respectively, relate to previously unrecognized tax positions of prior taxation years.

In the third quarter of fiscal 2009, the Canada Revenue Agency (CRA) completed its audit of the 2004, 2005 and 2006 taxation years and there were no significant adjustments to the Company's income tax returns. In fiscal 2008, the CRA completed an audit of the Company's income tax returns for the 2000, 2001, 2002 and 2003 fiscal years, the scope of which included a review of the Company's transfer pricing and the allocation of income between the Company's Canadian legal entity and its foreign subsidiaries. On December 10, 2008, the Company reached an agreement with the CRA, which resulted in a tax reassessment related to the restructuring of its international wholesale business and the related transfer of the Company's assets to its Barbados subsidiary, which occurred in fiscal 1999. The terms of the agreement were accounted for in fiscal 2008 through a charge to income tax expense of $26.9 million, including a provision for provincial taxes, and a reclassification of $17.3 million of future income tax liabilities to income taxes payable. There were no penalties assessed as part of the agreement, and there were no other significant income tax adjustments to reported taxable income for the years under audit. During fiscal 2009, the Company made payments of $24.8 million to the CRA and a provincial tax authority, as part of this agreement.

GILDAN

14. INCOME TAXES (continued):

The components of income tax (recovery) expense are as follows:

	2009	2008	2007
Current income taxes	$ (3,352)	$ 50,285	$ 4,104
Future income taxes	(2,434)	(15,885)	(8,919)
	$ (5,786)	$ 34,400	$ (4,815)

As at October 4, 2009, the Company has non-capital loss carryforwards available to reduce future taxable income for Canadian, and US tax purposes of approximately CAD$9.8 million and $20.3 million, respectively, expiring between 2022 and 2029.

The Company has not recognized a future income tax liability for the undistributed earnings of its subsidiaries in the current or prior years because the Company currently does not expect to sell those investments, and for those undistributed earnings that would become taxable, there is no intention to repatriate the earnings.

Significant components of the Company's future income tax assets and liabilities are as follows:

	2009	2008
Future income tax assets (liabilities)		
Non-capital losses	$ 9,261	$ 9,442
Reserves and accruals	5,094	5,690
Other	2,653	1,910
	17,008	17,042
Valuation allowance	(2,579)	(907)
	14,429	16,135
Property, plant and equipment, intangible assets, and other	(30,283)	(34,183)
Net future income tax liability	$ (15,854)	$ (18,048)
Presented as:		
Long-term assets	$ 7,910	$ 9,283
Long-term liabilities	(23,764)	(27,331)
	$ (15,854)	$ (18,048)

GILDAN

NOTES TO CONSOLIDATED FINANCIAL STATEMENTS

15. EARNINGS PER SHARE:

A reconciliation between basic and diluted earnings per share is as follows:

	2009	2008	2007
Basic earnings per share:			
Basic weighted average number of common shares outstanding	120,811	120,479	120,340
Basic earnings per share	$ 0.79	$ 1.21	$ 1.07
Diluted earnings per share:			
Basic weighted average number of common shares outstanding	120,811	120,479	120,340
Plus dilutive impact of stock options and Treasury RSUs	624	1,143	1,198
Diluted weighted average number of common shares outstanding	121,435	121,622	121,538
Diluted earnings per share	$ 0.79	$ 1.20	$ 1.06

Excluded from the above calculation for the year ended October 4, 2009 are 452,093 (2008 – 125,208) stock options and 236,934 (2008 – 25,575) Treasury RSUs which were deemed to be anti-dilutive. All the stock options and Treasury RSUs outstanding for fiscal 2007 were dilutive.

16. RESTRUCTURING AND OTHER CHARGES, AND ASSETS HELD FOR SALE:

	2009	2008	2007
Gain on disposal of assets held for sale	$ (619)	$ (526)	$ (1,530)
Accelerated depreciation	-	-	3,493
Asset impairment loss and write-down of assets held for sale	1,595	2,700	3,560
Employee termination costs and other benefits	2,180	400	13,619
Carrying and dismantling costs associated with assets held for sale	3,120	3,470	8,870
Adjustment for employment contract	(77)	(555)	-
	$ 6,199	$ 5,489	$ 28,012

In fiscal 2006 and 2007, the Company announced the closure, relocation and consolidation of manufacturing and distribution facilities in Canada, the United States and Mexico, as well as the relocation of its corporate office. In fiscal 2008, the Company announced the consolidation of its Haiti sewing operation, which was finalized in the first half of fiscal 2009, and the planned phase out of sock finishing operations in the U.S., which was finalized in the third quarter of fiscal 2009. The costs incurred in connection with these initiatives have been recorded as restructuring and other charges.

For fiscal 2009, restructuring and other charges totalled $6.2 million which included $3.7 million for the closure of the Company's U.S. sock finishing operations in the third quarter, and $3.2 million primarily related to facility closures that occurred in previous fiscal years, including carrying costs and asset write-downs relating to assets held for sale, net of a gain of $0.6 million on the disposal of equipment.

Restructuring charges of $5.5 million in fiscal 2008 included $2.1 million relating to the consolidation of the Company's Haiti sewing operation, and $4.5 million relating to facility closures which occurred in previous fiscal years, primarily for carrying and dismantling costs associated with assets held for sale, net of a gain on disposal of assets held for sale of $0.5 million. The Company also had a recovery of $0.6 million from the obligations accrued for the employment contract with the former Chairman and Co-Chief Executive Officer of the Company.

GILDAN

NOTES TO CONSOLIDATED FINANCIAL STATEMENTS

16. RESTRUCTURING AND OTHER CHARGES AND ASSETS HELD FOR SALE (continued):

The $28.0 million of restructuring charges incurred in fiscal 2007 relate primarily to the closures of the Company's textile facilities in Canada and the United States and its sewing facilities in Mexico as well as the relocation of its corporate office, resulting in employee termination costs of $13.6 million, an asset impairment of $3.6 million, an accelerated depreciation charge of $3.5 million, a gain on disposal of assets held for sale of $1.5 million, and other exit costs of $8.8 million.

Assets held for sale of $6.5 million as at October 4, 2009 (October 5, 2008 - $10.5 million) include property, plant and equipment relating to the closed facilities. The Company expects to incur additional carrying costs relating to the closed facilities, which will be accounted for as restructuring charges as incurred and until all property, plant and equipment related to the closures are disposed of. Any gains or losses on the disposal of the assets held for sale will also be accounted for as restructuring charges as incurred.

Accounts payable and accrued liabilities include amounts relating to restructuring activities and charges to comply with an employment contract, as follows:

Balance, September 30, 2007	$ 4,248
Employee termination and other benefits	400
Adjustment for employment contract	(555)
Foreign exchange adjustment	(95)
Payments	(2,005)
Balance, October 5, 2008	1,993
Employee termination and other benefits	2,180
Adjustment for employment contract	(77)
Foreign exchange adjustment	(25)
Payments	(2,385)
Balance, October 4, 2009	$ 1,686

17. OTHER INFORMATION:

(a) Supplemental cash flow disclosure:

	2009	2008	2007
Cash paid during the year for:			
Interest	$ 2,028	$ 7,866	$ 5,447
Income taxes	30,419	5,867	4,780
Balance of non-cash transactions:			
Additions to property, plant and equipment included in accounts payable and accrued liabilities	627	1,720	2,566
Proceeds on disposal of long-lived assets in other assets	808	1,382	1,855
Proceeds on disposal of long-lived assets in accounts receivable	456	-	1,050
Business acquisition in accounts payable and accrued liabilities	-	1,196	-
Reversal of valuation allowance on acquired future tax assets	-	-	7,340

GILDAN

NOTES TO CONSOLIDATED FINANCIAL STATEMENTS

17. OTHER INFORMATION (continued):

(a) Supplemental cash flow disclosure (continued):

	2009	2008	2007
Non-cash ascribed value credited to share capital from issuance of Treasury RSUs	2,759	190	226
Cash and cash equivalents consist of:			
Cash balances with banks	$ 92,608	$ 8,068	$ 9,250
Short-term investments, bearing interest at rates up to 0.12% at October 4, 2009 and up to 2.22% at October 5, 2008	7,124	4,289	-
	$ 99,732	$ 12,357	$ 9,250

(b) Depreciation and amortization:

	2009	2008 (recast note 1(b))	2007 (recast note 1(b))
Depreciation and amortization of property, plant and equipment and intangible assets	$ 65,407	$ 57,135	$ 37,268
Adjustment for the variation of depreciation of property, plant and equipment included in inventories at the beginning and end of the period	(2,437)	(957)	(1,837)
Depreciation and amortization included in the consolidated statements of earnings and comprehensive income	$ 62,970	$ 56,178	$ 35,431
Consists of:			
Depreciation of property, plant and equipment	$ 59,571	$ 52,887	$ 35,053
Amortization of intangible assets	3,197	3,070	150
Amortization of deferred financing costs and other	202	221	228
Depreciation and amortization included in the consolidated statements of earnings and comprehensive income	$ 62,970	$ 56,178	$ 35,431

(c) The following items were included in the determination of the Company's net earnings:

	2009	2008	2007
Defined contribution expense	$ 1,447	$ 1,827	$ 1,360
Research and development tax credits	-	-	(646)
Bad debt expense (recovery)	5,995	4,543	(1,300)

(d) During fiscal 2009, the Company expensed $7.1 million (2008 - $6.1 million; 2007 - $4.7 million) in cost of sales, representing management's best estimate of the cost of statutory severance and pre-notice benefit obligations accrued for active employees located in the Caribbean Basin and Central America. As at October 4, 2009, an amount of $9.5 million (2008 - $6.9 million) has been included in accounts payable and accrued liabilities.

GILDAN

18. RELATED PARTY TRANSACTIONS:

The Company has transactions with Frontier Spinning Mills, Inc., which manages the operations of CanAm. These transactions are in the normal course of operations and are measured at the exchange amount, which is the amount of consideration established and agreed to by the related parties. The following is a summary of the related party transactions and balances owed:

	2009	2008	2007
Transactions:			
Yarn purchases	$ 149,754	$ 138,642	$ 103,902
Management fee expense	750	750	750
Balances outstanding:			
Accounts payable and accrued liabilities	22,129	32,445	20,130

19. FINANCIAL INSTRUMENTS:

Disclosures relating to exposure to risks, in particular credit risk, liquidity risk, foreign currency risk and interest rate risk, are included in the section entitled "Financial Risk Management" of the Management's Discussion and Analysis of the Company's operations, performance and financial condition as at October 4, 2009, which is included in the Report to Shareholders along with these consolidated financial statements. Accordingly, these disclosures are incorporated into these consolidated financial statements by cross-reference.

(a) Financial instruments – carrying values and fair values:

The fair values of financial assets and liabilities, together with the carrying amounts included in the consolidated balance sheets, are as follows:

		2009		2008
	Carrying amount	Fair value	Carrying amount	Fair value
Financial assets				
Held-for-trading financial assets:				
Cash and cash equivalents	$ 99,732	$ 99,732	$ 12,357	$ 12,357
Loans and receivables:				
Accounts receivable - trade	159,645	159,645	206,276	206,276
Accounts receivable - other	7,117	7,117	9,557	9,557
Long-term non-trade receivable included in other assets	1,254	1,254	1,748	1,748
Restricted cash related to Prewett acquisition included in other assets	6,042	6,042	10,000	10,000
Forward foreign exchange contracts included in other assets	-	-	929	929

GILDAN

NOTES TO CONSOLIDATED FINANCIAL STATEMENTS

19. FINANCIAL INSTRUMENTS (continued):

(a) Financial instruments – carrying values and fair values (continued):

	2009		2008	
	Carrying amount	Fair value	Carrying amount	Fair value
Financial liabilities				
Other financial liabilities:				
Accounts payable and accrued liabilities	$ 124,378	$ 124,378	$ 149,344	$ 149,344
Long-term debt - bearing interest at variable rates:				
Revolving long-term credit facility	-	-	45,000	45,000
Other long-term debt	3,876	3,876	6,318	6,318
Long-term debt - bearing interest at fixed rates	511	511	1,686	1,686

The Company has determined that the fair value of its short-term financial assets and liabilities approximates their respective carrying amounts as at the balance sheet dates because of the short-term maturity of those instruments. The fair values of the long-term receivable, the restricted cash related to the acquisition of Prewett, and the Company's interest-bearing financial liabilities also approximate their respective carrying amounts. The fair values of cash and cash equivalents and forward foreign contracts were measured using Level 2 and Level 1 inputs, respectively, in the fair value hierarchy.

(b) Financial (income) expense, net:

	2009	2008	2007
Interest expense (i)	$ 1,824	$ 7,223	$ 4,898
Bank and other financial charges	1,039	946	1,239
Foreign exchange (gain) loss (ii)	(3,167)	1,071	(717)
	$ (304)	$ 9,240	$ 5,420

(i) Interest expense:

	2009	2008	2007
Interest expense on long-term debt	$ 1,800	$ 7,422	$ 4,997
Interest expense on short-term indebtedness	142	191	233
Interest income on held-for-trading financial assets	(103)	(413)	(460)
Interest income on loans and receivables	(80)	(80)	-
Other interest expense	65	103	128
	$ 1,824	$ 7,223	$ 4,898

Interest income on held-for-trading financial assets consists of interest earned from cash and cash equivalents invested in short-term deposits. Interest income on loans and receivables relates to interest earned on the Company's long-term receivable included in other assets.

GILDAN

NOTES TO CONSOLIDATED FINANCIAL STATEMENTS

19. FINANCIAL INSTRUMENTS (continued):

(b) Financial (income) expense, net (continued):

(ii) Foreign exchange (gain) loss:

	2009	2008	2007
(Gain) loss relating to financial assets and liabilities, excluding forward foreign exchange contracts	$ (220)	$ 674	$ (1,486)
(Gain) loss relating to forward foreign exchange contracts, including amounts realized on contract maturity and changes in fair value of open positions	(82)	2,084	(1,945)
Foreign exchange (gain) loss relating to financial instruments	(302)	2,758	(3,431)
Other foreign exchange (gain) loss	(2,865)	(1,687)	2,714
	$ (3,167)	$ 1,071	$ (717)

(c) Forward foreign exchange contracts:

As at October 4, 2009 the Company had no outstanding derivative financial instruments relating to commitments to buy and sell foreign currencies through forward foreign exchange contracts.

The following table summarizes the Company's derivative financial instruments at October 5, 2008:

October 5, 2008	Maturity	Notional foreign currency amount	Average exchange rate	Notional U.S. equivalent	Carrying and fair value Asset	Carrying and fair value Liability
Buy CAD/Sell USD	0-6 months	5,483	0.9302	$ 5,100	$ -	$ -
Buy EUR/Sell GBP	0-6 months	962	1.3740	1,322	-	-
Sell EUR/Buy USD	0-6 months	5,650	1.4591	8,244	472	-
Sell GBP/Buy USD	0-6 months	2,951	1.9177	5,659	457	-
				$ 20,325	$ 929	$ -

20. CAPITAL DISCLOSURES:

The Company's objective in managing capital is to ensure sufficient liquidity to pursue its organic growth strategy and undertake selective acquisitions, while at the same time taking a conservative approach towards financial leverage and management of financial risk.

The Company's capital is composed of net debt and shareholders' equity. Net debt consists of interest-bearing debt less cash and cash equivalents. The Company's primary uses of capital are to finance increases in non-cash working capital and capital expenditures for capacity expansion as well as acquisitions. The Company currently funds these requirements out of its internally-generated cash flows and the periodic use of its revolving long-term bank credit facility.

GILDAN

NOTES TO CONSOLIDATED FINANCIAL STATEMENTS

20. CAPITAL DISCLOSURES (continued):

The primary measure used by the Company to monitor its financial leverage is its ratio of net debt to earnings before interest, taxes, depreciation and amortization, non-controlling interest, and restructuring and other charges ("EBITDA"), which it aims to maintain at less than 3.0:1. Net debt is computed as at the most recent quarterly balance sheet date. EBITDA is based on the last four quarters ending on the same date as the balance sheet date used to compute net debt. The computation of net debt (cash in excess of total indebtedness) and EBITDA as at October 4, 2009, October 5, 2008 and September 30, 2007 were as follows:

	2009	2008	2007
Current portion of long-term debt	$ 2,803	$ 3,556	$ 3,689
Long-term debt	1,584	49,448	55,971
Less: cash and cash equivalents	(99,732)	(12,357)	(9,250)
(Cash in excess of total indebtedness) net debt	$ (95,345)	$ 40,647	$ 50,410

	For the last four quarters ended on		
	October 4, 2009	October 5, 2008	September 30, 2007
Net earnings	$ 95,329	$ 146,350	$ 129,062
Restructuring and other charges	6,199	5,489	28,012
Depreciation and amortization	65,407	57,135	37,268
Variation of depreciation included in inventories	(2,437)	(957)	(1,837)
Interest, net	1,824	7,223	4,898
Income tax (recovery) expense	(5,786)	34,400	(4,815)
Non-controlling interest in consolidated joint venture	110	230	1,278
EBITDA	$ 160,646	$ 249,870	$ 193,866
Net debt to EBITDA ratio	n/a	0.2:1	0.3:1

The terms of the revolving credit facility require the Company to maintain a net debt to EBITDA ratio below 3.0:1, although this limit may be exceeded under certain circumstances. The Company does not currently plan to refinance its revolving credit facility, or a portion thereof, with debt of longer maturities or to raise additional equity capital. In the first quarter of fiscal 2008, the Company used its revolving credit facility to finance the acquisition of Prewett.

In order to maintain or adjust its capital structure, the Company, upon approval from its Board of Directors, may issue or repay long-term debt, issue shares, repurchase shares, pay dividends or undertake other activities as deemed appropriate under the specific circumstances. The Company does not currently pay a dividend. However, the Company's Board of Directors periodically evaluates the merits of introducing a dividend.

The Company is not subject to any capital requirements imposed by a regulator.

GILDAN

NOTES TO CONSOLIDATED FINANCIAL STATEMENTS

21. SEGMENTED INFORMATION:

The Company manufactures and sells activewear, socks and underwear. The Company operates in one business segment, being high-volume, basic, frequently replenished, non-fashion apparel.

(a) Net sales by major product group:

	2009	2008	2007
Activewear and underwear	$ 795,535	$ 957,061	$ 826,252
Socks	242,784	292,650	138,177
	$ 1,038,319	$ 1,249,711	$ 964,429

(b) Major customers and revenues by geographic area:

(i) The Company has two customers accounting for at least 10% of total net sales:

	2009	2008	2007
Company A	18.6%	23.1%	23.1%
Company B	15.5%	13.6%	5.3%

(ii) Net sales were derived from customers located in the following geographic areas:

	2009	2008	2007
United States	$ 939,717	$ 1,125,961	$ 852,522
Canada	35,134	56,353	53,336
Europe and other	63,468	67,397	58,571
	$ 1,038,319	$ 1,249,711	$ 964,429

(c) Property, plant and equipment by geographic area are as follows:

	October 4, 2009	October 5, 2008
Caribbean Basin and Central America	$ 324,430	$ 325,670
United States	67,491	83,264
Canada and other	22,617	27,582
	$ 414,538	$ 436,516

Goodwill and intangible assets relate to acquisitions located in the United States.

22. COMPARATIVE FIGURES:

Certain comparative figures in the statement of earnings and comprehensive income have been reclassified as described in note 1(a). In addition, certain other comparative figures have been adjusted to conform to the current year's presentation including the reclassification of a non-trade accounts receivable balance of $6.3 million as at October 5, 2008 against accounts payable and accrued liabilities for which the Company has the legal right of offset and intends to settle on a net basis.

Appendix B

Time Value of Money: Future Value and Present Value

The following discussion of future value lays the foundation for our explanation of present value in Chapter 8 but is not essential. For the valuation of long-term liabilities, some instructors may wish to begin on page 758.

The term *time value of money* refers to the fact that money earns interest over time. *Interest* is the cost of using money. To borrowers, interest is the expense of renting money. To lenders, interest is the revenue earned from lending. We must always recognize the interest we receive or pay. Otherwise, we overlook an important part of the transaction. Suppose you invest $4,545 in corporate bonds that pay 10% interest each year. After one year, the value of your investment has grown to $5,000. The difference between your original investment ($4,545) and the future value of the investment ($5,000) is the amount of interest revenue you will earn during the year ($455). If you ignored the interest, you would fail to account for the interest revenue you have earned. Interest becomes more important as the time period lengthens because the amount of interest depends on the span of time the money is invested.

Let's consider a second example, this time from the borrower's perspective. Suppose you purchase a machine for your business. The cash price of the machine is $8,000, but you cannot pay cash now. To finance the purchase, you sign an $8,000 note payable. The note requires you to pay the $8,000 plus 10% interest one year from the date of purchase. Is your cost of the machine $8,000, or is it $8,800 [$8,000 plus interest of $800 ($8,000 × 0.10)]? The cost is $8,000. The additional $800 is interest expense and not part of the cost of the machine.

Future Value

The main application of future value is the accumulated balance of an investment at a future date. In our first example above, the investment earned 10% per year. After one year, $4,545 grew to $5,000, as shown in Exhibit B-1.

If the money were invested for five years, you would have to perform five such calculations. You would also have to consider the compound interest that your investment is earning. *Compound interest* is not only the interest you earn on your principal amount, but also the interest you receive on the interest you have already earned. Most business applications include compound interest. The table on the next page shows the interest revenue earned on the original $4,545 investment each year for five years at 10%:

EXHIBIT B-1 **Future Value: An Example**

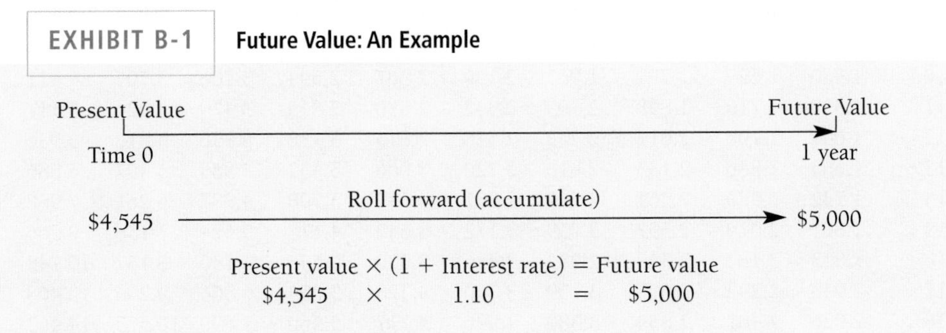

End of Year	*Interest*	*Future Value*
0	—	$4,545
1	$4,545 × 0.10 = $455	5,000
2	5,000 × 0.10 = 500	5,500
3	5,500 × 0.10 = 550	6,050
4	6,050 × 0.10 = 605	6,655
5	6,655 × 0.10 = 666	7,321

Earning 10%, a $4,545 investment grows to $5,000 at the end of one year, to $5,500 at the end of two years, and $7,321 at the end of five years. Throughout this appendix we round off to the nearest dollar.

Future-Value Tables

The process of computing a future value is called *accumulating* because the future value is *more* than the present value. Mathematical tables ease the computational burden. Exhibit B-2, Future Value of $1, gives the future value for a single sum (a present value), $1, invested to earn a particular interest rate for a specific number of periods. Future value depends on three factors: (1) the amount of the investment, (2) the length of time between investment and future accumulation, and (3) the interest rate. Future-value and present-value tables are based on $1 because unity (the value 1) is so easy to work with.

In business applications, interest rates are always stated for the annual period of one year unless specified otherwise. In fact, an interest rate can be stated for any period, such as 3% per quarter or 5% for a six-month period. The length of the period is arbitrary. For example, an investment may promise a return (income) of 3% per quarter for six months (two quarters). In that case, you would be working with 3% interest for two periods. It would be incorrect to use 6% for one period because the interest is 3% compounded quarterly, and that amount differs from 6% compounded semiannually. *Take care in studying future-value and present-value problems to align the interest rate with the appropriate number of periods.*

Let's see how a future-value table like the one in Exhibit B-2 is used. The future value of $1.00 invested at 8% for one year is $1.08 ($1.00 × 1.080, which appears at the junc-

EXHIBIT B-2 **Future Value of $1**

	Future Value of $1									
Periods	4%	5%	6%	7%	8%	9%	10%	12%	14%	16%
1	1.040	1.050	1.060	1.070	1.080	1.090	1.100	1.120	1.140	1.160
2	1.082	1.103	1.124	1.145	1.166	1.188	1.210	1.254	1.300	1.346
3	1.125	1.158	1.191	1.225	1.260	1.295	1.331	1.405	1.482	1.561
4	1.170	1.216	1.262	1.311	1.360	1.412	1.464	1.574	1.689	1.811
5	1.217	1.276	1.338	1.403	1.469	1.539	1.611	1.762	1.925	2.100
6	1.265	1.340	1.419	1.501	1.587	1.677	1.772	1.974	2.195	2.436
7	1.316	1.407	1.504	1.606	1.714	1.828	1.949	2.211	2.502	2.826
8	1.369	1.477	1.594	1.718	1.851	1.993	2.144	2.476	2.853	3.278
9	1.423	1.551	1.689	1.838	1.999	2.172	2.358	2.773	3.252	3.803
10	1.480	1.629	1.791	1.967	2.159	2.367	2.594	3.106	3.707	4.411
11	1.539	1.710	1.898	2.105	2.332	2.580	2.853	3.479	4.226	5.117
12	1.601	1.796	2.012	2.252	2.518	2.813	3.138	3.896	4.818	5.936
13	1.665	1.886	2.133	2.410	2.720	3.066	3.452	4.363	5.492	6.886
14	1.732	1.980	2.261	2.579	2.937	3.342	3.798	4.887	6.261	7.988
15	1.801	2.079	2.397	2.759	3.172	3.642	4.177	5.474	7.138	9.266
16	1.873	2.183	2.540	2.952	3.426	3.970	4.595	6.130	8.137	10.748
17	1.948	2.292	2.693	3.159	3.700	4.328	5.054	6.866	9.276	12.468
18	2.026	2.407	2.854	3.380	3.996	4.717	5.560	7.690	10.575	14.463
19	2.107	2.527	3.026	3.617	4.316	5.142	6.116	8.613	12.056	16.777
20	2.191	2.653	3.207	3.870	4.661	5.604	6.728	9.646	13.743	19.461

tion of the 8% column and row 1 in the Periods column). The figure 1.080 includes both the principal (1.000) and the compound interest for one period (0.080).

Suppose you deposit \$5,000 in a savings account that pays annual interest of 8%. The account balance at the end of one year will be \$5,400. To compute the future value of \$5,000 at 8% for one year, multiply \$5,000 by 1.080 to get \$5,400. Now suppose you invest in a 10-year, 8% guaranteed investment certificate (GIC). What will be the future value of the GIC at maturity? To compute the future value of \$5,000 at 8% for 10 periods, multiply \$5,000 by 2.159 (from Exhibit B-2) to get \$10,795. This future value of \$10,795 indicates that \$5,000, earning 8% interest compounded annually, grows to \$10,795 at the end of 10 years. Using Exhibit B-2, you can find any present amount's future value at a particular future date. Future value is especially helpful for computing the amount of cash you will have on hand for some purpose in the future.

Future Value of an Annuity

In the preceding example, we made an investment of a single amount. Other investments, called *annuities*, include multiple investments of an equal periodic amount at fixed intervals over the duration of the investment. Consider a family investing for a child's education. The Dietrichs can invest \$4,000 annually to accumulate a college fund for 15-year-old Helen. The investment can earn 7% annually until Helen turns 18—a three-year investment. How much will be available for Helen on the date of the last investment? Exhibit B-3 shows the accumulation—a total future value of \$12,860.

The first \$4,000 invested by the Dietrichs grows to \$4,580 over the investment period. The second amount grows to \$4,280, and the third amount stays at \$4,000 because it has no time to earn interest. The sum of the three future values (\$4,580 + \$4,280 + \$4,000) is the future value of the annuity (\$12,860), which can also be computed as follows:

End of Year	*Annual Investment*		*Interest*		*Increase for the Year*	*Future Value of Annuity*
0	—		—		—	0
1	\$4,000		—		\$4,000	\$ 4,000
2	4,000	+	(\$4,000 × 0.07 = \$280)	=	4,280	8,280
3	4,000	+	(\$8,280 × 0.07 = \$580)	=	4,580	12,860

These computations are laborious. As with the Future Value of \$1 (a lump sum), mathematical tables ease the strain of calculating annuities. Exhibit B-4, Future Value of Annuity of \$1, gives the future value of a series of investments, each of equal amount, at regular intervals.

What is the future value of an annuity of three investments of \$1 each that earn 7%? The answer, 3.215, can be found at the junction of the 7% column and row 3 in Exhibit B-4. This amount can be used to compute the future value of the investment for Helen's education, as follows:

Amount of each periodic investment	×	Future value of annuity of \$1 (Exhibit B-4)	=	Future value of investment
\$4,000	×	3.215	=	\$12,860

EXHIBIT B-3 Future Value of an Annuity

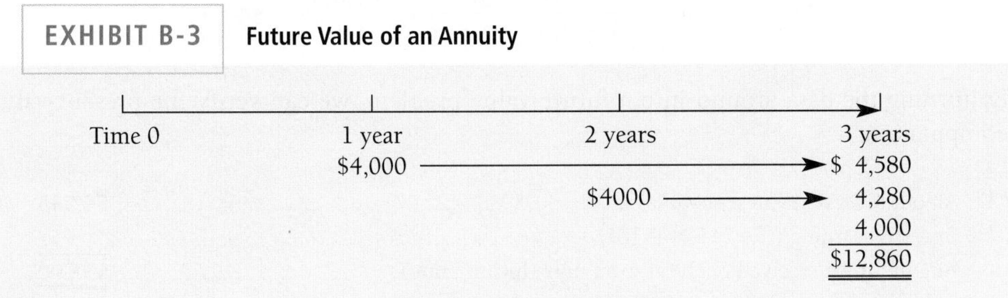

EXHIBIT B-4 **Future Value of Annuity of $1**

Future Value of Annuity of $1

Periods	4%	5%	6%	7%	8%	9%	10%	12%	14%	16%
1	1.000	1.000	1.000	1.000	1.000	1.000	1.000	1.000	1.000	1.000
2	2.040	2.050	2.060	2.070	2.080	2.090	2.100	2.120	2.140	2.160
3	3.122	3.153	3.184	3.215	3.246	3.278	3.310	3.374	3.440	3.506
4	4.246	4.310	4.375	4.440	4.506	4.573	4.641	4.779	4.921	5.066
5	5.416	5.526	5.637	5.751	5.867	5.985	6.105	6.353	6.610	6.877
6	6.633	6.802	6.975	7.153	7.336	7.523	7.716	8.115	8.536	8.977
7	7.898	8.142	8.394	8.654	8.923	9.200	9.487	10.089	10.730	11.414
8	9.214	9.549	9.897	10.260	10.637	11.028	11.436	12.300	13.233	14.240
9	10.583	11.027	11.491	11.978	12.488	13.021	13.579	14.776	16.085	17.519
10	12.006	12.578	13.181	13.816	14.487	15.193	15.937	17.549	19.337	21.321
11	13.486	14.207	14.972	15.784	16.645	17.560	18.531	20.655	23.045	25.733
12	15.026	15.917	16.870	17.888	18.977	20.141	21.384	24.133	27.271	30.850
13	16.627	17.713	18.882	20.141	21.495	22.953	24.523	28.029	32.089	36.786
14	18.292	19.599	21.015	22.550	24.215	26.019	27.975	32.393	37.581	43.672
15	20.024	21.579	23.276	25.129	27.152	29.361	31.772	37.280	43.842	51.660
16	21.825	23.657	25.673	27.888	30.324	33.003	35.950	42.753	50.980	60.925
17	23.698	25.840	28.213	30.840	33.750	36.974	40.545	48.884	59.118	71.673
18	25.645	28.132	30.906	33.999	37.450	41.301	45.599	55.750	68.394	84.141
19	27.671	30.539	33.760	37.379	41.446	46.018	51.159	63.440	78.969	98.603
20	29.778	33.066	36.786	40.995	45.762	51.160	57.275	72.052	91.025	115.380

This one-step calculation is much easier than computing the future value of each annual investment and then summing the individual future values. In this way, you can compute the future value of any investment consisting of equal periodic amounts at regular intervals. Businesses make periodic investments to accumulate funds for equipment replacement and other uses—an application of the future value of an annuity.

Present Value

Often a person knows a future amount and needs to know the related present value. Recall Exhibit B-1, in which present value and future value are on opposite ends of the same time line. Suppose an investment promises to pay you $5,000 at the *end* of one year. How much would you pay *now* to acquire this investment? You would be willing to pay the present value of the $5,000 future amount.

Like future value, present value depends on three factors: (1) the amount of payment (or receipt), (2) the length of time between investment and future receipt (or payment), and (3) the interest rate. The process of computing a present value is called discounting because the present value is less than the future value.

In our investment example, the future receipt is $5,000. The investment period is one year. Assume that you demand an annual interest rate of 10% on your investment. With all three factors specified, you can compute the present value of $5,000 at 10% for one year:

$$\textbf{Present value} = \frac{\textbf{Future value}}{\textbf{1 + Interest rate}} = \frac{\$5{,}000}{1.10} = \$4{,}545$$

By turning the data around into a future-value problem, we can verify the present-value computation:

Amount invested (present value)	$4,545
Expected earnings ($4,545 × 0.10)	455
Amount to be received one year from now (future value)	$5,000

This example illustrates that present value and future value are based on the same equation:

$$\text{Future} = \text{Present value} \times (1 + \text{Interest rate})$$

$$\text{Present value} = \frac{\text{Future value}}{1 + \text{Interest rate}}$$

If the $5,000 is to be received two years from now, you will pay only $4,132 for the investment, as shown in Exhibit B-5. By turning the data around, we verify that $4,132 accumulates to $5,000 at 10% for two years:

Amount invested (present value)	$4,132
Expected earnings for first year ($4,132 × 0.10)	413
Value of investment after one year	4,545
Expected earnings for second year ($4,545 × 0.10)	455
Amount to be received two years from now (future value)	$5,000

You would pay $4,132—the present value of $5,000—to receive the $5,000 future amount at the end of two years at 10% per year. The $868 difference between the amount invested ($4,132) and the amount to be received ($5,000) is the return on the investment, the sum of the two interest receipts: $413 + $455 = $868.

Present-Value Tables

We have shown the simple formula for computing present value. However, calculating present value "by hand" for investments spanning many years is time-consuming and presents too many opportunities for arithmetic errors. Present-value tables ease our work. Let's reexamine our examples of present value by using Exhibit B-6: Present Value of $1 given at the top of the next page.

For the 10% investment for one year, we find the junction of the 10% column and row 1 in Exhibit B-6. The figure 0.909 is computed as follows: 1/1.10 = 0.909. This work has been done for us, and only the present values are given in the table. To calculate the present value for $5,000, we multiply 0.909 by $5,000. The result is $4,545, which matches the result we obtained by hand.

For the two-year investment, we read down the 10% column and across row 2. We multiply 0.826 (computed as 0.909/1.10 = 0.826) by $5,000 and get $4,130, which confirms our earlier computation of $4,132 (the difference is due to rounding in the present-value table). Using the table, we can compute the present value of any single future amount.

Present Value of an Annuity

Return to the investment example on page xxx. That investment provided the investor with only a single future receipt ($5,000 at the end of two years). *Annuity investments* provide multiple receipts of an equal amount at fixed intervals over the investment's duration.

Consider an investment that promises *annual* cash receipts of $10,000 to be received at the end of each of three years. Assume that you demand a 12% return on your investment.

EXHIBIT B-5 **Future Value: An Example**

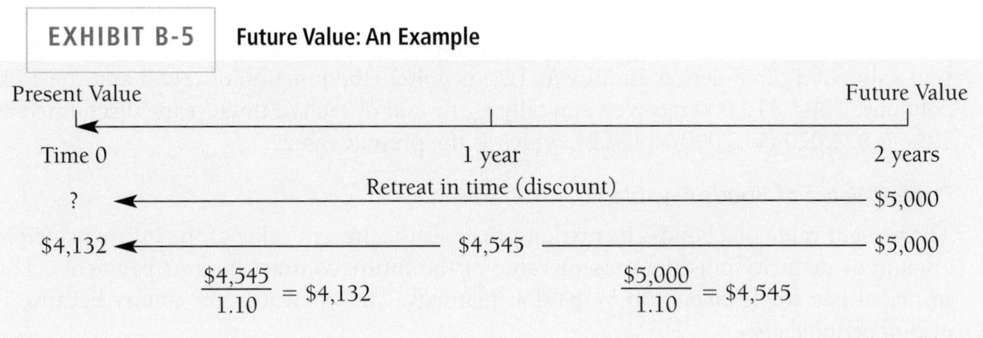

EXHIBIT B-6 **Present Value of $1**

					Present Value of $1				
Periods	4%	5%	6%	7%	8%	10%	12%	14%	16%
1	0.962	0.952	0.943	0.935	0.926	0.909	0.893	0.877	0.862
2	0.925	0.907	0.890	0.873	0.857	0.826	0.797	0.769	0.743
3	0.889	0.864	0.840	0.816	0.794	0.751	0.712	0.675	0.641
4	0.855	0.823	0.792	0.763	0.735	0.683	0.636	0.592	0.552
5	0.822	0.784	0.747	0.713	0.681	0.621	0.567	0.519	0.476
6	0.790	0.746	0.705	0.666	0.630	0.564	0.507	0.456	0.410
7	0.760	0.711	0.665	0.623	0.583	0.513	0.452	0.400	0.354
8	0.731	0.677	0.627	0.582	0.540	0.467	0.404	0.351	0.305
9	0.703	0.645	0.592	0.544	0.500	0.424	0.361	0.308	0.263
10	0.676	0.614	0.558	0.508	0.463	0.386	0.322	0.270	0.227
11	0.650	0.585	0.527	0.475	0.429	0.350	0.287	0.237	0.195
12	0.625	0.557	0.497	0.444	0.397	0.319	0.257	0.208	0.168
13	0.601	0.530	0.469	0.415	0.368	0.290	0.229	0.182	0.145
14	0.577	0.505	0.442	0.388	0.340	0.263	0.205	0.160	0.125
15	0.555	0.481	0.417	0.362	0.315	0.239	0.183	0.140	0.108
16	0.534	0.458	0.394	0.339	0.292	0.218	0.163	0.123	0.093
17	0.513	0.436	0.371	0.317	0.270	0.198	0.146	0.108	0.080
18	0.494	0.416	0.350	0.296	0.250	0.180	0.130	0.095	0.069
19	0.475	0.396	0.331	0.277	0.232	0.164	0.116	0.083	0.060
20	0.456	0.377	0.312	0.258	0.215	0.149	0.104	0.073	0.051

What is the investment's present value? That is, what would you pay today to acquire the investment? The investment spans three periods, and you would pay the sum of three present values. The computation is as follows:

Year	*Annual Cash Receipt*	*Present Value of $1 at 12% (Exhibit B-6)*	*Present Value of Annual Cash Receipt*
1	$10,000	0.893	$ 8,930
2	10,000	0.797	7,970
3	10,000	0.712	7,120
Total present value of investment			$24,020

The present value of this annuity is $24,020. By paying this amount today, you will receive $10,000 at the end of each of the three years while earning 12% on your investment.

This example illustrates repetitive computations of the three future amounts, a time-consuming process. One way to ease the computational burden is to add the three present values of $1 (0.893 + 0.797 + 0.712) and multiply their sum (2.402) by the annual cash receipt ($10,000) to obtain the present value of the annuity ($10,000 × 2.402 = $24,020).

An easier approach is to use a present value of an annuity table. Exhibit B-7 shows the present value of $1 to be received periodically for a given number of periods. The present value of a three-period annuity at 12% is 2.402 (the junction of row 3 and the 12% column). Thus, $10,000 received annually at the end of each of three years, discounted at 12%, is $24,020 ($10,000 × 2.402), which is the present value.

Present Value of Bonds Payable

The present value of a bond—its market price—is the present value of the future principal amount at maturity plus the present value of the future contract interest payments. The principal is a *single amount* to be paid at maturity. The interest is an *annuity* because it occurs periodically.

EXHIBIT B-7 **Present Value of Annuity of $1**

Present Value Annuity of $1

Periods	4%	5%	6%	7%	8%	10%	12%	14%	16%
1	0.962	0.952	0.943	0.935	0.926	0.909	0.893	0.877	0.862
2	1.886	1.859	1.833	1.808	1.783	1.736	1.690	1.647	1.605
3	2.775	2.723	2.673	2.624	2.577	2.487	2.402	2.322	2.246
4	3.630	3.546	3.465	3.387	3.312	3.170	3.037	2.914	2.798
5	4.452	4.329	4.212	4.100	3.993	3.791	3.605	3.433	3.274
6	5.242	5.076	4.917	4.767	4.623	4.355	4.111	3.889	3.685
7	6.002	5.786	5.582	5.389	5.206	4.868	4.564	4.288	4.039
8	6.733	6.463	6.210	5.971	5.747	5.335	4.968	4.639	4.344
9	7.435	7.108	6.802	6.515	6.247	5.759	5.328	4.946	4.607
10	8.111	7.722	7.360	7.024	6.710	6.145	5.650	5.216	4.833
11	8.760	8.306	7.887	7.499	7.139	6.495	5.938	5.453	5.029
12	9.385	8.863	8.384	7.943	7.536	6.814	6.194	5.660	5.197
13	9.986	9.394	8.853	8.358	7.904	7.103	6.424	5.842	5.342
14	10.563	9.899	9.295	8.745	8.244	7.367	6.628	6.002	5.468
15	11.118	10.380	9.712	9.108	8.559	7.606	6.811	6.142	5.575
16	11.652	10.838	10.106	9.447	8.851	7.824	6.974	6.265	5.669
17	12.166	11.274	10.477	9.763	9.122	8.022	7.120	6.373	5.749
18	12.659	11.690	10.828	10.059	9.372	8.201	7.250	6.467	5.818
19	13.134	12.085	11.158	10.336	9.604	8.365	7.366	6.550	5.877
20	13.590	12.462	11.470	10.594	9.818	8.514	7.469	6.623	5.929

Let's compute the present value of 9% five-year bonds. The face value of the bonds is $100,000, and they pay $4^1/_2$% contract (cash) interest semiannually (that is, twice a year). At issuance, the market interest rate is expressed as 10% annually, but it is computed at 5% semiannually. Therefore, the effective interest rate for each of the 10 semiannual periods is 5%. We thus use 5% in computing the present value (PV) of the maturity and of the interest. The market price of these bonds is $96,149, as follows:

	Effective Annual Interest Rate ÷ 2	*Number of Semiannual Interest Payments*	
PV of principal:			
$100,000 × PV of single amount at 5%		for 10 periods	
$100,000 × 0.614 (Exhibit B-6)			$61,400
PV of contract (cash) interest:			
$100,000 × 0.045 × PV of annuity at 5%		for 10 periods	
$4,500 × 7.722 (Exhibit B-7)			34,749
PV (market price) of bonds			$96,149

The market price of the bonds shows a discount because the contract interest rate on the bonds (9%) is less than the market interest rate (10%).

Let's consider a premium price for the 9% TELUS bonds. Assume that the market interest rate is 8% (rather than 10%) at issuance. The effective interest rate is thus 4% for each of the 10 semiannual periods:

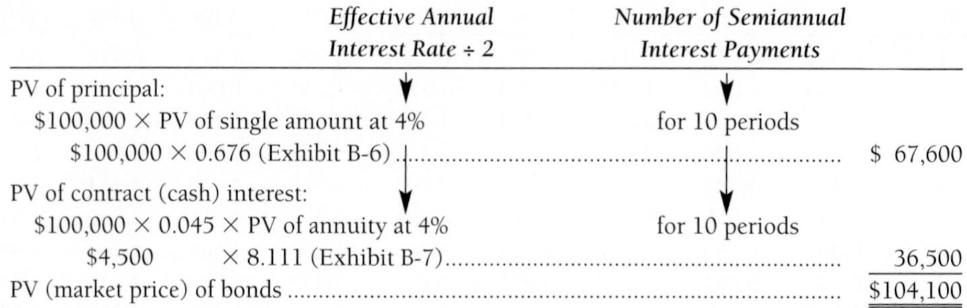

	Effective Annual Interest Rate ÷ 2	*Number of Semiannual Interest Payments*	
PV of principal:			
$100,000 × PV of single amount at 4%		for 10 periods	
$100,000 × 0.676 (Exhibit B-6)			$ 67,600
PV of contract (cash) interest:			
$100,000 × 0.045 × PV of annuity at 4%		for 10 periods	
$4,500 × 8.111 (Exhibit B-7)			36,500
PV (market price) of bonds			$104,100

We discuss accounting for these bonds on pages 412–414. It may be helpful for you to reread this section ("Present Value of Bonds Payable") after you've studied those pages.

Capital Leases

How does a lessee compute the cost of an asset acquired through a capital lease? (See page 420 for a definition of capital leases.) Consider that the lessee gets the use of the asset but does *not* pay for the leased asset in full at the beginning of the lease. A capital lease is therefore similar to an installment purchase of the leased asset. The lessee must record the leased asset at the present value of the lease liability. The time value of money must be weighed.

The cost of the asset to the lessee is the sum of any payment made at the beginning of the lease period plus the present value of the future lease payments. The lease payments are equal amounts occurring at regular intervals—that is, they are annuity payments.

Consider a 20-year building lease that requires 20 annual payments of $10,000 each, with the first payment due immediately. The interest rate in the lease is 10%, and the present value of the 19 future payments is $83,650 ($10,000 × PV of annuity at 10% for 19 periods, or 8.365 from Exhibit B-7). The lessee's cost of the building is $93,650 (the sum of the initial payment, $10,000, plus the present value of the future payments, $83,650). The lessee would base its accounting for the leased asset (and the related amortization) and for the lease liability (and the related interest expense) on the cost of the building that we have just computed.

Appendix Problems

PD-1 For each situation, compute the required amount.

a. Suppose Enbridge Inc. is budgeting for the acquisition of land over the next several years. Enbridge Inc. can invest $100,000 today at 9%. How much cash will Enbridge Inc. have for land acquisitions at the end of five years? At the end of six years?

b. Stedan Inc. is planning to invest $50,000 each year for five years. The company's investment advisor believes that Stedan Inc. can earn 6% interest without taking on too much risk. What will be the value of Stedan Inc.'s investment on the date of the last deposit if Stedan Inc. can earn 6%? If Stedan Inc. can earn 8%?

PD-2 For each situation, compute the required amount.

a. Suppose Rogers Communications Inc.'s operations are generating excess cash that will be invested in a special fund. During 2011, Rogers invests $5,643,341 in the fund for a planned advertising campaign on a new product to be released six years later, in 2017. If Rogers' investments can earn 10% each year, how much cash will the company have for the advertising campaign in 2017?

b. Rogers will need $10 million to advertise new software in 2011. How much must Rogers invest in 2011 to have the cash available for the advertising campaign? Rogers' investments can earn 10% annually.

c. Explain the relationship between your answers to *a* and *b*.

PD-3 Determine the present value of the following notes and bonds:

1. Ten-year bonds payable with maturity value of $500,000 and contract interest rate of 12%, paid semiannually. The market rate of interest is 12% at issuance.
2. Same bonds payable as in number 1, but the market interest rate is 14%.
3. Same bonds payable as in number 1, but the market interest rate is 10%.

PD-4 On December 31, 2011, when the market interest rate is 8%, Circle 4 Corp. issues $400,000 of 10-year, 7.25% bonds payable. The bonds pay interest semiannually.

Required

1. Determine the present value of the bonds at issuance.
2. Assume that the bonds are issued at the price computed in Requirement 1. Prepare an effective-interest-method amortization table for the first two semiannual interest periods.
3. Using the amortization table prepared in Requirement 2, journalize issuance of the bonds and the first two interest payments and amortization of the bonds.

PD-5 St. Mere Eglise Children's Home needs a fleet of vans to transport the children to singing engagements throughout Normandy. Renault offers the vehicles for a single payment of €630,000 due at the end of four years. Peugeot prices a similar fleet of vans for four annual payments of €150,000 at the end of each year. The children's home could borrow the funds at 6%, so this is the appropriate interest rate. Which company should get the business, Renault or Peugeot? Base your decision on present value, and give your reason.

PD-6 Surrey Pre-School Inc. acquired equipment under a capital lease that requires six annual lease payments of $40,000. The first payment is due when the lease begins, on January 1, 2011. Future payments are due on January 1 of each year of the lease term. The interest rate in the lease is 16%.

Required

Compute the cost of the equipment to Surrey Pre-School Inc.

Appendix C
Check Figures*

Chapter 1

S1-1 NCF
S1-2 a. $300,000 b. 200,000 c. 100,000
S1-3 NCF
S1-4 NCF
S1-5 NCF
S1-6 Net income $70
S1-7 R/E, end $260
S1-8 Total assets $140,000
S1-9 CB, Dec. 31, 2011, $19,000
S1-10 NCF
S1-11 NCF
S1-12 NCF

E1-13 NCF
E1-14 NCF
E1-15 NCF
E1-16 Telus Total assets $16,987 mil.
E1-17 2. $2,997.8 mil. 3. $1,836.4 mil.
E1-18 1. No net loss 2. No net loss 3. Net loss of $1 mil.
E1-19 1. Total assets $840,000 2. SE $400,000
E1-20 NCF
E1-21 R/E $25 mil.
E1-22 1. Net inc. before tax $9 mil. 2. Dividends $3 mil.
E1-23 Net cash provided by operations $360 thou. End Cash $125,000
E1-24 R/E, July 31, 2011, $5,900
E1-25 Total assets $44,100
E1-26 Net cash provided by operations $11,100. End Cash $8,100
E1-27 NCF
E1-28 NCF

Q1-29 a
Q1-30 a
Q1-31 c
Q1-32 a ($20,000 – $4,000 = $16,000)
Q1-33 b
Q1-34 d
Q1-35 b
Q1-36 b
Q1-37 d
Q1-38 b ($140,000 – $59,000 – $8,000 – $3,000 = $70,000)
Q1-39 a ($145,000 + $90,000 – $30,000 = $205,000)
Q1-40 c
Q1-41 c
Q1-42 a (Total assets $25,000 + $11,000 = $36,000)
Q1-43 c ($450,000 + $50,000 – $320,000 = $180,000)

P1-44A 1. Net inc. $28,000
P1-45A Chain Inc.
P1-46A 1. Total assets $99,000
P1-47A 1. Total assets $160,000
P1-48A 2. R/E, end. $116,000 3. Total assets $180,000
P1-49A 1. Net decrease in cash $41 mil.
P1-50A 1. b. $2.4 thou. g. $5,700 thou. m. $2,600 thou. s. $17,400 thou.
P1-51B 1. Net inc. $0.8 mil.
P1-52B Groceries Inc. ending assets $3,389 mil.
P1-53B 1. Total assets $114,000
P1-54B 1. Total assets $199,000
P1-55B 2. R/E, end. $90,000 3. Total assets $293,000
P1-56B 1. Net increase in cash $34,000
P1-57B 1. b. $5,850 thou. g. $15,400 thou. m. $3,670 thou. s. $43,490 thou.

DC1 NCF
DC2 1. Net inc. $0; Total assets $70,000
FOF 3. Amt. owed $171,623 thou.
FOA 2. Net earnings of $95,329 thou. is 34.8% decrease

Chapter 2

S2-1 NCF
S2-2 a. $12,000 b. $2,000
S2-3 Cash bal. $23,000
S2-4 NCF
S2-5 NCF
S2-6 2. A/P bal. $2,000
S2-7 3. Total assets $500
S2-8 T/B total $398 mil. NI, $31 mil.
S2-9 1. $95,000 4. $38,500
S2-10 NCF
S2-11 NCF
S2-12 Total debits $160,000

E2-13 Cash $10,000 Total assets $270,000
E2-14 NCF
E2-15 NCF
E2-16 2. a. $68,300 d. $57,300 ($50,000 + $7,300)
E2-17 NCF
E2-18 NCF
E2-19 2. T/B total $32,200 3. Total assets $30,700
E2-20 Cash bal. $10,700; Owing $30,600
E2-21 1. T/B total $71,200 2. Net inc. $14,300
E2-22 T/B total $94,200
E2-23 Cash bal. $4,200
E2-24 1. T/B total $27,500 2. Net income $8,500
E2-25 4. T/B total $14,400
E2-26 a. Cash paid $85,000
E2-27 1. T/B out of balance by $2,200 2. T/B total $118,200
E2-28 NCF

Q2-29 c
Q2-30 d
Q2-31 c
Q2-32 a
Q2-33 d
Q2-34 b
Q2-35 c
Q2-36 a
Q2-37 b
Q2-38 d
Q2-39 d
Q2-40 c
Q2-41 a
Q2-42 b
Q2-43 a
Q2-44 d
Q2-45 c
Q2-46 b
Q2-47 a
Q2-48 b

*NCF = No check figure

P2-49A NCF

P2-50A 2. Net inc. $8,900
4. Total assets 23,700

P2-51A 3. Cash bal. $7,700; A/P bal. $5,500

P2-52A 2. Total assets $56,500

P2-53A 3. Cash bal. $10,800; Amt. owed $35,600

P2-54A 3. T/B total $35,000
4. Net inc. $2,205

P2-55A 3. T/B total $116,800
4. Net inc. $1,400

P2-56B Total assets $292,000
Net inc. $33,000

P2-57B 2. Net inc. $16,400 4. Total assets $73,900

P2-58B 3. Cash bal. $32,500; A/P bal. $5,200

P2-59B 3. b. Total assets $56,400

P2-60B 3. Cash bal. $26,300; Amt. owed 30,000

P2-61B 3. T/B total $29,300
4. Net inc. $7,290

P2-62B 3. T/B total $174,600

DC1 3. T/B total $27,900
4. Net inc. $6,400

DC2 Net inc. $3,000; Total assets $21,000

FOF Cash $99.7 mil; A/R $166.8 mil.

FOA 3. Net sales decrease $211,392 mil.

Chapter 3

S3-1 a. Net inc. $50 mil.

S3-2 NCF

S3-3 NCF

S3-4 1. Prepaid Rent bal. $2,000
2. Prepaid Supplies $500

S3-5 3. $20,000 Carrying amount

S3-6 Income statement, $42,000,000; Balance sheet $2,000,000

S3-7 3. Interest Payable Dec. 31 bal. $1,500

S3-8 3. Interest Receivable Dec. 31 bal. $1,500

S3-9 NCF

S3-10 Prepaid Rent: a. $6,000 b. $0; Rent Expense: a. $0 b. $6,000.

S3-11 NCF

S3-12 Net inc. $3,500 thou.; R/E $4,800 thou. Total assets $97,900 thou.

S3-13 Retained earnings $4,800 thou.

S3-14 a. 1.24, b. 0.69 c. 0.02

S3-15 Net income as a % of revenue, 0.02

E3-16 NCF

E3-17 a. $10,000 b. $80,000

E3-18 NCF

E3-19 NCF

E3-20 NCF

E3-21 2. Net inc. overstated by $17,200

E3-22 NCF

E3-23 Carrying amount $48,000

E3-24 Service Revenue $15,700

E3-25 Net inc. $4,000 thou.; Total assets $22,200 thou.; R/E $6,800 thou.

E3-26 Sales rev. $20,900 mil.; other operating expense $4,200 mil.

E3-27 Mountain B/S: Unearned service rev. 3,000; Squamish I/S: Consulting expense $9,000

E3-28 1. B/S: Unearned service rev. $90 mil.

E3-29 Dec. 31, 2009, bal. of R/E $2,700 thou.

E3-30 NCF

E3-31 1. Total assets $39,100
2. Debt ratio Current Yr. 0.48

E3-32 1. 2011 Current ratio 2.0; Debt ratio 0.40; NI% of R 0.138

E3-33 7. Net inc. $1,200, Total assets $12,800; R/E $200

E3-34 2010: 1.868; 2011: 2.174

E3-35 a. Net inc. $108,000
b. Total assets $158,000
c. Total liabilities $13,000
d. Total shareholders' equity $145,000

Q3-36 b

Q3-37 b

Q3-38 a

Q3-39 b

Q3-40 d

Q3-41 d

Q3-42 c

Q3-43 c

Q3-44 c

Q3-45 d

Q3-46 b

Q3-47 c

Q3-48 a

Q3-49 d

Q3-50 c

P3-51A 1. $27 mil. 3. End. rec. $6 mil.

P3-52A 2. Cash basis—loss $700,
Accrual basis—inc. $3,240

P3-53A NCF

P3-54A a. Insurance Exp. $3,100
d. Supplies Exp. $6,600

P3-55A 2. Net inc. $6,000, Total assets $54,000; R/E $15,000

P3-56A 2. Total assets $68,600,
Net inc. $4,100

P3-57A 1. Net inc. $39,200, Total assets $47,000, Debt ratio 0.549

P3-58A 2. March 31, 2011 bal. of R/E 47,300

P3-59A 1. Total assets $83,300
2. Current ratio 2011, 1.60

P3-60A 1. 2011, 1.69
2. 2011, 0.571
3. 2011, 0.065

P3-61B 1. $15; 3. End. rec. $5

P3-62B 2. Cash basis—loss $2,700,
Accrual basis—inc. $1,100

P3-63B NCF

P3-64B c. Supplies Exp. $11,400
f. Insurance Exp. $2,700

P3-65B 2. Net inc. $19,800, Total assets $61,600, R/E $36,200

P3-66B 2. Total assets $30,400, Net inc. $25,500

P3-67B 1. Net inc. $78,600, Total assets $109,000

P3-68B 2. Dec. 31, 2011 bal. of R/E $16,800

P3-69B 1. Total assets $55,000
2. Current ratio 2011, 1.71

P3-70B 2011, Current ratio 1.36, Debt ratio 0.681, Net income as % of sales 0.036

DC1 1. $2,000 3. Current ratio 1.748

DC2 Net inc. $7,000, Total assets $32,000

DC3 1. $260,000 2. Shareholder Equity $148,000

FOF 5. 2009: Current ratio 4.17; Debt ratio 0.159

FOA 2. $59,571

Chapter 4

S4-1 NCF

S4-2 NCF

S4-3 NCF

S4-4 NCF

S4-5 Adj. bal. $3,005

S4-6 NCF

S4-7 $1,000 stolen

S4-8 NCF

S4-9 NCF

S4-10 NCF

S4-11 Cash available $4 mil.

S4-12 NCF

E4-13 NCF

E4-14 NCF

E4-15 NCF

E4-16 NCF

E4-17 NCF

E4-18 NCF
E4-19 Adj. bal. $1,150
E4-20 Adj. bal. $1,780
E4-21 NCF
E4-22 NCF
E4-23 NCF
E4-24 New financing needed $(64) mil.
E4-25 NCF
E4-26 7.37%
E4-27 NCF
E4-28 1. Cash available $45 thou. 2. Current ratio 1.60; Debt ratio 0.50

Q4-29 c
Q4-30 b
Q4-31 a
Q4-32 d
Q4-33 d
Q4-34 a
Q4-35 b
Q4-36 c
Q4-37 d
Q4-38 a
Q4-39 d
Q4-40 c

P4-41A NCF
P4-42A NCF
P4-43A 1. Adj. bal. $6,090
P4-44A 1. Adj. bal. $2,242.16
P4-45A NCF
P4-46A 1. (New financing needed) $(3,700) thou.
P4-47A NCF
P4-48B NCF
P4-49B NCF
P4-50B 1. Adj. bal. $5,960
P4-51B 1. Adj. bal. $8,239.00
P4-52B NCF
P4-53B 1. (New financing needed) $(5,490)
P4-54B NCF

DC1 Bookkeeper stole $1,000
DC2 NCF
FOF 1. Adj. bal. $99,732 thou.
FOA NCF

Chapter 5

S5-1 NCF
S5-2 Unrealized gain $4,000
S5-3 Dr. Unrealized Loss $6,000
S5-4 NCF
S5-5 2. A/R, net $62,500
S5-6 Dr. Uncollect.-Acct. Exp. $15,000
S5-7 3. A/R, net $184,000
S5-8 d. Uncollect.-Acct. Exp. $12,000
S5-9 3. A/R, net $123,000
S5-10 b. Dr. Cash $93,600
S5-11 3. $102,667
S5-12 c. Dr. Cash $6,480
S5-13 c. Nothing to report d. Interest rev. $200
S5-14 1. 0.95 2. 24 days
S5-15 2. Net inc. $4,424 thou. 3. 1.60

E5-16 3. B/S: Short-term invest. $195,000 I/S: Unrealized gain $10,000
E5-17 I/S: Div. rev. $500; Unrealized (loss) $(500); B/S Short-term invest $49,500
E5-18 Unrealized Gain on Invest. $5,000; Gain on Sale of Invest. $1,000
E5-19 NCF
E5-20 A/R, net $91,000
E5-21 3. A/R, net $49,500
E5-22 2. A/R, net $52,800
E5-23 3. A/R, net $224,850
E5-24 Unc. Exp. $150; Write offs $148
E5-25 Dec. 31 Dr. Interest Rec. $1,326
E5-26 I/S: Interest rev. $750 for 2010 and $250 for 2011
E5-27 NCF
E5-28 a. 1.89 b. 53 days
E5-29 1. 10 days
E5-30 Expected net inc. w/bank cards $129,800
E5-31 a. $28 mil. b. $11,148 mil.

Q5-32 c
Q5-33 c
Q5-34 d
Q5-35 b
Q5-36 $201,000
Q5-37 d
Q5-38 b
Q5-39 $1,000
Q5-40 c
Q5-41 b
Q5-42 a
Q5-43 a
Q5-44 Dr. Cash $10,450
Q5-45 a
Q5-46 c
Q5-47 c

P5-48A 3. $7,500 4. Div. rev. $260; Unrealized (loss) on invest. $(1,500)
P5-49A NCF
P5-50A 5. I/S: Uncollect.-acct. exp. $380
P5-51A 3. A/R, net: 2011, $221,000; 2010, $207,800
P5-52A 2. Corrected ratios: Current 1.48; Acid-test 0.75; 3. Net inc., corrected $82,000
P5-53A 2. 12/31/12 Note rec. $25,000; Interest rec. $82
P5-54A 1. 2011 ratios: a. 1.98 b. 1.14 c. 31 days
P5-55B 3. 40,000 4. Div rev. $1,250; Unrealized gain on invest. $2,500
P5-56B NCF
P5-57B 5. I/S: Uncollect.-acct. exp. $335 thou.
P5-58B 3. A/R, net: 2011, $109,200; 2010 $107,300
P5-59B 2. Corrected ratios: Current 1.39; Acid-test 0.85 3. Net inc., corrected $84,000
P5-60B 2. 12/31/11 Note rec. $20,000; Interest rec. $247
P5-61B 1. 2011 ratios: a. 1.87 b. 0.87 c. 35 days

DC1 Net inc. $223,000
DC2 2011: Days' sales in rec. 26 days; Cash collections $1,456 thou.
FOF 1. $50 thou. 2. Customers owed Gildan $166,762 (2009) and $215,833 mil. (2008) 3. Collected $1,077,007
FOA One day sales = $2,845 thou. Days in receivables = 67 days Acid-test ratio = 1.92

Chapter 6

S6-1 NCF
S6-2 GP $160,000
S6-3 COGS: Weighted-Avg. $3,760; FIFO $3,740
S6-4 Net inc.: Weighted-Avg. $3,060; FIFO $3,100
S6-5 Inc. tax exp: Weighted-Avg. $551; FIFO $558
S6-6 NCF
S6-7 COGS $421,000
S6-8 GP% 0.32; Invy TO 3.0 times
S6-9 $100,000
S6-10 c. $1,190 mil. d. $510 mil.
S6-11 1. Correct GP $5.7 mil. 2. Correct GP $5.1 mil.
S6-12 NCF

E6-13 2. GP $1,100 thou.
E6-14 3. GP $3,790
E6-15 1. COGS: a. $1,730 b. $1,760 c. $1,710
E6-16 $12.50
E6-17 2. Net inc. $132
E6-18 1. GP: FIFO $0.2 mil.; Weighted-avg. cost $0.6 mil.
E6-19 NCF
E6-20 NCF
E6-21 GP $45,000
E6-22 a. $475 c. $56 f. $2 g. $3; Myers (net loss) $(136) mil.
E6-23 Myers GP% 0.125; Invy. TO 17.9 times
E6-24 GP $16.3 bil.; GP% 29.7; Invy. TO 5.3 times
E6-25 $1,272 mil.
E6-26 $33,000
E6-27 Net inc.: 2012 $65,000; 2011 $69,000
E6-28 NCF
E6-29 1. $150,410 2. $152,750
E6-30 2011 ratios: GP% 0.202, Invy. TO 3.7 times

Q6-31 b
Q6-32 b
Q6-33 d
Q6-34 d
Q6-35 c
Q6-36 a
Q6-37 c
Q6-38 b
Q6-39 a
Q6-40 d
Q6-41 a
Q6-42 d
Q6-43 d
Q6-44 c
Q6-45 a
Q6-46 c
Q6-47 c

P6-48A 3. Net inc. $561,125
P6-49A 2. GP $2,409 3. $2,437
P6-50A 1. COGS: Weighted-Avg. $7,299; FIFO $7,200 3. Net inc. $2,450
P6-51A 1. GP: Weighted-Avg. $60,286; FIFO $60,785
P6-52A NCF
P6-53A 1. Chocolate Treats: GP% 12.5%; Invy. TO 17.9 times
P6-54A 1. $476,500 2. GP $332,000
P6-55A 1. $771,000 2. Net inc. $160,000
P6-56A 1. Net inc. each yr. $2 mil.
P6-57B 3. Net inc. $1,403,436
P6-58B 2. GP $1,173 3. $340
P6-59B 1. COGS: Weighted-Avg. $40,937; FIFO $40,530 3. Net inc. $10,829
P6-60B 1. GP: Weighted-Avg. $291,571; FIFO $299,500
P6-61B NCF
P6-62B 1. 2010: TC Motors: GP% 24.7%; Invy. TO 8.0 times; X-Country Trucks: GP% 33.8; Invy. TO 45.4 times
P6-63B 1. $2,442,000 2. GP $3,432,000
P6-64B 1. $802,000 2. $160,000
P6-65B 1. Net inc. (thou): 2011, $150; 2010, $320; 2009, $50

DC1 1. Net inc.: FIFO $370,300, Weighted-avg. $364,168
DC2 NCF
FOF 5. Inv. To 2.61, F.G. 3.5

Chapter 6 Appendix

S6A-1 NCF
S6A-2 2. $90,000 3. GP $50,000
E6A-3 COGS: Specific $2,890; Weighted-avg. $2,863; FIFO $2,800
E6A-4 4. $2,863
P6A-5 2. GP $2,843
P6A-6 2. GP $1,820 thou.

Chapter 7

S7-1 2. Carrying amount $3,389.8 mil.
S7-2 NCF
S7-3 Building cost $56,000
S7-4 Net inc. overstated
S7-5 2. Carrying amount: SL $21 mil.; UOP $22 mil.; DDB $15 mil.
S7-6 Dep'n.: UOP yr. 5, $2 mil.; SL $4 mil. DDB yr. 3, $3.6 mil.
S7-7 2. Save $787,500
S7-8 a. € = 1.25 mil. b. € = 3.5 mil. c. € = 2.857143 mil.
S7-9 Dep'n. Exp. $12,000
S7-10 1. $13,000
S7-11 NCF
S7-12 1. Goodwill $19.7 mil.
S7-13 1. Net inc. $2,100,000
S7-14 1. Net cash provided by investing $6 mil.

E7-15 Land $283,000 Building $3,820,000
E7-16 Machine 1 $25,000; 2 $41,700; 3 $33,300
E7-17 NCF
E7-18 2. Building, net $737,160
E7-19 Yr: SL $9,000, UOP $7,200 DDB $19,980
E7-20 I/S: Dep'n. exp.-building $6,000; B/S: Bldg., net $194,000
E7-21 CCA saves $2,250 cash
E7-22 Dep'n. yr. 12, $55,833
E7-23 Loss on sale $2,200
E7-24 Carrying amount $140,800
E7-25 NCF
E7-26 Amort. yr. 3, $200,000
E7-27 NCF
E7-28 1. Cost of goodwill $17,000,000
E7-29 NCF
E7-30 NCF
E7-31 Hours of usage 5,600
E7-32 Sale price $20.2 mil.
E7-33 Expected net inc. for 2011, $21,426
E7-34 2013 Effects on: 2. Equip. $50,000 under; 3. Net inc. $50,000 over; 4. Equity $50,000 under

Q7-35 c
Q7-36 a
Q7-37 c
Q7-38 b
Q7-39 c
Q7-40 c
Q7-41 d
Q7-42 b
Q7-43 d
Q7-44 b
Q7-45 b
Q7-46 c
Q7-47 c
Q7-48 a
Q7-49 d

P7-50A 1. Land $296,600; Land Improve. $103,800; Warehouse $1,241,000
P7-51A 2. A/Dep'n.-Bldg. $105,000; A/Dep'n.-Equip. $338,000
P7-52A Dec. 31 Dep'n. Exp.-Motor Carrier Equip. $58,667; Dep'n. Exp.-Bldgs. $1,050
P7-53A NCF
P7-54A 3. Cash-flow advantage of CCA $7,000
P7-55A 1. Carrying amount $41,497 thou.
P7-56A Part 1. 2. Goodwill $1.2 mil. Part 2. 2. Net inc. $2,480,000
P7-57A 1. Loss on sale $0.1 mil. 2. P,P,& E, net $0.7 mil.
P7-58B 1. Land $143,450; Land Improve. $86,000; Garage $654,000

P7-59B 2. A/Dep'n.–Bldg. $52,000; A/Dep'n.–Equip. $437,500

P7-60B Dec. 31 Dep'n. Exp.–Comm.; Equip. $4,000; Dep'n. Exp.–Televideo Equip. $1,333

P7-61B NCF

P7-62B 3. Cash-flow advantage of CCA $3,000

P7-63B 1.Carrying amount $2,131 mil.

P7-64B Part 1. 2. Goodwill $5,500; Part 2. 3. Amort. $300,000

P7-65B 1. Gain on sale $0.02 bil. 2. Prop,Pl,&Eq net $7.26 bil.

DC1 1. Net inc.: LPF $142,125; BA $128,250

DC2 NCF

FOF 4. Proportion of property, plant, & equipment used up in 2009, 37.7%

FOA 2. Amortization expense $3,197 thou.

Chapter 8

S8-1 3/31/12 Debits include Interest Exp. $250

S8-2 2. Interest exp. $250

S8-3 2. Est. Warranty Pay. bal. $50,000

S8-4 NCF

S8-5 NCF

S8-6 a. $897,500 b. $551,875

S8-7 NCF

S8-8 10/31/11 Interest Exp. $312

S8-9 1. 7/31/12 Bond carry. amt. $88,302

S8-10 3. Interest exp. 2012, $3,934

S8-11 1. $9,400 4. $355.00

S8-12 b. Interest Exp. $375

S8-13 EPS: A $3.11; B $2.25

S8-14 Times-int.-earned ratio 1.81

S8-15 Total liab. $501,000

E8-16 2. Warranty exp. $9,000; Est. warranty pay. $7,600

E8-17 Unearned subscr. rev. $500

E8-18 P/R tax exp. $9,000; P/R tax pay. $2,200

E8-19 3. Interest exp. for 2011: $1,250; for 2012: $1,750

E8-20 Income tax pay. $130,000; Income tax exp. $180,000

E8-21 2. Debt ratio 0.76

E8-22 Est. Loss $2,000,000

E8-23 Total current liab. $149,625

E8-24 12/31 Interest Exp. $2,625

E8-25 3. and 4. $316,000

E8-26 1. 12/31/11 Bond carry. amt. $372,660

E8-27 1. 6/30/11 Bond carry. amt. $553,125

E8-28 12/31/15 Bond carry. amt. $300,000

E8-29 1. Carry. amt. $296,850

E8-30 Sobeys ratios: Current 1.00; Debt 0.51; Times-int.-earned 9.49

E8-31 1. EPS: A $6.86; B $3.55

E8-32 Pay off $1 bil.

E8-33 1. Gain on derecognition $37 mil. 3. Debt ratio after 0.68

E8-34 5. 3/15/13 Bond carry. amt. $97,632

Q8-35 a

Q8-36 d

Q8-37 b

Q8-38 b

Q8-39 a

Q8-40 c

Q8-41 a

Q8-42 d

Q8-43 f

Q8-44 a

Q8-45 c

Q8-46 d

Q8-47 Interest Exp. $7,650

Q8-48 Interest Exp. $2,550

Q8-49 e

Q8-50 d

Q8-51 a

Q8-52 c

Q8-53 c

P8-54A e. Note pay. due in 1 yr. $20,000 Interest pay. $6,000

P8-55A 12/31/11 Warranty Exp. $3,800; 4/30/12 Interest Exp. $1,500

P8-56A 4. Interest pay. $5,667, Bonds pay., net $194,250

P8-57A 2. $583,800 3. a. $24,900 b. $24,000

P8-58A 2. 12/31/14. 4 Bond carry. amt. $589,001

P8-59A 1. 12/31/13 Bond carry. amt. $474,920 3. Convert. bonds pay., net $284,952

P8-60A NCF

P8-61A 4. Lease interest exp. $28,450 5. Lease payment $24,550

P8-62A 1. Total current liab. $129,000, Total LT liab. $633,000 3. Times-int.-earned ratio 4.3

P8-63B e. Long-term Note pay. due in 1 yr. $20,000; Interest pay. $2,083

P8-64B 12/31/11 Warranty Exp. $18,000 6/30/12 Interest Exp. $9,000

P8-65B c. Interest pay. $20,000 a. Bonds pay. $1,000,000

P8-66B 4. Interest pay. $7,000 Notes pay., net $289,000

P8-67B 2. $95,200 3. a. $4,600 b. $4,000

P8-68B 2. 12/31/14 Bond carry. amt. $483,439

P8-69B NCF

P8-70B 3. Dep'n. exp. $26,912 4. Interest expense $18,684 5. Lease liability $19,316

DC1 1. Ratios after: Debt 0.93 Times-int.-earned 1.3

DC2 1. EPS: A $4.78 B $4.54; C $4.63

FOF 4. 0.159

FOA 2. Est interest rate 6.58%

Chapter 9

S9-1 NCF

S9-2 NCF

S9-3 NCF

S9-4 NCF

S9-5 1. $1.80 3. 5,650

S9-6 NCF

S9-7 Total SE $1,246 thou.

S9-8 a. $585 thou. b. $3,011 thou. c. $4,257 thou.

S9-9 Overall, SE decreased $33 mil.

S9-10 R/E increased $50,000

S9-11 1. $150,000 4. Pfd. $450,000

S9-12 No effect

S9-13 BV per share $61.35

S9-14 NCF

S9-15 ROA 1.5%; ROE 4.1%

S9-16 Cash used by financing $(6.4) bil

E9-17 NCF

E9-18 2. Total SE $92,500

E9-19 Total SE $143,000

E9-20 Total PIC $1,045,000

E9-21 SE $(29) deficit

E9-22 Overall increase in SE $19,700

E9-23 NCF

E9-24 Total SE $4,285 mil.

E9-25 3. 564 mil. shares 4. $136 mil. 5. $6.00, $1,430

E9-26 2010: Pfd. $24,000; Com. $26,000

E9-27 2. Total SE $8,134,000

E9-28 a. Decrease SE $80 mil.

E9-29 Total SE $2,755 mil.
E9-30 1. $10.40 2. $10.27
E9-31 ROA 0.116; ROE 0.183
E9-32 ROA 0.062; ROE 0.100
E9-33 Cash used by financing $(2,273)
E9-34 c. Issued 500 shares
E9-35 NCF
E9-36 Div. $1,407 mil.
E9-37 12/31/11 Total equity $66 mil.

Q9-38 c
Q9-39 c
Q9-40 d
Q9-41 c
Q9-42 b
Q9-43 d
Q9-44 a
Q9-45 c
Q9-46 b
Q9-47 b
Q9-48 d
Q9-49 d
Q9-50 b
Q9-51 a
Q9-52 c
Q9-53 a
Q9-54 a
Q9-55 d
Q9-56 b
Q9-57 c

P9-58A NCF
P9-59A 2. Total SE $207,500
P9-60A Total SE $663,000
P9-61A NCF
P9-62A Total SE $7,290,000
P9-63A 4. $22,500
P9-64A 2. Total SE $92,800
P9-65A NCF
P9-66A 1. Total assets $439,000, Total SE $309,000 2. ROA 0.089; ROE 0.125
P9-67A NCF
P9-68B NCF
P9-69B 2. Total SE $323,800
P9-70B Total SE $540,000
P9-71B NCF
P9-72B Total SE $3,886,000
P9-73B 4. $183,700
P9-74B 2. Total SE $121,600
P9-75B NCF
P9-76B 1. Total assets $554,000, Total SE $290,000 2. ROA 0.090; ROE 0.107
P9-77B NCF

DC1 3. Total SE: Plan 1, $220,000 Plan 2, $230,000
DC2 NCF
DC3 3. Debt ratio, adjusted 0.869
FOF 1. 427,000 common shares 3. Avg share price $8.58
FOA 1. ROE 2009, 0.111; 2008, 0.199; 2. ROA 2009, 0.0892; 2008, 0.156

Chapter 10

S10-1 1. Unrealized Loss on Invest. $500 2. LT avail.-for-sale invest. $7,000
S10-2 1. Gain on sale $300
S10-3 3. LT Invest. bal. $42.6 mil.
S10-4 (Loss) on sale $(7.3) mil.
S10-5 NCF
S10-6 NCF
S10-7 2. Cash interest $70,000 4. Interest rev. $68,175
S10-8 c. Dr. Interest Rev. $1,825
S10-9 Nov. 10 FC Transaction Gain $400
S10-10 Aug. 28 FC Transaction Gain $4,000
S10-11 NCF
S10-12 NCF

E10-13 d. Loss on Sale $4,000
E10-14 2. Unrealized Loss $63,560 3. LT investments $242,644
E10-15 Invest. end. bal. $1,055,000
E10-16 Gain on sale $1,645,000
E10-17 2. LT investment, at equity $525,000
E10-18 2. Consol. total SE $321,000
E10-19 3. Interest rec. $350, LT invest. in bonds $18,214
E10-20 1. 4/30 FC Transaction Loss $888
E10-21 FC translation adj. $23,000
E10-22 Net cash (used)-invest. $(11.8) mil.
E10-23 NCF
E10-24 3. c. LT invest., at equity $755,000
E10-25 3. Accum. other comp. (loss) $(40) mil.

Q10-26 a
Q10-27 d
Q10-28 Gain on Sale $8,000
Q10-29 b
Q10-30 c
Q10-31 a
Q10-32 d
Q10-33 b
Q10-34 a
Q10-35 b
Q10-36 d
Q10-37 c

P10-38A 2. B/S: LT invest. at equity $523,300; I/S: Equity-method invest. rev. $178,500; Div. rev. $240; Unrealized (loss) $(2,600)
P10-39A 2. LT Invest. in MSC bal. $659,000
P10-40A 3. Consol. debt ratio 0.898
P10-41A Consol. total assets $907,000
P10-42A 2. B/S: LT invest. in bonds $622,031, I/S: Interest rev. $25,031
P10-43A 1. I/S: FC transaction gain, net $100
P10-44A 1. FC translation adj. $46,000
P10-45A NCF
P10-46B 2. B/S: LT invest., at equity $526,300, I/S: Equity-method invest. rev. $87,500; Div. rev. $750; Unrealized (loss) $(3,300)
P10-47B 2. LT Invest. in Affil. bal. $535,000
P10-48B 3. Consol. debt ratio 0.901
P10-49B Consol. total assets $976,000
P10-50B 2. B/S: LT invest. in bonds $445,304, I/S: Interest rev. $35,304
P10-51B 1. I/S: FC transaction gain $1,500
P10-52B 1. FC translation adj. $230,000
P10-53B NCF

DC1 NCF
DC2 2. Gain on sale $4,200 3. Gain on sale $80,000
FOF NCF
FOA NCF

Chapter 11

S11-1 NCF
S11-2 NCF
S11-3 Comp. inc. $18,000
S11-4 EPS for Comp. inc. $1.30
S11-5 Comp. inc. $21,000
S11-6 Est. value $44.83
S11-7 NCF
S11-8 2. Net inc. $82,500, Future tax liab. $5,000
S11-9 R/E, 12/31/11, $201,000
S11-10 1. $14,000 3. $18,720

E11-11 Comp. inc. $1,790 thou.
E11-12 1. EPS for comp. inc. $4.59 2. $57.57

E11-13 NCF
E11-14 6.3%
E11-15 $4.78
E11-16 EPS for comp. inc. $0.74
E11-17 Net inc. $450,000, Future inc. tax liab. $12,500
E11-18 2. $62,500 3. $52,500
E11-19 R/E, 12/31/11 $5=374 mil.
E11-20 Total SE 12/31/11, $2,010,000
E11-21 1. Total SE 12/31/11, $9,446 thou. 2. 44.3% 4. $10.00 per share
E11-22 NCF

Q11-23 b
Q11-24 b
Q11-25 d
Q11-26 a
Q11-27 b
Q11-28 c
Q11-29 c
Q11-30 d
Q11-31 a
Q11-32 b
Q11-33 d
Q11-34 c

P11-35A 1. Comp. inc. $37,900, EPS for comp. inc. $1.58
P11-36A R/E, 12/31/11 $115,100
P11-37A Est. value $637,500; Current mkt. price $640,000
P11-38A 1. EPS for comp. inc. $1.41 2. Est. value at 6% $26.17
P11-39A Comp. inc. $100,550, EPS for comp. inc. $2.39
P11-40A 1. $120,000 2. Cr. Future Inc. Tax Liab. $3,300 3. Net. inc. $87,100
P11-41A 1. $806 mil. 2. $5 per share 3. $10.00 per share 4. 7.8%
P11-42B 1. Comp. inc. $127,250, EPS for comp. inc. $4.88
P11-43B R/E, 4/30/11 $180,250
P11-44B Est. value $1,108,333, Current mkt. price $1,200,000
P11-45B 1. EPS for comp. inc. $0.92 2. Est. value at 7% $15.71
P11-46B Comp. inc. $80,500, EPS for comp. inc. $1.55
P11-47B 1. $185,000 2. Cr. Future Inc. Tax Liab. $3,750 3. Net. inc. $150,000
P11-48B 1. $537 mil. 2. $3 per share 3. $3.77 per share 4. 8%

DC1 Use $0.59
DC2 NCF
FOF NCF
FOA 2. Est. value at 6% 2009, $13.16 2008, $20.00

Chapter 12

S12-1 NCF
S12-2 NCF
S12-3 Net cash-oper. $70,000
S12-4 NCF
S12-5 Net cash-oper. $54,000
S12-6 Net cash-oper. $54,000; Net increase in cash $53,000
S12-7 a. $60,000 b. $20,000
S12-8 a. New borrowing $10,000 b. Issuance $8,000 c. Dividends $146,000

E12-9 NCF
E12-10 NCF
E12-11 NCF
E12-12 Net cash-oper. $11,000
E12-13 Net cash-oper. $48,000
E12-14 1. Net cash-oper. $99,000, Net increase in cash $27,000, Noncash inv. and fin. $50,000
E12-15 NCF
E12-16 a. $500 b. $11,000
E12-17 1. Gain $120 thou. 2. $240 thou.

Q12-18 c
Q12-19 a
Q12-20 b
Q12-21 b
Q12-22 d
Q12-23 c
Q12-24 c
Q12-25 financing; operating
Q12-26 c
Q12-27 d
Q12-28 b
Q12-29 a
Q12-30 c
Q12-31 a
Q12-32 a
Q12-33 a
Q12-34 d
Q12-35 d
Q12-36 a
Q12-37 a

P12-38A NCF
P12-39A 1. Net. inc. $51,667 2. Total assets $396,667 3. Net cash-oper. $(49,000); Net increase in cash $90,000
P12-40A Net cash-oper. $63,200 Net increase in cash $16,000 Noncash inv. and fin. $160,000
P12-41A 1. Net cash-oper. $76,900 Net (decrease) in cash $(4,100); Noncash inv. and fin. $101,000
P12-42A 1. Net cash-oper. $80,000 Net increase in cash $12,300
P12-43B NCF
P12-44B 1. Net. inc. $157,333 2. Total assets $340,333 3. Net cash-oper. $81,000; Net increase in cash $191,000
P12-45B Net cash-oper. $74,500 Net (decrease) in cash $(5,700) Noncash inv. and fin. $290,4000
P12-46B 1. Net cash-oper. $68,700 Net increase in cash $16,300 Noncash inv. and fin. $30,000
P12-47B 1. Net cash-oper. $90,600 Net increase in cash $13,100

DC1 (in thousands) 1. Net cash-oper. $132, Net (decrease) in cash $(46)
DC2 NCF
FOF 2. a. $1,087,390 thou. b. $904,767 thou.
FOA NCF

Appendix 12A

S12-A1 Net cash-oper. $110,000; Net (decrease) in cash $(20,000)
S12-A2 Net cash-oper. $13,000
S12-A3 Net cash-oper. $13,000; Net increase in cash $12,000
S12-A4 a. $699,000 b. $326,000
S12-A5 a. $68,000 b. $134,000

E12-A6 NCF
E12-A7 NCF
E12-A8 Net cash-oper. $21,000
E12-A9 NCF
E12-A10 1. Net cash-oper. $102,000; Net increase in cash $29,000
E12-A11 a. $50,000 b. $113,000
E12-A12 (in thousands) a. $24,637 b. $18,134 c. $3,576 d. $530 e. $73 f. $1,294

P12-A13 1. Net cash-oper. $95,700 Net (decrease) in cash $(2,700) Noncash inv. and fin. $79,400

P12-A14 1. Net. inc. $51,667 2. Total assets $396,667 3. Net cash-oper. $(49,000); Net increase in cash $90,000

P12-A15 Net cash-oper. $80,000 Net increase in cash $12,300

P12-A16 1. Net cash-oper. $55,800 Net (decrease) in cash $(2,000) Noncash inv. and fin. $99,100

P12-A17 1. Net cash-oper. $73,200 Net increase in cash $20,000 Noncash inv. and fin. $19,000

P12-A18 1. Net cash-oper. $30,000 Net increase in cash $7,600 Noncash inv. and fin. $142,800

P12-A19 1. Net. inc. $157,333 2. Total assets $340,333 3. Net cash-oper. $81,000; Net increase in cash $191,000

P12-A20 1. Net cash-oper. $90,600 Net increase in cash $13,100

P12-A21 1. Net cash-oper. $77,200 Net (decrease) in cash $(4,600) Noncash inv. and fin. $83,200

P12-A22 1. Net cash-oper. $40,400 Net increase in cash $4,100 Noncash inv. and fin. $48,300

Chapter 13

S13-1 2011 Net. inc. (increase) 9.2%

S13-2 2011 Sales trend 107%

S13-3 2011 Cash 2.13%

S13-4 Net. inc. % Porterfield 6.2%

S13-5 2008 Current ratio 1.21

S13-6 1. 2009: 0.48; 2008: 0.40

S13-7 a. 9.7 times b. 10.1 days

S13-8 1. 0.514 2. 11.5

S13-9 a. 3.1% b. 8.8% c. 16.3%

S13-10 1. EPS $4.85; P/E 16

S13-11 a. $3,855 thou. d. $873 thou.

S13-12 a. $562 thou. d. $3,768 thou. e. $1,294 thou.

S13-13 $570 thou.

E13-14 2010 WC (decrease) (5.4)%

E13-15 Net. inc. decreased 5.8%

E13-16 Yr. 4 Net. inc. trend 147%

E13-17 Current assets 24.6%, Total liab. 41.7%

E13-18 Net. inc. 20% both years

E13-19 NCF

E13-20 a. 1.67 b. 0.83 c. 4.4 d. 9.5 e. 38 days

E13-21 2011 ratios: a. 2.07 b. 0.91 c. 0.47 d. 4.13

E13-22 2011 ratios: a. 0.098 b. 0.132 c. 0.151 d. $0.67

E13-23 2011 ratios: a. 17.3 b. 0.014 c. $6.00

E13-24 Amazon $100 mil.

E13-25 Total assets $20,000 mil. Current liab. $6,800 mil.

E13-26 Sales $6,400 mil. Net. inc. $720 mil.

Q13-27 b

Q13-28 c

Q13-29 a

Q13-30 b

Q13-31 d

Q13-32 c

Q13-33 b

Q13-34 c

Q13-35 a

Q13-36 a

Q13-37 d

Q13-38 d

P13-39A 1. 2011 trends: Net sales 186%; Net. inc. 231%; Total assets 155% 2. 2011, 0.101

P13-40A 1. Net. inc. 10.7%, Current assets 77.1%

P13-41A NCF

P13-42A 1. Current ratio before 1.74 2. a. Current ratio after 1.84

P13-43A 1. 2011 ratios: a. 1.41 b. 2.24 c. 4.32 d. 0.173 g. 11.9

P13-44A 1. Video: a. 060 b. 2.16 c. 100 d. 0.68 f. 0.196 2. Video $29,700

P13-45A NCF

P13-46B 1. 2011 trends: Net rev. 134%; Net. inc. 205%; SE 147% 2. 2011, 0.111

P13-47B Net. inc. 5.3%, Current assets 75.0%

P13-48B NCF

P13-49B 1. Current ratio before 1.54 2. a. Current ratio after 1.44

P13-50B 1. 2011 ratios a. 2.04 b. 2.78 c. 10.8 d. 0.315 f. 16

P13-51B 1. Thrifty Nickel: a. 0.78 b. 2.32 c. 40 d. 0.41 h. 10.6 2. Thrifty Nickel $33,840

P13-52B NCF

DC1 NCF

DC2 NCF

DC3 NCF

FOF 2009 trend: Total Sales 159%; Net earnings 111%; Net cash-oper. 131%

FOA 2009 trend: Net earnings & comp. inc. 9.2%

Glossary

Accelerated depreciation method A depreciation method that writes off a relatively larger amount of the asset's cost nearer the start of its useful life than the straight-line method does.

Account The detailed record of the changes that have occurred in a particular asset, liability, or shareholders' equity during a period. The basic summary device of accounting.

Accounting The information system that measures business activities, processes that information into reports and financial statements, and communicates the results to decision makers.

Accounting equation The most basic tool of accounting: Assets = Liabilities + Owners' Equity.

Account payable A liability for goods and services purchased on credit and backed by the general reputation and credit standing of the debtor.

Accounts receivable An asset, amounts due from customers to whom a business has sold goods or services.

Accounts receivable turnover Measures a company's ability to collect cash from credit customers. Net sales divided by average net accounts receivable.

Accrual An expense or a revenue that occurs before the business pays or receives cash. An accrual is the opposite of a deferral.

Accrual accounting Accounting that records the impact of a business event as it occurs, regardless of whether the transaction affected cash.

Accrued expense An expense incurred but not yet paid in cash.

Accrued liability A liability incurred but not yet paid by the company.

Accrued revenue A revenue that has been earned but not yet received in cash.

Accumulated depreciation The cumulative sum of all depreciation expense from the date of acquiring a capital asset.

Acid-test ratio Ratio of the sum of cash plus short-term investments plus net current receivables to total current liabilities. Tells whether the entity can pay all its current liabilities if they come due immediately. Also called the *quick ratio*.

Adjusted trial balance A list of all the ledger accounts with their adjusted balances.

Adverse opinion An audit opinion stating that the financial statements are unreliable.

Aging of accounts receivable A way to estimate bad debts by analyzing individual accounts receivable according to the length of time they have been receivable from the customer. Also called *balance-sheet approach* because it focuses on accounts receivable.

Allowance for bad debts Another name for *Allowance for Uncollectible Accounts.*

Allowance for Doubtful Accounts Also called *Allowance for Uncollectible Accounts.*

Allowance for Uncollectible Accounts A contra account, related to accounts receivable, that holds the estimated amount of collection losses. Another name for *Allowance for Doubtful Accounts.*

Allowance method A method of recording collection losses based on estimates of how much money the business will not collect from its customers.

Amortization Allocation of the cost of an intangible asset with a finite life over its useful life.

Asset An economic resource that is expected to produce a benefit in the future.

Audit A periodic examination of a company's financial statements and the accounting systems, controls, and records that produce them.

Available-for-sale investment All investments held to earn dividend revenue and/or capital appreciation.

Bad-debt expense Another name for *uncollectible-account expense.*

Balance sheet List of an entity's assets, liabilities, and owners' equity as of a specific date. Also called the *statement of financial position.*

Bank collection Collection of money by the bank on behalf of a depositor.

Bank reconciliation A document explaining the reasons for the difference between a depositor's records and the bank's records about the depositor's bank account.

Bank statement Document showing the beginning and ending balances of a particular bank account and listing the month's transactions that affected the account.

Benchmarking The practice of comparing a company to a standard set by other companies, with a view toward improvement.

Board of directors Group elected by the shareholders to set policy for a corporation and to appoint its officers.

Bond market price The bond market price is the price investors are willing to pay for the bond. It is equal to the present value of the principal payment plus the present value of the interest payments.

Bonds payable Groups of notes payable (bonds) issued to multiple lenders called *bondholders.*

Brand name A distinctive identification of a product or service. See *trademark* or *trade name.*

Budget A quantitative expression of a plan that helps managers coordinate the entity's activities.

Bylaws Constitution for governing a corporation.

Callable bonds Bonds that may be paid at a specified price whenever the issuer wants.

Capital Another name for the *owners' equity* of a business.

Capital asset Another name for *property, plant, and equipment.*

Capital cost allowance (CCA) Depreciation allowed for income tax purposes by Canada Revenue Agency; the rates allowed are called *capital cost allowance rates.*

Capital expenditure Expenditure that increases an asset's capacity or efficiency or extends its useful life. Capital expenditures are debited to an asset account. Also called *betterments.*

Capital lease Lease agreement that meets any one of four criteria: (1) The lease transfers title of the leased asset to the lessee at the end of the lease term. (2) The lease contains a bargain purchase option. (3) The lease term is 75% or more of the estimated useful life of the leased asset. (4) The present value of the lease payments is 90% or more of the market value of the leased asset.

Carrying amount Amount of owners' equity on the company's books for each share of its stock.

Carrying amount (of a plant asset) The asset's cost minus accumulated depreciation.

Cash Money and any medium of exchange that a bank accepts at face value.

Cash-basis accounting Accounting that records only transactions in which cash is received or paid.

Cash budget A budget that projects the entity's future cash receipts and cash disbursements.

Cash equivalents Highly liquid short-term investments that can be converted into cash immediately.

Cash flows Cash receipts and cash payments (disbursements).

Chairperson Elected by a corporation's board of directors, usually the most powerful person in the corporation.

Chart of accounts List of all of a company's accounts and their account numbers.

Cheque Document instructing a bank to pay the designated person or business the specified amount of money.

Classified balance sheet A balance sheet that shows current assets separate from long-term assets, and current liabilities separate from long-term liabilities.

Clean opinion An audit opinion stating that the financial statements are reliable. Also called an *unqualified opinion*.

Closing entries Entries that transfer the revenue, expense, and dividend balances from these respective accounts to the Retained Earnings account.

Closing the books The process of preparing the accounts to begin recording the next period's transactions. Closing the accounts consists of journalizing and posting the closing entries to set the balances of the revenue, expense, and dividends accounts to zero. Also called *closing the accounts*.

Common shares The most basic form of share capital. Common shareholders own a corporation.

Common-size statement A financial statement that reports only percentages (no dollar amounts).

Comparability Investors like to compare a company's financial statements from one year to the next. Therefore, a company must consistently use the same accounting method each year.

Comprehensive income A company's change in total shareholders' equity from all sources other than from the owners of the business.

Computer virus A malicious program that enters a company's computer system by e-mail or other means and destroys program and data files.

Consistency principle A business must use the same accounting methods and procedures from period to period.

Consolidated statements Financial statements of the parent company plus those of majority-owned subsidiaries as if the combination were a single legal entity.

Contra account An account that always has a companion account and whose normal balance is opposite that of the companion account.

Contract interest rate Interest rate that determines the amount of cash interest the borrower pays and the investor receives each year. Also called *coupon interest rate* or *stated interest rate*.

Contributed capital The amount of shareholders' equity that shareholders have contributed to the corporation.

Controller The chief accounting officer of a business who accounts for cash.

Controlling interest Ownership of more than 50% of an investee company's voting shares.

Convertible bonds (or notes) Bonds (or notes) that may be converted into the issuing company's common shares at the investor's option.

Copyright Exclusive right to reproduce and sell a book, musical composition, film, other work of art, or computer program. Issued by the federal government, copyrights extend fifty years beyond the author's life.

Cost assumption Assumption that assets and services should be recorded at their actual cost when acquired.

Corporation A business owned by shareholders. A corporation is a legal entity, an "artificial person" in the eyes of the law.

Cost of goods sold Cost of the inventory the business has sold to customers. Also called *cost of sales*.

Cost-of-goods-sold model Brings together all the inventory data for the entire accounting period: Beginning inventory + Purchases = Goods available for sale. Then, Goods available for sale − Ending inventory = Cost of goods sold.

Cost principle Principle that states that acquired assets and services should be recorded at their actual historical cost.

Credit The right side of an account.

Creditor The party to whom money is owed.

Cumulative preferred shares Preferred shares whose owners must receive all dividends in arrears before the corporation can pay dividends to the common shareholders.

Current asset An asset that is expected to be converted to cash, sold, or consumed during the next 12 months, or within the business's normal operating cycle if longer than a year.

Current liability A debt due to be paid within one year or within the entity's operating cycle if the cycle is longer than a year.

Current portion of long-term debt The amount of the principal that is payable within one year. Also called *current installment of long-term debt*.

Current ratio Current assets divided by current liabilities. Measures a company's ability to pay current liabilities with current assets.

Days' sales in receivables Ratio of average net accounts receivable to one day's sales. Indicates how many days' sales remain in Accounts Receivable awaiting collection. Also called the *collection period*.

Debentures Unsecured bonds—bonds backed only by the good faith of the borrower.

Debit The left side of an account.

Debt ratio Ratio of total liabilities to total assets. States the proportion of a company's assets that is financed with debt.

Debtor The party who owes money.

Deferral An adjustment for which the business paid or received cash in advance. Examples include prepaid rent, prepaid insurance, and supplies.

Deficit Debit balance in the Retained Earnings account.

Denial of opinion An audit opinion stating that the auditor was unable to reach a professional opinion regarding the quality of the financial statements.

Deposit in transit A deposit recorded by the company but not yet by its bank.

Depreciable cost The cost of a capital asset minus its estimated residual value.

Depreciation Allocation of the cost of a plant asset over its useful life.

Derecognition The decision to pay off a bond before maturity.

Direct financing lease Substantially similar to a sales-type lease, except it is negotiated through a financial institution.

Direct method Format of the operating activities section of the statement of cash flows; lists the major categories of operating cash receipts (collections from customers and receipts of interest and dividends) and cash disbursements (payments to suppliers, to employees, for interest, and income taxes).

Direct write-off method A method of accounting for bad debts in which the company waits until the credit department decides that a customer's account receivable is uncollectible and then debits Uncollectible-Account Expense and credits the customer's account receivable.

Disclosure principle A business's financial statements must report enough information for outsiders to make knowledgeable decisions about the business. The company should report relevant, reliable, and comparable information about its economic affairs.

Discount (on a bond) Excess of a bond's maturity (par value) over its issue price.

Dividend Distributions (usually cash) by a corporation to its shareholders.

Dividend yield Ratio of dividends per share to the share's market price per share. Tells the percentage of a share's market value that the company returns to shareholders as dividends.

Double-diminishing-balance (DDB) method An accelerated depreciation method that computes annual depreciation by multiplying the asset's decreasing carrying amount by a constant percentage, which is two times the straight-line rate.

Double-entry system An accounting system that uses debits and credits to record the dual effects of each business transaction.

Double taxation Corporations pay income taxes on corporate income. Then, the shareholders pay personal income tax on the cash dividends that they receive from corporations. Canada's tax laws attempt to minimize double taxation.

Doubtful-account expense Another name for *uncollectible-account expense.*

Earnings management Occurs when managers record revenues and/or expenses inappropriately to meet profit objectives.

Earnings per share (EPS) Amount of a company's net income per share of its outstanding common shares.

Effective interest rate Another name for *market interest rate.*

Efficient capital market A capital market in which market prices fully reflect all information available to the public.

Electronic funds transfer (EFT) System that transfers cash by electronic communication rather than by paper documents.

Entity An organization or a section of an organization that, for accounting purposes, stands apart from other organizations or sections of an organization or individuals as a separate economic unit.

Equity method The method used to account for investments in which the investor has 20–50% of the investee's voting shares and can significantly influence the decisions of the investee.

Estimated residual value Expected cash value of an asset at the end of its useful life. Also called *scrap value* or *salvage value.*

Estimated useful life Length of service that a business expects to get from an asset. May be expressed in years, units of output, kilometres, or other measures.

Exception reporting Identifying data that is not within "normal limits" so that managers can follow up and take corrective action. Exception reporting is used in operating and cash budgets to keep company profits and cash flow in line with management's plans.

Expense Decrease in retained earnings that results from operations; the cost of doing business; opposite of revenues.

Extraordinary gains and losses Also called *extraordinary items*, these gains and losses are both unusual for the company and infrequent and are not determined by management.

Extraordinary item A gain or loss that is both unusual for the company and infrequent.

Face value of bond The principal amount payable by the issuer. Also called *maturity value.*

Fair value The amount that a business could sell an asset for, or the amount that a business could pay to settle a liability.

Fair value (of a share) Price for which a person could sell a share of stock.

Faithful representation The fundamental qualitative characteristic that accounting information is complete, free from bias, and without material error.

Fidelity bonds Insurance policies taken out on employees who handle cash.

FIFO (first-in, first-out) method Inventory costing method by which the first costs into inventory are the first costs out to cost of goods sold. Ending inventory is based on the costs of the most recent purchases.

Finance lease A lease defined by IFRS that transfers substantially all risks and rewards incidental to ownership of assets.

Financial accounting The branch of accounting that provides information to people outside the firm.

Financial statements Business documents that report financial information about a business entity to decision makers.

Financing activities Activities that obtain from investors and creditors the cash needed to launch and sustain the business; a section of the statement of cash flows.

Firewall An electronic barrier, usually provided by passwords, around computerized data files to protect local area networks of computers from unauthorized access.

Fixed asset Another name for *property, plant, and equipment.*

Foreign-currency exchange rate The measure of one country's currency against another country's currency.

Franchises and licences Privileges granted by a private business or a government to sell a product or service in accordance with specified conditions.

Free cash flow The amount of cash available from operations after paying for planned investments in plant, equipment, and other long-term assets.

Fraud triangle The three elements that are present in almost all cases of fraud. These elements are motive, opportunity, and rationalization on the part of the perpetrator.

Fraudulent financial reporting Fraud perpetrated by management by preparing misleading financial statements.

Generally accepted accounting principles (GAAP) Accounting standards, issued by the Canadian Institute of Chartered Accountants' (CICA) Accounting Standards Board, that govern how accountanting is practised in Canada.

Going-concern assumption Holds that the entity will remain in operation for the foreseeable future.

Goodwill Excess of the cost of an acquired company over the sum of the market values of its net assets (assets minus liabilities).

Gross profit Also called *gross margin.*

Gross profit Sales revenue minus cost of goods sold.

Gross profit method A way to estimate inventory based on a rearrangement of the cost-of-goods-sold model: Beginning inventory + Net purchases = Goods available for sale – Cost of goods sold =

Ending inventory. Also called the *gross margin method*.

Gross profit percentage Gross margin divided by net sales revenue. Also called the *gross margin percentage*.

Hedging To protect oneself from losing money in one transaction by engaging in a counterbalancing transaction.

Held-to-maturity investments Bonds and notes that an investor intends to hold until maturity.

Horizontal analysis Study of percentage changes over time through comparative financial statements.

Imprest system A way to account for petty cash by maintaining a constant balance in the petty cash account, supported by the fund (cash plus payment slips) totalling the same amount.

Income statement A financial statement listing an entity's revenues, expenses, and net income or net loss for a specific period. Also called the *statement of operations* or the *statement of earnings*.

Indirect method Format of the operating activities section of the statement of cash flows; starts with net income and reconciles to cash flows from operating activities. Also called the *reconciliation method*.

Intangible asset An asset with no physical form, a special right to current and expected future benefits.

Interest The borrower's cost of renting money from a lender. Interest is revenue for the lender, expense for the borrower.

Interest-coverage ratio Another name for the *times-interest-earned ratio*.

Internal control Organizational plan and all the related measures adopted by an entity to optimize the use of resources, prevent and detect error and fraud, safeguard assets and records, and ensure accurate and reliable accounting records.

Inventory The merchandise that a company sells; also includes raw materials for use in a manufacturing process.

Inventory turnover Ratio of cost of goods sold to average inventory. Indicates how rapidly inventory is sold.

Investing activities Activities that increase or decrease the long-term assets available to the business; a section of the statement of cash flows.

Investment capitalization rate An earnings rate used to estimate the value of an investment in the share capital of company.

Journal The chronological accounting record of an entity's transactions.

Lapping Fraudulent scheme to steal cash through misappropriating certain customer payments and posting payments from other customers to the affected accounts to cover it up. Lapping is caused by weak internal controls (i.e., not segregating the duties of cash handling and accounts receivable bookkeeping, allowing the bookkeeper improper access to cash, and not appropriately monitoring the activities of those who handle cash).

Lease Rental agreement in which the tenant (lessee) agrees to make rent payments to the property owner (lessor) in exchange for the use of the asset.

Ledger The book of accounts and their balances.

Lessee Tenant in a lease agreement.

Lessor Property owner in a lease agreement.

Leverage Earning more income on borrowed money than the related interest expense, thereby increasing the earnings for the owners of the business. Another name for *trading on the equity*.

Liability An economic obligation (a debt) payable to an individual or an organization outside the entity.

LIFO (last-in, first-out) method Inventory costing method by which the last costs into inventory are the first costs out to cost of goods sold. This method leaves the oldest costs—those of beginning inventory and the earliest purchases of the period—in ending inventory.

Limited liability No personal obligation of a shareholder for corporation debts. A shareholder can lose no more on an investment in a corporation's shares than the cost of the investment.

Limited liability partnership A business organization in which the business partnership (not the partners) is liable for the partnership's debts.

Liquidity Measure of how quickly an item can be converted to cash.

Lockbox system A system of handling cash receipts by mail whereby customers remit payment directly to the bank, rather than through the entity's mail system.

Long-term asset An asset that is not a current asset.

Long-term debt A liability that falls due beyond one year from the date of the financial statements.

Long-term investment Any investment that does not meet the criteria of a short-term investment; any investment that the investor expects to hold for longer than a year or that is not readily marketable.

Long-term liability A liability that is not a current liability.

Lower-of-cost-and-net-realizable value/ LCNRV rule Requires that an asset be reported in the financial statements at whichever is lower—its historical cost or its market value (current replacement cost for inventory).

Majority interest Ownership of more than 50% of an investee company's voting shares.

Management accounting The branch of accounting that generates information for the internal decision makers of a business, such as top executives.

Marketable security Investment that a company plans to hold for one year or less. Also called *short-term investments*.

Market interest rate Interest rate that investors demand for loaning their money. Also called *effective interest rate*.

Market price (of a share) Price for which a person could buy or sell a share of stock.

Maturity date The date on which a debt instrument must be paid.

Maturity value The sum of principal and interest on a note.

Misappropriation of assets Fraud committed by employees by stealing assets from the company.

Multi-step income statement An income statement that contains subtotals to highlight important relationships between revenues and expenses.

Net assets Another name for *owners' equity*.

Net earnings Another name for *net income*.

Net income Excess of total revenues over total expenses. Also called *net earnings* or *net profit*.

Net income as a percentage of sales revenue This ratio determines how much of the company's sales revenue ends up as net income.

Net loss Excess of total expenses over total revenues.

Net profit Another name for *net income*.

Net realizable value The amount a business could get if it sold the inventory less the costs of selling it.

Non-controlling interest A subsidiary company's equity that is held by shareholders other than the parent company.

Nonsufficient funds (NSF) cheque A cheque for which the payer's bank account has insufficient money to pay the cheque. NSF cheques are cash receipts that turn out to be worthless.

No-stated-value shares Shares of stock that do not have a value assigned to them by the articles of incorporation.

Note payable A liability evidenced by a written promise to make a future payment.

Objectivity principle See *reliability principle*.

Operating activities Activities that create revenues or expenses in the entity's major line of business; a section of the statement of cash flows. Operating activities affect the income statement.

Operating budget A budget of future net income. The operating budget projects a company's future revenue and expenses. It is usually prepared by line item of the company's income statement.

Operating cycle Time span during which cash is paid for goods and services, and these goods and services are sold to bring in cash.

Operating lease Usually a short-term or cancellable rental agreement.

Outstanding cheque A cheque issued by the company and recorded on its books but not yet paid by its bank.

Outstanding shares Shares in the hands of shareholders.

Owners' equity The claim of the owners of a business to the assets of the business. Also called *capital* for proprietorships and partnerships and *shareholders' equity* for corporations. Sometimes called *net assets*.

Parent company An investor company that owns more than 50% of the voting shares of a subsidiary company.

Partnership An association of two or more persons who co-own a business.

Password A special set of characters that must be provided by the user of computerized program or data files to prevent unauthorized access to those files.

Patent A federal government grant giving the holder the exclusive right for twenty years to produce and sell an invention.

Payroll Employee compensation, a major expense of many businesses.

Pension Employee compensation that will be received during retirement.

Percentage-of-sales method Computes uncollectible-account expense as a percentage of net sales. Also called the *income statement approach* because it focuses on the amount of expense to be reported on the income statement.

Periodic inventory system An inventory system in which the business does not keep a continuous record of the inventory on hand. Instead, at the end of the period, the business makes a physical count of the inventory on hand and applies the appropriate unit costs to determine the cost of the ending inventory.

Permanent account Assets, liabilities, and shareholders' equity.

Perpetual inventory system An inventory system in which the business keeps a continuous record for each inventory item to show the inventory on hand at all times.

Petty cash Fund containing a small amount of cash that is used to pay minor expenditures.

Phishing Creating bogus Web sites for the purpose of stealing unauthorized data, such as names, addresses, social insurance numbers, bank account information, and credit card numbers.

Plant assets Another name for *property, plant, and equipment*.

Posting Copying amounts from the journal to the ledger.

Private enterprises (PEs) Corporations whose shares are privately held either by its founders and/or by family members.

Preferred shares Shares that give their owners certain advantages, such as the priority to receive dividends before the common shareholders and the priority to receive assets before the common shareholders if the corporation liquidates.

Premium (on a bond) Excess of a bond's issue price over its maturity (par) value.

Prepaid expense A category of miscellaneous assets that typically expire or get used up in the near future. Examples include prepaid rent, prepaid insurance, and supplies.

Present value Amount a person would invest now to receive a greater amount at a future date.

President Chief operating officer in charge of managing the day-to-day operations of a corporation.

Pretax accounting income Income before tax on the income statement.

Price/earnings ratio Ratio of the market price of a common share to the company's earnings per share. Measures the value that the stock market places on $1 of a company's earnings.

Principal The amount borrowed by a debtor and lent by a creditor.

Prior period adjustment A correction to beginning balance of retained earnings for an error of an earlier period.

Private company Company that does not offer its securities for sale to the general public.

Property, plant, and equipment Long-lived assets, such as land, buildings, and equipment, used in the operation of the business. Also called *plant assets*, *fixed assets*, or *tangible capital assets*.

Proprietorship A business with a single owner.

Public company Company that offers its securities for sale to the general public.

Publicly accountable enterprises (PAEs) Corporations that have issued or plan to issue shares or debt in a public market.

Purchase allowance A decrease in the cost of purchases because the seller has granted the buyer a subtraction (an allowance) from the amount owed.

Purchase discount A decrease in the cost of purchases earned by making an early payment to the vendor.

Purchase return A decrease in the cost of purchases because the buyer returned the goods to the seller.

Qualified opinion An audit opinion stating that the financial statements are reliable, except for one or more items for which the opinion is said to be qualified.

Quick ratio Another name for the *acid-test ratio*.

Receivables Monetary claims against a business or an individual, acquired mainly by selling goods and services, and by lending money.

Relevance The fundamental qualitative characteristic of accounting information is capable of making a difference to the decision maker and has predictive or confirming value.

Reliability principle The accounting principle that ensures that accounting records and statements are based on the most objective data available. Also called the *objectivity principle*.

Remittance advice An optional attachment to a cheque (sometimes a perforated tear-off document and sometimes capable of being electronically scanned) that indicates the payer, date, and purpose of the cash payment. The remittance advice is often used as the source document for posting cash receipts or payments.

Repurchased shares A corporation's own shares that it has issued and later reacquired.

Retained earnings. The amount of shareholders' equity that the corporation has earned through profitable operation of the business and has not given back to shareholders.

Return on assets (ROA). See *rate of return on total assets*.

Return on common shareholders' equity Net income minus preferred dividends, divided by average common shareholders' equity. A measure of profitability. Also called *return on equity*.

Return on equity (ROE). See *rate of return on common shareholders' equity.*

Return on net sales Ratio of net income to net sales. A measure of profitability. Also called *return on sales.*

Return on sales Net income divided by sales. Measures how much sales revenue ends up as net income.

Return on total assets Net income plus interest expense, divided by average total assets. This ratio measures a company's success in using its assets to earn income for the persons who finance the business. Also called *return on assets.*

Revenue Increase in retained earnings from delivering goods or services to customers or clients.

Revenue principle Governs when to record revenue and the amount to record.

Sales-type lease From the point of view of the lessor, transfers substantially all the benefits and risks of ownership of the asset.

Segment of the business An identifiable division of a company.

Serial bonds Bonds that mature in installments over a period of time.

Shareholder A person who owns shares of stock in a corporation.

Shareholders' equity The shareholders' ownership interest in the assets of a corporation. Also called *owners' equity.*

Short-term investment Investment that a company plans to hold for one year or less. Also called *marketable securities.*

Short-term note payable Note payable due within one year.

Single-step income statement Lists all revenues together and all expenses together; there is only one step in arriving at net income.

Specific identification method See *specific-unit-cost method.*

Specific-unit-cost method Inventory cost method based on the specific cost of particular units of inventory. Also called the *specific identification method.*

Stable-monetary-unit assumption The reason for ignoring the effect of inflation in the accounting records, based on the assumption that the dollar's purchasing power is relatively stable.

Stated interest rate Interest rate that determines the amount of cash interest the borrower pays and the investor receives each year. Another name for the *coupon rate* or *contract interest rate.*

Stated value Arbitrary amount assigned by a company to a share of its stock at the time of issue.

Statement of cash flows Reports cash receipts and cash payments classified according to the entity's major activities: operating, investing, and financing.

Statement of earnings Another name for the *income statement.*

Statement of financial position Another name for the *balance sheet.*

Statement of operations Another name for the *income statement.*

Statement of retained earnings Summary of the changes in the retained earnings of a corporation during a specific period.

Statement of shareholders' equity Reports the changes in all categories of shareholders' equity during the period.

Stock Shares into which the owners' equity of a corporation is divided.

Stock dividend A proportional distribution by a corporation of its own stock to its shareholders.

Stock split An increase in the number of authorized, issued, and outstanding shares of stock coupled with a proportionate reduction in the share's book value.

Straight-line (SL) method Depreciation method in which an equal amount of amortization expense is assigned to each year (or period) of asset use.

Strong currency A currency whose exchange rate is rising relative to other nations' currencies.

Subsidiary company An investee company in which a parent company owns more than 50% of the voting shares.

Taxable income The basis for computing the amount of tax to pay the government.

Temporary account Revenues and expenses related to a limited period.

Term The length of time from inception to maturity.

Term bonds Bonds that all mature at the same time for a particular issue.

Time-period concept Ensures that accounting information is reported at regular intervals.

Times-interest-earned ratio Ratio of income from operations to interest expense. Measures the number of times that operating income can cover interest expense. Also called *interest-coverage ratio.*

Trademark, trade name A distinctive identification of a product or service. Also called a *brand name.*

Trading investment Share or bond investments that are to be sold in the near future with the intent of generating profits on the sale.

Trading on the equity Earning more income on borrowed money than the related interest expense, thereby increasing the earnings for the owners of the business. Also called *leverage.*

Transaction An event that has a financial impact on the business and can be measured.

Treasurer In a large company, the person in charge of managing cash.

Trend percentages A form of horizontal analysis that indicates the direction a business is taking.

Trial balance A list of all the ledger accounts with their balances.

Trojan horse A malicious program that hides within legitimate programs and acts like a computer virus.

Uncollectible-account expense Cost to the seller of extending credit. Arises from the failure to collect from credit customers. Also called *doubtful-account expense* or *bad-debt expense.*

Underwriter Organization that purchases the bonds from an issuing company and resells them to its clients or sells the bonds for a commission, agreeing to buy all unsold bonds.

Unearned revenue An obligation arising from receiving cash before providing a service.

Units-of-production (UOP) method Depreciation method by which a fixed amount of depreciation is assigned to each unit of output produced by the plant asset.

Unqualified opinion Another name for *clean opinion.*

Vertical analysis Analysis of a financial statement that reveals the relationship of each statement item to a specified base, which is the 100% figure.

Weak currency A currency whose exchange rate is falling relative to other nations' currencies.

Weighted-average-cost method Inventory costing method based on the weighted average cost of inventory during the period. Weighted-average cost is determined by dividing the cost of goods available for sale by the number of units available. Also called the *average-cost method.*

Working capital Current assets minus current liabilities; measures a business's ability to meet its short-term obligations with its current assets.

Index

A

F

J

K

S